The Mind and Society

A TREATISE
ON GENERAL SOCIOLOGY

by Vilfredo Pareto

Translated by Andrew Bongiorno and Arthur Livingston
with the advice and active cooperation of
James Harvey Rogers.
Edited by Arthur Livingston

Four volumes bound as two

Volume Three: Theory of Derivations
Volume Four: The General Form of Society

Published through the sponsorship of The Pareto Fund
Philip E. Allen, Founder and President
New York   San Francisco

DOVER PUBLICATIONS, INC.
NEW YORK   NEW YORK

Manufactured in the United States of America

Dover Publications, Inc.
180 Varick Street
New York 14, N. Y.

The Mind and Society

A TREATISE
ON GENERAL SOCIOLOGY

by Vilfredo Pareto

Volume Three: Theory of Derivations

CONTENTS

VOLUME III

THE MIND AND SOCIETY

Volume III: Sentiment in Thinking
(Theory of Derivations)

CHAPTER IX

Derivations

1397. We now come to derivations as defined in § 868. They account for the production and acceptance of certain theories, so these we shall now be considering from the "subjective" standpoint (§ 13). We have already come upon derivations in large numbers, though we have not always used that term for them. We shall continue to find them whenever we centre our attention on the ways in which people try to dissemble, change, explain, the real character of this or that mode of conduct.[1] Human beings are persuaded in the main by sentiments (residues), and we may therefore foresee, as for that matter experience shows, that derivations derive the force they have, not, or at least not exclusively, from logico-experimental considerations, but from sentiments.[2] The principal nucleus

1397 [1] In Chapter III we went at some length into the reasonings with which people try to make conduct that is non-logical seem logical. Those were derivations, and we classified a few of them from that particular point of view. We met others, again, in Chapters IV and V, considering them from other points of view.

1397 [2] Jeremy Bentham condemns political orators for using sophistries and fallacious arguments: *Traité des sophismes politiques* (Dumont text), Vol. II, pp. 129, 213, 3 [As is well known, nothing in Bentham's *Book of Fallacies* (*Works*, Vol. II, pp. 375 f.) exactly corresponds to Dumont's French, this form of Bentham's thought being known in English only in translation.—A. L.] Says Bentham: "Fortunately, an orator of that sort, however brilliant and talented, will never hold the forefront in a legislative body. He may dazzle, he may astonish, he may have a momentary success, but he inspires no confidence even in those for whom he pleads. The greater the experience one has with political bodies, the more clearly one realizes the soundness of Cicero's definition of the orator as an honest man trained in the art of public speaking: *vir bonus dicendi peritus.*" If Bentham means, as he seems to mean, that only the honest, loyal, straightforward orator achieves success, we get a proposition which experience belies a thousand times over, and the very case of Cicero might be cited in proof. Bentham heaps praises on Fox for the qualities mentioned; but Fox unquestionably was defeated in the English Parliament. His case would rather disprove the contention. If Bentham is thinking of the esteem that certain "good" people may have for an orator, he may or may not be right, according to the meaning one attaches to the term "good." That, however, would be shifting the point at issue, which is the basis of success in politics. [Bentham forgot, and Pareto overlooked, the fact that the celebrated definition of the ideal orator referred to is not Cicero's, but is attributed to the younger Cato by Quintilian, *Institutio oratoria*, XII, 1, 1: "*Sit ergo nobis orator . . . is qui a Marco Catone fini-*

in a derivative (a non-logico-experimental theory) is a residue, or a number of residues, and around it other secondary residues cluster. That group is produced, and once produced is consolidated, by a powerful force: the need that the human being feels for logical or pseudo-logical developments and which manifests itself in residues of the I-ε type. It is in those residues therefore in combination with others that derivations in general originate.

1398. Some distance back (Chapter II) we studied a large group of derivations that were designed to "explain" certain manners of dealing with storms: and we found that they originated in the human hunger for logical developments, or developments considered logical (§ 888) (residue I-ε). The nucleus of the act was faith

---

tur: vir bonus dicendi peritus."—A. L.] Elsewhere Bentham condemns politicians for opposing ministers in power and attacking measures which they themselves recognize as good, on the ground that it is their duty to remove from power persons whom they consider harmful to the country. "If the men you are attacking are what you say they are, they will not be long in supplying you with opportunities for fighting them without prejudice to your sincerity. If such legitimate opportunities fail you, your charges of incapacity or malpractice would seem to be either false or premature. If such measures are more often bad than good, public opinion must necessarily turn in your favour. [What a fine thing, but how imaginary, such a public opinion!] There can be no doubt that a bad measure is much easier to attack than a good one." That may be true in some ideal universe where everything makes for the best in a best of all possible worlds; but it seems not at all to square with experience in our real world. Bentham writes a whole book on political sophistries and is not aware that every now and then he himself unwittingly falls into the fallacy of mistaking effusions of his own sentiments and inclinations for conquests of experience. "The sophistry," he says, "supplies a legitimate presumption against those who use it. Only for lack of sound arguments does one resort to it. [That is based on the implicit assumption that logically sound arguments are more convincing than fallacies. Experience is far from showing that.] As regards measures that are in themselves sound it is useless, or at least it cannot be indispensable. [The same implicit assumption, and experience, again, in no sense concords with it.] The sophistry presupposes in those who use it, or in those who adopt it, either lack of sincerity or lack of intelligence." Bentham's assumption is that the person who uses a fallacy recognizes it as such (insincerity) or that, if he fails so to recognize it, he is wanting in intelligence. As a matter of fact many fallacies that are current in a given society are repeated in all sincerity by people who are exceedingly intelligent and are merely voicing in that way sentiments which they consider beneficial to society. Also implicit in Bentham's sermon is the assumption that lack of sincerity and lack of intelligence are uniformly harmful to society; whereas there are plenty of cases—to go no farther than diplomacy—where too much sincerity may be harmful, and other cases where a highly intelligent man may go wrong and do incalculable harm to a society by forcing certain logical policies upon it; whereas a stupid individual instinctively following beaten paths that have been counselled by long experience may be a blessing to his country.

in the efficacy of combinations (residue I-ζ): people felt instinctively that there *must* be some way of controlling storms. Around that nucleus clustered a number of residues relating to the mysterious effects of certain procedures, the mysterious workings of certain objects (residue I-γ); and the result was a variety of magical rites. In these other residues were incidentally involved—residues relating to unusual things and exceptional occurrences (I-$\beta2$), mysterious linkings of names and things (I-$\gamma2$), mystery in general (I-$\gamma1$), and even residues of generic combination (I-α). Eventually, and still incidentally, Class II residues (group-persistences) were introduced. A very populous family of such residues was obtained by resorting, in the quest for explanations, to personifications (II-η), such as divinities, demons, genii. Rare the case where a family of that sort does not figure somewhere in a group of derivations.

1399. We have already dealt with residues exhaustively, and so, as regards the derivation, our only problem would be to determine which residues are primary and which secondary. But that would give us the mere substance of the derivation, and derivations may profitably be considered from other points of view.

In the first place, with special reference to form, the relation of the derivation to logic has to be considered—whether, that is, it is a sound reasoning or a sophistry. That, however, would be a problem in logic (§ 1410), and we are not called upon to deal with it in any special way here. Secondly, there is a question as to the relation of the derivation to experimental reality. A derivation may be strictly logical and yet, because of some error in the premises, not accord with experience. Or again it may be logical to all appearances, yet in view of some indefiniteness in its terms or for some other reason have no experimental meaning, or a meaning that has only a very distant bearing on experience.[1] Now, all the while adding to our list of derivations, we must go on and examine them in particular from the subjective standpoint, from the standpoint of their persuasive force. Still left then will be a third problem, the question of their social utility.[2]

1399 [1] It was from this point of view that we considered a number of derivations in Chapters III, IV, and V, though we were not then calling them derivations.

1399 [2] To the question of utility we shall come in Chapter XII. In any event, to get a complete theory of derivations from the first two standpoints, Chapters III, IV and V have to be taken in conjunction with our argument here. Deduction re-

1400. Derivations will be differently classified according to the standpoint from which they are considered (§ 1480). Just here we are thinking of the subjective character of the "explanations" that are given, through derivations, of certain behaviour, certain ways of thinking; and of the persuasive force of such explanations. We shall therefore classify derivations according to the character of the explanation. Where there is no explaining there is no derivation; but the moment an explanation is given or sought, a derivation comes into play. The animal does not reason, it acts exclusively by instinct (§ 861). It uses no derivations therefore. The human being, however, wants to think, and he also feels impelled to keep his instincts and sentiments hidden from view. Rarely, in consequence, is at least a germ of derivation missing in human thinking, just as residues are rarely missing. Residues and derivations can be detected every time we look at a theory or argument that is not strictly logico-experimental. That was the case in Chapter III (§ 325), where we came upon the derivation in its simplest form, the pure precept, with no explanation or demonstration offered. It is the type of argument used by the child or the illiterate in the tautology: "We do thus and so *because* we do thus and so." Such a statement is a pure expression of residues of sociality (Class IV). It really means: "I do as I do (or others do as they do) because that is what is usually done in our community." Then comes a derivation somewhat more complex in that a show is made of accounting for the custom, and one says: "We do thus and so because that is what one *ought* to do." Such derivations are simple assertions. Let us put them in a class by themselves, Class I. But already in the second of the derivations mentioned an indefinite, somewhat mysterious entity, "duty," has put in an appearance. That is our first intimation as to a general manner in which derivations are elaborated: by appealing, that is, under one term or another, to various kinds of sentiments. But going on from there, people are not long satisfied with mere names such as "duty." They want something more concrete, and they also want somehow to account for their using the name. What in the world is this thing "duty" that has suddenly popped up? Every-

traces the inductive path in inverse direction. Anyone using the two methods successively must necessarily encounter some at least of the theories and arguments upon which he came in his first survey.

body has his answer—the illiterate, the educated man, the philosopher, all alike; and we go from the childish answer of the plain man to the abstruse, but from the logico-experimental standpoint no better, theory of the metaphysicist. A first step is taken by appealing to the authority of maxims current in the community that happens to be involved, to the authority of individuals, and, with new elaborations, to the authority of supernatural beings or personifications that feel and act like human beings. That gives us another variety, Class II. The thinking now grows more complicated: it becomes abstruse, abstract, as interpretations of sentiments, abstract entities, and the will of supernatural beings are introduced. That procedure may yield long long sequences of logical or pseudo-logical inferences and eventuate in theories that have the look of scientific theories. Among them are to be counted theologies and systems of metaphysics. Suppose we put them in a Class III. But we have still not exhausted our supply of derivations. Still remaining is a large class where we find proofs that are primarily verbal, explanations that are purely formal but pretend to pass as substantial—Class IV.[1]

1401. Suppose we go back for a moment and translate into the terminology of residues and derivations the matter we expounded in §§ 798-803, where we used letters of the alphabet in place of words. Concrete theories in social connexions are made up of residues and derivations. The residues are manifestations of sentiments. The derivations comprise logical reasonings, unsound reasonings, and manifestations of sentiments used for purposes of derivation: they are manifestations of the human being's hunger for thinking. If that hunger were satisfied by logico-experimental reasonings only, there would be no derivations; instead of them we should get logico-experimental theories. But the human hunger for thinking is satisfied in any number of ways; by pseudo-experimental reasonings, by words that stir the sentiments, by fatuous, inconclusive "talk." So derivations come into being. They do not figure at the two extreme ends of the line, that is to say, in conduct that is purely instinctive, and in strictly logico-experimental science. They figure in the intermediate cases.

1400 [1] We shall see as we go on (§ 1419) that these classes subdivide into genera, and we shall deal specially with each such genus in turn. But before we come to that, we had better consider other general aspects of derivations and derivatives.

1402. Now the only things of which we have any direct knowledge are the concrete reasonings that correspond to these cases. So we analyzed many of them, distinguishing an element that is virtually constant, *a,* from an element that is more variable, *b* (§§ 798 f.). Those elements we have named, respectively, *residues* and *derivations* (§ 868), and we have seen that the more important element as regards the social equilibrium is the residues (§ 800). But in that we go counter to common opinion, which is controlled by the notion that all conduct is logical, and is inclined to invert the relation and ascribe the greater importance to derivations (§ 1415). The person who is influenced by a derivation imagines that he accepts or rejects it on logico-experimental grounds. He does not notice that he ordinarily makes up his mind in deference to sentiments and that the accord (or conflict) of two derivations is an accord (or conflict) of residues. When, then, a person sets out to study social phenomena, he halts at manifestations of social activity, that is to say, at derivations, and does not carry his inquiry into the causes of the activity, that is to say, into residues. So it has come about that the history of social institutions has been a history of derivations, and oftentimes the history of mere patter. The history of theologies has been offered as the history of religions; the history of ethical theories, as the history of morals; the history of political theories, as the history of political institutions. Metaphysics moreover has supplied all such theories with absolute elements, from which it was thought that conclusions no less absolute could be drawn by pure logic. So the history of the theories has become the history of the deviations observable in the concrete from certain ideal types existing in the mind of this or that thinker. Not so long ago, some few scholars sensed that that procedure was taking them far afield from realities, and to get back to the real, they replaced such abstract "thinking" with a search for "origins," but without noticing that in so doing they were merely replacing one metaphysics with another, explaining the better known by the less known, and facts susceptible of direct observation by fancies which, for the simple reason that they related to times very remote, could not be proved; and meantime adding on their own account principles, such as unitary evolution, that altogether transcended experience.

1403. Derivations, in a word, are things that everybody uses. But the writers of whom we are thinking ascribe an intrinsic value to derivations and regard them as functioning directly as determinants of the social equilibrium. For us, in these volumes, they figure only as manifestations, as indications, of other forces that are the forces which really determine the social equilbrium. Very very often, hitherto, the social sciences have been theories made up of residues and derivations and furthermore holding in view the practical purpose of persuading people to act in this or that manner deemed beneficial to society. These present volumes aim instead at bringing the social sciences wholly within the logico-experimental field, quite apart from any purpose of immediate practical utility, and in the sole intent of discovering the uniformities that prevail among social phenomena (§ 86). If one is writing a book with a view to inducing people to act in a given way, one must necessarily resort to derivations, for they are the only language that reaches the human being in his sentiments and is therefore calculated to modify his behaviour. But the person who aims at logico-experimental knowledge and nothing else must take the greatest pains not to fall into derivations. They are objects for his study, never tools of persuasion.

1404. As regards the important rôle that we ascribe to sentiment in derivations, we meet here again a problem which we stated and solved in Chapter III. If the rôle that sentiment plays in derivations is really of such great importance, how can the many men of genius who have dealt practically and theoretically with human societies have failed to notice the fact? We must answer here again that the rôle played by sentiment has in fact been often perceived; but indistinctly, so that it has never been given a complete theory and its importance has never been accurately evaluated—and that for various reasons, prominent among which is the preconception that the leading rôle in human activity is played by logical thinking.

Here again let us look at a few examples of the way in which the subject has been conceived by one writer or another in the past.

1405. According to a very plausible theory Aristotle conceived of the enthymeme as a judgment that is combined with a statement of its reason.[1] The enthymeme of modern logicians is a syllogism

1405 [1] [*Century Dictionary, s.v. Enthymeme:* "In Aristotle's Logic, an inference from likelihoods and signs, which, with Aristotle, is the same as a rhetorical syllogism." Pareto wrote: "A judgment that rests on the cause that is the origin of it"—which I find not very lucid.—A. L.]

in which one of the premises is not stated. Let us accept the latter definition, and it will at once be apparent that the consequences we draw from it apply *a fortiori* to Aristotle's enthymeme.

1406. Derivations are often stated in enthymemic form. There are reasons for that. If we think of the art of rhetoric, there is first of all the fact that a piece of writing made up of syllogisms would be cumbersome, tedious, unreadable. Then there is a consideration of a more general order and which is as valid for the art of rhetoric as for a scientific argument (or one passing as such). The syllogistic form tends to reveal the logical weakness of a derivation—it stresses its fallacies. It is advisable, therefore, not to use it in arguments made up of associations of ideas or residues. The enthymeme ignores one of the propositions in the syllogism, and things may be so arranged that the proposition not stated is the one where the logical weakness is most apparent. As a rule the proposition suppressed is the major, in other words, the premise contains the middle term and the predicate. The conclusion that is sought contains the subject and the predicate, and the subject is of such importance that it is hard to suppress the minor in which it is contained. When the middle term is a non-experimental entity (§ 470), something is gained by suppressing at least one of the propositions which contain it.

1407. Take, for example, an enthymeme [of unknown authorship] quoted by Aristotle, *Rhetorica,* II, 21, 6: "Nourish not, being mortal, immortal wrath." [1] Taken literally the proposition is senseless. A man's wrath ends, evidently, when he dies and vanishes from the Earth. It is therefore useless to adjure him not to nourish immortal wrath. But the proposition means something altogether different: the advice is not to nourish a grudge for *too long* a time, not to nourish a *very long* wrath, which however is called "immortal." The basic residue, *a,* in the proposition is a residue of sociality (Class IV). The residue that is introduced for purposes of derivation is a residue linking names and things (I-γ). Two associations of ideas are so obtained: first, a repugnance to combining two contraries such as "immortal" and "mortal"; and second, a confusion between "immortal" and "very long." The weak point in the argument lies in just that confusion, and it must therefore be made as inconspicuous as possible.

1407 [1] Freese, p. 282: 'Αθάνατον ὀργὴν μὴ φύλασσε θνητὸς ὤν.

1408. The enthymeme just quoted is an enthymeme in the Aristotelian, but not in the modern, sense of the term. In the modern sense the complete syllogism would be: "Man is mortal. A mortal cannot nourish immortal wrath. Therefore a man cannot nourish immortal wrath." But that is not at all what the enthymeme was devised to show. The actual meaning was that a man cannot—or, rather, ought not—nourish a grudge for too long a time. If that meaning be stated in enthymemic form the wording will be: "Since man is mortal, he must not nourish wrath for too long a time"; and many persons will accept it in that form, because they will be impressed by the contrast between the *brief* life of a human being, and a *long*-protracted wrath. Now let us state the completed syllogism: "Man is mortal. A mortal must not nourish wrath for too long a time. Therefore man must not nourish wrath for too long a time." The assertion that "a mortal must not nourish wrath for too long a time" at once calls attention to the weak point in the argument. It had better be suppressed, therefore, to avoid the danger that its fallacy may be perceived, and so the enthymeme is used instead of the syllogism. That procedure is all the more useful in the Aristotelian sense of the enthymeme. If on asserting a judgment we limit ourselves to stating the reason that provokes, or apparently provokes, it and drop the intermediate propositions, we place ourselves in the more favourable situation for arguing by associations of ideas, by residues, as opposed to strictly logical argument. Aristotle instinctively sensed that when he said, *Rhetorica,* I, 2, 8 (Freese, p. 19), that the enthymeme was the orator's syllogism. He was also right, *Ibid.,* II, 21, 3 (Freese, p. 279), in viewing a maxim as a partial enthymeme. A maxim is, in fact, a syllogism reduced to lowest terms, so that nothing is left but the conclusion.

1409. One must avoid the pitfall of imagining that a maxim is accepted because it is part of an enthymeme and the enthymeme because it is part of a syllogism. That may be true from the standpoint of formal logic, but not as regards its persuasive force. Both maxim and enthymeme are accepted in view of the sentiments that they arouse, for intrinsic reasons, without reference to the completed syllogism (§ 1399). Aristotle, *Ibid.,* I, 2, 8-9 (Freese, pp. 19-21), reenforces the enthymeme with the example as a means of persuasion. The example is one of the simplest derivations. A fact is stated and then a residue of group-persistence (residue II-ε, persistence of uniformities, § 1068) is called in: the single case, that is, is represented as the general rule.

1410. In his *System of Logic,* Book V, Chap. I § 3 (p. 513), John Stuart Mill mentions—but rather by way of eliminating them from his purview—two other sources of error in addition to the logical fallacy, the one intellectual, the other moral. That approximately is the distinction we make between our derivations *B* and *b* (§ 803). Since he was dealing with logic Mill was right in not going into those sources of error. They are however of the greatest importance to the sociologist.

1411. When the logician has discovered the error in a reasoning, when he can put his finger on the fallacy in it, his work is done. But that is where the work of the sociologist begins, for he must find out why the false argument is accepted, why the sophistry persuades. Tricks of sophistry that are mere finesses in logic are of little or no interest to him, for they elicit no very wide response among men. But the fallacious, or for that matter the sound, theories that enjoy wide acceptance are of the greatest concern to him. It is the province of logic to tell why a reasoning is false. It is the business of sociology to explain its wide acceptance.

1412. According to Mill there are, in the main, two sources of ethical error: first, indifference to knowledge of the truth; and then, bias, the most common case being "that in which we are biased by our wishes," though after all we may accept agreeable and disagreeable conclusions alike provided they manage to arouse some strong emotion. Mill's "indifference" and "bias" would be what we mean by sentiments corresponding to residues. But Mill handles them very badly, being led astray by his preconception that only logical behaviour is good, beneficial, praiseworthy, whereas non-logical conduct is necessarily evil, harmful, blameworthy. He is not in the least aware that he himself does most of his thinking under the influence of just such a "bias."

1413. A person who is trying to prove something is almost always conscious of the purpose of his derivation. Not so, oftentimes, the person assenting to the conclusion that the derivation reaches. When the purpose is to justify some rule of conduct, the effort is to associate the norm with certain residues by more or less logical arguments if the primary aim is to satisfy the hankering for logic in the individuals who are to be influenced; by heaping up residues if the primary appeal is to sentiment.

1414. Arranging these procedures in order of importance, they may be represented as follows: 1. The purpose. 2. The residues with which we start. 3. The derivation. A graph will make the situation clearer. Let B stand for the purpose that is to be attained, starting with the residues R' R'' R''' . . . and working up to the derivations $R'rB$, $R'tB$, $R'vB$. . . . In the case of a moral theory, the purpose, let us say, is to establish the precept forbidding homicide. That objective can be reached by a very simple derivation, namely, the blood-taboo. One can also start with the residue of a personal god, and attain the objective by way of many different derivations. One may start with a metaphysical residue, a residue of social utility, a residue of personal utility, or some other residue, and get to the point desired by way of a literally huge number of derivations.

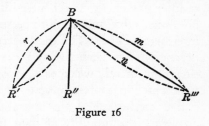

Figure 16

1415. Theologians, metaphysicists, philosophers, theorists of politics, law, and ethics, do not ordinarily accept the order indicated (§ 1402). They are inclined to assign first place to derivations. What we call residues are in their eyes axioms or dogmas, and the purpose is just the conclusion of a logical reasoning. But since they are not as a rule in any agreement on the derivation, they argue about it till they are blue in the face and think that they can change social conditions by proving a derivation fallacious. That is all an illusion on their part. They fail to realize that their hagglings never reach the majority of men, who could not make head or tail to them anyhow, and who in fact disregard them save as articles of faith to which they assent in deference to certain residues.[1][2]

1415 [1] Political economy has been and largely continues to be a branch of literature, and as such falls under anything that may be said of derivations. It stands as a matter of plain fact that economic practice and economic theory have followed altogether divergent paths.

1415 [2] Bayle, *Dictionnaire historique, s.v. Augustin:* "To anyone examining the question without prejudice and with the necessary competence, it is so evident that

1416. What we have just been saying leads to very important conclusions with reference to that "logic of sentiments" to which we alluded in § 480.

1. If the basic residue from which a derivation develops disappears and is not replaced by another, the purpose also disappears.[1] That is the usual case in logical reasonings based on experimental premises: that is to say, a scientific theory is discarded in the light of new facts. However, even in such a case it is often possible for a conclusion to hold its ground if the erroneous premises can be replaced by new ones. But in non-scientific reasonings what usually happens is that abandoned premises are replaced by new ones—one residue gives way to other residues. Only in the exceptional case does such substitution fail to occur. Between the two extremes come intermediate cases. The disappearance of the residue from which a derivation has been evolved does not eradicate the purpose entirely, but merely weakens it, saps its vitality. The ideal remains but is accepted with less fervour. It has been observed in India that native converts lose the morality of their old religion without acquiring the morality of their new customs and beliefs (§ 1741).

2. In the case of a scientific argument, if it can be shown that the conclusion does not follow logically from the premises, the argument

the doctrines of St. Augustine and Jansenius, Bishop of Ypres, are one and the same, that one can hardly keep one's temper at the thought that the Court of Rome could boast of condemning Jansenius and meantime keep the Saint secure in all his glory. The two things are altogether incompatible. Not only that: in condemning Calvin's doctrine of free-will, the Council of Trent necessarily condemned the doctrine of St. Augustine. . . . There are people who regard it as a very happy circumstance that the masses at large take such little interest in the vicissitudes of doctrine, are in fact incapable of doing so. If they did, they would be rising more often against theologians than against usurers. 'If you do not know,' they might say to them, 'that you are deceiving us, your stupidity deserves your being sent to till the soil. If you do know what you are doing, you deserve prison on bread and water for your wickedness.' . . . [In that Bayle is mistaken. A person may be as intelligent as one could wish and yet assent to contradictory derivations in the best of faith. That happens every day, and especially on such matters as "free will." Bayle is right in what follows:] But there is little to fear. All the masses ask is to be led along the beaten paths; and even if they wanted more than that, they would not be capable of mastering the subject. Their daily occupations have not permitted them to acquire sufficient competence for that."

1416 [1] That is a particular case of the general theory of the reciprocal influence of residues and derivations upon each other. That theory we shall elaborate in §§ 1735 f.

falls. But in an unscientific reasoning, if one form of derivation is demolished, another immediately is brought forward. If it is shown that the reasoning which connects a given residue with a given conclusion (the purpose) is unsound, the only result as a rule is that a new derivation takes the place of the old one which has been overthrown. That comes about because the residue and the purpose are the basic elements in such reasonings. The derivation is secondary, often very very secondary. The various Christian sects have doctrines as to good works and predestination that, from any logical standpoint, are altogether different and sometimes even antithetical or contradictory. Yet there is no difference between them as regards practical morals. A Chinese, a Moslem, a Calvinist, a Catholic, a Kantian, a Hegelian, a Materialist, all refrain from stealing; but each gives a different explanation for his conduct. In other words, it is a case of a number of derivations connecting one residue that is operative in all of them with one conclusion which they all accept. And if someone chances to invent a new derivation or refute one of the existing ones, his achievement has no practical consequences and the conclusion remains the same.

3. In scientific thinking the most stable conclusions are obtained by drawing strictly logical inferences from premises that have experimental verifications which are as nearly perfect as possible. In unscientific thinking the strongest conclusions are those which rest on powerful residues without any derivations. Next come conclusions that are obtained from strong residues supported, in the form of derivations, by residues which are themselves relatively powerful. In proportion as the distance between residue and conclusion lengthens, in proportion as residues are replaced by logical reasonings, the security of the conclusion lessens, except for some few scholars. The plain man is convinced by the plain Christian catechism, never by fine-spun theological disquisitions. The latter exert but an indirect influence at the most. The plain man, to be sure, admires them without understanding them, and that admiration serves to endow them with a prestige that is carried over to the conclusions. That was the case in our day with Marx's *Capital*. Some few Socialists in Germany may have read it, but those who can possibly have understood it must have been as rare as white blackbirds. But the devious and obscure disquisitions in the book were

admired at long range and so conferred prestige upon it. That admiration helped to determine the form of Socialist derivations, but not the residues or the conclusions, which existed before the book was written and will continue to be there after the book has been forgotten, and which are common both to Marxians and non-Marxians.

4. From the logical standpoint two contradictory propositions cannot hold side by side. From the standpoint of non-scientific derivations two apparently contradictory propositions can very well stand together in one individual, one mind. The following propositions seem to be contradictory: "It is wrong to kill," "It is right to kill"; "It is wrong to appropriate other people's property," "It is right to appropriate other people's property"; "Wrongs must be forgiven," "Wrongs must not be forgiven." And yet they can be accepted at one and the same time by one and the same person in virtue of interpretations and distinctions that serve to explain the contradiction away. So, from the logical standpoint, if $A = B$, it follows inexorably that $B = A$; but no such consequence is necessary in a reasoning by derivations.

1417. In addition to derivations made up of one group of basic residues and a second accessory group of residues used for purposes of derivation, one finds simple combinations of a number of residues or groups of residues that are brought together into a new unit group of residues. We also have the logical, or presumably logical, implications of considerations of individual or collective interest, but these are in the nature of scientific inferences, and we are not concerned with them here.

1418. The proof of a derivation is very often different from the reason for its acceptance. Sometimes again the proof and the reason may coincide. A precept may be demonstrated by appeal to authority and accepted in deference to the same authority, but then again the two things may be altogether at odds. When a person proves a proposition by taking advantage of the ambiguity of some term in it, he most assuredly does not say: "My proof is sound because of the trickery involved in my juggling of words." But the person who accepts the derivation is unwittingly taken into camp by that verbal trickery.

1419.   CLASSIFICATION OF DERIVATIONS

CLASS I: ASSERTION (§§ 1420-33)

I-α. Assertions of facts, experimental or imaginary (§§ 1421-27)
I-β. Assertions of sentiments (§§ 1428-32)
I-γ. Mixtures of fact and sentiment (§ 1433)

CLASS II: AUTHORITY (§§ 1434-63)

II-α. Of one individual or a number of individuals (§§ 1435-46)
II-β. Of tradition, usages, and customs (§§ 1447-57)
II-γ. Of divine beings, or personifications (§§ 1458-63)

CLASS III: ACCORDS WITH SENTIMENTS OR PRINCIPLES (§§ 1464-1542)

III-α. Accord with sentiments (§§ 1465-76)
III-β. Accord with individual interest (§§ 1477-97)
III-γ. Accord with collective interest (§§ 1498-1500)
III-δ. Accord with juridical entities (§§ 1501-09)
III-ε. Accord with metaphysical entities (§§ 1510-32)
III-ζ. Accord with supernatural entities (§§ 1533-42)

CLASS IV: VERBAL PROOFS (§§ 1543-1686)

IV-α. Indefinite terms designating real things; indefinite things corresponding to terms (§§ 1549-51)
IV-β. Terms designating things and arousing incidental sentiments, or incidental sentiments determining choice of terms (§§ 1552-55)
IV-γ. Terms with numbers of meanings, and different things designated by single terms (§§ 1556-1613)
IV-δ. Metaphors, allegories, analogies (§§ 1614-85)
IV-ε. Vague, indefinite terms corresponding to nothing concrete (§ 1686).

1420. Class I: *Assertion*. This class comprises simple narrations, assertions of fact, assertions by accord of sentiments. They are offered not as such, but in an absolute, axiomatic, dogmatic manner. They may be mere narrations or indications of experimental uniformities; but they are often so worded that it is not clear whether they are mere statements of experimental fact, or expressions of sentiment, or somewhat of both. In many cases, however, their composition may, to a certain degree of probability, be determined. Take the collection of maxims by Publilius Syrus. The first four are of the I-α type: "We mortal men are equally nigh unto death." "Expect from another what you have done to another." "Extinguish with tears the wrath of him who loves you." "To quarrel with a drunken man is to quarrel with one absent." Then comes a maxim of the I-β type: "It is better to receive a wrong than to inflict one." Then come four maxims again of the I-α type, and one of the I-β: "He who loves his wife licentiously is an adulterer." Finally a maxim of the I-γ type: "We all ask, 'Is he rich?' No one asks, 'Is he good?'" That maxim contains an assertion of fact (I-α) and a censure of the fact (I-β).[1] Or further, consider the maxims of Menander: "It is agreeable to pluck everything in its season" (I-α). "Neither do nor learn aught that is shameful" (I-β). "Silence is an ornament to all women" (I-γ).

1421. I-α: *Assertions of facts, experimental or imaginary.* The assertion may be subordinate to experience, and in that case it is a logico-experimental proposition and has no place among derivations. But the assertion may also subsist of itself by virtue of a certain inherent persuasiveness independent of experience. In that case it is a derivation.

1422. As we saw above (§§ 526, 1068), a simple narration and the assertion of a uniformity are different things. Both may belong to logico-experimental science or to derivations, according as they are subordinate to experience or subsist of themselves.

1423. Oftentimes a person following the method of the logico-experimental sciences will begin with a derivation and proceed to subject it to experimental test. In such a case the derivation is just an instrument of research and may have its place in logico-experimental science—though never as an instrument of proof or persuasion.

1424. When a uniformity is asserted on the basis of a fact, or a number of facts, the residue which is brought in for purposes of derivation is connected with a feeling that relations between facts of nature are constant (§ 1068). That procedure is scientific, provided one remember that there is nothing absolute about a uniformity so

1420 [1] [In Lyman, p. 13, the numbers of the maxims read in order, 1-5, 10; in Kremsier, they are, respectively, 2, 19, 12, 669, 343, pp. 1, 4, 3, 157, 69.—A. L.]

obtained. It is a non-scientific derivation of the I-β type if the constancy of natural "laws" is regarded as something absolute, or if the statement is in any way considered as transcending experience.

1425. The blunt assertion has little or no demonstrative value, but sometimes it has great persuasive force.[1] However, the assertion pure and simple is a rare thing, especially among civilized peoples. There is almost always some adjunct, some derivation, however rudimentary.[2]

1426. Frequent, on the other hand, in times past and present, is the re-enforcing assertion that is appended as a sort of exclamation to other derivations. In the Bible in issuing commands to His people

1425 [1] That is why we come upon the assertion here just as we came upon it some distance back (Chapter III) when we were investigating the ways in which people try to convince themselves and others that non-logical conduct is logical. We did not meet with it when we were considering demonstrations (Chapter IV).

1425 [2] Seneca discusses the utility of precepts in his *Epistulae,* 94. That is not our problem here, but some of his observations hit the mark as to the character and the appeal of the assertion: *"Adiice nunc quod aperta quoque apertiora fieri solent."* ("Then again what is obvious usually becomes more so.") He is met with the objection that if a precept is questionable it has to be proved, and in that case the useful thing is the proof, not the precept, and he replies: "What do you say to the fact that the very authority of the mentor has its effect (*prodest*) quite apart from any proof? So it is with the dicta of jurists, even when they give no reasons. Besides, the maxims imparted to us have a great weight all by themselves whether they are elaborated in verse or are compressed into the proverb in prose, such as Cato's famous maxim: *'Emas non quod opus est sed quod necesse est. Quod non opus est asse carum est.'* ("Buy not what you need but what you have to have. What you do not need comes dear at a farthing"—*Reliquiae,* 4 (8), p. 17.) So with the responses of oracles or things of that kind, such as *'Tempori parce!' 'Te nosci.'* What proof do you require when someone quotes to you lines such as: *'Iniuriarum remedium est oblivio,' 'Audentes fortuna iuvat,' 'Piger ipse sibi obstat'?* Such maxims need no advocate. They touch us in our inner emotions and stimulate us by their own natural force. [So Pareto. *"Natura vim suam exercente proficiunt"*: perhaps "by force of our very natures"; Gummere: "because nature is exercising her proper function"; Morell: "Let nature exert her own power, they cannot but do good."— A. L.] The seeds of all nobility lie in our souls, and they are stirred to life by the admonition, much as a spark when gently fanned unfolds its inner flame." To be quite exact the last sentences need retouching: "The seeds of *certain things* lie in our souls, and they are stirred to life by *simple assertions,* much as, etc." Seneca goes on to say: "Some things moreover are present in our souls but in a state of sluggishness, and they become supple and active (*in expedito*) when they are expressed in words. Some things lie scattered about so that an untrained mind cannot bring them together; and so they have to be assembled and organized before they can be useful and inspiriting to the soul." That is all very sound and well describes the effects of simple assertions.

through Moses, Jehovah now and again exclaims as it were by way of re-enforcement: "I am the Lord your God." [1] Frequent in our time are assertions to the effect that this or that measure means "progress" or "democracy" or that it is "broadly human" or "makes for a better humanity." The assertion is less a derivation, in just that form, than a mere device for evoking certain sentiments. But by being repeated over and over again, it eventually acquires a force of its own, becomes a motive of conduct, and is to all intents and purposes a derivation.

1427. The simple assertion also figures in the taboo without sanction, to which we have already alluded (§§ 321 f.). Simple derivations of that sort can be detected in a great many compound derivations—rare, indeed, the concrete derivation that fails to contain one. The arbitrary assertion generally finds some little place among experimental assertions; or else it creeps into an argument or dissembles its presence there to usurp for itself the assent that is accorded to the other propositions among which it lurks.

1428. I-β: *Assertion of sentiments.* The assertion may be an indirect manner of expressing certain sentiments, and it is accepted as an "explanation" by people who share those sentiments. In such a case, therefore, it is a mere manifestation of the secondary residues that go to make up the derivation.

1429. When a uniformity or precept is derived from an individual sentiment, the residue brought into play for purposes of derivation is the one that transforms subjective facts into objective realities (residue II-ζ, § 888) along, oftentimes, with residues of sociality (Class IV). A man sees other people run and he runs. That is an instinctive act, a reflex action such as is observable in animals. He hears someone shout, "Run!" and he runs. We are still in the same case. Ask him, "Why did you run?" and he answers, "Because I heard people shouting 'Run!' and I thought that one *ought* to run." In that we get a first glimmer of the derivation, which will become more complicated if the man undertakes to give a reason for the "ought." A man reading a poem exclaims, "It is beautiful!" Were he to say, "It seems beautiful to me," he would merely be stating a subjective fact. Using the language, "It is beautiful!" he makes the subjective fact objective.

1426 [1] Lev. 14:3, and *passim:* "And ye shall fear every man his mother and his father and keep my sabbaths: I am the Lord your God."

Furthermore, anyone hearing the exclamation has a feeling that anything that is reputed beautiful *ought* to make an impression of beauty upon him, a residue of sociality interposing. That is the reason why people as a rule share the tastes of the community in which they live.

1430. An assertion is accepted and gains prestige through the sentiments of various kinds which it excites in those who hear it, the sentiments so acquiring status as "proof." It convinces because it is stated in a doctoral, sententious tone, with great assurance, and in a choice literary language. It will be more effective in verse than in prose, in print rather than in manuscript, in a book rather than in a newspaper, in a newspaper rather than in the spoken word (§ 1157).

1431. The causes that account for the persuasiveness of the assertion fall into three categories: 1. A vague feeling that a person who expresses himself in such a form *must* be right. In that the derivation is reduced to a minimum and is to be taken as the distinctive type of the I-β variety. 2. A feeling that such a select form is authoritative. In that the derivation is somewhat more evolved and belongs to Class II (and see below, §§ 1434 f., authority). 3. The more or less vague notion that the authority is justified. The derivation still belongs to Class II (§ 1435), and may develop to the point of yielding a logical reasoning.

One might guess, in the abstract, that the sentiments in 3 gave rise to the sentiments in 2, and those in 2 to those in 1: that first, in other words, one is shown that certain circumstances confer authority; that then the authority is accepted in general terms; and that, finally, and quite apart from any authority, comes a feeling of reverence for the manner of expression used. That may sometimes be the process; but in reality the three groups are often independent, each having a life of its own; and when a relation does exist between 2 and 3, it is the reverse of the one indicated. In many cases the person accepting the assertion expressed in the forms mentioned does not do any very extensive thinking: he says, "I see by the papers . . ." and for him that is proof enough.[1] It is a I-β derivation,

---

1431 [1] *Journal des Goncourt,* Vol. V, p. 9 (Jan. 10, 1872): "Today the newspaper has replaced the catechism among the French. A leading article in the *Journal de Paris* by Tom, Dick, or Harry becomes an article of faith that the subscriber

but only in case the sentiment of respect for the printed or written word is made implicitly or explicitly to serve as an explanation or justification of the assent that is given to what is printed or written. If the sentiment is merely expressed (as when something printed or written is taken as a fetish, or amulet) or is merely regarded with reverence and no inferences are drawn from it, we get a residue that we discussed some distance back (§§ 1157 f., authority of symbols). The observation is of general bearing: a sentiment finds expression in a residue. If the residue is then used to explain, justify, demonstrate, we get a derivation. In the case where a person takes his opinions from the newspaper that he habitually reads, there figure, along with the I-β derivation, a cumulus of other derivations and residues, notable among which are residues of sociality (Class IV): the newspaper expresses, or is taken as expressing, the opinion of the community to which the reader belongs. In other cases the concept of authority figures (§§ 1157 f.), now in combination with the residue of sociality, now independently of it. Finally, in a case relatively rare, sentiments justifying the authority also come into play (§ 1432). But as a rule a person first has the sentiment of authority, and then goes looking for ways to justify it.

1432. From the logico-experimental standpoint, the fact that an assertion is made in a tone of great assurance may be an indication, slight though it be, that it is not to be doubted. The fact that it is made in Latin proves, unless it be a parrot-like repetition, that the person who makes it has a certain amount of education, and that may create a presumption of legitimate authority. In general, the fact that it is expressed in language that not everybody could use may be an indication, though often enough misleading, that it comes from a person better able than others to know what he is talking about. An assertion made in print, as in newspapers or books, may almost always be regarded as publicly made, and so as more readily susceptible of refutation than an assertion made in private and passing from mouth to mouth. So if the refutation fails to materialize, the printed assertion has greater plausibility than the spoken word. But people are seldom influenced by considerations of that kind. Not logico-experimental reasonings but sentiments prompt

accepts with the same absence of free thought that the mystery of the Trinity used to get from the old-fashioned Catholic."

them to lend credence to assertions that are made in those manners.

1433. I-γ: *Mixtures of fact and sentiment.* Our I-α and I-β varieties, which we separated in the abstract, nearly always appear combined in the concrete and so give rise to this present genus. To be sure, a person giving an explanation may, though such a thing rarely happens, be free of the sentiments he exploits in giving it. But in general the person who assents to it does share those sentiments—otherwise he would not give his assent. It follows from that that most Class I derivations in the concrete are of the I-γ variety, and that statements of fact and expressions of sentiment are so intimately blended in them as not easily to be distinguished. Often sentiments of authority figure.

1434. Class II: *Authority.* Here we get a tool of proof and a tool of persuasion. With authority as a means of proof we have already dealt (§§ 583 f.). Here our more particular interest is in authority as an instrument of persuasion. The various derivations in this class are the simplest next after assertions (Class I). As in many other derivations, the residues that are used for purposes of deriving are residues of group-persistence (Class II), II-ζ residues that represent sentiments as objective realities being supported by residues of other kinds, as, for instance, II-β residues (surviving authority of a dead parent, or of the forefathers), residues of tradition (II-α); of persisting uniformities (II-ε), and so on. As a rule Class I residues sooner or later come into play to elongate and complicate the derivation.

1435. II-α: *Authority of one individual or of a number of individuals.* An extreme case would be the derivation that is strictly logical. It is evident that in a given connexion the opinion of an expert has a greater probability of being verified by experience than the opinion of a person who is ignorant of the matters in hand or but slightly acquainted with them. That is a purely logico-experimental situation and we need not linger on it. But there are other kinds of derivations in which the individual's competence is not experimental. It may be assumed to exist from misleading evidence or be altogether fictitious. In the case least remote from the logico-experimental situation the authority is presumed on grounds that may or may not be sound, it being a question of a greater or lesser degree of probability (§ 1432). Next to that would come the case where the competence is stretched, through sentiments of group-persistence, beyond the limits within which it is experimentally valid. The situation dealt with in the familiar maxim, "Cobbler, stick to your last"—*Sutor, ne ultra crepidam*—is of all times and places.[1]

1436. Because he is a first-class politician, Theodore Roosevelt is sure that he also knows history; and he makes bold to deliver a lecture in Berlin in which he makes brilliant display of his perfect ignorance of Greek and Roman history. The university that once listened to the lectures of Mommsen confers on him the title of Doctor *honoris causa*. He makes the discovery—and it is a feat indeed—that the apothegm, *Si vis pacem, para bellum,* is George Washington's—and he becomes a corresponding member of the French Institute of Moral and Political Sciences.[a] Now indubitably Roosevelt is a past master in the art of manipulating elections. He knows all the ins and outs of publicity. He is not a bad hunter of the white rhinoceros. But how can all that make him competent to advise the English on how to govern Egypt, or the French on the number of children they should have? Undoubtedly political considerations and considerations of rather undignified adulation figured in the honours that were conferred upon Roosevelt by the French Institute and the universities of Berlin and Cambridge, to say nothing of flattery which he received from influential statesmen in the course of his rapid flight through Europe. But even where

1435 [1] Bentham, *Tactique des assemblées législatives,* Vol. II, pp. 23-24, expresses an altogether erroneous opinion: "Authority has been the support over countless centuries of the most discordant systems, the most monstrous opinions. [Such opinions are supported by residues and explained by derivations, among which the derivation of authority.] The religions of the Brahma, of Foh, of Mohammed, rest on nothing else. [Not at all! Authority is only one of many derivations that are called in to logicalize the various group-persistences.] If authority is a thing that cannot be questioned, the human race that peoples those vast territories has no hope ever of escaping from darkness." In that we get, first of all, the usual error of assuming that all conduct is logical and that beliefs are products of reasoning. The fact is—they are dictated by sentiment. Implicit, secondly, is a conflict between the Religion of Progress in which Bentham believes and the "superstition" of authority that he combats. To adopt the superstition would be tantamount to renouncing every hope of progress for the peoples of Asia; and since such a thing is inconceivable, the superstition has to be rejected. That is one of the usual confusions between the question of the utility of a doctrine and its accord with experimental facts.

1436 [a] [And yet why not George Washington, as well as some other modern? For the phrase has no classical authority. Vegetius, *De re militari,* III, *proemium,* said, "*Qui desiderat pacem, praeparet bellum*"; and Cicero, *Philippicae,* VII, 6, 19, "*Si pace frui volumus bellum gerendum est.*"—A. L.]

those considerations were not operative there was plenty of admiration for Roosevelt's fatuous chatter. The feeling was that there was a man who was man enough to get himself elected to the presidency of the United States and to make a terrible noise in that office, and that therefore he must surely be competent in any matter relating to the historical and social sciences. It was the feeling also that a man who is competent in one thing is competent in everything; along with a sentiment of generic admiration, which prevents people from distinguishing the respects in which a man is competent from the respects in which he is not.[1]

In a day gone by the prestige of the poet intruded upon every field of human activity, in many cases with some slight logico-experimental justification, since the poet was often a scholar. That consideration no longer applies to the poets and *literati* of our time. Yet in many cases such men are reputed authorities in matters altogether stranger to them. Here is a Brieux, who "solves" some "social question" for us in every one of his dramatic productions. He "discovers" a thesis that has been a commonplace from times most ancient and in the footsteps of Plutarch and Rousseau solemnly tells mothers that they ought to suckle their children. That wins him loud applause from hosts of men and women of no great brains. Anatole France is a novelist of the very first rank, a great stylist, and a master of literary form. He has written in marvellous language novels distinguished for a keen psychological insight and sagacious irony. In all such connexions his authority is not to be disputed. And then, one fine day, he takes it into his head to extend that authority to matters about which he knows much less. He sets out to solve questions of politics, economics, religion, history: he becomes Dreyfusard, Socialist, theologian, historian; and people flock in throngs to him in all of those varied metamorphoses. The sentiment of authority re-enforced by political passions was so strong in his case that it resisted all proofs to a contrary in itself more plau-

---

1436 [1] The public attentions showered on Roosevelt were to a certain extent logical actions. It was believed at the time in Europe that Roosevelt would again be President of the United States, and the idea was to work for favours from him. Those calculations went amiss, however: Roosevelt was not re-elected. To counterbalance such fawning, the Pope refused to receive Roosevelt, a Genoese nobleman denied him entrance to his palace, and Maximilian Harden wrote an article lampooning German adulators of Roosevelt.

sible. Andrew Lang, in his time, called attention to the serious and astonishingly numerous errors that France's *Jeanne d'Arc* contains, some childish, some unintentional, and some that cannot, unfortunately, be called unintentional. In spite of everything the book still has hosts of admirers and enjoys not a little prestige.[2]

1437. The residue of veneration (§§ 1156 f., inferiors for superiors) often contributes to lending weight to assertions. The sentiment may show varying degrees of intensity, running from simple admiration to deification outright. It serves for purposes of deriva-

---

1436 [2] Andrew Lang, *La Jeanne d'Arc de M. Anatole France,* pp. 95-102, Chap. IX, *The Forest of Errors* [Lang's review was written in French and seems never to have appeared as such, in English. It contained material that Lang had already put forward against Anatole France in *The Maid of France, Being the Story of the Life and Death of Jeanne d'Arc,* London, 1908.—A. L.]: France states that "the tax imposed . . . upon the population of Domremy amounted to not less than £220 in gold." Lang informed France before the definitive publication of the *Jeanne d'Arc* that "for the tax to have reached such a sum, we should have to assume that Domremy had as large a population as Orléans. . . . I had already called M. France's attention to this error, but it has not been corrected in the revised edition. . . . M. France obstinately maintains that a certain young woman whose son was godson to Jeanne 'ridiculed her because of her devoutness,' mentioning the testimony of the woman as proof. Now there is not a suggestion of any such thing in the woman's testimony; and I am not alone in having called M. France's attention to that fact. That is how he bases his work on 'the most reliable sources,' to use the words of his new preface, and 'interpreting them with all the insight of a real scholar,' to believe his good-natured critic, M. Gabriel Monod!" Lang notes other errors of minor importance but which go to show that France took the writing of his book not overseriously: "In a short passage from the celebrated letter of Gerson, every sentence as translated by M. France becomes nonsense. A versified proverb of Dionysius Cato, *'Arbitrii nostri non est quod quisque loquatur,'* becomes in the book of M. France, 'Our arbiters are not what each one says.' Of the false rumours current regarding Jeanne, Gerson says, *'Si multi multa loquantur pro garrulitate sua et levitate aut dolositate aut alio sinistro favore vel odio. . . .'* M. France translates that as follows: 'If several witnesses have testified to Jeanne's garrulousness, and to her frivolousness and shrewdness . . .'! In the sentence next following Gerson alludes to the words of the Apostle, *'Non oportet servum Dei litigare,'* and M. France translates, 'It is not meet to involve the servant of God in this question.' " Noting another important error on France's part, Lang comments: "While M. France was finding in Dunois's testimony things that were not there, it was quite natural that he should fail to observe that D'Aulon was a member of the Royal Council and had been summoned by the King along with the other Councillors to pass on Jeanne's first petition—a thing that must surely strike us as altogether natural. But it is very regrettable that after his attention had been called to these points by the 'praiseworthy conscientiousness of Mr. Andrew Lang,' he should have allowed his fabrication to stand in his revised edition." Though Salomon Reinach shows himself very kindly disposed towards Anatole France, he is forced to admit the latter's errors: *Cultes, mythes et religions,* Vol. IV, pp. 311-12: "I am going to say at the

tion in all its forms, but in the higher reaches it often appears as authority of verbal or written tradition.[1]

1438. With derivations of this II-α type are to be classed many pseudo-experimental assertions that are current in all periods of history and are repeated parrotwise by everybody. Sometimes they carry a suggestion of proof in some more or less intelligent, some more or less accurate, attestation; but oftentimes again they are destitute of even that support, and keep afloat no one knows how, without a shadow of foundation, whether experimental or otherwise. Examples without end might be mentioned. Open any book of ancient times and one will soon be encountered, and the chances are just as good among modern writings. We have seen many specimens already. Let us look at just one more. St. Augustine, *De civitate Dei,* XXI, 2, sets out to prove against unbelievers that the torment of hell-fire will really be visited upon the damned. He has been met with the objection that it is incredible that flesh should burn on for ever without being destroyed, and that a soul should suffer so much without dying. That difficulty he meets with the rejoinder that things just as marvellous have happened and that they would be incredible if they were not certainly true; and he mentions a long list of them. We need not go into the major issue, the argument

outset that M. Lang is often right in his criticisms of M. France, though he is inclined to attach a great deal of importance to small matters." But he concedes, p. 320, that France did not rectify errors that had been called to his attention: "In spite of the improvements M. France has made, his book is still very inaccurate. Perhaps we ought to assume that M. France shared his labours with others, using what we call a *'nègre,'* and not a very trustworthy *'nègre.'* " As regards the Cato proverb in dispute between Lang and France, France should have remembered that in the *Distica Catonis,* a work well known and greatly admired in centuries past, the proverb reads, III, 2:

> "*Cum recte vivas ne cures verba malorum:*
> *arbitrii non est nostri quid quisque loquatur.*"

("So long as you live rightly, give no thought to the words of the malicious. It is not within our power to control what people say.")

1437 [1] Maimbourg, *Histoire de l'Arianisme,* Vol. I, pp. 17-18: "I am well aware that one is not always obliged to believe in the extraordinary things called visions, especially when they are not vouched for by some celebrated author whose name is in itself genuine proof. But I am also not unaware that history, leaving us full liberty to believe what we will, cannot without excessive meticulousness (*délicatesse*) and without a certain meanness of spirit suppress visions that have been accepted as true for ages and ages and by people whom one could not accuse of frailty without losing one's own reputation."

being utterly fatuous on both sides. The question of the reality of hell-fire transcends the possibilities of experimental verification and experimental science can therefore in no way discuss it. But it is a very curious thing that nearly all the examples mentioned by the Saint are imaginary; so much so that had his own argument been made by an adversary, one might suppose that the intention was to disprove the miracles which the Saint thinks he is proving. Using the very same "facts," one might say to the Saint: "We accept your challenge: we grant that the miracles you speak of are as true as the wonders with which you compare them. But, alas, these too are false!" For one of the wonders in question, the allegation that the flesh of the peacock never rots, there is a pseudo-experimental basis. In the other cases the proof is by derivations based on authority.

The Saint, in all that, is a predecessor of our present-day worshippers of the goddess Science. He says that he believes only what is proved by the facts, so denying credence to pagan mythology. In our day, the convinced Positivist-Humanitarian asserts in his turn that he believes only what is proved by the facts and refuses credence to Christian mythology. Unfortunately, however, in the one case as in the other, the facts are pseudo-experimental and nothing more.

After all, some slight doubt as to the "facts" creeps into St. Augustine's mind, a thing that seems never to happen with our worshippers of democracy and humanitarianism. God's omnipotence is, at bottom, the best proof of miracles for St. Augustine. And in that he is right; for in taking the question out of the logico-experimental field, he avoids the objections of logico-experimental science, which, however, retain their full vigour against anyone who obstinately insists on remaining in that field.[1][2][3][4] (For footnotes 2-4 see pages 912-913.)

1438 [1] To begin with, the Saint asserts that he will take his stand in the experimental field: "Unbelievers will not allow us to ascribe this thing to the power of the Almighty, but challenge us to persuade them by some example." He undertakes to do so; but unluckily the unbelievers are such obstinate and perverse creatures that they demand proofs even of his new assertions: "We might tell them that there are animals which are certainly corruptible because mortal, yet which nevertheless remain alive in fire. We might tell them that a species of worm is to be found in hot springs which are so hot that nobody can touch the water without harm— whereas the worms not only live there without damage but cannot live anywhere else. But even if we told them such things they would not believe them unless we were able to produce them before their eyes [Unreasonable creatures!]; or if we were able to produce them or to prove them by trustworthy witnesses, they would

1439. The residue of authority comes down in derivations across the centuries without losing any of its vigour. After a talk in our day with an admirer of Eusapia Paladino, or Cesare Lombroso, or William James, one can only admit that it is as strong now as it ever

still not budge from their unbelief, but contend that anyhow such animals do not live for ever and that the heat occasions them no suffering." If such an objection was really raised, the Saint was right in rejecting it. But the existence of the animals still remains to be proved! Authority comes to the Saint's rescue: "According to writers who have investigated the nature of animals with the greatest care, the salamander lives in fire." And if a soul can suffer without perishing, lost souls can really suffer in hell-fire eternally. Then there is the fact that God can endow flesh with a capacity for not being consumed by fire, for he has made the flesh of the peacock immune to decay. On that point the Saint had made an experiment himself. He had set aside a piece of peacock's breast that had been cooked. After a long enough time for any other cooked meat to have rotted, the peacock's breast was brought to him. His sense of smell was in no way offended. Thirty days later it was found in the same condition, and so again after a year, except that by that time it was rather dry and shrivelled—*"nisi quod aliquantum corpulentiae siccioris et contractioris fuit."* Another marvel is the diamond, which resists iron and fire and any other force except ram's blood. When a diamond is set beside a loadstone the latter no longer attracts iron. But the unbelievers still stand adamant and will have the reasons for the miraculous things described by the Saint: "But when we assert divine miracles past or future and are unable to demonstrate them tangibly (*experienda*) before their eyes, the unbelievers insist on our explaining the reasons for them; and since we are unable to do that, surpassing as they do the powers of the human mind, they conclude that what we say is false. But in that case suppose they try themselves to account for all the wondrous things that we see or may see if we choose." So far the Saint is right. The fact that we do not know the cause of a thing proves nothing as to its reality. But the existence of the thing still has to be proved by direct observation. That is where St. Augustine falls short. Nearly all the things he represents as authentic facts are purely fantastic: 1. When the salt of Agrigentum (Sicily) is thrown into fire it melts as in water. In water it crackles as in fire. Pliny's account, *Historia naturalis,* XXXI, 41, 2 (Bostock-Riley, Vol. V, p. 505), is somewhat different: *"Agrigentinus ignium patiens ex aqua exsilet"* (resistant to fire it effervesces in water).   2. In the Garamantian district (Africa) there is a spring where the water is so cold by day that it cannot be drunk, and so hot by night that it cannot be touched. And *cf.* Pliny, *Ibid.,* V, 5, 6 (Bostock-Riley, Vol. I, p. 399): "At Debris there is a spring in which the water is boiling hot between noon and midnight and freezing cold for the same length of time from midnight till midday."   3. There is another spring in Epirus where, as is usual with other springs, a burning torch will go out if it is dipped in the water; but, as is not usual with other springs, an unlighted torch can be lighted by dipping it in the water. And *cf.* Pomponius Mela, *De situ orbis,* II, 3, 5; and Pliny, *Ibid.,* II, 106 (Bostock-Riley, Vol. I, p. 133). Lucretius tries to explain something very similar in *De rerum natura,* VI, vv. 880-89.   4. Asbestos is a stone found in Arcady. It is so called because once set on fire it can never more be extinguished. Pliny, *Ibid.,* XXXVII, 54 (Bostock-Riley, Vol. VI, p. 442), notes simply that it is a stone from Arcady. Solinus, *Polyhistor,* VII, 13 (Leipzig, pp. 74-75), says the same and adds: *"accensus semel*

was in the day when Lucian wrote his "Lover of Lies." Nor are the fabulous wonders that Lucian ridicules so very different from those current today, and in Lucian's time, as in ours, they were justified on the authority of people who were reputed to be intelligent and responsible. Long before Lombroso and William James ever prom-

extingui nequit." 5. The wood of a certain fig-tree in Egypt does not float in water: it sinks to the bottom, and then, after a certain time, it returns to the surface again. *Cf.* Pliny, *Op. cit.,* XIII, 14 (7) (Bostock-Riley, Vol. III, pp. 180-81). 6. In the Sodom district there are certain fruits that if touched with lips or hand, seeming to be ripe, vanish into smoke and ashes. *Cf.* Josephus, *De bello Judaico,* IV, 8, 4 (27) (*Opera,* Vol. V, p. 371; Whitson, Vol. V, p. 315). 7. In Persia there is a stone that catches fire if it is pressed hard between the hands. For that reason it is called "pyritis." *Cf.* Solinus, *Op. cit.,* XXXVII, 16 (Leipzig, p. 227); Pliny, XXXVII, 73 (Bostock-Riley, Vol. VI, p. 460): "Pyritis, though a black stone, burns the fingers when rubbed by them." 8. Also in Persia is a stone called "selenite." It has an inner brilliancy that waxes and wanes with the Moon. *Cf.* Pliny, *Op. cit.,* XXXVII, 67, 1 (Bostock-Riley, Vol. VI, p. 456): "Selenitis is white and transparent with a reflected colour like that of honey." 9. In Cappacodia mares are fertilized by the wind, but their foals live not more than three years. (*Cf.* § 927 [8].) 10. The island of Tilon in the Indies is blessed above all others, because the trees there do not lose their foliage. This last statement is the only one of the list that has the slightest probability of being true, provided it be taken as applying not just to one island but to all the tropics.

1438 [2 3] The Saint continues: "Hosts of things are recorded in books [Explicit derivations of authority.] not as having been done and then having passed away, but as still existing in their various localities, so that if anyone were minded and able to go there, he could see for himself whether they be true." There the derivation of authority is implicit. To say that anyone might go and see whether such wonderful things were true is equivalent, in that context, to saying that "it was believed" that such a verification was possible. As a matter of fact, a person actually going on such a mission could not possibly have verified facts that were not facts. But the obstinate unbelievers lay a trap for the Saint as regards the written record: "To this, perhaps, they will straightway answer that these wonders do not exist, that they do not believe in them, that those who have spoken and written of them have spoken and written falsely; and they argue that if such things are to be believed then one ought also to believe the other things that are described in those same books, such as the story that there was, or is, a certain temple to Venus where one may see a candelabrum with a lamp standing out in the weather, but which no storm, no rain, can extinguish." In that argument the Saint's critics were trying to place him in the dilemma either of denying the miracle of Venus and so discrediting the evidence he had adduced in behalf of his own wonders, or of admitting the existence of the gods of paganism. But he wriggles free by pointing out that he is not obliged to believe everything the heathen writers say: *"non habemus necesse omnia credere quae continet historia gentium";* for, as Varro notes, they are at variance with one another on many points. We believe, he says, the things that they do not dispute (*"quae non adversantur libris"*) and which we can prove by

ised to return after death and communicate with their friends, the wife of Euchrates had returned from the other world to have a talk with her husband. The philosopher Arignotus tells of even more marvellous things, and the incredulous Tychiades, betraying the fact that he does not take overmuch stock in them, is adjudged a man

good witnesses. He does not name his witnesses, however, any more than the worshippers of the modern goddess Science name theirs when they assert the equality or solidarity of all men. The Saint now resumes the offensive. With the miracle of the lamp of Venus he associates the many miracles of magic, which cannot be denied without offence to the authority of Holy Writ: "Either the lamp in question is devised by human art, with asbestos; or what is seen in the temple is the work of magic; or else a demon, going under the name of Venus, has wrought with such efficacy that this prodigy has been made manifest before all men and has endured." And he concludes that if magicians can do that much, we should be all the more ready to believe that God, who is so much more powerful than any magician, can work greater wonders still: *"quanto magis Deus potens est facere quae infidelibus sunt incredibilia sed illius facilia potestati"*—since He was the creator of that stone (asbestos) and of the virtues of other things, of the intelligence of the men who use such virtues in wondrous ways and of the angelic natures, which are far more powerful than all earthly creatures. But that is all a reasoning in a circle, a manner of thinking seldom missing in concrete derivations of the Augustinian type. To offer the testimony of the Scriptures to people who deny their authority, the miracles of a devil Venus to people who deny miracles, the might of the Christian God to people who deny His existence, is to take the conclusion of one's arguments for the premise.

1438 [4] As for St. Augustine's doubts: "I do not ask that these facts which I have mentioned be accepted out of hand (*temere*) as true. I do not believe them myself to the extent that no doubt whatever is left in my mind, except as to those things which I have experienced myself or which it would be easy for anyone to verify." An excellent resolve, to which unfortunately the Saint does not remain very faithful! In addition to wonders that are only partially true, he takes exception to two of the less credible marvels, the story about lighting the torch in the spring in Epirus, and the story about the fruit at Sodom. As for the spring in Epirus he confesses that he had known no eyewitnesses; but he had met people who had seen a similar spring at Gratianopolis (Grenoble). "As for the fruit-trees of Sodom, not only are they vouched for by books altogether trustworthy, but so many writers speak of them of their own experience that I cannot doubt them." Interesting the Saint's way of giving and taking back at the same time, a common device in many such derivations. It arises from the need of influencing sentiments, disregarding contradictions, which would become apparent enough in a logico-experimental argument. St. Augustine begins by representing his wonders as facts. He says indeed that anyone who chooses may verify them, and in the matter of the diamond he calls the jewellers of his city to witness. Then, when the effect of that has sunk in, he ventures a certain amount of doubt that he may save both the goat and the cabbages. So nowadays worshippers of solidarity begin by pointing to a solidarity-fact: and then when that has done its work, they deign to admit that their solidarity-fact is the opposite of their solidarity-duty (§ 450 [1]).

of poor sense in not deferring to such authority.[1] To find similar comments one has only to dip at random into any one of the many books that deal with marvellous occurrences.[2]

1440. Such beliefs still exist in our day. Many people believe in cures by prayer (§ 1695[2]). A great many live in holy fear of our hygienists, who are modern saints defending wretched mortals from the evil machinations of demons now become microbes. A text-book on morals (!) in use in public schools in France teaches that "to be in good health one must never touch alcohol or alcoholic beverages. One must never swallow a single drop of brandy, cordial, absinthe,

1439 [1] Lucian, *Philopseudes*, 17, 32 (Harmon, Vol. III, pp. 347, 369)—the incredulous Tychiades speaking ironically: "Oh, I said, how could I fail to believe Euchrates, son of Deinon, a man of sober years, who discourses with authority on any subject that happens to interest him—in his own house. . . . When Arignotus, a famous, nay an inspired, sage, began telling such tales, there was not one in the company who did not call me a lunatic because I took no stock in them. Imagine! Things vouched for by Arignotus! But I, without that much respect for his shaggy locks and great renown, I cried: 'O Arignotus, so you too—you promise us truth, and feed us prattle! You make the proverb come true, "We seek a treasure and ashes we find."' 'Very well,' answered Arignotus, 'if you believe not my words, nor Dinomachus, nor Cleodemus, nor Euchrates himself, come, tell us of a man of greater authority to gainsay what we have just said.' And I, 'Yes, by Jove, and a wonderful man—Democritus of Abdera!'"

1439 [2] Mentioning numberless cases where human beings had turned into wolves and then back into men again, Bodin expresses his astonishment that anyone could doubt a thing enjoying such universal consensus: *De la démonomanie*, II, 6 (Paris, f. 99; Frankfurt, pp. 239-40): "We read further in the history of Johann Tritheim that in the year 970 there was a Jew by the name of Baian, son of Simeon, who could turn into a wolf whenever he chose and also make himself invisible. Now that is a very strange thing, but I find it stranger still that there should be people who do not believe it, seeing that all the peoples on earth and all antiquity stand in agreement in the matter. Not only did Herodotus write of it 2,200 years ago [*Historiae*, IV, 105], and 400 years before the time of Homer, but there is Pomponius Mela [*De situ orbis*, II, 1, 13], there is Solinus, there is Strabo, not to mention Dionysius Afer, Marcus Varro, Virgil, Ovid, and countless others." Father Le Brun, *Histoire critique des pratiques superstitieuses*, Vol. I, p. 118, tries to steer a middle course. One ought not, certainly, believe everything, but "obstinacy in unbelief ordinarily comes of an excessive pride that inclines one to esteem oneself higher than the most respectable authorities and to prefer one's own lights to the wisdom of the greatest men and most judicious philosophers." Following just such principles Don Calmet remarks, *Dissertations sur les apparitions*, p. 63, that "Plutarch, a man of recognized seriousness and wisdom, often speaks of spectres and apparitions. He says, for instance [*Theseus*, 35], that at the famous battle of Marathon, against the Persians, several soldiers saw the shade of Theseus fighting with the Greeks against their enemies."

or apéritif." [1] There is no reason to suppose that the author of the text-book did not believe precisely what he says—otherwise the example would be truly deplorable in a text-book on "morals"! He believes—and his reader must believe by virtue of his authority—that to swallow "a single drop of brandy or cordial" will impair one's health. It is a very easy matter to test the assertion and see whether it be true that after drinking *a single drop* of liquor one feels that one's health has been impaired. In that case as in many others it will be apparent that experience gives the lie to the authority. But there is better yet. A certain individual declares as a fact of experience that if a man is a drinker his daughter will lose her ability to suckle a child and that that capacity is forever lost to succeeding generations. In this case the substitution of authority for experience is brazen and belies itself. To show experimentally that the capacity for nursing a child is lost forever to succeeding generations, the generations must, obviously, have been examined for a number of centuries at least. And how is that possible? Where are the statistics of centuries now past to show whether a man was or was not a drinker, or that the women descended from him were or were not able to suckle children? Let alone the fact that if what the gentleman in question says were true no wine-growing country would show a single woman able to nurse a child! A pair of eyes and a walk through such a district are all that is required to be convinced of the contrary. [2]

1440 [1] Bayet, *Leçons de morale,* p. 33, a text-book in the Aulard *Collection.* The Aulard in question is the same gentleman who rebuked Taine for insufficient scholarship and accuracy. It should be noted that a bill for "the defence of the lay school" recently brought before the Chamber of Deputies proposes a penalty for anyone daring to influence minors in the direction of disbelief in such fine doctrines.

1440 [2] For the hereditary effects of alcohol on mother's milk, see *Journal de Genève,* Apr. 29, 1909: "In collaboration with more than a hundred physicians from Switzerland and abroad [There you have the authority that requires deference from everybody.], he has studied 2,051 families. On the basis of very considerable data he concludes as follows: 'When the father is a drinker, the daughter loses her capacity to nurse a child and that capacity is irremediably lost for the following generations. [This gentleman may know little enough about the past, but he has learned all about the future—probably through some trance medium.] So with moderate drinkers (less than one litre of wine or two litres of beer *per diem*), the alcoholization of the father is the main cause of the woman's inability to nurse her children.'" There must be mighty few women in Germany who are able to nurse their children; for few the men in that country who do not drink as much as two litres of beer a day. As usual derivations serve equally well to demonstrate the pro

1441. And here is another gentleman who says—and he finds people to believe him—that a pint of wine or a quart of beer will diminish capacity for mental work by from 25 to 40 per cent. If that were true, German universities, where professors and students regularly drink more than that amount of beer or wine, would show a very small capacity for mental work. Abel, the great mathematician, actually abused alcoholic beverages. He should have turned out an idiot—but it is very hard to notice it. Bismarck, too, should have had a microscopic capacity for mental work.[1][2] (For footnote 2 see page 917.)

1442. Many of the believers in this modern Prohibitionist religion are bitterest enemies of the Catholic Church and ridicule its miracles, not observing that their own miracles are as miraculous as the Catholic, and that if belief in both sorts of miracles is dictated by sentiment it has, after all, its justification in authority. But there is a difference, and it is not in favour of the Prohibitionists. There is no means available today for proving by experiment that a miracle that took place ages ago was false. Whereas anyone can perform experiments or make observations to prove the falsity of the miracles of our present-day Prohibitionists.

1443. The residue of authority also appears in the devices that are called into play to discredit it. That fact is apparent enough in almost any quarrel on theological, moral, or political questions.

and the contra. When the idea is to induce mothers to nurse their own children, the argument changes, and complaisant statistics show just as convincingly that mothers are, or are not, able to supply their young with milk. *Ibid.*, Oct. 27, 1910: "Mlle. Louise Hedwige Kettler has observed some 1,700 maternity cases and reached many interesting conclusions. . . . Absolute inability on a mother's part to nurse her child must be considered very rare. 93.42 per cent of the mothers observed by Mlle. Kettler over a three years' period were able to attend to that duty. Physical causes preventive of such nursing are on the whole not very numerous. Mothers should look out. In their resorting to artificial feeding there is risk of their rearing a generation of women unable to nurse their children." One needs only a superficial acquaintance with Geneva to be certain that 93 per cent of the women in that town are not daughters of parents who drink neither wine nor other alcoholic beverages. But in the logic of derivations two contradictory propositions may be true at one and the same time.

1441 [1] The report of a lecture by a Geneva physician in the *Journal de Genève:* "With painstaking documentation and taking into account researches conducted at the Heidelberg School . . . Dr. Audéaud showed that the amount of alcohol contained in about half a litre of wine or two litres of beer was enough to diminish capacity for mental work by from 25 to 40 per cent. The falling-off is due to the paralyzing, stupefying effects of alcohol. They are observable for several days after

1444. From the logico-experimental standpoint the soundness of the proposition $A = B$ is independent of the moral qualities of the person who asserts it. Suppose tomorrow it should be discovered that Euclid was a murderer, a thief, in short the worst man that ever lived. Would such a thing in the remotest degree affect the validity of the proofs in his geometry?

1445. Not so, however, from the standpoint of authority. If the statement $A = B$ is accepted only in view of the authority of the individual who asserts it, anything that discredits that authority will also discredit the proof that $A = B$. One of the tricks of the debater, furthermore, is to locate in the field of authority a proposition that properly belongs in the logico-experimental field.

1446. For the very reason that they have no logico-experimental force such devices lose their effectiveness when they are used too freely. We know in our late day that when one theologian says of another that he is a rogue and ought to be in jail, all it means is that the two men have different opinions. When a newspaper calls a man in public life a malefactor, it means simply that the paper has reasons of personal or partisan interest for combating him, or even a different opinion. That method of discrediting authority may be an utter failure in politics at the present time.

the absorption of the poison. . . . Dr. Audéaud's results are the fruit of long years of laborious experiment and careful observations."

1441 [2] On Bismarck and alcohol see Busch, *Tagebuchblätter,* Vol. I, p. 68 (English, Vol. I, p. 58), Aug. 12, 1870: "Cognac, Bordeaux, and a light sparkling wine from Mainz stood on the table. Someone mourned the absence of beer. 'No harm!' cried Bismarck. 'Too much beer-drinking is deplorable from every point of view. It makes one stupid, lazy, good for nothing. Beer is responsible for all these democratic idiocies that are being passed around the tables in the cabarets. Take my word for it, a good rye-whiskey does much less harm.' " *Ibid.,* Vol. III, p. 280 (English, Vol. II, p. 519), Mar. 22, 1890: On his fall from power, Bismarck retires to Friedrichsruh and commissions Busch to move his effects thither: " 'There,' he said, 'are my maps. Put the letters inside and roll them up. . . . They will go along in the moving van with the other things. I have some three hundred trunks or boxes and more than thirteen thousand bottles of wine.' He told me he had a lot of fine sherry that he had bought when he was rich." Palamenghi-Crispi, *Carteggio di Francesco Crispi,* p. 446: "*Otto von Bismarck to Crispi,* Friedrichsruh, Jan. 7, 1890: 'Dear Friend and Colleague: I was deeply touched by the new proof of your friendship on learning that you have shipped to me a case of your splendid Italian wine. I appreciate it all the more since the high quality of last year's vintage leads me to look forward to all that it will be. A good wine is never without its influence on the quality of the drinker's statesmanship.' " Poor Bismarck! What a pauper in capacity for mental work he must have been!

1447. II-β: *Authority of tradition, usages, and customs.* Such authority may be verbal, written, anonymous, of a real or a legendary person. In such derivations residues of group-persistence play an important part. In view of them, "the wisdom of the forefathers" in a day gone by, the "traditions of the party" in our time, take on an independent existence of their own. Derivations by authority of tradition are exceedingly numerous. No city or nation but has its traditions. Even particular societies cannot do without them. They play an important rôle in all social life. To explain a thing by tradition is a very easy matter; for among the many legends that exist or can be invented if necessary one can readily be found that, in view of some resemblance more or less distant, some accord of sentiments more or less vague, can be made to fit the thing for which an "explanation" is sought.[1]

1448. Custom is at times indistinguishable from tradition; and not infrequently the person observing a given custom can give no other reason for his conduct than the fact that "that is what people do."

1449. Traditions may come to constitute independent residues (§ 877), and if these are at all powerful the society becomes, as it were, crystallized and rebuffs virtually everything new. But tradi-

---

1447 [1] Of that type are derivations 4, 5, 6, and 7 in the following example from Ovid, *Fasti,* IV, vv. 783-806. We saw in § 1266 [4] that Ovid is there describing the purification rites that were practised during the feast of the Palilia. He sets out to find their "origins," to "explain" them—in other words, he goes looking for derivations, and he finds no less than seven: 1. Fire purifies everything. 2. Water and fire are the opposite principles that constitute all things. 3. Those elements are the principles of life. 4. The fire and the lustral water commemorate respectively the adventure of Phaeton and Deucalion's flood. 5. Shepherds discovered fire with flint. 6. Aeneas ran through flames in his flight and they did him no harm. 7. In memory of the foundation of Rome when the hovels in which the Romans had lived up to that time were burned. This last is the explanation that Ovid himself prefers. The first three derivations derive their persuasiveness from certain metaphysical sentiments (III-ϵ); the last four, from tradition (II-β). Obviously still other derivations of the kind might be found—they are the variable element in the phenomenon. The need of purification (residues V-γ, restoration of integrity) and the instinct of combinations (residues Class I) are the constant element, and it is the more important one, the variable element deriving from it. Note further that within the constant element the need of purification, of restoring integrity, is the main thing, the combinations designed to satisfy it being secondary. So we get as a whole: 1. Residues made up of, *a,* main residues (purification) and, *b,* secondary residues (combinations). 2. Derivations designed to explain the sum of residues as a whole, and which, in general, aim at "explaining" the secondary residues, *b.*

tions are often mere derivations, and in that case the society can innovate little or much, and even in opposition to the substance of the tradition, the accord persisting in mere forms. That has been the case with many sects of Christianity.

1450. Derivations, as we have repeatedly remarked, are on the whole flexible, and derivations by tradition present that trait to a very conspicuous degree. In the book that creates a tradition one can find anything one pleases. The Greeks found everything imaginable in Homer, and the Latins, in Virgil. So Italians today find many things in Dante. The case of the Bible and the Gospels is truly remarkable. What has not been found in those books would be hard to imagine. Different and even contradictory doctrines have been based on them in vast numbers; and they furnish proofs for and against with equal ease.

1451. Of course every sect is convinced that it has the one "true" interpretation and scornfully rejects every other. But that sort of "truth" has nothing to do with experimental truth, and there is no standard of reference to help decide who is right. In such disputes there are advocates in plenty but no judges (§ 9).

1452. It may be determined, experimentally, that this or that interpretation departs from literal meanings. But the person of "living faith" is not worried by that. He disregards the literal sense quite deliberately. If the Song of Songs were part of some book other than the Bible, everybody would take it as a matter of course for a love-poem (§ 1627). Faith sees something else in it; and since it takes its stand outside experience, no objection can be raised against it by anyone electing to remain inside that field.

1453. So long as tradition serves merely for purposes of derivation, criticism of it has but slight effect on the social equilibrium. One could not go so far as to put it at zero, but, saving some rare exception, it is never very great.

1454. From the eighteenth century on the Bible has been attacked with a formidable artillery of science, scholarship, and historical criticism. It has been shown very convincingly that no end of passages in the book cannot possibly be taken in their literal senses. The unity of the Bible has been demolished, and in place of the magnificent edifice so greatly admired of yore only formless heaps of literary materials are left. And yet, reverence for the Bible has in no sense diminished, nor are believers any the fewer—they are still to be counted by the millions and millions; and then there are people who criticize the Bible as history but otherwise fall on their knees before it and worship it. Derivations change, residues endure.[1]

1455. Numbers of good souls in our time have imagined that they could destroy Christianity by proving the historical unreality of Jesus. They have made many fine holes in the water. They do not observe that their disquisitions never get beyond a very small circle of scholars, never reach the public at large, nor even the majority of believers. Ordinarily they persuade people who are already persuaded.

1456. So there have been people to imagine that by proving that Joan of Arc was a hysteric or a lunatic, they could destroy Catholic patriotism in France and so contribute to the stability of M. Clemenceau's *bloc* and the Radical-Socialist régime. They caught the ear only of the public that was already of their opinion. Far from dimin-

---

1454 [1] Gautier's *Introduction à l'Ancien Testament* is a book rich in learning and historical criticism. Now in his "conclusion," Vol. II, p. 507, he is replying to critics who have censured him on one point or another: "I wish finally to deal with one last notion that is continually recurring in the dispute now raging: [Higher] criticism, it is held, 'is attacking and ruining the authority of Scripture.' I have already had occasion to say that it is important before anything else to understand what one means by the word 'authority.' If one means external authority [A euphemism for objective statements.], the charge mentioned is well founded; but if the authority is of the domain of the inner life, of the spiritual order [Euphemism for subjective propositions. That language helps to conceal the *petitio principii* involved in the believer's believing in the Bible only what he reads into it, only what is already in his own mind.], one may baldly assert that the authority of the Bible is in no way compromised. [Quite so! A tautology is never false.] Everything depends on our being clear on one fundamental point, that the authority in religious matters is the authority of God, and in the more special sphere of evangelical truth, the authority of Christ. [Quite so! But now we must be shown how those two wills are to be recognized: if by criteria extrinsic to us, they may be independent of anything we think or say; if only by criteria intrinsic to us, we are merely baptizing our wills with the name of divine will.] That authority is exercised upon heart and conscience, though at the same time appealing to the whole sum of our faculties in virtue of the very unity of our being. It is something quite above discussions of a literary or historical order. It can neither be shaken nor consolidated by purely intellectual arguments. [Quite so, but only in the sense that residues are independent of logic. But we still have to be shown that they are "divine." And what if there were one or two "diabolical" ones among them, as certain heretics claim?] It is in no way affected by the fact that on problems of authenticity or historical exactitude solutions are reached which are at variance with traditional views."

ishing the admiration of their adversaries for Joan of Arc, they have helped to increase it.[1]

1457. Books that are viewed with reverence often end by acquiring mysterious powers and being used for purposes of magic. That has been the case with the Bible, with the poems of Virgil, and other books still.

1458. II-γ: *Authority of divine beings, or personifications.* If one were to keep strictly to substance, derivations of this variety would be classed with derivations by tradition, since really the will of a divine being or of a personification can be known only through human beings and by way of traditions. But looking at forms, the introduction of supernatural forces is important enough to merit classification by itself. The interposition of a deity gives rise to three different types of derivation: 1. Once the will of the deity is assumed to be known, a person may obey it out of simple reverence for the deity, without splitting hairs very finely as to the reasons for his conduct or, at the most, adding some few words on one's duty to respect it. That gives our present variety, II-γ. 2. Or a person may obey the divine will out of fear of some punishment that threatens transgressors of divine commandments. There individual interest comes in, and we get actions that are logical consequences of the premise. In cases where individual interest is replaced or supplemented by the community interest, derivations of that sort belong to our III-β (individual interest), or III-γ (collective interest) varieties. Or, finally, a person may accommodate his conduct to the divine will out of love for the deity, from a desire to act in accord with sentiments that the deity is assumed to feel, or on the belief that such conformity in itself and regardless of its consequences is good, praiseworthy, a matter of duty. That yields derivations of our III-ζ type (accord with supernatural entities).

1459. As we have repeatedly observed, in analyzing a thing we distinguish in the abstract elements that stand combined in the syn-

---

1456 [1] The importance that "free-thinking" worshippers of the goddess Science attach to the matter of Joan of Arc is something extraordinary. Needless to say, to those who believe in the divine mission of the Maid, as well as to those who make her a saint of the patriotic religion, every detail of her life is of the greatest interest. For the strict followers of experimental science, Joan of Arc is a historical figure like any other, and the problems raised in connexion with the minuter details of her life are of very scant significance.

thesis of the concrete. Concrete derivations in which a supernatural being figures very very often combine the first two types just mentioned, and in such a way indeed that it is difficult to distinguish them. Often also they bring in the third type; but that is already on the road to metaphysics and is more commonly the case with thinkers. Many individuals have a complex feeling of reverence, fear, and love for the supernatural being and they themselves would not be able to analyze it into simpler elements. Catholic controversies with regard to "contrition" and "attrition" are not unrelated to such distinctions as we have just been making between varieties of derivations.[1]

1459 [1] St. Thomas, *Summa theologiae, Supplementum, qu. 1, art.* 3 (*Opera,* Vol. XII, *Suppl.,* p. 4): "The principle of attrition is servile fear, but of contrition filial fear." *Canones et decreta Concilii Tridentini, sessio* XIV, 4 (Richter, p. 77; Schaff, Vol. II, pp. 144-46): "Contrition . . . is the sorrow and detestation of the soul for the sin that has been committed, accompanied by a resolve not to sin again. . . . But as regards that imperfect contrition which is called attrition, since it is commonly conceived either in consideration of the disgrace (*turpitudinis*) of sin or in fear of punishment in the other world, it [the Council] declares that if it precludes the desire to sin through hope of [God's] forgiveness it not only does not make man a hypocrite and a greater sinner but is a gift of God and an impulse from the Holy Spirit . . . with the help of which the penitent opens a way for himself to holiness (*justitia*)." Gury, *Casus conscientiae,* Vol. II, pp. 182-83: "Confession finished, Albert is asked by his confessor just why he feels sorry for his sins. The penitent answers: 'I am sorry for my sins because I am afraid that God will punish me in this life with tribulations or sudden death, and in the life to come with eternal torments.' 'Tell me, child,' says the confessor, 'was that the reason why you were sorry for your sins heretofore when you came to confession?' Albert nods. Whereupon the confessor adjudges those confessions invalid as wanting in divine love and inspired by nothing but fear. . . . Whence our Question I: *As to whether attrition be sufficient.* . . . And the answer is: Attrition is sufficient, and perfect contrition is not required for justification in the sacrament of penance." Ménage, *Ménagiana,* Vol. IV, p. 157: "M. Boileau Despréaux was calling one day on the late First President [Chief Justice] at Basville. Some casuists [Jesuits] were there, and they were vigorously contending that a certain well-known author had been right in publishing a whole book for the sole purpose of showing that we were not obliged to love God and that those who held the contrary were thrusting an unbearable yoke upon the Christian of which God had freed him by the new dispensation. The argument was waxing warm when M. Despréaux, who had so far said not a word, exclaimed, rising to take his leave: 'What a thought! So on the day of the Last Judgment Our Lord will say to the elect: "Come, you beloved of my Father, for you have loved me not. Always have you kept others from loving me, and always have you dealt roundly with those heretics who would have obliged all Christians to love me. But you, O accursed of my Father, get you into the outer darkness, for you have loved me with all your heart and you have begged and encouraged all others to love me." ' " And *cf.* Boileau, *Épitres,* XII, *Sur l'amour de Dieu.*

1460. In all three of these types of derivations it is important to observe the ways in which the divine will is supposed to be known or the accord with the deity's sentiments determined. Barring some few exceptions, they are generally simple in the first two types and much more complex in the third. The ancient science of divination had a special branch devoted to discovering the will of the gods.

1461. An abstract entity may sometimes provoke derivations of the type proper to a divine being. That is the case when, in virtue of residues of group-persistence, the abstraction is acquiring definite personality—is, so to say, a deity in the making.

1462. The derivation that appeals to the alleged will or sentiment of a supernatural being is the more persuasive, the stronger the residue corresponding to that being. The way in which the will or sentiments come to be known is quite secondary. There is always some expedient for making the deity will whatever the petitioner has most at heart (§ 1454 [1]). People often imagine that they act in one way or another in deference to the will of some supernatural being. Really they invent such a will as a result of their acting in that way. "It is God's will" (*"Dieu le veut"*), cried the Crusaders of old. Really they were under the sway of a migratory instinct such as the ancient Germans felt—a longing for adventure, a passion for something new, weariness with an orderly humdrum life, eagerness for easy money. If swallows could talk, they too might just as well say that they change climes twice a year in obedience to the divine will. In our day certain individuals appropriate the goods of other individuals, or aid and abet those who do, in obedience, they say, to the "laws of Progress," "Science," "Truth." Their real inspiration is a very natural hankering for the property in question or for the goodwill of those who are appropriating it. A new divinity has of late been enthroned on the Olympus of "Progress." It has been given the name of "Vital Interests" and it presides over international relations. In barbarous ages one people made war upon another, sacked its cities, and carried off what loot it could without any great palaver. In our day the same thing is done, but always in the name of "Vital Interests," and the new way represents, it is said, a great improvement in civilization. To the layman in such matters, the brigandage of European countries in China may seem no whit different from the raids of Attila upon the Roman Empire. But experts in the casuistry of derivations can see offhand that there is a world of difference between the two. So far "Vital Interests" has made few converts among footpads and other exponents of private initiative in brigandage. They are satisfied with a humbler divinity, and justify their exploits by saying that they are trying "to live their own lives." [1]

1463. Sometimes the complex derivation ends by acquiring independent status and comes to constitute a residue (§ 882) or else a simple derivation of the II-γ type here in hand. That is often the case with abstractions which are deified but not personified—a circumstance that prevents their being credited too explicitly with a personal will, so that they have to be satisfied with some "imperative" or other. Examples are abundant in all periods of history—there is a very interesting one in our own. The automobile enjoys the protection of Progress (which is a god, or what amounts to that) very much as the screech-owl enjoyed the protection of the goddess Athena in ancient Athens. Worshippers of the god Progress have to respect automobiles just as Athenians had to respect screech-owls. If in our day of triumphant democracy the automobile did not enjoy the protection of the god Progress, it would be proscribed. It is used chiefly by people of wealth, or at least by people in comfortable circumstances. It kills many children and not a few adults

1462 [1] For the comparison between the Crusaders and the ancient Germans, see Tacitus, *Germania*, 14: "If their home tribe (*civitas*) grows humdrum (*torpeat*) through a long period of peace and inactivity, not a few nobles and young men move on to other tribes which are at the time engaged in some war or other." Michaud, *Histoire des croisades*, 1877 ed., Vol. I, p. 28 (Robson, Vol. I, pp. 54-56): "Certainty of impunity, hope of a better lot, licentious hankerings and yearning for relief from most sacred burdens, attracted multitudes to the standards of the Crusade. Personal ambitions were not altogether stranger to their devotion to the cause of the Lord Jesus. If religion held out its rewards to those who went to fight in its behalf, fortune also promised worldly wealth and power [To such as were knights.]. Crusaders returning from the East spoke in glowing terms of the wonders they had seen, of the rich countries they had visited. It was generally known that two or three hundred Norman pilgrims had conquered Apulia and Sicily from the Saracens. . . . Robert of Friesland, second son to the Count of Flanders and therefore destined not to share in the property of his house, said to his father: 'Give me men and ships and I will go and conquer a state for myself from the Saracens in Spain.' That sort of harangue is common enough in the fiction of the Middle Ages and faithfully reflects prevailing states of mind: '*Beau sire, baillez-moi hommes suffisans pour me faire estat ou royaume.*' '*Beau fils, aurez ce que demandez.*' "

of the poorer classes and prevents the children of the poor from romping and playing in the streets. It fills the homes of poor farmers and country-dwellers with dust. All that is tolerated in deference to the god Progress (in appearances at least; in reality the interests of innkeepers and automobile manufacturers have a little something to do with it). The thing is carried so far that people who fail to admire the automobile are treated as heretics were treated in a day gone by. In Switzerland, the Grison Canton voted not to allow automobiles on roads built with public funds. Priests and worshippers of the god Progress at once went on the war-path and in horror truly holy loudly condemned such a heretical and sacrilegious act. The Confederation was hounded to compel a canton tainted with such dire heretical depravity to open its roads to automobiles; and with that in view an amendment to the federal constitution was proposed and it almost got to the referendum stage.[1]

It is interesting that in this connexion a derivation turns up that is commonly found in other religions: the individual is blamed for what actually is a consequence of the general order of things. An accident occurs. Actually it is a consequence of the great speed at which automobiles are allowed to run. But the blame is laid on the chauffeur, who is appropriately rebaptized for the occasion as a *chauffard*. In that way the real cause is kept out of sight and the danger of any reform avoided. So in countries where political cor-

---

1463 [1] Says Émile de Saint-Auban in *Figaro* (reprinted, *Gazette de Lausanne,* Mar. 29, 1912): "Let a school-teacher cuff a sulking schoolboy and he looks like a savage today: he has violated the rights of the brat and the citizen. He is a sinner against our accepted type of civilization. He is more vigorously denounced than his associate next door who denies his country in open class-room. But the hit-and-run driver (*écraseur*), who cultivates the seventy-miles-an-hour average in contempt of the insignificant pedestrian, is guilty of just a peccadillo. There is absolution, or almost that, for the automobile whose sins are mortal only for the silly people it kills. I personally witnessed the exploit of the tremendous auto-bus that went zigzagging down the rue Notre-Dâme-des-Victoires like a drunk on a tear (*comme un pochard*) and hit two children. Some who saw it were enraged. But one gentleman could not understand that: 'It's not the bus's fault!' he protested. 'That man is learning to drive!' The auto-bus was just going to school! The auto-bus was having the mumps! The remark took. A humourist got it into his column. What solicitude for human life!" As regards traffic legislation the Italian parliament looks after the interests of automobile manufacturers and companies with loving eye. In 1912 it passed a law depriving the pedestrian of what little protection he still had left under the old law against owners and drivers of automobiles.

ruption is rife frequent investigations and prosecutions are conducted in order to give the impression that the few gnats who get caught in the net are to blame and to prevent any discredit being cast on the system that is responsible as a whole.

1464. Class III: *Accords with sentiments or principles.* Oftentimes the accord is with the sentiments of the persons producing or accepting the derivation and merely that, but it is represented as an accord with the sentiments of all men, the majority of men, all good men, and so on. Such sentiments eventually become detached from the subject experiencing them and stand as principles.

1465. III-α: *Accord with sentiments* (of a larger or smaller number of persons). With these derivations we have already dealt (§§ 591-612) from the standpoint, more especially, of their relations to experimental reality. Some further remarks will be in point here as to the forms they assume.

1466. The accord with sentiments may arise in three manners, as was the case with deference to authority (§ 1458): 1. An individual may make his conduct conform with the sentiments, real or assumed, of human beings, or of mind in the abstract ("the mind"), out of simple reverence for the opinion of the majority or of experts who are spokesmen for "the mind." That gives us derivations of the III-α variety. 2. Or an individual may act as he acts out of fear of harmful consequence to himself or others; and so we get derivations of our III-β, III-γ, III-δ types (accord with individual interest; collective interest; legal principles). 3. Or finally an individual may be impelled to such conformity by a mysterious force—in an extreme case there is an "imperative" operating through occult powers of its own. That gives derivations of our III-ε and III-ζ types (accords with metaphysical and supernatural entities). Prominent here among the residues used for purposes of derivation are the residues of sociality (Class IV).

1467. With this III-α variety accord with the sentiments of the author of the derivation are also to be classed. He reasons not objectively but by mere accord of sentiments (§ 1454[1]), making lavish use of combination-residues (Class I). *A* bears some remote and fantastic resemblance to *B*. But that is enough for him. He uses *A* to "explain" *B* by a vague accord of undefined sentiments. When there is a certain amount of definiteness and the sentiments seek expression in metaphysical forms, we get derivations of our III-ε type. Often derivations by accord of sentiments take on a merely verbal form, the accord subsisting between the sentiments that are associated with this or that word. In that case the derivation belongs, strictly, to Class IV.

1468. In concrete cases the three attitudes distinguished in § 1466 are often combined; but the second (fear of consequences), which is very important when divine personifications are involved, is often barely perceptible or entirely missing in derivations by accord of sentiment, especially in those of the metaphysical type. Furthermore, in many derivations by accord of sentiments one notes a compact group of sociality residues (Class IV), sentiments of reverence for the community on the individual's part, a tendency to imitate, and so on. In that powerful aggregate lies the great sentimental force that impels people to accept opinions which enjoy the consensus of "the majority," or of "all" men.[1]

1469. The accord of sentiments often stands by itself, no explicit attempt being made to give an exact definition to the relationship in which it stands towards objective reality. It is for metaphysics to find that exact definition, and it often takes the form of an assertion that the accord in ideas is identical with an accord in the objects corresponding (§§ 594-95). The contention more or less is that "if a notion exists in the minds of all men, or of the majority of men, or in mind in the abstract (in 'the mind'), it necessarily corresponds to an objective reality." Often, however, that is not stated—it is tacitly taken for granted: in other words it is left implicit, not made explicit, no verbal form being given to the II-ζ residue to which it corresponds. Sometimes it is stated, now in one form, now in another, as something that is evident or axiomatic—a favourite method with metaphysicists. Then again a show of proof will be given for it, so lengthening the derivation. It will be said, for instance, that what exists in every human mind was put there by God and must therefore necessarily correspond to an objective reality. That is the favourite procedure of theologians, though it is used by other

---

1468 [1] That is the answer to the question raised in §§ 597-98 (as to the reasons for the wide-spread acceptance of certain metaphysical theories that are in themselves meaningless). Here we must confine ourselves chiefly to accords of sentiments that may be taken as operating of their own intrinsic force (III-α).

thinkers too. Then there is the very pretty theory of "reminiscence," and no end of metaphysical theories of the same sort.

1470. Suppose we look at a few concrete examples. For long ages great importance was attached to "universal consensus" as demonstrating the existence of the gods, or of God. That result may be obtained in the manner indicated. God first imprinted a certain concept on the human mind, which now in its turn reveals it to us; or, working the other way round, one may start with the concept and in virtue of some metaphysical principle conclude that God exists.[1] "Greeks and Barbarians," says Sextus Empiricus, "recognize that there are gods";[a] and Maximus of Tyre, *Dissertationes,* XVII, 4-5 (Taylor, Vol. I, pp. 6-7), adds to the list: "That is admitted by Hellene and Barbarian, by continental and islander, by wise man and dunce." Maximus admits that there is the greatest variety of opinion as to the nature of God and of what is "good" or "evil," "shameful" or "pure"; but in a discord so great, he says, all men agree that there is one single god, sovereign and father of all things, along with other gods, his children and helpers. An excellent example of a writer's objectifying a subjective theory of his own! How

1470 [1] Gousset, *Théologie dogmatique,* Vol. I, p. 325: "All races of men have preserved a more or less distinct conception of the oneness of God. As Bergier says, *Dictionnaire de théologie, s.v. Dieu:* 'It must be either that that idea has been engraved upon all minds by the Creator Himself or that it is a remnant of a tradition going back to the origins of the human race, since it is found at all times as well as in all countries of the Earth.' " Gousset, *Op. cit.,* p. 309: "Prophecies are possible . . . The Jews and the Christians have always believed in prophecy. The patriarchs and the heathen held the same belief. All peoples have preserved some memory of predictions foretelling a Messiah to whom the nations could look forward. . . . The possibility of prophecies must therefore be conceded. The peoples would never have agreed in believing them possible if the belief did not rest on tradition, experience, reason." It is the same with prophecy as with miracles. *Ibid.,* pp. 342-43: "Belief in the immortality of the soul goes back to the infancy of the world . . . it has been a fundamental dogma of religion with the Hebrews, the Christians and the patriarchs. The same belief is to be found among other peoples, even the most uncivilized peoples. . . . And that belief has been handed down to the moderns. When European travellers discovered America and other far-away countries, they found no race of people that did not have its conception of a life to come."

1470 [a] *Contradictiones,* IX, *Adversus physicos* II, *De diis,* 60 (565) (*Opera,* Vol. II, p. 565).

many people there were at that time who were far from seeing eye to eye with Maximus of Tyre![2]

1471. Maximus of Tyre tries to answer an objection that is generally raised in such cases: that, as a matter of fact, from the "all" who are said to hold certain views quite a few persons who do not hold them have to be excepted; and he extricates himself from the predicament with a form of derivation that is as general as the objection (§§ 592 f.): he bluntly bars them as unworthy of consideration. People who do not think as Maximus thinks are rabble, not to say worse: therefore all who are not rabble or worse agree with him:

1470 [2] Sextus, *loc. cit.,* continues: "Those who believe that there are gods justify their thesis on four grounds: one is the consensus of all men; the second is the order of the world; the third is the *absurdum* into which those who deny gods are drawn; the fourth and last is the confutation of those who deny. And they argue from common opinion, for all men, Greeks and Barbarians, believe that there are gods." Sextus's second reason is based on a Class II residue (group-persistence). Plato's proofs of the existence of gods, *De legibus,* X, 886 (Bury, Vol. II, p. 301), are: "First, the Earth, the Sun, and all the stars, the beautiful order of the seasons, the distinction of the years and months. And then, all men, whether Greeks or Barbarians, believe that there are gods." Many passages in works that go under the name of Plato express the contrary view that the opinion of the majority is worth little or nothing: *e.g., Alcibiades,* I, 110-11; and *cf., Laches,* 184 (Lamb, p. 27): "*Socrates:* 'What is to be judged rightly has to be judged by competence, I suppose, and not by numbers [of votes].' *Melesias:* 'Certainly.' " Cicero, *De natura deorum,* II, 2, 4, puts into the mouth of Lucilius Balbus arguments very much like Plato's. In his *Oneirocritica* (*Interpretation of Dreams*), I, 8, in distinguishing custom that is general from custom that is particular, Artemidorus mentions as general customs: worship and honour of the gods, "since no nation is without gods, just as none is without government," and then, on the same footing, the rearing of children, waking by day and sleeping by night, sexual love, eating, and so on. Delicious is St. Augustine in imagining, in a diatribe against the Donatists, *Epistolae,* LXXXIX, 5 (*Opera,* Vol. II, p. 311; *Works,* Vol. VI, p. 378), that the whole terrestrial globe thought as he thought as to the effectiveness of baptism. Eminent doctor that he was, he did not realize that the vast majority of men living on Earth at that time had not even dreamed of the existence of such a theological problem. "Some timid souls may chance to be influenced by what they commonly say of baptism [that it has to be administered by a priest of unblemished character] . . . for the whole world accepts the very obvious evangelical truth proclaimed by John when he says . . ." [Healy amends "the whole world" to "the whole Christian world."—A. L.] According to Plutarch, *De placitis philosophorum,* I, 6, 9 (Goodwin, Vol. III, p. 117), the idea of worshipping gods came from three sources: from the philosophers, through nature; from the poets, through poetry; and from the consensus of the practices of the cities.

"In course of time," he says, *Op. cit.,* XVII, 5, "there may have been two or three abject and stolid atheists, whose eyes see crosswise and whose ears hear amiss—spiritual eunuchs, idiots, sterile, fatuous people, so many lions without courage, so many bulls without horns, so many birds without wings! But even from them you will learn that the divine exists." Abuse of one's adversaries is fatuous from the logico-experimental point of view. It may be very effective indeed from the standpoint of sentiments.[1][2][3] (For footnote 3 see page 931.)

1471 [1] The circular argument is common enough even today, as examples in surfeit show; *e.g.,* Tolstoy, *The Four Gospels,* Vol. I, Preface, p. xx: "I have found good people, not in one, but in all churches and sects, and saw how they were all guided in their lives by one and the same idea, that had its foundation on the teaching of Jesus." Who are these "good people"? If Tolstoy is using the words in their ordinary meanings, he cannot be unaware that there are plenty of "good people" who are far from agreeing with him and who in particular withhold their assent from such of his doctrines as condemn all war, incite to evasion of military service, and under pretext of "non-resistance to evil" recommend leaving a free hand to criminals; and since he insists that those doctrines of his are based on "the teaching of Jesus" it is clear that not all "good people" live according to the teaching of Jesus. So if Tolstoy's statement is to be saved, the meaning of his "good people" has to be changed. For it to have any meaning, the class of people whom he styles "good people" has to be defined and the definition, furthermore, has to be independent of any acceptance or rejection on their part of his doctrine. For if the proviso that "good people" are people who live according to "the teaching of Jesus" as interpreted by Tolstoy creeps into the definition in any way at all, even implicitly, it will not be hard, it is true, to demonstrate that "all good people" live according to the "teaching of Jesus"; but the demonstration, it is no less true, will be a mere tautology. As a matter of fact Tolstoy and admirers of Tolstoy care not a fig for all that. With them sentiment takes the place of logic and observation of facts. They have a certain notion of what seems to them to be "good." First they exclude from the category of "good people" all individuals who have different notions. They, necessarily, are "bad people." On the other hand they believe, or imagine, that they are deriving their notions from the teachings of a man whom they revere, love, admire: really, they are making his teachings over to fit notions of their own. In the case of Tolstoy and his followers the man happens to be Jesus; but it would make no difference if he were some other person—Buddha, Mohammed, Socrates. Tolstoy's statement simply means: "By 'good people' I mean people who subscribe to doctrines in which I think I recognize the teaching of Jesus as I choose to conceive that teaching."

1471 [2] Plato, like Maximus of Tyre, gets out of the same predicament by abusing his adversaries: *De legibus,* X. There were those who denied gods and therefore made it necessary for him to prove their existence. He calls them insufferable people, properly to be hated. Wroth as he is against them, he musters his self-control and tries to give the floor to such corrupt, sensuous, and silly persons, some of whom go so far as to say that the stars are not divinities but masses of earth and stone! A fine example, that, of the difference between that knowledge

1472. The assertion that all peoples had some conception or other of gods was not left unanswered. It was doubted or even flatly denied. The question itself has little bearing on the matter here in hand. We need simply note that, as usual, "gods" and "God" are not very sharply defined terms. One can find or not find the concept in the mind of this or that people as one chooses.[1]

of "things in themselves," which the divine Plato had and which his modern imitators after him possess, and the experimental knowledge of modern astronomers. Neo-Hegelians would confer a great favour on us by explaining just how they reconcile the "absoluteness" of their knowledge with such changes in science. Or is it, perhaps, that they still hold to Plato's conception and think the stars are gods?

1471 [3] Bayle, *Continuation des Pensées diverses,* § 18, quoting Father Rapin, *Comparation de Platon et d'Aristote.* Says Rapin, p. 425, § 11: "This general consensus of all peoples, no one of whom has ever been found without belief in some god, is an instinct of nature and cannot be mistaken, being so universal. It would be silly to listen on such a matter to the opinions of the two or three libertines, at the most, who have denied the Divinity in every age in order to live more tranquilly in their licence." He had said just previously, p. 423, §§ 7-8: "That truth . . . is disputed only by a few minds that have been corrupted by sensuousness, presumption, and ignorance. Nothing more monstrous than atheism is to be found in nature: it is a mental disorder conceived in libertinage. No respectable, sane, and reasonable man will ever think of doubting religion." *Journal de Genève,* June 11, 1913, reporting the award of a prize of the French Academy to Romain Rolland: "The most inflexible opponent of Romain Rolland was, it is said, a member who years ago was one of the supplest and most emancipated intelligences of his time, but who with advancing age became so partisan in his views as to see in Tolstoy only an unfortunate who had gone morally bankrupt and was worthy at the most of pity." We are therefore placed in the dilemma either of accepting Tolstoy's theories, which many people regard as not at all sound, or of being declared "partisan." But why do people use such cardboard artillery? Evidently because there are other people who are as afraid of it as of the real, and who, instead of laughing as they ought, feel of their ribs at every detonation to make sure they have not been hurt.

1472 [1] Cicero, *De natura deorum,* I, 23, 62-63. Velleius had taken general consensus as proof of the existence of the gods. Cotta replies: "You say that the fact that that has been the opinion of all races and nations of men is sufficient reason for us to admit that there are gods. That would be a trifling argument even if it were not false. In the first place, how do you know what the ideas of the various races are? For my part I imagine that there are many people so barbarous that no conception of deity is to be found among them. And how about Diagoras, who was called an atheist, and after him, Theodorus? Did they not openly deny divinity (*nonne aperte deorum naturam sustulerunt*)?" Diodorus Siculus, *Bibliotheca historica,* III, 9, 2 (Booth, Vol. I, p. 156), asserts that some few Ethiopians denied the existence of gods. Miot remarks on the point in his notes to his translation of Diodorus, Vol. II, pp. 478-79: "The ancients believed that there was no people on the surface of the Earth that professed atheism, and the unanimous consensus of all peoples on the point has always been taken as one of the main proofs

1473. A further distinction seems to be drawn between "all peoples" and "all men"; for it would in fact be convenient to distinguish between simple souls who represent general opinion and certain individuals who are for ever splitting hairs. The atheists would fall within the latter group, and their opinions could then legitimately be met with the good sense of the majority.

1474. Again as usual, the derivation answers both "yea" and "nay"; and the failure of universal consensus has been used by some to impugn the existence of the gods and of moral laws. Plato accuses the Sophists of doing that. What in brief they seem to have said is that the gods did not exist by nature but by "art," being different among different peoples; that the beautiful is one thing according to nature and another according to law; that the just does not exist by nature, since men never agree as to what it is and make new laws every day.

1475. Majority consensus is often taken for granted—that is to say, it seems to be so obvious that things stand thus and so that one assumes, without feeling called upon to say as much, that things must seem thus and so to all men, or to the majority. Sometimes consensus is put forward explicitly as proof (§§ 592 f.). Then again it is in its turn demonstrated by reference to some other metaphysical principle. Such reasonings have ever been met in vain with the experimental fact that many general beliefs, such as astrology, have been mistaken. The metaphysical adjunct to the principle of universal consensus serves primarily to satisfy the demand of educated people for logical explanations.[1]

of the existence of God." That was written in the year of grace 1833! Two passages in Strabo's *Geographica* refer to godless peoples: III, 4, 16 (Jones, Vol. II, p. 109): "Some say that the Callaicans are atheists"; and XVII, 2, 3 (Jones, Vol. VIII, p. 147): "Some [peoples] of the torrid zone are deemed to be atheists." The passages have often been quoted against the proof by universal consensus of the existence of gods. But as evidence they are of little if any value. In the first place Strabo is very guarded in his assertion: "some say," "are deemed." Then even if he were altogether positive there would still be the question of his authorities. Finally—and it is the weightiest consideration—the existence or non-existence of universal consensus proves nothing.

1475 [1] Cicero uses both methods (offering consensus as proof, and proving the consensus with a metaphysical adjunct). Velleius says in *De natura deorum,* I, 17, 44: "That to which all men by nature consent is necessarily true (*De quo autem omnium natura consentit id verum esse necesse est*)." That might be sufficient in itself. Since he began by saying that all men have some notion of gods,

1476. Analysis of nearly all concrete derivations yields a derivation of universal consensus or a consensus of the majority, the honest, the wise, of the human mind, of Right Reason, of the balanced, sensible man, and so on. Very very often it is implicit: then again it is disguised under one form or another in impersonal expressions such as "It is believed," "It is understood," "It is thought," and the

the conclusion logically follows: "Therefore it must be admitted that there are gods (*Esse igitur deos confitendum est*)." But Velleius is not satisfied with that much: he wants further to explain, I, 16, 43, how and why men came by the notion, and he praises Epicurus for demonstrating the existence of the gods in an experimental manner that quite contrasts with the senseless vagaries of other philosophers: "For he was the first to see that there were gods from the fact that Nature herself had imprinted the concept of divinity on the minds of all men (*Solus enim vidit primum esse Deos, quod in omnium animis eorum notionem impressisset ipsa natura*)." He would be saying exactly the same thing had he said simply that the notion of divinity is present in the minds of all men; but he drags in our old friend Dame Nature, because that metaphysical entity gives a semblance of authority to his assertion. However he does not stop there: the notion is a "pre-notion," *loc. cit.*: "For what race, what family of men, is without as it were a foreknowledge of the gods quite apart from any learning? That is what Epicurus calls πρόληψις, in other words, a notion of a thing that is held in advance (*anteceptam*) by the mind and without which nothing can be known and no investigation, no argument, is possible." From that, and from the principle that everything enjoying universal consensus is true, Velleius goes on to infer, I, 17, 45, that the gods are immortal and live in bliss, just as he could infer any other pretty thing, if he chose: "From that we therefore conclude that the gods are blessed and immortal; for that same Nature which gave us our knowledge of the gods [Dame Nature is an accommodating soul and will say anything one would have her say.] has also graven it upon our hearts that they are eternal and blissful." Balbus repeats, II, 4, 12, that the main issue is agreed upon by "all men of all nations; for the belief that gods exist is innate in all men and as it were engraved upon their souls." The existence of the gods, he avers, II, 2, 4, is self-evident. Opinions differ as to what they are like, II, 5, 13, but no one denies their existence: "*Quales sint, varium est: esse nemo negat.*" However he allows himself to be enticed into giving a proof, II, 9, 23: "But though I began otherwise . . . and held that the point did not need discussion, since it was self-evident to everyone that the gods exist, I should nevertheless prefer that it be corroborated by reasons of physic." Cotta then makes a remark that should be repeated in every similar situation—that Balbus keeps bringing on new proofs because he feels that his demonstration has not been conclusive, III, 4, 9: "You have seen fit to prove the existence of the gods with those many arguments because you are not sure that it is all as obvious as you would like to have it." And he goes on flatly to deny that the opinion of the majority, or of all men, is to be considered, III, 4, 11: "Do you insist then that so many things should be determined by the judgment of the ignorant majority—you especially who keep repeating that the majority of men are altogether brainless?" This argument of Cotta's is most interesting, because it is of general bearing and applies to many other cases of the kind.

like; or by using epithets or names, "Such and such a thing is *X*," which means simply that the author of the derivation has found for the thing a name that fits the sentiments he happens to hold. Proverbs, adages, sayings, generalities, when offered as proofs, also as a rule conceal an appeal to a consensus, real or presumed, of the majority.

1477. III-β: *Accord with individual interest.* To induce a person to do a certain thing *A,* which he would not do of his own accord, various devices may be used and not all of them are derivations.

1478. Not derivations are the following: 1. The person does not know that it would be advantageous for him to do *A*. He is shown that it would be. To show just such things is the function of experience, of the trades, of science. Experience shows that one should save in times of prosperity in order to be prepared when hard times come. A trade will show how to get iron for a plough; science, how to realize now this purpose, now that. 2. The person is commanded to do *A* by an external and real authority wielding a real sanction (if the power or the sanction or both are unreal, we get a derivation.) It is the function of civil and criminal legislation to establish such real sanctions. Simple usage and custom also have sanctions, in the censure that falls upon the person who violates them and in the hostility he incurs from other members of his community. 3. The doing of *A* is required by the person's own temperament so that failure to do it brings him remorse or sorrow.[1]

1479. Derivations, instead, are the following: 4. The blunt assertion that doing *A* will be advantageous (in reality it will not be) to the person in question and that refraining from doing *A* will be detrimental to him.[1] This device corresponds to 1 above, provided the inferences are not logico-experimental. The typical case is the taboo with spontaneous sanction inherent in the taboo. The residues exploited in such derivations are those, on the whole, that are used in derivations of assertion (Class I) and authority (Class II). 5. Doing—or not doing—*A* is required by an external authority wielding a sanction—the power or the sanction, or both, being unreal.

1478 [1] [The elliptical argument in 3 will be clearer from rereading the first quarter of § 1400. The conduct here would be a purely instinctive matter. No derivation would figure until some explanation or justification were attempted.—A. L.]

1479 [1] Here we are considering from the standpoint of derivations, strictly, a particular case of a theory that is general. It will be elaborated later on in §§ 1897 f.

This device corresponds to 2 above, there both the authority and the sanction being real. 6. It is asserted, but cannot be proved, that the person will feel remorse or sorrow if he does, or does not, do *A*. This device corresponds to 3 above.

All these derivations are of great importance to human societies. They aim primarily at obviating possible conflicts between individual interest and the collective interest. One of the devices most commonly used to attain that end is to confuse the two interests by derivations, asserting that the interests are identical and that in working for the good of the community the individual is working for his own good (§§ 1903-98). Among the many derivations used for that purpose are the derivations which we are examining here. Identity of interests is obtained automatically through derivations 4 and 6, and through the interposition of an unreal power in the case of 5.

1480. In Chapter III (§§ 325 f.) we classified precepts and sanctions with special reference to the transformation of non-logical into logical conduct (§ 1400). Let us see the correspondence between that classification and the one given above. The cases in Chapter III were designated as *a, b, c, d*. In *a* no demonstration of the precept exists; *a* therefore involves not a derivation but residues. In *b* there is a demonstration, but it has been suppressed. If it is restored, and in the measure in which it is restored, *b* takes its place among the derivations, provided the demonstration is pseudo-experimental. In such a case it corresponds to method 4 above, or even to 6. If the demonstration is logico-experimental *b* corresponds to 1 and also to 3. In *c* the precept has a real sanction enforced by a real power. We are therefore in the case of 2. In *d* either the power or the sanction or both are unreal, and that class therefore corresponds to method 5. Suppose we now look more closely at devices 4, 5, and 6, each in turn.

1481. *Device 4: Pseudo-experimental demonstration.* The type is the taboo with sanction. We have already discussed the taboo without sanction (§§ 321 f.). The idea is that violation of the taboo exposes a person to disastrous consequences, such as befall a person who violates a prescription not to drink of a poisonous beverage. In both cases there are antidotes for avoiding consequences. In the case of the taboo both consequences and remedies are pseudo-experimental (4). In the case of the poison they are experimental (1). Thinking more particularly of residues we mentioned (§ 1252 [1]) certain remedies which were used on the Island of Tonga to obviate the untoward consequences of violating a taboo. In that connexion our main concern was with the restoration of individual integrity; and from that point of view we placed the violation of a taboo and its remedies on a par with the Catholic's violation of precepts of his religion, which he remedies by confession and penance. But from the standpoint of derivations, which we are considering here, the two cases have to be distinguished. The first envisages evils and remedies that though pseudo-experimental in substance are real in form, whereas the second envisages evils pertaining to a future life and therefore unreal, and remedies of a spiritual character—a sinner's contrition. The simple taboo is re-enforced with new derivations. Where some concept of a supernatural being is handy, it is associated with the taboo, as indeed with every other important operation in life. Then again the automatic functioning of the taboo is changed into an action that is artificially procured. Without waiting for the injurious effects of violation to ensue as a matter of course, a public authority provides for the punishment of the transgressor.[1]

1481 [1] Europeans are often misled in regarding the taboo as a consequence of the divine intervention. Really, the latter is a consequence of the taboo. Domeny de Rienzi, *Océanie*, Vol. I, pp. 53-54: "More than any other inhabitant of Polynesia the New Zealander is blindly obedient to *tapou* (taboo) superstitions, and that without having in any way kept any conception of the moral principle on which that practice was based. [He has not kept it because it never existed.] He believes simply that the *tapou* is pleasing to the *atoua* (God), and that is sufficient for him as a determining motive. [A derivation added to the taboo.] He is convinced, furthermore, that any object, whether a living creature or of inanimate matter, when tabooed by a priest is thenceforward under the immediate control of the divinity and by that very fact under interdict of any profane contact. [In all that the religious preconceptions of the European are apparent enough. De Rienzi talks of a "priest" and in the next breath notes that any chief may impose a taboo.] As one may well imagine, the taboo will be all the more solemn and impressive according to the importance of the person from whom it emanates. The plain man, who is subject to all the taboos of the various leaders in the tribe, can impose a taboo at the most upon himself. . . . The chiefs and *arikis* (priests), of course, always manage to get together to guarantee the full inviolability of the taboos. The chiefs are for the most part *arikis* themselves. At the very least the *arikis* are closely connected with the chiefs by ties of kinship or marriage."

1482. Reinach [1] is inclined to think that the biblical injunction to honour father and mother was a taboo. In its primitive form it was something to this effect probably: "Insult not (strike not . . .) thy father or thy mother, *or thou shalt die*" (the spontaneous consequence of the transgression). So too—still according to Reinach—touching the Ark of God resulted *ipso facto* in death. When Uzzah dies after touching the Ark (II Sam. 6: 6-7; I Chron. 13: 10-11) "it is not," says Reinach, "that the Eternal strikes the innocent Uzzah dead. Uzzah has committed an imprudent act. He dies very much as a man touching a live electric wire dies of the shock."

1483. The taboo of this type is very powerful because, directly and without any hair-splitting, it sets the residues of combination (§ 1416-3) in motion; and, in fact, its prevalence is observable not only in ancient times but in a day more recent.[1] On the other hand, such specific sanctions run the risk of being discredited by observation. So, as the use of logic and observation becomes more general, the taboo has to be transformed. In a first stage, the sanction is made more indefinite and therefore less susceptible of being discredited. In a second stage, a twin development takes place. The sanction is transferred to a supernatural world and so is able to serve just as well for plain and educated man alike. Then again a fog of metaphysics is draped about it, till it becomes incomprehensible and therefore irrefutable, since the existence of a thing cannot be disputed when nobody knows what it is. Among the ancients the fact that the wicked prospered in this world was an argument dear to the atheists as proving that there were no gods. The Christians broke that weapon in their hands. No one ever returned from Hell or Paradise to report just how the wicked and the good were faring; for, to tell the strict truth, the journey of Dante and other journeys of the kind do after all transcend the limits of the experimental world.

1484. King Rio-Rio abolished the taboo in Hawaii by publicly demonstrating that it could be violated without harmful consequences. His experiment had the effect he desired because physical

1482 [1] *Cultes, mythes et religions,* Vol. I, pp. 6, 4.

1483 [1] Bayet, *Leçons de morale,* p. 57: "To be happy one must love all men. But above all one must love one's parents." That from a non-religious, scientific ethics, a brand that is said to be a great improvement on the religious! M. Aulard's ethics makes a point, moreover, of never plagiarizing biblical morals.

consequences were involved. It would have failed had the threatened effects been supernatural or metaphysical.[1]

1485. The taboo or precept with supernatural sanction need not
concern us here; nor need we linger on those theories which,
through verbal or other sorts of sophistry, eliminate in reality that
individual interest which is said to be the one thing they hold in
view (§§ 1897 f.). Here let us keep strictly to derivations that present
the outstanding trait of reducing to the principle of individual interest conduct which seems to have no bearing whatever upon it.

1486. We may take Bentham's theory as typical. At first blush
that theory seems to obviate every possible misunderstanding and,

---

1484 [1] Domeny de Rienzi, *Océanie,* Vol. II, pp. 39-40: "The final abolition of
idolatry and the taboo was . . . the work of Rio-Rio, son and successor to the
great Tamea-Mea. . . . The suppression of the taboo, that time-honoured symbol of
inviolability, required still greater adroitness on Rio-Rio's part. He first began
working at the chief priest . . . and was lucky enough to win him to his idea.
In inaugurating the reform the taboo that affected women was first dealt with.
The King waited for a general holiday when the natives gathered in throngs about
the palace to attend the royal banquet. The rugs being arranged and the foods
appointed for the men set thereon, with the food for the women on other rugs,
the King came up, selected a number of delicacies that were forbidden the women,
went over to their side, and began to eat of them and to invite the women to
share. Straightway loud cries of horror arose on all sides: 'Taboo!' 'Taboo!' But
Rio-Rio paid no attention and continued eating. The priests came hurrying from
the *moraï,* whence they had been summoned by the crowd. 'That in fact is a
manifest violation of the taboo,' they said. 'But why do the offended gods not
inflict their own vengeance? . . . Either they are good-for-nothing gods or false
gods.' 'Come, ye people of Hawaii,' cried the chief priest at this point, 'let us
have done with this annoying, absurd, and barbarous form of worship!' And he
took a torch and himself set fire to the principal *moraï.*" The missionaries, says
De Rienzi, applauded. But could they have been sure that their own taboos
would have stood the test of experiment any better? Draper, *History of the Conflict
between Religion and Science,* p. 77: "Though her [Rome's] military renown
was thus recovered [after the victories of Heracleus], though her territory was re-
gained, there was something that the Roman Empire had irrevocably lost. Religious faith could never be restored. In face of the world Magianism had insulted
Christianity by profaning her most sacred places—Bethlehem, Gethsemane, Calvary
—by burning the sepulchre of Christ . . . by carrying off, with shouts of laughter,
the cross. Miracles had once abounded in Syria, in Egypt, in Asia Minor: there
was not a church which had not its long catalogue of them. Very often they were
displayed on unimportant occasions and in insignificant cases. In this supreme
moment, when such aid was most urgently demanded, not a miracle was worked.
Amazement filled the Christian populations of the East when they witnessed these
Persian sacrileges perpetrated with impunity. . . . In the land of miracles, amazement was followed by consternation—consternation died out in disbelief." And
see § 1948 [1].

as regards definiteness, to leave nothing to be desired. "I am a believer," says Bentham,[1] "in the principle of 'utility' . . . when I use the terms 'just,' 'unjust,' 'moral,' 'immoral,' 'good,' 'bad,' as collective terms standing for the concepts of certain pains and certain pleasures, without attaching any other sense to them, I want it distinctly understood that I take the words 'pain' and 'pleasure' in their ordinary senses, without inventing arbitrary definitions to except certain pleasures or deny the existence of certain pains. There is no subtlety in my use of the words and no metaphysics! There is no need of consulting either Plato or Aristotle. 'Pain' and 'pleasure' stand for what each person feels as such, the peasant as well as the prince, the plain man as well as the philosopher."[2]

1487. One could not speak more clearly! But at that point a problem at once arises, as is always the case in theories of that kind: "How reconcile the principle of absolute selfishness with the principle of altruism" (§ 1479) which Bentham is unwilling to abandon? Some get out of the difficulty by introducing sanctions of an earthly or supernatural power; some by changing the meanings of terms; some by resorting to the verbal subterfuges that Bentham scorns; some, finally, take back what they have conceded in deference to one principle in virtue of some other principle. And that is the method adopted by Bentham.

1488. Bentham's first step is to throw public approbation or disapprobation into the balance. That gets the altruistic principle in! But it is not enough. It has to be reconciled with the first principle (absolute selfishness). So Bentham points out that the disapprobation of others is harmful to the individual, so that it is to his advantage to avoid it.[1] And with that he has withdrawn the concession

---

1486 [1] *Traité de législation civile et pénale* (Dumont), Vol. I, p. 4 (Atkinson, Vol. I, p. 4).

1486 [2] He goes on to say, *Ibid.*, Vol. I, p. 317 (Atkinson, Vol. I, p. 268): "It is absurd to talk of human happiness save in terms of the desires and sensations that human beings actually feel. It is absurd to try and show by computation that a man ought to be happy when he knows that he is miserable." Yet that is the very thing that Bentham does. And *cf. Deontology,* Vol. II, p. 121: "Every man is able to form the best estimate of his own pleasures and his own pains."

1488 [1] *Deontology,* Vol. I, p. 84: ". . . It might happen that the act which promises the present pleasure might prove prejudicial to others in the society to which you belong, and they, having sustained an injury at your hands, would, if prompted by self-preservation alone, seek to avenge themselves by the inflic-

he has made. If a thief is told, "If your theft is discovered, you will be disliked and suffer from it," he can answer: "Weighing the pleasure I will get from the thing I want to steal against the probable pain I may suffer, I find the pleasure greater than the pain." In that case we can make no answer without going counter to the principle we posited, that "pain and pleasure are what each person feels as such," and without deserving the criticism that it is absurd to discuss the happiness of men otherwise than according to their own desires. One gets a clear conception of this theory of Bentham's in an imaginary practical situation which he devised. Really, it is one of the stories that are told to children to frighten them with the bogey-man. One of the best possible refutations of it was made by Mark Twain with his two playful stories of the good boy and the bad boy.[2]

tion of pain equal or greater in amount than the pleasure enjoyed." The fallacy lies in the assumed consequence: 1. It is not enough for people to be disposed to avenge themselves: they must also have the power to do so. Bentham treats those two things as one. 2. How can Bentham be sure that the pain which people who have sustained an injury at our hands may inflict upon us will be "equal or greater in amount than the pleasure enjoyed"? And what has become of the case where the pain would be less than the pleasure? 3. And suppose someone should say: "The actual pleasure that I experience from the conduct from which you are trying to persuade me to refrain is, in my estimation, greater than the future and merely probable pain which will be the consequence of it? According to your own principle it is absurd to try to deprive me of it by reasoning on my happiness otherwise than by consulting my own desires and inclinations." What could Bentham say in reply that would not involve him in a self-contradiction?

1488 [2] *Deontology,* Vol. I, pp. 118-20: "Timothy Thoughtless and Walter Wise are fellow prentices. Thoughtless gave into the vice of drunkenness. Wise abstained from it. Mark the consequence. 1. Physical sanction. For every debauch, Thoughtless was rewarded by sickness in the head; to recruit himself he lay in bed the next morning, and his whole frame became enervated by relaxation; and when he returned to his work, his work ceased to be a source of satisfaction to him." But Wise, whose health was not good, improves by temperance and is happy. "2. Social sanction. Timothy had a sister, deeply interested in his happiness. She reproved him at first, then neglected, then abandoned him. She had been to him a source of pleasure—it was all swept away." But what if he had had no sister? Or suppose he had one and she had stood by him? And what if she were the sort of person whom it is better to lose than to keep? Walter, instead, has a brother who has been indifferent to him but who eventually becomes very fond of him. "3. Popular sanction. Timothy was a member of a club which had money and reputation. He went thither one day in a state of inebriety. He abused the secretary and was expelled by an unanimous vote. The regular habits of Walter had excited the attention of his master. He said one day to his banker: 'That young man is fitted for a higher station.' The banker bore it in mind and on the

1489. So this first line of proof is not very convincing, and its weakness seems not to have escaped Bentham altogether;[1] for he resorted thereafter to a second proof, utilizing another principle, "the greatest happiness of the greatest number," and so calling into play our residues of sociality (Class IV).[2] In many connexions this

first opportunity took him into his service. He rose from one distinction to another and was frequently consulted on business of the highest importance by men of wealth and influence." One begins to suspect that Bentham must have been living in Cathay or the land of Cockaigne, where all well-behaved individuals were rewarded in that way. "4. Legal sanction . . ." Timothy is sentenced to deportation. Walter becomes a judge. It is now certain that Bentham was living in Cathay, or some other blessed country where sin is always punished and virtue recompensed. There are countries where things do not run that smoothly. "5. Religious sanction." Timothy lives in fear of the life to come. Walter looks forward to it with feelings of hope and peace. [For the Mark Twain allusion, see Index, *s.v. Clemens.*—A. L.]

1489 [1] *Deontology,* Vol. I, p. 52: "By accident, no doubt, good repute may attend upon ill-desert, and ill-repute upon good. But if this disastrous state of things be possible, if it sometimes be witnessed, its continuance is of rare occurrence. Were there even more truth in it than there is, the use of such an argument little becomes a moralist." So then, even if it is true, it must not be pressed; and that may very well be; but, in that case, Bentham ought to decide what he is trying to do—whether he is preaching a sermon or sustaining a scientific thesis.

1489 [2] *Deontology,* Vol. I, pp. 298, 319, 328; Vol. II, p. 11. Bowring, the collector and publisher of Bentham's works, appends to the first volume a "History of the Greatest Happiness Principle." Says he: "Dr. Priestley published his *Essay on Government* in 1768. He there introduced, in italics [p. 17], as the only reasonable and proper object of government, 'the greatest happiness of the greatest number.'" [The epithets "proper" and "reasonable" carry us back into the metaphysics that Bentham thought he was avoiding.] That theory went "beyond all notions that had preceded it. It exhibited not only happiness, but it made that happiness diffusive. It associated it with the majority, with the many." [Associated? It replaced one happiness with the other. For it is obvious enough that this second principle is in many cases antithetical to the first.] "The phrase 'greatest happiness of the greatest number' was first employed by Mr. Bentham in 1822, in his *Codification Proposal* (*Works,* Vol. IV, pp. 535 f.). Every suggestion there put forward is made to turn upon the requirements of the 'greatest happiness of the greatest number.'" Well and good, but that being the case, why do you pretend that every man is sole judge of his own happiness; or that one "may wear out the air with sonorous and unmeaning words: those words will not act upon the mind: nothing will act upon it but the apprehension of pleasure and pain." However, Bentham seems not to have been entirely satisfied with his new formula: "In the later years of Mr. Bentham's life the phrase 'greatest happiness of the greatest number' appeared on closer scrutiny to be wanting in that clearness and correctness which had originally recommended it to his notice and adoption . . . but though it . . . did not satisfy Mr. Bentham, one may doubt whether there be sufficient grounds for rejecting it." [Priestley's actual phrases, referred

new principle is antithetical to the first. By using the two principles together one eliminates but does not solve the ethical problem that Bentham had set himself, of finding a way in such cases to reconcile the individual's utility with the utility of the greatest number. We have here stumbled by chance upon one of those problems in which one feels intuitively that there is a certain "maximum" of happiness or advantage for the individual, and a similar maximum for the community. But like all intuitions, it leaves the subject as it were cloaked in fog.[3]

1490. Bentham makes a curious application of the principle of "the greatest happiness of the greatest number" to the matter of slavery. According to Bentham slavery might be defended if there were but one slave to each master.[1] That might lead one to suppose that he would end by proposing legislation in that direction. But no: he is in favour of the gradual abolition of slavery! That makes it clear enough that the derivation has a predetermined goal which it must willynilly attain, and Bentham, moreover, or at least his editor, does not disdain the procedure of appealing to the opinion of the greatest number and then excluding adversaries from that favoured list. Says he: "Slave-owners who have not been deprived of their good sense and humanity by personal interest readily admit the advantages of liberty over slavery." But Bentham had banished "good sense" and "humanity." What are they doing here? And besides, if the slave-owner were "humane," that alone would suffice to abolish

to by Bowring above, are: "the good and happiness of the members, that is of the majority of the members, of any state"; and, in italics, *"the good of the whole."* —A. L.]

1489 [3] We shall dispel the fog in due course (Chapter XII) by trying to reduce the conceptions involved to exact definitions.

1490 [1] *Traité de législation civile et pénale,* Vol. I, p. 323 (Atkinson, Vol. I, pp. 269-73). He had said just previously, p. 318: "In any case if slavery were established in such proportions that there would be but one slave for each master, I might hesitate before pronouncing on the balance between the advantage of the one and the disadvantage of the other. It might be that all considered the sum of happiness by that arrangement would almost equal the sum of pain. But that is not the way things go. The moment slavery is established it becomes the lot of the greatest number. . . . The advantage is all on the side of the one, the disadvantage on the side of the multitude." On that principle one might find a majority cannibalism defensible. The disadvantage would belong to the few, the advantage to the many.

slavery and no theory based on strict personal interest would be required.[2]

1491. Bentham's stumbling-blocks are primarily two: 1. He tries to make all conduct logical, and so loses touch with reality, many human actions being non-logical.[1] 2. He tries to reconcile by logic principles that are logically antagonistic, the egoistic and altruistic principles.

1492. The logico-experimental value of Bentham's theory is very slight;[1] and yet it enjoyed a great vogue. Why? For the same reason that other theories of the kind have met with similar success: because it combines residues of personal integrity with residues of sociality. That is enough for people and they are not very particular as to just how they are brought together—as to the derivation, in other words. Bentham is inclined to include animals in his "greatest number"; and so also is John Stuart Mill, who believes that "the general principle to which all rules of practice ought to conform, and the test by which they should be tried, is that of conduciveness to the happiness of mankind, or rather of all sentient beings."[2]

1493. Spinoza[1] has another very handsome derivation designed, as usual, to reconcile the egoistic and altruistic principles. "If two persons of the same mind (*natura*) come together, they form an individual twice as strong as either. Nothing, therefore, is more useful to man than man. Men, I say, can choose no course better calculated to preserve their being than to agree all in everything." If two men are starving and there is one loaf of bread, they would discover right

1490 [2] In *Op. cit.,* Vol. I, p. 11 (Atkinson, Vol. I, p. 10), Bentham disenfranchises the "arbitrary principles" of sympathy and antipathy, and condemns appeals to "Conscience or Moral Sense" and "Common Sense." At the time of his *Introduction to the Principles of Morality and Legislation* (*Works,* Vol. I), Bentham admitted the principles of sympathy and antipathy. He changed his mind later on and rejected them.

1491 [1] *Deontology,* Bowring's Preface, Vol. II, p. 11: "There are, properly speaking, but two parties in morals or politics and in religion. The one is for the unlimited exercise of reason, the other is against it. I profess myself of the former."

1492 [1] I have not the remotest intention of dealing with the intrinsic merits of Bentham's theory or any other in these volumes (§ 1404). I touch on the question of its accord with the facts only for the light it throws on the subject of derivations.

1492 [2] *Deontology,* Vol. I, pp. 13-15. For Mill, see his *System of Logic,* Bk. VI, Chap. 12, § 7 (p. 658). For a theory of Herbert Spencer designed to reconcile the egoistic and altruistic principles see my *Manuale,* Chap. I, § 29.

1493 [1] *Ethica,* IV, 18, *scholium* (Latin, p. 216; Willis, p. 575).

away that nothing is more detrimental to a man than another man. And the same sentiment would be shared by the man who found that the woman he loved had another lover. Both lover and starving man would suffer from the fact that other men were "of their same mind (*natura*)." But Spinoza drives ahead and says that from his principle it follows that "men who are governed by Reason [Needless to say anyone not agreeing with Spinoza is not 'governed by Reason.'], that is to say, men who seek their own welfare under guidance of Reason desire nothing for themselves that they do not desire for other men, and so are just, honest and of good faith." [2] So the derivation changes in form, but the substance is still the same: one achieves one's own welfare by achieving the welfare of others. The same argument recurs in other writers of the eighteenth century and turns up again in the modern doctrine of "solidarity." [3]

1494. Burlamaqui begins by finding a sanction for natural laws in the harm that comes in natural course upon those who violate them. That is a derivation like Bentham's. But, shrewd soul that he is, Burlamaqui has a feeling that one should not trust Dame Nature too implicitly to enforce her laws, the good lady having fits of absent-mindedness at times. So he brings in the sanction of a supernatural life, and, stepping outside the experimental world, evades the objections that might be urged against him within it. [1]

1493 [2] "*Si enim duo, exemplo gerendo, eiusdem prorsus naturae individua invicem iunguntur individuum componunt singulo duplo potentius. Homini igitur nihil homine utilius; nihil, inquam, homines praestantius ad suum esse conservandum optare possunt quam quod omnes in omnibus ita conveniant . . . ex quibus sequitur homines qui Ratione gubernantur, hoc est, homines qui ex ductu Rationis suum utile quaerunt, nihil sibi appetere quod reliquis hominibus non cupiant, atque adeo eosdem iustos fidos atque honestos esse.*"

1493 [3] *Cf.* Holbach, *Système de la nature*, Vol. II, p. 436: Chap. IX, *"The True Meaning of the System of Nature"*: "The purpose of man is self-preservation and to lead a happy life. Experience teaches him that other people are necessary to him. It shows him how he can make them useful to his designs. He sees what is approved and what causes displeasure. Such experiences give him a notion of what is just. Virtue, like wickedness, is not founded on convention but on relationships obtaining between the members of the human race. The mutual obligations of men derive from their need of using means apposite to the objectives which their nature sets them. It is by contributing to the happiness of others that we bind them to contribute to ours."

1494 [1] *Éléments du droit naturel*, Pt. I, Chap. 6: "A just remark that one may make . . . is that exact observance of natural laws is ordinarily accompanied by a number of very considerable advantages, such as a strong and healthy body, clarity

1495. Other writers, such as Pufendorf, Hobbes, Spinoza, and Locke, think that there is a sanction for natural laws in the fact that the individual who violates them does harm to society and consequently to himself as a member of society. That is all well enough in general (§ 2115), but the quantitative question, the amount of the individual's advantage, which is direct, and the amount of his harm, which is indirect, have to be considered. Instead of doing that those writers, and others too, resort to an argument that recurs in a vast number of derivations and which might be termed the "fallacy of apportionment." Given an individual who is a member of a community and who is doing a certain thing, *A,* that is harmful to the community, the idea is to show him that if he thinks of his own interest he will refrain from doing *A.* So he is reminded that as a member of the community he will share in the harm he does to it. The conclusion is that the conduct *A* is harmful to him, so that if he does *A,* it can only be out of ignorance. Whence the further conclusion, that the misapprehensions of men as to what constitutes their own good are the sources of all evil.[1]

and tranquillity of mind, the affection and goodwill of one's fellows. Violation of those laws is ordinarily attended by a number of disadvantages, such as physical weakness, diseases, prejudices and errors, the hatred and contempt of one's fellows. However, such natural rewards and punishments do not seem sufficient for establishing a very solid sanction for natural laws. For, firstly, the inconveniences ordinarily accompanying violation of natural laws are not always great enough to hold men to the path of duty. Secondly, it often happens that the good are unfortunate in this life, while the wicked enjoy the fruits of their crimes in peace. Thirdly, there are times even when the virtuous man cannot do his full duty and comply with natural laws without exposing himself to the greatest of natural misfortunes, to death." Burlamaqui then gives a long proof of the immortality of the soul and of the necessity of believing that God rewards the good and punishes the wicked, and finally concludes: "All we know, therefore, of the nature of man, the nature of God, and the designs He had in creating the human race [How on earth does Burlamaqui know what those designs were?], all concur in proving that there are natural laws, that they have a sanction, and that there is a future life where that sanction will be applied through rewards and punishments."

1495 [1] Novicow, *La morale de l'intérêt,* pp. 20, 49-56: "The fundamental basis of morality is absolute respect for the rights of one's neighbours. But it is in no sense out of love of one's neighbour that one should respect his rights, but only and strictly out of love for oneself. . . . The idea that one can get rich more quickly by robbing one's neighbour than by working seems to be true but is not really so. The directly opposite fact, that the quickest possible way to get rich is scrupulously to respect the rights of one's neighbours, is the only one that conforms to realities. [No one of course has ever been known to get rich except by strictly moral means!] . . . Every time a working-man uses violence to exact a wage

1496. The fallacy lies: 1. In disregarding amounts of gain or loss, on the assumption that *all* individuals are to act in one way or *all* in another, and in not considering the case where some individuals are to act in one way and some in another. 2. In going to extremes along the line of the above and considering gains only, or losses only. In fact, let us adopt the premise that if *all* individuals refrained

higher than the natural market-price [What on earth can such a natural market-price be?], he robs himself. Every time an employer uses violence to force on the worker a wage lower than the natural market-price, he robs himself. Try to imagine what the world would be like if men should find it more in conformity with their interests not to rob their neighbours and to refrain from doing so under any form whatsoever! From that moment there would be no more locks, no more strong-boxes, fortresses, battle-ships, no more watchmen, no more judges, lawyers, police, no more soldiers by land or by sea ([In a note]: I am speaking of civil actions of course—there would still be crimes of passion). In such a society there would be no litigations, no strikes, no sabotage, no lock-outs, no shady speculation. . . . In a word, in a non-robbing society, there would be the greatest and most rapid production that can possibly be attained on this earth, and wealth, therefore, would reach its culminating point. Now wealth, comfort, happiness, and interest are synonymous terms. But then again, morality and absolute respect for the rights of one's neighbour are also identical concepts. Since, therefore, our interests are best satisfied when our manner of conduct is the most moral, how can the identity of morality and interest be disputed? [The fallacy of the argument in general becomes strikingly apparent in a particular case:] Is it really to a judge's interest to accept a bribe? Certainly not, and when he does accept one, it is from his failure to understand that there is no advantage in his doing so. . . . Experience shows that judges draw the highest salaries in the very countries where they do not sell their consciences. . . . Incorruptibility on the part of judges contributes very considerably to increasing social wealth, and the greater the social wealth, the better paid can public officials be. So a judge who is ill informed thinks that he will get a larger return by selling justice. A judge who is well informed knows that it is just the contrary. But a judge who knows that he will get larger returns by avoiding corruption understands that it is to his interest to avoid corruption." Suppose we adopt the somewhat arbitrary premise that judges are better paid when there is no corruption, and keep to the logical errors in the argument. 1. The dilemma assumed by Novicow does not exist. We are not necessarily confined to a choice between a situation where *all* judges are corrupt and a situation where *no* judges are corrupt. There are intermediate situations. If all judges *but one* are incorruptible, the one enjoys the general advantage *plus* the individual profits of his corruption. If *all but one* are corrupt, the one suffers the general loss *plus* the particular loss of the profits of his corruption. 2. It is not enough to show that honest judges are better paid than corrupt judges. It must also be shown that the general gain is greater than the particular gain from the corruption. Honest judges receive, let us say, $10,000 a year, corrupt judges $2,000. But one of the corrupt judges is offered $30,000 for a decision. He would be the loser if he refused the money on the remote, in fact the very remote, and uncertain chance of some day being advanced to $10,000 a year.

from doing A, every individual as a member of the community would derive a certain advantage. But now if all individuals *less one* continue refraining from doing A, the community loss is very slight, whereas the one individual doing A makes a personal gain far greater than the loss that he incurs as a member of the community. The fact that the fallacy is not recognized at once is due to a residue which usually interposes in such arguments implicitly and gives rise to the first half of the fallacy. It is assumed, but not stated, that all individuals are to act like the individual doing A. In such a case the loss is distributed, while the direct gain, in great part at least, is eliminated. The answer would be that the person who does A in no sense wants others to do A. That answer, however, cannot be made without giving offence to the residue of equality and it is therefore lost sight of in the argument. Take a thief, for instance. Our idea is to convince him that stealing is against his personal interests. So we point to the loss that society in general suffers because of his theft, and explain that he too suffers his share of it. We might specify expenses for police, judges, prisons, and the like; or the losses resulting from lack of personal security. It is certain that if no one stole, society would be the gainer and that every member of society would share in the gain. But the thief can reply: 1. That the direct gain which he derives from the theft is greater than the indirect loss that he incurs as a member of society, especially considering the fact that if he refrained from theft it would by no means follow that everybody else would do the same. 2. That it is true that if everybody, or even many people, turned to thieving, his indirect loss in many cases would probably be greater than his direct gain; but that he has not the remotest intention of encouraging everybody to turn thief. In fact, what he earnestly hopes is that everybody else will be honest, and he the one thief.[1]

1496 [1] A jest that is variously recounted by various writers appears among the *Facetiae* of Poggio Bracciolini as follows, II, 158: "A usurer of Vicenza kept urging a monk of great reputation who was regularly preaching to the people to deliver some strong sermons on the subject of usury and roundly to condemn such a great vice, which was especially rife in that city; and he pestered the monk to the point of annoyance. One day, in surprise that he should be so insistent on having a trade by which he himself lived rebuked, a certain person asked him the reason for his great solicitude. And he: 'So many people are plying the trade of the usurer in this town that I am getting very few customers and am earning

1497. A similar derivation was for some time used in defence of "solidarity." All men were held to be interdependent—indeed, to give greater force to the argument, all Creation (§ 499), animals being made dependent on the vegetable world, and plants in turn on minerals. The conclusion was that since one individual is dependent on other individuals he can realize his own welfare only by working for the welfare of others. The trouble with the argument is that the enumeration is incomplete. There is the kind of dependence where *A* realizes his own welfare by working for the welfare of *B, C.* . . . But there is also the kind of dependence where *A* realizes his own welfare at the cost of *B, C.* . . . The wolf realizes its welfare by devouring the sheep, the slave-owner by exploiting the slave.[1] The argument in favour of solidarity is peculiarly childish, and could never have convinced anybody who was not already convinced.

1498. III-γ: *Accord with collective interest.* If the interest is real and the individual acts logically to favour it, there is no derivation: it is a case of plain logical conduct designed to attain an end desired by an individual. Class IV residues (sociality) do to be sure stimulate the individual in such conduct. More often, however, the objective end differs from the subjective purpose (§§ 13, 151), and we get non-logical conduct justified by derivations. This type of derivation is very generally used by people who want something and pretend to be asking for it not for themselves but in behalf of the community. A certain number of politicians want something for themselves. They ask for it in the name of party, city, country. Certain factory-hands want better conditions. What they demand is a betterment in the conditions of the "proletariat" or the "working-classes." A group of manufacturers want a favour from the government for their particular industry. They ask for it as a help to business in general or as a benefit to the working-classes. For more than a half-century past, "speculators" (§ 2235) have been astute enough to win favour after favour from our various governments, and bigger and bigger ones, by asking for them in the interests of the labouring classes or even in the "public interest."

nothing. If the others could be persuaded to go out of business, all their earnings would come to me.' " [*Cf.* Bandello, *Novelle,* Pt. III, no. 53, on the usurer Tommasone, this time at Milan.—A. L.]

1497 [1] For the detailed refutation see my *Systèmes socialistes,* Vol. II, pp. 225 f.

1499. Examples of that sort of derivation turn up before one has read very far in any article written in support of a protective tariff, or of an increase in public expenditures, or of one of the many measures whereby the "speculators" get their hands on money belonging to people who live on fixed, or virtually fixed, incomes (§ 2235). In politics all ruling classes have at all times identified their own interests with the "interests of the country." When politicians are afraid of a too rapid increase in the number of proletarians, they are for birth-control and show that Malthusianism is to the interests of public and country. If, instead, they are afraid a population may prove inadequate for their designs, they are against birth-control, and show just as conclusively that their interest is the interest of public and country. And all that is accepted as long as residues remain favourable. The situation changes as residues change—never in view of arguments pro or contra.

1500. This type of derivation is well known, so much so that virtually all other derivations are commonly brought under it, on the assumption, explicit or implicit, that a person who uses an unsound argument does so in bad faith, and would use sound ones if he were in good faith. That view is altogether out of touch with realities, as may readily be seen from the many exceedingly important derivations that we have been identifying in this chapter.

1501. III-δ: *Accord with juridical entities.* A person living in a civilized society becomes familiar with certain moral or juridical relationships that are continually shaping his life, with which his mind is gradually saturated, and which end by becoming part and parcel of his intellectual personality. Eventually, through group-persistences, through his inclination to take what is relative as absolute, he carries them beyond the limits within which they may have been valid. They were adapted to certain circumstances, certain cases, merely; he makes them serve all cases, all circumstances. So concepts of an absolute morality and an absolute law come into being. Then he goes on and imagines that those relationships which arose and developed in a given community existed before the community, nay, gave rise to it; and we get theories of a "pact," or "social contract," of "peace under law," of "solidarity," with its adjunct of the "debt to society" and the like. In another direction the juridical and moral relationships obtaining among human beings may be extended to animals, living creatures in general, and even inanimate things. Indeed the power that speech sometimes exercises over human beings is extended to things—whence the notion of the magical chant, and the spoken or written word becomes a potent instrument for working upon things and is thought capable of moving or halting the Sun and the other stars. A part is played in such phenomena by residues of our I-β1 variety (likeness and oppositeness) whereby, in view of certain analogies real or imaginary, the traits and properties of one object are carried over to another. The substance in such cases is supplied by group-persistences, the forms by the derivations that are devised to account logically for the non-logical conduct. In concrete cases we ordinarily get mixtures of non-logical conduct of one sort or another and derivations and logical conduct designed to derive some advantage from the non-logical conduct—the effort serving merely to demonstrate the existence of the non-logical conduct, since only something that exists can be used and turned to account. Given a group-persistence whereby juridical relationships are extended to cases with which they have nothing to do, individuals will turn up to take advantage of the situation for ends of their own; but it is evident that they could not do that if the group-persistence in question were not already there. The shrewd take advantage of any weapon that comes into their hands. In the Middle Ages prosecutions of animals and of persons who were dead were so exploited. Nowadays it is "solidarity." Tomorrow it will be something else.

The records show that juridical penalties have been inflicted upon beings other than human, in all countries, in all periods of history. There are examples in Athens and among the Hebrews in ancient times, and in Western countries in the Middle Ages and even in times more recent. As usual if we knew only one group of such facts, we should not be able to decide which of the elements in them was the constant element (residues) and which the variable (derivations). But the doubt vanishes as we examine the various known types and see that the derivations used for one type do not serve for others. In the case of the action for damages—the *noxalis actio*—in Rome, the group-persistence that is brought into play seems in the main to be the relationship of the head of the family to the *liberi* under his authority, or to his slaves.[1] If cases of that sort were the only ones known to us, we would not be able to say whether juridical actions were ever extended to animals. But, lo and behold, in Athens we come upon actions against animals independently of any owner; and even when the action is directed against the owner, the personality of the animal is the more prominent of the two.[2] Actions are brought even against inanimate things; and in opposing a decree designed to condemn without trial "whoever slew Caridemus," Demosthenes clearly compares procedure against an inanimate thing with procedure against a human being, holding that a man cannot be denied a guarantee which is accorded to an inanimate thing.[3] A law ascribed to Draco provided that a stone, or a piece of wood or iron, that had fallen and killed a person should be thrown out-

1501 [1] Daremberg-Saglio, *Dictionnaire, s.v. Noxalis actio:* "The proprietor is, in certain cases, responsible for damage done by his animals. According to the Twelve Tables, the animal had to be a quadruped. . . . Jurisprudence later extended the rule to damage caused by bipeds. The victim was authorized to prosecute the proprietor of the animal through a special action called *de pauperie* [damage done by an irresponsible party]. The proprietor had two options: either to give up the animal (*deditio noxalis*) or to repair the damage. The option of surrendering the animal applied the principle that the owner of a thing that had caused a damage could not be held liable beyond the value of the thing." In his *Manuel élémentaire de droit romain*, p. 393, note 4, Girard well points out how the theorists of Roman law tried to remedy by derivations certain consequences of that group-persistence which were considered harmful: "It is interesting to note the fruitless efforts of jurists under the late Republic to adapt those old procedures to more modern notions of responsibility, deciding that the damage must have been caused by the animal *contra naturam* and applying to fights between animals the principles of legitimate self-defence." Surrender of the animal still obtains under Burgundian law: *Lex Burgundiorum*, XVIII, 1 (Canciani, Vol. IV, p. 19): "If a horse has killed a horse or if an ox has gored or a dog bitten an ox so that it is incapacitated (*debilitetur*), the animal or dog against which the damage has been proved shall be handed over to the man who has suffered the damage."

1501 [2] Beauchet, *Histoire du droit privé de la république athénienne*, Vol. IV, p. 391: "In Athens the action called βλάβης [corresponding to the action *de pauperie* of the XII Tables] seems to have been brought rather against the animal than against the owner and with a view to permitting the victim of the tort to exercise the *vindicta privata* on the animal itself." The Athenian law requiring transfer of the offending animal to the offended party was ascribed to Solon. See Plutarch, *Solon, 24, 3* (a biting dog in question).

1501 [3] Demosthenes, *Contra Aristocratem*, 645 (Auger, Vol. VII, pp. 62-63): "If, therefore, it is not lawful to deny a trial to things inanimate and without reason which are subject to such indictment [homicide] . . ."

side the boundaries of the state.[4] The law like other ancient laws is quoted in Plato's treatise on *Laws,* IX, 873 (Bury, Vol. II, p. 267), where animals as well as inanimate things are mentioned as guilty of homicide. The corpse of a patricide had to be thrown outside the boundaries of the state in exactly the same manner (Bury, Vol. II, p. 259). Pausanias, *Periegesis,* VI, *Elis* II, 11, 5-7, relates that, at Thasos, one of the rivals of the champion runner, Theagenes, was in the habit of thrashing his statue every night, and that finally to punish the man it fell upon him and crushed him: "The children of the dead man then brought action against the statue for murder, and following one of the Draconian laws, the Thasians threw it into the sea." But a blight fell forthwith upon their territory, and the Delphic oracle declared that it was because the Thasians "had forgotten the greatest of their fellow-citizens." So they fished up the statue and re-erected it in its original position.[5] In Athens, finally, we come upon a mock trial for the murder of an ox. An ox was made to eat offerings of fodder that were deposited on an altar, and he was then killed. Then a trial was held before a court that had jurisdiction over murders committed by inanimate objects. Each of the actors in the drama in turn laid the blame for the murder on his neighbour, until only the ax with which the ox had been slain was left. The ax was thereupon condemned and thrown into the sea.[6] Phenomena of totemism may

1501 [4] Aeschines, *In Ctesiphontem,* 88, 244; Aeschylus, *Septem adversus Thebas,* v. 197 (203) (*Scholia prôta,* Butler, p. 53); Pausanias, *Periegesis,* VI, *Elis,* II, 11, 6; Suidas, *Lexicon, s.v.* Νίκων. Cases of that sort were archaic and of a religious character. They were tried, therefore, at the Prytaneum: Demosthenes, *Contra Aristocratem,* 645. Pausanias, *Periegesis,* I, *Attica,* 28, 11, mentions a common belief that certain inanimate objects brought about punishment for certain crimes automatically. And *cf.* Pollux, *Onomasticon,* VIII, 9, 90 (Dindorf, Vol. I, p. 137, and see note, Vol. V, p. 709), and 10, 120 (Dindorf, Vol. I, p. 147).

1501 [5] Suidas, *Lexicon, s.v.* Νίκων, substitutes that name for Θεαγένης. And *cf.* Eusebius, *Evangelica praeparatio,* V, 34 (*Opera,* Vol. III, pp. 395-98). Whether the story be pure fiction or legend based on a certain amount of historical fact makes no difference to us here. Our object is to discover the sentiments that were at work in the individuals who devised or accepted the story. Conspicuous enough in them is a persistence of associations whereby a statue stands in the same juridical relationships as a human being.

1501 [6] The ceremony was called the βουφόνια. Porphyry, *De abstinentia ab esu animalium,* II, 29-30, gives a detailed account of it, and it is referred to by other writers. Pausanias, *Periegesis,* I, *Attica,* 24, 4, cryptically chooses not to state the reason that was given for the rite. Efforts have naturally been made to guess it, and not a few suggestions have been offered—among them totemism. But to

possibly figure in it, but in any event it certainly shows an extension
to animals of juridical relationships that were established for human
beings. Pliny, *Historia naturalis,* VIII, 18 (Bostock-Riley, Vol. II,
p. 267), relates that in Africa lions were crucified in order to
frighten other lions.[7] A number of passages in the Bible clearly indicate that juridical relationships proper to human beings were extended to animals.[8] On those passages derivations which justified
similar extensions of juridical procedure were based in part, while
meantime there was no lack of ingenious derivations designed to give
the passages themselves logical significance. Famous the prosecution
conducted against the body of Pope Formosus:[9] "A formal trial of
Formosus was proclaimed by public crier. The deceased was cited to

tell the truth, nothing certain or even very probable can be known on such a
matter. To set out to guess at the combinations that underlie a given derivation
is altogether hopeless when there is no direct testimony, and hardly less so when
there is very little. For our purposes we can stop at the fact that a prosecution was
directed simultaneously against human beings and an ax, as codefendants. [And
cf. further Pausanias, *loc. cit.,* 28, 10.—A. L.]

1501 [7] "Polybius, who accompanied Aemilianus, states that when lions get old
they attack human beings, since they are no longer strong enough to hunt wild
prey. In such circumstance they begin to infest the cities of Africa, and he says
that he and Scipio saw some that had been crucified that others might be deterred
from their depredations by fear of similar punishment."

1501 [8] Gen. 9:5: "And surely your blood of your lives will I require. At the hand
of every beast will I require it, and at the hand of man, and at the hand of every
man's brother will I require the life of man." The animal is prosecuted quite independently of the owner. The animal that kills a man is held culpable and punished
as such. The owner is innocent: Ex. 21:28: "If an ox gore a man or a woman that
they die then the ox shall be surely stoned, and his flesh shall not be eaten; but the
owner of the ox shall be quit." Lev. 20:15-16: "And if a man lie with a beast, he
shall surely be put to death: and ye shall slay the beast. And if a woman approach
unto any beast and lie down thereto, thou shalt kill the woman and the beast:
they shall surely be put to death: their blood shall be upon them." So then, both
the woman and the beast! That delightful soul, Philo the Jew, works out a very
pretty derivation to account for these prescriptions: he imagines that the animal
is killed that it may not give birth to a monstrous lineage such as sprang from
the passions of Pasiphae and the bull: *De legibus specialibus,* III, 8 (Cohn, Vol. V,
pp. 162-64; Yonge, Vol. III, pp. 314-15): "So, whether a man or a woman be with
a quadruped, they shall be killed, human beings and quadrupeds alike; the males
because they have overstepped the prescribed bounds in contriving new forms of
lust and seeking a loathsome pleasure in unspeakably foul ways: the females because they have lent themselves to such iniquities, and to prevent them from giving
birth to such abominations as are commonly born of detestable crimes of that character."

1501 [9] Gregorovius, *Geschichte der Stadt Rom im Mittelalter,* Vol. III, p. 246.

appear in person before a Synod sitting as a Court of Justice. [As we shall see, animals were served with summonses in the same way.] It was February or March in the year 897. . . . The Cardinals, the Bishops, and many other Church dignitaries, assembled in Sanhedrin. The Pope's body, wrested from the tomb in which it had been lying for eight months, was clothed in the pontifical robes and seated on a throne in the Council hall. Pope Stephen's attorney arose and turned towards the horrible mummy—at its side sat a terrified deacon who had been designated to act as its counsel. [Animals too had their attorneys.] The prosecutor read the charges. Then the living Pope inveighed at the dead Pope in a mad violence: 'Why, ambitious man, didst thou usurp the Apostolic See of Rome, thou who wert Bishop of Porto?' The attorney of Formosus answered in his defence so far as terror did not paralyze his tongue. The dead Pope was convicted and his punishment fixed. [Animals were convicted and sentenced in the same way.] The Synod signed the decree of deposition and pronounced sentence of condemnation." The Inquisition also conducted many prosecutions against people who were dead. The purpose was to get possession of such property as the dead heretics had left to their heirs; and the means, popular beliefs and superstitions, not least among which the feeling that the juridical relationships of the living could be extended to the dead.

1502. In our Western countries prosecutions of animals occur all the way along from the twelfth century, and even before that, down to the eighteenth. Berriat Saint-Prix has compiled a list of such trials, chiefly for France.[1] Some took place before lay tribunals, others before ecclesiastical courts. In civil tribunals the procedure was the same as for human defendants.[2] Even before ecclesiastical tribunals

1502 [1] *Les procès et jugements relatifs aux animaux.* The catalogue is too long for reprinting here in full; just a specimen from the beginning and the end, giving the year, the kind of animal, and the locality: 1120, field-mice and caterpillars, Laon; 1121, flies, Foigny, near Laon; 1166, a pig, Fontenay, near Paris; 1314, a bull, Comté de Valois; 1386, a sow, Falaise; 1389, a horse, Dijon; 1394, a pig, Mortain; 1633, a mare, Bellac; 1647, a mare, Parlement, Paris; 1679, a mare, Parlement, Aix; 1690, caterpillars, Auvergne; 1692, a mare, Moulins; 17th century (end), pigeons, Canada; 1741, a cow, Poitou. In all ninety-two cases!

1502 [2] Cabanès, *Les indiscrétions de l'histoire,* Ser. 5, pp. 34-35: "Action was opened against the animal by criminal process and procedure developed as follows. A crime being reported, the delinquent animal was arrested and taken to the detention prison of the criminal court before which the preliminary investigation was

procedure was on the whole the same; but in many cases the process seems to be an afterthought, as a means of avoiding hitting innocent creatures with the fulminations of the Church; and there are cases where mention is made only of the condemnation and not of any trial.[3] Next, under pressure of the sentiment extending juridical re-

to be conducted. Affidavits were drawn up . . . and a thorough-going inquest opened. The facts being established beyond reasonable doubt, the prosecuting attorney, in other words, the official exercising the functions of state prosecutor within the feudal jurisdiction concerned, asked for the indictment and trial of the defendant. Witnesses were heard and after their testimony in the affirmative the prosecutor made his plea. The judge then rendered his verdict, declaring the animal guilty of murder and sentencing him to be strangled and then hung by the hind legs to an oak-tree or to the public gallows, according to local custom. . . . The formalities of criminal procedure were so strictly observed in some places that sentences would not be executed till a warrant had been read to the animal itself in its prison." Beaumanoir, *Coutumes de Beauvaisis*, II, 1944: "Some have [courts of] justice on their lands, and execute animals when they have killed someone. For instance, if a sow or some other animal kills a child, they hang it and drag it [at the tail of a horse]. But that amounts to nothing, for mute beasts have no understanding of what is right and what is wrong, and for that reason such justice is wasted." Trumelet, *Les saints de l'Islam*, p. 132, note: "There is a story . . . that one day the Calif, Omar-ben-el-Khoththah, cousin thrice removed to Mohammed, found a scorpion on the carpet that he used as his bed. He was seized with a doubt as to his right to kill one of God's creatures, and . . . to have peace with his conscience, he went to consult the Prophet, his relative, stating the case to him. After reflecting for some moments, Mohammed answered that he could not claim such right of destruction till the insect had thrice disobeyed him, that is to say, until he had bidden it thrice to be gone."

1502 [3] Étienne de Bourbon, *Anecdotes historiques*, §§ 303-05: "They say that animals are afraid of the sentence of excommunication and avoid it, as a result of example and divine miracles. I am told that at the time Pope Gregory IX was Legate of the Apostolic See in Lombardy before he became Pope, he visited a town where he found certain nobles (*maiores*) fighting, so that they interfered with his journey. He therefore excommunicated the leader of the dissension who was alone standing in the way of peace. That individual however snapped his fingers (*contempneret*) at the excommunication. Whereupon the many cranes who had been nesting on the towers and chimneys of his house departed thence and moved their nests to the house of the other leader in the feud aforesaid, who stood ready to obey the decision of the Legate. Seeing which the obdurate leader humbled his heart to the extent of asking absolution and doing the will of the Legate." In that we have a case of innocent animals shunning a person who has been excommunicated. Here now are cases where animals are themselves excommunicated! "I am likewise told that at Macon [in France] . . . many sparrows were in the habit of entering the Church of St. Vincent, dirtying the building and interfering with mass. When there seemed to be no way of keeping them out, the Bishop in that place . . . excommunicated them, threatening them with death if they went into the church again; whereupon they withdrew from the church and never again entered it. [To tell the unadorned truth, the poor sparrows were excommu-

lationships to animals, it was ruled that trial had to precede sentence. Then, incidental considerations contributed to prolonging procedure: first of all, the fees earned by lawyers and court attendants; and then again, as seems quite possible in times of increasing scepticism, Church authorities were not altogether convinced of the effectiveness of the ecclesiastical excommunication as an exterminator of pests, and they were not at all loath to allow proceedings to drag along, that the animals might disappear of themselves in natural course without putting excommunication to the test. It is difficult otherwise to account for the long protractions of trials, as in the case of which Menabrea gives a detailed description.[4] Menabrea puts

nicated without trial and Étienne himself is an eyewitness to the efficacy of the sentence:] I myself saw flocks of them nesting, flying, or sitting about the church, but never a one did I see inside, and it is common opinion in the town that if anyone catches a sparrow and takes it by force inside the church, it dies the moment it is inside. [The Bishop's excommunication is no whit more miraculous in its effects than Rousseau's social contract, which continues to have believers though it can boast no eyewitness.] I have also heard from a number of our friars that there was once a certain Bishop in Lausanne who had fishermen on the lake. One night he sent them out to fish for eels, and they set their nets in the lake and caught snakes along with the eels. One of the men crushed their heads with his teeth, thinking them eels, and in the morning when he saw that they were snakes he was so horrified that he died of his disgust. . . . Hearing which the Bishop excommunicated the eels in case they should remain any longer in those waters. However, they all departed thence and since that time, it is said, there have been no eels in the lake."

1502 [4] *De l'origine, de la forme et de l'esprit des jugements rendus au moyen âge contre les animaux,* pp. 7-23. It contains the record of a trial conducted in the year 1587 against a certain insect(Rynchites auratus—grape-vine weevil) that was ruining the vineyards at Saint-Julien near Saint-Jean de Maurienne. The same record is summarized and in part reprinted in a volume called *Curiosités des traditions, des mœurs, et des légendes,* pp. 429-31. "The vines [at Saint-Julien] are subject at certain intervals to depredations from a green beetle called the *amblevin* (vine walker ?) or *verpillon* (green-worm ?)." Court records of the year 1587 "show that forty-two years before (in 1545) a similar action had been entered between the same parties, but the destroying insects having disappeared, the plaintiffs had not seen fit to go on with the case. At that time a first hearing had been held for arbitration purposes before the Honourable François Bonnivard, doctor of laws, Attorney Pierre Falcon representing the insects, with Attorney Claude Morel as assistant counsel. Negotiations failing, the syndics of Saint-Julien brought action before the ecclesiastical judge (*Official*) at Saint-Jean de Maurienne, and entered formal suit." Expert testimony was heard, counsel on both sides summed up, "and the court issued an order temporarily setting aside the petition of the inhabitants of Saint-Julien, who had asked for the excommunication of the insects, and prescribing public prayers. . . . The action of 1545, which had been left in abeyance for forty-two years owing to the disappearance of the devastating insects, was reopened in 1587

within our reach many of the derivations that came to the fore in such trials. "An action initiated in 1451 . . . for the purpose of expelling the leeches which were infesting waters in the territory of Berne . . . furnishes very curious details as to the methods of process-serving in use in such cases. . . . In the case of an insect pest a process-server, or 'usher,' was sent to the place where the insects were at work, and they were summoned to appear in person before a magistrate on such and such a day at such and such an hour to hear sentence passed against them, ordering them to evacuate the fields on which they were trespassing within such and such a time, under penalty of the law. The insects failing to appear, the summons

when the unlucky Coleoptera had made a new invasion of the vineyards and perhaps a more alarming one than usual. This new case is entitled [in Latin]: 'Action of the Syndics of the Commune of Saint-Julien against brute animals, winged like flies, and of a green colour, commonly called *verpillons* or *amblevins*.' " The syndics request the Reverend Official " 'at his pleasure to appoint a new attorney to replace the former who had passed from this life by death, to designate in advance of trial a competent commissioner to inspect the damaged vineyards, the defendant party having been summoned to attend the inspection if it be his pleasure [No more, no less!], whereafter procedure shall be taken for the eviction of said animals by way of excommunication or interdict and all other due ecclesiastical censure, they, the syndics, signifying their readiness to appoint to said animals, on behalf of the commune, lands where they will have sufficient pasturage in future.' " The action develops. The attorneys present briefs. There are answers and rejoinders. Finally "the syndics could not have had any great confidence in the soundness of their case at law, since they saw fit to make a prime issue of the compromise that they had suggested at the outset of the action in a wholly secondary way." They convoked a meeting of the Commune " 'to the end of giving effect to earlier offers, by deeding to the weevils a place where said little animals would find sustenance.' . . . Each of those attending having expressed his opinion, all agreed to offer the weevils a piece of land situate above the village of Claret . . . 'of fifty-six acres (*sétérées*) more or less, and which attorneys representing said animals are willing to accept . . . said piece of land being occupied by several sorts of trees, plants, and foliage, such as ferns (? *foulx*), beeches (? *alagniers*), cherry-trees, oaks . . . in addition to grass and pasture, which are there in fairly good quantity.' In making that offer the inhabitants of Saint-Julien thought best to reserve the right of thoroughfare through said parcel of land for purpose both of reaching properties situate beyond, 'without however causing any damage to pasturage of said animals,' and of working certain 'mines of colour' (ochre), situate near by. 'And since,' they add, 'the place is a safe retreat in time of war, being well supplied with springs, which will also be of use to said animals,' they further reserve the privilege of repairing thither in case of necessary defence, promising on the terms specified to cause to be drawn up 'in favour of the insects herein named' a deed to said parcel of land 'in regular form and valid in perpetuity.' On July 24, Petremand Bertrand, attorney for the plaintiffs, produced in duplicate a copy from the minutes of the resolution adopted." He moves that, in case the defence fails to accept, " 'it shall be the pleasure of

was usually repeated, sometimes as many as three times in order that the contumacy might be better established. . . . As one may well imagine, the defendants always defaulted . . . and a curator (receiver) with power of attorney was appointed for the little animals. That officer swore to discharge his duties with zeal and fidelity, and ordinarily counsel was put at his service. It was while serving as defence attorney for the rats in the diocese of Autun that the famous lawyer Barthélemy Chassanée, who at the time of his death was Chief Justice of the Parlement of Provence, established his reputation. Although the rats had been served in due form, Chassanée did not rest until he had obtained an order that his clients be again summoned by the curates of each parish, because, as he set up, since the case interested all rats they ought all to be served. Having won that point, he undertook to show that the period of grace allotted them had been insufficient, that the court should have taken into account not only the distance of the places but also the difficulties of the journey to court, a difficulty aggravated by the fact that cats were always on watch and were blocking every hole big and little. In short, combining Bible with profane literature, piling text on text, and exhausting every resource of the learned eloquence of those days, he succeeded in having their date of appearance deferred. The case made Chassanée a much-sought attorney."

the Reverend Official to give judgment on the basis of his contention, to the effect that said defendants be ordered to quit said vineyards in the Commune, under injunction of never again trespassing thereon in future, under penalties of the law.' " On Sept. 3, "Antoine Filliol, attorney for the insects, notified his refusal in behalf of his clients to accept the offer made by the plaintiffs, inasmuch as the land offered was barren and of no yield (*cum sit locus sterilis et nullius redditus*), to which Petremand Bertrand replied that far from being barren, 'said land abounded in shrubbery and small trees well suited to the sustenance of the defendants.' The Official thereupon orders the papers filed. The part of the sheet on which the court's decision was entered has fallen prey to time; but enough is left to show that before finally disposing of the action, the Official appointed experts to report on the serviceability of the land offered the weevils." The notion of assigning to the insects a place where they could live is not confined to the action here in question. There are other examples. Hammerlein, a writer quoted by Menabrea, states that after a regular action at law, the inhabitants of Coire (Switzerland) provided certain Cantharides (Spanish beetles) with a place where they could live. "Even today," Hammerlein adds, "the inhabitants of the Canton make a formal annual contract with the beetles, handing over to them a certain parcel of land. So true is it that they are satisfied and never try to overstep the specified boundaries."

1503. That all seems ridiculous to us; yet who can be sure that some few centuries hence the disquisitions of our day on the subject of solidarity will not seem equally ridiculous, and that M. Léon Bourgeois's invention of a debt which is being forever cancelled and forever revived will not occupy an honoured place beside Chassanée's defence of the rats of Autun? There were jurists and theologians who thought that the procedures used against rational beings could not be extended to brute creatures, and among the theologians stood St. Thomas Aquinas, no less.[1] But nothing of that sort could put an end to such trials; any more than in our time demonstrations of the utter inanity of the "social contract," of "solidarity," "peace through law," "Christian Science," and other such vagaries can put an end to the use of their respective derivations. As usual, everyone sees the mote in his neighbour's eye, never the beam in his own.

1504. Derivations change in form to accommodate themselves to circumstances, but the goal to which they are expected to lead remains unchanged. Among the many theorists who have represented human society as originating in some convention, pact, or contract, not a few have talked as though they were describing a historical incident: certain human beings not as yet living in society came together somewhere one fine day and organized human society, very much as people in our day get together and organize a business corporation.

1503 [1] *Summa theologiae,* IIᵃ IIᵃᵉ, *qu.* 76, *art.* 2 (*Opera,* Vol. IX, p. 144: *Utrum liceat creaturam irrationalem maledicere*): "To curse irrational creatures as being creatures of God of the order of rational creatures (*ad rationalem creaturam ordinatae*) is blasphemy. To curse them for what they are is illicit [*i.e.*, sinful], since it is an idle fatuous thing." *Decretum Gratiani, pars* 2, *causa* 15, *quaestio* 1, *canon* 4 (Friedberg, Vol. I, p. 747): "An animal with which a woman has had to do is killed not as a culprit but as a reminder of the crime. Whence Augustine on Lev. 20:74, § 1: 'The question is: how can an animal as an irrational creature in no way susceptible to law be guilty of a crime? . . . We must suppose that the animals were ordered killed because once contaminated by such a shame they would ever be refreshing the distressing memory of it.'" Menabrea, *Op. cit.,* pp. 138-41, reprints the *Discours des monitoires avec un plaidoyer contre les insectes* by Gaspard Bally of Chambéry, a lawyer who lived in the second half of the seventeenth century. It contains model specimens of pleas for and against insects as well as for summings up by the bishop's counsel, and forms of sentences used by ecclesiastical judges. Counsel for the insects marshals no end of sacred and legal precedents, and concludes: "'For which reasons it is evident that these animals are to be acquitted (*sont en nous absolutoires*) and should be dismissed from action before this bar, that being our conclusion.'" But plaintiff's counsel replies: "'The principal reason

1505. That idea being obviously absurd, there came an effort to make it seem a little more rational by deserting the field of history. It was now said that the relationships that go to make up society exist not because such a constitution was ever actually voted by men not as yet living in society, but because they ought to be conceived as though such a constitution had been voted. "Rousseau," says M. Léon Bourgeois, "places the contract at the beginning of things; we place it at the end." [1] That is the way Rousseau's disciples are defending their master's theories today. But locate the social contract at the beginning of human society, in the middle, or at the end, the fact still remains that the contracting parties are disposing of things over which they have no control. Man is a social animal and cannot live by himself, save perhaps in some case where he is reduced to

alleged by the defence of these animals is that, being without the use of reason, they are amenable to no law, on the basis of the law *Cum mulier,* 1, 5, *qu.* 1, the law *Congruit in fin.,* and the law . . . *sensu enim carens non subiicitur rigori juris civilis.* However, we intend to show that such laws do not militate against the issue at present before the bar, for there is no claim for punishment for a crime that has been committed, but an injunction against the commission of crimes hereafter.' " He follows with abundant quotations from authorities of all sorts, and even refutes St. Thomas: " 'In rebuttal of the dictum of St. Thomas that it is not permissible to curse such animals if they be taken in themselves, we claim that in the matter in hand we take them not as animals merely, but as causing harm to human beings by eating and destroying the fruits that serve for their food and sustenance. But why do we hesitate when there are precedents in quantity where Holy Authorities have excommunicated animals that do harm to human beings?' " The Official ends his decision with the words: " 'In the name and by the power of the Father, God omnipotent, and the Son, by order to the purport of this sentence (*a monitione in vim sententiae huius*) that they shall depart from the vineyards and lands of this place, doing no further damage thereon nor elsewhere: if within the said number of days said animals shall not have obeyed this order . . . when the six days have elapsed, by the afore-mentioned power and authority . . . of the Holy Spirit . . . and the authority of the Blessed Apostles Peter and Paul, along with that which we exercise in this place, we serve warning in this script upon said worms and caterpillars and said animals by whatever name they are called . . . that within six days we herein place them under anathema and malediction.' " It is interesting that Bally's book, as he himself states, was printed with permission of the Senate of Savoy, "having been seen and examined by the gentlemen of that distinguished body and reported on with praise."

1505 [1] *Essai d'une philosophïe de la solidarité,* p. 46: "Then, it will be said, solidarity is the social contract! I am willing! I will keep the expression [He is right: they are all variations on the same musical theme.], on condition, however, that our social contract be not mistaken for Rousseau's. Rousseau's hypothesis—as he thought of it—was merely that, and not a fact of history."

extreme poverty. From the standpoint of formal logic, therefore, the argument cannot stand even in its new form.

1506. Nor is it easy to see why the contract should not hold just as well for animal societies such as the ants and the bees. If we assume that nothing but reasoning and logical thinking can hold human society together and prevent its dissolution, how explain the fact that the societies of ants and bees hold together and endure in time? But we say that such societies are grounded on instinct. How deny that that instinct plays its part in human societies as well?

1507. Rousseau's theory is essentially the theory of Hobbes. But, as ordinarily happens with derivations, those two writers arrive at opposite conclusions. Rousseau's theory is in vogue today because we are living in a democratic age. Hobbes's theory might again prevail tomorrow if a period favourable to absolutism should recur. And if times favourable to some other type of social organization should some day come, no time would be lost in finding a derivation that would still start with the premise of the social contract and reach conclusions in harmony with that new system. The point of departure and the goal are fixed because they correspond to certain residues that are the constant element in the movement. Only a little imagination is required to find a derivation that will bring the two points together. If one does not hit the mark, others will be devised; and so only they tickle certain residues in the people to whom they are addressed, there can be no doubt of their favourable reception.

1508. Theories of "peace through law" must be classed with this same variety (III-δ). The usual objection urged against them is that law with no force to uphold it is worth little or nothing, and that if force is used war, which was banished in one direction, comes back from some other. The objection is valid only in part. In the first place many norms of social life are enforced without any resort to violence, and it is not absurd to think that some at least, if not all, of the rules of a given body of international law can be enforced by public opinion, by the sentiments that are active in individual human beings. That to some extent is actually taking place already. In the second place war might not disappear, but it would occur less frequently, if there were an international power to enforce a given system of law, just as acts of private violence decrease in numbers in a society where there is a public police power to enforce its will upon individuals. But of far greater weight is an objection involving the term "law," which in the phrase "peace through law" corresponds to nothing definite. The so-called civilized nations are all occupying territories by force, and no other principle can be thought of to justify our present-day territorial divisions. The justifications which people have pretended to find resolve into sophistries that are not seldom frankly childish. If Poland had been stronger than Prussia, as it was in a day gone by, Poland might have conquered Prussia; but since Poland was weaker than Prussia allied with Russia and Austria, Poland was conquered by those three powers. If Russia had been stronger than Japan, Russia would have seized Korea; instead Japan annexed Korea by force of arms. That much and only that much is real: the rest is talk.[1]

1509. So as between the various social classes no principle of "right" can be found to regulate the division of social advantage. The classes that have the greater strength, intelligence, ability, shrewdness, take the lion's share. It is not clear how any other prin-

1508 [1] Worshippers of the god Progress used to assure us that the time was long since past when congresses of European diplomats could get together and settle the destinies of peoples as was done in 1815. Yet in 1913 a congress of diplomats in London settled the destinies of the Balkan peoples. It denied Serbia access to the Adriatic. It compelled Montenegro to relinquish the city of Scutari, which she had conquered. It settled the fate of the wretched inhabitants of the Aegean Islands, and so on and so on. If Montenegro had been stronger than Austria, Austria would not have compelled Montenegro to relinquish territory; Montenegro would have compelled Austria to do so. What rule can one imagine to show with equal clarity that Austria had a "right" to occupy Bosnia and Herzegovina and that Montenegro had no "right" to occupy Scutari? The hoary theory of "equilibrium" that was appealed to in times past to keep Italy a divided and subject country serves the new Italy quite as well, with the connivance of her former oppressor, to keep the Balkan peoples divided and subject. By what miraculous sophistry can it now be shown that to maintain equilibrium in the Adriatic Italy has a "right" to keep Greece from occupying territories of Greek nationality, while in virtue of that same rule of "right" Greece did not have the "right" to maintain the same hoary equilibrium by forbidding the occupation of Taranto and Brindisi by the troops of Piedmont and so preventing the establishment of the Kingdom of Italy? There is only one thing that accounts for the facts and that thing is force. If Greece had been stronger than Italy, and stronger than the countries that were acting as patrons of the new kingdom, Greece would have "maintained equilibrium" in the Adriatic in her own favour just as Italy is doing now because she is stronger than Greece. Because "a Mighty One, crowned with the token of His victory" [Dante, *Inferno*, IV, vv. 53-54] heard "the cry of anguish that is reaching our ears from all parts of

ciples of division could be logically established and even less clear how once they were established logically they could be enforced or applied in the concrete. Every individual certainly has his own principle for a division that would seem ideal to him. But such a principle is nothing more than an expression of his individual sentiments and interests which he comes to conceive of as a "right." It is just a case of the usual derivation whereby a name is changed to make a thing more acceptable to others.

1510. III-ε: *Accord with metaphysical entities.* In derivations of this type accords with certain entities foreign to the experimental domain are sought. As regards substance, an accord of sentiments, a combination of residues, is at work. The form however is supplied by the entities in question, and, without being supernatural, they are non-experimental. The residues used for purposes of derivation come chiefly from our II-δ (persisting abstractions), II-ε (persisting uniformities), II-θ (new abstractions) varieties, as usual combining in concrete cases with other residues. From the logico-experimental standpoint there is little or no difference between these derivations and derivations utilizing personified divinities (III-ζ).[1]

1511. Metaphysical derivations are primarily designed for the use and consumption of educated people. The plain man, in our

Italy" [words of Napoleon III], and because fortune favoured him on the battlefield, Italy was freed of the Austrian yoke; and it was not because of any differences in "right," but because no Mighty One heard the "cry of anguish" of the Balkans and the Aegean Islands, that those nations failed of a destiny similar to Italy's. The Italian Leopardi sang in Dante's language (*Batracomiomachia,* II, vv. 30-39) of the mighty feats of Austrian "crabs" intent upon "maintaining equilibrium" in Italy; just as now some Greek poet might sing in Homer's language of the no less admirable feats of Austro-Italian "crabs" in "maintaining equilibrium" in the Adriatic and other regions. A person judging the facts by the sentiments of nationalism will say, if he is an Italian, that Italy is "right" and Greece "wrong," and if he is a Greek he will invert the terms. A person judging the facts by the sentiments of internationalism or pacifism will place in the wrong the party whom he considers the aggressor, in the right the party whom he deems to be the victim of the aggression. But a person resolved to stick to the objective field will simply see in such things new instances of the struggles that have always raged between the peoples; and in such judgments, the usual translations into terms of "right" of the fact that certain things are in accord with certain sentiments, and into terms of "wrong" of the fact that certain things are not in accord with certain sentiments. He will, in other words, see just residues and derivations.

1510 [1] Religious tradition may even be combined with the most advanced metaphysics. "Christian Science" (§ 1695 [2]), for instance, might be defined as a sort of "biblical Hegelianism."

Western countries at least, is tending to revert from such abstractions to personifications. It would of course be absurd to imagine that any of our contemporaries picture "solidarity" as a beautiful woman, the way the Athenians thought of the goddess Athena. All the same, in the minds of our masses such entities as "Solidarity," "Progress," "Humanity," "Democracy," are far from standing on a par with pure abstractions such as a geometric surface, chemical affinity, or luminous ether. They abide in a far loftier realm. They are powerful entities that can work miracles for the good of mankind.[1]

1512. Interesting in this connexion is the evolution of Auguste Comte. Comte was driven by a peculiarly violent impulse to endow his abstractions with concrete traits. He even went so far as to personify Humanity as a "Great Being," to speak of the Earth as if it were a person, and to recommend worship of Space as his "Great Medium." As we have already pointed out (§§ 1070 f.), such sentiments form a jumbled mass in the minds of many people; and they are not in the least interested in breaking the aggregate up into its elements to determine just where abstraction ends and personification begins.

1513. This derivation figures in all reasonings that appeal to "Reason," "Right Reason," "Nature," "the goal of mankind" (or other such goals), "Welfare," "the Highest Good," "Justice," "Truth," "Goodness," and, in our day more particularly, "Science," "Democracy," "Solidarity," "Humanity," and the like. Those are all names that designate nothing more than indistinct and incoherent sentiments.

1514. Famous a metaphysical entity that was imagined by Kant and is still admired by many good souls. It is called the *categorical imperative,* and there are plenty of people who pretend to know what it is, though they can never make it clear to anyone who in-

---

1511 [1] Weber, *L'enseignement de la prévoyance,* p. 101: Of certain persons who busy themselves with loan funds and societies for mutual aid and cooperation, Weber says: "In their eyes, as well as for the vast majority of their associates, Mutual Aid and Savings are dogmas that one must not even try to understand, things that have special virtues, that are virtues in themselves, and are blessed with some mysterious power for healing the woes of mankind. Their idea seems to be that the important thing so far as they are concerned is to be an adept and a believer. After that one need simply bring an offering, some small personal contribution, to 'the movement,' to obtain extraordinary results, such as retirement pensions or unemployment insurance, at ridiculously small costs."

sists on remaining in touch with reality.[1] Kant's formula reconciles, as usual, the egoistic with the altruistic principle, which is here represented by "universal law," a notion pleasantly coddling to sentiments of equality, sociality, and democracy. Many people have accepted Kant's formula in order to retain their customary morality and yet be free of the necessity of having it dependent upon a personified deity. That morality may be made to depend upon Jupiter, upon the God of the Christians, upon the God of Mohammed, upon the will of that estimable demoiselle Milady Nature, or upon *Seine Hoheit* the Categorical Imperative of Kant. Whatever it is, it is all the same thing. Kant gives still another form to his phrase, to wit: *"Act as if the maxim of your conduct were to become, by your will, a universal law of nature."* A customary trait in all such formulae is that they are so vague in meaning that one can get out of them anything one chooses. And for that reason it would have been a great saving of breath to say, "Act in a way pleasing to Kant or his disciples," for "universal law" will in the end be dispensed with anyhow.

1515. The first question that comes into one's mind as one tries to get some definite meaning into the terms of Kant's formula is

1514 [1] In his *Metaphysik der Sitten*, pp. 45-46 (Semple, pp. 33-34), Kant serves warning that (Semple translation) "the ground of the difficulty of comprehending the possibility of the categorical imperative, *i.e.*, of the moral law, is very great: THE IMPERATIVE IS A SYNTHETICAL PROPOSITION A PRIORI; and as we felt so much difficulty in comprehending the possibility of this kind of proposition in speculative metaphysics, we may presume the difficulty will be no less in the practical. In this inquiry we shall examine whether or not the mere conception of a categorical imperative may not involve in it a general formula, furnishing us with that expression which can alone be valid as a categorical imperative. [The conception will certainly furnish one. The mere conception of a Jabberwock will also furnish the expression for a Jabberwock.] . . . When I represent to myself a hypothetical imperative, I do not know beforehand what it contains, till the ulterior condition on which it rests is put in my possession; but with the very conception of a categorical imperative is given also its contents [And given the conception of a Jabberwock, I at once know its make-up.], for the imperative can in this case contain only the law ordaining the necessity of a maxim to be conformed to this law; and since the law is attached to no condition which could particularize it, there remains no what [read whit] except the form of law *in genere* to which the maxim of an act is to be conformed; and this conformity is, properly speaking, what the imperative represents as necessary. The categorical imperative is therefore single and one: '*Act from that maxim only which thou canst will* [to become] *law universal.*' " [Kant's German: "*Handle nur nach derjenigen Maxime durch die Du zugleich wollen kannst, dass sie ein allgemeines Gesetz werde.*"]

whether: (1) the "universal law" is dependent upon some condition; or (2) whether it is unrestricted by any condition of any kind. In other words, can the law be stated in either of the following ways? 1. Every individual who has the traits M ought to act in a certain manner. 2. Every individual, regardless of his traits, ought to act in a certain manner.

1516. If the first form of statement be adopted, the law itself means nothing, and the problem then is to determine which traits M it is permissible to consider; for if the choice of traits is left to the person who is to observe the law, he will always find a way to select traits that will allow him to do exactly as he chooses without violating the law. If he wants to justify slavery, he will say with Aristotle that sòme men are born to command (among them, of course, the gentleman who is interpreting the law) and other men are born to obey. If he wants to steal, he will say that it may very well be a universal law that he who has less should take from him who has more. If he wants to kill an enemy he will say that revenge can easily be a universal law; and so on.

1517. To judge by the first application that Kant makes of his principle, he would seem to reject that interpretation. Making no distinctions between individuals, he concludes that suicide could not be a universal law of nature.[1]

1517 [1] Kant, *Metaphysik der Sitten*, p. 48 (Semple, pp. 34-35): "An individual harassed by a series of evils and sickened with the tedium of life proposes to commit self-murder but first inquires within himself to know if the maxim regulating such an act would be fit for law universal. [The reply would have to be in the affirmative if qualifications were admissible. One would say in fact: "All men—and they are in the great majority—who prefer living to dying will try to remain alive as long as they can; and those few who prefer dying to living will kill themselves." What is there to prevent that from being a "universal law"? So little to prevent it that that is what actually happens, and has always happened in the concrete. Kant fails to draw any distinction between those two sorts of people and so answers in the negative.] His intended maxim would be, to deprive himself of life whenever existence promised more of misery than of pleasure; and the question is, Can such a principle of self-love be regarded as fit for a universal law of nature? and it is instantly observable that an order of things whose law it were to destroy life [Note the impersonal mode of statement which is generally adopted by those who are manipulating the cards. The man who is contemplating suicide is not concerned with life in general, but with his own life in particular.] by force of the sensation intended for its continuance [If that is to stand, all qualifications have to be suppressed; for the function of the sensation in question might be to encourage continuance of living when its blessings outweigh its pains, and under no other

1518. So let us look at the second interpretation (where no distinctions or limitations in individuals are recognized). Kant's reasoning might seem able to stand after a fashion. But there is another trouble with it. Before it could stand, the whole human race would have to constitute one homogeneous mass, without the least differentiation in the functions of individuals. If distinctions are admitted, it is possible for some men to command and others to obey; but not if distinctions are not admitted, for there can be no universal law that all men should command and no one obey. A man wants to spend his life studying mathematics. If distinctions are in order, he may do so without violating the Kantian law, since it may well be a universal law that a person possessing certain traits M should spend his life studying mathematics, and that a person not possessing those traits should till the soil or otherwise employ himself. But if distinctions are not allowed, if, as in the case of the suicide, one refuses to divide individuals into classes, there can be no universal law that all men should spend their lives studying mathematics, if for no other reason, for the very good one that they would starve; and therefore *no one* could be allowed to spend his life in such mathematical studies.

Such implications are not noticed, because people reason on sentiments and not with the facts before their eyes.

1519. As metaphysicists habitually do, after giving what he says is to be a single principle, Kant begins filling out with other principles, which come bobbing up no one knows from where. In a third case that he considers, *Op. cit.*, p. 49 (Semple, pp. 35-36), still "a third [person] finds himself possessed of certain powers of mind [Those are qualifications, conditions. Why were they not mentioned in the case of the presumptive suicide? Why was it not said in his case, "A person finds himself possessed of a certain nature whereby life for him is a painful burden and not a pleasure"?] which, with some slight culture, might render him a highly useful member of

conditions.] could not be upheld [It could not be if there were no qualifications; it could be if there were qualifications.], but must return to chaos. Whence it results that such maxim cannot possibly be regarded as fit for an unvaried law of nature, but is repugnant to the supreme principle of duty." (Semple translation.) In spite of this eloquent sermon anyone nursing intentions of killing himself will make his bow to our dear and illustrious and no less impotent Categorical Imperative, and proceed to end all.

society; but he is in easy circumstances and prefers amusement to the thankless toil of cultivating his understanding and perfecting his nature." (Semple translation.) He wants to know whether the latter can be a universal law. The answer is in the affirmative, at least from a certain point of view: "He observes that [such] an order of things might continue to exist under a law enjoining men to let their talents rust (after the manner of a South Sea Islander) and to devote their lives to amusement." It would seem, then, if one would adhere strictly to the formula which Kant has posited as a single comprehensive principle, that since such a course of action can be a universal law, it should be permissible. But not so! "It is impossible for any one *to will* that such should become a universal law of nature, or were by an instinct implanted in his system [The formula does not mention any such "instinct."]; for he, as [an] Intelligent [being], of necessity wills all his faculties to become developed, such being given him in order that they may subserve his various and manifold ends and purposes." (Semple translation.) Here we have a principle altogether new: that certain things are given us (no one knows by whom) for certain ends and purposes.

In order to reason in that fashion one would have to modify the terms in Kant's formula and say: "Act only on a maxim that it would be your will at the same time to have become a universal law. However, do not let yourself be deceived by the possessive 'your.' To say 'your will' is just my way of saying. In reality it is something that must necessarily exist in a man, full account being taken of the capacities with which he is endowed, of his designs and purposes, and of many other fine things that will be explained to you at the proper time and place." That much granted, one might just as well, from the logico-experimental standpoint, do away with "will" altogether, for it is thrown overboard in any event. But not so from the standpoint of sentiment. The appeal to "will" serves its purpose in flattering egoistic sentiments and giving hearer or reader the satisfaction of having it reconciled with his sentiments of altruism. And other sentiments also are stirred by the maxim of "universal law": first, a feeling of satisfaction that there should be an absolute norm which is superior to captious wranglings and petty human altercations—something established by Nature; and then that sum of sentiments whereby we vaguely sense the utility of the principle that the decisions of judges should be based on reasons, on general rules, and that laws also should be made with reference to such rules and not against or in favour of any given individual.

1520. The utility, we may note in passing, is really there, for such general rules do, in spite of everything, serve as a check on mere whim, just as Kant's law itself does. But the gain is not after all so very great; for if he chooses, a judge can always find a way to give a semblance of generality to a partisan decision. If, as between three persons, *A, B,* and *C,* one is concerned to favour or to harm *A,* one seeks, and one always finds, some aspect wherein *A* is different from *B* and *C,* and the decision is based on that aspect and therefore given an appearance of generality. That is saying nothing of that much-followed method of deciding in general and applying in particular, now with, now without, indulgence. So all our codes contain a law that, in the general, punishes assaults and batteries. But in the particular, the courts shut one eye, and even two, in cases of assaults and batteries committed by strikers on non-unionized workers. In Italy, before the war of 1911 it was possible to insult an army officer without interference from the courts. A certain Deputy was able to slander an army officer on purely private grounds that had nothing to do with politics; and though he was convicted in a criminal court he did not spend a day in prison even after he had failed of re-election to the parliament. Then the war with Turkey came and the pendulum swung to the other extreme. At the Scala Opera House in Milan individuals were abused and beaten with impunity for mere failure to rise to their feet when the "Royal March" was being played.

1521. Theologians scan the heavens for the will of God, and Kant for the will of Nature. There is no escaping such speculations, which are as alluring as they are difficult and imaginary. "As regards the natural constitution of an organized being," says Kant, p. 13 (Semple, p. 5), "a being, that is, that has been constituted with a view to living, it is a fundamental position in all philosophy that no means are employed except those only that are most appropriate and conducive to the end and aim proposed. [A reminiscence of the time-honoured theory of final causes.] [1] If then the final aim of nature [What on earth can that be?] in the constitution of man (*i.e.,* a being endowed with intelligence and will) had been merely his general welfare and felicity [These are arbitrary assertions about the arbitrary purposes and intentions of an arbitrary entity.], then we must hold her to have taken very bad steps indeed in selecting reason for the conduct of his life." [2]

This whole argument develops by arbitrary assertions relating to altogether fantastic things. The only word to describe it is childish; and yet many people have accepted it and many still do, and it is therefore evident that with them it can only be a matter of

1521 [1] When a metaphysicist feels an urge to talk about the natural sciences coming over him, he ought to remember the proverb that speech is silver, silence gold. Metaphysics ought to remain in its own field without invading the domains of others. Yves Delage, *La structure du protoplasme et les théories sur l'hérédité,* p. 827, note: "Probably not a few of the arrangements that we deem useless or harmful look that way to us because of our ignorance of the services they render; but then again, just as probably, they may be as useless or detrimental as they seem to be. In any case it is for those who deny that to prove what they say. [They have to, if they are naturalists. Metaphysicists are privileged to assert without proof.] Most species get along more or less badly, more or less well. They are far from being what has been called an intricate machine where each part is perfectly adapted to its place and work in the great mechanism of Nature. Some have had good fortune in the sense that the variations by which they have been formed have created few embarrassments for them. That is the case with the fly. It has only to fly about, rest, rub its wings and antennae. It finds anywhere those nameless deposits from which it can suck the little it requires for subsistence. But those same blind variations have created lives that bristle with difficulties. That is the case with the spider, which is always faced with most perplexing dilemmas: no food without a web, and no web without food. It must be in the light to catch the insect, it must stay in the dark to escape the bird. Why so surprising then that under such conditions it came to develop the absurd instinct that drives the female to devour the male after copulation, if not before [Blessed Kantian Nature! What a shocking oversight!], an instinct, by the way, that selection for the good of the species would be greatly embarrassed to explain." St. Augustine, good soul, also needlessly borrows trouble by venturing into entomology, *De Genesi ad litteram,* III, 14, 22-23 (*Opera,* Vol. III, p. 245). Following a number of other metaphysicists, he explains that many insects originate in putrefaction: "Not a few of them are born of the waste matter of living bodies, such as excrement and exhalations, or from the decay of dead bodies. Some others come from the rotting of wood and plants." And he wonders how on earth they ever came to be created: "As for those that are born from the bodies of living creatures and especially of the dead, it is altogether absurd to imagine that they were created at the time when those creatures were created."

1521 [2] [Pareto read: "in selecting reason as the executrix of her intentions," and comments: *"That might be favourable to a theory of non-logical conduct."*—A. L.]

sentiments that are agreeably stimulated by that sort of metaphysical poetry. And that is further corroboration of the importance of derivations, though the measure of the importance is not the accord of the theory with the facts, but the accord of the theory with sentiments.[3]

1522. In general, as we have over and again cautioned, it is important not to stop at the form of a derivation, but to delve into the substance that the form covers, to see whether residues with an influence on the social equilibrium may not be lurking in it. We have seen many. Let us look at another—and it will not be the last. In August, 1910, the German Emperor made a speech at Königsberg

1521 [8] Kant goes on, *Op. cit.,* p. 15 (Semple, pp. 5-6), to give the reasons for that assertion: "For the whole rule and line of action necessary to procure happiness would have been more securely gained by instinct than we observe it to be by reason. [Kant knows that, but he does not reveal how he came by it, and he gives no proof.] And should her favoured creature have received reason over and above, and in superaddition to it, such gift could only have answered the purpose of enabling it to observe, admire, and feel grateful to the Beneficent Cause [Another very pretty entity.] for the fortunate arrangement and disposition of the parts of its system. . . . In a single word, nature [Alias Beneficent Cause.] would have taken care to guard against reason's straying into any practical department. . . . So far is this, however, from what is in fact observed, that the more a man of refined and cultivated mind addicts himself to the enjoyment of life and his own studied gratification, the farther he is observed to depart from true contentment." Mark the word "true." It means the contentment that Kant likes best: any other contentment would be "false." Those who have made the most extensive use of reason and then calculated the benefits they have derived from the arts and even from the sciences acknowledge that "they have felt a certain hatred of reason, because they could not conceal from themselves that upon a deliberate calculation of the advantages arising from the most exquisite luxuries, not of the sensory merely, but likewise of the understanding (for in many cases science is no more than an intellectual luxury), they had rather increased their sources of uneasiness than really made progress in satisfactory enjoyment, and felt inclined rather to envy than think lightly of those inferior conditions of life, where man comes nearer to the tutelage of instinct, and is not much embarrassed by suggestions of reason as to what ought to be pursued or avoided. [How could Kant ever have compiled any such statistics? This part of the derivation was designed to satisfy people (and they were numerous in Kant's day) who admired the "natural man" and were ever declaiming against civilization. Derivations have their eye on sentiments, not on facts and logic.] . . . For, since reason is insufficient to guide the will so as to obtain adequate objects of enjoyment and the satisfaction of all our wants, and innate instinct would have reached this end more effectually, and yet reason is bestowed on man as a practical faculty of action, *i.e.,* such a faculty as influences his will and choice, it remains that THE TRUE END [Again mark the adjective "true," for there is a "false" end as well—the end that Kant does not like.] FOR WHICH REASON IS IMPLANTED, is to produce a will good not as a means toward some ulterior end, but good in itself."

that attracted wide attention. Said he: "Here the Great Elector on his own authority declared himself sovereign. Here his son placed the royal diadem upon his head. Here again my grandfather, and again on his own authority, assumed the royal crown of Prussia, so clearly showing that he was receiving it not from a parliament nor from a popular assembly, but that he was receiving his power from the grace of God, that he regarded himself as the executor of the will of Heaven, and that, as such, he believed that he had the right to wear the Imperial crown. . . . Considering the fact that our neighbours have made enormous progress, we must be prepared. Only our preparedness will assure peace. That is why I am resolved to walk in the path appointed to me, I too an executor of the Divine Will, taking no thought of the petty questions of day to day, dedicating my life to the well-being and progress of my country and to its development under peace. But in so doing I shall need the help of every one of my subjects."

The speech is a derivation of our III-γ variety (collective interest).

The opposition parties bitterly assailed the Kaiser's utterance, denouncing it as "a rallying cry against the German masses and against popular representation" standing in flat contradiction with the "modern conception of the state"; as an appeal to the outworn principle of divine right as opposed to the "modern principle of the people's right."

Those are all derivations of our III-δ variety (juridical entities) with a drift towards the III-γ (collective interest); for the "right of the people" is not very different from the "divine right" of kings.

1523. We must not be led astray by the term "people," which seems to designate a concrete thing. Of course the sum of the inhabitants of a country might be called a "people," and a "people" in such a case is a real, concrete thing. But only in virtue of an abstraction wholly foreign to reality can such an aggregate be regarded as a person possessing a will and the power to express it. First of all, and in general, before that could be the case the group in question would have to be able to understand a given problem and be capable of volition in regard to it. That never, or almost never, happens. Then again, coming down to the particular, it is certain that some Germans approved of the Emperor's speech, just as others did not.

Why should those who did not be privileged to call themselves "the people"? Were not those who approved just as much a part of "the people"? The usual answer in such cases is that the term "people" means "the majority." But in that case, to be exact, the antithesis to divine right would be not "the right of the people" but "majority right." That statement of the concept is avoided in order not to impair its force. Nearly always the term "majority" is itself a new abstraction. The term generally indicates the majority of adult males, leaving out the women. However, even in that restricted sense no one knows, oftentimes, what exactly the majority wants. A solution of the problem is more or less approximated in countries that have the referendum. But even in those countries very considerable numbers of the adult males fail to vote, and it is only by a legal fiction that the will expressed by the voters—granted that they all have understood the question that has been put to them—is taken as the will of the majority. In countries where there is no referendum, the will of a small number of individuals is taken as equivalent to the "will of the people" only by a complicated series of abstractions, fictions, inferences.

1524. Believers in the "will of the people" quarrel back and forth very much like orthodox and heretic in any other religion. A profane observer might well believe that the plebiscites held in France under Napoleon III manifested the "will of the people." But he would be as guilty of heresy as those early Christians who thought that the Father must have existed before the Son. These plebiscites in no way manifested the "will of the people"! All the same, parliamentary majorities under the Third Republic do manifest that popular will. So there you are! But every religion has its mysteries; and this one is after all not deeper or darker than any other.

In any country, when election reforms are up for discussion, each party looks to its own advantage and works for the reform that it judges most favourable to itself, without an instant's worry over the sacrosanct "expression of the general will." [1] Many "liberals" are loath

1524 [1] Speaking in the French Chamber, Jan. 24, 1913, Premier Briand said: "The most urgent problem is election reform. At no time have I personally pronounced anathema on the vote by ,districts. I have always recognized the services that that system has rendered. I have always added that as a tool it was out of gear. I do not regard election reform as a matter of principle: it is a matter of tactic. The party in power must try to stay there in the interests of the country and the

to grant the ballot to women because they fear that women will prove "reactionary"; and many reactionaries are in favour of women's suffrage for the same reason. In France the Radicals have a holy horror of the popular referendum; the "general will" has to be expressed through their own lips—otherwise it is not "the general will." The extension of the franchise in Italy was certainly not un-influenced by the hope of certain calculating politicians that they could turn it to their own advantage. In Germany Bismarck ac-cepted an extended franchise as a weapon against the liberal *bour-geoisie*. It might seem that champions of proportional representa-tion were an exception to the rule; but many of them see in that reform a way of obtaining a humble seat at the governmental banquet-board without too lively a competition and without run-ning the risks of battle.

1525. The "modern conception of the state" is another abstraction. The conception voiced by the German Kaiser is held by many people living today. Why then is it not entitled to be called a "modern" conception? An enthymeme is involved. Suppose we state it: "The Kaiser's conception is contrary to the modern conception of the state; therefore it is bad." [The major premise has been suppressed.] The completed syllogism would be: [Major premise:] "Everything that is contrary to the modern conception of the state is bad." [Minor premise:] "The Kaiser's conception is contrary to the modern conception of the state." [Conclusion:] "Therefore the Kai-ser's conception is bad." The major premise was suppressed as call-ing attention to the weak point in the argument.

1526. Now let us turn aside from these derivations for a moment and look at the substance which they hide.[1] Every community has two sorts of interests—present interests, future interests. So in every business corporation a problem arises and has to be solved as to whether a larger or smaller portion of profits shall be distributed as dividends to stockholders or saved in order to strengthen the

nation that has put it in power [*Excitement in several sections of the Chamber*]. The party in power must actuate the instrument (! *réaliser l'instrument*) of justice and equity through its own agencies."

1526 [1] In so doing, we turn to a particular case of the general problem of social utility that we are to consider in detail in Chapter XII. Just here a very brief survey will suffice.

company. Various boards of directors will be inclined to solve the problem in different ways.

1527. In the case of a people the interests of a present generation often stand in conflict with the interests of future generations. Material interests, which entirely or almost entirely engross one element in the population, stand in conflict with interests of another kind—the future prosperity of the country—which are the major concern of another element in the population, and which the first element mentioned comes to sense only in the form of some residue of group-persistence.

1528. Different administrations will be inclined to attach differing importance to such interests. So the Roman Republic had, under that one name, different tendencies according as Senate or plebs prevailed. If one strips off the veiling of derivations, one finds in the German Kaiser's speech an assertion of the interests of the country as against the temporary interests of a part of the population. In the utterances of his critics one notes the reverse. Both the Kaiser and his critics express themselves through derivations that are calculated to stir emotions, for there is no other way of catching the ear of the masses at large.

1529. The Emperor's statement is much clearer than that of his adversaries. Take the sentence: "That is why I am resolved to walk in the path appointed to me, I too an executor of the Divine Will, taking no thought of the petty questions of day to day." If the phrase "executor of the Divine Will" be replaced by the phrase "representative of the permanent interests of the country," we get a proposition that is fairly close to the scientific type. The reason why the Emperor's critics are less clear is that the residue of patriotism is very strong in Germany; and no one is likely to state very bluntly that he prefers his own present interests to the future and permanent interests of the country. If one were trying to translate the Emperor's speech into terms of experimental science, one could do no better than recall the case of Bismarck. Had he, backed by the will of his sovereign, not governed against the will of the elective Chamber, it might never have been possible to create the German Empire. On October 7, 1862, the Prussian Landtag rejected the budget by a vote of 251 to 36. The temporary interests of a part of the population were in conflict with the permanent interests of the country. King

William made up his mind to side with the latter. On October 13, he prorogued the Landtag by a decree bearing Bismarck's signature, and thereafter governed without regard to the approval or disapproval of that body. From that point on one's argument would infer the future from the past. That is characteristic of reasonings in the experimental sciences. They seek knowledge of the future from what is known of the past. One uses that method when one inquires whether, under certain circumstances, one may expect that a policy that has been used in times past and then had certain consequences may again be used with the same consequences.

Now let us try to translate the position of the Kaiser's opponents into the language of experimental science. The most logical among them were the Socialists, who regarded Bismarck's policies in general as detrimental to them. They had been opposed to the interests that Bismarck had defended in 1862. Logically enough, they stood opposed to the same interests defended by the Kaiser in 1910. Their idea is that the present interests of the working-classes ought to prevail over all other sorts of interests. Since, in fact, that attitude is common enough in contemporary Europe, it would be no great stretch of the truth to call it the "modern conception of the state." And since the parliamentary form of government seems to favour that attitude, no great margin of error is involved in setting the parliamentary majority over against the rights of the sovereign.

Less logical is the opposition of the *bourgeois* parties to the Kaiser. They want at bottom precisely what he wants. However, they are pulled into opposition by a desire to satisfy a much larger number of sentiments, regardless of whether some of them may not be mutually inconsistent. That is a common course of action in politics and is oftentimes very helpful to a party.[1]

1530. Metaphysical entities may thin down to the vanishing point. In certain accords of sentiments they appear but faintly, serving merely to lend them a vague hue of intellectuality. They often figure in explanations of usages and customs. The Sun, for instance, is saluted, revered, worshipped, as the principle of all earthly life. It

1529 [1] A similar analysis might be made for most manifestations of social activity. Such analysis gives us some inkling as to the forces that are at work in determining the social equilibrium.

was once believed that one's life could be prolonged by a child-sacrifice, as though life were a fluid that might be piped, as it were, from one person to another. On the same theory, a man of sober years was able to imagine that he could prolong his life by sleeping beside a young woman. So resemblances oftentimes imaginary are transformed into metaphysical entities and serve to explain facts. In general the function of such entities is to give a semblance of logic to combination residues (Class I).

1531. The metaphysical concept may be taken for granted; and we then get derivations that are very close in type to those based on accords of sentiments (§ 1469) and may be indistinguishable from them. A striking example would be the case of the metaphysicist who refutes logico-experimental science with principles which that science denies, and insists at all costs on finding the absolute in reasonings which he is over and again told are irremediably relative. In a day gone by such people met experimental science with the argument, in their eyes unanswerable, that to obtain "necessary" consequences one had to have a principle superior to experience. It is a well-known fact that a human being may use altogether absurd derivations in one field and think soundly enough in some other. Otherwise one might wonder how a mind could possibly have been so obtuse as not to grasp the fact that experimental science does not have, does not seek, and does not want "necessary" consequences (§ 976); that it shrinks from the absoluteness implied in the concept of "necessity," and that it seeks nothing more than results that are valid within certain limits of time and space. Those estimable souls have of late come out with another fine discovery which an ever prolific race of parrots is ever and anon repeating. Experimental inferences based on a certain number of facts they meet with the argument that not "all the facts" have been examined, concluding, more or less explicitly, that such inferences are not "necessary" or not "universal." And so far so good! In saying that, they are in perfect agreement with the practitioners of experimental science. They are merely throwing their shoulders against an open door. The ridiculous thing about it is their imagining that they have made the discovery that experimental science does not do a thing which, in the clearest language possible, it says, repeats, and says over again that it is not trying to do. None so deaf as those who will not hear! If people persist in refusing to understand that experimental science seeks nothing that is "necessary" or "universal" or possessed of some other such trait of absoluteness, there is nothing to do but leave them to their blissful ignorance, and laugh at their assaults on experimental science as one laughs at Don Quixote's joustings with his windmills. Experimental science is in a perpetual state of flux for the simple reason that new facts are being discovered every day, so that every day the scientist is called upon to modify conclusions previously based on facts previously known. The scientist is like a tailor who makes a new suit of clothes for a child every year. Every year the child has grown, and every year the tailor must make a suit of different size. Let $A, B, C \ldots P$ stand for a series of facts so far known in a given science. Tomorrow new facts Q, R are discovered. The series has now lengthened: it has become $A, B, C \ldots P, Q, R$. The inferences that stood previous to the discovery of Q, R may be retained, or they may have to be modified little or much or abandoned altogether. That has been the procedure so far in all the logico-experimental sciences, and there is nothing to indicate any likelihood of a change.

1532. But that is not all. We cannot draw any "universal" inferences today because we are not in possession of the facts $Q, R \ldots$ which are going to be discovered tomorrow. And we may not even care to draw "general" inferences from the known facts $A, B, C \ldots P$. We may prefer to divide them into separate categories and draw certain "partial" inferences from the group A, B, C, other partial inferences from the group D, E, F, and so on. That is the general procedure in science, and it is the origin of all scientific classifications.

If we select the facts A, B, C and group them together as presenting a common trait X, and then state the proposition that they have the trait X, we are simply reasoning in a circle (§ 1166[1]). Real theorems, instead, are propositions like the following: A certain number of facts present the trait X. Wherever the trait X appears, the trait Y will be found too. We select animals that suckle their young and call them mammals. To say, then, that mammals suckle their young would be to reason in a circle. It is a theorem to say, A very large number of animals suckle their young. Or, Animals that suckle their young are warm-blooded. All that is exceedingly

obvious and exceedingly elementary, but it is for ever being forgotten, disregarded, overlooked, and merely in deference to a
derivation in which the principle of the absolute figures at least
implicitly, and under pressure of the sentiments that correspond to it.
The metaphysicist who is accustomed to reasoning in a certain way
becomes incapable of following a thought of an entirely different
character. He translates into his own language, and thereby deforms,
reasonings that are stated in the language of the experimental
sciences. That is a language altogether strange and incomprehensible
to him.

1533. III-ζ: *Accord with supernatural entities.* The exposition of
a theory, the written statement of it, may contain a larger or smaller
number of narrations of experimental facts; but the theory itself
lies in the conclusions that are drawn from such premises real or
imaginary. It either is or is not logico-experimental, and objectively
speaking, there can be no question of a more or a less. We can
know nothing of anything that happens outside the experimental
field, and therefore the problem of determining whether a theory
is more or less remote from experience does not exist objectively.
But the problem may arise in connexion with sentiments, and we
may ask whether certain theories seem, from the standpoint of
sentiment, to depart little or much from experimental reality. The
answer will differ with different classes of persons. In the first place
such people may be divided into two groups: *A,* persons who use
the logico-experimental method strictly in such an inquiry; and *B,*
persons who use it little or not at all. There are, besides, subjects
that admit of only one sort of explanation. Just here we are thinking of subjects in which experimental and non-experimental explanations are both possible.

A. We are not concerned with such people in these volumes. We
may disregard the handful of scientists who clearly distinguish what
is experimental from what is not. For them the order of theories, as
regards their experimental content, is simply: (1) Theories that are
logico-experimental; and (2) theories that are not.

B. But this group has to be divided into subvarieties, according
to the more or less extensive, the more or less perspicacious, the
more or less sensible, use that is made of the logico-experimental
method.

Ba. In our day, and to some extent also in the past, in the eyes of educated individuals who make a more or less extensive use of the logico-experimental method, and, indirectly, in the eyes of less cultivated individuals who live in contact with educated people and belong to their society, personifications represent the maximum departure from the experimental field, and abstractions the minimum —an attitude that is promoted by the confusion which is created, unconsciously or by design, between such abstractions and experimental principles. For such persons the experimental content seems therefore to decrease in the following order: (1) experimental facts; (2) pseudo-experimental principles; (3) sentimental or metaphysical abstractions; (4) personifications, divinities. To be sure, certain idiosyncrasies develop. The Hegelians, for instance, reduce everything to (3). But the followers of such doctrines are always few, in fact, very few; and the majority, even of educated people, do not understand what such talk is all about. The mysteries of metaphysics stand on a footing with the mysteries of any other religion.

Bb. When uneducated people are not influenced by daily association in the same social "set" with the cultivated and by the prestige of such people, the order is different. To them personifications seem to come closer, much closer, to reality than any other sort of abstraction. No great effort of the imagination is required to carry over to other beings the impulses and thoughts that we ordinarily observe in our fellows. It is much easier to conceive of Minerva than it is to conceive of Intelligence in the abstract. The God of the Ten Commandments is much more readily grasped than the Categorical Imperative. The order, as regards experimental content, therefore becomes: (1) experimental facts; (2) pseudo-experimental principles; (3) personifications, divinities; (4) sentimental or metaphysical abstractions. Here also idiosyncrasies appear. Mystics, theologians, and other such people bring everything—facts, principles, abstractions alike—down to one element: divinity. The followers of mystical and theological doctrines are much more numerous than the adepts of pure metaphysics. However, among civilized peoples they represent only a small percentage in the total population.

Bc. Finally, in the eyes of people who are incapable of dealing with theological, metaphysical, and scientific speculations, or who by choice or otherwise are ignorant of them or in any event disregard them, all that remains is: (1) Experimental facts; and (2) pseudo-experimental principles. Those two categories merge into a homogeneous mass in which, for example, experimental remedies and magical remedies figure side by side. Here too there are idio-syncrasies such as fetishisms and other beliefs of that kind. Large numbers, in fact very large numbers, of people, in times both past and present have been and still are able to adopt such ideas, which are hardly to be called doctrines.

1534. We have already seen that evolution does not follow a single line and that consequently we would be losing touch with realities if we imagined that a given people started in the state Bc, then went on to the state Bb, and finally reached the state Ba (§ 1536). But to get at the real situation, we are free to start with that hypothesis, correcting it as we progress in order to get closer to the facts. Let us suppose then, and strictly by way of hypothesis, that a given people develops successively through the three states Bc, Bb, Ba. From what has been said above it follows that the sum of non-logical actions in the state Bc, along with the rudimentary explanations that are given of them, will gradually produce ex-planations involving personifications, and then, in due course, meta-physical explanations involving abstractions. But once we have reached that point we have to stop, if we choose to consider a popu-lation as a whole. For let alone an entire population, not even any very considerable fraction of one, has so far in history been known to give strictly logico-experimental explanations of things, and so to have attained the state A. It is beyond our powers to foresee whether such a thing can ever happen. We can say, if we consider a small, in fact a very small, number of educated people, that in our time there are individuals who come somewhere near the state A; and it may well be—though we have no means of proving such a thing—that in the future an even larger number of persons may attain the state A to perfection.

Another consequence is that in order to be understood by the majority, even by the majority of educated people, a language cor-responding to the states Ba and Bb has to be used; whereas language peculiar to the state A is not; and cannot be, understood.

1535. The hypothetical situation just described deviates from the real situation in the following respects, chiefly: 1. We have been distinguishing subjects that admit of various kinds of explanations from subjects which admit of only one kind. In the concrete such subjects are intermixed and one moves by imperceptible degrees from one extreme to the other. 2. In distinguishing the states *Ba*, *Bb* and *Bc*, we have represented as discontinuous variations that are really continuous. In reality there is a countless number of intermediate states. That, however, is no great loss; for after all some such procedure nearly always has to be used in cases where mathematics cannot be applied. 3. Far more serious is the deviation re-

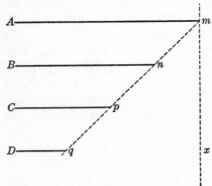

Figure 17

sulting from our taking a population as homogeneous, whereas in reality it is heterogeneous. It may be true enough that the state one class is in has its influence upon the state another class is in; but from that it by no means follows that the two states are to be taken as one. To divide society into an educated class and an uneducated class is a very crude device. In reality the classes that have to be taken into account are more numerous than that. To give graphic form to the above, let *A, B, C, D* . . . (Figure 17) stand for different strata in a given population. A certain evolution carries the stratum *A* to a position *m*. This change influences *B*, quite apart from the general effect of the historical evolution, and brings the stratum *B* to the position *n*. But the resistance of *B* also has its effect on *A*, so that the point *m* is determined not by the general direction of the evolution only, but also by the resistance of *B*. The same considerations apply, if we assume several strata *A, B, C* . . . instead of just two. In a word, the state of the population will be represented by the line *mnpq* . . . passing through the points *m, n, p, q* . . . at which points the various strata have severally arrived through the general effects of the evolution, and the reciprocal actions and reactions of the various strata. If only one stratum, for example *A*, be considered, the general result of the evolution—the general state of the population, that is—would be represented by the line mx, which may be something very different from the real state $mnpq$ . . . . 4. Still greater is the margin of error resulting from considering only one evolution, whereas there are several, and from taking it as progressing uniformly in a given direction, whereas its progress is generally undulatory. 5. Lastly, we are here studying derivations. We should not, therefore, be afraid of falling into the error of confusing the evolution of derivations with the general evolution of society, which embraces not only the evolution of derivations, but also the evolution of residues, of the effects of sentiments, interests, and so on, and of the logico-experimental sciences. All the same, it is well to keep that error in mind, for it is very commonly made, especially by people who do not clearly distinguish between logical and non-logical conduct.

1536. The hypothetical situation described above as regards a population as a whole was more or less vaguely perceived by Auguste Comte. It underlies, substantially, his famous theory of the fetishistic, theological, metaphysical, then positivistic stages. Comte envisages an evolution somewhat after the pattern Bc, Bb, Ba, A—but with the following reservations. In his *Cours,* Comte fell heels over head into error 5 above, mistaking the evolution of explanations of natural phenomena for the evolution of the social state. Later on, in his *Système,* he partly corrected the error, giving sentiment predominance over intellect (§ 286), but meantime falling into graver errors still (§§ 284 f.). Comte stood worlds removed from experimental scepticism, which in fact he hated cordially. He was a dogmatist, and so expounded his theory not for what it really was—a first and very gross approximation, but as something exact and absolute. And yet he had to some slight extent glimpsed error 3 above: it did not escape him that, in the fact, a certain intermixture of intellectual strata occurred.[1] In a word, going back to our Figure

1536 [1] Comte, *Cours de philosophie positive,* Vol. V, pp. 26-27: The various modes of human thought "not having all kept pace the one with the other, the result so far has been [The tone of a prophet appointed to regenerate the world.], in spite of the inclination of the human mind to unity of method and homogeneity of doctrine, that the metaphysical state of a given intellectual group has corresponded to the theological state of a later group less general and more backward, or to the positive state of an earlier group less complex and more advanced. That apparent confusion [He has just said himself that it is not apparent but real.] may indeed occasion in people who have not clearly grasped the principle [*Read:* "who do not accept Comte's chatter at face value."], an embarrassing hesitation as to the true philo-

17, in determining the state of a society made up of several strata *A, B, C* . . . Comte tries to substitute the line *mx* for the real line *mnpq* . . . and he clears his traces by considering the line *mx* as representing the "true philosophical character of the corresponding periods," whereas, the line *mnpq,* which actually corresponds to reality, he does not deem worthy of the epithet "true." Resort to such epithets is a general procedure, designed to leave an impression that many things are reducible to one only—the thing desired by the writer. And also general is the procedure of using successive assertions (derivations Class I), in lieu of logico-experimental proof— so hiding the flimsiness of the argument under a plethora of words.[2]

1537. Another very serious error on Comte's part lies in his giving a definition of the term "positive" philosophy, which in no way corresponds with the use that he makes of the term in the course of his writings.[1] According to the definition, "positive" philosophy would correspond to our state *A* above, and the development would be of

sophical character of the periods corresponding. But to anticipate or dispel it entirely, it is sufficient here to distinguish, in general terms, the intellectual group by which the real speculative stage of a given period ought more especially to be judged." And there we go galloping out of the experimental field! Never mind minor imperfections, such as his calling the "hesitation" "embarrassing"—why so embarrassing, after all?—and his allusions to a "philosophical character that is true" and a "speculative stage" that is "real"—how are they to be distinguished from others that are "false" or "unreal"? The more important point is that Comte takes for granted the thing that has to be proved: namely, that there is but one speculative stage at a given period of history. Several such stages exist simultaneously and it is hard to see why one should be called more "real" (*véritable*) than another.

1536 [2] *Op. cit.,* Vol. V, p. 27 (italics ours): "Now all *essential* considerations have worked together *of their own accord* in this connexion to indicate with utter clearness [So saith the prophet, and that is the end of the matter.] the more special and complicated order of fundamental concepts—in other words the body of moral and social ideas, as *always* being the one that is to constitute the *main* basis for such a decision, in view of their intrinsic importance, which is necessarily very great not only in the mental systems of almost all [ordinary] men [But that was the very thing that had to be proved.], but with philosophers themselves, as a result of their *rational* location at the extremity of the *true* encyclopaedic hierarchy, as outlined at the beginning of this treatise."

1537 [1] *Op. cit.,* Vol. I, Preface p. xiii and p. 3 (italics his): "I use the term 'philosophy' in the acceptation given it by the ancients, and specifically Aristotle, as designating the general system of human concepts. Appending to it the word 'positive,' I give notice that I am envisaging that special manner of philosophizing that lies in viewing theories of whatever order as purposing to coordinate observed facts. [That, really, would be the experimental method.] In the positive stage, the human mind comes to recognize the impossibility of obtaining absolute concepts. It aban-

the pattern *Bc, Bb, Ba, A*. But very shortly Comte's "positive" philosophy becomes a sort of metaphysics, the evolution halting with the series *Bc, Bb, Ba*, or, at best, allowing Comte some indulgence, with the series *Bc, Bb, Ba, Ba*1—*Ba*1 representing a stage where, in deference to sentiment, it is held that theories depart from the experimental field in the following order of increase: (1) experimental facts and "positive" interpretations of them (*i.e.,* "positive" metaphysics); (2) other metaphysical systems; (3) theologies. Noticeable in the *Cours* itself is a tendency on Comte's part not just to "coordinate" facts, as he promised, but to interpret them with reference to certain *a priori* principles present in his own mind. That is quite a different matter—it is nothing more nor less than what any other metaphysicist does. The whole *Cours* might be cited in proof. At every forward step one meets such adjectives as "true," "sane," "necessary," "inevitable," "irrevocable," "perfect," through which Comte tries to subordinate the facts to his ideas instead of coordinating the facts and subordinating his ideas to them.[2] But all that is noth-

dons the quest for the origin and destiny of the universe and for knowledge of the inner causes of phenomena, and tries merely to discover by the use of reasoning and observation combined their actual laws, in other words, their invariable relations of succession and likeness." And that again would be a definition of the logico-experimental method. To make it meticulously exact it might perhaps be better to say "observation and reasoning" instead of "reasoning and observation" and to suppress the adjective "invariable" before "relations." But if that is the point of departure, the point of arrival in the *Cours* itself, to say nothing of Comte's other works, is a faith which, substantially, differs little if at all from any other faith. *Cf.,* for example, *Cours,* Vol. VI, p. 858 (italics ours): "A *sound* appreciation of our nature, in which *vicious* and *wrongful* inclinations necessarily predominate at the outset [Who is to decide which inclinations are "vicious" and "wrongful"? Comte's own inclinations, of course!], will make commonplace and unanimous the *obligation* [Where does it come from? From whom does it emanate? Certainly it is not an experimental relation.] to exercise over our various inclinations a *wise* and *orderly* control that will be calculated to stimulate them and keep them within their respective channels. Finally, the *fundamental* conception, at once scientific and *moral* [The word "moral" is here suddenly appended to an inquiry that was advertised at the beginning as strictly scientific.], of the *true general situation* [What on earth can that be?] as the spontaneous leader of real economy, will *always* emphatically stress the *necessity* of constantly developing by *judicious* exercise of those *noble* attributes, no less of the heart than of the mind, that place us at the head of all living creation." All that patter may be anything one chooses to call it—but it is certainly not a search for experimental uniformities.

1537 [2] *Op. cit.,* Vol. VI, pp. 286-87: "This first scientific exercise of the abstract sense of evidence, *i.e.,* of the nature of proof and harmony, however limited in scope at first, was enough to provoke an important philosophical reaction, which, for the

ing as compared with the metaphysical expatiations that literally run riot in the *Système,* and especially in the deified abstractions of the *Synthèse.* Comte, in a word, underwent an evolution that may be roughly pictured as follows: 1. experimental, or better, pseudo-experimental explanations; 2. metaphysical explanations (at a time in his life when he was still giving predominance to thought over sentiment—see §§ 284 f.); 3. theological explanations (when he comes to give the pre-eminence to sentiment, and especially when, in the last stage of his evolution, the *Synthèse,* he deifies his abstractions). Comte's personal evolution, therefore, is directly opposite to the evolution that he represents human societies as undergoing.

moment favourable to metaphysical speculations only, was none the less a remote predecessor of the *inevitable* advent of a positive philosophy" by making sure of the early elimination of a theology then preponderant." In that Comte is evidently thinking of Newton and Newton's successors, forgetting all about the era of religious scepticism towards the end of the Roman Republic. The remarks that Cicero made in his *De natura deorum,* or Lucretius in the *De rerum natura,* by no means originated in mathematical research, yet they were aimed at polytheism and all religion. Sextus Empiricus lumps mathematicians and polytheists together in one simultaneous attack. Those, however, are mere errors of fact—we can overlook them. But where on earth did Comte discover that the "advent" of positive philosophy was "inevitable"? If that is not a mere tautology, a way of saying that what has happened had to happen—mere determinism, in other words—it indicates that Comte is subordinating his facts to certain dogmas. He adds: "In that, the ancient unity of our mental system, which down to that time had been uniformly theological, was irrevocably broken up." Again we may disregard the error of fact. But from what "coordination of facts" can Comte be inferring that such a break in the old uniformity was "irrevocable"? Lucretius was also of that opinion and gave Epicurus credit for the destruction of religion. And yet religion came to life again (assuming as a very lame hypothesis that it had ever died) and again prospered. Why should Comte be a better prophet than Lucretius? Then too the distinction that Comte tries to draw between a theological faith and a positive faith is altogether imaginary: "Theological faith, *always* bound up with some revelation or other [An error of fact: Comte is thinking only of Hebrew-Christian theology.] in which the believer has no share, is certainly something quite different from a positive faith which is always subordinate to a real demonstration, and is always open to examination under specified conditions [Worth a round of applause, that qualification! The Catholic Church is also open to examination, and specifies the conditions!], though they are products of that universal aptitude for trust [Authority. Comte wants to replace the Pope's with his own. That is all there is to that.] without which no society could subsist." And that is all very well; but only in the sense that the non-logical impulses in which authority originates are useful and indispensable to a society: it in no way follows that they will produce theories that square with the facts. Comte's "positivistic" faith may be more or less useful to society than what he calls a theological faith—that question remains open. But both types of faith lie outside the logico-experimental domain.

1538. We have lingered at some length on Comte's case because it illustrates a serious error that in our time especially is general—the assumption that the personification derivations are much farther removed from experimental reality than metaphysical derivations, the difference between them being simply a matter of form. Says Homer, *Iliad,* I, v. 5 and *passim:* "So was the will of Zeus accomplished." Say the moderns: "Thus were the requirements of Progress met." The two states of mind are the same. Whether "Progress," "Solidarity," "a Better Humanity," and so on are, or are not, personified matters little from the standpoint of experimental substance.

1539. As regards the form of the derivation, the personification deviates more widely from the metaphysical abstraction when the entity personified is assumed to manifest its will through revelation, tradition, or some other pseudo-experimental agency—the case of the II-γ derivations. But the personification tends to merge with the metaphysical abstraction when there is an effort to make the two accord with certain realities. Theologies and metaphysical systems are largely made up of derivations of that kind.

1540. One method for learning the divine will with which human actions must conform is very commonly followed. God is presumed to act like any human being of good sense and to want what a sensible man wants. In that way the divine will is deleted, substantially, from the conclusion, and only the will of the sensible man, or the man assumed to be such, is left (§ 1454 [1]). That is just another case of that general method of reasoning where a non-experimental X is eliminated (§ 480). Even when biblical revelation is resorted to, if there is any amount of loose or allegorical interpretation, the interpretation itself is eliminated in the end, and the accord substantially is with sentiments of the interpreter. It is interesting here as in other similar cases that a derivation is felt to be necessary instead of a bald assertion, though the latter from the experimental standpoint would have exactly the same value and would often, in fact, be better, since it could not be refuted. For that our I-ε residues (need of logical or pseudo-logical developments) are responsible.

1541. St. Augustine, *De Genesi ad litteram,* II, 1, 2 (*Opera,* Vol. III, p. 245), tries to explain the passage in Genesis which says that the firmament divides the waters that are below from the waters that are above: "Many indeed," he objects, "have asserted that because of their nature the waters could not abide on the sidereal heaven." He objects to answering with the principle of divine omnipotence: "Nor should they be confuted with the argument that, in view of the omnipotence of God for whom all things are possible, we are obliged to believe that water, though as heavy as we know and feel it to be, can hold its location (*superfusas*) above the celestial body where the stars are." Yet he would have been more prudent in following that line of argument than in letting himself be entangled in the somewhat fantastic physical explanations that he actually ventures upon.

1542. Again as usual, such derivations prove the yea and the nay equally well. The principle that God acts as a man of good sense serves to show that the Bible is "true," but just as well to show that it is false.[1] Needless to add that from the experimental standpoint neither the one proof nor the other has the slightest validity.[2] Even

1542 [1] The numberless "scientific" objections that are raised against religion are of that type. The only conclusion they can justify is that the content of the Bible and experimental reality are entirely separate things. Lefranc, *Les conflits de la science et de la Bible,* pp. 143-44 (I quote the book simply in view of the date of its publication, 1906): "If God called forth from nothingness those species which are alive and in full activity today with their present organs which have remained essentially unchanged, the Creation must have been overwhelming and complete at the very outset. [What creation is nobody knows, but Lefranc knows what it must have been like.] *Dixit et facta sunt! Deus creavit omnia simul!* It is inconceivable [But so many many things are inconceivable!] that the Almighty should have begun with timid efforts at first [How can Lefranc be sure they were necessarily timid efforts and not applications of far-sighted design? Was he there personally to see?], first making simple outlines, very unassuming in aspect and structure, and then going on with an unbroken sequence of violent assertions of force, continually remodelling His handiwork, changing His mind over and over again a thousand times to make it more perfect from day to day, like a craftsman unable to work out his plan, so creating and recreating one after another and for century on century as many as six hundred thousand different types, to keep to the animal kingdom alone. That childish conception carries its own refutation within itself."

1542 [2] During a session of the City Council of Milan, Dec. 31, 1912, a Socialist councilman made a fierce attack on the teaching of Christian doctrine in the schools, on the ground that it contained "absurd assertions belied by science." Among such he quoted the statement that the light came first and the Sun afterwards, he apparently having certain knowledge that the Sun came first and the light afterwards; whence it would follow that the Sun must have been created before all the other stars. That may in fact have been the case. But who told him so? However, suppose we assume that by "Sun" he meant all the stars, all luminous bodies. It would indeed seem natural that there should be first luminous bodies and then light, but,

from the merely logical standpoint, quite aside from any experience, the idea of an omniscient God cannot be reconciled with the idea that a human being can pass judgment on His work. An ignorant man is absolutely incapable of understanding what a scientist does in his laboratory, nor are a large number of such individuals any better equipped than one alone to pass such a judgment. That shows the fatuousness of the man of little knowledge in presuming to judge the work of anyone whose knowledge far surpasses his (§ 1995 [1]). It is the indispensable premise in all such judgments on personifications that the personification should be mentally, as well as in other respects, fashioned in the image of the person who creates it.

truth to tell, we know absolutely nothing about the matter. We do not know what "bodies" are nor what "light" is. Much less do we know in what relation, chrono- logical or otherwise, those entities may have stood "in the beginning." Christian "science" gives one solution, Socialist "science," apparently, another. Logico-experi- mental science knows nothing of either.

CHAPTER X

Derivations: Verbal Proofs

1543. Class IV: *Verbal proofs.* This class is made up of verbal derivations obtained through the use of terms of indefinite, doubtful, equivocal meaning and which do not correspond to any reality. If the classification were to be taken in a very loose sense, it would embrace nearly all derivations, and nothing would be gained by distinguishing Class IV derivations from the others. The definition must therefore be taken as applying to cases in which the verbal character of the derivation is very conspicuous, prevailing over other traits. In this class logical sophistries may be conveniently placed as regards their purely formal element, so far, that is, as they serve to satisfy the need of logical development that human beings feel (residues I-ε). But that element is nearly always incidental and does not determine the judgment of the person who accepts the derivation. The judgment results from an element of far greater importance— the sentiments that are stirred by the reasoning. Ordinarily such logical sophistries deceive no one who is not already disposed to be deceived. More exactly, there is no deception at all. The author of the argument and those who accept it are already in mutual agreement in virtue of an accord of sentiments, which they are merely supplementing, for good measure, with the dressing of the logical sophistry.

1544. The residues chiefly utilized for purposes of derivation in verbal proofs are the residues of our II-ζ variety (§ 888). They give body to an abstraction that has a name, endowing it with reality because it has a name. They also assume, *vice versa,* that a name necessarily has some real thing corresponding to it. Others of our Class II residues also figure, as well as residues of the I-γ type (mysterious linkings of names and things). In the special case still other residues may be involved. The residues indicate the desire to attain certain ends. That desire is humoured by a number of devices which language readily makes available.

1545. As we have time and again noted, the terms of ordinary parlance do not, in general, correspond to sharply defined things, and therefore all arguments in which such terms are used run the risk of being nothing but verbal derivations. There is least danger of that in scientific reasonings, for in such cases the thinker always has before his mind the things for which his terms are mere designations, mere labels. The danger is greater in derivations where the terms begin by not being just labels, and so on and on progressively till we get to metaphysical derivations, which are almost never wanting in the traits of the verbal derivation.

1546. When a term that can have more than one meaning is used in a syllogism, the syllogism may come to have more than three terms and so be fallacious. Very often it is the middle term that vitiates the syllogism by its indefiniteness. Such derivations vary from one extreme, where there is a simple play on words that no one takes seriously, to another extreme where a reasoning seems profound precisely because of its obscurity and indefiniteness. Take the argument, $A = X, X = B$, therefore $A = B$. If X has two meanings that cannot possibly be confused—for instance, the bark of a tree and the bark of a dog—we get a mere pun. But if X designates a fairly large and fairly vague aggregate of sentiments, certain sentiments prevail in the proposition, $A = X$, and certain other sentiments in the proposition, $X = B$. In reality, therefore, X is two different things: but people do not notice that and applaud the argument (§ 1607). If X is "Nature," "Right Reason," "the Good," or something else of that sort, one may be almost certain, not to say certain, that the argument is of the verbal type. Example: "One lives well according to Nature. Nature recognizes no private property. Therefore one lives well without private property." In the first proposition, the term "Nature" designates a vague sum of sentiments, distinguishes something that is in accord with our inclinations (what is "natural" to us) from something that we do only under compulsion (from what is foreign or repugnant to us), and instinctively we assent to the proposition that "one lives well according to Nature." The second proposition brings to the fore sentiments that distinguish things which the human being does (artificial things) from things that exist independently of human action (things that are "natural"); and there again the person following the lead of his sentiments will admit that private property is not a product of Nature, that Nature does not recognize it. Put the two propositions together and it logically follows that "one lives well without private property"; and if this proposition chances to harmonize with the sentiments of the person at whom the argument is directed, he will regard it as sound from every point of view. And perfect it is in the sense of humouring all the desires of the person who hears it, including his desire for a logical tinting—for some derivation or other (§§ 972, 1602).

1547. In concrete cases the Class IV derivations that we are here dividing into subvarieties are used together, and often also in combination with other derivations. Only by abstraction can we isolate the simple derivations of which the concrete derivation is compounded. That point must never be forgotten.

1548. The subgenera in Class IV (§ 1419) show derivations of two forms: in the first, procedure is from the thing to the term, in the second, from the term to the thing, real or imaginary as the thing may be. In concrete cases the two forms often mingle: after going from the thing to the term, one goes back from the term to something else. There are plenty of arguments that amount, substantially, to nothing more than that. As we saw in § 108, one may slip from the logico-experimental field both by using terms that correspond to entities not belonging in that field and by using indefinite terms which but loosely represent experimental entities. That is why we find the use of such terms among our derivations.[1]

1549. IV-α: *Indefinite terms designating real things; indefinite things corresponding to terms.* This is a very frequent type of derivation. It is seldom absent in derivations in the concrete.[1] Suppose we confine ourselves just here to a typical case.

1550. A celebrated fallacy, known as the sorites, very extensively exercised the logicians of a day gone by. You have a kernel of wheat.

1548 [1] We encountered many verbal derivations in Chapter V. In § 658 we illustrated the procedure from the thing to the name and from the name to the thing, and showed, in the paragraphs following, how errors—divergences, that is, between certain derivations and reality—arose in that way. Theories that infer the nature of a thing from the etymology of its name (§§ 686 f.) are in fact verbal derivations where procedure is from the name to the thing; and that direct etymological process also has its reverse (§ 691). Everything said on that subject in Chapter V must be taken as applying to the derivations we are considering here.

1549 [1] That is why we have already had to make frequent reference to it and shall have frequent occasion to revert to it hereafter.

Add another kernel to it. You do not have a heap. Add a third. Still you do not have a heap. Go on in that manner indefinitely, and you will come to the conclusion that a collection of kernels, no matter how large, is not a heap. The conclusion is evidently false. Where does the error in the reasoning lie? The fallacy is often stated the other way round: Reduce a heap of wheat one kernel at a time and the last kernel left is still a pile. Of the same nature is the fallacy of the man who loses the hair on his head one hair at a time, and is not bald so long as one hair is left. Cicero well notes that the fallacy may be made more general: "That," says he, *Academica,* II, 29, 92, "applies not only to a heap of corn, from which the name sorites [from σωρίτης, "heap of corn"] is derived; but to everything else, such as wealth and poverty, light and darkness, much and little, large and small, long and short, wide and narrow; for if we are questioned by imperceptible additions or subtractions we can give no answer." He extricates himself with a derivation of our IV-α variety, going from the thing to the name. He imagines that any word which exists must have something real corresponding to it: "Nature [When that lady comes dancing on the scene, the attendance of a fallacy may be taken for granted.] has given us no knowledge of the limits of things." So then, there is in fact a thing corresponding to the term "long"; but Madame Nature has not deigned to reveal to us the limits or boundaries of "long"; so we, poor devils, cannot tell it from "short." But what if, instead of things, there were nothing but sentiments corresponding to such terms? In that case, Dame Nature would be free of all blame, and the fault would lie with us for not managing to designate our sentiments with sufficient exactness. Chrysippus invented a device known as the "method of rest" to escape the dilemma. If you are asked, he suggests, whether three be few or many, before you come to the term "many," you should "rest." Whereupon Carneades objects that that will not prevent your being asked over again whether, by adding "one" to the number at which you "rested," you will have a "large" number. But along come the Sceptics, and take over the "method of rest" of Chrysippus and extend it to every argument. Carneades was using the sorites to prove that there were no gods.[1]

1550 [1] On the sorites see Ulpian, in *Digesta, lib.* L, *tit.* 16, sec. 177 (*De verborum significatione*) (*Corpus iuris civilis,* Vol. I, p. 969; Scott, Vol. XI, p. 284): "The

1551. Those philosophers who failed to find the error in this fallacy were misled by their habits of metaphysical thinking, and they could not recognize a particular error without admitting thereby that all their reasonings were fallacious. As a matter of fact the error in the sorites lies in the use of terms that do indeed arouse indefinite sentiments but otherwise correspond to nothing real. There is nothing objective corresponding to the terms "much" or "little," "large" or "small," "heavy" or "light," and so on. But the metaphysicist who might venture to concede that much would at once be faced with the objection to his own pretty structures that other terms such as "good" and "bad," "beautiful" and "ugly," "honest" and "dishonest," "just" and "unjust," "moral" and "immoral," belong to the same identical class (§ 963). The sorites must be met with the following: "Tell me what you mean by the term 'heap' or 'cumulus' (or whatever the term used), and I will give you an answer. If you tell me that a 'heap' is a thousand, or a thousand or more, kernels, when we get to nine hundred and ninety-nine and you add one more, I will say, 'There you have your heap!' But if you choose not to give strict definitions for the terms you are pleased to use in your argument, I for my part choose not to answer. It is for the person who wants an answer to state his question clearly." And that is the answer that must be made in our day to economists who go looking for the "cause" of "value." "Tell us, good people,

peculiarity of the cavil which the Greeks called the sorites is that the argument is led by very small changes in things that are evidently true to conclusions that are evidently false." Familiar the passage in Horace, *Epistulae*, II, I, vv. 45-49, where he shows by that method that no dividing line can be drawn between "ancient" and "modern," and that a horse's tail can be all plucked out one hair at a time, still remaining a tail. The Pseudo-Acron remarks: "The syllogisms of Chrysippus are pseudomenes and sorites" [missing in Paris, 1519]. As for the Sceptics and the "method of rest" see Sextus Empiricus, *Pyrrhonianae institutiones*, II, 22, § 253 (125) (*Opera*, Vol. I, p. 203): "Therefore whenever an argument is being worked out before us we shall suspend our assent to each and every proposition; and then when the argument is complete we shall set against it anything we see fit. For, in fact, if the dogmatists of Chrysippus are to teach that when an argument by the heap (sorites) is being worked out, one must hold one's tongue while the argument is in progress and refrain from assenting so as not to be led into an *absurdum*, it is much more advantageous for us who are Sceptics and are always on the watch for absurdities not to allow ourselves to be entangled in the lines of a reasoning, but to suspend our assent to each and every step until the whole argument has been set before us." For Carneades, see Sextus Empiricus, *Contradictiones*, IX, *Adversus physicos*, II, *De diis*, 190 (*Opera*, Vol. II, p. 611).

exactly what you mean by 'value.' Tell us how and why it should have *one* cause. Then we will answer, not before." To be sure, in ordinary parlance the term "value," like the term "heap," has an obvious meaning; but unfortunately the two meanings are equally indefinite, and that fact eliminates any possibility of using them in scientific thinking.[1]

1552. IV-β: *Terms designating things and arousing incidental sentiments, or incidental sentiments determining choice of terms.* Derivations of this type play an important rôle in judiciary eloquence and in politics. They are very effective in persuasion, and all the more because the sentiments that are set in motion by the language used work upon the auditor unawares. In the *Rhetorica,* III, 2, 10-14 (Freese, pp. 355-61), Aristotle gives good counsel on the subject: "If one would favour a thing, the metaphor must be chosen from what is best; if one would harm it, from what is worst." And then: "Epithets may be chosen from the worse or the degrading, as [Orestes] the 'matricide'; or from the better, as [Orestes] the 'avenger of his father.'" On similar grounds steadfastness in one's religion will be called "zeal" if the religion is orthodox, "obstinacy" if it is heretical. In the year 1908, the friends of the Russian Government called the judicial killing of a revolutionist an "execution," and the killing of a government official by a revolutionist a "murder." The enemies of the government inverted the terms: the execution was a "murder," the murder an "execution." A similar interchange is common between the terms "expropriation" and "theft."[1]

1551 [1] Pareto, *Systèmes socialistes,* Vol. I, pp. 338-40.

1552 [1] In the Italo-Turkish war of 1912, Arabs who brought information from the Turco-Arab camp to the Italians were called "informers"; those who carried information from the Italian camp to the Turks and Arabs, "spies." Bentham, *Tactique des assemblées législatives,* Vol. II, pp. 178, 163-66, 175: "The word 'persecution' does not appear in the dictionary of persecutors. All they know is 'zeal' for religion. When the Abbé Terray defaulted on public creditors he called it a 'reservation' (*retenue*). [In Italy a reduction of 4 per cent in the 5 per cent interest on the public debt was euphemized as a "tax on personal property."] In the nomenclature of moral beings there are terms that present the object pure and simple without adjoining any sentiment of approval or disapproval. Such would be 'desire,' 'inclination,' 'habit.' I call them 'neutral' terms. There are others that add a general idea of approbation to the main idea: 'honour,' 'piety.' Others supplement the main idea with an habitual idea of disapprobation: 'libertinage,' 'avarice,' 'luxury.' . . . In referring to the conduct, the inclinations, the motives of a given

Answering a Deputy before the Prussian Landtag in 1864 Bismarck said:[2] "The gentleman has rebuked us . . . for refusing to have anything to do with 'Germany.' There must be some extraordinary power in the term 'Germanic,' for everyone is trying to appropriate it. Everyone styles 'Germanic' anything that is useful to himself, anything that may be favourable to his party interest, and the meaning of the term is modified as the case requires. At one time it is 'Germanic' to oppose the Diet; at another it is 'Germanic' to favour a Diet now turned progressivist." In our day, if one would favour a thing, one must call it "modern," "democratic," "human," or even better, "broadly human," "progressive." Few people can resist such a bombardment. Keeping to the strict meanings of words, it would seem that a "free-thinker" should be a man who favours few or no restrictions on thinking (or better, on the expression of thought, since thinking to oneself is free, altogether free, and one could hardly agitate for the removal of restrictions that do not exist). As a matter of fact, a "free-thinker" is a believer who is bent on forcing his own religion upon others and on shackling the thinking of people who do not agree with him. If a person wants freedom in the sense of removing restraints from thought, he should be in favour of allowing uncramped discussion both for and against Catholicism. Our free-thinkers, instead, consent to attacks on Christianity, on Catholicism, but deny the privilege of defence. They insist on pro-

individual, is he an object of indifference to you? Then you use the neutral term. Do you wish to win him the favour of your auditors? Then you resort to the term that incidentally implies approbation. Will you have him despised or hated? You use the term that implies reproach. What does a man mean when he talks of 'good order'? Merely an arrangement of things to which he gives his approval and of which he declares himself a partisan." But how comes it that while so many writers all the way from Aristotle to Bentham have been sign-boarding the error in such sophistries, they continue to be so lavishly used? Simply because their force lies not in the argument, which, to tell the truth, is childish, but in the sentiments that they stir. If a theorem in geometry is shown to be false, that is the end of it— the matter is dropped. But if an argument in some social connexion is shown to be absurd, nothing whatever has happened—the argument continues to be generally used. The explanation of the difference is that, in the first case, reason controls, in the second, sentiment—sentiment re-enforced almost always by interests. From the sociological standpoint, therefore, such sophistries are to be judged not by their logical soundness, but by the probable influence of the sentiments and interests that they cloak.

1552 [2] Bismarck, *Ausgewählte Reden*, Vol. I, p. 73 (Jan. 22, 1864).

hibiting priests from teaching in the schools, and they demand a state monopoly of education, the better to impose their own theories and restrain thought in a direction that they consider good.[3]

1553. So in discussing freedom and the chains that shackle it, the nature of those chains is designedly left vague, and no distinction is drawn between chains that are voluntarily accepted and chains that are imposed by an external power—though the distinction is, substantially, essential.[1] One often hears reference to "papal" tyr-

1552 [3] I am not inquiring here whether that programme is, or is not, beneficial to society. I am merely saying that to proceed in that fashion is to distort the word "free" from its usual acceptation and give it an approximately opposite meaning. The National Congress of Free Thought, meeting in Paris in October, 1911, voted a resolution that read: "Faithful to the international ideal of progress and justice [That is a faith. It may be a good one. Other faiths may be bad. But it is none the less a faith and has nothing to do with free thought.], this Congress of Free Thinkers urges all associations of free-thinkers to make constant demand for the application *in toto* of the international conventions signed at The Hague. [What have those conventions got to do with free thought? A "free" thought should be at liberty to favour or oppose them as it saw fit.] Free-thought associations should urge Republicans elected to the government of the Republic to take the initiative in negotiations looking to the conclusion of new agreements for the limitation of military and naval budgets and the assurance of disarmament." A very pretty pair of handcuffs locked on in the name of freedom! Anyone whose thought is "free" has to be in favour of disarmament; and if a man believes that disarmament is dangerous for his country his thought is "enslaved"! Those are absurdities that require no refutation; yet there are people who fall under their spell. And how can that be? Simply because the meanings of the words have been changed, so that they function, not through their common meanings, but through the sentiments to which they appeal. The words "free-thought" set in motion a body of sentiments connected with a thought that is shackled to a humanitarian, anti-Catholic religion, and they therefore serve as labels for the dogmas of that religion.

1553 [1] In 1912 the Patriarch of Venice, following a doctrine of the Church Fathers, vigorously censured women who dressed in a manner that he thought immodest and suggestive, warned them that he would not admit them to the baptismal font with their children nor to communion, and actually withheld the latter rite from a lady who presented herself in a gown that he considered too low-cut. Newspapers at the time compared him to Senator Bérenger. But the two cases are entirely different and belong to categories that must not be confused. For the parallel it would be necessary for the government to compel women to attend the religious functions over which the Patriarch of Venice presides. But that was not the case. Those functions were attended only by people who chose to attend them, and the Patriarch had not the least power over anyone electing to disregard him; whereas the man Bérenger imprisons and fines people who disregard him and confiscates newspapers and books. In short, to say "If you want me to do *A*, you must do *B*" is one thing. To say "Whether you want to or not, I

anny, and the same term is used both when submission to papal authority is voluntary and when it is supported by the secular arm, though the two cases are radically different. In like manner, one often hears accusations of oppression against people who are trying to expel some individual member from a society of theirs. They are said to be "excommunicating" him, whether the excommunication involves penalties enforced by a public authority or has no other effect than expulsion from some private group. Yet those things also are altogether different. In France, excommunication in the Middle Ages and excommunication today are things that have the same name but nothing else in common. Today the non-Catholic laughs at being excommunicated and has no fears of being prosecuted by the government. But there are many persons who would like to invert the rôles and who demand in the name of "freedom" that the government interfere to force their society upon those who will have none of it. That is changing the sense of terms entirely. Keeping to literal meanings, a "free" state of things is a state in which a person chooses the company he will keep at pleasure, without forcing his upon others or having others force theirs upon him. And if one is going to call "free" a state of things in which a distasteful or repugnant company is forced upon one, why then, if one is to avoid misunderstandings, one had better find some other word to designate a state of things where one is not compelled to accept unwanted company.[2]

compel you to do *B*" is quite another. Sentiment does not bother with any such analysis and views the matter synthetically. The anti-Clerical censures the "intolerance" of the Patriarch of Venice and applauds Bérenger; and that is all a derivation, which means simply that the anti-Clerical dislikes the Patriarch and admires the Specialist in Purity.

1553 [2] In Germany a Protestant pastor, Mr. Jatho, who professes a Christianity all his own, preached a series of sermons on Goethe. They scandalized good Christians, and the consistory of the Rhineland and the High Council of the German Evangelical Church interfered. *Journal de Genève,* Feb. 23, 1911: "The Consistory has begged Mr. Jatho to declare that his sermons had been incorrectly reported and to pledge his word that he will deliver no more of that kind. The pastor has refused on both scores. He asserts he is the victim of anonymous charges and takes his stand behind the indelicacy of that procedure to avoid making any concessions. As a result charges have been lodged against him before the High Council of the Evangelical Church. . . . A coincidence, unfortunately, complicates the case still further. All Protestants have felt in duty bound to take a vigorous stand against the anti-Modernist oath. Mr. Jatho and his press have not missed the chance to say that an anti-Modernist oath was being demanded of him, and they

1554. The fate that has befallen the term "freedom" is, in truth, comical enough. In many cases nowadays the word means the exact opposite of what it meant fifty years ago; but the sentiments that it stirs are the same—in other words, it designates a state of things of which the average auditor approves. If Smith is interfering with Jones, Jones calls it "freedom" to escape from the interference. But if Jones in his turn gets control of Smith, he calls it "freedom" to tighten the ropes. In both cases the term "freedom" has the pleasantest associations for Jones. Half a century ago, in England, the "Liberal party" was the party that sought to reduce as far as possible such restrictions as to some extent deprived the individual of freedom to do as he pleased with his own person and property. Today the "Liberal party" is the party that is trying to increase the number of such restrictions. In those days the Liberal party was trying to reduce taxes. Today it is for increasing them. In France and Italy the liberals of the old days insistently demanded that the individual be permitted to work whenever he chose, and they spat poison at the "tyranny of kings and priests" which constrained them to be idle on Sundays and holidays.[1] In France, under the Restora-

tried to get the evangelical press to shower the Cologne preacher with the same inordinate praises it has been bestowing on the handful of priests who have balked at the anti-Modernist oath. Needless to say, the Protestant papers have side-stepped the issue, seeking and finding distinctions." He who seeks finds, and always finds as many distinctions as he happens to need.

1554 [1] La Fontaine, *"Le savetier et le financier"* (*Fables*, VIII, 2)—the poor cobbler speaking:

> ". . . *le mal est que toujours—*
> *et sans cela nos gains seraient assez honnêtes—*
> *le mal est que dans l'an s'entremêlent des jours*
> *qu'il faut chômer. On nous ruine en fêtes:*
> *l'une fait tort à l'autre, et monsieur le curé*
> *de quelque nouveau saint charge toujours son prône."*

("The trouble is—and but for that our earnings would be fair enough—the trouble is that days when we cannot work are mixed in all through the year. We are ruined by holidays, the one spoiling the other; and Father priest is always loading down his weekly scolding with some new saint.") When the "seventh day's rest" —which was, after all, nothing but the Lord's Day observance—was put into force in Milan, a poor cobbler whose shop had been closed hung a string of shoes over his shoulder and went about the streets in quest of customers crying, "I have to eat on Sunday as well as on other days." In former times abstinence from labour was enforced by government and clergy. In our day it is enforced by governments and by associations of one sort or another; and to the days of rest required by

tion, "liberals" and government fought a war to the death on that issue, and people still remember the fiery pamphlets that Courier wrote on the subject.[2] As late as 1856 dread of seeing the Sunday holiday become a matter of law prompted the Senate of the Empire, ordinarily a tame and submissive body, to resistance—"strong feelings" will move even a lamb to rebellion. According to Ollivier,[3] Senator Lavalette "proposed that the oath taken by the Empress-Regent, in conformity with the *senatus-consultum* of 1813, should be re-enforced with an oath 'guaranteeing respect for the provisions of the Concordat, including the organic law and freedom of worship.' The blow was aimed directly at the Empress, who was suspected of favouring the suppression of civil marriage, compulsory Sunday closing, and the whole list of 'ultramontane extravagances.'" When the bill went to vote, the amendment was defeated by 64 to 56. Now, everything has changed. "Liberal" doctrine demands enforcement of rest on the Lord's Day, though as a sop to the anti-Clericals the phrase has become "weekly day of rest" (*repos hebdomadaire*). "Ultra-liberals" demand that state inspectors be appointed to prevent citizens from working behind closed doors in their own homes. To justify such procedure they resort to a residue[4] of the IV-$\beta2$ variety (enforced uniformity): to permit a person to work on certain days is an infringement on the "liberty" of people who prefer not to work on those days, whence one can argue logically that Sunday idleness is enforced by law in the name of freedom. Some liberal who has read Hegel will even add that in so doing "the state is creating freedom."[5] The term "freedom" as used in that derivation has three

law must be added those enforced by violence on strike-breakers, and those connected with political strikes, and strikes of "protest," solidarity, and so on. The difference lies in the fact that in our day a person is constrained to act contrarily to his own will in the name of "freedom," the term so acquiring a meaning directly opposite to its primitive meaning.

1554 [2] *Pétition à la Chambre des députés pour les villageois que l'on empêche de danser (Œuvres complètes,* p. 84): "Gentlemen, those who are so bitter against working on Sundays want high salaries, vote increases in the budget, and put indigent taxpayers in jail. They expect us to pay more and to work less each year."

1554 [3] *L'Empire libéral,* Vol. IV, p. 11.

1554 [4] [Pareto wrote "derivation"—a *lapsus linguae.*—A. L.]

1554 [5] The argument reduces to an *absurdum* on one's noting that it applies to every case where conflicts arise in the exercise of freedom of action by numbers of persons. A law might be passed to compel violin-teachers to give lessons free because for them to accept fees would be an "infringement on the liberties" of

different senses: 1. A vague meaning as a personified abstraction. 2. A definite meaning, as a capacity to act or not to act. And this second subdivides into two: (2-*a*) such capacity in a given individual; (2-*b*) such capacity in individuals other than he. The four capacities often stand in conflict, so that a measure that safe-guards the one interferes with the others. The derivation takes advantage of the quadruple meaning to bring under "freedom" in the first sense what is valid for it in one of the three other senses only. Sometimes the better to dissemble that manoeuvre in verbal hide-and-seek an epithet is attached to the term "freedom" in the first meaning (§ 1561). The derivation here in question asserts that Sunday closing "safe-guards liberty." That identifies "freedom" in the first sense with "freedom" in the sense 2-*b*. One might just as readily equate the first meaning with the 2-*a* sense, and then the Sunday-closing law would be an "infringement on liberty." The practical conflict is settled by neither of those derivations, but by inquiring whether, with a view to certain ends, it is desirable to favour 2-*a* at the expense of 2-*b*, or 2-*b* at the expense of 2-*a;* and in so doing one would be stepping from the domain of derivations over into the domain of logico-experimental thinking.

1555. That disposes of the relation of the derivation to logico-experimental reality. Why, we may now ask, is it used? What can be the cause of such obstinate insistence on designating different, nay opposite, things by a single term? Nothing more nor less than a desire to exploit the agreeable sentiments that the term suggests—the same reason that prompted the Roman Empire to go on calling itself a republic. And then, too, though in a very secondary way, a

---

people who want to learn the violin but cannot afford to pay. It is therefore a duty of the Never-Sufficiently-Praised State to "create" said "freedom" of violin-study. In the same way, if a lady refuses to requite a suitor, she is depriving him of free action in loving her, is, in other words, infringing on his "freedom" of action. The law therefore should "create freedom" in sex by at once coming to the rescue and compelling the lady to be merciful to anyone who desires her. But, it will be objected, such "liberties" are not as respectable as the freedom of persons not to work on the Lord's day and who ought to be working if others are to work. And the objection is sound enough; but to take that ground forces us to inquire whether, with a view to certain definite ends, it is desirable, or whether for one reason or other we are inclined, to favour the one or the other of these respective freedoms to do or refrain from doing; and that would at once take us entirely outside the field where it is possible to speak of "infringements on freedom" or "creations of freedom."

certain sense of decency in our politicians. Burning today the idols they worshipped yesterday, emulating the "reactionary" governments which they were wont of yore to vilify, they are concerned to create an impression that they still cherish the principle which they found so convenient when they were fighting those governments. As for the justification of which we have been speaking, it is used, as other derivations of the kind are used, to attach the favourable and indefinite sentiments aroused by "freedom" in the generic (*i.e.,* 1) sense to "freedom" in the special senses 2-*a* or 2-*b*, as the case requires.[1]

1556. IV-γ: *Terms with numbers of meanings, and different things designated by single terms.* This derivation is used either directly, to give one meaning to a proposition which is going to be used in another meaning (§ 491 [1]), or indirectly, to avoid a contradiction between two propositions by breaking up one or more terms in them into two or more meanings. It is also used to lengthen a bald assertion (§ 1420) somewhat and give it the semblance of a logical reasoning. Instead of saying simply, $A = B,$ one says, $A = X;$ and it is then assumed implicitly by accord of sentiments, or stated explicitly, that $X = B;$ and so it results that $A = B.$ From the logical standpoint the detour is no whit better than the short cut (§ 783); but it is effective from the standpoint of sentiments as satisfying the hankering for pseudo-logical expatiation.[1]

1555 [1] Among the many amazing travesties of the term "liberalism" one of the most striking is an equation brought into play by the Italian Premier Salandra, some years ago. Outlining his policy before the Chamber of Deputies on Apr. 6, 1914, he said: "To my mind liberalism in Italy means patriotism [*Applause*]." The item should be added to some future dictionary of synonyms! But perhaps the Italian Premier meant simply that "liberal and patriotic" was a phrase used to designate a certain group of politicians. In that case he was, alas, not far from the truth. The phrase is very truly a euphemism that the party of our "speculators" (§ 2235) in Italy is pleased to take as its name.

1556 [1] The Pythagorean tradition seems to have set up as its ethical rule a striving to be like the gods (Themistius, *Orations,* XV, 192; Dindorf, p. 236). Hierocles located perfection in that likeness: *Commentarius in Aureum carmen,* vv. 63-66: [The *Carmen* reads (Lowe translation): "These [the mystic rules of nature] if to know thou happily attain, soon shalt thou perfect be. . . ." Hierocles paraphrases merely: "Mortals are kin to God, in that nature reveals everything to them."—A. L.] Stobaeus, *Eglogae physicae et ethicae,* II, 7 (Heeren, Vol. II, p. 66), quotes a saying of Pythagoras: "῍Επου θεῷ": "Follow thou God." If the god in question were the god of the multitude, the norm alluded to would be adding something to the simple assertion of a precept: it would, that is, be saying that the

To this variety belong the many sophistries in which the middle term is broken up into two meanings, and those other equally numerous sophistries in which one term is used in two successive meanings so that the argument moves in a circle. A very common type runs as follows. It is asserted that all *A*'s have the opinion *B*. Here *A* is used in a vague generic sense merely conforming with the

precept is in accord with the conception that the plain man has of the god. So also if the will of the god were known through sacred books, tradition, or in some other such way, something would still be added to the plain assertion of the precept. But when the author of the precept is himself also determining the nature and the will of the god, to invoke the god serves only to lengthen the journey in arriving at the precept; and whether he states the precept directly, or indirectly asserts that it originates in a likeness to the god, or in a divine will which he, the author, determines, is one and the same thing. The Pythagorean tradition did in fact make a difference between the gods of the plain man and the gods of Pythagoras. Hieronymus relates (Diogenes Laertius, *Pythagoras,* VIII, 21; Hicks, Vol. II, p. 339) that in Hell Pythagoras saw "the soul of Hesiod chained to a bronze pillar and shrieking aloud, and the soul of Homer hanged to a tree with snakes about it, as punishments for the things they had said of the gods." Just so Plato amends in his own fashion the conception which plain people, the poets, and other sorts of writers had of God; and in the *Respublica,* III, 3, he rejects and condemns a number of the opinions current on the subject of the gods, rebukes Homer for his accounts of certain incidents, and concludes, 388A: "If, then, friend Adeimantus, our young people hearken diligently to such stories without scorning them as unworthily told, hardly any one of them on reaching manhood will deem them unworthy of himself and condemn them." In *De legibus,* IV, 716 (Bury, Vol. I, pp. 295-97), he says that like loves like and that if a man would be loved of God he must strive to make himself like God; "and according to this maxim the temperate man is beloved of God because like unto Him; the intemperate man is not like unto Him and is unholy." But which god should a man strive to resemble? Not the god of Homer, but God as Plato chooses to fashion Him! Homer's Zeus was making no great show of self-restraint when, *Iliad,* XIV, he tried to possess Hera on Mount Ida without retiring to his quarters; and only because Plato rejects and condemns the Homeric and other adventures of Zeus can he call him "temperate." His reasoning is very much as follows: "A man must do so and so because he must be like unto the god whom I imagine as doing so and so"; and the logico-experimental force of the argument is in no way superior to the simple declaration, "A man must do so and so." But matters do not stand that way as regards sentiment. It is better to string the derivation out as far as possible in order to reach as many sentiments as possible, much as in a piece of music variations are made on one same theme. And here comes Stobaeus, *Op. cit.,* 66, quoting Homer, whose support it is just as well to have when one can, and then adding: "And so also Pythagoras said, 'Follow thou God,' evidently not with the eyes and as a guide, but with the mind, and harmoniously with the beautiful order of the world, the which is set forth by Plato according to the three parts of philosophy: physically, in the *Timaeus* . . . ethically in the *Republic,* logically in the *Theaetetus.*" And everybody is satisfied!

sentiments of the average auditor, who therefore as a rule asks no questions. But if one does ask for a definition of the A's, an answer, more or less verbose, involved, inexplicit, is made, to the effect, substantially, that the A's are those who hold the opinion B, A in that way taking on a new meaning. So the argument simmers down to the statement that those who hold the opinion B hold the opinion B.[2]

1557. The use that is made of the term "solidarity" (§§ 449 f.) would be a good example of the direct resort to such a derivation. Champions of "solidarity" themselves confess that the word is used in very different senses. Says Croiset:[1] "Everybody is using it, and by dint of using it, everybody is forgetting to ask just what it means. Now if one examine closely, one perceives without much trouble that it is applied to very different things. There is, first of all, a solidarity *de facto* that is merely the reciprocal interdependence of divers associated elements. In law, for instance, a state of 'solidarity' exists between debtor-partners when each of them is responsible for the debt of all. In biology a state of solidarity is said to exist between the parts of an organism when modifications undergone by one member have counter-effects upon all other members."[2] Croiset errs in putting two very different things together. A man is condemned to have a hand cut off. If a state of solidarity in the legal sense existed between the two arms, in the sense that they are both liable

1556 [2] We have given many examples of arguments of that type, *e.g.*, §§ 592-93.

1557 [1] In Bourgeois, *Essai d'une philosophie de la solidarité,* Preface, p. vi.

1557 [2] Croiset continues (*Ibid.*, Preface pp. vi-viii): "The solidarity of which our moralists and politicians are now talking so glibly is a very different thing, or at least a much more complex thing. [They admit that now, the sly foxes, but for a long time they tried to keep up the confusion. Now that that game is failing to work, they are changing the tune for the same old song:] When one speaks, as M. Léon Bourgeois speaks, of the social debt of individuals, it is not a question of a common debt to an outsider, but of a reciprocal obligation among associates, which is an altogether different thing. [Yes, but for a time the estimable champions of solidarity tried to make out that they were the same thing.] When the example of biological solidarity is pointed to, that is far from meaning that individuals in society are subject, like the cells in a living organism, to a sort of external natural fatality which they can do nothing but recognize. [But in that case, why all the patter about "universal solidarity"—the solidarity of animals with plants and plants with minerals?] The concept of solidarity is in reality envisaged as a principle of conduct, moral conduct, as a means of stimulating in individuals an aspiration to a higher justice [Just how is the height of this or that justice to be

for payment of the common debt, half the hand on one arm ought to be cut off and half the hand on the other arm. Yet only one of the two arms pays the common debt. So the two arms are not in a state of solidarity, in the legal sense, though they may be in such a state, as M. Croiset says, as "parts of the same organism." Croiset then proceeds very ingeniously to explain why the term "solidarity" has enjoyed such a great vogue, finding it, substantially, vague enough to allow anybody to make it mean anything desired—a sound observation, and generally valid for derivations containing vague or ambiguous terms.[3] That is why such terms are the best possible for derivations, the worst possible for scientific thinking. If sentiments are to be stirred and realities concealed, it is well that terms be not too precise. If the point is to discover actual relations between facts, terms had better be as exact as possible. Preachers of solidarity were acting very wisely therefore in using a vague language. But that fact alone, if there were no other evidence, would suffice to show the fatuousness of their claim that they were giving us a scientific theory.

1558. An example of the indirect use of the IV-γ derivation would be the precept "Thou shalt not kill." It is established by giving a general meaning to the term "kill," in order to take advantage of the blood-taboo, which forbids the shedding of human blood in gen-

---

measured in feet and inches?] and as a rule that is calculated to facilitate their reaching it. [How many things in just one word! Solidarity! Magical term indeed! And still M. Croiset has left out something. Solidarity also stands for a desire on the part of certain politicians to get a following, and for the verbal sops that are handed out to the mob by democratic metaphysicists. Croiset rightly concludes:] It is therefore evident that the word 'solidarity' has taken on a wholly new meaning in that connexion, and that in spite of the identity in words moral solidarity is something profoundly different from biological or juridical solidarity"—which, in their turn, as we have just seen, are also different things.

1557 [3] Croiset, *loc. cit.*, p. x: "The word 'solidarity,' taken over from biology, fitted in marvellously with that vague but deep-seated yearning [for oneness of all individuals in some whole]. The word 'altruism' was out of the question. It was too great a barbarism ever to have made its way into ordinary parlance. [There was another reason: the word "altruism" could never have led anyone to believe that the Moon was made of green cheese, that, in other words, "solidarity" was a scientific theory.] The term 'solidarity' was furthermore rather vague, as being taken over from a field where it had an exact meaning to another field where, in fact, the problem was to acclimatize it. So people were free gradually to bring under it all those still hazy ideas which older words, more definite in meaning as a result of long usage, were not so well fitted to express."

eral, or at least the blood of members of one's own community. But
lo, the case arises in which one has to say "Thou shalt kill!" To be
rid of the contradiction the term "kill" is not restricted in meaning, and the two propositions then become: "One should not kill
except under certain circumstances," and "One should kill under
certain circumstances." In that way the contradiction disappears, to
be sure; but in such an explicit wording the two statements mean
little or nothing. That is why they are not put directly in that form.

1559. Pacifists have a formula: "International disputes should be
settled by arbitration, by the international Court at The Hague, and
not by war," and that they call "peace under law." In 1911 Italy declared war on Turkey without in the least concerning herself with
arbitration or with the international Court at The Hague. Pacifists
abroad stood loyal to their formula and condemned the Italian Government; but a number of Italian pacifists stood by their government, because in going to war it had vindicated "Italy's good right."
It goes without saying that if some other country, X, had been in
Italy's situation, a number of pacifists in that country would have
said what the Italian pacifists said, while the Italian pacifists would
have stood by their formula and condemned the government of the
country X.[1] For those pacifists who approve of wars, the theoretical

1559 [1] At the Peace Congress held at Geneva in September, 1912, a number
of French pacifists stood out for the use of airplanes in warfare, whereas pacifists
from other countries were for prohibiting them. By a coincidence that may not
have been fortuitous, France was at that time the country best prepared for aërial
warfare. English pacifists who condemned the Italian conquest of Libya were
highly indignant because the Congress expressed the hope that England would
withdraw from Egypt. Will ever logician be so subtle as to explain why a conquest
of Egypt should be according to "right" and a conquest of Libya contrary to
"right"? The Italian "war-pacifists" of 1911 had preached, or had applauded those
who preached, that Julius Caesar, Napoleon I, and other conquerers were mere
"assassins" and that there were no "just" wars, unless, perhaps, wars in self-
defence. Then one fine day they change their allegiance and ask us to admire
other conquerors as heroes, and applaud other wars of conquest as "just," without
telling us how conquerors and wars that are to be condemned are to be distinguished from those which are to be applauded. Instead of enlightening those who
disagree with them, they abuse them. Before burning her heretics, the Holy
Catholic Church at least taught them the catechism! The Italian "war-pacifists"
were so indignant at their sometime comrades, the "peace-pacifists," that had
they been able they would have challenged them to mortal combat. And they
took that position, they said, in defence of their country's honour. But was not
"the country's honour" the very cause of many of the wars they had previously

formula would seem, therefore, to be: "International disputes must be settled by arbitration, except when it is to the advantage of a country minded to fight to settle them by war." But when the formula is stated in that way, who is not a pacifist? In reality, as we have many times seen, the whole manoeuvre is dictated by sentiments and not by any logical reasoning.

1560. In that same case we get a good example of the divergences that are possible between the accord of a theory with reality and its social utility. The Italian pacifists divided into two camps: on the one hand, those who approved of the Libyan war and might be called "war-pacifists"; on the other, those who stood by their pacifist doctrines and might be called "peace-pacifists." The "war-pacifists" were certainly wrong from the logical standpoint. They may have been right from the standpoint of their country's advantage. The "peace-pacifists" were no less certainly right from the standpoint of logic and loyalty to principles. They may have been wrong from the standpoint of national utility.[1]

1561. A widely used method for splitting terms into double meanings is to qualify them with certain epithets, such as "true," "right," "honest," "noble," "good." So an *A* that is "true" comes to be dis-

condemned? To justify his war of 1870, Ollivier writes in *L'Empire libéral,* Vol. XIV, pp. 558-59: "Faced with the choice between a war of doubtful outcome and a dishonourable peace, *bellum anceps an pax inhonesta,* we were forced to pronounce for war—*nec dubitatum de bello.* 'For peoples as for individuals there are circumstances where the voice of honour must speak louder than the voice of prudence' (Letter of Cavour to Arese, Feb. 28, 1860: *Lettere edite ed inedite,* Vol. III, pp. 220-23.) Governments fall not only from defeat on the battle-field. Dishonour also destroys them. . . . A military disaster can be repaired. . . . Dishonour accepted in acquiescence is a death from which there is no resurrection." Cavour was a man bitterly hated by our pacifists. Why was he wrong? And why were they right when they found it convenient to repeat his precise words? Was Rome right or wrong in warring upon the nations of Mediterranean Africa and conquering them? If she was right, what becomes of the beautiful doctrine of pacifism, and how is it to be distinguished from a doctrine that is non-pacifistic? If Rome was wrong, how can countries that are today doing the very same thing be right? To answer with the national anthem or by abuse of one's critics may be a good way to rouse emotions; but it is not in the least logical, nor in the remotest degree rational.

1560 [1] This is not the place to solve the problem of utility that is involved in this special case. It is sufficient for our purposes here that the two solutions mentioned should in fact be possible. Farther along (§§ 1704 f.) we shall see just what residues underlay the above derivations, and one aspect of utility we shall discuss in Chapter XII.

tinguished from a mere *A,* and the difference between them may amount to oppositeness. In that way the contradictions in uses of the term "freedom" are evaded (§ 1554): "true freedom" is something very different from plain ordinary "freedom." Sometimes "true freedom" is the exact opposite of plain "freedom." To work when you choose to work is just "freedom"; but to work only when someone else wants you to work is "true freedom." To take a drink of wine when you choose is just "freedom"—it was the freedom the Czar granted to the Finns. To be forbidden to touch lips to a drop of wine is "true freedom"—it was the freedom the "liberal" assembly of Finland would have granted to that country had it not been prevented from doing so by the Czar's despotism.

1562. The epithet "true" is helpful because, as we saw of the term "solidarity," meaning little or nothing it can be made to mean anything desired.[1] Then if some indiscreet soul insists on knowing what, after all, one of said epithets means, he is promptly served with a neat reasoning in a circle. Do I wish to give the term *A* the meaning of the term *B?* I simply say that the "true" *A* is *B.* But some bore may ask, "How distinguish the 'true' *A* from the *A* that is not 'true'?" I answer in a more or less wordy manner that the only *A* that can be properly called "true" is the *A* that is *B.*

1563. So someone will assert that "reason" leads to a conclusion *B*—the existence of God, let us say, or "solidarity." But the atheist, or the anti-solidarist, replies, "My reason does not lead to any such conclusion!" But he is told, "Because you do not use 'right' reason." "But how is 'right' reason to be distinguished from the reason that is not 'right'?" "Very easily: 'Right' reason believes in God (or in solidarity)."

1564. All the Christian sects have had their martyrs, and each has considered its own martyrs the only "true" ones. St. Augustine de-

---

1562 [1] In his early day, Cicero, *Academica,* II, 46, 142, notes several meanings in which the term "true" was used. From his time to ours the list has constantly been lengthening: "Pythagoras is of one view, that the opinion of each individual is truth to him; the Cyrenians of another, that there is no criterion of judgment apart from inner intuition (*permotiones intimas*); and Epicurus of still another, for he located all judgment in the senses, in our perceptions (*notitiis*) of things and in pleasure (*voluptate*). Plato, however, held that the whole criterion of truth, and the truth itself, have nothing to do with opinions and feelings (*adductam* misprint for *abductam*), but are prerogatives of thought and of the mind."

clares flatly: [1] "Heretics, furthermore, all suffer [*i.e.*, martyrdom] in behalf of error and not of the truth, for they lie against Christ Himself. Whatever things the impious and the heathen suffer they all suffer in behalf of falsehood." [2] It goes without saying that "truth" is what St. Augustine believes in, and "error," any other belief. Bayle clearly perceived the fallacy in a reasoning of the type of St. Augustine's that was designed to show that the orthodox were right and the heretics wrong in persecuting dissenters. [3] That fallacy, centuries and centuries old as it is, is at all times fresh and retains the full vigour and vitality of youth. It did yeoman's service for the Christians in persecuting the pagans, for the Catholics in persecuting the Protestants, and *vice versa,* for the various Protestant sects in persecuting one another, for all Christians in persecuting free-thinkers, and now for the free-thinkers in persecuting Christians, and especially Catholics. Under the Second Empire in France there were objections to Renan's appointment as a teacher. Under the Third Republic the same objections are urged against the appointment of Father Scheil (§ 618 [2]). But the Empire was doing wrong because it was on the side of error; and the Republic right because it is on the side of truth. Many Italians also reason as follows: "Catholics have no right to teach in the schools because they teach error. Only free-thinkers have a right to teach, because they teach the

1564 [1] *Sermones,* CCCVII: *In natali martyrum* (*Opera,* Vol. V, p. 1450), III, 4.

1564 [2] [The argument is in reply to the pagan rejoinder that the sufferings of the martyrs proved merely that they were on a par with the worst criminals, who were also cruelly put to death.—A. L.] *"Omnes haeretici etiam pro falsitate patiuntur non pro veritate, quia mentiuntur contra ipsum Christum. Omnes pagani impii quaecumque patiuntur pro falsitate patiuntur."* But how identify the "true" martyr? A very simple matter! He is the one that has died for the truth: *"Ergo ostendamus illos veraces. Iam ipsi se ostenderunt quando pro veritate etiam mori voluerunt"* ("Therefore we show that they were the true ones, or rather they have shown themselves true in being willing to die for the truth"). So the martyr proves the truth of the faith—he is its witness; and the faith proves the genuineness of his martyrdom.

1564 [3] *Commentaire philosophique,* Pt. III, § 17 (p. 461): "'It is wrong to use force only when those who are in the truth are forced to embrace error. Now we have not forced anybody from the truth into error. We, the orthodox, have forced you, heretics or schismatics, to move over to our side. We have therefore done no wrong. But you would be doing wrong if you were to force us.' Is that not the fallacy known as the *petitio principii?* It can be met in no better way, in the case in point, than to change the minor from negative to affirmative, and conclude directly against the one who has used it."

truth." Some generations back, the opposite reasoning was the prevailing one. So the wise change as the times change.[4] The Clericals used to say, and the liberals are today repeating, that the freedom that should be allowed is freedom to do "good," not freedom to do "wrong," the freedom that is "truth," not the freedom that is "error." Needless to add, what is "good" and "true" for the ones is "evil" and "false" for the others and *vice versa*. The terms "truth" and "error" have as many meanings as there are parties; and only in virtue of a IV-β derivation are they preferred to their equivalents: "What I believe" and "What I do not believe."

1565. Derivations of our IV-γ variety generally involve Class II residues (group-persistences). The ideas and sentiments engendered in us by a given term remain operative even after an epithet has been attached to the term, and may even grow in potency if the epithet is opportunely chosen. If "freedom" is a good thing, how much better must "true freedom" be! If "reason" cannot lead astray, how much safer the guidance of "right reason"!

1566. "This doctrine is true; hence it can, and ought to be, enforced." Most propositions which are stated in that form involve the use of an ambiguous term. The individuals upon whom the doctrine is to be forced in no wise admit that it is "true": they call it "false." The sound form of statement would be: "This doctrine is the truth for us; therefore we can, and ought to, enforce it." But in this latter form it is far less persuasive than in the other.

1564 [4] Socialists expel from their party—in other words, they "excommunicate" —persons who do not subscribe to their party's platform; and the practice is indispensable to them, as it is to anyone who is trying to build up a party. However, certain members of the Socialist party insist on barring Catholic priests from teaching in the schools because they are not "free" to think as they choose, but are obliged to follow the teachings of the Church. That "obligation" on the part of the Catholic priest is identical with the Socialist's "obligation." Both have to subscribe to the dogmas of the group to which they belong under pain of expulsion from it. It follows that if such an "obligation" precludes efficient teaching, it is desirable, for the sake of efficient teaching, that both should be denied the right to teach. If it is no such obstacle, it is desirable that both should be allowed to teach. Sentiment, however, draws the distinction. Those who like priests and dislike Socialists say that priests ought to be allowed to teach and Socialists be barred. That more or less is what happens in Germany. Those who dislike priests and like Socialists say that priests should be barred and Socialists accepted. And that is what is going on in France. Ingenuous souls, simpletons, and idiots are then fed with the notion that it is all being done out of love for the "ethical State," or Madame Liberty.

1567. In theoretical derivations the meaning given to the noun "truth" oscillates between two extremes. On the one hand "truth" signifies accord with the facts—what is sometimes called "experimental" and "historical" truth. On the other hand, it designates mere accord with certain sentiments, which carries with it the assent of the believer.[1] Between these two extremes there are any number of intermediate significations. Accord with facts may be a consequence of scientific experiment and observation, of researches in what is called historical criticism. Or it may result merely from the impressions that the facts make upon the minds of one or more persons in view of the sentiments they engender. In that again there are intermediate degrees between the extremes: now a scientific or historical scepticism that is ever checking impressions on impressions and so trying to accommodate them as closely as possible to facts; now a faith so robust that facts can in no way shake it, the impressions which they make being always distorted as much as is required to make them square with the faith. The science of mechanics from Aristotle to Laplace, natural history from Pliny to Cuvier, Roman history from Livy to Mommsen, Greek history from Herodotus to Grote, Curtius, and others, have progressed from this last extreme to the first; and the term "truth" has constantly changed in meaning all along the line (§§ 776 f.).[2]

1567 [1] If a person has a religious or metaphysical faith, he says that the "truth" which is to be found at that extreme is "superior to," "higher than," the truth located at the other extreme. It is a logical consequence of the Hegelian's belief that his religion, his metaphysics, his "science" (§§ 19 f.), are "superior" to experience. Materialists invert the relation, but their "experience" is itself just a form of religion. Really they are comparing two "truths" both located at our second extreme.

1567 [2] Just one among hosts of examples: Merle d'Aubigné, *Histoire de la Réformation*, Vol. I, p. 1: "A weakened world (a) was tottering on its foundations when Christianity appeared (b). The national religions that had satisfied the fathers had ceased to satisfy the children (c). . . . The gods of all nations had been transported to Rome and had lost their oracles there (d) as the peoples had their freedom (e). . . . Soon the narrow conceptions of nationality fell with their gods. The peoples blended one into another (f). In Europe, Asia, Africa there was now but one empire (g). The human race (h) began to be conscious of its universality, its unity." If one fix one's attention on historical realities, the following remarks will at once suggest themselves: a. What does D'Aubigné mean by "the world"? He seems vaguely to mean the Roman world, the Mediterranean area, but then again he seems to be thinking of the whole globe. When he says "a weakened world" he is probably thinking of the Roman world, for it hardly seems

1568. As we have already seen (§ 645), in repeating a story a person uses language somewhat different from what he heard, and he thinks that he is reporting the "truth," in the sense that the language he uses makes the same impression upon him as the language he heard. The precise words uttered in a long conversation cannot possibly be remembered. What sticks in the memory is the impression one had of it, and that impression is what one tries to reproduce in setting out to repeat the conversation. If one has done that successfully one feels in all good faith that one has "spoken the truth." In practice, before courts of justice, such approximate reproduction is usually adequate for ordinary purposes. If it seems insufficient in

possible that he could have been thinking of China, Japan, Germany, and the many other countries. *b.* Why "weakened"? At the time when Christianity appeared the Roman Empire was very strong and prosperous. It was rather after the triumph of Christianity that the Empire "weakened." Many pagan Emperors dictated peace to the barbarians at the point of the sword. Many Christian Emperors bought peace with gold. *c.* D'Aubigné forgets that if Christianity was quite willing not to be a national religion, it ended by being one. Islamism, instead, is essentially non-national even in our day; and of Islamism far better than of Christianity might one say that it appeared in a "weakened" (Roman) world. *d.* The Delphic oracle was very famous in antiquity. Did it really pass out of existence because its god had been transported to Rome? Where can D'Aubigné have found evidence of any such transfer? *e.* D'Aubigné is trying for a literary effect by balancing the oracles of the gods against the liberty of the peoples. Historical realities have quite gone out of his mind. *f.* What peoples? He must be thinking of the peoples who were conquered and made subject by the Romans, forgetting all about the Barbarians, the Chinese, Japanese, Hindus, Africans, Americans . . . mere bagatelles, they! *g.* Here D'Aubigné is surely naming the whole by the part. He could not have been unaware that the Roman Empire was very far from extending over all Europe, all Asia, all Africa. *h.* But if the preceding stricture is sound, how can it now occur to him to think of mentioning the "human race"? If our assumption was unsound, if D'Aubigné really meant *all* Europe, *all* Asia, *all* Africa—never mind about America and Oceania—he can then, it is true, allude in all strictness to the "human race"; but just as truly he will be talking nonsense. A person who shares D'Aubigné's faith does not notice such obvious departures from reality in reading his history, any more than a lover notices the freckles on his sweetheart's face. Of such a lover Lucretius in his time wrote, *De rerum natura*, IV, vv. 1160-72:

> "*Nigra melichrus est, immunda ac fetida acosmos,*
> *caesia, Palladium, nervosa et lignea, dorcas,*
> *parvola pumilio, chariton mia, tota merum sal . . .*
> *cetera de genere hoc longumst si dicere coner.*"

("Is she black? She is blond as honey! Is she unclean, uncouth? She is pleasantly négligée! Has she green eyes? She is Minerva! Is she stiff and wooden? She is a gazelle! A puny dwarf, she is one of the Graces—and what wit! . . . But were I

some respect, the court can ask the witness to make himself more clear.

1569. As is well known, ancient historians have a mania for giving the orations that they allege were delivered by one character or another in their story. Even Polybius, who is otherwise so conscientious, follows that practice.[1] He repeats verbatim the oration which Cornelius Scipio delivered before his army on the eve of the battle on the Ticinus, III, 64, 3-11 (Paton, Vol. II, pp. 155-57). Now it is altogether certain that Polybius could not have known the contents of that speech, word for word. It cannot be an accurate reproduction of the incident, but a mere formulation of the impression left with Polybius by stories he had heard of it. The same may be said in general of the stories told by the ancient historians, and of not a few accounts by moderns. They report impressions more often than facts. At times such impressions come fairly close to historical reality, then again they vary from it and may end by having no relation to it whatever.

1570. This extreme is illustrated by the impressions that Jean Réville describes,[1] in connexion with the problem of the Fourth Gospel: "Concluding his study of the Prologue of the Fourth Gospel, M. Loisy says of the Evangelist:[2] 'He is not writing a history of Jesus but rather a treatise on knowledge of Jesus.' I hold instead

to give the whole list of such things, the task would be long indeed.") [Lucretius is mimicking the Greek affectations of love-making in the Roman Mayfair of his day: *melichrus* is μελίχροος, *acosmos*: ἄκοσμος, *Palladium*: Παλλάδιον, *dorcas*: δόρκας, *chariton mia*: χαρίτων μία.—A. L.] Molière imitates the passage in *Le misanthrope*, Act. II, Scene vi, when he says of lovers:

> "*Ils comptent les défauts pour des perfections,*
> *et savent y donner de favorables noms:*
> *la pâle est au jasmin en blancheur comparable;*
> *la noire à faire peur une brune adorable.*"

("They count defects so many perfections and manage to give pleasant names to them. Pale, she is comparable in whiteness to the jasmine; and black enough to frighten, she is an adorable brunette!")

1569 [1] However, he condemns, *Historiae*, XII, 25, 4-5 (Paton, Vol. IV, pp. 369-71), the use of orations by Timaeus as excessive and in fact seems (XII, 25, 3) to condone the practice only as a means of portraying sentiments and manners. And *cf.* Thucydides, *Historiae*, I, 22, 1.

1570 [1] *Le quatrième Évangile*, pp. 113-14, note.

1570 [2] *Le Prologue du quatrième Évangile*, p. 266.

that he intended to write a history, but history as an Alexandrian understood history, which is something radically different from what we mean by history. . . . The aim of the Gospel, the aim of the Prologue itself, is historical—that is the fact that must not be lost sight of. However, the Evangelist writes history as all men who were imbued with the Alexandrine spirit in his day wrote history, with a sovereign contempt for concrete material reality, as was the case with Philo or St. Paul. In the view of those great minds, history was not a pragmatic narrative of events, a faithful reproduction of details, a careful chronology, an integral resurrection of the past. The historian's task was to emphasize the moral and spiritual values of facts, their deeper significance, that element of eternal truth [Another kind of truth!] which is present in each contingent and ephemeral phenomenon in history. For them history becomes one vast allegory, one perpetual symbol of which only the inner value has any importance. Such a point is difficult for us moderns to understand—our manner of thinking is entirely different; but it was clarity itself to those who lived in intimate association with Philo and most of the early Christian writers." From the scientific standpoint there are a number of sound remarks in this passage, along with a surplusage of derivations foreign to science. Réville feels called upon to assure us that Philo and St. Paul were "great minds," though there are plenty of people who regard them as inconsequential chatterboxes—and that is not a problem to be treated offhand. But such praise comes strangely indeed from Réville at a moment when he is presenting them to us as men of very ordinary minds as historians. He might at least have drawn such a distinction himself! But that is all a derivation of our IV-β variety. Réville wants to have the protection of incidental sentiments to offset the disastrous effects of the facts themselves; then shortly we see a very respectable entity step forward—the "function of the historian." Those "great minds" understood that function in the sense of writing history without regard to facts. That granted, one might wonder why the *Arabian Nights* should not be classed with the histories. There are, it would seem, "contingent and ephemeral phenomena in history," and other phenomena that are not such. Which, pray, would they be? Réville does not say. Nor can one ever imagine what that "eternal truth" might be, of which, it seems, a quantity small or large is present in every "historical phenomenon." Hannibal marched into Italy with his army. That is a historical fact. But who can say just how much "eternal truth" it contains? Such talk is arrant nonsense.

1571. After alluding to prevailing doubts as to the historical reality of the biblical Flood, M. Loisy [1] adds: "The story of the Creation is true, even though it contains no history and is framed in a cosmogony that is no longer accepted today. Who knows but that in the chapters following there may be stories which are also true in their way, though they do not contain all the materially exact historical elements which we would like to find in them (§ 774)?" [2] Evidently in all this passage the word "true" has, for the writer, a different meaning from the one it has when we say, "It is 'true' that Garibaldi landed in Sicily in 1860." But until he tells us the precise sense he chooses to give to the word, we can neither accept nor

---

1571 [1] *Études sur la religion chaldéo-assyrienne,* Vol. IV, pp. 152-53.

1571 [2] There is a similar derivation in another work by Loisy, *Études bibliques,* pp. 131-32: "One cannot say, however, that the Bible contains errors in astronomy. That would be at once unjust and naïve. Before we could have a right to charge the Bible with an error of that sort, an inspired author would have to make it apparent, in some passage or other, that he is trying to force this or that conception of the universe upon his reader as a certain truth. [Another kind of truth! How many many kinds there are!] But none of the sacred writers ever betrayed any intention of giving lessons in astronomy." Loisy does not care to have the unfavourable sentiments associated with the word "error" come into play where the Bible is concerned. He calls in a derivation, in order to confuse "objective error" with "subjective error" and bring those two different things under a single name. Had he chosen to express himself clearly he might have said: "The fact that the Bible contains assertions which do not correspond to the facts (objective errors) does not justify the conclusion that the writer was trying to make anyone believe that they corresponded to the facts, or even that he thought they did himself (subjective error)." But that concedes the presence of the objective error, a fact, after all, which Loisy does not care to deny. He is however unwilling to use the word "error." Loisy's position, which as a matter of fact is the position of many exponents of the "higher criticism," has not, to tell the truth, any great probability; but it cannot, strictly speaking, be disputed. Suppose a naturalist is discussing preparations for dinner with his wife and says, "For fish, instead of smelt, I suggest we have lobster." The statement would contain an objective error: a lobster is not a fish. There is no subjective error, however, because the naturalist knows very well that a lobster is not a fish and he also knows very well that he would look ridiculous to his wife if he were to say, pedant-fashion, "For fish, instead of smelt, a fish, I suggest we have a crustacean—a lobster." All the same, even granting that, the fact still remains that his first statement contained an objective error.

reject the conclusions in which it figures, provided, of course, we intend to remain in the logico-experimental field. If we abandon that field for the field of sentiment, we will accept or reject them according to the vague sentiments that the word chances to arouse in us.[8] But note, meantime, how everything in the passage works in to intensify the appeal to sentiment. Loisy tries in every way to profit by the favourable sentiments that the term "true" arouses. He speaks of a "story that is true even though it contains no history and no historical elements that are materially exact." Why the "materially"? If the word "true" is taken in the sense of "accord with the facts," how can a story be "historical" and not "materially exact"? It might be historical as a whole and not be exact in parts, but that is not what Loisy seems to mean. Had he meant that he would not have spoken of "stories that are true in their way." Julius Caesar was or was not a dictator. In the first case, Caesar's dictatorship is a historical fact; in the second case it is not. In the first case, it is accurate to say that he was a dictator; in the second it is not. One cannot imagine what the following proposition could mean: "To say that Caesar was not a dictator is a story true in its way, even though it does not contain the materially exact historical elements which we would like to find in it." And indeed it is hard to guess just what Loisy was trying to say. He may have meant that there are stories in the Bible which do not correspond to historical, experimental, reality, but which do correspond to certain things lying outside the

1571 [8] Rousselot, *Études sur la philosophie dans le moyen âge,* Vol. II, pp. 14-15: "At the time when Christianity appeared, sentiment had been stifled or vitiated in the peoples. . . . Then came Christianity with all its blessings, to warm hearts and strike a note from the religious chord before which the other two [intelligence and will] fell silent. But truth residing only in a reality that is complete [An unintelligible proposition.], the time came when intelligence and will, after expiating, so to speak, their shortcomings by a long submission, again demanded the right to occupy the place that belonged to them. [So then: because the "true" can reside only in a "reality" that is "complete," intellect and will ask back a certain place that belongs to them.] So, among thinking people, first Nominalism arose, as a first manifestation of independent intelligence—we know what our judgment is to be of it; then Realism as a higher and worthier, but no less exclusive, manifestation [Why "higher"? And as for the "worthiness," who is to be judge of it?], which, accordingly, could not yield an exact formula for the truth, for truth demands harmony, and at that time there was nothing but antagonism." But when and where did our estimable Dame Truth ever file her demand for "harmony," and what on earth is "harmony" anyhow?

pale of experience that the sentiment functioning in certain individuals thinks it knows. If that is really what he had in mind, he would have been clearer had he stated it in some such way. But from the standpoint of derivations it was wise in him not to do that, in order not to lose that retinue of pleasant sentiments which Dame Truth always has in attendance on her.

1572. In a chapter replete with reticences, Monsignor Duchesne exerts himself to justify, without seeming to, the ancient persecutions of the Donatists.[1] Apropos of the famous letter of St. Augustine to Vicentius, he writes: "In still other ways, through controversial pamphlets, local conferences, sermons, letters, the bishops did all in their power to set forth the truth and get it before the Donatist public." Even for Monsignor Duchesne the "truth" in question is, evidently, different from the "truth" which St. Augustine and other Holy Fathers "set forth and got before the public" when they denied the existence of antipodes. To avoid misapprehensions, Monsignor Duchesne might, in place of "truth," have used the phrase: "What Catholics believe to be the truth." But that wording would have defeated his purpose of creating a confusion between "subjective truth," a truth recognized by certain individuals only, and "objective truth," which is tested by its accord with the facts, and so nursing in his reader a sentiment of disapprobation for the Donatists as individuals capable of denying objective truth.

1573. By resorting to terms that are ostensibly objective but actually subjective, these derivations may be used to prove both sides of a question equally well. The derivations that Monsignor Duchesne calls in to justify the persecutions of the Donatists in Africa are the very ones that are being used in France today to justify persecutions of Monsignor Duchesne's coreligionists. Monsignor Duchesne begins by rebuking the Donatists for their hostility to the Catholics. So the French free-thinkers rebuke the Catholics for hostility to themselves and the Republic. In Africa a Catholic bishop of Bagai was mishandled by Donatists. In France Dreyfus is said to have been abused by Catholics. Says Monsignor Duchesne, Vol. III, p. 130: "Their backs to the wall, the Catholic episcopate [The French republican government.] recollected that there were laws

1572 [1] *Histoire ancienne de l'Église,* Vol. III, pp. 130 f.

against instigators of schism [Against religious congregations.], and that, at bottom, the whole Donatist Church [The majority of the religious congregations.] was one vast infraction of the law." Of the penalties prescribed for heretics in the Theodosian Code Monsignor Duchesne remarks, p. 131: "They would have been very severe had the heretics been peaceable citizens [Had Catholics kept out of politics, one might have said in France—had Catholics not been "intriguing monks" (*moines ligueurs*), Waldeck-Rousseau actually said.]; but considering the temper of the Donatists and the extravagances in which they indulged under the eye of complaisant authorities, they were not severe enough." [But, considering the temper of the clericals and the outrages they committed against Dreyfus, Jews, Protestants, and free-thinkers, under the benignant eye of complaisant authorities, they were not severe enough.] Monsignor Duchesne congratulates himself, p. 133, on the results of the persecution, just as M. Combes was satisfied with the outcome in France: "It cannot be denied that official pressure had far-reaching and beneficial consequences. The fanaticism of the Circumcellians [Of Waldeck-Rousseau's *"moines ligueurs"*] was not shared by all Donatists [By all French Catholics.] Not a few sensible persons among them were aware of the ineptitude of their schism [Of Papal infallibility, one might say, for France.] and were waiting only for a pretext for breaking loose from it. Many were Donatists by habit, by family tradition, without knowing why, without ever having devoted serious thought to the matter [Anti-Clericals speak of Catholics in just those terms.] Others were kept in the sect only by fear of violence from the fanatical wing. In a word, the interference of the state tended far less to molest people in their conscience than to deliver them from an unbearable oppression." That was exactly what Waldeck-Rousseau, Combes, and all the French anti-Clericals said and repeated. Nor has there been any lack of metaphysicists to assure us that in persecuting Clericals the French Government was "creating freedom."

1574. Those gentle peace-loving Catholics of St. Augustine's sought nothing, says Monsignor Duchesne, but unity in faith. But what did Combes want? Said he in a speech before the Senate (June 24, 1904): "We believe that it is not fantastic of us to regard it as desirable and practicable to do for the France of our time what the

Old Régime so well achieved for the France of old. One king, one faith! Such the watchword, then! And it was a tower of strength to our monarchical governments. Our task is to find for ourselves a similar watchword that will correspond to the requirements of the present age." Monsignor Duchesne, Vol. III, p. 127, mentions a certain popular song that "Catholic children sang about the streets, so popularizing the cause of unity." In twentieth-century France, *La Lanterne* and other anti-Clerical newspapers played just that rôle. Under Louis XIV, in the Cévennes district, the Royal Dragoons also exerted themselves actively in behalf of religious unity.

1575. There are so many kinds of truth in this world that there may well be one to fit the relationship that obtains between Monsignor Duchesne's narrative and the facts as related by St. Augustine, along with the comments that the Saint makes on them. But that truth certainly is not of the historical variety, and St. Augustine's text and the prose of the modern writer leave altogether different impressions with us. The fact is, St. Augustine has something greater and better in view than the suppression of "an infraction of the law." The doughty Saint elaborates a finished theory of persecution. He compares the schismatic to a patient suffering from hysteria [1] and recommends the use of force as a cure for both. He does not admit that a man has a right not to be "forced into holiness," [2] and he proves his point with many deftly chosen quotations from the Bible. That gentle soul would exile and fine dissenters that they may learn to prefer what they read in the Scripture to the "gossip and slanders of men"—said "gossip and slanders" being so called, of course, by the learned St. Augustine, the able scientist who read in Scripture that there were no antipodes, contrarily to the "gossip and slanders" of ignoramuses who said there were. [3] And that no shadow of doubt as to his meaning may be left, he adds: "And in truth, that I have said as well of all Donatists as of all heretics who are Christians by sacrament yet depart from Christ's truth or from

---

1575 [1] *Epistolae*, XCIII, 1-2 (*Ad Vicentium*) (*Opera*, Vol. II, pp. 322-23; *Works*, Vol. VI, p. 397).

1575 [2] *Ibid.*, 2, 5 (*Works*, p. 399): "*Putas neminem debere cogi ad iustitiam.*"

1575 [3] *Ibid.*, 3, 10 (*Opera, loc. cit.*, p. 326; *Works*, p. 403): "*. . . ut coercitione exsiliorum atque damnorum admoneantur considerare quid quare patiantur, et discant praeponere rumoribus et calumniis hominum* [Healy: "mischievous and frivolous human fables."] *Scripturas quas legunt.*"

Christian unity."⁴ That the Saint held any such doctrine would not be remotely suspected by a person reading Monsignor Duchesne's history without going back to Augustine's text. And he cannot claim that the Saint's doctrine is a matter of no importance. Monsignor Duchesne knows perfectly well that when Protestants were being persecuted in France under Louis XIV, the Archbishop of Paris published translations of two of St. Augustine's letters to justify the new persecution on the precedent of the old. Nor can he be unaware that Bayle took advantage of that publication to pen an eloquent defence of toleration.⁵ It would have been well for Monsignor Du-

1575 ⁴ *Ibid.*, 3, 10 (*Works*, p. 404): "*Et hoc quidem vel de omnibus haereticis qui Christianis sacramentis imbuuntur et a Christi veritate sive unitate dissentiunt, vel de Donatistis omnibus dixerim.*" The Saint goes on to say, 5, 16 (*Opera, loc. cit.*, p. 329; *Works*, p. 409) that the important question is not whether one is, or is not, constrained, but whether the constraint is toward good or toward evil: ". . . *sed quale sit illud quo cogitur utrum bonum an malum.*" It is the same old story: I set out to force a person to do what I like. What I like I call "good," what he likes "bad"; and then I tell him that he has no right to complain since I am forcing him into what is good," *Epistolae*, CLXXIII, CLXXXV (*Opera*, Vol. II, pp. 753-57; *Works*, Vol. XIII, pp. 346-53; *Opera*, Vol. II, pp. 792-815; *Works*, Vol. III, pp. 479-520). Delightfully, the Saint adds (after a number of theological considerations on baptism), LXXXIX, 6 (*Opera*, Vol. II, p. 312; *Works*, Vol. VI, p. 379): "And yet, though such a luminous truth [A pretty name that the Saint has found for his own patter.] strikes the ears and hearts of men, such a whirlpool of evil habit has engulfed them that they prefer to resist all reasons and authorities rather than defer to them. They resist in two ways, now raving in their fury, now sulking in inaction (*saeviendo aut pigrescendo*)." That too is perfectly clear! And then we are given to understand that the Catholics were on the defensive! It takes courage to pretend that a man who is "sulking in inaction" (*pigrescendo*) is attacking someone!

1575 ⁵ *Commentaire philosophique*, Pt. III, Preface: "So let us glance at the two 'Letters' of this Father [St. Augustine] which the Archbishop of Paris has had printed in a special pamphlet in a new French translation. . . . The pamphlet is entitled as a whole: 'Consistency of the Conduct of the Church of France in Bringing back the Protestants with the Conduct of the African Church in Bringing back the Donatists to the Catholic Church.'" Combes might have published a pamphlet supplementing these two "consistencies" with still a third: the consistency with St. Augustine's doctrine of the measures of the French anti-Clericals in bringing back Catholics into the fold of the Radical-Socialist church. Admirers of St. Augustine must not forget the proverb that one reaps as one has sown. Blood-thirsty as his successors may have been, the Saint was much more mild. He urges Donatus, the proconsul in Africa, to repress the Donatists but not to kill them (*Epistolae, C. Donato proconsuli Africae, ut Donatistas coerceat, non occidat*) (*Opera*, Vol. II, p. 366; *Works*, Vol. XIII, p. 26). He, as he elsewhere shows, is satisfied if they kill themselves, to escape the persecution that he is aiding and abetting: *Epistolae*, CLXXXV, 3, 14 (*Opera*, Vol. II, pp. 798-99; *Works*, Vol. III,

chesne to make known his views on all that, instead of resorting to the lean pretext of an "infraction of the law" in order to evade the issue.

1576. Monsignor Duchesne is also silent on the cupidity of the Catholics for the property of the Donatists. St. Augustine records the fact and gives what one must judge an exceedingly feeble excuse for it.[1] He points out that Donatists who returned to the fold got

pp. 490-91): "If however they choose to kill themselves to prevent the deliverance [from error] of those who have a right to be delivered . . ." [Pareto renders: "to prevent us from persecuting the others."—A. L.] And he concludes, "What therefore shall be the stand (*quid agit*) of brotherly love as between fearing the temporary fires of the stake for the few or sending all into the eternal fires of Hell?" ("*Quid agit ergo fraterna dilectio: utrum dum paucis transitorios ignes metuit caminorum, dimittit omnes aeternis ignibus gehennarum.*") Those few words state the whole program of the Inquisition. *Cf. Contra Gaudentium*, I, 24 f. (*Opera*, Vol, IX, pp. 707 f.).

1576 [1] *Epistolae*, CLXXXV, 9, 35-36 (*Opera*, Vol. II, pp. 808-09; *Works*, Vol. III, p. 508): "They reproach us with being greedy for their property and confiscating it. . . . But the Christian Emperors have commanded by their religious laws that all property held in the name of churches of the Donatist sect should go over to the Catholic Church with the churches themselves." So in our day in France the property of the religious congregations "went over" to the government—and also it seems, in great part, to the liquidators, and to the politicians who were their accomplices. Another passage in St. Augustine contains an indirect admission of such spoliations (*Ibid., loc. cit.*, 9, 41; *Opera*, pp. 810-11; *Works*, pp. 511-12), with a biblical paraphrase from the Wisdom of Solomon, 5: 1. On the Day of Judgment, he says, "the pagan shall not stand in boldness before the face of the Christian, who made no account of his labours in destroying his temples and robbing him of his idols. But the Christian shall stand in great boldness before the face of the pagan who made no account of his labours in scattering the bones of the martyrs. [What an effective metaphor for getting into another person's pocket!] So the heretic will stand in boldness before the face of the Christian who made no account of his labours when the laws of the Catholic Emperors prevailed. But the Catholic will stand in great boldness before the face of the heretic who made no account of his labours when the madness of the impious Circumcellians prevailed." Gaudentius, the bishop of the Donatists, says of the Catholics according to St. Augustine, *Contra Gaudentium*, I, 36, 46 (*Opera*, Vol. IX, p. 754): "But those who are wrongfully withholding the property of others do not know this." The Saint, replying, does not dispute the fact of the possession, but merely insists that the Donatists are not "the righteous" (*justi*) to whom Scripture alludes: "It is a question," he says, "of righteousness (*justitia*), not of money." And that may well be, but meantime the Catholics were pocketing the cash, and the Donatists, it seems, should have been satisfied, for it is written: "The righteous shall spoil the ungodly" [Wisdom of Solomon, 10:20: '*Labores impiorum justi edent*']; and because the Catholics were inspired not by any design of greed but by zeal in repressing error: *In talibus quippe omnibus factis non rapina concupiscitur sed error evertitur*. And, besides, the Catholics seized the properties of the heretics with every intention of restoring them the moment the heretics were converted.

their properties back, and pretends not to understand what the quarrel is about when he objects that greed for the possessions of the Donatists is inconsistent with a desire to convert them; for the charge was brought not as to properties of Donatists who recanted but as to properties of non-recanters. To justify the persecution St. Augustine uses metaphors that are far-fetched to a degree: "Was I called upon," he cries to the Donatists, "to oppose this measure, just to save you properties that you say are yours and enable you to proscribe Christ in all security? Just to enable you to make your testaments according to Roman law while with your slanderous insults you were tearing to shreds the Testament bequeathed to your fathers and founded on divine law? [Note the play on the double sense of "Testament" and the offer of the pun as an argument.] . . . Just to enable you freely to buy and sell while daring to divide what the sold Christ had bought?" [2] And so the Saint goes on piling up antitheses that are based on double meanings of words and other cavillings. These wretched and inept arguments have been admired by many people; and that, as we have so often said and repeated in similar cases, shows the great power that sentiments have.[3] At bottom St. Augustine's argument comes down to this: "You hold a belief that we consider erroneous; therefore we are justified in doing anything to bring you over from your belief, which we think bad, to our belief, which we think good. And you have no cause for complaint, since you can escape your plight by adopting our view." But in that form the argument has far less persuasive force than the form used by St. Augustine, where "truth" and "error," "good" and "bad," are palmed off not as subjective but as objective entities.

1577. Of course a person sharing St. Augustine's faith cannot grant that the terms in question are subjective. But if he will have them objective at all costs, he might still admit, without derogating

1576 [2] *Epistolae*, XCIII, 5, 19 (*Opera*, Vol. II, p. 331; *Works*, Vol. VI, p. 411): "*Ita sane huic provisioni contradicere debui ne res quas dicitis vestras perderetis et securi Christum proscriberetis? ut iure Romano testamenta conderetis et iure divino patribus conditum Testamentum ubi scriptum est: 'In semine tuo benedicentur omnes gentes'* [Gen. 26:4] *calumniosis criminationibus rumperetis? ut in emptionibus et venditionibus liberos contractus haberetis et vobis dividere quod Christus emit venditus auderetis?*"

1576 [3] [Pareto says, "and that shows the fatuousness of derivations"— apparently a *lapsus linguae.*—A. L.]

one whit from his faith, that their objectivity is something different from the objectivity of a chemical or physical experiment. That admission would be enough to eliminate all conflict with experimental science, which concerns itself strictly with facts of this latter type.

1578. At other times the confusion between the many kinds of truth arises without any preconceived design on a writer's part to take advantage of it—merely as a reflection of a similar confusion prevailing in his own mind. He is seeing the facts through a coloured glass and describing them as he sees them. He tells us what the good is, as he sees things, and goes to no pains to investigate the relations of that good to experimental reality. When Renan speaks of the "ineffable truth" of the sayings of Jesus in the Gospel according to Matthew,[1] he is evidently attaching to the term "truth" an entirely different meaning from the one he would give it in speaking of a chemical or physical experiment. But no one knows to just what objective reality the word as he uses it corresponds. The chances are that it merely corresponds to certain sentiments he feels. It is, at any rate, apparent enough from his writings that in his case "historical truth" is one thing and "scientific truth" quite another. He observes, *loc. cit.*, p. xlvii, that two accounts of the same episode given by two eyewitnesses are essentially different, and asks: "Must we on that account give up all the colouring in the two stories and keep to the bare statement of the facts as a whole? That would be suppressing history!"[2] No, it would merely be suppressing historical romance. If a person refuses all history because he cannot have it complete in every detail, he is refusing to take the less because he cannot have the more. But, *vice versa,* a person accepting the less that is certain by no means contracts thereby an obligation

1578 [1] *Vie de Jésus,* Preface, p. xxx.

1578 [2] The whole passage reads: "In almost all ancient histories, even histories far less legendary than the Gospels, matters of detail are subject to endless doubt. Whenever we have two accounts of one same episode, they rarely agree. Is that not good ground for very grave doubts when we have only one? The chances are that of the anecdotes, speeches, witticisms, handed down by the historians not one is strictly genuine. Were there stenographers present to record such fleeting words? Was a historian always on hand to note the gestures, the facial expressions, the sentiments, of the people in question? One need only try to get at the truth as to just how some episode or other has taken place in our day. One will not succeed. The accounts two eyewitnesses give of one same event present essential differences. Must we on that account, *etc.*? . . ."

to accept the more which is uncertain or even manifestly contrary to the fact. Of no event in the past can we have a complete description; but we must at least try to determine what we do know about it and what we are obliged to discard. There are, moreover, different planes of probability. It is almost certain that the battle of the Ticinus took place. It is very doubtful whether, before that battle, Cornelius Scipio delivered the oration which Polybius ascribes to him (§ 1569). It is virtually certain, at any rate, that there were some differences between the words uttered by Scipio and those reported by Polybius. It is virtually certain—not to say certain outright, in the ordinary sense of the term—that a man named Julius Caesar once lived. It is very very doubtful that Romulus was a person equally real. We cannot therefore put things so different into the same class. Such ambiguities are useful from the standpoint of derivations. From the logico-experimental standpoint they cannot be tolerated. Give any name one chooses to the accord between a story and fact: call it "historical truth," call it by some other name—that is a matter of little importance. But unless one would chatter to no purpose, the name, whatever it be, must be different from the name one uses for the miracles of the various religions, the legends of folk-lore, prophecies and portents, and stories of the type of Aladdin's marvellous lamp. Some of these stories may have, if one will, a "higher" truth than experimental truth—that is not the question. What is important is that that *truth,* however superior it may be, should have a name to distinguish it from our modest, inferior, commonplace, "experimental truth." [3]

1578 [3] There are many other "truths," and very pretty ones. Writing of Tolstoy in the *Corriere della sera,* Nov. 21, 1910, Antonio Fogazzaro, the novelist, says: "He created truth and never seemed to care about creating beauty. He seemed almost to disdain Art as something inferior, as something human and not divine. But of the whole Truth he was the voice, as it were, and the flame, not only of the truth that the artist pantingly pursues, but also of that moral truth which glows resplendent in the soul that it has permeated. The True and the Good were one with Tolstoy. Not everything, to be sure, that seemed Good and True to him seems Good and True to me, or to numberless others who feel the passion of the Good and the True." Fogazzaro prints the word "true" sometimes with a capital, sometimes with a small letter. Whether there be a difference, and just what, in the two cases is not very clear. Dame Truth has a voice and a flame. That seems to be very consoling to Fogazzaro. To us it is merely obscure. There is a certain "moral truth which glows resplendent in the soul that it has permeated." That is under-

1579. The Abbé de Broglie [1] exemplifies very fairly a subjective conception of prophecies. Abraham Kuenen had shown that certain prophecies in the Bible do not accord with the facts. Father de Broglie replies: "Kuenen starts out with a false conception of prophecy. He assumes that the prophetic texts have only one meaning, that the meaning has to be clear, that it has to be the meaning which the prophets and their contemporaries gave to it. He does not recognize any fulfilment unless events conform to the meaning so established." Such, in fact, is the meaning used in the objective reasonings of historical criticism and of logico-experimental science in general. [2] The Abbé de Broglie meets Kuenen with subjective considerations that may perfectly well be accepted so long as they are kept distinct from those of the logico-experimental type. Such a distinction is essential unless we are to talk to no purpose. Says he: "The true conception of prophecy is quite different." And as usual the term "true" leads to an argument in a circle. That would not be the case if, instead of saying the "true conception," the Abbé had said "my conception" or "the Catholic conception," or the equivalent. But he does not do that because his derivation needs the word "true" in order to arouse certain sentiments. The Abbé continues: "It is a word of God addressed to future generations and not to be understood until after the event. It is an enigma the key to which

standable. Everybody finds resplendent a truth with which he has been "permeated." The trouble is, not everyone is permeated. And what does it mean to "create truth"? Truth ordinarily is discovered, asserted, proclaimed. Fairy-stories and old wives' tales are "created" and very easily. It might be objected that such criticisms miss the point in Fogazzaro's article in that they approach from a logico-experimental point of view a paragraph designed exclusively to act upon sentiment. And that would be true. Our criticisms aim at nothing else than at demonstrating the sentimental value of the passage. Writings of that kind are ridiculous from the logico-experimental standpoint. They may be very effective as appeals to sentiment. In that appeal the value of derivations resides.

1579 [1] *Les prophètes et la prophétie,* p. 194.

1579 [2] Gousset, *Théologie dogmatique,* Vol. I, pp. 312-13, begins: "But for a prophecy to stand the test it must in the first place have indicated the event predicted in a definite and exact manner so that the application of the prophecy is not a matter of arbitrary choice." Excellent! That is the logico-experimental manner of reasoning. But, alas, Gousset at once withdraws the concession he has made: "All the same, prophecy does not have to be absolutely clear. It need simply be clear enough to have attracted the attention of men and be understood when it has been fulfilled."

is to be supplied by the event." [3] Thinking in objective terms, one has to admit that along that line pagan prophecies were as good as the Christian. The riddle of the "wooden wall" that was to save the Athenians was even clearer than many biblical prophecies, and in our day trance quacks and fortune-tellers also favour us with "prophecies that come true," being understood only by people who are minded to understand them and not till after the predicted event has taken place. The Italian "dream-book" infallibly foretells the numbers that are to be drawn at a lottery. But, unfortunately, not till after the drawing do we understand, in general, what numbers should have been played—a defect that proves most costly to our poor gamblers. A certain Guynaud went to the pains of writing a book to show that all the prophecies of Nostradamus had been fulfilled; and his arguments are neither better nor worse than other disquisitions of the kind (§§ 621 f.). [4] But as everybody knows and

1579 [3] Guillaume de Jumiège, *Histoire des Normands,* p. 313. A mysterious individual is asked whether Count Rollon's line is to endure very long: "He refused to make any answer and began merely to draw something like lines in the ashes on the hearth with a little stick which he held in his hand. His host then insisting very obstinately on getting him to say what was to happen after the seventh generation, he began with the same wooden stick to erase the lines he had drawn in the ashes. Whence it was inferred that after the seventh generation the duchy would be destroyed, or at least would have to undergo great trials and tribulations, the which in fact we have seen to be fulfilled in large part, those of us who have survived King Henry, who was, as we can show, the seventh in descent in that line." Paulin Paris, *Les romans de la Table ronde,* Vol. II, pp. 56-57 (The magician Merlin declares): " 'Henceforward I shall not speak before the people or at court save in obscure words, nor will they know what I mean until they see it come to pass.' " Merlin, says Paris, "kept his word to the letter, and all soothsayers before and after him have followed that same policy." That, in fact, was an excellent precaution on Merlin's part, and it may be recommended in full confidence to all our estimable prophets and fortune-tellers.

1579 [4] *La concordance des prophéties de Nostradamus avec l'histoire,* pp. 115 f. One "verification" chosen at random, *Centurie III, Quatrin 91:*

> *"L'arbre qu'avoit par long temps mort seiché*
> *dans une nuit viendra à reverdir:*
> *chron. Roi malade: Prince pied attaché:*
> *craint d'ennemis fera voiles bondir."*

("The tree that had long since dried up and died will leaf out again in the course of a night. Chron.: King sick; Prince tied at the foot; fear of foes will set sails a-bounding.") "Explanation: Historians are quite in agreement as to the veracity of the matter of this prophecy, but not as to the day or the month of its fulfilment. Favyn . . . reports [*Histoire de Navarre,* p. 868] that the day after St.

as the proverb says, hindsight is better than foresight—*del senno di poi son piene le fosse!* Even when the divergence between the prophecy and the fact is altogether patent, the Abbé de Broglie makes one more attempt at reconciliation and ends by saying that

Bartholomew, Aug. 25, 1572, an old tree known as 'the Hawthorne' which had long since dried up and died was found to be entirely green the morning after the night of Sunday-Monday. . . . That proves today the truth of the first two verses. . . . However, Jean le Gaulois claims that that did not take place till September of that same year, 1572. . . . But whether the miracle occurred the day after St. Bartholomew or a week or more later is of no importance today. It is enough for us that Nostradamus had predicted it. [As for the two following lines:] There are also signs of the veracity of the predictions of Nostradamus, inasmuch as Charles IX, some time after the occurrence of the miracle in question, fell sick . . . of a chronic ailment, a sort of quartan fever. As for 'the Prince tied at the foot,' that meant that M. the Duc d'Anjou would, as he actually did and also about that same time, tie himself to the foot of the walls of La Rochelle. The last verse . . . meant that in fear of the enemies of France the King would fit out a great naval force." See also Nicoullaud, *Nostradamus et ses prophéties.*

In his *Bickerstaff Papers* Swift delightfully satirizes such mongers of prophecy. He pretends in person of Bickerstaff to make a number of prophecies, one among others foretelling the death on a certain day of Partridge, the almanac writer, and the Cardinal de Noailles. He assumes that the fulfilment of the prophecy has been disputed and replies: "With my utmost endeavours I have not been able to trace above two objections ever made against the truth of my last year's prophecies. The first was of a Frenchman, who was pleased to publish to the world 'that the Cardinal de Noailles was still alive notwithstanding the pretended prophecy of Monsieur Biquerstaffe.' But how far a Frenchman, a Papist, and an enemy, is to be believed in his own cause against an English Protestant who is true to the government, I shall leave to the candid and impartial reader. [Arguments of the type are still being put forward in our day in all seriousness.] The other objection . . . relates to an article in my predictions which foretold the death of Mr. Partridge, to happen on March 29, 1708. This he is pleased to contradict absolutely in the almanack he has published for the present year. . . . Without entering into criticisms of chronology about the hour of his death, I shall only prove that Mr. Partridge is not alive." Arguments follow parodying the arguments used on such occasions, among others this one: "Secondly, Death is defined by all philosophers a separation of the soul and body. Now it is certain that the poor woman who has best reason to know, has gone about for some time to every alley in the neighbourhood and sworn to the gossips that her husband had neither life nor soul in him. Therefore, if an uninformed carcass walks still about and is pleased to call itself Partridge, Mr. Bickerstaff does not think himself any way answerable for that." As to the precise moment of Partridge's death: "Several of my friends . . . assured me I computed to something under half an hour; which (I speak my private opinion) is an error of no very great magnitude that men should raise a clamour about it." Virtually what Guynaud says of the dead tree.

Apollo's oracle *"Aio te, Aeacida, Romanos vincere posse"* ("I say, O son of Aeachus, that you the Romans can defeat") also was not understood till after the fact. Pyrrhus took it to mean that he was to defeat the Romans. Instead he was

if no fulfilment is to be recognized, one can still suspend judgment in the premises.[5]

1580. The question often arises, "How should history be written?" In the first place the term "history" is ambiguous. It may designate two very different kinds of composition according to the purpose one has in view. 1. The purpose may be purely scientific: to describe facts and the relations between them. Suppose, to avoid misunderstandings, we call that "scientific history." 2. Then there may be no end of other purposes: the purpose of amusing, which is envisaged in the "historical novel"; or the didactic purpose of portraying the past in such vivid colours that it will impress itself upon the mind, with a sacrifice if necessary of accuracy to colour. That is the object in histories that more or less closely ape the historical novel. Or there may be a purpose of social or some other sort of utility, where the idea is to arouse, provoke, foment certain senti-

defeated by them—all because of the ambiguity of the infinitive construction in Latin! But oh, those annoying sceptics who fail to grasp the nature of "true" prophecies! They make the point that the Pythia never spoke Latin in her oracles. Says Cicero, *De divinatione*, II, 56, 116: "In the first place Apollo never spoke Latin. In the second place the prophecy in question was never known to the Greeks. In the third place, Apollo had ceased making versified responses in the day of Pyrrhus. Finally, even though, as Ennius has it, the stolid line of Aeachus were always better of brawn than of brain,

> '. . . *Stolidum genus Aeacidarum!*
> *Bellipotentes sunt magis quam sapientipotentes,*'

Pyrrhus would have had sense enough to know that the ambiguity in the line 'you the Romans can defeat' promised no better for him than for the Romans."

1579 [5] *Op. cit.*, pp. 121-24: "Kuenen notes a fact still stranger. When the New Testament writers need to use an Old Testament text in a sense contrary to the natural meaning of the terms, they are not afraid to alter it, suppressing sentences, clauses, and words that determined the original meaning. [The Abbé mentions a case where St. Paul certainly altered a biblical text.] This passage is extremely strange and perplexing. St. Paul seems to declare that Moses said something that he obviously did not say. Nevertheless, as one looks attentively into the matter, the difficulty lessens. . . . [And a very captious exegesis proves that St. Paul is, at bottom, right. All the same, the good Abbé is not easy in his conscience:] In spite of these interpolations one difficulty still remains. St. Paul's way of quoting the Old Testament is certainly free to a degree, and it is apparent that he is giving a lesson in dogma, not a grammatical commentary on the text. [What he is giving is not a grammatical commentary but a false text.] Solutions for such difficulties may be sought. However, if they seem to us inadequate, we can still fall back on a resort that the Pope himself has suggested to us: suspense of judgment: *cunctandum a sententia*. One may wonder, indeed, whether such procedure is not the wisest when we are faced with texts like the one just mentioned."

ments such as patriotism, loyalty to this or that political system, enthusiasm for some noble and useful enterprise, the sense of honesty, and so on. Such purposes are envisaged in compositions that stand midway between scientific history and historical romance. It is characteristic of them that they manage to colour their facts in the proper direction and, as occasion requires, suppress them.[1] One must however manage to diverge from experimental reality without being caught telling lies; and that task is frequently made easy by the fact that before the author deceives his readers he deceives himself: he sees reality in the colours in which he paints it.

There is another ambiguity in the question, "How ought history to be written?" The term "ought" may refer to the purpose itself, or to the means that are to be used in attaining it. The question may mean: 1. Which of the purposes mentioned "ought" one, must one, is it better to, select? 2. The purpose decided upon, what means "ought" one, must one, is it better to, use in attaining it? The first of these two propositions, like all others of its tribe, is elliptical:[2] the special purpose in view of which history "ought" to be written in this or that manner is not stated. One may ask: What course had historians better follow with a view to promoting the material, political, or other prosperity of a country, social class, political system, and so on? Or: How and when is it advisable to use the different sorts of history? Is it better to use just one or all of them in different proportions, according to different social classes or the differing social functions of individuals? Then again, one may ask: In a given country, at a given time, what sort of history had better be used in the elementary schools, the secondary schools, the universities, to secure this or that specific advantage for society as a whole, for a part of society, for this or that political system, and so

1580 [1] In a perface to his *Geschichte des deutsch-französischen Krieges von 1870-71,* p. xi (English, Vol. I, p. viii), Marshal von Moltke states his own views as to his purposes in writing: "The things that are published in a military history always undergo a certain adaptation (*wird . . . appretiert*), according to the success that has been achieved. But loyalty and love of country require one not to damage the respect with which the victories of one's arms have clothed this or that individual person." That is excellent. It makes his purpose clear: he is to describe facts, but taking into account the social effects that may be involved in his narrative. [The preface in question is, however, by Major von Moltke, the Marshal's son, and the remark is quoted as oral.—A. L.]

1580 [2] Pareto, *Manuale,* Chap. I, § 40.

on? The second question mentioned—the question as to means—is of a technical character. There is a declared purpose and to ask what means "ought" to be used is to ask what means are best suited to attaining the purpose.[3]

The question "How *ought* history to be taught?" merges for the most part with the question as to purpose, for history is generally written with a view to teaching—as a means, that is. In any event, the same remarks apply to it. Ordinarily the types of history that we have distinguished are not so separated, and compositions calling themselves history are mixtures of the various types, with copious addenda of ethical considerations.

1581. In all the above we have been speaking from the objective point of view. Considered from the subjective standpoint, the questions are, on the whole, well stated and there is no ambiguity; for

1580 [3] Strange as it may seem, a number of different histories may be current in one same country at one same time. The history of the Risorgimento that is taught in Italian schools differs in many respects from the actual history that is so well known. In February, 1913, the German Emperor delivered an address before the University of Berlin. In it he said: "To the Prussian people it was vouchsafed to redeem itself from its misfortunes because of its faith. There is a tendency in people nowadays to believe only what can be touched with the hands and seen with the eyes. There is a disposition to lay greater and greater obstacles in the way of religion. Let me say then: soon after the reign of the Great King [Frederick II] came the catastrophe of 1806. That was because Prussia had lost her faith and in it we can only see the hand of God, and not the hand of men. But that disaster was the birth of the German nation, and in that God has shown that He was protecting Germany. Let our young men temper their steel in the fire of faith! With such arms we can dash forward, full of confidence in the divine power." The *Berliner Tageblatt* observed in comment: "The Emperor says that Prussia lost her faith soon after the death of Frederick II and was for that reason defeated in 1806. One cannot help remarking that the victorious Frederick II was surely not a hero in matters of the faith; whereas Prussia was defeated under the reign of a most pious prince. Verily it is a risky business to measure historical events on the yardstick of devoutness." The criticism is sound from the standpoint of experimental history, but not as regards stimulating sentiments in a country, which was the sole purpose the Emperor had in view. From the experimental standpoint the Emperor's address is so wild that when he speaks of "the hand of God" one can only think of Fucini's verse on the aurora borealis: "That? . . . That was the finger of the Omnipotent!" [*Poesie,* 30, p. 64.] But what weight will experimental truth have in the balance on the day when the German warriors go marching forth to death? When, furthermore, some people think they are using experimental truth, they are really doing nothing more than exploiting another religion; and religion for religion, the religion of the German Emperor seems better under the circumstances than many others in that it fortified, instead of depressing, the sentiments required by men who were destined to die on a field of battle. Consider, now, the devotees of the "Dreyfusard" religion

they mean, at bottom: "Just which of your sentiments accord with the sentiments aroused in your mind by the terms, 'writing' or 'teaching,' 'history'?"

1582. Since the problem when so stated has but one solution, many people imagine that it also has but one solution when considered from the objective standpoint; and if they chance indeed to be in some doubt, they are not likely to discover the various objective solutions. A writer who is producing a more or less adulterated history rarely, in fact almost never, is in the slightest degree aware of the alterations of fact that he is making. He is stating the facts exactly as he sees them, without taking any pains to determine whether he is seeing them as they actually are. He would be surprised if he were to be asked: "Tell us, at least, whether you are writing scientific history, or history with an element of romance, or history with a

in France, who profess to be, but are not, devotees of experimental science. Millerand was beyond question the best Minister of War that France had had for many many years. He did everything in his power to lay the foundations for victory, just as André had been laying the foundations for defeat. But Millerand committed sacrilege against the Dreyfusard holy of holies by making Du Paty de Clam an officer in the reserves. From the experimental standpoint the effect of that appointment on preparedness for war was absolutely nil; but from the standpoint of the religion of the "intellectuals" it was a very serious crime, and to expiate it Millerand had to resign his post. To generalize, accordingly: A Minister of War in France ought to realize that whether or no he concerns himself with the defence of his country is a matter of little importance to anyone—and in fact André continued as Minister of War for a long time—but as to the sublime dogmas of the holy Dreyfusard, the holy humanitarian, religion, hands off! After all, the official history of the French "intellectuals" comes no closer to actual history than the history of the German Emperor! Of the Du Paty de Clam incident and the debate that ensued in the French Chamber, *Liberté* writes, Feb. 2, 1913: *"How we are getting ready!* Another day wasted! . . . We challenge anybody to find a good excuse for the debate that so excited the Chamber yesterday. It was a matter of determining whether a certain officer of the Territorial Army was to be left in charge of some little railway station in the suburbs in the event of war. The question engaged the whole attention of our six hundred representatives, while matters of gravest concern to our national defence were left in abeyance. The German Government is rushing its organization of a new and formidable army. France sits engrossed with the insignificant case of M. Du Paty de Clam! The situation, nevertheless, is very simple. M. Millerand stated it from the rostrum with absolute frankness. The order he issued was a matter of routine already arranged for by his predecessor. He felt himself in duty bound to keep a promise made by the latter. That is the whole story." So from the experimental point of view the official history of the French "intellectuals" stands on a par with the history of the German Emperor. It differs from it only in that it is an impediment to national defence, while the Kaiser's is a spur to it.

purpose polemical or otherwise." And he would probably reply: "I am writing history, and that is the end of it." As we have often noted, when a person is thinking scientifically he distinguishes, he separates, things that persons unaccustomed to such thinking confuse, at least to some extent.

1583. Even the person seeking the method of teaching history best calculated to achieve the greatest possible social benefits must believe, or pretend to believe, that there is but one solution. No more than an actor in a play can he interrupt his performance to inform his audience that what he is telling them is a fraud. He, like the actor, must lose himself in his part and sincerely feel everything that he is saying.[1]

1584. The expression, the "highest good," or even the plain "good," has numberless meanings, and every philosopher defines it as he best pleases.[1] What such definitions have in common is a nucleus of certain agreeable sentiments, which are left over after disagreeable sentiments, or sentiments so regarded, have been thrust aside. At one extreme we get the plain sensual pleasure of the moment. Next some consideration of future pleasure or pain creeps in. Then comes the influence that people surrounding a man have upon him. Then the individual himself contrasts sensual pleasures and the pleasures or pains deriving from certain residues, especially those of Classes II and IV (group-persistences, sociality). Such things become predominant, and matters of sense incidental. Then sensual pleasures disappear entirely or almost so, and we finally get to another extreme where all pleasure is located in an annihilation of the senses, in a future life, in something, in a word, that transcends the experimental domain.

1585. So far we have been looking at the individual from the out-

1583 [1] Along that line we enter a practical field quite different from the one in which we are interested here.

1584 [1] Cicero, *Academica,* II, 43, 132, notes the importance of defining what one's "highest good" is to be, "because one's whole scheme of life is bound up with the definition one gives of the highest good: those who dissent from it, dissent from one's scheme of life." Now indeed we are in for it, if we have to discover what the "scheme of life" is! It was a good two thousand years ago that Cicero was voicing such doubts, and they have not yet been dispelled. Will they be in another two thousand years? Meantime people have got to live, and live they do without bothering their heads too much over the "highest good," which remains a pretty plaything for the metaphysicists.

side. He himself, in his own mind, almost never sees things in just that way. First of all, as is generally the case with sentiments, where we go looking for sharply defined theories the individual actually has nothing but a blur of undefined or no more than verbally defined sentiments. And that is the case not only with the plain man, but with educated, nay, with very scholarly persons as well. So it comes about that the commentators go racking their brains with might and main to discover the idea a writer had in mind, and almost never succeed in finding it;[1] nor is that surprising, nor should the failure be ascribed to any deficiency on their part: They are simply hunting for something that does not exist (§§ 541-1, 578). Then again, as we have so many times remarked, when a person sets out to give an exact and logical form to the sentiments that he is experiencing, he is prone to assign an absolute value to what is merely relative, to represent as objective what is strictly subjective. So when a person is catering to one of the numberless groups of sentiments mentioned, he will not express his state of mind by simply describing how he feels; he will represent his feeling as something absolute and objective. He will never say: "For me, to my mind, this or that seems to be the 'highest good.'" He will say—a quite different matter, "This is the highest good," and then produce a flock of derivations to prove it.

1586. The derivation will be partly justified by the fact that in addition to the subjective phenomenon just noted, there are objective phenomena that also have to be considered. A certain group of sentiments, *A,* being active in an individual, the following problems arise: At a given moment and in a given connexion, what effect will the presence of A have upon the individual? Likewise, what will be the effect upon other given individuals, upon a given community? These problems constitute, at bottom, the theory of the social equilibrium, and they are exceedingly hard to solve. We must try therefore to simplify them, since that is about all we can do, at a greater or lesser sacrifice of exactitude.

1587. We can get a first simplification by eliminating the specific

1585 [1] Generally speaking, interpreters of the thought of this or that philosopher might repeat what, according to Cicero, *Academica,* II, 45, 139, Clitomachus said of Carneades—that he "had never been able to make out what Carneades really thought" (*quid Carneadi probaretur*).

individuations of individual, community, time—by considering, in other words, certain average and general phenomena; but to avoid serious pitfalls we must, after that, not forget that on that basis our conclusions also will be average and general. One may, for instance, say: "The present pleasure may be compensated by the future pain," and that will be an elliptical way of saying that "For many men, in general, there is a compensation between present pleasure and future pain." One may say: "To many people, in general, the momentary pleasure may bring serious pain through loss of the esteem and consideration (in general) of the other individuals in the community." But it would be a mistake to draw any particular conclusion from that general proposition—to say, for instance: "For John Doe the present pleasure may bring serious pain through loss of the esteem and consideration of Messrs. $M, N, P. \ldots$" In point of fact it may well be the case that John Doe cares not a fig for such esteem and consideration in general, or for the esteem and consideration of Messrs. M, N, P in particular.

1588. Effects upon communities are often more or less vaguely designated by such terms as the "prosperity" economic, military, political, and so on, of a nation; or the "welfare" from the standpoint of finances, dignity, public esteem, and so on of a family, or some other restricted social group. When we cannot have the more, we must perforce content ourselves with the less; and the solution of such problems, though not altogether exact, may nevertheless lead to sociological theories that, in general and on the whole, are not too greatly at variance with the facts. For the time being, we must consider ourselves fortunate if we can roughly solve them, at least in part. At some future time, as science gradually progresses, we can try to state and solve them more exactly.

1589. But with people who do not stick to the methods of experimental science, such problems are not stated even in the relatively inexact manner just noted, but in altogether indefinite terms. People ask what the individual "ought" to do, without drawing the very elementary distinctions between his direct "good," his indirect "good," his "good" as a member of a community, and the "good" of the community. They may, perhaps, as an extreme concession, specify the "good of the individual," or the "good of the country" to which he belongs—and what luck if they do not go on to the "good of humanity." But forthwith, in that outlook, the residues of sociality press to the fore, and instead of trying to solve the problem as now stated, they deliver themselves of a sermon showing that the individual *ought* to sacrifice his own "welfare" to that of humanity.

1590. All that comes out in the derivations, whereby, starting with sentiments present in the individual, with certain residues, that is, one ends by showing that he "ought" to act in a manner considered good by the author of the derivation—it never diverges very widely from the manner accepted by the society in which the author lives. Ordinarily the point of departure and the point of arrival are known in advance. The derivation follows some path, any path, that will bring the two points together.

1591. The derivation that exploits the phrase "highest good," or just plain "good," puts the whole story into that phrase or word—the groups of sentiments from which the start is made and all that is possible of the results that it is purposed to achieve. One of the derivations most frequently used, in fact, starts with the sentiments of egoism to arrive at altruistic conduct as its goal.

1592. Something similar has happened in the case of political economy. Literary economists, unable to get hold of any definite concept of the economic equilibrium, put into the term "value" everything they could cram into it as regards both factual data and the objectives they desired to attain. So the term "value" became, though in lesser proportions, a *quid simile* of the term "highest good."

1593. Philosophers, ancient and modern, to say nothing of the theologians, have stopped at no pains to discover what that blessed "highest good" might be; and since it is a subjective thing, in great part at least, each of them has readily found what he pleased. The extreme where the momentary sensual pleasure is exclusively contemplated—an extreme achieved not even by a dog, for he too has his dog's way of considering future pains and pleasures—has no defenders, or at least none to speak of. One may even doubt whether the adages that might be quoted in favour of it are to be taken as more than mere jests.[1]

1593 [1] The *Greek Anthology*, VII, 325 (Paton, Vol. II, pp. 174-75), has an epigram to which Cicero alludes in *Disputationes Tusculanae*, V, 35, 101, and which

1594. The first addendum to the sentiment of momentary sensual pleasure may be a consideration of the consequences, themselves sensual, of such pleasure. To tell the truth, no human being could seem to be so stupid as to overlook them entirely. A person capable of that would be the sort of person who would knowingly drink a poison just because it tasted good. The question, therefore, is merely how far such consequences are to be considered.

1595. Among the Cyrenians, who preached the pleasure of the moment as the "highest good," consideration of consequences was not carried very far, but it was nevertheless emphatic. To judge by the little we know of him, Aristippus would have a man remain at all times master in his mind of the sentiments of momentary sensual pleasure to which he yields.[1] That is the purport of his famous witticism as to the courtesan, Lais, "I am possessed of her, not by her." [2] Other refinements are now in order, always with a view to

was humorously suggested as a fitting epitaph for the tomb of Sardanapalus (licentious king of Assyria): "What I ate and drank and enjoyed in gay lust, that do I possess. All else of many other good things have I lost." Cicero comments, quoting Aristotle: "What else would you suggest for the tomb of an ox, let alone a king!" Extant also is a rejoinder by Crates of Thebes, *loc. cit.,* 326: "What I learned and thought and enjoyed in the companionship of the Venerable Muses, that do I possess. All else of many other good things has vanished in smoke." In a dispute with Archytas, Polyarchus remarks, Athenaeus, *Deipnosophistae,* XII, 64, 545, that to his mind the doctrine of Archytas strays far indeed from Nature: "For Nature, so far as she can make herself known to us, enjoins us to pursue pleasure, and that, she says, is the part of the wise man."

1595 [1] In view of the conflicting accounts we have of the incident, it is hard to know just what view Aristippus held. Certainly ancient writers took it for granted that there was a philosophical system placing the highest good in the moment's pleasure. Whether the theory is to be ascribed to Aristippus or to someone else is of no significance for our purposes here. Aelian, *De varia historia,* XIV, 6, declares in the clearest possible terms that Aristippus advised consideration only of the present and disregard of past and future. The kind of present in question is indicated in Athenaeus, *Deipnosophistae,* XII, 63, where Aristippus is said to have "approved of the life of lust, holding it to be the purpose of living and the thing wherein beatitude lay"; with the further comment that Aristippus recognized only the pleasure of the moment. Diogenes Laertius, *Aristippus,* II, 87-88 (Hicks, Vol. I, p. 217), says that according to the Cyrenians "the purpose [of living] was the particular pleasure, and happiness the sum of particular pleasures." And he adds that according to Hippobotus, "pleasure was a blessing even if derived from degrading things." Aristippus asserts, *loc. cit.,* 93 (Hicks, p. 221), that "nothing is by nature just, honourable, or degrading, but is so by law and custom."

1595 [2] Athenaeus, *loc. cit.:* Ἔχω καὶ οὐκ ἔχομαι. Diogenes Laertius, *loc. cit.,* 75 (Hicks, p. 203): Ἔχω Λαίδα ἀλλ' οὐκ ἔχομαι. Ménage cavils and proposes taking Ἔχειν in the sense of νικᾶν "to overcome": "What, therefore, Aristippus says is that over-

ulterior pleasures beyond those of the moment. So it was said of Aristippus in his day that he advised against doing anything contrary to the laws because of the penalties involved and, some writers add, because of one's reputation [3]—but that takes us into another field. Going on in that fashion one may, by using the apposite derivations, reach any point one wishes.

1596. When sensuous pleasure is represented as the highest good —"*extremum autem esse bonorum voluptatem*" [1]—already at work is one of our IV-γ derivations (multiple meanings of terms), which pretends to explain one term that is indefinite, obscure, by equating

come by his money Lais, whom we know to have been a woman of very difficult access . . . offered herself to him, but that he was not overcome by lust, as is the common case with the intemperate (τοῖς ἀκρατέσι)." But the sense is very clear. Ἐχω in Greek means to "possess," in the double sense common to Italian, French and English, of "to own," "to occupy," and to have carnal intercourse with a woman, to have her as wife or mistress. The passive Ἐχομαι has meanings corresponding to the active, and Plato, *Respublica*, III, 4, 390C, uses the verb in the very sense it has in the apothegm of Aristippus. Plato there rebukes Homer for portraying Zeus in lecherous mood and "saying that he was more possessed by passion (ὑπὸ ἐπιθυμίας) [for Juno] than he had been at any time since they first united behind the backs of their beloved parents" (*Iliad*, XIV, vv. 294-96). So Aristippus was not "possessed" in that way by his passion for Lais. Lactantius Firmianus, *Divinae institutiones*, III, 15, 15 (*Opera*, Vol. I, p. 223; Fletcher, Vol. I, p. 173), quotes the remark of Aristippus, but altogether failing to understand it. [This stricture seems undeserved. Lactantius understands but embroiders.—A. L.] Cicero, *Epistulae ad familiares, Paeto*, IX, 26, 2: "Listen to the rest. Cytheris [mistress of Mark Antony] had the place [at dinner] next beyond Eutrapelus. I can hear you thinking: 'The great Cicero was a guest at such a dinner?' . . . I never suspected, I assure you, that she was to be there—and yet, Aristippus the Socratist never batted an eyelash when he was taunted with a passion for Lais! 'I am possessed not by her but of her!' he said (the thing sounds better in Greek)." Diogenes Laertius, *loc. cit.*, 69 (Hicks, p. 199): "Once as he [Aristippus] was entering a courtesan's house, a young man in his company evinced some shame; and he remarked: 'The shame is not in going into such a place, but in being unable to go out.'" Persius, *Saturae*, V, v. 173, also calls that man free who can leave a courtesan's house in full possession of himself (Ramsay: "entire and heart-whole"):

". . . *Si totus et integer illinc*
    exieras . . ."

1595 [3] Diogenes Laertius, *loc. cit.*, 93 (Hicks, pp. 221-23). That however is inconsistent with what Aristippus is said, *Ibid.*, 68 (Hicks, p. 199), to have replied to a question as to what philosophers were good for: "If all laws were abolished, we would still live as we do now." However, we are not interested here in what Aristippus really thought, but merely in certain derivations: whether they be his or of someone else is of little moment.

1596 [1] Cicero, *De finibus bonorum et malorum*, I, 12, 40.

it with another also indefinite and obscure. The "pleasure" that figures in the formula mentioned is not the ordinary pleasure which everybody knows, but another that has still to be defined. Cicero, *De finibus bonorum et malorum,* II, 3, 6, turns the point to jest: "Then, said he, laughing: 'A fine idea, that the very man who says that pleasure is the goal of all our hopes, the last, ultimate Good, should not know what it is!'" And he goes on to say, *Ibid.,* II, 3, 8, that the terms *voluptas* in Latin and ἡδονή in Greek are perfectly clear, and that it is not his fault if he fails to understand them as they are used by Epicurus, but the fault of Epicurus in distorting them from their ordinary meanings. And so far, so good. But Cicero's criticism is more far-reaching than he is aware of, for it applies to all metaphysical disquisitions, Cicero's own not excepted. And not to go farther afield, when he sets out to show, *Ibid.,* II, 8, 23, that pleasure is not the highest good, he says of men who coddle all their sensuous impulses: "I shall never admit that such roués live either well or happily." [2] In that he leads the reader astray through the double meanings in to live "well" or "happily." Those terms may refer either to the sensations of the roués or to Cicero's own. He should rather have said: "Roués consider their manner of livin, good and conducive to happiness. But if I were to live my life in that way, I should not consider it such." Cicero adds, *loc. cit.,* 24: "Whence it follows, not that pleasure is not pleasure, but that it is not the highest good." [3] That is true, or false, according to the person. For the high liver, pleasure is the highest good; for Cicero it is not the highest good; and this last phrase all along refers to something that is not clearly enough defined. [4]

1596 [2] *"Hos ego asotos bene quidem vivere aut beate nunquam dixerim."*

1596 [3] *"Ex quo efficitur non ut voluptas non sit voluptas, sed ut voluptas non sit summum bonum."*

1596 [4] There are five parts to Cicero's argument: 1. A philological question, II, 4, 13: ἡδονή should be rendered in Latin as *voluptas:* "By that term all Latins the world over mean two things, and to wit: a feeling of joy in the spirit, and a pleasurable excitation of body." On that point Cicero seems to be right: ἡδονή in Greek and *voluptas* in Latin seem in fact to have just those meanings. 2. A question as to Epicurus's manner of expressing himself, II, 5, 15. Epicurus uses the term ἡδονή in a sense different from the meanings stated: "Whence it comes about not that we do not sense the term in its usual force (*non ut nos non intelligamus quae vis sit istius verbi*), but that he speaks in a manner of his own, ignoring ours (*sed ut*

1597. We have the proposition, $A = B$, and we want A to be equal to C. There are two ways of going about it. Either we may respect the first statement and alter the meaning B, so that it becomes equivalent to C; or we may negate the statement and replace it with $A = C$. This situation is general and accounts for large numbers of derivations.

1598. The derivation tends to grow in length because, along with "pleasure," it is better to take residues of group-persistence into account ("justice," "honesty," and so on) and residues of personal integrity ("honour," "self-respect" . . .) either with reference to the individual, by including those residues in the mass of sentiments that he is said to experience, or with reference to his fellows, to his community, by introducing into the derivation some hint as to the

ille suo more loquatur, nostrum negligat)." And there again Cicero is right, but much too right for his own thesis. The fault of Epicurus is the fault of all metaphysicists, Cicero not excepted; for he too *suo more loquitur, nostrum negligit,* if by "our way" we mean the way of anyone who disagrees with him. 3. A question as to the relations of sentiments aroused in certain persons by certain terms. The sentiments suggested respectively by the terms "pleasure" and "highest good" do not accord in the case of Cicero—his own testimony is adequate proof of that. Nor do they accord in the cases of certain other persons, as may be verified by observation. On that point too, then, Cicero is right. 4. A question as to the relations between sentiments or between things in the minds of *all* men. Not explicitly, but implicitly after the manner of many many metaphysicists, Cicero leaps over from the contingent to the absolute. For the same reason that Cicero's own testimony is sufficient to show that the terms "pleasure" and "highest good" do not make the same impression on him, the testimony of a person who disagrees with him has to suffice as evidence that the two terms do make an identical impression upon that person. And just as observation shows that many people agree with Cicero, observation also shows that many people think otherwise. Cicero therefore is in error in ascribing a universal, absolute value to a proposition that has a particular, contingent value only. 5. A sophistical argument to eliminate dissenters, and so again to get the contingent back to the absolute. Here too Cicero's reasoning is packed with unstated assumptions, as is common with metaphysicists. It is intimated that there really are things called "pleasure" and "highest good," things that are of common knowledge; and if some empty-headed individual chooses to deny their existence, we need no more take account of his chatter than of the ravings of some lunatic to whom it might occur to deny the existence of Carthage. In other words, Cicero intimates the universality of his proposition by raising the question as to what "people say." "People" means "everybody," and when everybody says the same thing, the thing must be as everybody says it is—as when everybody says that the Sun gives heat. As many incidental considerations as rhetoric can furnish are then brought in. So there Cicero is wrong, but neither more wrong nor less wrong than any other metaphysicist.

ideals one would attain. This process also yields theories in large numbers.[1]

1599. In his *De finibus bonorum et malorum,* II, 3, 8, Cicero takes up the view of Hieronymus of Rhodes that the highest good was freedom from all pain. He censures Epicurus, II, 6, 18, for not making up his mind; for, says he, Epicurus ought either to accept the term "pleasure" in its ordinary sense—the sense of Aristippus, Cicero calls it—or else take the term in the sense of absence of pain, or else combine the two things and so get two ends or purposes. II, 6, 19: "And in fact many great philosophers have made such combinations of the objectives of the good. Aristotle combines the exercise of virtue with a lifetime of perfect prosperity; Calliphon, sensuous pleasure with good repute; Diodorus [of Tyre], freedom from pain with the same good repute. Epicurus would have achieved the same result had he combined this opinion, here, of Hieronymus, with the old view of Aristippus." Cicero then counts up, II, 11, 35, and finds that, with reference to the highest good, there are three opinions which omit consideration of good repute—opinions of Aristippus (or Epicurus), Hieronymus, and Carneades (for Carneades the highest good lay in enjoyment of the principles of nature: *"Carneadi frui principiis naturalibus esset extremum"*); another three that combine good repute with some other thing—opinions of Polemon, Calliphon, and Diodorus; and one only, an opinion fathered by Zeno, which locates the highest good in good repute and decorum.

1600. According to St. Augustine, Varro computed a far longer list of possible opinions, reaching the very respectable number of two hundred and ninety-eight; but these were reducible to twelve if one tripled [by permutations with virtue] the four things: pleasure, repose, pleasure combined with repose, and the "primary goods of Nature." Varro throws out the first three of these, not from any disapproval of them, but as comprised under the "primary goods of nature" (a very handsome, but a very obscure entity), and thus is left with three possible opinions, to wit: the quest for the "primary goods of nature" as a means of attaining virtue, then virtue as a means of attaining the "primary goods of nature," finally virtue for

1598 [1] We need not deal with them here in detail since our present aim is merely to get a better understanding of the character of such derivations.

its own sake. St. Augustine has his fun with all such verbal drool and firmly and flatly sets up a supreme good of his own, eternal life; and a supreme evil, eternal death.[1] And there we are at the other extreme in such derivations.

1601. The nucleus of sentiments corresponding to the different meanings attached by metaphysicists and theologians to the term "true" is chiefly made up of concepts that meet no opposition in the minds of persons using such words. Hence the notion that the "good" and the "true" are equivalents arises spontaneously; for they are both groups of sentiments that encounter no opposition in the minds of such persons. In the same way, the equivalence may be extended to what is called the "beautiful." Was ever the man to find a thing "good" and "true" without also finding it "beautiful"? Whatever enters his own mind must also be present in the minds of all other men, especially if he is a metaphysicist or a theologian; and if there be someone so unfortunate as to differ with him, that person surely can hardly be called a man; so it straightway follows that the universe agrees with him, and the force and lustre of his sublime theories are enormously enhanced. In case such marvellous brains are unable to agree the one with the other—well, in days gone by they persecuted, imprisoned and sometimes burned, each other. In these milder times, they are satisfied with calling each other names.

1602. Another pretty entity sports the name of "Nature" and, along with its adjective "natural," and something or other called the "state of nature," it plays an important part in derivations. Those terms are all so vague that oftentimes not even the person who uses them knows just what meaning he is trying to convey.[1] In his daily life the human being encounters many things that are inimical to

---

1600 [1] *De civitate Dei*, XIX, 1, 4 f.: "*Si ergo quaeratur a nobis quid civitas Dei de his singulis interrogata respondeat ac primum de finibus bonorum malorumque quid sentiat, respondebit aeternam vitam esse summum bonum, aeternam vero mortem summum malum.*" In the *Summa theologiae*, IIᵃ IIᵃᵉ, qu. 27, art. 6 (*Opera*, Vol. VIII, p. 229), St. Thomas says: ". . . for the supreme good of man lies in the cleaving of the soul unto God (*in hoc quod anima Deo inhaereat*)."

1602 [1] In the *Retractationes*, I, 10, 3 (*Opera*, Vol. I, p. 600), St. Augustine cautions that his dictum about there being no natural evil—"*nullum esse malum naturale*"—might be misunderstood by the Pelagians. He used the term "natural" as referring to that nature which was created without sin—the nature that is "truly and properly" the nature of man: "*ipsa enim vere ac proprie natura hominis dicitur.*" By analogy, says he, we also use the term as designating man's nature at birth.

him, either doing him harm or causing mere annoyance through certain circumstances which he considers artificial. Such the depredations of highwaymen, the wiles of thieves, the tyrannical acts of the rich and powerful, and so on. If all such circumstances are eliminated, we are left with a nucleus that we will call "natural," as opposed to the "artificial" things we have discarded; and it must necessarily be good, nay, perfect, since we have thrown out everything that was bad in it (§ 1546). That, in fact, is the reasoning of all metaphysicists or theologians, of the followers of the Physiocrats, of Rousseau and other dreamers of that type. They do not say: "Here is a state that we call 'natural.' From observations by such and such scientists who have seen and examined it, it is known to present such and such traits." What they do is to start with a present state, eliminate from it everything they dislike, and then foist the term "natural" on what is left. Rousseau, indeed, who is still admired, not to say worshipped, by many people, candidly confesses his indifference to the facts (§ 821); and even more indifferent to them was that Holy Father who praised the beautiful order which God had bestowed on Nature and gravely assures us that in Nature all little animals make their societies in peace and concord.[2] He had never seen spiders eating flies, nor birds eating spiders, nor had he read Virgil's description of bees swarming to battle![3] But then again, nothing is more diverting than the manner of thinking of those who deride "Catholic superstition" but pay reverent homage to the superstitions of the Rousseaueans.

1603. De Rémusat[1] enumerates at least four senses in which

1602 [2] St. Clement the Roman, *Epistulae ad Corinthios,* I, 20, 10 (Gebhardt-Harnack, p. 39): Τά τε ἐλάχιστα τῶν ζῴων τὰς συνελεύσεις αὐτῶν ἐν εἰρήνῃ καὶ ὁμονοίᾳ ποιοῦνται.

1602 [3] *Georgics,* IV, vv. 67-70:

> "Sin autem ad pugnam exierint (*nam saepe duobus*
> *regibus incessit magno discordia motu*),
> *continuoque animos volgi et trepidantia bello*
> *corda licet longe praesciscere.* . . ."

("But when they rush forth to battle (for discord and noisy tumult often arise from there being two kings) one can sense straightway and even from afar the temper of the swarm and its quivering eagerness for combat.")

1603 [1] *Œuvres de Cicéron,* Vol. IV, p. 411 (Lecler, Vol. 27, pp. 95-96).

Cicero uses the word "Nature" in his essay on *Laws*.[2] 1. A general meaning: Nature as the sum total of the facts of the universe. 2. A particular meaning: Nature as the constitution of each individual being. 3. Another meaning, which Rémusat explains as "a personal, individual sense that is never more than implicitly defined, and transpires only from a knowledge of his doctrine [A fine expedient for starting arguments!]: The nature of a being is that which makes it what it is, its *law*. It is 'good,' accordingly: it is the being's perfection, as witness the following phrases: '*Ad summum ·perducta natura*,' I, 8, 25; '*ducem naturam*,' I, 10[3]—and there are others. So the expression 'natural law' is not without consequence, for it implies that the law exists of itself, that it is a part of the general law of beings. [There are people who claim they understand that!] See: '*Natura constitutum*,' I, 10, 28; '*quod dicam naturam esse, quo modo est natura, utilitatem a natura*,'[4] I, 12, 33." 4. A certain potency: "By a vague derivative from this meaning, Nature is further pictured as a distinct, active force that produces and conserves the world . . . '*Natura largita est, docente natura*,' I, 8, 25-26; '*eadem natura*,' I, 9, 26; '*natura factos, a natura dati, natura data*,' I, 12, 33." What a treasure-store such a term must be for derivations the reader may easily imagine. It means everything—and nothing!

1604. With Aristotle, Dame Nature changes altogether in aspect. The Stagirite begins by noting, *Naturalis Auscultatio*, II, 1, 1 (Wickstead, Vol. I, p. 107),[1] that natural beings have within themselves a

---

1603 [2] We can touch on them here but briefly, but the reader would do well to look at them in the original.

1603 [3] [Rémusat's reference is erroneous. There is no such phrase in *De legibus*, I, 10. In I, 6, 20 Cicero says, "*natura qua duce*."—A. L.]

1603 [4] [Another mistake by Rémusat: Cicero's phrase was "*utilitatem a iure*."—A. L.]

1604 [1] We need not here inquire whether or not the attribution of this treatise to Aristotle is sound. We call it Aristotle's because it is generally reprinted under his name. But instead of to Aristotle, ascribe it, let us say, to X, and our remarks will stand just the same, since they bear only on the derivation objectively considered. [Pareto amuses himself throughout these volumes by questioning the authenticity of the various works of Aristotle, but he seems to be nodding here. The *Naturalis auscultatio* is none other than the *Physica*, the authenticity of which has never been questioned. One may picture Pareto working from one of his countless notes, coming upon this reference to Bekker's *Aristotelis Graece*, Berlin, 1831, pp. 192-93, with the title written in Greek, Περὶ φυσικῆς ἀκροάσεως (*De naturali auscultatione*), and confusing it momentarily in his mind with one of the *Opuscula* of Aristotle of

principle of motion or of rest: whereas a bed, a garment, or some other object of the kind, has no such principle, because it does not tend to change. From that it follows, II, 1, 2 (Wickstead, Vol. I, p. 109), that "nature is the principle and cause of motion and of rest in entities in which said principle is present primitively and not contingently." [2] Then he gives another definition, II, 1, 10 (Wickstead, Vol. I, p. 113): "In one sense we may call nature the primal matter that exists in entities which have within themselves the principle of motion and change. Otherwise, we may call it form and character [species] according to definition." [3] There are people even today who imagine they understand such talk and who admire it. Says Barthélemy Saint-Hilaire: "I do not hesitate to say of the *Physics* that it is one of Aristotle's soundest and most considerable

dubious authenticity, *e.g.,* the *De mirabilis auscultatione.* Everywhere else Pareto refers to the *Physica* as the *Physica.*—A. L.]

1604 [2] Plutarch, *De placitis philosophorum,* I, 1 (Goodwin, Vol. III, p. 105), begins by noting, very properly, that it would be absurd to talk about "nature" without first explaining what is meant by the term. And to do so he says: "According to Aristotle (*Physica,* II, 1, 15; Wickstead, Vol. I, p. 115) 'nature' is the principle of motion and rest in bodies in which it exists primitively and not contingently." That makes everything clear! But later on, in the same treatise, Plutarch gives different definitions, I, 30 (Goodwin, pp. 131-32): "Empedocles says that 'nature' is naught but the combination and separation of elements . . . Anaxagoras, that 'nature' is combination and dissolution; in other words, birth and destruction."

1604 [3] Ἄλλον δὲ τρόπον ἡ μορφὴ καὶ τὸ εἶδος τὸ κατὰ τὸν λόγον. It is not easy to divine what all that means. At bottom there seems to be a dispute as to whether "nature" is matter or form, and the apparent conclusion is, I, 1, 15, that it is form: Ἡ ἄρα μορφὴ φύσις. However, we are shortly thereafter advised that "form" and "nature" have two senses, since privation is a sort of form. All of which is mere prattle. St. Thomas, *Summa theologiae,* Iᵃ IIᵃᵉ, qu. 31, art. 7 (*Opera,* Vol. VI, p. 221), tries to clarify the Master: "I answer by saying that a thing is called 'natural' which is according to nature, as he [Aristotle] says, *Physica,* II, 4-5. In man, however, nature may be taken in two ways: in the one sense, inasmuch as intellect, reason (*intellectus et ratio*), is the outstanding trait in man, since by it he is given his place in species. From that standpoint, those human pleasures may be called 'natural' which apply to what is proper to a man according to reason. So delight in the contemplation of truth and in acts of virtue is natural to man. [What a pity our criminals do not find things so!] In man considered as partaking of reason, nature may be taken, in another sense, as that which is common to man and other things, and especially as that which is not subordinate to reason." Nature, therefore, means white and black. But that is not the end of it: of the two species of pleasures, some are natural in one sense, but not natural in another: "As regards both these pleasures some are unnatural, simply speaking, but natural (*connaturales*) in certain relations (*Secundum utrasque autem delectationes contingit aliquas esse innaturales simpliciter loquendo, sed connaturales secundum quid*)." Verily one could go no

works." [4] However, as regards the philosopher's definition of nature, Saint-Hilaire, good soul, has some hesitation, pp. xxxii-iii: "I should not care to maintain that that definition is beyond all criticism. . . . Aristotle himself undoubtedly found it inadequate, for he tries to sound it somewhat deeper. Since he recognizes two essential elements in being, matter and form, along with privation, he wonders whether the true nature of beings be matter or form. [How is true nature to be distinguished from the nature that is not true?] He is inclined to think that the form of a thing rather than its matter is its nature, for matter is in a way only potency, whereas form is act and reality." An excellent example of verbal derivation—an endless string of words that do arouse certain sentiments but correspond to nothing real.[5]

farther than that in depriving a term of definiteness. One must learn how to be satisfied! St. Thomas also has had his commentators. Here is one: Goudin, *Philosophia juxta divi Thomae dogmata* (Brourard), Vol. II, p. 198: "So the word 'nature' can be understood in four ways: 1. In the sense of nativity. So the first-born is chief among his brothers 'by nature,' that is to say, by order of birth, and the Apostle says [Ephes. 5: 6] that 'by nature we are children of wrath,' that is to say, by conception and nativity, whence we derive sin. 2. In the sense of matter and form. So man is said to be made up of two partial natures. 3. In the sense of the essence of the thing. So we say that the angelic nature or essence is superior to human nature. 4. In physic, nature is taken for the intrinsic principle of movement and rest in the things about us." It does not occur to these good souls that to give the same name to things so vastly different is an excellent device for never being understood.

1604 [4] *Physique d'Aristote,* Vol. I, Preface, p. iv.

1604 [5] Earlier in his Preface, p. iii, Saint-Hilaire had said: "The theory of motion is so truly the necessary antecedent to physics that when Newton is laying the mathematical foundations of natural philosophy toward the end of the seventeenth century, his immortal book is nothing more or less than a theory of motion. ([In a note:] He says so himself in the preface to the first edition of the *Principia*.) In his *Principles of Philosophy* Descartes had also placed the study of motion at the head of the Science of Nature. So, two thousand years before Descartes and Newton, Aristotle had proceeded exactly as they proceeded, and if his work is to be fairly appraised, it will be recognized as of the same family and in more than one respect to have nothing to fear from the comparison." We may let that pass as regards Descartes. As for Newton, the difference between his *Principia* and Aristotle's *Physica* is the difference between day and night. It is true, alas, that here and there in the *Principia* a little metaphysics creeps in—it is like the barren rock that holds the experimental gold, and metaphysicists, of course, grasp at the rock and leave the gold. Says Newton in his Preface: "Since the manual arts are primarily concerned with the moving of bodies, Geometry is commonly applied to mass and Mechanics to motion. In that sense rational Mechanics will be the science, accurately stated and demonstrated, of the movements resulting from certain forces, and of the

1605. From the way in which the group of sentiments corresponding to such expressions as "purpose of life," "highest good," "right reason," "nature," has been built up, it is readily understandable that such terms may be equated with one another, since they represent, with no little vagueness, a single cumulus of sentiments. So the Stoics could say that the "purpose of life," the "highest good," was to live according to "nature." Just what that "nature" is nobody knows, and better so; for it is the various indefinite meanings that are associated with the term that win acquiescence for the Stoic maxim and others of the kind. In fact, according to Stobaeus, *Eglogae physicae et ethicae,* II, 7 (Heeren, Vol. II, pp. 132-35), Zeno began with a language even more indefinite, holding that the purpose of life was to live harmoniously; and that, Stobaeus adds, "means living according to one plan and harmoniously. But those who came after him, by way of improvement, explained it as meaning 'living in harmony with nature.' . . .[1] Cleanthes was the first . . . to bring in nature, and he ruled that the purpose was to live in harmony with nature." And going on equating terms corresponding to this or that sentiment, the Stoics came to assert that the goal was "happiness"; and "happiness" was "to live according to virtue, harmoniously, or, what amounts to the same thing, to live according to nature."

1606. It will also help to pay special attention to the principles of sociality and altruism, and by no means to forget right reason. All those pretty things we can cram into the concept of "nature" and say with the Stoics, following Diogenes Laertius, *Zeno,* VII, 88 (Hicks, Vol. II, pp. 195-97): "Hence the purpose of life is to live in accordance with nature, in other words, in accordance with one's own nature and with the nature of the universe, doing nothing that the common law ordinarily prohibits, which law is right reason that reaches everywhere and abides with Zeus who through it governs

forces required for certain movements." Of such things Aristotle talks not at all, but of matters quite different.

1605 [1] Τὸ δὲ τέλος ὁ μὲν Ζήνων οὕτως ἀπέδωκε, τὸ ὁμολογουμένως ζῆν. Τοῦτο δ' ἐστὶ καθ' ἕνα λόγον καὶ σύμφωνον ζῆν. Οἱ δὲ μετὰ τοῦτον, προσδιαρθροῦντες, οὕτως ἐξέφερον, ὁμολογουμένως τῇ φύσει ζῆν. The word ὁμολογουμένως properly means "suitably," "harmoniously," "concordantly," "conformably," and is therefore somewhat vague unless the thing with which the harmony or suitableness prevails is specified. Zeno's meaning would accordingly be: to live suitably, harmoniously, and so on; and one might even say perhaps, temperately, moderately.

all existing things. And that same law is the virtue of the happy man and the happiness of life when, that is, all is done in a harmony of the individual temperament with the will of the ruler of all things. And therefore Diogenes expressly declares that the ideal of life is right thinking in the choice of what is according to nature, and Archidamus, living in fulfilment of all duties." [1] That is a good example of the verbal derivation. Words are heaped on words, till one gets a hotchpotch containing a little of everything.

1607. These reasonings are of the following type. One sets out to prove that $A = B$. One begins by demonstrating that $A = X$, because the sentiments associated with A and X are in accord. Meanwhile pains are taken to select an X so indefinite that while the sentiments associated with it are in accord with the sentiments associated with A, they also accord with the sentiments associated with B. In that way an equation is established between X and B. But since it has already been granted that $A = X$, it follows that $A = B$ —the thesis that was to be demonstrated. This reasoning follows the lines of the one we examined in §§ 480 f., where the equation $A = B$ was proved by the elimination of a non-experimental entity, X. As in other cases, the introduction of a vague term imperfectly corresponding to a real thing has similar effects to the interposition of a term corresponding to an entity that stands altogether apart from the experimental field (§§ 108, 1546). A neat example is the case of "solidarity" (§§ 1557 f.). There X (solidarity-fact) is, really, as the authors of the argument confess, the opposite of B (solidarity-duty). Yet the proposition $A = X$ (*i.e.,* that solidarity-fact prevails among men) serves to demonstrate that $A = B$ (solidarity-duty must prevail among men). From the standpoint of formal logic, arguments containing the indeterminate X are syllogisms with more than three terms, the middle term X becoming multiple in virtue of its very indefiniteness, often without one's being able to determine just how many meanings it has. If, furthermore, X transcends experience, we get for the syllogism, in addition to the cause of error just mentioned (which is nearly always present), a major term and a minor term

---

1606 [1] Clement of Alexandria, *Stromata,* II, 19 (*Opera,* Vol. I, p. 1046A; Wilson, Vol. II, p. 59), imagines that the "nature" of the Stoics is none other than God: "Therefore the Stoics opined that the purpose of life was to live according to nature, very properly using the term 'nature' for 'God.' "

that have no meaning, as relating facts that are experimental with non-experimental entities (§ 474).

1608. Rousseau says that "the general will," X, cannot fall into error, A. To demonstrate that proposition he regards all citizens as constituting one single person, as having the same will; and the proposition means—for that matter giving a special twist to the term "error"—that a person is sole judge of what, to him, is agreeable or disagreeable. The proposition is acceptable in that form. But at that point a modification is introduced into X, and necessarily so; for a body of citizens acting as a single person is a thing that does not exist. It is asserted, without proof of any kind, that the general will, X, is expressed by the sum of particular wills when the citizens in question vote without communicating with one another. But that too is impossible; so X must suffer a further modification. Resting content with the little that is to be had, it is assumed that X is the sum of particular wills when there are no intrigues and no electioneering by private interests. That gives an equation between the general will, X, and the vote of the citizens, B, when the vote is without intrigues and electioneering. But we have seen that $X = A$. So $A = B$; and the conclusion is that there can be no error, A, in a decision of the citizens, B, when the vote is held apart from intrigue and pressure of private interests. This game is all to the liking of Rousseau's admirers, and they go on playing at it. Still again X is modified, and once the opinion of the majority (?) of the electors, it now becomes the opinion of the majority of those elected. Such the evolution of one of the sublimest dogmas of the democratic religion! [1]

1608 [1] In the *Contrat social*, II, 1, after showing how the social contract is drawn, Rousseau adds: "The first and most important consequence of the principles above established is that the general will can alone direct the forces of the State according to the purposes for which it was established, the common weal." How can that be? II, 4: "If the State or City is just a moral person deriving its life from the union of its members, and if the most important of its concerns is its own preservation, it needs a universal power of compulsion to move and arrange each part in the manner most advantageous to the whole. Just as Nature gives each individual absolute power over all his members, so the social pact gives the body politic absolute power over all its members, and it is that power directed by the general will which bears . . . the name of sovereignty. . . . Why else is the general will always right, why else do all invariably wish for the welfare of each individual among them, unless it be that there is no one who does not take the words 'each individual' to himself and does not think of himself in voting for all?" The general proposition, $X = A$,

1609. This argument is accepted by many people, not because of its intrinsic logico-experimental value, which is zero, nor for any lack of intelligence on the part of those who assent to it—some of them are very intelligent indeed. To what, then, is the success of

is now established: the general will, *X*, in other words, is always right, *A*. Following a method customary among metaphysicists and very dear to them, Rousseau attributes a characteristic to the general will before explaining at all definitely what that entity is. Now we proceed, II, 3, to modify *X*: "It follows from what has just been said that the general will is always right and always tends to the public welfare; but it does not follow that the deliberations of the people always have the same rectitude. A man always wants what is good for him, but he does not always know what it is. The people is never corrupted but is often deceived, and then only does it in appearances seek what is evil. [The modification in the meaning of "error." We shall return to the point presently.] There is often a great difference between the will of all [One of the forms of *X*.] and the general will [Another form of *X*.]: The latter envisages only the common interest; the other envisages private interest and is only a sum of particular wills [Watch the juggler's ball—it is slipping from one box to the other!]: but strip those same wills of the more and the less that cancel each other [For them to do that, the less would have to be equal to the more, otherwise there would be a remainder; but the divine Rousseau cares not a fig for such petty details.] [Pareto seems to misunderstand Rousseau's passage, which means not that the less cancels the more, but that a larger or smaller number of particular wills cancel each other: the French reads: *"Otez de ces mêmes volontés les plus et les moins qui s'entredétruisent."* To amend Pareto's stricture one might say against Rousseau that when a certain number of particular wills cancel each other, the dark horse wins; but the dark horse may represent a particular interest.— A. L.] and the general will is left as the sum of the differences. [Now the ball has slipped from the box on the right to the box on the left. But keep your eye on it. It will soon be doing something cleverer still: a real state, *B*, is going to be described for the purpose of equating it with one of the indefinite abstractions, *X*, just proffered.] When after sufficient enlightening the people deliberates, if the citizens have had no intercommunication [How can they be enlightened if there is no intercommunication? It must be an internal spontaneous sort of enlightenment!], the great number of little differences [Who told Rousseau that they were "little"?] will always yield the general will [*i.e.*, *X*.], and the decision will always be a good one. [Even when the people votes to burn a witch?] But when there is electioneering by partial associations at the expense of the great association, the will of each clique becomes general as regards its members, particular as regards the State. . . . Finally, when one such association is so large that it overbalances all the others, one gets as a result not a sum of little differences but one single difference. Then no general will is possible, and the view that triumphs is a particular view." A person knows what he likes or dislikes, but he may err through ignorance. Provision is made for eliminating this difficulty by asking that the people be not deceived and that they be adequately enlightened. The deception on that basis is always an intrusion from without. If the citizens were not deceived, they would always judge rightly; but the majority err because they are unable to discern the truth. However, in order to understand, they need only to be "enlightened." Rousseau's City contains no people who cannot understand. It being thus demonstrated: (1) that the general will is

the derivation due? To numberless causes. I will mention just a few: 1. People who are, or think they are, a part of a majority readily assent to a theory which, as they understand it, seems to represent their judgment as infallible.[1] 2. Shrewd schemers who are the gainers from protective tariffs and other measures, and politicians who win power, honours and wealth through popular suffrage judge theories of whatever kind not by their intrinsic soundness but by their capacity for winning the votes on which said schemers and politicians depend. Is it any fault of theirs if voters dote on absurdities? Aristippus was criticized for throwing himself at the feet of the tyrant Dionysius. But he replied: "I am not to blame! Blame Dionysius, for having his ears on his feet!" 3. Individuals who do not belong to the majority but are hostile to their superiors in the social scale flirt with those who they believe are in the majority in order to combat their superiors or merely to spite them. 4. Some few individuals who are religiously-minded to a very high degree accept this particular dogma of the democratico-humanitarian religion, just as they would accept any other. In pagan times they might have been priests of Cybele. In the Middle Ages they would have been friars. Today they are worshippers of "the People." 5. Many persons of limited understanding accept the opinion of the community, large or small, in which they live; and they readily pass from admiration of Bossuet to admiration of Voltaire, Rousseau, Tolstoy, or anyone else who happens to achieve fame or reputation. 6. Other persons, who judge theories much as an untrained amateur judges music, consider this theory good simply because it stimulates their sentiments agreeably. Other causes might be identified by considering the many classifications that might be made on the basis of the differing manners in which interests and sentiments influence the opinions of men.

1610. Our IV-γ derivations present an extreme case where mere verbal coincidences are observable. In the year 1148, "a Breton gentleman by the name of Éon de l'Étoile was brought before it [the

always right; (2) that the general will is expressed by the vote of well-informed citizens who have had no communication with one another, the conclusion logically follows that the decision in question is always right.

1609 [1] [Pareto wrote—rather obscurely, I find: "which they understand in the sense of their own infallibility."—A. L.]

Council of Rheims], a man almost illiterate, who said he was the son of God and the judge of the living and the dead, being led to such belief by the rough resemblance of his name to the Latin word *Eum* which appears in a sentence used at the end of exorcisms, *per eum qui judicaturus est,* and at the end of prayers, *Per eundem . . .* Absurd as this fantastic reason was, it none the less enabled him to swindle many ignorant people in the remoter districts of France, and notably in Brittany and Gascony." [1] Ambiguousness in terms and statements is an excellent device for interpreting oracles and prophecies; and with the further support of metaphors (IV-δ) and allegories (IV-ε), one would have to be an idiot indeed not to find a way to infer anything one chose from such pronouncements. Starting with reasonings of this kind, which are ostensibly offered in all seriousness, we gradually get to mere jests, such as the answer *"Domine stes securus,"* which was given to a person asking whether he could live in security from his enemies. The response could be interpreted to mean that he could, in fact, feel secure. But it could also mean the opposite: *"Domi ne stes securus"* ("Feel safe not even at home").

1611. The explanations that have been given of the term "demons" furnish an interesting example of IV-γ derivations following the twin route from the thing to the word, and from the word to the thing.

1612. 1. *From the thing to the word.* The term δαίμονες as used by the Greeks designated certain imaginary entities, which varied according to the times and the writer. In Homer δαίμων is often confused with the notion of θεός, or better, with the notion of the god's activity. It has been said—though far from proved—that the activity so designated was an evil one. In Hesiod, the δαίμονες have an intermediate status between gods and men, but they are all beneficent. As time went on, this intermediate character admitted of a distinction between good demons and bad demons. Milords the philosophers would have their say, and their ethical sensibilities being outraged that popular religion should ascribe both good and evil conduct to the gods, they thought they could be rid of the em-

1610 [1] Fleury, *Histoire ecclésiastique,* Vol. XIV, pp. 619-20; and see Labbe, Vol. XII, pp. 1659-60.

barrassment by foisting the wicked conduct upon the "demons."[1] The derivation in this case is something like the one that distinguishes a "right reason" that never errs from a plain ordinary reason that does sometimes falter. On this theme of divine misconduct numbers of writers expatiated, and the demons they invented were perverse beyond all words.

1613. 2. *From the word to the thing.* The Christians found the term δαίμονες ready-made, and they took advantage of it to retrace the road from the word to the thing. The Greeks had first taken gods and demons together. Then at a certain moment they came to distinguish them in order to pack exclusively upon the demons sins and crimes of which the gods could hardly be exculpated.[1] The Christians were quick to seize upon the point, and creating a confusion, either in good faith or by design, between the old and the new senses of the term "demon," they made bold to conclude that by very confession of the pagans the gods were maleficent beings. In that way the derivation turned all in favour of the Christians, who could point to witnesses and proofs of their own theology in the camp of their adversaries. Plato, good soul, had told a number of idiotic stories about demons in his *Symposium*. Minucius Felix took the greatest pains not to ignore such a treasure and he appeals

1612 [1] Plutarch, *De defectu oraculorum,* 15 (Goodwin, Vol. IV, p. 20): "Certain it is that all the stories of rapings, vagabondings, flights, and labours in slavery that are told in the myths and sung in the hymns are things that happened not to gods but to demons; and they are told to show the virtue and power of the latter. Wherefore Aeschylus should not have said [*Supplices,* v. 222]: 'Chaste Apollo, god exiled from heaven,' nor Sophocles through Admetus [*Fragmenta,* 65, 2; Musgrave, Vol. II, p. 275]: 'My cock [husband] hath led him [the god] to the mill.'" The text of this last in Plutarch is certainly corrupt. Admetus cannot be the speaker, but, at the most, Alcestis, his wife. [So Pareto. Goodwin renders: "My cock by crowing led him to the mill." Grotius, quoted by Musgrave: *"Meus se sponte pullus ad molam salsam tulit."*—A. L.]

1613 [1] Grote, *History of Greece,* Vol. I, pp. 426-27: "This distinction between gods and daemons appeared to save in a great degree both the truth of the old legends and the dignity of the gods: it obviated the necessity of pronouncing either that the gods were unworthy, or the legends untrue. Yet although devised for the purpose of satisfying a more scrupulous religious sensibility, it was found inconvenient afterwards, when assailants arose against paganism generally. For while it abandoned as indefensible a large portion of what had once been genuine faith, it still retained the same word *daemons* with an entirely altered signification. The Christian writers in their controversies found ample warrant among the *earlier* pagan authors for treating all the gods as daemons—and not less ample warrant among the *later* pagans for denouncing the daemons generally as evil beings."

to Plato's authority to show that the spirits which animated the statues of the gods were demons.[2] Lactantius Firmianus also thinks that the gods of the pagans are demons, and turning to the heathen, he bids them, "if they refuse to believe us, to believe their Homer, who classes the great Zeus among the demons, as indeed others of their poets and philosophers do who use the terms demons and gods in the same manner, the first being the true name and the latter false."[3] Tatian makes Zeus king of the demons.[4] He may be right, for of Zeus or demons alike we know nothing and experimental science is without means of any sort for determining whether Tatian is uttering truth or rubbish.

1614. IV-δ: *Metaphors, allegories, analogies.* If offered in mere explanation, as a means of conveying some conception of an unknown, metaphors and analogies may be used scientifically as a way of getting from the known to the unknown. Offered as demonstration, they have not the slightest scientific value. Because a thing, *A,* is in certain respects similar, analogous, to another thing, *B,* it in no sense follows that all the traits present in *A* are present also in *B,* or that a given trait is one of those particular traits whereby the analogy arises.

1615. Resort to metaphor and analogy may be direct or indirect. *A* and *B* have in common the trait *P,* in virtue of which *A* is analo-

---

1613 [2] Minucius Felix, *Octavius,* 26, 12; 27, 1 (Randall, p. 397; Freese, p. 77): "What about Plato, who thought it was difficult to discover God, but speaks glibly (*sine negotio*) of angels and demons, and in his *Symposium* even tries to determine their nature? For he claims there is a substance partly mortal, partly immortal, in other words, intermediate between matter and spirit and formed of a mixture of earthly weight and heavenly lightness; and from it, he says, we get our [original] inclination to love, and he says that it makes its way into human hearts, stirring our senses, shaping our emotions, and inspiring our passions. Those unclean spirits, the demons, as the Magi, the philosophers, and Plato show, lurk under consecrated statues and images and by their afflation gain the prestige of the god as present in person, meantime inspiring soothsayers, haunting shrines, animating the fibre of entrails, controlling flights of birds, determining lots, and uttering oracles that are for the most part steeped in lies (*falsis pluribus involuta*)."

1613 [3] *Divinae institutiones,* IV, *De vera sapientia,* 27, 15 (*Opera,* Vol. I, p. 387; Fletcher, Vol. I, p. 281): "*Si nobis credendum esse non putant, credant Homero qui summum illum Iovem daemonibus aggregavit, sed et aliis poetis ac philosophis qui eosdem modo daemones modo deos nuncupant, quorum alterum verum, alterum falsum est.*"

1613 [4] *Oratio adversus Graecos,* 8 (Migne, p. 823; English, p. 12): Καὶ μήτι γε οἱ δαίμονες αὐτοὶ μετὰ τοῦ ἡγουμένου αὐτῶν Διὸς . . .

gous to B and may be taken metaphorically as B's equivalent. But B also has a trait Q, which is not present in A; but the equivalence of A and B suggests the inference that A also has the trait Q. This is the most frequent case of the reasoning by analogy; because the fallacy is less likely to be noticed if care is taken not to separate P from Q and to speak in such terms as not to betray the fact that A is taken as the equivalent of B only in view of the common trait P.

For the indirect reasoning: A is analogous to B in view of a certain trait, P, common both to A and to B. B is analogous to C in view of a common trait, Q, which is not present in A. The argument is: $A = B$, $B = C$, therefore, $A = C$ (§ 1632). This case is not so frequent, because the form the argument assumes tends to arouse suspicion of a fallacy. To dissemble it more effectively it is better to avoid as far as possible any suggestion of the syllogistic form, and so to use the IV-β derivation that persuades by dint of the accessory sentiments associated with this or that term.

1616. Derivations by metaphor, allegory, and analogy are much used by metaphysicists and theologians. The works of Plato are one string of metaphors and analogies offered as proofs. He writes the *Republic* to discover what is "just" and what "unjust" and solves the problem by analogy. To begin with, he sets up (II, 10, 368E) an analogy between the search for justice and the reading of a script. Is not a piece of writing more readily deciphered when it is written in big letters? Let us look, therefore, for something in which "justice" appears in "big letters." Justice is present both in the individual and in society. But society is larger than the individual. It will therefore be easier to discern justice in society. And he runs on in that tone through the whole book. In the *Phaedo,* 71, Plato gives a celebrated demonstration of the immortality of the soul: "*Socrates.* Tell me, as regards life and death—would you not say that life is the contrary of death? *Cebes.* Certainly. *Socrates.* And that the one is born of the other? *Cebes.* Yes. *Socrates.* What, then, is born of the living? *Cebes.* The dead man. *Socrates.* And of the dead? *Cebes.* One has to agree—the living. *Socrates.* Of the dead, then, O Cebes, are born the living, and all that has life. *Cebes.* So it would seem. *Socrates.* So then our souls [after death] are in Hades? *Cebes.* I should assume so."

1617. In the days of the dispute over investitures, Pope and Emperor hurled metaphors at each other while waiting for more concrete weapons to decide the issue. Famous the metaphor of the two swords: "On the basis of the words of the Apostles [*sic*] to Jesus Christ [Luke 22:38], 'Lord, behold, here are two swords,' a theory was erected that the two swords meant respectively the temporal power, called the material sword, and the ecclesiastical power, called the spiritual sword. In just that sense St. Bernard wrote in one of his letters to Pope Eugene, *Epistolae*, CCLVI: 'Both swords belong to Peter, the one to be drawn at his command, the other by his own hand whenever necessary. The sword less evidently becoming to Peter he was bidden to return to its sheath. It belonged to him, but he was not to draw it with his own hand.' " [1] The Emperor's supporters did not admit that the "material sword" belonged to the Pope: "Whence the Pope's authority to draw a death-dealing sword as well as the spiritual sword? Pope Gregory the First says that if he had chosen to slaughter the Lombards they would then have had neither king nor dukes. 'But,' he adds, 'because I fear God, I will have no part in the death of any man.' Following this example, all the Popes who succeeded him contented themselves with the spiritual sword, down to the last Pope Gregory, in other words, Hildebrand, who was the first to gird on the mili-

---

1617 [1] (*Opera*, Vol. I, p. 463): "*Exserendus est nunc uterque gladius in passione Domini, Christo denuo patiente ubi et altera vice passus est. Per quem autem nisi per vos? Petri uterque est: alter suo nutu alter sua manu quoties necesse est evaginandus. Et quidem de quo minus videbatur de ipso ad Petrum dictum est: 'Converte gladium tuum in vaginam.' Ergo suus erat et ille sed non sua manu utique educendus.*" Says Fleury, *Histoire ecclésiastique*, Vol. XIV, p. 581: "This allegory of the two swords, which was to become so famous in course of time, had already been stressed in a work of Geoffrey, Abbot of Vendôme. St. Bernard carries it much further here." In another address to Pope Eugene, *De consideratione*, IV, 3, 7, St. Bernard exhorts him to use the material sword: "Why should you be trying again to usurp a sword which of yore you were bidden to return to its sheath? Those who deny that it is yours seem to me to pay insufficient heed to the Lord's words. For He said: 'Put up thy sword into the sheath' [John 18:11]. The sword, therefore, was yours, to be drawn, mayhap, at your bidding though not by your hand. Otherwise, if that same sword also in no sense belonged to you, when the Apostles said 'Here are two swords,' He would not have answered 'It is enough,' but 'It is too many.' Therefore, both the spiritual and material swords belong to the Church, the latter to be drawn on behalf of the Church, the former by the Church, the former by the hand of the priest, the latter by the soldier at, of course, the beck of the priest and the command of the Emperor."

tary sword against the Emperor." [2] Other pretty metaphors were brought into play: "Gregory VII, successor to St. Peter, and vicar of Jesus Christ on earth, thought himself authorized to chastise the successors of Nimrod, who in his eyes were naught but rebellious angels. Did not the soul prevail over matter, the Church over lay society, and the priesthood over the Empire, as the Sun over the Moon and gold over lead?" [3] These two metaphors—the comparison of the papal power to spirit and lay powers to matter; and the comparison of papal power to the Sun and lay powers to the Moon, were widely used. St. Ives resorts to the first in his letter to Henry, King of England, and it is upheld by the Saint of Aquino.[4]

1618. Another metaphor considers the Church pictured as a man as wedded to the State pictured as a woman.[1] Nor should we forget

1617 [2] Fleury, *Op. cit.,* Vol. XIV, p. 76.

1617 [3] Jules Zeller, *Histoire d'Allemagne,* Vol. III, p. 321.

1617 [4] *Epistolae,* CVI (*Ad Henricum Angliae regem*) (*Opera,* Vol. II, p. 125): "Just as the senses of the body (*sensus animalis*) should be subject to reason, so earthly power should be subject to ecclesiastical rule, and unless the earthly power is ruled and inspired by ecclesiastical discipline, it would be no better than the body apart from rule by the soul." In the *De regimine principum,* III, 10 (*Opuscula,* 20; *Opera,* 1570 ed., Vol. XVII, p. 177, 2B-C), St. Thomas contradicts those who hold that the words of Jesus which gave Peter authority to bind and to loose applied only to the spiritual domain: "For if it be said that they refer to the spiritual power alone, that cannot be, because the corporeal and the temporal depend on the spiritual and the internal as the activities of the body on the powers of the soul."

1618 [1] Phillips, *Du droit ecclésiastique,* Vol. II, pp. 473-75: "The position of Church and State has of late been likened to the union of the man and the woman in marriage. The comparison certainly suggests a number of perfectly sound reflections . . . though one must be careful not to get things upside down as would be the case if, on the mistaken analogy of the [gender of the] words, the Church were to be taken as the feminine element and the State as the masculine. Matters have to stand just the other way round." The creation of woman corresponds to the creation of the temporal order. The divine order "appears at first only in the background and as it were asleep. [A very pretty metaphor.] The temporal order is drawn forth from it during its slumber. The human race awakens in the new Adam and the divine order salutes the temporal as flesh of its flesh, bone of its bone. Thenceforward, both of them, united one to the other as the bride to the husband, are to reign together over the world." But what a power in the metaphor! In its name, O ye heretics, shall ye be burned, or at least imprisoned! Phillips couches a history of the relations between Church and State in the same figures: first the Church asks the hand of the State in marriage: "It is, after a fashion, the period of courtship." In a second period, Church and State have married and are living in perfect bliss: "There may be, as in marriage, some occasional misunderstanding but, the two spouses sincerely intending to abide together in Jesus Christ, such difficulties are soon smoothed out. Finally the temporal power draws apart from the

that other, which used the name of St. Peter to prove that the Church and the Papacy were founded on the authority of Jesus and which has been the occasion for spilling no end of ink.[2]

1619. Various peoples have books that are sacred or greatly revered, such as Homer among the Greeks, the Koran among the Moslems, the Bible among Jews and Christians.[1] The book may be taken literally; but sooner or later someone tries to find out whether it may not have some meaning other than the literal.[2] That may be

faith of the Church and the obedience it owes the Church in divine matters." That is the third phase, the separation stage. Three situations arise: "1. The wife [*i.e.*, the State] becomes entirely freed of dependence on her husband [the Church], severing the conjugal knot of her own accord. 2. She breaks up the marriage and hurries into a second union, exalting her new husband to domestic authority and oppressing her legitimate spouse with his help. 3. She refuses to recognize the absolute authority of the one who has detached her from her husband, but she remains cool to this latter, or indeed, if she does become reconciled to him, demands recognition of the other on the same footing." A clear case of polyandry.

1618 [2] Phillips, *Op. cit.*, Vol. I, pp. 53-55: "That utterance, 'Thou art Peter,' made Simon the foundation of the Church, the rock that supplied the keystone for the divine edifice." Unfortunately, the metaphor has given rise to endless dispute: "How many differing interpretations have been given for the words *Petrus* and *Petra*, which were used in the Greek translation to render the word *Cephas*, the only one that appears in the Syriac original as well as in Persian, Armenian, and Coptic translations! The difference arises from the fact that in Greek the word πέτρα, of feminine gender, could not be applied to a man. The translator therefore was forced by the genius of his language to change the physiognomy of the word in order to adapt it to the use he was obliged to make of it: whence πέτρος, twice repeated, instead of πέτρα. That explanation, so plausible in itself, has been accepted by the bitterest adversaries of the primacy of St. Peter. What inference can therefore be drawn from a purely syllabic, a purely external, difference? Can one say, to carry it into the very meaning of the terms, that πέτρα means a great rock, while πέτρος suggests the image of a pebble? That interpretation, which some recent lexicographers have adopted, is . . . devoid of any basis. We will grant it, nevertheless, if one insists, but on one condition that cannot be disputed us: namely, that if πέτρος means a pebble, that little pebble becomes, through the transmutation thrust upon it by Jesus in changing it to πέτρα, a great and solid rock."

1619 [1] We have already examined metaphorical explanations (Chapter V), chiefly with a view to seeing whether and how one could get back from them to the facts in which they originate. Here we are considering them chiefly as means of arriving at certain desired conclusions.

1619 [2] Berg, *Principes du droit musulman*, pp. 3-4: "The Koran or 'the Book' (*al-Kitab*), is the supreme, the fundamental law for the Mussulmans. . . . The fundamental principles of law have had to be deduced by jurists from the relatively few decisions rendered in the Koran. Such decisions all bear on special cases, and they would often lead to absurd consequences if the rigorous implications were not evaded by all the hair-splitting that casuistry can marshal [Derivations]. One could hardly imagine the strange embarrassments in which one would find oneself if one

done in the plain intent of discovering such a meaning, as is sometimes the case with scholars. But generally some definite purpose is
held in view, and what is sought is not what is in the book, but
some device for bringing the book into accord with the purpose—
some interpretation, some derivation that will serve to reconcile two
things that are pre-established with equal definiteness: on the one
hand, a text, and, on the other, the notion for which a justification
is sought (§§ 1414, 1447). For such a quest, the symbolical and allegorical methods of interpretation offer ready and effective tools.[3]

1620. If there were a norm of some sort for determining just what
symbol, just what allegory, a given statement, A, must necessarily
represent, the symbolical or allegorical interpretation might fail to
hit the facts and so not be "true," but it would at least be definite.
As a matter of fact, no such norm exists. The selection of the symbol
or allegory is at the pleasure of the interpreter, and it is often based
on far-fetched, childish, absurd resemblances, so that the interpretation becomes altogether arbitrary and indeterminate. That is now
evident to everybody in the allegorical interpretations that have been
made, let us say, of the Homeric poems. There is not a person left
in the world today who takes them seriously. Yet so great is the
power of the sentiments that incline people to yield to that type of
derivation that the Modernists of our day have been able to revive
the method of allegorical interpretation for the Gospels and find
people to admire them.

1621. We are speaking, remember, at all times and exclusively
from the standpoint of logico-experimental science, and any excursions whatever into the realms of faith are forbidden us. If loyalty
to a faith requires a certain interpretation it is not for us to say
whether it be right or wrong; indeed, the terms "right" and "wrong"
have no meaning in such a case; or, if they do have, it is something

kept to the letter of the Koran instead of to the spirit of the particular passage. . . .
The Koran is not only a book inspired by Allah. It is the book eternal, increate
like Allah himself, and only one copy of which was revealed to the Prophet. ([In a
note:] Allah Himself is supposed to be speaking in the Koran.) Whence the conclusion that not only the substance but the form of the Koran is sacred and infallible
and that all criticism is forbidden. That doctrine has, to be sure, long since found
its adversaries in Islam itself (the Mu'tazilites, for instance); but it is still generally
current today and gives rise to the most outlandish predicaments."

1619 [3] We say nothing here of interpretations such as those of Palaephatus with
which we have dealt elsewhere (§ 661).

quite different from the meaning they have in the logico-experimental field. If someone says that faith compels him to believe that the Song of Songs tells the story of the love of Christ for His Church, we have no objection. A question of that character entirely transcends the limits of our inquiry here. But if he sets out to demonstrate his interpretation with logico-experimental arguments, he will in so doing be entering our field, and we are free to appraise his arguments by the norms of the logico-experimental sciences. In the same way, we are not here discussing the social utility that certain interpretations, certain doctrines, may have.[1] An interpretation may be absurd from the experimental standpoint or from the standpoint of formal logic, and be (or not be) beneficial to society. That has to be decided in each particular case.

1622. Allegory is often resorted to because of an impulse human beings feel to embellish the stories they tell, even when they have no definite purpose in doing so. There are writers who cannot tell a story without dotting it spontaneously, and perhaps unconsciously, with allegories. But more often the allegory is used to attain some purpose, to reconcile theories with theories, theories with facts, and so on.

1623. Striking the case of St. Augustine, who begins with allegory and ends with literal meanings, whereas ordinarily procedure is in the opposite direction. The Saint needed allegory in his fight with the Manicheans, and used it, coming to the sense which he called "literal" in another connexion.[1] We must not allow ourselves to be deceived by that term, however. St. Augustine regards a figurative meaning also as "literal," and that serves his purpose quite as well as allegory in getting any meaning he chooses out of Holy Writ. When, in the *De Genesi ad litteram,* II, 13, 27 (*Opera,* Vol. III, p. 245), the pious Doctor says that "light" means the "spiritual creature"; when he says, IV, 9, 16, that the Lord's rest on the seventh

---

1621 [1] We shall come to that subject in Chapter XII.

1623 [1] *Retractationes,* I, 18 (*Opera,* Vol. I, p. 613): "When I was writing my two books against the Manicheans, I was dealing with the words of Scripture according to their allegorical signification and did nòt dare to expound such great secrets of natural things according to the letter." And *Ibid.,* II, 24 (*Opera,* Vol. I, p. 640): "I have called these books [*De Genesi*] 'On Genesis, according to the Letter'—not, that is, according to the allegorical meanings, but according to the actual happenings (*secundum rerum gestarum proprietatem*)."

day must be taken as meaning that "repose in Himself with the blessings of the Holy Spirit" which God bestowed on "rational creatures, among them man"; when he says, IV, 35, 57, that the first day which God made is "the spiritual and rational creature, and namely the supercelestial angels and the virtues"; and when he speaks in similar terms in other places, we have to understand that if he is not using allegories, he is using metaphors, or symbols, or some other interpretation of the kind—all of which are substantially as remote from literal meanings as the boldest allegories could ever be.

1624. As regards the narratives in the Gospels, St. Augustine accepts them as history and allegory side by side; and that theory is professed by many people. In the miracle, according to St. Augustine, there is the historical fact and also a lesson for mankind: "We find that three dead persons were visibly brought back to life by Our Lord." [1] For the Saint that is historical fact. But he adds: "What Our Lord Jesus Christ did physically He desired us to understand in a spiritual sense also. . . . Let us therefore see what He desired to teach us in raising three persons from the dead." That is all perfectly clear. The historical fact and the allegory go hand in hand, and we cannot therefore ask whether it was the writer's intent to relate a historical episode or to impart an allegorical lesson. No dilemma arises for the very reason that the two things can stand side by side. In reality that very often happens, and a writer either does not know or else forgets just where his story ends and allegory begins, and is himself unable to distinguish the one thing from the other. That, *a fortiori,* frustrates any effort an outsider might make later on to draw any such distinction. For that reason the task that our Modernists, returning to efforts made in olden times, have set themselves in reinterpreting the Gospel according to St. John seems altogether fatuous. Sometimes a writer himself distinguishes the story he tells from the allegorical moral that may be derived from it. Both may, in his mind, be foreign to reality, as in an animal dialogue with a moral; and in that case there is no difficulty, from the logical standpoint. But an author may also regard his story as a narrative of real fact and nevertheless interpret it in an allegorical

1624 [1] *Sermones* (*Opera,* Vol. V) *XCVIII* (*De verbis Evangelii Lucae VII, et de tribus mortuis quos Dominus suscitavit*), III, 3; IV, 4.

manner.[2] In such a case the logical nexus that he establishes between the fact and the allegory is not easily determined. But the difficulty largely arises in our own minds from an ingrained habit we have of insisting on finding exactness where there may never have been any, where, that is, the author of story and allegory may himself have been satisfied with a vague nexus.

1625. From the allegory that is intentional and clearly taken as unreal—*e.g.,* the allegory used by a poet—we go on by imperceptible degrees to the allegory that a writer uses unwittingly and which blends with reality in his mind. That is often observable when language is called upon to express some vigorous sentiment that gives form and animation to epithet, image, and allegory; and legends also not seldom originate in just that way.[1] This is one of

1624 [2] No end of examples might be mentioned. In the *Violier des histoires romaines,* fiction, and facts that the writer regards as historical, appear side by side, and he gives allegorical interpretations of both: *L'exposition moralle sur le propos.* According to St. Augustine, he says, Chap. 22, p. 74, the heart from the corpse of some Roman Emperor or other could not be consumed on the pyre because the Emperor had been poisoned: "Then the people took the heart out of the fire and bathed it with theriaque [Venetian treacle]. In that way the poison was driven out and when the heart was returned to the fire, it burned at once." For the writer that is historical fact. And he continues: *"Moral explanation of the above:* Morally speaking, the hearts of sinners that have been poisoned by mortal sin cannot be kindled and enlightened (*esprins et illuminés*) by the fire of the Holy Spirit save by that theriaque which is penitence."

1625 [1] Rocquain, *Notes et fragments d'histoire,* pp. 128-32, *Du style révolutionnaire* (In question, the writings of revolutionary leaders of 1789): "In the qualifiers which he ordinarily adds to the terms he uses he gives them a letter, a sign, that brings them before the mind in a more striking manner. Is it a question of duty? It is 'sacred.' Of selfishness? It is 'blind.' Of treachery? It is 'black.' Of patriotism? It is 'burning.' . . . As a result of the same tendency, the strongest words are invariably chosen to express any given state of mind. . . . After that it is only a step to giving life to words, or better, to the ideas they translate. That step is forever being taken in the writings of those days. In using the expressions 'body politic' or 'body social,' which the Revolution borrowed from the period just preceding, there is no stopping at the cold designations which those terms taken together make. The social body lives. It has arteries and veins through which a blood now vigorous, now impure circulates. . . . Ideas are not merely endowed with life. They are personified. Abstract terms, of such frequent use in those times, as I have noted, terms such as 'justice,' 'liberty,' 'reason,' and others of the same sort, stand for living beings that speak, move their eyes, act. . . . Personality is ascribed not only to abstractions of that kind which were, so to speak, the divine emblems of the Revolution. At that time, when France was prey to foreign wars as well as to civil discord, 'country' is a favourite theme in public utterances and appears with all the traits of a living being. . . . It is understandable, also, that under pressure of the

the many cases in which, as we have seen, terms are vague because the limits of the sentiments with which they are associated are also vague. The real character of a thing is not sharply distinguished from its allegorical character any more than the objective character of a personification is distinguished from its subjective character (§§ 1070 f.). It is hard to say whether the ancient Greeks took the "baneful dream" in the *Iliad* (οὖλον ὄνειρον, II, v. 6) in a strictly allegorical sense, rather than in a sense mingling the allegorical and the real.

1626. In this connexion we have more and better than mere probabilities: we have well-authenticated facts, and since they come from times such as ours, when the scientific spirit and the methods of historical criticism are in pre-eminent vogue, we may hold *a fortiori* that similar things must have happened in times when science and criticism were missing. One such case, indeed a most interesting one, is that of Auguste Comte's *Synthèse subjective*. On the one hand, Comte presents his notions not as realities but as useful fictions; but then he becomes so pleased with them that he mistakes them for realities.[1] In Comte's case, we are in a position to know the path,

prevailing passions the Revolution should personify the things it hates as well as the things it likes. 'There stands Fanaticism!' cries the Committee of Public Safety of refractory priests whom it is accusing of trying to arouse public opinion. 'There she stands, watching, waiting for her credulous victims, the palm of martyrdom in her hand.' Fanaticism, Federalism, and other objects of revolutionary hatred ordinarily figure as 'monsters'; and such 'monsters' live in 'lairs' into which the Revolution, like a modern Hercules, makes its way to fell and capture them. . . . As a result of their propensity to vivify, to personify, ideas, the writings of those times offer not so much pictures as living pictures."

1626 [1] Here is an example, pp. 8-11: "It being forbidden us ever to aspire to absolute notions, we can set up the relative conception of external bodies by endowing each of them with the faculties of sense and action, provided we deprive them of thought, so that their volition is always blind. [So, on pretext of our ignorance of the absolute, we treat fiction and reality on the same plane.] Confined to the Great Being, assisted by his worthy servants and their free auxiliaries, intelligence, spurred by sentiment, guides activity in such a way as gradually to modify a fatality, all of whose agents tend constantly to the good, without being able to know its conditions. By dispelling theological prejudices that represented matter as essentially inert, science tended to restore to it the activity that fetishism had spontaneously hallowed. . . . [So fiction is blended with reality, and to justify the confusion, Comte adds:] It could never be proved that a given body does not sense the impressions that it undergoes and does not will the actions which it performs; though it shows itself devoid of capacity to modify its conduct according to circumstances, which is the

AT (§ 636), that leads from certain facts, *A,* to a theory, *T* (Figure 18). Suppose some centuries hence knowledge of that path has been lost, and that all that is left is a certain theory which asserts that the Earth wisely prepared the conditions required for the existence of a certain Great Being. In that case, interpreters of the myth will come forward. A few of them will set out merely to discover *A* and very probably go wrong and get something quite different from *A*. Many, many others will start out from said worshipful theory, *T*, but with the idea of arriving at certain conclusions, *C,* which they want to reach; and the better to get there, they will invent all manner of beautiful and apt derivations obtained by ingenious allegorical and metaphorical interpretations.

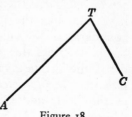

Figure 18

1627. The interpretations of this variety which have been used to reconcile the Scriptures with experimental fact are too well known to require any extensive comment here—we have already encountered the truly remarkable example of the Song of Songs (§ 1452). Since, by chance or otherwise, that work had found its way into the Scriptures, it had to be moral in content and beautiful in a literary sense, as could readily be shown by allegory, metaphor, and other

chief trait of intelligence." And so the metaphor becomes reality, since no one can prove that it is not reality! One cannot prove that Zeus does not exist—therefore Zeus exists! What are the "sensations" that a body receives from "impressions" upon it? What is its "will"? What its "conduct"? No one can prove that the sea does not "sense the impression" of a ship, or that the sea does not "will" the things that it does to the ship, simply because no one can prove the incomprehensible and the absurd. Once started along that path, Comte goes galloping ahead, writing less poetically but not less mythologically than Hesiod: "Forced to be continually subject to the fundamental laws of planetary life [What in the world can such a "life" be?], the Earth, when she was intelligent [That, probably, was in the days when animals could talk.], was able to develop its physico-chemical activity in such a way as to perfect the astronomical order by changing its principal coefficients. Our planet was so enabled to make its orbit less eccentric and thereby more habitable, by managing to execute a long series of explosions such as have produced the comets (according to the most credible hypothesis). Prudently repeated, those same shocks, seconded by vegetative mobility [Another wonderful thing—but again, what is it?], also succeeded in making the inclination of the terrestrial axis more congenial to the future requirements of the Great Being." And Comte runs on chattering in the same tone page after page.

such devices.[1] Such proofs come down to us in abundance from every period of history. Gautier classifies them as follows: "1. *Political allegory*. This theory has never had any great number of adherents. It is represented by a series of individual hypotheses that look to the history of Israel for the key to the Song. . . . 2. *Theocratic allegory*. Interpreters who have taken this point of view have had, like the preceding, the merit of not overstepping the boundaries of the old dispensation. According to them the Song of Songs describes the reciprocal loves of Jehovah and Israel. In the detail the greatest variety of interpretation prevails. . . . 3. *Messianic or Christological allegory*. . . . The Song hails the wedding of the Bride and Groom—of Christ, the divine leader, and His Church. . . . 4. *Mystical allegory*. With this mode of interpretation we quit the domain of history . . . to enter the inner sphere of the relations of the soul to God. . . . It is not surprising to find it adopted and developed in monastic circles. Interestingly also, it happens to be in high favour in the Greek Church."[2] To his list Gautier

1627 [1] Gautier, *Introduction à l'Ancien Testament,* Vol. II, pp. 126-38: " 'Song of Songs' means the most beautiful, the most perfect of songs, *the* song among them all. The title is a tribute paid to the superiority of that poem over all other poems."

1627 [2] Gautier is a Protestant. Suppose we listen to what a Catholic writer has to say: *Dictionnaire encyclopédique de la théologie catholique, s.v. Cantique des Cantiques:* "The Song of Songs is to be explained either literally, or 'typically,' or allegorically." The author of the article rejects of course the first two methods: "Theodore, Bishop of Mopsuestia, was the first to sustain the literal explanation, but Theodoret rebukes him, and his interpretation was rejected by the second Council of Constantinople. . . . The 'typical' interpretation lies in keeping the literal, the obvious text, but in considering and interpreting the events described as symbols of higher truths. Hugo Grotius was not the first to try that method. . . . He had been anticipated by Honorius of Autun, who applied the canticle literally to Pharaoh's daughter and allegorically to the Christian Church. Grotius [*Annotationes ad Canticum canticorum* (*Opera omnia theologica,* Vol. I, p. 267)] regards Solomon's love for the daughter of the King of Egypt as the incidental subject of the poem, but at the same time as the 'type' of the love of God for the children of Israel." The article goes on to refute that theory. "So only the allegorical meaning is left. But the partisans of the allegorical interpretation in their turn follow different routes. Some see in the Song Solomon's love for wisdom, others his love for Israel, others still Hezekiah's yearning for the reconciliation of the divided kingdoms; the old Jewish interpreters, the love of Jehovah for Israel; the older Christian commentators almost unanimously, the love of Christ for His Church." St. Augustine says in his *Speculum de Cantico Canticorum* (*Opera,* Vol. III, p. 925): "And we come finally to the book of Solomon called the Song of Songs. But what abridgment could we make of it here, since every line of it glorifies in figurative language, and foretells with prophetic loftiness, the holy endearments of Christ and the Church."

adds still another interpretation: "Realizing the difficulties that stand in the way of ascribing a religious intent to the author of the Song of Songs, but loath, nevertheless, to deny any religious status whatever to a book found in the Bible, a number of theologians have resorted to a fine distinction. That is the case with Franz Delitzsch and Zoeckler. They do not claim that the author of the Song set out to write an allegory: he merely purposed, they say, to sing of human love. But, they add, it is no less permissible and even enjoined upon us to ascribe a spiritual, religious, meaning to the poem. Its presence in the Bible proves that that is the will of God. In that case . . . it is no longer a question of allegory, but of a 'typical,' or 'typological,' interpretation." [3] Verily human beings must have a deal of time to waste to squander so much of it on such trifling speculations. Our contemporaries, it is true, are showing less interest in theological ramblings of this type, but only to turn to metaphysical speculations. And if that is not wolf, it is gray dog.

Renan also has his interpretation, and it is nothing but a particular application of his general method of dealing with Christian antiquities. These he deprives of everything supernatural and mystical, leaving, and even glorifying, their ethical implications: if they are not divine, they are at least surpassingly moral! To that trick Renan's work owed its huge success. At one extreme stood believers, at the other, unbelievers, atheistic or Voltairean. In between came hosts of people who were unwilling to go to either extreme and

1627 [3] Gautier, *Op. cit.,* p. 138, also examines the theory that the Song of Songs is a drama, and concludes: "This dramatic reconstruction of the Song of Songs seems to me unacceptable. I do not believe one can ever get from the poem, in any manner at all plausible, what partisans of the dramatic interpretation claim they see in it. . . . Now that the allegorical meaning is finding fewer and fewer friends, they are wondering whether some religious or at least moral tendency cannot be detected in the canticle if it be interpreted as a drama. Glorification of true love, opposition to sensuous passions and vulgar enjoyments, the superiority of monogamy over polygamy, the eulogy of marriage, constancy in love, conjugal fidelity, the triumph of a sincere and profound sentiment over the allurements of wealth and royal pomp—there is the list of themes that have seemed worthy of being celebrated and which have been designated as the inspirations of the poet of the canticle." Gautier favours the view that the canticle is a collection of nuptial songs. That view is supported by one consideration of great weight: the fact that it is obtained by the comparative method (§§ 547-48), explaining the past by customs observable in our day. However, it is still doubtful whether the origin and character of that literary fragment have really been hit upon, and fortunately humanity can live on without having the doubt dispelled.

were therefore in a mood to accept a system that was more or less sceptical but paid all due respect to established beliefs, which did away with the supernatural but spared the sublime—which followed, in a word, that middle course on which so many people are satisfied to remain. Humanitarians are never energetic enough to give up an old belief entirely; they merely reject such parts of it as do not square with their own beliefs. Just as the Christians saw demons in the pagan gods, our humanitarians see ethical travesties in the old theology. From that point of view it might be said that Renan, John Stuart Mill, Auguste Comte, Herbert Spencer, and many others, were Christians without a Christ; but in other respects, they show divergences: they share the same residues, their derivations are different. For Renan, *Le Cantique des cantiques,* p. 137, "the Song of Songs is neither mystical, as the theologians would have it, nor scandalous, as Châteillon believed, nor purely erotic, as Herder thought: it is moral. It is summarized in one verse—the seventh of Chapter VIII, the last in the poem: 'Many waters cannot quench love, neither can the floods drown it; if a man would give all the substance of his house for love, it would utterly be contemned' [Renan: "He would buy only shame"]. The subject of the poem is not the sensual passion that oozes about in the seraglios of the degenerate Orient, nor the dubious sentiment of the Hindu or Persian quietist who hides a hypocritical effeminacy under a mendacious front. It is true love." If that is enough to make a poem moral, there is plenty of morality in the collection of amorous epigrams in the *Greek Anthology*—V, 29, for instance. There the poet Cillactor remarks (Paton, Vol. I, p. 143) that "if one asketh the price of a kiss, it becometh bitterer than hellebore." Or V, 267, where a young man protests that he loves a girl but says he does not marry her because she is not rich enough. The poet Agathias tells him (Paton, Vol. I, p. 267): "Thou art deceived. Thou dost not love. How can a soul enamoured be so good at arithmetic?" [4] Piepenbring

---

1627 [4] Renan, *Ibid.,* Preface, pp. xi-xii: "I know that several passages in my translation will seem somewhat shocking to two classes of people: first to those who admire in antiquity only things that more or less resemble the forms of French taste; then, those who view the canticle only through the mystic veil that the religious consciousness of the ages has draped about it. These latter, of course, are the persons whose habits I am the least inclined to flout. Only in fear and trembling does one ever lay hand to those holy texts which have inspired and sustained the

also breaks a lance in defence of the Song of Songs.[5] He takes the view of Budde that Solomon and the Shunamite are allegorical figures, the first typifying glory, the second, beauty. "Following Wettstein, Budde further makes it clear that the canticle is just a collection of nuptial hymns. . . . The compiler of the collection may well have designed its publication to protest against polygamy and eulogize the mutual affection of husband and wife. Such an intent would lend a tone of moral earnestness to these pages, in spite of the over-crude realism one encounters in them." What ingenious reasons one can dig up, so only morality be saved! Here is one of the many cases where the arbitrary character of the derivation is patently manifest.[6]

hope of an eternal life." Crocodile's tears, more or less! Renan is so sensitive in such matters that farther along, p. 43, he does not even venture to quote the Bible! "Sulem, or Sunem, was a village of the tribe of Issachar, home of a certain woman, Abishag the Shunamite, whose adventures, as recounted in I Kings 1:3 and 2:17 f., are not without their points of resemblance to the ones that make up the scheme of our poem. We read, in fact, in the first of the passages mentioned, that the servants of David, in circumstances too greatly at variance with our notions of propriety to be stated here, sent out a call for the fairest maiden in all the tribes of Israel." We are certainly in a bad case if historians are to mention only such circumstances as do not diverge too widely from our present-day morality! Renan is hiding something that everyone knows. The translators of the King James Version were not as squeamish as the fashionable Parisian. They translate, I Kings 1:2: "Wherefore his [David's] servants said unto him: Let there be sought for my lord the king a young virgin: and let her stand before the king, and let her cherish him, and let her lie in thy bosom, that my lord the king may get heat." Sometimes Renan goes to even greater extremes: Sorel, *Le système historique de Renan,* Vol. I, p. 48: "Some years ago, M. Pascal, professor at Catania, called attention to a curious example of Renan's far-fetched translations (Carlo Pascal, *L'incendio di Roma e i primi cristiani,* p. 30)." It was a question of a series of double meanings that Renan insisted on seeing in the sign *domus transitoria,* which keeps appearing on certain buildings of Nero's time in Rome.

1627 [5] *Histoire du peuple d'Israël,* pp. 703-05.

1627 [6] Piepenbring concludes: "We are quite willing to grant that the collection [the Song of Songs] contains nothing that is immoral or even indecent. . . . We feel nevertheless that something is to be said for those among the ancients and moderns who have thought or still think that the poem is out of place in a sacred anthology or in a book designed for edification." In our ethical (in words) and democratic age, it is only natural that ethical and democratic interpretations should be the order of the day. Piepenbring, p. 703, quotes the view of Reuss: "As regards his public preachment of morality, the author of the Song of Songs intended to attack polygamy, eulogize conjugal fidelity, inspire admiration for virtue victorious over seduction, and make himself the mouthpiece of democratic indignation at corruption in high life." How many wonderful things in that poor little text! Why not also dig out of it something in favour of universal suffrage or world peace?

As regards another book in the Bible, the Book of Ruth, Piepenbring, following

1628. Suppose we resort to a graph, as we did in § 636. Let T be the text of the Song of Songs, A, its origin; C, the inference one is bent on deriving from T. A person using a derivation would often-

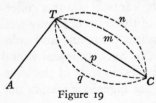

Figure 19

times have us believe that C is the same as A. C must necessarily be an edifying thing. The only problem is to find a road that will take us from T to C. Some will follow the allegorical path TmC, and show that the canticle symbolizes the love of Jesus for His Church. Some will follow the line TnC, and show that it celebrates types of glory and beauty. Some will follow the line TpC and show that the poem hails the victory of love over wealth. Someone, finally, hits on the line, TqC, and interprets the Song as a eulogy of monogamy. One may go on in that way indefinitely, and in all confidence that whatever the moral inference, C, one may desire to arrive at, one will never fail to find some road that will lead to it from T.

other writers, exerts himself to show that it must have had a moral purpose. It is clear enough that he and the writers he follows can only be seeking some path which will get them from the text to their heart's desire—in other words, a derivation; and since he who seeks in such a matter always finds, they readily discover that the Book of Ruth is a plea for a humane and universal religion. Says Piepenbring, *Op. cit.*, pp. 606-07: "The true purport of the Book of Ruth was not divined till very recently in our own time. . . . Its intent and meaning have been missed by numbers of modern 'higher critics' following the grammatical and historical method. Reuss in particular went completely off the track and gave the book a wholly artificial interpretation. The explanation we have given and the date we assign to the composition of the book are justified by abundant proofs in the special monographs we have so often quoted of Kuenen, Cornill [*Einleitung in das Alte Testament*, pp. 240-42; Box, pp. 254-56], and Wildeboer [?, p. 488]." The Book of Ruth may have all conceivable merits save possibly the merit of clearness, if it has taken the world some two thousand years to discover what it means! But lo—now, at last, we are privileged to know the great secret: "The Book of Ruth," says Piepenbring, "is in reality a very precious pendant to the reform of Esdras. It shows that the Jewish world as a whole did not allow itself to be carried away by the intolerant exclusive spirit of that scribe. . . . We learn in that way that mixed marriages which had been fought bitterly and in the mass by Esdras and his associates were justified not only from the standpoint of passion and interest but from the standpoint of justice and equity. At bottom, the author of the Book of Ruth placed the spiritual ties of religion above ties of blood, ascribing more importance to truly pious conduct than to flawless genealogy, and anticipating the doctrine of the Gospels that it is not necessary to be descended from Abraham in order to be a true believer." It cannot have been altogether by chance that such a

1629. Sometimes, and especially in olden times, the derivation becomes truly fantastic, as witness St. Bernard's long commentary on the Song of Songs. In it the fanciful manufacture of allegories oversteps all bounds. I select a few at random. There is the line: "My mother's children fought against me." [1] First, the Bride—that is to say, the Church—exclaims that she has been persecuted.[2] How can that be? Nothing simpler! "Annas, Caiaphas, and Judas Iscariot were children of the Synagogue, and the Church, which was also a child of the Synagogue, they cruelly beset at the time of her birth, crucifying her founder, Jesus. And so the Lord accomplished through them at that time what he had foretold of yore through the prophet, saying: 'I shall smite the shepherd and disperse his sheep.' . . . Of these, then, and of other such people who are known to have resisted the Church ye may consider that the Bride saith: 'My mother's children fought against me.' " [3]

Ecclesiastes and Ecclesiasticus have also exercised the commentators not a little. The latter was classed by the Protestants among the Apocrypha, but Ecclesiastes has held its place among the books of the biblical canon.[4] Epicurean maxims certainly abound in Eccle-

meaning should have been discovered in a humanitarian and democratic age such as our own. Gautier, *Introduction à l'Ancien Testament*, p. 152, says with much good sense: "To discover the provocation and purpose of the Book of Ruth, there is no need of resorting to ingenious and far-fetched conjectures. One has only to think of the fondness of Orientals for dramatic, striking stories that stir the emotions and are handed down from one generation to another." But that would be something far too simple for an inveterate interpreter.

1629 [1] Following the Vulgate, 1:5: "*Filii matris meae pugnaverunt contra me.*" King James Version, 1:6: "My mother's children were angry with me."

1629 [2] *In Cantica sermones*, 28, 13 (*Opera*, Vol. IV, p. 928): "*Adiiciens siquidem 'Filii matris meae pugnaverunt contra me,' persecutionem passam se esse aperte significat.*"

1629 [3] *Op. cit.*, 29, 1: "*Annas et Caiphas et Iudas Iscarioth filii synagogae fuerunt et hi contra Ecclesiam aeque synagogae filiam in ipso exortu ipsius acerbissime pugnaverunt, suspendentes in ligno collectorem ipsius Iesum. Iam tunc siquidem Deus implevit per eos quod olim praesignaverat per Prophetam, dicens: 'Percutiam pastorem, et dispergentur oves.' . . . De his ergo et aliis qui de illa gente Christiano nomini contradixisse sciuntur, puta dictum a sponsa: 'Filii matris meae pugnaverunt contra me.' "*

1629 [4] As regards Ecclesiasticus, one may read in an essay, "*Les livres apocryphes de l'Ancien Testament,*" which accompanies *La sagesse de Jésus fils de Sirach*, published by the Biblical Society of Paris, pp. 391-92: "The son of Sirach is not innocent of selfishness. The precepts of wisdom that abound in his book betray a too absorbing concern with personal interest. Even love of pleasure finds some echo

siastes, but the commentators twist them by ingenious interpretations into religious precepts. St. Jerome uses two methods in chief. On the one hand he assumes without trace of proof that the author is not speaking for himself when he recommends conviviality at table.[5] Then again he distorts to a spiritual significance what is obviously said in a material sense. So the reference to eating and drinking must be taken spiritually, and when the author speaks of embracing a woman, he must be understood as meaning the embrace of wisdom. On that basis Ovid's *Art of Love* could be turned into a moral and religious tract.[6]

1630. The Modernists found themselves confronted with the difficulties that had beset the path of their predecessors of old, in their effort to reconcile a traditional faith with a new one; and to surmount them they resorted to the identical devices that had been in

in his heart and he expresses himself in many places like a disciple of Epicurus. . . . However, such blemishes should not be exaggerated. On the whole the book is packed with good sense, uprightness, charity, piety."

1629 [5] *Commentarius in Ecclesiasten*, 9:7 (*Opera*, Vol. III, p. 1082): "*Go thy way, eat thy bread with joy, and drink thy wine with a merry heart.* Such, he says, the talk of some people—Epicurus, Aristippus, the Cyrenians, and other such cattle among the philosophers (*ceteri pecudes philosophorum*). But after pondering the matter diligently I find, not, as some falsely conclude, that all things are governed by chance and that a capricious fortune is at play in human affairs, but that all things happen by judgment of God."

1629 [6] *Ibid.*, 8:15 (*Opera*, Vol. III, p. 1079): "*Then I commended mirth, because a man hath no better thing under the sun than to eat and to drink and to be merry.* That we have interpreted more fully above, and now strictly we say that he prefers to the troubles of the world the pleasure of eating and drinking, fleeting and soon ended as such pleasure may be. . . . But this interpretation, taking the text as it is written, would prove that they that mourn and do hunger and thirst are the wretched ones, while Our Lord in the Gospel [Matt. 5:4, 6] calls them blessed. Let us therefore take the food and drink spiritually. . . . For [Matt., Chapter 9; Eccl. 3:11-13] the Lord's flesh [*i.e.*, communion] is the true food and His blood the true drink." *Loc. cit.*, p. 8 (Eccl. 3:1, 5) (*Opera*, Vol. III, p. 1036): "*To everything there is a season . . . a time to embrace, and a time to refrain from embracing.* The meaning is clear following the simplest interpretation (*juxta semplicem intelligentiam*): that one should attend to the matter of offspring and then again to continence, so harmonizing with what the Apostle says [I Cor. 7:5]: 'Defraud ye not one another except it be with consent for a time.' [Then comes an even stranger explanation:] Or else, that there was a time for embracing when the precept [Gen. 1:28] 'Be fruitful and multiply and replenish the earth' was in force. And after that, when that had been done, came a time to refrain from embracing. If, however [This is the best of all!], we choose to rise to loftier altitudes, we see Wisdom embracing those who love her . . . clutching them with her very nails to her bosom in tight embrace (*strictiori complexu*)."

use centuries and centuries before. The point of departure of the Modernists is the Holy Writ of the Christians, which they are bent on preserving; the point they desire to reach, a reconciliation of faith with "Science" and Democracy. As for "Science" they say, it is true, that they are immune to St. Gregory's rebuke of "moulding the heavenly pages of Scripture to philosophical doctrine"; but in actual fact they do everything in their power to effect that accommodation. That and no other is the origin of a certain "inner Christian experience," which they have fished up in caricature of the "experiment" known to chemistry, physics, and the other natural sciences.[1] As for Democracy, holy of holies, they betray their real thought clearly enough and but ill conceal their eagerness to win honours and favours of her.[2] But said blessed Democracy already has cor-

1630 [1] [Buonaiuti], *Il programma dei Modernisti: risposta all'Enciclica di Pio X, 'Pascendi Dominici gregis,'* p. 121 (Tyrrell, pp. 124-25): "As we have already said, in full accord with contemporary psychology Modernists sharply distinguish between science and faith. The mental processes that lead to science and those which lead to faith seem to them wholly foreign to each other, and independent." Excellent! But why such a great fuss, then, on the part of the Modernists, to reconcile science and faith? And one of their most revered leaders, M. Loisy, asks flatly, *L'Évangile et l'Église,* Preface, p. xxxiii: "Can conscience very long keep a God unknown to science, and will science forever respect a God of whom it has no knowledge?"

1630 [2] The same *Programma,* pp. 123-24 (Tyrrell, pp. 127-29), says of the Church (and Clericalism): "What popularity can petty and decrepit oligarchies of aristocrats give the Church, when in exchange for a little pomp they force upon her customs and procedures that are openly at war with the trend of the modern world? We understand that, and we speak our mind frankly: We are tired of seeing the Church reduced to a mere bureaucracy, jealous of powers she still retains and eager to regain powers she has lost. . . . The Church should feel a longing to embrace those currents of unwittingly religious feeling which are fostering the rise of democracy. She should find a way to merge with democracy, in order to give it a chance to succeed through the beneficent influence of her restraints and the stimulus of her moral leadership, which alone can impart lessons in abnegation and unselfishness. The Church should honestly recognize that in democracy a loftier expression of her own Catholicity is being formulated. And then democracy, in its turn, will come to feel the attraction of the Church as embodying the continuity of that Christian message in which democracy itself has its remote but none the less genuine origins." And one is tempted to add: "And then democracy, in its turn, will bounteously recompense deserters from the Catholic Church." However, once upon a time there were priests in France who in a similar frame of mind made common cause with the Third Estate to organize the National Assembly and so contributed to bringing on the Revolution. But they were sadly disappointed. Some of those good souls did not even collect Judas's thirty pieces of silver, but had to find their sole recompense in exile, prison, and the guillotine.

ralled the goddess Science for her Pantheon. What is to be done in that case? Nothing simpler! What on earth else were allegory and metaphor invented for? And lo, here cometh M. Loisy reviving under label of "modern" the old exegesis of Philo the Jew and denying the historicity of the Christ of John's Gospel![3] However, M. Loisy gives and takes away at one and the same time. Allegories and symbols are beautiful things, but after all reality is not to be despised: "The death of Jesus, accordingly, is a historical fact the reality of which has not undergone any transfiguration. But it belongs to faith not as a natural death, but as a voluntary death, as the outstanding symbol of redemption."[4] Hidden in a fog so thick, M. Loisy's idea is hard to capture: "Likewise, if one understands science as science is understood by the moderns, and with them by the scholars of Modernism, it is evident that science in itself [How is science in itself to be distinguished from plain ordinary science?] cannot be subordinated to faith, even though scientific labour, in so far as it emanates from a moral being, may be wholly inspired, one may even say governed, by the influence of faith." That is all a riddle! If "scientific labour" is inspired and governed by faith, how can the science which is the product of that work help being subordinate to faith? If you "inspire and govern" a workman, it would seem that what he produces would be subordinate to you. Epithets of course are, as usual, on hand to facilitate changes in the meanings of words and lift them from Earth to the clouds. Loisy's "science in itself" must be at the very least an own cousin, if not a born sister, of "right reason." Another beautiful unknown is "scientific work in so far as it emanates from a moral being." It would

1630 [3] Loisy, *Autour d'un petit livre,* pp. 93-95: "This Christ, to be sure, is not a metaphysical abstraction, for he is alive in the soul of the Evangelist. But this altogether spiritual and mystical Christ of faith is an undying Christ independent of the limitations of time and earthly existence. . . . John's narratives are not a history but a mystical contemplation of the Gospel. His harangues are theological meditations on the mystery of salvation. . . . The Christian Church allegorized the Old Testament. It did not refrain from allegorizing the Gospel narratives. . . . One must not find it surprising, therefore, that critical exegesis should discover allegories in the Fourth Gospel. . . . Was not allegory, in the eyes of Philo of Alexandria, the key to the Old Testament, the natural form of divine revelation? And is not the influence of Philoism on John beyond dispute?"

1630 [4] Loisy, *Simples réflexions sur . . . l'Encyclique "Pascendi Dominici gregis,"* pp. 170-71.

seem that the scientific achievement of formulating a mathematical theorem, or a uniformity in chemistry, physics, astronomy, or biology, would remain the same whether they "emanated" from moral or from immoral beings. How separate the sheep from the goats? Was Euclid a moral being, or was he not? We do not know! And do we care, if it is a question of judging his geometry? As compared with these foggy phrases of M. Loisy's, the papal encyclical, which he sets out to answer, reads like a model of clear statement, and in view of that very clarity it fails according to the Modernists accurately to represent their views, which mean and do not mean a thing at the same time.[5]

1631. A similar problem had to be solved by M. Léon Bourgeois and his brethren in "solidarity." There the point of departure was

---

1630 [5] *Acta pontificia*, October, 1907: *De Modernistarum doctrina . . . Pascendi dominici gregis*, p. 379: "So much . . . for the Modernist considered as a philosopher. If now, going on to consider him as a believer, we ask how, in Modernism, the believer is differentiated from the philosopher, we must observe that though the philosopher recognizes the reality of the divine as the object of faith, he will find that reality nowhere save in the soul of the believer, as an object of sentiment and profession. Whether or not it exists in itself independently of such sentiment and profession is a matter of indifference to him. [That is a good statement of the attitude of a person desirous of remaining within the field of logico-experimental science—save for the mention of a certain "reality of the divine," which is a non-experimental entity. But the Modernist cannot stick to the logico-experimental field, for there he would never establish his much-desired contact with Democracy, holy of holies, who does not frequent the sidewalks in those precincts. The Modernist, therefore, is a believer, and the encyclical goes on to show how the Modernist sets the believer over against the "philosopher":] The believer, on the contrary, holds as an unquestionable certainty that the divine reality really exists in itself and in no way depends upon the person who believes it. If we should go on to ask on what the believer's conviction is based, the Modernists reply: On *individual* experience. But if, in so saying, they part company with the rationalists, they fall into the opinion of the Protestants and the pseudo-mystics." It is in that, according to M. Loisy, that the encyclical seems to err. That is not the view of the Modernists, he says. But what their view actually is we cannot know unless Loisy expresses himself a little more intelligibly, clarifying the fog that enwraps a "science in itself," a "scientific work in so far as it emanates from a moral being," and many other obscurities of the kind. The encyclical further declares that science must be subordinate to faith. And since that statement is perfectly clear, perfectly clear also can be the answer of anyone who has resolved to keep to the field of logico-experimental science, and declares that he is in no way concerned with what faith, be it Catholic, Protestant, Moslem, Humanitarian, Democratic, or any other whatsoever, may try to prescribe for him in that field. Though from that it would by no means follow that under certain circumstances it may not be *useful* to believe that science should be subordinate to faith.

the present social system, and the goal to be reached a sort of middle-class Socialism. To effect the passage, derivations of various kinds were called in, among others a very pretty metaphor about a debt that is forever being paid but which is forever being reincurred so that it is always there (§ 1503). It all sounds like a jest, yet childish as it is, the argument is offered in all seriousness. Involved in the case is one of our III-δ derivations (juridical entities) that degenerates into a IV-δ or purely verbal derivation. The idea of a debt that is reincurred as fast as it is paid is juridical only in appearances: it is merely verbal.[1]

1632. For an example of the indirect use of metaphor, we may turn to the treatise *De baptismo,* 1, of Tertullian (*Opera,* Vol. IV, p. 157; English, Vol. I, pp. 231-32). He is attacking a woman, Quintilla by name, who has been preaching against baptism. He answers with an argument of the type described in § 1615: Quintilla, *A,* is a viper, *B,* because—he does not make the point, but we get it—because Quintilla has, in common with the viper, the characteristic, *P,*

1631 [1] *Essai d'une philosophie de la solidarité,* pp. 65, 77: "It must be positively understood that man cannot acquit himself once and for all, for the future as well as for the past. He must keep acquitting himself endlessly. Day by day he contracts a new debt that day by day he must pay. The individual must acquit himself at each moment, and so at each moment he reachieves his freedom." An individual, referred to in the text as *X,* was seized with panic lest, should his "debtors" clear their obligations, he should not be able to get anything more out of them—a situation that would in fact be defeating the practical purposes of "solidarity"! Said Monsieur *X:* "From the moral point of view, does not the notion of the acquittal of social debt lead, or possibly lead, to selfishness? When I have paid my debt, I am free. But am I not free also as regards human kindness, brotherly love? And would not that persuasion induce a certain dryness of heart?" Have no fear, good souls! The debts of your debtors are of a nature so marvellous that if they paid them in as many millions as there are grains of sand on the sea-shore they could never be free of them. M. Léon Bourgeois answers in fact: "That might be the case if the acquittal were a sweeping one covering everything for all time. [The reader will note the absence of any specification of amounts large or small.] But I have covered that point: A man is never completely freed. By the very fact that he goes on living, he acquires a new debt, a feeling that he owes something to his fellows, that they are his creditors, for ever laying hold on him!" Lucky for us that that blessed debt does not follow us after death, so that we are still allowed to think of the Grim Reaper as a Liberator! Meantime, supposing the debtor refuses to pay and tells Her Holiness Democracy to go West along with her prophets? Simple enough! Force is then called in! But in that case, why not resort to force in the first place without so much beating about the bush? Perhaps because chicanery is easier to use than force?

of being poisonous. The viper likes to live in dry places. That is a characteristic, *Q,* which is apparent enough in the viper but which is not so clearly apparent in Quintilla. But in view of Quintilla's resemblance to the viper, it is assumed that she must also affect the arid and loathe dampness and water, *C.* Then Tertullian repeats implicitly an argument of the same kind for the Christians. Christians are Christians because they have been baptized. People are baptized with water; therefore, anyone who is an enemy of water is an enemy of Christians.

One may doubt whether human being could ever have offered such a silly argument in earnest. But it may well have persuaded through the sentiments incidentally associated with the terms in which it is couched, proving acceptable as a medley of IV-β derivations.[1]

1633. Tertullian's treatise *On Baptism* is a veritable mine for derivations, and to note a few of them here will be a not altogether profitless digression. There were those who voiced their wonder that a few drops of water could confer the blessing of eternal life. Tertullian replies, Sec. 2, by pointing to pagan mysteries parallelling Christian baptism—a derivation based on analogy (derivation IV-δ) and authority (derivation II-β).[1] Next he inquires why it is that

---

1632 [1] "While living of late in that same place a certain viper [Quintilla] from the Gaian [Cainite] heresy laid hold on many people with her venomous doctrine [Heresy is poisonous, the viper is poisonous, therefore the heretic is a viper.], overthrowing more particularly the rite of baptism. That is all natural enough [Since the woman is a viper, she acts like a viper.]; for as a rule vipers, asps, and striped snakes (*reguli serpentes*) prefer arid waterless places. [A more effective manner of statement than by mentioning just the viper. In virtue of the incidental sentiments aroused, to yoke the asp and other snakes with the viper leaves the impression that the snake of heresy belongs with it just as well.] But we are little fishes. [In virtue of baptism. In his *De resurrectione carnis,* 52 (*Opera,* Vol. III, p. 251; English, Vol. II, p. 11), Tertullian says: "There is one sort of flesh—the flesh of fowls of the air, and that is the flesh of the Martyrs who aspire to loftier heights. Then there is the flesh of fishes who are nourished by the water of baptism."] We were born in water [Spiritually, that is, the water making us Christians.] following our Ἰχθύς, the Lord Jesus Christ, and we are saved only as we remain in the water. [A new metaphor: "to remain in the water" means to remain in the state of grace conferred by baptism.] That monster of a woman [Quintilla] therefore, who would have no right to teach even if she taught the truth (*cui nec integre quidem docendi ius erat*), knew it would be a fine way to destroy little fishes to take them out of the water." The logical inference from the argument by metaphor.

1633 [1] Returning to the same subject, *Ibid.,* 5, he cautions that the lustral waters of the heathen do not have the saving powers of Christian baptismal water

water is considered worthy of regenerating the Christian, and he answers with analogies involving residues of our I-β type (similarity, oppositeness). Then we get combinations of IV-δ (analogy) and III-α (accords of sentiment) derivations. First of all, says Tertullian, the origin of water has to be taken into account (*Opera*, Vol. IV, p. 159; English, Vol. I, p. 233): "In the beginning, it is written, God created Heaven and Earth. And the Earth was without form and void; and darkness was upon the face of the deep. And the Spirit of God moved upon the face of the waters. Therefore, O Man, must thou revere water, first for its antiquity, and then for its worthiness, since the Divine Spirit preferred it to all other elements for His throne." So he runs on, tossing many other beautiful bouquets to water, and stopping only in fear lest by continuing in the same vein he finish by making a panegyric on water instead of on baptism. All the same, a moment later, *Ibid.,* 9, he cannot resist the temptation to list other noble traits of water, and he shows that "water was very dear to God and His Christ." Water was used in Christ's baptism. He changed water into wine. He bade His disciples quench their thirst with water eternal, and among the acts of charity listed the offer of a goblet of water to the beggar. The conclusion is, *Ibid.,* 3, that there can be no doubt, since God made use of water in so many ways, that water should be used in His sacraments, and that "that which governs earthly life should have power to confer the heavenly."

1634. Tertullian then resorts to a derivation of the III-α type (universal consensus). He quotes, *Ibid.,* 5 (*Opera,* p. 152; English, p. 237), the belief that unclean spirits dwell upon the waters, and supports it by observing that persons who are killed, crazed, or terrified by water are called respectively nympholeptics, lymphatics, hydrophobics. That is one of the IV-δ derivations, the existence of a metaphorical term being taken as proof that a corresponding thing exists in reality. Having so established that unclean spirits dwell upon the waters and that they can harm people, Tertullian concludes, *Ibid.,* 4, with another IV-δ derivation: "It will not be difficult to believe that the holy angel of God doth apply water to the salvation of men,

($ 1292). The appeal to authority, therefore, serves merely to show that, in general, water can do wonderful things. In particular, of course, not all waters have that efficacy.

since the angel of evil, as is his profane habit, turneth the same elements to the hurt of man." The IV-δ derivation is itself re-enforced
with another of the IV-β type (accessory sentiments) that involves
residues of our I-β type (unusual occurrences).

1635. The compound derivation type, which is so naïvely manifest
in Tertullian's argument, figures in a manner now more, now less
dissembled in huge numbers of reasonings: one finds, that is, a IV-δ
derivation (metaphor, analogy), re-enforced by IV-β derivations
(accessory sentiments) that bring into play a great variety of residues and especially residues of Class I (combinations).

1636. Allegories and metaphors can be met with other allegories
and metaphors. Frequently enough an unscientific argument will
be victoriously refuted by an argument equally unscientific. What,
from the logico-experimental standpoint, may be a mere war of
words may, from the standpoint of doctrinal propaganda, be tre-
mendously effective in view of the sentiments that are called into
play.

1637. Opponents of the death-penalty have a commonplace based
on a metaphor. They say that the infliction of the death-penalty is
"legal murder," and that "Society" so meets one murder with another.

1638. People go even farther in that direction. Anatole France
says that the only way that has been found to punish thieves and
murderers is to imitate them and that, at bottom, justice serves
merely to double the number of crimes.[1] To be sure, from the logico-

---

1638 [1] *Opinions sociales,* Vol. II, pp. 196, 209, *La justice civile et militaire:* "I am
so far opposed to theft and murder that I cannot endure even legalized copies of
them and I am pained to see that the courts have found nothing better as a punishment for thieves and murderers than to imitate them. [A IV-γ derivation—terms
with varying meanings.] For, really now, Tournebroche, my boy, what is a fine
or an execution except a theft or a murder carried out with ceremonious pre-
meditation? Do you not see that, for all of the airs it puts on, our system of justice
amounts only to the shameful thing of avenging a wrong by a wrong, one wretched
act by another, and serves only to double, out of love of symmetry and balance, the
number of crimes and felonies?" Anatole France assumes that he is answering a
charge that he is "taking the part of thieves and murderers" and in that assumption we already get the beginning of the derivation. It is of little importance to the
public on just whose side M. France and his humanitarian friends desire to stand;
but it is of great importance that thieves and murderers should not be allowed to
run the streets in deference to the kind-heartedness of M. France and his friends.
Going on, France makes a prison warden his spokesman and has that character

experimental point of view, such verbiage is worth exactly as much as the chatter that is used to show that "Society" has a "right" to impose fines and inflict the death-penalty. But along with such problems of figures of speech there are other problems involving things. As a favour to Anatole France suppose we give identical

repeat commonplaces long familiar in humanitarian literature. So, he confides, "the longer I live, the more clearly I see that there is no such thing as a criminal—there is just an unfortunate." That may well be, but it is essential to know just what he means by "criminals" and what by "unfortunates." Let us imagine the case of a person who wants mad dogs and disease-bearing rats to be free to circulate at will, and is accused, as Anatole France assumes, of "siding with dangerous pests." He can reply: "I am so far opposed to killings by mad dogs and disease-bearing rats that I am pained to see that men have found no better way of defending themselves than by imitating mad dogs and disease-bearing rats in inflicting death on those animals. The longer I live the more clearly I see that among animals there are no 'criminals,' but just 'unfortunates.' " But here is the point, good man! For our part you may call mad dogs and disease-bearing rats criminals, unfortunates, or anything you please, provided you allow us to rid ourselves of them. And call thieves and murderers anything you please—call them saints at a venture—so long as you excuse us from living in the company of such "saints." That is all we ask of you. One need only open the morning newspaper to find an account of some laudable feat on the part of one of those "unfortunates" towards whom Anatole France has feelings of such pitying benevolence. I choose one at random: *Liberté*, Jan. 14, 1913: *"Girl used as target by thugs:* At Saint-Ouen, opening off No. 42 avenue des Batignolles, is a narrow blind-alley, lined with cottages. They are the homes of humble working-people with many children. The Paches are one of the most interesting of such families, since the father is a cripple from an accident at his work and can do only odd jobs. He has, however, managed to support his family of four children, and even to build a little house of his own on a microscopic plot at the end of the alley. The oldest of the children, Marcelle, has just reached her fifteenth birthday. She is in every respect the 'little mama' that is so frequently to be met with in poor and numerous families. Up at dawn, she makes breakfast for 'her babies,' then takes them all neatly dressed to day-school. Then she goes to a shop where she works all day, coming home at night to get supper for the family. Yesterday evening at seven o'clock, the 'little mama' went out to the end of the alley to draw water from the fountain there. A gang of young men stopped some yards away from the group formed by Marcelle and the 'big mothers.' 'Ready now!' cried one of the gangsters. It was a signal. A number of shots rang out one after the other. The 'little mama' gave a cry and sank to the pavement. A bullet had struck her in the middle of the forehead. The gangsters had merely used her as a target for revolver practice! The people of the neighbourhood came running. Marcelle was picked up from a pool of blood, while someone ran for Dr. Perraudeau. . . . The physician declared the child seriously injured and sent her to the Bichat hospital, where she was admitted." According to the theory of Anatole France, the "unfortunate" party in this case would be not the girl who was shot but her assailants. To the little girl people need not give a thought; much less should any measures be taken to prevent the recurrence of such incidents: only the footpad should have the benefit of "society's" tender solicitude.

names to the things that people have so far called now a "theft" and now a "fine," now a "murder" and now a "legal execution." However, it at once develops that if we are to understand each other, we have to make plain exactly what we are talking about. Suppose, then, we affix an asterisk to the term "theft *" when it designates a "fine," and an asterisk to the term "murder *" when it designates an infliction of the death-penalty. Now the problem of choosing names is not the only one. Suppose we should say to a man: "It is murder to kill your son. It is murder also to kill the bandit who is trying to kill your son. You therefore will not care whether you kill your son or the bandit." He, we may be sure, would answer: "The name is of no consequence to me! I am going to kill the bandit and save my son!" Names are of no consequence to human society either. Among the thing-problems that are here involved, two, in chief, are noteworthy: 1. How does it happen that the majority of civilized nations have met "theft" with "theft *," "murder" with "murder *"? 2. Are those measures effective, neutral, or positively harmful to the welfare of such societies? Obviously problems of that kind are to be solved only by considering things—not by considering the names of things. One must study the facts and not the metaphors of men of letters. The derivation used by M. Anatole France is copied from a general derivation that is very widely used among humanitarians. It tags the label of "unfortunates" upon criminals, and then, profiting by the ambiguous meanings of the term, concludes that criminals deserve "society's" most loving care.[2] Such the inspiration of certain books, such as Victor Hugo's *Les misérables,* with which literary men make fortunes by coddling humanitarian instincts in the public. The mad dog too is an "unfortunate"; and in his case, too, "society" has found nothing better to do than to match the death that he inflicts upon others with the death which is inflicted upon him. And that may well be an effective means of

---

1638 [2] This is a particular case of another very common derivation whereby agreeable names are given to people or things if the intent is to favour them, disagreeable names if the intent is to oppose them. At the present time in France, a defence counsel never breathes the word "crime" in connexion with a client. As Mme. Miropolska said in a lecture, *Liberté,* Feb. 19, 1913: "There are words that a lawyer never utters—'crime,' for instance. A defendant never answers for anything more than an 'act.' The talent of the defender lies in getting the jury's sympathy for all the circumstances that justify and simplify that 'act.'"

ridding society of the nuisance of certain criminals who are much more dangerous than mad dogs. The humanitarian fever has now become so acute that those who suffer from it are no longer satisfied with the supply of thrills offered by the present, but go hungrily delving into history, even into the history of the remote past, to find outlets for their idiotic sentimentality; and since men of talent are always on hand to provide what the public wants, we are witnessing most astonishing manifestations of sentiment in favour of criminals of generations past. One can hardly say whether it is in facetious satire of the humanitarian fever now raging, or out of love of paradox, or for both those reasons, that an eminent lawyer, M. Henri Robert, is going back to the somewhat stale case of Lady Macbeth to work up a stirring defence of that celebrated murderess, so stirring indeed that a humanitarian mob is already howling for her acquittal and rehabilitation. But there is better yet. A number of well-meaning individuals have just formed a committee to review the trial of the notorious Madame Lafarge that took place during the reign of Louis Philippe. Some day we shall probably read in the advertising columns of the newspapers: "A suitable reward will be paid to the person suggesting the *cause célèbre* that will make the best plaything for our habitual sobbers."[3]

1639. We have seen how a description, or a story, originating in a real fact of history and undergoing successive alterations, modifications, transformations, finally emerges as a legend. All the way along that path, allegories, metaphors, symbols, are grafted upon it,

1638 [3] See Henri Robert, *La défense de Lady Macbeth* and *L'affaire Lafarge*. Sorel, *Indépendance*, Oct. 10, 1912, p. 38: "The books that have been written to prove the innocence or guilt of Dreyfus fail altogether to satisfy people of any great amount of critical insight. That is readily comprehensible. The writers of such books work very much after the manner of certain scholars who go delving into the archives to review condemnations of the distant past. Everybody is now agreed as to the fatuousness of such enterprises. [Too benevolent a judgment on our times.] Legal experts [Not all! Not all!] rightly hold that, in matters of crime, intelligently conducted debates held shortly after the fact are alone likely to yield sound verdicts. The historian, however, does not stand entirely disarmed in the presence of old cases. He may determine in the light of the science of institutions whether procedure has been in accord with the spirit of the law. In case of a negative answer, he may pronounce that there is a presumption of error." That however is a road bristling with difficulties, and the probability of the presumption so obtained is very slight.

and so the legend grows and evolves, diverging more and more from the historical fact from which it sprang.[1]

1640. And that is the case of procedure from the thing to the word. But legends also grow by the converse procedure from the word to the thing—the legend, that is, having no slightest foundation in fact, is created out of whole cloth on the basis of certain words. It also happens, in the concrete, that the two methods are followed side by side. A real incident gives rise to a story. Then the story is altered, modified, embroidered with metaphor and allegory. Then the metaphors and allegories are taken as representing real things. The procedure, that is, is from words to things which are imaginary; but these are forthwith taken for real things, and serve in turn as points of departure for new stories and new metaphors— and so on indefinitely.

1641. The need human beings feel for exercising their faculties of reasoning and logic (I-ε residues) is of such effect that when their attention is caught by some term, T, they insist on explaining it—

1639 [1] In his *Dictionnaire historique, s.v. Tanaquil,* Bayle quotes a passage from Pliny, *Historia naturalis,* VIII, 74 (Bostock-Riley, Vol. II, p. 336): "Marcus Varro relates as an eyewitness that in his day in the Temple of Sancus one could still see wool on the distaff and spindle of Tanaquil, also called Gaia Cecilia, and in the Temple of Fortune, a waved royal robe which she had made and which Servius Tullius had worn. Hence the custom that when a young woman is married, she carries in her wedding-march a dressed distaff and a loaded spindle. Tanaquil invented the art of making the straight tunic such as is worn by young men and newly married girls along with the plain white toga." Bayle also calls attention to a passage in Plutarch, *Quaestiones Romanae,* 30 (Goodwin, Vol. II, p. 221), where a second answer is suggested for the question: "When a bride is introduced [to her home] why is she expected to say: 'Where thou art Gaius, there shall I be Gaia'?" Says Plutarch: "Is it perhaps because Gaia Cecilia, wife to one of the sons of Tarquinius, was a matron beautiful and pure? A bronze statue to that matron was erected in the temple of Santus [The name is variously spelled.]; and there, also, once upon a time, were treasured her sandals and her spindles, the former as a symbol of her domestic virtues, the latter of her industriousness." After a digression upon other matters, Bayle continues: "A Frenchman writing in the sixteenth century [Fr. Tillier, of Tours, *Philogame, ou l'ami des noces,* Paris, 1578, p. 120] comes out with a statement that he would have found it impossible to prove. 'The Tarquins,' says he, 'had had a statue erected in their palace, with nothing but a pair of house-slippers, a distaff, and a spindle. That was to encourage successors of their family to imitate their assiduous meticulousness in frugality (*en mesnageant*) and in keeping to their home.' Such the fate of Pliny's account of the statue of Tanaquil! Everyone takes it upon himself to alter some detail or other in a story he tells. So facts are distorted and rapidly degenerate in the hands of those who quote them."

that is to say, on drawing more or less logical derivations from it. So it comes about that from the same T one writer will arrive at certain things, A, which are altogether imaginary; and another, at still different things, B, likewise imaginary; and still other writers will use other derivations. The things A, B . . . derived from T

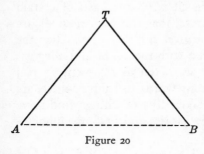

Figure 20

sometimes bear resemblances to each other, and the resemblance may even be considerable. When only A and B are known, there is no way of telling whether B is established by means of A, copying A in part; or whether A is established by means of B, copying B in part; or whether A and B are independent, having a common origin, T.[1] There are examples of each of those phenomena; and a choice between them *a priori* is impossible: we have to fall back on observation of fact and see which of the paths, TA, TB, AB, has actually been followed—sometimes they may all three have been used. Situations of this kind arise in investigations as to literary sources. Nowadays there is too much of an inclination toward guess-work in that field, and many researches of that type rest on exceedingly slim foundations.[2]

1641 [1] Renan, *Histoire du peuple d'Israël*, Vol. V, p. 70: "Resemblances are not proof of deliberate imitation. The scope of the religious imagination is not very broad—intertwinings arise in the very nature of things. One same result may have altogether different causes. All monastic rules are alike. The cycle of pious inventions offers scant variety." What Renan says here of religious institutions applies equally well to institutions of other sorts.

1641 [2] Let us, as usual, fall back on the method suggested in § 547. *Journal de Genève*, Feb. 26, 1913: "The literary reporters of German Switzerland have just fought a great battle—with windmills. They have been the victims of a hoax. M. Loosli had solemnly asserted in a long magazine article that the real author of the works of Jeremias Gotthelf was not Albert Bitzius, but a friend of his, J. U. Geissbühler. The declaration had aroused lively excitement among the outstanding critics and the 'Gotthelf question' had become a subject of passionate discussion in the newspapers. Now in the last number of *Heimat und Fremde*, M. Loosli explains that the idea of his practical joke came to him in the course of a conversation with a friend on the Bacon-Shakespeare controversy. M. Loosli had remarked to his companion on the ease with which the genuineness of the literary work of any writer could be disputed fifty years after his death. All one had to do was to put out some absurd statement with an air of authority. The

1642. If A is anterior in time to B, many literary historians will regard B out of hand as an imitation of A. We have seen cases (§§ 733 f.) where the absolute falseness of such an inference is clearly apparent. The mere fact that A resembles B and is anterior to B in time does not warrant any conclusion as to any dependence of B upon A. Other facts, other observations, are required.

1643. Well known the fact that the Fourth Gospel is widely different in style from the other three—it contains much more metaphysics, much more symbolism, than they contain. Now the author

world of literary pontiffs could then be relied on to grasp at it and discuss it with all the seriousness imaginable. His companion remaining unconvinced, M. Loosli made a bet that he could prove it and at the height of the season sent to the magazine in Berne the article that set all the Swiss press agog. Before publishing his article, however, he took the precaution to deposit with a notary a sealed envelope containing the following statement: 'Bümplitz, Jan. 4, 1913: I have this day drawn up, under title of "Jeremias Gotthelf—A Literary Riddle," an outline that I intend to publish and in which I show that the real author of the works of Jeremias Gotthelf was not Albert Bitzius, but his contemporary and friend, J. U. Geissbühler. This I have done with the idea of demonstrating by a practical example how easy it is to devise ridiculous hypotheses in the field of philology and for the pleasure of having a laugh at the expense of the scholars who will attack my article. I desire to give a lesson to philologists, because in my judgment they are betraying art and poetry. I am this day depositing this explanation with the notary Gfeller at Bümplitz and I shall publish it when the time comes. This I do to avoid any misunderstanding of my conduct and to protect the memory of Albert Bitzius from overzealous philologists. C. A. Loosli.' That document was supplemented by another: 'I, the undersigned, certify that the document herewith has been lying under seal in my office from Jan. 4, 1913, to the present time. Bümplitz, Feb. 15, 1913. Office of Public Notary Gfeller, Luthi, public notary.' The theory put forward by one of the victims of the jest that M. Loosli had gone off at half-cock and then tried to save his face by pretending that he had been joking has therefore to be discarded. In his new article the jester, M. Loosli, rubs it in: 'My article,' he writes, 'contained as many absurdities as words. It cannot bear examination and be taken seriously by any sensible person. Anyone at all wide-awake should have seen at once that it was a hoax. In spite of all that, I have before me articles with judgments like these: "A very plausible hypothesis" (*Frankfurter Zeitung*); "Bitzius the man may not be affected by M. Loosli's declarations, but Bitzius the poet will surely be, for just as Homer was not the man who . . ." (*National Zeitung*).' M. Loosli continues: 'The *Nachrichten* of Zürich and the *Bund* naturally devoted full-fledged articles to my "revelations" and the question was discussed at length by the Swiss press generally, and even abroad. The public had its hankerings for a sensation satisfied, and the name of Gotthelf, which is ordinarily of as much public concern as a dill-pickle, is today in every mouth. As I had foreseen, the national vanity was pricked and a most impressive group of Gotthelf specialists have been given an opportunity to display their learning in this battle with a ghost.' "

of the Fourth Gospel may well be narrating in a way of his own facts of which he had the same knowledge as the other three evangelists (he may, that is, be working from fact to theory). But it may just as well be that he got his facts at second hand and is giving his own metaphysical interpretation of them (that he is working from theory to fact). Nor is it by any means impossible that he is working in both those ways at the same time.[1]

1644. St. Paul in his day alludes to a certain "deceitful learning" (Ephes. 5:6 ["vain words"]), which may have been something along the lines of what was subsequently known as Gnosticism, something like the embellishments in the Fourth Gospel. We are not inquiring here as to whether there may have been some direct connexion between Gnosticism and the Fourth Gospel or whether the two things arose independently from the general human need of ratiocination, of giving a metaphysical elaboration to history or legend; or whether, finally, they arose in some other manner. Here we are looking at them as mere facts; and we note that they show a certain gradation, the maximum metaphysical development appearing in the Gnosis.[1]

1645. The terms "Gnosis," "Gnosticism," are not very definite. Suppose we ignore Clement of Alexandria, in whose eyes the true Gnostic was the Catholic, and keep to the heretical sects. There are numbers of such. Even Manicheism has its connexions with the Gnosis.[1] Let us keep, in fact, to the Valentinian Gnosis, as the type

1643 [1] I have no slightest intention here of going into these problems in themselves, nor of adding one chapter more to the many that have already been written on this subject. I am viewing the case in a very restricted aspect, as an example of derivations.

1644 [1] Buonaiuti, Lo gnosticismo, p. 124: "Gnosticism is a gigantic manifestation of a morbidly exhilarated religious psychology. [That is to say, it shows on a larger scale mental processes that are observable in many other manifestations of religion.] From humble beginnings it little by little grew to alarming proportions under the favourable conditions supplied by the intellectual atmosphere that prevailed in Rome during the second and third centuries. It serves no purpose, therefore, to break it up, dissect it, analyze it into its various coefficients. It is a complex phenomenon deriving its substance from a thousand sources and protruding its insidious tentacles upon a thousand different temperaments."

1645 [1] Our knowledge of Gnostic doctrine is derived almost exclusively from what its Christian adversaries say of it; but, from the little that is to be gathered from other sources, it seems that on the whole the Christians gave a fairly accurate picture of it. That at least seems to be indicated by Gnostic fragments recently recovered. We are in no sense interested here in the difficult, and for the present

of the species. In it one notes broad traces of procedure from the word to the thing. Words become persons, and the person retains a sex corresponding to the grammatical gender of the word. These entities of differing sex once created, they are made to copulate and give birth to new entities, which are not distinguishable from the words that serve as their names. Then the legend grows more and more elaborate. The entities have all the characteristics of the words, and live and act according to those traits. Numbers have their rôle in the legend. Whether deriving it from the Pythagoreans or other-wise, the Valentinians have a notion that there is something real corresponding to some perfection or other which they manage to see in numbers, and to that perfection they assign a place in their legend. Certain entities called "Aeons" play a leading part in Gnostic doctrine. It proves impossible to determine what on earth was meant by the word. But that need not distress us. Very probably the Gnos-tics did not know themselves.[2]

partly unsolvable, problems that arise in connexion with Gnosticism and the Gnostics. We are not writing the history of the doctrine. We are merely looking for examples of derivations. Amélineau, *Les traités gnostiques d'Oxford*, p. 39: "The publication of these two treatises seems to me in every respect important. In them we have two Gnostic documents of the second century, two works that are genuine in spite of the absence of any author's name and whatever the view one take of them. They enable us to study Gnosticism directly, test the assertions of the Church Fathers, determine that they were most often intelligent epitomizers speaking always in good faith, but that often also they did not grasp the ideas of the Gnostics and occasionally distorted their meanings, not deliberately but by mis-take." The Fathers gave a more rational, or rather a less absurd, semblance to the vagaries that are now accessible in the documents published by Amélineau. For example, p. 9: "What is the issue in this second treatise? In the first place, it is a question of the initiation that Jesus gives to His disciples in order to perfect their possession of the Gnosis, of the 'passwords' which He imparts to them, to enable them to traverse one world after another and finally to reach the last where the Father of all Fatherhood, the God of Truth, abides. The word 'mystery' must here be taken as referring either to the mysteries of the initiation, or to the mysteries of each Aeon, which is made up of a number of mysterious regions them-selves inhabited by hosts of powers, the ones more mysterious than the others. . . . The word Logos must be taken here as referring not to the Aeon-Logos, but to the passwords, the great and mysterious passwords that the Word gives to the Gnostics that they may reach the abode of the God of Truth after making their way through all the aeons, without, meantime, suffering in any respect from the con-duct of their inhabitants. The title of this second treatise is nothing more than one of those plays on words which were so dear to the Egyptians."

1645 [2] The principal meaning of αἰών seems to be a great, an immense, expanse of time—eternity. We say principal, not primary; for here we are classifying things,

1646. St. Irenaeus of Marseilles gives an account of the Valentinian system. He wrote in Greek. Only fragments of his text are still extant, but an old Latin translation is available. Here I shall translate from the Greek, and since the genders of the Greek words are lost in English and are frequently different in Italian or French, I shall mark them as (*m*) or (*f*) according as the Greek word is masculine or feminine. "It is said that at a height invisible and incalculable there abideth a perfect pre-existing Aeon. This also . . . [lacuna in ms.] they call First Father and Abyss (*m*) . . . [lacuna] Being infinite, invisible, eternal, increate, he did abide at rest and in perfect peace for infinite time eternal. With him did abide Idea (*f*)

not debating origins. Hesiod, *Theogonia,* v. 609 (White, pp. 122-23): ἀπ᾽ αἰῶνος: "From the most remote times." In the *Timaeus,* 37D, Plato says that God created the heavens "to make of them a mobile image of eternity": εἰκὼ . . . κινητόν τινα αἰῶνος ποιῆσαι. Aristotle, *De coelo,* I, 9, 11: "It is an aeon, having taken its name from its ever being" [Hardie-Gaye, Vol. III, p. 279a: Aiôn: "duration, a name based upon the fact that it *is* always—durable, immortal and divine."] There are other abstract meanings of the kind indicating long spaces of time, such as a century, a human lifetime. In a chapter of the *De fide orthodoxa,* II, 1, which he entitles Περὶ αἰῶνος (*De saeculo sive aevo*), St. John Damascene notes all those various senses (*Opera,* Vol. I, p. 862; Salmond, p. 18). A bare hint of personification is detectable in Euripides, *Heraclidae,* v. 895 (900) (Coleridge, Vol. I, p. 179), where αἰών, "Time," is said to be a "child of Saturn" (Cronus). One may also take the passage in the sense of "the succession of the ages born of time": "For Fate-Which-Leads-To-The-End, and Time, the child of Cronus, bring forth many things." That is a poetic personification, such as Claudian uses in his panegyric *De consulatu Stilichonis,* II, vv. 424-27 (*Carmina,* Vol. II, p. 32):

> "*Est ignota procul nostraeque impervia menti—*
> *vix adeunda Deis—annorum squalida mater,*
> *immensi spelunca* aevi, *quae tempora vasto*
> *suppeditat revocatque sinu. . . .*"

("Far away, unexplored of man, nay inaccessible to our minds and hardly approachable of the gods, is the dark and uncouth Mother of the years, the grotto of endless Eternity which supplies the cycles of time, calling them forth from its own infinite bosom.") Arrian, *Epicteti dissertationes,* II, 5, 13, seems to take the word "aeon" in the sense of an immortal being: Οὐ γάρ εἰμι αἰὼν ἀλλ᾽ ἄνθρωπος: ("For I am not an aeon, but a man"). ·Tatian, *Oratio adversus Graecos,* 20 (Migne, p. 851; English, p. 26), alludes to αἰῶνες in a context that does not make his exact meaning clear, though he seems to be thinking of "worlds," "regions": "For the sky is not infinite, O human, but finite and circumscribed; and above it are better aeons, which suffer not change of season whereof our various diseases spring, but have full enjoyment of a mild clime, of perpetual day, and of a light inaccessible to men." There have been two types of translation for the word "aeons" in this passage. Puech, for example, *Recherches sur le discours de Tatien,* p. 134, renders it by "worlds" and annotates: "*Aeones* 'centuries,' 'worlds' is one of the words

whom they also call Grace (*f*) and Silence (*f*). And at a certain time it was his pleasure that said Abyss should be made manifest as the principle of all things. This emanation (which he had been pleased to put forth) he did place as seed in the matrix, as it were, of his companion Silence (*f*). And she did receive said seed and did conceive and gave birth to Mind (or Reason) (*m*), one like and equal unto him who had begotten him and alone encompassing the greatness of his father. This Mind (*m*) they also call the Only-Begotten, father and principle of all things. And at the same time was begotten Truth (*f*). This, then, is the primal and first-born Pythagorean quaternion, which they call also the root of all things: and to

Tatian uses in common with the Gnostics." Otto, for the other type, renders, p. 91, by "centuries" (*saecula praestantiora*), as does Migne's editor also, p. 851. The latter explains: "It is a question of Paradise, which he locates in a land far better than ours." That would indicate that even those who translate "aeon" as *saeculum*, "century," may think of it as a world, a region. With the Gnostics the Aeons become persons and regions, and they are also considered under various aspects. In his diatribe *Adversus Valentinianos*, 7 (*Opera*, Vol. II, p. 116; English, Vol. II, p. 128), Tertullian says of the god: "Considering him in terms of substance they call him 'perfect aeon' (Αἰῶνα τέλειον); and in terms of person, 'first principle,' Προαρχή, 'principle,' Ἀρχή, and also 'Abyss,' 'Bython,' a name in no way suitable to a being inhabiting regions so sublime." Amélineau, *Les traités gnostiques d'Oxford*, p. 23 (Jesus taught His disciples that after death they would traverse the aeons): "There . . . we get the numbers corresponding to each world of seals, that is to say, the magic words which a person had to have and know in order to enter each aeon. . . . We also learn the 'apologies' that had to be recited, the words, that is, which had to be uttered in order to convince the Aeons that there was no trickery in one's possessing the number and the seal. . . . Use of the number, the talisman, had marvellous effects. When the soul presented itself in a given world all its Archons, all its Powers, all its denizens, in a word, came running toward it, ready to wreak all the chastisement the soul's temerity had incurred. But it pronounced the number, showed the talisman, recited the formula, and straightway Archons, Powers, inhabitants, gave ground before it, taking flight towards the West." *Idem, Notice sur le papyrus gnostique de Bruce*, pp. 194-95 (Jesus says to his disciples): " 'I will now give you the "apology" for all these places of which I have given you the mysteries [passwords] and the baptisms. . . . When you have left the body and perform these mysteries for all the aeons and all those who are in them, they will retreat [before you] until you come to these six great aeons. They will flee to the West, to the left, with all their Archons, and all who are in them.' " To recapitulate: the term "aeons" seems to have had three meanings for the Gnostics: (1) a metaphysical meaning with some bearing on eternity; (2) a meaning that tends to make an aeon a person; (3) a meaning that tends to make an aeon a place. But such meanings are not kept distinct. The metaphysical trait is extended to persons and places, the persons are something like places, and the places act like persons.

wit: Abyss (m) and Silence (f), and then Mind (m) and Truth (f)." [1] After this first quaternion there comes another made up of: The Word (m) and the Life (f), and Man (m) and the Church (f). The two quaternions added together yield an octad (ὀγδοάς), which, it would seem, must have been a very pretty thing. The Word and the Life beget another ten Aeons whose names I may be spared from giving here; and copulating with Dame Church (Ἐκκλσία) Milord Man begets a baker's dozen more. The Aeons, all told, are thirty and make up the Pleroma. [2] Then comes a long

1646 [1] Irenaeus, Contra haereses, I, 1, 1 (Migne, pp. 446-47; Keble, pp. 3-4): Λέγουσι γάρ τινα εἶναι ἐν ἀοράτοις καὶ ἀκατονομάστοις ὑφώμασι τέλειον αἰῶνα προόντα· τοῦτον δὲ καὶ [lacuna] Προπάτορα καὶ Βυθὸν καλοῦσιν [lacuna] ὑπάρχοντα δ' αὐτὸν ἀχώρητον καὶ ἀόρατον, ἀίδιόν τε καὶ ἀγέννητον, ἐν ἡσυχίᾳ καὶ ἠρεμίᾳ πολλῇ γεγονέναι ἐν ἀπείροις αἰῶσι χρόνων. συνυπάρχειν δ'αὐτῷ καὶ 'Εννοίαν, ἣν δὴ καὶ Χάριν καὶ Σιγὴν ὀνομάζουσι. καὶ ἐννοηθῆναί ποτε ἀφ'ἑαυτοῦ προβαλέσθαι τὸν Βυθὸν τοῦτον ἀρχὴν τῶν πάντων. καὶ καθάπερ σπέρμα τὴν προβολὴν ταύτην (ἣν προβαλέσθαι ἐνενοήθη) καὶ καθέσθαι, ὡς ἐν μήτρᾳ, τῇ συνυπαρχούσῃ ἑαυτῷ Σιγῇ. ταύτην δὲ ὑποδεξαμένην τὸ σπέρμα τοῦτο, καὶ ἐγκύμονα γενομένην ἀποκνῆσαι Νοῦν, ὁμοῖόν τε, καὶ ἴσον τῷ προβαλόντι, καὶ μόνον χωροῦντα τὸ μέγεθος τοῦ πατρός. τὸν δὲ Νοῦν τοῦτον καὶ Μονογενῆ καλοῦσι, καὶ πατέρα καὶ ἀρχὴν τῶν πάντων. συμπροβεβλῆσθαι δὲ αὐτῷ 'Αλήθειαν· καὶ εἶναι ταύτην πρῶτον καὶ ἀρχέγονον Πυθαγορικὴν τετρακτὺν ἢ καὶ ῥίζαν τῶν πάντων καλοῦσιν. ἐστι γὰρ Βυθὸς καὶ Σιγή, ἔπειτα Νοῦς καὶ 'Αλήθεια. On the epithets "First Father and Abyss" (Προπάτορα καὶ Βυθόν) Grabe notes: "Synesius, bishop of Ptolemais, not only used poetical licences in his hymns but adapted almost all the mataeology of the Valentinians to true theology singing the orthodox faith in heretical words. These two epithets, for instance, he applied to God the Father as in Hymn II, v. 27 (Opera, p. 317; Fitzgerald, Vol. II, p. 374): 'Paternal Deep' βυθὸς πατρῶος (profundum paternum); III, v. 147 (Opera, p. 321; Fitzgerald, Vol. II, p. 377): 'Fatherless First Father' (προπάτωρ ἀπάτωρ) and IV, v. 69 (Opera, p. 336; Fitzgerald, Vol. II, p. 384): 'Beauty unsoundable' (βύθιον κάλλος: immensa pulchritudo)." It is instructive to compare this description with the one in the Bruce papyri: Amélineau, Notice, pp. 89-92: "It [he] is the First Father of all things, the Prime Eternal, the King of the Unattainable [those who cannot be touched], the Gulf of All Things. . . . It [he] has been given no name since it [he] is unnamable and unthinkable. . . . The second place is called Demiurge, Father, Logos, Source, Mind, Man, Eternal, Infinite. It [he] is the prop [column], the overseer, the Father of all things, the Ennead which issued from the Father without beginning, father and mother to itself, the one which [whom] the Pleroma girt about the twelve abysses. The first abyss is the universal source from which all sources have issued. The second abyss is the universal wisdom, source of all wisdoms." And so on and on. The other abysses are: "Universal Mystery; Universal Gnosis; Universal Purity; Silence; Universal Essence before All Essence; the Propator; the Pantopator or Autopator, Omnipotence, the Invisible Truth." [Another truth to add to the long list we have already seen.—A. L.]

1646 [2] Amélineau, Les traités, etc., pp. 24-25, thinks he can identify three different pleromata in the Bruce papyri: "The word Pleroma has, I think, three very different meanings, or at the very least two that are certain. It seems to me first

story about the "passion" of Sophia (f)—Wisdom.[3] It must derive
from the Valentinians, who believed that Abyss had begotten a son
agamogenetically. It tells how Sophia "tried to emulate her father
and herself engender without a mate, that she might perform a feat
in no way inferior to her father's. She did not know that only he
who is increate, principle, root, altitude and abyss, can engender
without a mate." [4] Hera also was minded to emulate Zeus, who had
given birth to Athena all by himself, and without consort with any
mate she bore Hephaestus (Vulcan), who, saving the detail that one

to designate the aggregate of worlds, including our Earth; but on our Earth it is
applicable only to psychics qualified for admittance to some of the prerogatives
of the true Gnostic, and of inspired individuals (pneumatics) who enjoy those
prerogatives by essence. The 'hylics' are not of that number, because they belong
to the evil creation, or 'essence of the left,' to use their expression, and are to be
destroyed, annihilated. I would not be too positive about this understanding of the
word 'Pleroma.' It is not categorically established. It seems however to be the one
that is implied by the texts, especially the two here in hand. In any case, it is certain
that the word 'Pleroma' designates the intermediate and upper worlds taken together, in other words all the intermediate aeons between our Earth and the higher
Pleroma including the aeons of the latter Pleroma itself. Finally, the term
'Pleroma' is often used as a designation for the upper world alone. That upper
world is called the 'Aeon of the Treasure,' and the Treasure, like all treasuries,
contains a number of precious articles—sixty aeons, to be specific."

1646 [3] Cf. [Origen ?], Philosophumena, VI, 2, 30: It was the last of the
twenty-eight Aeons, "being female and called Sophia (θῆλυς ὢν καὶ καλούμενος Σοφία)."
Here the explicit attribution of sex leaves no room for doubt.

1646 [4] Philosophumena, VI, 2, 30. Other versions differ from this one and are to
a greater extent allegorical. Irenaeus, and Tertullian who follows him (Adversus
Valentinianos, 9-10; Opera, Vol. II, pp. 119-21), relate that Sophia desired to encompass her father's immensity. Unable to realize that ambition she began to
pine, and would have vanished altogether had not Limit ("Ορος [m]) come to the
rescue. Some Valentinians say that in the course of that arduous quest she bore
Cogitation (f) (or "Passion": ἐνθύμησις [f]); others, that the offspring was Matter-
without-Form, a female entity (Iraeneus, Op. cit., I, 2, 2; Migne, pp. 455-58;
Keble, p. 6).

It would seem that Gnostics were still to be found as late as the nineteenth century and that they were well acquainted with Sophia. Jules Bois, Les petites
religions de Paris, p. 176, puts the following words into the mouth of one Jules
Doinel, a Gnostic: " 'Do you know,' asked the Apostle, 'why we suffer and are so
often bad? The Demiurge, not God Himself, created the world. This Demiurge, a
clumsy workman in the service of Sophia, soul of the Universe, who fell through
her noble desire to know too much, made us in his own image and it was not a
very beautiful one. But Sophia took pity on us. By her decree, one of her tears
dropping from heaven took up its abode in our human clay. Demiurge got even
by binding man to the flesh, and he will never get free of it except through knowledge of his destiny, through the Gnosis."

of his legs was shorter than the other, was an up-and-doing god. Poor Sophia had no such luck: "She produced only what she could produce, namely, substance, formless and chaotic; and that is what Moses says: 'The earth was without form and void.'" [5] And that is far from being the end of the story.

1647. The polemist of the *Philosophumena* is interested chiefly in the metaphysical allegories of the Valentinians and declares, VI, 2, 29, that Valentinus got his doctrine, not from the Gospels, but from Pythagoras and Plato.[1] St. Epiphanius, for his part, fixes on the personifications and declares, *Panarium adversus haereses,* I, 3 (*Opera,* Vol. I, p. 478), that they repeat the genealogies of the pagan gods as reported by Hesiod, Stesichorus, and other poets.[2] Those two manners of approaching the Valentinian doctrine have each their modicum of truth; but we must not be forgetting that all meta-physical dreamers have a common fountain-head of inspiration, as

1646 [5] *Philosophumena, loc. cit.*

1647 [1] Tertullian, *Adversus Valentinianos,* 1 (*Opera,* Vol. II, p. 110; English, Vol. II, p. 120), compares the Valentinian mysteries with the Eleusinian: "*Eleusinia Valentiniani fecerunt lenocinia* (practised the Eleusinian whorings)."

1647 [2] The Bruce papyri give comical details of personification: Amélineau, *Les traités,* pp. 91, 97-99: "The light of his [its] eyes reaches forth from the regions of the outer Pleroma and the Word issues from his [its] mouth. . . . The hairs of his [its] head are equal in number to the hidden worlds. The lineaments of his [its] countenance are the image of the aeons. The hairs of his [its] beard equal in number the number of the outer worlds." All names become things: "There is also another place that is called 'Abyss' and there there are three Paternities. . . . In the second Paternity there are five trees with a table in the midst thereof, and enthroned on the table is a Word, the Unigenitus (*Monogenes*) having the twelve countenances of the Mind (*Nous*) of all things, and the prayers of all creatures are laid before him [it]. . . . And this Christ has twelve countenances. . . . Each Paternity has three countenances." This whole passage on the "Second Place" Buonaiuti, following Carl Schmidt [*Gnostische Schriften,* p. 278], translates as follows: *Lo gnosticismo,* p. 211: "The second place is the one called Demiurge, Father, Logos, Source, Nous, Man, Eternal, Infinite. He is the Pillar, the Super-visor, the Father of all things. He is he upon whose head the Aeons form a crown and he doth sparkle with their rays. The lineaments of his countenance cannot be seen in the outer worlds, which do yearn at all times to behold his face, for they would know him, since his Word hath come unto them and they would behold him. And the light of his eyes doth penetrate to the innermost places of the outer Pleroma, and the Word doth issue from his mouth, and doth reach forth above and below in all directions. The hairs of his head are equal in number to the hidden worlds, and the lineaments of his countenance are the reflection of the Aeons; and the hairs of his beard are equal in number to the number of the outer worlds."

do all creators of legend.[3] It is therefore difficult to determine just how far they are copying one another and to just what extent the ideas they express are spontaneous and original in each (§§ 733 f.).

1648. Certainly there are many cases where direct proofs of plagiarism, interpolation, falsification, are available; and others where evidence likewise direct creates great probability of imitation. But when direct proofs are altogether lacking, it is unjustifiable to infer imitation from resemblances alone. It is often difficult, for instance, to identify the reciprocal imitations of neo-Orphism and Christianity and distinguish elements of spontaneous origin from those which were merely copied.[1] Those scholars, Hebrew and Christian, who thought Plato had imitated the sacred writings of the Jews were on the wrong track. But their thesis could easily be made over into something in harmony with the facts, if one were to say that Hebrews, Christians, writers such as Plato, the Orphic poets, and so on, derived their notions from a common fund of residues and derivations. That is alone enough to explain resemblances between doctrines of independent origin. When, in course of time, such doctrines come into contact with elements of the same sort that have developed independently elsewhere, imitations occur sometimes by deliberate design, sometimes unconsciously.[2]

1647 [3] [*I.e.*, Class I and Class II residues, and IV-δ derivations.—A. L.]

1648 [1] One of the Orphic theogonies has some points of resemblance to the Gnostic; but that lone fact is not enough to show whether and to what extent there has been imitation. Daremberg-Saglio, *Dictionnaire, s.v. Orphici:* "The final version [of the theogony of the rhapsodes] seems to belong to a fairly late epoch, but the essential elements in the system may be very ancient and go back in part as far as the sixth century [B.C.]. Here is a résumé of the theogony: In the beginning was Cronus, or Time, and he produced Aether and Chaos whose marriage resulted in the Cosmic Egg, a huge silver egg. From it issued a god of many heads—they were heads of animals. At once male and female he contained all things in germ. He was called Phanes, but he also had other names: Protogonus, Ericapaeus, Metis, Eros. At the time when the god left the Cosmic Egg, its upper half became the firmament, its lower half the Earth."

1648 [2] Aristobulus, a Hebrew philosopher quoted by Eusebius, *Evangelica praeparatio,* XIII, 12, declares that Plato evidently utilized the books of the Hebrew law. Justin Martyr, *Apologia,* I, 59, 60 (Migne, pp. 415-19; Davie, pp. 45-46), mentions doctrines that Plato got from the Bible, and in his *Cohortatio ad Graecos,* 14 (Migne, pp. 267-70; missing in Davie), he decides that Orpheus, Homer, Solon, Pythagoras, and Plato all had access to the histories of Moses by way of the Egyptians. The Aristobulus in question was a first-rate falsifier of texts. He quotes writers as best suits his purpose and in one case has the impudence to tamper with a verse of

1649. The Valentinians waver between abstract combinations of elements and sexual unions. In that they are like many other systems which try to avail themselves of the powerful residue of sex, stripping the latter, it may well be, of any suggestion of licentiousness. In a fragment by Valentinus, which owes its preservation to its quotation by St. Epiphanius, the two sexes stand combined in the Aeon, who is represented as a male-female (ἀρρενόθηλυς); but then again Valentinus speaks of copulations of Aeons in the ordinary terms of intercourse between earthly males and females, with the saving qualification that such divine intercourse is "incorrupt." [1]

Neo-Orphism also wavers between allegory and personification, and as in many other doctrines one meets now personified beings, now plain metaphysical abstractions. [2]

Homer. Homer relates, *Odyssey*, V, v. 262, that Ulysses completed preparations for leaving Calypso's island by the *fourth* day: "It was the fourth day, and everything had been done by him." However, Aristobulus wants to show that the pagans also regarded the *seventh* day as holy, and so blithely substitutes ῞Εβδομον for Τέτρατον and makes Homer say that everything had been done by the seventh day. Eusebius, pious rascal that he was, quotes Aristobulus and pretends not to notice the falsification [*Evangelica praeparatio*, XIII, 12 (*Opera*, Vol. III, pp. 1097-98)]. But Aristobulus goes even that one better. He invents verses outright as occasion demands, and again Eusebius quotes them without a quaver. It should not be overlooked that those two gentlemen were great hands at harping on "morality."

1649 [1] St. Epiphanius, *Panarium adversus haereses, lib.* I, *tomus* II, *Haeresis* 31, 5, *Ex Valentiniano libro* (*Opera*, Vol. I, pp. 482-83)—in question a male and a female Aeon: ". . . and so they united in coition incorrupt, in embrace everlasting" (καὶ συνήεσαν ἑαυτοῖς ἀφθάρτῳ μίξει, καὶ ἀγηράτῳ συγκράσει). Just previously, adverting to a similar union, he had said: καὶ αὐτὴ αὐτῷ μιγεῖσα . . . ("and she, uniting with him . . ."). The verb μίγνυμι is the ordinary Greek term for commerce between the sexes. A pamphlet of Victorinus of Pettaw, entitled *Adversus omnes haereticos,* which was once mistakenly attributed to Tertullian, declares, § 1 (*Corpus,* p. 215; Thelwall, p. 650: Tertullian, English, Vol. III, p. 261): "This individual [Nicolas] says that Darkness had lusted with Light in a foul and obscene passion, and modesty forbids me to mention the filthy loathsome things that were born of that lechery. Then there are other obscenities. For he talks about certain Aeons that are born of shame, about execrable and obscene mixtures and minglings, and about things even more disgusting that come of them."

1649 [2] Daremberg-Saglio, *Dictionnaire, s.v. Orphici:* "Not content with transforming myths into symbols, the Orphics invented and adopted gods that were altogether abstract, gods without legends and without features of individuality, being mere metaphysical expressions of Orphic conceptions of cosmogony. Among this number were some of their most devoutly worshipped gods, such as the cosmic Eros, Protogonus, Metis [Cunning], Mise [Hate], Mnemosyne, Phanes [Light]. One need only consider the etymologies of these names to be sure that they were mere symbols without concrete substance or reality, the terms of metaphysics simply being deified."

1650. Another pleasant individual is that Justinus whom we know through the *Philosophumena,* V, 4, 26. He comes out with three increate principles of all things, and fancifully pictures just how they managed to produce Creation. In this system, as in the Valentinian doctrine, the allegory has an eye on the Bible.[1] But long before that, and without any help from Hebrew Scripture, Hesiod had mythologized on the manner of creation;[2] and such cosmogonies are avail-

1650 [1] "There are three increate principles of the all, two male and one female. Of the male one is called Good. He alone is so called, for he is prescient of all things. The other is father of all created things. He seeth not, foreseeth not (*imprudens*), knoweth not. The female foreseeth not, and she is prone to wrath, and deceitful [double], in all things like unto the monster of Herodotus [*Historiae,* IV, 8]: a maiden down to the private parts, a snake there below, as Justinus saith. And the maiden is called Edem and Israel. Such, saith Justinus, are the principles of the All, the root and source from which all things have come; and other than these there are none. And the unforeseeing (*imprudens*) father did look upon the semi-maiden, and he desired her. This father, saith Justinus, is called Eloim. Nor less was the desire for him of Edem. And so did lust unite them in one single enamoured embrace. Of which commerce with Edem did the father beget himself twelve angels. And the names of the paternal angels are . . . And of the maternal angels which Edem likewise made subject unto her the names are . . ." And know ye also that the trees of the biblical Paradise are allegories of these same angels. The tree of life is Baruch, Number Three among the paternal angels; the tree of knowledge of good and evil is Naas, Number Three among the maternal angels. Eloim and Edem produced all things: human beings come of the human part of Edem the part above the groin; animals, and all the rest, come of the bestial part—the part below the groin.

1650 [2] *Theogonia,* vv. 116-36: "And so first was Chaos, and then Earth-of-the-Broad-Bosom, ever the firm throne of the All [An interpolation reads: "of the Immortals who hold the snowy peaks of Olympus"], and Tartarus dark in the recesses of the spacious Earth, and Eros, who is the fairest of the immortal gods, who banishes the cares [or else, "loosens the limbs"] of all gods and men. . . . And of Chaos and Erebus was black Night born, and of Night, thereafter, were Aether and the Days born, she having known Erebus and conceived of him. And verily the Earth first of all bore the starry Uranus [the Sky], her equal, that he might envelop her all about . . . and of embrace with Uranus did she conceive Oceanus-of-the-Deep-Whirlpools, and Coëus, Creïus, Hyperion, Iapetus, Theia, Rhea, Themis, and Mnemosyne, Phoebus-of-the-Golden-Crown, and Thetis-the-Lovely." These verses of Hesiod have caused a great to do among commentators and philosophers in general. Diogenes Laertius relates, *Epicurus,* X, 2 (Hicks, Vol. II, pp. 529-31), that Epicurus turned to philosophy because neither Sophists nor grammarians had succeeded in explaining to him just what Hesiod's Chaos was. Sextus Empiricus, *Contradictiones,* X, *Adversus physicos,* I, 18 (636) (*Opera,* Vol. II, p. 678), repeats the same anecdote, adding a number of details. According to Sextus Hesiod gave the name of Chaos to the place that contains all things. Hesiod's ancient scholiast transmits several views on the same Chaos, among them an etymology deriving the term from χεῖσθαι, to amass, accumulate, spread out: παρὰ τὸ χεῖσθαι Χάος γένετο. According to another interpretation, ascribed to Zenodotus, Hesiod's Chaos is the atmosphere

able in surfeit from all times and peoples. Even a writer of the nineteenth century, Charles Fourier, was minded to have his own; and if anyone else should care to try his hand at world-building, he could easily have his way by proper resort to verbal allegory.[3]

1651. Verbal allegories figure largely in the controversy between the Realists and the Nominalists. As is well known, surrendering to that mighty current which rushes down across the centuries from remotest times to our own day, the Realists thought that abstractions

(ἀήρ). Coming down to critics of more recent date, Guyet notes: "Χάος γένετ': that is, the sky, the air, the immensity of the atmosphere, uncircumscribed immensity, universal space." Two other writers, who insist on reading their Hesiod Bible in hand, go deeply into the matter of chaos. Was it created or increate? Leclerc inclines to the second view because, if one were to adopt the other, one might ask the poet: "By whom was Chaos created?"—"The author of the Clementine Homilies therefore interprets ἐγένετο as though Hesiod had written ἐγεννήθη, 'Chaos was engendered.' " But that is a fatuous splitting of hairs. Quoting the passage from Hesiod, he says, VI, 3: " 'was made.' Evidently he means that the elements originated as created things and had not existed from eternity as increate things. But if that had been the meaning of the poet one would have had to devise some cause whereby he could say that Chaos was engendered. For when one says that it was 'made' one immediately meets the objection 'By whom?' nothing being 'made' without a maker." But Robinson, pp. 356-57, is not of that opinion: " 'Ητοι-γένετ': renders: 'First then Chaos was engendered,' as also below, 137, 930. So the ancients understood the passage, not reading 'was,' fuit, as does Leclerc." Robinson supports his interpretation by various authorities and concludes: "Such the darkness in which they grope, who, denying the cause of all things, set out to explain the origin of the world on other hypotheses. The same question, 'By whom was it produced?' necessarily must recur time after time until one arrives at some supreme, increate cause."

Today we laugh at such fatuous pedantries to which experimental science has at last put an end. But if ever the sway of such science comes to be extended over sociology and political economy, people will laugh just as heartily at many disquisitions, metaphysical, ethical, humanitarian, patriotic, and the like, which are to be found in the literature of those subjects in our time.

1650 [3] Fourier, Traité de l'association domestique agricole, Vol. I, pp. 521-27 (italics Fourier's): "The planets being androgenous like the plants, they copulate with themselves and with other planets. So the Earth, copulating with itself and fusing its two typical aromas, the masculine coming from the North Pole and the feminine from the South Pole, produced the cherry, a subpivotal fruit of the red fruits and attended by five fruits in the scale, as follows: copulating with Mercury, its principal and fifth satellite, the Earth engendered the strawberry; with Pallas, its fourth satellite, the black currant or cassis; with Ceres, its third satellite, the thorny currant." Now for the properties of such offspring: "The cherry, the subpivotal fruit of that series (modulation) by copulation of the Earth with itself is created of North Pole, with male aroma, and of South Pole, with female aroma. A symbol of the tastes of childhood, the cherry is the first fruit of the pleasant season. It

and allegories were real things.[1] From the logico-experimental point of view such a controversy may last indefinitely, and in fact has (§§ 2368 f.), there being no judge to settle it. At bottom both the Realist and the Nominalist are merely describing their own sentiments. They are therefore both "right," and the conflict between their theories is a conflict between sentiments. Individuals according to their private tastes will prefer now one theory, now the other, or even some intermediate one; but once a person has made his choice there is no way left to lock another person in the dilemma of either accepting his theory or rejecting logico-experimental fact. Overlooking the shifting nebulous character of the two theories, which necessarily excludes them from the logico-experimental field, we might say that the Nominalists seem to come the closer to experimental science. But the latter cannot entertain a proposition asserting the "existence of individuals." Such a theorem altogether transcends the experimental domain, and the term "existence," used in that manner, belongs properly to metaphysics. Experimentally speaking, to say that a thing exists is merely to say that it is part of the experimental world.

stands in the order of crops where childhood stands in the order of ages. . . . The strawberry, given by Mercury, is the most precious of the red fruits. It pictures childhood to us as raised to harmony in the industrial groups. . . . The thorny currant, that grows with separate berries, is a product of Ceres. It pictures the child that is repressed, held aloof from pleasures, morally harassed, educated apart from others. . . . The black currant, the cassis, is the gift of Pallas or Aesculapius, who always modulates on the side of the bitter tastes. The plant represents poor ill-bred children. That is why its black fruit, emblematic of poverty, is of a bitter unpleasant savour."

1651 [1] In his essay *De generibus et speciebus* (*Ouvrages inédits,* pp. 513-25) Abélard states a Realist position: "Opinions differ according to the person. . . . Some imagine that there are certain universal essences which they think are present essentially in each single individual. . . . Each individual is made up of matter and form. Socrates, for instance, is made up of matter—man, and of form—Socraticity, Plato of a similar matter—man, but of a different form—Plato-ness; and so on for other individual men. And just as the Socraticity that formally constitutes Socrates exists nowhere outside of Socrates, so that essence of a man which sustains the Socraticity in Socrates exists nowhere except in Socrates, and so on for all individuals. I therefore say that the species is not that essence of a man which is present only in Socrates or in any other individual, but the whole aggregate (*collectio*) brought together from other individuals of the same nature; which aggregate (*collectio*) taken as a whole, though essentially multiple, is nevertheless called by the authorities one species, one universal, one nature, just as a people though made up of many individuals is said to be one."

1652. But, in this connexion (§ 2373), there is another problem that belongs wholly to experimental science, the question as to which of the two courses had better be followed if one is trying to discover the uniformities that prevail among facts: 1. Shall one study individuals directly, classifying them by different norms according to the results desired; then consider as a means of inference the sum of common characteristics that a class presents; and, finally, when a theory is obtained, ascertain whether it reproduces the individual facts which it is supposed to explain? 2. Or shall we study an aggregate of characteristics not sharply defined, not clearly determined, resting content if the name that is given to it is in tune with our sentiments; then inferring from such study the characteristics of, and the relations between, the individuals whom we believe, or assume, to be parts of that aggregate; finally, taking the logical inferences that are drawn from it as proofs and otherwise paying no attention to experimental verifications? Experience in the sciences as they have developed has given its answer. All the uniformities that we have come to know have been obtained by following the first method. The second has usually led to theories that do not square with the facts. Past experience teaches, accordingly, which course ought to be followed if one would have theories that do square with the facts. Nominalist theories add a metaphysical element, often small, to an experimental element, often considerable; whereas Realist theories generally do the opposite; [1] and it is evi-

1652 [1] Hauréau, *De la philosophie scolastique,* Vol. I, pp. 234-35, 243: "We count Guillaume de Champeaux among those scholastic doctors who showed the keenest attachment to realized abstractions. Even when beyond real beings one assumes one or several problematical or imaginary beings, one may still be a very moderate Realist. But the greatest extravagance, the most absolute and intemperate thesis of Realism, lay in denying the conditions of existence to everything that exists and ascribing them exclusively to what does not exist. Guillaume de Champeaux, in our judgment, did nothing less than that. . . . According to the Nominalists universals *in re* are merely the more or less general attributes of individual things: the similarity among substances is in their manner of being. . . . According to our Guillaume, the universal *in re,* considered as the most general thing, is substance, or first and only essence, which does not contain the principle of distinction within itself but takes on individual forms as extrinsic accidents." What on earth is that "first and only essence"? A *quid simile* of the "Abyss" of the Gnostics? Rousselot, *Études sur la philosophie dans le moyen âge,* Vol. I, pp. 253-55: "Let us briefly recall the thesis of Nominalism. Roxellinus had said: Individuals are realities and constitute the essence of things: the rest is only an abstraction, a play of language, a sound of the voice, a *flatus vocis.* Shocked, and rightly so, at the proposition, Guillaume de

dent that they move in a world quite different from the world of experimental reality.[2]

1653. Allegories are a product of human fancy, and therefore have a certain likeness when produced by people of the same race, of related races, and sometimes even of whatever race. The stories of the Creation that are told by one people or another are all of a kind, because they conceive of the Creation as something after the manner of the procreation they have before their eyes. Spontaneously, therefore, and not by any reciprocal copying, they invent male and female beings, masculine and feminine principles, which produce all things by a sexual process. Frequently, nay preferably, they hatch the world and things in the world from an egg; imagine one being or one principle as at war with another being, another principle; make them love, hate, enjoy, suffer. In some particular case one such story may have been copied to a greater or lesser extent from another, but similarities may be present even where there has been no imitation.[1]

1654. Believers will say that such stories resemble one another because they are recording one single event, the memory of which has been handed down in various ways. That may well be. But such a problem overreaches the experimental field, and we have no means of solving it.

Champeaux . . . combats that doctrine and substitutes for it one directly opposite and quite as sweeping. . . . The universal *par excellence,* the absolute universal [What is that?] if I may be allowed the expression, is a substantial reality [Which may be captured in the same world as the monster half girl, half snake, of Justinus the Gnostic.]; for with Guillaume de Champeaux the idea of substance and the idea of reality must not be separated [Before deciding whether they stand united or separate we have to know what they are.] and it is from the house-top of that ontological principle that he proclaims the reality of universals and denies the reality of the individual." There are people who reason like that in the world today.

1652 [2] Diogenes Laertius, *Diogenes,* VI, 53 (Hicks, Vol. II, p. 55): "Plato speaking of his 'ideas' and chancing to use the terms *tableness* and *gobletness,* 'I,' said Diogenes, 'O Plato, see your table and your goblet, but your *tableness* and your *gobletness* in no wise do I see.' And Plato: 'And rightly so; for you have the eyes that see tables and goblets; but the mind that sees *tableness* and *gobletness,* that have you not.'" Both were right. Plato's followers are entitled to see what they please. Their talk may have its use as derivation—it is fatuous and sottish in every respect of experimental science.

1653 [1] Dhorme, *Choix de textes religieux assyro-babyloniens,* Preface, pp. x-xii: "How and by whom was the world made? The various cosmogonies answer that

1655. Allegories and metaphors usually figure in the formation of legends, but that does not enable us to conclude that a given legend is necessarily a mere allegory, and much less the allegory that we might find it plausible to imagine. Legends contain, in addition to allegories and metaphors, historical (or pseudo-historical, fictional) elements, and at times imitations and reminiscences are also present. Metaphor and allegory very probably played a considerable part in the development of the Valentinian Gnosis, but exactly what rôle we have no way of knowing. Our information comes almost exclusively from writings of its adversaries; but even if we had access to the original texts, we should be in no better position to decide just what the metaphorical element was, just what the allegorical. Quite probably the very authors of those theories did not know themselves—to judge, at least, by the few facts we do have.

1656. We have to proceed from the known to the unknown; and available in fact are not a few examples of the formation of such legends. We have seen the one Charles Fourier produced. His is a medley of stories and metaphors, and it is not very clear whether Fourier himself was aware of the precise bounds of the various ingredients he was utilizing. The part played by the Aeons for the Valentinians is played by the planets for Fourier. Like the Aeons,

question. Detectable in each of them are influences of the environments in which they originated. . . . The interposition of the divinity is clothed with more or less mystical traits that serve to fix the theological conception in the popular imagination. [As a matter of fact, just the other way round.] The 'Poem of Creation' . . . is, from that point of view, of the major interest. Not satisfied with running down the genesis of heaven and earth, it goes back to the time when 'none of the gods had been created' and displays a veritable theogony before us. The gods will issue in successive pairs [Personification, male and female, is rarely missing.] from a primal couple, Apsou, the ocean that surrounds our land, and Tiâmat, the 'tumultuous sea whose waters mingle into one.' . . . If the 'Poem of Creation' is steeped in mythological and popular ideas, the 'Chaldaean Cosmogony' tells a more abstract and theological story of creation. The world still comes from the sea, but we are not made witnesses of the births of any gods. If the Babylonians considered their national god, Marduk, as the author of the world and of mankind, it is quite natural that the Assyrians should have entrusted that rôle to Asur, their god. . . . That other legends of the Creation must have been current is proved by the fragmentary 'Creation of Animate Beings,' where we see a collaboration of gods in the formation of heaven and earth. Along with these cosmogonies of the scholarly tradition there were other hypotheses as to the origin of the world. Some of them are a part of general folk-lore."

they pair off and engender the various things that constitute the universe.[1]

1657. If we did not know how Fourier's theory was built up, and if we set out, on its being given us as a bald fact, to guess its origins, we would obviously go wrong in assuming: first, that Fourier intended to write pure history, or second, that he was using pure metaphor. As a matter of fact he stands between the two extremes. The facts are there, from his point of view; but the words in which he states them are the proof of their existence, because of the sentiments aroused by the metaphors, which in turn are suggested by the words themselves (derivation IV-β).

1658. If, therefore, we happen on a theory of that type, we may, in default of direct proofs to the contrary, regard it as at least possible that the theory was built up after the manner of Fourier's.

1659. Another example. Enfantin, the Father Supreme of the Saint-Simonian religion, discovers a new trinity and hails its transcendent beauties with all the enthusiasm of a neophyte. There is no reason in the world for questioning Enfantin's good faith. He is naïvely making us witnesses of the birth of a theology. Saint-Simon and his disciples had in mind the notion of the Catholic Trinity and perhaps also the perfection of the number three so dear to the pagan gods. Without their dreaming of such a thing that notion prompted them to evolve a whole string of trinities. Then, one fine day, they "discover" them, are struck with wonder, find them in accord with

1656 [1] Fourier, *Théorie des quatre mouvements,* p. 57: "It is a joy for God to create and it is to His interest to prolong the act of creation. [So far, a simple narrative without metaphor; but the story now suggests an analogy:] If the conception, gestation, and parturition of a human being require a duration of nine months, God must have used a corresponding length of time to create the three realms. [Now a narrative that is altogether capricious:] Theory estimates that period as 1/192 of the social cycle (*carrière*), which gives 450 years, more or less, for the duration of the First Creation. [And now a passage where metaphor, analogy, narrative, are jumbled together, Fourier apparently not in the least distinguishing between the different things:] All creation is effected through the conjunction of a boreal fluid, which is male, with an austral fluid, which is female." ([In a note:] "The star can pair: 1. With itself, from the North and South poles, like plants. 2. With another star, by emanations (*versements*) from opposite poles. 3. With some intermediary (the tuberose is engendered by three aromas: Earth-South, Herschel [Uranus]-North, Sun-South). A planet is a being with two souls and two sexes and procreates like the animal or plant by the combination of two generative substances. The procedure is the same in all nature.")

their sentiments, and their admiration knows no bounds at such beautiful, such profound, disquisitions.[1]

So, we may guess, the Valentinian Gnostics had in mind mythological notions such as one finds in Hesiod, and, in addition, certain of the metaphysical ideas of Plato, Pythagoras, or others. With those materials, and quite unconsciously, they worked up a theogony of their own. We in our time recognize the various ingredients, analyze them, separate them one from the other, and gratuitously ascribe to the Gnostic writers intentions and conceptions that they may never have had.

1660. One last example: a story of beer changing into wine, as told by Eginhard (Einhard).[1] Eginhard evidently believes that he is recounting a fact. Not only does he eschew any admixture of

1659 [1] Enfantin, *Religion Saint-Simonienne: Réunion générale de la famille,* pp. 69-70 (italics and capitals Enfantin's): "At the time when Eugene and I were laying the first foundations of the trinary dogma in its theological form, we had not as yet come to understand how deeply that dogma had been FELT BY SAINT-SIMON in his NEW CHRISTIANITY. Your father RODRIGUES alone kept repeating to us that that book contained the loftiest teaching which it was given to man to receive. And we ourselves, when we were carried in the course of our labours to investigating the scientific make-up of the trinitarian doctrine of the Christians and the ancient doctrine, soon came to justify the problem of the Trinity in our own eyes as the most significant that the human being could propound to himself. One of us let fall this sentence, which was afterwards repeated in Eugene's letters: *One who fails to understand the Trinity fails to understand God.* That was a real revelation as regarded doctrine. All those who heard it, and your father RESSEGUIER in particular, found some difficulty in comprehending its full scope. It was not till then that on re-reading the NEW CHRISTIANITY we saw that the idea of the Trinity figured on every page in it under a thousand different forms, such as MORALITY, *Dogma, Ritual,* FINE ARTS, *Science, Industry.* Great was our astonishment that we had been going over and over that eternal problem of humanity so many times without noticing that it had to be solved by us. At the same time all the sentences, all the indications, which had made no impression upon us at the time of *The Producer,* now strengthened us—Eugene and me—in the belief that our formula for the pantheistic trinitarian dogma was the true formula of Saint-Simon."

1660 [1] *Historia translationis beatorum Christi martyrum Marcellini et Petri,* IV, 44-45 (*Opera,* pp. 268-72; Wendell, pp. 57-59). Eginhard sets out for Court from the church where the bones of the saints Marcellinus and Peter are cherished. He reaches a certain locality on the Rhine when the following adventure befalls him: "After our supping, which had consumed a part of the night, I had retired with my attendants to the chamber whither I was appointed to rest. But the servant who was wont to prepare our drink hastened into the room as though he had some strange thing to tell. I looked at him and asked: 'What wouldst thou? For thou seemest to have something thou wouldst impart unto us.' Whereupon he: 'Two

metaphor but he vainly wonders what the significance of the prodigy may be—what allegory may be inferred from it. Now suppose
we did not have Eginhard's naïve confidences but knew only his
story of the bald fact. Our aim is to get from his story to what actually happened, and we argue, as M. Loisy argues regarding the
miracles in the Fourth Gospel, that the miracle as told by Eginhard
is "unintelligible, absurd, ridiculous as fact, unless we see in it the
bold manipulation of a trickster" (§ 774). We shall have plenty of
ways for discovering some "easy and simple interpretation" of the
miracle, and need only make our choice among numberless metaphors all equally probable. But in such case our error would be
apparent enough; for, far from intending to speak in metaphors,
Eginhard went looking for one and confesses that he failed to find

miracles have been wrought before our eyes, and of them would I speak unto you.'
And when I had bidden him speak, he said: 'When ye rose from table and entered
into your chamber, I and my companions withdrew into the nether store-room,
which is under the dining-hall. We had begun to give beer to the servants who
besought us of it, when there entered a servant sent thither by some of our companions and holding a flask, which he begged us to fill. The which when we had
done, he asked that we give him also of this beer to drink; and we gave him of it
in a vessel that chanced to lie empty on the cask of the beer. But as he put the vessel to his mouth to drink, he cried out, amazed: "Forsooth, this is wine, and not
beer." And when he who had filled the flask, drawing the same from the tap from
which he had given the man to drink, began charging him with falsehood, the
man cried: "Take it, and taste, and then shalt thou see that I spake not falsehood
but the truth." And the man took it and tasted, and likewise vowed that the drink
had the taste of wine, not of beer. And then a third, and a fourth, and all others
who were there did each taste, and stood amazed, and so drank they all that was
in the cask; and each of them who tasted bore witness that the taste was of wine
and not of beer.' " And then the same servant relates the second miracle—a case
where a candle first falls to the floor without being touched and goes out; and then,
after an utterance of the names of Sts. Marcellinus and Peter, is relighted of its
own accord. Eginhard goes on to say: "Whereupon I bade the man who had told
me these things to retire into his own chamber. And lying on my bed to rest and
turning many thoughts in my mind, marvelling, I began to speculate as to what
this transmutation of beer into wine, that is to say, of an inferior liquid into a better, could signify or portend; and why the prodigy should have occurred in that
way and in that place, that is to say, in a house of the King rather than in the man-
sion where the holy bodies of those blessed Martyrs lay, who through the power
of Christ had worked those miracles. But though however long and diligently I
pondered, it was not given me to solve the problem of a certainty, still I had and
shall always have it for a fact that that Supreme Power whereof it is held that these
and other like miracles come, never doth anything, nor permitteth anything to happen, without cause in those creatures which, I doubt not, abide under his providence
and government."

one. The same may be the case with allegorical interpretations of the Fourth Gospel. If the story of the water changed into wine as told in that Gospel is not a narrative of fact but an allegory for the "replacement of the Law by the Gospel," why should not Eginhard's story represent, not what was fact in his mind, but any allegory we choose? The persons who vouched for the incident to Eginhard had the Gospel miracle in mind; and, naturally, without the least intention to deceive, they reported what in good faith they believed to be fact. Why may similar causes not have operated to give us the accounts of miracles in the Fourth Gospel?

1661. This mania for trying to translate into allegory all stories that seem to us to lie outside the real world has no experimental foundation whatever. On the contrary, examples in abundance make it plain that many writers who report miracles believe in all good faith that they are recounting actual happenings and that such metaphors as may be detected in a story are introduced unconsciously by the author and not of any deliberate intent. And in other cases, even if metaphors are deliberately introduced, they are mere appendages to the fact and in no wise alter its actual or assumed reality.

1662. We have already seen (§§ 1623-24) that St. Augustine admits the literal and the allegorical interpretation side by side. St. Cyprian takes a very clear position as to the miracle of the water changed into wine. For him it is a matter of actual fact, but the miracle was wrought in order to "teach and show" (*docens et ostendens*) certain things.[1] Altogether arbitrary, therefore, is the system some would follow today, inverting that relation and assuming that a writer cannot have believed in the reality of facts which happen also to be susceptible of allegorical interpretation.

1663. With so obvious an example before our eyes, how can we assert without trace of direct proof that the author of the Fourth Gospel followed a procedure wholly different from St. Cyprian's and distinguished what the Saint combines? So long as we have no evidence on the point and follow the mere probabilities, these will

---

1662 [1] *Epistolae*, 63, 13, *Ad Caecilium, De sacramento Domini calicis* (*Opera*, p. 383; Wallis, Vol. I, p. 216): "In making wine out of water, Jesus was teaching and showing that the Gentiles were to succeed [to Abraham's inheritance] and that we shortly would attain by merit of faith to what the Jews had lost: He showed, that is, that when the Jews departed from the wedding-feast of Christ and His Church a great throng of Gentiles would flock to attend it in their places."

be quite in favour of a resemblance between the procedure of the author of the Fourth Gospel and St. Cyprian's.

1664. Another example from the same saint (he could supply us with them to the heart's content) confirms such vague mixtures of actual or assumed reality and metaphor. Cyprian says: "That is why the Holy Spirit came in the form of a dove. The dove is a simple, joyous bird, not bitter with gall, not cruel in its bites, not savage in its clawings." [1] Either words have lost all meaning and the texts we have are valueless, or else we are constrained to admit that St. Cyprian believes that the Holy Spirit actually assumed the form of a dove; and the things he adds to his description serve to show the considerations prompting the transformation but not in any way to cast doubt upon it (*loc. cit.*): "loving human dwellings, knowing the association of one home; when they have young, bringing them forth together, and when they fly abroad, flying side by side." (Wallis.) [2]

1665. Derivations with metaphors are frequently for the benefit of educated people, but often also they serve half-educated people to harmonize faith with logico-experimental science. Anything in a story or theory that seems impossible to accept from the experimental standpoint is at once set down as metaphor. The difference between faith and this semi-scepticism lies in the fact that faith believes in the historical truth of the story and adds the metaphor: what actually happens is a "sign" that teaches us something. Semi-scepticism does not believe in the historical reality of the story. It does not add metaphor to fact, but substitutes it for fact—the metaphor only is real, the fact imaginary. As for experimental science, it is not called upon either to accept or to reject the conclusions whether of faith or of semi-scepticism. Such things lie outside its domain. It confines itself to rejecting conclusions that are based on sentiment alone and have no experimental foundation.

1666. In Chapter V (§§ 635 f.) we mentioned two problems that

---

1664 [1] *De unitate ecclesiae*, 9 (*Opera*, p. 506; Wallis, Vol. I, p. 384): "*Idcirco et in columba venit Spiritus sanctus. Simplex animal et laetum est, non felle amarum, non morsibus saevum, non unguium laceratione violentum.*"

1664 [2] St. Augustine, however, says, *De symbolo, Sermo ad catechumenos*, X, 20 (*Opera*, Vol. VI, p. 649): "So the Spirit appeared in a dove but was not a dove." So one eats one's cake and has it too! It was, and yet it was not, a dove! The next step is to go farther still and see a mere allegory in the dove.

arise in connexion with theories. There we dealt with the first of those problems (relations of a theory to experimental fact) and in this present chapter we deal with the second (means of arriving at pre-established conclusions, persuasiveness). It now remains for us to consider the two problems together, epitomizing the observations that may be made on each of them separately. Suppose we take concrete cases as types: 1. A story that is purely mythological, such as the story of Aphrodite and Ares in the eighth book of the *Odyssey*, vv. 266-366. 2. Some wholly allegorical fable, where animals are made to talk—the fable of the wolf and the lamb, let us say. 3. The Valentinian Gnosis (§§ 1645 f.). 4. Fourier's theory of creations (§§ 1650[8], 1656[1]). 5. Comte's theory of the Earth and the Great Being (§ 1626[1]). 6. The theory of the Realists (§ 1651). 7. The theory of "solidarity."

1667. As regards the first problem, as regards their relations to fact, all those types stand on a par: their logico-experimental value is exactly zero. They in no way correspond to experimental facts. As regards the second problem, as regards the methods by which implications are drawn from them, and their persuasive force, we may distinguish: (*a*) the structure of the derivation; (*b*) the manner of its acceptance.

1668. *a. Structure of the derivation.* The seven types noted have one common characteristic: the arbitrary use of certain non-experimental entities. Tertullian, seeing the mote in his neighbour's eye, challenges the Valentinians to prove their statements as to their "Abyss," and takes no stock in what they say: "As though they could ever prove its existence, if they define it as we know that it has to be defined!" Bravo! As if figments of the human fancy could ever be proved to exist! To prove the existence of their Abyss, of Hesiod's Chaos, of gods and goddesses, of copulations of planets, of Fourier's sentient Earth, of universals, of talking animals, is something altogether impossible.

1669. But there are degrees in the arbitrary—which has its limits in the sentiments associated with words and in certain conventions as to their use. In Fourier's creations the arbitrary element seems great indeed. When the Gnostics represent beings with masculine names as copulating with beings of feminine names they expose to their reader's gaze facts that are well known to everybody. Whereas in Fourier one does not readily see just how and just why the Earth copulates with herself and with Pallas. The North Pole and the South Pole are both cold. It is not self-evident therefore why the fluid of the North Pole should be male and that of the South Pole female. But keeping to the terms "North" and "South" in themselves, we do understand that the warm South may somehow suggest a mild feminine nature. An arbitrariness somewhat less extreme but nevertheless considerable figures in mythological compositions. Certain conventions have, of course, to be respected; but within those limits the myth may assume as many different forms as one may choose. In fables, again, where animals talk, the arbitrary element is no less striking than in modern novels. The *Roman de Renart* is an excellent example of the very great variety such fables may take on. In Hesiod's theogony there is less, though still a great deal, of the arbitrary. One can see that sentiment will readily grant that Chaos, and even Love, existed before anything else. That the Earth should have produced the Sky, or the Sky the Earth, and that Earth and Sky should unite to produce many other things— that too is sentimentally intelligible. But why Coëus, Creïus, Hyperion, and so on should figure among such things, sentiment can hardly suggest. The arbitrary plays a still lesser rôle in the writings of the Valentinian Gnostics. Sentiment easily understands that the origin of all things should be pre-existent in a region very remote and unnamable, nor are the names "Abyss" or "First Father" inappropriate to such an entity. All such words are chosen for the simple reason that they arouse sentiments that accord with a feeling we have that we know nothing of the principle of the all. The story of Sophia's striving to know her father's face awakens in us a sense of the yearning men feel to know what is beyond experience. We understand by analogy that tears go with humid matter, laughter with light, and so on (§ 670). The analogies with Pythagorean perfections in numbers or with the numerical values of letters, superficial and arbitrary as they are, still awaken some response in human emotions. In Comte's mythology the status of the arbitrary element is not greatly different from its status in Gnostic theory, but it is not so conspicuously obtruded. And very much the same may be said of the theory of "solidarity." The object, in two words, is to persuade people who have money to share it with the followers of certain politicians; so the resort is to "solidarity," to a debt that is being constantly liquidated and constantly revived. As a matter of fact, entities altogether different could have served just as well—Marx's "surplus value," for instance, or anything else of the kind. The arbitrary element diminishes as we pass on to the Realists. It is understandable that to individuate Socrates one should resort to a certain Socraticity (§ 1651 [1]) and that sentiment should be tickled to have an explanation so adequate. How satisfying to know that a lamb chop is the manifestation of lamb-chopness! It is noteworthy, however, that the metaphysicist no less than the ignoramus orders the former for dinner, and he would find the latter a slim diet indeed.

1670. Suppose we look at the same derivations from the standpoint of personification. In narratives of the type of the love-story of Aphrodite and Ares, the personifications are fully worked out, to such an extent indeed that they are readily mistakable for historical narratives somewhat altered. Personification is likewise complete, though altogether artificial, in fables involving animals that talk. The Valentinian Gnostics flounder about like fleas in tinder among the difficulties of harmonizing personifications with allegories, going back and forth from the ones to the others and then round again, without ever finding a place where they can stop. When they have endowed one of their entities with sex, they would seem to have personified it; but then back they go from personification to abstraction, changing the Aeon into a male-female "principle" (Irenaeus, *Contra haereses*, I, 1, 1). However they do not stick to the abstraction. Soon again they begin talking of a generative process that is effected by the deposit of something like seed in something like a matrix, and of entities that fertilize, conceive and bring forth young.[1] Then they try to shed the material connotations by talking

1670 [1] The Greek text and the translation of Irenaeus, *Contra haereses*, I, 1, 1, are given in § 1646. The ancient Latin translator understands the passage thus: *"Prolationem hanc praemitti volunt et eam deposuisse quasi in vulva eius quae cum eo erat Sige* [*i.e.,* Silence]. *Hanc autem suscepisse semen hoc et praegnantem factam* [How could an abstraction ever get with child? All the terms here in question apply to human women.] *generasse Nun."* Tertullian, *Adversus Valentinianos,* 7 (*Opera,* Vol. II, p. 116; English, Vol. II, p. 129), reads: *"Hoc vice seminis in Sigae suae veluti genitalibus vulvae locis collocat. Suscipit illa statim et praegnans efficitur et parit."* The Valentinians do not seem to have been all of the same opinion: *Philosophumena,* VI, 2, 29: "Many differences are to be noted among them. Some, in

of a coition that is "incorrupt" (§ 1649). But as regards creation they also dispense with the sexual union: "They say that humid substances were born of the tears of Achamoth, luminous substances of his smile, solid substances of his gloom, and the mobile of his fear." In short they waver between literal meanings and metaphor, between personifications and allegory, without ever fixing once and for all on any definite attitude.

1671. Metaphor, as is well known, easily leads to personification, and many many examples of such developments are available. The personifications in Comte's mythology are very like the personifications of the Gnostics, with the difference that Comte begins by saying that his are fictions, but then proceeds to forget that and talks of them as though they were actual persons. Personification amounts to nothing in the theory of solidarity; nor does it play any part in the theory of the Realists. But that is true only as regards forms, not as regards substance. After all, the Abyss of the Valentinians and the universal essence of the Realists are the same actor in different costumes. All things proceed from the one as they do from the other, and such origin is conceived either by resort to a greater degree of personification, as in generation by the Aeons, or by dispensing with personification, as in Abélard's "accidents of the universal essence." One may add, if one chooses, Hesiod's Chaos or any other entity of the sort; for, whether all things proceed from an Abyss, from universals, from a Chaos, or from some other such entity, the same sentiments are satisfied and one gets theories that various persons will accept according to their individual preferences.

1672. Transformation of metaphors—not into persons as just above, but merely into objective realities—is largely if not altogether missing in mythological stories and animal fables.[1] Slight if any

order to keep the Pythagorean dogma of Valentinus in all respects intact, regard the Father as sexless, wifeless (*unfeminine*—Ἀλήθυς?) and solitary. Others deeming it impossible that a male should have engendered all things by himself, are forced to provide him with a mate, Sige (Silence, *f.*)."

1672 [1] Piepenbring, *Théologie de l'Ancien Testament,* pp. 129, 120: "The *maleach of the Lord:* If the revealed God is identified with the glory, name, or countenance, of God, so He is with the *maleach,* or, to follow the usual translation, the Angel of the Lord, or Jehovah. . . . It is easy to be persuaded that there is a close analogy between the Angel of the Lord and His Countenance. . . And that analogy perfectly explains the identification of the *maleach* with God Himself. . . . There are passages, nevertheless, where God and His *maleach* are contradistinguished as two

traces of it are detectable in Fourier's mythology. In the Valentinian Gnosis, as we have just seen, metaphors are mixed and mingled with personifications till it is difficult, not to say impossible, to separate them. Comte, for his part, first tries to keep them distinct, then combines them, and ends in personification pure and simple. Metaphorical entities reign sovereign in the theory of solidarity and among the Realists.

1673. Merging of metaphor and reality is the rule with persons who reason on sentiment. In the case of metaphysical and theological dreamers things, symbols, metaphors, allegories, all make one jumble in the mind. It is out of the question to reason in earnest with people who use terms so vague, so nebulous, that not even they know what they mean. Here, for instance, is M. Léon Bourgeois, who expatiates, mouth agape, on the notions implicit in his concept of interdependence, as "filling the moral idea with a new content." That string of words means exactly nothing: M. Bourgeois's moral idea is filled with a new content in the same way that Sige was fertilized by the Abyss of the Gnostics. Had he lived in the day of the Valentinians M. Bourgeois might perhaps have personified his metaphors.[1]

1674. All these types of verbal derivations with metaphors are of common use in metaphysics—oftentimes they predominate over everything else—and in the metaphysical parts of theologies, where, however, they are generally incidental. A word awakens certain

different persons, and on one occasion the identification and distinction stand side by side in the same passage. An angel of Jehovah, also called a Man of God, appears to Samson's parents (Judges 13:3, 6 f.). He is definitely distinguished from Jehovah (13:8 f.; 16:18 f.); yet after his disappearance, Manoah says to his wife (13:22): 'We shall surely die, because we have seen God.' Theologians have been to great pains to determine just what the Lord's *maleach* was, but they have reached widely divergent conclusions." And how otherwise, when they go looking for a single objective thing where all there is is a multiplicity of subjective things? Dugas-Montbel, in his *Observations sur l'Iliade*, Vol. I, pp. 145-46 (*Iliad*, III, v. 105), notes of an expression used by Homer: " 'Fetch the might of Priam hither' means 'Fetch Priam hither.' In the same way Homer says 'might of Hercules' for 'Hercules.' The term is frequent in Homer, and many other poets have imitated it from him. . . . The Latins have similar locutions, using, that is, a distinctive trait of the person for the person himself. . . . Thence doubtless have come such locutions in our modern languages as 'his Majesty,' 'his Eminence,' 'his Grace,' 'his Highness.' "

1673 [1] *Essai d'une philosophie de la solidarité*, p. 38: "We change nothing, I again insist, in those general principles of morality and right; but to follow an expression that I have kept and which admirably expresses what we have in mind,

sentiments; it is transformed into a thing; and, thereupon, one readily believes that the sentiments so awakened are produced by that thing. Poetry, literature, eloquence, even ordinary conversation, cannot do without such transformations, for they would otherwise fail in their principal purpose, which is the stirring of sentiments. So people acquire certain habits of thought and take them with them when they turn to science, where the object is not, ostensibly at least, to play on sentiments but to establish relationships between facts.

1675. *b. Acceptance of the derivation.* As regards the credence that human beings lend to derivations, the following traits stand out. Animal fables have never been taken as literally true. The mythologies of the Valentinians, of Comte, and Fourier, have had a certain number of believers. So also the metaphors of solidarity. Much more numerous, among educated people, are those who believe in a more or less mitigated Realism. Of the three types just mentioned, the first has had the largest following—mythological narrative, that is. For us, in our day and age, Greek mythology is a collection of pretty stories; but it was accepted as truth for centuries by vast numbers of human beings, and we, for our part, have merely replaced it with other mythologies of the same type. The number of believers increases beyond the maximum for the simple types as we move on to compound types, especially to composites arising in combinations of the first and last types, that is to say, the combination of the mythological narrative with the metaphors of Realism. Most religions are built up in just that way.

1676. As regards the sentiments that are coddled by the seven types in question (§ 1666), the instinct of combinations is satisfied chiefly by the first. In children and in not a few adults it is satisfied also by the second; but with many people the moral instincts are

---

the concepts that we have derived from our recognition of the interdependence that prevails among men *fill*—as M. Darlu says—fill the moral idea with a content altogether new." So then—the general principles of morality are in no way changed, but the moral idea is nevertheless filled with an entirely new content! If it is new, one would expect it to show some change, as compared with the old; and if there has been no change, how on earth can it be new? The brain that can make head or tail of that is a brain indeed. Bourgèois further explains: "There is something in these facts that clarifies and broadens old conceptions of right, duty, justice." So then, it was not true that nothing had been changed! The change would lie in that very "broadening"!

specially stirred—in other words, Class II residues are brought into play. The sixth type and, in more general terms, metaphysical reasonings at large, satisfy the need of logical explanation that educated persons feel (residues I-ε). So also for the seventh type and other doctrines of the kind, which dissemble brute appetite under ratiocination. The third, fourth, and fifth types aim to satisfy the instincts for combinations and logical reasoning both at the same time. They must have achieved their purpose only in part; for actually they survived but for very brief periods of time and won relatively few adherents. Religions that have endured for long periods of time and enjoyed large followings must have realized their purpose better. The ancient religion of Rome was supplanted by Greek religion because it gave no satisfaction whatever to the rationalizing instinct.[1] Neo-Platonism succumbed to Christianity because it gave no satisfaction to the demand for concrete combinations. So Modernism today, reviving the allegorical methods of Philo, makes no progress among the plain people because it satisfies the intellectual requirements of a mere handful of cerebrators. Theology is no longer in style even when it comes garbed in democratic toggery.

1677. Since personification satisfies a demand for the concrete and allegory a demand for abstraction, derivations tend to use the two together, so far as possible, in order to profit by both. But it is not easy to keep them in harmony. In that connexion the Catholic Church shows surpassing wisdom and sagacity in shrouding the accord in mystery. The Fourth Gospel is a necessary complement to the first three in satisfying the full religious requirements of men; and the Catholic Church very wisely condemns the interpretations of the Modernists, just as it has condemned, at one time or another, other systems that have aimed at distinguishing historical reality from allegory. The Church condemned the fancies of the Gnostics because they tipped the scales too far in one direction; but it has always accepted, to some moderate extent, allegorical interpretations that satisfied a demand for reasoning and inference. From that point of view St. Thomas stands really on a plane of his own. Is

1676 [1] The "because" here and in the sentence following must be taken as indicating prominent, but by no means exclusive, causes. Such summary modes of expression are indispensable if one would avoid cumbersome prolixities; but they can never be very exact. There is no danger of going astray if one at all times bears the interdependence of social phenomena in mind.

there anyone who could be compared with him? He satisfies in the best possible way the various requirements for concreteness and for abstraction, yet manages with consummate skill to side-step the discrepancies that are forever cropping up between reality and allegory.

1678. There is another very important aspect under which derivations have to be considered: and that is the judgment that is to be passed upon them in their relations to reality, and that not only as regards their accord with experience, but also as regards their bearing on individual or social utility.[1]

1679. There are those who are disposed to consider nothing but logical conduct, regarding the non-logical as originating in absurd prejudices and calculated to do nothing but harm to society. So there are those who will consider a doctrine only from the standpoint of its accord with experience and declare that any other way of regarding it is absurd, fatuous, harmful. That theory shocks the sentiments of many people and furthermore does not square with the facts, which clearly demonstrate that doctrines (derivations) that transcend experience are expressions of sentiments, and that these in turn play an important part in determining the social equilibrium (§ 2206). The theory is therefore false, in the sense of not squaring with the facts. But where does the error lie?

1680. The adversaries of those who disparage theories they deem unreal deny the alleged unreality. They feel instinctively that to consider such theories mere strings of words without effect on society is false and, in an effort to restore them to a dignity they deserve, exert themselves to make them seem real at any cost, or else superior to reality (§ 2340). But that is another error, which in its turn offends the sentiments of people who live in a world of practical realities, and these again reply by demonstrating the logico-experimental ineptitude of the revered derivations. Hence those perpetually recurrent swings of the pendulum, which have been observable for so many many centuries, between scepticism and faith, materialism and

1678 [1] We have already dealt with the first subject at length (Chapters IV and V) in our discussion of the way in which logical and non-logical conduct is to be viewed; but it remains for us to add a few remarks that could not be opportunely made until the exposition of theories just given had been completed. Nor shall we have exhausted the subject when we have made them. It will still remain for us to study various concomitant fluctuations in the vogue of derivations and in other social phenomena. To that we shall come in Chapter XII (§§ 2329 f.).

idealism, logico-experimental science and metaphysics (§ 2341).

1681. And so it is, considering for the moment only one or two of such oscillations,[1] that in a little more than a hundred years, and, specifically, from the close of the eighteenth to the beginning of the twentieth century, one witnesses a wave of Voltairean scepticism, and then Rousseau's humanitarianism as a sequel to it; then a religion of Revolution, and then a return to Christianity; then scepticism once more—Positivism; and finally, in our time, the first stages of a new fluctuation in a mystico-nationalist direction. Leaving the natural sciences aside and keeping to social theory, there has been no notable progress in one direction or the other. In a word, if faith is just a harmful prejudice, how comes it that it has survived over so many centuries, constantly reshaping itself and constantly reappearing, after its enemies, from Lucretius on, had thought they had vanquished it for all time? And if scientific scepticism is really so futile, so inconclusive, so harmful to human society, how comes it that it can return to fashion every so often in the plain good sense of a Lucian, a Montaigne, a Bayle, a Voltaire? How comes it that the progress which cannot be discerned in social opinions is indisputably real in the natural sciences?

1682. If one is disposed to keep strictly to the facts, an error will be apparent in both views, in that they both reduce to one unit things that have to be kept distinct. The accord of a doctrine, or theory, with fact is one thing; and the social importance of that doctrine, or theory, quite another. The former may amount to zero, the latter be very great; but the social significance does not prove the scientific accord, just as the scientific accord does not prove the social significance. A theory may not correspond to objective fact, may indeed be altogether fantastic from that standpoint, and yet meantime correspond to subjective facts of great moment to society (§ 843). A person aware of the social importance of a mythology will have that mythology real. A person who denies the truth of a mythology will also deny its social value. But the facts clearly show that mythologies have no reality and at the same time have the greatest social importance. Feelings are so strong on this point that people are persuaded that the day of the mythologies is definitely over, that myths are but ghostly memories of a past for ever dead, and so

1681   [1] We shall study them in their general traits hereafter (§§ 2329 f.).

deliberately shut their eyes to facts truly vast in numbers which show that mythologies are still alive and flourishing. So also there are people who believe that the achievements of logico-experimental science in the course of these many centuries amount to nothing, and that to know realities we can again go back to the dreams of a Plato revamped by a Hegel.

1683. The fluctuations observable in social opinions result theoretically (§§ 2340 f.) from a clash of two opposing forces: the correspondence of the derivations with reality on the one hand, and their social utility on the other. If the two things cogged together perfectly, a continuous movement ultimately leading to the absolute predominance of the resultant of the two forces would not be impossible; but since, instead of working in harmony, they are discordant, antagonistic, and since both a complete desertion of reality and a complete disregard of social utilities remain if not impossible, at least difficult, it necessarily follows that in regard to social matters theory oscillates like a pendulum, now swinging in one direction, now in the other. That is not the case with the natural sciences, because the theories of mathematics, chemistry, astronomy, and so on, have in our day at least a scant, if any, bearing on social questions; and so the pendulum swings farther and farther in the direction of logico-experimental science, without encountering any force, or at least any appreciable force (§ 617), tending to push it back in the direction of metaphysical, theological, or like derivations. Such forces have manifested themselves in certain instances in times past, as in ancient Athenian prosecutions for impiety or in the case of Galileo, but in the end they languished as not corresponding to any actual social utility; or—to state the situation more exactly, since social utility plays only a part, though a very considerable part, in the matter—because such forces did not correspond to sentiments with which men could not dispense short of serious alterations in the social equilibrium.[1]

1683 [1] There are still traces of such forces, nevertheless, owing to the fact that individuals who devote themselves to the natural sciences live in the same world as other men and cannot altogether escape being influenced by the various oscillations that disturb it. So at the present time a counter-offensive by metaphysics is observable in the theories of mechanics. Examine, for instance, Lémeray, *Le principe de relativité,* pp. 98, 31. The author has been examining a hypothetical case where two observers, both in motion, exchange signals by carrier pigeon and adds: "Now the

1684. Some reader may perhaps have regarded my exposition of Gnosticism just above as quite superfluous and have asked: What has such nonsense got to do with sociology? Such nonsense enters the field of sociology because it expresses sentiments that are still powerfully active in present-day society. Even disregarding such manifestations as the theories of Saint-Simon, Fourier, Comte, or humanitarian Socialism, we can any day, in England and the United States, observe the appearance and prosperous growth of Christian sects which, from the experimental standpoint, are no less absurd than Gnosticism; and to such Anglo-Saxon phenomena we must add the neo-Buddhism, the Theosophy, the Spiritualism, the Occultism, that have been winning converts all over Europe. Anyone desirous of convincing himself that moderns are no whit less adroit than the ancients in peddling balderdash as sublime truth need read, among the hosts of books available, only a volume by Sinnett on *Esoteric Buddhism*.[1]

conclusion we have just reached as regards the pigeons the principle refuses to accept in the case of light. [And of course we can only bow the knee to the will of Monsieur Principe.] In fact, the two relations (1) give us T_1 and T_2 as functions of T and v: we might decide, that is, which of the two observers was at rest vis-à-vis of space—a proposition that has no meaning [Exactly what used to be said of not a few propositions that are now commonplaces.], just as in the case of the pigeons, the relations (1) show which of the observers is at rest vis-à-vis of the Earth." This argument starts on a par with many other metaphysical reasonings—for a few examples see §§ 492-506—except that it has been decorated with mathematical embellishments. But mathematics cannot themselves confer reality upon a hypothesis that is devoid of any! Among the implications of the "principle of relativity" one notes "that different observers of one system [one of two systems in motion] on seeing *one same* observer from the other system go by, will note that he goes less rapidly than they; and one observer, seeing the different observers of the other go by in succession, will note that they age more rapidly than he." The system where one ages less rapidly will be in danger of overcrowding by women—they will flock to it as to a bargain-counter. Once one goes excursioning outside the experimental world, it is certain enough that one can prove anything one chooses. Since my aim in these volumes is not to preach, but merely to look for the uniformities that prevail among social facts, I may without harm, and in fact I must, keep the pendulum altogether swung in the direction in which it swings in the natural sciences (§§ 86,1403).

1684 [1] Pp. 47-48: "By what prophetic instinct Shakespeare pitched upon 7 as the number which best suited his fantastic classification of the ages of man is a question with which we need not be much concerned, but certain it is that he could not have made a more felicitous choice. In periods of seven the evolution of the races of man may be traced, and the actual number of the objective worlds that constitute our system, and of which the Earth is one, is seven also. Remember, the occult scientists

1685. Renan was always in the habit of holding with the hare and running with the hounds. After describing the nonsense of the Gnostics and telling the touching story of Sophia's passion, he somewhat inadequately states a notion that has its element of truth when he praises such portions of those ancient fancies as tended to exhilarate certain sentiments. He would have been much closer to the facts had he expressed himself subjectively instead of objectively, and said that the sentiments which were satisfied by Hesiod's *Theogony* and other such productions, as well as by the Gnostic myths which he, Renan, describes, are still active in many people of our day and express themselves in much the same ways as they did of yore. If a person is trying to preach to people in order to steer them into paths that he considers best, he will condemn or praise such sentiments and the various expressions of them. If one is concerned strictly with science, one will merely describe them and then try to establish their relations to other social facts.[1]

know this as a fact, just as the physical scientists know for a fact that the spectrum consists of seven colours, and the musical scale of seven tones. There are seven kingdoms of Nature—not three, as modern science has imperfectly classified them. . . . Seven rounds have to be accomplished before the destinies of our system are worked out. The round that is at present going on is the fourth. . . . An individual unit, on arriving on a planet for the first time, has to work through seven races on that planet before he passes on to the next, and each of those races occupies the Earth for a long time." How many fine things such good people know! But there sit the neo-Hegelians, telling us that "there is no thought that is error" (§ 1686 [1]). So the "thought" of these Buddhists cannot be error; and if anyone should dispute that and give a preference to neo-Hegelian thought, who on earth would there be to settle the quarrel?

1685 [1] Renan, *L'église chrétienne*, p. 175: "There is surely an element of greatness in these strange myths. [Instead of making an objective assertion of that sort Renan should have said: "There are people who find something great in such myths, and that fact should be taken into account even by people who consider them fatuous absurdities."] When one is dealing with the infinite, with things that can be seen but through a glass darkly, with things that cannot be said in words without falsifying them [A detour designed to give the impression that he is returning to the experimental field while carefully keeping outside of it.], pathos even has its charm. [For some people, not for others.] One enjoys it as one enjoys an unhealthy poem, of which one disapproves as taste, but which one cannot but find stirring. [That may be true of Renan and of people like him. It was not true of Lucian nor of people like Lucian. The usual error of representing what is subjective as objective.] The history of the world conceived as the agitation of an embryo aspiring to life, painfully attaining to consciousness, disturbing everything by its contortions, its very travail serving as the cause of its progress and tending to the full realization of vague yearnings for the ideal—that would be a fair picture of the story we tell at

1686. IV-ε: *Vague, indefinite terms corresponding to nothing concrete*. This is the extreme limit in verbal derivation, and it ends as a mere jingle of words.[1] Among such derivations a few are for the consumption of the ignorant, who halt in stupefaction before the strangeness of the terms, and imagine that they must conceal some profound mystery.[2] Most, however, are for the use of metaphysicists, who feed on them day in and day out and end by imagining that they stand for real things. The torrent of such verbiage rushes tumultuously down across the ages from a remote antiquity to our own day. Sometimes it swells, overflows, floods everything; then again it shrinks to the confines of its normal bed; but it persists at any rate, and that shows that it must satisfy some human need, as do songs, poetry, romance.[3] Every age has its fads as to language. At the present moment [1913] in Italy, the term *"superare"* (to overpass) and its derivatives *"superatori"* (those who overpass) and *"superamento"* (the act of overpassing) are being

times to express our views on the development of the infinite." Who is "we"? Surely not everybody! There are plenty of people who care not a fig about the "development of the infinite"; many others who do not know what that jabberwock may be, and still others who laugh aloud at mere mention of its name.

1686 [1] *Voce*, Jan. 28, 1914 (Fazio-Allmayer is analyzing Gentile's *Riforma della dialettica hegeliana*): "Gentile's philosophy is a living philosophy, it is an ethical vision of the world. He has therefore felt no need of elucidating the import of this identity of history and philosophy. The philosophy that is identical with history is the philosophy which is life, and that life is the ethical life, and the ethical life is the realization of liberty, and liberty is the assertion of the real as self-consciousness. The fundamental thesis of this new history is that thought is act, in other words, concreteness, and that therefore there is no thought which is error and no nature which is not thought. Thought-act, the actuality of thought, actual idealism, have now become terms that everyone thinks he readily understands [No, no, no! There are plenty of people who are sure they understand not a syllable in such jumbles of words.], but which, alas, go wandering meaningless about the philosophical world of today. The ease with which some people think they have disposed of them is a sign of that."

1686 [2] There is a story, truth or fiction as it may be, that one day the French Academician Népomucène Lemercier, on being reviled by a woman of the markets, replied: "Hush, you old catachresis!" At which devastating epithet, the harpy was taken aback and thought it best to say no more. [It must be supposititious. The story is also Italian. In Tuscany, the woman, unabashed by the epithet, answers: "So is your mother—till I have a chance to look it up in the dictionary!"—A. L.]

1686 [3] As for the present, just one more example, from the hosts available—Fazio-Allmayer in *Voce*, Dec. 19, 1912: "Hegel drew distinctions between logic, the history of philosophy, the philosophy of history. So he distinguished God, the human spirit, the world of nations. But in that way immanence and liberty are not

bandied about on all hands.[4] Exactly what they mean nobody knows, but it must be something very impressive, for at the mere sound of such words adversaries quail, stand as though struck dumb, and know not what answer to make. And what in fact would you, gentle reader, say if you were told that a theory of yours had been "overpassed"? But may the god of metaphysics grant that the theorem of the square of the hypotenuse be not "overpassed"—otherwise, farewell to geometry! Other terms at this moment in fashion in Italy, in the favourable sense, are: "living," "dynamic," "spiritual." They stand in antithesis to various words in a bad sense: "dead," "static" (and "stasis"), "mechanical," from which last, a verb, "to mechanize," has been heroically coined. What answer, gentle reader, would you make if someone should suddenly tell you that what you say is "dead" while what he says is "living"? Or assures you that you are "mechanizing in stasis" what he is "spiritualizing in the dynamic"?[5] If you are clever enough to understand

truly attained. They are achieved only as the world of nations and the human world, in their development, that is to say, in their auto-creation, are the creation of God Himself, absolutely existing being, liberty. [So far this hotchpotch of words is incomprehensible. What follows is clearer:] And that is the very thing that Hegel wanted to prove. *If he did not succeed,* it means simply that we have to work at the problem further. And that is a task for us Italians." Here a trait that is usual in metaphysical derivations comes into clear prominence. Allmayer knows what the conclusion of the proof is to be. All that he is looking for is the proof. Just how he knows that his proposition is so sound if neither Hegel nor any other philosopher has ever been able to prove it is not so clear. May it not, perchance, be a matter of faith?

1686 [4] *Cf.* Natoli, *Voce,* Dec. 19, 1912: "Few writers have, within such a brief time since the publication of a book, aroused to any extent comparable with Croce, along with admiration, a vague feeling of discontent, a vague, almost abstract, yearning for 'overpassing.' " In Croce's defence against his "overpassers," one might aptly quote a remark he made in the *Voce* some time ago—such a remark as he only could make—on this matter of "overpassing": "These fine terms, 'overpass,' 'overpassing,' and so on, have as much meaning as the words *'funicolì, funicolà'* in the Neapolitan song—only the Neapolitan song is less tiresome and more intelligible."

1686 [5] Platon in *Indépendance,* February, 1913 (pp. 85-86): "How warmly M. Sabatier glows at the spectacle of history! Overflowing with satisfaction, full of himself, he cries, *L'orientation religieuse de la France actuelle,* pp. 153, 156, 159: 'We have introduced the concept of Life into history, and that simple introduction of Life into History socializes history in all directions, makes it over into a philosophy, a religion, an ethical system [And also a thing devoid of meaning.], a foundation of foundations for individual political education.' Or again: 'We are partakers of the Truth, of the Life, of the Revelation. . . . The Church had talked to

that, you will also be clever enough to squeeze some sense out of the following lines from Swinburne's "Nephelidia":

> Surely no spirit or sense of a soul that was soft to the spirit and soul of our senses
> Sweetens the stress of surprising suspicion that sobs in the semblance and sound of a sigh;
> Only this oracle opens Olympians in mystical moods and triangular tenses:
> "Life is the lust of a lamp for the light that is dark till the dawn of the day when we die."

Aristophanes, *Ranae*, vv. 1195-1242, says in ridicule of Euripides that after almost any one of his verses one may add, by way of conclusion: "He lost his bottle." In just that way any word that has

us of tradition and of its value in religious instruction. To us *life* reveals its power in all spheres, and showing us what we are, suggests to us all what we ought and are able to become.' Well, let M. Sabatier glow and gloat—we have nothing to say on that point. That is an aesthetic matter. But let him try to 'make history over into a philosophy, a religion, an ethical system,' and it becomes an altogether different matter. That and no other is the question at issue between him and the Papacy. What is the position of the Papacy, except that history needs a philosophy, a religion, an ethical system in order to be an 'acceptable history,' a history worthy of man and humanity?" Logico-experimental science is entirely neutral in that dispute, if for no other reason, for the reason that there is no judge to decide it (§§ 17 f.). In addition to the two kinds of history mentioned by M. Platon, there is a third kind, and it is the only kind in which experimental science can take any interest: it is the kind of history that purposes solely to describe the facts and to discover the uniformities that prevail among them. Pray note that in so saying, we are distinguishing, not comparing. We are not in the least saying that this third variety is *superior* to the other two kinds—from our point of view, such a statement would have no meaning. We are simply saying that in these volumes we prefer to confine ourselves to this third kind. Anyone sharing that preference with us is welcome to join our company. Anyone not sharing it had better seek other company—and we will have two watch-fires. In M. Sabatier's text the word "life" is written sometimes with a capital sometimes with a small initial. The things those two forms stand for are probably different; but just what the difference is, I could not say; and one may wonder whether the writer who used them would be able to do so either. I would guess, merely, that the "Life" which is honoured with a capital initial must be something better than the "life" which is not so decorated. There may be the same difference between M. Sabatier's "History" and his "history." As for "Truth," she is an old acquaintance of ours, and we have encountered her frequently in these pages. She is a creature who has nothing whatever to do with experimental truth; but she is of a nature so lofty that her beauty transcends all things.

no meaning in the concrete may be somehow fitted into any argument whatsoever.[6]

1686 [6] One might imagine the following dialogue: *A.* "Two and two make five." *B.* "I beg your pardon—I thought two and two made four." *A.* "They used to, but now that theory has been overpassed. It is a doctrine accounted for in the chemical formula of the solidifying or congealing preparate." *B.* "I do not understand." *A.* "No great harm! You have mechanized, materialized addition; you are satisfied with a crude calculatory formula." *B.* "I am more puzzled than ever." *A.* "I see that I must speak more plainly. The addition 'two plus two make four' is dead. It represents a stasis in thought. We demand a living addition, which aspires dynamically to the loftiest altitudes of human thought. And to typize history to some extent . . ." But Heaven help us now, if the enemy artillery is to be re-enforced by a "typize" as well! [The passage from Swinburne, above, was ingeniously found by Mr. Bongiorno. Pareto had used a nonsense rhyme that has been current for a generation in Italy, and which seems to emanate from some comic weekly:

> *"Come nave che esce dal porto*
> *navigando con passo scozzese,*
> *è lo stesso che prendere un morto*
> *per pagarlo alla fine del mese."*

M. Boven, *Traité,* pp. 1108-09, substituted the pleading of the two lords before Pantagruel, Rabelais, *Œuvres,* Paris, 1854, pp. 110-13.—A. L.]

CHAPTER XI

Properties of Residues and Derivations

1687. Given certain residues and certain derivations, two sorts of problems arise: 1. Just how do such residues and derivations function? 2. What is the bearing of their action on social utility? Ordinary empiricism deals with the two problems at one time, either failing to distinguish them or distinguishing them inadequately (§§ 966 f.). A scientific analysis has to keep them distinct; and it is essential, if one is to avoid falling into ready error, that while one is dealing with the first one's mind should not be encumbered with the second. Here for the moment we shall ignore the question of social utility and consider the various elements that determine the forms of society, chief among them, residues and derivations, intrinsically.[1]

1688. But before we go any farther, a few cautions will be in point as to our manner of expressing ourselves. In the first place, as regards derivations, we have used the term to designate a phenomenon that for the purposes of our study henceforward had better be divided into two. There is the derivation proper and the manifestation to which it leads: there is, in other words, a demonstration, or rather a pseudo-demonstration, and then a theorem, or pseudo-theorem. This latter may remain unchanged while the derivations that lead up to it show endless variation. For instance, in the derivation that is designed to demonstrate the existence of a solidarity-

1687 [1] The examination of residues and derivations that we have just completed has acquainted us with the manifestations of certain forces which influence human society and consequently with those forces themselves. So step by step we are gradually approaching our goal, which has been to discover the form that society assumes in virtue of the forces acting upon it. The road is a long one, but there is no way of shortening it if we insist on accepting no guides but the facts. We have identified and classified residues and derivations and in so doing we have also learned something about their properties. The time has now come to go into the matter of their properties in detail. If we are to discover the form that society assumes we must obviously consider in the mass all the elements which determine that form. But before we can do that we have to examine those elements severally and certain of their combinations. That is our task in this present chapter. We shall come to the social organism as a whole in our next.

right there is a distinction between the manifestation of that belief [1] in the mind of the person resorting to the derivation, and the proof that is given of it, that is to say, the derivation proper. The proof may vary while the manifestation remains unchanged, and sometimes the proof may be repeated in an imitative way by a person whose mind is otherwise free, or virtually free, of the manifestation—people often repeat mechanically and without great conviction talk that is in fashion in the society in which they live (§§ 2004 f.). We shall continue, as in the past, to designate the phenomenon as a whole by the term "derivation." When we find it important to distinguish the two aspects we will designate them respectively as "manifestation" [2] and "derivation proper." Analyzing "derivations proper" we find, first of all, as the foundation for all the rest, the need of logical developments that human beings feel; then residues of combination (Class I) whereby that need is satisfied; finally residues from all the other classes that are used as instruments of persuasion. Analyzing "manifestations," we get an underpinning of residues—analysis of manifestations, in fact, was our method of looking for residues in the chapters preceding. Such residues have, as a logical varnish, a supplement of derivations proper and reasonings of different kinds. In the concrete case, furthermore, disposed about the principal residue is an array of secondary or incidental residues.

1689. The main error in the thinking of the plain man, as well as in metaphysical thinking, lies not only in an inversion of terms in the relationship between derivations and human conduct—the derivation being taken, in general, as the cause of the conduct, whereas really, the conduct is the cause of the derivation—but also in ascribing *objective existence* to derivations proper and to the residues in which they originate.

As we have already cautioned in § 94 and § 149, we attach no metaphysical significance to the expression "objective existence," and it would therefore be well if we made clear in just what sense

1688 [1] [Pareto wrote: "manifestation of such existence," which I find unintelligible.—A. L.]

1688 [2] [The "manifestation" would really be a "derivative" (§ 868), and why Pareto discards that term, which is quite his own, for an obscurer "manifestation" must remain a mystery. *Cf.* § 1826.—A. L.]

we are using it here. Take, for instance, "natural law," or the "law of nations." In the minds of vast numbers of persons the concepts of certain relationships between human beings are welcomed as agreeable, whereas the concepts of certain other relationships are rejected as disagreeable. Concepts of the former type do not differ very widely from certain other concepts that are commonly designated by the adjectives "good," "honest," "just," whereas they conflict with the concepts designated by the opposite adjectives, "bad," "dishonest," "unjust." Now there is nothing wrong in designating that first group of concepts, vague as they are, by the expression "natural law," nor in describing the situation by the statement that the concept of natural law "exists in the minds of men." But from that point people go on to conclude that the thing called natural law must necessarily *exist,* and that the only question is to discover what it is and define it accurately. If we were to meet that view with the theory that "subjective existence" does not necessarily imply "objective existence," we should be involving ourselves in a metaphysical argument—the sort of thing we are trying to avoid. Our answer is quite another. It is, in the main, that in the statements in question, the word "exist" is used to express two different things.

To make the point clearer, suppose we follow a parallel line of reasoning. It is an undisputed fact that in the minds of many persons, and specifically, persons called chemists, the concept of sodium chloride is accepted along with other concepts of chemical reactions and is correlated with them. There is nothing to prevent our stating that situation by saying that the concept of sodium chloride "exists in the minds of men." From that it is possible to conclude—though in actual practice the opposite course is followed, that a thing called sodium chloride must "exist."

The two reasonings have, it is true, one point of similarity. But in another respect, they are altogether different. With chemists, the consequences logically following from the concept of sodium chloride have such a great probability of being verified in practice that they may be designated as "certain," as that term is used in ordinary parlance. The consequences logically following from the concept of natural law are seldom verified in practice. More frequently they fail of verification altogether. The chemist does not say: "Sodium chloride in solution *ought* to precipitate silver nitrate." He says

—a very different matter—that sodium chloride in solution *precipitates* silver nitrate. The champion of natural law cannot use this latter form of expression; he must at all times rest content with the former. A glance at history is enough to show that natural law is just a rubber band: the powerful can stretch it to whatever length they choose.

We need not go too far afield. In the year 1913 certain of the European Powers decided that it would be a good thing if there were a principality of Albania. They allowed Montenegro to lay siege to Scutari, and then one fine day ordered that country to desist. Montenegro refusing, the same Powers, without any declaration of hostilities, sent war-ships to blockade the Montenegrin coast and they captured the private yacht of the King of Montenegro. Could anyone tell us what "right" the Powers in question had to do such a thing, and especially what "right" they had to Albanian territory and to Scutari—unless, of course, we are to use the word "right" in the meaning it has in the fable of the wolf and the lamb? It is evident that the Powers in question were able to do what they pleased with the "law of nations." But they could not have done what they pleased with reactions in chemistry. With all their armies and navies they could not have kept sodium chloride in solution from precipitating a solution of silver nitrate.

From the practical standpoint, therefore, there is an essential difference between the two cases in question. The "existence" of sodium chloride and other chemical bodies is one thing, the "existence" of "natural law," the "law of nations," or other entities of the kind is quite another thing. And likewise different in the two cases are the logical inferences that may be drawn from them. In chemistry I draw the logical inference that a certain weight of sodium chloride contains a definite weight of chlorine. I perform an analysis and verify my inference. Not so when the logical inference is to be drawn from entities of that vague and indefinite variety known as the "law of nations," "natural law," and the like. Still keeping to Montenegro, the British Foreign Secretary declared that Montenegro could not be permitted to occupy Scutari because the population was not of the same race, did not speak the same language, did not have the same religion. It would seem, therefore, that a country does not have the "right" to occupy another country when the latter presents those differences. Now let someone ask whether the Hindus are of the same race, language, and religion as the English; and if the answer is no, it must remain a mystery why Montenegro does not have the "right" to occupy Scutari while the English have the "right" to occupy India.[1]

In general terms, when we say that the concept of natural law "exists" in the minds of men, what we mean is that in the minds of certain numbers of individuals there is a concept to which that name is given. A practical test can be made of that, and it will be seen to succeed. Moreover one may draw the inference from that fact that in arguing with certain persons in the intent of persuading them, it would be well to take account of the fact that that concept is present in their minds. And there too the practical test turns out well. That is why the powerful, instead of saying simply that they want a thing, go to the trouble of devising sophistries to show that they "have a right" to it: they imitate the wolf's palaver with the lamb. The proposition that natural law "exists" in the minds of men is therefore of the same character as the assertion that the concept of sodium chloride "exists" in the minds of certain men, except that the latter statement is something much more definite. Likewise similar is the proposition that a thing called sodium chloride "exists." But the proposition that "natural law" "exists" is of an entirely different character.[2] For that proposition to belong to the other class it

1689 [1] An official *communiqué* issued by the Russian Government to justify its veto of the Montenegrin occupation of Scutari was couched in the following language: "Furthermore the population of Scutari is in the majority Albanian and that city is the see of a Catholic bishopric. It must, in this connexion, also not be overlooked that the Montenegrins have never been able to assimilate several thousands of Catholic or Mussulman Albanians who have settled on the frontiers of Montenegro." Substitute Russia for Montenegro, and Poland for Albania in the argument. Its validity will of course not be altered. Russia is Orthodox, Poland is Catholic, Russia has never managed to assimilate the Poles. But though the reasoning is identical, the conclusions are different: Montenegro does not have the "right" to occupy Scutari. Russia has the "right" to occupy Poland.

1689 [2] That is all we mean when we say that "natural law" *does not exist:* what we mean is that such an entity cannot be used in a reasoning in the way that sodium chloride or other things of that kind can be used. We do not in the least intend to adopt, either as equivalents or as consequences, the following propositions: (1) That the concept of natural law "does not exist" in the minds of certain men; (2) that that concept plays no part in determining the form of society; (3) that mankind would be better rid of it as a foolish, non-existent thing. Indeed we deem

would be necessary: (1) That there be some possibility of defining the meaning of the expression with reasonable definiteness; (2) that logical inferences from such a definition should be verifiable in practice. Neither of those conditions is fulfilled. In fact, we showed in Chapter IV that one can never know with any definiteness at all what a writer means when he uses the expression "natural law." And there are proofs without end to show that from that expression one may logically infer what *ought* to happen according to this or that writer, but never what actually happens.[3] It follows that entities of that sort can be of no use whatever when the purpose is to de-

that the propositions directly contrary to those three are in accord with the facts, namely: (1) that the concept of natural law "exists" (*i.e.,* is present), though in a very indefinite way, in the minds of certain men; (2) that that concept (or rather, the fact that that concept is present in the minds of certain men) plays a part in determining the form of society; (3) that in many cases, the fact that such a concept has been present in the minds of certain men has been beneficial to society. Let us add one more: (4) that the belief that natural law "exists" (or the belief that the concept of "natural law" can play in an argument the part that is played by concepts such as sodium chloride) has frequently proved beneficial to society, though such belief is in complete disaccord with the facts.

1689 [3] Metaphysicists and literary economists have hit on a very pretty derivation to meet objections of this type. They say that economic, moral, and social "laws" differ from "natural laws" in that they have exceptions, while the latter do not. Suppose we disregard the consideration that a "law" that has exceptions, that is to say, a uniformity which is not uniform, is an expression devoid of meaning (§ 101), and keep to the force of the argument. We may as well admit that, as regards forms, it is invincible. If one grants to a person who is stating a law that his law may have its exceptions, he can always meet every fact that is adduced against him with the excuse that it is an "exception," and he will never be caught in the wrong. And that is exactly what literary economists, moralists, and metaphysicists do: They proclaim "laws" and then do what they please with them, taking advantage of indefiniteness in terms, exceptions, and other subterfuges of the kind, to bend their laws to their every wish and whim.

Unfortunately for their thesis they are altogether too right if they follow that path: a law of that kind has no significance, and knowledge of it is not of the slightest use. A person might say that it rains only on even days in the calendar and then meet facts to the contrary by saying that rains on odd days are exceptions. Another might assert that it rains only on odd days, and meet objections in the same way. Reasoning in that fashion, both would be right, and neither "law" would teach one a single thing. To make it helpful, there has to be some obstacle, a restriction of some sort on the free manipulation of the "law." One might assert that the facts against the "law" are much less numerous than the facts in favour of it. The "law" has to be stated in language definite enough to be interpreted by persons other than the author of it. The conditions considered necessary for the verification of the "law" have to be at least suggested. And so on and so forth.

termine what actually happens. We regard them merely as manifestations of sentiments.[4]

1690. Returning to the matter of our modes of expression, we must further note that since sentiments are manifested by residues we shall often, for the sake of brevity, use the word "residues" as including the sentiments that they manifest. So we shall say, simply, that residues are among the elements which determine the social equilibrium, a statement that must be translated and understood as meaning that "the sentiments manifested by residues are among the elements which stand toward the social equilibrium in a relationship of reciprocal determination." But that statement too is elliptical and has again to be translated. Let us beware of ascribing any objective existence (§§ 94, 149, 1689) to our residues or even to sentiments. What we observe in reality is a group of human beings in a mental condition indicated by what we call sentiments. Our proposition must, therefore, be translated in the following terms: "The mental states that are indicated by the sentiments expressed in residues are among the elements that stand in a relation of reciprocal determination with the social equilibrium." But if we would express ourselves in a language altogether exact, that is still not enough. What in the world are those "mental states" or, if one will, those "psychic conditions"? They are abstractions. And what underlies the abstractions? So we are obliged to say: "The actions of human beings are among the elements that stand in a relationship of reciprocal determination with the social equilibrium. Among such actions are certain manifestations that we designate by the term "residues" and which are closely correlated with other acts so that once we know the residues we may, under certain circumstances, know the actions. Therefore we shall say that residues are among the elements that stand in a relation of reciprocal determination with the social equilibrium."

It is well enough to say all that once, just to fix with strict exactness the meaning of the terms we use; but it would be useless, tire-

1689 [4] It was for such sentiments that we went looking in Chapters VI, VII, and VIII, as belonging to that group of things which can be used in determining what actually happens. For the same reason, in Chapters IX and X we studied the disguises under which such sentiments are hidden from view. And in doing that we were following the procedure of the scientist who first determines the composition of a chemical body, and then the form in which it crystallizes.

some, and altogether pedantic to be for ever talking with such prolixity. That is why we replace the proposition just stated with its shorter original form: "Residues are among the elements that determine the social equilibrium." [1]

Derivations also manifest sentiments. Directly, they manifest the sentiments that correspond to the residues in which they originate. Indirectly they manifest sentiments through the residues that serve for purposes of derivation. But to speak of derivations in place of the residues they manifest, as is done in ordinary parlance, might lead to serious misapprehensions, and we shall refrain from doing so in all cases where any doubt as to the meaning of a statement is possible.

The subject being very important, it will not come amiss to offer some further elucidation. We observe, for example, a number of cases in which a hen defends her chicks, and we epitomize our observation of past facts, our forecast of future facts, and our guess at a uniformity, by saying that "the hen defends her chicks," that present in the hen is a sentiment that prompts her to defend her chicks, that that defence is the consequence of a given psychic state. So we observe a number of cases in which certain individuals sacrifice their lives for their countries; and we epitomize our observation of the past fact, our forecast of future fact, and our conception of a uniformity embracing large numbers of individuals, by saying that "Human beings—or some human beings—sacrifice their lives for their countries," that present in them is a sentiment which prompts them to sacrifice their lives for their countries, that such sacrifice is the consequence of a given psychic state.

But in human beings we further observe certain facts that are a consequence of their using language and are therefore not observable in animals: human beings, that is, express in language certain things which we associate with the facts that are observable when they sacrifice their lives for their countries. They say, for instance,

---

1690 [1] Nor can the short cut result in any harm if attention is paid to the exact sense we give to the terms we use. In the same way pure economics uses the term "ophelimity" and mechanics the term "force," which, in their relations to the economic and mechanical equilibria respectively, correspond to the term "sentiment" ("residue") in its relations to the social equilibrium. The theory of choices stated in my *Manuale* corresponds to the remarks we make here for the purpose of eliminating the term "sentiment" (§ 2409).

"Dulce et decorum est pro patria mori"; and we say that they express in that way a certain sentiment, a certain psychic state, and so on. But that is not very exact, for the propositions that we take as expressions of a sentiment (or better, of a sum of sentiments), a psychic state, and so on, are multiple and diverse. It was by separating in them elements that are constant from variable elements that we got residues and derivations and said that the residue expresses that sentiment, that psychic state, and so on. But in so saying we are adding something to the facts. All that experimental observation shows is a set of simultaneous facts—men dying for their countries and using certain modes of speech.[2] We may state that situation in

1690 [2] Between the statements *D* and the conduct *A* there may be a direct relation, *DA*. That, in fact, is the only relation envisaged by people who reduce all social phenomena to logical conduct. But the actual relation, as a rule, is different: that is to say, both statements and conduct have a common origin, *O*. Such common origin, which is generally unknown, may be called a "sentiment," a "psychic state," or

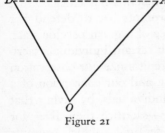

Figure 21

something else of the sort; but to give an unknown thing a name does not in the least increase our knowledge of it.

One might further assume that *D* stands for residues and *A* for derivations, and repeat the above: Residues and derivations have a common origin, *O*, unknown. To get at the residues we establish, theoretically, a relation *AD;* and then, to get the derivations from the residues, we similarly establish the relation *DA*. But the actual relations are *OD, OA*.

Going back to the analogies suggested in § 879 between language and other social facts, we may assume that *D* represents word-roots and *A* the words in a language. The philologist, working as above in the case of residues and derivations, posits a theoretical relation, *AD*, deriving roots from the words; and then, in the same fashion, a relation *DA*, deriving words from the roots. But in actual fact our languages have not been developed by deriving words from roots, though once they have been fully developed, such a thing may happen in a few rare cases at the instance of grammarians or scholars. Generally speaking, words originated spontaneously in the population at large, and the same forces that produced the words gave rise to their roots at the same time; that is to say, the actual relations, *OA, OD*, prevailed. Sometimes, as in cases of onomatopoeia, we are able to get a picture more or less exact of the origin, *O,* of a family of words, *A,* and its roots, *D;* but most often by far such origins remain absolutely unknown: all we know is the family of words, philologists abstracting the root. Investigations have been made into the "origins" of languages—efforts have been made, that is, to discover *O*. But such researches have so far been of no use either to grammar or to lexicography, though both those sciences have profited by knowledge of roots. In the case of Greek, grammar and dictionary stop at roots, and there would have been no

the following propositions, which start close to reality and gradually get farther and farther away from it: 1. Observable side by side are *acts* of self-sacrifice for country and expressions of approval or praise for such acts. Such expressions have an element in common. We call it a residue. 2. Human beings sacrifice themselves for country and have a sentiment, manifested by residues, which spurs them to such conduct. The divergence from reality lies in the term "sentiment," which has an element of vagueness. Then again, the uniformity is stated without limitations, whereas some limitation is essential. Finally, even the assumption that conduct is always inspired by sentiment is open to question. 3. Instead of saying, *"and* have a sentiment . . .", the form is, *"because* they have a sentiment . . ."

scientific grammars or dictionaries yet had philologists insisted on waiting till they had discovered "origins." Just so, in sociology, there may be cases where we catch some glimpse, remote and imperfect as it may be, of the origin, O, both of the residues, D, and of the derivations, or conduct, A; but in by far the greater number of cases, we know very much what the philologist knows: that is to say, only the derivations, or conduct, A, whence, theoretically, we infer the residues, D, and then re-deduce from the residues, D, the derivations and conduct, A, considering, in other words, the relations AD and DA, though the actual relations remain OA and OD.

Many many investigations in sociology are like philological speculations as to the "origins" of languages. They aim at discovering the "origins" of social phenomena, and so have been of little use to science.

Our aim in these volumes is to constitute a science of sociology by stopping at residues just as the philologist stops at roots, the chemist at elements (simple bodies), the student of celestial mechanics at universal attraction, and so on. As regards our modes of expression, when we say elliptically that residues determine conduct, we substitute, for the sake of simplicity, the relation DA, which is theoretical only, for the actual relations, OA, OD. In other words, we do as the philologist does when he says that a family of words, A, originates in a root, D, or that certain tenses of the verb are *formed* from the indicative radical, certain others from the aorist radical, and so on. No one has ever taken such a statement to mean that the Greeks got together one day, agreed upon certain aorist roots, and then derived aorist verb-forms from them. Neither should anyone take our statement that residues *determine* conduct in any such absurd sense.

Had we been following the deductive method, the matter treated in this note would properly have been part of the text and have found its place towards the beginning of our study. But it would have been difficult to grasp in that place because of its newness. The deductive method lends itself especially to a subject-matter that is already in part commonplace and well known. When a subject is entirely new, the inductive method is the only one that can adequately prepare a reader to grasp it clearly and understand it thoroughly. That is why the inductive method was followed in treatises such as the *Politica* of Aristotle, the political writings of Machiavelli, Adam Smith's *Wealth of Nations,* and other similar works in one field or another.

The term "because" takes us still farther away from reality, in that it asserts a relationship of cause and effect, and we have no certain knowledge that any such relation exists. 4. Human beings *believe* it their duty to sacrifice themselves for country; *therefore* they sacrifice themselves. . . . In that we get very very far from reality, assuming that the conduct is the consequence of certain beliefs and so substituting logical for non-logical conduct. This fourth manner of statement is the usual one, but it easily leads astray, even if we bear in mind that it is only another form for 1. There is no objection to the use of 2, provided we bear in mind that, strictly speaking, we are always to check it by reference to 1.[8] The third manner, 3, is also serviceable; but we must always remember that it really stands for 1, and be on our guard against drawing logical inferences from the term "because" that appears in it. The term "sentiments," "residues," and so on, are convenient makeshifts in sociology, just as the term "force" has proved convenient in mechanics. They may be used without untoward results if the realities to which they correspond are always kept clearly in mind.

1691. *Residues in general.* In identifying and classifying residues we considered them without regard to the intensity of the sentiments that are manifested through them and independently of the number of persons in whom they are to be met with. In other words, we dissevered them by a process of abstraction from the concrete individuals to whom they belong. We must now take account of all such circumstances.

Suppose, first of all, we consider the matter of intensities. It is important to distinguish between the intensity proper of a residue and the intensity that it derives from the general tendency of the individual to be more or less energetic. A person may have a strong sense of patriotism but still be a physical coward. In that case he will fight less effectively for his country than a man whose patriotism is much less virulent but who is a man of courage. If a person has a strong combination-instinct, but is inclined to indolence, he will utilize fewer combinations than a person in whom that instinct is not so strong but who is inclined to be active. We may therefore conclude that certain circumstances which we may

1690 [8] In point of fact, we have used form 2 freely in this work and shall continue to do so, especially in an equivalent variant relating conduct and residues.

designate by the term "strength," or its opposite "weakness," raise or lower the general level of this or that residue.[1]

1692. Then suppose we look at residues with respect to the concrete individuals to whom they belong. Let us assume that in a certain locality at a certain time a thousand cases of the phenomenon *A* are observable; in another place, or at another time, a hundred cases of the phenomenon *B*; finally in still a third locality or time, one single case of the phenomenon *C*. In our previous chapter, to get at the residues involved, we compared *A* with *B* and *C* on the look-out for a constant element, disregarding the numbers of cases of *A*, *B*, *C*. Now, however, we must direct our attention to this aspect of the matter, considering, that is, the distribution of residues.[1]

1693. Under a static aspect, we must consider: (1) The distribution of residues in a given society; and (2) their distribution in the different strata in that society. From a dynamic point of view we have to see: (1) how, approximately, residues vary in time, whether as a result of changes in the individuals belonging to one same social stratum, or of changes caused by a mixing of social strata; and (2) how each of those two things arises.

1694. Due attention must be paid, moreover, to the rhythmical movement that is observable in all social phenomena (§ 2329). A phenomenon that is virtually constant is not represented by a straight line, *mn* (Figure 22), but by an undulating curve, *svt*. A phenomenon of increasing in-

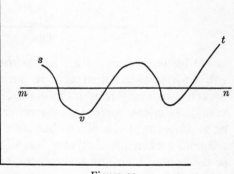

Figure 22

1691 [1] The difficulty lies in the ambiguity of the term "strong." It may apply to the intensity of a residue in an individual as compared with the intensity of other residues in the same individual, or as compared with the intensity of the same residue in other individuals.

1692 [1] However, we cannot go too far in this direction, for we lack as yet a theory for the division of society into classes. Here, therefore, we can merely broach

tensity (Figure 23) is represented not by a straight line, *ab,* but by an undulating curve, *rpq.* Lines such as *mn* and *ab* represent the *mean movement* of the phenomenon, and that movement we now propose to examine (§ 1718).

1695. *Distribution and change in society as a whole.* We are not here inquiring as to the causes that determine the character of a society—whether race, climate, geographical situation, fertility of soil, possibilities of economic productivity, or the like. We are look-

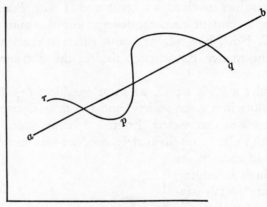

Figure 23

ing at historical societies as facts, without any concern, for the present, with origins. Observable in such historical societies are phenomena that vary little in substance, but widely in forms. As the various religions succeed one another in history, their forms may be as different as one please, but after all they are all expressions of religious sentiments that vary but slightly. The same may be said of the various forms of government, each of which explicitly or implicitly has its own "divine right." The modern free-thinker enforces, in the name of Science, Holy of Holies, a morality but slightly differing from the code that the God of the Israelites proclaimed for His people, or the code that the Christians received from their God; or the codes that now one, now another, of the ancient peoples received from gods or from lawgivers legendary or divine. Nor is there any very appreciable difference, either, in the derivations by which

the subject, going into it more fully in our next chapter, XII, after we have established such a theory (§§ 2025 f.).

the imperative and absolute character of all such ethical systems is justified.[1]

Similar uniformities are observable even in phenomena much less important. In ancient times people who were sick made pilgrim-

1695 [1] We have already given many examples. Here is another that may serve as typical of a very very large class. The derivations it uses serve, in general, for other cases without end.

The use of absinth had been prohibited in Switzerland, and Swiss temperance fanatics were vexed because the courts were not showing themselves very severe in dealing with violations. A newspaper wrote in that connexion: "Under a system of absolute monarchy, the will of a single individual is forced upon a whole nation. That single will may offend the sentiment of a people. It may flout legitimate traditions and customs. It may be in arrears or in advance of the period in which it is manifested. When a divergence of views arises between a monarch and his people, it becomes difficult to enforce the law. Quite otherwise the situation in a republic. There the people is the sovereign. Its rulers are not forced upon it—it chooses them itself. And under the system of direct democracy, a system such as ours, the citizens themselves determine the constitutional principles on which the country is to be governed. The constitution cannot be amended without the assent of the majority of the voters, who are always consulted in such a matter. The laws themselves, which are worked out by legislative bodies after public discussion and within constitutional limits, become obligatory only when the people has approved them formally or tacitly; it can assert its right to the referendum. It even possesses the right of initiative in legislation. So all the legal provisions that govern the conditions of social life are passed through the sieve of public discussion. Only those measures acquire force of law which correspond to the will of the people at the moment of their proposal. All antiquated conceptions are thrust aside, premature reforms are postponed. General obedience is required only of those laws and constitutional principles which have found favour with the majority of voters."

A number of points deserve comment here. 1. The careless attitude, as usual, of religions towards facts. Let us accept for the moment the comparison that is set up between the bad laws that presumably are peculiar to absolute monarchies, and the excellent laws that certainly, according to this editor, are peculiar to democracies. From that it would follow that Roman law as exemplified in the imperial Institutes should be greatly inferior to Athenian law. But is that really the case? 2. The fallacy, very widely resorted to, whereby "the people" is confused with a "majority of the people" and—what is even worse—with a "majority of the voters." As a matter of fact the prohibition of absinth was not voted by the majority of the Swiss people, but by a majority of the small fraction of that people which participated in the voting. How in the world that number, which was much smaller than the majority of the people, becomes equivalent to "the people," is a mystery that may well stand on a par with the mystery of the Holy Trinity. And how in the world the will of that small number becomes equivalent to the "will" of "the whole people" is another mystery, less mysterious, to be sure, than the one just mentioned, but fairly mysterious at that. It may be said that citizens who did not vote were wrong in not doing so, and that may well be; but it is not the point in question here. They may be as much at fault as one please; there may be excellent legal reasons why their preferences should not be taken into consideration; but all that

ages to the temples of Aesculapius in order to regain their health. They were succeeded in the Middle Ages by devout Christians who prayed to their saints for health and visited shrines and relics. Nowadays they would recognize descendants in the throngs that flock to Lourdes, in the devotees of "Christian Science," or even in those humbler souls who fatten the purses of medical quacks. We have no accurate statistics to show the exact numbers of such persons and therefore whether and to what extent their relative proportion to population has changed. Certain it is that the proportion has been and remains a very considerable one, that it has never been and is

does not change a minority of a "people" into a majority, nor reveal what the will of those who were guilty of not voting actually was, great though their crime may have been in not doing so. 3. The derivation which assumes that a person belonging to a community can be oppressed only by an absolute sovereign, never by a majority of which he is not a part. The justification for such a distinction is to be found only in a "divine right of the majority," or something of the sort. If an individual is absolutely averse to doing a certain thing, and disregarding the sentiments of reverence in deference to which he subordinates his will to the will of others—what difference can it make to him whether the thing is required of him by a Roman Emperor, a mediaeval king, a parliament, or some other authority? "When a divergence of views arises between a monarch and his people [The usual sophistry of treating the people as a unit.], it becomes difficult to enforce the law." And what if the difference of opinion arises between a majority and a minority? "Quite otherwise the situation in a republic." Really? The history of the Athenian and Roman republics tells just the opposite story. History may be wrong, of course, the way geology was wrong in its conflict with the Book of Genesis. "There the people is the sovereign." Or would not the sovereign be, rather, questions of "irregularities" aside, the majority of the voters? "Its rulers are not forced upon it—it chooses them itself." The pronoun "it" here refers to the people. In reality—still apart from irregularities—it refers to the majority, often a very slim majority, of those voting. 4. The derivation that a person who is forced to act in accord with the will of a majority—even granting that it is the majority that makes the laws—acts according to his own will as the will of the people of whom he is a part. Take a group of twenty-one persons. Eleven of them decide to eat the other ten (something of the sort has actually happened in cases of shipwreck). Shall we say that such a decision "corresponds to the will of the people," that the people is αὐτόφορβος—self-eating—and that each of the persons eaten will have to say as much before being put to death, and agree that the "will of the people" is his will? 5. Observable not only in the case mentioned, but in numberless others, is a theory similar to the Catholic theory of contrition and attrition (§ 1459). It is not enough that the citizen submit to the will of the majority through fear of the punishments the latter may visit upon him; he must also pay worship to its divine will.

As usual, to avoid misunderstandings, let us caution that all the above has nothing whatever to do with the essentially different question as to whether it may not be better for a community that the public should be given to understand that such divine rights exist, and that it be convinced of their existence.

not now small. If one may guess that it has decreased in our day as compared with times past, we have no conclusive proof of the fact. Since we cannot have the much, it is our part to rest content with the little, which, after all, is better than nothing.[2]

1696. And to such things still others of the same brand have to be added. In the temples of Aesculapius treatment was not exclusively a matter of supernatural forces or, if one will, of suggestion; it was often, in parts at least, material and therefore genuinely medicinal. So from that standpoint if one takes the cures of Lourdes or the treatments of Christian Science, and other such sects, as a

1695 [2] Christian Science is an attractive theory that perhaps cures all diseases and which certainly enriched its founder, Mary Baker G. Eddy. To avoid any chance of misrepresenting the doctrine I put before the reader an "explanation" of it furnished by a writer who is kindly disposed toward it. Byse, *La science chrétienne,* p. 22: "We have to deal with three enemies, in chief: sin, pain, death. Not only are they a perpetual threat to us, sometimes overwhelming us: their very existence is a riddle to our reason and an insult to our faith. How can the evil that reigns in the world under those three forms go back to the Creation? How reconcile it with a supremely good and powerful God? All the suggestions that have been put forward to solve that agonizing problem are more indicative of the embarrassment of the thinkers than satisfying to the intelligence. And now comes Mrs. Eddy and cuts the Gordian knot with one slash of the sword. Those formidable foes are mere phantoms. To see them vanish like fog one has only to tear the terrifying mask from their features and say to each one of them: 'You do not exist.' [A long theological divagation follows. We need not dwell on it. Let us see what happens in the real world, pp. 26-27:] The cures of Christian Science are to be counted by hundreds, thousands, tens of thousands. . . . Their genuineness is vouched for by all the guarantees that can reasonably be asked for. [Equally numerous and well established were ghost phenomena and the feats of witchcraft and magic.] . . . That is why they meet neither raillery nor incredulousness in Anglo-Saxon countries. Ever since the third century of our era Christianity has been neglecting its rights and its duty as regards disease. It is time we were coming to our senses. That is why on the cover of *Science and Health* there is a crown hung over a cross with an inscription written about it: 'Heal the sick, raise the dead, cleanse the leper, cast out devils.' Mrs. Eddy took that surprising command of the Saviour in earnest and now sees herself rewarded for her trust. Like the Master she is curing 'all sorts of diseases and infirmities,' and her pupils have learned to do likewise." But she never "mastered well that art" as regards herself. She died! *Medice, cura te ipsum!* Some of her disciples, either more stupid or more logical than others, said that she *could* not be dead, since that would have been inconsistent with her doctrine, which denies the reality of death. They therefore looked for her resurrection. Needless to say, they are still looking. William James, in a spirit of professional jealousy perhaps, did not take kindly to Mrs. Eddy. M. Byse talks back to him, p. 35: "The celebrated psychologist, I am sorry to say, treats this vast and subtle subject very superficially." Perhaps in fear of the Latin's sense of ridicule, M. Byse does not go into details as to the manner in which diseases are cured. We are there-

term of comparison, one might conclude that there has been retrogression rather than advance as regards any increase in the scientific element.[1] In the miracles at Lourdes, and in the practices of Christian Science, there is no trace of medical treatment. Of it, indeed, Chris-

fore obliged to depend on other sources. A correspondent of the *Resto del Carlino*, Vol. XXV, No. 330, met devotees of the new science in Berlin. They were people who were swallowing rigmaroles of the following order: "You say that a tumour gives you great pain. The tumour is merely a sign of your belief in pains as caused by inflammations and swellings, and that belief you call a tumour." Mrs. Eddy, one may conclude, was a consummate Hegelian, but only as regards diseases, not as regards money. "Imagine that you are not ill, but be sure to pay in money that is not imaginary." Mayor, *Mary Baker Eddy, et la Science chrétienne*, pp. 123-28, 224-29: "The treatment that is designed to destroy the false belief of the patient must therefore be purely mental, and partly silent, and it may even be given at a distance. . . . Cases have been mentioned where patients have been cured without even suspecting that they were under treatment. . . . The practitioner mentions disease only to deny it, his one purpose being to provoke a realization of its unreality. Tumours, ulcers, inflammations, boils, deformed joints, pains of all sorts, are nothing but depressing images born of the Spirit of Death and to be dissipated by the Divine Spirit. . . . [*Quoting from Mrs. Eddy:*] 'Summoned for a case of childbirth, in other words, the birth of a divine idea, the practitioner will try to banish all preoccupation with material things, that everything may take its course in a natural manner. . . . Born of the Spirit, born of God, the child cannot cause its mother pain.' " Mrs. Eddy gives her ideas gratis. Now let us see what she takes in return: "All such books are sold at prices which may seem high in view of the fact that publication costs have been reduced to a minimum. . . . Book-reviewers [Who were not at first favourable.] have now changed their tune and are showing themselves full of deference for the Mother of the Scientists, who on her side knows how to appreciate the favours that are done her. . . . The net profits from the sale of the book that was 'offered to the hungry' [That is what Mrs. Eddy calls her dupes.] may be estimated at present at about $2,000,000. The author's royalties have amounted to $1,000,000, the Church's share to $800,000. One may doubt whether any writer ever earned greater royalties than the Prophetess of idealistic asceticism." Mrs. Eddy was shrewder or luckier than the run of faith-curers, who also heal all sorts of diseases. She was certainly luckier than poor Cagliostro and other adventurers of that kind. Centuries and centuries have passed since Lucian wrote his *Pseudomantis* or *False Prophet;* but the book is contemporary history of ours, as true now as ever, in spite of the fact that devotees of the god Progress would give us to understand that their divinity has extirpated "superstition."

1696 [1] To mention the whole list of modern sects that have a medical slant would be too much for us, but I cannot resist setting down one more example. *Liberté,* Oct. 27, 1913 (article by "Séris"): *"The Antoinist Cult:* 'Father Anthony' was a 'healer' along the lines of Jake the Zouave. He made prodigious cures. He died last year at Jemmapes-lez-Liége, in Belgium. Now a religion has risen from his ashes. The 'Antoinist Cult' has its priests and its following and they are growing in numbers. 'Mother Anthony,' in other words, 'Father Anthony's' widow, has inherited the curative powers of her late husband and is doing business at the old stand with the assistance of an individual in long hair and whiskers who has

tian Scientists strongly disapprove. However, one cannot stop at that. Cures effected by magic, relics, and other fantastic instrumentalities were very numerous in a day gone by; and that fact would probably force us to the opposite conclusion that science after all has made some gains.

barbered himself up to look in all respects the prophet. This gentleman is not the 'Father.' His mission is to evangelize the masses, for 'Mother' has nothing to do but make grimaces and gestures. The Antoinists have built a little church in Paris in the Maison Blanche quarter, at the corner of the rue Vergniaud and the rue Wurtz. Instead of window-panes there are whitewashed squares. There are no crosses, no statues, no religious pictures or symbols of any kind. The walls are bare outside as well as in. There are, however, inscriptions, such as this one, on the front of the building: '1913: The Antoinist Cult.' Inside, and located near the entrance as though for a sort of battle-flag, there is another: 'Father Anthony, the Great Healer of Humanity, for Such as Have Faith.' At the end of the auditorium, a philosophical thought: 'There is one Remedy for Humanity: Faith. Of Faith Love is Born. Love reveals God Himself to us in our Enemies. Not to Love our Enemies is to Fail in Love of God, for the Love we have for our Enemies is what makes us worthy of serving Him. That is the one Love that wins Love for us, for it is pure and of the Truth.' There are no altars in the Church. There is a pulpit at the end of the room, a wooden structure, very plain. Nailed to the face is a wooden frame painted white, with a glass. It holds a little tree, something like a Japanese tree. An inscription in white letters imparts that it is the 'Tree of Knowledge of Life and Evil.' It is the one symbol used in the Antoinist Cult. It is to be seen again on a steel plaque that is fitted to a staff and is held aloft by an attendant—a sort of beadle. The attendants all wear uniforms that are black throughout, long afternoon-coats that are severely buttoned to the chin. They wear tall hats, of half-length, with flat brims—very much the sort of hat that Alexandre Duval designed, but minus the suggestion of *chic*. This forenoon there was a large audience for the dedication of the Church, all the more since 'Mother' was to work cures. An old woman, held up by two friends, made her way to a row of seats appointed for patients in front of the pulpit. Every step she took cost her an effort and a groan, but her eyes shone with a feverish brilliancy. She walked with shoulders bent, and was finally settled in a chair. An attendant strikes a gong three times, some distance apart, as at elevation in the mass. A door opens and 'Mother' appears. She is an old lady neatly dressed in black. Her widow's weeds are pinned to her bonnet. She walks up the steps to the pulpit, her hands folded. There she stiffens in an ecstatic pose, then slowly raises her arms and draws them apart. Her lips mutter incomprehensible words. Then she brings her hands together, darts them first to the right, then to the left, then throws herself flat on the platform, face down. That is the whole show. Resuming her normal self, 'Mother' walks down the stairs and leaves the auditorium, followed by 'Father,' who has stood motionless near the pulpit in an inspired attitude during this whole 'consultation.' 'Mother's' destination is a wooden shack behind the church, something like the tool-houses where city gardeners keep their tools. The aged patient musters all her will and rises; but her exhilaration has vanished suddenly. She leaves as she came, supported by her two friends. A young woman takes her

1697. It is further to be noted that the treatments practised in the temples of Aesculapius are not completely represented in modern times by the miracles at Lourdes, the treatments of Christian Science, and other phenomena of the kind. To such are still to be added the practices of those many medical quacks whom Daudet happily dubbed "deathers" (*"morticoles"*). In their regard the credulity of the ancients has its perfect counterpart in the credulity of the moderns. At no time in history have quacks flourished more abundantly on the money of simpletons than they do today; and in many countries the law protects such priests of the goddess "Science" just as religiously as it protected priests of the pagan gods of old— sometimes even more so. Believers gather in droves in those clinics and sanitoria which are the temples of the modern quack. Some of them get well, if Mother Nature chances to look upon them with kindly eye; but all of them contribute to the collection-box of the high-priests of the goddess "Science" and their acolytes—

place. She is carrying in her arms a little girl, four or five years old and frightfully thin. All the life in the child seems to have gathered in her eyes. Her arms and legs hang listlessly from her body. As she doubles over her mother's left arm she seems as limp as a piece of cloth. Indifferent to everything that is going on around her, she keeps her eyes fixed on the ceiling. The young mother's dismay transpires through the waxy pallor of her features. She keeps wiping her forehead with her handkerchief to remove the great drops of sweat that stand out like glass beads. The same ceremony is repeated: three strokes on the gong, a second appearance of the old lady, the same scene over again without a single variation—it is the prescription for every case. Then the mother carries her child out again, the same rag of a girl she had been before. Not a trace of comment in the congregation. The audience has looked on at all that in a sort of stupor, a sense of acute distress checking any thrust of irony. People have gathered in groups on the sidewalks outside. I hear a fat man with rum on his breath remark to an attendant, 'Why not, if a person has faith?' Then, locking arms with the other, he adds: 'Come on, *copain!* Let's have another glass. It will brace us up.' "

Every now and then something happens to show the fatuousness of such beliefs. In 1913 the actress Nuscha Butze-Beerman died in Berlin. *Corriere della sera,* Dec. 13: "Nuscha had been suffering from diabetes since the previous summer. She had been under the care of a physician and had followed the prescribed treatment; but later she fell into the hands of a *Gesundbeterin,* in other words, one of those female faith-curers who treat diseases by prayer. The actress neglected her medical régime and placed her whole reliance on the virtues of will-power and prayer. She grew steadily worse and a few days ago she was too weak to get to the theatre. Her practitioner, however, told her that she must not allow herself to lose heart; that she must always remember that mind knows not pain. She need simply say a prayer and go to her performance. The actress went, but half-way through her act collapsed, and never recovered consciousness."

among whom, let us not fail to count the pharmacists who sell their drugs at 1000 per cent profit; and the inventors of those patent medicines which shoot across the sky of publicity like meteors, cure every conceivable disease for more or less extensive, and often very brief, periods of time, and then are gone; not without leaving huge fortunes in the pockets of certain traders on public credulity who exploit the poor in spirit under the kindly eye of the legislator. And there is no argument, no fact, however obvious, however striking, that can avail to open the eyes of the fools who are thus fleeced.[1]

Confessors were accused in days of old of extorting legacies from the dying under threat of eternal punishment. Today our "deathers" go that one better. They get all they can from a patient before he dies, then fleece his heirs by presenting exorbitant bills for services rendered, relying upon the probability that to avoid litigation and suspicion of ingratitude towards the dead the heirs will submit to the blackmail and come forward with the money. In order to secure the good-will of our humanitarians, the better to go on with their practices of extortion under respectable auspices, these latter-day saints render free services to the poor, just as in former times saints of the monastic orders doled out broth to the poor from huge cauldrons in front of convent gates. When faith lost some of its hold upon the masses, this latter custom was ridiculed as "broth-charity." In our day faith in medical quackery is so strong that no

1697 [1] There have been and still are priests and physicians worthy of all honour, consideration, and respect, men who lend their help and advice to those who ask for help and advice, and aim not at all at imposing their will by force or by fraud upon those who disagree with them. What we say of our "deathers" must not in any way be taken as applying to those kind-hearted and learned physicians who modestly, scientifically, diligently, honestly, go about healing the sick and alleviating the pains of a suffering humanity. See Dr. Bourget, professor at Lausanne, *Quelques erreurs et tromperies de la science médicale moderne, passim.* In his *Beaux dimanches,* pp. 178-79, the same writer stresses the prevalence of superstition in the present-day public: "The simple-minded public believes the power of the physician much more extensive than it really is. That is why it asks impossible things of the doctor, whom it almost looks upon as a magician. For people of real religious faith it would be more logical to ask such cures of the God they worship, for in His power they must, I suppose, blindly believe. In a goodly number of organic diseases a real cure could result only from a miracle. The physician, for his part, cannot work miracles. Let us expect of him therefore nothing more than he can do." Along with many exaggerations there are also some truths in a book by Soller and Gastine, *Défends ta peau contre ton médecin.*

equivalent in blasting jest has gained universal currency to their discomfiture.[2] The priest was sure he knew the "absolute" and therefore did his best to force it upon others. Many of our doctors imagine, in spite of the repeated refutations they get from experience, that their science has achieved a certitude which in reality it is still far from attaining, and try to force upon a reluctant public their presumptuous will of today, which was not their will of yesterday and will not be their will of tomorrow.[3] In the eighteenth century in Italy and in France the "spiritual director" was supreme. Today the "deather" has superseded him. In both forms of superstition, women as a rule, and a few men of no great brains, most readily swallow the bait. Just as in the old days the spiritual director tyrannized over families, sowed dissension in homes, and brought wives and husbands to ruin, so do not a few "deathers" in our day. And where persuasion is not sufficient, the majesty of the law comes to the rescue. Catholic priests forbade their charges to eat meat during Lent, and they collected fees for procuring dispensations from such

1697 [2] The tale of Boccaccio, *Decameron,* I, 6, "in the which an honest man confounds the wicked hypocrisy of the monks with a witticism" may be applied, *mutatis mutandis,* to the hypocrisy of our humanitarian "deathers." The Academy of Medicine in Paris has asked for a law forbidding pharmacists to fill a doctor's prescription more than once. The silly rascals who support such measures say that their aim is to safe-guard "hygiene." Really their aim is to safe-guard the pocket-books of the "deathers," who in that way will get their fee for a new consultation every time a patient needs to have his prescription refilled.

There is nothing these fellows will not think up to make a little money. In 1913 in Italy a law was passed which had no other purpose than to help the pharmacists in their fleecing of the sick; and a cabinet minister was brazen enough to declare that the purpose of the law was to protect patients from low-grade remedies and notably from "foreign patent medicines," which, it seems, were bad if sold by grocers but excellent if sold by pharmicists. Anyone interested may prove to his own satisfaction that at Geneva the cost of drugs was from 20 to 50 per cent lower than it was in Italy; and who could be convinced that Swiss drugs are of an inferior grade? Assertions of that sort, so obviously at variance with the facts, go well enough on the lips of a minister in a "speculator" government, and they make fit fodder for a superstitious public. As a matter of fact all such things are mere survivals, under different forms, of ancient superstitions, for the purpose of extracting money from geese.

1697 [3] Many reputable physicians know and say how much of the uncertain there still is about their trade; but it is interesting to note how few of them dare oppose those among their colleagues who are disposed to force such uncertainties upon unwilling citizens. That is the case because worship of the god State is required not only of believers but of sceptics as well.

prohibitions. In some localities today our "deathers" have procured the passage of laws that forbid their patients to drink wine or other alcoholic beverages except as remedies, of which they, the "deathers," are the exclusive purveyors, and not without fees that are much higher in many cases than the bribes taken by the priests of yore. The clergy used to take it upon themselves to prohibit and permit marriages as they chose; and they demanded money for dispensations in cases where there was a prohibition. Today certain humanitarians are proposing that marriages be allowed only on a doctor's certificate of health. That would be a new source of gain for our "deathers." [4]

1698. Hosts of other facts of the same sort might be marshalled and all of them go to show that superstitions which might readily be supposed to have vanished long since have in reality merely changed their forms and are still alive under new guises. From the Middle Ages on to our time, the influence of magic on human societies has lessened, even if we reckon in the count its legacies to

---

1697 [4] In countries where prohibitionist legislation is rife, the "deathers" derive large incomes from prescriptions for alcoholic beverages, which they pretend are to be used for medicinal purposes only. That is one of the reasons why so many doctors are prohibitionists. *Cf.* Felice Ferrero, in the *Corriere della sera,* June 2, 1913 (the United States in question): "Teetotalism is so persistent and aggressive, and the bad repute into which it has succeeded in throwing King Alcohol is now so deep-rooted, that the whole country is affected by it in a more or less conspicuous way. [An exact parallel to the religious hypocrisy that prevailed in olden times. The reaction will come, but its hour is not yet at hand, and no Molière has so far written the Tartuffe of prohibitionism.] Not that Americans consume no alcoholic beverages. Quite the contrary: they drink, and they drink much more than is considered advisable even by people who refuse to admit that alcohol is a poison. But people who drink feel somehow called upon to explain and almost to offer excuses when they are screwing up their courage to perpetrate the dastardly act. Save for the sacred precincts of the clubs, where things are done behind friendly walls that no one would dare do in light of day, there is not one man in a thousand who has the courage to say frankly with Anacreon: 'Let my friends cease annoying me. They are free to do what they will. As for me, I drink.' There are those who drink 'by doctor's orders.' There are those who 'do not refuse a glass' for the sake of 'good fellowship.' There are those who drink 'a sip now and then.' Apparently there is no one who drinks for the most obvious reason of all—the pleasure of taking a drink." [The late Felice Ferrero lived for many years in Middletown, Conn. This description of the "American" attitude towards drinking, which denizens of the metropolitan and urban areas of the United States in 1935 may find naïve, is very accurate, so far as my own memory serves, for what one might call the "provincial" America of twenty years ago.—A. L.]

mind-readings, spiritualisms, telepathies, and other systems of thau-maturgy; but the domain from which it was banished has been partly occupied by the goddess Science.[1] Taken all in all, in the departments of the arts and sciences development has certainly been in the direction of an increase in the importance attached to experimental methods; but the evidence in favour of such an evo-lution is not so good if we turn to the fields of politics and social organization. It is significant that simple combinations foreign to scientific experience are far from having disappeared from modern social life; in fact, they persist in great numbers, thriving in pros-perous exuberance. Since simple combinations, in great part at least, are based on I-δ residues (need for combining residues), it is safe to say that that group of residues as a whole has changed much less than would seem to be the case at first sight.

1699. Then again, experimental science itself originates in the instinct of combinations and corresponds to Class I residues. But that is the one point such science has in common with the vagaries

1698 [1] Theosophists are not so few in numbers in Europe, and their literature is truly vast. Many people "believe in" spirits, double personalities, and the like. Darlès, *Glossaire raisonné de la théosophie, s.v. Extériorisation:* "The human body has about it a sort of vapoury envelope. It is called 'perispirit' by Spiritists, 'aetheric fluid' by Occultists. During the life of the body it serves to connect body and soul. After death when the material physical body is dissolved, broken down, oxidized, the individuality comes to possess an 'aetherized' body, which Occultists call 'the aetheric double.' It also is 'exteriorized' force. When we are wrapped in a slumber of sufficient depth our astral body, our aetheric fluid, detaches itself and goes to the goal of our desire, our will. That detachment takes place unconsciously in everybody; only, some individuals do not suspect any such thing and consequently conserve no memory of it, whereas others do remember and regard as a dream the scenes, the activities, the journeys they knew in the astral body; for man lives on the astral plane as well as on the physical plane. . . . ' "Sensitives," advanced me-diums, psychometrists, occultists,' says Ernest Bosc, *Dictionnaire d'orientalisme, d'occultisme et de psychologie,* Vol. I, p. 336, 'can detach their astral, their aetheric, double from the physical body even while awake, and adepts or initiates of Occult-ism who are very advanced are even able with the help of the aetheric fluid to ma-terialize the psychic [*physique,* misprint] body (move that is from the sthulic to the astral plane) and appear to friends, acquaintances, strangers, far from their bodies.' " Suppose we append a bit of explanation for those who do not know what the planes in question are: *"Sthula or Sthule:* matter: the Sthulic plane is the Physical Plane. . . . The cosmos is made up of seven planes, each divided into seven sub-planes." But no—it would take too much space to give them all. The reader desirous of making all their acquaintances had better refer to the books themselves. I will close with the "astral plane": "Astral Plane, also called the For-

of magic and other fantastic systems. If that fact is overlooked, one might imagine that Class I as a whole had been enormously strengthened in the course of past centuries, cutting in on the domain of Class II residues (group-persistences). Such a strengthening there has certainly been, but closer examination shows that the gain has been smaller than would seem. The combinations of experimental science have been vastly expanding all the way down to our own times, but for the most part they have occupied territory formerly held by the combinations of trial-and-error empiricism, magic, theology, and metaphysics. From the standpoint of social utility that displacement in combinations is very advantageous; but as regards the rôle played by residues in human conduct it is evident that the compensation has been very considerable also, so that the class as a whole has changed much less than the two elements of which it is made up; and considering Class I as a whole, it is apparent that, substantially, it changes but slightly and very slowly.

1700. The same may be said of the other classes of residues. Sup-

mative Plane, whence man gets his astral body. The Kamaloka, or place of passions and desires, is located on the Astral Plane. To it man repairs, after death. It corresponds to the Purgatory of the Catholics." Side by side with these new forms of old vagaries a few of the old forms here and there themselves survive. Periodically in the newspapers one may read accounts of witches, sorcerers, and other such persons. I select at random from the *Corriere della sera,* Aug. 31, 1913: *"Mysterious Rain of Stones Halted by Sacrifice of Two Cats:* At Termo d'Arcola, near La Spezia, a strange thing recently occurred that has given those innocent ruralites a great deal to talk about. . . . On July 21 last, a certain Irma Dal Padulo, eleven, while walking home from school noticed that a rain of stones was falling about her on the deserted country road. The stones had the peculiarity of being very hot. . . . On the following morning, however, the rain began again the moment the girl rose from her bed, and in spite of the vigilance of her parents and neighbors it lasted almost the whole day. Wherever the girl went stones began falling about her, without however hitting her, and they were always hot. The thing kept up for several days. Numbers of persons went to the village to witness it, among them Signor Luigi Parioli, city councillor of Vezzano Ligure, two women, and one of Irma's brothers. [It all reads like a story from the *Malleus maleficarum,* save that, with the passing of the years, the Devil has retired, relinquishing his rôle to spirits.] Someone suggested [Some Clerical, no doubt.] that the girl be treated with an exorcism by the village priest; but the exorcism was without result. [How hath the Devil fallen!] The family could not imagine what saint to turn to next, when a fellow-townsman [Probably an anti-Clerical—certainly a man with a sense of up-to-dateness.] suggested that a spiritualist *séance* be held in the Dal Padulo home. The suggestion was taken, and it seems that the table, speaking in the tiptological code, ordered that two cats be killed and buried in a certain place. That was done and the rains ceased forthwith."

pose, for instance, we consider Class II (group-persistences). The II-β variety in that class (relations of living and dead) has by no means disappeared. Indeed it was through observation of present-day phenomena that we were able (Chapter VI) to strip it clear of the derivations which in former times had hidden it from view. But there can be no doubt that it figures much less extensively in our times than in a remote era, when worship of the dead was virtually the only cult our Graeco-Latin ancestors knew; or in the Middle Ages, when the chief concern of the living seems to have been to endow masses for the dead. We may confidently assert, therefore, that the importance of residues of our II-β variety has greatly diminished in the course of the centuries.

1701. But that falling-off has been balanced, to some extent at least, by intensifications on the part of other varieties in the same class, so that the class as a whole has not greatly changed. The gods of Graeco-Latin polytheism came little by little to occupy the territory left vacant by a waning worship of the dead; and they in their turn were displaced by the divinities and saints of Christianity. In the sixteenth century the Reformation waged bitter war on the cult of relics, and especially on the rites practised in the Roman Church for the mitigation of punishments after death. Yet, at bottom, the Reformation merely replaced the old group-persistences with new ones. Life at Geneva under Calvin was much less free, much more extensively governed by ultra-experimental considerations, than life in Rome ever had been under the rule of the Popes; and taken all in all, Protestantism was much more narrow-minded, much more oppressive, than the Catholic Church had been in countries where the Reform superseded Catholicism; while Catholicism, on its side, under the impact of the attack upon it became less tolerant, less indulgent, more aggressive. In a word, in the days of Leo X and before the day of Luther, Rome enjoyed a freedom of thought and speech which vanished, quite, in Protestant countries and therefore in Catholic countries also. Protestants themselves point out that their Reformation tended to stimulate the "religious spirit." Which is another way of saying that it extended the influence of the Class II residues.

1702. Many other observations confirm these inferences. Thinking of logical forms primarily, there seem to be very great differences between the various competing religions; but attending chiefly to sentiments, one perceives in all of them varying forms of a single substance. In Europe, in the second half of the nineteenth century, Socialism made room for itself by crowding back some of the prevailing faiths such as Catholicism and nationalism, and assimilating others, such as humanitarianism and a so-called Liberal Christianity (which is not so very Christian and not at all liberal).[1] Later on, towards the beginning of the twentieth century, came a counteroffensive by the religions differing from Socialism.[2] The tide of positivistic humanitarianism receded a little. Socialistic religious sentiment lost ground, as did also, and to a greater extent indeed,

1702 [1] For many such people Christ has been stripped of all divine attributes and is to be applauded only as a Socialist or humanitarian teacher. Not a few go farther still. In November, 1912, while the Balkan War was raging and Christians under Turkish rule were trying to rid themselves of Mussulman oppression, an internationalist Socialist congress convened at Basel to pass furious resolutions denouncing that war. One of the most influential orators there was Jaurès. He had already published a number of articles in defence of Turkey. All the same, the Parochial Council of Basel put the cathedral of that city at the disposal of the congress, in other words, of people who were defending the Crescent against the Cross. To be sure, middle-class cowardice, which prompts many individuals to kotow to the Socialists and become their adulators, had something to do with such action; but it cannot be taken as the only cause, especially if one consider the approval of the action of the Catholics that was voiced in many quarters. A correspondent of the *Journal de Genève* wrote from Basel, Nov. 27, 1912: "What will distinguish the Socialist convention at Basel will be, not so much the lip-service to humaneness that is paid in its resolutions, as the fact of its gathering in the cathedral, that noble and trustful gesture on the part of our religious and political community towards partisans of peace. . . . That gesture symbolized the city's attachment not to the revolutionary International but to international peace and social peace among the classes in the various countries." Now the people who met in the Basel Cathedral were champions of the "class struggle," which was one of their dogmas, yet aiding and abetting them is represented as a symbol of "attachment to social peace"! Of the many absurd derivations that we have had occasion to note in course of these volumes, this certainly is not the least ridiculous. The Armenian Christians, who first endured the massacres of Abdul Hamid and then the massacres of the "Young Turks," might have found the Turkish peace that was preached from a still-Christian Cathedral at Basel but little different from what Galgacus (Tacitus, *Agricola*, 30) said of the Roman peace: *"Ubi solitudinem faciunt, pacem appellant"!*

1702 [2] In view of the scant variability of classes of residues taken as a whole, such a thing might have been foreseen. *Cf.* my *Systèmes*, Vol. II, p. 419: "It may well prove that in certain countries the Nationalists, the Imperialists, and the Agrarians will be the only parties capable of resisting Socialism, and *vice versa*. The choice in that case would be confined to those parties."

secondary religions such as liberalism,[3] humanitarianism, Tolstoyism, and the like; while nationalism underwent a remarkable revival, Catholicism prospered once more, the various metaphysical
systems emerged from their eclipse, and even magic and astrology
again made room for themselves.[4]

1703. The differences in intensity observable in the increasing
popularity of some derivations and the decreasing popularity of
others is a certain index of differing intensities in the residues to

1702 [3] The term "liberalism" is used here to designate the doctrines of the old
Liberalism (the historic Left), which aimed at reducing the number of restrictions
on the individual; not that newer liberalism which, aiming at multiplying such
restrictions under the old name, professes doctrines altogether new as compared
with what was formerly called liberal.

1702 [4] One may read expensive advertisements of magicians and astrologers in the
newspapers. It is certain that such individuals would not continue going to that
expense if there were no profit in it. We are therefore safe in concluding that many
people bite at their bait. There are special catalogues devoted to books on magic
and astrology, and every day new publications of the kind are added to the old
lists. Here, as one among a host, is a specimen of a "psychic" publication (in
French): *"Infallible Counsel within Everybody's Reach as to How to Sow the
Seeds of Love and Sympathy about One and Win Happiness for Oneself and.
Others*. Psychic Bureau, 98 rue Blanche, Paris, 1st edition, 25,000 copies." Then,
pp. 2-7: "The means that we would reveal to our readers for winning love and
happiness are obtained from magic Perfumes and astrological Stones. . . . The
chief magical perfumes are seven in number. Each of them corresponds to an
essential heavenly body . . . the Sun, the heliotrope; the Moon, the iris; Mercury,
sweet broom . . . Our readers, men and women, already know how important it
is for them to use the particular perfume of the heavenly body that exerts the
predominant influence upon their destinies. The day is past when astrological
science was the object of contempt and disdain. In that branch of knowledge of
the occult, as in every other, our age has witnessed a magnificent rebirth. No one
in this day and age would venture to question the fact that the planets influence
the Earth, the Earth's inhabitants, and everything on or inside it. [That derivation
stands on a par with Hegel's notion that comets influenced the quality of wines
(§ 510).] Be it a question of reproduction in animals, of germination in plants, of
disease in man, the influence of the Sun has to be recognized. Who would ever
think of doubting the power of the Moon over the tides [This good soul must
have about the same conception of Moon and tides as the Chinese—or Hegel.], over
periods in women, and certain mental diseases, and the deadly effect of red moons
on the sprouts of young plants. [The method of reasoning usual in metaphysicists
who look into their own egos in order to determine the experimental relationships
between facts.] One often hears people ascribing their preferences to chance. They
will say, for instance: 'Strange—but why do I dislike white so?' 'Why do I prefer
the rose, of all flowers?' 'Why is vervain my favourite perfume?' There is no
chance in such things. The fact is that such people sense vaguely, instinctively,
what is best suited to them. A mysterious voice is telling them what is best suited

which they correspond. That was clearly apparent in Italy in the period around 1913, where a rapid rise in the Nationalist tide kept pace with a decline no less rapid in the Socialist religion. The same trend was noticeable also in France, where the rise in tide of new faith was a matter not only of nationalism, but also, though in smaller proportions, of a Catholic revival. In Germany too Socialism fell off somewhat.[1] In England any gains by one of the so-

to them. [A reasoning that would seem for all the world to ape Bergson's line of argument in discovering an "instinctive me." What Bergson says is not so intelligible as the above, but experimentally it stands on a par with it.] . . . What we have said of perfumes also applies to precious stones. Of all earthly substances none have stronger sympathies for sidereal substances than genuine precious stones. It is a matter of common knowledge that the diamond is under the despotic sway of the polar star." And in that Hegel is evidently "overpassed" (§ 1686) in his vagaries on the diamond (§ 504).

The magical rites of the witch in Theocritus have counterparts in our own time. See, for instance, Papus, *Peut-on envoûter* (can spells be cast on people)?

1703 [1] The *Giornale d'Italia,* Sept. 15, 1913, carried an account by Cabasino-Renda of the Socialist Congress at Jena, which was in session at the time: "The German Socialist party is in decadence. That fact is frankly admitted by the Executive Committee in the long and detailed report that it is today presenting to the congress. The report evinces a mood of deepest gloom. The enrolment of new converts is at a standstill, a thing that has never happened before since the foundation of the party. During the past year only 12,000 new members were enrolled, a ridiculous figure relatively. Hitherto the number has always exceeded 130,000. Another very interesting fact: Of the 12,000 new members this year 10,000 are women, a circumstance that will fill feminists with a very legitimate pride but which gives the party leaders little cheer, since, in electoral terms at least, they find in this year's enrolment only two thousand persons who can be accounted as usable material. In many districts—more than a hundred—membership has actually decreased, and the slump affects all parts of Germany but especially Prussia.

"Socialist leaders are trying to find some comforting explanation for this very alarming development. They say that it may be due to the hard times which have been afflicting Germany this year. That argument, however, shows not a few wrinkles. The history of the Socialist party indicates, to the exact contrary, that during hard times in the past Socialist gains have stood in direct ratio to the distress and discontent. They also say that 'the party's propaganda in the press has been neglected.' But another section of the same report shows that expenses for agitation have been considerably higher this year than in previous years. As regards the Socialist newspapers, one notes a development that is in perfect harmony with the slump in new enrolments: subscriptions have fallen off perceptibly. The *Vorwärts* alone has lost 8,400 subscribers in the past nine months, and lesser papers as many as 5,000. Another circumstance completes the picture of decline in the German Socialist party: the number of votes it has polled at elections has fallen off, whereas past years have shown steady increases (up to the fabulous figure of 4,000,000—including sympathizers, of course; for the party has fewer than 1,000,000 actual members). In the thirteen local elections held this year the Socialists have

cial religions have been made at the expense of one or more of the others; but in that country the gains went to Socialism, the losses, to nationalism and liberalism. Since the present trend in England, in one of its aspects, nationalism, is in a direction counter to the general trend on the Continent, one may surmise that it will not hold very long. The transformation of Japan in the course of the nineteenth century is a most interesting case. There derivations change, but sentiments and residues still endure, expressing themselves in part in different ways. Class II (group-persistences) changes little if at all; but certain subvarieties in the class vary, the change in certain instances being very considerable.[2]

1704. The case of Italy is worth considering more in detail, not so much because of the magnitude and intensity of the movement—

had, with one single exception, many fewer votes than in past years; and they were defeated in almost every case. Of course, to infer from all this that the German Socialist party is falling to pieces would be a gross mistake; but we may assert in all confidence that having attained its peak in the elections of 1911, Socialist power is now on a declining curve. To justify the party's vote in favour of appropriations for increased armaments, Socialist leaders say that 'had they thrown their weight to the Opposition, the Government's bills would have been in danger of defeat, and that would have meant an immediate dissolution of the Reichstag.' So—the Socialists were against any dissolution of the Reichstag! They did not care to enter a general election on a platform that, logically, should have been altogether in their favour: a billion for new military expenditures! There could be no clearer demonstration of the present exhilaration of German national sentiments, and of the predicament of a Socialist party, which feels that not even under circumstances so exceptionally favourable could it maintain, in a new struggle, the position that it won at the last elections through a combination of circumstances which will never return." [Of this last, really, we cannot be sure. It will all depend on future developments.]

1703 [2] La Mazelière, *Le Japon,* Vol. V, pp. 7-10: "In that country where, for a moment, everything seemed to be going to pieces, one single institution held its ground, its prestige enhanced by the collapse of everything else. That was the monarchy, strengthened now by hatred of the foreigner, by revolutionary passions that had identified the monarchical cause with democratic reforms, by the mystical character which the Restoration had assumed. There were thirty millions of human beings who had no religion left and wanted one. So they began worshipping their Emperor. . . . So love of the Emperor was intensified by all other loves, worship of the Emperor by all other religious aspirations. . . . In the turmoil of hatreds and schisms that had resulted from the strife of civil war, the Imperial cult became the one focus of union for all Japanese. . . . Officers of foreign armies who saw Nogi's soldiers advance to the storming of Port Arthur, or Oku's men at Liao-Yang, all use the same expression: it was fanaticism." La Mazelière wrote these lines in 1910. Two years later, on the death of the Mikado, General Nogi committed hara-kiri, adding further confirmation to La Mazelière's picture.

for history shows movements of far greater scope and violence—but because it took place in our own time under our very eyes and we are therefore better able to sound its character. We are not interested just here in the rôle political and financial interests may have played in the movement, nor in deciding whether and to what extent sentiments sprouted like tender plants under the watering of a beneficent political and financial dew.[1] Here we are considering sentiments as they stood previous to that time (1913), and trying simply to see how Class II residues varied in distribution and how such changes were largely hidden from view under a mask of derivations.[2]

The first symptoms of the movement were discernible as early as 1908. By 1911, its existence was unmistakable. At that time religious exhilaration in large numbers of Socialists, liberals, humanitarians, Tolstoyans, and so on, assumed the new form of a nationalist, militarist enthusiasm. A fairly significant symptom of the decline of Socialist sentiment among Socialist leaders could be noted in the ratification by the Chamber on February 23, 1912, of a royal decree proclaiming the annexation of Libya. In the vote by roll-call thirty-eight Deputies were against, thirty-three of them Socialists. In the vote by ballot, only nine were against. It follows that a certain number of Deputies were of such lukewarm Socialist or Nationalist faith as to vote against the Socialist party's policy when they could do so secretly, and against the Nationalist policy when called upon to do so openly. It all reminds one of Machiavelli's sage remark (*Deca,* I, 27) that "very rarely do men manage to be altogether rascals or altogether upright." [3]

1704 [1] To those matters we shall come in due time in Chapter XII.

1704 [2] In this connexion we shall be adding a number of considerations to the remarks we made in §§ 1559 f.

1704 [3] *Corriere della sera,* Feb. 25, 1912: "At roll-call the 'nays' numbered 38, to wit, 33 Socialists, 2 Constitutionalists . . . 3 Republicans. . . . The vote by secret ballot showed 9 'nays,' though, as proved by the official minutes of the session, 22 Deputies who had voted against the bill on roll-call were present. The names of the 9 who voted 'nay' are of course not known; but it is clear enough that 13 of those who had at first been opposed changed their attitudes and voted for the bill when they were in a position to cast a secret ballot and were safe from any group control embarrassing to the free exercise of conscience. . . . This incident is unprecedented, unique, and must be taken as the index of a state of mind that is extraordinarily significant. Evidently those thirteen Deputies did not have the courage of their convictions. . . . Their group demanded that they come out

1705. Most interesting in view of the contrasts involved was the change from pacifist militancy to militarist militancy. Conditions of public health in Italy (cholera) happened to be such as to prevent foreign delegates from attending the peace-lovers' convention in Rome that Italian pacifists were all for holding while the expedition to Tripoli was being brewed. Had it not been for that, the chief business of that convention would have been to listen to panegyrics on war delivered by Italian pacifists. With few exceptions they were all set to strike up in chorus.[1]

1706. As usual, and in accord with the endless array of examples that we have already seen, derivations came running to the rescue to show that war in this special case was not in any sense inconsistent with general pacifist doctrine. That is one of the very numerous cases where the incidental character of the derivation becomes strikingly evident, as not determining events but as being determined by them. The classic example, of course, would be the very ancient fable of the wolf and the lamb.

1707. The Italo-Turkish war was brought on by a sum of interests and sentiments, just as the colonial wars of all the great European Powers have been brought on, for the past century at least. Italy was merely treading, somewhat tardily, a broad path that had

against the bill and they sacrificed their convictions to appearances. In the secrecy of the ballot they could be sincere, and then and then only were they sincere [Who can say that? They might very well have refrained from voting. The truth is they were spinning like weather-vanes, not knowing where they were at.], dropping the masks that they had been craftily wearing. But what a humiliation in a courage so secret! What a confession of weakness in such an act of sincerity!" But after the elections of 1913 came—as usual from the masses—a wave of faith; and the newly elected Deputies showed themselves violent defenders of their party.

1705 [1] Among those to be mentioned on the roll of honour as standing faithful to their professed doctrines and refusing to let themselves be swept away like chaff in the wind of war enthusiasm, were Deputy Napoleone Colajanni, Edoardo Giretti, a lawyer, and Professor Arcangelo Ghisleri.

Shortly afterwards, in 1912, the Italian pacifists petitioned the Minister of Public Instruction "to request teachers in the public schools to give talks on February 22 [the day when the conclusion of peace with Turkey was to be celebrated] showing how love of peace can and ought to go hand in hand with love of country" (*Corriere della sera,* Feb. 3, 1912). The minister was well aware of the absurdity of setting out to glorify a war in the name of peace! He may also have been deterred by a sense of the insult he would have been offering to freedom of thought on the part of Italian school-teachers by requesting them in an official order to address their pupils in a manner so fraught with bad faith. At any rate he replied

been opened for her by other countries; and very possibly she could not have refrained from doing as she did without serious disadvantage to herself. If that simple truth had been stated, it would have described the actual causes of what was happening. But the Italian pacifists saw fit to resort to derivations calculated to satisfy sentiments corresponding to Class II residues.

1708. To wit: 1. *Sentiments of justice.* In the ultimatum sent to Turkey by the Marchese di San Giuliano mention was made of injustices perpetrated by Turkey to the damage of Italy. It was alleged, for instance, that an Italian girl had been abused. The logical conclusion from that would have been to demand that reparation be made for the wrongs suffered, that the girl be handed over to Italian authorities. But, by a very special kind of reasoning, the conclusion was reached that Italy should conquer Tripoli. As for the girl who had been raped, having performed patriotic service as a pretext, she disappeared from view and was never heard of again.

2. Atrocities that Turco-Arab combatants were alleged to have perpetrated on Italian dead, wounded, and prisoners. These came in very handy. But in strict logic, a cause ought to antedate its effects. Strange indeed to give as the cause of a war incidents that could occur only after and in consequence of a declaration of war.

to Professor de Gubernatis as follows: "Assuredly the noble ideal of peace among the peoples—peace, be it understood, with honour and justice—smiles upon our spirits even in these days when Italy is being called upon to safe-guard her own vital interests and at the same time the interests of civilization by force of arms. [The spirits of the Romans were enlightened by the same smile as they went about conquering the Mediterranean world. So was the spirit of Napoleon I as his armies overran Europe.] But surely, sir, it cannot escape a man of your acuteness that a public demonstration in favour of peace made at this time would, in spite of any reservations that might be attached to it, lend itself to distorted and embarrassing interpretations. . . . [So the Minister dismantles the Professor's derivation. But he has one of his own:] The Romans closed the temple of Janus only when the enemy had been defeated. So shall we celebrate the festival of peace once more [Here perhaps the Minister is somewhat ironical. He too reminds one of the phrase of Tacitus (§ 1702 [1])] when the blood of our soldiers, the flower of the youth of Italy, shall have won for our country the recognition of her good right and the respect of the whole world; and it will be a sincere festival, one deeply felt by all." Substantially, stripped of its rhetorical frills and furbelows, the Minister's idea was that there would be plenty of time to glorify peace when war had brought home all the bacon it was expected to deliver—a very sound notion, for that matter. But it is as old as the world and has been held by very warlike peoples; so that it was really quite superfluous to fish up a high-sounding theory of pacifism just to express it once more.

3. Italy's obligation to free the Arabs from Turkish oppression. To be sure the Arabs did not care to be freed, but that was a matter of little or no importance: they *had* to be "freed" willynilly. As a pretext for conquering Greece ancient Rome thought up the notion of "freeing" Greeks. Modern Rome, much more modest, was satisfied with "freeing" Tripolitan Arabs. Sophistries and derivations live long long lives!

4. In a very subordinate way, some slight appeal was made to sentiments of national integrity. The annexation of Tripoli and Cyrenaica to Italy having been proclaimed, Arabs who refused to submit became "rebels." One may be a pacifist and still demand that a "rebellion" be suppressed.

5. There was some slight allusion to Christian sentiments, but that dangerous tack was soon abandoned as tending possibly to give the impression that the war was a conflict between Christianity and Islam.

6. More positive the appeal to sentiments of present-day religions. In times past the religion of Christ used to be set up against the religion of Mohammed. So in our time, and in the same way, fealties to the god Progress and to Civilization, Holy of Holies, are set over against the "superstitions" of "backwardness," "stagnation," "barbarism." The Italian pacifists took out and dusted off an age-old theory that Christian peoples should not make war upon Christians, but might well fight infidels.[1] We were told that the peace movement meant peace among "civilized" nations, not peace between civilized nations and "barbarous" nations. This new theory is much more vague than the old, for, after all, it is an easy matter to determine whether or not a nation is Christian, in forms at least. But how are we to know whether a nation is "civilized" and especially whether it be sufficiently civilized to be entitled to peace instead of war? The *Berliner Post* would have Germany appropriate the colonies of Portugal in order to substitute a "healthy" German civilization for a "corrupt" Latin civilization. Many Germans firmly believe that there is but one civilization, the German—that all the rest is barbarism. Ought we to accept that theory? Who is to settle a problem so arduous? It is new only in form. The sub-

---

1708 [1] The idea goes very far back. The ancient Greeks also used to say that Hellenes should not make war on Hellenes, but might well fight Barbarians.

stance of it is already present in the question which Saladin puts to Melchisedech the Jew in one of Boccaccio's tales, *Decameron,* I, 3: "I would fain know of you which of the three laws you judge the true: the Jewish, the Saracen, or the Christian?" Is Japan a civilized country or a barbarous country? Is it permissible or not permissible, according to pacifist doctrine, to wage war on Japan? And the difficulties multiply as we go on to empires that comprise numbers of nations, some of which are reputed civilized, others barbarous. France is certainly a civilized country. Does she cease to be such in view of her African and Asiatic possessions? And what of England? And Russia? Obviously such a theory can only be brought forward for mere purposes of partisan convenience in debate. It is neither true nor false: it is simply devoid of meaning.

7. Nor is any more sense discernible in another fine contraption of our pacifists, who explain that their peace means peace among countries in Europe and, we may take for granted, countries of the Americas. But does the word "European" refer to race, or to territory? If it refers to race it justifies, it is true, Italy's war against Turkey; but it would just as well justify a war against the Magyars or the Russians, among whom there are Tartars and Tartars. If it relates to territory, Turkey's territory lies both in Europe and Asia, as do England's, Russia's, and the territories of other countries; and the pacifist theory ends by not applying to anybody.

We will say nothing of minor derivations, such as the doctrine of "historical destiny," the argument based on the ancient dominion of Rome in Africa, and others fashioned of like rhetoric.

1709. Most beauteous among all such beautiful contrivances must be reckoned the contention that pacifism really means that war can be waged whenever war is considered advantageous to one's country. If this be granted, it would be difficult indeed to find one person in the whole world who is not a pacifist; for, after all, where find the dolt to say: "I am for war because I believe it will be disastrous to my country"? And why, if the patriots of a country *A* have the right to make war, should not the patriots of a country *B* have an equal right? And if the right be granted to all countries, what in the world can be the use of pacifism? The estimable pacifists in question never wearied of praising arbitration and Hague tribunals which prescribed that nations should appeal to them before entering upon a war. Then they turned around and supported their own government, which snapped its fingers at Hague tribunals and international arbitration. But in that case, where is our much esteemed "Peace through Law" to lay her head? The real dispute between pacifists and non-pacifists is not as to whether a man ought to do what is beneficial or what is detrimental to his country. The question is whether war is at all times harmful, save when waged in self-defence, as non-Italian pacifists aver, and as Italian pacifists also averred before the war of conquest in Tripoli supervened: or whether wars, even wars of conquest, may not sometimes be beneficial, as the adversaries of pacifism contend. Similarly there is a real issue between pacifists and non-pacifists as to whether the rules of "law" are adequate for settling international quarrels, as the pacifists assert, or whether, as non-pacifists claim, war is sometimes indispensable for that purpose. If it be granted that war is to be waged whenever a nation prefers it to arbitration, it is impossible to find anyone who is not a pacifist.

Fully to appreciate the fatuousness of the arguments adduced to justify the Italo-Turkish War, one should notice that once the war had ended in complete victory—or was said to have—the Italian Government showed not the slightest interest in such reasons or pretexts. The war was said to have been inspired by a sense of justice, by a desire to obtain redress for wrongs done to Italian citizens. No such wrong was ever righted. Quite to the contrary, new and more serious wrongs resulted from the expulsion of Italian citizens from Turkish territories. Nor were they righted. The sentiments of pity for peoples oppressed by the Turks, and especially the very lively sentiment of pity felt for the Arabs, who, after all, were delighted with their "oppression," were not extended to Christian peoples who had decided to rid themselves of Turkish domination. Indeed, Italy made peace with Turkey at the moment best calculated to help the Turks to the disadvantage of those peoples. As for the god Progress, the goddess Civilization, and others of that tribe, the Italian Government took no further notice of them, unless one is to say that in the war between Turkey and the Balkan and Hellenic peoples Holy Progress, and Civilization, Holiest of Holies, were on the side of Turkey. Finally, if Turkey had to be considered a non-European country in the war with Italy, and therefore a proper enemy for a European Power, in her war with Bulgaria, Serbia, Montenegro, and Greece, she must by some adroit legerdemain have suddenly become a European country against which war could not be waged, so that in view of that marvellous transformation Italy had to conclude peace at the earliest possible moment.

1710. These derivations, so utterly illogical and sometimes indeed so ridiculous, all lead up eventually to one same conclusion; and it is therefore evident that they were concocted with a view to that conclusion, and not thought out independently of any conclusion, the latter resulting from them. And it is further apparent that here, as we have seen to be true in many other such cases, they are merely the incidental element, the principal element lying in the sentiments and interests that gave rise to the conclusion which the derivations are an effort *a posteriori* to justify. So the variety that the derivations seem to show, but which is only apparent, disappears, only the substance being left, which is much more constant than the derivations, and is in fact the underlying reality. It often happens, in general, that statesmen ascribe to their conduct in public utterances causes that are in no sense the real ones; and that is especially the case when they allege general principles as motives (§ 1689).[1]

1710 [1] In 1912 the Italian Government withheld its *exequatur* from Monsignor Caron, who had been appointed Archbishop of Genoa by the Pope. There seems to have been quite a story behind the incident. It was hinted that Monsignor Caron had had a finger in the removal from Genoa of Father Semeria, a clergyman tainted to some slight extent with Modernism and who had a powerful following among many ladies highly placed in Genoese society. However, on all that we have no documents and therefore cannot go into it. We can consider the reasons which a minister in the then government, Signor Finocchiaro-Aprile, put forward before the Chamber in its session of Feb. 10, 1913, in justification of the refusal of the *exequatur*. He alluded to certain newspapers which were favouring the restoration of the temporal power, and charged Monsignor Caron—without producing any great proof—with aiding and abetting that campaign. And he concluded: "In dealing with circumstances such as those confronting us today, what must prevail over everything and everybody is a supreme consideration of state interests whereby no civic recognition can be accorded to anyone who, in a vague hope of restorations that are impossible, fails to render to the State the homage that is its due." Now in that we have the statement of a general principle. Had it come from a Prussian Minister of State there would be nothing to say to it, for in Prussia the Government does exclude from state offices, including university professorships, all persons who "fail to render to the State the homage that is its due." But no Italian politician can climb as high as a ministerial portfolio and not know that the Italian Government regularly awards appointments to Socialists who declare publicly and repeatedly that they are determined to destroy the *bourgeois* State and that they

1711. With reference to the greater or lesser degree of resistance offered by the various forms of religious sentiment to the wave of Nationalism that began to sweep Italy in 1911, it is to be noted that not a few Socialists remained loyal to their doctrine of opposition to *bourgeois* wars. So again almost all the Mazzinian Republicans stood firm against what they regarded as a monarchical enterprise. Meantime, Italian pacifists turned belligerent in great numbers, while the humanitarians and the Tolstoyans crawled into their shells and uttered not a sound. That therefore is the order in which those beliefs should be ranked, on the score of strength—in Italy, at least, and at the present time (1913). In other countries, too, I dare say, the order would not be greatly different.

1712. As regards Class III residues, devotion to the rites of Christian worship has diminished among modern civilized peoples; but it has been in part superseded by worship of Socialist and humanitarian saints, and especially by worship of the god State and the god People. One can detect no substantial difference between the festivals of a Catholic saint and the celebrations in honour of Rousseau's bicentenary for which the French Government appropriated thirty thousand francs. It is natural enough that in the eyes of the humanitarian the Catholic saint should be accounted an impostor, and Rousseau one of the greatest of men. It is also quite as natural that the Catholic should invert those judgments. But that very difference in opinions shows the similarity of the sentiments by which humanitarian and Catholic are alike moved. The old Catholic "processions" have all but disappeared; but they have been replaced by political and class "parades" and what the Latins call "manifestations." Protestants do not go to mass as Catholics do, but they go to the prayer-meetings of their several sects (which are often as noisy as "revivals"), and they join free-thinkers in swelling audiences at spiritualistic meetings. English and American Protestants sing hymns at the top of their lungs. Many of them break away from Christian worship; but their old religious fervour merely turns to "social," humanitarian, patriotic, or nationalist enthusiasms, and of

nourish not "vague hopes of restorations that are impossible" but positive hopes of downright destruction. The Minister was not telling the exact truth, therefore, in asserting that his conduct was determined by the general principle he stated. He is mindful of his principle only when he finds it politically convenient, and forgets it when he fears that it may be politically embarrassing.

such there are brands to suit all tastes. The god People has not a single unbeliever left. Individuals may, as is the case with other gods, differ as to the forms that his worship shall take, but not as to the obligation of worship. And where is the man who does not feel the need of shouting aloud that everything must be sacrificed to the "good of the People"?—shouting it in words, that is, for as regards deeds it is often an entirely different matter. It is a race among all parties to get there first in paying homage to "the People." The *Knights* of Aristophanes mirror with equal truth to life the situation in ancient Athens and the situation observable among us today. There is not a reactionary, however extreme, who dares speak ill of the god People. It took an eccentric like Nietzsche to dare such a thing, and it makes him look like the exception that proves the rule. Careful thinkers who are convinced in their heart of hearts of the ineptitude of the new religion dissemble such atheism, just as their predecessors dissembled unbelief in the days when it was a crime to doubt the "truths" of the Christian religion. They speak of "abuses" in democracy just as people of former times spoke of "abuses" in the clergy. They thrash the saddle, knowing well that they cannot thrash the horse.[1]

In a word, the Class III residues may have changed considerably in form, but as regards substance much less, especially when the class is considered as a whole.

1713. As regards Class IV, one might suppose that that group has shown a great increase as against a simultaneous and no less impressive falling off in Class V residues. For many persons it is an article of faith that in our day the "social sense" has greatly increased, while "individualism" has lessened. But, substantially, matters do not stand that way. The change is oftentimes a mere change in

1712 [1] The parties hostile to "the *bourgeoisie*" are constantly declaring in their books, pamphlets, and newspapers that it is their intention to annihilate said *bourgeoisie* root and branch. But show me a single *"bourgeois"* who in a fit of pique or even in jest dares reply: "You say you want to destroy us? Come ahead— and we will do some destroying too." The God of the Christians has blasphemers among His faithful. The god People counts not a one, let alone among his faithful, not even among those who take no stock in him. Humanity has its "misanthropes," but "the People" has no "misodemes." There is no one bold enough to display hatred, or antipathy, or repugnance, or even mere indifference, to it. And all that seems so obvious, so natural, that no one ever gives a thought to it. Indeed to mention it seems as useless as to say that a human being walks on two legs.

forms. In times past sentiments of subordination found their expression in the submissiveness of the lower classes to the higher; today they manifest themselves, as regards the lower classes, in submissiveness to the leaders of strikes, trade-unions, political parties, and as regards the higher, in submissiveness to "the People," which is fawningly blandished as no absolute monarch of past centuries ever was.[1] In those days, moreover, kings received stinging rebukes from the Popes now and again and met opposition in their nobilities. In our day no one has the courage to find fault with "the People," to

1713 [1] Michels, *Zur Soziologie des Parteiwesens*, pp. 64-67 (Paul, pp. 64-66): "*The masses need something to worship.* . . . The adoration the militants have for their leaders generally remains a latent thing. It betrays itself in barely perceptible ways, such as the respectful tone in which the leader's name is mentioned. . . . In 1864 the inhabitants of the Rhine district welcomed Lassalle like a god. . . . When the *fasci,* the first organizations of farm-labourers, were formed in Sicily (1892), men and women had an almost supernatural faith in their leaders. Mixing together in their simple-mindedness the social question and their religious habits, they often carried crucifixes in their parades side by side with the red flag and placards inscribed with maxims from Marx. . . . In Holland, when Domela Nieuwenhuis, a Deputy, left the prison where he had been confined, he received from the people, as he himself relates, honours such as no sovereign had ever received. . . . Such attitudes in the masses are observable not only in so called backward countries. . . . All the proof we need is the idolatry with which the Marxist prophet, Jules Guesde, is worshipped in the North, the most highly industrialized section in France. Even in the manufacturing districts in England the masses at this late day àre still welcoming their leaders with enthusiasms that remind one of the times of Lassalle. Worship of leaders endures after they have died. The greater among them are frankly sanctified. . . . Karl Marx himself has not escaped that sort of Socialist canonization, and the fanatical zeal with which certain Marxians are still defending him is something very like the idolizing of Lassalle in a day long past."

Maurice Spronck, *Liberté,* Nov. 17, 1912. (In France school-teachers were rebelling against the politicians: the snake had bitten the fakir. Of a session of the Chamber during which the crisis was under discussion, Spronck writes): "In the eloquent but slightly vague address of M. Paul-Boncour one point stands out as strikingly sound, and we gladly take upon our own shoulders all that the speaker said as to those responsible for the present unrest in the schools. 'These groups of teachers,' he declared, 'arose not only with the full knowledge of those in power but with their full approbation, and not so long ago the annual celebrations they held were held under the auspices of the men most highly placed under republican rule.' Nothing could hit the nail more squarely on the head. Not only did high government officials tolerate, not only did they encourage, the development of the old-fashioned plodding schoolmaster into a political courtier, but they did so in terms that in a measure, one must admit, extenuate the worst aberrations, the most absurd irregularities, in these poor souls who now have to be brought back to good sense and discipline. No sovereign of the farthermost regions of ancient Asia was ever courted, flattered, cajoled, boot-licked, as were those unfortunate

say nothing of offering open resistance. All of which does not mean that "the People" of today is not duped, deceived, and exploited by its leaders as much as the Athenian Demos was exploited by sycophants and demagogues in its day and as in more recent times princes were fleeced by their courtiers.[2] In many national parliaments it is not difficult to perceive through the fog of political derivations the substance of private interests for which the given régime is maintained. The fact is well known, and one may find the proofs of it in any number of publications of one sort or another.[3]

young men, who, to the still greater damage of their mental health, had chosen the honourable profession of instructing the young only to see permanently prostrate in obeisance before them politicians and would-be politicians in uncountable numbers. To make sure of their services at election time, government officials have literally crawled at their feet. Observe, moreover, that that atmosphere still continues about the school-teacher, and that at this very moment when there are signs of a reaction against an intolerable state of affairs, we are being offered a law that, under false pretences of protecting a secular school-system, is making a sort of sacerdotal caste of our teachers, sacrosanct and untouchable." During that same session a Socialist Deputy reproached the Government for not continuing to blarney the school-teachers. M. Compère Morel: "So long as the teachers served the Radical party, you buried them in flowers. Now that they are deserting you, you are treating them as enemies [Hisses. Applause]." In Italy the Government buys the votes of a number of Socialist Deputies by according pecuniary favours to certain Socialist cooperatives. A socialist Deputy in Rome owes his seat to the votes of employees of the Royal House. Journal des Goncourt, Vol. VIII, p. 22 (Feb. 28, 1889): "I note in this evening's Temps a sentence addressed to working-men by President Carnot: 'I thank you from the bottom of my heart for the welcome you have just given me, my dear friends—for you are my friends since you are working-men.' [As everybody knows, Carnot was assassinated by a "working-man" who seems not to have been so much of a "friend."] I wonder whether, in the whole history of the world, a courtier of king or emperor ever uttered a sentence to equal in cravenness that sentence of a courtier of the people."

1713 [2] Courier, Simple discours . . . (anent a subscription for the purchase of Chambord [the palace of Francis I]) (Œuvres complètes, pp. 47-54): "Chamber, antechamber, and gallery repeated: 'Master, all is yours,' which was the courtier's way of saying 'All is ours,' for courts give all to princes the way priests give all to God." Today our politicians, who are the legitimate descendants of the old courtiers, say the same things to "the People," which has succeeded the King; and one may say with Courier: "Chamber, Senate, and Press repeat: 'Master, all is yours,' which is the politician's way of saying 'All is ours'; for politicians give all to the People the way courtiers gave all to the princes of yore, and the way priests gave all to God."

1713 [3] For instance [Ciccotti], Montecitorio ("jottings by one who has been there"), pp. 56-57: "But the Italian bourgeoisie [Being a Socialist, Ciccotti ascribes to the capitalist class a trait that is characteristic of everybody.], whence the greater number of the Deputies derive both as a class and as an emanation, . . . does not

What with books, pamphlets, reviews, and newspapers, such publications would fill a large library. But the most important of them are the official minutes of parliamentary investigations. These are difficult to procure and no one reads them, but they may help some

feel the need and perhaps does not have the capacity for developing within itself those convictions and aspirations which would divide it into parties, and so, on a basis, at the very most, of divisions that are nominal more than anything else, it lives on in a state of political anaemia. Such being the situation, such the atmosphere in political and social life, since some centre must nevertheless be found, it is sought, naturally, and found in the constituted authority, in the Government, which exists inevitably . . . and which, in virtue of its control over a whole concatenation of interests, is in a position to satisfy appetites, coddle ambitions, manufacture majorities. But to seek a centre outside oneself is to place oneself in just that position of servitude in which the majorities at Montecitorio stand toward the ministers whom they ostensibly create but by whom really they are themselves created and controlled. The very populous class of 'ministerials' along with the ministries themselves live their lives in more or less complete oblivion of politics (using that term in the sense of statesmanship, an activity that is good and beneficial to the country), trusting in the ministry and blindly following it in deference to a sum of emotions made up of gratitude, hopes, fears, and worries as to personal interests." And see also by the same writer, Ciccotti, *How I Became and Ceased to Be Representative for Vicaria* (*Come divenni, etc.*). In his *Così parlò Fabroni* (Thus spake Fabroni), Roberto Marvasi describes how Naples was handed over to the Camorristi by the Government, pp. 10-13: "For the purpose of preventing the re-election of Ettore Ciccotti as Deputy from the district of Vicaria . . . many members of the Camorra were excused from compliance with the requirements of the 'special surveillance' [probation] to which they had been sentenced. Others received licences for carrying fire-arms or business licences; still others were placed on parole from prison or even pardoned outright. Such the soldiers who fought a battle that was ostensibly being staged in defence of civilized institutions. . . . In this unconfessable enterprise, criminals joined forces with the infantry and cavalry, and the latter bivouacked about the streets and squares of the city, charging suspicious voters with galloping horses. . . . A 'State Camorra' is certainly something quite original, and the spectacle of a government making a formal contract of partnership with the underworld and ordering of it *a job lot of crimes* [italics Marvasi's] is certainly an amazing one." Marvasi concludes, p. 283: "I confess that my purpose has been to call attention to the situation now prevailing in the country in its bearing on the capitalist system and the political system that are sapping the country's vitality." In that Marvasi is confusing two things that are entirely distinct: (1) A description of fact, which seems to be, in great part at least, accurate and sound; (2) the cause of those facts, which he locates in the "capitalist system." This latter is an assertion unsupported by scientific proof and it can find its place only in a Socialist theology.

Facts without number serve to show that for many people in the governing classes politics is simply the art of looking out for the interests of certain voters and the representatives they elect. In them Class I residues are absolutely dominant, while Class II residues tend to be weak. Many Deputies call themselves anti-Clericals yet get themselves elected by Clerical votes. Here is an incident that is

future historian to repeat a remark that Sallust, *Bellum Iugurthinum*, XXXV, 10, puts into the mouth of Jugurtha in comment on Rome: *"Urbem venalem et mature perituram si emptorem invenerit"*—"A city ripe for the destruction and up for sale, if only it

typical of a huge category of facts. In February, 1913, a certain Deputy made a fiercely anti-Clerical speech before the Italian Chamber. It came to light that he had been elected by Clerical votes. In that connexion the *Giornale d'Italia* commented (Feb. 18, 1913): "The president of the Catholic Voters' Union, Count Gentiloni, calls attention to this curious fact: that Deputy X elected at Y by the Catholic vote and with the support of the Catholic Bishop, has been functioning in Rome, in virtue of a special understanding with Ernesto Nathan, no less, as an anti-Clerical. Man of good sense that he is, Count Gentiloni naturally admonished the Bishop to keep a closer eye on the conduct of his Deputy and the scolding has caused quite a flurry among the Clericals. With that we need not concern ourselves. What does interest us is the case of the Deputy from Y, for it is just another of those daily incidents to which the political deportment of a number of Deputies is treating us. There are Deputies who change personalities on the trains that carry them from their district capitals to Rome. At home, in their counties, the gentlemen in question are most obsequious to Catholics, Catholic platforms, Catholic authorities; but once they are through the portal of the station in Piazza Termini in Rome, they suddenly become transfigured in a Pentecost of purest anti-Clericalism; and continuing, nevertheless, whenever necessary, to commend to the good graces of the ministry any priest in their district who chances to have some favour to ask of the Minerva [Ministry of Public Education] or of the Department of Religion and Worship, they take part, politically, in every demonstration of anti-Clericalism, especially—we need hardly say—if it is a mere matter of oratory. . . . For another particular speciality of our professional anti-Clericals is to exterminate Clericals by word of mouth, but carefully to avoid performing any act that might really damage Clerical activity and Clerical propaganda. The anti-Clericalism of Signor Finocchiaro-Aprile, to mention one, is of just that type: his speeches are numerous, impetuous, fierce; but look for administrative, and especially legislative, acts corresponding, and you do not find them, unless a fine chance to do a little anti-Clericalism comes along by refusing Monsignor Caron an *exequatur* and so doing a favour to the great majority of Genoese (and Italian) Catholics! The president of the Catholic Voters' Union has, therefore, it would seem, made a move towards introducing a little sincerity and honesty into our electoral morals, and for that our best praise. But we do not believe that he will at all succeed. This system of double-dealing comes in altogether too handy for both the Deputies and the Clericals—for the Deputies because it assures them votes; for the Clericals because it assures them that they will be let alone."

For such general situations everybody tries to find particular causes, and finds one that suits his sentiments. At the present time [1913] in France, many people are attributing this same evil to the system of electing Deputies by plurality votes; and they contend that proportional representation would be an effective remedy. Noting that the Chamber of Deputies never succeeds in approving the budget on time, Berthoulat writes, *Liberté*, Feb. 18, 1913: "What an arraignment this Chamber of the plurality ballot (*petit scrutin*) has made of itself! So, in eight months' time, it has not been able to patch together a bad budget! We are thinking of appropria-

could find a buyer." [4] Now and then a "scandal" occurs such as the bank scandals in Italy and the Panama scandal in France. An investigation is held, and it serves, if for nothing else, to give the public at large the impression that what is really the rule is just an excep-

tions, the taxation aspect of the subject not having been even broached as yet, for statesmanship with our district Deputies begins and ends with asking for greater and greater expenditures to fatten their followings with. . . . All the same, what is the essential and abiding justification for the parliament's existence? Is it not the same as for the old States General, which had, in their time, an intermittent mandate to protect the taxpayer from the demands of the Crown for money? Now, as a consequence of the strange and lamentable confusion of powers that is inherent in the present [republican] régime, our Deputies have stepped into the shoes of the Prince. Their ever present concern is to loosen our purse-strings to give free play to their grasping hands. But the maintenance of their principalities being bound up, thanks to the ethical code of a rotting ballot system, with the healthiest traditions of organized pillage, they work day and night at pillaging. Last summer the Government took the precaution to announce its budget very early. That is why the men from the sticks and swamps (*les hommes des mares*) have been sitting and sitting over the carving-up of France. Every one of them, almost, wants his slice for his particular pack, just as each one of the knights-banneret of the electoral fief has to have something to feed to his troop of retainers. So they all, one by one, interminably, have been asking for the floor to be sure of having their share in the scramble for five billions and a half."

Ciccotti's pamphlet on his experiences at Vicaria ought to be transcribed in its entirety here, so packed is it with data of the greatest interest to experimental sociology. Unfortunately we shall have to confine ourselves to the following quotations. Pp. 58-60: "But these increasingly frequent ministerial crises serve to turn up the man who is shrewdest, most energetic, and most accomplished in applying the inexhaustible resources of the Government to his own advantage; who gets the greatest hold on the press by making the wisest use of secret funds; who shows himself most adaptable, pliable, and skilful in organizing that chain of patronage which runs from minister to Deputy and from Deputy to election district; who tabulates, documents, and files away within reach the 'records' of friends and enemies alike, so that he may be able to control them and even blackmail them as occasion arises; who makes friends with people who have connexions at Court; and who so succeeds in showing himself able, omnipotent, indispensable, and in creating for himself a title to virtually absolute rule, which, in the form of a more or less disguised dictatorship, endures for years now under his own name and now under the names of his figure-heads. . . . Meantime such portion of this interplay

1713 [4] *Liberté,* Feb. 16, 1913: "Deputy Colly, who never minces words, remarked yesterday to his colleagues in the Chamber: 'Oh, we have not a very good reputation in the country at large. But when voters in my district tell me that the parliament is rotten and the Deputies so many roisterers and drunkards, I answer: "If the Deputies are good-for-nothings, the reason is that the voters who elect them are no whit better." ' " As we have noted often already, such literary phrases, which put a situation in a nutshell, have the merit of presenting a vivid picture, though the picture is not altogether exact, overstepping the literal truth now more, now less.

tion. Then shortly the troubled waters return to their customary calm; and since forces that are constant prevail in the end over forces that are temporary, the politicians return to their wonted ways and not infrequently a politician who has been severely damaged by an investigation again is able to become a cabinet minister, and even Premier of a country;[5] and meantime the so-called life-saving operations that are involved in such things increase the power of those who hold the whip-hand.

In general, opposition parties are the ones to impute misdeeds to individuals who are in power, and they believe that in so doing they give proof conclusive that it would be to the public interest

of combination and makeshift as can and must be exposed to light of day; that visible form which these intrigues, these veerings and tackings, have to assume if they are to get results and be widened in scope, and all along dissembled; the manners in which conflicting interests have to compromise, clash, and make up under the public eye—all such things transpire from the debates in the parliament, from the speeches that are made on that floor. The spoken word is the means of winning public favour [In more general terms, the derivation is a means of stirring sentiments.], of attracting, or it may be of diverting, public attention; and, to an even greater extent, it is a means of simulating and dissimulating, of attacking and defending. And all that goes on in the realization or semi-realization on the part of everyone that it is, after all, mere ceremony, mere stage-play. The Deputies will all tell you, if you ask them, that a speech is not going to change a situation [They recognize *practically* the truths that we have been expounding in these volumes *theoretically*.], that it will not shift one vote, not amount in a word to a tinker's dam. And yet the speaking goes on, in real earnest sometimes. [Derivations have been used since the beginning of the world.] An ingenuous soul may at times even have some illusion as to the immediate effects of a speech he has made, while men of passionate faith cherish the illusion, or comfort themselves with the thought, that everything comes to an end in the form in which it manifests itself, but that nothing in the end is lost. . . . Most parliamentary orators, however, feel more or less consciously that whenever they make a speech before the Chamber they are mere actors reciting their parts on a stage." At his trial before the French Chamber on one occasion on a charge of extorting money from the Panama Company for political purposes, Rouvier, it will be remembered, retorted: "If I had not done what I did, not a man of you would be here!" Well known the fact that the big banks of France are forced to contribute to the election funds of the party in power, and that some of them also give money to an opposition party that seems to have a chance of soon assuming power. The funds they use for such purposes are kept secret, so that the banks will always be in a position to make a denial if a newspaper, as sometimes happens, gets hold of the facts.

1713 [5] See, for example, Palamenghi-Crispi, *Giovanni Giolitti*. In France Rouvier became a minister again after the Panama affair. In England Lloyd George retained his post in the cabinet after an investigation of stock speculations which he had made and denied that he had made, so that he was placed in the position of having to admit that he had told an untruth.

to drive such men from office. Friends of the victims issue denials, look about for extenuating circumstances, or, with greater success, find ways of "hushing everything up." Individuals who know the ins and outs of the government admit the wrongdoing when they are speaking as man to man with their friends; but they add that such things do not make it any the less to the public interest that their friends should be kept in power.[6] Needless to say, when an opposition party comes to power and those in power become opposition, there is an inversion of arguments as well as of rôles. It may well be that all such things are "good," in that they serve to keep alive certain sentiments which are beneficial to society; but with that matter we are not concerned just here (§ 2140).[7]

1714. We have, in our day, under new forms, a feudalism that substantially is the counterpart of the old.[1] In the days of the old

1713 [6] Sometimes this manoeuvre takes place in broad daylight. The Italian Chamber answered the charges that Cavallotti was pressing against Crispi with the resolution that "it was not called upon to consider the *moral question*." The English House of Commons met the charges proved against Lloyd George with the dictum —and in words very thinly veiled—that a blow struck at that minister would be a blow struck at the party governing the country.

1713 [7] Here we have merely been trying to see how certain residues vary. The reader must not attribute to our remarks any broader bearing than belongs to them in that limited reference. He must not gather, even by inference, that we are either condemning or approving the facts alluded to from the standpoint of social utility. All that we have proved is that the arguments which are used to disguise such facts are, as a rule, derivations.

1714 [1] Not a few election districts in Southern Italy are veritable fiefs and something of the sort is observable in France. *Gazette de Lausanne,* Nov. 22, 1912 (article by F. C.): "The trial that has just taken place before the Yonne Criminal Sessions throws a distressing light on political morals in the French departments. . . . In the little district capital of Courson-les-Carrières, two lists of candidates were competing at the last municipal elections, one headed by the retiring mayor, M. Bouquet, Councillor-General, the other by M. Jobier, Sr., conservator of mortgages in Paris. The day before elections, M. Jobier went to a little hamlet in the district to hold a meeting. On his way back to his home he passed a number of gangs of ruffians of more or less threatening demeanour. Chancing to step aside from his company for a moment, he was struck from behind with a cudgel that stretched him on the ground in a serious condition. His son rushed to his side, found him in a pool of blood, and started in pursuit of the ruffians, discharging in their direction a revolver he was carrying on his person. The bullet hit a bakery-worker, one Saligot, killing him instantly. The Yonne jury acquitted young Jobier, who, however, had spent several months in prison awaiting trial. . . . Everywhere the same situation seems to prevail. In the Municipal Council yesterday a member on the Right raised the issue of the poor-relief budget in connexion with the conduct of the poor-children's physician for the Commune of Étang-sur-Arroux (a good name for a

feudalism the lords called their vassals together to wage a war, and if they won, they paid them in booty. In our day, politicians and labour leaders operate in the very same way. They marshal their gangs at election time (§ 2265) to browbeat their opponents and so procure the advantages that go to the winning side. In the old days vassals refusing to follow their lords to war were punished, just as the *crumiri* in Italy, the yellows (black sheep, blacklegs) in England, the foxes (*renards*) in France, the "scabs" in the United States, are punished today for refusing to march in industrial wars. The feelings that are aroused in loyal "militants" today by the "treason" of these people who refuse to be organized are exactly the feelings that people in the Middle Ages felt for the "felony" of a vassal. The privileges that the nobles enjoyed in those old days have their counterparts in the immunities as regards the courts and the tax-collector which are at present enjoyed by Deputies to the parliament and in

backwoods' constituency). The doctor had exerted pressure on voters by threatening to withdraw from them the children in his charge if they voted the wrong way. The charge was so strongly substantiated that the Council of the Prefecture felt obliged to quash the election, though it is not much inclined to take such measures. Naturally when M. Billard brought the matter up on the floor, the members on the Left began crying 'slander,' but, unluckily for them, a Socialist who chanced to be a native of the district in question rose from his bench and declared that the facts were exactly as charged. M. Mesureur had to back down, beat about the bush, beg that such an exception not be taken as the rule, give his word of honour that the bureau's physicians in the majority were meticulously loyal to their professional obligations. But that is not so. The placing of homeless children is a well-known device for influencing elections. It is cynically practised and oftentimes admitted. The Department of Public Charities, under the presidency of one of the outstanding Freemasons of the day, has become a mere vote-factory. . . . Returning to the case of young Jobier—the boy did what he did at one of those moments when there is no weighing of pros and contras, when one listens to instinct in its most spontaneous and praiseworthy impulses. In similar circumstances I am sure that anyone would have done what he did. But that is not the question: the drama has its lessons. The court trial showed that at Courson-les-Carrières political passions had been whetted to a paroxysm. It was shown that members of the Councillor-General's party had been singing songs in which the elder Jobier was referred to as 'Cholera,' and that not a few had gone so far as to say, 'We've got to kill the Jobiers.' On the other hand, the prosecution described the chief of the Jobier dynasty as a 'tough old bird,' a tyrannical old man in whom ambition stopped at nothing. Why, in any event, were all those people fighting so bitterly? For ideas? By no means! They all held the same ideas. They were Radical-Socialists on both sides. Indeed the one who stood farthest to the Left was a conservator (of mortgages, at least!). They were fighting for the possession of power, for the possession of the town hall! An unpleasant job, the town hall! Agreed! But in a social system

smaller but by no means inconsiderable measure by such of their constituents as are on the side of the party in power.[2]

1715. In olden times the requirement of uniformity asserted itself in certain regards; nowadays it asserts itself in certain other regards, but the requirement is still there. Requirement of uniformity as regards Christian beliefs has diminished everywhere, and in some countries it has virtually disappeared, whereas in economic, social, and humanitarian matters the requirement of uniformity has been growing progressively stronger to the point of absolute intolerance. People in the Middle Ages insisted on religious unity but tolerated personality of law and differing systems of government for different towns, districts, and provinces in a given state. Modern peoples liberally tolerate religious differences, but insist, in words at least, on uniformity of laws for persons, localities, and districts. The ancient Athenian was forbidden to introduce new gods into the city, but he was permitted, apart from certain religious observances, to work whenever and however he chose. In many countries today the law gives not a thought to new gods, but rigorously prescribes the days

where one has to be either abuser or abused, the town hall becomes the stronghold whence one carries on one's depredations in all security. It becomes the feudal castle where one quarters one's vassals and stores one's booty. It is the holy ark of clan and tribe. To hold it or not to hold it is to be or not to be."

The two incidents are merely typical of thousands and thousands of similar ones observable in France and Italy.

1714 [2] The *Giornale d'Italia,* Oct. 10, 1913, prints a list of the declared professional incomes of members of the parliament, taken from the *Riforma sociale.* There were twenty-two lawyers with incomes of 10,000 lire or over. The largest income declared was 30,000 lire. Forty-two lawyers declared from 5,000 to 9,000 lire, forty-two others from 2,000 to 4,800 lire. Twenty-one other lawyers (poor chaps!) earned only from 700 to 1,900 lire. Seven others do not appear in the personal property list at all! Then come seventeen physicians. " 'Incidental incomes' do not appear in the list. Only one is as high as 10,000 lire. Three others amount to 6,000 lire or over. From the 6,000-lire level there is an abrupt drop to 4,000 and under, and then on down to a minimum of 1,000 lire." Engineers and architects: "They are few in number, and only one of them has any considerable income (25,000 lire)." A number of the Deputies mentioned in the list are well-known men; and it is a matter of common knowledge that their professions yield them larger incomes than the amounts declared, twice as much, three times as much, perhaps five times as much. The same applies to members of the Italian Senate. How comes it that members of the parliament can get such false returns accepted by the tax authorities? A writer in the same paper (Oct. 12, 1913) explains the mystery: "In connexion with our advance notice on the results of the interesting investigation which the *Riforma sociale* will publish in its forthcoming issue, Signor Antonio Corvini, president of the Direct

and hours during which a man may work. The ancient Roman was required to respect official worship, but he could drink as he pleased. Today not a few countries have abandoned official worship (or at least lay no stress upon it) but forbid the use of alcoholic beverages. The Inquisitors of the Catholic faith diligently inquired into offences against their holy religion. Our present-day teetotallers and sex-reformers no less diligently inquire into offences against the holy religion of abstinence from wine and women. And if the effects of these respective inquisitions are different, that is due first of all to the fact that our times are in general less severe in their punishments for all crimes; and secondly to the fact that if our modern inquisitors are not lacking in the will, they are lacking, to an extent at least, in the power to wreak their will. On the other hand modern policing is more efficient than policing in the old days, and repression has therefore gained in extension what it has lost in intensity, so that the sum of the sufferings inflicted in this way upon mankind still remains very considerable.[1]

Tax Commission for the Province of Rome, transmits a communication which we print herewith in its essential paragraphs. Says Signor Corvini: 'In the performance of their difficult duties the tax commissioners have never had, and do not now have, any sense of tenderness or any reverential fears as regards Deputies and Senators. If, therefore, the low tax-assessments of many such gentlemen are to be deplored, the blame must be placed on other procedures and other persons. The public should know, in fact, that if the Commissioner fixes a definite sum as an acceptable income for a person, that person has the right to appeal to one or more higher commissions, which are the final, and not always the dispassionate and disinterested judges in the controversy. Unfortunately, in Italy such local and provincial Appeal Commissions are direct creations of local party organizations, these in their turn being creatures of the Deputy or Senator, who thus obtains, without any angelic benevolence on the part of the tax commission, anything he wishes, or anything he believes to be fair to himself. There is one defect that is common to the whole administrative system in our country: the imposition and superimposition of political influence upon all the organs of the executive branch.' " In its session of June 25, 1914, Deputy E. Chiesa reminded the Italian Chamber that a number of Deputies were paying personal property taxes on returns that were evidently lower than their actual incomes. His remarks attracted harsh retorts and criticisms altogether irrelevant to the matter in hand; but no one dared deny or even question the truth of the charges.

1715 [1] In Italy, in 1910, the Knight Commander Calabrese, Deputy Crown's Attorney and chairman of a subcommittee for the drafting of a bill relative to control of the press, proposed requiring that bonds of from 500 to 10,000 lire should be posted by all persons intending to publish newspapers, that newspaper editors be at least high-school graduates, and that "supervising commissions" be created to keep watch over newspapers and prevent them from publishing anything "contrary to

As a result of that undulating movement in social phenomena to which we have had frequent occasion to allude, one notes at the present time a return to the state of mind that prevailed in France at the time when Flaubert's *Madame Bovary* and other "immoral" books were being prosecuted, and in Italy too one notes a recrudes-

public peace, good morals, and civic and domestic virtue." Such commissions were to serve their decisions by constable on editors and managing editors of newspapers, who would be required to print them in the next following issue of their paper under penalty of a fine of 200 lire. Commendatore Calabrese even played schoolmaster to the proposed commissions as to manner of procedure and wrote: "Instead of striving to exert a calming influence upon the public, instead of acting as a moderator, the present-day newspaper capitalizes and whets public excitabilities. It seems to me to give excessive relief to anything that is dramatic, passionate, or romantic, stressing criminal trials and murders, even if they take place in the backwoods of China or Patagonia." It might be objected that one swallow does not make a springtime, and that the whims and fancies that chance to flit through one eccentric mind should not be taken too seriously. But these pleasant contrivances of Calabrese prompted the *Corriere d'Italia* to make a reportorial investigation, and many persons of prominence were found to sympathize with Calabrese's general feeling, though differing with him as to means. So the swallows were not just one, but a whole flock. Said Senator Filomusi-Guelfi, a professor of the philosophy of law: "My work as a philosopher and jurist is based upon the fundamental concept that law has its basis in morality; and it therefore seems logical that any attack made upon morality should be dealt with by law. And since the press in our day is missing no occasion or pretext for violating the norms of morality, the conduct of the press ought also to be subjected to some new and more effective sanction. For us Italians censorship has an odious past, an unpleasant tradition. It reminds us of old errors, old oppressions, old and outlandish intolerances. It recalls Spain to our minds and the era of Spanish influence. In a word, its efficacy is always an open question. In my opinion, therefore, what we need is not a censorship. We need to think up more energetic laws, measures that will provide for exemplary sentences and punishments for the more characteristic violations of the rules and laws that safe-guard morality. In my opinion the law should adopt a frankly punitive attitude, which, from the very nature of the juridical factor, would prove to be spontaneously preventive."

In June, 1914, a Republican newspaper in Ancona published an article that seems to have been held offensive to the memory of Victor Emmanuel II, who, to tell the truth, now belongs to history. Had the article been taken for what it was, a political utterance, the newspaper could not have been confiscated; and had the authorities chosen to prosecute, they would have had to bring the case before Criminal Sessions, where, in all probability, the paper would have been acquitted. By a clever sleight-of-hand, the Government chose to view the article as an "offence against decency," at the very least changing what was secondary into what was primary. In so doing, it was able to suppress the paper, have it convicted by government judges, and, in addition, behind closed doors. It is interesting that when, under identical circumstances in France in the days of the Restoration, Courier was accused of "offending public morals" by publishing a pamphlet that was obviously political, the Government did not dare conduct his trial behind closed doors.

cence of prosecutions of that type. The criticisms that are being made- in France of literary productions styled "immoral" recall, though in a much less marked degree, the attacks that were made on the *Camille* (*La dame aux camélias*) of Alexandre Dumas the younger.[2] In England a bishop rises to criticize the songs of Gaby

1715 [2] The censorship made three reports advising prohibition of the production of the play, which was finally allowed by Minister Morny. *La censure sous Napoléon III. La dame aux camélias*, Vol. I, p. 10: "This summary, though very incomplete in the twin respect of the incidents and the scandalous details that enliven the plot, will none the less suffice to show how very shocking this play is from the standpoint of public decency and morality. It is a picture in which the choice of characters and the baldness of the colouring overstep the most liberal limits of what can be tolerated on the stage."

Yet nowadays the play is produced everywhere without being found in the least shocking. The history of *La dame aux camélias* is an interesting example of the utter fatuousness of the efforts governments sometimes put forth to influence morals by attacking derivations (§ 1833). Hallays-Dabot, *La censure dramatique et le théâtre*, p. 15: "*Camille* was long under the ban. A revolution was required to get it on the stage. The *coup d'état* of December 2 and the advent of M. de Morny to the ministry determined its fate. By our time [1871] the public has grown familiar with spectacles of an equivocal world that has invaded and one might almost say absorbed the stage in the course of the past eighteen years. . . . But twenty years ago vice had a less brazen, more homelike demeanour, manifesting to a certain extent its shame for its degradation. The numberless reclamations of lost women in the novel and on the stage had not yet put it on a pedestal."

Dabot's terms have to be inverted: Changes in morals had stimulated a florescence of such novels and dramas. Dabot himself gives the proof for that in his *Histoire de la censure théâtrale en France*. After Thermidor, says he, p. 196, "the censorship allows a more pronounced reaction to begin in public spectacles. Following all the fluctuations in opinion and all the shifts in politics, the stage will be now royalist, now republican, according to the party in power." And p. 220: "Under the Empire [Napoleon I], the censorship was supported by the public in its efforts to purify stage morals. A strange reaction had occurred. For more than ten years past the theatres in Paris had been showing every conceivable debauch of the imagination, all conceivable shamelessness. Now lassitude, disgust, had laid hold on audiences, and they rapidly slipped down the opposite incline till they had now reached an intolerant prudery. [The case of our virtuists today.] The better-educated kept all their admiration for great tragic sorrows. The masses would listen only to heavy sobbing melodrama. People no longer cared to laugh. And it is curious to see how uneasy the censorship grew at this prudery in the theatre public."

Dumas's play has been the *bête noire* of no end of writers who are labouring under the illusion that morality can be enforced by suppressing this or that derivation. Viel Castel, *Mémoires sur le règne de Napoléon III*, Vol. II, pp. 34-36, Wednesday, Feb. 11 [1852]: "Last evening I attended the production of a play of Alexandre Dumas the younger, at the Vaudeville. Our theatres are subject to a censorship that is established for the purpose of obliging them to respect decency, good morals, and public respectability. [In his memoirs, Viel Castel describes the "good morals" of his time as extraordinarily bad.] The play in question, *La dame aux*

Deslys, and would have them kept from the public. These, at bottom, are all expressions of one same sentiment: an inclination on the part of certain individuals to force their own "morality" upon others. Among such are many hypocrites, but also many persons who are acting in all good faith. The state of mind of these latter seems to be as follows: They have within them a number of group-persistences, which are so active and powerful as entirely to control their minds. That is what we call "faith." The objects of such faiths may differ. Let us designate them, in general form, as *A*. The person who has the faith ascribes an absolute value to *A,* and banishes from his mind every doubt, every consideration of opportuneness, any appreciation of other facts that have to be considered. To force someone else to have one's own faith in *A,* or at least to act as if he did, is, at bottom, merely forcing him to seek his own and other people's welfare, is merely giving concrete form to the absolute good. *Compelle intrare!* As for the substance of what happens, it matters little whether *A* be the faith of Anytus or Meletus, the faith of St. Augustine or Torquemada or Senator Bérenger, the faith of an educated individual or an idiot, of a statesman or a *littérateur,* of the many or the few. What varies is the derivations that are used in the effort to represent the dictates of the faith in question as demonstrations of a "knowledge" which is nothing but sheer ignorance.[3]

camélias of Alexandre Dumas the younger, is an insult to everything for which the censorship is expected to enforce respect. The play is a disgrace to the age that endures it [Exactly what our Paladins of Purity say of other works of art today.], the government that tolerates it, the audiences that applaud it. [Just what has been said of the audiences that applaud *La Phalène* and other such plays.] . . . The whole play reeks with vice and debauchery. All the characters (*acteurs*) are monstrous. Even those the author tries to make attractive are disgusting. . . . There is no question of my summarizing the play—it is filthy beyond words; but the spectacle offered by the audience is more so. The police, the Government, are tolerating these outrages. They seem not to be aware that that is the way the demoralization of a people is brought on."

In 1913 the French Academy refused to participate in the observance of the bicentenary of Diderot. Perhaps we ought to thank the Academy for not resolving that his works should be burned and people put into prison for daring to prefer them to the insipidities of not a few Academicians one might mention.

1715 [3] It is a curious fact that when their own faiths are not concerned practical men sometimes perceive these truths quite clearly. Bismarck, *Gedanken und Erinnerungen,* p. 499 (Butler, Vol. II, p. 169): "In politics as in the religious sphere, the conservative can meet the liberal, the royalist the republican, the believer the unbeliever, only with one theme that has been bandied about with all the countless

Observe that the oscillatory movement develops about a general line that indicates, for our time, an average diminution in intensity. Alas and alack! The day is no longer when a cup of hemlock is promptly passed to the man who does not think as some "moralist" thinks, and when a slow fire is lighted under anybody who differs with some Dominican of the virtuistic faith!

1716. If the feudal lord be compared with the man of wealth of today, it is apparent that the sentiment of individual integrity has declined considerably. But if the comparison be extended to all classes in society, it is just as apparent that, by way of compensation, that sentiment has awakened and grown powerful in the lower classes, which at no time in history, not even in the day of the Latin and Greek democracies—especially if one think of the slaves and freedmen—had a sense of personal dignity at all comparable with what they have at present. So the protection of sentiments of integrity in the criminal has nowadays reached a degree of intensity far higher than anything heretofore witnessed in our Western countries. As regards the repression of crime, the "individual"—to use the jargon now current—was once sacrificed to "society"; nowadays "society" is sacrificed to the "individual." Authorities in former days were not so sensitive about punishing the innocent provided no guilty person escaped. Today people make nothing of letting a culprit escape, not only to save the innocent, but just to pamper humanitarian sentiments.[1] The same persons may be seen appealing to

variations of eloquence [That utterly simple remark contains the germ of our whole theory of residues and derivations.]: 'My political convictions are sound, yours are false,' 'My belief is pleasing in God's sight, your unbelief leads to damnation.' It is understandable, therefore, that religious wars should arise from differences of religious opinions and that party struggles in politics, even if they are not settled by civil war, should at least result in the suppression of those limits which the decency and self-respect of well-mannered people maintain in the social life that is foreign to politics." Bismarck was thinking particularly of politics, but his remark applies to the domains of religion, morality, and so on, just as well. And he concludes very truly: "But the moment a man can say to his conscience or to his group that he is acting in the interest of his party [In the general form, "of his own faith."], any infamy is winked at as permissible or at least excusable."

1716 [1] Examine almost any catalogue of books and pamphlets of our day, and one will find any number devoted to ways and means of helping criminals, or effecting their moral reform, or to proposals of new measures in their favour, such as pardon laws, indeterminate sentences, probation, non-registration of sentences in judicial records, and so on. But look for books or pamphlets devoted to saving honest men from murderers, thieves, and other criminals and one will find but

the "rights of society" as against the individual when it is a question of fleecing their neighbours of their possessions, and the "right of the individual" as against society when it is a question of safe-guarding the criminal—one of the many cases where contradictory derivations may be seen in use by the same individual at the same time. We must not, however, stop at derivations. We have to go on to look for the sentiments that they veil. In this case they are evident enough: They are, simply, sentiments favourable to a certain class of persons who desire to relieve others of their possessions and to commit crimes with impunity. Sometimes there is merely a difference in forms. John Doe belongs to the populous class of the poor. He desires to appropriate an object that is the property of Richard Roe, who belongs to the less populous class of the rich. He can attain his purpose in two ways: 1. He can have the law award him possession of the object, and for that purpose it is better for him to appeal to the rights of the majority as against the minority, a notion that he states as a right of "society" as against the "individual." [2] 2.

few, in fact, very very few. Non-registration of sentences in judicial records is an excellent device for misleading the honest citizen, who may so be induced to admit the honourable criminal into his home or at any rate employ him, so giving him an opportunity to resume his praiseworthy activities. But that is of no concern to anybody: the important thing is to be kind to the criminal and shield his personal integrity. Union Suisse pour la Sauvegarde des Crédits, Genève, *Report* of Feb. 23, 1910, p. 34: "We have several times had occasion to call attention in our reports to the difficulties we meet in the matter of judicial antecedents. Business men who are about to make connexions with a person as regards employment, or some other service requiring implicit trust, insist on knowing with just whom they have to deal. Jurists writing on the question claim that individuals convicted of crimes should not be reminded of them, and that point of view is shared generally by persons interested in sociology or social work (*patronage*) but not connected with business. There is no basis for reconciling the two views, the business man being exposed to loss in unwittingly giving his preference to a man with a record, while the others, for the most part of the liberal professions, are never called upon to take such people into their own employ."

1716 [2] Bayet, *Leçons de morale*, p. 114 (capitals and italics Bayet's): "Certain persons claim that it is proper to rob people who are very rich and possess great fortunes though they have never worked. . . . Those who say that are wrong. Undoubtedly it is NOT JUST that one should be rich without working. Neither is it just that those who work should be poor, *and everybody should wish there should be a change in that*. But for a change to come, it is sufficient to elect *Deputies* and *Senators* who are friends of the working-men who are poor. Such Deputies will then make laws so that each person will be more or less rich according to the way he works. Meantime the rich must not be robbed."

Note that the reason given for refraining from theft is merely one of expediency:

He can appropriate the thing directly. But in that case, John Doe no longer is a member of the more populous class of society, but of the least populous. The democratic derivation cannot therefore be used as it was before. One may use the term "poor" as equivalent to the term "society," but however great the sottishness and stupidity that wins acceptance for certain derivations, the term "society" cannot possibly be equated with our estimable criminal class. Another derivation has therefore to be devised for the purpose; and it is easily obtained, nowadays, by asserting the "rights" of the individual criminal as against society. If, in the first case, an innocent person is made to suffer, the comment is: "Too bad! But the good of society overbalances everything else." In the second, if an innocent person is made to suffer, the comment is: "Such a thing cannot be tolerated: let society go to smash, but let no innocent man be harmed." [3] If

it is better not to lay hands directly, just now, on what in a short time will be obtained through the law. The opinion expressed in this manual of Bayet's is important because the book is in general use in elementary schools in France and because a law has been proposed that punishes anyone venturing to condemn the instruction furnished in the lay schools too openly by imprisonment for from six to thirty days and by a fine of from 16 to 300 francs. . . . Commenting on this law, which was sponsored by a cabinet minister, M. Viviani, Berthoulat writes in *Liberté*, Nov. 10, 1912: "In a word, under pretext of secular defence, M. Viviani, who is a fiery libertarian, is coolly suppressing freedom of speech, press, and thought. Henceforward there is to be a 'Primary Syllabus' which, along with its pontiffs, it will be forbidden to criticize on pain of having to deal with the police." We are not here inquiring, remember, whether such a law would be beneficial or harmful to society. We are simply producing evidence as to the intensity of certain sentiments.

1716 [3] Most medical experts—or alienists, or psychiatrists, as they like to be called —when retained by the defence in criminal prosecutions make a business of accusing "society" of not having been as considerate as it might have been of the poor criminal. Such estimable souls are confusing the study of lunacy with the study of the essentials of human societies. Typical of this sort of rant is the plea made before the Assizes at Naples by an alienist retained to defend the Farneris woman (Yvonne de Villespreux), who had killed her lover, as reported in the *Giornale d'Italia*, May 18, 1913: "'Follow her briefly as a little girl: an infancy unbrightened by one ray of mother's love, by any moral guidance, by a single lofty sentiment. Professor P— has told you that she is lacking in any moral sense. And your moral sense, how did you acquire it? She can have no such sense, if she has been deprived of everything essential to its development and growth. All through her life she has always met obstacles to her innermost, but as yet undeveloped, sentiments; and consequently she may have known the concept of society, not love of society. She fell, as any man, any woman, must fall if they have lived as she lived. She presents many anthropological traits of degeneracy. They have only a limited value, but they probably had their influence on this woman's manner of living, and her very impulsiveness is correlated with the feeble development in her of that moral sense which is the high-

one would have concrete illustrations of these two manners of reasoning, used, though opposites, by the same persons, he has only to read the outpourings by French humanitarians and Socialists at the time of the Dreyfus affair.[4]

est expression of feeling. The moral sense implies, however, a profound respect, and a great love, for society. But what respect, I ask you, what love, could this woman have for society? What did society ever do for her? When the moral sense is missing, the responsibility nearly always lies with society, as a biological consequence, I mean. She is also subject to hysteria, to hysteria in that broad sense, as Professor P— has told you, which makes her unstable, changeable, in all her ideas, there being no organization of them; and her mental products are the result of that very disorganization.' [Suppose we agree that "the responsibility lies with society" every time some criminal is found wanting in a moral sense. But is "society" also responsible every time an alienist is found wanting in a scientific sense (§ 1766 [1])? Even the testimony of the expert for the prosecution had so little to do with medical science that he earned a reprimand from the presiding judge. Said he:] 'I should have preferred not to appear in this case, but since I could not get excused, I am forced to open my remarks by drawing a picture that will bring out the moral physiognomy of this wretched woman and set the environment in which she grew up in its true light. You have heard how she was cared for as a child by a certain woman named Giordano, who took her into her home and played the part of step-mother in her life. The Giordano woman had none of the tenderness of a mother, and the poor child in her charge was frequently obliged to go without food, endure all sorts of ill treatment, and listen to the degrading insult that she was nothing but

---

1716 [4] Similar things are also observable in other countries. As above noted (§ 1638), many people go looking about for historic convicts to "rehabilitate," with the idea of attracting attention to themselves and so winning fame and profit. Of the attempted "rehabilitation" of the Lafarge woman, Maurice Spronck writes in Liberté, Feb. 5, 1913: "In Mussulman countries there are monks, the 'howling' or 'spinning' dervishes, whose main occupation consists of whirling, on certain occasions, round and round and faster and faster like a top, shouting meantime at the top of their lungs, Allah ou! Allah ou! Sooner or later, those who practise this noisy rotative gymnastic fall into a pious trance where they see the gardens and cool springs of Mohammed's Paradise and houris waiting on the faithful. Anybody can see that after a person has spun and shouted long enough, he ought to be able to see almost anything he chooses. In the same way, when people have shivered and shouted long enough over some criminal case they know nothing in particular about, they are very likely to enter a state of beatitude where all sorts of hallucinations are possible. Justice and Truth descend from the clouds, Light sets itself in motion. This is the lay form of ecstasy, the only kind of ecstasy becoming to scientific minds emancipated from all outworn superstitions. The only question of any importance now is to decide whether Mme. Lafarge makes a good subject for the cultivation of ecstatic crises. We, personally, are not so sure. In the first place she has been dead quite some time. The few pictures we have of her show her gowned in a fashion long out of date. Besides, it is hard to unchain any very profound passions of a political or religious character in connexion with her adventures. Most inopportunely, she was a Clerical, if we are to judge by her correspondence with a

We have identified the sentiments with which the derivations start, but we must not stop there: we must still see why those particular derivations are used and not others. For surely it is not just for the fun of being inconsistent that two contradictory derivations

a bastard.' *The Court:* 'But, Professor P——, you cannot go on in that fashion. Your task is to state the evidence from which you have inferred these elements.' *Professor P——:* 'But, Your Honour . . .' *The Court:* 'No, no! You cannot go on along that line. You are to state the facts on which you base your findings.' *Professor P——:* 'But the facts have been stated in the evidence. I am concerned to get a complete picture of the defendant before the Court.' *The Court:* 'But that is permissible only on the basis of sworn testimony.' *Professor P——:* 'Very well, I will say nothing of her early years. We know that at the age of thirteen she was homeless, and destitute of every help and guidance along the pathway of life. So she found herself alone in the world, and that first day, she appealed to a girl friend to help her get to France to look for an uncle, her mother's brother. But that favour she could not obtain. Instead she went to Turin, where she found work as a maid. But she was not fitted for such work . . .' *The Court:* 'But who told you all that?' *Professor P——:* 'Mlle. Farneris herself.' *The Court:* 'Well?' *Professor P——* (continuing): 'Her mistress was a quick-tempered woman. One day she threw a candlestick at her. Mlle. Farneris fled the house, and she met a man on the staircase.' *The Court:* 'But you cannot say such things! How can you possibly continue in that fashion?' "

In any event, we still have not been shown why people who, be it through fault of "society," happen to be "wanting in a moral sense" should be allowed freely to walk the streets, killing anybody they please, and so saddling on one unlucky individual the task of paying for a "fault" that is common to all the members of "society." If our humanitarians would but grant that these estimable individuals who are lacking in a moral sense as a result of "society's shortcomings" should be made

---

number of priests, which one of our literary reviews has just published. What can one expect to do with a woman who is not even a victim of the Jesuits? Careful study of her case might have attracted the attention of specialists in the history of manners or in psychology. That was already a distressingly small group. As it is, the 'review' of her case, worked up in public meetings, will attract only a few 'intellectuals' from among the Anarchists—a slender phalanx, and all the slenderer since said 'intellectuals,' really, are finding in the ordinary course of our daily life far more exciting occasions for exercising their wits and coddling their temperaments. At this very moment a number of them are founding an association to establish the right of any citizen to make his abode a place of refuge for a murderer or burglar the moment he makes profession of Anarchistic faith. In days like these, with that perfect security in the streets with which the emasculation of crime-repression has blessed us, no more timely measure could indeed be imagined. The protectors and friends of our more formidable cut-throats certainly ought to be assured that they have the protection of the law and that the police are not to be allowed to molest them. One such philanthropist at least is at present seated in the pen in Criminal Sessions on a charge of complicity after the fact in a murder. Obviously if the jury finds him guilty, it will be a much more timely task to rehabilitate that pleasant character than to go bothering about Mme. Lafarge and the exact quantity of arsenic that was present in her husband's viscera.' "

are simultaneously used. Some reason there must be, and it can be no other than a desire to influence the sentiments of the persons listening to the derivation. It is true enough that it expresses certain sentiments, but it is further intended to work upon certain others. There is no doubt, in the case mentioned, as to the sentiments upon which the derivations are designed to work. As regards the first derivation, they are sentiments corresponding to the interests of the poorer portions of the population, and already present in these in

to wear some visible sign of their misfortune in their buttonholes, an honest man would have a chance to see them coming and get out of the way.

The Farneris melodrama had its epilogue. "Society," so direly at fault in its treatment of the woman, redeemed its shortcomings, in part at least, by providing her with experts for a masterly defence and with jurymen who considerately acquitted her and let her go scot-free. Not only that. After the verdict, the presiding justice gave her a very wise fatherly talk exhorting her to "redeem herself by work"; and to give her a chance for such redemption, some well-intentioned ladies of the social set called for her in an automobile and drove her to a shelter. If some poor mother of a family—of the kind that chooses to stay at home and rear her children decently instead of taking to vice and then laying the blame on society—chanced to hear or see all that, she must have reflected that the "shortcomings of society" are not always unmitigated evils; and if she saw and heard what came of it all, she must have understood that if once upon a time the converted sinner was with some reason preferred to the spotless soul, nowadays, thanks to this new religion of the god Progress, conversion is no longer necessary. In fact, the *Giornale d'Italia* reports the sequel of the story in the following terms: "Naples, May 30. Our readers will remember the language in which the President of the Assizes exhorted Mlle. Villespreux, immediately after her acquittal, to take up a life of work that would redeem her. They will also remember how a committee of society ladies interested themselves in procuring her admittance to a shelter that looks after women released from prison. That day Mlle. Villespreux excused herself with a few words of thanks, explaining that she had to go back to the prison for her clothes. But on leaving the prison again, she refused to accompany the representatives of the shelter and went away alone. Nothing more was heard of her that day; but the next it was learned that she had gone back to the via Chiaia, next door to the house where Ettore Turdò was killed and in the very house of the man who had testified at the trial that Yvonne was a good girl and that she stopped with him whenever she returned to Naples from her trips to music-halls in other cities. That was the house she went to after being acquitted of a crime and after, as she said, thirty-eight months of mourning for poor Turdò. But after all, why should all that be wrong, or rather, why should such a thing be taken in an unfavourable sense? Mlle. Farneris still has time to devote herself to work and to begin her life of redemption, starting perhaps from the very house where she should have closed her life of shame. However, we should be failing in a duty were we to refrain from reporting this last phase of her melodrama, just as during the trial we reported everything that tended to favour her acquittal. The news, we might add, has occasioned great surprise about town." Those who were surprised must have been either very great humanitarians or very great fools. Or maybe both.

very considerable proportions are sentiments of individual integrity. As regards the second, there may be, in the case of this or that politician, some idea of winning the favour of certain criminals of exceptional talent as vote-getters or the support of the relatives and friends of such men.[5] But that is the least important element in-

1716 [5] Illustrations without end might be mentioned. I will give two typical examples, the first, where a single criminal is involved, the second where it is a "gang." *Liberté,* Mar. 29, 1913: "*Creil.* The constabulary at Creil have just arrested an individual whose Odyssey is no ordinary story—André Pavier, 27, who escaped in 1911 from the Douera penitentiary in Algeria. Pavier hails originally from Saint-Denis. Coming of military age, he was enlisted in the colonial infantry, fell into breaches of discipline that got him before a court-martial, punched the Judge Advocate, was sentenced to death, had the sentence commuted to five years in prison, and wound up in the penitentiary at Douera. He had served all but two years when one day he profited by a moment's distraction on the part of his sergeant, felled a native soldier who was on guard at the prison with a blow on the head, got to the sea-shore, leapt into a row-boat belonging to the prison, and made the open sea without being hit by the bullets that sped after him. . . . He was picked up two days later, more dead than alive, by some Spanish fishermen who set him ashore near Valencia. Pavier lived from then on by stealing. He soon reached the frontier, made his way across France carefully steering clear of Saint-Denis, and stopped at Lille in June, 1912. There he was arrested for stealing food and was given six days in jail, though nothing was discovered as to his record. Thereafter Pavier settled at Villers-Saint-Paul, near Creil, getting a job in a factory located near the railway line that runs from Creil to Compiègne and working there three months. It was at Villers that he was arrested. Some days ago—he makes a point of his influential connexions—Pavier wrote to a Deputy to ask whether the parliament had not passed an amnesty bill covering offences such as his. The Deputy very politely answered that no amnesty had been voted and ended his letter with urgent advice that his correspondent should be extra careful if he did not wish to be found out. The Deputy's letter fell into the hands of the police and that was the way Pavier was discovered."

Liberté, Apr. 6, 1912, "*Marne Rioters Pardoned.*" The article is too long to be transcribed entire, though that would be valuable as showing the general features of such cases, which are to be observed not only in France but in Italy and other countries. We suppress proper names. One of the chief mistakes people make in such matters is to blame some specific individual for things that are consequences of the way in which society is organized. The person in question here was a cabinet minister. "After he had kept an eye on the progress of the judiciary investigation and narrowed the circle of penal severity to a number of heads that had been lifted too conspicuously against the background of fire that had consumed mansions and wine-cellars, it still devolved upon him to rescue the last soldiers of the riot who had been condemned in the courts of the Marne and in the Assizes at Douai. Now that has been attended to. Not one breaker of hogsheads, not one plunderer is left in the jails of the Republic. Senator X has paid his debt of political gratitude to the rioters. The judiciary investigation of these disturbances and crimes was a calvary of anguish. Taking things in their order: the complaint was filed with the guardian of seals—at the time, M. Perrier—May 20, 1911. The papers did not reach the prose-

volved, and if the derivation is used, it obviously must correspond to the sentiments of a large number of individuals. Such sentiments are mainly sentiments of personal integrity, which, it is felt, must not be offended even in the case of a criminal. Never in any period of history have criminals been allowed to be insolent to their judges as they are in our time. There are trials in criminal courts today where the rôles of the presiding judge who questions and the defendant who answers seem to be inverted.[6] This view of the matter

cutor's office till a week or ten days later, since the order of the investigating judge was not handed up till June 3. What state were they in when they reached Rheims? The Government had prevented several important documents from coming into the hands of the investigating judge during the inquest. Did it not make sure as to anything tending to show political responsibilities in the affair? In any event, despite the manoeuvres of M. Vallé and the governmental pressure, which echoed to the very doors of the inquest, some dozens of the rioters were remanded to the Assizes or tried before lower criminal courts. Seven were convicted at Douai and sentenced to terms varying from four years down to a month. The Appellate Division, for its part, affirmed thirteen sentences imposed by the lower courts, raising seven of them from ten to eighteen months. . . . And what are we to say of the acts that brought their authors before the bar of justice? The reviewing orders of the Court of Assizes and the indictments and complaints against the rioters tell the story. The first was accused of deliberately setting fire to the Gallois house and of pillaging in the Bissinger house. He was seen on the roof of the former 'tearing up tiles and throwing lighted grape-vines inside the building.' Fire broke out at once and the house was burned to the ground. The second was accused of pillaging in the houses. . . . 'Red flag in hand, he led the rioters to the doors of the houses,' and they were broken in. The third worked for two hours at the safe in the Bissinger house before he finally succeeded in getting into it with the help of a pickax. Then he burned deeds, account-books, and all business papers. The fourth lent a hand in the sacking of the Bissinger house. The fifth led the sacking of the Ayala and Deutz houses, breaking down a picket-fence to get into those places. . . . The pardons were dated February 9. On February 15, acts of sabotage at Pommery, on the twenty-first, twenty-second and twenty-fifth, further sabotage at Hautvilliers, Cumières, and other places."

Such the currency in which politicians pay their constituents, exactly as brigand chieftains used to pay their confederates.

1716 [6] We will say nothing of certain cases, such as that of Mme. Steinheil, where the defendant enjoys political "influence" or the protection of persons highly placed. They have no bearing on the point here at issue. But in other cases, where no such patronage or "influence" figures, defendants may be seen "talking down" to judges on the bench. Just one example from the record of the trial of the Bonnot-Garnier "gang," Paris, February, 1913: "*Q. The Court:* You were being persecuted in your home town because of your ideas? *A.* [*Callemin*, alias *Raymond La Science*]: You said this was not a political case. Yet you do nothing but talk politics—Anarchism. *Q.* You mean I am inconsistent. Well, what do I care? I choose to conduct my examination of you the way I please. *A.* Well, I will not answer then, whenever *I* please—that's all. *Q.* That is your look-out. [In fact Callemin lets a number of

is further confirmed by the extraordinary repugnance people of our time feel for corporal punishments, which are falling into disuse for the sole reason that they are insulting to "human dignity," because, in other words, they involve supreme offences to individual integrity.

To conclude, then: Considering substance rather than the derivations that disguise it, it would seem that in our day Class V residues (personal integrity) have rather augmented than diminished in intensity as compared with the residues of our Class IV (sociality).

1717. The residues of our Class VI (sex) are probably among the least variable of residues. There are changes in the veilings that disguise them, and changes also in the amount of hypocrisy they provoke; but no appreciable changes are apparent as regards substance (§§ 1379 f.).

1718. For a given society, therefore, we may establish the following scale of variations, increasing from the first to the last categories: (1) Classes of residues; (2) the genera in such classes; (3) derivations. A graph (Figure 24) may make the relations between classes and genera clearer. The movement in time of a class of residues may be represented by the undulating curve MNP; certain genera are represented by the curves, also undulatory, $mnpq$, $rsvt$. The waves are smaller for the class than for many of its genera. The mean movement of the class, which, let us say, is in a direction of increase, is represented by AB; and the same movement in the genera, some of which are increasing, others diminishing, by ab, xy. The variation represented by AB is much less wide than the varia-

questions pass without an answer. Then come other questions, which he answers with his usual insolence. The Court questions the veracity of one such answer, and Callemin flies into a fury.] *The Court:* I am doing my duty. *Callemin:* But not fairly. Someone wrote somewhere: 'I call a cat a cat and Rollet a rascal!' You are acting, you are, in the completest bad faith. *The Court:* Your insults do not affect me." In olden days steps would have been taken immediately to halt such behaviour towards a court. At a certain point in the examination of another defendant, the attorney for the defence also took a hand at berating the same unlucky judge: "The court-room is in a hubbub to a purport that is not quite clear. Presiding justice Cominaud decides to stop it: *The Court:* I cannot allow demonstrations against these defendants. *Maître de Moro-Giafferi:* They are demonstrating against *you.* This is an audience of admirable generosity [*sic,* not "imbecility"!]. *The Court:* I cannot allow demonstrations either for me or for or against you." Truth compels me to add that Judge Cominaud was not even jailed for contempt.

tions in some of the genera, *ab, xy*. On the whole, there is a certain compensation between genera and it is owing to such compensations that both the variation represented by *AB,* and the amplitude of fluctuation on the curve *MNP,* are attenuated as regards the class as a whole.

As regards social phenomena in general, this undulatory movement creates difficulties that may become quite serious, if one is to gauge the movement of a sentiment, quite apart from occasional, temporary, or incidental fluctuations. If, for example, one should

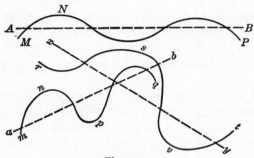

Figure 24

compare the position *r* with the position *s,* to get the general trend of the residue, one would conclude that the sentiment was growing in intensity, whereas the line *xy* shows that, on the average and in general, there is a diminishing intensity. And similarly if one were to compare the position *s* with the position *v* one would register an intensity diminishing at a much faster rate than on the average and in general is actually the case, as shown by the line *xy.*[1] When a development is susceptible of measurement and we have observations extending over long periods of time, it is fairly easy to eliminate such difficulties. By interpolation one may determine the line, *xy,* about which the intensity is fluctuating and so discover its mean general direction.[2] This is much more difficult when accurate meas-

1718 [1] *Cf.* Pareto, *Manuale,* VII, § 47.

1718 [2] One is sometimes able to push the inquiry further and separate the various elements in a situation. Many phenomena involve variations in different entities. For example, if the concrete development is represented (Figure 25) by *mnpqrstv,* one observes: (1) That that line fluctuates about the undulatory line *MNPQ;* (2) that the latter in turn fluctuates about the line *AB.* In other words there are fluctu-

urements for a sentiment are not available or cannot be made, for then we are obliged to replace accurate mathematical quantities with estimates in which arbitrary statement, individual impression, and perhaps even fancy, play a more or less important part. Such estimates must therefore be subjected to the severest examination and no possible verification ignored.

1719. Little or no compensation takes place among the different classes of residues. It would seem, at first sight, that there were some between Class VI residues and other religious residues, and in that, indeed, one might be enabled to see the reason why so many religions make war upon the sex religion in hopes of fattening on its

ations of different amplitude, namely: 1. fluctuations of brief duration, represented by the line *mnpqrstv;* (2) fluctuations of medium amplitude, represented by the line *MNPQ;* (3) fluctuations of maximum amplitude represented by the line *AB;* and so on. Interpolation enables us to distinguish these different types of fluctuation: Pareto, *"Quelques exemples d'application des méthodes d'interpolation à la statistique," Journal de la Société de statistique de Paris,* November, 1897: "When this formula is applied to the figures yielded by statistics, it is observable, in general,

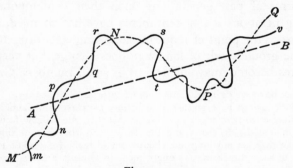

Figure 25

that the simple curves that are successively obtained do not approach the real curve in a uniform manner: the *precision* begins first by rapidly augmenting; then there is a period of slow augmentation, then another of rapid augmentation, and so on. These periods of slow augmentation in precision divide off the great groups of sinuosities mentioned—in other words, they separate the group of more and more particular influences that are influencing the phenomenon. [An example is given—population in England—and the article concludes:] It is seen that the indices of precision increase rapidly as far as the index Δ_3; after that, much more slowly. One finds, therefore, in the case in hand, that population is influenced by a first group of forces that give the phenomenon the form indicated by the first four terms of formula 2. The other terms represent 'perturbations,' 'irregularities.' " We shall meet other examples in the pages following (§§ 2213 f.).

spoils. But it becomes apparent on closer examination that the war is between derivations and not between residues. The other religions do not destroy the residues of the sex religion: they annex them, merely changing the forms in which they are expressed.[1]

1719a. An observation of the sort already made in regard to non-logical actions (§ 252) and in other similar connexions might occur to one with reference to the slight change that the passage of time occasions in residues. If residues really change so slowly, how can the fact have escaped the many talented writers who have studied the various aspects of human society?

The answer is: It did not escape them; only, as happens in the early stages of every science, they stated the fact in vague terms and without aiming at any great scientific exactness. The saying *Nil novi sub sole,* along with other apothegms of the kind, itself voices the perception, more or less veiled by sentiment, that there is something, at least, that is constant in social phenomena.[1] The implicit premise in the pedantry of grammarians who strive to force language forms of past generations upon their contemporaries and younger generations is that sentiments have not changed, and will not change to the point of requiring new language-forms to express them. The groundwork of language does change, but very slowly. Neologisms become unavoidable, but in small numbers. Grammati-

---

1719 [1] That point we dealt with amply in Chapter X.

1719a [1] Such sayings have given rise to literary paradoxes and fantasies without end. They have often been taken in the sense that there are no new facts, which is false. And in that the deficiency and the danger of such vague maxims becomes apparent: one may get anything one chooses out of them (§§ 1558 f., 1797 f.). As an example of such paradoxes, one might mention Fournier's, *Le vieux-neuf: Histoire ancienne des inventions et découvertes modernes:* By far-fetched comparisons, and remote and often imaginary analogies, Fournier shows, p. 1, that "there is nothing new save what has been forgotten." For one of the many literary fancies, see Bergerat, *Théophile Gautier,* p. 118: "*Bergerat.* Do you think the language of the sixteenth century adequate for expressing everything? In a word, do you accept neologism? *Gautier.* Are you referring to the necessity of finding names for the so called inventions and pretended discoveries of modern times? Yes, someone has said that: 'New things, new words.' You know my opinion on that subject. There are no new things. What is called progress is nothing more than the rebringing to light of some neglected commonplace. I imagine that Aristotle knew as much as Voltaire, and Plato as M. Cousin. Archimedes had very certainly found a way to apply steam to locomotion long before Fulton and Solomon de Caus. If the Greeks disdained taking advantage of it, it was because they had their reasons for doing so."

cal forms are modified, but substance endures through the ages. A long line of writers imitated the ancients and some pedants indeed even tried to prescribe that imitation. That would not be understandable unless such persons and the publics they addressed had had sentiments very kindred to those voiced by the ancients.[2] However, quite aside from the matter of imitation, how could we still enjoy the poems of Homer and the elegies, tragedies, and comedies of the Greeks and Latins if we did not find them expressing sentiments that, in great part at least, we share? Aeschylus, Sophocles, Euripides, Aristophanes, Plautus, Terence, Virgil, Horace, and other writers of Graeco-Latin antiquity—are they foreigners whom we no longer understand? Do we not find in Thucydides, Polybius, Tacitus, and other ancient historians, descriptions of things that reveal, under different, sometimes very different, guises, a fund of human sentiments identical with what we observe today? All thinkers who have pondered social phenomena at all deeply have not seldom been led to detect in them certain elements that are variable and certain others that are relatively stable. All we have been doing in these volumes is to offer a scientific formulation of the concept, just as the chemist who "discovered" aluminium and calcium carbonate was merely giving a scientific formulation to notions that had existed long before him and, in fact, ever since human beings had been able to distinguish between clay and limestone.[3]

1719a [2] Dugas-Montbel, *Observations sur l'Iliade,* Vol. I, pp. 70-71 (*Iliad,* II, v. 38): "The Latin poet [Virgil] almost always swings into the movement of the Homeric phrase, that being the expression of the soul which never changes. The manners, customs, habits of men are for ever being modified by civilization, but passions do not vary with the centuries: the voice of the heart is the same in all ages. So it is with all the poets. When Racine imitates Homer, it is the rhythm of the phrase he catches, steeped as his poetry is in the manners of his own age and in the ideas of a vastly different society. [The critic mentions imitations of *Iliad,* V, 116-17 by Virgil and Boileau; then, Vol. I, p. 230:] Neither Virgil nor Boileau mentions 'the thighs of the sheep and the goats covered with thick fat'—they share the ideas of their own times. But they follow Homer in everything touching expressions of the soul. That is the real imitation, the only one that genius can permit itself. [And on *Iliad,* VI, v. 303 (Vol. I, p. 296):] If the imitators of Homer differ from him as regards details of manners, customs, and usages, they insist on following him with happy fidelity in everything touching the expression of sentiment. This cannot vary, the human heart remaining at bottom for ever the same."

1719a [3] There are utopians who set up a certain "human nature" as the foundation for their studies of society, and to uphold one reform or another that is suggested by their fertile imaginations. Such writers instinctively recognize, without

1720. The fact that classes of residues change but slightly or not at all in a given society over a given period of time does not mean that they may not differ very widely in different societies.[1]

1721. The differences between Sparta, Athens, Rome, England, and France that we noted in Chapter II were nothing but differences in intensities of Class I and Class II residues; and it is interesting to note that the conclusions which we now reach through our theory of residues are the very ones which were at that time forced upon us by a direct examination of the facts independently of any general theory of any kind.

1722. Now that we have such a general theory, suppose we go back again to the matter there treated directly (§§ 172-74) and formulate our conclusions in more general terms. Back there we said: "Let us assume that in the case of two peoples Y is identical in both and X different in both. To bring about innovations, the people in whom X is feeble wipes out the relations $P, Q, R \ldots$ and replaces them with others. The people in whom X is strong allows those relations to subsist as far as possible and modifies the significance of $P, Q, R \ldots$" Now we can say: "Let us assume that in two peoples Class I residues (combinations) are of equal strength and Class II residues (group-persistences) of unequal strength. To bring about innovations, the people in which Class II residues are the weaker wipes out the groups P, Q, R both in substance and in name and replaces them with other groups and other names. The people in which Class II residues are the stronger also makes substantial changes in the groups $P, Q, R \ldots$ but allows names to subsist as

being aware of as much, that there is a constant element in social phenomena solid enough to serve as a groundwork on which to develop their dreams. But they glimpse the scientific truth here in question about as much as the man who thinks the Sun dives into the ocean every evening succeeds in glimpsing the movements of the heavenly bodies.

1720 [1] One such case we examined in Chapter II. Back there, in order not to anticipate the results of our investigation here, we used a different terminology. We said in § 172: "There is a very important psychic state that establishes and maintains certain relations between sensations, or facts, by means of sensations $P, Q, R \ldots$" Now we can say that the maintenance of such relations is a group-persistence; and such phenomena we examined at length in Chapter VI. In § 174 we spoke of a force X uniting sensations $P, Q, R \ldots$ Now we can say that that force is a force that keeps the groups from disintegrating, that its measure is the measure of the intensity of the group-persistence. The force Y (§ 174) that prompts innovations corresponds to Class I residues (combinations).

far as possible, resorting, for that purpose, to opportune modifications in derivations, so as to justify, be it fallaciously, the use of the same names for different things." That is the rule, one might add, because, in general, derivations change much more readily than residues and because movement as usual takes place along lines of least resistance. The relative proportions of the various classes of residues in the different peoples are perhaps the best indices of the social states of those peoples.

1723. *Distribution of residues and change in residues in the various strata of a given society.* Residues are not evenly distributed nor are they of equal intensities in the various strata of a given society. The fact is a commonplace and has been familiar in every age. The neophobia and superstition of the lower classes has often been remarked, and it is a well-known fact of history that they were the last to abandon faith in the religion which derived its very name, paganism ("ruralism"), from them. The residues of widest diffusion and greatest intensity in the uneducated are referable to Classes II and III (activity), whereas the opposite is often the case with the residues of our Class V (individual integrity).

1724. Dividing society into two strata, calling one the "lower" and the other the "higher," brings us one step closer to the concrete than we were in thinking of society as a homogeneous unit, though it still leaves us far enough removed from anything concrete, anything real. To get a closer approximation, we should have to divide society into a larger number of classes, in fact, into as many classes, roughly, as there are differing traits in human beings.[1]

1725. *Relations between residues and conditions of livelihood.* Useful classifications of residues may be based on the different occupations of human beings. Such too have been familiar from most ancient times; but almost always those who have utilized them have confused two very different things: (1) The simple fact of a difference in residues corresponding to a difference in occupation or mode of life; and (2) appraisal of the ethical, political, social value, and so on, of the various residues. Often indeed, the observation of fact appears merely as an incidental implication of such appraisal.

1726. Cato the Elder says in praise of tillers of the soil, *De re*

1724 [1] In order not to stray too far afield from the matter here in hand, we must postpone that inquiry till later on, §§ 2025 f.

rustica, proemium: "Our farmers furnish very strong men and brave soldiers, men who earn their bread in manners most honourable and above reproach; and they who till the soil do not cherish evil thoughts." [1] And that is an indirect way of saying that residues present in farmers are different from the residues present in other citizens. Cato's last phrase implies a faint perception that country people are less prone to innovations, that in them Class II residues are of greater importance than in other sorts of people.

1727. Similar observations have been commonly made in all periods of history with regard to merchants, soldiers, magistrates, and so on. There is a general recognition that, on the whole, sentiments tend to vary with occupation. Along that line, the so-called theory of economic materialism might be linked up with the theory of residues by correlating residues with economic status; and as far as it goes such a correlation would undoubtedly be sound. It goes wrong, however, in isolating economic status from other social factors, towards which, on the contrary, it stands in a relation of interdependence; and, further, in envisaging a single relation of cause and effect, whereas there are many many such relations all functioning simultaneously.

1728. Such remarks might be grouped with the many others that stress the influence of soil, climate, and so on, upon the traits of peoples. Hippocrates deals with such influences at length in his treatise *On Airs, Waters, and Places.* The correlations he sets up between human character-traits and living-conditions are probably mistaken; but they none the less recognize differences in temperaments as independent of will, of thought, and of level of enlightenment. The differing temperaments of Europeans and Asiatics he explains by differences in soil and climate supplemented by differences in institutions; and not satisfied with generic differences, he goes into the particular differences of the particular peoples. As a matter of fact, few writers, if any, deny differences in traits between different peoples; the disagreement arises as to the causes—not as to the fact. Almost unique is the conception of the Emperor Julian, who

1726 [1] And so Euripides, *Orestes,* vv. 918-20 (Coleridge, Vol. II, p. 309), contrasts a good farmer with the politician who is the bane of a town: "He is not a man of fair aspect; but he is a manly fellow, and rarely frequents the city and the circle of the market-place. He is one of those peasants who of themselves are able to save a country." Aristotle too expatiates at length on the same theme (§ 274).

thought that the temperamental diversities of the various peoples were due to the diversities in the divine beings appointed to rule them. It is interesting however that, among such divinities, he includes the Air and the Earth.[1]

1729. Unaware of the inconsistency with his own theory, which attaches supreme importance to logical conduct (§§ 354 f.), Buckle [1] follows Hippocrates in his views as to the influence of climate and soil—he adds food-supply as depending on climate and soil—upon the temperaments of peoples, their manners and customs and levels of civilization. Here again it is to be noted that the correlations established by Buckle may be partly sound, partly mistaken; but that, in any event, he views human conduct as being determined by residues, and not by derivations, and varying as residues vary. Buckle also knows the origin of such residues. We are chary about following him down that path, deeming it the wiser part to leave matters of origin to future investigations.

1730. Many other writers might be mentioned in this connexion. Let us stop at Demolins,[1] who thinks he has shown that the civilization of a people is determined by the route it has followed in its migrations. His books make pleasant reading. They are as seductive as a siren's song, the arguments seeming faultless and irresistibly conclusive. And yet at the end one wonders—can it really be that an itinerary of migration, most often a mere matter of guess-work on our part, is alone enough to account for all the traits a people shows, independently of any other factor? And then one notices

---

1728 [1] St. Cyril, *Contra impium Iulianum*, IV (*Opera*, Vol. IX, pp. 719-22) (quoting Julian): "If God has not assigned to each people a ruler subordinate to Him, either angel or demon, whose function it is to guide and supervise particular kinds of souls, so that differences in customs and laws arise, I should like to be shown what other cause could have brought such differences about." The Emperor was controverting Christians who sought to explain differences in laws and customs by the confusion of tongues at the Tower of Babel. He points out that similar differences are also apparent in physique: "If one consider how greatly the Germans and the Scythians differ from the Libyans and the Ethiopians, can such differences be ascribed to a naked order [to world-order all by itself], without regard to atmosphere, the location of their lands and the disposition of stars in the firmament?" St. Cyril replies that Christians attribute differences in customs and manners of living to differing temperaments [inclinations of will] and differing ancestral traditions.

1729 [1] *History of Civilization in England*, Vol. I, pp. 39 f.
1730 [1] *Les grandes routes des peuples.*

that the force of the reasoning depends more upon the talents of the writer than upon the cogency of his facts and his logic, and we begin to put question-marks where we have been putting periods. There again we leave to future investigations the task of determining the influence that a migration route may have had upon the characteristics of a civilization. We are satisfied, just here, with the fact that, to an extent at least, such traits are not dependent on reasoning, on human logic, on *knowledge* of certain ethical systems, certain religions, and so on, that, in other words—to repeat a thing we have already said over and again—they depend much more largely on residues than on derivations; without, for that matter, precluding that in a minor way derivations also may have had their influence.

1731. The theories just mentioned were attempts to explain social phenomena by relationships of cause and effect. They are like the theories that were commonly current in political economy prior to the synthesis of pure economics. They are not altogether false—they have a part, sometimes a very considerable part, that accords with experience. But they also have a part that is altogether at odds with experience, and that is due chiefly to the fact that they neglect the interdependence of social phenomena, and in two ways: (1) By envisaging only one "cause," where there are many many causes; (2) by again considering only one cause, but putting it in a relation of cause and effect with other phenomena, whereas their real relation is one of interdependence giving rise to a series of actions and reactions.[a]

In general, social phenomena, like economic phenomena, show undulatory forms of development; so that the relationships between the undulations have to be taken into account above all else. Suppose we have two phenomena with measurable indices that are the ordinates of two curves (§ 1718[2]), and that we are trying to find the relationship between them. If we insist on taking every minutest fluctuation into account, the problem is altogether unsolvable. But we can get an at least roughly approximate solution if we resign ourselves to considering only the more marked fluctuations, the general development of the phenomena. This general direction can be

1731 [a] [Pareto's phrasing of 2, which I find opaque, has been rewritten in translation to clarify the meaning.—A. L.]

determined by two methods. The first, which is very imperfect from the experimental standpoint, is to substitute for the concrete phenomenon certain abstract entities that are assumed to represent it more or less adequately. So we say that the height of tides depends upon the attraction of Sun and Moon. No such "height" exists: there are heights in infinite numbers, according to the points considered. So when we say that the exchange rate of a country's currency depends upon the status of the debts and credits the country has with foreign countries, we are correlating two abstract entities. There is no such "rate of exchange." There is an infinite number of rates, sometimes a different rate for every actual contract. There is no status of debts and credits, but an infinitude of debts and credits, every passing moment witnessing the appearance and disappearance of some one of them. Economists say that a given commodity on a given market at a given time could not possibly have more than one price. Such statements are abstractions that at times approximate reality and at times vary widely from it and do not describe it at all save in a very rough way. So supply and demand in a given commodity on a given market are abstractions; and the same may be repeated in general for all the entities considered in political economy. Monsieur Jourdain talked prose without knowing it. So persons who deal with entities of that sort make interpolations (§ 1694) without knowing it. But it is always better to proceed in full knowledge of what one is about. We had better look more closely therefore at the second method for determining trends in certain phenomena. The method is to determine curves to represent the phenomena, then to interpolate those curves, and finally determine the relations between the average movements (§ 1718 [2]). But in all that we must guard against a new error into which one may easily fall. This second method must not result in our neglecting the first, for both may be made to contribute to the sum of our knowledge. The results yielded by surveying come closer to realities than the results yielded by topography, which in their turn are more concrete than the results of geodesy; but that is no reason for ignoring or abolishing geodesy in favour of topography, or topography in favour of surveying. The empirical theory of tides brings us closer to the concrete than does the pure astronomical theory; but that is no reason for scrapping the latter. We are not called upon to ignore abstract economics because we are studying undulations in economic phenomena empirically.[1]

It is interesting that each of the methods in question can be profitably developed both in the abstract and the concrete directions. When Newton's theory of tides develops into the theory of Laplace, the development is in the abstract direction. When empirical observations of the heights of tides in different harbours develop into the theories of Thomson (Lord Kelvin) and G. H. Darwin, the

1731 [1] Hatt, *Des marées,* pp. 9-11: "Newton was the first to give an exact explanation of the cause of the tides. The considerations that he developed are of two sorts. He first imagines a circular canal surrounding the whole earth, roughly analyzes the horizontal movement under the influence of the heavenly bodies of the molecules contained in it, and then observes that it has to involve an alternate rising and falling of level. But he considers the question in a much loftier perspective in getting at the analytical theory of the phenomenon. Ignoring the molecular movement, Newton looks for the momentary picture of equilibrium that the water-mass would assume under the influence of the attractive force of one heavenly body, and determines the shape and dimensions of its surface—an ellipsoid with the long axis constantly pointing towards the star. As a consequence of the Earth's movement, the distortion makes the round of the Earth in twenty-four hours, the level rising and falling at each point twice a day. But the hypothesis on which Newton's theory rests is not consistent with the rapidity of the movement. [That has been a reason not for rejecting mathematical theories of tides, but for perfecting them.] The water-molecules, drawn at every moment to a new position of equilbrium, evidently tend to overpass it and develop fluctuations determined by the laws of dynamics. The problem of the tides therefore requires assistance from the theory of the movement of liquids on which Laplace's analysis rests. [So in mathematical economics there was a move from Cournot's theories to present-day theories, and so there will be from present to future theories.] Book IV of the *Celestial Mechanics* is entirely devoted to a theoretical and practical examination of the oscillations of the sea, and we may say that the pure theory has suffered no appreciable modifications since it was established on its foundations by the great analyst; but the general solution of that difficult problem still remains to be discovered. Despite all the efforts of mathematicians, theory has so far proved unable not only to adapt itself to the infinite variety of conditions on the Earth but even to approach the question otherwise than in the very simple situation of a spheroid entirely covered with water. But if we envisage practical aspects of the matter, the analysis has been extraordinarily productive. The general principle of a correspondence between periodic forces and marine movements that it brought to light [In mathematical economics, the principle of mutual dependence that we are here extending to sociological phenomena.] served as point of departure for the study of the tides at Brest, to which the fourth and almost all the thirteenth book of the *Celestial Mechanics* are devoted. On the same principle Sir William Thomson in England based his method of harmonic analysis, a theory that is as remarkable for its simplicity as for its inflexible logic and which seems destined to serve as crown for the whole edifice of the empirical study of tides, as offering a more effective instrument of investigation for resolving the complex movement of the sea into its elements."

development is in the concrete direction. When the old economy is supplemented with the chapter on mathematical economics, the development is in an abstract direction. When economic and social phenomena are considered together (§ 2292 [1]), as we are considering them here, the development is in the concrete direction.[2] Now all that is beyond the comprehension of vast numbers of persons whose critical sense is wholly vitiated by preconceptions or downright ignorance, and who have no notion whatever of the logico-experimental character of the social and economic sciences. Their disquisitions sometimes remind one of a person trying to find recipes for cooking in a mathematical text-book or geometrical theorems in a cook-book.[3]

1732. We must therefore be careful not to fall into errors of that sort ourselves and for that reason always bear in mind that when, for instance, we refer to the influence of residues upon other social facts, our attention is centred on one aspect of the situation only;

1731 [2] One same scientist may develop a theory in the two directions. After working out an abstract formula for tides, *Traité de mécanique céleste*, II, Bk. IV, 216, 241, Laplace remarks in connexion with one of its corollaries: "Now we shall shortly be seeing that this result is contrary to observed facts, and however far the formula above is extended, it does not succeed in satisfying all observed phenomena. Irregularities in the depths of the ocean, its manner of distribution over the Earth, the location and slope of its shores, their relation to neighbouring coasts, the resistance that the waters meet, all such causes, which cannot be reduced to measurement, modify the oscillation of the great fluid mass. We can therefore merely analyze the general phenomena that ought to result from the attractions of Sun and Moon and draw from observation the data indispensable for completing the theory of the ebb and flow of the sea in each seaport. . . . [Then, after stating his formulae:] Now let us compare these formulae with observations. Early in the last century and at the initiative of the Academy of Sciences a large number of observations of the ebb and flow of the tide were conducted in our harbours. They were continued each day at Brest for six consecutive years, and although they are still far from satisfactory, they make up by their number and in view of the height and regularity of the tides in that harbour the most complete and useful collection that we have of that kind. It is with the Brest observations, therefore, that our formulae will be compared." A splendid illustration of the method to be followed, adding, perfecting; there is no destroying (§ 1732).

1731 [3] Protectionist derivations lend themselves much better than the scientific theories of political economy to the defence of the protectionist system. There are excellent subjective reasons why a person deriving or hoping to derive some direct or indirect advantage from protective tariffs should give his preference to derivations. But no such reasons exist for the person who is merely trying, in an objective spirit, to discover the relations obtaining between facts.

and that there is another aspect involving not only the influence of those facts upon residues, but of all factors, including residues, upon each other reciprocally (§§ 2203 f.).

There are various ways of envisaging interdependent phenomena. Suppose we classify them: 1. Relations of cause and effect, only, may be considered, and interdependence wholly disregarded. 2. Interdependence may be taken into account: 2a. Relations of cause and effect are still considered, but allowance is made for interdependence by considering actions and reactions, and by other devices. 2b. One may work directly on the hypothesis of interdependence (§§ 2091 f.).[1] The soundest method, undoubtedly, is the one we designate as 2b, but unfortunately it can be followed in but relatively few cases because of the conditions that it requires. Essential to it, in fact, is the use of mathematical logic, which alone can take full account of interdependencies in the broadest sense. It can be used, therefore, only for phenomena susceptible of measurement—a limitation that excludes many many problems, and virtually all the problems peculiar to sociology. Then again, even when a phenomenon is in itself measurable, serious difficulties arise as soon as it becomes at all complex. An interesting example of that may be seen in celestial mechanics, where insuperable difficulties still stand in the way of determining the movements of many bodies of about equal mass when some of the interdependencies can no longer be regarded as perturbations. Pure economics goes so far as to state the equations for certain phenomena, but not so far as to be able to solve

1732 [1] Very often the chronological order of the three methods is different from the one noted here, where the scale is drawn from the most erroneous to the most perfect. Sometimes the chronological order is, more or less, 1, 2b, 2a. That was the case in the history of political economy. The old economy followed 1. On the advent of mathematical economics there came a leap to 2b. Now, thanks to the conquests of mathematical economics, economists may follow the method 2a. Two economic treatises based on considerations of cause and effect may differ radically. If such considerations are not supplemented by considerations of interdependencies, if the study of actions is not followed by studies of reactions, and especially if principal phenomena are not distinguished from secondary, the procedure is 1, and results are almost always vitiated by serious errors. If, however, in deference to the achievements of mathematical economics, 2b, considerations of cause and effect are used, but with due account taken of interdependencies by studying actions and reactions and by distinguishing between principal and secondary phenomena, the procedure is 2a and results may closely approximate realities.

them, at least in their general form.[2] So as regards the economic and social sciences, the 2*b* method remains as an ideal goal that is almost never attained in the concrete.[3] Shall we say, on that account, that it is useless? No, because from it we derive, if nothing more, two great advantages. 1. It gives us a picture of a situation, which we could get in no other way. The surface of the Earth does not, to be sure, have the shape of a geometric sphere; and yet to picture the Earth in that way does help to give some notion of what the Earth

1732 [2] See Pareto, *Manuale*, Chap. III, §§ 217-18. Not a few economists have made the mistake of imagining that the theories of pure economics could directly control the concrete phenomenon. Walras thought he could reform society on that basis [*Éléments d'économie politique pure*, Preface, p. xv, and pp. 277-80]. On that point see Boven, *Les applications mathématiques à l'économie politique*, p. 112 and *passim*.

1732 [3] Pareto, *Manuale*, Chap. III, § 228: "The chief advantage derived from the theories of pure economics lies in their providing a synthetic conception of the economic equilibrium, and at the present time there are no other means of attaining that end. But the phenomenon envisaged by pure economics diverges, now little, now much, from the concrete phenomenon, and it is for applied economics to study those divergences. It would be futile and not very intelligent to pretend to regulate concrete phenomena according to the theories of pure economics. . . . [Very very often the theories of sociology will be found in the same boat.] The conditions that we have found for the economic equilibrium give us a general conception of that equilibrium. . . . To discover what the economic equilibrium was, we tried to see just what forces determined it. We must further caution that the identification of those forces is in no sense designed to supply a numerical calculation of prices. Suppose we are placed in the situation most favourable for such a calculation: suppose we have overcome all our difficulties as to knowledge of the data involved in the problem. . . . Such assumptions would be absurd and still they would not be adequate for making a solution of the problem practically possible. . . . If all those equations [in the equilibrium] were really known, still the only means humanly available for solving them would be to watch the practical solutions provided by the market in terms of certain quantities at certain prices." As I have elsewhere shown (in my article, "*Économie mathématique*," in the *Encyclopédie des sciences mathématiques*) [and see above, § 87 [1]], only an infinitude of index-functions could show how the economic equilibrium is actually determined. The selection one makes from among them is a question of expediency merely. In particular, the purpose of our selection of lines of indifference is not at all to find some practical measurement of ophelimity; but merely to bring into relation with the conditions of the equilibrium and with prices certain quantities that may *theoretically* be assumed to be measurable. Similar reservations are pertinent in the case of sociology. The purpose of that science is not to reveal the future in detail. It is not "carrying on" for the Delphic Oracle nor is it competing for business with prophets, sibyls, soothsayers, trance-mediums or fortune-tellers. Its object is to determine in their general form the uniformities that have obtained in the past and those which are likely to prevail in the future, and at the same time to describe the general characteristics of all such uniformities and their mutual relations.

is like. 2. It sign-boards the path we have to follow if we are to avoid the pitfalls of method 1 and so approximate realities. Even a beacon we shall never reach may serve to indicate a course. By analogy we can carry over the results achieved by mathematical economics into sociology and so equip ourselves with concepts that we could get in no other way and which we can proceed to verify on experience, to decide whether they are to be kept or thrown away. 3. Finally, the concept of interdependence, imperfect though it be, is a guide to using 2a, which tries, through use of relations of cause and effect (§2092), to produce results that are at least something like what we would have got by following 2b; and it helps to avoid the errors inherent in 1, which is the least perfect of the three, the most exposed to error.[4] In our present state of knowledge the advantages of method 2b are therefore not so much direct as indirect. That method is a light and a guide to save us from the pitfalls of 1 and to beckon to a closer approximation of reality.[5] This is not the place to linger on details of the method 2a.[6] We will simply note, because the point will be of use to us presently, that the method 2a proves to be workable when we have a principal phenomenon that exactly or approximately assumes the form of a relationship of cause and effect, and then incidental, secondary or less important phenomena with which interdependence arises. When we are able to reduce a situation to that type, which after all is the type of celestial mechanics, we are in a fair way to understand it. With just such a reduction in mind, we saw that residues were much more stable than derivations, and we were therefore able to regard them as in part "causes" of derivations, but without forgetting secondary effects of derivations, which sometimes, be it in subordinate ways, may be "causes" of residues. Now we are seeing that the different social classes show different residues, but for the moment we

1732 [4] The errors in question have been admirably elucidated in Sensini's *La teoria della rendita.*

1732 [5] Pareto, *"Le mie idee," Il divenire sociale,* July 16, 1910: "Pure economics is only a kind of book-keeping, and the books of a business enterprise never give the true *physiognomy* of that enterprise. . . . Economics is a small part of sociology, and pure economics is a small part of economics. Pure economics, therefore, cannot of itself give rules for dealing with a concrete situation, nor can it altogether give the *feel* of that situation."

1732 [6] With them we shall deal more amply farther along, §§ 2091 f.

are not deciding whether it is living in a certain class that produces certain residues in individuals, or whether it is the presence of those residues in those individuals that drives them into that class, or, better yet, whether the two effects may not be there simultaneously.[7] For the present we are to confine ourselves to describing such uniformities as are discernible in the distribution of residues in the various social classes.

1733. Data in abundance are available on that point. They are not very exact, often coming forward under literary or metaphysical guises. From them, nevertheless, we are able to infer with reasonable probability that for the various strata in society the scale of increasing variability noted above (§ 1718) still holds valid: (1) Classes of residues; (2) the genera of those classes; (3) derivations. But the variability is greater for a given social stratum than for society as a whole, since as regards the latter compensations take place between the various strata. There are, furthermore, social categories comprising few individuals within which variations may be wide and sudden, whereas they are slight and gradual for the mass of the citizenry. The higher classes change styles in dress much more readily than the lower classes. So they change in their sentiments and, even more, in their ways of expressing their sentiments. Changes in style in the various branches of human activity are followed much more closely by the wealthier, or higher, than by the poorer, or lower, classes. Not a few changes, indeed, remain within the confines of the higher classes and often fail to reach the lower because they have disappeared in the higher before reaching the lower.

1734. Unfortunately, history and literature give a better picture of the states of mind, the sentiments, the customs of the few individuals located in the higher strata of society than of those same things in the larger number of individuals belonging to the lower strata. In that fact lies the source of many serious errors. There is a temptation to extend to a whole population, or the larger part of it, traits that are characteristic of a small, perhaps an insignificant, number of individuals. And failure to take account of changes in the composition of the higher classes due to class-circulation leads to the

1732 [7] To all that we shall come in the next chapter.

further error of mistaking changes in the personnel of a class for changes in the sentiments of individuals. In a closed class, X, sentiments and expressions of sentiments may change; but if the class X is open, a further change results from changes in the composition of the class; and this second change depends, in its turn, upon the greater or lesser rapidity of the circulation.

1735. *Reciprocal action of residues and derivations.* Residues may act (*a*) upon other residues; (*b*) upon derivations. So likewise derivations may act (*c*) upon residues; (*d*) upon derivations.[1]

Of the influence in general of residues upon derivations, *b*, we have nothing further to say here, having already dealt with that subject throughout the course of these volumes and shown that, contrary to common opinion, residues exert a powerful influence on derivations, derivations a feeble influence on residues.[2] It remains for us to speak only of the special case where certain fluctuations in derivations correspond to fluctuations in residues. But we cannot do that as yet for lack of a number of concepts that we shall not acquire till further along (§§ 2329 f.). Let us devote our main attention therefore to the relationships *a, c, d*.

1736. *a. Influence of residues on residues.* It will help, first of all, to distinguish residues *a, b, c . . .* corresponding to a given group

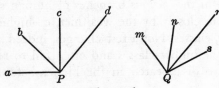

Figure 26

of sentiments, *P*, from residues *m, n, r, s . . .* corresponding to another group of sentiments, *Q*. The residues *a, b, c . . .* corresponding to one same group *P* go fairly well together—they are not too discordant, not too openly contradictory. On the other hand such discord, such contradiction, may prevail between residues *a, b, c . . .*, corresponding to *P*, and residues *m, n, r . . .* corresponding to *Q*.

1735 [1] Here we are considering such effects intrinsically only, without regard to any bearing they may have on individual utility or the utility of society.

1735 [2] It was with a view to showing that that we began this study with an investigation of non-logical conduct.

Since all we know of such residues we know through derivations, we shall likewise find derivations that are not too discordant and derivations which frankly disaccord. Still other discordant derivations arise through the importance of influencing various sorts of individuals who are equipped with various other sorts of residues (§ 1716).

1737. *Discordant residues and their derivations.* Contradictory derivations expressing residues that are also contradictory are oftentimes observable in one same person, who either fails to notice the contradiction or tries to remove it by resort to more or less transparent sophistries.[1] Of that we have given many proofs, but further elucidation will not come amiss in view of the importance of having the fact clearly appreciated. Let us take a number of groups of residues, each group corresponding to certain complexes of sentiments. It will be found that the reciprocal influence of the groups, when they are not in accord, is generally slight in everybody if there is any at all, mutual effects appearing only in educated people in sophistical efforts to reconcile derivations arising from the groups. Uneducated people for the most part are not worried at all by such contradictions.

1738. Generally speaking, save for persons who are in the habit of indulging in long and complicated ratiocination, the individual makes no effort to harmonize discordant derivations. He is satisfied if they fit in with his sentiments or, if one will, with the residues corresponding to his sentiments. That is sufficient for the majority of human beings. Some small few feel a need for logic, for pseudo-scientific ratiocination, which impels them to refined disquisitions tending to harmonize one derivation with another. But as com-

---

1737 [1] In his *Dictionnaire historique, s.v. Lubienietzki, remarque (E)*, speaking of a religious persecution, Bayle observes: "I doubt whether there was ever a subject more fertile in rejoinders and counter-rejoinders than this one. It can be twisted over and over again now in one direction, now in another. So a writer will tell us today that the Truth has only to show her face to put Heresy to rout, and tomorrow that if Heresy is allowed to go on talking everybody in the world will be affected. [The first derivation reflects, in the main, a group of residues associated with the authority of one's own religion, and the reverence in which it is held (II-a, II-δ, V-a, etc.); the second reflects sentiments associated with the requirement of uniformity (IV-β, IV-$\beta 2$)]. One day truth will be pictured as an impregnable stronghold, the next, as something so frail that it cannot be exposed to the hazards of debate, that such a shock would shatter it in the minds of the public."

pared with the bulk of a population, theologians and metaphysicists have always been very few in numbers.

1739. Historians and literary critics often try to ascertain *the thought* of a writer or a statesman. Researches of that kind presuppose that such a "thought" exists, and that may sometimes be the case. More often it is not. If such thinkers would but examine their inner selves, they would find plenty of contradictory notions in their own minds, without needing to go elsewhere. If one is a "determinist" he will see that he often acts as though he were not; and the one who is not, that he often acts as though he were. Nor would they fail to observe that for many moral precepts they have personal interpretations which differ to some extent from the views of other people. To be sure, their own interpretations are the "good" ones, and others "bad"; and that may well be, but it merely confirms the fact of the difference; and for the person who has one of the other interpretations, there is a contradiction between the formal precept and the manner in which the critic in question interprets it. In a happy moment a person will assert that anyone who follows the precepts of religion and morality is certain of a happy life in this world. In a moment of gloom he will exclaim with Brutus, "Virtue, thou art but a name!" What is such a person's "real thought"? He has two thoughts; and he is equally sincere in expressing them, contradictory though they be.[1]

1740. *Reciprocal influence of residues corresponding to a given sum of sentiments.* Such influence may arise in three ways, which it is important carefully to keep distinct. Let P be a psychic disposition corresponding to a sum of sentiments that are manifested by the residues $a, b, c, d. \ldots$ Those sentiments may be of differing intensities, a situation that we state elliptically by saying that the residues are of differing intensities (§ 1690).

1741. 1. If for some reason or other P, the common source of the residues, increases in intensity, all the residues, $a, b, c \ldots$ will also increase in intensity, becoming $A, B, C \ldots$ and conversely if P

1739 [1] Facts of that kind are of great importance in determining social phenomena. We must therefore not rest content with merely asserting them. We must adduce ample proofs. That justifies the interest we have shown and will continue to show in many petty incidents on which, had we no such purpose in view, it would be a waste of time to linger.

diminishes in intensity. Among the reasons for the rise or fall of intensity in *P* may be an increase or a decrease in a group of residues, *a,* which reacts upon *P.* In that case the rise or fall in *a* occasions a rise or fall in all the groups, *b, c, d. . . .* In the case of a community at large such effects are often gradual and not very considerable, since, as we have seen, a class of residues as a whole varies slowly and but slightly. In a single individual it may be far stronger and more rapid. That would be the case with the Hindu converts to Christianity whom we mentioned farther back (§ 1416) as losing the morality of their old religion without acquiring that of the new. That was the case too with the degenerate Sophists of ancient Greece; and there are other examples. In such cases, certain residues, *a,* are destroyed,

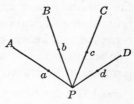

Figure 27

and the whole group, *b, c, d . . . ,* is weakened in consequence.

1742. 2. In many cases a group of residues increases at the expense of other groups of the same class—the instinct of combinations, for example, which may turn to some new kind of combinations; and in such case we get a new distribution among *a, b, c . . .* without any variation in *P.* Combining effects 1 and 2, we get a number of permutations. For instance, *a* increases and that occasions an increase in *P* and consequently also in *b, c. . . .* But the increase in *a* is obtained by usurping—among other things—a part of what belonged to *b, c. . . .* So, finally, a group, *b,* may increase because what it loses to *a* it more than regains through the increase in *P;* and another group, *c,* may decrease because what it loses to *a* is greater than what it regains through *P;* and so on.

1743. 3. There might well be a direct action of *a* upon *b, c . . .* without any mediation through *P.* This third situation is readily confused with the first. The visible fact may be that when *a* became *A, b* was seen to become *B; c, C;* and so on; and reasoning *post hoc, propter hoc,* the inference might be that the movement *a* to *A* was the "cause" of the movement *b* to *B, c* to *C,* and so on, and so the presumption of a direct relation, *ab* or *ac . . . ,* becomes natural.

1744. Ordinary observation gives a special form to this reasoning, with the customary substitution of logical for non-logical conduct. It is assumed that *a* has a logical origin, *P;* and so, if *a* is modified to

A, it is because the logical origin, *P,* has been re-enforced, and the changes of *b* to *B, c* to *C,* follow as a matter of course. It is argued, for instance: "A religiously-minded person refrains from wrongdoing because he knows that God punishes sin. If, therefore, we foment the religious sentiment, *a,* we shall get as a consequence increased honesty, *b,* morality, *c,* self-respect, *d,* and so on." The facts have shown that any such reasoning is erroneous, and readers of these volumes now know that the fallacy lies in the failure to distinguish non-logical from logical conduct.[1] The reasoning would become sound if instead of trying to intensify *a* one tried to intensify *P.* The situation can be stated, imperfectly it may be, but yet in such terms as to give a vivid image of it, if one says that the conduct

1744 [1] That was a common error of governments in olden times, and in a day quite recent it was observable in France as a special trait of the policies of the Restoration and the Second Empire. Two further errors usually go with it: (1) A belief that the religious sentiment may be awakened in people who do not have it, and intensified in people who have it, by using force upon dissidents and punishing them; and (2) a tendency to identify the religious sentiment in general with the religious sentiment attached to a given faith in particular. So governments wear themselves out in efforts to force a religion, *X,* upon their subjects, and if they get any results at all, it is the result of enforcing hypocrisy and so promoting the many evils that go with hypocrisy. But even if they were in a measure successful, that would be of little or no service as regards the end they held in view in undertaking to enforce the religion *X* as a means of improving the morals and loyalty of their subjects. That is not saying that when a religious sentiment is a spontaneous manifestation of good morals and loyalty in a people, it is not better not to offend it if one's aim is to encourage those manifestations (§ 1753). Modern governments endorsing the religion of Progress disdainfully reject any help from the old religion, *a,* in regulating civil life. But they replace it with others. Many of them are inclined to assign the function to the sex religion, *f,* so repeating a common mistake of governments of the past. It is, in fact, usual for individuals who are upright and temperate in the various aspects of their activity to evince the same qualities in the domain of sex; and it is not difficult to show, therefore, that, in general and on the whole, observance of the rules of the sex religion, *f,* goes hand in hand with observance of the rules of a religion, *a,* of decency, *b,* morals, *c,* honesty, *d,* and so on. But that easily leads to the mistake of taking *f* as at least a contributory "cause" of *a, b, c, d.* . . . Because that error is a very very common one, we have repeatedly marshalled proofs to show that *f* is not a cause, nor even a contributory cause, of *a, b, c.* . . . That error is usually coupled with another more serious one, which, really, follows from it: the belief that by influencing *f* one can influence *a, b, c* . . . till one arrives at the extreme absurdum that if sex hypocrisy can be enforced by law one can get a good, honest, clean-living citizenry. Nevertheless, the countless and most striking disproofs of the doctrine that historical experience provides do not suffice to budge the race of sex-fanatics and the plain man in general from that utterly false notion.

in which b, c, d . . . originate is in some respects similar to the conduct in which a originates. If we call all such conduct "religious" and the complexes a, b, c, d . . . "religions," we can then say that to stimulate growth in one such "religion" is of scant influence upon the other religions; but if one can procure increased intensity in the sentiments of group-persistence, P, in which they all originate, an effective influence will be exerted upon them all. With most people the reasoning is the direct reverse: that to stimulate a given religion is an effective way to stimulate growth in others.[2]

1745. But the fact that one demonstration offered for a direct influence of one residue upon other residues is fallacious in no wise precludes the possibility of cases in which such an influence exists, and we have to look for evidence of it directly to the facts. However, it is not easy to find. Oftentimes when we think we have it, it is still possible to interpret it as an influence of the first type; and we are left in doubt as to any conclusion. But there are plenty of cases that clearly indicate the independence of the residues a, b, c . . . the well-known fact, for instance, of brigands being devout Catholics, and other facts of the same sort. In such cases, b, c, d . . . seem to be in no way related to a. Confining ourselves to certain probabilities, we may say that the direct influence, when there is any, arises chiefly between residues that are closely related, or at least among residues of the same genus; seldom among residues of different genera or different classes. The person who already believes in a number of silly stories will readily believe one more. That might seem to be a case of direct influence; and yet one might say that belief in silly stories is an expression of a psychic state that will incline the person to believe in one more.

1746. *c. Influence of derivations on residues.* This problem is close kin to the one just discussed. Derivations are manifestations of sentiments, and the influence of derivations on residues is therefore similar to the influence of Class III residues and I-ε residues on other residues. Only because of this latter influence do derivations have any perceptible effects in determining the social equilibrium. A derivation which merely satisfies that hankering for logic which the human being feels, and which neither is transmuted into sentiments nor re-enforces sentiments, has slight if any effect on the

1744 [2] We shall revert to this matter farther along (§§ 1850 f.).

social equilibrium. It is just a superfluity: it satisfies certain sentiments, and that is all. Briefly, but not in strict exactness, one may say that in order to influence society, theories have to be transmuted into sentiments, derivations into residues. It must not however be forgotten that that holds true only for non-logical conduct, not for conduct of the logical variety.

1747. Generally speaking, a derivation is accepted not so much because it convinces anybody as because it expresses clearly ideas that people already have in a confused sort of way—this latter fact is usually the main element in the situation. Once the derivation is accepted it lends strength and aggressiveness to the corresponding sentiments, which now have found a way to express themselves. It is a well-known fact that sentiments upon which the thought recurrently lingers manifest a more exuberant growth than other sentiments on which the mind does not dwell (§§ 1749, 1832); but that, as a rule, is something secondary as compared with the other phenomenon. For the very reason that derivations exert influence only through the sentiments which they stir, persons who are alien to such sentiments, either as not sharing them or from having experienced and then forgotten them, find it difficult to appreciate the practical importance of certain derivations; so they accuse those who suppress them of lack of intelligence, whereas the only lack perhaps may lie in strategy.[1]

1747 [1] Examples are legion. We may take as typical the case of a play by Collé, *La partie de chasse de Henry IV,* which has been interpreted at one time or another in directly opposite fashions according to prevailing sentiments. Hallays-Dabot, *Histoire de la censure théâtrale en France,* pp. 85-86: "One measure of severity one is at a loss to understand unless one is keenly alive to the state of mind prevailing toward the end of the reign of Louis XV, and the difficulties the government was meeting. I refer to the interdiction of the *Hunting-Party of Henry IV.* Collé's play is the most inoffensive thing imaginable . . . but look a little closely at it and it becomes a most serious matter—everybody is worried. It is deemed hardly proper to put on the stage an ancestor of the King, a sovereign who is only fifty [*sic*] years distant in history. [There we have the play judged anti-monarchical in general. It will also be found hostile to the particular government holding power at the time.] The sensation produced by another play, *Théagène et Chariclée,* betrays the state of excitement and hostility in the city. A measure of success had just previously attended a tragedy of Leblanc, the *Manco-Capac,* a dull enough play, but full of declamations against royalty, and it had to be lightened by some four hundred lines before it could be played at Court. [So there was the Court, running to hear a play that was aimed at the King! When a strong current of sentiment is taking shape, it sweeps even people who have everything to fear from it off their feet.] Profiting by those precedents, the Government saw in Collé's play just what the public would be

1748. From a logico-experimental standpoint, the only way to refute an assertion, *A,* effectively, is to show that it is false. When logical conduct is involved that is done by logic and by observations of fact (§ 1834). Not so from the standpoint of sentiments and in

looking for in it—an allusion by force of contrast, a pretext for a demonstration. Henry IV was at the time what he was later on, a banner, an emblem, of liberal, democratic, light-hearted royalty. Henry IV will be king of the theatre on three separate occasions: first, at the opening of the reign of Louis XVI, then, just after the fall of the Bastille and the establishment of the constitutional oath, and, finally, on the return of the Bourbons in 1814. At those moments he will be hailed as the sovereign incarnating the dreams and hopes of a people's imagination. At other times, just to the contrary, and notably under Louis XV, the personality of Henry IV will be not a flattery but an epigram. His ideas will be set up against the ideas of the day and enthusiasm for the man of Béarn will be just a war-machine of the opposition. In that alone are the real causes of the great success of Collé's *Hunting-Party* and the basis for its suppression to be sought. . . . Efforts were made many times [under the First Empire] to revive [Duval's] *Édouard [en Écosse]* [suppressed after the first performance, Feb. 17, 1802], and the *Hunting-Party of Henry IV.* During the declining years of Louis XV, Henry IV was, as we have seen, a monarchical mask for the *philosophes* who were plotting the overthrow of the monarchy. Now on a stage in Paris Henry IV would have been the white flag around which all malcontents would gather." Welschinger, *La censure sous le premier Empire,* p. 226: "Napoleon kept an eye on the theatre both at short and at long range. He wrote Fouché from Mainz, Oct. 3, 1804: 'I see they have played the *Hunting-Party of Henry IV* at Nantes. What good there is in that I cannot see . . .'"—and the seditious play was at once suppressed. But the Restoration came and the play was "formally" revived, Hallays-Dabot, *Op. cit.,* pp. 225, 239, 291: "All the plays hitherto forbidden, the *États de Blois, Henri IV et d'Aubigné,* all plays dealing with the man from Béarn, were now to be authorized. It would be hard to say how many times Henry IV was put on the stage during that period. He was to be seen somewhere every evening. From the Comédie Française to the Franconi, it was just one chorus of adulation, and the secret of it all events have now revealed to us. Henry IV was the emblem of monarchy and he had further suffered humiliation at the hands of the previous régime. . . . [Shortly the public tires of him:] The *États de Blois* was revived on May 30, 1814. Raynouard's tragedy had a half-hearted success—enthusiasms were already cooling. Legislation on the press was brewing. The public was beginning to weary of the dithyrambs which had been declaimed, sung, danced, played, mimed, on every stage in Paris ever since April [§ 1749]. . . . [And now for Louis Philippe:] Napoleon now takes on the stage the place that Henry IV had occupied in 1755, 1790, 1814, and 1815. He appears simultaneously in all the theatres, and the public waxes as excited over the Emperor's grey coat as it had of yore over the white plume of Navarre. . . . [Of the *"Widow of Malabar"* [by Scribe and Mélesville], a play of Louis XVIII's time, Hallays-Dabot remarks, *Op. cit.,* p. 123:] That play had always been regarded as a rather tedious portrayal of Hindu manners. No one had recognized the Catholic clergy in those priests in Brahman garb. Now that people are excited and on the watch for every word, every turn of expression that they can grasp, everything becomes allusion. The clergy is aroused and M. de Beaumont calls on the King."

the case of non-logical conduct. Reasonings and experimental observations have very little influence on sentiments and non-logical conduct, individual inclination being a very great, not to say the only, influence. Sentiments therefore must be met with sentiments. An absurd derivation may perfectly well serve to refute another absurd derivation, though that would not be the case from the logico-experimental point of view. Indeed silence may be an effective instrument for sapping the strength of an assertion, *A,* whereas a refutation, triumphant though it be from a logico-experimental standpoint, may serve to spread instead of clip its wings (§ 1834).[1]

1748 [1] Hallays-Dabot, *Histoire de la censure théâtrale en France,* p. 275: "To that period [around 1827] belongs a prohibition by the censorship that is gaily recounted year after year in many little sheets as a model of the innate ineptitude of the censors. It seems that in a certain vaudeville sketch there was reference to making a salad and the writer had put into it 'Capuchin's beard,' a sort of wild chicory. The censor insisted on a different recipe and pitilessly vetoed any sort of 'monk's beard.' An amusing story! But however fastidious the cutting, I must confess I have never found it as ridiculous as people are pleased to suppose. One has only to think of the battle of epigrams, puns, pin-pricks, stupid jests, that was fought each day by Government and Opposition, that period of the Restoration furnishing the most complete example of that sort of thing. One has only to remember that ten newspapers delivered broadsides every morning against the *capucinades* of the court of Charles X—that was the term then current. . . . And then one may wonder whether the writer in question was as innocent as was pretended of any hostile thought when he put 'Capuchin's beard' into a salad then in vogue. And one may wonder whether the minister who approved the cut, in itself so childish, was altogether wrong in mistrusting a public that made any simple declaration from the quai Voltaire a pretext for a noisy riot." So Hallays-Dabot manages to clear the minister on the count of stupidity. But the charge of bad strategy still stands, for Hallays-Dabot ought also to remember what was being said along the quai Voltaire about the effects of such censorings. Las Cases, *Mémorial de Saint-Hélène,* Vol. II, p. 107: "Speaking of the works that were censored or forbidden by the police under his rule, the Emperor said that having nothing to do while he was on the island of Elba, he had amused himself by skimming some such works and that oftentimes he could not guess the reasons of the police for prohibitions they had ordered. Then he went on to discuss the question of freedom or limitation of the press. It was, he said, an endless question, admitting of no half-way measures. The great difficulty lay not in the principle itself but in judging the circumstances to which the principle, taken abstractly, had to be applied. By inclination, the Emperor said, he was for unrestricted freedom." By no means a unique case. Looking at things in a certain perspective, many practical men perceive the fatuousness of chasing derivations, but that does not prevent them from following the cry when caught in the passions of the moment. Welschinger, *La censure sous le premier Empire,* pp. 235-36: "It is interesting to note that Napoleon was as keenly concerned with the theatre as with politics. What phase of life, for that matter, did that universal mind not embrace, what slight detail did not

1749. To argue about a thing with a person, in terms whether favourable or unfavourable, may arouse in him an inclination—if he hasn't it already—to interest himself in that thing; if he already has the inclination, it may whet it.[1] It is an interesting fact that with

have its interest for him—things that would nowadays bring a smile to the lips of our statesmen? In a letter from Potsdam, Oct. 25, 1806, he approves the cancellation of the ban laid on a ballet, *Return of Ulysses,* and asks Fouché to get a detailed report on the performance and attend the first night himself to make sure there was nothing wrong in it." Noble worries for an Emperor and one of his ministers! Of verses of Marie-Joseph Chénier alluding to Tacitus [*Épître à Voltaire, Œuvres,* Vol. III, pp. 101-02.], Welschinger relates, p. 149: "Tacitus! That name had a way of angering the Emperor. His public disapprobation of Dureau de Lamalle's translation and his prohibition of the Tragedy *Tibérius* are sufficient indications of his dislike for the Roman historian. . . . [Napoleon was minded to put Chénier in prison, but Fouché dissuaded him:] 'All Paris will work to get him out. He is not popular, but he will be pitied if he is in jail. Sire, let us not make our enemies interesting!' [The key-verse of Chénier read: *"Tacite en traits de flamme accuse nos Séjans."*] [Not even the classics were spared by the Imperial censorship:] 'Most surprising changes,' says Bourdienne, 'were made in the plays of our great masters by poets hired for the purpose, and Corneille's *Héraclius* was produced only in mutilated form.' The censor, Lemontey, said to a caller one evening: 'Are you going to the *Théâtre Français* this evening to hear Racine revised by Lemontey?' That was not just a pleasantry. It was the exact truth. The great poet of Louis XIV had been roughly handled by the censor no less than any scribbler under the Empire. The Prompter's Library at the Comédie Française has a copy of *Athalie* that bears the most unmistakable traces of it and enables one to imagine what cuts must have been made in other tragedies of Racine. . . . [Welschinger gives specimens of such deletions. But there is worse: the censor replaces verses of Racine with his own!] In *Athalie,* II, vii, the censor deletes four verses (116-19), fearing lest an allusion to the Pretender be seen in them; but then to tie up the passage with what follows, he suppresses the hemistich *'Que Dieu voie et nous juge'* and replaces it with a hemistich of his own: *'Je connais votre attente,'* so that Athalie can cry in the verse following *'Mais nous nous reverrons. Adieu! Je sors contente. . . .'* In *Athalie,* IV, iii, twenty-five verses fall under the censor's scissors; but that leaving no rhyme for the line *'Prêtres saints, c'est à vous de prévenir sa rage,'* the censor follows with a line of his own: *'De proclamer Joas pour signal du carnage.'* " The time Napoleon spent in keeping an eye on the theatre, the press, and Mme. de Staël, he could certainly have better spent on affairs of his Empire. But he had a mania that has been the mania of many another statesman. Such men can never learn that the art of government lies not in trying to change residues but in skilful manipulation of existing residues. If only they would lay aside their preconceptions and condescend to take some notice of history, they would see that in persecuting derivations in order to modify residues governments waste enormous amounts of energy, inflict untold sufferings on their subjects, compromise their own power, and achieve results of little account.

1749 [1] Speaking in *L'Empire libéral,* Vol. VI, p. 346, of the acrimonious attacks of the clergy on Renan's *Life of Jesus,* Ollivier says: "The results the bishops achieved were not what they expected. Lesseps once told me that the chief item in

many people of a contradictory turn of mind to condemn a thing is a surer way of gaining its acceptance than to praise it. In certain matters also, and notably in matters of sex, a certain instinct of perverseness is awakened in that way, so that the individual is stimulated to do the very thing one would dissuade him from do-

his expense account for advertisements [The word was a euphemism.] in England in favour of the Suez Canal was *the amounts he paid for attacks on himself* [italics Ollivier's]. Renan protested. 'You are wrong,' his friends assured him. 'Attacks alone attract attention. Then they are forgotten and nothing is remembered except the name or the act attacked.' Each pastoral of the bishops increased the circulation of the book, and many a person who would not have noticed the publication said to himself: 'Well, if that book is so wicked, I guess I must read it.' Far from extinguishing the torch, they had lighted it." Charpentier, *Carpentariana,* pp. 337-38: "La Mothe le Vayer having written a book that was not selling, his publisher came to him and complained, begging him to make up for it by doing something else. He told the man not to worry, that he had enough influence at Court to get his book suppressed, and that once that was done, he would sell all he cared to print. He had the book suppressed, and things turned out as he had predicted: everyone hurried to get a copy of the book, and the publisher was obliged to get out a new edition at once in order to provide everyone with copies." *Prosecution of the* Chansons *of P. J. Béranger (Procès faits . . .)*, pp. 74-76 (Dupin speaking for the defence): "The idea is to halt the circulation of a book of poems, and public curiosity is aroused to the highest pitch! The idea is to do away with certain features that are regarded as harmful, and ephemeral as they were by nature, they are made as eternal as the history with which they are associated! . . . If there were any doubt of that, it would be a simple matter to consult experience. It would bear witness that all prosecutions of this kind have produced results contrary to those expected. M. de Lauraguais wrote to the Parlement of Paris: 'Honour to burned books!' He might have added: 'Profits to writers and publishers!' A single detail will suffice to prove it. In 1775 some satirical verses had been published against the Chancellor, Maupéou. . . . To ridicule a Chancellor, or even a mere registrar of deeds, was a serious matter in those days. Hurt to the quick, Maupéou stormed at the writer, threatening him with all his wrath if ever he were detected. To escape the ministerial whirlwind the rhymster fled to England, whence he wrote to Maupéou enclosing a new satire in verse. 'Monseigneur,' said he, 'I have never wanted more than a modest income of 3,000 francs. My first song which displeased you so much has earned me a capital of 30,000 francs from the sole fact of your displeasure. Invested at 5 per cent that gives me half my amount. Please, sir, show the same wrath against this new satire which I send you. That will complete the revenue. I desire and I promise you that I will write no more." Belin, *The Trade in Prohibited Books in Paris, 1750-1789 (Le commerce, etc.)*, pp. 109-10: "It was easy to determine that to proscribe a work was to call attention to it, that the prohibition aroused curiosity and served merely to multiply surreptitious editions that were dangerous from the inferences that were drawn from all the mystery. So a little pamphlet entitled *So Much the Better for Her,* which Choiseul hesitated for some days before condemning, sold up to 4,000 copies 'under the cloak' during the first fortnight but ceased making any noise once it was permissible to offer it

ing.[2] In such matters when silence actually leaves the individual in ignorance it is oftentimes about the only effective means of dealing with him. Silence with regard to persons is very effective in political connexions also. There are many situations where it is better for a politician to be attacked and reviled than to hold no place in public attention. For the same reason an occurrence of little or of no im-

publicly for sale (Favart to Durazzo, 1760, Favart, *Mémoires et correspondance littéraires*, Vol. I, p. 99). So the *Secret Memoirs* reported in 1780: 'There has been a great demand for a pamphlet entitled *Essay as to the Judgment to be Passed on Voltaire* since it has been suppressed by decree of the Council (XIV, 4).' Voltaire was quite right in saying, Letter to Voisenon, July 24, 1756 [*Œuvres*, Vol. XI, p. 789]: 'A censure from those gentlemen merely sells a book. The publishers ought to pay them to burn everything they print.' Extract from the *Pot pourri, Étrennes aux gens de lettres*, quoted by Metra [*Correspondance secrète politique et littéraire*, Vol. IV, p. 293]: 'Burning was for a book what election to the Academy was for the man of letters.' Diderot, *Letter on the Book Trade* (*Lettre, etc.*, p. 66): 'The severer the proscription, the higher the price of the book, the greater the eagerness to read it, the wider its sale, the more it was read. . . . How often might not the publisher and the author of a licenced book have said to the magistrate, had they dared: "Please, gentlemen, a little proclamation condemning me to be tonged and burned at the foot of your great staircase!" When sentences against a book were being cried, the type-setters in the printing establishments would exclaim: "Good! Another edition!" ' " Hallays-Dabot, *La censure dramatique et le théâtre*, p. 61 (in question Claretie's *Les gueux*): "The censorship adjudged the play inoffensive. It was therefore required to appear before the public as a play much talked of in advance by part of the press but without the anticipatory sympathy that attends victims of the censorship. . . . It was a virtual failure." The deletion of a number of lines in Victor Hugo's *Marion de Lorme* was enough to lend popularity to others that were supposed to summarize them. I say "supposed," for the famous verses read:

> *"De l'autre Marion rien en moi est resté.*
> *ton amour m'a refait une virginité."*

("Of the other Marion nothing is left in me. Your love has given me a second virginity.") Now the poet says in a note: "The author's manuscript contained four verses that were suppressed in the stage version and which we think should be printed here. At the odious proposal of Laffemas, Marion turns without answering toward Didier's prison and says:

> *'Mon Didier, près de toi rien de moi n'est resté,*
> *et ton amour m'a fait une virginité.' "*

Had the lines not been censored no one probably would have remembered them.

1749 [2] In a day gone by many libertines felt more deeply stirred by love-affairs with nuns than with ordinary women, and cases might be mentioned where lovers insisted that their lay mistresses wear monastic habits. In England in our day certain persons are being led in a spirit of contradiction to break rules that there is an effort to enforce by law and which would probably be respected if no prohibition existed.

portance that serves to make him a topic of general discussion may be the starting-point for his success. Many many lawyers, Gambetta, for instance, owe their start towards fame and power to some clamorous trial. To minimize the importance of an incident or a fact it is somewhat less effective but still helpful to say nothing of it,[3] the efficacy depending on whether or not in that way the public can be kept from concentrating upon it, either because many people

1749 [3] Many religious organizations make a practice of saying nothing of occurrences that might occasion scandal. Such things are commonplace in the Christian Church and other religions of that kind. I will give one example from the Dreyfusard religion of certain French intellectuals. On M. Millerand's reinstatement of Du Paty de Clam in the territorial army (§ 1580 [3]), a writer in the *Gazette de Lausanne,* Feb. 3, 1913, reports: "The truth is, it was all a trade, the promise to M. Du Paty to reinstate him being given against his promise to desist from his appeal, which was embarrassing because it rested on a charge that was true. Amid applause from the Left, M. Jaurès made a fiery protest that the deal should not go through, that M. Du Paty was to be told: 'You can justify yourself as you see fit!' Now let us go slowly. That there should have been no such deal is very possible. The bargain that was struck was nothing to boast of, but that M. Du Paty was to be left the task of clearing himself, no, no, and again no! It was the work of a moment to determine whether M. Du Paty had been cashiered on the basis of a forged document, and if so—and it was so—he was entitled to fair treatment. The mind refuses to admit that men who have done themselves honour by their attitude in a tragic campaign should not have seen that it was as intolerable that M. Du Paty should be the victim of a forged document as it was that Captain Dreyfus should be the victim of the secret production of forged and criminal documents." If, now, one turns to the many Dreyfusard or humanitarian newspapers of those days it will be seen that, in general, they maintain scrupulous silence as to any forgery. They could have denied that the document was a forgery; they could even have declared it genuine—what is not justifiable in defence of a faith? As a matter of fact they preferred to say nothing.

Here, in a connexion altogether different, is an instance that is typical of a large number of cases. In the years 1912 and 1913 it was considered patriotic in Italy to make the state budget show surpluses that did not really exist. A number of important newspapers abroad faithfully reported the statements issued by the Italian ministries anent such balances and glossed them copiously with interviews by leading financiers in praise of such striking achievements in finance. But then scholars, such as Giretti and Einaudi (§ 2306 [1]), went to work and showed that the surpluses in question were fictitious, that there had been deficits instead. Those same newspapers said nothing. And so far, so good: the papers may have known nothing of the researches of mere scholars. But what they could not have missed, in view of the eminence of the individual and the platform from which he spoke, was the incisive criticism of such doings delivered in the Chamber of Deputies by Signor Sonnino. Yet those papers still held their peace! And lo, the strange coincidence! Gossip had it that those papers were partly owned by "speculators" who thought it better for their activities on exchange that no publicity be given the matter at just that moment.

never hear of it, or because those who do, observing no interest in it, come to ignore it themselves.[4] Silence as to theories and arguments that have to be combated is also more or less effective according as it succeeds or fails in causing them to be ignored, forgotten, or belittled, and oftentimes is far more devastating than any refutation could possibly be. In the same way, repetition, though it has not the slightest logico-experimental validity, is more effective than the soundest logico-experimental demonstration.[5] The asseveration influences sentiments and modifies residues; the demonstration appeals to the reason and may in the very best case modify derivations: it has little effect upon sentiments. It is significant that when a government or a financial institution wishes to have some measure defended by the newspapers it has in tow, the arguments it uses are frequently—one might almost say always—far from being the ones best calculated to show the advantages of the measure. Generally the cheapest verbal subterfuges are called into play—derivations based on authority, and the like. But that does not matter. More often than not it is the best way. The important thing is to have a derivation that is simple, and readily grasped by everybody, even the most ignorant people, and then to repeat it over and over and over again.[6]

1749 [4] This is not just the place to consider how and when such results are achieved. Here we are concerned strictly with the manner of working of residues, and not with the ways in which the organization of society permits the realization of this or that purpose.

1749 [5] Ollivier, *L'Empire libéral*, Vol. V, p. 138: "Endless repetition has to be one of the familiar demons of the man who would influence a distraught or indifferent crowd. An idea does not begin, I will not say to be understood, to be even perceived until it has been repeated thousands of times. Then the day finally comes when that good Panurge of a demos finally hears, understands, warms to you, congratulates you on having so well divined and expressed his thought, and there you are popular. The publicist who really knows his trade repeats the same article for years. The special pleader must do that too."

1749 [6] That is the case also with many critics of current developments in social or economic science, persons who are unacquainted with the first principles of those sciences, yet not a few of whom have made counterfeit reputations as experts. They use certain types of derivations (they are always the same) that are well suited to their own ignorance and to brains that can swallow them. I will specify a few such types: 1. *The book is badly written.* It is easy in any language to find some case where the use of a word is doubtful and call it a mistake. But even if it were obviously wrong, what has that to do with the logico-experimental validity of a proposition? If a theorem of Euclid's is stated in barbarous or illiterate language, does it cease to be true? No; but to refute it one has to be a mathema-

1750. Oftentimes, to refute an absurd argument, and as soundly as one may wish, proves to be a means of accrediting it if it chances to correspond to sentiments powerfully active at the moment (§ 1749 [1]). The same is also true, of course, of reasonings that are sound from the logico-experimental standpoint, and in general, of attacks of all sorts and persecutions of theories, opinions, doctrines. Whence the illusion that "truth" has some mysterious capacity for triumphing over persecutions. That notion may accord with the facts in the domain of pure logico-experimental science; but it less often

tician, whereas to say that "the style is bad" one need only be a fool. 2. *The book contains nothing new.* In its extreme implication the derivation implies an accusation of plagiarism. It would be difficult to find a writer of any worth or repute who has not been the victim of such charges. In a tale of Boccaccio, *Decameron,* I, 82, Messer Erminio de' Grimaldi asks Guglielmo Borsiere to tell him of "something that has never been seen," so that he could have a picture made of it. To which Borsiere replies: "I do not believe I could show you anything that nobody has ever seen, unless it should be a sneeze or something of that sort; but if you will, I will show you something [*i.e.,* courtesy] that I do not think *you* have ever seen." Like tart retort might be made to many such critics. 3. *The work contains many mistakes*—and pains are taken not to designate them, in hopes that people will accept the criticism without testing it. Then again alleged errors are pointed out; and when it is shown that they were not errors, the rectification is ignored in hopes that people will not hear of it or at least disregard it. That was the case with our estimable M. Aulard, who said nothing in reply to Cochin's drastic rejoinder (§ 537 [1]). 4. *Personal attacks upon the writer, criticisms of things irrelevant to the problem in hand, and other digressions.* 5. *Intromission into matters of science of sentimental considerations of a political or other such character.* An individual, who thinks himself an "economist," objected to mathematical economics because, as he maintained, it could never be made "democratic." Another rejected it, stated in a way of his own, as not calculated to bring "a little more justice into the world." Another, who seemed somewhat of a stranger to the subject he was discussing, prattled about "a school" of mathematical economics that was based on premises of "individualism" (a synonym for the Devil among such people) and contrasted it with another school, a product of his own imagination, which would be based on considerations of "collectivism." 6. *The writer has not said everything: he has neglected to quote certain books and state certain facts.* Such criticism would be sound if the sources and facts overlooked or neglected were calculated to modify the writer's conclusions; it is fatuous if the conclusions stand in any event. People inexperienced in scientific investigation cannot understand that a great mass of detail may hinder, instead of aiding, the discovery of that general average form of a phenomenon which is the only thing the social sciences are looking for (§ 537). 7. *The writer is made to say things he never dreamed of saying by interpreting in sentimental, political, ethical, and similar senses things that he said in a strictly scientific sense.* The temptation is to judge others by oneself. People who have never acquired the habit of scientific thinking cannot imagine anyone else thinking in that detached way.

accords and often frankly disaccords with the facts in the case of reasonings to any extent depending on sentiment.

1751. These effects of refutations and persecutions may be called indirect; and so may the effects of silence. If they are applied to a class of facts at all numerous and important and to sentiments that are at all powerful, they leave unsatisfied, in view of such sentiments, the sentiments corresponding to Class III (activity) and I-ε (need of logic) residues, while the very fact of restraint intensifies the eagerness for that satisfaction. That is especially conspicuous in matters relating to sex: and it is everyday experience that reticence in such matters tends to enhance interest in them. But it is no less true in religious and political matters. If people are forbidden to attack a dominant religion or an existing political régime, any slightest criticism, any attack however insignificant, stirs the public deeply. When criticism is permitted and is a matter of everyday occurrence people become calloused and ignore it. That results from the two elements that we saw figuring in the effects of derivations (§ 1747). When people are constrained to silence, sentiments are pent up within them and burst into expression at the first favourable opportunity; and that may be furnished by the appearance of certain derivations, which sweep all before them and once accepted lend new force and aggressiveness to the sentiments. Finding those two elements in combination in the concrete, we have no way of telling how they can be distinguished; and our inclination to reduce all our conduct to logic inclines us to attribute to the second element (force of derivations) a greater weight than it actually has, even if we do not give it all the credit. The verifications that we are able to make on the concrete chiefly concern the synthetic phenomenon where the two elements stand combined, whereas we can separate them only by analysis. In France towards the end of the eighteenth century, the attacks of Voltaire, Holbach, and other philosophers on the Catholic Church corresponded to a complex of circumstances unfavourable to Catholicism which is not operative in the case of similar attacks today. In the eighteenth century the situation in some part doubtless is really to be ascribed to the influence of anti-religious literature; but the major factor, beyond any doubt, was the manifestation of sentiments already active in people (§§ 1762 f.). In countries such as Germany where nothing can be published against the sovereign, any criticism however slight that is made of him is greedily devoured by the public. In countries such as Belgium where one may say anything one chooses about the sovereign, no attention is paid to anything written against him.[1] Very instructive is what took place in France in 1868, when the Empire, after a long muzzling of the press, gave it a little freedom. Not only the fierce assaults, but attacks that seem rather trivial to us today, were eagerly taken up by the public.[2]

1752. Silence, refutation, persecution, all have direct effects and indirect effects (§ 1835); and the resultant is a question of quanti-

1751 [1] Numberless examples are available from all periods of history. Tacitus in his day gives one, *Annales*, XIV, 50: Fabricius Veiento, a court favourite, had written a satire against the Senate and the pontifices. Prosecuted by Nero, he "was convicted and exiled from Italy, and his books were ordered burned. Sought after and greedily read so long as they were obtainable only with danger, they were forgotten as soon as it became again permissible to own them" (§ 1330 [3]). Hallays-Dabot, *Histoire de la censure théâtrale en France*, p. 265: "The Restoration Government went so far wrong as to put an absolute ban on Voltaire. His works were never to be named. . . . Such a radical suppression was a nuisance. More than that it was not very shrewd. What was the result? Four years were spent in careful watching for the marked foe, ears erect at the slightest allusion. Then one day, in 1826, at the Odéon, an oversight allowed a valet in outlining an itinerary to pronounce the lines:

> 'Le Pont Royal! Fort bien! . . .
> d'un écrivain fameux voici le domicile:
> de Voltaire! A ce nom le monde entier . . . Mais chut!
> la maison de Voltaire est loin de l'Institut.
> La voici! . . .'

Voltaire! Voltaire's house! The two words were like a match touched to a magazine. The floor leapt to its feet in an uproar and the play was interrupted by round after round of applause."

1751 [2] The first number of Rochefort's *Lanterne* (Paris, May 31, 1868) begins as follows: "According to the Imperial Almanach France has 26,000,000 subjects, not counting subjects of dissatisfaction." The witticism made a hit and was repeated from one end of France to the other. Who in our day would pay any particular attention to a jest of that kind made at the expense of a French ministry? The *Lanterne* had admirers even in the monarch's entourage. *Journal des Goncourt,* Vol. VI, p. 11 (Feb. 6, 1875): "Speaking of the infatuation of all Imperial society at Fontainebleau for Rochefort's *Lanterne,* Flaubert told of a jest of Feuillet's. Flaubert had seen everybody reading the sheet, and finally he noticed that a master of the hounds on mounting his horse for the hunt stuffed a copy into his coatpocket. Somewhat irritated, he asked of Feuillet: 'Do you really consider Rochefort a man of talent?' The Empress's novelist looked about to right and left. Then he answered: 'For my part, I find him very ordinary, but I should not care to be heard saying so. They would think me jealous.' "

ties. At one extreme, the direct effect is far greater than the indirect; then gradually along the scale the one increases at the expense of the other, till at an opposite extreme the indirect effect far exceeds the direct. At the first extreme we may locate measures bearing on small numbers of facts and not involving powerful sentiments, the measures, for example, that are taken against small political, religious, or moral minorities. At the opposite extreme stand measures directed at large numbers of facts and involving powerful sentiments; and an example there would be the measures that are taken, and ever in vain, to prevent manifestations of the sexual appetite.

1753. In past centuries, in Europe, it was generally believed that government, religion, and morality could not endure unless expressions of thought were held in leash; and events following on the Revolution of '89 seemed to demonstrate the truth of that theory; so it came into vogue again during the first decades of the nineteenth century. Then one by one restrictions on the free expression of thought gradually lapsed again; and in our day, save in matters pertaining to the sex religion, they have in great part disappeared, and government, religion, and morality continue to flourish; and the theory would seem therefore to be exploded. But such judgments are too absolute, because the circumstances under which the theory is applied have changed. To withhold freedom of thought from people who feel no need of it has no effect of any kind. To withhold it from people who do "demand" it leaves desires unsated, so that they deepen in intensity, and so, as happened in France towards the end of the eighteenth century, the granting of freedom has effects of great intensity that are deleterious to the institutions of the past. But such effects gradually lessen in intensity and in the end freedom comes to have but slight effects on sentiment. When freedom is the rule, it functions chiefly through derivations, and they, as we already know, do not, on the whole, exert any great influence. But for that very reason, it then becomes the wiser policy to pass over a fact or a theory in silence, since that is one of the cases where the direct effect far exceeds the indirect.[1]

1753 [1] With the above we reach a point where examination of the ways of achieving ends, of "virtual movements," should begin, and to those problems we shall come presently (§§ 1825 f.).

1754. So far we have been speaking as though society were a homogeneous unit; but since that is not the case, what we have said can apply only, and only approximately, to a population group that may without going too far astray be regarded as a homogeneous unit. To determine effects upon a population as a whole, effects upon its various strata (§§ 2025 f.) have to be taken into our calculation. That explains a development which has been long recognized empirically: the differing effects, that is, of freedom of thought upon the educated and the uneducated portions of a population respectively.[1]

1755. The influence exerted by great newspapers in our time is a good illustration of the influence of derivations. It is a matter of common observation that their power is great. But that does not come of any special facilities which they possess for forcing their points of view upon the public, nor of the logico-experimental validity of their reasonings—these are often childish enough. It is all due to the art they have developed for working at residues through derivations. Speaking in general, the residues have to be there in the first place. That fact determines the limits of the newspaper's influence; it cannot go counter to sentiments: it can only use them for one purpose or another.[1] By rare exception, and in a very long run, some new residue may be manufactured and one that has apparently died out be revived. This fact of playing upon residues further explains why opposition newspapers are sometimes supported by parties in power.[2] From the logical standpoint such a

1754 [1] That too is a subject with which we shall be in a better position to cope later on and specifically in the chapter next following.

1755 [1] Robert de Jouvenel, *La république des camarades,* pp. 248, 252: "It is said that newspapers make public opinion. The reverse is no less true. A reader is quite ready to accept the opinion of his newspaper, but the newspaper chooses the opinion that it judges best fitted to please the reader. . . . Luckily the questions on which the public voices its attitude are few in number. It may have very positive opinions but they are few. So long as those few are never shocked, one may guide one's readers where one wills in all others."

1755 [2] Bismarck was very adept in the art of using newspapers both at home and abroad. Ollivier, *L'Empire libéral,* Vol. XIV, p. 49, tries to acquit his ministry of the charge of unskilful management of the press: "Bismarck had much the greater influence with the press, for he could count on at least one paid writer on every paper to follow his orders. Since we knew who some of them were, we were in a position to use them for keeping track of the intentions of their paymaster. [Ollivier was a naïve soul. Bismarck's intentions may have been altogether differ-

thing would seem absurd. How could a government be so silly as to pay money to people who are working against it? But once one thinks of sentiments, the advantage of the practice is apparent. In the first place the ministry makes sure that the newspaper it buys

ent from the ones he allowed his paid agents to betray.] Furthermore Bismarck had in hand not only all the Prussian press but most of the papers in Germany and Austria, and so, to a much greater extent than we, he had means of creating both in France and in Europe generally any trend of opinion he pleased." *Ibid.,* Vol. XII, pp. 304-05: "Bismarck's method was most ingenious. On occasion the French Government had had some paper abroad in its pay. That had not proved very profitable, for the fact of the paper's venality soon came to light, and no further importance would be attached to its opinions. [Those times were different. In our day such a thing would cast no discredit on a paper.] Bismarck did not buy papers. He bought *one writer* on *each* important paper, the editor-in-chief whenever possible [Nowadays nobody is bought, directly. The pressure is applied through financiers who own stock in the corporation that owns the paper.] or, that failing, some ordinary reporter whom no one suspected of 'connexions.' The man so bought was regularly conspicuous for the virulence of his patriotism [A significant touch! That is the way of opposition papers in domestic politics.], and in very timely ways, as best suited the purposes of Prussian policy, he would rouse or quiet public emotions. [So again, in internal politics.] That system was much more effective and much cheaper. I know the names of the wretches who were so employed by German money. I had rather not divulge them." Bismarck worked the newspapers in the same way even after 1870. Busch, *Tagebuchblätter,* Vol. II, p. 394 (English, Vol. II, pp. 95-96), Feb. 20, 1873: "It appears from a report of Arnim's of the seventeenth of last month that he has engaged a certain [Rudolf] Lindau, brother of the dramatist and critic, and afterwards councillor of the Embassy in Berlin, to furnish him with detailed reports from the French press. In a despatch of the eighth instant the ambassador states that Lindau has asked not to be deprived of the assistance of Beckmann. . . . Arnim strongly supported their request 'in the interests of the service.' Lindau must have someone at his disposal who would understand the more compromising portion of the whole arrangement. . . . Besides, neither Herr Lindau nor any other official at the Embassy was in a position to deal with all the material, and to furnish full and satisfactory reports on the press, and at the same time to write articles himself for the German, Italian, and Russian newspapers." Bismarck rejected the device proposed, which shows simply that he preferred some other. With his crude outspokenness Bismarck makes no secret of the money he spent on the French press. *Cf.* his *Gedanken und Erinnerungen,* p. 508 (Butler, Vol. II, pp. 179-80), Arnim's prosecution in question: "At no time during his trial did I mention the fact that certain amounts—6,000 or 7,000 thalers—which had been set aside to have our policy defended in the French press, he used to attack our policy and make trouble for me in the German press." So the Prussian press, therefore, would seem to have been, in part at least, as venal as the French. Such confessions on the part of outstanding leaders in public life are precious evidence in that they establish facts which otherwise would remain doubtful so long as they were known only through the gossip that is bandied about. In 1913-14, for instance, it was persistently rumoured that the German Government was paying out large sums of money for attacks by French newspapers on army legislation in

will hold its tongue at the right moment, that it will not rouse every sleeping dog, that it will steer its readers towards venting their spleen in ways less dangerous to the government than others. Then again, there are moments when violent agitations lay hold on a country. At such times a spark will set off the magazine, and it is better to be sure no opposition paper strikes it. Thirdly—and this is exactly what powerful financial syndicates have in view, when, like governments, they subsidize apparently hostile newspapers— there are ways of opposing certain measures, certain proposals for legislation, which may influence sentiments quite as favourably as the best defence, if not more so. Fourthly, to have a subsidized opposition newspaper at one's beck and call provides a means, and often the only means, of getting before an adverse party statements that they would not read in newspapers favourable to a government or to a financial syndicate, or which they would suspect for the very reason that they were.[3] Another important means of exerting

France. We have no way of knowing to just what extent such charges were well founded. We may know some years hence, when and if we get revelations such as Ollivier's and Bismarck's. Busch, *Tagebuchblätter*, Vol. III, p. 243 (English, Vol. II, p. 428), Sept. 28, 1888, gives details on Bismarck's shrewd use of the press (an alleged diary of Emperor Frederick in question): "I myself consider the Diary even more genuine than you do. . . . [Bracketed clauses in quotations from Busch are omitted from the published German text.—A. L.] He [the Emperor Frederick] was far from being as clever as his father, and the father was certainly not a first-rate politician. It is just that which proves its genuineness to me. But at first we must treat it as doubtful. . . . [The following (English, Vol. II, p. 435, Sept. 28, 1888) is entirely omitted in German.—A. L.]: On that occasion he also repeated his plan of campaign with regard to the publication in the *Deutsche Rundschau*: 'First assert it to be a forgery, and express indignation at such a calumny upon the noble dead. Then, when they prove it to be genuine, refute the errors and foolish ideas that it contains.' "

1755 [3] Busch, *Tagebuchblätter* (English, Vol. II, p. 471; Passage omitted from German), quotes a letter from William I to Bismarck dated April 8, 1866, in which the King complains of an article against the Duke of Coburg (in the *Kreuzzeitung*). Bismarck replies: "I confess frankly that the main part of this article was written at my instance, as I—like every one of my colleagues—while having indeed no influence over the *Kreuzzeitung* to prevent their insertion of matters to which I object, have yet enough to secure the insertion of what is not directly opposed to its own tendencies." The *Siècle* was one of the two republican newspapers tolerated in France after the *coup d'état* of 1851. It received patronage and subsidies from Napoleon III. Ollivier, *L'Empire libéral*, Vol. IV, p. 17: "The *Siècle* did not belong to a business man, but it was a going concern yielding large profits. That compelled the editor always to be very careful when conducting an opposition—opposition was its reason for existence—in order to

influence through newspapers is to "hush up" certain facts, certain arguments, certain discussions, certain publications. Often all a government or a financial syndicate asks of a newspaper on which it exerts influence is silence.[4]

Almost all great newspapers, not excepting a goodly number that are professedly Socialist, have connexions, direct or indirect, with the plutocracy that is the ruling power in civilized countries today, and with the governments in which it plays a part (§ 2268[3]).[5] It is interesting that that situation should have been realized instinctively by the French General Federation of Labour and stated in a mani-

avoid suspension, which would have spelled ruin for the stockholders. [Nowadays what a newspaper fears is not suppression but the loss of the subsidies, direct and indirect, that it receives from financial powers, and also that falling-off in circulation which is certain to result from any opposition to a pronounced trend in public feeling.] M. Havin was made for that difficult manoeuvre . . . which was in no way irreconcilable with the Empire. . . . The *Siècle* [in 1858, Vol. IV, p. 69] was saved only by a personal appeal by Havin to the Emperor. . . . Havin [Vol. XI, p. 122] was a very wide-awake person . . . maintaining almost friendly relations with the ministers, and posing as an anti-Clerical to escape having to seem anti-dynastic" § 1755[4]).

1755 [4] I prefer examples from the past as less likely to stir the feelings of readers living today. Ollivier, *L'Empire libéral,* Vol. VI, pp. 212-13: "They [the Government's commissioners in the Legislative Body] did not have such smooth sailing when it came to refuting charges as to stock manipulations that the 'Company of the South' was alleged to have worked on its own shares in agreement with the Crédit Mobilier. . . . [An account of that fraudulent operation follows.] I denounced that stab in the back (*coup de Jarnac*). . . . The Government's commissioner, M. Dubois, a very fine gentleman, outdid himself with explanations, which explained nothing and, not only that, implied admission of most of the facts revealed. . . . The directors of the 'Company of the South' were nevertheless clever enough to prevent [the minutes of that session] from appearing in any of the papers in Paris."

1755 [5] In his *1896-1901: petits mémoires du temps de la Ligue,* pp. 209-21, Henry de Bruchard deals with a number of democratic newspapers that defended Dreyfus. I omit names, because here we are interested in social phenomena, not in persons. As I have said, one of the commonest mistakes in matters of this kind, is to accuse particular individuals of things that are general. Of persons who wrote for those papers in all good faith, Bruchard says: "I imagine they were themselves aware of their own imprudence and of the extent to which they were dupes. In any event those mandarins of letters must have been able to appreciate how little concerned with the dignity of their profession their anonymous masters were. Ask those haughty independents who edited their papers, and why it took them so long to discover that the editor was always chosen without their knowing who made the choice! They know at this late day that the founder and backer was M. L——, former chief of police and organizer of the League for the Defence of Jews. And to think that some of them still professed to be revolutionaries! But they had to earn

festo that the Federation published on the occasion of the Balkan War of 1912.[6] We are not interested here in the form in which the sentiment was expressed, in the derivation, which was as absurd as any other, but only in the sentiment, altogether unreasoned, in-

their bread and butter, and others just had to write from a mania for seeing their names at the end of an article. It was a form of humbug, and one had to put up with everything! They accepted the editorship of a certain P——. Now P—— is one of the big shareholders in *Humanité!* Does he still represent L—— and his heirs? That question was not raised at the last Socialist convention, yet it was the one issue that should have been raised!" And to what advantage? If you get rid of one, another takes his place. If that is the organization of society, there will never be any shortage on the side of personnel! In 1913, as president of a parliamentary commission, Jaurès made every effort to save the plutocrat and demagogue Caillaux from deserved rebuke for trying to influence the courts in favour of Rochette, through his friend and crony, Monis. All parties try to use the newspapers for their own purposes, and the papers, in turn, extort favours by threatening to attack or promising to defend now one minister, now another. If a person wants to have a newspaper of his own, he has to face huge expenditures, and they would be net losses were they not offset by compensations in the shape of honours pure and simple in the case of some few (very few) politicians; of honours plus money in the case of most politicians, most political financiers, trust magnates, political attorneys, "fixers," "speculators." Palamenghi-Crispi, *Giovanni Giolitti,* pp. 76-77: "Crispi was unique among the politicians of his time in this respect also: Ascribing to the newspaper the great importance that it in fact has in modern life, he always wanted to have a paper in which he could say what he had to say. But instead of shouldering off the expense of such a thing upon some group of business men, as so many others have done (it would be easy to give names), he always paid the bills himself with his own money. Only by rare exception would some friend help. So it came about that he was often faced with debts that he was pinched to pay, and had sometimes to resort to loans from banks, which he was always careful to settle. Everyone knows the high cost of newspapers that are exclusively devoted to politics. The *Riforma* alone, the organ of the historic Left, which defended Liberal ideas and Liberal statesmen over a period of thirty years, absorbed about 1,200,000 lire from the fruits of Crispi's devoted [That adjective is perhaps superfluous.] labours." *Giornale d'Italia,* Nov. 23, 1913: "Another nomination [for the Senate] that is being talked about— on what foundation we do not know—and which would greatly please the Reformists [Socialists], is the name of the Milanese banker Della Torre, who has been and is *magna pars* financial in Socialist and democratic newspapers—democratic in a Reformist sense. Della Torre is, in a word, the deity of 'blocist' high finance and may some day be called a pioneer, the day that is, when high finance in Italy, hav-

---

1755 [6] The C.G.T., as they call the Federation in France, held a congress at Paris, Nov. 24, 1912, to declare its opposition to the war. It adopted the following resolutions: "Recognizing that mobilization must be paralyzed at all costs, the Congress declares that the most effective means must be tried in order to attain that end. The Congress therefore resolves that, in order to cripple the harmful influence of the bourgeois press, printers and printers' hands should be urged to destroy the presses of newspapers unless they can be utilized for our cause."

stinctive. All that we have been saying is a matter of common knowledge, and, in private, no one playing any part in public life or in high finance is so naïve as to deny it; but in public those same leaders try to look shocked and hypocritically say that such talk is bosh.[7] But the amusing thing is that the person who knows such

ing seen which way the wind is blowing, joins the *bloc* as its elder sister in France did." Della Torre was in fact named Senator along with two other Socialists, and the *Corriere della sera*, Nov. 25, 1913, writes: "Giolitti today unlocked the doors of the Senate to Karl Marx, who was behaving a bit too obstreperously up in the garret [Giolitti had said before the Chamber that now at last the Socialists "had laid Marx away up in the garret."] and disturbing the peace of mind of people who thought they had adroitly kidnapped him. . . . Three Socialists are not, after all, a strong dose . . . and they will not give any great annoyance either to the Government, to which they owe such a debt of gratitude [And *vice versa.*], or to the *bourgeoisie.* . . . Since the Senate is a legislative body, it too should have representatives of all political tendencies, and it is therefore not a bad idea that, just as Radicals are now quite numerous in the Senate, Socialists also should find their place thither—Socialists at least from among the favoured few who are well acquainted with stairways at the Quirinal and who in practice show themselves disposed to 'be reasonable.' It is a real pity that the Senate cannot be seasoned also with a pinch or two of republic; but Republicans, fortunately, never cause any alarm and, unfortunately, are most pig-headed about their doctrinal chastity. [And so cannot have a newspaper, since they insist on paying for it themselves.] . . . The Senate must in fact be de-aged. Or rather, let us call a spade a spade: The Senate too must be put to some use. That language is more exact and more faithfully describes the reality of things. [Very true.] If in an honestly democratic spirit one should set out in earnest to make the Senate genuinely representative of all the currents in the nation's thought, there could be but one logical conclusion: to face the issue of an elective Senate fairly and squarely. . . . It is true that in that case there would be a more generous sprinkling of Socialists at Palazzo Madama [the Senate building] and governmental munificence would no longer be called upon to manifest its selfish sympathy with extremist parties." Early in October, 1918, the following item appeared in the newspapers: "The great liberal organ in England, the *Daily Chronicle,* has been bought by Sir Henry Dalziel and a few friends for £300,000. . . . The new proprietor is a wealthy newspaper man and member of Parliament for the Liberals. He is known especially as an intimate friend and loyal supporter of Lloyd George both in Parliament and in the press. In that chiefly lies the political significance of the purchase of the *Daily Chronicle,* a paper that had seemed tolerably lukewarm toward Lloyd George of late, and was leaning rather towards that wing of the Liberal party that recognizes Asquith as its leader. It is announced that the policies of the paper will not be changed, but it is probable that under its new ownership it will vigorously support Lloyd George."

1755 [7] In May, 1913, a Florentine newspaper that was discontinuing publication explained how during its thirty-three years of existence it had been sustained by the various successive governments. Almost all the great Italian newspapers maintained a silence of holy chastity on the incident, which might have been of greater interest to their readers than many insignificant items of news that they did pub-

facts in general nevertheless has faith implicit in his own newspaper on matters in which he can have no doubt as to the part
played by the pocket-books of international finance. During the
Balkan War the news published in many papers had much less to
do with facts as they were than with the facts as coloured in the
interests of this or that "scheme" on the part of international finance;
and yet the news they printed was accepted as news by persons who
were perfectly well aware of the resourcefulness and power of those
influences.[8] Plutocratic demagogues, such as Caillaux and Lloyd
George, are praised by newspapers of great reputation in deference to
the clink of the arguments that Figaro found so irresistible. Many
of the small fry take the bait—and that is nothing to wonder at;
but plenty of big fish too are hooked, and that is not so easy to understand. It is true that the big fellows often profess to believe many
things that they find it to their interests to believe.

1756. There are one or two types of derivations that are widely
used for influencing the ignorant more particularly. They are to be
noted in orations addressed of yore to the masses in Athens and
Rome. They play a much more important rôle in the modern newspaper. One of the most frequent is designed to bring sentiments of
authority (residue IV-ε2) into play. The derivation might be stated
in logical form as follows: "A certain proposal, A, can be sound only
if it is made by an honest man. The person who is making this proposal is not an honest man (or, he is being paid to make it). Therefore the proposal A is detrimental to the country."[1] That of course

lish. They probably remembered most opportunely the adage: *De te fabula narratur.*
The Belgian Government has published a list of the newspapers that were subsidized by King Leopold to praise his administration in the Congo or at least to say
nothing as to its crimes. Some future historian of the present plutocratic régime in
the civilized countries of the West will get some most instructive data from that
publication.

1755 [8] In Italy plenty of attention was called to the fact in the case of newspapers
hostile to Italy; but nothing was said of the pro-Italian papers, though their policies
were dictated by the very same forces that determined the policies of the opposition
press.

1756 [1] Oftentimes the argument runs: "The person who is making the proposal
A today was opposed to it some time ago." That is supposed to prove that the proposal A is not sound. Never mind the fact that a man may honestly change his mind
as circumstances change—Bonghi used to say, in that connexion, that only an animal never changes its mind. But even if it were shown that the person proposing A
has changed not in view of any intrinsic merit in A but in hopes of deriving some

is absurd; and anyone so arguing abandons the rational domain therewith; but not so for the auditor, who is persuaded not by the force of the logic but by associations of sentiments. Quite instinctively he realizes that he is incapable of judging directly whether A is good or bad for his country, that he must therefore rely upon the judgment of someone else; and in accepting such a judgment, he prefers to have it from a person whom he deems worthy of his esteem. This derivation is oftentimes the only one that certain newspapers use. They never admit that there are problems of things. They answer all questions by abusing persons. Jugglers of pens naturally find it easier to call names than to think logically, and their tactics often prove successful because the public that feeds on such writing is an ignorant public, and forms its opinions more by its sentiments than by its brains. But the cord breaks when the bow is drawn too taut. In a number of countries abuse and slander of men in public life have ceased to be effective. They were more so in the days when courts afforded protection against them and they were therefore less common.

1757. A considerable group of such derivations aims at utilizing the sex residues. It was a rule with few exceptions in centuries past for members of a dominant religion to accuse dissenters of immorality (§§ 1341 f.). Ignoring the fact that such charges were nearly always false, let us assume that they were true. In that case the derivation would have a logical element, being soundly urgeable against anyone preaching a certain morality and then deporting himself against it. But that logical element vanishes when the derivation is turned against statesmen or heads of governments (§ 2262). Facts clearly show that there is not the slightest connexion between a man's sex morality and his worth as a statesman or as an

---

personal advantage from A, that would still be nothing against A. It would simply be taking us back to the personality derivation mentioned above. The fact that such derivations can have no weight in the judgment that is to be given of A is all the truth there was in the defence Caillaux's friends made for him against the attacks of M. Calmette in *Figaro*. It is undeniable that the advantages or disadvantages accruing to a given society from an income-tax levy have nothing, absolutely nothing, to do with the domestic, moral, and even statesmanlike qualities of the individual proposing one. But to inflict the death-penalty on a person for using those fallacious derivations seems to be too severe a punishment; and if the practice should become so general as to be applied by every citizen, few newspaper editors, and indeed few writers, would be left alive.

occupant of a throne. Yet it is an argument that is almost invariably used against such persons by their enemies, and where hatreds are intense some charge of incestuous sex relations becomes the rule. Ordinary politicians have the honour of being treated in that respect on a par with sovereigns.[1]

1758. Generally speaking, derivations that exploit sex residues have the advantage of being difficult to refute and of depreciating the victim even if the refutation by some singular chance is perfect. It was long asserted, though in no way proved, that Napoleon I had relations with his sisters. In the eyes of many people, that accusation all by itself was enough to condemn him as citizen, as public servant, as head of the state. So in days gone by a charge of heresy, even when unproved, was sufficient to make a man at least suspect to good Catholics. Heresy in matters of sex holds in our day the place held by heresy of yore in matters of Catholic doctrine.

1759. Verbal derivations are also great favourites with the newspapers. In the days of the Restoration in France anything not to the liking of the dominant party was called "revolutionary," and that was enough to damn it. Nowadays it is called "reactionary," and that too is enough to damn it. Such arguments by epithet bring sentiments of party and sect into play (residues Class IV, sociality).

1760. There is not much competition in the field of large-scale journalism, because the cost of establishing a newspaper of that type

1757 [1] Sorbière, *Sorberiana, s.v. Anabaptistes* (pp. 15, 17-18): "Extravagant tales are current even in Holland as to the Anabaptists, who none the less are good people. They are said, among other things, to hold meetings at night and take advantage of the darkness to mingle promiscuously. That is altogether false and has no basis except a tale of John of Leyden, King of Münster, and the fact that a hundred years or more ago there were some few who believed that in order to be saved one had to go stark-naked like Adam before the Fall, whence they were called 'Adamists.' . . . So far as I know, there has been nothing of the sort since, and intelligent people in Amsterdam ridicule the absurd stories that have been spread abroad. All the same I remember that at Paris a certain Soubeyran averred that he had attended one such meeting at night and had had the daughter of his host who thereafter refused him at home what she had granted him in the name of Christian love. There is nothing surprising in the fact that there should be liars now and then. What is more so is that an imposture should spread so easily in the credence of a whole people, as is the case in this matter. And then there is the story of the girl with a pig's snout, a print of whom was sold to every cobbler in Paris and Holland. In Amsterdam she was generally supposed to live in a house on the Keyssergraft. However, no one could ever point it out—and that was enough to show that the story was false."

is enormous. It may, therefore, be a very good idea to have several such papers at one's disposal, and better yet if they belong to different parties. The powerful financial combinations of our day have come to understand that thoroughly and, taking advantage of the impersonal character of the corporations that own newspapers, they strive to gain control within such corporations and shrewdly make use of them.[1] Gossip mentions a number of newspapers as belonging to opposite and even hostile political parties, but operated by one same newspaper trust; and for not a few such rumoured facts there is fairly adequate proof. The function of such trusts, fundamentally, is to exploit the sentiments of people who read newspapers. The power they wield is something like the power formerly wielded by the Jesuits, but it is vastly more extensive.[2]

1760 [1] Speaking of protectionist newspapers in England in his article, "*La logica protezionista,*" p. 856, Einaudi remarks: "Such the language in which they venture to describe agriculture in England today. . . . The *Times,* unfortunately, has fallen into the hands of the same great 'yellow' journalist who is at the head of the *Daily Mail* and a 'combine' of imperialistic protectionist newspapers. Rider Haggard is a man of the sensational school, the school of those newspaper men in Italy who described the agricultural marvels of Libya before the war and during the first months of the war."

1760 [2] Robert de Jouvenel, *La république des camarades,* pp. 201-09: "The manager of a newspaper is rarely a newspaper man. [That may be overstating a little.] He is almost never a politician. He is, most often, a man interested in public contracts. He is always a business man. [As we have often remarked, there is, in general, an element of truth in rhetoric of that type.] Sometimes the newspaper is his only business, then again it is only one branch of a main business. In either case, the newspaper business involves the turnover of a great commercial establishment. [That is true of large countries where plutocracy is dominant.] There are papers [in France] whose annual business amounts to more than $6,000,000. A third-class daily represents an outlay of $300,000 a year. To handle such a budget it is not enough to have imagination, wit, or even talent. . . . In 1830 a newspaper was a matter of four small pages—the two sides of one sheet. It contained a few poorly paid or unpaid articles, no despatches, no costly news, no illustrations. It cost 5 cents. Today most newspapers are of six, eight, ten, or twelve pages. They are illustrated with costly pictures. They carry articles by Academicians or other outstanding individualities for which high prices are paid. They print columns of despatches some of which cost several francs per word. They are sold to retailers at a fifth of a cent per copy. How then do they live? They live by their advertising, unless, of course, they live by their 'deals.' A newspaper can do without writers and reporters, it can even do without appearing. [Jouvenel explains that paradox in a note: "There is somewhere or other a cemetery for suspended publications. Some enterprising business man owns their titles, has them printed at the top of columns in some other paper, and so collects the proceeds of outstanding contracts for advertising. It is a flourishing business."] It cannot do without 'publicity.' . . . Before coming

1761. Returning now to the matter of the relations between derivations and residues in general—one oftentimes imagines that derivations have been transformed into residues, whereas the reverse is really the case, residues manifesting themselves through derivations (§§ 1747, 1751). That mistake is the more readily made in view of the way in which we come by our knowledge of social phenomena. Most of our information is derived from the written word. It is therefore easy to mistake the effect for the cause and assume that the literary expression is the cause, whereas it is nothing but the effect.

1762. It is observed that at a certain moment a given idea makes its appearance in literary productions and then develops and flourishes exuberantly. We seem to be describing the facts accurately when we say that literature has planted that idea in the minds of men. That may sometimes be the case, but the reverse is the more frequent case. In other words, sentiments already present in the minds of men have inspired the literature and then nursed it to prosperous vogue (§ 1751). Residues of our IV-ε2 variety, sentiments of authority, then intervene to lead us further astray. When we are reading a great writer, it seems evident enough that only such a man could have the power to shape society in that way, his way.

1763. When one reads Voltaire, it is natural enough to conclude that he was the artisan of the unbelief so prominent in the people of his time. But pondering the matter a little more closely, we can only wonder how it could have come about, if that is the general rule, that the writings of Lucian, which are in no way inferior to Voltaire's on the side of literary quality and logical effectiveness, failed to have an influence as great as Voltaire's, that Lucian stood alone in his unbelief while faith and superstition were increasing all about him. There is no way of explaining such facts, and many

to any decision, the manager of a paper, be he an angel with wings, has to consider two essential requisites: 1. He must not offend those who have the news to give out—all the powers, that is, in politics or public administration. 2. He must not offend those who have 'publicity' to give out, in other words, all the powers in business and finance. [Not all, to be strictly exact: only those with which the newspaper is working.] Newspapers are called 'governmental' when they are servile. They are called 'independent' when they are merely 'governmental.' An 'opposition paper' is a paper that is flirting with the ministry in power. Some few organs have no connexions with the Government in any way through anybody, but no one of course would ever make the mistake of taking them seriously."

others of the kind, except by assuming that the seed that is sown bears fruit, or fails to bear fruit, according as it falls on congenial or uncongenial soil. The *philosophes* of the eighteenth century in France revived arguments that had already been used against Christianity by Celsus and the Emperor Julian. Why did they succeed where their predecessors failed? Obviously because there was a difference in the minds of the people whom they addressed. But that is not all. Had Voltaire been the chief artisan of the ideas prevalent among his countrymen, those ideas should not have weakened in intensity so long as his literary labours continued. Yet towards the end of Voltaire's life, while his fame was still soaring, one notes the rise of a movement directly opposite to his tendencies: the educated classes were turning to Rousseau. Rousseau, in his turn, was doing little more, on the whole, than to state derivations that corresponded to residues that Voltaire had left unstirred. To that Rousseau owed the favour with which the public showered him, just as Voltaire owed the popularity he had enjoyed to derivations corresponding to other residues. Those writers did not create the public sentiments of their day. The sentiments created the reputations of those writers. So much for the main element in the phenomenon (§ 1747); for the facts clearly show that the writing of such men was not entirely and absolutely without effect, that it did amount to something. But, as compared with the other, this latter effect seems something quite secondary.

1764. What we have just been saying relates to the effectiveness of certain reasonings, but it has nothing to do with the intrinsic value of the reasonings in themselves. It is obvious that the scientific genius of a Newton, the military skill of a Napoleon or a Moltke, the diplomatic talent of a Bismarck, the literary value of a Lucian or a Voltaire, have nothing to do with residues. But for the activity of such men to have any notable effects, they must encounter favourable circumstances in their respective societies through the presence of certain residues. Had Newton lived in the Middle Ages, he might have produced some mere work in theology. Had Voltaire lived in the day of Lucian, he would have had no following. Had Bismarck lived in a country controlled by democratic or plutocratic politicians, and had he managed to get as far as a seat in a Parliament, he would have seen a Depretis or a Giolitti preferred to him in Italy, a Rouvier or a Caillaux in France.

1765. Still another cause of the error of assigning too great an importance to derivations as regards determining the social equilibrium is a temptation we feel to ascribe objective existence to certain ideas, principles, dogmas, and then to reason as though they functioned by themselves independently of residues. Class II residues (group-persistences) are largely responsible for that illusion. The metaphysical entities they create are altogether similar to the gods of the theologians, and function in the very same manner. Few the histories in a day gone by that could narrate a course of events and consider their mutual relations without dragging in gods somewhere, somehow, and few the histories in our day which fail to assume implicitly or explicitly that principles and theories serve to shape human society.

1766. *d. Influence of derivations on derivations.* On this subject we touched in our study of derivations, noting that when a type of derivation comes into vogue, derivations of the same type come forward in great numbers. The residues of sociality that encourage people to be like their fellows, to imitate them, serve to give a common form to certain derivations. If, moreover, in virtue of strong feelings a person has been prevented from perceiving the fallacy of a certain argument in a certain case, he readily fails to perceive the same fallacy in other cases where he is not strongly influenced by his feelings. That favours the growth of derivations of the type of the derivation used in the special case.[1] Furthermore, less intellectual effort is required to imitate than to create. That is why minor writers are constantly repeating phrases, formulas, and arguments used by authors of greater reputation and prestige.

1767. Of great importance is a reciprocal tendency in derivations

---

1766 [1] A few centuries back almost all the derivations that were used in social or pseudo-scientific matters were combined with considerations of Christian theology; nowadays they are combined with considerations of humanitarian theology. The old ones often seem absurd to us; ours will seem just as absurd to people of future generations, when some other theology has superseded the humanitarian. A few centuries ago everything was explained by "original sin." Nowadays everything is explained by "the shortcomings of society" (§ 1716 [3]). In the future there will be some other explanation, equally theological and, from the experimental standpoint, equally inept.

to eliminate, in appearances at least, any substantial contradiction that may exist between them.[1] Once a derivation is accepted, it comes about that among educated persons—literary men, theologians, metaphysicists, pseudo-scientists and the like—there will be some who insist on drawing logical inferences from it. Such inferences stray farther and farther afield from the residues corresponding to the derivation in which they originated, and therefore farther and farther afield from realities. Let A stand for certain sentiments, certain residues, to which a derivation, S, corresponds. So long as that correspondence remains unaltered, S is a way of stating a real fact, and differs from it only in form. But a logical inference, C, drawn from S, may, in point of substance, lose contact with A and seriously so (§ 2083). That situation presents itself under various forms: 1. *Lack of definiteness.* The derivation S, stated in ordinary language, sometimes fails to correspond to anything definite and is accepted only in virtue of a vague accord with certain sentiments. It therefore cannot serve as a premise for any reasoning at all strict (§§ 826 f.). 2. *Lack of correspondence.* In the very best case, even when there is correspondence between S and A, the coincidence is never perfect, and the inferences logically drawn from S do not accordingly apply to A. Taking the two forms together, we may say therefore that through lack of definiteness or correspondence on the part of S, no accurate inferences can be drawn from it, or, if so drawn, they are not valid for A. 3. *Complexity of sentiments.* The group of sentiments, A, is never sharply defined, and the lack of correspondence between A and S is due, therefore, not only to imperfect correspondence between the definite elements in A and S, between the nucleus of the fog of sentiments and S, but also to the complete lack of correspondence between S and the indefinite elements in A, between S and the fog that hangs about the nucleus A. 4. *Interdependence of groups of sentiments.* The group A is not independent of other groups, $M, P, Q. \ldots$ In the individual, these groups have adapted themselves after a fashion

1767 [1] We have already dealt with this tendency at length, noticing the error of many educated persons in imagining that because they themselves feel an urgent need, apparent or real, for logic the same need is felt, and to the same extent, by everybody. That among other reasons is why they devise "scientific" religions, in the belief that in so doing they are satisfying a public demand. As a matter of fact such religions remain for the exclusive use and consumption of their few founders.

to getting along together and cohabit in a sort of harmony; but the harmony vanishes in their respective logical implications. Many Christian feudal lords of the old days harboured a sentiment, A, connected with the forgiveness of wrongs and enforced by religion, along with a sentiment, M, which was enforced by the exigencies of practical life, by a sense of personal honour, and even by a desire for vengeance. But the relatively peaceful cohabitation of those two sentiments would have vanished in their logical corollaries if from A, on the one hand, the feudal baron had drawn the conclusion that it was his duty patiently to put up with every insult and every wrong without defending himself; and if from M, on the other, he had drawn the conclusion that the Gospels, of which M takes no account, were silly and fatuous books. 5. *Correspondence between theories and social facts.* If the correspondence between A and S were perfect in each individual, it would also be perfect in the community composed of such individuals, and the conduct of the community could be logically inferred from S. Knowledge of political and social forms would in that case be easy. It is in fact no very difficult task to identify the derivations that are current in a society, and if knowledge of political and social facts could be derived from them logically, social science would develop under difficulties no greater and no different than those encountered by geometry. As everybody knows, that is not the case. To reason geometrically in social matters is to depart, much or little, from realities. But it is a mistake to lay the blame for that on the reasoning; it is the premise that sets us on the wrong road. And it is likewise a mistake to try to evaluate the social importance of a residue by the correspondence of the inferences drawn from it with realities; for the importance of a residue lies chiefly in its correspondence with the sentiments that it expresses.[2]

1767 [2] Renan, *Histoire du peuple d'Israël,* Vol. V, pp. 349-50: "How, after all that, can Philo remain a Jew? That would be hard to say, were it not well known that in a question involving one's mother-religion, the heart has touching sophistries to reconcile things that have no connexion with each other. [The case of Philo is not, as Renan seems to think, a particular case. That happens in general. And we can do without the "touching."] Plato loves to illustrate his philosophical positions with the most attractive myths of the Greek genius. Proclus and Malebranche both think they are following their ancestral religions, the one in writing philosophical hymns to Venus, the other in saying Mass. Inconsistency in such connexions is piety. Rather than abandon a belief that is dear to one, any false identifica-

We have already dealt frequently and at length with problems arising in connexion with the first four of these forms. It still remains for us to consider those peculiar to the fifth; but they are part of a more general problem that we must now examine.

1768. *Relations of residues and derivations to other social facts.* We have seen (§§ 802-03) that there is a certain correspondence between the logico-experimental sciences, which begin with experimental principles, *A,* and from them, by rigorous logic, draw the inferences *C,* and social reasonings, which start with residues, *a,* and from them, through derivations, *b,* which are compounds of residues and logic, reach inferences *c.* The conclusions of the logico-experimental sciences—overlooking, for the moment, cases where observations of fact are not exact and the logic unsound—will surely accord with the facts, since the principles *A* picture the facts exactly and the reasoning is faultless. But the same cannot be said of social reasonings; for we have no way of knowing in just what relation the residues, *a,* stand towards the facts, nor the value of the reasoning, *b,* in which other residues figure. And yet daily experience shows that many such reasonings lead to inferences that do accord with the facts. That cannot be doubted, once we reflect that they are the only ones that have been used in social life, and that if they led to results which did not square with the facts, all societies would long since have been annihilated. How then can it be that conclusions drawn from residues should so accord with the facts?

1769. The solution of this problem is to be sought in the relationship in which residues and derivations stand towards social facts. If residues were expressions of those facts in the way in which the principles of the experimental sciences are expressions of fact, and if the derivations were strictly logical, the accord between the con-

tion, any convenient twist, is admissible. Moses Maimonides will use the same method in the twelfth century, upholding both the *Torah* and Aristotle—the *Torah* interpreted after the manner of the Talmudists, Aristotle after the materialist fashion of Averroës [§ 1931 [2]]. The history of the human mind is full of such pious paradoxes. What Philo did nineteen hundred years ago, many honest minds are doing in our day under the sway of a resolve not to abandon beliefs that are regarded as something ancestral. [Still representing as particular a trait that is general for every type of derivation.] The most perilous acrobatics are risked in order to reconcile faith and reason. [In general terms, to reconcile derivations based on heterogeneous residues.] After obstinately rejecting the results of science, people reverse positions when the evidence is overwhelming and coolly say, 'We knew that before you did.' "

clusions and experience should be certain and perfect. If the residues were selected at random and the derivations likewise, accord would be exceedingly rare. So then, since accord is frequent but not invariable, residues and derivations must occupy some middle ground between the two extremes. It is to be noted that a residue which is at variance with experience may be corrected by a derivation which is at variance with logic in such a way that the conclusion is brought back to something like experimental fact. That comes about because in performing non-logical actions under guidance of instinct human beings approximate experimental fact (§ 1782) and then quite undesignedly correct by poor reasonings inferences drawn from a residue that is at variance with reality.

1770. The problem here in question is an aspect of an inquiry still more general, as to how, namely, the forms of living beings and societies are determined. Such forms are not creatures of chance—they depend upon the conditions in which individuals and societies live; but the precise nature of that dependence we do not know, since we have been obliged to reject the Darwinian solution, which had its answer to that question. But if we cannot solve the problem altogether, we can at least identify certain properties of forms and residues. It is evident first of all—and that was the element of truth in the Darwinian solution (§§ 828, 2142)—that forms and residues cannot stand too openly in conflict with the conditions in which they are evolved. An animal that has gills, only, cannot live in dry air; and an animal that has lungs, only, cannot live continuously submerged. So human beings endowed with anti-social instincts, only, could not live in society. One may go one step farther and recognize that there is a certain adaptation between forms and environment. The Darwinian solution errs in regarding the adaptation as perfect; but that does not preclude there being a certain rough adaptation. It is certain that animals and plants have forms that are partly, and sometimes wonderfully, adapted to the conditions under which they live. So it cannot be denied that peoples have instincts more or less adapted to their modes of living. But that, notice, is just a relation between two things. It by no means follows that the one thing is a result of the other. We see that the lion lives on prey and has powerful weapons with which to capture it; but that is not saying that it lives on prey *because* it has such weapons; or that it has such weapons *because* it lives on prey. A warlike people has warlike instincts; but that is not saying that it is warlike because of those instincts, nor that it has those instincts because it is warlike.

1771. That gives us a solution, a very rough one to be sure, of our problem: Social reasonings yield results that are not too greatly at variance with realities because their residues, both those which inspire the derivations and those which they utilize, stand more or less related to realities. If the basic residues do come close to realities and derivations are moderately logical, we get results that, as a rule, are not too greatly at variance with realities. If the primary residues go astray, they are corrected by the other residues that inspire sophistical derivations as a means of getting back to realities.

1772. Now let us look at some other aspects of the situation. As for the correspondence between residues and other social facts, we can repeat what we said in § 1767 as to the correspondence between derivations and residues, namely: 1. That certain residues have very slight correspondence with the facts upon which social organization depends, and so cannot in any way be made to correspond to logico-experimental principles derived from those facts. 2. That even the residues which have a certain rough correspondence with the facts that determine the organization of society and which roughly correspond to logico-experimental principles inferred from those facts, do not correspond perfectly to the facts and are altogether lacking in the definiteness required for such principles.

As regards derivations, they overstep reality, as a rule, in the direction in which they are headed, whereas they rarely stop short of it. Three principal forms may be noted in that phenomenon. In the first place, in virtue of a tendency in sentiment to go to extremes, there is a definite tendency in derivations to evolve into idealizations and myths: a local inundation easily becomes a universal flood— the advantage accruing to a society from following certain practices develops into a divine code of commandments or into a categorical imperative. In the second place, the fact that if a derivation is to be accepted and impressed on the mind it has to be stated in striking language has the effect of concentrating stress on the principal element, while secondary elements are neglected. A principle is stated without regard to those modifications and exceptions which would make it more comfortable to realities. The maxim is, "Thou shalt not kill," a statement that far oversteps the rule of conduct which one is aiming to establish and which would have to be stated in a great many more words if one were to specify in just what cases and under just what circumstances one must not kill, in what other cases one may kill, and in what other cases still one must kill. The injunction is, "Love thy neighbour as thyself"; and that too oversteps the rule, which is really being set up in order that the people living in a given community may practice mutual goodwill. In fine, the efficacy of a faith in spurring men to vigorous action is the greater, the simpler, the more nearly absolute, the less involved in qualification, the less ambiguous, it is, and the farther it stands removed from scientific scepticism. And from that it follows that the derivation, so far as it aims at spurring men to action, uses simple principles that overstep realities and aim at goals that lie beyond them, sometimes far far beyond. In a word, to get back from derivations to realities certain allowances almost always have to be made.

The qualities that make a good derivation out of a reasoning are oftentimes the opposite, therefore, of the qualities which would make it a sound logico-experimental reasoning; and the nearer it comes to one of those limits, the farther it gets from the other. But the logico-experimental reasoning is the one that corresponds to reality; and therefore if people acting on derivations approximate reality, it is clear that the divergence existing between derivations and reality must somehow or other have been corrected. The correction is obtained through the conflict and composition [1] (§§ 2087 f.) of the many derivations current in a society. The simplest, but also the least frequent, form in which this process manifests itself is in the case of two directly contradictory derivations, A and B, where A oversteps reality in one direction and B in another; so that when A and B are at work simultaneously they come closer to reality than either of them taken singly would do. The derivation A, for instance, bids people to love their neighbours as themselves, and the derivation B enjoins the vendetta as a duty. The more complex, but also the more frequent, form is the case where there are many derivations, $A, B, C \ldots$ that are not directly contradictory, and which,

1772 [1] [A technical term, not to be taken in its ordinary senses.—A. L.]

when combined and mutually composed (§§ 2087 f., 2152 f.), give a resultant that approximates reality more closely than any one of them singly; and examples would be the many derivations concerning the law of nations, patriotic selfishness, the independence of the courts, reasons of state, abolition of interest on money, the advantages of increasing the public debt, and so on, which are all derivations observable among all civilized peoples.

1773. *Effects upon conclusions of divergences between residues and logico-experimental principles.* Suppose we are reasoning by the logico-experimental method. Taking certain residues, *a*, as our premises we reach the conclusions *c*. If we reasoned in the same way with strictly experimental principles, *A*, we should reach the conclusions *C*. Now our aim is to determine the relationships existing between conclusions *c* and *C*. To do that we have to know the relation between residues *a* and principles *A*. Now let us take a hypothesis that is actually verifiable in certain instances. We assume, that is, that *a* coincides with *A* within certain limits only and overreaches *A* beyond those limits; in other words, that certain residues, or the propositions that express them, represent reality within certain limits only. What conclusions may be drawn from such propositions? We first have to specify whether the limits are known or unknown. If they are known, the problem is solved forthwith. The conclusions derived from the propositions will be true within the limits within which the propositions are valid. Scientific theories are all of that type, limits being more or less broadly drawn.

1774. If the limits are not known the problem becomes much more difficult and is often unsolvable. Unfortunately, in the case of social reasonings, of reasonings by derivations, the limits are but vaguely known, when not entirely unknown. So we have to rest content with solutions that are crudely approximative. We may say that conclusions in accord with the facts may be drawn from propositions which are true within certain vaguely known limits, provided the reasoning *does not depart too radically* from the situation in which the propositions are true. That is very very little, and it can be accepted only because a little is better than nothing.

1775. *Examples.* We know that when the temperature of water rises from 4° to 100° Centigrade under a barometric pressure of 760 mm. of mercury, its volume increases. In this case the limits within which the proposition is true are definitely determined, and we are warned not to extend it beyond those limits. In fact, between 0° and 4° water decreases instead of increasing in volume. When we say that in a given society it is a good thing to allow a majority of citizens to decide on social measures, we do not know within what limits the proposition accords with the facts (we are here disregarding the lack of definiteness in the proposition itself). It is probable that if one were to ask whether it would be advantageous to allow half the people in a society plus one to decide to kill and eat the other half less one, the answer would be in the negative. But the reply would very likely be in the affirmative if one should ask whether or not it would be *advantageous* to allow a majority of one to decree a law regulating automobile traffic. Within certain limits the proposition may therefore be in accord with the facts; whereas within others it might not be. But what are those limits? We are not in a position to give a satisfactory answer to such a question.[1]

1776. Where science fails, empiricism comes to the rescue. Empiricism plays, and will continue to play, for a long time to come, a very important part in social matters: and it often corrects deficiencies in premises (§ 1769). If a person has a good topographical chart and knows how to use it accurately, he will be sure to find his way from one place to another. But the road will be found just as well, and perhaps better, by an animal guided solely by instinct, and by a person who also follows it instinctively from having been over it a number of times. If a person has a poor topographical chart and reasons on it in strict logic, he will probably find his way less readily than persons in those extreme cases. Ancient geographers used to

1775 [1] One group of derivations pretends to answer the question by restating it as a problem of "rights" on the part of the individual as against "rights" on the part of the "State." That solution is like explaining why water rises in a pump by the theory that Nature abhors a vacuum—that is to say, it explains facts not by other facts, but by imaginary entities. No one can say precisely what the "State" in question may be, much less what its "rights" are, and what the "rights" of the "individual." The mystery and darkness increase if one inquires as to the relations between such "rights" and various utilities. Finally, assuming that the problem of terms is solved, no one can say how the theoretical solution can be applied in the concrete. The solution therefore is seen to be merely the expression of a pious wish on its author's part; and he might have stated it outright, without going so far afield to dig up those very pretty but very obscure entities.

say that the Peloponnese was shaped like the leaf of a plane-tree.[1] If a person starts out on that premise and reasons logically, he will know less about the topography of the Peloponnese than a person who has a modern regulation map and even, let us say, just a moderately bad sketch of that country. Very close to these latter, as regards conformity with experience, stands the person who decides haphazard. Next in order come those who follow residues and derivations, and they are like the person who knows that the Peloponnese has the shape of a plane-tree leaf. Finally comes the merely practical man, and he is like the ignorant person who has no map at all but has traversed the Peloponnese from end to end. These two sorts of persons oftentimes obtain results that are not very greatly at variance with experience.

1777. Propositions that are not epitomes of experience pure and simple, as experimental principles are, are sometimes called *false* propositions. What can be got out of them? First we have to explain the term "false." If by "false" one means a proposition that is utterly at variance with the facts, there is no doubt that reasoning conducted logically on false premises will yield conclusions that will also be false (at variance with the facts). But the term "false" often indicates a false explanation of a real fact; and in that case it is possible, within certain limits, to draw from such propositions conclusions that are *true* (which accord with the facts).

1778. *Examples.* Once upon a time to explain how a pump sucks water it was said that "Nature abhors a vacuum." The fact was real, the explanation false; but the explanation will lead to conclusions that are verifiable by experience. Fill a bottle with water, press a finger over the mouth, immerse the neck in water, and remove the finger. What will happen? The answer is: The water will remain suspended in the bottle, for if it came out, the bottle would be left empty; and we know that that is impossible, since Nature abhors

---

1776 [1] Eustathius, *Commentarius in Dionysium Periegetem* (*Orbis descriptio, v.* 157), pp. 111, 245: "Ye should know that just as the Euxine is comparable to a bow, so many other places are diversely representable by a certain similitude. So history says that the Egyptian delta is triangular. . . . Thus is Alexandria represented by a chlamys [a military cloak]; Italy by an ivy-plant; Spain by an ox's hide; the island of Naxos by a vine-leaf; the Peloponnese by a leaf of the plane-tree; Sardinia by a human footprint; Cyprus by a sheep's hide; Libya by a trapeze; and so other lands the ancients pictured otherwise."

a vacuum. We perform the experiment and see that the conclusion is in accord with the facts.

Now let us perform the same experiment with a tube of mercury a metre long, one end of the tube being open and immersed in a mercury bath. The conclusion now fails of verification, for the mercury drops in the tube and leaves part of it empty. Now if that were a fact of social life instead of physics, there would be no end of new derivations put forward to explain it. One might show, by using a very pretty and very ingenious reasoning of the sort used in theories of natural law, that Nature's abhorrence of a vacuum ceases at about 760 mm. of mercury. It is known that the number 7 is a perfect number and so also the number 6. Put two such perfect numbers side by side, and they would surely give a very perfect number indeed, and Nature's love for it might well vanquish her abhorrence of a vacuum. If the height of the mercury were stated in inches or in some other system of measurement, no difficulty would arise on that account. Many writers (§ 963), among them Nicomacus of Gerasa, would show us how to find the perfection in the number we should then get. If someone were to object that when the experiment is performed with water the height at which Nature's abhorrence of the vacuum ceases is much greater than in the case of mercury, we could answer that that is only fit and proper, since, after all, water is "the best of the elements" and should therefore have greater privileges than mercury. And such a reasoning would be quite as sound as an argument by M. Léon Bourgeois in favour of solidarity.

To explain why one "ought" to be hospitable to strangers the Greeks, who were pagans, used to say that strangers came of Zeus, and Christians quoted the Gospels, where it is written that he who receiveth a stranger receiveth Christ.[1] If one infers from such propositions that it is "useful" to show hospitality to strangers, one gets a proposition that might be in accord with the facts in the case of the ancients and, though not by any means to the same degree, in the case of the moderns. The conclusions would be something like the conclusions we reached for the bottle full of water. If we should go on and draw the inference—which also follows logically—that

1778 [1] Matt. 25:35, and 38-40: "I was a stranger and ye took me in," *etc.*

strangers are to be honoured as ambassadors from Zeus, according to the Greeks, and as Christ in person according to the Christians, we would get a conclusion that has never squared with the facts among either Greeks or Christians.

We may therefore say, reasoning very roughly, that from the derivations current in a given society one may get conclusions that will be verified by experience, provided (1) We *make a certain allowance* in such derivations, which customarily overstep the limits actually aimed at (§ 1772); provided (2) the reasoning does not stray *too far* from conditions in that society; provided (3) the reasoning that is premised on the residues corresponding to the derivations is not pushed to its *extreme logical limits*. The expressions, "a certain allowance," "too far," and "extreme limits" are not very definite because the limits within which the derivations (or the residues that engender them) correspond to the facts are not precise; and also because in ordinary language derivations are stated in a manner that is not very strict, if at all so. This last reservation might perhaps be more clearly worded if we said that reasoning on derivations must be more apparent than real, and that actually it is better to let oneself be guided by one's sense of the residues than by plain logic.[2]

1778 [2] In respect of form this experimental conclusion looks something like the conclusion of certain metaphysicists who have intuition with or without intellect as a means of knowing the "truth." It is different however in substance. 1. First of all, there is a difference in the use of the term "truth." For the metaphysicist it designates something independent of experience, beyond experience; for the experimental scientist it designates mere accord with experience. To make the point clearer, let us use a crude but expressive parallel. The individual is like a photographic film, which when exposed in a given place, receives an impression of things, of "facts." The derivations through which he voices his impressions correspond to the developing of the film. The metaphysicist would have the film, after it has been developed, show things, "facts," that were not present in the place where the film was exposed, but which are just as "real"—in fact, as some say, they are the only "reality." The experimentalist expects the developed film to show nothing but an image of the things, the "facts," that were present in the place where the film was exposed. 2. Then there is the usual difference between the metaphysical absolute and the experimental relative. The metaphysicist thinks his intuitive operations guide him to "absolute truth." The scientist accepts his only as an indication of what reality may be, an indication that it is the exclusive prerogative of experience to confirm or refute.

To return to the analogy just suggested: After the film has been developed, the metaphysicist thinks that it corresponds perfectly with reality. The experimentalist knows that there are countless divergences between the two. We will say nothing

1779. Towards the end of the nineteenth century in France the revolutionary party thought best to avail itself of the talents of certain theorizers who were called "intellectuals" and who, in fact, pretended to submit practice to the test of the conclusions that they reached logically from certain principles of theirs (§ 1767 [1]). Such "intellectuals" naïvely thought they were enjoying the admiration of certain groups who actually were using them as mere tools: and in their self-conceit they contrasted the splendours of their logic with the darkness of the "prejudices" or "superstitions" of their opponents. In point of fact, they were straying much farther from realities than their opponents. Some of the "intellectuals" in question started with the principle that no innocent person must ever be condemned, and went on to the most extreme implications of that premise, refusing to see anything else (§ 2147, example II). It may very well be that such a principle may be a useful one for a society to have; but it is also true that it is useful only within certain limits. If one is to reject that reservation, one must choose one of the two following lines: (1) Either one must deny that there is any divergence between observance of the principle and the prosperity of a nation; or else (2) declare that one is to disregard the question of prosperity and be satisfied with just following the principle. Neither of these paths could the said "intellectuals" be induced to take, for they were really far less logically-minded than they were willing to appear; and both propositions might more fitly have been classed with the "superstitions" so fiercely reproved by the "intellectuals," for, after all, the first does not differ very greatly from the assertion that God rewards the good and punishes the wicked; and the second could be congenial only to the fanatical ascetic who despises all earthly

of the fact that the film shows what exists in space as existing in a plane, that it fails to show the colours of the various objects, and so on. There are other more special differences still, as for example whether some living being may have moved, or a leaf been stirred by the wind, while the film was exposed. By a very extraordinary coincidence there happens to be a real case corresponding to the very comparison we instituted for mere purposes of clarity. Many people have believed that photographs have recorded the "astral doubles" of human beings and animals. They have shown the photographs of a human being with a spot near by, or of pheasants with another spot, and the spot they call the "astral double" of the human being or the pheasant. Such photographs all beginners make, when they have not yet learned to take photographs and develop films without spots. How many such spots have been palmed off as real things by metaphysicists and theologians!

goods. That kind of politics was a politics for children; and our "intellectuals" were less in touch with realities than many practical politicians of no education worth talking about.

1780. The derivation route may be followed in the inverse direction, that is to say, from certain manifestations one may infer the principles from which they logically follow. In the logico-experimental sciences if the manifestations are in accord with the facts, the principles of which they are regarded as consequences will also be in accord with the facts. Not so in reasonings by derivation; there the principles of which the manifestations would be the logical consequence may be altogether at variance with the facts (§ 2024).

1781. Here comes a Tolstoyan who condemns all wars, even a strictly defensive war. The principle from which that doctrine is deduced is that to be happy human beings "ought not to resist evil." But the residue that is so expressed is something quite different; it is a subjective residue, instead of being an objective residue. In order to keep in accord with the facts, the Tolstoyan ought to say: "I imagine that I should be happy if I did not resist evil." That does not prevent someone else from being unhappy if he does not resist evil. To change his proposition from subjective to objective, the Tolstoyan ought to show—a thing which he does not and cannot do —that others ought to make themselves unhappy to please him. The Tolstoyan who reasons with strict logic draws from the principle that human beings "ought not to resist evil" inferences that may reach the extreme of absurdity. The Tolstoyan who is not altogether out of touch with realities sacrifices logic, follows the guidance of his sentiments—among them the instinct of self-preservation and the preservation of society—and arrives at less absurd conclusions. In fact, if he knows how to use his subtle casuistry skilfully and is not loath to disregard strict logic, he may even arrive at conclusions that accord with the facts.

1782. So, summing up many things in one, to reason in such cases in strict logic leads to conclusions at variance with the facts; to reason with serious lack of logic and with evident fallacies may lead to conclusions that come much closer to the facts.

1783. That proposition will provoke the indignation of many persons who imagine that reason and logic are the guides of human societies; and yet those same people unwittingly accept under other forms propositions that are its equivalents. Theory, for instance, has always been contrasted with practice by everybody everywhere, and even the people who are pure theorists in certain matters recognize the utility and the necessity of practice in other matters. Such propositions are derivations that take account of the following facts: 1. When theory starts with rigorously scientific propositions, it isolates by abstraction a phenomenon that in the concrete is combined with other phenomena. 2. When theory starts with empirical propositions that are true only within certain limits, there is in reasoning a temptation unwittingly to overstep those limits. 3. When theory starts with derivations, the latter, being, as a rule deficient in definiteness, cannot be taken as premises for strict reasoning. 4. In the same case, we know little or nothing of the limits beyond which a derivation ceases to be true, even if it is not in all respects false. In view of all these difficulties and others still, the practical man, following residues, frequently arrives at conclusions that are much better verified by the facts than the conclusions of the pure theorist reasoning in strict logic.

1784. In the field of politics the theorist has not as yet been able to vindicate himself, as he has done in many trades. The empiricist has seen a thing happen under certain circumstances; but circumstances in the future will differ widely from them, and he can predict nothing with regard to what is going to happen; and even if he tries, he will certainly go wrong, save in some few instances where he will guess aright by merest chance. But if the theorist has at his disposal a theory that is not too imperfect, he will predict things that closely approximate what is actually to occur.

1785. In the Middle Ages master-masons built marvellous edifices by rule of thumb, by empiricism, without the remotest knowledge of any theory as to the resistance capacities of building materials—merely by trying and trying again, rectifying mistakes as they went along. Now thanks to such theories, modern engineers not only eliminate the losses incident to the old mistakes, but erect buildings that the master-masons and other artisans of past centuries could not possibly have built. Practice had taught physicians certain remedies that were oftentimes better than those recommended by quacks or alchemists. Sometimes again they were altogether worthless. Nowadays chemical theories have eradicated not all, but a very large number, of those mistakes, and biology has made it possible to make better use of the many substances that chemistry places at the disposal of medicine. Only a few years back, in making cast iron in a blast-furnace it was wiser to follow the directions of an empiricist than the prescriptions of theory. Today the iron industry is no longer carried on without consultant chemists and other theorists. The same may be said of the dyeing industry and of many others.

1786. But in politics and political economy the day is still far distant when theory will be in a position to lay down useful prescriptions. It is not merely the difficulty of the subject that holds us off from that goal, but also the intrusion of metaphysics and its reasonings, which might be better termed vagaries; and the singular fact that that intrusion has its advantages, since reasoning by metaphysical or theological derivations is the only kind of reasoning that many people are capable of understanding and practising. In that the conflict between *knowing* and *doing* stands out in striking relief. For purposes of knowing, logico-experimental science is the only thing of any value; for purposes of doing, it is of much greater importance to follow the lead of sentiments. And just here, again, another important fact comes to the fore: the advantage, as regards eliminating that conflict, of having a community divided into two parts, the one in which knowledge prevails ruling and directing the other in which sentiments prevail, so that, in the end, action is vigorous and wisely directed.

1787. So, in politico-social prognoses, there are many cases in which results in accord with facts are more readily reached by following the lead of residues than by taking derivations as guides. It follows that in such cases forecasts will be the better the fewer the derivations mixed in with the residues. Conversely, when the purpose is to obtain scientific propositions, to discover the relations between things, between facts, to abstract a phenomenon from the concrete the better to examine it, that purpose will be the better attained the less one is influenced in one's reasoning by residues, the more exclusively the reasoning is logico-experimental, residues being considered as external facts purely and simply and never allowed to master one's thinking. In two words: Inferences in the practical field are the gainers from being essentially synthetic and inspired by residues; scientific inferences, from being essentially analytical and based on nothing but observation (experience) and logic.

1788. Using the ordinary terms, "practice," and "theory," practice is the better the more practical it is and theory the better the more theoretical it is. Altogether wretched, in general, are "theoretical practices" and "practical theories."

1789. Practical men are often tempted to formulate theories of their conduct, and usually they are worth little or nothing. Such people know how to act, but not how to explain *why they act*. Their theories are almost always derivations bearing not the remotest resemblance to logico-experimental theories.

1790. The conflict between theory and practice sometimes takes the form of an absolute denial of theory. A certain "historical school," for instance, has denied not only that there are economic theories, but even that there are laws in the economic field (§§ 2019 f.). If, with that start, the followers of the school had confined themselves to practice, they might have carved niches for themselves among our statesmen, instead of turning out the mere sophists and chatterboxes they in fact proved to be. There was probably a large element of truth in the substance of their doctrines, their error lying principally in their manner of stating it. What they should have said was that the theories of political economy and sociology are not as yet capable of yielding a synthesis of social phenomena and giving reliable forecasts of the future in the domain of the concrete; and that, as has been the case in other departments of human knowledge, until theory has made greater progress we had better place our main reliance on practice and empiricism.

1791. But the partisans of the "historical school" were primarily theorists. Their criticisms of the theories of political economy were theoretical in character. They called them "practical" in the belief that by changing them in name they would also be changing them in substance. Actually their theories are much worse than the theories of political economy, being based on ethical derivations devoid of the slightest definiteness and having little or nothing to do with fact; whereas economic theories have at least some basis in fact and sin only in being incomplete and unable to yield a synthesis of concrete social phenomena. The theories of political economy are

merely imperfect. The theories of the "historical school" are erroneous and oftentimes fantastic.

1792. Striking the contradiction in these self-styled "historians."
On the one hand they assert that there are no laws, no uniformities,
either in political economy or in sociology. On the other, they reason
in a manner that necessarily presupposes the existence of such laws.
To begin with, what is the use of all their studies in history if there
are no uniformities and if, therefore, the future has no connexions
with the past? That would be a mere waste of time, and it would
be far better to read fairy-tales or story-books than to study history!
But if one believes that norms for the future can be derived from
the past, one recognizes by that very fact that there are uniformities.

Then again, thinking more especially of the substance, one sees
very readily that the error of those good souls lies in their never having managed to grasp the fact that a scientific "law" is nothing but
a "uniformity." Their minds perverted by the vagaries of their metaphysics and their ethics, their determination aroused to find derivations that will justify certain currents of sentiment and please a
public as ignorant as they of every principle of scientific method,
they imagine that economic and social laws are mysterious and
mighty creatures which are bent on forcing their rule upon society;
and they rise in wrath against such pretensions, especially on the
part of "laws" that do not meet with their approval; though they
joyfully admit such pretension on the part of the imaginary "laws"
of their metaphysics and their ethics. They are mere believers in a
religion different from the religion that they are combating. They
deny the supposedly absolute "laws" of their adversaries. But such
deities they replace with others that are just as far removed from the
logico-experimental domain. The "laws" of political economy and
sociology annoyed them. They did not feel themselves the men to
refute them, and strangers as they were to scientific method, they
could not get it through their heads that neither the old "laws," nor
"laws" of any other kind, can have any absoluteness. To remove the
obstacle that towered before them, therefore, they acted like the believers of any new religion who destroy old altars to erect new ones,
as the Christians did when they proclaimed that the pagan gods
were but empty phantoms and that their God was the one living

and true God. Nor did they fail to supplement their conviction in faith by pseudo-reasonings designed to show that their religion was much more rational than the old one. Such nonsense acquires and holds prestige because it chances to accord with the sentiments and the ignorance of the people who listen to it. That explains why "historians" in the field of economics are able with little or no opposition to continue repeating, like parrots, that economic and social laws suffer "exceptions," whereas, they say, scientific laws do not. They do not know, they do not even suspect, that their "exceptions" are nothing but phenomena due to the operation of causes alien to those which science, by its process of abstraction, chooses to consider, and that such interposition of alien causes is as commonplace in chemistry, physics, geology, and all other sciences, as it is in economics and sociology. The differences are quite other than they imagine. They lie in the degree of difficulty experienced in separating in the abstract, or even materially, certain phenomena from certain other phenomena. Among such differences in degree it is interesting to note that sciences such as geology, which have to rely chiefly on observation (as distinguished from experiment), cannot separate one phenomenon from other phenomena materially, as do sciences such as chemistry, which are in a position to make extensive use of experiment (as distinguished from simple observation). From that point of view, political economy and sociology are more like geology than like chemistry (§§ 97-101).

1793. Napoleon's hatred of "ideology" is a striking instance of the conflict between theory and practice. In a reply to the Council of State at its session of December 20, 1812, he ascribes the misfortunes that had afflicted France to "ideology," and contrasts "ideologies" with the study of history.[1] Excellent this last remark, as a plea for the resort to experience, which is the source and fountain-head of all knowledge. But for that very reason it stands in contradiction

1793 [1] *Moniteur universel,* Paris, Dec. 21, 1812: "All the misfortunes that our beautiful France has been experiencing have to be ascribed to 'ideology,' to that cloudy metaphysics which goes ingeniously seeking first causes and would ground the legislation of the peoples upon them instead of adapting laws to what we know of the human heart and to the lessons of history. Such errors could only lead to a régime by men of blood, and they have in fact done so. Who cajoled the people by thrusting upon it a sovereignty it was unable to exercise? Who destroyed the sacredness of the laws and respect for the laws by basing them not on the sacred prin-

with Napoleon's own appeal to the "sacred principles of justice." That too belongs to pure metaphysics and in making it Napoleon, unwittingly to be sure, was merely setting one "ideology" over against another. And when he asserts that the "ideology" of the others is the cause of the misfortunes of France, he is stating a theory that may or may not be in accord with the facts but which in any case remains a theory.

1794. The same thing happens with many writers. They reject theories in words, but in the fact merely set one theory against another. Taine, for instance, *Ancien Régime,* Bk. III, Chap. IV, sec. 1 (Vol. II, p. 47), lays a share of the blame for the French Revolution on the "mathematical method," by which he means the use of pure logic: "In conformity with the habits of the classical mind and the precepts of the prevailing ideology, public policy was fashioned on the model of mathematics. One takes, all by itself, a simple, very general principle that is readily accessible to observation, familiar to everyone, and is grasped without difficulty by the most inattentive and ignorant schoolboy." In point of fact not only the theory of the Revolution, but all theories, are fashioned in just that way (overlooking the gratuity about the ignorant schoolboy). The inference one should draw from the fact is that no theory, even when it is based on experimental principles, as rarely happens (§ 1859) with social theories, can all by itself picture the complicated phenomena that we find in the concrete, and that therefore after breaking up phenomena into their elements by scientific analysis and studying them in their various parts, we have to put them together again and so get a synthesis that will yield the concrete phenomenon. Taine has nothing of that sort in mind. He notes an error in French thinking and tries to show that it was responsible for the disasters of France, and going on along that line he evolves a theory that is as abstract, as unilateral, as "mathematical," as the theories he is deploring and which is false into the bargain, in that it mis-

ciples of justice, on the nature of things and the nature of civic justice, but simply on the will of an assembly made up of individuals who are stranger to any knowledge of law whether civil, criminal, administrative, political, or military? When a man is called upon to reorganize a state, he must follow principles that are for ever in conflict. History draws the picture of the human heart. The advantages and disadvantages of different systems of legislation have to be sought in history."

takes what is effect for what is cause, or, rather, what is effect for what is actually a relationship of interdependent facts.[1]

1795. Certainly what Taine calls the "mathematical method" did not produce any French Revolution. Never never has any method had any such capacity. In reality there was, in France, a certain state of mind that expressed itself on the theoretical side in a "method" which Taine describes, and on the practical side in acts which prepared the ground for the Revolution.

1796. That vague, indistinct feeling which sets theory over against practice—substantially, it is an intuitive perception that to keep close to realities one had better reason on residues rather than on derivations—comes to light in still other ways. Of the same type is the maxim that it is better in everything to follow the "golden mean"; or the adage that rules (derivations) should be interpreted according to the "spirit" and not according to the letter, which, oftentimes, is just another way of saying that rules ought to be interpreted in the manner most satisfactory to the person quoting the maxim.

1797. *Derivations of indefinite meaning and their adaptation to specific ends.* As we have seen (§ 1772), derivations usually overstep the limits of reality. Sometimes, as also in the case of myths, people do not mind that. But then again, as happens with pseudo-experimental derivations, there is an effort, now by one device, now by another, to effect a certain accord with reality. One of the most widely used and most effective of such devices is to take advantage of the vagueness of the language in which the derivation is stated. There is hardly a prescription of a moral or religious character that

1794 [1] Taine makes no distinction between a "simple datum" (*"une donnée simple,"* loc. cit.) derived from experience and a "simple datum" derived from sentiment. Yet such a distinction is indispensable as marking the boundary-line between the logico-experimental sciences and sentimental literature, metaphysics, theology (§§ 55-56). Adam Smith and Rousseau likewise draw inferences from simple principles; but Adam Smith uses principles that epitomize experience, however inadequately, while Rousseau deliberately (§ 821) holds his principles aloof from experience. From that it follows that the inferences which may be drawn from the principles used by Adam Smith have a part, small or large, in common with experience; whereas the implications of Rousseau's principles float in a nebulous realm of sentiment far removed from the world of experience. The same may be said of other principles that certain writers have tried to palm off as experimental when actually they are not.

can be followed to the letter. That fact clearly emphasizes the gulf that separates derivations from reality and the adaptability of derivations to realities in virtue of their lending themselves to arbitrary interpretations. They can be used only as clues to the residues that they express, never as premises for strict logical reasonings that are calculated to yield conclusions which accord with reality.

1798. Theological and metaphysical believers will not admit any such thing. They maintain that their prescriptions are clear, specific, unexceptionable, and in exact correspondence with realities. They are never willing, however, to accept all the consequences that may be drawn from them. Now in order to refute an implication of a reasoning one must either deny the premises or find some flaw in the method by which the conclusions were drawn. Believers refuse to follow the first course. They are necessarily forced, therefore, to adopt the second. That is why some of them bluntly deny that one can reason logically on such premises as theirs, and demand that they be taken not "according to the letter," but "according to the spirit"; while others, again, instead of rejecting logic take it for their ally and call upon casuistry to furnish a means of keeping the premises and escaping this or that one of its consequences. Finally come others who simply wipe the annoying problem off the slate and assert that nothing "exists" except concepts of the "human mind," by which they mean their own mind, and that that mind "creates reality." On that basis it is evident enough that there can be no divergence between their ideas and reality. And that, in fact, is one of the best ways ever devised for getting rid of all objection from experimental science (§ 1910).[1]

1798 [1] Sometimes they meet their adversaries with the charge that they are not thinking according to the rules of metaphysics. So astrologers might embarrass an astronomer by saying that his thinking does not follow the rules of astrology. If a person accepts a given science, S, and wishes merely to change some of its consequences, he must obviously reason according to the rules of the science S. But if a person considers the science S inconclusive, silly, fantastic, he must no less obviously refrain from reasoning according to rules that he thereby rejects; and it is childish to accuse him of not knowing them because he does not use them. It is not difficult to see why a person who is defending a fantastic theory thinks it important to pretend that his theory cannot be questioned unless its norms and principles are accepted. In that way, he entrenches himself in an impregnable citadel. But the choice of weapons belongs to the person who uses them, not to the person who is their target. It may well be that the astrologers would be the gainers if they could

1799. Religions are idealistic; nor could they be otherwise without ceasing to be religions and losing all their effectiveness, all their social utility. They overstep realities, yet they have to live and develop in a real world. So they are obliged perforce to find some way to bring idealism and reality into harmony; and it is there that non-logical actions come to the rescue and, then to justify them, derivations and casuistry. That not seldom is the source of bitter rebuke to a religion from its adversaries, though really they ought to praise it for managing to preserve the stimulus of its idealism by reconciling it with the requirements of reality; and all the more so since they themselves in due course resort to similar means and expedients, so clearly showing that such devices are indispensable. Of such situations one could give examples without end from all countries and all religions. Here we will mention just a few from our Western countries and the Christian religion.[1] As everybody knows, as Christianity gradually won converts in the Roman world it had to relax in its primitive strictness and tolerate failings that at first it had fiercely condemned. Many conversions, furthermore, were largely superficial, mere changes in form rather than in substance. That was the case especially with conversions of Barbarians in the

be fought only under the rules and principles of astrology. But they have to resign themselves to seeing the fatuousness of their pseudo-science, its norms, and its principles, brought to light by a comparison of its results with experimental facts.

1799 [1] Christianity was originally a religion of the poor, the improvident, the peace-loving—people who scorned material goods. In course of time it readily adapted itself to societies where there were wealthy people, people who did think of the morrow, rapacious seekers after the good things of this world, fighters. The adaptation was made possible by derivations; but the derivations also had some effect upon the substance of things and produced new consequences such as the Inquisition and a series of religious persecutions. We still lack good histories of such events, histories written without polemical intent, showing no bias either for or against Christianity or any one of its sects, and without design of praising or condemning this or that social or moral institution. The Marxist religion absolutely condemns interest on capital; but the practical effects of the condemnation are not appreciably greater than the effects of the condemnation levelled at interest of yore by the Christian Church. In both the older and the newer religions there are persons who live apart from the world and loyally observe their dogmas; but such as play a part in the direction of public affairs manage very well at reconciling dogmas with practical necessities. To say nothing of Catholic princes, the Popes themselves borrowed money on interest. Nowadays, in countries where Socialists play a part, small or large, in public affairs, they are not in the least opposed to what are frequently enormous increases in the public debt. There is no lack of municipalities administered by Socialists that contract debts and pay interest on them. In such cases, as in

days when the Roman Empire was falling. One may see from St. Gregory of Tours (§ 1379 [3]) how thin the Christian varnish lay over Frankish kings and Barbarian chieftains who were adapting the new religion to their fierce warlike natures. That indeed was the reason why the western districts of the Mediterranean basin were better able to resist Asiatic invasions than the lands in the East, where the inhabitants were by nature milder and were growing still more so. A people of ascetics and monks, such as would have resulted had the derivations of the primitive Christians been literally followed, could not have been a warlike people; and it is hard to see how a people who literally "resisted not evil" could have resisted invaders of their own country. Fortunately for the peoples of the western Mediterranean, Christian derivations in no way enfeebled their bellicose instincts, but merely tempered excessive manifestations of them that might have proved disastrous. Something of the same sort, though in lesser proportions, may nowadays [1913] be observed in the contrast between France and Germany. In France, a democratico-humanitarian religion is dominant, and it seems to be unfavourable to any fostering of the warlike qualities of the French. In Germany, a patriotic religion prevails, and it is stimulat-

the old, derivations turn up in the pinch to justify the violation of the dogma. The Catholics excogitated that most ingenious of derivations about the three contracts. Socialists, whether because less ingenious or more modest, simply say that they cannot refrain from borrowing money until interest on loans has been generally abolished, and with that very convenient excuse handy they can go blithely on till the day one hears in the vale of Jehosaphat

> ". . . the sound of the angelic trump
> When comes the Doomsman of the dread Assize . . .
> To thunder to eternity their doom."
> —Dante, *Inferno*, VI, v. 99 (Fletcher)

If the dogmas of the humanitarian religion were followed literally in practice, they would lead directly to the destruction of human societies. But when these blessed humanitarians get into a government, they often find convenient ways of forgetting them, and without the slightest scruple they destroy people whom they call barbarians or else hold them in cruel servitude, a servitude oftentimes more cruel than what used to be known as slavery. But the god Progress will have his victims, like the gods who preceded him in the pantheon of civilized peoples. If equality, which is a dogma of the modern democratic religion, were ever made effective, human societies would probably revert to a state of savagery; but luckily for us, it keeps to its throne among the derivations, where it reigns sovereign, while in the practical world the most extreme inequalities prevail and they are not less extreme, different as they may be in forms, than the inequalities observable in ages past.

ing those qualities.[2] Our estimable moralists are wont to speak with horror of the warfaring prelates and mail-clad barons of the Middle Ages; yet they should be reminded that had the sentiments which found expression in that fashion chanced to fail, the countries of Western Europe would have suffered the same fate as the countries of Asia Minor and European Turkey; and our philosophers, instead of talking nonsense at their comfort and leisure in our civilized countries, would be serving as bellhops to some Asiatic satrap. Other good people are righteously indignant at the Roman pontificate because in the Middle Ages or a little later it was not sufficiently religious, not sufficiently "Christian," as they say, and because it found ways of opportunely reconciling Christian derivations with social and political exigencies. But that was the very reason why our present civilization was able to be born again after the fall of Graeco-Latin civilization and then go on to grow and prosper. A person who spurns the benefits of that civilization and condemns it may also spurn and condemn its origins. Not so the person who accepts it, praises it, enjoys its comforts; for, as Dante says, "the contradiction consenteth not" that one should accept the end without accepting the means as well.[3]

1800. Most of the precepts in the Gospels are poetical derivations that express certain residues; and it has been for the very reason that they are lacking in definiteness and are often contradictory that they have proved acceptable to all sorts of peoples in so many different periods of history. In times when Class I residues predominate, they are interpreted in such a way as to make them compatible with civilized living. When group-persistences (residues Class II) and ascetic residues are the dominant ones, everything possible is done to stick to their literal meanings and turn them against the progress of civilization. Take, for example, the precept not to economize, to think no more of the morrow than do the birds of the air

1799 [2] This particular contrast may be more of form than of substance, something merely temporary reflecting one of the many oscillations that are observable in social phenomena.

1799 [3] We are not saying that everything connected with this enterprise of reconciling certain religious and moral derivations with practical life was all to the good of society. There were respects in which it was beneficial, respects in which it was detrimental. We are merely saying that the beneficial aspects were of greater weight than the harmful.

or the lilies of the field.[1] If that precept were taken literally, all saving of wealth would disappear, and the civilized peoples would relapse into savagery. Precepts stated in that fashion, if they are to be taken at all strictly, are valid only for the improvident and the shiftless. In every civilized society, therefore, they have to be corrected by a certain amount of interpretation. The precept of Jesus has been generally taken to mean that one should give more thought to the soul than to the body; but in that case where do the birds and the lilies come in? Have they souls for which they care more than they do for their bodies?

1801. St. Jerome's remarks on the point are interesting.[1] At bot-

1800 [1] Matt. 6:19-34. There are a number of variants, but they make no essential difference in the meaning: "Lay not up for yourselves treasures upon earth, where moth and rust doth corrupt, and where thieves break through and steal. . . . Therefore I say unto you: Take no thought for your life, what ye shall eat, or what ye shall drink; nor yet for your body, what ye shall put on. Is not the life more than meat, and the body than raiment? Behold the fowls of the air: for they sow not, neither do they reap, nor gather into barns; yet your heavenly Father feedeth them. Are ye not much better than they? And why take ye thought for raiment? Consider the lilies of the field, how they grow; they toil not, neither do they spin. Therefore take no thought, saying, What shall we eat? or, What shall we drink? or, Wherewithal shall we be clothed? For after all these things do the Gentiles seek: for your heavenly Father knoweth that ye have need of all these things. Take therefore no thought for the morrow: for the morrow shall take thought for the things of itself. Sufficient unto the day is the evil thereof."

1801 [1] *Commentarii in Matthaeum* (6:19-34) (*Opera,* Vol. VII, pp. 43-46): "1. *Ne soliciti sitis . . . quid manducetis neque corpori vestro quid induamini:* some manuscripts add: 'or for what ye shall drink.' We are not altogether freed of attention to the lot that nature has assigned to all beasts and animals and which is common to man. We are taught not to let our minds be absorbed (*ne solliciti simus*) in what we eat. Since we win our bread in the sweat of our faces, we have to labour. It is our engrossment (*sollicitudo*) in such things that should be mastered (*tollenda*). As for the reference to food and raiment, we are to take it as applying to carnal food and raiment; but we should always be solicitous as to spiritual food and raiment. 2. *Is not the life more than meat and the body more than raiment?* What He means by that is that if a man has been attentive to the higher duties (*maiora*) he will certainly fulfil lesser ones. 3. (6:26) *Behold the fowls of the air* (*Respicite volatilia caeli*). The Apostle tells us that we should know no more than is good for us. That lesson should be kept in mind in connexion with this passage; for there are some who would go beyond what the Fathers say and, in trying to soar aloft to the stars, sink to the depths. They say that the 'fowls of the air' are angels of Heaven and other powers in the service of God, who are fed by God's providence without taking any thought 'for themselves. If the passage means what they say it means, how comes it that it is asked of men: 'Are ye not much better than they?' It is better therefore to take it simply: for if the birds of the air are fed by God's providence quite apart from worries and troubles, if they are today but

tom, he would take St. Matthew's words in the sense that we should, of course, work to earn our daily bread but in no way worry about the future.

1802. Pure asceticism, which figures not only in Christianity but in many other religions, tends to shun hard work; and there have been people in all ages who have lived in idleness as parasites on society. That manner of living results from certain sentiments, not from reasoning—the latter comes in *a posteriori* to supply a logical justification for the conduct. As regards his earning a livelihood, Diogenes lived more or less the way a Capuchin friar lives, but the reasons he gave for his conduct were not the ones that are put forward by the friar. When, moreover, such theories have implications that clash too violently with the requirements of individual or social life, they are necessarily modified to take account of them. There have at all times been saints, hermits, fanatics, who have insisted on following the words of the Gospels to the letter; and at the same time there have been people alive to the requirements of civilized living who have sought to find fairly liberal interpretations of them.

1803. It seems that in the days of St. Augustine there were those who followed the words of Jesus in their literal rigour, and used them to refute St. Paul's exhortation to labour. St. Augustine for his part [1] experiences not a trace of difficulty in reconciling precepts so antithetical, and by an ingenious feat in logical acrobatics invokes the contradiction itself to show that there is no contradiction. He says, in substance: "You tell me that *A* contradicts *B?* Not so; that

tomorrow are no more, if they have no immortal soul and will not live forever when they have ceased to be, how much more should men who have promise of eternity be submissive to the will of God? 4. (6:28) *Consider the lilies of the field:* He showed that the soul (King James Version: the life) was more than meat by the simile of the birds. So now he shows that the body is more than raiment by the things following. 5. (6:31) *Wherefore take ye no thought, saying What shall we eat:* He grants that those whom He forbids to worry about the future should be attentive to present things. So the Apostle said, I Thess. 2:9: '. . . labouring night and day because we would not be chargeable unto any of you . . .' The 'morrow' in Scripture is to be taken as any time in the future. 6. (6:34) *Sufficient unto the day is the evil thereof:* Here He uses 'evil' (*malitiam*) not as the contrary of virtue, but for travail, affliction, the troubles of the world. . . . The worries of the moment are therefore sufficient unto us. Let us refrain from thought of future things, since it will be vain (*incerta*)."

1803 [1] *De sermone Domini in monte secundum Matthaeum,* II, 17, 57 (*Opera,* Vol. III, p. 1295; *Works,* Vol. VIII, p. 109).

merely proves that *B* has to be taken in some other sense than the literal." St. Augustine evidently takes the Scriptures as constituting a whole in which the parts can never be inconsistent: they contain no contradictions, because no such contradiction *can exist*.[2] He confides, *Retractationes*, II, 21 (*Opera*, Vol. I, p. 638-39), that he was writing his treatise *On the Labour of Monks* because there were not a few among such who were refusing to work, on the plea that in that they were obeying the Gospel. The Saint shows them that they were wrong and involved in a contradiction, in that they themselves were not following the Gospel precept to the letter.[3] All that he

1803   [2] After quoting St. Paul's exact words, the Saint adds: "To those who fail to read his words aright it might seem that the Apostle were failing to keep the precept of the Master when He says 'Behold the fowls of the air for they sow not, neither do they reap nor gather into barns,' and 'Consider the lilies of the field, how they grow. They toil not, neither do they spin.' In the passage in question the Apostle teaches that they should work, labouring with their hands that they might have wherewith even to give unto others (I Thess. 2:9). He often says of himself that he wrought with his hands that he might not be chargeable to any man (II Thess. 3:8). Of him it was written, Acts 18:3, that he joined Aquila because he was of the same craft, that they might work together to earn a living. And in that he seems not to have imitated the fowls of the air and the lilies of the field. [It would seem so, in very truth. And yet—not so:] It is sufficiently apparent from these and other similar passages in Scripture that what Our Lord condemns is not the provision a man makes for himself by human means, but rather service of God in purport of such things [*i.e.,* as a way of making a living] so that one aims in one's labour not at the kingdom of God, but at a comfortable living (*acquisitionem*)." If St. Matthew really meant that, he may have had many excellent endowments, but certainly no great knack for clear expression of his thoughts.

1803   [3] "I was constrained of necessity to write my book *On the Labour of Monks*, for when there began to be monasteries in Carthage, some of them provided for themselves with the work of their hands in obedience to the Apostle, others elected to live on the alms of the devout, doing nothing to obtain their requirements either in whole or in part, believing, nay boasting, that in that they were the better observing the precept of the Gospel, where Our Lord says, Matt. 6:26: 'Consider the birds of the air and the lilies of the field.' Wherefore, even among laymen, who were simple souls but animate of living faith, there broke out fierce contentions that disturbed the peace of the Church." In the *De opere monachorum*, 23, 27 (*Opera*, Vol. VI, p. 569; Haddan, p. 517), the Saint says further: "Now forsooth they bring forth the Gospel of Christ against the Apostle of Christ. Truly marvellous the industry of these time-wasters who out of the Gospel would raise an impediment to the very thing which the Apostle prescribed and did to the end that the Gospel itself should have no impediment. And yet if we were to constrain these people to live according to the literal words of the Gospel, as they understand them, they would be the first to essay persuasion of us that those words were not to be understood as they understand them. For in truth they say that they must not work, because the birds of the air neither sow nor reap, which Our Lord gave us as an example to

shows by that, really, is that to follow the precept to the letter would be very difficult, not to say impossible. He in no wise shows that the meaning is different from the obvious meaning of the terms used. To clear his traces, the Saint changes the meaning of the Gospel text altogether. Says he: "The whole precept, then, comes down to this rule: that even in being provident we must think of the kingdom of God, and that in soldiering for the kingdom of God we should not linger on thoughts of amassing material goods." [4] Similar interpretations are to be found in the writings of other Holy Fathers, who go looking for ways to reconcile the Gospel text, which is after all clear enough, with the requirements of a civilized society.[5]

St. Thomas has an ingenious interpretation with which he designs to eat his cake and have it too. He states the question: "What

the end that we take no thought of these necessary things. But why do they not attend to what follows? For it is not only written that 'they sow not, neither do they reap,' but it is further added: 'nor gather into barns.' Which barns may be said to be either granaries or pantries. Why, then, do they wish to have hands idle but pantries full? Why do they gather in and save for their daily needs the things that they receive of the work of others? Why do they grind? Why do they cook? For verily the birds do not so."

1803 [4] *De sermone Domini, etc.*, II, 17, 58 (*loc. cit*). [The Saint's idea, in a nutshell, is that monks are violating the precept of Jesus when they practise the monastic profession as a way of getting a living without work; they are not disobeying the precept when they create and save wealth for the better service of God.—A. L.] A sermon attributed to St. Augustine, but which seems to be apocryphal, comes closer to the literal meaning of the Gospel text. In it the precept is taken as condemning greed, merely, and as a promise that God will take care to provide His faithful with material goods. In another sermon entitled *Eleemosinae efficacia: Inanis est avarorum providentia, Sermones* (*Opera,* Vol. V), CCCX, he writes: "Give alms! Why do you fear? He who made you His favourite petitioner (? *qui te praerogatorem constituit*) will not fail you. For His is the voice that chides untrustfulness in the Gospel, saying, 'Consider the fowls of the air for they sow not neither do they reap,' nor do they have wine-cellars or pantries, yet 'your Heavenly Father feedeth them.'" Perhaps; but when the snow is on the ground the poor birds get hungry, and not a few die; and such as live near human habitations are happy indeed to be fed on what human providence has in store.

1803 [5] Anselme of Laon [Pareto attributes this work to Anselm of Canterbury. I follow Migne.—A. L.], *Enarrationes in Evangelium Matthaei, VI* (6:25) (Migne, p. 1312): "*Ideo dico vobis: Ne soliciti sitis, etc.* And since you cannot serve God and mammon, be ye not solicitous [take no thought] of temporal wealth for the sake of food and raiment. There are two kinds of solicitude, the one arising from external circumstance, the other from the evil in man (*alia est rerum alia ex vitio hominum*). Solicitude arises from external circumstance in that we cannot have bread unless we sow, labour, and do other such things. Such solicitude the Lord does not forbid, for He says: 'In the sweat of thy face shalt thou eat bread. [That

thought shall one take of the morrow?" [6] Following his usual custom, he begins by bringing out the arguments in favour of the solution that he is later to reject, and which, in the present case, is that one should take thought for the morrow. In favour of that solution we get: 1. The passage on the provident ant in Prov. 6:6: ["Go to the ant, thou sluggard: Consider her ways and be wise."] 2. Providence is an aspect of prudence, which is a virtue. 3. The passage in John 12:6, from which it would appear that Jesus had a moneybag, which He entrusted to Judas ["For he had the bag and bare what was put therein"]; and another, Acts 4:34-35, where the Apostles are said to have kept the proceeds of the sale of the lands that were laid at their feet. "Hence it is permissible to take thought of the morrow. Against which stand the words of the Lord (Matt. 6:34): 'Take therefore no thought for the morrow.' . . . *Conclusion*: Man should take thought for the future at proper and opportune times, but not except at such times." [7] Of this invention of a "proper and opportune time" there is no trace in the Gospel; and much less of the further elucidations that St. Thomas proceeds to give: "There is a care proper to every season; so in the summer there is the care of reaping, in the autumn the care of gathering the grapes. If someone should be solicitous about the harvest in early summer, he would be taking undue thought for the morrow. Such a solicitude, therefore, being superfluous, the Lord prohibits when He says: 'Take therefore no thought for the morrow.'" As for the

shows that there are contradictory passages in the Old and New Testaments. It does not change the meaning of Matthew's words.] Labour and providence are therefore allowed us. But there is a certain superfluous solicitude that arises from the evil in men, when, not trusting in the goodness of God, they lay aside more provision and money than is necessary, and are intent on that to the extent of dismissing spiritual things from their minds. That is forbidden." The distinction between the two solicitudes is made by this Anselme—there is no trace of any such thing in Matthew. St. John Chrysostom also escapes in a similar way. After quoting the Lord's words about the fowls of the air, he adds, *Homilia XXI in capitulum Matthaei VI*, VI, 3 (4) (Gaume, Vol. VII, p. 309b; Prevost, p. 149a): "What, then? There must be no sowing, doth He say? Not that men must not sow, doth He say, but that one should not be absorbed in the thought [of sowing]; not that one should not work, but that one should not degrade oneself, and torment oneself, with worldly striving."

1803 [6] *Summa theologiae*, II[a] II[ae], qu. 55, art. 7 (*Opera*, Vol. VIII, pp. 402-03: *Utrum aliquis debeat esse sollicitus in futurum*).

1803 [7] "*Conclusio. Oportet hominem tempore congruenti atque opportuno non autem extra illud tempus de futuris esse sollicitum.*"

example of the ant, the answer is "that the ant's care is proper to the season and is therefore given us to imitate." When such a powerful mind as St. Thomas is found stooping to such wretched verbiage, one is really forced to the conclusion that the enterprise of harmonizing the letter of the Gospel precept with the necessities of practical life is a desperate one indeed.[8]

1804. In the fourth century of the Christian era the heresy of the Massalians (Pray-ers), also called Euchites (*Praecatores, Orantes*), and Enthusiasts, broke out. The Massalians were said to have been pagans originally,[1] and that may well be; for, after all, residues of asceticism are observable among the pagans as well as among Christians. Later on, at any rate, there were Christian heretics of the same persuasion. They refused to perform manual labour and spent their time praying and sleeping.[2] The Catholic Church has always held aloof from such extravagances. It repudiated the Massalians, therefore, and made at least an effort to discipline the contemplative life. The Church, however, has been called upon to combat such tendencies in all periods of its history.

1805. Specially interesting from that standpoint is the controversy of the Church with the Franciscans, who tried to dictate to the Church, but whom the Church managed to assimilate and use for its own purposes—one of the many examples that serve to show that the art of governing lies in manipulating residues, not in trying to change them.

1806. The twelfth and thirteenth centuries witnessed a rebirth of civilization in Italy and in France, which, as is always the case, expressed itself in an intensification of Class I residues, which began

1803 [8] [Pareto seems to overlook Anselme's phrase *"desperantes de bonitate Dei"* (§ 1803 [5]), which shows the ethical derivation for this Catholic view of "thought of the morrow."—A. L.]

1804 [1] St. Epiphanius, *Panarium adversus haereses, lib.* III, *tomus* II, *Haeresis* 80, 1-2 (*Opera*, Vol. II, pp. 755, 758): . . . ἀλλὰ μόνον Ἕλληνες ὄντες ("but being only Greeks"). Later on they called themselves Christians.

1804 [2] Theodoret, *Ecclesiastica historia,* IV, 10 (*Opera,* Vol. III, pp. 1142-43; Jackson, p. 114); and *Compendium haereticarum fabularum,* IV, 11 (*Opera,* Vol. IV, pp. 430-31): St. John Damascene, *De haeresibus,* 80 (97) (*Opera,* Vol. I, p. 731): "They avoid all manual labour as not befitting the Christian and unbecoming in him." St. Augustine, *De haeresibus ad Quodvultdeum,* 57 (*Opera,* Vol. VIII, p. 41): "The Euchitae are said to believe that it is not lawful for monks to do any work to earn their living, and so to have adopted the monk's profession in order to be free of all work."

more vigorously to dispute the dominance of group-persistences (Class II residues). The clergy were at that time the only intellectual class in society, and they were gradually approximating lay society in their morals. Moralists at the time described the development as a "perversion" of morals in the Catholic clergy; and so they were to describe it again, later on, during the Renaissance and at the time of the Protestant Reformation. They were right, if one adopt the standpoint from which they view the situation. But there is another point of view as well—the matter of progress in civilization. From this latter standpoint the so-called perversion of morals in the clergy represented a "betterment" in the conditions of life in society, which either ceases to progress or else actually retrogresses the moment morals are "corrected" or "reformed" through any considerable increase in certain Class II residues and in IV-ζ residues (asceticism). Not that good or bad morals in the clergy have any direct influence on progress in civilization. They are merely an index of the power of certain Class II residues, just as the rise of the mercury in a thermometer is not the cause of the rise in temperature but merely an index of it. In the twelfth and thirteenth centuries a tide of religious feeling, welling up then as it always does from the lower classes, arrested the progress of civilization; just as a tide of religious feeling represented by the Protestant Reformation was again to arrest it, though for a brief moment, later on. The mediaeval tidal wave left the Inquisition on the beach. The tidal wave of the sixteenth century left the Jesuits. Both waves set back for many generations that freedom of thought (Class I residues) towards which society had been advancing at the time when they occurred. Such are the facts, though they appear under greatly distorted forms in the various derivations (§§ 2329 f.).

1807. One of the greatest distortions—and with it it is timely for us to deal in particular at this point—views such phenomena as the consequences of certain logical interpretations of Scripture or other reasonings of the kind. Another, and certainly a not inconsiderable distortion, arrays on the one hand a Papacy resolved to govern despotically and enforce its "superstition," and on the other hand the heretics, who demand "liberty" and freedom of scientific thought. In point of fact "superstition" or, if one will, "religious sentiment" was more intense in the heretics than in the Papacy. They granted less liberty and, wherever they prevailed, they imposed very burdensome restrictive norms inspired by their ascetic spirit.[1] It should not be overlooked, further, that such tidal waves of religious feeling (prevalence of Class II residues) occurred both in the orthodox and in the heretical or schismatic sectors of Christendom; and that is even clearer proof that orthodoxy, heresy, and schism were alike mere veils hiding one common substance.

1808. Distortions of this kind underlie the many different interpretations of the facts. Enemies of the Papacy necessarily approve of all heretics, all schismatics; and it is amusing to see free-thinkers, who are avowed enemies of all religion, or profess to be, go into ecstasies of praise for individuals who sought to impose exceedingly strict and rigorous religious forms. How many modern admirers of Calvin that reformer would have persecuted and oppressed had they lived in his time! Villari calls himself a "positivist." He admires Savonarola for no other reason than that he was an enemy of the Pope. But if Villari had lived under the rule of that friar, neither he nor his "vanities" would have escaped with unruffled fur. After all, Pope Borgia persecuted neither literature nor science, while Savonarola, had he been able to have his way, would have destroyed all profane literature and all science, with the possible exception of theology, if that can be called a science. We are not asking here whether such a thing would have been "good" or "bad." We are simply calling attention to the contradiction involved in simultaneously admiring "free science" and the overbearing tyrannical superstition of a man like Savonarola.

1809. The tidal wave of religious feeling that broke in the Middle Ages manifested itself partly in heresies, such as the Albigensian, and partly in pious "works" such as the founding of the mendicant orders, which, if not exactly orthodox, were such at least in appearances. St. Francis of Assisi has had admirers all the way along to our

1807 [1] Speaking of the Franciscan intransigents in his *Eresia nel medio evo,* p. 518, Tocco says: "Underneath these petty pretexts the intransigents were really aiming much higher: to a declaration, namely, that the kind of life prescribed in the Rule did not differ from the evangelical life; that that was the life that Jesus and the Apostles had led, and that that was the life that not only the Friars Minor, but all Christians, since they must take the Gospel as the rule of their lives, should lead; which was another way of saying that not only the clergy but all Christendom ought to be turned into one vast Franciscan convent."

day, and can even count some now among votaries of the god Progress. He founded an order of friars for whom the Gospel verses about the fowls of the air and the lilies of the field were, or were supposed to be, a strict rule of life. It is evident that such persons can function only as exceptions in a civilized society. If the Franciscans are to live by alms, there must be other people to provide the alms; and if they are not going to take thought for the morrow, there must be people to do that thinking for them. They can be improvident only if they have a society of providents to live in—otherwise they all starve and the game is up.

1810. The attitudes of the various Popes towards the Franciscan movement were determined by a variety of causes. Religious sentiments (Class II residues) were not altogether without effect, and they were especially conspicuous under Celestine V. But the more influential residues were those of Class I. The Pope had to solve a problem that rulers are very frequently called upon to face: to find ways, through appropriate combinations and for the purpose of fighting their enemies, to avail themselves of the sentiments that might make new enemies for them, or be of service to enemies who were already there. Waves of religious fanaticism and superstition were beating high upon the dikes of the Papacy; and it sought materials for strengthening its ramparts of that very fanaticism, that very superstition. And so it is that the policy of the Papacy with regard to the Franciscans, which to the superficial glance seems vacillating and contradictory, proves on a deeper analysis of its substance, and with due allowances for exceptional cases such as that of Celestine V, to have been in all respects consistent and consistently aimed at one objective. The Popes favoured the Franciscans to the farthest limits of orthodoxy. When the Franciscans overstepped those limits, they repressed them. The Popes were willing to use them as auxiliaries. They could not tolerate them as enemies. They were glad to use them against heretics, and against rich and powerful elements in the clergy who were disposed to assert their independence of the Holy See. Moral reform was a good weapon for fighting such churchmen. But reform had to stop at the point beyond which the Holy See itself would have been hurt. In the end this latter conception prevailed; for, as always happens, the pretended return to the Gospel ended in being only a mask for heresy.[1] That indeed is the real reason why so many new admirers of St. Francis have come forward in our day. They are simply enemies of the Papacy and use praises of St. Francis as a weapon in their war.

1811. Active in them also is a residue of democratic humanitarianism, which was even more conspicuous in their predecessors—not only those Franciscans who were sticklers for the letter of the Rule, but the Catharists and other sects of the kind. At bottom the activities of both were in the direction of destroying civilization, representing as they did a predominance of Class II residues, which are always so powerful in the lower strata of society.

1812. Innocent III saw the absurdity of the Rule of St. Francis and was in doubt whether to approve or reject it.[1] "Certainly," says Tocco,[2] "he could not reject these new forces which had unexpectedly come to his aid in his fight on heresy; nor is there any doubt that he gave his blessing to the Mendicant of Assisi without forbidding him to go forward with his work. But he never was easy in his mind as to the Rule, which he thought did not take due account of the real needs and tendencies of human nature, nor did he ever consent to issue a bull approving it." Pope Honorius III took that step in 1223. He saw a new power rising and designed to take full advantage of it.

1810 [1] We have a long letter of John XXII in which he voices keen displeasure at the disobedience of the Minorites and rebukes them for trying to free themselves of the control of the Holy See. Baronio (Rinaldi), *Annales ecclesiastici, anno* 1318, XLV: ". . . such mental cases run in this wise (*sic sunt casus mentis*): that first the unfortunate spirit swells with pride, then by an unhappy gradation, not to say by a headlong plunge, it moves on to contention, and from contention to schism, from schism to heresy and from heresy to blasphemy."

1812 [1] Fleury, *Histoire ecclésiastique,* Vol. XX, Preface, pp. xii-xiii (speaking of the Franciscans): "It would, it seems, have been to the greater advantage of the Church for bishops and Popes to have applied themselves in earnest to reforming the secular clergy and putting it back on the footing of the first four centuries, without calling on these outside troops [the Franciscans] for help, so that there would have been but two sorts of persons sacred to God: clerics appointed to supervise the education and conduct of the faithful and absolutely subject to the bishops, and then monks holding entirely apart from the world and busied exclusively with praying and labouring in silence. In the thirteenth century, however, the idea of such perfection had been forgotten, and the impressive thing was the disorder to be seen before one's eyes: the greed of the clergy, their expensive living, their effeminate voluptuous habits, which had also spread to the endowed monasteries."

1812 [2] *Op. cit..*, p. 428.

1813. The Popes were not the only ones willing to use the religious enthusiasm of the Franciscans for their own ends. The Emperor Frederick II had the very same intention, and he had no religion to speak of, being, as a type, the exact opposite of Celestine V.[1] Such the substance over which a veil of derivations was spread. Suppose now we look at it more closely.

1814. Immediately after the death of St. Francis, and perhaps even earlier, contention arose in the order between those who wished to follow the Rule—or, if one will, the precept of Jesus—to the letter, and those who were disposed to reconcile both Rule and Gospel with the requirements of life in society.[1] In course of time the order was broken up into three branches: the "Little Friars" (*Fraticelli*) and the "Spirituals" (*Spirituali*), both strict observers of the Rule, but holding different theological views; then the "Conventuals"

1813 [1] Preaching a return to "evangelical poverty" was ever the favourite weapon of the enemies of the Papacy and Frederick II also used it. Tocco, *Op. cit.,* pp. 447-48: "As regards the secular clergy, Frederick's language is no different from the language of the intransigent Franciscans, as witness his letter to the King of England, Huillard-Bréholles, *Historia diplomatica Frederici Secundi,* Vol. III, p. 50: 'The primitive Church, in the days when she was producing in such fertility the saints who are listed in the calendar, had been founded on poverty and simplicity. But at no later date could anyone establish any foundation save that which had been laid and established by Our Lord. Now because they are wallowing in wealth, lolling in wealth, building in wealth, there is fear lest the wall of the Church be tottering and lest when the wall has been thrown down the fall of the whole ensue.'" And to combat Frederick, Gregory IX favoured the intransigent party among the Franciscans. Tocco, *Op. cit.,* pp. 445-46: "I think it probable that the Pope broke with the Franciscan General for political reasons. As we have already seen, the General was equally acceptable both to Gregory and to Frederick, and Salimbene tells us that he often acted as mediator between them. Perhaps in these dealings he may have shown himself more favourable to the Imperial cause. . . . In view of that Gregory surrendered to the intransigent party and not only deposed the unlucky General, but had him expelled from the order and solemnly excommunicated him, and worse certainly would have befallen him had not Frederick taken him under his protection. The shrewd Emperor, lying under a charge of heresy, found it to his advantage to have on his side a comrade of St. Francis who a few years before had been held in high esteem by the Pope himself."

1814 [1] Somewhat later, in 1311, a similar difference is defined in a bull by Clement V: *Clementis Papae V Constitutiones, lib.* V, *tit.* XI, *De verborum significatione, cap.* I, *Exivi de paradiso* (Friedberg, Vol. II, p. 1193): "In view of that a very knotty question arose among the friars as to whether they were bound by profession of the Rule to the strictly meagre or 'poor' use of property requisite for sustaining life (*ad arctum et tenuem sive pauperem usum rerum*), some of them believing and saying that they had made a very strict renunciation in their vow as

(*Conventuali*) who interpreted the Rule somewhat liberally.[2] Pope Celestine V allowed another order to secede from the Friars Minor, to be known as the Friars of Pope Celestine (Celestines) or Poor Hermits. This order too was uncompromising as to observance of the Rule. That Pope was a simple soul and very devout. He did not last long on the throne of St. Peter. On the other hand Pope Boniface VIII, who replaced him, was a shrewd diplomat and persecuted the Poor Hermits.[3]

1815. In a word, since it was impossible to live without property and without providence, some subterfuge had to be found for interpreting the Gospel precept and the Rule of St. Francis in such a way that they would not jar too violently with property and providence. Derivations, as we have seen, are like rubber bands and can be stretched to mean anything desired. It was therefore not dif-

regarded ownership of property, so that the strictest frugality and meagreness were prescribed for them as regarded its use [*i.e.,* quite apart from ownership]; others holding to the contrary that they were bound by their profession to no practice of poverty (*ad nullum usum pauperem*) not expressly prescribed in the Rule, though they were indeed bound to the moderate observance of temperance to the same extent as other Christians and, concededly, more so."

1814 [2] Tocco, *Op. cit.,* p. 500, note: "*Liber sententiarum inquisitionis Tholosanae,* p. 326: 'He said that he had heard from certain Friars Minor about the so-called Spirituals of Narbonne and so he thought that things were in such a state that the Friars Minor ought to be divided into three parts, namely, into the community of the order that wishes to own barns and cellars, then the Brothers (Friars) and Little Brothers who are in Sicily under Fra Enrico de Ceva, and finally the friars called Spirituals or Poor Friars and also Beguines. And they [the friars in Narbonne] had said that the first two divisions were destined to decline and be destroyed as not observing the rule of the Blessed Francis, but that the third part, since it observed the evangelical rule, was to endure to the end of the world.' "

1814 [3] Fleury, *Histoire ecclésiastique,* Vol. XVIII, pp. 535-43: "Those among the Friars Minor who professed greatest zeal for strict observance did not fail to profit by the favourable attitude of Pope Celestine towards austerity and reform. They therefore sent two of their number to him, Fra Liberatus and Fra Pier de Macerata. They called on the Pope . . . and requested that with his authorization, which no one would dare dispute, they should be allowed to live according to the purity of their rule and the intent of St. Francis. That they readily obtained. But the Pope further granted them permission to live together wheresoever they chose in order to be at liberty to practise their strict observance. . . . And he ordered that they should no longer be called Friars Minor but Poor Hermits, and later on they came to be called the Hermits of Pope Celestine [Celestines]. So, though Celestine's intentions were of the purest, the simplicity in which he lived his whole life, his inexperience, and the feebleness due to age, led him into making many mistakes. . . . Boniface began his pontificate by revoking the favours that Celestine had granted through the abuse people had made of his simplicity."

ficult to find, let alone one device, any number of devices. The principal ones enjoined observance of the letter on the friars, while other persons did the owning and the saving for them. Gregory IX assigned that function to "dummies," who were outsiders. John XXII assigned it to Superiors in the Order, to whom the ordinary friars owed obedience. That he did because his enemies were using the point of the "dummies" as a weapon against him; but had he chosen, he could have stuck to Gregory IX's interpretation and made it mean whatever he pleased.

1816. The derivation contrived by Gregory IX was an ingenious one. The Rule forbade the friars to receive money. How then were they to buy or sell? Very simple! A person not bound to observe the Rule receives the money and spends it for the friars! The friars must hold no property of their own. How then can they own both real and personal property? No difficulty! Some other persons hold the bare title, and the friars enjoy the use of the property. So too other persons are prevented from appropriating the property the friars are using. They stick to the Rule, resisting nobody who would rob them; but along comes the titular owner and does the resisting. Tolstoy, in his day, got along in just that fashion. He never "resisted evil," he never repelled the thief who would despoil him. But his wife was there, resisting, repelling, and managing the property on which her husband lived and had his being.

1817. Innocent IV, in 1245, and Nicholas III, in 1279, gave sounder form to the theory. Pope Nicholas says that a distinction has to be made between ownership, possession, and usufruct (usufact), that there can be no calling that bars the use of the things necessary for subsistence. He shows at great length that, in spirit, the Rule of St. Francis conceded such use. The Rule says that friars may own breviaries. That means usufruct of breviaries and other books required in the performance of divine offices. The Rule allows the brothers to preach: "The which of a certain presupposes knowledge; and knowledge requires study, and one cannot suitably study without the use of books. From all the which it appears that the Rule grants the friars the use of things necessary to feeding and clothing themselves, to the observance of divine worship, and to learned study." Anyone desiring to make a gift to the friars means to make a gift to God, "nor is there person to whom, in the stead of God, one may more fittingly transfer ownership than to the Holy See and the person of the Roman Pontiff, Vicar of Christ, who is the father of all men and especially of the Friars Minor." [1] With the ordinance, *Exivi de paradiso* . . . of Pope Clement V, we go back for a brief spell to literal interpretation, and once more their lords and ladyships, the birds who are fed by divine Providence, come on the scene.[2] Then came Pope John XXII, who was more keenly awake to the exigencies of practical life; and since he had grounds for dissatisfaction with the dissident Friars Minor, he turned against them. He found no trouble in putting his finger on the weak spot in Gregory's derivation and showing how ridiculous it was to divorce ownership from usufact as regards things that are consumed; for it truly is a laughable thought that the ownership of a piece of bread should be of some other person than the one who eats it. Since the quarrel among the Franciscans had degenerated, as things have a way of going in such cases, into childish disputes as to the cut and the length of Franciscan habits, John XXII decreed, in a constitution of 1317, that it was for the Superiors of the Franciscans to determine the cut of habits and the quality of cloth, and to lay in stores of grain and wine, further reminding the brethren that the principal virtue they were expected to show was obedience.[3] But the

---

1817 [1] Boniface VIII, *Sexti decretales, lib.* V, *tit.* 12, *De verborum significatione, cap.* 3: *Exiit qui seminat* (Friedberg, Vol. II, p. 1109). And he continues with this specification: "And that the ownership of such things may not seem to be uncertain and since the property that is offered, granted, or given is acquired by the son for the father, by the slave for the master, by the monk for the monastery, we, therefore, by this present constitution forever valid, rule (as our predecessor of blessed memory Pope Innocent, fourth of that name, is known to have ruled) that the proprietorship and ownership of utensils, books, and furnishings present and future, which said Orders or said friars shall lawfully hold or of which they shall have usufruct, fully and freely belongs to us and to the Roman Church."

1817 [2] Clement V, *Constitutiones, lib.* V, *tit.* 11, *De verborum significatione, cap.* 1: *Exivi de paradiso* (Friedberg, Vol. II, p. 1198): "Inasmuch as the aforesaid saint [Francis], both in the examples he set in his life and through the words of his Rule, made it clear that he desired that his brothers [friars] and sons, should, trusting in Divine Providence, turn all their thoughts to God, who feeds the fowls of the air which neither sow nor reap nor gather into barns, it is not plausible that it was his intent that they should have barns or cellars, since they should hope to be able to live their lives through daily mendication."

1817 [3] John XXII, *Extravagantes, lib.* XXII, *tit.* 14, *De verborum significatione, cap.* 1: *Quorundam exigit* (Friedberg, Vol. II, p. 1222) (The ordinance was proclaimed more than once and therefore bears various dates posterior to 1317): "By

Franciscans were not hushed. They made bold to defy the Pope's expressed will, and he was accordingly moved to expand his derivation.[4] He revoked the bull of Nicholas III; and then, in the bull *Ad conditorem,* he asserted that it was, in general, altogether permissible for one Pope to revoke the ordinances of his predecessors and demonstrated the ineptitude of distinguishing between owner-

the authority of these presents we commit it to the judgment of said ministers, guardians, and wardens to consider, determine, and rule as to the length, breadth, thickness, thinness, shape, cut, or whatever similar attribute, of the habit, cowl, or inner tunic that all Friars Minor of said order shall wear. . . . In the matter of the petition (*consilio*) of our afore-said friars, we likewise and in the same form by authority of these presents commit it to the judgment of the said ministers and wardens to consider, determine, and rule as to how, when, where, and how often they shall obtain and store up grain, bread, and wine for the subsistence of the friars and as to the quality thereof and also as to whether it shall be stored and kept in said barns and cellars. . . . For it is to the hurt of religion if subordinates are withdrawn from their proper obedience. Great is poverty but greater is purity (*integritas*), and greatest of all is obedience if it be perfectly observed. For poverty rules material things, purity the flesh, but obedience the mind and soul which, as it were unbridled (*effraenes*) and impatient of external control, it humbly brings under the yoke of the will."

1817 [4] In 1318, in Marseilles, four Friars Minor chose to go to the stake rather than obey the Pope. The sentence of condemnation, quoted by Tocco, *Op. cit.,* p. 516, says of them: "They asserted that the Most Holy Father John XXII did not have and does not have the authority (*potestatem*) to make the statements, commitments, and orders contained in a certain constitution or decretal beginning *Quorundam exigit* . . . and that they were not called upon to obey said Pope (*Domino Papae*). Brought into our presence, they protested orally and in writing that they stood by their protests and intended to stand by them till the Day of Judgment . . . to wit, that that which is against the observance and sense (*intelligentiam*) of the Rule of the Friars Minor is consequently against the Gospel and the faith—otherwise it would not be exactly what the Gospel rule was (? *alias non esset penitus quod regula evangelica*), and that no mortal would be able to compel them to lay aside their short tight habits." John XXII, *Extravagantes, lib. XII, tit. 14, De verborum significatione, cap. 5: Quia quorundam mentes* (Friedberg, Vol. II, p. 1230). The Pope rebukes and condemns the attitude of those who do not bow to his ordinance *Quorundam exigit,* and says of the Friars Minor: "To impugn the aforesaid constitutions on the grounds mentioned, they are reported to have made public use of the spoken and written word. Anything, they say, in the spheres of morals and faith that the Roman Pontiffs have once decided through the key of knowledge remains immutable, so that it is unlawful for a successor to cast doubt upon it or rule to its contrary; though they say the situation is different in things that they [the Roman Pontiffs] have ordained through the key of power. They say that the following words are contained in the confirmation of the Rule of the Order of the Friars Minor by Honorius III, Gregory IX, Innocent IV, Alexander IV, and Nicholas IV, our predecessors as supreme pontiffs: 'This is the evangelical rule of Christ and one that imitates the Apostles in that it recognizes no

ship and usufruct in the case of things that are physically consumed.[5] He accordingly repudiated ownership of the property of the Friars Minor, which they claimed was his, and handed it back to the friars themselves to dispose of through their Superiors.[6] Such great fluctuations in interpretation show how truly insuperable the difficulties were in the way of reconciling the theoretical strictness of the Franciscan Rule with practical life. In the case of the Franciscans we see them enlarged, as it were, under a lens, but they are no less discernible in such doctrines as pacifism, humanitarianism, and non-resistance to evil, and they also arise, though in differing and sometimes in minor proportions, in almost all ethical doctrines, all theories of natural law, and other theories of the kind, which can be defended only by resort to ingenious, nay, thaumaturgic sophistries and interpretations that strip them of every speck and particle of definiteness.

individual or common property (*nihil habet proprium vel commune*), but they have simple usufact (*usum facti*) in the things they use.' To all that they go so far as to add that the afore-said Supreme Pontiffs and many general Councils have ruled by the key of knowledge that the poverty of Christ and the Apostles consisted perfectly in an expropriation of temporal ownership of a civil or worldly character and that their sustenance consisted of nothing but pure usufruct. From that they try to conclude that it has not been and is not lawful for the successors [of those Popes] to make changes in any respect against those premises."

1817 [5] John XXII, *Extravagantes*, VI, 3, 14: *Ad conditorem canonum* (Friedberg, Vol. II, p. 1225). The following summary of the ordinance is supplied by Lancelotto in *Corpus iuris canonici accademicum*, Basel, 1783, Vol. II, p. 395 (*Institutiones iuris canonici*): "The Supreme Pontiff refutes the assertion that ownership of the property coming into the possession of the Friars Minor has been held by the Roman Church, simple usufact thereof being reserved to said friars in the constitution *Exiit qui seminat*. He shows by many reasons that they cannot have simple usufact in anything; and he rules that furthermore the Roman Church shall have no right or title of ownership in things that thenceforward shall be given or offered to said friars." Of commodities for physical consumption the Pope says: "For who could be of mind so unsound as to believe that so great a father ever meant to hold that in the case of an egg, a piece of cheese, a crumb of bread, or of the other victuals that are oftentimes given to such friars for consumption on the spot (*e vestigio*), the ownership belongs to the Roman Church, the use to the friars?"

1817 [6] John XXII, *Extravagantes, lib.* XXII, *tit.* 14, *cap.* 3: *Ad conditorem canonum* (Friedberg, Vol. II, p. 1225). The Pope expresses his eagerness to get back to verities of fact and have done with fictions that might bring discredit upon the Church. Then he concludes: "Regarding the opinion of our friars, we declare by this edict for all time valid that in the property which hereafter shall be given or offered to or otherwise acquired by the afore-said friars or order of friars (with the exception of churches, oratories, workshops, dwellings, and vessels, books and vest-

1818. In our day Tolstoy has furnished some fresh samples of absurd derivations in his theory of non-resistance to evil. More or less like him are those anti-militarists who would disarm their own countries and dream of a universal peace, and further splendour is added to that egregious company by our enemies of alcoholic beverages and amorous pleasures—in fact, all material pleasures—and by our ultra-hygienists who live in holy horror of the microbe.

1819. Many among all such are those who as preachers preach well, but as practitioners practise badly. Words are one thing, actions quite another. At best the more scrupulous among them try to reconcile words with conduct. Often the person who admires and hails Tolstoy's evangelical doctrine that we should not defend our property against those who would relieve us of it shows himself, when

ments dedicated or to be dedicated to divine offices, which shall come to them hereafter and to which the afore-said difficulties do not extend—wherefore we do not wish this constitution to apply to them) the Roman Church acquires no right or title whatsoever in virtue of the above-mentioned ordinance or of any other ordinance proclaimed specially on this matter by any of our predecessors, but that such ordinances shall in this regard be held henceforward as null and void." On this point there was a long and acrimonious dispute between the Pope and the Franciscans, the latter supported by Ludwig of Bavaria; for, as usual, a real issue lay concealed under the derivations—in this case the quarrel between Papacy and Empire. The Pope deposed and excommunicated Michael of Cesena, General of the Franciscans. He then published the celebrated bull *Quia vir reprobus,* in which subtly and at length he refutes the former General's animadversions, and which is evidently a comprehensive treatise on the whole matter. It is interesting to note that the Pope perceived the ineptitude of taking a natural law, or law of nations, as the basis of legality. However, he wanted to keep a natural law all the same, so he went looking about for a derivation suited to the purpose and, as always happens, readily found one, making human law a corollary of divine law: "That no property right in temporal things could have been given to man by any human law, but only by divine law, is evident; for it is granted that no one can give anything away unless he be the owner of it, or by the will of the owner. There is no doubt that God is the owner of all temporal things whether by right of creation, since He created them out of nothing, or by right of manufacture, since He made them of His materials. It follows that no king could rule as to ownership of such things save by will of God." Admitting the premises, the syllogism is perfect; and if logic had anything to do with such things, we should have to recognize that the Pope's reasoning shows not a wrinkle: "Whence it is evident that neither by natural primeval law—if it be taken as that law that is common to all living creatures, though such a law does not legislate (*nihil statuat*) but merely inclines or guides living creatures in common to the doing of certain things —nor by law of nations, nor by the law of kings or emperors, was property ownership in temporal things introduced, but it was conferred upon our first parents by God who was and is the owner of them."

it comes to conduct, a relentless creditor who will not let a debtor get away with a farthing, finding, as occasion requires, no end of pretexts to justify such procedure amply.[1] There are pacifists and anti-militarists a-plenty who nevertheless will have their own countries great and powerful in war and who can fish up the most ingenious arguments in praise of "wars to end war." How many the people who would prohibit the use of alcohol, but themselves consume, for their health, they say, ether, morphine, or cocaine, or drink enough tea to contract a malady that has been named "teaism." And how many others go out with their mistresses on their arms to work in campaigns "for the elevation of morals" or the suppression of the "white-slave trade," and then justify themselves by the claim that they have a right to "live their own lives."

1820. Eusebius, *Evangelica praeparatio*, XIV, 7 (*Opera*, Vol. III, pp. 1211-12), repeats after Numenius an anecdote, fictitious beyond a doubt, but which shows as under a magnifying glass the issue here in point. Numenius relates that one Lacides, who was being secretly robbed by his slaves, observed that the good things in his pantry kept disappearing but could not discover what was becoming of them. He chanced to hear a discourse by Arcesilaus on the impossibility of our understanding anything. He was convinced forthwith, and in his turn began professing the doctrine that we can know nothing for certain, adducing in proof his own experience with his pantry. One of his hearers, who knew the trick the slaves were using, revealed it to him, whereupon the good man took measures to lock his pantry more securely. But the slaves, nothing daunted, broke the seals and then brazenly told their master that being certain of nothing, he could not be certain, either, that he had put seals on the pantry. The game lasted a long time to the damage and rage of poor Lacides; until he threw philosophy by the board one day and said to his slaves: "Young men, in the schools we reason in one way; but at home hereafter we are going to live in quite another."

1821. Once one is started on the road of derivations it is easy to

1819 [1] There is nothing new under the Sun. This type of person has his counterpart among the devout in all countries in all periods of history. The religious fanatics of the past and our present-day humanitarians are of the same breed. See, in § 1172 [1], the quotations from Molière and the *Sorberiana*.

go to ridiculous extremes. In the sixteenth century one Simon Gedik made a rejoinder in all earnestness to a book which set out to show that women did not belong to the human race—*mulieres non esse homines*—though it was just a satirical jest at the expense of the Socinians.[1]

1822. Another important illustration of the ways in which people try to escape the logical consequences of certain principles is the case of morality. Civilized peoples naïvely imagine that they follow in practice the principles of a certain theoretical ethics. In point of fact, they act very differently indeed and then resort to subtle interpretations and ingenious casuistries to reconcile theory and practice that are ever and anon discordant.

1823. At every step in the history of the civilized peoples we find applications of the principle that the end justifies the means, and those who assert the principle explicitly are not the ones who make most lavish use of it. Every sect, every party, accuses its adversaries of immoral acts, while it fails altogether to see its own. How loudly have "liberals" not decried the misdeeds of "reactionary" governments, only to do worse themselves! In Italy the older governments were accused of "speculating in immorality" in conducting lotteries, but the highly moral government that succeeded them has main-

---

1821 [1] Bayle, *Dictionnaire historique, s.v. Gediccus, remarque* (A): "The author of the dissertation has no special grudge against women. He abuses them just incidentally and quite indirectly. His principal aim is to ridicule the system of the Socinians and their way of playing wtih the most positive texts of God's Word touching the divinity of the *Verbum*. A journalist noted the fact long long ago. Here is what he said, *Nouvelles de la république des lettres*, July, 1685, p. 802: '. . . The Socinians pay with such wretched sophistries that they were once shown that with their glosses one could eliminate from the Scriptures every passage tending to prove that women are human beings—I mean, of the same species as men. That was the subject of a little book that appeared toward the end of the last century. . . . A certain Simon Gedik, Prime Minister of Brandenburg, wrote an answer [*Defensio sexus muliebris*, The Hague, 1638, new ed., 1707] in all seriousness, failing to catch the intent of the author, which was to write a violent satire against the Socinians.' Dobeneck used the same device, but quite unavailingly, against Luther, writing books by Luther's method, and proving by passages from Scripture that Jesus Christ was not God at all, that God had to obey the Devil and that the Holy Virgin did not preserve her virginity." "Théophile Raynaud," Bayle continues, "had just given [*Erotemata de malis ac bonis libris*, III, 3, no. 514 (*Opera*, Vol. XI, p. 366)] a fine example of the power of verbal trickery, showing that if one were to follow the principles of certain censors the Apostles' Creed would not contain an item that could pass the censorship."

tained and continues to maintain that form of gambling. Judges penalize gamblers in the name of a government that derives an annual income of tens of millions from the lottery.[1] In France and other countries horse-racing takes the place of the lottery. The Austrian censors were ridiculous, but not more ridiculous than Luzzatti, in distributing fig-leaves right and left to statues in public museums. The Neapolitan Bourbons, it is said, were friendly with the Camorra; but the government that succeeded them does not disdain to show its benevolence to the same "gangs," in order to get parliamentary elections to its liking.

1824. There are hosts of estimable people who have not a word of censure for the men who cast ballots for absentees and for the dead in southern France, yet who fly into a fury, and in utter good faith, at the mere thought of a Jesuit's contending that the end justifies the means. Among the people in Italy who tolerated the un-

---

1823 [1] Martello, *"Considerazioni in difesa del giuoco d'azzardo,"* pp. 491-92: "I have said that the lottery is a game of robbery. I was not speaking metaphorically. That was the literal truth. The lottery is a game of robbery because it does not limit its winnings, as roulette, which is a game of pure chance, does. It keeps 85 of the 90 numbers in the urn in its own favour. In roulette the person who bets 1 franc on one colour wins 1 franc; on 6 numbers, he wins 5 and gets back his own; on the 'dozen' or 'column' (12 numbers), he wins 11 and gets back his own. Anyone who bets 1 franc *en plein,* who bets, that is, 1 franc on any one number of the 36, wins 35 and gets back his own. Anyone who desires to bet on the bank bets on zero. The Royal Lottery pays 10½ times the stake to the winner of the 'simple draw.' If it operated on the same principle as roulette, it would pay 18 times the stake—in other words, as many more times the stake as there are more probabilities in its favour (17 + 1). To the winner of the 'specified draw' *(estratto determinato)* the Royal Lottery pays 52½ times the stake, instead of 90 (a 41.67 per cent robbery, if you please). From that point on the robbery grows by leaps and bounds: to the winner of the *ambo* [two-number series] it pays 250 times the stake, instead of 400½ times (a 37.58 per cent robbery); to the winner of a *terno* [three-number series] it pays 4,250 times the stake, instead of 11,748 times (a 63.82 per cent robbery); to the winner of a *quaterno* [four-number series] it pays 60,000 times the stake, instead of 511,038 (an 88.26 per cent robbery). . . . Observe, moreover, that whatever the stake may be for any ticket *(terno, quaterno, cinquina)* the Royal Lottery refuses to pay the winner more than 400,000 lire; so that the person who stakes 100 lire on a *quaterno* ought to receive a sum amounting to 511,038 times the stake, or 51,103,800 lire; but since the winner of the *quaterno* receives a sum amounting to 60,000 times the stake, a 100-lire ticket ought to bring him 6,000,000 lire. In point of fact, in virtue of the limitations shown above, he receives only 400,000 lire, and the robbery, therefore, amounts to 93.33 per cent. But that is not all. The Royal Lottery will not pay more than 6,000,000 lire to cover all the winnings from a single drawing on all the frames in the king-

lawful appropriations revealed by the bank investigations, and who continue to tolerate similar "graft," are to be found honest citizens who believe that they are faithfully following the principles of a theoretical morality. Among the people in France who approved of the State's Attorney-General, Bulot, when he declared that magistrates must bow to the *"fait du prince"* under penalty of dismissal, are to be found individuals of at least average morality who believe in all good faith that the present government has done away with the abuses of justice which disgraced the old governments and that if there were privileged persons under the monarchy, under the Republic there is equality before the law; nor is their faith in any way shaken by cases such as the Rochette or Mme. Caillaux affairs.[1]

1825. *Measures for attaining a given end.* So far our concern has been with real movements. Let us now turn to a problem pertaining to virtual movements and inquire as to what occurs when residues or derivations are modified (§§ 133-34).[1]

dom; and if the gains of any one drawing should amount to a sum greater than 6,000,000 lire, all the gains of all the tickets sold in all offices would be reduced in corresponding proportions. In that case the robbery has no fixed percentage, but it is greater than the percentage indicated above according to the sum above 6,000,000 lire that the gains may total. By this trick the state takes yearly a sum of over 90,000,000 lire from the meagre resources of the most numerous and least pecunious portion of the Italian population." Such the "ethical state," such the "state of right," of our moralists!

1824 [1] For Bulot's remark see Pareto, *Manuale,* Chap. II, § 50 [1]: *"Sembat:* The State's Attorney has also spoken of some 'higher interest' in this case. Am I to infer that there is a 'reason of state' to which a magistrate is required to bow? *Bulot.* On pain of dismissal! Of course! (*Laughter*)." In 1914 a parliamentary investigating commission established that a French Attorney-General and a president of a Court of Appeals had bowed before the *"raison d'état"* incarnate in the person of one Monis, and had favoured one Rochette, against the evidence and the law. At that time many people were surprised and others were shocked at this practical application of a theory that had been stated in words years before by State's Attorney Bulot, which was perfectly well known to them, and which is continually being applied by all parties in power in France (§ 2262 [2]). Here we are merely trying to call attention to the gap that exists between theory and practice, and at the same time to the illusion under which people are labouring in believing that the two things coincide. We are not passing judgment of any kind on the effects, whether socially beneficial or otherwise, of such disaccord, nor on the effects beneficial or otherwise of its being generally known or unknown to the public at large.

1825 [1] We shall conduct this research by considering certain groups of residues and derivations separately (§ 1687). That will give us a part of the phenomenon, but only a part. To grasp it in its entirety we shall have to take all the elements acting upon society and consider them as a whole. That task we reserve for our next

1826. We must keep before us here the classification of derivations outlined above in § 1688: *derivations proper* and *manifestations* corresponding respectively to demonstrations and doctrines. Let us take a group of sentiments, *P,* which gives rise to residues or, better, to groups of residues, *a, b, c.* . . . From one of these, *a,* we obtain, by way of derivations proper, *m, n, p* . . . manifestations or doctrines, *r, s, t* . . . and so for the other groups, *b, c.* . . . Only for the sake of simplicity do we take a single group of sentiments. In

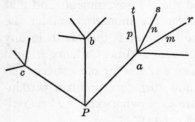

Figure 28

reality we ought to consider larger numbers of them, their effects appearing now distinct, now combined in certain groups of residues. However, such a synthetic view can readily be obtained from the elements that we are about to set forth.

1827. We may distinguish various cases of virtual movements. 1. The case where *a* is suppressed is the simplest. That suppression involves the suppression of manifestations *r, s, t* . . . and that would be the end of it were it not that there are other groups like *a* that remain intact. When that is the case, the manifestations *r, s, t* do disappear, but others of the same type are still left. Furthermore the disappearance or weakening of the group *a* may be offset by a reenforcement in other residues of the same class (§ 1742), or by the development of new ones.

1828. In that we are simply restating in different terms a situation which we noted above when we said that in a community at all large a class of residues taken as a whole varies but little, much less than single genera and species.[1]

chapter, where (§ 2087) we shall study the composition of certain forces that we here consider separately. Fundamental to our present research is the inquiry we completed above in §§ 1735-67, as to the reciprocal influence of residues and derivations, but whereas at that time we were trying to determine the general character of that influence, here we are trying to see what it must be like in order to realize certain specified purposes.

1828 [1] The point is of great importance, but to treat it with the thoroughness it deserves would require as much space as this entire sociology. We must therefore halt in our advance along that road, all the more since we have still a number of other very important problems to examine and into them as well we shall be unable to go as deeply as we would wish.

1829. 2. What happens if one or more of the derivations proper, *m, n, p* . . . is modified or destroyed? That question we have already answered in its general form, finding that in many cases derivations (or, more exactly, the complex of derivations proper and manifestations) were of secondary importance as compared with residues, while the rôle of derivations proper was still less significant and often times negligible. The production of such derivations is a very easy matter, and if one is refuted another takes its place forthwith and there is no change whatever in the substantial situation. However, that is just a first approximation. Secondary as the influence may be and at times very feeble, the derivations proper can never be absolutely without influence. To get a second approximation, therefore, one would have to see what that influence is.[1]

1830. 3. What happens if one or more of the manifestations *r, s, t* . . . are modified or eliminated? To answer the question one has to recall all that we have learned, from examples without end, about reciprocal influences of the residues *a* and the manifestations *r, s, t.* . . . The principal and by far the most important influence is that of *a* on *r, s, t.* . . . A whole class of residues (activity residues, Class III) are driving the individuals who have them to produce those manifestations. If that influence were the only one, if there were no other similar pressures, the elimination of *r* would have no other consequence than the disappearance of *r*. Conversely, if some public authority or other compelled individuals to perform *r,* the only effect of the compulsion would be the appearance of *r*.

1831. That that is the main element in the situation is shown by the fact that if a person believes in a religion he feels a need for performing the rites of its cult, whereas, conversely, to enforce observance of a cult upon persons without the corresponding religious sentiments by no means engenders such sentiments in them.

1832. But in addition to this principal element there is a secondary one—a reverse action, namely, of *r* upon *a*. 1. Spontaneous manifestations of certain sentiments have the effect of strengthening them. Religious sentiment inspires people to perform the rites of a cult, and the performance intensifies the religious sentiment

---

1829 [1] There again considerations of space prevent our dwelling too long on the subject in these volumes. We must rest content with a few glimpses.

(§ 1747). Manifestations that are not spontaneous may sometimes have similar effects, generally very feeble ones; but they also have other effects in a contrary direction, in reaction to the violence to which the individual has to submit. In certain cases such effects may be very considerable. 2. If certain manifestations, *r,* are suppressed spontaneously, the effect may be the reverse of what it was in the case of spontaneous performance: the sentiments corresponding to *a* may, that is, be weakened. A similar effect, also very considerable in certain cases, takes place when manifestations are scoffed at with impunity. Ridicule is a weapon that often (not always) proves effective in weakening residues of group-persistence. The situation where manifestations are suppressed by force is a complicated one.[1] In general one might say that if the sentiments corresponding to the manifestations that are suppressed are at all strong, sentiments are strengthened as a reaction to the suppression.[2] If, instead, the sentiments are weak, they may in the long run be weakened. Again in general, the use of force to prevent overt scoffing at certain observances is more effective than the use of force to impose them. To protect certain group-persistences (Class II residues) directly is of little avail. To protect them indirectly by forbidding overt expressions of disrespect towards them may often be most efficacious. That is a particular case of the general rule that it is wiser and easier for a government to exploit existing residues than to modify them (§ 1843).

1833. The reason why strong sentiments are strengthened is that, in reality, the manifestation *r* is not suppressed; it merely ceases to be public. But it endures in private, perhaps only in the secret of the individual heart, and the sentiments are re-enforced by the very obstacles that are thrown in the way of their expression. With that qualification, therefore, one may say that to suppress *r* always

---

1832 [1] A particular case of that we examined in §§ 1752 f.

1832 [2] [*From the French ed.:* Literary observations in this sense abound. One thinks of the well-known lines:

"*L'absence est à l'amour ce qu'est au feu le vent;*
il éteint le petit, il allume le grand."

("Absence is to love as wind to fire: the little one it extinguishes, the great one it rouses.")]

weakens *a* to a greater or lesser extent, provided the suppression is real and extends to the individual's inner thought.[1]

1834. We now have the general explanation of the particular case examined in §§ 1748-54 above. If in the logico-experimental sciences an assertion, *A,* is effectively refuted by showing that it is false (§ 1748), that happens because the manifestation, *r,* the act of assertion—comes to an end, and because it has no sentiments, *a,* of any particular strength to support it. The rule is proved by the exception, when a scientist is swayed by personal vanity or some other sentiment, and holds to *A* without regard to the logico-experimental value' of its demonstration. If, in matters involving sentiment and non-logical conduct, opposition to the manifestation *r* does not deprive it of its vitality (§ 1748), that is due to the fact that the sentiments manifested by *r* are not weakened, but, in some cases, strengthened (§§ 1749-50).

1835. What we called (§ 1751) the indirect effect of refutations and persecutions is the effect of attacking manifestations that we are considering here, the manifestation comprising the two elements noted in § 1747—the manifestation of sentiments or concepts previously existing and corresponding to *a,* and the effect proper of the derivation (§ 1751).

1836. The sentiments that we call "strong" considering a population or a social class as a whole, may be so intrinsically, or because they are stirred by a large number of pressures, or because they are shared by a large number of individuals. And so for sentiments that we speak of as "weak." That is why, in § 1752, we took account not only of the intrinsic strength of sentiments, but of the more or less extensive numbers of facts and individuals that are affected by this or that measure.

1837. When the external suppression of *r* intensifies *a,* it follows, as a consequence, that *s, t* . . . are also intensified—that, in other

---

1833 [1] [*From 1916 ed.:* To many people it is a matter of no consequence as regards the social equilibrium, whether a derivation lapses from currency because it is rejected by the public or because it is condemned by some public authority. The two cases are, however, radically different. In the first case the lapse indicates that a change is taking place in the social equilibrium; in the second, it merely indicates a desire on the part of public authorities to change a situation by action that, more often than not, will prove ineffective.]

words, there are cases where the weakening or elimination of one manifestation, r, has the effect of intensifying other manifestations, s, t. . . . That effect is very like the effect that results when one group of residues is weakened and other residues are intensified, by way of compensation. Both those effects may be observable simultaneously.

1838. From what has just been said a number of important consequences as regards virtual movements follow. Suppose we arrange them under four heads:[1]

α. If a government desires to suppress a certain group of residues, a, it can do so most effectively by destroying, if possible, all individuals who show such residues. The effectiveness of this measure is illustrated by Spain, where the Inquisition succeeded in extirpating heresy and free-thought. Had the Roman State been able to deal with Christianity in similar fashion, it would probably have been successful in extirpating it. It failed in that because the residues, a, that found expression in Christianity, r, were the same residues that found expression in the cult of Mithras, s; in the solar (Osiris) cult, t; in Neo-Platonism, v; in Philo's mysticism, x; and in many other ways, y, z, . . . and the Emperor Julian, a great enemy of the Christians, shared those residues with them. All the manifestations r, s, t, v, x, y, z . . . , so different in appearances, for the most part belonged to the one group of sentiments, a, which were shared by so many people that to destroy a would have meant destroying the entire population, virtually, of the Roman Empire, an enterprise manifestly impossible. The Emperor Constantine acted more wisely than his predecessors. He did not apply himself obstinately to destroying or modifying the sentiments a. He exploited them as instrumentalities of government (§ 1843).

1839. Suppression of the residues a may occur spontaneously, and in that case we get real, instead of virtual, movements. Events that deeply impress a population modify sentiments in the individuals who have witnessed them very considerably. But when those individuals are all, or almost all, dead, their successors know of those events only by hearsay or tradition and are much less deeply impressed by them. In that sense, one may say, roughly, that the in-

1838 [1] a, §§ 1838-41; β, §§ 1842-49; γ, §§ 1850-59; δ, §§ 1860-62.

dividuals who harboured the sentiments corresponding to the group *a* have disappeared.[1]

1840. A similar situation arises when, instead of disappearing, individuals harbouring the sentiments *a* come on the scene. That is what took place in the Roman Empire when the ancient population of Latium, and indeed of Italy, gave way to a population of freedmen or other sorts of people hailing chiefly from the East. It is very inexact to speak of an invasion of the Roman Empire by Christianity. That invasion was not an invasion of ideas, of derivations; it was an invasion of human beings who brought with them residues that found expression in Christian derivations. The ancient peoples of Rome, Latium, and Italy had certain residues with a certain religion corresponding. The Orientals had different residues with, therefore, different religions corresponding. Rome conquered them by force of arms and enslaved them; but in course of time they became her freedmen, and then her citizens, and she allowed the conquered peoples to flock to Rome from all the subject provinces, even from the despised Judaea. Not only Greece, therefore, but Asia, Africa, and the Barbarian countries imported their sentiments, and the ideas or derivations corresponding, into Rome. The Romans of the Empire, not only in the days of its decline but in its period of glory, had nothing but a name in common with the people who had conquered the Mediterranean basin.

1841. Many people imagine that *a* can be suppressed by effecting a change in education. That method may be fruitful of results if the effect of the altered education is carried on through the individual's life. Otherwise it is of little or no avail. The future Christians were educated in pagan schools. The Jesuits played schoolmaster to most of the leaders among the enemies of Catholicism in France, towards the end of the eighteenth century, as well as to most of the

1839 [1] By 1911 the greater part of the individuals in France who were full-grown at the time of the War of 1870 had passed from the scene; and to that fact was due, in part at least, the reawakening of nationalism in the country. In the same way, in Italy, by the year 1913 most of the individuals who had directly suffered from the Austrian domination in Italy had disappeared; and that made it easier for the Italian Government to treat Arabs who were defending their native land as rebels, and to try to maintain an "equilibrium in the Adriatic" by forcing the Greeks of Epirus to submit to domination by the Albanians, exactly as the Italians of Lombardy and Venetia had once been forced under an Austrian yoke.

leaders of the French Revolution. That does not prove that the effect of education is zero. It shows that it is just one among the many that figure in the resultant registered in human conduct.

1842. β. With a view to influencing *a*, governments ordinarily attack the manifestations *r, s, t.* . . . That policy is inspired not so much by any logical thinking as by the non-logical pressure of sentiments that are shocked by the manifestations *r, s, t.* . . . The derivation most commonly invoked runs: "The sentiments manifested in *r* are harmful to society; therefore I will suppress *r.*" A logico-experimental reasoning would have to add: "because by suppressing the manifestation *r,* I shall be destroying the sentiments that find their expression in *r.*" But that is the weak spot in the argument, for it is by no means certain that to suppress the manifestation of a sentiment is to destroy the sentiment itself.

1843. A truly imposing mass of fact stands there to show the scant efficacy of trying to influence residues by attacking their manifestations or, what is worse, derivations inspired by them. Did the severities visited upon expressions of thought in the press serve to prevent first the French Revolution, then the fall of Charles X in France, then the revolutionary disturbances that swept all Europe in '31? Then, again, the disturbances of '48, the growth of revolutionary parties under Napoleon III, and the uprising in Russia after the Japanese War? And how ever could a press be more thoroughly muzzled than it was in Russia at that time? At the apex of his power, and still haloed by his victories over France and his foundation of the German Empire, Bismarck seems to have tried to destroy the residues underlying Socialism and Catholicism by suppressing their manifestations in their respective parties. Yet he achieved the precise opposite—he strengthened them. The Socialist party began polling the largest vote in Germany; and Catholicism, in the party of the Centre, often won preponderant positions in the German Government.[1] Shrewd practical man that he was, Bismarck

---

1843 [1] In 1871, the "Old Catholic" movement started in Bavaria and the Bavarian Prime Minister, Lutz, opened hostilities on the Roman Curia. Says Lefebvre de Béhaine, *Léon XIII et le prince de Bismarck,* pp. 19, 48, 51: "Though on many occasions afterwards Prince von Bismarck declined responsibility for that aggressive policy, it is hard to grant that he experienced any displeasure at seeing it initiated by the Minister of Public Worship in one of the most important of the Catholic states in Germany. . . . As early as 1874, in other words before the end

himself finally came to recognize the mistake he had made in the *Kulturkampf.*[2] The government of Emperor William II very opportunely reversed tactics and, instead of combating or trying to modify the residues expressed in Catholicism, began utilizing them as tools of policy. It was unable, or unwilling, to do the same with the sentiments manifested by the peoples in Alsace-Lorraine and Poland; and in those instances its failure was as complete as in the case of the *Kulturkampf* (§ 2247[1]). The example of Poland indeed is truly typical. In that case, one country had been divided into three parts. In the two parts under the dominion of Russia and Prussia, the governments tried to combat or modify sentiments, and their policies were utterly futile and ineffective. In the section under Austrian dominion the government took advantage of the same sentiments

of the third year of the campaign against Rome, attentive observers could foresee that the results of the campaign would be dubious, and it was noted that Prince von Bismarck was manifesting less enthusiasm for the idea of a national German Church. . . . The conflict was to continue violent for a number of years; and circumstances unforeseen by the National Liberals had to supervene before Prince von Bismarck definitely dissociated himself from a policy that had at first appealed to him but which seemed doomed to failure after the Catholic elements in the Empire had answered threats against them by sending to the Reichstag a minority that had acquired great importance under the name of the Group of the Center, whereas the National Liberals were meeting stiffer and more enthusiastic opposition every day from Progressives and Socialists." Bismarck, *Gedanken und Erinnerungen,* p. 646 (Butler, Vol. II, p. 339): "One should think back to the time when the Center, strong rather in the support of the Jesuits than of the Pope, re-enforced by the Guelphs (and not only by those in Hanover), the Poles, the Alsatian Francophiles, the Radical Democrats, the Social Democrats, the Liberals, and the Particularists, all united in one same sentiment of hostility to Empire and Dynasty, possessed, under the leadership of this same Windthorst who had become a national saint since his death, as he was before, a safe and aggressive majority that served as an effective check to the Emperor and the confederated governments."

1843 [2] To tell the truth, Bismarck's mistake seems rather to have lain in an error of political tactics than in any failure to appreciate the strength of residues or the importance of using them. In fact, both before and after the *Kulturkampf,* he showed that he had the knack of using residues without trace of scruple. The fanatical "intellectuals" who supported the *Kulturkampf* imagined that Bismarck shared their beliefs. Really he was just using those gentlemen as his tools. Busch, *Tagebuchblätter* (English, Vol. I, p. 220; passage omitted from German), Nov. 8, 1870: In October, 1870, rumours were rife that the Pope was leaving Rome: " 'They would not like to see him go,' added Hatzfeldt; 'it is in their interests [of the Italians] that he should remain in Rome.' The Chief:—'Yes, certainly. But perhaps he will be obliged to leave. But where would he go? Not to France, because Garibaldi is there. He would not like to go to Austria. . . . There remains for him but Belgium or North Germany! As a matter of fact, he has already asked whether

as instruments of policy, and its work met striking success.[3] Rome enjoyed the favour and goodwill of the peoples she conquered precisely because she respected their sentiments. English rule in India continues to endure on the same grounds; and for identical reasons Tunis is of all the French colonies the one where French rule is most popular and most willingly accepted, for there the sentiments, usages, and customs of the natives have been best respected. Peoples more readily submit to heavy burdens than to offences against their manners and customs, however slight and insignificant these may seem to be. The revolt of the Sepoys in India was provoked, it is said, by a rumour that the English were tying their cartridges with strings greased in pork-fat (in those days the cartridge was torn open with the teeth before being emptied into the gun). Minor acts of arbitrary disregard in matters of language, religious usage, and, in Oriental countries, behaviour toward women, are tolerated grudg-

we could grant him that asylum. I have no objection to it—Cologne or Fulda. It would be passing strange, but after all not so very inexplicable, and it would be very useful to us to be recognized by Catholics as what we really are, that is to say, the sole power now existing that is capable of protecting the head of their Church. Stofflet and Charette, together with the Poles and their Zouaves, could then go about their business. We should have the Poles on our side. The opposition of the ultramontanes would cease in Belgium and Bavaria. [There speaks the statesman who knows the art of using residues.] . . . But the King will not consent. He is terribly afraid! He thinks all Prussia will be perverted and he himself would be obliged to become a Catholic. . . . I told him, however, that if the Pope begged asylum he could not refuse it. . . . And, after all, even if a few people in Germany became Catholic again (I should certainly not do so), it would not matter much, so long as they remained believing Christians. People ought to be more tolerant in their way of thinking!' [Such a declaration by a practical man should be pondered; it is rigorously scientific (§ 1851).] The Chief then dilated on the comic aspect of this migration of the Pope and his cardinals to Fulda, and con-

---

1843 [3] Even in the case of Poland Bismarck seems to have seen clearly at one time. Busch, *Tagebuchblätter*, Vol. I, p. 554 (English, Vol. I, p. 308), Dec. 20, 1870: "'You have no idea,' said the Chancellor, 'how pleased the Poles are when they see that someone knows their mother-tongue. Not long ago I ran into some poor devils in a military hospital. When I addressed them in Polish I could see their pale faces brighten to a smile. Too bad their general-in-chief does not know their language!' That was an indirect thrust at the Crown Prince, who had the command of the Polish forces. He picked up the Chancellor's allusion with a smile: 'That is just like you, Bismarck,' he said. 'You are always harping on that. But I think I have told you times without end that I do not like that language and refuse to learn it.' 'All the same, my lord,' Bismarck replied, 'the Poles are good soldiers and fine fellows.'" Great military leaders, such as Caesar and Napoleon, have been past-masters in the art of using sentiments in their soldiers.

ingly. But we must not forget that what may seem slight and insignificant from the logical standpoint may be serious, nay, most important, from the standpoint of sentiments. Governments that are not aware of that attain results directly opposite to their aims. In 1913 the German Chancellor explained to the Reichstag that his difficulties with the inhabitants of Alsace-Lorraine arose from the fact that they preferred their French to their German cousins. That being so, the art of government lies in finding ways to take advantage of such sentiments, not in wasting one's energies in futile efforts to destroy them, the sole effect of the latter course very frequently being only to strengthen them. The person who is able to free himself from the blind dominion of his own sentiments is capable of utilizing the sentiments of other people for his own ends. If, instead, a person is prey to his own sentiments, he cannot have the knack of using the sentiments of others, and so shocks them to no

cluded: 'Of course—the King could not see the humorous side of the affair. But if only the Pope remains true to me, I shall know how to bring His Majesty round.' " *Ibid.*, Vol. II, p. 111 (English, Vol. I, p. 390), Jan. 30, 1871: "The Chief had told the Frenchman, among other things, that to be consistent in one's policy was frequently a mistake. . . . One must modify one's course of action in accordance with events, with the situation of affairs . . . and not according to one's opinions. One must not impose one's feelings and desires upon one's country." Lefebvre de Béhaine, *Op. cit.*, p. 25 (speaking of the outbreak of the *Kulturkampf*): "Was not the moment propitious in Germany for beginning the *Kulturkampf*, the outlines of which had already been drawn by Lutz? Would not Rome retreat at that warning? Everything leads one to believe that that was Prince von Bismarck's hope early in the year 1872. That thought came out in the speeches he delivered before the Prussian Chamber on January 30 and 31 during the debate on the budget of the Ministry of Public Worship. Alongside the rebuke addressed to the clerical party for working to mobilize the Center group with a view to waging a more effective war on the new state of things [In that the real cause of the war that Bismarck is about to declare.], alongside the usual denunciations of the old Rhenish confederacy, certain words of the Chancellor might have been read as indicating a disposition on his part to enter on negotiations with the Vatican." The Pope showed himself not too pliant and Bismarck set out to combat him; but being a wise and a practical man, he soon realized that he had better things to do than waste his energies in fatuous arguments in theology. In 1885 he submitted his dispute with Spain over the Caroline Islands to the Pope's arbitration. Lefebvre de Béhaine, *Ibid.*, pp. 198, 220: "On May 26, 1886, the King of Prussia proclaimed a law in fifteen articles that abrogated a certain number of items in previous laws, known as the *Maigesetze* and dating for the most part from the years 1873-75. . . . Today the Catholic Church is enjoying a profound peace in Germany. It is free in its teachings and has been liberated from all the impediments that it seemed likely to be called on to suffer twenty-five years ago."

purpose and fails to derive any advantage from them. The same may be said, in general, of the relations between ruler and ruled. The statesman of the greatest service to himself and his party is the man who himself has no prejudices but knows how to profit by the prejudices of others.

1844. Facts connected with the sex religion furnish another excellent example of the futility of attempts to destroy residues by suppressing the manifestations that they provoke. It is doubtful whether over the course of the centuries the hosts of laws and measures against sex immorality have had the slightest effect upon it; so true is it that, if one were not on one's guard against any reasoning *post hoc, propter hoc,* one would be tempted to say that where legislation against immorality is most severe, there immorality is most rampant. We may see under our very eyes that measures designed to suppress a manifestation, *r,* serve only to strengthen other manifestations, *s, t.* . . . Whenever war is declared on Cythera, Sodom, Lesbos, and Onan gain in vogue. In the countries where public women are hunted down under pretext of suppressing the "white-slave trade," adultery and annual marriages dissolved by easy divorces flourish and prosper.

1845. In many situations dealt with by criminal law we have manifestations of the same sort. Thefts and murders are not, of course, theoretical manifestations; but it does not follow on that account that they are independent of sentiments and are not manifestations of them. For that reason they present a number of traits of the type just considered.

1. As a result of the part that non-logical impulses play in them, they have little to do with reason. Threat of punishment is of little avail in checking felonies or crimes of passion, so called, because, barring exception, such crimes originate in strong sentiments leading up to non-logical conduct. In the minor crimes sentiments are less influential, and the part played by logic is correspondingly greater; threat of punishment is more successful in controlling misdemeanours than murders.

2. The main cause of crimes, still barring exception, lies in the prevalence of certain sentiments, *a.* The theory that there are born criminals merely adds to that that the individual derives his sentiments from heredity. The theory seems to be in part sound, but it

could hardly be accepted as comprehensive; for the sum of circumstances of time, place, and so on, in which the individual has lived, have certainly modified some at least of the sentiments with which he was born. But as contrasted with the theory of responsibility, so called, which reduces all conduct to logic, the theory of the born criminal looks like the truth contrasted with error.

3. Among the least disputable facts of social science is the fact that, so far in history, the effects of penalties as designed to reform the criminal, and especially as regards major crimes, have been exceedingly scant even when, as is frequently the case, they have not made the criminal worse. That is all in accord with the general law that forcibly to suppress the manifestations of a given group of sentiments is often of little or no effect as regards diminishing the intensity of sentiments in that group, and sometimes it enhances them. Many efforts have been made to remedy that defect in criminal legislation, and, to tell the truth, with no very appreciable results; and the slight, or rather the insignificant, progress that has been made has been made through influencing sentiments, *a*.

1846. 4. The only procedure that has proved effective in decreasing the number of crimes is to rid society of criminals—the procedure described as α in § 1838.

5. It is certain, moreover, that the general status of sentiments in a community has its effect on crime. There are communities of thieves, communities of swindlers, communities of murderers, and so on. In other words, the groups of sentiments, *a, b* . . . differ according to peoples, places, and times, and often there are compensations between the various genera.

1847. 6. Erroneous, therefore, are all those reasonings which, from the fact that a penalty is ineffective from the standpoint of logical conduct, conclude that it is ineffective in general. It is erroneous, for instance, to argue that the death-penalty is ineffective because logically, directly, it does not restrain a man from committing murder. The penalty works in a different way. In the first place— and the fact cannot be questioned—it does away with the murderer and rids society of at least a few of the persons who have a fondness for killing their neighbours. Then again it serves indirectly to invigorate sentiments of horror for crime. That can hardly be doubted, once one thinks of the effectiveness of so called laws of honour, which are without direct penal sanctions but produce such an atmosphere through apposite sentiments that the majority of men are loath to transgress them. So the Sicilian will hardly ever disregard the prescriptions of *omertà,* because he has inherited or acquired sentiments which accord with those rules and the punishments that are visited on infractions maintain and intensify those sentiments.[1]

To infer, for another example, that the so-called probation law is innocuous from the assumed fact—the real fact is probably different—that it has not increased the number of second offenders, is also to reason erroneously. Modifications in sentiments take place slowly, sometimes very very slowly. Generations must pass before the effects of that law, or any other law of the sort, can be known with certainty. Recidivity, moreover, is not the only factor to be taken into account—there is criminality in general. The effect of the probation law extends beyond the criminal whom it protects. The population at large grows accustomed to thinking that a first crime may be committed with impunity; and if that manner of thinking becomes ingrained in sentiment, diminishing the aversion for crime that the civilized human being instinctively feels, criminality may increase in general without any corresponding increase in recidivity. The whole-hearted punishment of crimes that took place over long periods of time in centuries past has contributed to the maintenance of certain sentiments of aversion to crime, and those sentiments we now find active in men. It will be another long time before they can be destroyed. Those nations which are nowadays indulging in an orgy of humanitarianism are acting like the prodigal son in frittering away the fortune he had inherited from his father.

1848. In § 1832 we discussed the effects produced by the possibility of showing overt disrespect for certain manifestations of sentiment. Mild laws in general, the probation and suspended-sentence law in particular, whereby society tends virtually to grant a citizen

1847 [1] [*From the 1916 ed.:* According to the rules of *omertà* a member of the Maffia or some other association of the sort pledges aid and fidelity to his comrades. If they get into trouble with the public authorities or the courts, he must do nothing to their disadvantage. Least of all can he ask the courts to settle any differences he may have with them. When an attempt is made on his life, he may avenge himself if possible, but in no case is he to make a complaint to the police.]

the right to commit a first crime; the extreme mercifulness of courts and juries; the kind-hearted patience of magistrates who allow criminals to show contempt for them in public court (§ 1716[6]), and sometimes to utter personal insults and ridicule the penalties with which they are threatened; the comforts that have been provided in certain "modern" prisons, where, under pretext of "reclaiming" the criminal, society shows him every consideration and gives him greater ease than oftentimes he could have in his own home; the mitigation of penalties already mild; frequent commutations and pardons—all such things allow a large number of individuals to think lightly of crime and punishment of crime and to glory as strong and free-thinking men in their lack of aversion to crime and in their contempt for punishments that in many cases are more imaginary than real. The humanitarian religion strengthens these sentiments, supplying the derivations in which they are expressed and the myths that go to make up their theology.

1849. 7. Similar, in general, is the effect of theologies and of metaphysical, or other, moralities, all of which, in so far as they are derivations proper or manifestations of derivations have little or no direct effect on crime. In so far as they are manifestations of sentiments they seem to have effects, which, however, are largely attributable to the sentiments themselves (§ 1860). It follows that, ignoring such indirect effects, little or nothing is to be gained by trying to influence theories. The little gain that can be made in that way is due to the reaction of the derivations upon the sentiments from which they derive and then to the influence of those sentiments upon crime.[1]

1850. γ. Likewise in any inquiry as to the effects resulting from a modification in a we are confronted with a particular case of the general uniformity obtaining in the action of residues corresponding to a given sum of sentiments (§§ 1740 f.). Governments that are working upon a in one way or another should understand that, awares or unawares, they are influencing other residues of the same class.[1] Sometimes they are aware of it, and that is why governments

1849 [1] In that we have a particular case of the general law that we found prevailing as to the influence of residues and derivations.

1850 [1] The French Government either was not aware of that truth or else disregarded it when, in trying to deal with certain religious sentiments that it con-

have patronized this or that religion out of considerations of policy. To justify that course they have used, in addition to the fallacy already examined in § 1744 in which logical conduct is envisaged instead of the non-logical, the argument that in protecting one genus of residues protection is also extended to all other genera of residues dependent upon a given sum of sentiments (§ 1744). Commonly used for that purpose are variations on the following type of derivation: "The religious individual possesses sentiments that I desire to have in good citizens. I must therefore have everyone believe in the religion X, which I have selected and which I will protect." Suppose we disregard questions as to the efficacy of the protection, which usually consists in interference with religious manifestations. That problem we have just discussed. Let us assume for the moment that the interference is really effective and proceed from there.

1851. The logico-experimental reasoning corresponding to the derivation just stated would be: "The religious person possesses sentiments that I desire good citizens to have; but a person can be devout only if he possesses the sentiments of a specified religion; therefore I will encourage the sentiments of that religion in my citizens." The proposition "A person can be religious only if he has the sentiments of a specified religion" is completely discredited by experience, and many practical men know that (§ 1843[2]), even if they see fit not to admit as much in public. Many religions that are different in forms are manifestations of substantially identical religious sentiments. The religious spirit, moreover, is ordinarily stronger in heretics than in the followers of an established orthodoxy protected by a government. Such a government is, to be sure, protecting a given theology and specified forms of worship, but mean-

sidered harmful, it unintentionally damaged other sentiments of the same group, among them the sentiment of patriotism, which, certainly, it had no intention of impairing. In 1912, the French school-teachers assembled in convention at Chambéry voiced sentiments of hostility to patriotism. Many politicians marvelled at such a thing. But they might readily have foreseen it by giving just a thought to the work they had themselves been doing. But if the germ inoculated by the French "intellectuals" found a favourable medium in a few school-teachers, it found a sterile environment in the French population at large, especially in the lower classes. Religious sentiments linger most tenaciously in those classes under one form or another, and they are the source of those occasional tides of religious feeling which rise and engulf the higher classes. That is what happened in France with respect to sentiments of patriotism in the years 1911 and 1912.

time it is persecuting the very religious spirit that it set out to foster. A double error is involved in the policy: in the first place, it confuses derivations and residues, in the manner just stated, mistaking theology for the religious spirit; then it confuses certain specified residues with other residues of the same genus or kindred genera. If the residues underlying a number of different religions are a_1, a_2, a_3 . . . and if the whole sum of sentiments upon which those religions depend is strengthened (§ 1744), there will be an increase in the religious spirit. But if a_1 is strengthened at the expense of a_2, a_3 . . . the religious spirit is not necessarily intensified; it may actually be reduced. To see how ineffective governmental protection is as a means of strengthening religious residues, one has only to compare the present state of Catholicism in the United States, where all Christian sects enjoy the amplest freedom, with the state of that same religion in France at times when it enjoyed governmental protection, as under Napoleon III. Another example would be Rome under papal rule, where there was vigorous suppression of manifestations contrary to Catholicism, yet Catholic religious residues were very feeble.[1]

1852. The error just elucidated has been sensed by many people, but that perception, ordinarily, instead of being stated in logico-experimental form has taken the form of a derivation that, from the logico-experimental standpoint, is as erroneous as the theory which it is used to combat. Dissenters have vaunted the "truth" of their heresies as contrasted with the "error" of established religions. They have set their own devoutness over against the lukewarm faith of their adversaries. They have shown that as citizens they were just as good as orthodox believers, in fact even better. And then along came the metaphysicist and the theorizer to apply their ingenuity to the subject, fishing up from somewhere a "right" of the individual conscience as against public authority; a sacrosanct "freedom of thought" that is of such a lineage that it can be invoked for oneself while being denied to others; a "tolerance" that the orthodox must have for the dissenter, but which the dissenter is under no obligation to have for the orthodox; and no end of other such contrivances.

1851 [1] The extent to which the religious spirit in the city of Rome had degenerated by the year 1830 or thereabouts may be measured to some degree by the obscene satirical sonnets in Roman dialect of Belli (*Sonnetti romaneschi*).

Such doctrines have at times succeeded in winning wide acceptance; not by the soundness of their logic but by their correspondence with sentiments that, originating under changing social conditions, eventually have come to conflict with the sentiments that were preponderant in a day gone by and which confused the religious spirit in general with some one of its manifestations; and then again by their correspondence with sentiments originating in intensifications of the instincts of combination and similar variations in other residues.

1853. At this point it is in order to draw a distinction of great importance. We have shown that if the purpose is to obtain the advantages of devoutness the person whose function it is to regulate the conduct of others should be somewhat, nay, very largely, indifferent to religious forms; but the demonstration does not hold for those who are to perform the conduct; and it would be a serious error to consider it valid for them. Quite to the contrary, obstinate devotion to one's own faith and aversion to the faiths of others is generally an index of strong convictions, and an indication further that the desired effects of devoutness will be rendered. One might say, elliptically, that it is better for the person in whose conduct one is interested to have such obstinacy and such aversions, provided one is thinking not of the derivations through which those attitudes are expressed, but of the sentiments that stimulate the religious conviction (§ 1744). If one should say that it "would be well" for people to be tolerant of the differing beliefs of others, meanwhile maintaining strong convictions as to their own, there could be no objection except that such a pious wish would be assuming as absent a tie, a correlation, that is ordinarily present in religious phenomena. It is likewise advisable that the person who is utilizing the religious convictions of others for social purposes should not himself adopt certain extreme manifestations of that religious zeal; for ardent believers at times manifest their faith in manners quite irrational or even frankly ridiculous.[1] Similarly, again, if one were to say—as

1853 [1] A phenomenon depending on the residues of Class III (activity). Human beings, like animals, feel a need of expressing their sentiments by actions that it is impossible to connect with the sentiments themselves by any logical or rational nexus. The dog sees its master and wags its tail. No logical connexion between the wagging and the dog's affection for its master can be established. If dogs had moralists, the latter would probably demonstrate by any amount of fine-sounding

many actually do say—that it "would be well" for people to refrain from such manifestations, still feeling their own faiths none the less strongly, the answer would be the same: that there can be no objection to such a recommendation, except that to imagine that it can be carried out presupposes the absence of a tie, a correlation, ordinarily found present in religious phenomena. That does not prevent anyone from trying to attenuate the strength of the ties: one may still strive to diminish the intolerance arising from certain sentiments and to correct the absurdity and nonsense in certain of their manifestations. One goes wrong when, disregarding the presence of the ties, one condemns them and sets out to eliminate the consequences of sentiments that one is trying to conserve.[2] The difference just noted between the person who is regulating conduct and the person who is performing it is of a general character. We shall see many other examples of it.

1854. It was for mere convenience of expression that we have just been using the term "religion," which is not and cannot be

balderdash that to wag one's tail in such circumstances is altogether ridiculous; but the dogs would let them talk on and continue showing their affection for their masters by wagging their tails. Human beings act in the very same fashion.

1853 [2] Not seldom the manifestations of sentiment on the part of the Pan-Germanists are altogether irrational and exceedingly ridiculous. Now level-headed Germans may be eager to weaken the tie that connects those manifestations with patriotism in such a way that the patriotism will be as ardent as before and the manifestations will cease or diminish in numbers and virulence. But so long as that correlation subsists, the person who wants his patriotism must also resign himself to the manifestations of it. In France a reawakening of patriotism was observable as early as 1912 and it is still continuing at this moment (May, 1914), attended by blatant manifestations on the stage and in literature. Not a few moralists in France are scandalized at this "noisy jingoism" and are inveighing against it, so betraying a belief on their part that such manifestations being fatuous prattle, the sentiments from which they derive must be equally so. Such a blunder is worthy of such people, who are repeatedly showing their ignorance of the correlations obtaining among social facts. It is all well enough to prefer that powerful sentiments should not be accompanied by manifestations that are not strictly rational and that the sentiments expressed through Class III residues (activity) should accordingly be attenuated in virulence; but so long as they retain their vigour, the person who will have his sentiments must resign himself to accepting their manifestations also. It is of course true that among said moralists in France there are humanitarians who would abolish the sentiments as well. They dare not say so in fear of public censure, but at heart they deplore the existence of patriotism, sometimes consciously, sometimes unconsciously, and dream of universal brotherhood. Not daring to combat the sentiments of patriotism openly, they turn to fighting the manifestations of it.

accurately defined. We must therefore be on our guard against any misapprehension that might arise from the haziness in its meaning. The complexes called "religions" are made up of residues and derivations. There are residues that are common to all of them, other residues that are peculiar to particular religions. That is the chief reason why they cannot be brought under a single definition. Endless in number the definitions hitherto proposed, and over them people have quarrelled for centuries without coming to any conclusion. Other definitions will be brought forward in the future, and people will argue about them as well as about those of the past, so long as human beings shall continue to feast themselves on fatuous arguments of that type. As we already know, with religions as with all other doctrines, social values depend to a very slight extent upon derivations and to a very large extent upon residues. Several religions present an important group of residues, made up principally of group-persistences, which correspond to sentiments of discipline, submission, subordination. That fact has been more or less intuitively perceived by one government or another and such governments have tried to protect religion in order to have loyal citizens. The sentiments in question find their chief form of expression in acts of worship; and from that it follows that from the standpoint of social utility forms of worship, rites, are much more important than theology. That view is contrary to common opinion, but it accords with the facts.

1855. The great social value of the religion of ancient Rome lay in the very fact that that religion was almost exclusively made up of rites and consequently contained a maximum of useful elements. Among the Christian sects Catholicism is far more effective than any other for purposes of maintaining discipline.

1856. At this point an objection suggests itself spontaneously to the mind. Italy is a Catholic country, and yet sentiments of obedience to law are much less powerful there than they are in Prussia, a Protestant country. To make the objection stronger suppose we disregard the fact that Prussian Lutheranism of all the Protestant sects has laid greatest stress on discipline, and confine ourselves to the consideration, which happens to contain the solution of the problem, that observable in Prussia is the simultaneous prevalence of a number of kindred groups of residues, notable among them residues expressing themselves in the monarchical faith and in the military spirit, to say nothing of submission to public authority. In Italy such residues are weak. In Prussia they are very strong. In that we have one of the many cases where one set of residues may be seen gaining in vigour at the expense of kindred groups.

1857. The habit people have of paying their chief or exclusive attention to derivations leads to their calling different things by the same name. A complex, for instance, where the derivations are all alike comes to look like a single religion; whereas if we consider the different residues that induce its acceptance by different kinds of people it is seen to consist of several. Take the case of Socialism. In the lower classes, which look to that religion for betterment in their conditions of living, Socialism is chiefly accepted in virtue of residues of personal integrity and, in addition, on grounds of interest. In the upper classes we find, first of all, people who are using Socialism for their personal ends. Their conduct is predominantly logical—we will therefore not linger upon it. Then again we find people who are inspired to accept Socialism chiefly by residues of sociality, among which residues of asceticism not seldom play an important part. Considered, therefore, from the standpoint of residues, the Socialist religion of such people is altogether different from the Socialist religion of the masses.

So for other religions—the Catholic, for instance. Ignoring, as usual, individuals who use that faith for personal ends, there remain under a single canopy of derivations a number of religions differing according to the residues that are brought into play; and among them we find a class of residues in which the residues of asceticism play a far more important part than all other groups. That fact has been clearly perceived by the men who have governed the Catholic Church; and they have found ways to recognize without changes in derivations many varieties of residues, through a secular clergy, a regular clergy, a laity, various orders of friars, and so on. And in that we have another example that as usual shows that the art of governing consists in knowing how to take advantage of the residues one finds ready to hand (§ 1843).

1858. From the standpoint of social utility, the ascetic residues are not beneficial—they are positively harmful. It is very probable, therefore, that the Socialist religion of the lower classes is socially beneficial, while the ascetic Socialism of the upper classes is socially pernicious. Proletarian Socialism may be at bottom revolutionary, but it is not in the least opposed to discipline, in fact stresses it; and the authority of Socialist leaders is often far better respected than the authority of government officials. The Socialist religion is a great school of discipline, and one may even go so far as to say that, from that standpoint, it runs a close second to Catholicism. It has served to strengthen Class V residues (personal integrity) in people of the lower strata of society. Better than any legislative enactment—not excepting compulsory education—it has succeeded in raising the molecules in an amorphous mass of humanity to dignified status as citizens, and in so doing it has increased the capacities for action of society as a whole. Ascetic Socialism, on the other hand, tends to debilitate every sort of energy. When at all effective it weakens Class V residues in the higher strata of society, and of the few individuals who accept it in good faith it makes cowards and dolts who are useless to themselves and to others, so that if—as fortunately does not happen—they were assigned any important rôle in the government of society they would lead it to ruin. The practice of such a religion by such individuals has no greater utility than the macerations practised by the anchorites of yore in the African deserts. Standing apart from real interests, ascetic Socialism prevents social conflicts from finding solutions on the basis of a balance among such interests, and so occasions useless wasting of energies. In a word, the religion of the proletarian, revolutionary Socialist has contrary effects to the religion of the "intellectual" and "evolutionary" Socialist. That truth is intuitively perceived by *bourgeois* statesmen, who flirt with upper-class Socialism in order to use it for their own ends, while they fiercely combat the Socialism of proletarian type, which they know would prevent them from continuing to live on their countries.[1] And it is also sensed by not a few proletarian Socialists, as when they "decline to cooperate" with "capitalists" and "intellectuals," and refuse to abandon the "class-struggle." The same

1858 [1] That very thing happened in Italy in the elections of 1913. Characteristic the case of Rome, where the "transformist" Socialist, Bissolati, was elected to the parliament thanks to the support of the Government and to votes of dependents of the royal house, defeating the revolutionary Socialist, Cipriani. Bissolati had had the same support in the previous elections against Santini, a Conservative.

may be said of Syndicalism and Anarchism, or of other sects of the kind that will gradually replace them. As we shall see farther along (§§ 2170 f.), the use of force is indispensable to society; and when the higher classes are averse to the use of force, which ordinarily happens because the majority in those classes come to rely wholly on their skill at chicanery, and the minority shrink from energetic acts now through stupidity, now through cowardice, it becomes necessary, if society is to subsist and prosper, that that governing class be replaced by another which is willing and able to use force. Roman society was saved from ruin by the legions of Caesar and Octavius. So it may happen that our society will one day be saved from decadence by the heirs of the Syndicalists and Anarchists of our day.

1859. The weakness of the humanitarian religion does not lie in the logico-experimental deficiencies of its derivations. From that standpoint they are no better and no worse than the derivations of other religions. But some of these contain residues beneficial to individuals and society, whereas the humanitarian religion is sadly lacking in such residues. But how can a religion that has the good of humanity solely at heart, and which is called "humanitarian" for that very reason, be so destitute in residues correlated with society's welfare? The answer to that objection we already know (§ 1779). The principles from which the humanitarian doctrine is logically derived in no way correspond with the facts. They merely express in objective form a subjective sentiment of asceticism. The intent of sincere humanitarians is to do good to society, just as the intent of the child who kills a bird by too much fondling is to do good to the bird. We are not for that matter forgetting that humanitarianism has had some socially desirable effects. For one thing it has contributed to the mitigation of criminal penalties; and if among these some were beneficial, so that society has suffered from the mitigation, there were others that were useless, so that by their mitigation society has gained (§ 1861). But on the other hand, humanitarianism is worthless from the logico-experimental point of view, whether because it has no slightest intrinsic soundness of a scientific character, or more especially because even if, on an assumption devoid of any probability, it had some points of soundness, that fact would not help as regards spurring human beings to the re-

quired activities, for human beings are guided primarily by sentiment. A similar judgment may be passed upon the work of our
"intellectuals" as leading to few results that are beneficial and to
many that are very bad; because, from the standpoint of sentiments, they shut their eyes to realities as the latter stand reflected in
many sentiments that they condemn from failure to grasp their
rôle in society; and because, from the standpoint of logico-experimental science, they reason not on facts but on derivations, and from
the latter draw, by a logic inopportunely thorough-going, inferences
that are altogether at war with the facts (§§ 1782 f.). And so for
the democratic religion in general. The many varieties of Socialism,
Syndicalism, Radicalism, Tolstoyism, pacifism, humanitarianism,
Solidarism, and so on, form a sum that may be said to belong to the
democratic religion, much as there was a sum of numberless sects
in the early days of the Christian religion. We are now witnessing
the rise and dominance of the democratic religion, just as the men
of the first centuries of our era witnessed the rise of the Christian
religion and the beginnings of its dominion. The two phenomena
present many profoundly significant analogies. To get at their substance we have to brush derivations aside and reach down to residues. The social value of both those two religions lies not in the least
in their respective theologies, but in the sentiments that they express.
As regards determining the social value of Marxism, to know
whether Marx's theory of "surplus value" is false or true is about as
important as knowing whether and how baptism eradicates sin in
trying to determine the social value of Christianity—and that is of
no importance at all. Certain extravagances on the part of Syndicalism do not prove the social worthlessness of the democratic
religion, any more than certain extravagances on the part of the
Franciscans prove that Catholicism is socially worthless. The theory
of solidarity and the cosmogony of the Bible both lie equally far
distant from the domains of experimental reality; but that in no
wise diminishes the social importance of the religions to which
those theories belong. As we have time and time again insisted,
the experimental fatuity of those derivations and others of the kind
does not in any sense permit us to conclude that they are harmful
or even merely useless. There is little if any connexion between the
two things. The similarity between certain Christian and certain

democratic derivations explains why those two religions come to merge in certain sects such as the Tolstoyans, the Christian Democrats, the Liberal Protestants so called, Modernists, our latter-day admirers of St. Francis, and so on. Brushing derivations aside, we place ourselves in a position to see the great social transformation that expressed itself in the origin of Christianity, and the equally great social transformation that is now in progress and is finding its expression in the democratic religion. To determine the relations between those transformations and social utility is a very serious and a very difficult problem; and to solve it we need a theory of social utility that is far less rudimentary than any that at the present time we could sketch even in outline. But at any rate we are safe in saying that we will get a first approximation to a solution by leaving derivations out of our calculations; for their influence is secondary and therefore to be considered only in later and finer approximations. On the other hand, we must not fail to consider the sentiments manifested by the transformations in question; and we must consider them not objectively, apart from individuals, but in their relations to individuals; for the same sentiments may be useful to some individuals and detrimental to others. Among the things to ignore, finally, are secondary questions such as the "sincerity" of this or that follower of the one or the other religion. Every religion has its parasites; but that is a secondary matter with little bearing upon the social value of a religion. Those of our contemporaries who do not share the democratic faith are in the same situation on the whole as were those pagans of old who witnessed the inundation of the ancient world by Christianity. Some people now vainly imagine, as those pagans imagined, that they can effectively check the progress of the religion they are fighting by refuting its derivations. Others find those theories so absurd that they disdain giving a thought to them. And in that again they are following a precedent set by some of their ancient precursors.[1] But

1859 [1] Boissier, *La fin du paganisme*, Vol. II, pp. 243-44, expresses his surprise that Macrobius does not so much as mention Christianity, which in his day was sweeping Rome. "Our surprise is only the greater when we observe the same silence in almost all the pagan writers of the time, the grammarians, the orators, the poets, and even the historians, though it seems very strange that an event such as the triumph of the Church could be disregarded in an account of that past. Neither Aurelius Victor nor Eutropius mentions Constantine's conversion, and one gets the

usually both these moderns and the ancients are to be found adopting other derivations that are in no way better than the ones they reject. It occurs to few, one might say to none, to ignore derivations altogether and apply themselves exclusively to facts and the relations that obtain between them.

1860. δ. Lastly, one may be trying to abolish a certain manifestation, *r*, while retaining other manifestations, *s*, *t* . . . or, conversely, to establish *r* without giving rise to *s*, *t*. . . . Such a thing is always very difficult and often impossible. Before human beings will really and regularly perform the conduct *r*, they must be imbued with the sentiments underlying the residues, *a*, of which *r* is the consequence. If they have those residues, *s*, *t* . . . will also put in an appearance along with *r*; if they do not have them, there will be no *r*, but also no *s*, and no *t*. . . .

1861. Suppose our idea is to abolish the penalties, *r*, inflicted by one or another religion on crimes of thought and heresy, and meantime to retain very heavy penalties, *s*, *t* . . . for theft and murder. Such a thing is not impossible—there stands the example of ancient Rome; but it is a very difficult matter, for it took the so-called civilized peoples of Europe centuries and centuries to achieve it. Indeed even among those peoples the disappearance, or virtual disappearance, of *r* has been attended by a marked enfeeblement in *s*, *t* . . . and that because the group of residues, *a*, on which all penalties depended, was modified in the direction of a strengthening in the sentiments of pity for criminals who broke the laws in force in society. Certain interests, moreover, develop counter to the various religions; and that explains why there has been a greater mitigation in penalties for crimes of heresy than for other crimes. After the fall of the Second Empire in France the interests of the Republicans conflicted with the interests of the Catholics. As a result penalties for offences against the Catholic Church, and by extension, against all Christian churches, were abolished. The Empire, meantime, had

impression from them that all the *principes* of the fourth century were continuing practice of the ancient cult. Certainly no mere chance brought them all to omit reference to a religion they detested. It was by design: it was an understanding, the significance of which could escape no one. Silence, haughty, insolent, became with them the last protest allowed the proscribed religion. That tactic, for that matter, was nothing new in Rome. From the very first day, high society in Rome had made it a habit to fight Christianity with contempt."

made itself champion (in words) of the sex religion; the Republic therefore granted greater liberties in that field; though afterwards, when the policies of the Empire had ceased to be an issue, a slight reaction followed.[1]

1861 [1] Some pages back (§ 1716 [6]) we quoted one of the numberless instances where in deference to humanitarian sentiments magistrates and juries allowed criminals to insult judges on the bench and their attorneys to dispute rulings by presiding magistrates in open court. Suppose here we show a contrast dating from a day when tender hearts were not blinding the eyes of magistrates. Edmond Goncourt, *Journal des Goncourt*, Vol. I, pp. 42-45 (Feb. 20, 1853), tells how he and his brother were indicted and brought to trial, in 1853, for reprinting in a newspaper a poem that had appeared without anyone's protesting in a book by Sainte-Beuve that had won a crown from the French Academy: "Finally our case was called. 'Prisoners to the dock!' ordered the presiding magistrate. The order caused a sensation among the spectators. The dock was the detention pen for thieves! Never had a press case even when tried in Criminal Sessions won a reporter a 'Prisoner to the Dock!' . . . The acting State's Attorney opened. In an access of raging eloquence he pictured us as men without faith or honour, as sneaks and vagabonds without family, without mothers, without sisters, without respect for womanhood and, for a peroration to his arraignment of us, as apostles of physical love." The lines that had so stirred the wrath of the acting prosecutor ran:

> *"Croisant ses beaux membres nus*
> *sur son Adonis qu'elle baise,*
> *et lui pressant le doux flanc,*
> *son cou douillettement blanc*
> *mordille de trop grand aise."*

Something far worse than any crime of Bonnot, Garnier and Company! Goncourt continues: "Then our attorney arose. He was just the defender we had been looking for. He was far from repeating the pleas of Paillard de Villeneuve in defence of Karr, by making bold to demand of the court how it dared to prosecute us on the charge of an article that was itself not under prosecution and the author of which was not in the dock beside us. He groaned, he wept over our crime, representing us as callow youths, not all there in the upper story, in fact a little off." The Court finally denounced the article, but acquitted the defendants as guiltless of any "intent to insult public decency and sound morals." "In spite of anything that may be written or said, the undeniable fact is that we were prosecuted in a police court, seated in the dock with a policeman on either side of us, for quoting five lines of Tahureau as printed in the *Tableau historique et critique de la poésie française* by Sainte-Beuve, a work crowned by the Academy." Fools of the breed that forgathers in societies for the improvement of morals may consider the publication of such lines a crime as serious as murder or burglary; but that cannot possibly be admitted from the standpoint of social utility.

And here, now, is an example from the field of politics. Ollivier, *L'Empire libéral*, Vol. IV, pp. 373-74. Ollivier was attorney for Vacherot, who was being prosecuted for inciting his countrymen to hatred and contempt of the government in a book called *La démocratie*: "I began my rebuttal as follows: 'Gentlemen, in matters of this sort the first requisite is extreme cautiousness. I shall make no answer to the

1862. The situation is no more different as regards place than as regards time. In France offences against the Christian Church are entirely exempt from penalties. In England there are still some few survivals of punishment for blasphemies. Crimes of sex heretics are less zealously ferreted out and more lightly punished in France than they are in England. Similar differences may be noted as regards common crimes, which are treated with much greater leniency in France than in England. Such contrasts result from the fact that human beings do their thinking not with the methods of the logico-experimental sciences but in deference chiefly to sentiment (§§ 826 f.).

1863. *Difficulties in law-making.* The obstacles that stand in the way of making a law perfectly adapted to a purpose which the legislator has in view are of two kinds. In the first place, one has to decide what the law is to be, and to do that solutions are required not only for the particular problem which we have just been considering (§ 1825), but for the other more general problem as to the indirect effects a measure will have, the problem, in other words, of the composition of social forces (§ 2087). Even assuming that the law-maker is to reason logico-experimentally, he will find that the necessary scientific elements for solving such problems are at present lacking, though one may reasonably hope that as sociology progresses it will some day be in a position to supply them.

1864. But we are still nowhere—the law now has to be applied

offensive parts of the prosecutor's address. His appeal to passions was out of place here. In entering this enclosure you who are our judges and we who are defending this book should all remember that we are nothing but mouthpieces, interpreters, of the law.' The presiding justice interrupted me: '*Maître* Ollivier, you have said something improper. Withdraw it!' I replied calmly and in surprise: 'Your Honour, I have said nothing improper. I was still under the sway of the words I had been listening to.' The president retorted: '*Maître* Ollivier, you said that the Ministry of Justice had made an appeal to passions. That is an impropriety. Withdraw it!' . . . The Court left the bench, returning a moment later. . . . [Ollivier was again requested to withdraw his remark. He refused:] Then, without leaving the bench, the Court sentenced me to suspension from practice for three months and adjourned Vacherot's case for a week to give him time to choose another attorney." If acts that only sectarian fanatics and a servile magistracy consider crimes cannot be distinguished from acts so regarded by the reasonable desire that almost every human being feels not to be murdered, plundered, or robbed, it might in many cases be the lesser evil if humanitarians would exercise their indulgence upon the former rather than upon the latter.

practically! That can be done only by influencing interests and sentiments; and it must not be forgotten that the derivations which will have to be used for that purpose are something altogether different from the logico-experimental reasonings that served to discover the law best suited to a given end. One has only to examine the reasons that have been put forward in times past in behalf of this or that social enactment to see how fatuous they have been; that frequently people have aimed at one objective and attained another; and that in the few cases where those in power have realized a given purpose, they have carried their publics with them by professing different purposes from the ones they realized and by cajoling them with reasonings of a variety suited to the public understanding, in other words, with arguments that are childishly inadequate from the logico-experimental point of view. If, furthermore, in working for a given objective, one is in a position to influence interests and sentiments, to modify them, the modification may have, in addition to the effects desired, other effects that are not in the least intended; so that one still has to consider both the intended and the incidental effects and see just what the social utility of their resultant will be. That is like the problem that practical mechanics solves in the construction of a machine. The machine transforms part of the energy it consumes into a desired effect, part it wastes, and the part it uses advantageously is often very small as compared with the part it wastes.

1865. So social enactments have, in general, some effects that are beneficial and others that are negative or harmful; but if one will have the ones, one must of necessity put up with the others.[1]

1866. When the engineer has found the best machine, he has little difficulty in selling it, and even without dispensing with derivations altogether, he can for the most part utilize arguments that are logico-experimental. Not so the statesman. For him that situation is precisely reversed. His main resort must be derivations, oftentimes absurd ones. He can use logico-experimental arguments only by exception. The choice of a machine is primarily a logical act. There is no harm in showing, therefore, that, let us say, a steam-engine

1865 [1] And here again one has to consider not only direct effects, which we are at present examining, but indirect effects, with which we shall deal in the chapter next following.

converts only a small part of the heat generated in its fire-box into useful labour. Such an admission is in fact helpful, as pointing the way to increasing the proportion of energy profitably consumed. If the choice of a machine were a non-logical act, chiefly, if sentiment played any notable part in it, an absurd theory asserting, for instance, that the steam-engine wastes not the smallest particle of fuel-energy might be used to great advantage (§§ 1868 f.). To sell a machine, there has to be someone interested in selling it. To win approval for a social enactment, it is much more important—it is absolutely necessary—that it have a champion. In both cases individual interest is a powerful factor; but where social measures are concerned, sentiment is the factor most powerful by far, especially if the sentiment be "aroused" to the point of becoming a religion. In that case, it had better express itself in enthusiastic derivations that overreach cold realities, something very different from the sceptical thinking of the logico-experimental sciences. All the same those sciences are exerting some influence in our time, since they are accepted by the generality of men as derivations. Progress in the logico-experimental sciences has bred a sentiment of reverence for them, and that sentiment has to be satisfied. But that is no very difficult task, for the plain man is satisfied if his derivation has a remote, indeed a very very remote, semblance of being "scientific."

1867. What we have just said with regard to the sentiments manifested by derivations is commonly recognized in the perception that enthusiastic derivations are better calculated than cold reasoning to influence human conduct. This elliptical form of statement may be passed, provided it be clearly understood that the capacity in question lies not in the derivations but in the sentiments underlying them (§ 2085).

1868. The capacity for influencing human conduct that is possessed by sentiments expressed in the form of derivations that overstep experience and reality throws light upon a phenomenon that has been well observed and analyzed by Georges Sorel, the fact, namely, that if a social doctrine (it would be more exact to say the sentiments manifested by a social doctrine) is to have any influence, it has to take the form of a "myth." [1] To restate in that

1868 [1] Sorel, *Réflexions sur la violence,* pp. 92-94 (164-67) (Soule, pp. 133-36): "Experience shows that constructions of a future indefinitely located in time may be

language an observation that we have many times made, we may say that the social value of a doctrine, or of the sentiments which it expresses, is not to be judged extrinsically by the mythical form that it assumes (they assume), which is only its means (their means) of action, but intrinsically by the results that it achieves (they achieve).

1869. Since the situation here is not an easy one to grasp, a graph may help to make it clearer. The picture we set before the reader is a very crude affair. Too exacting a scrutiny would even prove it fallacious, but it will nevertheless serve to clarify the more precise statement that is possible with words. Ignoring the case where people think they are going in one direction and are actually going in another (§ 1873), let us keep to the case where they are going to some extent at least in the direction desired. An individual finds himself, let us say, at *h,* where he is enjoying a certain amount of utility represented by the index *ph.* The idea is to induce him to go on to *m,* where he will enjoy a greater utility, *qm.* To state the matter to him in that fashion would amount to little in the way of rousing him to action. It is wiser, therefore, to put before his eyes the point *T,* located at quite a distance from the curve *hm* on the tangent *hT,* where he would enjoy an enormous, though altogether fantastic, utility, *rT.* The result now is somewhat analogous to what happens in the case where a material point

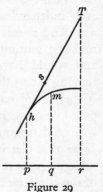

Figure 29

is moved by a tangential force, *hT,* along a curve, *hm.* That is to say, the individual aspires to *T,* and moves towards *T,* but, hampered by all sorts of practical ties (correlations, checks) he cannot hold to the tangent *hT.* He is forced to keep to the curve and ends up at *m,* whither, however, he might never have gone had he not been stimulated by a tangential impulse along the line *hT.*

very effective and involve very few embarrassments when they are of a certain character. That is the case with myths that chance to embrace the strongest tendencies of a people, party, or class, tendencies that in all the circumstances of life are for ever presenting themselves to the mind with all the assertiveness of instincts, lending an aspect of full reality to those hopes of imminent action on which reforms of the will are based. We know, for that matter, that these social myths in no way prevent people from managing to profit by all the observations they make in the

1870. Evidently, in order to determine the conditions under which the individual will be situated at m one need not bother with T. The index rT is at bottom arbitrary and has no relation to the real index, mq, except the fact that progress in the direction of both T and m lengthens the index of which the value was ph. Furthermore, it is altogether immaterial that T should be imaginary and impractical, so long as m, for its part, is concrete and real.

1871. A being capable of non-logical conduct only could be pushed from h to m unawares. But the human being is a logical animal. He wants to know *why* he is moving in the direction hm. And so a person who is moved by instinct, interest, or other pressures along the course hm exercises his imagination and hitches his wagon to the star T. Then, through group-persistences, the imaginary goal T acquires potency as sentiment in him and comes to serve, even independently of other causes, to urge him along the course hm. And it exerts the same influence upon other individuals, who find the sentiment ready-made in the society in which they live, and would have no other reasons, or very indifferent ones, for moving along the line hm. In so far as the imaginary objective, T, is mere explanation, it satisfies the human desire for logical, or pseudo-logical, ratiocination, but it can do little or nothing in the way of determining conduct. As an explanation it has the limited value that derivations have as approximating logico-experimental reasonings more or less closely. The extent to which the trend, hm, of the curve more or less approximately coincides with the trend, hs, of the tangent is the measure of the correspondence of the derivations with realities.

1872. The fact that m and T are different things and that to get

course of their lives nor from fulfilling their normal functions [Composition of social forces.]. That can be shown by numberless examples. The first Christians looked for the return of Christ, and for the total collapse of the pagan world followed by the establishment of the Kingdom of the Saints, by the end of the first generation. No such catastrophe occurred, but Christian thought took such advantage of the apocalyptic myth that certain scholars of our time contend that the whole preachment of Jesus bore on that theme alone. . . . One may readily see that actual developments in the Revolution in no way resembled the enchanting pictures that had enthralled its first converts. But could the Revolution have triumphed without such pictures? . . . Myths have to be thought of as instruments for influencing the present, and any discussion as to ways of applying them materially to the course of history is devoid of sense."

to *m* one must aim at *T* has many consequences in addition to those just noted, and we shall have occasion to advert to them in pages hereafter.

1873. It may, and sometimes actually does happen, that things develop not in the manner pictured in Figure 29, but in a manner pictured in Figure 30. The individual desirous of moving along the line *hT* in order to improve his situation, moves instead from *h* to *f* and so lessens his utility; which, from the index *ph,* diminishes to the index *vf.* Such, among others, are cases where the derivations have no correspondence with reality whatever, where, that is, the

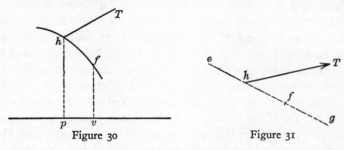

Figure 30   Figure 31

route *hT* cannot be imagined as coinciding with the route *hf* even roughly or even for the shortest distance. Oftentimes, further, the impulse to move towards *T* actually carries one in an entirely different direction.[1] To grasp this situation more clearly we may again have recourse to a crude graph. Figure 30 may be thought of as representing a vertical cross-section of the surface *hf* over which the individual has to move. Let us look at a horizontal projection of that same surface, as in Figure 31. The point *h* is stimulated by a force moving in the direction *hT;* but it encounters certain obstacles (prejudices, sentiments, interests, and the like) that force it to move along the line *ehfg;* and so, under pressure of the force *hT,* it moves not at all towards *T* but brings up at *f,* in something like the movement of a ship tacking against the wind.[2]

1874. We have seen what may conceivably happen. It remains to determine what actually does happen in the concrete. If we consider history as a whole it is at once apparent that—be it indeed within

---

1873 [1] That is the case which we decided to ignore at first (§ 1869).

1873 [2] The substance of this paragraph will serve us again later on (§§ 2148 f.) in examining phenomena of the same sort.

narrow limits—acts which have ideal goals, T, or are performed as if they had, must also in many cases achieve results that show a gain in individual and social utility—must, in other words, lead to a point, m (Figure 29), where the indices of utility tend to rise. In point of fact, non-logical actions are still very numerous and still very important in our time; and they were far more so in times past. The impellent of many such actions, the ideal, T, at which they aim, is stated in theological, metaphysical, and like derivations; while the practical purpose of human beings is the welfare and prosperity of themselves and their societies. If the two goals were antithetical, if the person aiming at the ideal, T, never attained practical benefits, it would never have been possible for societies that have made such great efforts to attain T to subsist and prosper. Going back to Figure 29 (§ 1869), observed fact shows that there must have been many many cases in human history in which things followed very much the course pictured in that figure; that is to say, aspiring to T, people must have looked to their interests and gone to m; for if, in almost all cases, things had gone the way of Figure 30 (§ 1873), if, that is, in striving for T people had always reached f to their loss, human societies would have to show continuous decline. That has not been the case, and the hypothesis must therefore be abandoned.

1875. If that all goes to show that people have aimed at imaginary goals and frequently attained real advantages, it by no means follows that that has always been the case. So we have before us still unsolved the problem as to when and within what limits the two aims coincide, given the circumstances of place and time in which the given case arises. Nor do we know either whether, when, and to what extent it may be desirable to substitute an imaginary aim for a real aim. But before attacking those problems and examining the various solutions that have been proposed for them, we are obliged to halt on a matter of more general bearing.

1876. *Ideals and their relations to other social facts.*[1] Suppose we

1876 [1] We are to examine these problems qualitatively just here, coming to quantitative considerations in the next chapter (§§ 2121 f.). There too a definition of the term "utility" will be supplied. For the time being it will be sufficient to think of that term as indicating a certain entity that is correlated with other social facts and is susceptible of increase and decrease. If we had been following the deductive method and working from the general to the particular, we should have begun with

have a society made up of individuals whose conduct, in part, envisages certain ideal principles, T, either observing certain ideal norms, or else performing non-logical actions that to an observer seem to be consequences of such norms, such principles. Now we want to determine the character and the consequences of the conduct performed and its bearing on various utilities (§§ 2115 f.). Two problems at once arise: 1. What are the facts, in reality? 2. How do they look to observers viewing them from the outside, and especially to the authors of theories and doctrines? In the case of writers and specialists, the solutions of the problems are, in great part at least, explicit; but for human beings in the mass they are often implicit, that is to say, without formulating the solutions they in fact find people conduct themselves as though they were acting with reference to them. One might better say, to avoid the usual danger of mistaking non-logical for logical conduct, that the conduct of people is such that in seeking a logical principle as a premise for it one is led to one of those solutions. The logical principle, it follows, is merely an inference drawn from the conduct by the observer, and is not at all a principle on which the individual bases his behaviour logically (§§ 2147 f.). Another problem further arises: 3. What manner of viewing facts is most desirable for individuals, society, and so on (§§ 2115 f.)? But that problem may be included in the preceding if one think of a given belief as to facts as an ideal, T, so corresponding to the first problem thus stated. And that also prepares us to see that there is still a fourth problem, corresponding

the subjects we deal with in Chapter XII, coming down from them to the matters here in hand. But that method is not the best suited to a sound understanding of our subject. It is the qualitative problem that confronts us in the concrete whenever we touch upon social matters. That was virtually the only problem ever considered in times past, as it continues to be for almost all writers today. So the concept of utility presents itself in a somewhat vague and uncertain manner, as happens with all concepts of the kind. Down to a few years ago writers did not feel the need of any greater precision. In the case of a special variety of utility, the utility considered in political economy, the need came to be felt some time ago and gave rise to the theories of pure economics. In this study we are trying to extend a similar exactness to other sorts of utility, and we are following the same course that was followed in economics, working, that is, from the better known to the less known, from the more imperfect to the less imperfect, from the less exact to the more exact. That manner of exposition is less succinct and polished than the deductive method, which works in the opposite direction; but it is much clearer, much easier, and much more helpful for the person who desires to master a subject.

to the second above, and which can be stated in the question: 4. How actually has the relation between utility and the manner in which individuals interpret facts been viewed by people, and especially by writers? Just here we are interested in problems 1 and 2 only.[2] They suggest the following subjects for our examination:

I. The ideal, T (§§ 1877-78)

    I-1. First problem (§ 1877)
    I-2. Second problem (§ 1878)

II. Relations between T and m (§§ 1879-91)

    II-1. First problem (§§ 1879-82)
    II-2. Second problem (§§ 1883-91)

        II-2a. T and m are not distinguished or are at least regarded as approximately identical (§§ 1883-84)
        II-2b. The ideals, T, are distinguished sharply and *a priori* from the utility, m (§§ 1885-91)
        II-2b-α. Only certain purposes T are considered (§ 1886)
        II-2b-β. The imaginary purposes, T, and the utility, m, are set flatly in opposition (§ 1887)
        II-2b-γ. Intermediate cases (§§ 1888-91)

III. How T is associated as an effect with certain causes (§§ 1892-93)

    III-1. First problem (§ 1892)
    III-2. Second problem (§ 1893)

IV. Character of the routes by which the ideal is reached (§§ 1894-95)

    IV-1. First problem (§ 1894)
    IV-2. Second problem (§ 1895)

1877. I: *The ideal (purpose)*, T. It lies outside experience.[1]

I-1: *First problem.* In the case of animals T seems to be an instinct pure and simple. It may also be an instinct with human be-

---

1876 [2] We have many times already alluded to problems 3 and 4 without so designating them explicitly; and we shall have further occasion to sound them in the course of this work. Further along (§§ 1896, 1932), we shall discuss them somewhat generally and in a particular case.

1877 [1] Logico-experimental purposes that are realized through the arts and sciences do not fall within our present purview.

ings in some few cases; but usually it is expressed in the form of residues at least, and, to satisfy the need of logic felt by the human being, in the form of manifestation-derivations (§ 1688).[2] It is essential to distinguish the purpose, T-α, that an individual has of his own accord from the purpose, T-β, that others may try to induce him to have. That distinction is of immense importance in human societies because of the conflict the individual feels between his own advantage and the advantage of other individuals or society. The history of morals and law is, one may say, the history of the efforts that have been made to reconcile, by fair means or foul, those two sorts of utility. In animals the conciliation is effected by instinct, and marvellous indeed the conciliation that is achieved between the utility of the young and the utility of the parents. Oftentimes it involves the sacrifice of the latter to the former. Something of the same sort happens in human beings; but their hunger for ratiocination prevents them from stopping at purely instinctive acts and leads them on into the spacious field of derivations.

1878. I-2: *Second problem.* People who stop to consider the ideals (purposes) *T* have viewed them in general as absolute, or at least as experimental, principles, so ascribing an ostensibly real form to imaginary principles. That has been the case not only in virtue of the tendency of the residues of group-persistence, of which the *T*'s are made up, to assume absolute forms or at least an appearance of concrete reality, but also in virtue of the practical advantage of not allowing a doubt of any kind to lodge in the mind of the person who is to be persuaded, and of utilizing, for that purpose, the force which absoluteness, or at least the presumed reality, confers upon principles. Both motives are still active in our day, the second, in fact, is gaining in strength with the progress of science, which is conferring greater and greater authority upon reality. It is not probable that either of them will disappear in any near future. One may predict that there will continue to be absolute *T*'s and imaginary *T*'s represented as real; for barring some change in the ties we see functioning about us at present, society will never be able to subsist without them (§§ 2143 f.). Writers who are unwilling to

---

1877 [2] [Pareto is speaking somewhat loosely. Strictly, manifestation-derivations, *i.e.,* derivatives, express the residue directly, the demand for logic being met by derivations proper (§ 1688).—A. L.]

lose touch with the real world altogether are forced to recognize the presence of such ideals in the past and at present. Some, however, say that they will gradually disappear and that at the end of social evolution mankind will have nothing but experimental aims.

1879. II: *Relations of the purpose (ideal),* T, *to the point,* m, *that individuals actually attain, and to various utilities.*

II-1: *First problem.* The solution of the objective problem is to be gathered from the whole sum of investigations that we are now completing. It was partly to obtain such a solution that we felt obliged to go so deeply into residues and derivations, for the purpose of discovering the substance underlying outward forms. We may say, in brief, that to aim at an imaginary objective, T, in order to attain a real end, m, is frequently an indispensable yet none the less an imperfect means of achieving m. To use it is like using a machine which transforms only a part of the total energy that it consumes into serviceable energy (§§ 1864 f.). So if someone were to assert that to replace the struggle to attain imaginary objectives, T, with efforts to attain ends that were experimental, real, would result in an elimination of waste and an increase in advantage to society, he would not be going wrong. But neither would one be going wrong in saying that to use machines that transform the whole of their consumed energy into useful work would eliminate economic waste and redound to the economic advantage of society.

1880. But we still have to know whether such a thing is possible—the most important problem for those of us who do not care to live in the clouds. As we have already noted (§§ 130 f.), if all the ties in a social system hold their own, what is does not differ from what might be; and *possible* cases are cases in which we assume as non-existent certain ties that are actually found missing in real cases (§§ 2143 f.).

1881. That is admitted in substance, or at least implicitly admitted, by those who would replace imaginary ideals with real purposes and so render social life logico-experimental throughout. But as a rule they recognize only one tie—ignorance. Ignorance being eliminated, they have no doubt that society will follow the course they think is the best. The tie of ignorance may legitimately be said to have been suppressed, at least in great part; for it is certain that there are educated people in our time just as there have been educated people in the past; and in society as a whole knowledge has increased in the course of the ages. So far, therefore, no obstacle blocks our path; but one rises insuperable in that part of the argument which holds that the tie of ignorance is the only tie that has to be removed before the conclusion is possible. If the most intelligent people we know—the "best-educated," to use a current term—were also the people who make most extensive use of logico-experimental principles in social matters to the exclusion of all other principles, it would be legitimate to conclude that, in course of time, such people would reject everything of a non-experimental character; and that other people, more or less their equals in knowledge, would also be more or less like them in their exclusive acceptance of logico-experimental principles. But the facts do not stand that way. If theologians have diminished in number among our educated people and lost much of their power, metaphysicists, properly so called, are still prospering and enjoying fame and influence, to say nothing of those metaphysicists who call themselves "positivists" or under some other name are merrily overstepping the boundaries of the logico-experimental. Many scientists who are supremely great in the natural sciences, where they use logico-experimental principles exclusively or almost so, forget them entirely when they venture into the social sciences.[1] As regards the masses in the large, what one

---

1881   [1] A chemist or a physicist would be amused if an amateur who had never made a special study of chemistry or physics should presume to pronounce judgment on problems connected with those sciences. And yet such scientists, without ever having read a book in the social sciences, set themselves up as oracles in connexion with most knotty social problems (§§ 1435 f.). One of them confidently decides that it would be a great misfortune for humanity if Germany did not become mistress of Europe, making her "civilization" triumphant over Russian "barbarism." He seems not even remotely to suspect that to determine the effects upon human evolution of German predominance, or Russian predominance, in Europe is about as difficult a task as to determine the constitution of matter. That comes about because the scientist, following the objective method in his chemistry or physics, unwittingly falls under the spell of the subjective method in turning to the social sciences. When he is talking about the structure of the atom, he keeps to what experience has taught him and discards sentiment. When he pronounces on Socialism, imperialism, German "civilization," Russian "barbarism," and so on, he merely voices the sentiments which those words or phrases awaken in him, and cares not a fig about experience (historical observation and the like), of which he is almost always totally ignorant. That anomaly is all the more striking when we see novelists, poets, and playwrights pronouncing *ex cathedra* on social and economic matters on which they are grossly uninformed. What connexion can there be between writ-

observes is an unending alternation of theologies and systems of metaphysics rather than any reduction in the total number of them (§§ 2329 f.). That fact we have repeatedly stressed, and do so here again in connexion with 2.

1882. Our conclusions, therefore, will be that the pursuit of certain imaginary aims, T, has been in the past, continues in the present, and will probably continue in any near future, to be very advantageous for human societies (§ 1932); that oftentimes there may be several concurrent aims, T, T', T'' . . . widely differing as regards derivations, but equivalent, or almost so, as regards their social utility (§§ 1740, 1850 f.); but that all that in no way proves that the pursuit of other imaginary, theological, or metaphysical aims may not have been detrimental to society in the past, or may not be in the present or future (§ 1873, Figure 30). Questions as to the utility of ideals cannot be answered in general. One must specify which ideals one is considering, and then go on to determine their relations to other social facts; and that must be done not only qualitatively, but quantitatively as well (§§ 2142 f.). And one must further determine whether there may not be some proportion between the pursuit of imaginary ideals and the pursuit of logico-experimental aims that is more useful to society than any other proportion. Nor is that yet all. Society is a heterogeneous affair and that fact cannot be ignored. The investigation therefore has to be made for each of the various social classes in turn.[2]

1883. II-2: *Second problem.* Just here we are interested in the substance, rather than in the forms, of the doctrines that have been current as to the relations of T and m. When they make any extensive use of derivations they are better analyzed in connexion with III and IV.

II-2a: T *and* m *are not distinguished or are at least regarded as*

ing a successful play and objectively solving a problem in social science? There is a connexion, all the same! And that is where sentiment comes in. The notions such people express in regard to social problems are absurd, fatuous, idiotic, from the scientific standpoint. But from the standpoint of sentiment, they will please the same audiences that have applauded their plays. Such a public is, for the most part, incapable of grasping a logico-experimental argument; but it feasts on sentimental utterances that are suited to its mental powers. Such is the world, and one cannot imagine how and when it is ever going to change.

1882 [2] We are to do that in the chapter next following.

approximately identical. That can be done in two ways: *A.* One believes that the pursuit of the ideal is the best way of attaining one's own and other people's advantage—one aims at *T* and attains *m.* *B.* Conversely, one may believe that one is aiming at an ideal, whereas one is really looking to one's own advantage or to the advantage of others—one aims at *m* and preaches *T.* All that, however, is very hazy and indefinite in the mind, as we shall better see in a less general case (§§ 1897 f.), the various utilities in particular being oftentimes confused.[1]

A. [The conscious purpose is *T.* What actually is attained is *m.*] Such doctrines are far more numerous and more important than other sorts; for almost always the purpose of a doctrine is to persuade individuals to aim at an objective that yields an advantage to other individuals or to society. If *T*1 be the selfish purpose that yields the advantage, *m*1, of the individual, and *T*2 the altruistic pur-

1883 [1] Here is an example that may serve as typical of vast numbers of such reasonings. On Jan. 20, 1914, the French ministry introduced before the two Chambers and successfully passed a bill appropriating 20,000 francs for a national funeral for General Picquart. A member in the Senate rose to inquire just what services that general had rendered the country. The premier, M. Doumergue, replied: "You ask me what services General Picquart has rendered the country: he believed in immanent justice and truth!"

What "immanent justice and truth" may be no one knows exactly, and M. Doumergue perhaps less than anybody else. Still, there are so many kinds of truth that such a handsome thing as "immanent truth" may well have its place among them. Let us ignore these goat's-wool subtleties, as Rabelais would have called them, and concede without debate the existence of the respectable entities called "immanent justice and truth," and go on to see what meanings M. Doumergue's statement may have had. We may classify them roughly as follows:

a. There is an implicit principle from which one may infer that a real advantage, namely, national welfare, will be obtained.

a-I. The advantage lies in winning the victory in case of war.

a-I-1. A general who believes in "immanent justice and truth" is better fitted than an other sort of general to discharge his function, which is to lead his troops to victory in case of war. Picquart held the belief in question; therefore he must have contributed to assuring victory for his country in case of war. M. Doumergue, notice, did not refer to the belief as an adornment over and above Picquart's merits as a soldier. Of those merits he said nothing; and wisely, for what more he could have said in Picquart's favour than what he said is very little indeed. A writer in the *Gazette de Lausanne,* Jan. 21, 1914, who was nevertheless kindly disposed towards Picquart, wrote: "One may wonder—and the question has been passionately argued —whether the hero of the Dreyfus affair was as soundly inspired in accepting the compensation that the abrupt development in events brought his way. The very peculiar prestige which haloed that attractive and rather enigmatic figure could only

pose yielding the utility $m2$ of other individuals or society, one may say that the purpose of many many ethical theories is to merge $T1$, $T2$, $m1$ and $m2$, into a single homogeneous mass. If the prime stress is laid on the utility, $m1$, of the individual, and the aims $T1$, $T2$ and the utility $m2$ are represented as so much like it as to be identical with it or almost so, we get the seeds that will sprout, by appropriate derivations, into the various "utilitarian" ethical systems that have flourished from the earliest historical times down to our own

suffer some diminution when the man agreed to become a cabinet minister like any other and to submit, to an extent at least, to the limitations that the fact of belonging to a political party necessarily involves. All the same, those who followed General Picquart's activities in the Ministry of War at close range know that his transfer to the rue St. Dominique meant a sort of perpetual conflict for him, in which his instinctive independence of character was more than once at swords' points with the passwords of party spirit. Thoroughly and justly to appraise his rôle during that period, a sharp line of demarcation has to be drawn between what he had to grant under pressure from his friends, and notably the deplorable reduction of drill-periods for reservists, and the services he rendered the army, most important here the uncompromising resolve he manifested during the debates on the Artillery Appropriations bill. It appears, on the other hand, that he was not entirely successful in exercising the high command entrusted to him. Through a succession of circumstances he had missed the experience of intermediary commands and suddenly found himself faced overnight with difficulties he was not accustomed to meeting. His technical knowledge and an amazingly cultivated mind better equipped him for directing certain services of the General Staff than to command large units in the field. That perfect gentleman, whose smile was so engaging and whose thought so ornate, was more of a scholar than a soldier. To look at him one had the impression that the personality which his moral courage illumined with such splendour was hardly cast for the career he followed."

It would still seem therefore that belief in "immanent truth and justice" were the chief requisite in a general. Was it from holding that belief that Philip of Macedon defeated the Athenians at Chaeroneia, that Alexander the Great routed the Persians, and Hannibal won his victory at Cannae? Hannibal's defeat at Zama must perhaps have been due to some backsliding; but we may guess that Moltke was a virtual fanatic to win as he won at Sedan. With all that it seems a little hard to agree; so that the experimental basis of our syllogism collapses.

α-I-2. One may conceive of the effects of believing in immanent justice and truth in somewhat more general and somewhat less personal terms, and those estimable entities are then to be counted among the gods-protectors of peoples. If the Israelites were shielded in battle by their Jehovah, if Rome owed her victories to her divinities, if the God of the Christians protected them against the Moslems, and the god of Mohammed the Moslems against the Christians, one may readily admit that the godhead Immanent-Truth-and-Justice can protect a people too. However, it is hardly probable that such a notion of divine interposition could have figured explicitly among the theories of a free-thinker such as M. Doumergue.

α-I-3. Belief in such entities may inspire men to achievements that will make victory certain. That has been the case with many such beliefs; but it is not at all

and find literary expression all the way along from the fables that were current in the infancy of the race down to the complicated disquisitions of Bentham and the Positivists. Most human beings are unable to forget their own utility, m_1. They must therefore be shown that it is to their interests to aim at T_2 and attain m_2. If the main

apparent that the belief in Immanent-Truth-and-Justice is to be counted among them. It has the ear-marks of being just a rhetorical belief of certain men of letters. That certainly was not what M. Doumergue meant.

Being unable to show the utility of the belief as guaranteeing victory, suppose we look about for some other utility.

a-II. The national utility envisaged is not of the military type, but some other.

a-II-1. It is more profitable to pursue certain "moral" principles than material prosperity.

a-II-2. The utility of having a certain form of government is superior to the utility of winning a war. Those two principles M. Doumergue and those who applauded him may well have had in mind, but it would have been difficult to get a clear statement of them out of those gentlemen. Our many difficulties in demonstrating the utility of the principle may be obviated if we move on to another order of ideas:

β. Observance of the principle stated is an end in itself independent of any consideration of utility.

β-I. Our sole concern must be to satisfy "immanent justice and truth": Do what you ought, come what will! That, substantially, is the rule-of-life of all faiths that are at all vigorous—it was the rule of the Christian martyrs. It is not apparent however that M. Doumergue and his friends bear any close resemblance to Christian martyrs.

β-II. We must not worry about war—there is not going to be a war, anyhow! So the important thing is not to have generals who are good fighters on the field of battle, but generals who follow the "moral" principles of the party in power. A believer in "immanent truth and justice" must be preferred to an able general. At the head of our army we want not a Napoleon Bonaparte, but a St. Francis of Assisi who holds a paid-up membership in the Radical party. Something like that may well have been in the minds of M. Doumergue's friends. One must not forget that they wanted André for their Minister of War and Pelletan for their Minister of Marine and that those two gentlemen utterly disorganized the national defence of France. M. Doumergue's party, moreover, opposed the three-years law and in every way showed itself hostile to the army.

So now we are getting closer to the realities underlying the derivation "immanent truth and justice":

γ. It is a mere euphemism for the interests of a group of politicians and "speculators" (§ 2235). Those individuals found in the Dreyfus affair a ladder for climbing into power, making money, and winning public honours, with the support of a few "intellectuals" who swallowed the bait that was dangled before them and took the euphemisms, immanent truth and immanent justice, for realities.

M. Doumergue's derivation has therefore to be translated into the following language: "Picquart served our interests, and we are honouring him that we may induce others to do as he did. For the country's defence we care not a hang. Come what may, we stand by our interests, and the interests of our party."

stress is laid on T_2, often represented as identical with T_1, and m_1 and m_2 are represented as more or less identical with T_2 and T_1, we get in germ the many theological and metaphysical systems of ethics. In order to bring T_2 and m_1 closer together to the point of identity, theological moralities resort to sanctions emanating from their particular deities. Metaphysical ethics replace gods with some imperative or other (§§ 1886, 1938)—and with no great success, one must add.

1884. B. The schemer consciously aims at m and preaches T; but the same thing is also done by many individuals who are in all good faith. Cynically selfish people are rare and downright hypocrites equally so. The majority of men merely desire to reconcile their own advantage with the residues of sociality (Class IV); realize their own happiness while seeming to strive for the happiness of others; cloak their self-seeking under mantles of religion, ethics, patriotism, humanitarianism, party loyalty, and so on; work for material satisfactions while seeming to be working only for ideals. In that way, furthermore, such men are able to win the support of people who are attracted by the beauty of the ideal, T, but who would be indifferently, if at all, interested in the humble, earthly purpose, m. That is why they go rummaging about for theories adapted to the achievement of their purpose, and find them without difficulty; for the market is glutted with theories manufactured by theologians, moralists, social writers, and other people of the kind, who keep their counters covered with an article so greatly in demand, and so are able to attain their own advantage while seeming only to be in quest of the sublime.[1]

1884 [1] The nineteenth century yielded a rich harvest of such derivations in the course of the conflict between working-men and "capitalists" (who are really *entrepreneurs*). The situation, substantially, is that between those two sorts of people there is the usual conflict of interest that arises between any two parties drawing up a contract in the economic field. Each, in other words, tries to bring the grist to his own mill, each tries to make his own share as large as possible. Such the objectives for which they strove and are striving. But outwardly they said and still say, and many believed and still believe, that their aim was and is the ideal, T.

From the manufacturers' side we did not get such very subtle reasonings. They pointed to their concern for the welfare of the working-classes, the "legitimate" remuneration due to men who made an enterprise prosper by the art of combinations, the social advantages of economic freedom, which they always remembered when fixing wages and always forgot when fixing prices.

From the working-men's side came a flood of subtle theories that were agitated

1885. II-2*b*: *The purposes,* T, *are distinguished sharply and* a priori *from the utility,* m. Ordinarily it is only in appearances that writers deal with the ideals *T* in general. Actually what they have chiefly or exclusively in view is certain particular purposes, *T*, of their own.

1886. II-2*b*-α: *Only certain purposes,* T, *are considered.* The writer disregards the utility, *m*, or at the most thinks of it as a thing of little or no account. So we get theological or metaphysical systems of ethics that overlook utility altogether and set forth in absolute terms what people *ought* to do; and also ascetic, mystical systems, and others of that kind. Owing to the power that ascetic residues normally have these latter have their social importance, though much less so than ethical systems of type I (§ 1877). Asceticism is generally an end in itself; but, in virtue of the supernatural sanctions that it ordinarily invokes, it may sometimes develop into some-

by "intellectuals" and accepted by the working-people in blind faith and without any comprehension of them. From the Socialistic utopias down to Marxism and democratic or Socialistic radicalism, one finds vast numbers of doctrines that all use draperies of gay colours to hide the very simple resolve to demand "a larger share in the proceeds of economic production." But to state the idea in such simple terms would weaken the case of the people who use it; for it would cost them the support they derive from the ideal character of a purpose and the backing of those good souls who succumb to the lure of such theories. So in our derivations we will appeal, as usual, to one sentiment or another. We will call the demands of the workers "claims" to give the impression that they are demanding only something that belongs to them—and that will win us the support of Class V residues (individual integrity). However, so simple a suggestion will not be enough: we had better get the I-ε residues (logic) on our side; so we will evolve theories about the "total product of labour," "surplus value," the need of having "a little more justice in the world," and so on. The longer in words and the more difficult to grasp such theories are, the more glamorously ideal will they make the objective at which we say we are aiming.

But disregarding their fatuity as arguments and looking only at their substance, one soon observes that it has been to the advantage of the working-classes to aim, in that fashion, at fantastic ideals; for, in virtue of the stubborn battle that they have fought for them and which they might perhaps not have fought under any other inspiration, and thanks to valiant aid from the allies whom they have recruited through the ideal character of their purposes, the working-classes have managed to improve their lot very appreciably in the course of the nineteenth century. As regards a nation or society as a whole, it is much more difficult to decide whether or not that change has been for the better. An affirmative answer would seem to be the more probable; but to prove it we should have first to consider the problem of social and economic evolution synthetically; and that we cannot do till our next chapter.

thing that has the look of a theological system, advocating, that is, an imaginary utility instead of the real utility, m. Such appearances are deceptive, for in view of the criterion we are using for our classification here, m is essentially real.

1887. II-2b-β: *The ideal,* T, *and the utility,* m, *are set flatly in opposition.* Writers commonly express themselves as though they were considering all possible imaginary ends, whereas, at bottom, they are contemplating certain specific ends only, which they desire to replace with other ends equally imaginary. The conflict resulting is between two theologies, two metaphysics, and not between theology and metaphysics on the one side and logico-experimental science on the other. Here are to be classed purely ascetic doctrines that cherish no ideal of other-worldly happiness but are ends in themselves, deliberately ignoring utility. And here too belong pessimistic systems which hold that no matter what the ideal pursued mankind will never achieve "happiness" (which in that case is a synonym for utility).

1888. II-2b-γ: *Intermediate cases.* T and m are not distinguished *a priori;* they are taken as different things that may stand now in one, now in another, relation to each other. If such relations are experimental, the logico-experimental solution is correctly perceived—in other words, our solution II-1 is reached. If they are non-experimental or are established *a priori,* we get various derivations. Noteworthy among these are such doctrines as separate the imaginary objectives, T, into two groups, one of which, Th, is said to be infallibly beneficial, the other, Tk, infallibly harmful, very very harmful. Needless to say, the good ones, Th, are the ones that accord with the religion of the given writer. This case very often blends with the cases preceding; for as a rule writers by no means admit that there is any such division of the imaginary or merely ideal ends, T, into the two classes, Th and Tk. For them there is but one class, Th, and the ends Th are the only ends that really exist. They, therefore, are "real" ends, "true" ends, the ends Tk being nonexistent, "unreal," "false." Since the purposes Th are the only real ones in the eyes of such writers, the category Th takes the place of the category T, to which we alluded in the preceding cases, and is identical with it.

1889. Phenomena of that sort are observable in history whenever attempts are made to replace one religion with another. In such cases they are readily recognized. They are a little less obvious when materialistic and positivistic doctrines, or others of the kind, open fire on all "religion"; yet a glance at all close readily reveals that such doctrines differ from the religions which they are attacking not in substance but in name only, and that, really, what is represented as a conflict between "Reason" and positive religions is just a conflict between theologies. One should not forget that if "Reason" is nowadays being invoked against Christianity, it was invoked by Christianity against paganism in a day gone by and that the modern theology of Progress is new only in part, in other parts merely repeating the ideas of the past in different language.

1890. In the theology of Progress, the history of humanity is chiefly, and perhaps exclusively, the history of a struggle between a principle of "evil," called "superstition," and a principle of "good," called "Science." To write history is simply to paraphrase a verse of Lucretius, *De rerum natura*, I, v. 101: *"Tantum religio potuit suadere malorum."* The religion of Progress is polytheistic. "Superstition," queen of darkness, mistress of evil, has a retinue of inferior deities, and, as is usually the case, there are some among them who increase in prestige while others wane or even vanish from the earth. At one time the *auri sacra fames* held first place in the hierarchy; now that demon is quoted very low. In the heyday of Christian fervour "Pagan Superstition" was in the ascendant as opposed to "True Religion." In modern times "Private Property" came to dispute the primacy of "Superstition," and Rousseau berated the poor thing with appalling invectives. But in the days of the French Revolution "Superstition" resumed her former throne, this time with an ample household of paladins, and to wit, kings, nobles, and priests. Then theoretical speculations had their turn again, and "Capitalism" succeeded "Private Property" much as Jupiter succeeded Saturn of old. Blessed the man who holds such a key of knowledge! Every mystery, past, present, or future, yields to the magic password "capitalism." Capitalism, and capitalism alone, is the cause of poverty, ignorance, immorality, theft, murder, war. Little avails it to produce the catalogues of those disciples of Messalina who have been numerous in every age. It remains an article of faith that if there were no capitalism all women would be chaste and prostitution would be abolished.[1] Nor does it avail to point to savage peoples who spend their lives in constant warfare. This new faith requires one to believe that without capitalism there would be no wars of any kind, though there are plenty of Socialists who fight in wars nowadays and then excuse themselves with the casuistic plea that they are opposed to wars in general but in favour of the particular war that happens to be to their liking. If there are paupers, illiterates, hoodlums, degenerates, drunkards, lunatics, spendthrifts, thieves, assassins, conquerors, capitalism alone is to blame. The reasoning by which all that is proved is the usual *post hoc, propter hoc.* Our society is "capitalistic." Its ills therefore originate in "capitalism." There are, of course, other arguments too, but they come down, at bottom, to the plain assertion that if people had all the things they wanted they would not resort to crimes and cruelties in order to procure them. Granting, then, that "capitalism" alone prevents people from having all the things they want, it remains demonstrated that capitalism is the root of all evil.

1891. Over against the principle of evil is set the principle of good, which in a day gone by was "True Religion" and is nowadays "Science." "Science" too surrounds herself with minor deities such as "Democracy," "Humanitarianism," "Pacifism," " Truth," "Justice" —all those entities, in short, which are deemed worthy of the epithet

1890 [1] Well known the fact that there are married women with large incomes who nevertheless sell themselves to add to the luxuries they already enjoy. It is answered that the poverty and the wealth produced by capitalism have the same effect. That may be so. Let us see: If the explanation is sound, the situation in question ought not to arise among people who have just modest incomes. Unfortunately that is not the case. The woman of the petty *bourgeoisie* sells herself to get a stylish hat; the society woman sells herself to get a string of pearls—but they both sell themselves. The conclusion has to be that if all individuals in a given community had exactly the same income, there would still be women ready to give themselves to the men who were disposed to supply them with the things they want. The objection is urged, of course, that our society is corrupt because of the existence of the capitalistic system; and that objection cannot be answered, for it is an article of faith and faith transcends experience. Other fanatics, of the breed that organize leagues against obscenity and the "white-slave trade," and societies for the "improvement of morals," deliberately shut their eyes to the light from such facts. It is an article of faith with those innocent souls that the man always seduces the woman, and that women therefore must be protected. Yet anybody willing to go to the trouble of reading the newspapers and following cases in the courts will find that it is more frequently the woman who misleads the man. Everywhere, in cases of the unfaithful clerk, the dishonest cashier, the absconding banker, the army officer

"progressive," and which, like the angels of light fighting the angels of darkness, fight other entities called "reactionary" and defend and preserve our wretched humanity from the wiles of such demons.

1892. III: *How* T *is associated as an effect with certain causes.* III-1: *First problem.* We have already seen one of the ways in which that is done—by trying to create a confusion between the ideals and the utilities. But that is not the only way. Ideals and interests may be identified by other devices; and then, in addition to interests, people have passions and sentiments with which ideals may be correlated. Furthermore, as regards means of effecting the union of ideals and other facts, there is not only persuasion but also constraint. The latter asserts itself in the hostility that is shown to individuals who violate the usages, customs, norms, that prevail in a given society, and it is applied practically in penal law. With it we are not concerned here. As regards means of persuasion, there are the numberless productions of literature, from simple fairy-stories all the way along to the most complicated theological, ethical, metaphysical, "positivistic," and like disquisitions. As we have over and again repeated, the persuasive force of such productions resides not in the derivations, but in the residues and interests that they call

turned spy, some woman is involved, and we get new confirmation of the judge's apothegm, *"Cherchez la femme."* The needs of such women are not the needs of a modest comfortable standard of living, but the needs of extravagance and display; and it is to satisfy such demands that men are often led to steal, betray, and sometimes commit murder. If there must be this craze for protection, why worry so much about the seduction of women and so little about the seduction of men? Why is there no ingenious brain to invent some other stupid phrase like the "white-slave trade" to apply to the case of the poor white man? Only a sick or childish mind can imagine that it is just the material requirements of getting a living that drive women to prostitution. With many women it is a case of vanity and love of extravagance. Not a few others turn to the occupation out of indolence; and, in higher social circles, there are those who like the profession the way a hunter likes hunting and the fisherman fishing. There too there is no lack of facts for those who choose to see them. How many the prostitutes who have been forcibly redeemed by simple-minded uplifters and provided with respectable and comfortable livings, only to desert them and return to their old occupation for which they felt an incurable homesickness? But many people refuse to see these facts, and others like them, because they are not telling the truth when they say they are trying to fight prostitution for the benefit of womanhood and to destroy the "white-slave trade" for the benefit of said "slaves." Really all they are doing is coddling a theological antipathy to pleasures of the senses.

into play. It follows that only those works of literature will live which associate ideals with powerful residues and important interests. Such residues are always available from some one of our classes. Very effective are certain residues of group-persistence, which, taken either singly or in combination with other residues (among which chiefly those of sociality), supply the many entities with which human beings have peopled their divine, metaphysical, and social Olympuses. We may therefore foresee that ideals, T, will usually be associated with such entities; and that is precisely what happens in the case of theological and metaphysical systems of ethics and in those moralities which are based upon reverence for tradition and ancestral wisdom—today represented by the infallibility of Progress—and for the usages and customs of tribe, city, nation, or race. In these latter cases, residues of sociality play a prominent part; and ascetic residues (IV-ζ) play the leading rôle in ascetic systems.

If we are to remain in touch with realities, it must not be forgotten that many ideals, T, that state rules of conduct are, if not in form, in substance at least, given—are, that is, products of the thinker's society, in which he finds them ready-made, and not products of his theoretical meditation. The quest, therefore, is not for the ideal, T, but, T being given, for something with which it may be correlated, and for the means of effecting the correlation (§§ 636, 1628). The ideal at which the individual is invited to gaze varies but little in time, as regards substance, at least; the residues to which it is tied vary somewhat more; the derivations and pseudo-scientific reasonings serving to associate ideals and residues, much much more.

1893. III-2: *Second problem.* In doctrines, in general, when ideals do not stand by themselves as absolutes they are considered consequences of theological or metaphysical principles or of interests; and the result is those various moralities which we discovered in germ in examining the relations of T and m (§§ 1883 f.). As for the nature of the correlation, it is bluntly represented as rigorously logical, and nowadays as scientific or even experimental. So the ideal, T, is made to look like the statement of a theorem; and miraculous the regularity with which it always manages to contain something that was already present in the mind of the searcher, and not infrequently in the opinions of the community to which he belongs.

There is no chance that the theoretical moralist will ever end up with a theorem that conflicts with his own conscience; and very rarely with a theory conflicting with the ethics of the society in which he lives. Conversely, if it is shown that a certain ideal, T, is not a logical consequence of experimental, or at least "rational," principles, it is assumed as proved that it can only be harmful; and there again it is a marvel to behold how regularly the ideals that are so discovered to be contrary to experience, or at least to "reason," are the ideals of which the moralist disapproves or which run counter to the ethics of his community.

1894. IV: *Character of the routes by which the ideal,* T, *is reached.* IV-1: *First problem.* This properly is an examination of derivations. We have already completed it in great part and need not dwell further upon the subject here.[1]

1895. IV-2: *Second problem.* We are also familiar already with the attitude that is taken toward such devices in statements of doctrine; for we have repeatedly explained, and just above recalled, that pseudo-scientific derivations and reasonings are represented as logico-experimental, and that that procedure, though scientifically untrue, may frequently lead to results that are socially beneficial.

1896. And now briefly for problems 3 and 4 as stated in § 1876. 3. *What manner of viewing facts is desirable for individuals, society, and so on?* Our main concern is with problem II-1 (§ 1876). For the present let us confine ourselves to stating it.[1] It must not be taken as relating to doctrines in themselves, apart from the individuals who profess them, but as relating to the doctrines as viewed in connexion with individuals and their functions in society. That fact has always been perceived more or less vaguely by empiricists. It is now denied *a priori* by the theology of "equality." Using terms of

1894 [1] We first encountered (§§ 306 f.) the devices that are used to give an appearance of logic to non-logical conduct performed with the ideal, T, in view. Such devices are resorted to with the explicit, but more often implicit, intention of representing T and m as identical. Logical conduct leads to m. If it is to lead to T as well, T, logically, must be indistinguishable from m. Later on, in our examination of derivations in general, we came upon other devices, and found them to be particular instances of facts that are general. We shall be meeting other particular instances very shortly (§§ 1902 f.).

1896 [1] We might repeat that the solution has to come from the sum of investigations which we have been conducting in these volumes. This problem we shall treat more specially in our next chapter.

ordinary language, which, however, may be misleading because of their inexactness, one might say that it may be best for people to regard as "true" doctrines that are "false." Trying to come closer to realities by using expressions somewhat more exact, we might say that it may be beneficial to society for people to regard as in accord with experience (or with reality) doctrines that show no such accord.

4. *How has the relation between utility and the manner in which facts are interpreted been viewed by people, and especially by writers?* Here again empiricists have sometimes vaguely perceived a solution very like the logico-experimental solution just referred to. Very few theorists, on the other hand, have had any inkling of it, most of them accepting solutions corresponding to II-2*a*. They have confused "truth" and "utility," holding that it is always useful to individuals and community that people should view the facts under their "true" aspect. If "truth" there means conformity with experience, the proposition is false, as empiricists of all times have readily seen. If, as usually happens, "truth" means conformity with certain nebulous ideas of the writer, the proposition may approximate experience or be altogether at variance with it, according as the utility of such ideas approximates experience or diverges from it (§§ 1773 f.). Other ideals besides "truth" may be confused with utility—very frequently so, "justice." It is asserted, for instance, that only what is "true," "just," "moral," and the like, is "useful." Nowadays the theology of "equality," which is an aspect of the theology of Progress, shrinks with horror from the idea that it may be a good thing for individuals to have a variety of different doctrines and pursue differing ideals according to their functions in society.[2] To get a better understanding of the general theories just stated, and in view of their great importance to sociology, it will be well for us to analyze a particular case.

1897. *Relations between observance of the norms of religion and morality and the attainment of happiness.*[1] People have at all times

---

1896 [2] The other solutions are of less account and we need not dwell upon them here. We can go no farther along this line at present because we have no exact notions as to what the various utilities are (§§ 2115 f.). We shall therefore return to this subject in the next chapter.

1897 [1] One should re-read at this point the remarks we made in § 1876 [1].

wondered whether individual or community realized happiness by following such rules. The problem is a more limited one than the preceding. In the first place, we are not inquiring as to general relationships, but asking merely whether or not happiness is realized. That eliminates theological or metaphysical solutions of our II-2*b* type (§ 1876), which envisage "duty" without reference to utility. We can consider only such solutions as take account of some utility or other, be it real or imaginary.[2] In the second place, the ideals, T, envisaged in the broader problems just examined not only comprise observance of the rules of religion and morality, but are, in general, all that is counselled or required by a faith or a vigorous sentiment. We therefore find among them other norms that are current in society and deriving from tradition or some other such source, along with sentimental, ideal, mythical, or other similar objectives. In a word, utility here appears under a special form: the form of "happiness."

1898. To solve the particular problem that we have set ourselves we must first give greater exactness to our statement of it. We may disregard the very serious lack of definiteness in the terms "religion" and "morality," since they are not essential to the problem. Things would still be the same were we to speak of the observance of certain rules, to be designated by any names one chose and therefore also by the quite nebulous terms "religion" and "morality." But there are two points in the statement where the vagueness is important and cannot be disregarded. The first is the meaning of the terms "happiness" and "unhappiness"; and we shall see that people have availed themselves of that vagueness in those very terms in order to get the solutions of the problem that they desired (§ 1904). The other is the vagueness as to who is to apply the norm and who to attain the "happiness" or "unhappiness." In that connexion the following distinctions are in order.

I. The conduct and the realization of happiness or unhappiness may be viewed as united in the same person or persons. One may ask, that is: If a person scrupulously observes the rules of morality

---

1897 [2] Efforts are frequently made to confuse the two kinds of solutions, for it is not comfortable to leave "duty" floating in the air in that fashion, without any bearing whatever on the real world. Solutions $B2$, $B3$ and $B4$ of § 1902 are designed to produce just that confusion.

and religion will *he* necessarily be happy—and if he violates them, unhappy? Or one may ask: If the individuals constituting a community observe or violate the afore-said rules will *they* be happy or unhappy?

II. The individuals who observe, or violate, the rules may be different from the individuals who profit, or suffer, in consequence. Practical investigations have chiefly considered cases where an individual observes or violates certain rules and his descendants, or his fellow-townsmen or, more generally, other people belonging to his community profit or suffer in consequence of his conduct.

1899. To give an affirmative answer to the question as to whether, by following the rules of religion, morality, tradition, individuals are themselves happy and procure the happiness of their neighbours, is generally advantageous to society. Such a remark carries us into problem 3 of § 1876; and if we would reason in a severely scientific manner, we should keep it sharply distinct from problems 1 and 2 with which we are dealing here. Ordinary reasoning, which rests primarily on accords of sentiment, usually fails to make the distinction; and for that very reason, from the very fact that questions altogether distinct are dealt with concurrently, affirmative solutions are available in much greater numbers than negative solutions; and they are deemed worthy of approval, whereas negative solutions and even such as cast suspicion of doubt upon the affirmative are deemed reprehensible.

1900. It may be worth while observing that to give an altogether affirmative answer to the two questions in § 1898-I is to give an answer that is at least partially negative to the questions in § 1898-II, and *vice versa.* In fact, if a man can profit or suffer *only* by his own conduct, by observing or violating certain precepts, that is, it follows that he cannot profit or suffer by the actions of others. And, conversely, if he can profit or suffer by the conduct of others, it follows that he does not profit or suffer *only* by his own.

1901. That is so simple and self-evident that, keeping to strict logic, one can hardly understand how it could possibly be forgotten or overlooked. And yet it is overlooked or forgotten by hosts of writers; and the reason is the reason that we have so often had occasion to stress: the dominion of sentiment, which puts logic to flight and prevents a man from remembering the principles of which his conduct is presumably the logical consequence. Such principles are visible only to the disinterested observer. They remain implicit for the individual concerned (§ 1876).

1902. Suppose we see just what solutions have been offered for the problems just stated, whether they have been considered together or kept distinct; and first of all let us classify them:

AFFIRMATIVE SOLUTIONS (§§ 1903-98)

(Particular cases of the general theory II-2a (§§ 1876, 1883)):

A. Verbal solutions (§§ 1903-29)

    A1. Begging the question (§§ 1904-12)

    A2. Change of the meanings of precepts or norms from objective to subjective (§§ 1913-18)

    A3. Casuistry: interpretations of precepts and norms (§§ 1919-29)

B. Objective solutions. Terms "happiness" and "unhappiness" taken in their ordinary senses (§§ 1930-98)

    B1. Assertions of perfect accord (§§ 1934-76)

    (And, to evade exceptions:)

    B2. Happiness and unhappiness removed in space and time (§§ 1977-88)

(Particular cases of the general theory II-2b-α (§§ 1876, 1886)):

    B3. Happiness and unhappiness located outside the real world (§§ 1989-94)

    B4. No interpretation is discoverable—inscrutable are the ways of the Lord (§§ 1995-98)

NEGATIVE SOLUTIONS (§§ 1999-2001)

(Particular case of the general theory II-2b-β (§§ 1876, 1887)):

C. Absolute negation: pessimism (§§ 1999-2000)

(Particular case of the general theories I-1 (§§ 1876, 1877) or II-2b-γ (§§ 1876, 1888)):

D. Qualified negation. Two different situations that may have certain points in common (§ 2001)

The solutions *B1* and *C* originate in the fact that each considers one group of residues exclusively. The solutions *A, B2, B3,* and *B4* originate in an effort to reconcile contradictory derivations based on different groups of residues. Solutions of the *D* type include, in addition to intermediary solutions of the other varieties, the scientific solution, which aims exclusively at discovering uniformities. Let us now examine these various types of solutions.

1903. *A. Verbal solutions.* They belong to the large class of verbal derivations that we analyzed in Chapter X; and the cases we are to consider are just particular cases of that general phenomenon.

1904. *A1: Begging the question.* One takes advantage of the lack of definiteness in ordinary language (§ 1898) to make the term "happiness" signify the state resulting from the observance of certain principles. That much granted, it is evident that if the happy man is the man who observes certain principles, the man who observes those principles is the happy man. The same thing can be repeated for a community, a country, and so on.

1905. Diogenes Laertius states the views of the Stoics in the following terms: "Of existing things they say that some be good, some evil, some indifferent. Good, accordingly, are virtue, justice, wisdom, temperance, and other such things; evil the opposites thereof, and to wit, folly, injustice, and others; and indifferent those things which work neither benefit nor hurt, such as life, health, physical pleasure, beauty, strength, wealth, glory, noble birth; and indifferent likewise, the opposites of these, namely, death, disease, physical pain, ugliness, weakness, poverty, obscurity, lowliness, and other like things." [1] That granted, it is easy to prove that we ought to seek

---

1905 [1] *Zeno,* VII, 101-02 (Hicks, Vol. II, pp. 207-09): Τῶν δὲ ὄντων φασὶ τὰ μὲν ἀγαθὰ εἶναι, τὰ δὲ κακά, τὰ δὲ οὐδέτερα. Ἀγαθὰ μὲν οὖν τάς τε ἀρετὰς, φρόνησιν, δικαιοσύνην, ἀνδρείαν, σωφροσύνην, καὶ τὰ λοιπά· κακὰ δὲ τὰ ἐναντία, ἀφροσύνην, ἀδικίαν, καὶ τὰ λοιπά· οὐδέτερα δὲ ὅσα μήτε ὠφελεῖ μήτε βλάπτει, οἶον ζωὴ, ὑγίεια, ἡδονὴ, κάλλος, ἰσχὺς, πλοῦτος, εὐδοξία, εὐγένεια· καὶ τὰ τούτοις ἐναντία, θάνατος, νόσος, πόνος, αἶσχος, ἀσθένεια, πενία, ἀδοξία, δυσγένεια, καὶ τὰ τούτοις παραπλήσια. In the *De finibus bonorum et malorum,* III, 8, 27-28, Cicero states: *"Deinde quaero quis aut de misera vita possit gloriari aut non de beata? De sola igitur beata."* Tacitus, *Historiae,* IV, 5: "He [Helvidius Priscus] followed doctors of philosophy (*sapientiae*) who accounted honourable things as the only good ones, and dishonourable things as the only bad ones, and power, nobility, and other things external to the mind, as neither good nor bad." Plutarch, *De Stoicorum repugnantiis,* 13, quotes Chrysippus to this effect: "The good is desirable, the desirable pleasing, the pleasing laudable, the laudable beautiful [becoming]" (Τὸ ἀγαθὸν, αἱρετόν· τὸ δ'αἱρετὸν, ἀρεστὸν· τὸ δ'ἀρεστὸν, ἐπαινετόν· τὸ δ'ἐπαινετὸν, καλόν). (Goodwin, Vol. IV, p. 440: "What is good is eligible, what

good things, eschew the bad, and ignore the indifferent; but in saying that, all that we are saying is that by acting on certain norms one attains the ideal of acting on those norms. That is all undeniable, but it tells one exactly nothing. It is true that in the argument of the Stoics there is a little something more. They intimate, by an association of ideas, that we *ought* to act so and so, and the moral adjunct serves to conceal the tautology. Unfortunately, the supplement is a purely metaphysical one.

1906. There is the further effort to confuse the "good things" as they are newly defined with "good things" as ordinarily understood. Following that line, in expounding the doctrine of the Stoics, Cicero has them say: "I ask you, furthermore, who could really glory in the pursuit of a life of wretchedness, and not a happy life?"[1] By that he tries slyly to leave the impression that the happy life is "glorious," forgetting that "glory" was reckoned by the Stoics among the indifferent things.

Once one has left the field of reality to go wandering in imaginary worlds, one had better not stray from them if one would avoid inevitable mishaps and contradictions that will sometimes look ridiculous. Hegel's metaphysics continues to flourish, while his "philosophy of nature" is defunct. He took a false step when he entered

---

is eligible is acceptable, what is acceptable is laudable, and what is laudable is honest.") The argument gains in persuasive force from the many simultaneous senses of the term καλόν—beautiful, noble, honest, honourable, glorious. Plutarch gives a second quotation that falls in with our verbal solutions, A. Says he: "The good is delightful, the delightful praiseworthy, the praiseworthy beautiful" (Τὸ ἀγαθὸν, χαρτόν· τὸ δὲ χαρτὸν, σεμνόν· τὸ δὲ σεμνὸν, καλόν). There again accessory connotations of terms do a rushing business: χαρτόν is everything that makes one, or ought to make one, happy; and it is assumed that no one will have the effrontery to deny that one ought to be happy in the "good." The word σεμνόν [from the root of σέβομαι, "to feel awe," "to worship"] has meanings stretching all the way from "venerable," "honourable," "worthy of honour," to "magnificent" and "surpassingly beautiful." And where the lunatic to deny that what is "magnificent," or "worshipful" (σεμνόν), is also "beautiful" (καλόν)?

1906 [1] [The whole passage reads: "Their arguments conclude, therefore: Anything that is good is in all respects praiseworthy, but what is praiseworthy is in all respects honourable. Anything good therefore is honourable. Does that seem sufficiently convincing? . . . I ask you furthermore, who could really glory in a life of wretchedness, and fail to glory in a happy (*beata*) one? Only in the happy one, therefore! Whence it follows that the happy life is worthy of being, so to say, gloried in, which can really (*iure*) be the lot only of the life that is honourable. Whence it follows that the honourable life is the happy life."—A. L.]

on paths where ingenious metaphysical inanities dissolve in the light of experience.

1907. Not a few writers of the ancient world ridiculed the chatter of the Stoics and their resolve to seem what they were not. Athenaeus, *Deipnosophistae*, IV, 47, gives it as a doctrine of the Stoics that "the Wise Man can do all things well; he can even cook a dish of lentils sensibly"; and replying to the Stoic doctrine that wealth is nothing, he quotes, III, 63, lines of Theognetus to the effect that "the books of the Stoics" had been the ruin of one of the speakers in the dialogue who took that position.[1] Horace also, *Saturae*, I, 3, vv. 121-36, makes fun of the Stoics for being mendicants and posing as kings.[2]

1908. The author of the *Treatise in Defence of Noble Birth* (*Pro nobilitate*), which is generally attributed to Plutarch (*Fragmenta et spuria*, pp. 61-80), facetiously describes the conflict that arose between the metaphysical divagations of the Stoics and realities (XVII, 2): "But neither he [Chrysippus] nor any of the Stoics need to be of noble birth; for they are followers of a philosophy that can, as they boast, provide them with everything as with a magic wand, and make them magnates, nobles, dandies, kings. But magnates of wealth, they go begging a meal of others. Kings, they are obeyed

---

1907 [1] Vv. 121-36: Ἀντέστροφέν σου τὸν βίον τὰ βιβλία ("Books have ruined your life"; Yonge: "Your books have turned your whole head upside down.")

1907 [2] Vv. 124-26:

> "... Si dives qui sapiens est
> et sutor bonus et solus formosus et est rex,
> cur optas quod habes?"

("If he who is wise is rich, and a good cobbler, and the one handsome man, and a king to boot, why dost thou seek what thou hast?") Horace has someone answer that the wise man is a good cobbler the way a singer is a good singer, even when he is not singing; that is to say, the wise man has all the best qualities latent within him. And then back comes Horace, vv. 133-36:

> "... Vellunt tibi barbam
> lascivi pueri, quos tu nisi fuste coerces,
> urgeris turba circum te stante miserque
> rumperis, et latras, magnorum maxime regum!"

("Mischievous boys pluck at thy beard, and didst thou not keep them off with thy staff, thou wouldst be trampled on and crushed by the crowd that surrounds thee; and in thy rage dost thou bark like a dog, O thou greatest of great kings!") Then, vv. 137-38, he shows the Stoic going to a cheap bath-house for the despicable price of a farthing ("*dum tu quadrante lavatum rex ibis*").

by no one. Possessing all things, they are dependent on the rest of us, and barely manage to pay their rent at the quarter-term."

1909. In the same way those good souls who go about saying that "the external world does not exist"—and that may even be so, for experimentally such a jumble of words means nothing—take their stand in a fantastic world that has nothing to do with practical life (§§ 95, 1820). Metaphysical concepts of that type have attained their maximum development in the doctrines of Christian Science, according to which, if one would escape suffering from an illness one need only persuade oneself that the disease does not exist (§ 1695 [2]). To tell the truth, an idea that does not exist for a person is for him non-existent. But that is a mere tautology; and history shows that in general certain concepts force themselves upon individuals, try as they may to evade them. The followers of Mary Baker Eddy, who founded Christian Science, were within their rights in rejecting the idea that she could die and in holding that that idea did not exist for them. But the day came when the concept of her death forced itself upon them—or, to state the situation more exactly, when their concept could no longer accord with other concepts to which we ordinarily give the name of death. That fact is enough for us and spares us the pains of arguing the metaphysical question as to the existence or non-existence of "death."

1910. It is likewise true that, for a given person, history is nothing more nor less than the concept of history which he has in his mind, and that if he is lacking in certain notions the portion of history which corresponds to them is for him non-existent. But it is also an observable fact that the ideas which a man may thus hold stand more or less at odds with other ideas that he may subsequently acquire, according to their greater or lesser correspondence with what we call historical facts (§ 1798). A Pole may never have heard of the partition of his country, and he may imagine that it is still an independent kingdom. For such a person the partition of Poland is non-existent; and it may remain non-existent for him for a long time, for a whole lifetime—if he is kept shut up in a lunatic asylum and never returns to the state commonly known as the state of sanity. But once he returns to the latter state, new ideas begin to conflict with the idea he has been holding and they cure him of it. That is the fact we commonly observe, and it is sufficient for us.

We may leave it to others to amuse themselves deciding whether the external world does or does not exist.

1911. Of the *A*1 variety also is an argument by Epictetus.[1] He begins by dividing things into two categories: "Things which are under our control, and things which are not. Under our control are: opinions, impulses, desires [appetites], aversions, and, in short, every act of our doing. Not under our control are: our bodies, wealth, fame, public distinctions, and, in short, everything which is not of our doing. Those things which are under our control are, by their proper nature, free, unchained, untrammelled; those which are not under our control are inert, slavish, bound, alien [under the control of others]." That much granted, the rest could not be simpler: "If that only which is yours [things under your control] you consider yours, and that which is alien [not under your control], not yours, as yours it is not, no one will ever constrain you nor bind you; nor will you rebuke or accuse any man; for you will do nothing against your will, nor have injury of anyone; and you will have no enemy, since no evil can be inflicted on you." It is true, of course, that if you say that you do whatever you are forced to do of your own accord, you may claim that you are doing nothing against your will. So argued the person who on being thrown from his horse remarked, "I was just dismounting."

1912. The doctrine of Epictetus and others of the sort, such as the Christian's resignation to the will of God, are not scientific doctrines: they are consolations for people who cannot, or will not, fight. It is certain that pain is often alleviated by not thinking about it and trying to imagine that it does not exist; and something of the sort is observable again in our time, in Christian Science; just as there are instances where the physician, and more likely the quack, alleviates pain by his simple presence. The favour with which the doctrine of Epictetus was welcomed was one of the many symptoms presaging the imminent vogue of Christianity.

1913. *A*2: *Change of the meanings of precepts or norms from objective to subjective.* In the *A*1 type the tautology arose from changes in the meanings of the terms "happiness," "unhappiness," "the good." In this variety it results from changes in the meanings of the precepts. Needless to say, if we consider only such rules as the

1911 [1] *Dissertationes,* I, 1-3. See Pareto, *Manuale,* Chap. I.

individual observes with pleasure, we may unhesitatingly assert that he experiences pleasure in observing them.

1914. If we look at torture objectively, we may say that, in general, it is a misfortune for human beings to suffer torture; but if, subjectively, we consider the Christian martyr's feelings, we see that it is a blessing in his eyes to be tortured for his faith.

1915. When it is asserted that he who does evil cannot be happy because he suffers remorse, it is implicitly assumed that the wrong-doer is capable of remorse. But it is not hard to see that in many individuals remorse is either a sentiment present in negligible quantities or not existing at all, and for such people, therefore, the penalty threatened is almost if not altogether a matter of indifference.[1]

1916. The majority of men and women who set out to reform society assume, at bottom, that society will be made up of individuals endowed with the sentiments and ideas with which they choose to endow them, and only under those conditions can they promise such persons happiness.

1917. Certain Protestant sects that no longer admit the divinity of Christ are propagating a doctrine that is altogether subjective. They say that Christ is the type of the perfect man. That is just an idea of theirs; and they have no way of combating anyone who might say, to the contrary, that He is the type of the imperfect man. But such a weapon is available for anyone who believes in the divinity of Christ; for that divinity is an objective thing, independent of individual opinion, and the unbeliever can therefore be threatened with action on the part of the objective entity. But how threaten him with the action of something that depends upon himself, and which he can accept, modify, or reject, as he pleases? Furthermore

---

1915 [1] Cicero, *De finibus bonorum et malorum*, II, 16, 51-53: "And so, Torquatus, when you said that Epicurus declared that one could not live happily unless he lived honourably, wisely, justly, I had the impression that you were boasting. There was so much power in your words because of the majesty of the things they stood for, that you looked taller to me. . . . All the same, the deterrents you mentioned are trifling and very weak—all that about wicked men being tormented by their consciences, and then by their fear of the punishment that overtakes them or which they fear may sometime overtake them. The wicked man must not be thought of as a timid weak-minded creature who is always tormenting himself, whatever he does, and fearing everything. Think of him rather as a person who is always shrewdly calculating his interest, crafty, wide-awake, sly, always figuring how he can sin again secretly, without witnesses or accomplices."

as regards the Old Testament, those same people beg the question: They deny divine inspiration to such portions of the Old Testament as they deem to be inconsistent with their own ethics. After that, of course, they can safely conclude that their ethics accords with divine inspiration.

1918. The power that precepts have in a given society at a given time lies chiefly in the fact that they are accepted by the majority of individuals comprising that society, and that individuals who violate them experience a sense of discomfort, find themselves ill at ease. Such precepts are merely an expression, and no very exact one, of the residues operating in that society. It is therefore bootless to inquire whether observance of them is a source of pleasure to the majority of individuals constituting the society and violation a source of pain. If that were not the case, the precepts would not express majority residues, would not, in other words, be the rule in the community. The problem that has to be solved is quite another. From the standpoint of individual pleasure (ophelimity), the question is what effect the precepts have upon individuals not possessing the residues expressed in the precepts and how dissidents are to be persuaded that they will experience a pleasure, or a pain, that they do not directly feel. From the standpoint of utility the question is whether observance of the precepts is useful to individual, community, nation, and so on, in the sense given to the term "utility," as, for instance, material prosperity, if material prosperity is regarded as "useful." If an animal is prevented from following an instinct, it may experience a sense of discomfort; but in the end, possibly, its material welfare will be enhanced. If a statesman violates some norm that is widely accepted in the community in which he lives, he may experience a feeling of discomfort, and in the end his conduct may prove detrimental to the community, but it may also prove to be an advantage. Those are the situations which it is important to examine.

1919. *A3: Casuistry: interpretations of precepts and norms.* It is to escape such sentiments of discomfort, experience in their stead the pleasurable sentiments ensuing on observance, and at the same time achieve the advantages of violation, that casuistry and interpretation are resorted to—a procedure furthermore that is necessary if certain sentiments are to be satisfied and one is not to stray, in appearances at least, from the logical implications of the derivations. In that way one gains the advantage, small or great, of being and not seeming, of looking out for oneself yet of standing, in the eyes of people who at times readily swallow sophistries and more frequently still need only an excuse for believing, as strict observers of morality and the proprieties and therefore deserving of the public's benevolence. That may sometimes be done of design, but sometimes also in all good faith. Through the casuistries that are used by governments and countries to justify this or that conduct on their part, the *salus populi suprema lex* often enough transpires. If that fact were stated bluntly, it would be a sound logical justification, and we would so get one of the negative solutions, *D*. But one is reluctant to offend believers in affirmative solutions, so one tries to reconcile the irreconcilable by representing the *D* solutions as affirmative.[1] Furthermore, those who accuse and rebuke governments and countries for violating certain norms rarely make clear just what solution they are adopting; they do not make clear, that is, whether they deny that the *salus populi* lies in a violation of the norm, and accept one of the affirmative solutions; or whether, accepting the solution *D* and rejecting the *salus populi,* they would—even at the risk of serious damage and possibly of complete ruin—adopt one of the metaphysical or theological solutions (§ 1897) and have the norms obeyed; or whether, finally, rejecting the solution *D,* they locate the *salus populi* in adherence to some solution such as *A2, B2, B3*. They try to persuade, instead, by a simple vague accord of sentiments. With the effective aid of casuistry and interpretation one may assert that the observance of certain precepts, certain norms, *always* redounds to the material welfare of individuals, communities, countries, the human race. It is preached in general that one should always keep one's promises; but then, in the particular cases in which it is found advisable not to keep them, excellent pretexts are never wanting for avoiding that duty.

1920. The history of Rome furnishes specimens of such interpretations in abundance. Thanks to them the Romans were able to act in bad faith and persuade themselves all the while that they were acting in good faith. One example will suffice—the trick by which

---

1919 [1] [Literally Pareto said: "One tries to reconcile the irreconcilable by confusing these with the solution *D*."—A. L.]

the Romans deceived the Numantians, while nevertheless preserving every semblance of good faith. By virtue of that excellent piece of casuistry Rome saved an army which might have been destroyed, and saved her face by offering to surrender a consul for whom she could have had no possible use as a general. The Numantians refused the princely gift. Mancinus, the general, returned to Rome, and what is more, got back his seat in the Senate (Pomponius, in the *Digesta*, L, 7, 17 (18), *Corpus iuris civilis,* Vol. I, p. 955; Scott, Vol. XI, p. 239). Such the miracles that can be wrought if one has a knack for casuistry.[1]

1920 [1] Mommsen, *Römische Geschichte,* Vol. II, p. 14 (Dixon, Vol. III, pp. 14-15): "On a mere rumour, which proved to be false, that the Cantabrians and Vaccaei were marching to the relief of Numantia, the army evacuated its camp during the night without orders and took refuge behind the lines that Nobilior had built sixteen years before. Informed of the flight, the Numantians at once started in pursuit of the Romans and surrounded them. The Romans now had no alternative except cutting their way out, sword in hand, or making peace on terms that would now be dictated by the enemy. The consul was an honest man, weak, and of obscure name. Fortunately Tiberius Gracchus was quaestor of the army. Worthy heir of the prestige of his father, who had once been the masterly organizer of the Province of the Ebro, he exerted pressure on the Celtiberians and at their instance the Numantians rested content with an equitable peace to which all the high officers in the legions subscribed. But the Senate at once recalled its general, and after a long debate brought before the people a motion that the precedent of the Treaty of the Caudine Forks should be followed in the case. The treaty, that is, should not be ratified, and responsibility for making it should be thrown back upon those who had signed it. Following the rule of law, the whole corps of officers should have been hit, without exception, but thanks to their powerful connexions, Gracchus and the others were saved. Mancinus, unluckily for him, did not belong to the high aristocracy. He alone was designated to pay for his own and the common mistake. That day witnessed the spectacle of a Roman of consular rank being stripped of his insignia and led before the outposts of the enemy. The Numantians refused to receive him (for that would have meant recognition of the abrogation of the treaty), so that the degraded general spent a whole day in front of the city gates, naked, with his hands tied behind his back." Florus, *Epitoma de Tito Livio,* I, 34, 5-8 (II, 18, 5-8; Forster, p. 153): "They decided [in the case of Pompey] to make a treaty though they might have won a crushing victory. Then Hostilius Mancinus too they so harassed with continuous slaughter that everybody fled at sight or sound of a Numantian soldier. Yet in his case also they preferred to make a treaty, being satisfied with the proceeds of the booty, though they might have been cruel and exterminated his army. But no less outraged at the disgrace and humiliation of this Numantine treaty than at the treaty of the Caudine Forks, the Roman People expiated the discredit of the present crime by surrendering Mancinus." Florus is so convinced of

1921. The story of the Caudine Forks seems to have been copied from the story of Numantia.[1] If the story is true, it furnishes proof that such casuistry was a common thing with the Romans; if the story is false, it serves that purpose even better; for in fabricating such a story the Romans must certainly have taken pains to turn out what seemed to them a good story; and their copying from accounts of the treaty of Numantia shows that they found nothing in those negotiations discreditable to the reputation for honesty which they were concerned to preserve and of which they were wont to boast. That view is confirmed by Cicero; for in the treatise that he wrote to teach us poor mortals our duties, he points approvingly to the conduct of the Romans in the episodes at the Caudine Forks and at Numantia. But Cicero was keen enough to see that to have done honestly by the Numantians the Romans should have handed over to them not the consul only, but the entire army, replacing it

the honesty of that procedure, that he goes on to exclaim, I, 19, 1 (Forster, p. 157): "To that extent was the Roman People handsome, distinguished, loyal, pure, magnificent!" Really, if the rules of justice and honesty can be manipulated in that fashion, there can be no doubt that observance of them will always redound to the material prosperity of a people. Velleius Paterculus, *Historia Romana*, II, 1, 4-5: "That city [Numantia] whether because of its military ability, or the incompetence of our generals, or the indulgence of chance, reduced, along with others of our generals, Pompey, a man of great fame and the first of our consuls from the Pompeian gens, to make a very humiliating peace, and to a no less base and cowardly one, the consul Mancinus Hostilius. Influence saved Pompey from punishment, Mancinus, his sense of shame, for on his own motion he was sent to Numantia that he might be handed over to the enemy by our heralds, naked, with his hands bound behind his back. But just as had happened at the Caudine Forks, the enemy refused to receive him, saying that a violation of faith by a people could not be atoned for by the blood of one man." Those Numantians were good fighters but very ordinary casuists.

1921 [1] In his *Storia di Roma*, Vol. I, pp. 498-500, Ettore Pais considers the document that Livy quotes regarding the peace of the Caudine Forks as fictitious: "The story was invented to extenuate the moral responsibility of the Romans, who were later on accused of having turned their backs on the traditional good faith of which they were wont to boast. Livy's long narrative [*Ab urbe condita*, IX, 1-12] is only one of the many ornaments of the rhetoric, or pseudo-pragmatic, of the annalists, designed to render less dishonourable first the defeat and then the treachery of the Romans. . . . But it would be idle for us to show at any length that Livy's account of the negotiations is unhistorical. A learned and penetrating critic of our day has noted that all details in the story were borrowed from later history, and especially from the treaty of peace concluded with the Numantians by the consul Hostilius Mancinus (137 B.C.)."

in the situation in which it stood when it was extricated by a pact that the Romans refused to live up to.[2]

1922. In our day the famous "Ems despatch" has given rise to a debate resplendent with most handsome bits of casuistry. Says Welschinger:[1] "In his *Wegweiser*, or criticism of Bismarck's *Reflections and Reminiscences* (pp. 118-19), the historian Horst-Kohl considers it 'an extraordinary fact' that King William should have authorized his minister to communicate the Ems despatch to the ambassadors and the press. 'The form,' he says, 'was the business of the minister; and our social democracy, which is no worshipper of country, is indescribably insolent in speaking of a falsification of the Ems despatch, since Bismarck was acting simply in obedience to a royal command with the consent of Moltke and Roon, and under violent pressure from a sentiment of honour to the highest degree aroused. Bismarck foresaw the injury that was being done to our development as a nation by our increasing inclination to be too accommodating. Convinced that the abyss which had been opened between North and South by the differences in dynasties, manners, and customs could be bridged only by a national war fought in

---

1921 [2] *De officiis*, III, 30, 109 (In question the tribunes and consuls, T. Veturius and Sp. Postumius, who were handed over to the Samnites at the Caudine Forks): "They were surrendered . . . in order that the treaty of peace with the Samnites might be repudiated, and Postumius himself, who was to be the victim, was the proposer of the bill and spoke in support of it. The same thing was done years later by Caius Mancinus, who concluded a treaty with the Numantians without the authorization of the Senate. He too spoke in favour of the bill [ordering his surrender to the Numantians] which F. Furius and Sextus Atilius introduced [before the *comitia*] in compliance with a resolution of the Senate. The bill was passed and he was handed over to the enemy. He deported himself much more honourably than Quintus Pompey, who in the same situation refused his assent, so that the bill did not pass." This manipulation of the principle of public honour was thought to be justified by legal analogies: Cicero, *Pro Aulo Caecina*, 34, 99: "A Roman citizen is surrendered that the state may be released from its pledge. If he is accepted, he belongs to those to whom he has been delivered. If they do not accept him, as the Numantians did not accept Mancinus, he retains his status unchanged and his rights of citizenship." [In the *De Officiis* Cicero recounts with explicit disapproval another example of Roman sharpness. Appointed to arbitrate a boundary dispute between the people of Naples and the people of Nola, the Roman representative urged moderation upon both parties and procured their signatures to contracts accepting much less territory than they were entitled to. The result was that a large area was left between the boundary accepted by Nola and the boundary accepted by Naples, and this was occupied forthwith by the Roman People.—A. L.]

1922 [1] *La guerre de 1870*, Vol. I, pp. 124-26.

common against an enemy who for centuries had ever stood prepared, he gave the official communication *a particular turn* [This
historian would probably find nothing wrong with Pascal's famous
"Mohatra contract" in the *Provinciales!*] that put the French in the
painful dilemma either of declaring war themselves or bowing to
the . . . affront that Bismarck had contrived to give them.' " [2] All of
which reminds one of the famous "mental reservations" of the man
in Pascal's *Provinciales,* who was asked, "Has So and So passed this
way?" and replied, "No!" meaning "up his sleeve." Bismarck did not
falsify the Ems despatch—he merely gave it *a particular turn!* It may
well be that the German social democracy is "no worshipper of
country"; but Horst-Kohl certainly seems to be no worshipper of
truth; and by "truth" we mean experimental truth; for there are so
many many "truths" that among them there may easily be one for
the personal use and consumption of the historian Horst-Kohl.[3]

1923. Then, a breath later, the same "historian" turns champion
of the strictest morality.[1] " 'If the war broke out through any fault
of the Germans, then the French are absolutely justified in complaining of so brutal an enterprise and in demanding the return of

---

1922 [2] [Pareto used a French translation that gave a "particular turn" to Kohl's
German. Kohl said not *"eine besondere Fassung,"* but simply *"eine Fassung,"* a
small difference that considerably alters the stress.—A. L.]

1922 [3] Welschinger makes Bismarck out a strong-willed, far-sighted man, who
prided himself on having "retouched" the despatch in such a way as to render war
inevitable. He unintentionally praises him when he says: "The *Hamburgische
Nachrichten,* the Prince's paper, unequivocally recognizes that in altering the
despatch Bismarck had forced France to take the initiative in the war and responsibility for it and that he had so done a great service to the Fatherland. Had he
acted otherwise the war would not have taken place. The war was absolutely
necessary for establishing a united Germany. Had that opportunity been allowed
to escape, some other pretext would have had to be found, a less adroit one perhaps, which might have cost Germany the sympathies of Europe.' Bismarck jest-
ingly replied to a newspaper man who was expressing astonishment at his expedient: 'Oh, if that one had missed fire, some other would have been found.'
'Blessed,' says Hans Delbrück, 'blessed the hand that falsified the Ems despatch!' "
Hohenlohe, *Denkwürdigkeiten,* May 6, 1874, Vol. II, p. 119 (Chrystal, Vol. II, p.
109): "At table Bismarck revived memories of 1870—his discussion with Roon
and Moltke, who were beside themselves at the resignation of the Prince von
Hohenzollern and the King's good-natured assent; then the Abeken despatch and
the abridgment of it that he, Bismarck, had made and which rendered war unavoidable." But rhetoricians, sophists, and casuists have their uses, because they
bake a bread that is suited to the teeth of the mass of people in a population.

1923 [1] Welschinger, *loc. cit.,* p. 126.

Alsace-Lorraine, which is now in our hands, as the prize of victory.' " If Horst-Kohl really believes what he says, he is a man of extraordinary ingenuousness. How many changes would have to be made in the boundaries of modern countries if each of them were called upon to restore all territories conquered in wars for which it was responsible! But there are people who listen approvingly to such twaddle, and that is why it is worthy of attention. There are, there have always been, there always will be, powerful individuals—princes, nations, aristocrats, plebeians, parties large, parties small—who disregard the laws of morality; and to defend their conduct there always are, always have been, always will be, casuists in abundance who stand at all times ready to produce, now in good faith, now in bad, now for love and now for money, justifications of the requisite cleverness and resonance. However, only those who can say *quia nominor leo* enjoy the privilege of violating norms and finding obliging casuists to show that they are observing them. As a matter of fact, the reasonings of those worthy gentlemen convince in general only people who are already convinced, or whose vision is clouded by some strong sentiment—by a worship, let us say, of the sort mentioned by the casuist Horst-Kohl. Their influence, therefore, is slight, though it may serve to re-enforce the sentiments already existing that win them favourable reception in the first place. Conversely, condemnations of the powerful for violations of the rules of ethics are approved and adopted chiefly by people who are already their competitors or enemies, and who are inspired by sentiments of the same kind as the defenders and friends of the victims, though in a contrary direction. As for the powerful themselves, they pay little attention to such wars of words, to which they listen only for the slight utility that may chance to derive from them. They let others talk, while they go on doing.[2]

1923 [2] Notable among the moralists mentioned are the many who believe or at least assume that the gods of ethical systems avenge wrongs exactly as do the gods of theology. The influence of such people, so far as derivations have influence, is bad for the parties and countries to which they belong, in so far as they tend to hamper suitable preparations for the resort to force, which after all is the *ultima ratio* in such disputes, and to dissipate in fatuous chatter energies that might more wisely be expended in action. Woe unto the party that counts upon ethics to win the respect of its adversaries; and more luckless still the country that trusts its independence to international law rather than to force of arms. To persuade a people that the victories in civil or international conflicts go to virtue and

1924. There is a gradation between the cases where the interpretation is made in good faith and the cases where it is made in bad faith. These latter are very very numerous; and if they are more frequently observable among the ancients than among the moderns, that is due probably to the mere fact that the ancients were less hypocritical than the moderns.

1925. It is hard to believe that certain pretexts were ever put forward in good faith. Fearing the Epirotes, the Acarnanians besought Rome for protection and the Roman Senate accordingly sent ambassadors to admonish the Aetolians "to withdraw their garrisons from the cities of Acarnania in order that they might be free who alone did not ally themselves with the Greeks against Troy, ancestress of Rome" (Justin, *Historiae Philippicae*, 28, 1; Clarke, p. 221). How opportune for the Romans this sudden remembrance of their mythological lore! The books of Polyaenus and Frontinus on *Stratagems* are full to the bindings of deceptions of every kind, and wisely did Virgil remark that in war one depends either on valour or on treachery.[1]

1926. No one can imagine why authorship of the maxim that the end justifies the means should ever have been credited to the Jesuits. It is as ancient as any known literature, and is just another of the interpretations advanced in the effort to reconcile practice with theory. According to Plutarch, *Agesilaus,* 23, Agesilaus discoursed admirably on justice and set it above utility, in words, inverting the terms only in his deeds.[1] Judith also thought that in getting rid of

not to cunning is to lead it to ruin by distracting it from adequate precautions against cunning and from those long and laborious preparations which alone can lead to victory. It is, in short, like persuading an army to use cardboard cannon instead of steel. "Intellectuals" pride themselves on such idle chatter because they are manufacturers and sellers of artillery of the cardboard variety—not of the steel.

1925 [1] *Aeneid,* II, v. 390: *Dolus an virtus, quis in hoste requirat?* "Be it trickery, be it valour—who cares, in the case of an enemy?" Servius annotates (Thilo-Hagen, Vol. I, p. 281): "Something seems to be missing, as for instance: 'Who ever asks in the case of an enemy whether virtue or treachery is best in war?' "

1926 [1] "Phoebidas having done the cruel deed of occupying the Cadmeia in time of peace, all the Greeks were wroth, and above all the Spartans, especially those among them who were hostile to Agesilaus. And angrily they inquired of Phoebidas by whose order he had done that thing, turning their suspicion upon Agesilaus himself. But Agesilaus did not hesitate to say openly in defence of Phoebidas that one ought to consider whether such a deed were profitable, for

Holofernes the end justified the means, and on that account, partly, the Protestants have banished her book from their Bible (leaving in other things quite the equal of Judith's guile).[2]

1927. The festival of the Apaturia at Athens was probably nothing more than a festival of the phratries or clans; but the Athenians invented an etymology that made it a glorification of fraud. As the story runs, ownership of certain territories in dispute between the Athenians and the Boeotians was to be settled by a combat between the kings of the two peoples. "Thymoëtes, at that time king of Athens, was afraid to fight and abdicated his throne in favour of anyone willing to do battle with Xanthus, king of the Boeotians. Melanthus, excited by the prize of a throne, accepted the duel, and the contracts were drawn. At the moment of joining with his adversary, Melanthus spied as it were the figure of a beardless man following in the train of Xanthus; and he cried aloud of a breach in the pact, since Xanthus had someone to aid him. Knowing nothing of such a thing, Xanthus was surprised and turned around, and straightway Melanthus ran him through with a lance. . . . Whereafter the Athenian, at the bidding of an oracle, reared a temple to Dionysus Melanthidos [Bacchus of the Black Goat-Skin] and every

whatever was profitable to Sparta was done rightly even without orders. . . . Yet in his words he always asserted that justice was the first of all the virtues. . . . Not only did he save Phoebidas. He also persuaded the city to take the misdeed upon itself and hold the Cadmeia. . . . Shortly therefore the suspicion arose that the thing had indeed been done by Phoebidas, but that Agesilaus had counselled it." Xenophon, *Hellenica,* V, 2, 32: "Agesilaus nevertheless said that if a man had done aught to the harm of Lacedaemon, he would be justly punished; but that if the deed were good, it was the law of the forefathers that it should be done without orders." Yet Xenophon also says, *Agesilaus,* 10, 2, that Agesilaus was the type of the virtuous man: "The virtue of Agesilaus seems to me to be a model for those who desire to be virtuous; for who, by imitating the pious man, would become impious or the just man, unjust?" In private matters as well, Agesilaus was no stickler for niceties. Plutarch, *Agesilaus,* 13, 5 (Perrin, Vol. V, pp. 35-37): "In every other respect he was a strict observer of the law; but in matters regarding friends he considered too much justice an affectation. Often quoted in this connexion is a brief note that he addressed to Hidrieus of Caria: 'If Nicias is innocent, acquit. If he is guilty, for my sake acquit. In any event, acquit.' "

1926 [2] Judith, 9:10-3: She prays God: "Smite by the deceit of my lips the servant with the prince and the prince with the servant. . . . And make my speech and deceit to be their wound and strife." Why should this book not have its place among the books that justify the Christian experience? There are so many people who think just as Judith thought, in time of war!

year celebrated a feast in his honour; and they sacrificed also to Zeus the Deceiver, because they had profited by treachery in that duel." [1] Rare the mythological or historical narrative of antiquity in which treachery does not play some part, and ever with more praise than blame.

1928. In the *Iliad*, II, v. 6, Zeus is not ashamed to send a "baneful dream" to Agamemnon to tell him lies and mislead him. The Greeks promise to save Dolon's life and then kill him. In the *Odyssey*, XIII, vv. 256-86, Ulysses utters as many falsehoods as words and Athena is delighted. Even Dante, *Inferno*, XXXIII, v. 150, resorts to a mental reservation when he promises to remove the "hard veils" of ice from Fra Alberigo's face. Asked afterwards to fulfil his promise, he refuses with the excuse:

> *E cortesia fu lui esser villano.*[1]

With such a wealth of interpretations at one's disposal, one may justify any conduct one chooses, and the same individual may successively assert contradictory things without the slightest scruple as to his logic.[2]

1927 [1] *Cononis narrationes*, 39 (Photius, *Myriobiblon*, pp. 446-47). See also the scholiast of Aristophanes, *Archanenses*, v. 146, and *Pax*, v. 890 (Dübner, pp. 7, 391, 625; 198, 475, 625); Suidas, *Lexicon, s.v.* 'Απατούρια; Harpocratio, *Lexicon in decem oratores, s.v.* 'Απατούρια, and Polyaenus, *Strategematon*, I, 19. Pausanius, *Periegesis*, II, *Corinth*, 33, 1, speaks of a temple to Athena Apaturia (the Deceiver) reared by Aëthra, who was tricked by Athena into commerce with Poseidon. Strabo, *Geographica*, XI, 2, 10 (Jones, Vol. V, p. 201), mentions a temple to Aphrodite Apaturia. According to the myth, says Strabo, the Giants were intending violence to the goddess. She calls Heracles to her aid and hides him in a cave. Then she promises to offer herself to each of the Giants in turn; and as each enters, Heracles "treacherously" (ἐξ ἀπάτης) slays him.

1928 [1] "And discourtesy to such a man was courtesy."

1928 [2] Montaigne, *Essais*, II, 12: "Some pretend to the world that they believe what they do not believe. Others, and in greater number, pretend it to themselves, not being keen enough to see just what it means to believe. And then we find it strange if we see that in the wars that are oppressing our country at this moment, events are for ever fluctuating and that change is the ordinary and common rule! The reason is that we bring nothing to the matter save our own interest. The Justice that is with one of the parties is there only as an ornament and covering. She is indeed much touted; but she is not welcome there, nor is she lodger or bride there. She is as it were on the lips of the advocate, not as in the hearts and affections of the party. . . . Those who take religion on the left, those who take it on the right, those who say it is white, those who say it is black, use it in manners so similar for their purposes of violence and ambition, and they behave so much alike

1929. Our Machiavelli's one wrong, if wrong one must call it, was in manifesting his contempt for such idiocies when he wrote:[1] *"How the use of treachery in waging war is a thing of glory.* Albeit the use of deceit in any connexion is a reprehensible thing [That he says just as an excuse for what he is going to say, and so does not mind the contradiction.], nevertheless in the conduct of war it is a laudable and glorious thing, and he that vanquishes the enemy by treachery is praised likewise as he who vanquishes him by force of arms. The which may be seen through the judgments of those who write the lives of great men . . . the ensamples whereof abound so that I shall repeat none of them. This only will I say, that I do not mean that the deceit whereby one breaks the given word and the plighted troth is a thing of glory, for if it wins you a state and a crown, as aforesaid, it never wins you glory. [Note the reason why Machiavelli counsels abstention from a particular kind of treachery.] . . . *For one's country has to be defended either in honour or in dishonour, and in whichever wise is well defended.* . . . When the utter safety of one's country is at issue, there should be no question of justice or injustice, pity or cruelty, honour or dishonour, but, thrusting aside every other consideration, one should embrace that counsel only which saves the country and preserves its freedom; which thing has been proclaimed by the French [In our day the Germans.] in word and ensampled in deed in defence of the majesty of their king and the might of their realm." (§§ 1975[2], 2449).

1930. *B: Objective solutions.* Rhetorical and philosophical divagations are largely a luxury, and practical life demands something else. People want primarily to know how they should conduct them-

as regards extravagances and injustices, that they make it dubious and difficult to believe that there is as much difference in their opinions as they pretend. . . . See the horrible impudence with which we marshal divine arguments, and how sacrilegiously we drop them or pick them up according as fortune has changed our situation in these public storms. Take the solemn proposition as to whether it is permitted a subject to rebel and take up arms against his prince in defence of religion, and remember on what lips its affirmative was to be heard last year as the main buttress of a party! And the negative, the buttress of what other party! And now from what quarter the affirmative and the negative are being sounded and propounded—and are arms any less noisy for the one cause than for the other? And we burn people for saying that truth must be subject to the yoke of our need! Yet how much worse than merely saying it is France doing!"

1929 [1] *Deca,* III, 40, 41.

selves in order to achieve "happiness" in the ordinary sense of the word as material well-being. They need answers therefore to the objective problems that arise in that connexion. The masses at large pay little attention to the sources of their rules. They are satisfied so long as society has rules that are accepted and obeyed. In the opposition that is aroused by any violation of them the sentiment chiefly manifested is hostile to any disturbance of the social equilibrium (residue V-α). That sentiment is prominent in our most ancient biblical texts, and in general in the primitive periods of all civilizations. It appears in almost unmixed form in the feeling that the violation of a taboo necessarily entails harmful consequences. It figures again in the notion that anything that is legal is just, which, substantially, is another way of saying that whatever is legal should voluntarily be respected, that an existing social equilibrium should not be disturbed. Any intrusion on the part of reasoning is arrested by the strength of the sentiment supporting existing norms and also by their social utility. Reasoning therefore abandons logic and experience, turns to sophistry, and so manages to force itself upon sentiment without too great offence to the latter. The mixture of sentiment and sophistical explanation is essentially heterogeneous, and that accounts for the amazing contradictions that are never lacking in such reasonings.[1] Around the equilibrium residue as a nucleus other residues cluster, and notably those of the II-ζ (sentiments taken as objective realities) and of the II-η (personifications) varieties.

1931. These objective solutions, for the very reason that they are such, are easily contradicted by the facts. The masses at large do not mind that, not attaching any great importance to theories and accepting objective solutions that are visibly contradictory without giving a thought to their inconsistency. Thinkers, theorists, and individuals accustomed to logical meditation insist on knowing the sources of the norms that they are told should be observed, and never rest till they have found origins for them, though these exist, ordinarily, only in their own minds. Such people, moreover, are restless, annoyed, pained, at certain apparent discords between theory and fact or between one theory and another, and do everything

1930 [1] We encountered a number of examples in our study of derivations (§§ 1481 f.).

in their power to attenuate, eliminate or dissemble them. In general they do not altogether abandon objective solutions, especially solutions of an optimistic trend, but strive by appropriate interpretations to explain away, or at least to explain, the exceptions that undeniably are there.[1] So we get our B_2, B_3, and B_4 types of solutions, which, starting out from the experimental field, finally end by deserting it altogether.[2] The same grounds enable us safely to predict that in a given society of a certain stability the residues that we find operative will for the most part be residues favourable to its preservation; and they also enable us to predict that in such a society affirmative solutions to our problem will be the ones most widely current and most readily accepted; while such of its individual members as feel a need for logical, or pseudo-logical, developments will be using every means within reach and resorting to every device of ingenious sophistry to eliminate very obtrusive con-

1931 [1] That is a particular case of the use of derivations which we discussed above in §§ 1737 f.

1931 [2] Maimonides excellently describes the hotchpotch of varying doctrine that he himself was so familiar with, *Guide of the Perplexed,* III, 17, Theory V (Munk, Vol. III, p. 125; Friedländer, Vol. III, p. 72): "Here then is a succinct epitome of these differing opinions: All the varied conditions under which we find individual human beings are regarded by Aristotle as due to nothing but pure chance, by the Ashariyah as products of pure [divine] will, by the Mu'tazilites as products of [divine] wisdom, by us [Jews] as the consequences to the individual of his works. That is why, according to the Ashariyah, God may cause the good and virtuous man to suffer in this lowly world and then damn him for all eternity to the fire that is said to be in the other world, for, one could say, God has *willed* it so. But the Mu'tazilites think that that would be an injustice, and that a being that has suffered, be it even an ant, as I have said [For the quotation see § 1995 [2].] . . . will have a compensation, the divine wisdom making him suffer that he might have a compensation. We, finally, hold . . ." [For the quotation see just below, § 1934 [1].] The theory of "final causes" also is a device for eliminating contradictions. Applied to the conduct of the individual, it asserts that the purpose of such conduct, whether the individual knows it or not, is always the individual's "good" or the "good" of the community, and by arguments that are sometimes ingenious, but quite often absurd and childish, it goes on to discover that "good" where no such thing exists. Following that method, it is easy to show that all actions leading to one same goal can never be contradictory. The theory has the nine lives of a cat. Demolished at one point, it bobs up at another, undergoing the most varied metamorphoses. As has often been remarked, Darwinism degenerated into an application of final causes to the forms of living beings. Metaphysicists make wide and various use of the theory as applied to conduct (§ 1521), nor do theologians by any means disdain it. To have their turn with it, a number of writers have fished up a certain "excogitation" and other delightful contraptions of that sort.

traditions between solutions and experience. That, in fact, is actually the case. We have already seen how derivations are used to create confusions between individual welfare and the welfare of the community, and how that is done in order to encourage individuals to work for the good of the community, believing, even when it is not true, that they are working for their own good. In such cases that is as beneficial socially as it is false experimentally.

1932. In order at this point will be a few remarks on solutions to our problems 3 and 4, to which we alluded in general terms in § 1896. The larger and more effective portion of the residues prevalent in a society cannot be altogether unfavourable to its preservation; for if that were the case, the society would break down and cease to exist. Residues must, in part at least, be favourable to the preservation of society; and it is in fact observable that the residues operative in a given society are largely favourable to it. It is to the advantage of that society, therefore, that neither such residues nor the precepts (derivations) which express them should be impaired or minimized. But that is best accomplished if the individual judges, believes, imagines, that in observing those precepts, in accepting those derivations, he is working for his own welfare. Speaking, then, in general and very roughly, disregarding possible and in fact numerous exceptions, one may say that it is advantageous to a society that, at least in the minds of the majority of individuals not belonging to the ruling class, problem 3 should be answered in the sense that facts should be viewed not as they are in reality, but as they are transfigured in the light of ideals. Therefore—passing from the general to the particular case here in hand, the relations of moral conduct to happiness—it is advantageous to society that individuals not of the ruling classes should spontaneously accept, observe, respect, revere, love, the precepts current in their society, prominent among them the precepts called—roughly, inadequately, to be sure —precepts of "morality" and precepts of "religion"—or we might better say of "religions," including under that term not only the group-persistences commonly so named, but many other groups of similar character. Hence the great power and the great effectiveness of the two forces, morality and religion, for the good of society; so much so that one may say that no society can exist without them, and that a decadence in morals and religion ordinarily coincides with a decadence of society.[1] Human beings, therefore, from the remotest times from which their thoughts have come down to us, have not gone wrong in solving problem 4 in the sense that it is better for people to understand facts not as they are in reality, but as they are pictured in the light of ideals; and—using terms of ordinary parlance—in ascribing the highest importance to "morality" and "religion," meaning in general the moralities and religions of their own particular times and countries; while a very small number of perspicacious and far-sighted persons were ascribing great importance to "moralities" and "religions" in general, so coming closer to reality, where the importance actually belongs to certain group-persistences and to the non-logical conduct that is their consequence, implicit or explicit. But for the very reason that there has always been a gap more or less wide between them and reality, it cannot be said that in passing that judgment on "moralities" and on "religions" in general, and worse still, on particular moralities, particular religions, they have not sometimes overreached the truth, so doing harm to society though aiming only at its welfare. They have generally gone wrong in trying to justify their adherence to their particular solutions of problem 4, almost always giving reasons that were in some respect fallacious even when not imaginary and fantastic. But that, after all, is a merely theoretical error, and therefore of little importance; for, whatever the reasons, effects remain. But seriously harmful, at all times then and now, is the error of identifying morality and religion with some special morality and some special religion, so giving to derivations an emphasis that belongs only to residues. So it has come about that whenever the champions of such theories have had a clear field that particular error has led to enormous wastage of energies in efforts to achieve results of little or no consequence, and has occasioned untold and altogether futile sufferings for many many human beings. And so also it has happened that when such champions have met with resistance, their antagonists also have conceived the mistaken notion of extending to all group-persistences, to non-logical conduct of all kinds, the objections that could justly be urged against the enforcement of a specific derivation originating in certain specific group-

1932 [1] Note that the problem is here being solved qualitatively only (§§ 1876 [1], 1897 [1]). Quantitative considerations will be introduced in Chapter XII.

persistences. If a given group-persistence, Q, which is beneficial to society, finds expression in the derivations A, B, C, D . . . it is usually detrimental to a society to try to enforce a specific derivation, A, to the exclusion of the others, B, C . . . whereas it is beneficial to a society that individuals should adopt the derivations most acceptable to them, thereby showing that they are harbouring the residue, Q, which alone—or almost alone—is the important thing.[2]

1933. Negative solutions are not seldom capricious manifestations of pessimism, outbursts on the part of individuals who have been hurt or vanquished in the battles of life. They do not assume popular forms very readily. Scientific solutions, which are not expressions of sentiment but arise from observations of fact, are very rare. When they are put forward, they are correctly understood by very few people; and that exactly was the fate of the scientific portions of Machiavelli's theories (§ 1975). Optimistic and pessimistic solutions may exist side by side, for, as we have frequently seen, contradictory residues may be active simultaneously or successively in the same individual. The masses at large ignore such contradictions; the educated try to eliminate them, and the effort leads to one or another of our solutions.

1934. *B1: Assertions of perfect accord.* I cannot aver that a perfect accord, an accord embracing all the consequences, all the corollaries, that might be drawn from it, has ever been explicitly asserted. The assumption of accord appears implicitly, however, in utilitarian systems of ethics (§ 1935). There is no lack of other doctrines that assert the accord in general, as an abstract theory, without going to any great pains to determine just what consequences

---

1932 [2] We have frequently pointed to the logico-experimental weakness—the absurdity even—of certain derivations; but we have also given repeated warnings that in so doing we had no intention of minimizing in the slightest the social utility of the residues of which they were manifestations. That usefulness is likewise not affected when we point to the harm that is done by trying to enforce certain derivations. What we have said as to the experimental ineptness of the derivations of certain religions and the harm that is done in trying to force some of their derivations upon a public must not be understood, as is commonly the case, in the sense that the group-persistences functioning in those religions are not beneficial but harmful. Among such religions we even include the sex religion, with which we have frequently had to deal because of absurd and pernicious derivations connected with it.

would necessarily follow.[1] Very very often such doctrines are merely manifestations of vigorous sentiments that mistake desires for realities, as regards either the welfare of the individual or the welfare of society; or else manifestations of a resolute faith in certain entities or principles altogether foreign to the experimental world. Frequently, in fact almost always, they are stated in terms devoid of any exactness, and while taken literally they seem to assert something indubitable, the ambiguity of their language, their many exceptions, their shifting interpretations, sap the substance of the precept and draw the teeth of the assertion that the precept is conducive to the welfare of the person observing it.

1935. From ancient times down to our own there have been theories holding that violations of the norms of morality and, among the ancients, more particularly of the norms of religion, result in

1934 [1] Maimonides, *Guide of the Perplexed,* III, 17, Theory V (Munk, Vol. III, pp. 127-27; Friedländer, Vol. III, pp. 72-73) (continuing quotation in § 1931 [1] above): "We [the Jews], finally, hold that everything that happens to a man is a consequence of what he has come to deserve, that God is above injustice and punishes him only among us who has earned punishment. That is what the law of Moses, our Master, literally says, to wit, that all depends on merit; and to that purport also our doctors in general rule. They expressly state that there is 'no death without sin, and no punishment without transgression.' And further they say: 'To man is measured with the measure he hath himself used'—the text of the Mishnah. They everywhere declare that for God justice is an utterly necessary thing, in other words, that He rewards the pious man for his acts of piety and uprightness even when they have not been enjoined on him by a prophet, and that He punishes each wicked act that an individual has committed even when it has not been forbidden by a prophet." On the maxim "No punishment without transgression," Munk, the French translator of the *Guide,* comments, p. 127, note: "The commentator, Schem Tob, rightly points out that that doctrine is refuted by the Talmud itself in the same place, that it is a popular doctrine that is taught to the Jewish masses, but that the Talmudists did not pretend to represent it as an unquestionable truth." In his *Politica,* I, 3 (Lyons, p. 8), Justus Lipsius quotes approvingly a dictum of Livy: "Those who cherish the gods meet fortune in all their concerns, those who scorn the gods, misfortune"—"*Omnia prospera eveniunt colentibus deos, adversa spernentibus.*" Similar ideas are to be observed in hosts of writers of the past. Whether that was or was not their actual opinion, they deemed it decorous and profitable to say it was. The passage from Livy appears in *Ab urbe condita,* V, 51, 5, and Livy himself adds an empirical illustration that Justus Lipsius does not quote. In an oration to the Romans, Camillus says: "Consider from the beginning the events happy and unhappy of these past years, and you will find that all has gone well with us when we have followed the gods, badly when we have ignored them." He goes on, 6-10, to specify the war with Veii and the invasion by the Gauls, remarking that the former ended happily because the Romans heeded warnings from the gods, the latter disastrously because they disregarded such admonishments.

unhappiness in this world, and observance of them in earthly happiness. Specially interesting is one type of theory, the "utilitarian" ethics, so called, which views morality as merely the expression of a sound conception of utility. A dishonest act is merely the consequence of a mistaken conception of utility. A more perfect accord between morality and utility could not be imagined; for it is the strictly logical accord of conclusion and premise in a syllogism. Those theories have a scientific look and are made up of derivations with which we have already dealt (§§ 1485 f.). They come into special favour with people who aim at making human life completely rational and at banishing non-logical conduct, and so readily find places in the theologies of Reason, Science, and Progress.

1936. In other theologies, and in general in doctrines which do not reject the ideal element, one meets theories that are different from those just mentioned and which sometimes take on a semblance of science. They do not reject, in fact they often stress, metaphysical and theological elements. In general, keeping to the broad lines such theories have in common, one notes the following traits: 1. Punishment of violations is frequently pushed to the fore, while rewards of observance are relegated to the background. That is probably due to the fact that in human life pains are more numerous and more keenly experienced than the good things. 2. The two sorts of problems mentioned in § 1898 are usually confused. One might, in all strictness, assert that an individual acting in conformity with the norms of morality and religion can, while achieving his own happiness, in no way do harm to those committed to his care or in any way related to him. But that is rarely asserted. It is taken for granted rather than stated, being left in an implicit nebulous form. There is much talk of rewards and punishments; but it is not made clear whether they will go to the person who has done the good or evil deed or will extend to others. As regards the person himself, pains are taken not to forget a way out, by postponing to some indefinite time his garnering of the fruits of his conduct—it is not made clear, in other words, whether the idea is to resort or not to resort to the exceptions of our group *B2*. 3. If one chose to be punctiliously exact, one would have to note a confusion in assigning to one *same* individual an act that he has performed at one moment and the reward or punishment due him after a certain lapse of time.

When the reasoning here in question is used, it is implicitly assumed that the individual is one and the same in successive periods of time. That cannot be granted as regards the physical body; though if one admits a metaphysical entity called "soul" or otherwise, which remains the same while the body changes, the unity of the individual may be conceded; otherwise, if one is disposed to stickle for strictness, one has to specify in just what sense such a unity is conceived. 4. These theories commonly present in great abundance and in striking forms the contradictions alluded to above (§ 1931). They advance propositions and then implicitly or even explicitly proceed to contradict them, now asserting that every individual's happiness or unhappiness is the result exclusively of his own conduct; then a little later making some statement from which it is apparent that he suffers or prospers from the conduct of others. Oftentimes such things are stated explicitly—and no one seems to care about the inconsistency. In reality, just as they think of the individual as a unit throughout the various stages of his life, so they are often led to taking the family, a given community, the nation, or humanity at large as a unit. In that residues of group-persistence are at work, for their function is to transform such groups or associations of ideas and acts into units. In times remotely past many people did not even think of raising the question as to whether or not the family was to be considered a unit for purposes of reward or punishment. So now many people do not think of asking whether or not the material group that we call an individual should be regarded as a unit in time (§ 1982).

1937. Many of the theories here in question pay no attention to such problems, and in asserting that "everybody" suffers or profits by his or her conduct, they leave the meaning of the term "everybody" undefined. Then when an effort is made to define it, we get the theories of the $B2$, $B3$, and $B4$ varieties (of which hereafter, §§ 1977-98). Definiteness and logic are gravely lacking in connexion with all such matters; though the deficiency is readily understandable if one but thinks of the inconsistencies that prevail among the residues active in the same individual, and the individual's desire to surmount them—in appearance if nothing more. Sometimes, when the contradictions involved are habitual and trite, there is no trace of any desire to eliminate them, and that not only with the non-compromiser, who sees only one side to all questions, but even with the plain man. In the long run the inconsistencies are lost sight of—they come to seem natural. Most people fail to notice them at all, and act as if they did not exist. That is a very general fact and may be observed in every department of human activity. Many people, for instance, assume implicitly or explicitly that it is possible to change, to altogether determine, the conduct of human beings by reasonings, or by exhortations addressed to the sentiments. At the same time they recognize the existence of traits such as are described explicitly in books along the lines of the *Characters* of Theophrastus, La Bruyère, and others, and implicitly in literary works too numerous to count, from the *Iliad* and the *Odyssey* down to modern novels, and which, for that matter, are revealed to us in our daily dealings with our neighbours. Now those two ways of viewing things are quite contradictory.[1] The spendthrift and the miser,

1937 [1] We have already seen many examples of disquisitions to the point. Here is one more, of a very very common type: Pseudo-Turpin, *Les fais et les gestes le fort roy Charlemaine,* pp. 232-33 (*Charlemaine,* of course, is Charlemagne): "The next day, on the point of three, came Agoulant [a Saracen] to Charlemaine to receive baptism. At that time Charlemaine and his men were seated at table. Said Charlemaine: 'Those whom you see gowned in silk, all red, are the bishops and priests of our faith, who preach to us and impart the commandments of Our Lord. They absolve us of our sins and bestow on us Our Lord's benedictions. Those whom you see in black habits are monks and abbots. . . . And those next to them in white habits are called canons of the chapters (*réglés*).' Then Agoulant looked in another direction and saw thirteen paupers clothed in tatters and eating on the floor without table or table-cloth and with very little to eat and drink. And he asked Charlemaine what people they were. 'They,' he answered, 'are people of God, messengers of Our Lord Jesus Christ, whom we feed each day in honour of the Twelve Apostles.' Then answered Agoulant: 'Those who are sitting about you are very fortunate. They eat and drink liberally and are gowned well and nobly. And why do you suffer those who you say are messengers of your God to be hungry and uncomfortable and so poorly clothed and seated so far from you and so badly served? One does a great insult to one's Lord in treating his messengers in that way. Your religion which you say was so good clearly shows by what I see that it is false.' Whereat he took leave of Charlemaine and went back to his people and refused the holy baptism which he had decided to receive and the next day ordered a battle against Charlemaine. Then the Emperor understood that he had refused baptism because of the poor whom he had seen so badly served, and for that reason Charlemaine commanded that the poor in the army should be decently clothed and sufficiently provided with wines and meats." Boccaccio's Jew, *Decameron,* I, 2, reasons in a manner directly opposite to Agoulant's. He goes to Rome, notes the contrast between the evangelical purity that the Church preached and the immorality of the Roman Curia, and asks to be baptized, deeming that

we may guess, have heard arguments and sermons in goodly number against their sins. If they have not reformed, if lectures and sermons have had no effect upon them, it is evident that something else is determining their conduct and that that something else is strong enough to offset reasoning and sermonizing. If, in spite of all that has been said and written against intemperance, and in spite of all that has been done to suppress it, there are still drunkards galore, we have to recognize the presence of a force that makes for intemperance and overbalances contrary forces. In propounding a theory of non-logical actions in these volumes we have been doing nothing more than giving scientific form to ideas that are more or less vaguely present in the minds of all or almost all men, ideas that many writers have stated more or less clearly, and which facts without number do not permit us to ignore. We are not denying that reasonings and sermons may have their influence on people (§§ 1761 f.). We do assert that their influence is not the exclusive or, in many cases, the preponderant influence; that they are not the only elements which determine human conduct; that other elements intervene, elements not belonging to the categories of reasonings and sermons, or of derivations either. Now many people deny that in theory, but deport themselves in practical life as if they admitted it—and they do not notice the contradiction. Now and then a writer will observe that contradiction, or some other like it, and draw upon it for literary effects, ranging from the simple jest to the full-fledged psychological portrait. Inconsistencies between religion and practical life have inspired countless intellectual productions that arrive now at the one, now at the other, of the opposite conclusions, according to the purpose the author has in view and according as he gives first place to religion or to practice. The writer is against the practical if he holds that practical life should

the Christian faith must be truly divine, since it is strong enough to resist such causes of dissolution. Those are legends, tales, of long ago, but if anyone imagines that the substance revealed under those forms no longer exists in our day, he need only gaze about him to find similar inconsistencies very readily. Names only have changed. Out of the twilight of the ancient gods new gods have arisen: the radiant sun of Science, Progress, Democracy; the brilliant planets of that solar system called Truth, Justice, Right, Exalted Patriotism, and others still; the luminous satellites that take the name of Organization, Civilization, Nationalism, Imperialism, Xenophobia, Solidarity, Humanitarianism, and so on, world without end. These new religions are as packed with contradictions as the old.

be conducted in strict accordance with religious theories. That is the theme of preachers, ascetics, saints, and extremists of every kind. He is against religion if he holds that the necessities of life are sovereign over doctrine, and is disposed to attack religion at its weakest point. And that is the theme of atheists, materialists, the "libertines" of a day gone by, and generally of people who have only a lukewarm faith or no faith at all. Between the two extremes fall our casuists who, by dint of ingenious sophistries and acrobatic interpretations, strive to reconcile the irreconcilable. Phenomena of the same kind arise in the relations between religion and ethics, the latter being sometimes regarded as a simple appendage to religion, then again as an independent entity that must necessarily be in harmony with religion, and then finally, in a counter-direction, as opposed to religion or to some one religious sect. At one moment in history religion will be found passing judgment on morality, at another moment, morality on religion. The early Christians maintained that morality demonstrated the superiority of their religion over paganism. The pagans retorted—to no great effect—that patriotism demonstrated the inferiority of Christianity to paganism. Christians and pagans, as well as the various Christian sects, have hurled charges of immorality back and forth at one another and used and abused that type of argument. It was one of the antagonisms between the severities of religious precept and the necessities of practical life that inspired Pascal to write his *Lettres provinciales,* a book that is admirable from the literary standpoint but false from the standpoint of experimental reality, for it limits itself to denouncing the sophistries of the casuists, but puts nothing in their stead, so allowing the contradiction between doctrine and practical necessities to subsist dissembled. The reasonings of the casuists have no logical value. Pascal's precepts have no practical value. Contradictions between law and practical life, and especially between international law and the necessities of statecraft, have existed from time immemorial: they literally swarm in Graeco-Roman history; they are interwoven with religious questions in the Middle Ages; they persist in huge numbers in the centuries succeeding, and are far from lacking in our own day. We are dealing, in short, with a very general phenomenon, of which the cases we are examining here are particular instances.

1938. The notion of reward or punishment following on conduct has, besides its pseudo-experimental form, two other forms that frequently merge into one: the metaphysical and the religious. In the metaphysical form reward or punishment necessarily follows the conduct—just why, to tell the truth, is not very clear. This form is often dissembled in our times under a pseudo-experimental garb, but it remains substantially the same. In the religious form the reason why the reward or punishment necessarily follows is known: it is by will of a divinity. But that interpretation opens the door to the divinity's caprice; and generally he is not content with being a more or less strict custodian of morality, but acts also on his own account, avenging offences or omissions that affect him personally with as great severity as he avenges offences or omissions affecting morality—and not seldom with more.

1939. When religious sentiments are strong, no one finds anything to criticize in that situation, but let them grow weaker, let sentiments of benevolence towards one's fellows gain in strength, and an effort is made to restrict as far as possible, and sometimes to the point of elimination, this latter aspect of the divinity's action. Then it is said that a religion is the more "advanced," the more "perfect," the more the divinity busies himself with moral questions to the disregard of everything else. But it is not ordinarily realized that when religion goes in that direction, the limit that the "perfect religion" approaches is non-religion, and the confusion of religion with metaphysics (§§ 1917, 1883).

1940. And now it is only fair that we should begin furnishing proofs of the assertions we have been making; and the reader must not be annoyed if in so doing we have to turn to details in themselves rather insignificant, for he will remember that theories have no other value than their capacity for picturing facts—whether the facts be great or small does not matter—and that facts are the only things that give theories value or deprive them of it. To tell the truth, if one were to set out to give all the proofs, one would find oneself obliged to quote the whole of history. There being no room here for that, we can only do the next best thing, and select a few cases that may serve as typical.

1941. Examples of inconsistencies may be found in virtually every author who asserts the accord here in question. Sometimes the contradition is explicit, that is to say, in a given work certain passages will be found to contradict certain other passages; then again, the contradiction is implicit—it is apparent, that is, in the inferences that are to be drawn from one passage or another.

1942. Examples of the explicit contradiction are to be found in Hesiod's *Works and Days*. Many passages indicate that author's conviction that the wrongdoer is always punished. So, vv. 265-66: "He bringeth evil upon himself who wrongeth another." Hesiod devotes three more verses, 267-69, to showing that Zeus has an eye on everything; and then, without any transition, he asserts, vv. 270-73: "Now, verily, not I shall be just among men, nor my son; for woe unto the just man if the unjust hath the greater right." [1]

1943. Contradictions of that type abound in the moralists. We are told, for example, in *Ecclesiasticus* 1 : 16, that "Wisdom filleth the house with all things"; and then that "the wisdom of the poor man doth exalt him and seateth him among the mighty." But how can that be? If the poor man was left poor, his wisdom could not have filled his house with all things.

1944. Of the implicit contradiction, I will give an example from the ancient Hebrews. They believed, on the one side, that Jehovah always rewarded the just ("righteous") and pious man with worldly goods, and punished the unjust and impious by taking such goods away; [1] and, on the other, that the poor man enjoyed the favour of

1942 [1] The verse following, 274, seems to be a gloss interpolated in the text: "But methinket not that that be the will of Zeus the High Thunderer." But be it the will of Zeus or not, the fact noted by Hesiod still remains. Other verses also stand in contradiction. In many places Hesiod insists that the man guilty of an injustice does not escape the punishment he deserves and that the just man is rewarded; whereas in describing the iron age in which we, presumably, are living, vv. 190-93, he says: "No longer in grace will be the man faithful to his oath, nor the just man, nor the good. Honour rather will be unto him who is guilty of maleficence and hurt; right will stand in might and reverence will be no more."

1944 [1] Piepenbring, *Théologie de l'Ancien Testament*, p. 208: "It comes out clearly from the above, and from all documents of the first two periods, that the Israelites believed only in an earthly remuneration for human acts. In the prophets, with whom the punishment of sin on the one hand and hope of future salvation on the other play such an important part, there is not the slightest trace of the notion that sin may be punished and virtue rewarded in another life. According to the general opinion of the Hebrews, God recompenses good works and punishes evil in this world. Every misfortune is a divine punishment brought down upon one by unfaithfulness, every blessing a reward deserved through fidelity. In a word,

Jehovah.[2] The two propositions lead to contradictory conclusions. From the first, one infers that the rich man ought to be just ("righteous"), pious, and pleasing in the sight of the Lord, and the poor man unjust, impious, displeasing to Jehovah. The inference from the second is the exact reverse. The contradiction was a glaring one and could not escape Hebrew thinkers, who exerted themselves in various ways to be rid of it; but of that we shall speak later on (§ 1979).[3]

1945. Peoples have imagined, and still imagine, that they win their wars with the help of their gods. The group of associated sensations called a people is regarded as a unit, and the conduct of each single individual making up the aggregate is instrumental in attracting or alienating the favour of the gods. Sometimes the conduct of a single individual is sufficient to cause a punishment, and much more rarely a reward, for the group as a whole. Sometimes it would seem as though the number of individuals had to be large enough to constitute a considerable portion of the group.

1946. As for the gods, every people may have its own, and the victorious people wins for itself and its gods, who are enemies of other peoples' gods, and these must be in no way worshipped. The type of that case would be the "jealous God" of the Hebrews. Then again, peoples waging war upon each other may have each its own gods, or gods in common; but in either event, each people had better pay worship not only to its own gods, but to the gods of the other also; and typical of that situation would be the Greeks and the Romans with their gods. The *Iliad* has made ideas of that sort generally familiar. Finally, again, there may be only one god for two or

there is an exact relationship between misfortune and culpability, good fortune and merit." (Quotation continued in § 1976 [1].)

1944 [2] Renan, *Vie de Jésus*, p. 180: "The prophets, real tribunes and in a sense the boldest of tribunes, had thundered incessantly against the great and established a strict relationship on the one side between the words 'rich,' 'impious,' 'violent,' 'wicked,' and on the other between the words 'poor,' 'gentle,' 'humble, 'pious.' "

1944 [3] Bayle, *Dictionnaire historique, s.v. Malherbe, remarque* C (quoting Racan, *Vie de Malherbe*, p. lxxii): "Whenever beggars assured him that they would pray for him, Malherbe would answer that he did not think they had any great influence in Heaven, considering the wretched estate in which it had left them in this world, but that he did wish that M. de Luyne, or some other favourite, would put in a word for him."

more belligerent peoples, and it is assumed that he decides in favour of one as against the other according to certain rules that are not very clearly determined but which among modern peoples tend to merge with the norms of "morality," or "justice," as understood on each side. Typical of such situations would be struggles between two or more Catholic or two or more Protestant peoples. In wars between Catholics and Protestants in a day gone by, it was easy to set one belief over against the other; but of late, warring peoples have been talking rather as though there were no difference in beliefs and a common God had to decide whom to favour, with the rules of "morality" and "justice" as His sole guide. All that, I need hardly add, does not bear the most casual examination from the logico-experimental point of view.

1947. In 1148 the city of Damascus was besieged by the Crusaders, who were repulsed and had to retreat. Christians and Moslems alike made each their own god responsible for what happened, and each side interpreted what happened to its own advantage. On that point one may compare the story of Guillaume de Tyr with accounts by Moslem writers.[1]

1948. The God of Israel was not a little capricious. The God of the Christians, who succeeded him, not seldom acts in ways not readily comprehensible. He begins by giving a victory to the Crusaders, who are defending His faith; then withdraws His aid because—we are told—of their sins; and it would seem that His wrath

---

1947 [1] Guillaume de Tyr, *Histoire des croisades,* III, 10-11: "It seemed that the city could not avoid falling very soon into the power of the Christian people through the patronage of the divinity. But He who is 'terrible in His designs upon the sons of men' (Ps. 65:4 ?) had decided otherwise. I have just said that the city was under very close siege and that the inhabitants had lost all hope of defence and salvation . . . when, as a punishment of our sins, they came to base some hope on the cupidity of our soldiers. . . . Meantime the Emperor Conrad, seeing that the Lord had withdrawn His favour from him and that he was in no condition to do anything of advantage to our realm, caused his ships to be put in order, took leave of Jerusalem, and returned to his own states." Now, on the Moslem side, the *Book of the Two Gardens,* Vol. IV, p. 59: "The Mussulman population evinced very keen joy at the success that Allah had vouchsafed them, and offered numerous thanksgivings to Heaven, which had hearkened favourably to the prayers that had been made during those days of trial. Allah be praised and blessed! Shortly after that sign of divine patronage, Nur ed-din came to the relief of Mo'in ed-din and effected a junction with him in a village in the neighbourhood of Damascus."

must still endure to this late day, for the Sepulchre of the Saviour continues in the hands of the infidel.[1]

1949. Needless to recall, because too well known, the old ordeals and "judgments of God," which, if we keep to derivations, are closely related to the theory that God punishes evil conduct and

1948 [1] Draper, *History of the Conflict between Religion and Science,* pp. 77, 91, speaks of the conquest of Jerusalem by Kosroès [This quotation has already been given in part in § 1484 [1].—A. L.]: "In face of the world Magianism had insulted Christianity, by profaning her most sacred places—Bethlehem, Gethsemane, Calvary —by burning the sepulchre of Christ, by rifling and destroying the churches, by scattering to the winds priceless relics, by carrying off, with shouts of laughter, the cross. Miracles had once abounded in Syria, in Egypt, in Asia Minor; there was not a church which had not its long catalogue of them. Very often they were displayed on unimportant occasions and in insignificant cases. In this supreme moment, when such aid was most urgently demanded, not a miracle was worked. Amazement filled the Christian populations of the East when they witnessed these Persian sacrileges perpetrated with impunity. The heavens should have rolled asunder, the earth should have opened her abysses, the sword of the Almighty should have flashed in the sky, the fate of the Sennacherib should have been repeated. But it was not so. . . . [Speaking now of the conquest of Jerusalem by the Saracens:] The fall of Jerusalem! the loss of the metropolis of Christianity! In the ideas of that age the two antagonistic forms of faith had submitted themselves to the ordeal of the judgment of God. Victory had awarded the prize of battle, Jerusalem, to the Mohammedan; and, notwithstanding the temporary successes of the Crusaders, after much more than a thousand years in his hands it remains to this day." Draper errs in imagining that the Saracen victory was ever taken by Christians as proof of the superiority of Mohammedanism over Christianity. Never never have human beings used as much logic as that! Bayle, *Dictionnaire historique, s.v. Mahomet, remarque* P. "[Bellarmino and other Jesuit controversialists] have even been so rash as to count prosperity among the signs of the true Church. It might easily have been foreseen that that would elicit an answer, for by those two signs the Mohammedan Church will pass more appropriately than the Christian as the true Church." Bayet, *Leçons de morale,* p. 156. Probably with a view to discrediting Christianity, Bayet supplies a great deal of statistic that would seem to have little to do with a treatise on ethics: "The religion with the greatest number of followers is Buddhism. There are about 500,000,000 Buddhists. [Really? Bayet has counted them?] Next comes Christianity, which is divided into three branches: 217,000,000 Catholics, 127,000,000 Protestants, and finally 120,000,000 human beings who belong to the Russian Church." Bayle, *Op. cit., s.v. Mahomet II, remarque* D: "I have noted that as regards triumphs the star of Mohammedanism has prevailed over the star of Christianity [That could not be said today.], and that if one had to judge the quality of those religions by the glory of temporal successes, Mohammedanism would pass as the better. The Mohammedans are so sure of that that they advance no stronger proof of the justice of their cause than the striking successes with which God has favoured it . . . [Then quoting Hottinger, *Historia orientalis,* p. 338:] 'The success of infidel arms is another argument they use to stress the truth of their religion. Believing that God is responsible

rewards the good. Bayle [1] alludes to an incident that may serve as an example of the comical inconsistencies involved in that theory. The Chevalier de Guise, son of the Duc de Guise, who had been assassinated at Blois in 1588, killed the Baron de Lux in a street in Paris on January 5, 1613. The Baron's son challenged the Chevalier to a duel, and was also killed by the latter. "People," says Bayle, "did not fail to notice the inequitableness of the outcome in two encounters in which the points of justice seemed to be the same. If the Chevalier was entitled to success in his first duel because he was trying to avenge his father's death, he should have lost in the second where it was a question of squaring accounts with the son of the man he had slain. Yet luck was with him in the second as well as in the first. That surprised many people and aroused considerable discussion. However, generally speaking, affairs of that sort are settled according to the mores and the lesses of skill, courage, and physical strength in the participants, or by fortuities of circumstance, and not by the mores and the lesses of right on each side."

1950. In our day it is no longer believed that God indicates the side that is in the right by the outcome of private duels; but it is still more or less believed that He does so in wars between nations. A "just" war must, for many persons, be a victorious war; and, conversely, a victorious war must necessarily be a "just" war. Many Germans were, and still are, convinced that they won the War of 1870 because the Lord elected to award the victory to Germanic "virility" as against Latin "decadence." That may well be; but it may also be that the genius of Bismarck, Moltke, and Roon, as well as the stupid humanitarianism of Napoleon III, his ministers, his democratic opposition, and not a few French conservatives, may have had something to do with the German victories.[1]

for all good happenings, they conclude that the greater their success in their wars, the more clearly God indicates that He approves of their zeal and their religion.' " [A very free translation: Hottinger says: *"Secundum motivum est victoria eorum continua contra christianos, quod aliquos multum movet. Unde victores se nominant et gloriantur quasi victores totius mundi."*—A. L.]

1949 [1] *Op. cit., s.v. Guise (Charles de Guise, duc de Lorraine), remarque* F.

1950 [1] Busch, *Tagebuchblätter,* Vol. I, pp. 103, 106, 332 (English, Vol. I, pp. 80-81, 204; French, Vol. I, pp. 64, 67, 172-73), Aug. 24, 1870: "Count Waldersee for his part was eager 'to see that Babel [Paris] completely destroyed.' The Chancellor interrupted: 'That in fact would not be a bad idea, but it is impossible for many reasons, the main one that too many Germans from Cologne and Frankfurt have

1951. It is always a good thing for peoples to believe that their gods are fighting on their side (§ 1932). The King of Prussia was altogether wise in proclaiming a day of prayer in his decree of July 21, 1870. Said he: "I must first thank God that at the first signs of war one single sentiment welled up in all German hearts, the sentiment of a general rush to arms against oppression and the sentiment of an inspiring hope in the victory which God will grant to our just cause. My people will stand by me in this war as of yore it stood by my father who sleeps in the Lord. In Him I put my every hope, and I beseech my people to do likewise."

But God was being invoked in the same manner on the other bank of the Rhine, just as Homer's gods in their time had been invoked both by Greeks and Trojans. Napoleon III addressed the French people with the words: "God will bless our efforts. A great people defending a just cause is invincible." The God of the Christians failed to heed the prayer of the French, and led their army to Sedan, just as the Zeus of the *Iliad* failed to heed the prayers of the Trojans and countenanced the destruction of their city. Ollivier, under whose premiership the "just," but, alas, ill-fated War of 1870 was declared, took comfort in the thought that if "justice" had not been rewarded that time, it would be at some future time, at least. He writes: [1] "By an intolerable piece of insolence he [Bismarck] forces into a war a sovereign who has been systematically pacific [In that the Emperor's original sin.] since the Italian campaign [The origin of French misfortunes, as Thiers clearly saw.], without whose acquiescence [This the unpardonable sin.] he would not even have tempted fortune at Sadowa [Where he defeated Austria, laid the foundations for the defeat of France and the downfall of the tender-hearted Napoleon III.] and who, ever favourable to the independence of nations [Sacrificing his own country to those utopias.],

considerable funds invested there.' . . . Some distance beyond Saint-Aubin, I [Busch] noticed on the side of the road a milestone with the indication: 'Paris, 241 kilometres.' So we were that near already! Thirty-two German miles from Babel!" . . . Oct. 29, 1870: " 'She [the Countess von Bismarck] is quite well now,' the Minister [Bismarck] answered, 'only, she is still suffering from her ferocious hatred of the Gauls. She would like to see them all shot and stabbed to death, down to the little babies, who, after all, cannot be held responsible for having such abominable parents.' " The Countess von Bismarck and her husband considered themselves, and perhaps were, good Christians.

1951 [1] *L'Empire libéral*, Vol. I, pp. 30-31.

had decided, in spite of the alarums of his diplomats [Who saw a little light where that blind man could not be made to see anything.], to place no obstacle in the way of the free development of Germany and so to add one more service to those already rendered by a generous France to the Germanic peoples in 1789, 1830, and 1848. [Those good German souls probably deserved rewards for their virtues; but it was hard on the French to have to foot the bill in the form of those five billions paid to Germany as an indemnity.] 'Ingratitude,' said Cavour, 'is the most odious of sins.' It is also the clumsiest of calculations. [A gratuitous assertion on Ollivier's part, without the slightest hint of a proof.] Bismarck designed to drown in the blood of a common victory the antipathies of the states of the South, which were still smarting under their recent defeat. Far more effectively than that dangerous remedy, a little patience would have quieted the excitement. [Another assertion without hint of proof.] A German unity achieved without dismemberment of France, certain as it would have been of a peaceful future, might have proved a common blessing for all, and not a calamity. God sometimes punishes by the gift of success. The future will tell!" Wait, nag of mine, the grass will some day grow! Meantime, while that future punishment is coming in its own good hour, and which will fall upon posterity anyhow, the Frenchmen of Ollivier's day are suffering, and the Germans of his day are gloating! Compare that insipid ethical disquisition with Bismarck's realistic analyses, and one readily sees how and why Bismarck was to defeat Ollivier.[2]

1951 [2] Ollivier's history, notice, was a work in seventeen volumes, and pretended to be a scientific study. It was therefore something entirely different in character from the proclamations of William I and Napoleon III previously quoted, and from other such expressions, where the purpose was not to discover truth, but to rouse popular emotions and guide them into what were regarded as proper channels. Bismarck goes about things in quite a different way in judging the conduct of Napoleon III. Busch, *Tagebuchblätter,* Vol. I, p. 55 (English, Vol. I, p. 44; French, Vol. I, pp. 30-31), July 27, 1870: " 'His policy has always been stupid. The Crimean War was diametrically opposed to the interests of France, who needed an alliance or at the very least a good understanding with Russia. And so with the war in Italy. There he built up a rival for himself in the Mediterranean, North Africa, Tunisia, and so on [Bismarck said that in 1870; he saw far and clearly.], who some day may perhaps be dangerous. [Omitted from French:] The Italian people are much more gifted than the French; only less numerous. The war in Mexico and France's attitude in 1866 were also blunders, and there can be no doubt that in the hurricane that is breaking today, the French themselves feel that they are committing

Welschinger, a writer who is far from being in complete agreement with Ollivier, also says in his turn:[3] "The memory of the War of 1870 and the Treaty of Frankfurt that was its lamentable sequel will for a long time to come—saving reparations, which lie in the secret bosom of eternal Justice—be a cause of bitterness between the two nations." So, besought for aid by two opposite sides, "eternal Justice" did not know which way to turn and ended by preferring the side that had the larger army and the better prepared, and was led by the better generals.

1952. History shows that, as a rule, that is the side she prefers. When the Theban army broke Spartan power at Leuctra, it was effectively aided by "eternal Justice," who had decided at last to avenge the two daughters of Scedasus—girls who had been raped, ages earlier, by a number of Spartans (§ 2437[2]), and their tombs were located on the field where the battle of Leuctra took place. Such intention on the part of the supernatural powers had been announced before the battle; but as Grote wisely observes:[1] "While others were thus comforted by the hope of superhuman aid, Epaminondas, to whom the order of the coming battle had been confided,

one last blunder.'" Bismarck was right, but he disregarded certain circumstances that explain and extenuate. It is very true that the Crimean War was an error in French foreign policy, but it proved very useful as regarded domestic policy, giving the government of Napoleon III a halo of glory so sadly lacking to the régime of Louis Philippe. Furthermore, the error in foreign policy might easily have been corrected by an alliance with Russia after the victory. The war in Italy arose from a combination of humanitarian enthusiasms on the part of Napoleon III and interests of international "speculators," who were beginning in those days operations which have become so extensive and influential in ours. The Mexican venture was primarily a manifestation of pathological humanitarianism. There is no excuse for the attitude of Napoleon III in 1866. It was, as usual, the attitude of a humanitarian with few brains. Thereafter things happened in a whirl. France looked like a ship blown rudderless over a stormy sea. Under the Republic, French foreign policy was far superior to what it had been under Napoleon III, and for the very reason that it was more like Bismarck's realistic policy. That alone would more than justify one's preferring the Republic to the Empire [in France]. The Republic's domestic policy has not measured up to the standards of its foreign policy, and there is therefore a danger that the foreign policy may be paralyzed by the domestic. However, if the Republic is neglecting military preparedness, the Empire was even more neglectful in that respect, and was more to blame, for it had the power to force measures that far-sighted republicans, such as M. Poincaré, cannot obtain.

1951 [3] *La guerre de 1870,* Vol. II, p. 56.
1952 [1] *History of Greece,* Vol. X, p. 178.

took care that no human precaution should be wanting." That, perhaps, was what spurred "eternal Justice" to action, and it is most assuredly the thing that always should be done under similar circumstances. It is well enough to talk of "eternal Justice," but it is better to make one's preparations as though she did not exist.

1953. Nowadays many individuals who have ceased to believe in the supernatural have changed just the outward form of the derivation, replacing divine justice with a certain "immanent justice" or a "justice immanent in things," which is a very handsome, but a rather vague, entity. "Immanent Justice," however, prefers to operate in private business rather than in martial enterprise, perhaps because she counts not a few pacifists among her worshippers (§ 1883[1]).

1954. It is certain that among the ancient Hebrews and the Greeks and Romans, the conduct of the divinity did not always dovetail exactly with the upholding of morality and justice. There was an added something, designed to assert some sort of divine prerogative. That fact is distasteful to certain theorists, who would be better satisfied if the discrepancy did not exist. So they bluntly deny it, disregarding the contradictions, patent or veiled, into which they fall. That is why they happen to give such splendid examples of this sort of contradiction, and the more splendid, the more intelligent, the more reasonable and the better informed the writer happens to be.

1955. With the Church Fathers, and so on down to the Catholic theologians of our day, considerations of faith allowed no opening for the admission that the God of the Old and the New Testaments could ever do anything that was not perfectly moral and just. By this or that interpretation, therefore, they modify the counter-conceptions that are stated in the Scriptures. That is no concern of ours here, as taking us, to an extent at least, outside the experimental field. We will note that among the Liberal Protestants there are those who describe the ideas of the ancient Hebrews from an experimental point of view.[1]

1956. We are obliged, however, to linger for a moment on the

1955 [1] Piepenbring, *Histoire du peuple d'Israël*, p. 245: "Really, as a consequence of this supreme power, Jahve extends favour or mercy to anyone He sees fit, like the despots of the ancient Orient, who also enjoyed manifesting their power."

fact that in our day, in such a deluge of science and criticism, many people profess an intention of remaining inside the logico-experimental field, but shut their eyes to facts and foist upon peoples of the past manners of thinking that in reality they never had. That comes about because where sentiment is rampant the critical sense falters or even fails. Maury, for instance, one of the best of scholars on classical antiquity, expresses himself in the following terms:[1] "Chastisement from Heaven threatened transgressors of the laws of morality, just as there was recompense for good deeds. The *Ion* of Euripides ends with an address that is put into the mouth of the Chorus and declares that in the end the good find the reward of virtue and the wicked just penalties for their crimes—an idea which is to be found as far back as the days of Homer. Divine vengeance, which is nothing but the deity's resolve to let no crime go unpunished, nothing but the deity's implacable aversion to wrongdoing, always reaches the criminal. . . . The ancient myths depicting merely physical phenomena in the form of symbols or allegories give way to more moral myths, where the purpose is to emphasize this formidable principle of the inevitableness of divine vengeance."

1957. If one were to stop at that very authoritative opinion, one would get the impression that the Greeks, and, in particular Euripides, were inclined to solve our problem in the affirmative, that they believed the gods always rewarded the good and chastised the wicked. A direct examination of the facts leads to a far different conclusion.[1]

1958. In the first place, in Euripides himself, the purport of not a few passages is directly opposite to Maury's view. In *Helen* the Chorus says that he does not know whether a god, or a non-god, or someone betwixt and between, governs happenings in this world,

<hr />

1956 [1] *Histoire des religions de la Grèce antique,* Vol. III, pp. 48-49.

1957 [1] The Chorus in the *Ion* reads, vv. 1621-22 (Coleridge, Vol. I, p. 317): "Since in the end the good obtain what they have deserved, so the wicked, as is natural, can never be happy." Maury also quotes a Chorus in the *Bacchae,* vv. 882-87 (Coleridge, Vol. II, p. 114): "Slowly but surely cometh the power of the gods, and chastiseth those who cherish iniquity and in their folly refuse worship to the gods." Here too, after all, the reference is to people who manage to obtain the favour of the gods or else incur their wrath; but it is not clear whether because of virtue or wickedness.

since one sees them ever fluctuating now this way, now that.[1] Worse still, in *The Madness of Hercules* the Chorus says that the good fare no better in this world than the wicked.[2]

1959. Then, looking more closely at the tragedy quoted by Maury, the *Ion,* one can hardly say that the conclusion of the Chorus is so very moral. Apollo violates the virgin Creusa and begets a son of her, Ion by name. To conceal her involuntary infidelity, Creusa exposes the infant among the foundlings. Apollo proceeds to lie to Xuthus, Creusa's husband, and misleads him into believing that Ion is his own child, and the god naïvely explains that his purpose in the deceit is to provide a rich and illustrious family for Ion. Creusa does not know that Ion is the child she abandoned, nor Ion that Creusa is his mother. Believing him a bastard of her husband, as the god has averred, she tries to poison him, and he, to get even, tries to kill her. But she recognizes her child from a certain box he carries, and Athena comes forward to dispel all doubt and confirm Ion's true descent.

1960. It is not apparent just where, in all that, "the good" come in to get "in the end the reward of their virtue." We will say nothing of Apollo, who is a very fair scoundrel; but not even Creusa seems any more virtuous than the rest. One could hardly describe her attempt to poison Ion as a virtue. The best that can be said for her is that she succeeded in seducing a god. Poor Xuthus has done no harm to anyone; and his reward is to be presented by the god with a bastard not his own. Ion is a good enough fellow, if we overlook his little slip in trying to murder Creusa—he does neither good nor evil otherwise. Decidedly, the choice of such a play to show how the "good" are rewarded and the "wicked" punished can hardly be called a convincing one.

1961. As a matter of fact, the tragedy leads, substantially, in an

1958 [1] *Helena,* vv. 1137-43 (Coleridge, Vol. I, p. 358): "Who of mortal men, having searched the ultimate purpose of things, can aver that he doth find therein a thing that is god, not a god, or an intermediate being [demon], forasmuch as the designs of Heaven do turn now hither, now thither, issuing in happenings unforeseen?"

1958 [2] In *Hercules furens,* vv. 655-58 (Coleridge, Vol. II, pp. 191-92), he says that the good ought to have a double youth and be born again after dying, the wicked living only once: "No boundary of the gods doth sever the good from the wicked."

altogether different direction: it shows that the protection of the gods is a good thing to have. But it does not say that the protection is won by virtue. That fact is more strikingly evident—and Maury should have noted the point—in the *Hippolytus*. The unfortunate Phaedra did not "cherish iniquity," to use Maury's words; nor was she neglectful in worship of the gods. Aphrodite admits that Phaedra had built her a magnificent temple; but she cheerfully sacrifices her to her own thirst for vengeance on Hippolytus. The goddess expressly declares, vv. 47-50 (Coleridge, Vol. I, p. 76): "Verily a noble woman is Phaedra, but none the less shall she perish; for no hurt of hers shall stay me that mine enemies sate not my vengeance." When passages of that sort stand before one's eyes, one's reason has to be under the sway of a sentiment indeed before they can be quoted to exemplify that "divine vengeance, which is nothing but the deity's resolve to let no crime go unpunished."

1962. Maury is far from being without good company. Even in our day there are hosts of people who themselves deem it a good thing to believe that virtue is rewarded and wickedness punished and accordingly imagine that they find that idea expressed in all ages, among all peoples, and even in writers whose thinking runs quite in the contrary direction. It is important to note such facts, because they indicate the strength, even in our day, of the residues of Class II (group-persistences). A scientist writing the history of morals in a given country is unable and unwilling to confine himself to his quest for uniformities. He feels under some imperious constraint to laud *his own* morality, *his own* political faith, *his own* religion; so he steps aside from the field of scientific investigation, mounts the pulpit, and begins to preach.

1963. In a book which, for that matter, contains a wealth of accurate observation and sound inference, one reads:[1] "The essence of religious faith, as professed by every intelligent being during the best days of Greece, may be summarized briefly as follows: There is a body of divine beings whose power is exercised over nature and humanity, from whom good and evil derive, and whose favour we can either win or alienate as we choose. The way to be pleasing to them and make them propitious to us is, on the one hand, to per-

---

1963 [1] Schoemann, *Griechische Alterthümer*, Vol. II, p. 119.

form in their honour the religious ceremonies to which they have always been accustomed and the requirement of which they themselves have laid upon us; and, on the other, to deport ourselves properly, performing our duties to our state and our fellows, duties that also either have been laid down for us as commandments by the gods or by human beings inspired of the gods, or are revealed to each of us by reason and conscience." In all that, substitute the word "God" for "gods," and one gets the Christian's view of the Christian's religion. Schoemann is simply transporting that view back into the past, thereby furnishing another of the many examples of group-persistences (Class II residues); and his readers get the impression that the "eternal truths" of *their* morality and *their* religion may indeed have been obscured by polytheism, but nevertheless subsisted in the conscience of every "intelligent being." And what, pray, of people such as the atheists and the sceptics who did not believe all those pretty things? A twist of the wrist and they are put out of court in virtue of our epithet "intelligent": we deny them membership in the category of intelligent beings, and all is well (§§ 1471, 1476). Where ever in the Greek authors did Schoemann find that to have the gods "propitious" one needed *only* to perform the religious ceremonies prescribed for their worship and do one's duties? What ceremonies in honour of the gods had the daughter of Agamemnon neglected to perform, in what duties towards her fellows had she been remiss, that the gods should have bidden her father to offer her in sacrifice? And Megara, wife of Hercules, and their children—for what backsliding in ceremonies or duties had they deserved death at the hand of Hercules? Euripides represents the Fury, whom Iris, at Hera's bidding, had commissioned to deprive Hercules of his reason, as loath to execute so dastardly a command, yet finally obeying; and it seems that the Athenian public found nothing objectionable in the tradition that the poet followed. How and when had Hector sinned against the gods or his fellows that he should be slain by Achilles? And why should his body have been dragged around the walls of Troy? And so on and on. One could continue marshalling such legends indefinitely, did not the above suffice. To be sure, Plato repudiates them and condemns them, and of him, perhaps, Schoemann may have been thinking. But in that case he should have mentioned Plato by name and not gone talking about "every intelligent being."

1964. Decharme quotes a fragment of *The Heliades* (*Daughters of Helios*) by Aeschylus that reads: "Zeus is the aether. Zeus is also the Earth. Zeus is also the sky. Zeus is all things and that which is above all things."[1] And Decharme then adds: "There is nothing loftier than a doctrine such as that, and nothing, at the same time, more contrary to popular religion. . . . This wholly new conception of Zeus, which at the time could have been the dream only of a few great minds, enables us to appreciate the extent to which the religion of Aeschylus surpassed that of his time." We may disregard the subjective portion of the statement; the author has a certain ideal and calls those who stand more or less close to him "great minds." Let us look only at the facts. Is it, after all, true that the tragedies of Aeschylus contain the conceptions alluded to, and not the conceptions of the ordinary Greek religion? To tell the truth, the solution of that problem would be of little moment to us if it were a question merely of determining the personal opinions of Aeschylus. But the fact that opinions were expressed in his tragedies and that his tragedies were well received by Athenian audiences, points the way to the residues by which the Athenian public was swayed—and that is of greater importance to us.

1965. Evident in the trilogy of the *Oresteia* is the conflict between a conception of a spontaneous, automatic consequence of crime, and a conception of a judgment that one might make of it, taking account of the circumstances under which it was committed. One might say, indeed, that the purpose of the trilogy was to state the problem arising in that conflict and solve it. As will be remembered, the Erinyes are frustrated by Apollo, which implies that the second notion prevails over the first. However, the first is far from yielding the ground entirely, and Apollo's pronouncements are far from conclusive.[1]

1964 [1] [*Fragmenta*, 34 (70), Smyth, Vol. II, p. 403.] Decharme, *La critique des traditions religieuses chez les Grecs*, p. 102.

1965 [1] *Eumenides*, vv. 658-66. According to Apollo a mother is just the nurse of a child, the real parent being the father; and in proof he adduces a mythological argument: a male, he says, may become a father without the concert of a female, for Athena was born of Zeus without ever being nourished in a womb.

1966. Passages in the trilogy that bear on the subject may be grouped in three categories:

1. Passages which assume that murder engenders murder or, in general, that violations of certain norms lead to other violations— and that, quite apart from any idea of "justice" or "injustice," or at least laying slight and insignificant emphasis upon that idea. After Clytemnestra has killed Agamemnon the Chorus lays the guilt for the murder on an evil genius that has made its way into the house of the children of Tantalus; and Clytemnestra says, *Agamemnon,* vv. 1475-80: "Rightly hast thou uttered judgment through the words of thy lips, naming the thrice-gravid demon of this line. For he doth breed in our bowels a lust for blood; and ere the olden woe hath spent itself, behold, new blood!" And then come bits like the following (*Choëphoroe* (*The Mourners*), v. 48): "What expiation is there for a blood fallen on the earth?"[1] . . . "The murderer must pay his debt."[2] Electra asks the Chorus what she must wish for her father's assassins, *Choëphoroe,* vv. 119-21: "*Chorus.* That to them go a demon or a mortal man. *Electra.* A judge or an avenger, sayest thou? *Chorus.* Pray only, someone who will slay them in their turn."[3]

In a word, the fatality that broods over the line of the Atreïdes is a derivation from the conception of a necessary link between crime and its consequences. Like all derivations of the kind, it is not very definite, and not very logical; and thence the difficulties one encounters the moment one sets out to determine exactly what, in particular, the author's doctrine was and, worse still, in general, what people of the time understood by the word "fate"; for one is hunting for something that does not exist, in other words, for a definite doctrine, and no such doctrine is there. It is not, be it remembered, that good necessarily engenders good, and evil evil. A belief of that sort would presuppose, implicitly at least, a sentiment of "justice." Instead, evil may originate in the good. Aeschylus states that opinion clearly, though, to be sure, disagreeing with it. The Chorus says, *Agamemnon,* vv. 750-60: "An ancient rule hath been a long time among mortals: a great and consummated happiness of

---

1966 [1] Τί γὰρ λύτρον πεσόντος αἵματος πέδῳ.

1966 [2] *Agamemnon,* v. 1562: ἐκτίνει δ'ὁ καίνων.

1966 [3] The last line reads: 'Απλῶς τι φράζουσ', ὅστις ἀντάποκτενεῖ.

man doth procreate, and endeth not seedless; but from good fortune springeth everlasting misery. But my sense doth differ from the general. Iniquity in time mature doth breed its like; but a house that is truly just is blessed with a fair progeny." And the Chorus continues, paraphrasing these first lines. Aegisthus alludes to the successive crimes, bred one of the other, which weigh upon the house of Atreus. Whatever the circumstances, the necessary and inevitable consequence of homicide is a stain upon the killer, be he guilty or not guilty, be the killing deliberate or involuntary (§ 1253). Aeschylus, however, has doubts on that point. The Chorus in the *Eumenides,* v. 430, says that Athena cannot judge Orestes, since he is unclean from homicide and therefore incompetent to take an oath. But Athena replies: "Thou dost prefer the word of right to the deed thereof";[4] in other words, "Thou dost prefer the forms of justice to the substance thereof." It is well to note that the problem stated in those terms is not solved and that Athena is expressing just an opinion, because the trial proceeds, Orestes asserting and proving that he has been purified; because, in other words, the obstacle alleged by the Eumenides has been removed.[5]

1967. 2. Passages in which the idea of justice is the main one. In the first place, the whole trilogy leads up to the triumph of that idea over ancient usages: the new gods vanquish the ancient goddesses and become their masters. Then again, the conception of fatality is frequently made to accord with the conception of "justice." We have just seen conflicts between the two ideas. Aeschylus, *Choëphoroe,* vv. 59-64, settles them in favour of "justice." "A god and a sovereign god is success ($\epsilon\dot{v}\tau v\chi i\alpha$) among mortals. But promptly do the scales of justice tip for those who dwell in the light. Those who dwell on the bourne betwixt the light and the darkness suffer more tardily; and there are those who abide in everlasting night." The Eumenides, *Eumenides,* vv. 313-20, boast that they are the dispensers of justice: "Our wrath assaileth not the

---

1966 [4] Κλύειν δικαίως μᾶλλον ἢ πρᾶξαι θέλεις.

1966 [5] Orestes says, *Eumenides,* vv. 445-52: "I am tainted of no crime nor soiled are my hands as I sit by thine image." And he proves it: "I will give thee a firm proof of these things," the proof being, substantially, as follows: The law enjoins silence upon the person who has not cleansed himself, and he has cleansed himself with blood and with water. The talk is all about one thing: the mechanical efficiency of expiatory blood and water.

man who protendeth hands undefiled, and he doth live out his days secure. But the culprit who hideth blood-stained hands, as doth this man [Orestes], to him do we reveal ourselves in our good time, true witnesses for the slain, avengers of blood." [1]

Both these two types of passages are alike in that they indicate punishment as the inevitable consequence of crime. They differ as to the manner in which the punishment comes about. But if every crime leads to misfortunes, not all misfortunes are born of crimes: that is to say, punishments are inflicted for deeds that are not violations of the norms of justice and morality and, conversely, some violations go unpunished. And so we get a third group of lines:

1968. 3. Passages where the idea of "justice" is entirely absent. Clytemnestra describes the destruction of Troy, the slaughter of the vanquished, the pillaging, the burning, *Agamemnon,* vv. 338-40. But all that is nothing: "If the victors revere their tutelary gods and the temples of the conquered land, they shall not in their turn be vanquished." [1]

1969. The envy of the gods, about which the writers of ancient Greece had so much to say (§ 1986), also figures in the trilogy. Agamemnon, *Agamemnon,* vv. 946-47, fears he will offend the gods by treading purple carpets; and the Chorus remarks, vv. 1001-07, that happiness breeds misfortune, that human prosperity is ever coming to grief on some hidden shoal. He counsels, therefore, as the part of prudence, that one should throw away some portion of one's possessions.

1970. The conflicts here in question are discernible in the words uttered by Zeus in the first canto of the *Odyssey;* and Eustathius rightly perceived that they raised the problem of the good or evil which an individual brings upon himself by his own conduct, and of the good or evil that the gods, or Fate, bring upon him independently of any conduct on his part. Zeus begins by complaining, I, vv. 32-41, that men lay the blame for their woes upon the gods,

---

1967 [1] *Eumenides* (supplement), vv. 732-33, reads: "At the time and day appointed doth the mortal who spurneth the gods sustain his punishment." *Cf.* Euripides, *Bacchae,* vv. 882-90, quoted above, § 1956 [1]; and Solon, *Elegiae,* XIII (IV), vv. 27-32 (for quotation see § 1980 [5]).

1968 [1] In a fragment of the *Niobe* (Smyth, Vol. II, p. 432), it is said that "evil thoughts doth the god inspire in the minds of men when he would ruin a lineage utterly."

whereas they really bring them upon themselves.[1] The theory is obvious: Punishment is the fruit of crime, and Zeus is sole witness of things that happen. Athena in reply, I, vv. 45-62, puts forward another theory: the woes of men *ought* only to be punishments for their evil deeds. Aegisthus was justly punished. But Ulysses has done no wrong. He ought not be punished by being kept far from his homeland. Zeus again has his say, I, vv. 63-75. He has by this time forgotten his declaration that mortals are wrong in laying the blame for their woes upon the gods. He now says that the woes of Ulysses are due to the wrath of Poseidon, who is tormenting him for putting out the eye of the Cyclops. Yet in that act Ulysses could in no sense have sinned against the norms of justice! And so we get a third theory: The woes of men come upon them partly because they do foolish things, and partly because they are tormented by some god quite apart from any wrong they have done. The other gods, it is true, do what they can to embarrass Poseidon in behalf of Ulysses; but they lift not a finger to help the poor Phaeacians, whom also Poseidon is punishing, not for any wrong they have done, but quite to the contrary, for their good deed in helping Ulysses back to his home in obedience to the divine precept that would have strangers regarded as coming from Zeus!

1971. With these passages and others of the kind before one, it

1970 [1] "For from us they say that evils come, and they themselves of their folly have evils beyond what fate hath ordained. E'en now against fate hath Aegisthus taken the wedded wife of the son of Atreus and him hath he slain on his return, knowing well the dire disaster that awaited him; for we had sent Hermes, shrewd slayer of Argus, unto him and admonished him that he slay not Agamemnon and woo not his wife, for on him would fall the vengeance of Orestes of the line of Atreus, when he, become of age, should return to his homeland." The god's remarks are to be taken in the following sense: "For from us they say that evils come, whereas they of their folly," etc. That eliminates a formal contradiction between this declaration by Zeus and a subsequent ascription of the misfortunes of Ulysses to the wrath of Poseidon. But the substantial contradiction remains; for, after all, even if only a portion of mortal woe comes from the gods, mortals have not been shown wrong in complaining of the gods for sending that portion. Cf. *Iliad,* XXIV, vv. 527-32, and Plato's remarks on the subject in the *Respublica,* II, 18, 379. Plato concludes, II, 19, 380A, that no one should be allowed to say that Zeus is the author of the evils that befall men; and that even if he be responsible, what he does is righteous and just, as serving to improve the wicked by chastising them. And no poet, he goes on to say, should be allowed to teach that a man so punished is unfortunate. In Plato, metaphysics is superimposed upon theology, and Zeus is little more than an executor of the sentences of metaphysics (§ 2349 [1]).

is hard to understand how Girard could say [1] that, in the *Odyssey*, "if there is an idea on which the whole sequence of events visibly depends, it is that on the one hand, men draw chastisement upon themselves by their persistence in evil and that on the other, a brilliant reward is held in store for energetic and patient virtue." A brilliant reward indeed was handed out to the wretched and virtuous Phaeacians! The contradictions in the first canto seem not to have been observed by whoever wrote the poem. Later on doubts arose and efforts were made to solve the problems to which they give rise. In his commentary on *Odyssey*, I, v. 34, Eustathius ascribes the misfortunes of human beings on the one hand to Zeus and Fate, whom he regards as one, and on the other to the imprudence, or better, to the recklessness (ἀτασθαλία) of men who sometimes work their own undoing. He seems chiefly to consider whether the misfortunes are independent of what men do, or dependent on conduct.[2]

1972. The example just given is one of the many many that might be offered to show that oftentimes to go looking for *the idea* a writer has in a certain piece of literature is a bootless task, and for the reason that, in such cases, there is no single idea (§ 541) in the mind either of the writer or of the public he addresses. Both writer and public follow the lead of sentiment, which is satisfied with propositions that are undefined and sometimes accepts them even when contradictory. There are two sentiments in people: a sentiment inspired by "deserved" misfortunes, and a sentiment inspired by "undeserved" misfortunes. If *every* misfortune is said to be deserved, only the first sentiment may be operative in certain circumstances, the second remaining inactive. Conversely, if it be a ques-

1971 [1] *Le sentiment religieux en Grèce,* p. 97.

1971 [2] As examples of misfortunes not dependent on what men do, Eustathius, Vol. I, p. 14, calls the attention of the Greeks to their own "Hippolytus, who suffered unjustly at the hands of the Cyprian," to "Heracles, who was persecuted by the wrath of Hera," to Bellerophon, Euchenor, and Ulysses. As examples of men responsible for their own mishaps, he mentions Aegisthus; then the comrades of Ulysses, who feasted on the cattle belonging to the Sun; Achilles, who had the option of growing old on Phthios or dying young at Troy; Alexandrus (Paris), who deserted Oenone to abduct Helen; finally, Elpenor, who met his death while heavy with wine [by falling off the roof of Circe's palace]. All of those suffered through their own imprudence or recklessness: ἐξ οἰκείας ἀτασθαλίας οὗτοι πάσχουσιν. It is interesting that Eustathius treats on the same footing criminals such as Aegisthus and Paris, merely imprudent men such as Elpenor, and men of high aspiration such as Achilles.

tion of misfortunes brought upon the innocent by fate, the second sentiment comes into play and the first remains inactive.

1973. That must be kept in mind in speaking of the gods and of fate, of the conflict between "justice" and "fatality." The Emperor Julian ridicules the God of the Hebrews for losing His temper at very slight provocation; but he forgets that the gods of paganism were not slower to wrath. As a matter of fact, human beings are accustomed to ascribe to their gods the character traits of powerful men.[1]

1974. Bayet's booklet, *Leçons de morale,* which I quote so often because it is in general use in French public schools and therefore contains theories that are safe-guarded by the law "for the protection of lay education," starts out by giving an affirmative solution to the problem as to whether virtue leads to happiness. We are told in fact, pp. 1-2, 26 (italics and capitals Bayet's): "Good actions are those which are *useful* to us: that is to say, those which make us REALLY HAPPY. Bad actions are those which are *harmful* to us: that is to say, those which will make us UNHAPPY. It may be said therefore that morality teaches us *what we should do in order to be truly happy.*"[1] The person therefore who follows the teachings of

1973 [1] Julian is quoted by St. Cyril, *Contra impium Julianum,* V (*Opera,* Vol. IX, p. 746): "What provocation could be more frivolous than the one which here kindles God's wrath, if this writer is to be believed!" In point is the incident recounted in Num. Chapter 25, where God slays thousands of the Israelites because they had been marrying women of the Moabites and worshipping the gods of such wives.

1974 [1] Bayet further avers, p. 6, following Hesiod, he says (see § 1942), that "those who heed the teachings of morality are *always happy.* Peace reigns in their land. They are not called upon to endure the frightful sufferings of war [Of course, no moral country has ever been the victim of another country's aggression.] . . . the Earth provides them with food in abundance. The bees give them honey. The sheep give them their wool. They are always rich and free from worries. [In that the goddess Science really seems to be stealing the business of old-fashioned Superstition (§ 1984).] But when men do not heed morality, *misfortune* falls upon them." Farther along, p. 163, Bayet describes the misfortunes of the Protestants under the reign of Louis XIV. If it be granted that "those who heed the teachings of morality are always happy," it necessarily follows that the Protestants, who were certainly unhappy, had not heeded the teachings of morality. There are not a few formal contradictions as well. On p. 146 one may read: "ONE SACRIFICES ONESELF when one consents to be unhappy that others may be happy. . . . In self-sacrifice one not only makes others happy: ONE IS HAPPY ONESELF." The same individual is therefore happy and unhappy at the same time.

morality will be *truly* [Mark the word!] happy. But to dispel every doubt Bayet, after stating his general theory, proceeds to a particular case: "It is said that it is *our duty not to lie.* That means that if we lie we shall, *sooner or later* [Mark the restriction!], be unhappy and that if we refrain from lying, we shall be TRULY HAPPY." Finally, in case there be somebody who has not yet understood, he adds: "It is *as stupid and as dangerous* not to heed the teachings of MORALITY as it is not to heed the teachings of MEDICINE." Excellent! The theory as stated is clear. But a little further along, p. 26, the writer quotes a remark of F. Buisson, to the effect that in a day gone by the French serfs (*manants*) were "bent to the ground, dirty, underfed, and taxed in produce and labour at their lord's caprice." In other words, they were unhappy. So, if the individual who observes the norms of morality is always happy, the French serfs must have been a bad lot indeed. But that, certainly, is not what Bayet intended to say! There is better yet. As we saw above (§ 1716 [2]), Bayet finds that present conditions in society are not just and that "everyone should desire a change." But if the theory just stated is true, it follows that if the poor nowadays are unhappy, it is because they do not observe the norms of morality. The remedy for their troubles would therefore be to begin observing them; for, as Bayet says, "morality teaches us what we should do in order to be truly happy." But is that the author's conclusion? Not in the least! He has forgotten what he said back there. His remedy now is to vote for the Deputies and Senators of the Radical party (§ 1716 [2]). But if that is necessary and enough to achieve greater happiness for the poor, why did Bayet begin by saying that their happiness depended on observance of the norms of morality? He might, it is true, reply that in his judgment to vote for the Deputies and Senators of the Radical party is a norm of morality. That rejoinder would take us back to our solutions *A*1 (*petitio principii*). If everything that is capable in an author's judgment of achieving happiness is said to be "moral," one may surely conclude that, still according to that author, whatever is moral achieves happiness. The begging of a question always gives an indisputable syllogism. Bayet's "Science" is probably that estimable entity which has been deified during these late years; but it has nothing whatever to do with logico-experimental science. Many centuries intervened between the date when Homer wrote the first canto of the *Odyssey* and the day when Bayet gave his booklet to the world. The literary value of the two things may be different, but the same inconsistencies are present in both. It is true that the author of the *Odyssey* was not so presumptuous as to pretend that he was dispelling the darkness of "superstition" with the transparent radiance of a "Science" sacrosanct.

1975. What consequences follow when the person observing or violating the norm is different from the persons who derive the advantages or suffer the penalties resulting from his conduct (§ 1898-II)? When that question arises a writer will either completely disregard the problem of the correspondence of the conduct to the happiness or unhappiness of the individual, or merely hint in some roundabout way at an implicit solution. In our day that is the case especially in the relations between rulers and ruled; and, in general, writers seem to incline more or less implicitly to one of the two following theses: (1) That rulers are obliged to comply with existing norms—that that is all there is to it, that the question of consequences is irrelevant; or (2) that rulers may violate such norms for the public benefit—but that is taken for granted without too much analysis and sometimes, indeed, is glossed over with assertions to the contrary. In one way or another the necessity of solving the problem of the correspondence of conduct to consequences is evaded.[1] Anyone viewing the facts objectively, anyone not minded

---

1975 [1] The *Anti-Machiavel,* ascribed to Frederick II of Prussia, takes the position, Preface, pp. viii-ix, that history ought to ignore bad rulers: "Only the names of good princes should be preserved in history, the others with their indolence, their injustices, their crimes, should be allowed to die for ever. History-books, it is true, would be fewer on that basis, but humanity would be the gainer, and the honour of living in history and seeing one's name pass on from future ages to eternity would be the recompense of virtue alone; Machiavelli's book would cease infecting the schools of politics; contempt would be visited upon the self-contradictions in which it is always involved; and the world would be convinced that the true policy of kings, based exclusively on justice, prudence, and goodness, is in every way preferable to the disconnected and horrible system that Machiavelli had the effrontery to offer to the public." In very truth one good way to defend a thesis would be to suppress knowledge of the facts that tend to demolish it. Bayle, *Dictionnaire historique, s.v. Machiavel, remarque* E: "Boccalini claims that since the reading of history is permitted and recommended, it is a mistake to condemn the reading of Machiavelli. That is a way of saying that history teaches the same maxims as the *Prince* of that author. In history they are to be seen as put into practice, whereas they are merely counselled in the *Prince*. That may be the reason why many

deliberately to shut his eyes to the light, is forced willynilly to recognize that it is not by being moralists that rulers make their countries prosperous. But he says nothing, or else apologizes for what he says, by laying the blame for the facts on a "corrupt" humanity. Yet not even in that way will he escape the charge of immorality that was hurled at Machiavelli for merely stating uniformities which anybody can verify by a glance at history (§ 2459).[2] Machiavelli has been accused of plagiarizing Aristotle and other writers. The fact is, he happens to coincide with such of them as have described realities. The case of Machiavelli shows how hard it is to make a scientific analysis. The run of men are incapable of keeping separate two inquiries that are altogether distinct; 1. The examination of what we have called (§ 129) real movements, which is a study of facts and their relations. Are the facts as stated by Machiavelli true or untrue? Are the relations that he finds between them real or unreal? Those questions seem to have no interest for many writers who attack Machiavelli or defend him, their whole attention centring on the following: 2. The examination of what we have called

intelligent people deem that it would be desirable if no history were written (see Mascardi, *Dell' arte historica*). [In fact, if the term of comparison between theory and reality can be suppressed, the theory can be constructed at pleasure.] But look out—our Florentine is accused of enriching himself on the spoils of Aristotle! . . . Gentillet accuses him of plagiarizing Bartoli. I am surprised that no one says he stole his maxims from the Angelic Doctor, the great St. Thomas Aquinas. You may read in Naudé's *Coups d'état* [Williams, pp. 16-18] a long passage from the commentary of Thomas Aquinas on Book V of Aristotle's *Politics*. Monsignor Amelot proves [*Examen du* Prince *de Machiavel*] that Machiavelli is only a pupil or interpreter of Tacitus."

1975 [2] Among the many pertinent passages in Machiavelli I will refer again, for the moment, to the two quoted above (§ 1929). Ariosto also says, *Orlando Furioso*, IV, 1:

> "Though an ill wind appear in simulation,
> And for the most such quality offends,
> 'Tis plain that this in many a situation
> Is found to further beneficial ends,
> And save from blame and danger and vexation,
> Since we converse not always with our friends,
> In this less clear than clouded mortal life,
> Beset with snares and full of envious strife."   (Rose)

For Machiavelli further, *cf. Deca,* II, 13: "I hold it very true that seldom if ever do men of low estate rise to high place without use of force and deceit, unless such place has been devised to them by gift or inheritance, some other having come of it. Nor do I believe that force alone will ever be found to suffice, but it will be easily

(§ 130) virtual movements, which concerns the measures suitable for attaining certain ends. Assailants of Machiavelli accuse him of inciting princes to become tyrants. His defenders reply that he merely shows how a prince can attain that objective, but without commending it. The accusation and the defence may stand side by side, but neither has anything to do with the problem of determining what is going to happen under certain hypothetical circumstances. Practical man that he was, Machiavelli chose to consider a concrete case, which so becomes a particular instance of the general inquiry. He wrote *The Prince;* but he might have written a *Republic* along the same identical lines and to some extent did so in his *Deca,* or *Discourses on the First Ten Books of Livy.* Had he lived in our day, he might have studied the parliamentary system. The problem he set himself was to discover the best means available to princes for

found that deceit alone may suffice. . . . And the very things which princes are forced to do in the beginnings of their increase, republics also are forced to do, until such time as they be grown powerful and able to stand on force alone. . . . It is evident that the Romans in their early increase showed no lack of fraud, which has always of necessity been used by those who from lowly beginnings would rise to exalted station and which is the less reprehensible the more covert it is, as was that of the Romans." *Il principe,* § 15: "But it being my intent to write something of profit to men of experience in such matters, I have deemed it the wiser part to follow rather the effectual truth of things than the imagination thereof. And verily many have imagined republics and principalities that man has never seen, nor known of in the fact; for betwixt the manner in which men live and the manner in which they ought to live there is a distance so great that the man who abandons what is done in favour of what ought to be done learns rather his ruin than his preservation; for he who would in all circumstances make profession of virtue cannot but come to ruin amidst the many who are rascals." To that the *Anti-Machiavel,* pp. 167-68, replies: "Machiavelli contends that it is not possible to be altogether good in this world, the human race being as wicked and corrupt as it is, without perishing. I say, instead, that if one is not to perish, one must be good and prudent. Men ordinarily are neither altogether good nor altogether wicked. [The writer either does not know or is pretending not to know that those are Machiavelli's very words, *Deca,* I, § 27. *Cf.* § 1704.] But wicked, good, and indifferent will all alike support a prince that is powerful, skilful, just. I had much rather wage war on a tyrant than on a good king, on a Louis XI than on a Louis XII, on a Domitian than on a Trajan; for the good king will be well served and the tyrant's subjects will join my troops. . . . No good and wise king was ever dethroned in England even by a great army. All their bad kings succumbed to competitors who never began a war with as many as four thousand trained troops. Do not therefore be dishonest with rascals. Be virtuous and intrepid with them. And you will make your people as virtuous as you are. Your neighbours will be eager to imitate you and the rascals will tremble."

holding their power; and he took two hypothetical cases—the case where the prince has newly acquired power and the case where the power has been inherited. He might have made similar investigations along the same lines for other types of political organization; and still along the same lines, he might have broadened the scope of his inquiry and considered the means most suitable for acquiring economic or military power, political influence, and other things of the kind. In so doing he would gradually have gone on from the particular concrete case that he actually examined to the general problems of virtual movements which sociology considers today. That would not have been possible in his time, just as it would not have been possible in the day of his one great predecessor, Aristotle—the social sciences had not as yet been born. That fact only emphasizes the extraordinary force of Aristotle's genius and still more of Machiavelli's, in that they were able to attain such heights with the very imperfect materials supplied them by the knowledge of their time. But it also serves to emphasize the stolid ignorance of certain of our contemporaries who are not capable even of grasping the importance of the problem studied by Machiavelli, and who try to meet him with a mass of ethical and sentimental chatter that has no scientific status whatever, though they are ridiculous enough in their presumption to imagine they are experts in the political and social sciences. An amusing instance would, again, be Ollivier.[3] He

1975 [3] Just a few examples of Ollivier's general approach to history: *L'Empire libéral*, Vol. V, pp. 61-66, 257-78 (we are not considering the accuracy of Ollivier's assertions, of course—we accept them at face value, as hypotheses for discussion): "Napoleon III had come back from Italy in the consciousness of being bound to a vigorous act of capital importance: the reorganization of his army. It was urgent to correct defects that the prestige of victory hid from the public, but which he had, so to say, touched with his hand. It was a laborious task. The laxity in atmosphere due to the habits contracted in Africa was easy to remedy. . . . Much more difficult the problem of increasing contingents in case of war. . . . [Ollivier goes on to describe the efforts made in that direction and claims that an excellent reorganization of the army had been planned.] But to carry out that fundamental reform, money was needed, a great deal of money. Now the Minister of Finance, the Budget Commission, and the Legislative Body were all for economies. Had the Emperor come to ask for new credits to any considerable amount, there would have been a riot and not only from the Opposition. He would have met in the Legislative Body as stubborn a resistance as was beginning in Prussia against the Regent's plan for military organization along the same lines as Randon's. [Randon was the French War Minister.] There was this difference in the two situations. The resistance in Prussia had more strength at its disposal than was the case in France. A long and mighty

tries—not very hard—to establish the concordance of good works with happiness by postponing the happiness to some future time (§ 1951); but that point with him is more or less incidental. The bulk of his seventeen-volume history is zealously devoted to present-

effort and doubtful of outcome was required in Prussia to rouse the Deputies in the Landtag. The Emperor, on the other hand, was in a position to checkmate ill will in the Legislative Body with no great difficulty. It would have made a noise, but it would have voted the money. But while the Regent in Prussia threw himself head down into the parliamentary fray, risking everything, the Emperor stopped short at the distant glimpse of a battle. The why of that difference in conduct holds the secret of what was afterwards to happen."

"What was to happen afterwards" was all in Prussia's favour, and supremely disastrous to France: It is therefore self-evident that France would have been the gainer if rôles had been inverted, if, that is, her rulers had done what the Prussian Regent did and the rulers in Prussia what the Emperor of the French did. Ollivier however proceeds, p. 65, to state his conception of the reasons for those differences in the respective procedures: "William was getting ready for a war that he wanted in order to establish Prussian supremacy in Germany. Napoleon III did not think that he needed another war to maintain his moral [sic!] supremacy in Europe— the only supremacy he desired. [It was, and no mistake about it, a disaster for France that her sovereign should be forgetting force to that extent and thinking only of "morality."] . . . The Emperor could see no cause for a war, in whatever direction he looked. . . . Germany was hostile but powerless. [A fine statesman not to know that one must trust not to the weakness of the enemy but to one's own strength!] He alone could create a cause of war by trying to seize Belgium or the Rhine. . . . Had he harboured that calculation, he would surely have braved the Legislative Body's resistance to a costly reorganization of the army. But he was thinking less than ever of expansions and aggressions. [But other people were, and to ignore that fact may have been very moral but it was certainly very short-sighted.] He expressed the literal whole of his thought in his address to the Legislative Body: 'I sincerely desire peace, and I shall neglect nothing to maintain it.' " What a pity it did not occur to some Deputy to interrupt and shout at him: "Si vis pacem, para bellum!" Ollivier draws the picture of an estimable private citizen and an utterly wretched statesman. Everything he says sounds praises of the former and damnation of the latter (§ 2457). And that is not all. Here we are at the Mexican venture. Ollivier washes the Emperor clean of any charge of deciding on that expedition for financial reasons, and adds, p. 257: "And there was no motive of ambition either." Nor was he tied to the Empress's apron-strings, pp. 257-58: "There has been more specious allusion to the influence of the Empress. . . . Her imagination was of a chivalric turn and flared up at these distant glimpses of glory and honour. She used her eloquence and her seductive charms to convince the Emperor. He was all the more accessible to such pressure in that he had private sins to obtain her forgiveness for. [Exemplary such remorse! But it is not so exemplary to make one's country pay the ransom for one's sins. Henry IV of France had his petticoats too, but that did not prevent him from being a good statesman and a good general.] However, he did not follow her lead blindly, any more than he did anybody else's. . . . [But here, at last, are the reasons for the expedition, according to Ollivier:] His real motive was different. He was inconsolable at not having realized his pro-

ing Napoleon III as a perfect gentleman. Since, however, it is not to be denied that fate was not kind to the Emperor Louis Napoleon, it would seem proved, if one is to accept Ollivier's assertions with eyes closed, that good works are not necessarily conjoined with good

gramme 'From the Alps to the Adriatic' and blotted from the history of his race the stain of Campo Formio. [What a tender conscience: remorse for his private sins is not enough. He is remorseful for the sins of his forefathers, and does penance for them, or rather has the country he is governing do the penance.] But resolved never again to enter Italy, he was looking about for means of obtaining what he no longer intended to take by force. [What a gentle kind-hearted soul, and what an ass!] He had proposed to the English Foreign Office to suggest a sale of Venetia in concert with him. . . . In obtaining a throne for the Archduke Maximilian, Napoleon III saw an unexpected opening for the liberation of the captive province. He hoped that Francis Joseph would be pleased at the gift he was making his family and later on consent, perhaps, to let go of Venetia in exchange for an expansion on the Danube. 'The ghost of Venice stalks the halls of the Tuileries,' Nigra wrote to Ricasoli, 'and the spectre has taken Napoleon III by the hand and led him to sign the order to overthrow Juarez to make room for the Austrian Archduke.' " That ghost must have said to him: "Till we meet again at Philippi-Sedan!" Bismarck knew the art—and a rich harvest it bore the country he was ruling—of laying such ghosts. But there is still no end. The war of 1866 supervenes. Napoleon III declares his neutrality and so allows Prussian power to grow to gigantic proportions. He had forgotten the warning issued by Machiavelli in the *Deca* II, § 22: "Pope Leo did not yield to the wishes of the king [of France], but was persuaded by his councillors, so it was said, to remain neutral, on the ground that it was not to the interest of the Church that either the King or the Swiss should become powerful in Italy, and that if the country were to be restored to her ancient liberties, she must first be freed from the mastery of them both. . . . And no case could be more opportune than the present, since both were in the field, and the Pope's forces were well ordered to appear anew on the borders of Lombardy . . . and the battle was going to be a bloody one to both sides and the victor would be so weakened that the Pope could easily assail and vanquish him, so remaining to his glory lord of Lombardy and arbiter of all Italy. How mistaken that opinion was appeared from the event; for the Swiss being defeated after a desperate battle, the armies of the Pope and the Spaniards, far from adventuring to attack the victors, made ready for flight" (§ 2472). Describing the events of 1866 Ollivier has a glimmer of the realities. Says he, Vol. VIII, pp. 189-200: "In view of the disappointments that had followed on the spectacular gesture in Italy, it seemed imprudent, to say the least, to set out just as spectacularly to regulate in advance the results of a war in which we were having no part." But then straightway he falls back into the dark again, and resumes dreaming. He quotes an article of his own in which he advanced principles to which he ever after adhered: "Where Right stands is clear. In Italy Right stands with the army advancing to the deliverance of Venice. In Germany it stands with the army under Austrian leadership that is advancing to protect Frankfurt and deliver Dresden. Right does not allow us to lay hand to the Rhine provinces. Right forbids Prussia to seize Hanover, Hesse, and the Duchies, and Austria to keep Venice." How many many places for the most estimable Monsieur Right to keep an eye on! But when the cannon thundered at Sedan, Metz, and Paris, Monsieur Right

fortune. Furthermore, in the passage in which he trusts to the future to change bad luck to better, he does not at all make clear just how the future is going to right the wrongs of people who will be dead before the change for the better comes. He does not seem to have a very definite theory (§ 1995 [3]), nor does he try to explain the discrepancy between the misadventures of the French in 1870 and the exemplary conduct of their Emperor before that time. Are we to understand that it is the case—only the other way round—of the Achaeans, who suffered so grievously from the pride of Agamemnon? Or are we to adopt some other explanation? Ollivier does not notice that the justifications that he makes of Louis Napoleon's conduct from the standpoint of personal morality constitute a thorough-going condemnation of that sovereign's conduct as a statesman.[4]

1976. People of vigorous faith generally regard the supreme good as incarnate in their faith and are therefore led to believe that observance of its norms necessarily brings happiness. All the same, when the term "happiness" stands for something tangibly existing in the experimental world, the assertion of perfect accord between observance and happiness, or between violation and unhappiness, is too frequently contradicted by observation of fact to win any wide assent.[1] But ways are found to eliminate the conflict by suitable

was nowhere to be found; and seeing that no one had heeded his prohibitions regarding Hanover, Hesse, and the rest, he refused in a pet to interfere with the annexation of Alsace-Lorraine. There would still be a long story to tell, but enough for the present. Farther along (§§ 2455 f.) we shall return to these same facts and consider them from another standpoint.

1975 [4] Ollivier himself shows him as absolutely destitute of foresight on many occasions: for instance, *Op. cit.*, Vol. V, p. 67: "Bent nevertheless on carrying out the policy of army decentralization that had been haunting his mind ever since the Crimean War and which was the only means of effecting a rapid passage from a peace footing to a war footing, Napoleon III directed Randon to execute it without any increase in credits, and since it was impossible on that basis, that amounted to abandoning it. And in fact, from that time on, neither Emperor nor minister paid any further attention to it." Only a half-wit would consider a thing indispensable and then order it to be carried out under conditions known to be impossible. And yet Napoleon III was an intelligent man; but if he saw the better, he followed the worse under the influence of sentiments that were active in him—sentiments corresponding to residues of Class II (§ 2454 [3]).

1976 [1] Piepenbring, *Théologie de l'Ancien Testament,* pp. 208-09 (continuing the quotation in § 1944 [1]): "For a long time these ideas seem to have raised no serious objection, for none is met with in the more ancient texts. But as the events of his-

explanations, and to the production of them many persons have addressed themselves from ancient times down to the present. Now and then theorizers will cut an argument out of whole cloth; more often, and also with better results, they borrow them from certain expressions of residues found ready to hand. Group-persistences, for instance, lead people to think of this or that community as a unit; and the theorist can avail himself of that fact to explain how members of it may suffer harm without doing anything to deserve it. All he needs is to lay the blame for the trouble on some other person in the group (§ 1979).

1977. *B2: Happiness and unhappiness removed in space and in time.* A person performs the conduct *M*, which is said to be followed by a happening, *P*, it also being possible for *P* to occur by chance. It is evident that the longer the lapse of time between the conduct, *M*, and the happening, *P*, the greater the probability that *P* will happen by chance; in fact, if the lapse of time is at all long, the chances that *P* will happen are so great as to amount virtually to certainty. If a person with a weakness for predicting lottery numbers does not confine himself to a single drawing but asks for a century's time for a given number to be drawn, he can be almost certain, not to say certain, that his prediction will come true. In the same way, if the prophecy has a long and indefinite time in which to come true, there is no danger of being belied by the outcome in predicting

tory and of individual lives came to be better observed and more thoughtfully pondered [It was not so much the observation as the reflection that was lacking. Besides, the general form of statement is defective: those who pondered and those who gave the matter no thought were different people.] it was seen [Not by everybody.] that experience gave the lie at every step to the theory of remuneration, that many rascals were lucky in life, many virtuous people unfortunate. Whence a great embarrassment for those who did not shut their eyes to the facts [The very distinction that should be drawn.], a pitfall to cause the believer to stumble and fill him with doubt. That difficulty made itself especially felt beginning with the time of the Captivity. At that time therefore the most earnest efforts were made to overcome it." (Quotation continued in § 1979 [1].) Cicero, *De natura deorum,* III, 32, 81, after a list of examples exclaims: "But the day would be too short for me to enumerate the good men who have had bad fortune, nor any less so if I were to mention all the rascals who have prospered." In his treatise *On Tardy Punishments of Guilt* (*De sera numinis vindicta,* 4; Goodwin, Vol. IV, pp. 144-45), Plutarch piles derivation on derivation to show that the conduct of the deity is always just, not forgetting to keep the road home clear by remarking that the ways of the Lord are inscrutable (a *B4* solution, § 1902).

that if a country does wrong it will sooner or later be punished, and if it conducts itself nobly, rewarded. No nation in the course of years and centuries is in all respects fortunate or in all respects unfortunate; and any prophet who is not under restrictions of time will always find the reward or punishment he is looking for.

One way of removing in space and in time the fortunes and misfortunes that come to human beings is to say that if a man happens to be unlucky, it is all to his advantage as serving to correct him of some fault or sin, or leading others to improve themselves; and much more rarely, it is said, if a scoundrel has a stroke of luck, that his prosperity will prove to be his undoing, since he will be blinded by his success and so rush to his ruin, or else that it will help to discredit material prosperity in the eyes of others by showing that even a rascal can enjoy it (§ 1995 [3]).

1978. In view of the brevity of human life, an individual is less likely than a country to find the desired correspondence in time between conduct and its consequences. Nevertheless it is rare enough for an individual A to be altogether fortunate, altogether unfortunate; so for the person also the desired correspondence will be found between this or that act on his part and its reward or punishment. We get accordingly a large number of theories that defer the given individual's retribution in time, and a large number of others holding that a man's troubles work for his regeneration and so, if he will only wait, turn out to his advantage. Anyone speaking at a given moment and declaring that the future will tell whether a bad deed is punished, a good deed rewarded, cannot be definitely silenced by experience; for the future is as unknown to us as it is to him. But if he is stating a theory in general terms, if he understands it as applying to the past—and that is the way it is usually understood—we ought by this time to know just what punishments or rewards have been allotted before death to the people we know about; and proceeding in that fashion one finds that the theory is in no wise verified by experience. That is not noticed by persons swayed by sentiment; and the case is like the one discussed in § 1440 [2], where we found people believing that the female descendants of men who drink wine lose the ability to suckle children, regardless of the fact that if that theory were true, not a woman capable of suckling children could any longer be found in vine-growing countries.

1979. We will find it all the easier to discover some blessing or misfortune to correlate with some specific act if we broaden the scope of our quest from a single individual to a number of them. Powerful residues incline people to think of the family as a unit, and we can avail ourselves of that circumstance to find among a man's descendants some individual who has received the reward or punishment for his conduct. Success in such a quest is certain. When in the long course of the ages has a man's posterity been known to be uniformly fortunate, or uniformly unfortunate? [1]

1979 [1] Piepenbring, *Théologie de l'Ancien Testament,* pp. 208-10 (continuing the quotation in § 1976 [1]): "The difficulty may perhaps have been glimpsed in an earlier period and efforts made to obviate it by saying that God punishes the sins of the fathers in the children and rewards posterity for the fidelity of the forbears. [Interesting the attempt at justification that Piepenbring then makes:] And one must say that that principle has some foundation in the law of solidarity and heredity that can be seen operating in everyday experience, where children often suffer from the faults of their parents or benefit by their virtues." Piepenbring does not notice that what he is proving is not at all what he pretends to be proving; he is merely showing that there is a nexus between a child's status and his father's conduct. What he is promising to show is that the nexus is of a certain particular kind. It may well be that the vices and virtues of parents always have consequences for their children; but that does not prove that the sins of parents always have evil consequences for the children—a usurer or a burglar may leave his son a wealthy man; nor that the virtues of parents always have good consequences for their children—a philanthropic father who sacrifices himself for the good of others may leave his child in want. To show that the sins of the fathers are punished, and their virtues rewarded, in their children, such cases have to be eliminated—a fact that Piepenbring completely disregards, so giving another example of the lack of logic in these matters. He continues: "But that relatively ancient principle also raised objections and inspired the sarcastic proverb in Jer. 31:29 and Ezek. 18:2: 'The fathers have eaten sour grapes and the children's teeth are set on edge.' It was met with the thought that each individual bore the penalties for his own sin (Jer. 31:30: "Everyone shall die for his own iniquity"; Ezek. 18:3: "The soul that sinneth, it shall die"). That was a way of sustaining the traditional point of view and avoiding an explanation that attenuated at least the difficulty which the problem raised. But in that case, how surmount the difficulty? It was preached that man has no right to question God, the creature the Creator, the work its maker (Is. 29:16: "For shall the work say of him that made it: He made me not?" 45:9 f.: "Woe unto him that striveth with his maker"; Jer. 18, 6: "As the clay is in the potter's hand, so are ye in my hand") [Our *B4* solution—inscrutable are the ways of the Lord]; that far from being righteous (just), man was in reality sinful (Ezek. 18:29 f.: "Are not your ways unequal?" 23:17 f.; Is. 58:3 f.) [Solution *A,* a verbal solution.], or else that the prosperity of the wicked was only a fleeting thing and always led up to a disastrous ending, whereas the misfortunes of the righteous can be but transitory (Ps. 73:16-24: "Thou didst set

1980. Dionysius the Elder, tyrant of Syracuse, committed every kind of crime and sacrilege and gaily laughed at it all. Returning to his capital after pillaging the temple of Proserpine at Locris, his ship had favourable winds, and he remarked to his friends: "See what a good voyage the immortal gods themselves vouchsafe the blasphemer!" In reporting this anecdote Valerius Maximus mentions other examples of impiety and concludes: "Albeit Dionysius paid not the penalty due him, he suffered in the infamy of his son after his death the punishment which in this life he evaded. If slowly divine wrath proceeds to its vengeance, it compensate tardiness with severity." [a] In Horace, a dead man, Archytus, asks a sailor to cover his bones with a little sand and assures him that if he refuses he will leave behind him a crime for his children to expiate.[1] L. Cor-

them in slippery places"; 9:18 f.; 37; 49; 55:23; 64; 94:8-23; Prov. 23, 17 f.: "Thine expectation shall not be cut off"). [A B2 solution—happiness removed in space and time.] In some passages the writer even rises to the notion [Note the ethical connotation in the term "rises," which is foreign to the experimental domain.] that misfortune has salutary effects on a man just as correction is salutary for the child (Prov. 3:11 f.: "My son, despise not the chastening of the Lord"; Deut. 8:2-5: "Forty years in the wilderness to humble thee"; Lament. 3:27-30). [Again B2.] In Isaiah, finally, comes the thought that the righteous may be called to suffer for the wicked and so to spare them merited punishment (Is. 53:5: "He was wounded for our transgressions"—[B2.]). . . . The problem mentioned so concerned and so embarrassed Hebrew thinkers that one of them felt impelled to sound it to the bottom and devote the whole Book of Job to it"—[A B4 solution, i.e., no solution is found: inscrutable are the ways of the Lord. All this great varying of derivations is a quest for a way of reaching a point that is determined in advance (§§ 1414, 1628)].

1980 [a] De dictis factisque memorabilibus, I, 1, Externa exempla, 3.

1980 [1] Oda, I, 28 (2), vv. 10-11 (30-31):

>   "Negligis immeritis nocituram
>   postmodo te natis fraudem committere forsan."

("You think it a light matter to commit a wrong that can only do harm to your innocent children after you.") However, the passage is variously rendered. The Pseudo-Acron comments (Paris, 1519, p. 36): "Fraudem committere: either that in his eagerness to go on trading he will commit an act of deceit that will affect his posterity, or that a crime of such inhumanity [inhumanitatis: Paris, 1519, reads better: inhumati piaculum: failure to perform burial] would harm his children; or, in order to keep him from considering too long he [the poet] threatens that the man himself will after all suffer the punishment for his crime." Another scholiast, Porphyrio, says (Paris, 1519, p. 37): "Negligis immeritis nocituram: The order is 'you think it a light matter to commit a wrong.' But the meaning is: you take me lightly, and you think it will be easy to trick me. But the deceit will fall upon those born of you, in other words upon your children." There is no doubt in any event as to the punishment falling upon the children.

nelius Sulla passed his whole life in unbroken prosperity, but Faustus Sulla, his son, was slain by the soldiers of Sittius, and Publius Sulla, his grandson, was among Catiline's accomplices.[2] Dining with one of his veterans at Bologna, Augustus asked him whether it were true that the man who had been the first to lay hand to the image of the goddess Anaitis in Armenia had died paralyzed and blind.[3] The veteran replied that Augustus owed his dinner to one of the goddess's legs; that he, the veteran, had been the first to lay ax to the image and that all he owned had come of that bit of plunder. If we knew the history of all the descendants of the veteran in question, we could no doubt find one who had been a victim of some misfortune, and we could imagine that his bad luck was the penalty for his ancestor's crime. Just so when the unhappy Croesus lost his kingdom and his liberty, he sent ambassadors to Delphi to rebuke Apollo for the misfortunes that had come upon him. The god, answering through the lips of the Pythia, did not accuse

---

1980 [2] Seneca, *De consolatione, ad Martiam,* 12: "I will begin with a most happy man. Lucius Sulla lost his son, but that fact did not attenuate his malice (*militiam* misprint for *malitiam*) nor his fierce vigour against his enemies at home and abroad, nor did it cast suspicion of inappropriateness upon the name [*Felix*] which he impudently (*salvo*) borrowed from the son he had lost. Nor did a Sulla so truly *Felix* ever fear the wrath of the mortals on whose sufferings his own excessive good fortune rested, nor the envy of the gods, who were insulted by it" (*quorum illud crimen erat:* Lodge: "whose crime it was that Sulla was so happie"). Pliny, *Historia naturalis,* VII, 44 (Bostock-Riley, Vol. II, pp. 190-91): "One man so far, Lucius Sulla, has presumed to take the name of Felix, but in his case it came drenched in civil blood from the ruins of his country." Pliny, however, adds that Sulla died unhappy because of the hatred of his fellow-citizens and the sufferings of his last illness. Duruy, *Histoire des Romains,* Vol. II, pp. 712, 715 (Mahaffy, Vol. II, pp. 722-25, 728), takes a wider sweep: "In human affairs, justice sometimes leaps a generation. [A very interesting uniformity of which Duruy fails to give the slightest proof.] It was at Pharsalia thirty years afterwards [after Sulla's death] that the Roman nobility expiated Sulla's proscriptions." Ethical declamations such as these still circulate under the name of history. Duruy is even worried about the remorse that Sulla should have felt, but which seems not to have troubled him. He observes that for the Romans a striking success justified everything and adds: "That is why the terrible dictator died without remorse. And so it will be with all those who interpose a false principle between their science and their conduct." The inference, and certainly not the one Duruy intended, would be that it is a good thing to have "false principles" if one wants to be happy. But the question is not whether a man's happiness is due to "false principles," but whether he can be happy in spite of his misconduct, leaving other people, his family, his caste, his country, or perhaps humanity at large, to pay the penalty for his sins.

1980 [3] Pliny, *Historia naturalis,* XXXIII, 24.

Croesus of ever having sinned against gods or men. He said: "The lot decreed by Fate cannot be voided even by a god. Croesus hath been smitten for the sin of his ancestral parent of the fifth generation." Had he chanced to enjoy a uniformly happy life, his son might have been called upon to suffer the penalty for the crime of an ancestor of the sixth generation; and so on indefinitely.[4]

1981. Notwithstanding iniquities too numerous to count, the Romans enjoyed long centuries of prosperity; but nothing prevents one from assuming that retribution came in the Barbarian invasions. So the Mohammedan invasions of a later date may have punished the sins of the Christians, and the Christian invasions of Moslem lands today the sins of the old Mohammedans. He who seeks finds, and with no great effort.

1982. The "responsibility" for crimes, as well as "rewards" for good behaviour, may not only pass on to posterity but be extended to communities variously constituted. Wide-spread among the

1980 [4] Herodotus, *Historiae*, I, 91. In reporting the legend Herodotus finds nothing to criticize in it. Larcher, however, in a note to his translation of the passage, quotes a remark by Cicero, *De natura deorum*, III, 38, 90: "Do I understand you to say that the power of the gods is such that even if a man has escaped punishment for his crimes by dying, those punishments fall on his children, grandchildren, and descendants? O wondrous equity of the Gods! Would any state tolerate the proposer of a law of that kind, so that a son or grandson would be condemned if his father or grandfather had committed a crime?" Larcher himself adds: "The philosopher Bio (Plutarch, *De sera numinis vindicta*, 19; Goodwin, Vol. IV, p. 171) had preferred to ridicule that idea. 'If a god,' he said, 'were to punish children for the crimes of their father, he would be more ridiculous than a doctor giving somebody a medicine because his father or grandfather had at one time been sick.' People were still without a sound notion of the Divinity in the day of our historian. There was none such except among the Jews." And he quotes Deut. 24:16 and Ezek. 18:20, but forgets many other passages to the contrary, and notably, Ex. 20:5: "For I the Lord thy God am a jealous God, visiting the iniquity of the fathers upon the children unto the third and fourth generations of them that hate me." Another example of the way in which a virulent sentiment leads the mind astray. Larcher certainly knew the passage in Exodus and others of that sort in the Bible, but he disregards them in deference to sentiment. [Awkward paragraphing led Pareto into telling the anecdote of Croesus and his oracle twice in this paragraph. I eliminate the first account in the translation.—A. L.] Solon, *Elegiae*, XIII (IV), *On Righteousness*, vv. 27-32 (Bergk, Vol. II, p. 43; Edmonds, Vol. I, pp. 127-28): "The man with a wicked heart does not for ever remain in secret, but in the end reveals himself utterly. The one has his merited punishment sooner, the other later. If it seems that some escape and are not overtaken by the pursuing destiny of the gods, they are smitten in the end. The price of their misdeeds their innocent children pay, or later, perchance, their grandchildren."

ancients was the belief that a man's sins were visited upon all his fellow-citizens. Rome even managed to benefit by the rascality of some of her consuls, but she never made a theory of it. When ancient writers fail to evince any reluctance in admitting that children should pay the penality for the parent, they are evidently regarding the family as a unit represented by the paterfamilias; and similarly, when they speak of a city's being smitten for the misdeeds of one of its citizens, they are thinking of the city as a unit.[1] "Just" in both cases is the punishment of the whole for the sin of the part, much as a person's whole body suffers "justly" for the deed of the hand. In that lies the main residue (group-persistence), and only incidentally is it used for the derivations that are designed to reconcile the punishment (or rewarding) of the group with the guilt (or merit) of the individual. Furthermore, what we call "guilt" is identified, to some extent, at least, with an uncleanness that alters the integrity of the individual, his family, and the various groups to which he belongs. Thence quite spontaneously comes a feeling that the integrity has to be restored as regards not only the individual but also his family and his other affiliations of one sort or another (§§ 1231 f.)

1983. Interesting among the various derivations just alluded to is one to the effect that a city is justly punished for the crimes of any one of its citizens, since it could have avoided the penalty by chastising the culprit itself.[1] Incidents in plenty betray the artificial character of that derivation. Oftentimes a city or a community suffered the punishment before it knew of any crime or offender, and therefore was quite unable to punish the offender directly or expiate the crime in any way. Ancient legends recite hosts of instances where nations are punished for unknown crimes that are not revealed till afterwards by prophets or soothsayers. The Achaeans were completely in the dark as to why the plague was ravaging their camp, and before they could learn the reason Calchas, protected by Achilles, had to reveal that Apollo was angry, and the cause of his wrath

---

1982 [1] Plutarch, *De sera numinis vindicta*, 15-16 (Goodwin, Vol. IV, pp. 166-68).

1983 [1] Glotz, *La solidarité de la famille dans le droit criminel en Grèce*, pp. 563-64: "That a city should speedily be punished for the crime of a citizen or ruler is only just and is easily understandable. Responsible to the gods, the state had only to purge itself by a measure of public safety, a 'noxal' repudiation through death or banishment."

(Iliad, I, vv. 93-100). Furthermore, not even after the revelation has been made does it even remotely occur to anyone that the Achaeans should have inflicted some punishment or other on Agamemnon, and the plague ceases not because of any such punishment—there was none, either before or after—but because of the satisfaction given to Apollo. Agamemnon decides to restore Chryseis to her father of his own accord, because *(Iliad,* I, v. 117) "He wishes his people safe that it perish not," [2] and he squares accounts by taking Briseis away from Achilles. How could the Thebans have avoided being smitten by the plague, when they were utterly ignorant of the crimes of which Oedipus had unintentionally become guilty? In fact the oracle of Apollo does not tax them with any fault. It merely prescribes an expiation, the way a physician might prescribe a medicine for a patient.[3]

1984. If a nation could suffer by the misconduct of its king, it could also benefit by his good conduct. Hesiod describes the happiness of peoples ruled by just kings, and their unhappiness if ruled by unjust ones. In his case, the notion that the conduct of kings is punished or rewarded in their peoples merges with the experimental notion that the welfare or unhappiness of a people depends upon its having a good or a bad government.[1]

1983 [2] Βούλομ' ἐγὼ λαὸν σόον ἔμμεναι μὴ ἀπολέσθαι. Dugas-Montbel annotates, Vol. I, p. 23: "Zenodotus suppressed this line as expressing too commonplace an idea; but taking it in connexion with what goes before, the thought gains in loftiness from the sacrifice Agamemnon is making, since he consents to return his captive only to help his people. I do not think the criticism of Zenodotus can be subscribed to, and none of the modern editors accept it." Considerations as to the "commonplaceness" or "loftiness" of this or that "thought" are foreign to Homeric times. Agamemnon could not have spoken differently; he is simply making clear why he does what no one could have compelled him to do.

1983 [3] Sophocles, *Oedipus rex,* vv. 96-98 (Storr, Vol. I, pp. 12-13): "Phoebus our king doth bid us drive forth, and no longer support, so long as it be inexpiable, a pollution (μίασμα) which this land doth sustain."

1984 [1] Hesiod, *Opera et dies,* vv. 260-61:

... ὄφρ' ἀποτίση
δῆμος ἀτασθαλίας βασιλέων.

("So long as the people pays for the recklessness of its kings.") Elie Reclus, a writer who cannot be so very well grounded in his antiquity, pictures the Greek king as something like a Negro chief procuring rain and all sorts of good things for his subjects by magic. Says he, *Les primitifs,* pp. 271-72: "Men [according to certain ancient writers] would ask nothing better than to riot in debaucheries and roll in crime, were it not for the monarchs who repress greed and violence and bridle the nations with laws. In those conceptions it is not always easy to distinguish between

1985. The groups that suffered for the guilt of a member could be more or less fortuitous. Accidental companionship with the wicked could hurt. That may happen in the experimental world under certain circumstances. A person violating the norms of prudence inside a powder-magazine may bring death to everybody in its neighbourhood. It is assumed that the same thing happens in other cases where there is no experimental demonstration. Caught in a storm at sea, Diagoras was taxed by the sailors on his ship with being the cause of their misfortune. He replied by pointing to other ships that were also in danger on the same course and asking whether his accusers thought those ships too had a Diagoras aboard.[1] The answer would seem conclusive to many people; but it was not. If it be assumed that the atheism of Diagoras could harm people who were with him on the same ship, it is just as easy to assume that it could harm everybody in his neighbourhood, even though they were on other ships. It is a question only of more or of less, of extending or restricting the area within which the impiety of Diagoras had the effect of causing a storm.[2]

the cases where the god delegates his powers to man and where man receives his powers from the god. That is why Hindu doctrine taught that Indra never rains on a realm that has lost its king. Ulysses, the crafty Ulysses, explained to the chaste Penelope, *Odyssey*, XIX, v. 108: 'Under a virtuous prince the earth bears barley and grain in plenty: the trees are laden with fruits, the sheep bear many coats a year and the sea teems with fish. A good leader means all that to us.' " If Reclus had examined the text he was quoting and grasped its meaning, he would have seen that it does not say that "a good leader means all that to us," but makes the blessings originate ἐξ εὐηγεσίης, which means, beyond question, "from his good government [his good leading]." The text earlier explains that this king "governeth with justice"—εὐδικίας ἀνέχῃσι; and that for that reason "the people doth prosper under him"—ἀρετῶσι δὲ λαοὶ ὑπ' αὐτοῦ.

1985 [1] Cicero, *De natura deorum*, III, 37, 89: "*Idemque* [*Diagoras*], *cum ei naviganti vectores adversa tempestate timidi et perterriti dicerent non iniuria sibi illud accidere* [No wonder such a thing was happening to them.], *qui illum in eamdem navem recepissent, ostendit eis in eodem cursu multas alias laborantes, quaesivitque num etiam iis navibus Diagoram vehi crederent.*"

1985 [2] Horace, *Oda*, III, 2, vv. 29-32:

> ". . . *Saepe Diespiter*
> *neglectus incesto addidit integrum:*
> *raro antecedentem scelestum*
> *deseruit pede poena claudo.*"

("Often has a slighted Jupiter classed the innocent man with the blasphemer. Rarely has Punishment, even be she slow of foot, failed to overtake the rogue accursed who has gained a start upon her.")

1986. The "envy of the gods" ($\phi\theta\acute{o}\nu o\varsigma$ $\theta\epsilon\tilde{\omega}\nu$) did not allow a man to live a whole lifetime in happiness, and it extended to his posterity and his community. It is curious to note that Plutarch rebukes Herodotus for believing in such a thing, *De Herodoti malignitate,* XV (Goodwin, IV, p. 337), but then gives an example of it himself from the life of Aemilius Paulus.[1] In this, as in other instances of the kind, Class II residues are working. Paulus Aemilius and his children are taken as one unit and no one thinks of distinguishing the children from the father. The group, the aggregate, must not be altogether fortunate and is smitten, in fact, in one of its parts.

1987. Modern theorists are in the habit of bitterly reproving ancient "prejudices" whereby the sins of the father were visited upon the son. They fail to notice that there is a similar thing in our own society, in the sense that the sins of the father benefit the son and acquit him of guilt.[1] For the modern criminal it is a great good fortune to be able to count somewhere among his ancestry or other relations a criminal, a lunatic, or just a mere drunkard, for in a court of law that will win him a lighter penalty or, not seldom, an acquittal. Things have come to such a pass that there is hardly a criminal case nowadays where that sort of defence is not put forward. The old metaphysical proof that was used to show that a son should be punished because of his father's wrongdoing was neither

---

1986 [1] *Aemilius Paulus,* 35, 36 (Perrin, Vol. VI, pp. 447-51). In a speech to the Roman People Paulus Aemilius explains how extraordinarily favourable Fortune had been to him and the army in the war against Perseus and in everything else down to his return home. Then he adds, 36, 4-5: "Nevertheless, having come hither safely and seeing the city full of joy and well-being and busily applied to the performance of the sacrifices, I did not on that account cease to hold Fortune suspect, knowing full well that the great favours she grants unto men are not pure and undefiled nor without taint of divine envy. Nor was I freed of the fear that my soul had conceived at these things, in sore dread lest some public calamity impend, until I had experienced a grievous misfortune about my own private hearth. For in these sacred days I have buried, one after the other, those noble sons who were all I had left to succeed me."

1987 [1] As usual (§ 587) derivations prove the pro and the contra equally well. With Plutarch, *De sera numinis vindicta,* 16 (Goodwin, Vol. IV, p. 167), the sins of the father are disasters for the son, the justification being, he says, that children inherit more or less of their father's character. In the eyes of our modern humanitarians the sins of the father benefit the son by winning him, in case he commits a crime, a lighter penalty or an acquittal, for, say our humanitarians, the father's sins diminish the son's "responsibility."

more nor less valid than the proof used nowadays to show that the punishment which otherwise he deserves should for the same reasons be either mitigated or remitted. When, then, the effort to find an excuse for the criminal in the sins of his ancestors proves unavailing, there is still the recourse of finding one in the crimes of "society," which, having failed to provide for the criminal's happiness, is "guilty" of his crime. And the punishment proceeds to fall not upon "society," but upon some one of its members, who is chosen at random and has nothing whatever to do with the presumed guilt.[2]

1988. The concept of "solidarity" that makes the good incur the punishment of the wicked appears here and there in antiquity and later on becomes fundamental in Catholicism. To steal the thunder of the "Solidarists" and Socialists Brunetière used to lay great stress on the point.

1989. B_3: *Happiness and unhappiness located outside the real world*. From the standpoint of formal logic, solutions of this type are incontrovertible. As we have time and again repeated, experimental science can have nothing whatever to do with anything transcending the experimental domain. Its competence ends at the boundaries.

1990. We might recall here, as a matter of purely experimental competence, that the theory that supernatural retribution and recom-

---

1987 [2] The classical case is that of the starving man who steals a loaf of bread. That he should be allowed to go free is understandable enough; but it is less understandable that "society's" obligation not to let him starve should devolve upon one baker chosen at random and not on society as a whole. The logic of the situation would seem to be to acquit the starving man and have society pay the baker for the stolen loaf. Another case by no means hypothetical: A woman aims a revolver at her seducer, misses him, and hits a third party who has nothing to do with the quarrel. A sympathetic jury acquits her. Let us grant that the woman is excusable as a victim led to crime by her lover's misdeeds. Yet why should the penalty for the man's rascality devolve upon a third party who is absolutely innocent? To satisfy sentiments of languorous pity humanitarian legislators approve "probation" and "suspended sentence" laws, thanks to which a person who has committed a first theft is at once put in a position to commit a second. And why should the luxury of humaneness be paid for by the unfortunate victim of the second theft and not by society as a whole? In general, assuming that, as some say, the crime is more the doing of society than of the criminal, it is sound enough to conclude that the criminal should be set free or made to pay some very light penalty; but the same reasoning exactly leads to the conclusion that the victim of the crime should, within the limits of the possible, be indemnified by society. As it is, the criminal only is looked after and no one gives a thought to the victim.

pense were inventions of potentates designed to control their peoples, cannot stand. The notions of such retribution and recompense exist independently of any preconceived design. They are associated with those residues of group-persistence whereby human personality endures after death. Practical men have, of course, taken advantage of such ideas, just as they have of other sentiments in society. Theorists too may have used them to solve their particular problems, and have given them literary, metaphysical, or pseudo-scientific forms. But they did not invent them: they merely gave shape to a matter already existing and, like the men of affairs, utilized them for their personal ends.

1991. Maimonides acquaints us with the theory of a Moslem sect, called the Qadarites, and another called the Mu'tazilites, who carried the solutions of our $B2$ and $B3$ types to their extremest limits.[1] Ordinarily people do not go so far. What we get, rather, is huge numbers of explanations that are of mixed type and, more especially, vague and indefinite.

1992. More or less of the mixed type are interpretations that do not defer the consequences of an act to an imaginary world, but rest content with relegating them to the realm of the possible. It is said, for instance: "This individual is happy, but he might have been happier"; "It is hard on this man, but it might have been worse." The scope of the possible is not definable, and so one can prove anything one chooses. Pleasant rhetorical disquisitions in all periods of history have been devoted to this theme.

1991 [1] Maimonides, *Guide of the Perplexed*, III, 17, Theory IV (Munk, Vol. III, pp. 122-23; Friedländer, Vol. III, p. 70): "If a man has an infirmity by birth though he has not yet sinned, they say that that is a consequence of Divine Wisdom and that it is better for that individual to be deformed in that way than to have had a perfect constitution. [Solution $B2$ (§ 1978).] We do not know in what his advantage lies [Solution $B4$.], though the thing has happened to him not as a punishment but for his good. [$B2$.] They make the same answer when a good man perishes. It is that he may have all the greater recompense in the other world. [Solution $B3$.] They go even farther with their absurdities. When they are asked why God is just towards man without being so towards other creatures, and for just what sin an animal has its throat cut, they resort to the ridiculous answer that that is better for the animal, that God will reward it in another life. [$B3$.] Yes, say they, even the flea and the louse that have been killed are to have their recompense for that from God; and so if the mouse that has been torn to pieces by cat or hawk is innocent, Divine Wisdom, they say, has required that it be that way with that mouse, and God will make amends to it in another life for what has happened to it in this." (§ 1934 [1].)

1993. A hermit, once upon a time, was condemning the judgments of God because he saw men who lived wickedly blessed with many goods and prosperous, and men who lived virtuously cursed with many woes. An angel came to him and led him to the abode of another hermit who had lived long years in penance but was now minded to return to the temptations of the world. The angel threw the hermit—the latter—over a precipice; and pointed out that his death, which was apparently in ill keeping with his righteous life, was really its reward, as it transported him to eternal beatitude. And so, going on, the angel showed the hermit other instances where an apparent evil proved really to be a blessing, and *vice versa*.[1]

1994. Let no one imagine that our own age does not produce its fairy-tales of the same sort. When our teetotallers are invited to gaze upon men who have lived to advanced old age or given proof of extraordinary physical or intellectual prowess despite their addiction to wines or other alcoholic beverages, they answer that if such men had been temperate they would have lived to even greater age or been physically and intellectually even more remarkable. A rather handsome type of the virtuist once said in a lecture: "We hear of supreme statesmen and soldiers who were not chaste men, and of heroic generals who were not chaste men. That is true, but had they been chaste men they would have been greater men than they were." In reasoning, or rather ranting, in such fashion, people forget that the burden of proof rests with the person who makes the statement and that appealing merely to the possible is a good way to mistake fire-flies for lanterns.

1993 [1] Étienne de Bourbon, *Anecdotes historiques*, § 396: "A variant of this celebrated apologue has been published by Thomas Wright, *Latin Stories*, No. 7, pp. 10-12 [*De angelo qui duxit heremitam ad diversa hospitia*] following English manuscripts. It is also to be found in the *Gesta Romanorum* (a collection of the fifteenth century) [Dick, No. 220, pp. 234-37; Swan, No. 80, Vol. I, pp. 274-80], in Méon's *Nouveau recueil de fabliaux et contes*, Vol. II, pp. 216-35, in the sermons (*Conciones*, Turin, 1527) of Albert of Padua, a preacher of the fourteenth century, in the English poems of Thomas Parnell [*The Hermit*], and in the *Magnum speculum exemplorum*, Douai, 1605, Vol. I, p. 152. It supplies the theme for an incident in M. de Voltaire's *Zadig*, Voltaire replacing the angel with another hermit. Le Clerc, *Histoire littéraire de la France*, Vol. XXIII, p. 128, thinks he can connect it in origin with the old 'Lives' of the anchorites of the desert. It seems in fact to have come from the East. It appears in many Oriental collections and even in the Koran, XVIII, 64. And *cf.* Luzel, *Légendes chrétiennes de la Bretagne*, Saint-Brieuc, 1874, p. 14 [read *Légendes chrétiennes de la Basse Bretagne*, Vol. II, pp. 1-11]."

1995. *B4: No interpretation is discoverable—inscrutable are the ways of the Lord.*[1] We can say simply that we cannot know why an act leads to certain consequences and shrug our shoulders as to whether they be "just" or "unjust." That seems to be the conclusion reached in the Book of Job, and such was the doctrine of the Ashariyah, as described by Maimonides.[2] Now if a person sits with his mouth closed, nobody can object to what he is saying. In the same way there could be no objection to a person's going no farther than saying that he knows nothing about the ways of the Lord, provided he sticks to that doctrine consistently. But that, as a rule, is not the case. A writer will start out by showing that he knows all the ins and outs of "the ways of the Lord," and only when he is pressed with objections does he come out with the claim that the Lord's ways are inscrutable. Of that procedure we have an instance in the arguments of St. Augustine that may well serve as typical of its class. It is a general procedure, however, and is frequently encountered in the writings of theologians and other thinkers.[3]

1995 [1] Dante, *Paradiso*, XIX, vv. 79-81: "Now who art thou that with vision of a span wouldst sit upon a bench and judge a thousand miles away?" (Norton.)

1995 [2] *Guide of the Perplexed*, III, 17, Theory III (Munk, Vol. III, p. 121; Friedländer, Vol. III, pp. 69-70): "Members of that sect claim that it has been God's pleasure to send prophets, to command, forbid, terrify, inspire hopes or fears, though we have no power to act ourselves. He may therefore require impossible things of us, and it is altogether possible that even though obeying a commandment we may be punished or, disobeying, rewarded. In a word, it follows from that view that the acts of God have no final purpose. They carry the load of all such absurdities for the pleasure of safe-guarding that opinion, and they go so far as to hold that if we see an individual who was born blind or a leper and can ascribe to him no previous sin that could have made him deserve such a lot, we are to say: 'That is God's will'; and there is no injustice in it, for they hold that God is at liberty to inflict torments on the man who has not sinned and shower blessings on the sinner."

1995 [3] In all the works of St. Augustine there is a continuous swinging back and forth between an assertion that the ways of the Lord are unknowable and the claim that they are perfectly well known to St. Augustine: *Contra adversarium legis et profetarum* (*Opera*, Vol. VIII, p. 605), I, 21, 45: "The Apostle cries (Rom. 11: 33-34): 'O, the depth of the riches both of the wisdom and knowledge of God! How unsearchable are His judgments and His ways past finding out! For who hath known the mind of the Lord? or who hath been His counsellor?' " In the *De civitate Dei,* all of Chapter XX is a disquisition on the inscrutability of the Lord's ways. Both good men and evil, the Saint says, partake of this world's goods; then: "We really know not of what judgment of God this good man be poor and this wicked man rich; why the one rejoices who, it would seem, should be in torment because of his corrupt living, whilst the other dwells in sorrow, who would seem to merit happiness for his commendable behaviour." And he recites many parallel cases. "If,"

1996. The inconsistency of saying that one does not know what one pretends to know very well is ordinarily not noticed because of a controlling sentiment. At bottom the reasoning is of the following type: "*A* ought to be *B*. If observation does not show that, I am at a loss to tell why; but that does not lessen my confidence that *A* ought to be *B*." When it assumes that form, experimental science can find no fault with it, for the reason we have so often mentioned, that it joins no issue with faith. But oftentimes the form, implicitly at least, is a different one, approaching the following type: "*A* = *B*. If that fact is not observable, we labour under an illusion, for in reality, in a manner unknown to me, *A* = *B*." When *A* and *B* fall within the domain of experience, logico-experimental science is competent to deal with such a proposition. If it observes that *A* is not equal to *B*, it cannot admit that *A* = *B*, nor does it care whether one can or cannot determine the cause of that fact.

1997. In this case, again, the proposition that "the ways of the Lord are unknowable" was not invented by the theorists who have

he says, "that were the constant rule, if all the wicked were at all times prosperous, and all the good unfortunate, one might assume that the cause was a just judgment of God, compensating worldly blessings and sorrows with blessings and sorrows eternal. But it also happens that the good enjoy worldly blessings and that the wicked are visited with worldly sorrows; wherefore all the more are the judgments of God unfathomable, and His ways unsearchable." That much clear, the Saint, it would seem, ought to stop and try no farther to fathom the unfathomable designs of God. But not at all! From beginning to end in his book the Saint fathoms and fathoms, quite as if they were discoverable. By the end of Chapter XX, he has adopted one of our solutions, *B*3, and predicts that on the Day of Judgment we shall see the justice of the judgments of God, even of those judgments the justice of which is at present hidden from our eyes. Specially interesting his frantic efforts to find justifications for the fact that the Barbarian invasions had smitten the good as well as the wicked. First he resorts to a solution of our *B*2 type: "Those evils," he says, I, 1, "are to be ascribed to Divine Providence, which is wont to use wars to correct and punish the sinfulness [corruption] of men"; then, suddenly, he switches to one of our *B*3 solutions, averring that Providence sometimes afflicts the righteous, allowing them thereafter to pass on to a better world, or even to remain in this world if he has designs for their further service (*B*4). He dwells on the point that the pagan temples did not save the lives of their worshippers, whereas Christian asylums were respected. That takes us altogether away from the matter of the relations between good conduct or sinful conduct and rewards or punishments. The temples seem to work their effects in virtue of some intrinsic property, very much like lightning-rods, some of which are effective, others not. Then back we go to the thorny problem of the blessings of the wicked and the sorrows of the good, I, 8: "It hath pleased divine Providence," he says, "to prepare future blessings for the good which the wicked shall not have, and for the wicked sorrows which shall

utilized it. They found the sentiment, which is associated with Class II residues, ready-made in the masses at large, and one after another they have taken advantage of it, giving its manifestations, to be sure, such forms as they pleased.

1998. Close kin to solutions of this type are metaphysical solutions such as Kant's "categorical imperative," which posit a certain conception of "duty," without going on to tell what happens to the person who snaps his fingers at his "duty" and ignores it. Such solutions are not free from the usual inconsistencies, since they assume as known everything of which the author approves, bringing in the unknown only when it becomes necessary to answer the objections that may properly be urged. A type of such reasonings would be the following: "*A ought* to be done because it is a consequence of *B*." "And why *ought B* to be done?" "Because it is a consequence of *C*." And so on until one asks, let us say, "Why ought *P* to be done?" The answer to that question is a categorical imperative. These metaphysical solutions are, in general, for the use and consumption of metaphysicists. Practical men and the masses at large take little notice of them.

not come nigh the righteous." That is a *B3* solution. But Augustine does not discard the *B1* type completely; after all, he says, the good are not without some sin: "They are afflicted, together with the wicked, not because they lead as bad a life as the wicked, but because they are no less enamoured of life in the flesh." Then he shows, I, 10, that the saints lose nothing in losing temporal blessings (*A1*) and that good Christians, for their part, cannot mourn such loss without manifesting an inclination to sin. The pagans were noting the fact that even nuns consecrated to God had been violated by the Barbarians. The Saint discusses that point at length, tacking and luffing as usual between solutions of our various types. He draws, I, 26, a distinction between material and spiritual virginity (a verbal solution of the *A1* type) and says that only the material could have been violated by the Barbarians, not the spiritual. Why, he asks, I, 28, did God permit such outrages to holy women? He begins with a *B4* solution: "the judgments of God are unfathomable, His ways unsearchable." But he keeps fathoming and searching all the same, and with no great effort hits on a *B1* solution: Had the nuns in question not perhaps sinned through pride in their virginity? *"Verumtamen interrogate fideliter animas vestras ne forte de isto integritatis et continentiae vel pudicitiae bono vos inflatius extulistis, et humanis laudibus delectatae in hoc etiam aliquibus invidistis"* ("envying others in your delight in human praises"). In any event, those who have not sinned may consider that God sometimes permits evil that He may punish it on the Day of Judgment (*B3*). But unsatisfied, evidently, with that answer, he reverts to a *B1* solution: Those nuns who had made no boast of their chastity had perhaps some secret vanity that might have eventuated in vainglory had they escaped, amidst so many calamities, the humiliation that they actually experienced. In his twisting and

1999. *C: Absolute negation: pessimism.* Such solutions count for little in the social equilibrium. They are never popular. They have vogue primarily among men of letters and philosophers, and are valuable only as manifestations of the psychic state of this or that individual. In moments of discouragement many people repeat, as we saw, with Brutus, "Virtue, thou art but a name." Many people enjoy reading the pessimistic poems of Leopardi just as they enjoy listening to a well-written tragedy. But neither poem nor tragedy has much influence on their conduct.

2000. Oftentimes pessimism acts as a spur to material enjoyments, and many people of literary inclinations will repeat the maxim: "Let us eat, drink, and be merry, for tomorrow we die." In Russia, after the war with Japan, there was a movement for revolution, with eager hopes of an exciting future. The revolution was put down, the hopes were dispelled. A period of discouragement followed, with a marked impulse towards purely physical enjoyments.

2001. *D: Qualified negation: two different situations that may have certain points in common.* If the reader has attentively considered the many facts we have been assembling—and to them others, many many others, might readily be added—he will already

turning from one solution to another, unable ever to settle upon an idea that is even remotely definite, St. Augustine is a model of which copies too numerous to count are to be found all the way along down to modern times, to say nothing of the copies that will be provided by the future. In § 1951, we quoted Bismarck's French antagonist, Ollivier, to the effect that ingratitude is sooner or later punished. Now that theory is clear and definite. Do not be ungrateful—if you are, you will be punished. If, in spite of your ingratitude, you are at present soaring on the wings of success, look out—do not trust in it: God (or some metaphysical entity) is granting it to you today, the better to punish you tomorrow. That is a solution of the B2 type. Barring the difference between the person who is rewarded for his conduct and the person who is punished for the conduct of someone else (§ 1975), the theory has the merit of justifying possible divergences between good works and the attainment of happiness. But further along, Ollivier switches from that solution to another. Says he, *L'Empire libéral*, Vol. III, p. 590: "Just as evil is sometimes crowned with a success that is a scandal to justice, so the good sometimes leads only to undeserved reverses. In that lies a dispensation of Providence that eludes our understanding"—a solution of the B4 type. It would seem that Ollivier, whenever he finds it convenient, does know the designs of Providence, and so he knows that, sooner or later, Providence always punishes the wicked. But when his convenience lies in another direction, he says that he does not know the designs of Providence. If he does not know them, how does he know that Providence is going to punish the wicked at some future time? If he knows that Providence is going to punish the wicked at some future time, how can he say that he does not know its designs?

have perceived the scientific solution of the problems stated in § 1897.

As regards the first, strict observance of the norms prevailing in a given community has certain effects that are advantageous to the individual, to the community, and to individual and community; and then again other effects that are disadvantageous (§§ 2121 f.). Ordinarily the advantages outweigh the disadvantages. Both advantage and disadvantage, however, can be determined only by an examination of each particular case.

As regards the second problem, it is to a certain extent beneficial to believe that observance of the norms prevailing in a community is always advantageous to individual and community, and that that belief should be neither doubted nor controverted. That attitude too has its drawbacks, but ordinarily the favourable effects overbalance the bad, and again in order to determine what they are an analysis of each particular case is necessary.

Returning to the more general problems stated in § 1897, we may repeat to the letter everything that we have just said, replacing the term "norms" with the expression "the residues operative in a community, and their consequences." After that, we have to restate the different solutions given to those problems by theologies and metaphysical systems. As for the first, metaphysical systems, and the theologies of religions self-styled as "positive," usually hold that to act in accord with the existing residues which they accept, and with the consequences of those residues, can only have effects that are "good," "just," "beneficial." But the theologies of Progress and of Reason, Holy of Holies, declare that to act according to those residues (they call them "prejudices") and their consequences can only have effects that are bad, harmful, pernicious. Logico-experimental science, as usual, accepts neither the one set nor the other of those dogmatic assertions, but insists on testing each particular case by experience, which alone can determine the utility or harmfulness of certain modes of conduct.

2002. The examination we have just completed supplies an excellent example of certain doctrines that are experimentally unsound but nevertheless have their great social utility. For more than two thousand years moralists have been investigating the relations presumably subsisting between strict observance of the norms of ethics and the consequent happiness or unhappiness of individuals or communities. They have not yet succeeded either in finding a theory that squares with the facts or in stating a theory that is definite in form and exclusively made up of terms designating experimental entities. They keep repeating the same things over and over again. A theory is demolished, then bobs up again, to be demolished a second time, and so things go on unendingly (§§ 616 f.). Even in our day, when historians and other practitioners of the social sciences set out to judge human conduct according to "morality," they refrain from stating, as they should, which solution of the problem they are adopting. They leave their solution implicit, veiled in a nebula of sentiment, a procedure that enables them to change it at their convenience and often to have two or more contradictory ones in succession. That conclusions drawn in such fashion from premises that are left unstated and therefore uncertain, impalpable, nebulous, must have scant logico-experimental value is readily understandable; and such conclusions win acceptance in virtue of sentiment, and nothing else. The disputes that rage in connexion with them are mere wars of words. If the ethics of Aristotle is compared with modern ethical systems, one sees at once that the difference between the two is enormously less than the difference between Aristotle's physics and modern physics. And why? It cannot be claimed that the men who have dealt with the natural sciences have been individuals of greater genius than the men who have dealt with ethics. Not seldom one and the same author—Aristotle, for instance—has written on both physics and ethics; and then again, history furnishes no indication whatever of any such differences in mental ability. A cause of the unequal progress in those different researches might be sought in their intrinsic difficulty: one might say that chemistry, physics, and geology have advanced more rapidly than ethics because their problems are not so difficult. Socrates happened to say that they were more difficult [1]—and they surely are as compared with reasonings based on sentiment. But leaving Socrates aside, how explain the fact that down to about the fifteenth century physics, chemistry, and the other natural sciences had made no greater progress than ethics? If they were the easier, how is it that they failed to produce results before that time? The fact is that the

2002 [1] Xenophon, *Memorabilia*, I, 1, 11-13.

natural sciences marched *pari passu* with ethics, and sometimes even fell behind, so long as they used the same theological, metaphysical —in other words, sentimental—method that ethics used. But they parted company with ethics and rapidly advanced when they changed procedure and began to use the experimental method. It is therefore evident that the unequal progress of ethics and the natural sciences must be due principally to the difference in methods.

But we are not through with our question-marks yet! Why that difference in methods? Granted that it may have been due in the first place to mere chance! But why has it held its ground for centuries, as it still continues to do? The Athenians were as angry at Anaxagoras, who said that the sun was a red-hot stone, as they were at Socrates, who preached an ethics of which they did not approve. In times nearer our own, the "errors" of Copernicus, reiterated by Galileo, were as zealously persecuted as the moral "errors" of the heretics. Why now is there a free field for "errors" of the first kind, while "errors" of the second kind are persecuted by public opinion at all events and to some extent also by public authority? It is evident that the difference in effects must be an indication of forces that are different also. Prominent among these forces must be counted social utilities. Experimental researches, even if imbibed or practised by the masses at large, have proved beneficial; whereas ethical researches have, under the same circumstances, proved harmful in that they are for ever shaking the foundations of the social order. And in that we have proof and counter-proof of the consequences that ensue when experimental truth and social utility coincide or diverge (§ 73).

2003. *Propagation of residues.* If certain residues are modified in certain members of a community, the modification may spread directly, by imitation. But that case is hard to distinguish from the case where the diffusion takes place indirectly by virtue of changes in certain circumstances, which modify residues in certain individuals and then gradually in others. All the same, it is easy to determine that the second case is much the more frequent of the two, for modifications in residues are seen to go hand in hand with modifications in economic, political, and other circumstances.

2004. *Propagation of derivations.* Here too there are analogous situations. Since residues are among the chief circumstances determining derivations, the three following cases may arise: 1. There may be propagation by imitation or in other direct ways. 2. There may be propagation through modifications in the residues corresponding to the derivations. 3. There may be propagation through other circumstances affecting the community at large.

It is important to remember that the same residue, A, may produce many derivations, $S, S', S'' \ldots$ (§ 2086), and that choice between these may be determined by a variety of causes, even by very slight ones—caprice, fashion, circumstances of insignificant importance. The same may be said of the various manifestations of certain residues, certain sentiments. Familiar the fact that every so often some form of suicide comes into vogue, so manifesting a sentiment of weariness with life.[1]

2004 [1] In the fifteenth, sixteenth, and seventeenth centuries the finger of Satan was seen in everything. If a hail-storm came, if some animal or a human being fell sick or, what is worse, died under circumstances at all strange, some sorcerer or sorceress had to have been at work. The man who was keeping a black cat or black dog in his house was harbouring the Devil; and if—Heaven forefend!—he also kept a toad, no reasonable doubt whatever was left that he was the sorcerer. After the Eulenburg case in Germany, any two men seen walking together in that country were suspected of degenerate relations. After the Paternò trial in Italy, any man seen frequently with a woman was suspected of living upon her shame. In 1913 an army officer was tried in Milan on an accusation brought by fellow-officers of his, who had become obsessed with just such suspicions, though the trial proved that they had no foundations whatever in fact. If those individuals had been living in the sixteenth century, they would have accused their colleague, with the same conviction and the same reasonableness, of being in the pay of Satan. A suicide that took place in August, 1913, gave a writer in the *Giornale d'Italia* (Aug. 27, 1913) occasion to make certain reflections that clearly show the fluctuating instability of public feeling. We quote the article here, suppressing names as usual, since we are interested in the facts strictly in the abstract: *"A suicide not for love . . .* What took place on the occasion of this suicide is something worthy of examination by experts in mob psychology. At first everybody was filled with a sense of profound pity for the woman who had so tragically cut short her days and for the man who was left to mourn her. A drama of the heart was suffused with a perfume of romance, and that excited the sensibilities of the public and stirred its emotions. Then the rumor spread that X [the suicide's last lover] was showing himself indifferent to the violent end of his mistress, and a veritable right-about occurred in public opinion. All the sympathy turned to the woman, all the suspicions upon the young man. People began to ask why Z [the suicide] had killed herself, and they laid the blame on X, who had driven her to that act by his cruel indifference—perhaps to be rid of her. From there they went on to insinuate, though in veiled ways, that he had been living on the poor woman's shame, and the wildest, most astonishing conjectures became current. The confusion was worse confounded by a statement made by Y [representative of Z's family]; and that gentleman for a day or two enjoyed

2005. From that it follows that imitation, conversely to what happens with residues, plays an important rôle in the propagation of the forms of derivations and of certain other manifestations of residues. All the individuals who speak a given language express almost identical sentiments in terms on the whole similar. In the same way all individuals who live in a given environment and are affected by its many influences are inclined to manifest almost identical sentiments in very similar forms. The similarity extends to the derivations, or manifestations, of different residues. Suppose the derivations $S, S', S'' \ldots$ correspond to the residue A; the derivations $T, T', T'' \ldots$ to the residue B, the derivations U, U', U'' to the residue C, and so on. Then, let us imagine that $S, T, U \ldots$ are somehow similar, are of the same general character, and that we can say the same for $S', T', U' \ldots$ then for $S'', T'', U'' \ldots$ and so on. Now if it happens, as a result of certain circumstances, even circumstances in themselves insignificant, that S is chosen to express the residue A, it will also be likely that T will be chosen to express B, U to express C, and so on—in other words, the terms will be chosen from the similar series, $S, T, U. \ldots$ In different circumstances, at some other time, the terms selected will be those of the similar series $S', T', U'. \ldots$ And the same will be the case for other series. That is what actually happens. We observe that during a certain period in history theological derivations, $S, T, U \ldots$, are in fashion and that at another period they give way to certain metaphysical derivations, $S', T', U'. \ldots$ Not so long ago, a series of "positivist" derivations was in vogue, and a series of Darwinian derivations, which were used to explain everything and

a real popularity and was the object of demonstrative expressions of sympathy which came altogether as a surprise to him. But the truth began to transpire. Letters of Z began coming to light. They showed clearly that the cause of the suicide had not been love. A few days before deciding to take the fatal step, the woman herself declared that she loved no one. Then public conjecture turned to the part money may have played in the affair; but positive information emanating from X's family and an agreement concluded with Y [the representative of Z's family] showed that those conjectures were altogether unfounded. What, then, was the kernel of the affair? The suicide was the whim of a hysterical woman hungry for pleasures, luxuries, and the excitements of a varied and adventurous life; and she had not had the stamina to endure a moment of unjustified discouragement. Investigations by the police authorities will lead to nothing. The only blame that can be attached to X is that he did not act with enough decision in keeping a revolver out of reach of a woman who had the soul and the brain of a child."

more besides. Concrete situations are complicated. Imitation plays a more or less important part in them, but many other circumstances also have their influence (§ 1766).

2006. Marxism gave rise to an infinitude of similar derivations, S'', T'', U'' . . . , designed to explain all social phenomenon by "capitalism" (§ 1890). In that instance imitation is evident enough. Such derivations express residues depending chiefly upon social and economic circumstances, but those same residues might just as well have been expressed in other derivations. It has been due chiefly to imitation that the derivations S'', T'', U'' . . . have been chosen.

2007. That must be kept in mind when we are trying to get at residues through derivations. Great social currents often produce general changes in derivations, leaving residues unaffected. Of that we have encountered many examples in the course of these volumes. One period in history may use the derivations S, T, U . . . and another the derivations S', T', U' . . . and, keeping to forms, we might conclude that a great change has taken place, that the two periods represent two quite different epochs in civilization; whereas, at bottom, it is a case of residues that are the same, or almost the same, expressing themselves in different forms at different times.

2008. The examples above would be particular cases of phenomena much more general that may be observed when religious, ethical, metaphysical, or mythical derivations are adapting themselves to the necessities of practical life. Theories cannot be entirely severed from the practical. There must be a certain adjustment between them, and that adjustment is effected by a series of actions and reactions. As we have seen in every page of these volumes—and contrarily to ordinary opinion, especially the opinion of moralists, men of letters, and pseudo-scientists—the influence of practice upon theory is, in social matters, much greater than the influence of theories upon practice. It is the theories that make the adjustment to practice, and not practice the adjustment to theories. But that does not mean—and that fact too we have repeatedly stressed—that theories have no influence on practice. All that it means is that ordinarily the influence of theories upon practice is much weaker than the influence of practice upon theories—a quite different matter. An examination of the latter influence, therefore, taken by itself, often gives a first approximation to concrete realities that could never be had from an exclusive consideration of the influence of theories upon practice.[1]

2009. *Interests.* Individuals and communities are spurred by instinct and reason to acquire possession of material goods that are useful—or merely pleasurable—for purposes of living, as well as to seek consideration and honours. Such impulses, which may be called "interests," play in the mass a very important part in determining the social equilibrium.

2010. *The economic sphere.* That mass of interests falls in very considerable part within the purview of the science of economics, on which we should enter at this point had that science not already produced a very important bibliography of its own to which we need merely refer. Here we shall confine ourselves to a few remarks on the relations of the economic element to the other branches of sociology.

2011. *Pure economics.* Just as a "pure jurisprudence" might deal with the inferences that are logically to be drawn from certain principles of law, so the function of "pure economics" is to find the inferences deducible from certain hypotheses (§ 825). Both of these two sciences are valid in the realm of concrete fact, inasmuch as the hypotheses or principles that they posit play a preponderant rôle in concrete phenomena. The historical evolution of human knowledge resolves itself into a movement outwards, which proceeds by analysis from the concrete to the abstract, followed by a movement backwards, which proceeds by synthesis from the abstract to the concrete. Starting with the practical necessities of measuring the surfaces of fields and other lands, people go on to abstract researches such as geometry, arithmetic, and algebra; and then they go back from those abstract researches to the arts of the surveyor and the cartographer. We have three treatises on "economics" in ancient Greek, two of them attributed to Aristotle (the *Oeconomica,* though one, at least, is not his), and the other to Xenophon (the *Oeconomicus*).

2008 [1] This single remark is enough to demonstrate the futility of many many books addressed to the study of political or social phenomena, not to mention works on economics. I took it into account in my *Manuale* by considering an objective and a subjective aspect in every phenomenon.

They consist of practical considerations on the art of domestic government for individuals and cities. From such considerations one goes on to the abstractions of pure economics. From "pure economics," now, the question is to get back again to the study of concrete situations. But knowledge of such realities will not be attained by trying to give the practical characteristics of ancient economics to the abstractions obtained by analysis; just as knowledge of geodesy and the art of surveying was not obtained by trying to give concreteness to Euclid's geometry. The course that has been followed in a great many such cases is altogether different; it lies, fundamentally, in a synthesis of a number of theories.

In every period of history there have been people to proclaim the uselessness of abstract researches. In a certain sense they have been right. Oftentimes, any one among such researches, taken by itself apart from the rest, has little or no bearing on practical needs. They acquire practical utility only when they are taken in the mass—and because of the habits of mind that they inculcate. From that standpoint, "pure economics," taken by itself, is of no more use than any number of theories in geometry, arithmetic, algebra, mechanics, thermodynamics, and so on, which are taught in all schools of engineering today. As regards direct utility, the study of exchange in pure economics is like the study that is made in every course in physics of a body falling in a vacuum—similar in its merits and in its defects, in its usefulness and its uselessness. A feather falling through the air does not follow the law of bodies falling in a vacuum, any more than this or that exchange in actual practice follows the uniformities discovered by pure economics. The case of the feather does not prove that the study of mechanics is useless, just as failure to meet the actual requirements of exchange does not prove the uselessness of pure economics (§ 87 [1]).

2012. Theory has usually appeared after the art; the disquisitions of the Roman jurists came after the judgments rendered by the Roman praetors. So the work of Adam Smith followed on numberless treatises on practical economic problems, and the works of Walras and Edgeworth in pure economics came after numberless treatises on theoretical and practical economics.

2013. Given certain creatures who have appetites or tastes and who encounter certain obstacles in their attempt to satisfy them, what is going to happen? The question is answered by pure economics, and it is a science of great scope, owing to the no scant variety in tastes and the enormously great variety in obstacles. The results that it achieves form an integral and not unimportant part of sociology, but only a part; and in certain situations it may even be a slight and negligible part, a part at any rate that must be taken in conjunction with other parts to yield the picture of what happens in reality.

2014. *Applied economics.* Just as one proceeds from rational mechanics to applied mechanics by supplementing the former with considerations on concrete problems, so one proceeds from pure economics to applied economics. Rational mechanics, for instance, yields a theory of leverage. Applied mechanics tells how to construct a lever that one can use. Pure economics determines the function of money in the economic sphere of life. Applied economics describes monetary systems now in existence, monetary systems of the past, their transformations, and so on. In that way we get closer to the concrete, but we do not reach it. Applied mechanics describes how the parts of a steam-engine function; but it is the part of thermodynamics to show how steam functions; and then we have to resort to many other considerations, the economic included, before we can make a wise choice of a power-plant. Applied economics supplies a bounteous store of information as to the nature and history of monetary systems; but to know how and why they arose, we have to appeal to other sources of knowledge. Ignoring geology and metallurgy, which we have to consult to find out how precious metals have been obtained, and confining ourselves to social forces only, we have still to learn how and why certain governments have falsified their currency, and others have not; how and why the gold monometallism of England exists side by side with the bandy-legged bimetallism of France, the silver monometallism of China, and the paper monetary system of Italy and other countries. Money is an instrument of exchange and as such is studied by economics. But it is also an instrument for levying taxes without suspicion on the part of the public at large that it is being taxed; and in that connexion the study of money belongs to the various branches of sociology. We have purposely chosen an instance in which the economic element is by far the preponderant one. In others the gap between theory and practice is more conspicuous. Pure economics shows that the *direct*—mark the restriction—the direct effect of protection by customs tariffs is a destruction of wealth. Applied economics confirms that inference. But neither pure nor applied economics can explain why English free trade prevails side by side with American, German, and other numerous protections, all differing in the degree to which protection is carried and in their methods of application. Worse still, nobody understands why English prosperity has increased under free trade, while German prosperity has increased under protection (§§ 2208 f.).

2015. Hearing, on the one hand, that according to economic theories the effect of protection was the destruction of wealth, and seeing, on the other, that protectionist countries nevertheless prospered, many people were at their wits' ends, and not knowing the real causes of the paradox, excogitated imaginary ones. Some branded as erroneous economic theories that they were not even able to understand. Others condemned any sort of social theory—except the one they happened to hold. Some turned disciples of Don Quixote (who knew how to make a balsam that was excellent for Don Quixotes, but deadly to Sancho Panzas), and came out with some "national economy" or other that would be profitable to themselves and their friends. Others, unable to find a reason for what was, went around dreaming as to what ought to be. Some deserted the treacherous ground of economics and took their stand in the swamps of ethics and metaphysics, and others and others and others went wandering in other directions, now this way, now that; but all the ways they went were equally far distant from the one way that could have led to the goal—the experimental study of those social forces which influence the economic factor in life and modify it.

2016. The science of the classical economists, to describe it briefly, applied itself, in part at least, to the examination not only of what was but also of what ought to be, so, to a greater or lesser extent, substituting sermonizing for the objective study of facts. Such a procedure is excusable in the first economists; and, in fact, at the time of Adam Smith and Jean Baptiste Say it would have been difficult to follow any other course. In those days all civilization seemed to be undergoing a new birth, materially and intellectually. Misery, ignorance, and prejudice belonged to the past. The future was for prosperity, knowledge, rational behaviour. A new religion was daz-zling the minds of men. "Science," Holy of Holies, was casting non-logical conduct into the outer darkness, leaving Logic and Reason, Holiest of Holies, as sole dwellers on Olympus. In addition to such general causes there were others of a particular character; for economic science had taken a gigantic step forward, something com-parable to the advance in physics and chemistry. It seemed natural, therefore, that the analogy should be carried farther, that only ignorance could defend the older economic, physical, and chemical fancies against the new theories, that the older economic doctrines should give way to the modern, much as the theory of the phlogiston had given way to the theory of equivalents. In those circumstances the chief function of the economist was to dissipate "ignorance" by teaching and preaching the "truth."

That conception of things seemed to find a decisive and brilliant experimental confirmation in the success of Cobden's League. There, people could say, you have predictions come true! The learned elo-quence of Cobden and his friends had dissipated the darkness of ignorance, defeated and abolished protection, and established free trade, whereat England had prospered incredibly. Everywhere leagues in imitation of Cobden's came into being; and it really seemed as though the whole economic structure of the world were to be made over in the directions indicated by the economists. But not one of the leagues in question achieved results even remotely comparable to Cobden's. For a short time it could be legitimately hoped that the failure was due to the difficulties that lay in the way of teaching the ignorant. But that excuse is no longer valid, and it is evident even to the blind that if the ignorant do not learn, it is because they will not. Blame for the failure was laid on the poli-ticians also, for leading the ignorant astray with their chicanery, and that, one must say, squares to a very considerable extent with the facts; but there is still the mystery as to how and why the politicians came to be able to wield the power they wielded—and in that we get one of those situations where the economic problem is evidently subordinate to the sociological problem.

2017. The classical economists envisaged what ought to be; de-termined on it by logic, starting with very very few principles; and —since the logic and the principles were valid for the whole terraqueous globe—found laws that were no less comprehensive in their validity. But then, when they found their conclusions at war with the facts, it became necessary to locate the error, and, as usual, they thought they could find it in the premises and in the theory. These, therefore, they declared false—they were only incomplete—and set out to reject them entirely, whereas they should have tried to fill them out.

2018. Suppose a geometrician discovers the theorem of the square of the hypotenuse. He rightly concludes that a right-angled triangle with sides three and four metres long respectively will have a hypotenuse five metres in length. He then decides to transfer the results of his theory into practice and says: "No matter how the three sides are assumed to be measured, the three numbers indicated will always result." An observer in Paris sets out to verify the statement. He takes a piece of string and without stretching it at all measures off two sides, one three metres, the other four metres, in length. Stretching the string as tight as he can, he finds his hypotenuse is 4.60 metres in length. In London another observer proceeds with a string the other way round, and for sides of three and four metres finds a hypotenuse of 5.40 metres. The results of the theory do not accord with the facts! To re-establish the accord it is necessary simply to *add* to the geometric theory specifications as to manners of measuring the sides, which specifications may in their turn give rise to various theories. The sum of such theories plus the geometric theory will enable one to explain and *foresee* facts such as the outcomes of the experiments in Paris and London.

2019. But instead of supplementing the theory in that way, certain persons come forward, who knows from where, and in order to re-establish the accord deny the existence of geometry outright, and reject the theorem of the square of the hypotenuse because it has been obtained by an "abuse" of the deductive method and fails to take due account of ethics, which is so very very important to humanity. Incidentally, even if there could be some theorem of the sort, they deny that it could be the same in both Paris and London. So they proclaim the substitution of "national" geometries, differing with each country, for "universal" geometry, and conclude that instead of worrying over geometric theories people ought simply to write the "history" of all the measurements of right-angled triangles ever made. And if somewhere, sometime, in measuring a right-angled triangle, a boy has blown his nose and failed to count his centimetres correctly, they write an inspiring dissertation on the "ethics" of blowing one's nose and describe the boy at length, noting whether his hair was red or black and other fascinating details of the kind. That, with but very little caricature, is a picture of many writings of the "historical school" of political economy (§§ 1790 f.).

2020. For some time that school enjoyed a thriving success through causes foreign to logico-experimental science. It was a reaction of nationalistic against cosmopolitan sentiments, and in general of the sentiments of group-persistence (Class II) against sentiments connected with the instinct of combinations (Class I). Its ethical element gave rise to academic Socialism, which satisfied the hankerings of certain middle-class rationalists who were unwilling to go as far as the cosmopolitan doctrines of Karl Marx. But it also had effects with a bearing on logico-experimental science, though remaining outside the experimental field. By setting up another error against the error of classical economics it called attention to both. Directly, in view of its ethical inclinations, it was less experimental than the classical school; but indirectly, through the stress it laid on history, it served to demolish an edifice that was in a fair way towards overreaching experience and soaring off into nebulous realms of metaphysics.

2021. Marx too thought he was getting closer to realities in rejecting the theory of value and replacing that very imperfect concept so widely current in his day with another, even more imperfect, which was, at bottom, a copy for the worse of Ricardo's. With his theory of "surplus value" he too introduced ethical considerations into places where they did not belong. His sociological work, on the other hand, is better, and by far. He too helped to tear down the ethico-humanitarian edifice of a classical economics based on middle-class interests; and his notion of the "class-struggle" emphasized the absolute necessity of adding new notions to the concepts of economics if one were to arrive at knowledge of concrete realities. As for Marx's ethics, it was no better than the *"bourgeois"* ethics, but it was different; and that was enough to open the way to a perception of the errors in both.

2022. Evident in many other ways, too numerous to mention here, became the need of adding new considerations to those used in certain economic theories if one were to get closer to concrete realities. To one such way we alluded above (§§ 38, 1592)—the effort to obtain such a supplement by taking advantage of the indefiniteness of the term "value." In that the error lies not so much in the end as in the means, a means so indirect and leading over a road so long, so tortuous, so broken by pitfalls, as never to get one to the desired destination. It would be something like setting out to learn all Latin grammar by studying the conjunction *et!* It is true enough that all roads lead to Rome; but that particular road was long indeed and hardly passable. A number of economists today are aware that the results of their science are more or less at variance with concrete fact, and are alive to the necessity of perfecting it. They go wrong, rather, in their choice of means to that end. They try obstinately to get from their science alone the materials they know are needed for a closer approximation to fact; whereas they should resort to other sciences and go into them thoroughly—not just incidentally—for their bearing on the given economic problem. The economists in question are bent on changing—sometimes on destroying—instead of supplementing. So they go round and round like squirrels in their cages, chattering forever about "value," "capital," "interest," and so on, repeating for the hundredth time things known to everybody, and looking for some new "principle" that will give a "better" economics—and for only a few of them, alas, does "better" mean in better accord with the facts; for the majority it means in better accord with certain sentiments they hold. Even with those few their effort, for the present at least, is doomed to disappointment. Until economic science is much farther advanced, "economic principles" are less important to the economists than the reciprocal bearings of the results of economics and the results of the other social sciences. Many economists are paying no attention to such interrelations, for mastery of them is a long and fatiguing task requiring an extensive knowledge of facts; whereas anyone with a little imagination, a pen, and a few reams of paper can relieve himself of a chat on "principles."

What was just said applies also to many other doctrines that purport to give theories of the phenomena of human society (§§ 2269, 2273). Any given social science, unless it is purely and exclusively descriptive, unless it confines itself to saying, "In such and such a case A was observed, and simultaneously B, C, D . . ." and refrains from drawing the slightest inference from that concurrence and from passing judgment on it in any way at all, necessarily rests on solutions of problems belonging to a category of which the general type would be: "In what mutual correlation do A, B, C stand to each other?" And that type differs only in form from the following, which envisages virtual movements (§ 136): "If A arises in a situation where it was not observable before, or observable as changed in its old situation, what other facts, B, C . . . , have arisen or changed with it? If B arises in a situation where it was never observable before, or arises in modified form in its old situation, what other facts, A, C . . . , have arisen or been modified with it?" And so on for C, D[1]. . . . To visualize the situation more readily, suppose we

2022 [1] Here we have one of the many cases in which mathematical language enables one to achieve an exactness and a rigour impossible in ordinary language. Let x, y, s, u, v . . . be indices of the magnitudes of $A, B, C.$ . . . The *relations* (as we call them in the text) between A, B, C . . . are then given by certain equations:

$$\text{System 1: } \phi_1 (x, y \ldots) = 0 \qquad \phi_2 (x, y \ldots) = 0. \ldots$$

All the quantities x, y . . . may be functions of the time t, which may, moreover, figure explicitly in the System (of equations) which we have numbered 1. This system, if we assume the time as variable, represents the relationships of A, B, C . . . and the evolution of those relationships in time. Only a knowledge, vague and imperfect as it may be, of System 1 enables us to have any knowledge at all of those relationships and their evolution in time. Most writers do not take account of that system, in fact are not even aware of its existence. But that does not prevent their taking it, unwittingly, as the premise of their thinking. If it is assumed that the number of equations in System 1 is equal to the number of unknowns, the unknowns are all determined. If it is assumed that the number of equations is smaller than the number of unknowns—which amounts to suppressing, hypothetically, some *condition* (§ 130) that really exists—s, u, v . . . may be taken as independent variables, equal in number to the number of equations suppressed, and x, y . . . may be assumed to be functions of those independent variables. If we differentiate equations 1 with reference to the independent variables, we get a second system:

$$\text{System 2: } \begin{cases} \dfrac{\delta \phi}{\delta x} dx + \dfrac{\delta \phi^1}{\delta y} dy + \ldots = 0 \\ i = 1, 2 \ldots \end{cases}$$

The total differentials dx, dy . . . represent virtual movements that arise when it is assumed that the independent variables, s, u, v . . . , are changed into $s + ds, u + du$. . . . These virtual movements are determined by the equations in System 2. In mathematics, the Systems 1 and 2, or the systems into which they may be assumed

reduce the general case of relationship to the particular case of a relationship of cause and effect between A and B, C. It is evident that any social science proposing to determine the effects of the interposition of the cause, A, has to be in a position to recognize the effects, B, C. . . . That problem differs only in form from the following: "If A is brought in or is modified, what effects, B, C . . . , will arise or be modified?" Solutions of these problems may be asked of the various branches of the social sciences and of their synthesis expressed in sociology. But many writers who deal with the social sciences, far from having an even vaguely approximative notion of the solutions, are incapable of understanding how problems should be stated and are not even aware that they exist. The purpose of their researches is, in general, to find arguments that will support doctrines which they get from the intellectual set to which they be-

as transformed, are equivalents. Transition from the first to the second is effected through differentiation, from the second to the first through integration. Very frequently the second system is much more easy to establish directly than the first. If nothing is known of those two systems, nothing is known either of the relations that may obtain between A, B, C. . . . If something is known about those relations, something by that very fact is known about the Systems 1 and 2. To establish the relations by considering not what is, but what "ought" to be, is to replace with products of the imagination the Systems 1 and 2 that are yielded by experience and to build on clouds. If there is only one independent variable, s, it is generally called the "cause" of the "effects" x, y . . . and its increase, ds, is called the "cause" of the virtual movements dx, dy. . . . When relations of cause and effect are alone considered, what takes place, from the mathematical standpoint, is a reduction of the Systems 1 and 2 to the following, or other equivalent systems:

System 3: $\phi_1 (x, s) = 0$ $\qquad$ $\phi_2 (y, s) = 0$ . . .

System 4: $\dfrac{\delta \phi_1}{\delta s} ds + \dfrac{\delta \phi_1}{\delta x} dx = 0$ $\qquad$ $\dfrac{\delta \phi_2}{\delta s} ds + \dfrac{\delta \phi_2}{\delta y} dy = 0$ . . .

These two systems are much easier to deal with than the systems 1 and 2, whether in ordinary or in mathematical language (§ 2092 [1]). It is advisable, therefore, to replace Systems 1 and 2 with them as often as possible. In some cases such substitution yields a solution at least approximate of the problem that is being dealt with. In other cases the substitution cannot be made, and then to replace the Systems 1 and 2 with the Systems 3 and 4 is impracticable because it would give results that have nothing in common with reality. From the mathematical standpoint the integration of System 2 does not, as we have seen, reproduce System 1 only, but yields more comprehensive solutions, one of which is the System 1. To determine System 1 exhaustively, therefore, other considerations have to be brought in. So the integration of System 4 not only reproduces System 3, but also introduces arbitrary constants that have to be determined by other considerations. That, after all, is very

long or with which they are currying favour; from governmental ministries that hire them or with which they would "stand well"; from the political or social parties with which they are affiliated; from theological, metaphysical, ethical, patriotic, or other beliefs that they happen to hold.[2] They are advocates, rather than impartial judges. If they like *A,* the only question is how to show that all its consequences are infallibly "advantageous"; if they dislike *A,* "dis-

generally the case in applications of mathematics to concrete facts. Even in the elementary problems of algebra, when a solution is given by an equation of the second degree, one often gets one root that is suitable to the problem and another that has to be rejected as unsuitable. I make this remark here because of the inept objection of a certain writer, who imagines that equations of type 2 cannot represent the solution of an economic problem, because they yield multiple solutions, whereas there can be but one actual solution. To obtain a clearer understanding of the general theory here set forth, one might study a particular case, such as the determination of the economic equilibrium, with a system of the type 2. That I do in the appendix to my *Manuale,* and in an article already mentioned (*"Economie mathématique"*) in the *Encyclopédie des sciences mathématiques.*

From the strictly mathematical point of view the independent variable in 3 and 4 may be changed, taking x instead of s, for instance. In such a case, in the terminology of ordinary language, s would correspond to the "effect" and x to the "cause." Such an interchange in terms is at times admissible, at other times not; for in ordinary language, "cause" is not just an independent variable; it has other characteristics besides—it has, for instance, to be anterior in time to its "effect." So selling-price may be considered as the "effect," and cost of production as the "cause"; or the relationship may be inverted, and cost of production may be considered as the "effect" and selling-price as the "cause"; for in that case there is a sequence of actions and reactions which enable one to assume at pleasure that supply precedes demand or that demand precedes supply (§ 2092[1]). In reality there is a mutual correlation between demand and supply, and that correlation may be stated theoretically by the equations of pure economics. However, as regards terminology it would not be possible to invert in that way such a correlation as the freezing of water in a pipe, called the "cause," and the bursting of the pipe called an "effect," and to say that the bursting of the pipe is the "cause" of the freezing. But if, terminology aside, we consider only the experimental relationship between the two facts, taken apart from all other facts, it is altogether possible to infer the bursting of the pipe from the freezing of water, and *vice versa.* In reality there is a mutual correlation between the temperature that turns water into a solid and the resistance of the container that holds the water. Resorting to mathematical language, the science of thermodynamics is able to state that interrelation in exact terms. Ordinary language, instead, states it roughly.

2022 [2] If many "economists" have repropounded and continue to repropound the theory of fiat money (Pareto, *Cours,* § 276), it is not so much from any ignorance on their part of economic science as from eagerness to please the ministries and political parties that use currency issues as a means of levying taxes surreptitiously.

advantageous"; never of course even defining such terms or stating just what utility (§§ 2111 f.) they have in mind.[3]

Sometimes the better of such writers barricade themselves in some one department of science and try to refrain from any venturing into departments in which they sense that a danger lurks. So classical economists stoutly maintained that they kept strictly aloof from questions of politics.[4] Others arrive at an identical point by adhering, whether through prejudice, ignorance, mental indolence, or some other brain condition, to ready-made solutions bearing on certain subjects.[5] So many economists accept the solutions of current morality without subjecting them to an even casual examination. In former days they accepted the sanctity of private property, and now that the wind is changing they fall under the spell of a more or less diluted Socialism. Many writers take for granted the absolute power of an entity that they call the "State," especially of a certain "ethical State"; study under the microscope the insignificant effects of the incidences of an income-tax and disregard the more important influences that permit a government to impose an income-tax or prevent it from doing so; lose their way in complicated calculations of compound interest—on the assumption that money-savers arrive at their decisions by a logic that they have never never used—and overlook the "effects" of the income-tax on class-circulation

2022 [3] Oftentimes they defend their views by resorting to the fallacy called *ignoratio elenchi*—evasion of an answer. If doubts are expressed as to the reality of the relationships that they pretend to establish between A and B, C . . . they reply that such doubts emanate from heretics of the predominant religion (in days gone by, Christianity and the monarchical faith; nowadays the religion of Progress and Democracy), or from bad citizens, poor patriots, or immoral, disreputable individuals. Now the question really is not who is voicing them, but whether the doubts are justified or dispelled by experience. There would be no fallacy if it were possible to establish an identity between experimental reality and the beliefs of the numerous religions, the no less numerous moralities, the various kinds of patriotism —beliefs frequently in contradiction one with another—and the various conceptions of honesty, and so on, that human beings hold. But not always is any such identity alleged, and when it is, no experimental proof is, or can be, given of it; whereas proofs to the contrary abound.

2022 [4] A scientist of great merit, G. de Molinari, editor of the *Journal des économistes,* never ceased repeating to his contributors: *"Surtout, pas de politique!"*

2022 [5] The author of these pages fell at one time into that error and must humbly plead *mea culpa.* However, he has done his best to mend his ways: *Errare humanum est, perserverare diabolicum!*

(§§ 2025 f.) and the "effects" of class-circulation on the income-tax. Not long ago it was an article of faith with such men that the income-tax "ought" to be proportional; nowadays with their successors, it is an article of faith that it "ought" to be progressive. Oftentimes, individuals who concern themselves with such matters do not know that such changes in doctrines take place in correlation with other social facts, or at least they err grotesquely as to the nature of that correlation. In such ways and others still are the interdependencies of social phenomena disregarded or misconstrued, and at the present time that is one of the most serious obstacles to progress in the social sciences.

2023. In solving problems such as the one stated in § 2013 we have to consider not just the economic phenomenon taken by itself, but also the whole social situation, of which the economic situation is only a phase. Evidently, the general state, X, of a country may be analyzed into two states; an economic state, A, and a non-economic state, B. Let us assume that the economic state, A, develops into A'. If we grant that knowledge of that development is sufficient to determine the general social state, X', which results from the change, we therewith admit that A and B are independent, that it is possible to cause variations in A without affecting B, and conversely. If we do not admit that, neither can we grant that knowledge of A' is enough to supply full knowledge of X'. Before we can have that, we must know what B has been doing, that is to say, we must know B'; and we cannot know B' unless we know the mutual relationship of A and B. A number of economists have reasoned, not analytically but on the gross concrete, as if A and B were independent, thinking that they could study A without reference to B. That cannot be laid up against the founders of the science, for problems have to be studied one at a time, and an investigation of the influence of the single element A is a necessary preparation for the investigation of the combined influence of A plus B. Champions of the economic interpretation of history had the great merit of perceiving the correlation of A and B, but fell into the error of interpreting it as a cause-and-effect relationship, where A was the "cause" of B. Nor can they, in turn, be blamed too severely for that; for before the real character of the correlation of A and B could be determined, it was necessary to know that the correlation was there. Now that progress in science has demonstrated the correlation, there is no excuse for economists to continue in ignorance of it, nor are they excusable in giving the correlation a form that it does not have in reality.[1]

2024. Much has been done for the investigation of the economic phase of society, and that much we shall utilize for a knowledge of that special element in social life as a whole, taken apart from other elements. In utilizing writings on economic science, we shall find it advisable to eliminate everything relating directly or indirectly to ethics, if for no other reason, for the reason that not being engaged in a special study of the ethical aspects of their subject, writers accept and use indefinite ethical terms that, as we have shown repeatedly and at length, will yield any meaning one chooses. We shall also eliminate everything that sounds like counsel, admonition, or preaching, or is designed to encourage this or that practical conduct. Matters of that kind are foreign to science and have to be kept out of scientific research, if one would avoid serious mistakes.

2025. *Heterogeneousness of society and circulation among its various elements.*[1] We have more than once found ourselves called upon to consider the heterogeneous character of society, and we shall have to consider it all the more closely now that we are coming to our investigation of the conditions that determine the social equilibrium. To have a clear road ahead of us, it would be wise to go into that matter somewhat thoroughly at this point.[2]

Whether certain theorists like it or not, the fact is that human society is not a homogeneous thing, that individuals are physically, morally, and intellectually different. Here we are interested in things as they actually are. Of that fact, therefore, we have to take account. And we must also take account of another fact: that the social classes are not entirely distinct, even in countries where a caste system prevails; and that in modern civilized countries circulation among the various classes is exceedingly rapid. To consider at all

2023 [1] In our chapter next following we are to examine society as a whole, taking the interdependence of *A* and *B* into account in its real form.

2025 [1] A first rough sketch of the theory I am about to set forth was published in my *Systèmes socialistes.*

2025 [2] The matter of social heterogeneousness and the question of circulation among its various elements might be examined separately and apart from each other; but since the phenomena corresponding to them appear in combination in the concrete, there will be advantages in considering them together, so avoiding repetitions.

exhaustively here this matter of the diversity of the vastly numerous social groups and the numberless ways in which they mix is out of the question.[3] As usual, therefore, since we cannot have the more, we must rest content with the less and try to make the problem easier in order to have it the more manageable. That is a first step along a path that others may go on following. We shall consider the prob-

2025 [3] Even if it could be done, it would be better, for the reasons stated in § 540, not to carry the investigation beyond certain limits. When a number of elements, $A, B, C \ldots P, Q, R, S \ldots$, are influencing a situation, it is important to have at the outset an idea, be it a very rough idea, of the quantitative total of such influences and then go on to consider just certain elements, $A, B \ldots P$, the influence of which is considerable, disregarding other elements, $Q, R. \ldots$ So we get a first approximation, which may be succeeded by other approximations, if there is anybody disposed, equipped, and at liberty to make them. Many people are not aware of that—an ignorance that has a number of causes, among which it may be worth while to note the following: 1. Habitual addiction to absolute, metaphysical considerations, and verbal derivations of the sort that have been dealt with throughout the course of these volumes ("natural law" or other such entities), considerations and derivations that are something altogether different from the quantitative notions of the experimental sciences. 2. An inclination to look, in history, primarily for the anecdote and the ethical judgment. An element, Q, which may be having a virtually zero effect upon the phenomenon in hand, may show a very considerable index from the standpoint of anecdote or ethics. Protestantism in its early phases has very fair indices of an anecdotal, moral, and theological character. Its effects upon the ruling class in France were practically nil, on the ruling classes in Prussia very considerable. Protestantism should therefore be disregarded in studying the French ruling classes, but taken into account in studying the ruling classes in Prussia. There are people who go even farther along that path of error and place a scandalous love-affair of Julius Caesar's on a par with his campaign in Gaul, or Napoleon's alleged licentiousness on a par with his genius as a strategist. Those are the people who for centuries have been pretending that the great and significant changes in human society have not seldom been due to the whim of a sovereign, the caprice of some female favourite, or other such spicy details of little or no moment. In the nineteenth century such people seemed to be losing prestige; but of late they have come into vogue again, curtaining the vacuum of their derivations with pompous verbal flourishes. 3. The presumption that to get the theory of a situation one must have "all the facts," down to the most insignificant. If that were true, it would not be necessary to draw any distinctions in the series $A, B \ldots P, Q \ldots$ and such elements would all have to be placed on a footing. Another consequence would be that not a single natural science could exist; for all the natural sciences are in a perpetual state of development and came into being at a time when any number of terms in the series $A, B \ldots P, Q \ldots$ were unknown. What is more, we do not know all such terms even now—and never shall. The pretension in question may be excusable in Hegelians, who withhold the name of science from Newton's astronomy; but it becomes somewhat ridiculous on the lips of people who admit that astronomy is a science and ought to know, or be silent until they learn, that Newton founded modern astron-

lem only in its bearing on the social equilibrium and try to reduce as far as possible the numbers of the groups and the modes of circulation, putting under one head phenomena that prove to be roughly and after a fashion similar.[4]

2026. *Social* élites *and their circulation.*[1] Suppose we begin by giv-

omy at a time when among the things that were then unknown and are now known is to be counted the existence of a major planet, no less—the planet Neptune—and many small planetoids. But such considerations can hardly be grasped by people who have not mastered the fundamentals of the experimental method— or at least forget them when they begin chattering on social science. As we declared very early in these volumes (§ 20), our purpose in them is to build up a sociology on the model of the experimental sciences and not on the model of the science of Hegel, Vera, or any other metaphysicist—in fact it is our firm intention to keep as far away as we possibly can from such "science." 4. And finally, intellectual laziness, which is ever inclining people to take the smoother and less fatiguing road. The effort required to bring important facts, $A, B \ldots P$, under a theory, or merely to determine their significance, is greater than the effort required to find one such fact, and greater, far far greater, than the effort required to find one of the less important facts, $Q, R \ldots$ Indeed, some of those facts are the more easily determined in proportion as their influence upon a given situation is slight. Infinitely less intellectual effort is required, and less genius, to add one more observation of fact to the facts that Kepler had before him in his study of Mars than is required to discover, as Kepler discovered, the approximate shape of the orbit of Mars. In Newton's time only a little patience was required to add a new observation to the many then available as to the celestial bodies; but it took the genius of a Newton to formulate a theory of universal gravitation. In the social sciences it takes little talent to find some detail of fact that a writer has overlooked. The plain man —and many persons who are scientists in one subject or another are plain men in sociology—has convenient encyclopaedias for such things, and a "library rat," a bookworm, can even go to the original sources. Hardly more effort is required to write a history according to an ethics dictated by a man's own sentiment, and to criticize everybody else who does not follow him in their beliefs. But it is a different matter to find an experimental theory that, as a first approximation, manages to correlate the more important facts, $A, B \ldots P$; and people who are not fitted to make that effort should turn their talents to more congenial pursuits.

2025 [4] A general theory, of which the one with which we are dealing is only a particular case, may be found stated in Sensini's *"Teoria dell' equilibrio di composizione delle classi sociali."*

2026 [1] Kolabinska, *La circulation des élites en France*, p. 5: "The outstanding idea in the term *'élite'* is 'superiority.' That is the only one I keep. I disregard secondary connotations of appreciation or as to the utility of such superiority. I am not interested here in what is desirable. I am making a simple study of what is. In a broad sense I mean by the *élite* in a society people who possess in marked degree qualities of intelligence, character, skill, capacity, of whatever kind. . . . On the other hand I entirely avoid any sort of judgment on the merits and utility of such classes." [The phrase "circulation of *élites*" is well established in Continental literature. Pareto himself renders it in Italian as "circulation of the élite (selected, chosen,

ing a theoretical definition of the thing we are dealing with, making it as exact as possible, and then go on to see what practical considerations we can replace it with to get a first approximation. Let us for the moment completely disregard considerations as to the good or bad, useful or harmful, praiseworthy or reprehensible character of the various traits in individuals, and confine ourselves to degrees —to whether, in other words, the trait in a given case be slight, average, intense, or more exactly, to the index that may be assigned to each individual with reference to the degree, or intensity, in him of the trait in question.

2027. Let us assume that in every branch of human activity each individual is given an index which stands as a sign of his capacity, very much the way grades are given in the various subjects in examinations in school. The highest type of lawyer, for instance, will be given 10. The man who does not get a client will be given 1 —reserving zero for the man who is an out-and-out idiot. To the man who has made his millions—honestly or dishonestly as the case may be—we will give 10. To the man who has earned his thousands we will give 6; to such as just manage to keep out of the poor-house, 1, keeping zero for those who get in. To the woman "in politics," such as the Aspasia of Pericles, the Maintenon of Louis XIV, the Pompadour of Louis XV, who has managed to infatuate a man of power and play a part in the man's career, we shall give some higher number, such as 8 or 9; to the strumpet who merely satisfies the senses of such a man and exerts no influence on public affairs, we shall give zero. To a clever rascal who knows how to fool people and still keep clear of the penitentiary, we shall give 8, 9, or 10, according to the number of geese he has plucked and the amount of money he has been able to get out of them. To the sneak-thief who snatches a piece of silver from a restaurant table and runs away into the arms of a policeman, we shall give 1. To a poet like Carducci we shall give 8 or 9 according to our tastes; to a scribbler who puts people to rout with his sonnets we shall give zero. For chess-players we can get very precise indices, noting what matches, and how

ruling, "better") classes." It is a cumbersome phrase and not very exact, and I see no reason for preferring it to the more natural and, in most connexions, the more exact, English phrase, class-circulation.—A. L.]

many, they have won. And so on for all the branches of human activity.

2028. We are speaking, remember, of an actual, not a potential, state. If at an English examination a pupil says: "I could know English very well if I chose to; I do not know any because I have never seen fit to learn," the examiner replies: "I am not interested in your alibi. The grade for what you know is zero." If, similarly, someone says: "So-and-so does not steal, not because he couldn't, but because he is a gentleman," we reply: "Very well, we admire him for his self-control, but his grade as a thief is zero."

2029. There are people who worship Napoleon Bonaparte as a god. There are people who hate him as the lowest of criminals. Which are right? We do not choose to solve that question in connexion with a quite different matter. Whether Napoleon was a good man or a bad man, he was certainly not an idiot, nor a man of little account, as millions of others are. He had exceptional qualities, and that is enough for us to give him a high ranking, though without prejudice of any sort to questions that might be raised as to the ethics of his qualities or their social utility.

2030. In short, we are here as usual resorting to scientific analysis, which distinguishes one problem from another and studies each one separately. As usual, again, we are replacing imperceptible variations in absolutely exact numbers with the sharp variations corresponding to groupings by class, just as in examinations those who are passed are sharply and arbitrarily distinguished from those who are "failed," and just as in the matter of physical age we distinguish children from young people, the young from the aged.

2031. So let us make a class of the people who have the highest indices in their branch of activity, and to that class give the name (§ 119) of *élite*.

2032. For the particular investigation with which we are engaged, a study of the social equilibrium, it will help if we further divide that class into two classes: a *governing élite,* comprising individuals who directly or indirectly play some considerable part in government, and a *non-governing élite,* comprising the rest.[1]

2032 [1] Kolabinska, *Op. cit.,* p. 6: "We have just enumerated different categories of individuals comprising the *élite.* They may also be classified in many other ways. For the purpose I have in view in this study it is better to divide the *élite* into two

2033. A chess champion is certainly a member of the *élite,* but it is no less certain that his merits as a chess-player do not open the doors to political influence for him; and hence unless he has other qualities to win him that distinction, he is not a member of the governing *élite.* Mistresses of absolute monarchs have oftentimes been members of the *élite,* either because of their beauty or because of their intellectual endowments; but only a few of them, who have had, in addition, the particular talents required by politics, have played any part in government.

2034. So we get two strata in a population: (1) A lower stratum, the *non-élite,* with whose possible influence on government we are not just here concerned; then (2) a higher stratum, *the élite,* which is divided into two: (*a*) a governing *élite;* (*b*) a non-governing *élite.*

2035. In the concrete, there are no examinations whereby each person is assigned to his proper place in these various classes. That deficiency is made up for by other means, by various sorts of labels that serve the purpose after a fashion. Such labels are the rule even where there are examinations. The label "lawyer" is affixed to a man who is supposed to know something about the law and often does, though sometimes again he is an ignoramus. So, the governing *élite* contains individuals who wear labels appropriate to political offices of a certain altitude—ministers, Senators, Deputies, chief justices, generals, colonels, and so on—making the apposite exceptions for those who have found their way into that exalted company without possessing qualities corresponding to the labels they wear.

2036. Such exceptions are much more numerous than the exceptions among lawyers, physicians, engineers, millionaires (who have made their own money), artists of distinction, and so on; for the reason, among others, that in these latter departments of human activity the labels are won directly by each individual, whereas in the *élite* some of the labels—the label of wealth, for instance—are hereditary. In former times there were hereditary labels in the

parts: one, which I will call *M,* will contain those individuals in the *élite* who share in the government of the state, who make up what may be more or less vaguely called 'the governing class.' The other part, *N,* will be made up of the remainder of the *élite* when the part *M* has been set off from it."

governing *élite* also—in our day hardly more than the label of king remains in that status; but if direct inheritance has disappeared, inheritance is still powerful indirectly; and an individual who has inherited a sizable patrimony can easily be named Senator in certain countries, or can get himself elected to the parliament by buying votes or, on occasion, by wheedling voters with assurances that he is a democrat of democrats, a Socialist, an Anarchist. Wealth, family, or social connexions also help in many other cases to win the label of the *élite* in general, or of the governing *élite* in particular, for persons who otherwise hold no claim upon it.

2037. In societies where the social unit is the family the label worn by the head of the family also benefits all other members. In Rome, the man who became Emperor generally raised his freedmen to the higher class, and oftentimes, in fact, to the governing *élite*. For that matter, now more, now fewer, of the freedmen taking part in the Roman government possessed qualities good or bad that justified their wearing the labels which they had won through imperial bounty. In our societies, the social unit is the individual; but the place that the individual occupies in society also benefits his wife, his children, his connexions, his friends.

2038. If all these deviations from type were of little importance, they might be disregarded, as they are virtually disregarded in cases where a diploma is required for the practice of a profession. Everyone knows that there are persons who do not deserve their diplomas, but experience shows that on the whole such exceptions may be overlooked.

2039. One might, further, from certain points of view at least, disregard deviations if they remained more or less constant quantitatively—if there were only a negligible variation in proportions between the total of a class and the people who wear its label without possessing the qualities corresponding.

2040. As a matter of fact, the real cases that we have to consider in our societies differ from those two. The deviations are not so few that they can be disregarded. Then again, their number is variable, and the variations give rise to situations having an important bearing on the social equilibrium. We are therefore required to make a special study of them.

2041. Furthermore, the manner in which the various groups in a population intermix has to be considered. In moving from one group to another an individual generally brings with him certain inclinations, sentiments, attitudes, that he has acquired in the group from which he comes, and that circumstance cannot be ignored.

2042. To this mixing, in the particular case in which only two groups, the *élite* and the non-*élite,* are envisaged, the term "circulation of élites" has been applied [1]—in French, *circulation des élites* [or in more general terms "class-circulation"].

2043. In conclusion we must pay special attention (1), in the case of one single group, to the proportions between the total of the group and the number of individuals who are nominally members of it but do not possess the qualities requisite for effective membership; and then (2), in the case of various groups, to the ways in which transitions from one group to the other occur, and to the intensity of that movement—that is to say, to the velocity of the circulation.

2044. Velocity in circulation has to be considered not only absolutely but also in relation to the supply of and the demand for certain social elements. A country that is always at peace does not require many soldiers in its governing class, and the production of generals may be overexuberant as compared with the demand. But when a country is in a state of continuous warfare many soldiers are necessary, and though production remains at the same level it may not meet the demand. That, we might note in passing, has been one of the causes for the collapse of many aristocracies.[1]

2045. Another example. In a country where there is little industry and little commerce, the supply of individuals possessing in high

2042 [1] [And most inappropriately, for, in this sense, the phrase never meant more than circulation within the *élite*. Furthermore, the *élite* is not the only class to be considered, and the principles that apply to circulation within the *élite* apply to circulation within such lower classes as one may choose for one purpose or another to consider.—A. L.]

2044 [1] Kolabinska, *Op. cit.,* p. 10: "Inadequate recruiting in the *élite* does not result from a mere numerical proportion between new members and old. Account has to be taken of the number of persons who possess the qualities required for membership in the governing *élite* but are refused admittance; or else, in an opposite direction, the number of new members the *élite* might require but does not get. In the first case, the production of persons possessing unusual qualities as regards education may far surpass the number of such persons that the *élite* can accommodate, and then we get what has been called an 'intellectual proletariat.'"

degree the qualities requisite for those types of activity exceeds the demand. Then industry and commerce develop and the supply, though remaining the same, no longer meets the demand.

2046. We must not confuse the state of law with the state of fact. The latter alone, or almost alone, has a bearing on the social equilibrium. There are many examples of castes that are legally closed, but into which, in point of fact, new-comers make their way, and often in large numbers. On the other hand, what difference does it make if a caste is legally open, but conditions *de facto* prevent new accessions to it? If a person who acquires wealth thereby becomes a member of the governing class, but no one gets rich, it is as if the class were closed; and if only a few get rich, it is as if the law erected serious barriers against access to the caste. Something of that sort was observable towards the end of the Roman Empire. People who acquired wealth entered the order of the curials. But only a few individuals made any money. Theoretically we might examine any number of groups. Practically we have to confine ourselves to the more important. We shall proceed by successive approximations, starting with the simple and going on to the complex.

2047. *Higher class and lower class in general.* The least we can do is to divide society into two strata: a higher stratum, which usually contains the rulers, and a lower stratum, which usually contains the ruled. That fact is so obvious that it has always forced itself even upon the most casual observation, and so for the circulation of individuals between the two strata. Even Plato had an inkling of class-circulation and tried to regulate it artificially (§ 278). The "new man," the upstart, the *parvenu,* has always been a subject of interest, and literature has analyzed him unendingly. Here, then, we are merely giving a more exact form to things that have long been perceived more or less vaguely. Above, in §§ 1723 f., we noted a varying distribution of residues in the various social groupings, and chiefly in the higher and the lower class. Such heterogeneousness is a fact perceived by the most superficial glance.

2048. Changes in Class I and Class II residues occurring within the two social strata have an important influence in determining the social equilibrium. They have been commonly observed by laymen under a special form, as changes in "religious" sentiments, so called, in the higher stratum of society. It has often been noted that there were times when religious sentiments seemed to lose ground, others when they seemed to gain in strength, and that such undulations corresponded to social movements of very considerable scope. The uniformity might be more exactly described by saying that in the higher stratum of society Class II residues gradually lose in strength, until now and again they are reinforced by tides upwelling from the lower stratum.[1]

2049. Religious sentiments were very feeble in the higher classes in Rome towards the end of the Republic; but they gained notably in strength thereafter, through the rise to the higher classes of men from the lower, of foreigners that is, freedmen, and others, whom the Roman Empire raised in station (§ 2549). They gained still further in intensity in the days of the decadent Roman Empire, when the government passed into the hands of a military plebs and a bureaucracy originating in the lower classes. That was a time when a predominance of Class II residues made itself manifest in a de-

---

2048 [1] Many writers who are not equipped with this general conception fall into contradictions. Sometimes the clarity of the facts forces itself upon them; then again preconceptions will blur their view of things. Taine is an example. In the *Ancien régime* he well notes (Chap. III) that the mind of the masses at large is steeped in prejudices (is, in our terms, under the sway of Class II residues). On that basis he should go on and conclude that the French Revolution was a particular case of the religious revolution, where popular faith overwhelms the scepticism of the higher classes. But, consciously or otherwise, he succumbs to the influence of the preconception that the higher classes are educators of the masses, and views unbelief and impiety in the nobility, the Third Estate, and the higher clergy as among the main causes of the Revolution. He notes the difference between France and England in that regard and seems on the verge of ascribing to that circumstance the fact that the revolution which occurred in France did not occur in England. Says he, Bk. IV, Chap. II, sec. 1 (Vol. II, p. 118): "In England [the higher class] speedily perceived the danger. Philosophy was precocious in England, native to England. That does not matter. It never got acclimated there. Montesquieu wrote in his travel note-book in 1729 (*Notes sur l'Angleterre*, p. 352): 'No religion in England. . . . If anyone brings up the subject of religion, he is laughed at.' Fifty years later the public mind has about-faced: 'all those who have a tight roof over their heads and a good coat on their backs' [The expression is Macaulay's.] have seen what these new doctrines mean. In any event they feel that speculations in the library must not become preachings on the streets. [They and Taine therefore believe in the efficacy of such preachings.] Impiety seems to them bad manners. They regard religion as the cement that holds public order together. That is because they are themselves public men, interested in doing things, participating in the government and well taught by daily personal experience. . . . [Yet a few lines before that Taine had refuted himself:] When you talk religion or politics with people, you find their minds almost always made up. Their preconceptions,

cadence in literature and in the arts and sciences, and in invasions by Oriental religions and especially Christianity.

2050. The Protestant Reformation in the sixteenth century, the Puritan Revolution in Cromwell's day in England, the French Revolution of 1789, are examples of great religious tides originating in the lower classes and rising to engulf the sceptical higher classes. An instance in our day would be the United States of America, where this upward thrust of members of lower classes strong in Class II residues is very intense; and in that country one witnesses the rise of no end of strange and wholly unscientific religions—such as Christian Science—that are utterly at war with any sort of scientific thinking, and a mass of hypocritical laws for the enforcement of morality that are replicas of laws of the European Middle Ages.

2051. The upper stratum of society, the *élite*, nominally contains certain groups of people, not always very sharply defined, that are called aristocracies. There are cases in which the majority of indi-

their interests, their situation in life, have convinced them already, and they will listen to you only if you tell them aloud things they have been thinking in silence." If that is so, the "preachings in the street" to which Taine alludes ought not to be very effective, and if they are, it cannot be that people "will listen to you only if you tell them aloud things they have been thinking in silence." As a matter of fact, it is these latter hypotheses that the more closely approximate experience. The mental state of the French people towards the end of the eighteenth century had been but little affected by the impiety of the higher classes, any more than the mental state of the Romans had been affected by the impiety of the contemporaries of Lucretius, Cicero, and Caesar, or the mental state of the European masses by the impiety of the nobility and higher clergy at the time of the Reformation. Belin, *Le commerce des livres prohibés à Paris de 1750 à 1789,* pp. 104-05: "One may assert that the works of the philosophers did not directly reach the masses or the lower *bourgeoisie.* The working-men, the tradesmen, did not know Voltaire and Rousseau until the time of the Revolution, when their tribunes began to gloss them in inflammatory harangues or to translate their maxims into legislation. When they stepped into the limelight they had certainly not read the great books of the century, though they could not have missed entirely the more celebrated of the literary quarrels. The true disciples of the *philosophes,* the faithful patrons of the pedlars of forbidden literature, were the nobles, the abbés, the members of the privileged classes, idlers about the parlours of society who were on the look-out for some distraction from their relentless tedium and threw themselves headlong into philosophical discussions and soon let themselves be vanquished by the new spirit [That is all borne out by experience; the following less so.], without foreseeing the remoter consequences of the premises that they were adopting so gaily. . . . [Belin makes a further point:] The privileged for that matter were the only ones who could afford the exorbitant prices that any lover of forbidden books had to pay."

viduals belonging to such aristocracies actually possess the qualities requisite for remaining there; and then again there are cases where considerable numbers of the individuals making up the class do not possess those requisites. Such people may occupy more or less important places in the governing *élite* or they may be barred from it.

2052. In the beginning, military, religious, and commercial aristocraries and plutocracies—with a few exceptions not worth considering—must have constituted parts of the governing *élite* and sometimes have made up the whole of it. The victorious warrior, the prosperous merchant, the opulent plutocrat, were men of such parts, each in his own field, as to be superior to the average individual. Under those circumstances the label corresponded to an actual capacity. But as time goes by, considerable, sometimes very considerable, differences arise between the capacity and the label; while on the other hand, certain aristocracies originally figuring prominently in the rising *élite* end by constituting an insignificant element in it. That has happened especially to military aristocracies.

2053. Aristocracies do not last. Whatever the causes, it is an incontestable fact that after a certain length of time they pass away. History is a graveyard of aristocracies. The Athenian "People" was an aristocracy as compared with the remainder of a population of resident aliens and slaves. It vanished without leaving any descent. The various aristocracies of Rome vanished in their time. So did the aristocracies of the Barbarians. Where, in France, are the descendants of the Frankish conquerors? The genealogies of the English nobility have been very exactly kept; and they show that very few families still remain to claim descent from the comrades of William the Conqueror. The rest have vanished. In Germany the aristocracy of the present day is very largely made up of descendants of vassals of the lords of old. The populations of European countries have increased enormously during the past few centuries. It is as certain as certain can be that the aristocracies have not increased in proportion.

2054. They decay not in numbers only. They decay also in quality, in the sense that they lose their vigour, that there is a decline in the proportions of the residues which enabled them to win their power and hold it.[1] The governing class is restored not only in num-

---

2054 [1] To that point we shall return presently (§§ 2190 f.).

bers, but—and that is the more important thing—in quality, by families rising from the lower classes and bringing with them the vigour and the proportions of residues necessary for keeping themselves in power. It is also restored by the loss of its more degenerate members.

2055. If one of those movements comes to an end, or worse still, if they both come to an end, the governing class crashes to ruin and often sweeps the whole of a nation along with it. Potent cause of disturbance in the equilibrium is the accumulation of superior elements in the lower classes and, conversely, of inferior elements in the higher classes. If human aristocracies were like thorough-breds among animals, which reproduce themselves over long periods of time with approximately the same traits, the history of the human race would be something altogether different from the history we know.

2056. In virtue of class-circulation, the governing *élite* is always in a state of slow and continuous transformation. It flows on like a river, never being today what it was yesterday. From time to time sudden and violent disturbances occur. There is a flood—the river overflows its banks. Afterwards, the new governing *élite* again resumes its slow transformation. The flood has subsided, the river is again flowing normally in its wonted bed.

2057. Revolutions come about through accumulations in the higher strata of society—either because of a slowing-down in class-circulation, or from other causes—of decadent elements no longer possessing the residues suitable for keeping them in power, and shrinking from the use of force; while meantime in the lower strata of society elements of superior quality are coming to the fore, possessing residues suitable for exercising the functions of government and willing enough to use force.

2058. In general, in revolutions the members of the lower strata are captained by leaders from the higher strata, because the latter possess the intellectual qualities required for outlining a tactic, while lacking the combative residues supplied by the individuals from the lower strata.

2059. Violent movements take place by fits and starts, and effects therefore do not follow immediately on their causes. After a governing class, or a nation, has maintained itself for long periods of time on force and acquired great wealth, it may subsist for some time still without using force, buying off its adversaries and paying not only in gold, but also in terms of the dignity and respect that it had formerly enjoyed and which constitute, as it were, a capital. In the first stages of decline, power is maintained by bargainings and concessions, and people are so deceived into thinking that that policy can be carried on indefinitely. So the decadent Roman Empire bought peace of the Barbarians with money and honours. So Louis XVI, in France, squandering in a very short time an ancestral inheritance of love, respect, and almost religious reverence for the monarchy, managed, by making repeated concessions, to be the King of the Revolution. So the English aristocracy managed to prolong its term of power in the second half of the nineteenth century down to the dawn of its decadence, which was heralded by the "Parliament Bill" in the first years of the twentieth.

The Mind and Society

A TREATISE
ON GENERAL SOCIOLOGY

by Vilfredo Pareto

Volume Four: The General Form of Society

CONTENTS

VOLUME IV

amples. Equilibrium in the various social strata. Effects that the
means used for maintaining that equilibrium have upon Class I
and Class II residues and consequently upon the social equilibrium itself. Examples. Evolution of Roman society and analogies with similar developments in modern societies. The trends
toward crystallization and free initiative are mutually successive phenomena. That is just a particular case of the general
law that social movements progress in waves.

THE MIND AND SOCIETY

Volume IV: The General Form of Society

CHAPTER XII

The General Form of Society

2060. *The elements.* The form of a society is determined by all the elements acting upon it and it, in turn, reacts upon them. We may therefore say that a reciprocal determination arises. Among such elements the following groups may be distinguished: 1. soil, climate, flora, fauna, geological, mineralogical, and other like conditions; 2. elements external to a given society at a given time, such as the influences of other societies upon it—external, therefore, in space; and the effects of the previous situation within it—external, therefore, in time; then 3: internal elements, chief among which, race, residues (or better, the sentiments manifested by them), proclivities, interests, aptitudes for thought and observation, state of knowledge, and so on. Derivations also are to be counted among these latter.

2061. These elements are not independent: for the most part, they are interdependent. Among them, morever, are to be classed such forces as tend to prevent dissolution, ruin, in societies that endure. When, therefore, a society is organized under a certain form that is determined by the other elements, it acts in its turn upon them, and they, in that sense, are to be considered as in a state of interdependence with it. Something of the sort is observable in animal organisms. The form of the organs determines the kind of life the animal leads, but that manner of living in its turn has its influence upon the organs (§§ 2088 f.).

2062. In order thoroughly to grasp the form of a society in its every detail it would be necessary first to know what all the very numerous elements are, and then to know how they function— and that in quantitative terms. It would, that is, be necessary to assign indices to the various elements and their effects and to know just how they are correlated—to establish, in a word, all the conditions that determine the form of the society; and they, being quantitively considered, would be stated in the form of mathematical equations. The number of equations would have to be equal to the number of unknowns and would determine them exhaustively.[1]

2063. An exhaustive study of social forms would have to consider at least the chief elements that determine them, disregarding those elements only which seem to be of secondary or incidental influence. But such a study is not at present possible, any more than an exhaustive study of plant or animal forms is possible, and we are therefore obliged to confine ourselves to a study covering a part only of the subject. Fortunately for our project, not a few of the elements have an influence upon human proclivities and sentiments, so that by taking account of residues we indirectly take account of them as well.

2064. The influence of the first group of elements (soil, climate, and so on, § 2060) is undoubtedly very important. A comparison of the civilizations of peoples of the tropics and peoples of temperate zones would be enough to show that; and many books have been written on the subject, but so far with no great results. We shall make no direct examination of such influences here, but account for them indirectly by taking as data of fact the residues, proclivities, and interests of human beings who are subject to them.

2065. To go farther still in our avoidance of difficulties, we shall confine our investigations to the peoples of Europe and of the Asian and African sections of the Mediterranean basin. That will free us of the many serious—and unsolved—questions that are connected with race. We must necessarily take account of the influences upon

2062 [1] Still left would be the practical difficulty of solving the equations, a difficulty so great that it may well be called insuperable if one is to consider the social problem in all its ramifications. In my *Manuale,* Chap. III, §§ 217-18, I noted that fact as regards the economic system, which is only a small fraction of the social system as a whole. From the standpoint, therefore, of a complete general solution of a position of equilibrium, or some other such problem, knowledge of the equations would be of no help. But it would be of great help in solving particular problems, as has proved to be the case in pure economics. Even imperfect knowledge of the equations would give at least some hint as to solutions for the problems: (1) of determining certain properties of the social system (it has already enabled us to determine certain properties of the economic system); and (2) of determining the variations of certain elements in close proximity to a real point for which the equations are more or less approximately known. Those, at bottom, are the problems which we are setting out to solve in this chapter. Our lack of any exact knowledge of the equations we make up for by such knowledge as we can have of their nature and of the relationships that they establish among the various elements in the social system.

a given people of other peoples, for the various peoples of the regions indicated have at no time in history been entirely isolated. But military, political, intellectual, economic, and other kinds of power through which those influences have been exerted depend upon elements such as sentiments, state of knowledge, and interests; and the influences, therefore, may be inferred, in part at least, from those elements.

2066. But however many, however few, the elements that we choose to consider, we assume at any rate that they constitute a system, which we may call the "social system"; and the nature and properties of that system we propose to investigate. The system changes both in form and in character in course of time. When, therefore, we speak of "the social system" we mean that system taken both at a specified moment and in the successive transformations which it undergoes within a specified period of time. So when one speaks of the solar system, one means that system taken both at a specified moment and in the successive moments which go to make up a greater or lesser period of time.

2067. *The state of equilibrium.*[1] If we intend to reason at all strictly, our first obligation is to fix upon the state in which we are choosing to consider the social system, which is constantly changing in form. The real state, be it static or dynamic, of the system is determined by its conditions. Let us imagine that some modification in its form is induced artificially (virtual movements, § 130). At once a reaction will take place, tending to restore the changing form to its original state as modified by normal change. If that were not the case, the form, with its normal changes, would not be determined but would be a mere matter of chance.

2068. We can take advantage of that peculiarity in the social sys-

2067 [1] Since pure economics began considering a "state of equilibrium," many writers have talked of that state without having any precise notions as to what it is. Not accustomed to defining strictly the terms they use, they of course feel no particular need of a rigid definition when they come to this one. Even worse is the attitude of people who imagine that they can grasp the nature of the "equilibrium" in question sentimentally, so putting the word in that class of metaphysical terms where "the good," "the beautiful," "the true," and company stand in awful array. So the strangest conceptions are for ever coming forward, things bordering on the ridiculous. Needless to add, we are here using the word "equilibrium" as a mere label, convenient for indicating certain things that we shall in due course be careful to define exactly.

tem to define the state that we choose to consider and which for the moment we will indicate by the letter X. We can then say that the state X is such a state that if it is artificially subjected to some modification different from the modification it undergoes normally, a reaction at once takes place tending to restore it to its real, its normal, state. That gives us an exact definition of the state X.[1]

2069. The state X is ever in process of change, and we are not able, nor do we care, to consider it that way in all its minute detail. If we desire to figure on the fertility of a piece of land, we do not set out to watch how the grain grows in the sown field every minute, every hour, every day, or even every month. We take the annual crop and let it go at that. If we want to figure on the element of patriotism, we cannot follow each soldier in every move he makes from the day when he is called to arms to the day when he falls on a battle-field. For our purposes it is enough to note the gross fact that so many men have died for their country. Or again, the hand of a watch moves and stops, stops and moves, yet in measuring time we disregard that circumstance and figure as though the movement of the hand were continuous. Let us therefore consider successive states $X_1, X_2, X_3 \ldots$ reached at certain intervals of time that we fix on for the purpose of getting at the states which we choose to consider and which are such that each one of the elements that we elect to consider has completed its action. To see the situation more clearly, we might look at a few examples. Pure economics affords a

2068 [1] Somewhat similar to the artificial changes mentioned are those occasional changes which result from some element that suddenly appears, has its influence for a brief period upon a system, occasioning some slight disturbance in the state of equilibrium, and then passes away. Short wars waged by rich countries, epidemics, floods, earthquakes, and similar calamities would be examples. Statisticians long ago observed that such incidents interrupt the course of economic or social life but briefly; yet many scientists, who have worked without the concept of equilibrium, have kept meandering about in search of imaginary causes. Mill, for one, wondered why a country afflicted for a short time by the curse of war soon returned to its normal state; while other economists, such as Levasseur, came out with a mysterious "law of compensation" (see Pareto, *Manuale,* Chap. VII, § 79). The equilibrium of a social system is like the equilibrium of a living organism, and of the latter it was noticed in very early times that an equilibrium that has been accidentally and not seriously disturbed is soon restored. In those days the phenomenon was, as usual, given a metaphysical colouring by reference to a certain *vis medicatrix naturae.*

very simple one. Let us take a person who in a given unit of time—every day, we will say—barters bread for wine. He begins with no wine, and stops bartering when he has a certain quantity of wine.[1] In Figure 32, the axis of time is Ot, and ab, bc, cd, de . . . are spaces representing equal units of time. The axis of the quantities of wine is Oq. At the beginning of the first unit of time, the individual has no wine—his position is at a; at the end he has the quantity bX_1 of wine—his position is at X_1. Exactly the same transaction is repeated

every day, and at the end of every day, or of every unit of time, the individual's position is at X_1, X_2, X_3. . . . All those points fall within a line, MP, parallel to Ot, and the distance between the two lines is equal to the quantity of wine that the individual acquires through ex-

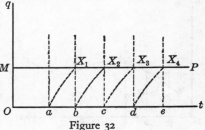

Figure 32

change each day. The line MP is called the line of equilibrium and, in general, is the line determined by the equations of pure economics.[2] It does not have to be a line parallel to the axis Ot, for there is no reason why exactly the same transaction should be repeated every day. It may, for example, be the line MP in Figure 33: ab, bc, cd . . . are still equal units of time, but at the beginnings of the various periods the individual's position is at a, s, r, d, u . . . and at the ends at X_1, X_2, X_3, X_4, X_5. . . . The line $M X_1, X_2, X_3, X_4, X_5$ . . . is still called the line of equilibrium. When it is said that pure economics gives the theory of the economic equilibrium, it means that pure economics shows how the final positions,

2069 [1] This is a case of exchange between two individuals, one of whom has no wine and a given quantity of bread, and the other no bread and a given quantity of wine. This elementary problem gave rise to the theories of pure economics. We consider it here merely for convenience of exposition; but what we say may easily be extended to the much more complex problems examined by pure economics.

2069 [2] A number of the economists who founded the science of pure economics thought of determining only the line aX_1, without even specifying that it was to be considered strictly within a unit of time. They cannot be censured for that. It is the general rule in the development of every science that pioneers consider the main elements in a phenomenon and leave it to their successors to complete their calculations and make them more exact.

X_1, X_2, X_3 . . . are reached from the points *a, s, r, d, u* . . . and nothing more.[3] Now let us consider the more general case. In Figure 33, *ab, bc, cd* . . . are no longer equal to one another, but represent different periods of time, which we choose in order to examine a phenomenon at the end of each of them, the length of the period being determined by the time required for an element to complete the particular action that we have chosen to consider. The points *a, s, r, d, u* . . . represent the state of the individual at the beginning of the action; X_1, X_2, X_3 . . . the state of the individual when it is completed. The line M X_1, X_2 . . . P is the line of the state X (§ 2076).

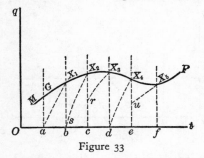

Figure 33

2070. That definition is identical, barring the mere difference in form, with the one given in § 2068. In fact, if we start in the first place with the definition just given of the state X_1, we see that the action of each element having been completed, society cannot of itself assume any form other than the form X_1, and that if it were made artificially to vary from that form, it should tend to resume it; for otherwise, its form would not be entirely determined, as was assumed, by the elements considered. In other words, if society has reached a point, X_1 (Figure 34), following such a path, aX_1, that at X_1 the action of the elements which we choose to consider is complete; and if society is artificially made to vary from X_1, the variation can be brought about only: (1) by forcing society to points such as *l, n* . . . which are located outside the line aX_1; or (2), by forcing it to a point *m* on the line aX_1. In the first case, society should tend to return to X_1; otherwise its state would not be completely determined, as was assumed, by the elements considered. In the second case, the hypothesis would be in

2069 [3] In the example chosen, the individual successively traverses the distances aX_1, bX_2 . . . , but there could be other examples in which he would traverse the distances GX_1, X_1X_2, X_2X_3 . . . on the line MP. In that case, MP would no longer be the line uniting the extreme points, X_1, X_2, X_3 . . . at which the individual arrives at the end of every unit of time, but the line actually traversed by the individual. However, in economic and social matters phenomena generally occur somewhat after the manner shown in the examples mentioned.

contradiction with our assumption that the action of the elements is complete; for it is complete only at X_1, and is incomplete at m; at the latter point the elements considered are still in action and they carry society from m to X_1.

Using the definition we gave in § 2068 as the point of departure, we see, conversely, that if after society has been artificially made to vary from the point X_1, it tends to return to X_1, the phenomenon indicates one of two things: either, as in the first case above, that society has been brought to the points l, n . . . which are different from the points determined by the elements considered, or that society has been brought to a point m, at which the action of the elements considered is incomplete. If instead of reaching the points X_1, X_2, X_3 . . . successively the system were to traverse the line X_1, X_2, X_3 in a continuous movement, there would be nothing to change in the definitions just given. One would need

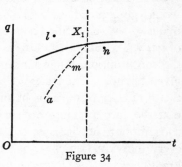

Figure 34

merely to say that if the system were made artificially to deviate from the line X_1, X_2 . . . it would tend at once to return to it; and that if the effect of the elements is to impel the system along that line, their action would not be complete unless the system were located on that line, and on no other.

2071. So we get the precise and rigorous definition that we said (§ 123) we were intending to give of the state we are about to consider. To become more familiar with it let us now look at some analogies, much as one looks at a sphere to get some conception of the shape of the Earth.

For a concrete example, the state X is analogous to the state of a river, and the states X_1, and X_2 . . . to the states of the same river taken day by day. The river is not motionless; it is flowing, and the slightest modification we try to effect in its form and in the manner of its flow is the cause of a reaction that tends to reproduce the original state.

2072. For an abstract case, to which we alluded in § 121, the state X that we are considering is analogous to the state of dynamic equilibrium in a physical system, the states X_1, X_2 . . . to successive positions of equilibrium in that system.[1] The state X, one might also add, is analogous to the state of equilibrium in a living organism.[2]

2073. We might look for analogies in a field closer to our own. The states X_1, X_2, X_3 . . . are like the states that pure economics considers in an economic system; and the analogy is so close that the states of the economic system may be regarded as particular cases of the general states of the sociological system.[1]

2074. There is another analogy that we cannot disregard if we would go somewhat deeply into this matter. The state X is analogous to the state called a *statistic* equilibrium in the kinetic theory of gases. To make that clearer, suppose we consider a particular case, the consumption, for instance, of cigars of a given quality within a given territory. The states X_1, X_2, X_3 . . . represent, hypothetically, the annual consumptions of such cigars. Let us begin by assuming that they are all more or less equal. Then we would say that the consumption of cigars is constant. By that we do not mean that every individual smokes the same number of cigars each year. We know very well that such numbers vary widely. But the variations more or less offset one another, so that the resultant is zero or, to

2072 [1] That fact was not noticed by a certain good soul, who for reasons best known to himself imagined that the economic equilibrium was a state of immobility and therefore to be condemned by every loyal worshipper of the god Progress. Many people talk just as wildly when they set themselves up as judges on the theories of pure economics without taking the trouble to study the subject, on which they are eager to talk, imagining that they can grasp it by a hasty and cursory reading of books that they understand upside down because their minds are packed with preconceptions, and because they are interested not in calm and thoughtful scientific research, but in rendering a service to their particular social faith. In that way they miss many golden opportunities to be silent. Quite a number of the books, pamphlets, prefaces, and articles on pure economics that have been published in a recent past are not even worth reading.

2072 [2] Such an equilibrium is evidently a dynamic one. If biology were as backward as the social sciences, some very knowing individual might write a treatise on *positive* biology and evince surprise and pain that anybody could think of life as in a state of equilibrium, in other words of immobility, since life is movement!

2073 [1] This matter is not easy to grasp. A reader desirous of gaining a clear conception of the sociological states, X_1, X_2 . . . , and of the possible ways of determining them, should first study the similar situations that are considered in the theories of pure economics. It is better always to proceed from the easier to the more difficult, from the better known to the less well known.

be more exact, approximately zero. To be sure, it may happen that so many of these variations will be in the same direction that the resultant will no longer be approximately zero, but such a probability is so slight that we need not consider it; and that is what we mean when we say that the consumption is constant. If, instead, the probability is not so slight, fluctuations around the constant total of consumption will be observable, such fluctuations following the law of probabilities. But suppose X_1, X_2, X_3 . . . represent increasing consumptions. We can then repeat, with the proper modifications, everything we have just said. We are in no sense assuming that the individual consumptions are on the increase. We know they are extremely variable. We are speaking of a *statistic* equilibrium, where variations offset one another in such a way that the resultant is an increasing total consumption. And such increasing total consumption may have a probability so great as to eliminate fluctuations depending on probabilities; or a probability not so great, and then fluctuations will occur. So, in preparing ourselves by studying particular cases of that sort we find it easy to grasp the general significance of X_1, X_2, X_3 . . . for consumptions varying in any manner whatsoever.

2075. Extend to an entire social system what we have seen to hold for a system of consumers of one brand of cigars, and the result will be a clear conception of the analogy we have in view for the states X_1, X_2, X_3. . . .

2076. We could continue to designate the social states that we elect to consider (§ 119) with the letters X, and X_1, X_2 . . . , but that manner of designating things soon begins to weary and one would prefer to have them given names. We could choose a name at random, but it is perhaps better to borrow it from something more or less like the thing we intend to designate by it. So, stopping at the mechanical analogy, we will call the states X and X_1, X_2 . . . *states of equilibrium*. But the meaning of the term as we use it has to be sought strictly within the definitions that we gave in §§ 2068-69, due attention being paid to the argument in § 2074.

2077. We have now simplified our problem by deciding to consider certain successive states instead of the numberless imperceptible mutations that lead up to them. We now have to go on along that path and try to reduce the problem of mutual correlations and the number of elements that we are to consider to greater simplicity.

2078. In our study we stop at certain elements, just as the chemist stops at chemical elements; but that in no sense means that the elements at which we stop are not reducible to a smaller number, or even, at a hazard, to one; just as the chemist does not claim that the number of chemical elements is not still further reducible or indeed that some day they may not be recognized as different manifestations of one single element.[1]

2079. *Organization of the social system.* The economic system is made up of certain molecules set in motion by tastes and subject to ties (checks) in the form of obstacles to the acquisition of economic values. The social system is much more complicated, and even if we try to simplify it as far as we possibly can without falling into serious errors, we at least have to think of it as made up of certain molecules harbouring residues, derivations, interests, and proclivities, and which perform, subject to numerous ties, logical and non-logical actions. In the economic system the non-logical element is relegated entirely to tastes and disregarded, since tastes are taken as data of fact. One might wonder whether the same thing might not be done for the social system, whether we might not relegate the non-logical element to the residues, then take the residues as data of fact and proceed to examine the logical conduct that originates in the resi-

2078 [1] There are those who regard economics as a branch of psychology, and again those who would bar "individual" psychology from economics, deeming it a sort of metaphysics, and confine attention strictly to the "collective" facts of production and exchange. Such a question is generally more of words than of facts. All human conduct is psychological and, from that standpoint, not only the study of economics but the study of every other branch of human activity is a psychological study and the facts of all such branches are psychological facts. The distinction that some would like to draw in economic exchange between the "individual" and the "collective" fact is childish. Every human being consumes bread on his own account, and it is ridiculous to imagine that a hundred human beings eat bread "collectively" and are fed, while no one of them eats bread "individually" and is fed. On the other hand all studies of human activity, whether labelled psychological or otherwise, are studies of facts, since facts are the only thing known to us; and the psychology of a human being remains an unknown so long as it is not made manifest in facts. The principles of an economic psychology or of any other psychology can be *deduced* only from facts, as are the principles of physics and chemistry, the principles of gravitation, and so on. Once the principles are obtained in that fashion, or even merely by way of hypothesis, their consequences are drawn, and if such consequences are verified by the facts the principles are established (§§ 2397 f.). A very general view of common well-known facts gave English

dues. That, indeed, would yield a science similar to pure, or even to applied, economics. But unfortunately the similarity ceases when we come to the question of correspondences with reality. The hypothesis that in satisfying their tastes human beings perform economic actions which may on the whole be considered logical is not too far removed from realities, and the inferences from those hypotheses yield a general form of the economic phenomenon in which divergences from reality are few and not very great, save in certain cases (most important among them the matter of savings). Far removed from realities, instead, is the hypothesis that human beings draw logical inferences from residues and then proceed to act accordingly. In activity based on residues human beings use derivations more frequently than strictly logical reasonings, and therefore to try to predict their conduct by considering their manners of reasoning would be to lose all contacts with the real. Residues are not, like tastes, merely sources of conduct; they function throughout the whole course of the conduct developing from the source, a fact that becomes apparent in the substitution of derivations for logical reasonings. A science, therefore, based on the hypothesis that logical inferences are drawn from certain given residues would yield a general form of the social phenomenon having little or no contact with reality—it would be a sociology more or less like a non-Euclidean

writers the concept of a "final degree of utility," and Walras the concept of "rarity" [*Éléments d'économie politique pure*, pp. 21, 22, 466]. The inferences drawn from those principles were found to accord approximately with the facts, and the principles were therefore considered acceptable within certain experimental limits. From the concept of a final degree of utility Edgeworth derived his lines of indifference to picture simple economic facts. I inverted the problem, and from lines of indifference derived the concepts that correspond to the final degree of utility, or "rarity," or "ophelimity"; nor did I fail to remark that instead of lines of indifference I might just as well have considered other economic factors, such as the laws of supply and demand, and derived from them the concept of ophelimity, of which for that matter they may just as well be taken as consequences. But in all this inferring back and forth, a great many precautions have to be taken that I have explained, and which seem to be entirely unknown to many writers treating on such matters with a very scant acquaintance with them. The residues and derivations that we have just been considering in sociology ought, in part at least, to be considered as concepts analogous to the concept of "ophelimity" in economics. From an examination of the facts we were led, by induction, to formulate those notions; then, following an opposite course, we drew inferences from them, and because the inferences were found to be in approximate accord with the facts, the concepts from which they had been drawn were held to be established.

geometry or the geometry of a four-dimensional space. If we would keep within realities, we have to ask experience to acquaint us not only with certain fundamental residues, but with the various ways in which they function in determining the conduct of human beings.[1]

2080. Let us consider the molecules of the social system, in other words, individuals, who are possessed of certain sentiments manifested by residues—which, for the sake of brevity, we shall designate simply as residues. We may say that present in individuals are mixtures of groups of residues that are analogous to the mixtures of chemical compounds found in nature, the groups of residues themselves being analogous to the chemical compounds. We have just examined (Chapter XI) the character of such mixtures and groups, and we found that while some of them appear to be virtually independent, others also are correlated in such a manner that an accentuation in the one is offset by an attenuation in others, and *vice versa*.[1] Such mixtures and groups, whether dependent or independent, are now to be considered among the elements determining the social equilibrium.

2081. Residues manifest themselves through derivations. These are indications of the forces operating upon the social molecules. We have divided them into two categories (§ 1826): derivations proper and the manifestations in which they eventuate. Here, for the sake of a comprehensive view, we shall take them both together.

2082. Common opinion attaches great importance to derivations and among them to derivations proper,[1] to theories, as determining social forms. Contrarily to that view, we have seen as the result of long and far-reaching researches that their direct influence on such forms is slight—a fact that is not perceived because there is a tendency to ascribe to derivations effects which really are referable to

2079 [1] It was to show that very thing that we have had to make our long study of residues and derivations. Some of my readers may have judged it superfluous. And yet it was not, because the conclusion to which it led is an indispensable groundwork for the theory that we are about to set forth with regard to the general form of society. Furthermore, since our conclusions deviated in many respects from views that are generally held, it seemed better to buttress them with facts in very great abundance.

2080 [1] We shall be meeting other forms of dependence presently (§ 2088).

2082 [1] [So Pareto. Apparently a slip, for manifestation-derivations, *i.e.*, theories.— A. L.]

the residues that they manifest. Before derivations can acquire any considerable efficacy they have to be themselves transformed into sentiments (§ 1746), and that does not happen so readily.[2]

2083. In this matter of derivations, the capital fact is that they do not correspond exactly to the residues in which they originate (§§ 1767 f., 1780 f.). In that lie the chief obstacles to the constitution of a social science; for derivations only are known to us, and we are sometimes at a loss as to how to find our way back from the derivations to the residues that underlie them. That would not be the case if derivations were of the same nature as logico-experimental theories (§§ 1768, 2007). Derivations, furthermore, contain many principles that are not explicitly stated, which are taken for granted, and as a result they are gravely lacking in definiteness (§ 2002). The uncertainty is greater in the case of derivations proper than in the case of manifestations, but it is not wanting in the latter also. To remedy that difficulty, we have to collect large numbers of derivations associated with one same subject-matter, and then find in them a constant element that can be distinguished from variable elements.

2084. Even when there is some rough correspondence between derivation and residue, the derivation usually oversteps the terms of the residue and oversteps reality (§ 1772). It indicates an extreme limit of which the residue falls short, and very very often contains an imaginary element that states a goal far beyond the goal which would be set if it expressed the residue exactly (§ 1869). If, furthermore, the imaginary element expands and evolves, the results are myths, religions, ethical systems, theologies, systems of metaphysics, ideals. That happens more especially when the sentiments corresponding to derivations are intense, and the more readily, the greater the intensity.

2085. So, using the sign of the thing for the thing itself, one may say that human beings are spurred to a vigorous manner of action by derivations. But such a proposition, taken literally, would be far from the truth, and has to give way to the less foggy statement that human beings are spurred to a vigorous manner of action by the sentiments that find expression in derivations (§ 1869). In many

2082 [2] [Croce expresses this idea in the form: to be effective "thought has to be warmed by love." Two poles of the Italian temperament!—A. L.]

cases the use of either of the two forms of statement is a matter of indifference—the cases, chiefly, where there is a certain correspondence between derivations and conduct. A correspondence subsisting between the conduct and the sentiment betrayed by the derivation, there is also correspondence between the conduct and the derivation, and *vice versa*. But in other cases, to use the first proposition instead of the second is to go woefully astray, and those are cases, chiefly, where in their eagerness to influence conduct people imagine that they can attain that end by changing derivations. Modification of the sign does not in the least modify the thing to which the conduct corresponds, and therefore not the conduct either (§§ 1844 f.).

2086. In trying to get back from derivations to residues, it must not be overlooked that a given residue, *B,* may have any number of derivations, *T, T′, T″* . . . (§§ 2004 f.), that are readily interchangeable. So: 1. If *T* appears in one society and *T′* in another, one cannot conclude that the two societies have different corresponding residues: they may have the same residue, *B* (§§ 2004 f.). 2. To replace *T′* with *T* is of little or no avail as regards modifying social forms, since the substitution has no effect on the residue *B,* which plays a much more important part than the derivations in determining those forms (§§ 1844 f.). 3. But the fact that the subject of the conduct considers or does not consider the substitution a matter of indifference may have its effect, not through that opinion as such, but through the sentiments that it manifests (§ 1847). 4. The derivations *T, T′, T″* . . . may show reciprocal contradictions. If two logico-experimental propositions were contradictory they would destroy each other. Two contradictory derivations not only may subsist simultaneously but may even reinforce each other. Sometimes other derivations are brought in to eliminate the contradiction and establish harmony, but that is of quite secondary importance. People experience little difficulty in devising and accepting sophistical derivations of that type. They feel a certain need for logic, but readily satisfy it with pseudo-logical propositions. For that reason the intrinsic logico-experimental validity of derivations *T, T′, T″* . . . , usually has little to do with their influence on the social equilibrium.

2087. *Composition of residues and derivations.* We have so far been considering separate groups of residues. Now let us see how they work when they are taken together. The situation in one of its aspects bears some analogy to the compounding of chemical elements, and under another aspect, to the composition of forces in mechanics. Speaking in general terms, suppose a society is being influenced by certain sentiments corresponding to the residue groups A, B, C . . . manifested through the derivations $a, b, c.$ . . . Now let us give each of those groups of residues a quantitative index corresponding to the intensity of its action as a group. So we get the indices $\alpha, \beta, \gamma.$ . . . Let us further designate as S, T, U . . . the derivations, myths, theories, and so forth, that correspond to the residue groups, $A, B, C.$ . . . The social system will then be in equilibrium under the action of the forces α, β, γ . . . which are exerted approximately in the direction indicated by the derivations S, T, U . . . due account being taken of counter-forces. In that we are merely restating what we have just said in a new form.

2088. Keeping to this new form we get the following propositions: 1. One cannot, as is usually done, estimate the effects of each group of residues, or variations in the intensity of the group, taking the group all by itself. If the intensity varies in one group, variations, generally, must occur in other groups if the equilibrium is to be maintained. That is a different sort of dependence from the one mentioned in § 2080. Different things have to be designated by different names. Suppose, then, we use the term *dependence, first type* for the direct dependence between various groups of residues, and the term *dependence, second type* for the indirect dependence arising from the proviso that the equilibrium has to be maintained, or from some other requirement of the kind. 2. The real movement takes place according to the resultant of the forces α, β, γ . . . and in no way corresponds to the imaginary resultant—if there be such a thing—of the derivations $S, T, U.$ . . . 3. The derivations show only the direction in which certain movements are tending to evolve (§ 2087); but that direction is not, generally speaking, the direction that would be indicated by the derivation taken in its strict literalness, as would be the case with a logico-experimental proposition. We have frequently seen that two contradictory derivations can hold side by side, a thing that would be impossible in the case of two logical propositions. The two propositions $A = B$ and $B <> A$ are logically contradictory and so cannot both be true. But as derivations they can get along together perfectly well and mean one and the same thing, namely, that the *A*'s are trying to rule the *B*'s, using the first proposition to weaken the resistance of people who, though not partisans of the *B*'s, would not like to see them reduced to subjection; and using the second proposition to inspire those who are already partisans of the *A*'s to action. 4. Ordinarily, if the social system does not move in the direction indicated by the residues, *A*, to which the force α corresponds, the reason is not that there has been direct resistance to *A*, and much less that the derivation *S* corresponding to *A* has been refuted; but that the movement in accord with *A* has been deflected under the influence of the residues *B, C*. . . . It is important to distinguish, among these latter, the residues belonging to various classes (§ 2153-4 °); for owing to the tendency of the class as a whole to remain virtually constant, one should be on watch for the action rather of the various classes than of each single residue.[1]

2089. Better to picture the difference between interdependences of the first and the second types, one might consider a given society. Its existence is in itself a fact, and then we have the various facts that are taking place within it. If we look at the first fact and these latter facts simultaneously, we will say that they are all interdependent (§ 2204). If we separate them, we will say that the latter facts are all mutually dependent (dependence, first type) and are furthermore interdependent through the first fact (dependence, second type). We can also say that the fact of the existence of society results from the facts observable within it, that, in other words, these latter facts determine the social equilibrium; and, further again, that if the fact of the existence of a society is given, the facts arising within it are no longer altogether arbitrary but must satisfy a certain condition, namely, that the equilibrium being given, the facts which determine it cannot be altogether arbitrary.

Let us look at a few illustrations of the difference between interdependences of the first and second types. The inclination of the Romans towards formalism in practical life tended to produce, maintain, and intensify formalism in religion, law, and politics; and *vice versa*. That would be an interdependence of the first type. But we get an interdependence of the second type in the fact that the inclination of the Romans to independence managed to survive owing to the fact that political formalism averted the dangers of anarchy. That was what actually happened down to the last years of the Republic. The inclination of the Romans to political formalism weakening about that time (chiefly because the old Romans had given way to people of other stocks), their inclination to independence was also weakened, and they were obliged to accept imperial despotism as a lesser evil. Had it not given ground in that way, Roman society would have broken down either through internal revolutions or through foreign conquest, exactly as happened, and for identical reasons, with Poland. In this case there is no direct interdependence between Class II residues (inclination to formalism) and Class V residues (inclination to independence)—which would be a dependence of the first type. There is an indirect interdependence, arising from the fact that for the Roman community at that time and under those circumstances, the position in which the index of the inclination to independence (residues of personal integrity) remained constant while the index of political formalism (residues of group-persistence) fell off, was not a position of equilibrium (interdependence, second type).

2090. From the manner of operation of interdependences of the second type it is evident that their effects oftentimes become much less promptly manifest than the effects of interdependences of the first type—for a change in the equilibrium must first have occurred and then have had its repercussions on other residues. For the same reasons, interdependences of the second type will play a more important rôle than those of the first type in the rhythmical character of social movements (§ 1718).

2091. We have already discussed (§ 1732) various ways of taking account of interdependences. To follow the better, the $2b$ method, one would have to be able to assign an index to each of the interdependent elements correlated and then proceed by mathematical logic to determine the indices through a system of equations. That has been possible in pure economics, but, for the present at least, it cannot be done in sociology; and we are consequently thrown back on less perfect methods (§§ 2203 f.).

2092. Since we are here using ordinary instead of mathematical language, it will not perhaps come amiss to give a very simple example of the method $2a$ (consideration of cause-and-effect relations as modified by actions and reactions) that illustrates its relation to the method 2b (direct consideration of interdependences). Let x and y be two quantities in a state of interdependence. Using mathematical language, we would say, according to the method 2b, that there is an equation between the two variables x and y, and that would be the end of it. But using ordinary language we have to follow the method 2a, and say, therefore, that x is indeed *determined* by y, but that it also *reacts* upon y, so that y in its turn is dependent upon x. We could, notice, invert the terms and say that y is indeed determined by x, but then also *reacts* upon x, so that x is dependent upon y. When applied to equations, this method sometimes yields the same results as the method 2b, but sometimes it does not. It is better therefore, in general, to be very cautious in using the method 2a in place of the method 2b, and in any event carefully to scrutinize the consequences of substitutions.[1]

2092 [1] Let us assume that the selling-price, p, of a certain commodity, when the quantity sold is x, is given by the equation:

$$(1) \qquad p = 15 - 0.4x$$

and that the production-cost, q, of the same commodity, when produced in the quantity x, is given by the equation:

$$(2) \qquad q = 9 + 0.2x$$

The producer will stop at the point where selling-price is equal to production-cost, that is to say, at the point where we get the equation:

$$(3) \qquad p = q$$

The practical man acts in such a way as to solve these equations by trial and error—unwittingly, in other words, he uses a method equivalent to the method 2b of § 1732. In that way it will be found that for $x = 10$ one gets $p = 11$ and also $q = 11$—in other words, selling-price is equal to production-cost.

Suppose, now, that following the method 2a, we try to substitute a study of a sequence of actions and reactions for a direct solution of the equations 1, 2, and 3, for the method 2b, that is. In doing that, we may follow two courses:

I. We may begin with sales, considering the price as the *cause* of the sale of the quantity, and then consider that quantity as the *cause* of production cost. If the cost proves not to be equal to the assumed selling-price, we consider it as a new selling-price that will be the *cause* of the sale of a new quantity, which in its turn will be the *cause* of a new production-cost, and so on. Algebraically that is equivalent to taking the equations 1 and 2 in the following order and form:

$$(4) \qquad x_1 = 37.5 - 2.5p_1 \qquad q_1 = 9 + 0.2x_1$$

Taking $p_1 = 9$, we get $x_1 = 15$; then, from the second equation, we get $q_1 = 12$. Taking q_1 for p_1 in the first equation and giving the index 2 to x, we get $x_2 = 7.5$. Substituting that value in the second equation and giving the index 2 to q as well,

2093. Let us assume, by way of hypothesis, that it has been possible to assign certain indices, $x_1, x_2 \ldots$, to sentiments; certain others, $y_1, y_2 \ldots$, to economic conditions; certain others, $z_1, z_2 \ldots$, to customs, laws, religions; and still others, $u_1, u_2 \ldots$, to intellectual conditions, scientific knowledge, technical capacity, and so on. Using mathematical language we can say that the state X, defined in § 2068, is determined by a number of equations equal to the number of the unknowns, $x_1, x_2 \ldots, y_1, y_2 \ldots, z_1, z_2 \ldots, u_1, u_2 \ldots$, and so on. And we can say that the states $X_1, X_2, X_3 \ldots$ defined in § 2069 are determined in the same way.

2094. Moreover, considering the dynamics of the system, we can say that likewise determined is that movement which, *if there were no variation in the circumstances* indicated by the parameters of the equations, would carry the system successively to the positions $X_1, X_2, X_3. \ldots$ If such circumstances were to vary, the movement would change also, and the successive positions would be $X_1, X'_2, X'_3 \ldots$ as in Figure 35.

Figure 35

we get $q_2 = 10.5$. Putting that value for p_1 in the first equation, and giving the index 3 to x, we get $x_3 = 11.25$. This latter value substituted for x_1 in the second equation will yield $q_3 = 11.25$. We may go on in that way indefinitely and so get the following successive values for p and x:

| $p =$ 9 | 12 | 10.5 | 11.25 | 10.875 |
| $x =$ 15 | 7.5 | 11.25 | 9.375 | 10.3175 |

Those values will constantly approach the values obtained by solving the equations 1 and 2 directly—by the method 2*b*, that is. Those values were:

$$(5) \qquad p = 11 \qquad\qquad x = 10$$

II. Instead of beginning with sales, we may begin with production. The price, q, will be taken as the *cause* of the production, x; then, going over to sales, the quantity x is taken as the *cause* of the selling-price. That is equivalent to taking the equations 1 and 2 in the following order and form:

$$(6) \qquad x_1 = 5q_1 - 45 \qquad\qquad p_1 = 15 - 0.4x_1$$

Starting with one of the values we found above, with $x_1 = 7.5$, and making the calculation by the same method, we get the following successive values for p and x:

| $p =$ 12 | 9 | 15 | 3 |
| $x =$ 7.5 | 15 | 0 | 30 |

Instead of approaching the values (5) obtained from the solution of the equations 1 and 2, they get farther and farther away. It follows that in adopting that course the method 2*a* cannot be used instead of the method 2*b*.

Let no literary economist try to see the reason for that fact in the circumstance

2095. We may assume a certain number of unknowns as given, provided we suppress an equal number of equations. We might, for example, assume as given certain sentiments corresponding to the indices $X_1, X_2. \ldots$ Then the movement that leads to the positions $X_1, X_2, X_3 \ldots$ would be the movement that would take place if those sentiments remained constant; whereas the movement $X_1, X'_2, X'_3 \ldots$ would be the movement occurring if the sentiments varied.

that in procedure I the point of departure was sales, whereas in procedure II it was production; and then say that since production has to precede sales, it is no wonder that the first procedure leads towards the solution, the second away from it. The reason is quite different. Take, in general terms, two equations:

$$(7) \qquad x = f(y) \qquad\qquad y = \phi(x)$$

The two procedures have this in common, that an arbitrary value is given to one of the variables in one equation; the value of the other variable is derived in terms of it, and then substituted in the other equation, and so on. They differ according to the variable that one gets as the function of the other. From the equations (7) it is possible to derive:

$$(8) \qquad y = \bar{f}(x) \qquad\qquad x = \overline{\phi}(y)$$

Following procedure I, we will solve equations (7); and following II, equations (8). Take x_0, y_0, as the values that satisfy equations (7). Substituting for y in the first an arbitrary value $y_1 = y_0 + b_1$, we get for x a value $x_1 = x_0 + a_1$. If b_1 is sufficiently small, it will be possible to assume, approximately:

$$x_0 + a_1 = f(y_0) + b_1 f'(y_0)$$

Substituting in the second equation, we get the values:

$$y_2 = y_0 + b_2, \text{ and approximately:}$$
$$b_2 = b_1 f'(y_0) \phi'(x_0)$$

If the successive values of y, and therefore also of x, are to approach values that solve the equations (7), then in absolute value b_2 has to be less than b_1; that is to say, we have to have:

$$(9) \qquad |f'(y_0) \phi'(x_0)| < 1$$

Similarly, if one were to follow procedure II, indicated by equations (8), we should have to have:

$$(10) \qquad |\bar{f}'(x_0) \overline{\phi}'(y_0)| < 1$$

But it is known that:

$$\bar{f}'(x_0) = \frac{1}{f'(y_0)} \text{ and that } \phi'(y_0) = \frac{1}{\phi'(x_0)}$$

Hence the value of the first member of equation 10 is equal to unity over the value of the first member of 9. That is why, if this last is less than unity in absolute value, the second is greater; that is to say, if the first procedure approaches the values x_0, y_0, the second moves away from them, and *vice versa*. If $f(y_0)$ is virtually constant, it varies but slightly as y varies very considerably, in the first equation; and y varies

2096. If we suppress one or more equations of the system determining the equilibrium and the movement, an equal number of unknowns will remain indeterminate (§ 130), and we shall be in a position to consider virtual movements; in other words, we can produce variations in certain indices and determine the others. The interdependence of the elements will come out as that is done.[1]

but slightly as x varies very considerably in the second, while the relations in which the opposite takes place must be avoided. One may also hope to reach a solution of the problem by following the method 2a if one of the relations, for example the second equation in (7), is of very very slight importance as compared with the first, if, that is, $\phi'(x_0)$ is very small. We have simplified the problem as far as possible, but in general, among the interdependent quantities we get equations of the form:

$$f_1(x, y, z \ldots) = 0 \qquad f_2(x, y, z \ldots) = 0$$
$$f_3(x, y, z \ldots) = 0 \ldots$$

and it is much more difficult to know which procedure to follow in order to use the method 2a in place of the method 2b.

2096 [1] Every proposal to modify the existing social order in any way whatever is, at bottom, a proposal to modify this or that one of the conditions determining that order; and inquiries into the possibility of such modifications of the social order are inquiries into the possibility of modifying the conditions that determine it. People who preach aim at modifying residues, but they never, or almost never, attain that end. They do, however, and with no great difficulty, attain another, which is modification in the manifestations of existing residues. Take a community that is keenly dissatisfied with its government, the dissatisfaction being vague and general and venting itself in various ways that are frequently at loggerheads. A preacher arises and gives distinct and exact form to the residue, concentrating its manifestations upon one point. Ties and conditions are changed, and the social order adapts its form to the new ties and conditions. Those who pass laws and get them enforced sometimes aim at modifying residues, but they often find that they have worked to no purpose. If they have force at their disposal, they may modify certain ties and create others, but only within certain limits. Even the despot encounters such ties; he has to find ways to get approval of his policies from those who are upholding him by force: otherwise he is either not obeyed or else is overthrown. Then, too, a despotic government is no more able than a free government to enforce measures that are in too violent a conflict with the residues functioning in its subjects. It is not enough to proclaim a law—the law has to be enforced; and observation shows that many laws fail of enforcement because the people who are charged with their application are weak in resolve, while resistance on the part of those who are to obey is energetic. From that standpoint a despot often has far less power than a free government, since the measures dictated by the latter usually express the will of a party and consequently find many supporters to look after enforcement; whereas there may be few, very very few, supporters for the measures of a despot. He may enforce his will by energy and exertion in certain particular cases, but not in very many, for that would be a task far beyond the powers of a single individual. The people about him nod their heads but do not obey, and his prescriptions are left a dead letter. That is the case too, on a much smaller scale, in the relations between

2097. Using ordinary language, we may say that all the elements considered determine the state of equilibrium (§ 2070); that there are certain ties (§ 126); and that if, by way of hypothesis, some of the ties are suppressed, we will be in a position to consider hypothetical changes in society (virtual movements).[1] And the better to understand the interdependence that becomes apparent at once in mathematical language, we may add that sentiments *depend* on economic conditions, just as economic conditions *depend* on sentiments; and that there are similar correlations among the other elements.

2098. Examination of the facts allows us to go farther than these general considerations. Using mathematical language, we may say

a government minister and his subordinates. Here is an instance that may serve as a type. Persano, *Diario,* Pt. III, pp. 88-90. We are in October of the year 1860. Persano is received in audience by Cavour and the following dialogue ensues: "[Cavour] 'I wish you were to be in the Chamber today. There may be questions from the floor, and your presence there would be desirable. Unfortunately, on your promotion you ceased to be a member. That is a nuisance—it annoys me!' [Persano] 'Promotion, Excellency? What promotion?' 'Why, your promotion to vice-admiral.' 'I have never received notification of any such promotion.' 'Never?' 'Never, Excellency.' 'In point of fact, we have been at a loss to explain your silence on the matter, and your continuing to sign yourself "Rear-admiral." But what has been going on? We sent you a notification of your promotion while you were still at Naples!' 'Oh, Excellency, one of the usual intrigues of underlings.' [But Cavour instantly found a way to take advantage of the slight, as the alert and skilful statesman will always do.] [Cavour] 'I have written to Lanza [the president of the Chamber] not to announce your promotion, since you have not received it. So you will attend the session. There may be some explanations to make, and it would be a good idea if you were there.' " The man who had been disobeyed was no less than Cavour and at a time when the Kingdom of Italy was being founded through his efforts!

In place of all these ties, so numerous, so varying, so complicated, worshippers of the goddess Reason see only one, the state of knowledge and the logical consequences of knowledge, thence going on to imagine that the modes and forms of society are determined by reasoning. That notion is highly pleasing to "intellectuals," for they are manufacturers of reasonings, and every manufacturer sings the praises of his own wares. But in that they fall into a truly childish error. Never mind the fact that their "reasonings" are usually derivations, and that the slight efficacy they do have rests entirely on the residues which underlie them. Even if they were sound logico-experimental reasonings, in fact for the very reason that they were such, they could do little or nothing as regards modifying the forms of society that stand in correlation with quite different facts of far greater importance.

2097 [1] That is what reformers do, without saying so, in building their imaginary Utopias. The man who can do what he pleases with the sentiments of human beings can also, within certain limits determined by other conditions, give society any form he pleases.

that the variables do not figure in the same way in all the equations, or, to put the situation more exactly, may approximately be assumed as not figuring equally in them all.

2099. In the first place, groups differ in degree of variability. One group is so stable that it may, approximately and over a not very extensive period of time, be taken as constant (geographical conditions, climate, soil, and so on), and the quantities that figure in such a group may be counted, approximately, in the group of constants. Another group varies to some slight extent (classes of residues, for instance). It may be taken as constant over a short period of time, but without overlooking the fact that it does vary in course of time. Another is quite considerably variable (education level, for instance). Another shows a maximum variability (derivations).

2100. Approximately, again, the equations that determine the equilibrium can be divided into groups in such a way that interdependences with other groups can be disregarded. There are good examples of that situation in pure economics where there may be equations of only two variables. In that case one of them may be said to be determined by the other.

2101. Using ordinary language, we may say that in determining the equilibrium certain elements may be considered as constant over fairly long periods of time, others as constant over periods not so long, but still not short, others as variable, and so on. We can add that, roughly at least, as a first approximation, the interdependence may be considered within certain groups of elements only, the various groups being taken as independent. If one such group is reducible to two elements and one of the two elements may be called constant, or practically so, that element may be taken as the *cause*, the other as the *effect*.

2102. If, by way of hypothesis, the geographical situation of Athens and its commercial prosperity in the age of Pericles are taken apart from other elements, the geographical situation may be said to be the *cause*, the prosperity the *effect*. But that group has been arbitrarily constituted by ourselves. Had two elements been indissolubly united, there should never have been any change in the second, since there has been no change in the first. But since the second has undergone a change, it could not have depended exclusively on the first. It was not in other words, the *effect* of that *cause*.

2103. Another example—the case of ancient Rome. If we form a group made up of morals on the one hand, and political and economic prosperity on the other; and if we assume, by way of hypothesis, that morals were better at the time of the Punic Wars than they were at the end of the Republic; and if we assume, for still another hypothesis, that the morals are the constant element as compared with the element represented by the prosperity, we can say in company with many writers that good morals were the *cause* of Rome's prosperity. But along come those same writers, or others, and tell us that the prosperity of Rome was the *cause* of the corruption of morals. In the ordinary sense of the word "cause," this latter proposition contradicts the other. They can stand side by side if the relationship of cause and effect is dropped, and interdependence only is envisaged. In this form the relationship between the morals and the prosperity of a nation could be stated as follows: Good morals increase prosperity, prosperity *reacts* upon morals and corrupts them.[1]

2104. It is readily apparent that instead of considering a group of two elements, we may consider a group of a larger number of elements and then numbers of groups, each made up of a number of elements. That is a method—and it is at present the only one at our disposal—for obtaining approximate solutions that will be made more exact as the number of the elements and groups considered is expanded (§§ 2203 f.).

2105. *Properties of the social system.* A system of material atoms and molecules has certain thermic, electrical, and other properties. So a system made up of social molecules also has certain properties that it is important to consider. One among them has been perceived, be it in a rough and crude fashion, in every period of history—the one to which with little or no exactness the term "utility," or "prosperity," or some other such term, has been applied. We must now dig down into the facts to see whether something definite can be found underlying these vague expressions, and its character determined.[1]

2103 [1] Neither this latter proposition nor the two preceding square with the facts —but we do not care to go into that just here.

2105 [1] What we are about to do is something like what the physicists did when the ordinary vague notions of "heat" and "cold" were replaced by the exact concept of "temperature."

2106. Take the things called economic, moral, and intellectual prosperity, military and political power, and so on. If we would deal with them scientifically, we must be able to define them rigorously; and if we would introduce them into a determination of the social equilibrium, we must find some way, be it by mere indices, to make them correspond to quantities.

2107. That has been possible in pure economics and that is why that science has made such progress. But it cannot be done as readily for sociology. Again as usual, we must get around the difficulty by substituting rough approximations for the precise numerical data that we cannot have. So if a person had no table of vital statistics at his disposal he would have to rest content with the rough approximation of knowing that mortality is high in the years of infancy, then diminishes, and rises again in old age (§ 144). That is little, very little indeed, but it is better than nothing; and the way to increase the little is not to throw it away, but to keep it and make successive additions to it.

2108. If we ask, "Is Germany today, in the year 1913, more powerful in prestige and in a military sense than she was in 1860?", everyone will answer yes. But if we go on to ask just how much more powerful she is, no one will be able to answer. We can do the same with other questions of the kind; and it is taken for granted that the things called military power, political prestige, general intelligence, and so on are susceptible of increase or decrease without our being able to represent them in their various stages by exact figures.

2109. Even less definite are the entities called the prosperity and the power of a country, which are the sum of the various capacities just mentioned. Yet anybody can see that the prosperity and power of France are greater than the prosperity and power of Ethiopia, and that French prosperity and power are greater now, in the year 1913, than they were immediately after the war of 1870. Everyone understands, without any requirement of numerical definiteness, that there was a difference between the Athens of the age of Pericles and the Athens of the period following the battle of Chaeroneia, between the Rome of Augustus and the Rome of Augustulus. Even differences far less marked are perceptible and roughly evaluable; and for all of our lack of numerical precision, we still have an impression of the situation that does not go very far wide of the facts. Then we can go on into the details and consider the various elements in the complex.

2110. To get a more exact picture, one has to state just what norms—they have to be to some extent arbitrary—one intends to follow in determining the entities that one is trying to define. Pure economics has succeeded in doing that. It has taken a single norm, the individual's satisfaction, and it has further set down that of that satisfaction he is the only judge. So economic "utility" or "ophelimity" came to be defined. But if we set ourselves the problem, after all so simple, of ascertaining quite apart from the individual's judgment just what is most advantageous to him, it soon appears that we require a norm, and that it has to be arbitrary. Shall we say, for instance, that it will be to his advantage to suffer physically for the sake of a moral satisfaction, or shall we say the opposite? Shall we say that it is better for him to seek wealth exclusively, or to apply himself to something else? In pure economics we left the decision to him. If now we are going to deprive him of that function, we must find someone else to whom it can be assigned.[1]

2110 [1] In setting out on his inquiry into the nature of the "best republic," Aristotle clearly saw that such problems had to be solved. *Politica,* VII, 2, 1 (Rackham, p. 539): "It remains for us to see whether the same happiness should not be attributed to the individual as to a city. But that doubt is dispelled, for every man confesses that it is the same. For whosoever says that the individual is happy where he has wealth says also that that city is happy on Earth that has wealth. And whosoever praises the tyrannical life as blessed also holds that city most blessed which rules most peoples. And if there be he who says that the individual is happy if he has virtue, so he calls the city happy if it is virtuous."

Now we would stop at that point. That is to say, we have noted these and other similar opinions as to the state towards which the city should be guided, and we would then look for the characteristics common to all such states. Aristotle goes further than that. He determines what state one *ought* to prefer, VII, 1, 1 (Rackham, p. 533): "If one would soundly ascertain what the best state is he must first determine what the best life is." With that, we leave the field of the experimental relative to go wandering compassless in the field of the metaphysical absolute. In reality Aristotle does not determine his absolute—a thing that would be impossible. He merely finds the solution to the problem that best accords with his own sentiments and with the sentiments of people who agree with him, with the usual adjunct, more or less implicit, of the derivation that everyone agrees, or at least *ought* to agree, with him, and the tautology that every respectable man thinks as he thinks, since those who do not are not respectable. But in Aristotle, along with the metaphysicist, there was also the scientist with an eye to experience. So, in IV, 1, 2-4 (Rackham, pp. 277-81), he returns from the field of the absolute to the field of the

2111. *Utility*. Whoever the judge we choose, whatever the norms we decide to follow, the entities so determined have certain common properties, and we shall now look at them. Once we have fixed upon the norms we elect to follow in determining a certain state as the limit that an individual or a community is assumed to approach, and once we have given numerical indices to the different states that more or less approximate the limit state, so that the state closest to it has an index larger than the index of the state farthest removed, we can say that those indices are indices of a state X. Then, as usual, for the purpose of avoiding the inconvenience of using mere letters of the alphabet as terms, we will substitute some name or other for the letter X, taking the name, again as usual, in order to avoid a jargon too baroque, from something of kindred nature. When we know, or think we know, just what thing is advantageous to an individual or a community, we say that it is "beneficial" for both individuals and communities to exert themselves to obtain it, and judge the utility they enjoy the greater, the nearer they come to obtaining it. By simple analogy, therefore, and for no other reason, we shall apply the term "utility" to the entity X just described.[1]

2112. We must not forget that, for the very reason that the name is derived from a mere analogy, the "utility" so defined may on occasion roughly accord with the "utility" of ordinary parlance, but

relative and remarks that the majority of peoples cannot organize along the lines of the "best commonwealth," and that a form of government suited to peoples actually existing has to be found. He then very soundly adds: "For one should not only speculate as to the best government [republic] but also as to the government that is possible and which likewise can be common to all [cities]." He is also aware that it is not enough to just imagine the best form of state, but that ways have to be found to get the form one proposes accepted. However, he soon goes astray again, and for the usual reason of giving the major rôle to logical conduct and imagining that a lawgiver can shape a state according to his own pleasure. All the same, the knowledge he has of practical politics later constrains him to add that "to reform a state is no less serious a task than founding a new one."

2111 [1] If it could be known what the metaphysicists ever mean when they speak of the "purpose" or "end" a human being is made for, that "end" might be taken as one of the states X; and the letter X could then (still by analogy) be replaced by the word "end," and one could say that the state X was the "end" towards which individuals and communities tend or "ought" to tend. That "end" might be absolute, as it usually is with metaphysicists, but it could also be relative if it were left to the judgment of certain individuals to determine it. A state more closely approaching that "end" would have a higher index than a state that did not come so close to it.

then again be in disaccord, and to such an extent as to mean the flat opposite. For example, if we take a state of material prosperity as our limit state for a people, our utility will not be greatly different from the entity that practical men designate by that name, but it will differ widely from the ideal envisaged by the ascetic. Conversely if we take the state of perfect asceticism as the limit state, our "utility" will coincide with the entity to which the ascetic aspires, but will differ altogether from the ideal of the practical man. After all, since human beings are in the habit of designating opposite things by the same name, we are left a choice between two modes of expression only: (1) We can resolutely eschew ordinary language and give different names to the different things—since these are very numerous, we will get, in consequence, many many coined words. Or (2) we can keep the same names for the things, with the warning that the names designate those things only in general, like the name of a class of objects, like the term "element" in chemistry, the term "mammal" in zoology, and so on; and that the species within the class will be fixed subject to the criterion we have chosen in defining the term "utility."

2113. It is undoubtedly most unfortunate that a single term should designate different things; and it would therefore be better to avoid using the term "utility" in the sense defined in § 2111, which coincides with one of the senses of the term in ordinary language, and to substitute a new term for it, as has been done in economics, where "ophelimity" has been distinguished from "utility." I believe that the time will come when it will be necessary to do that. If I refrain from doing it here, it is from sheer terror of overabusing coined words.[1]

2114. The mere coining of a term will not extricate us, of course, from all our difficulties. Even when we consider some particular

2113 [1] I say that, but I am sure I am wrong. There may be no way of reconciling the literary approach to sociology with the scientific approach. Once one sets out to study sociology on the models of chemistry, physics, and other sciences, it is perhaps the wiser part courageously to accept the sort of terminology that has shown itself unavoidably requisite in those sciences. Anyone desiring to apply himself to them has to familiarize himself with a certain number of baroque technical terms—know, for example, their systems of measurement and the meanings of such units as "dyne," "barye," "erg," "joule," "gauss," "poncelet," and so on. That is much more complicated than remembering the meanings in which I use the terms "residues"

utility with reference to its end, the utility of material prosperity, let us say, we find there are other utilities of different kinds from the standpoints of individuals or communities, the ways in which they are attained, the notions people have of them, and other circumstances of the sort.

2115. The important thing, first of all, is to distinguish cases according as we are thinking of the individual, the family, a community, a nation, the human race. And not only are the utilities of those various entities to be considered; a further distinction has to be drawn between their direct utilities and the utilities that they derive indirectly through their mutual relationships. So, disregarding other distinctions that it might be of advantage to make, and keeping to such as are absolutely indispensable, we find ourselves obliged to deal with the following varieties:

a. Utility to the Individual:

  a-1. Direct

  a-2. Indirect, resulting from the fact that the individual is part of a community

  a-3. Utility to an individual, as related to the utilities to others

b. Utility to a Given Community (For this variety the same distinctions, *a-1, a-2, a-3,* serve.)

and "derivations." Even in ordinary literary essays it is wise not to imitate the writers alluded to by Boileau (*Épître* X), who condemned

> ". . . *la métaphore et la métonomye,*
> *grands mots que Pradon croit des termes de chymie.*"

The "energy" of mechanics must not be confused with the "energy" of ordinary parlance, nor is it excusable to imagine that a mechanical "live force" is a force that is alive. If one would know the meaning of "entropy" one had better glance at a treatise on thermodynamics. Chemistry, for its part, uses new terms by the hundreds, and chemists are sometimes obliged to give them synonyms for ordinary use. So in pharmacy the euphonious "hexamethylentetramine" has been replaced by "utropin," which at least has the merit of being a few letters shorter. To study chemistry one has to turn to a treatise on chemistry—plain good sense and etymology are of no help. That is unfortunate, but that is the way it is. No breed of literary chemists exists. To study sociology one has to turn to a treatise on that science and resign oneself to not trusting etymology and plain good sense. That, too, is unfortunate, in that it prevents the very numerous race of literary economists and sociologists from understanding the subject. For that matter, their breed is destined still to thrive for some time to come, since its existence corresponds to a certain social "utility" (§ 2400 [1]).

b-1. Direct utility to communities, considered apart from other communities

b-2. Indirect utility, arising by reaction from other communities

b-3. Utility to one community as related to the utilities to other communities

Far from coinciding, these various utilities oftentimes stand in overt opposition.[1] Sometimes explicitly, more often implicitly, all of them are usually brought down to one—by theologians and metaphysicists, out of a love for the absolute, which is one; by moralists, in order to induce individuals to concern themselves with the good of others; by statesmen, to induce the individual to blend his own advantage with the public advantage; and by other sorts of people for reasons of like character.

2116. Without departing from the logico-experimental domain, further distinctions may be drawn and the different utilities considered in two ways: as one of the members of the community pictures them to himself, and as an outsider views them, or a member of the community trying as far as he can to render an objective judgment. An individual who has a vivid sense of the direct utility, *a*-1, and little or no sense of the indirect, *a*-2, will simply look to his own convenience and not concern himself with his fellow-citizens; whereas a person judging that individual's conduct objectively will see that he is sacrificing the community to his own advantage.

2117. Nor have we yet done with our distinctions. Each of the varieties indicated (§ 2115) may be considered with reference to time—in reference to the present, that is, and to one point or another in the future; nor will the conflicts between those various utilities be found any less sharp than between the others, nor can there be less difference as regards the person who judges them under sway of sentiment and the person who views them objectively.

2118. Suppose, to give the discussion a more concrete form, we consider one of the utilities in particular, material prosperity, let us say. In so far as human conduct is logical, one may hold, strictly, that the man who goes to war and does not know whether he will fall in battle or return home is acting out of considerations of individual utility, direct or indirect, for he can compare the probable

2115 [1] Of such situations we have already seen many examples (§§ 1975 f.).

utility accruing to him if he returns safe and sound with the probable damage he will suffer if he loses his life or is maimed. But that argument ceases to hold for the man who marches to certain death in defence of his country. He is deliberately sacrificing individual utility to national utility (the case of the subjective utility mentioned in § 2117).

2119. In the majority of cases a man makes such a sacrifice in virtue of a non-logical impulse, and subjective considerations of utility have nothing to do with it—the only consideration applying being the objective consideration of the on-looker. That is the case with animals, many of which instinctively sacrifice themselves for the good of other animals of their kind. The hen dying in defence of her chicks, the cock in defending the hen, the bitch in defending her pups, and so on, sacrifice their lives for the utility of their species and as a matter of instinct. Very prolific species of animals endure only through sacrificing the individual. Rats are killed by the thousands, yet there are still rats. The Phylloxeron has defeated man and taken possession of his vineyards. The utility of today is frequently in conflict with the utility of days to come, and the conflict gives rise to phenomena that are well known under the names of providence and improvidence in individuals, families, and nations.[1]

2120. *Net utility*. Taking account of the three types of utility noted (§ 2115) in the case of a single individual, we get as a result the net utility that the individual enjoys. He may, on the one hand, suffer a direct damage and on the other hand, as a member of a community, secure an indirect advantage; and the latter may be so great as more than to offset the direct damage, so that in the end there is a certain gain for a remainder. So for a group. If we could get indices for these various utilities, and take their sum, we would have the total or net utility of the individual or group.[1]

2119 [1] [Another striking example from the animal world would be the sea-gull. A sea-gull always screams at sight of game. If he could control himself, he could enjoy the prey all to himself and derive a very considerable individual advantage, especially when food is scarce. Instead his cry attracts all the gulls in his flock, and nine times out of ten the discoverer of the game is not the one who eats it. The utility of this instinct to the flock is obvious, though it violates every commonsense principle of "rugged individualism."—A. L.]

2120 [1] [The sea-gull derives a very considerable net utility from his instinct. If he usually loses the fish he discovers himself, he is often able to steal the fish some

2121. *Maximum utility* of *an individual or group.* Since the utility just mentioned has an index, it may, possibly, in a certain state have a larger index than in a state more or less close to it—that is to say, it may have a maximum. People sense problems of that type in practical life, be it intuitively and in a vague way. We encountered one along our own path when we were inquiring as to the utility the individual might derive from observance of certain rules prevailing in his society (§§ 1897 f.), or, more generally, the utility that he might derive from aiming at certain ideal ends (§§ 1876 f.). At that time we considered only the qualitative solution of the problem, and not even with that could we go very far, since we lacked a rigorous definition of utility. We must therefore return to that subject here.

2122. When we consider a definite species of utility with reference to an individual, we get indices of partial utilities and also an index of the total net utility; and that is what makes it possible to estimate the utility which the individual enjoys under given circumstances. Furthermore if, as circumstances vary, the index of his net utility, which began by increasing, ends by decreasing, there will be a certain point at which it reaches a maximum. All the problems that we stated previously in qualitative terms (§§ 1876 f., 1897 f.) then become quantitative and involve problems of maxima. Instead of asking whether an individual achieves his own happiness through observing certain norms, we ask whether and to what extent his ophelimity increases, and once on that road, we end by asking how and when such ophelimity attains its maximum.

2123. The particular problems stated in § 1897 are comprised in the more general problems stated in § 1876, and these in turn are part of a still more general category. If the state of an individual depends upon a certain circumstance to which variable indices may be assigned, and if for each of those indices we can know the index of net utility for an individual (or for a group considered as an individual), we shall be able to determine in what position of the individual (or community) that utility reaches a maximum.

2124. Finally, if we repeat that operation for all the circumstances

comrade discovers. This instinct functions in the sea-gull, be it noted, with an ideally Paretan indifference to ethics, for the tie of good manners is normally absent among sea-gulls.—A. L.]

upon which the social equilibrium depends, all ties being known, we shall have that many indices from which we can select one index that will be greater than all the indices which stand anywhere near it, and it will correspond to the maximum of utility, due account being taken of all the circumstances mentioned.

2125. Difficult as these problems may be practically, they are theoretically easier than others on which we must now touch.

2126. So far we have considered the maxima of utility of an individual and of a community taken apart from other individuals and communities. Still left is the problem of those same maxima when individuals or communities are taken relatively to one another. For the sake of brevity we shall speak only of individuals in what follows, but the reasoning will apply just as well to comparisons of distinct communities. If the utilities of single individuals were homogeneous quantities and could therefore be compared and reduced to a sum, our study would not, theoretically at least, be difficult. We would simply take the sum of the utilities of the various individuals and so get the utility of the community they constitute —and that would be taking us back to problems already examined.

2127. But the business is not so simple. The utilities of various individuals are heterogeneous quantities, and a sum of such quantities is a thing that has no meaning; there is no such sum, and none such can be considered. If we would have a sum that stands in some relation to the utilities of the various individuals, we must first find a way to reduce those utilities to homogeneous quantities that can be summed.

2128. *Maximum of ophelimity* FOR *a community in political economy.* A problem of just that character arose in economics and had to be solved by that science. It will be well to consider it briefly, that we may be the better prepared to solve the more difficult sociological problem. In economics the equilibrium can be determined provided we stipulate that every individual achieves the maximum of ophelimity. The ties can be posited in such a way that the equilibrium will be perfectly determined. If, now, certain ties are suppressed, the perfect determination will come to an end, and the equilibrium will be possible at an infinite number of points at which maxima of individual ophelimities are attained. In the first case, only movements leading to the determined point of equilibrium were possible; in the second, other movements also are possible. These are of two quite distinct types. Movements of a first type, *P*, are such that, beneficial to certain individuals, they are necessarily harmful to others. Movements of a second type, *Q*, are such that they are to the advantage, or to the detriment, of all individuals without exception. The points *P* are determined by equating with zero a certain sum of homogeneous quantities dependent on heterogenous ophelimities.[1]

2129. Consideration of the two types of points, *P* and *Q*, is of great importance in political economy. When the community stands at a point, *Q*, that it can leave with resulting benefits to all individuals, procuring greater enjoyments for all of them, it is obvious

2128 [1] Pareto, *"Il massimo di utilità* per *una collettività in sociologia,"* Giornale degli economisti, April, 1913, pp. 337-38 [This article was overlooked by Rocca-Spinedi, *Bibliografia di Vilfredo Pareto.*—A. L.]: "Let us begin by recalling the economic problem. If we have the individuals 1, 2, 3 . . . for whom the elementary ophelimities of the commodity *A* are ϕ_{1a}, ϕ_{2a} . . . and if the variations of the total ophelimities that each one enjoys are $\delta\phi_1$, $\delta\phi_2$ . . . one considers the expression:

$$(1) \qquad \delta U = \frac{1}{\phi_{1a}}\delta\phi_1 + \frac{1}{\phi_{2a}}\delta\phi_2 + \dots$$

Variations arising along the route that leads to the point of equilibrium are indicated by *d*. If the equilibrium is determined on the condition that each individual achieve the maximum of ophelimity, we get, for the route that leads to the point of equilibrium:

$$(2) \qquad d\phi_1 = 0 \qquad d\phi_2 = 0 \dots$$
$$(3) \qquad dU = 0 = \frac{1}{\phi_{1a}}d\phi_1 + \frac{1}{\phi_{2a}}d\phi_2 + \dots$$

The points determined by the equations (2), supplemented by the equations of the ties, are points of equilibrium in the system, and for them we get: $dU = 0$. If some of these ties are removed, it will be possible to consider other variations, δ, and for them δU may or may not be zero. Let us call points at which δU is zero points of the type *P*, and points at which δU is not zero points of the type *Q*. Points of the type *P* have one important peculiarity. Since the elementary ophelimities, ϕ_{1a}, ϕ_{2a} . . . , are essentially positive, if the equation

$$(4) \qquad \delta U = 0 = \frac{1}{\phi_{1a}}\delta\phi_1 + \frac{1}{\phi_{2a}}\delta\phi_2 + \dots$$

is to be satisfied, some of the total ophelimities $\delta\phi_1$, $\delta\phi_2$ . . . must necessarily be positive and some negative: they cannot all be positive nor all negative. That peculiarity may be again expressed in the following manner: The points of the type *P* are such that we cannot deviate from them to the benefit or detriment of all the members of the community—we can deviate from them only to the benefit of some individuals and the detriment of others.

that from the economic standpoint it is advisable not to stop at that point, but to move on from it as far as the movement away from it is advantageous to all. When, then, the point *P*, where that is no longer possible, is reached, it is necessary, as regards the advisability of stopping there or going on, to resort to other considerations foreign to economics—to decide on grounds of ethics, social utility, or something else, which individuals it is advisable to benefit, which to sacrifice. From the strictly economic standpoint, as soon as the community has reached a point *P* it has to stop. That point therefore plays in the situation a rôle analogous to the rôle of the point where the maximum of individual ophelimity is attained and at which, accordingly, the individual stops. Because of that analogy it has been called *point of maximum ophelimity* FOR *the community*. But, as usual, nothing is to be inferred from the etymologies of those terms (§ 2076); and to escape the ever present danger of falling into errors of that kind we shall continue to call that point the point *P*.[1]

2129 [1] Failure to distinguish between the maximum of ophelimity *for* the community and the maximum of ophelimity *of* each individual in the community has led certain writers to regard my demonstrations of my theories concerning the maximum of ophelimity *for* the community as reasonings in a circle. As a matter of fact, in the case of free competition, the equations of economic equilibrium are obtained by positing the condition that each individual attains the maximum of ophelimity; so that if one were to infer from those equations that every individual achieves the maximum of ophelimity, one would obviously be reasoning in a circle. But if, instead, one asserts that the equilibrium determined by the equations has the peculiarity of corresponding to a point of equilibrium *for* the community, that is to say, to one of the points that we have just designated as *P*, one is stating a theorem that has to be demonstrated. The demonstration I gave first in my *Cours* and then in my *Manuale*.

The error of regarding my argument as a reasoning in a circle has its foundation, really, in the work of Walras, who, in fact, never dealt with a maximum of ophelimity *for* a community, but always exclusively considered a maximum of ophelimity for each individual. Boven, *Les applications mathématiques à l'économie politique*, pp. 111-12: "Walras develops [*Éléments d'économie politique pure*, pp. 77-87] what he calls the Theorem of Maximum Utility of Commodities. That so-called proof is a splendid example of the vicious circle. One has only to judge for oneself. The problem is to determine under just what conditions the two individuals exchanging will obtain the maximum satisfaction of their needs. The premise with which we start is as follows: (Walras, *Ibid.*, p. 77): 'Assuming that he effects the exchange in such a way as to satisfy the greatest possible total of needs, it is certain that p_a being given, d_a is determined by the proviso that the sum of the two surfaces shall be the maximum. And that condition is that the relation of the intensities r_{a_1}, r_{b_1}, of the last needs satisfied by the quantities d_a and y, or of the rarities after

2130. If a community could be taken as a single individual, it would have a maximum of ophelimity just as a single individual has; there would, that is, be points at which the ophelimity *of* the community would attain a maximum. Those points would not be the same as the points Q indicated in § 2128. Since, in fact, advances from those points can be made with resulting benefit to all the individuals in a community, it is obvious that the ophelimity of the community might be increased in that fashion. But it cannot be said that such points would coincide with the points P. Let us take a community made up of just two persons, A and B. We can move from a point P, adding 5 to A's ophelimity and taking 2 from the ophelimity of B, and so reaching a point s; or adding 2 to A's ophelimity and taking 1 from B's, so that a point t is reached. We cannot know at which of the two points, s, t, the ophelimity *of* the community will be greater or less until we know just how the

exchange, shall be equal to the price p_a.' Let us assume that that condition is met. . . . If it is certain that that equation is forced upon us, and if it is taken as our hypothesis, there is no need whatever of covering four pages with calculations just to discover that 'two commodities being given on a market, the maximum satisfaction of needs, or the maximum of actual utility, is attained for each bidder when the relation of the intensities of the last needs satisfied, or the relation of rarities, is equal to the price. . . .' To be sure there is no mistake in the argument, nothing that vitiates the theory, since the solution that is reached is none other than the hypothesis with which we started. But it is astonishing that Walras should have succumbed to such an illusion. One would willingly believe that it was an oversight on his part. But that is not the case. The tautology was called to his attention several times and by the most appreciative critics, but Walras simply would not see it that way. And in that we come upon a most interesting thing—the violence of the sentiments that were driving the illustrious economist to preach a practical doctrine. He wanted the public interest to be demonstrated mathematically, at all costs. He was resolutely bent on showing that free competition was good and monopoly bad."

Those strictures in no way detract from Walras's great merit in having been the first to state the equations of the economic equilibrium in a particular case, just as criticisms that might be made of Newton's theory of light or, what is worse, of his comments on the Apocalypse, do not detract from the admiration due to the immortal founder of the science of celestial mechanics. People who are ever confusing the prophet with the scientist are not aware of that. It may well be that the dogmas of a religion, being reputed absolute, do not change as the years go by. But scientific doctrines are in a perpetual state of flux and, now by an author himself but at any rate always by others, they are forever being modified, amplified, given new forms, and even new content. Believers in the Apocalypse may be eager to count Newton as one of them. Believers in the humanitarian or Socialist religion may strive to make capital out of the name of Walras. But such wretched pettifogging does no harm either to Newton or to Walras.

ophelimities of A and of B are to be compared; and precisely because they cannot be compared, since they are heterogeneous quantities, no maximum ophelimity *of* the community exists; whereas a maximum ophelimity *for* the community can exist, since it is determined independently of any comparison between the ophelimities of different individuals.

2131. *The maximum of utility* FOR *a community, in sociology.*[1] Now let us take all that over into sociology. In so far as he acts logically, every individual tries to secure a maximum of individual utility, as explained in § 2122. If we assume that some of the ties imposed by public authority are suppressed without being replaced by others, an infinite number of positions of equilibrium with the provisos of individual maxima as indicated become possible. Public authority interposes to require some and prohibit others. Let us assume that it acts logically and with the sole purpose of achieving

2131 [1] (Continuing the quotation from my article, *"Il massimo di utilità* per *una collettività,"* in § 2128 [1] above): "The quantities $\delta\phi_1$, $\delta\phi_2$ . . . are heterogeneous and therefore cannot be summed, for such a sum would be without meaning. But let us assume for a moment that they are not heterogeneous and that the equation

$$(5) \qquad \delta H = \delta\phi_1 + \delta\phi_2 + \cdots$$

does mean something. In that case it would represent the variation of ophelimity of the community considered as a single person; the proviso $\delta H = 0$ would correspond to the proviso of a maximum of ophelimity for that imaginary person, and the points P would therefore be the points of maximum ophelimity for such a person. The purpose in considering the quantities

$$(6) \qquad \frac{1}{\phi_{1a}}\delta\phi_1, \quad \frac{1}{\phi_{2a}}\delta\phi_2 \cdots$$

is to avoid the difficulty arising from the heterogeneous character of the ophelimities $\delta\phi_1$, $\delta\phi_2$ . . . and to make it possible, by the fact of their being homogeneous, to take their sum. The quantities (6) are that because, in virtue of the equations of the equilibrium, they all represent quantities of a single commodity A. It is evident that if there were some other way of rendering the heterogeneous quantities $\delta\phi_1$, $\delta\phi_2$ . . . homogeneous by multiplying them, let us say, by certain positive quantities a_1, a_2 . . . consideration of the sum

$$(7) \qquad \delta V = 0 = a_1\,\delta\phi_1 + a_2\,\delta\phi_2 + \cdots$$

would yield somewhat the same results as consideration of (4) [§ 2128 [1]] and determine certain points of the type P from which departure cannot be made to the advantage, or detriment, of *all* the members of the community. Economics does not require this other manner of assimilating the variations in ophelimity, and therefore does not look for one. But sociology does, and it therefore seeks and finds. An individual (equation 1) sets out to act in such a way that all his fellow-citizens shall achieve the greatest possible good, without anyone's being sacrificed. The expres-

a certain utility. (That rarely is the case; but that fact we need not consider here, since we are envisaging not a real, concrete situation, but a theoretical, hypothetical one.) In such a case the government must necessarily compare—we need not now ask with reference to what criteria—the various utilities. When it shuts a thief up in prison, it compares the pain that it inflicts upon him with the utility resulting from it to honest people, and it roughly guesses that the latter at least offsets the former; otherwise it would let the thief go.[2] For the sake of brevity we have here compared two utilities only. A government of course—as best it can, and that is often badly enough—compares all the utilities it is aware of. Substantially, it

sion (7) exists subjectively for him; that is to say, he experiences the variation $\delta\phi_1$ directly and imagines the variations $\delta\phi_2$, $\delta\phi_3$. . . . The coefficients a_2, a_3 . . . serve to effect the transition from the quantities $\delta\phi_2$, $\delta\phi_3$ . . . , which are objective and heterogeneous, to the quantities $a_2\ \delta\phi_2$, $a_3\ \delta\phi_3$ . . . which are subjective and homogeneous. Humanitarians 1, 2, 3, who dislike to see the criminals 4, 5, 6 in jail, giving not a thought to the victims 7, 8 . . . will assign high coefficients to the quantities $\delta\phi_4$, $\delta\phi_5$, $\delta\phi_6$, and coefficients of approximately zero to the quantities $\delta\phi_7$, $\delta\phi_8$. . . . In that way, however, there are as many equations (7) as there are individuals, namely:

$$(8) \qquad 0 = a'_1\ \delta\phi_1 + a'_2\ \delta\phi_2 + a'_3\ \delta\phi_3 + \ldots$$
$$0 = a''_1\ \delta\phi_1 + a''_2\ \delta\phi_2 + a''_3\ \delta\phi_3 + \ldots$$
$$0 = a'''_1\ \delta\phi_1 + a'''_2\ \delta\phi_2 + a'''_3\ \delta\phi_3 + \ldots$$

And the heterogeneity, eliminated from the quantities in the single equation, turns up again in the quantities of the different equations. To render these homogeneous, they have to be multiplied again by certain coefficients β'_1, β''_1, β'''_1 . . . determined with an objective purpose in view—the prosperity of the community, let us say. Suppose a government believes that the prosperity of the community demands the extermination of criminals. It will then resign itself to inflicting pain on kind-hearted humanitarians; it will, in other words, assign very low coefficients β'_1, β''_1, β'''_1 . . . to their pains, and fairly high coefficients, β^{VII}_1, β^{VIII}_1 . . . to the pain of the victims of the criminals. Now that, thanks to the coefficients, the quantities corresponding to the equations (8) have become comparable, their sum can be taken after they have been multiplied by β'_1, β''_1 . . . and we get:

$$(9) \qquad 0 = M_1\ \delta\phi_1 + M_2\ \delta\phi_2 + M_3\ \delta\phi_3 + \ldots$$

The equation (9) will determine points of the type P analogous to the points P determined by the equation (4) [§ 2128 [1]]. A government that has fixed on the equation (9) will have to carry the movement of the community on till one of the points P is reached; and there it will stop, for if it went any farther it would become involved in a self-contradiction, sacrificing people who it believes should not be sacrificed."

2131 [2] The comparison is usually made with derivations, comparing ideal purposes rather than actual positions. To tip the scales in favour of honest people, it will be said that "the criminal deserves no mercy," which means, at bottom, that it is better

does at a guess what pure economics does with scientific exactness: it makes certain heterogeneous quantities homogeneous by giving them certain coefficients, thence proceeding to add the resulting quantities and so determine points of the type P.

2132. All that is sensed more or less vividly, more or less vaguely, in practical life; and it is said that a government ought to stop at the point beyond which no "advantage" would accrue to the community as a whole, that it ought not to inflict "useless" sufferings on the public as a whole or in part, that it ought to benefit the community as far as possible without sacrificing the "ideals" it has in view "for the public good," that it ought to make efforts "proportionate" to purposes and not demand burdensome sacrifices for slight gains. The foregoing definition is designed to substitute exact conceptions for such expressions of common parlance, which are deficient in all exactness and, in view of that vagueness, misleading.

2133. In pure economics a community cannot be regarded as a person. In sociology it can be considered, if not as a person, at least as a unit. There is no such thing as the ophelimity of a community; but a community utility can roughly be assumed. So in pure economics there is no danger of mistaking the maximum of ophelimity *for* a community for a non-existent maximum of ophelimity *of* a community. In sociology, instead, we must stand watchfully on guard against confusing the maximum of utility *for* a community with the maximum of utility *of* a community, since they both are there.

2134. Take, for instance, the matter of population increase. If we think of the utility *of* the community as regards prestige and military power, we will find it advisable to increase population to the fairly high limit beyond which the nation would be impoverished and its stock decay. But if we think of the maximum of utility *for* the community, we find a limit that is much lower. Then we have to see in what proportions the various social classes profit by the in-

to assign a coefficient of zero, or almost zero, to his discomforts. Conversely, to tip the scales in favour of the criminal, it will be said that "to understand all is to forgive all," that "society is more responsible for the crime than the criminal is," so disregarding the sufferings of honest people, which are given coefficients approximating zero, while the discomforts of the criminal take the foreground through high coefficients. Many derivations that are habitually used in discussions on social subjects can be translated into just such terms.

crease in prestige and military power, and in what different proportion they pay for it with their particular sacrifices. When proletarians say that they refuse to have children because children merely increase the power and profits of the ruling classes, they are dealing with a problem of maximum utility *for* the community—the derivations they chance to use, such as derivations of one religion or another, or of Socialism or pacifism, are of little importance—the thing to look for is what lies underneath. The rejoinders of ruling classes oftentimes show a confusion of a problem of maximum utility *of* the community and a problem of maximum utility *for* the community. They also try to bring decisions down to a question of a maximum of individual utility, trying to make the "subject" classes believe that there is an indirect utility which, when properly taken into account, turns the sacrifice required of them into a gain. That may actually be the case sometimes, but not always; there are many cases where, even taking very liberal account of indirect utilities, the result shows not an advantage, but a sacrifice, for the subject classes. In reality, in cases such as these, non-logical impulses only can serve to induce the subject classes to forget the maximum of individual utility, and work for the maximum of utility *of* the community, or merely *of* the ruling classes—and that fact has not infrequently been sensed, intuitively, by the latter.

2135. Let us imagine a community so situated that a strict choice has to be made between a very wealthy community with large inequalities in income among its members and a poor community with approximately equal incomes. A policy of maximum utility *of* the community may lead to the first state, a policy of maximum utility *for* the community to the second. We say *may,* because results will depend upon the coefficients that are used in making the heterogeneous utilities of the various social classes homogeneous. The admirer of the "superman" will assign a coefficient of approximately zero to the utility of the lower classes, and get a point of equilibrium very close to a state where large inequalities prevail. The lover of equality will assign a high coefficient to the utility of the lower classes and get a point of equilibrium very close to the equalitarian condition. There is no criterion save sentiment for choosing between the one and the other.

2136. There is a theory—we are not now concerned with the extent of its correspondence with the facts—according to which slavery was a necessary condition of social progress; because, so the argument runs, it enabled a certain number of individuals to live lives of leisure and consequently devote themselves to intellectual pursuits. Granting that contention, for a moment, if one person desires to solve a problem of maximum utility *of* the species and considers that utility and nothing else, he will decide that slavery has been a benefit; on the other hand, if another person desires to solve a problem of the same sort, and envisages nothing but the utility of the human beings who are reduced to slavery, he will decide that slavery has been an evil, meantime overlooking a number of indirect effects. We cannot ask who is right, who wrong. Such language has no meaning until a criterion has been selected for guiding a comparison between the two decisions (§ 17).

2137. We are to conclude from that not that problems simultaneously considering a number of heterogeneous utilities cannot be solved, but that in order to discuss them some hypothesis which will render them commensurate has to be assumed. And when, as is most often the case, that is not done, discussion of such problems is idle and inconclusive, being merely a play of derivations cloaking certain sentiments—and those sentiments we should alone consider, without worrying very much about the garb they wear.

2138. Even in cases where the utility of the individual does not stand in conflict with the utility of the community, the points of maximum of the one do not ordinarily coincide with the points of maximum of the other. Let us go back for a moment to the particular case examined in §§ 1897 f. Taking a given individual, let *A* be the extreme point representing strictest observance of every precept obtaining in his society; *B*, another extreme point representing violation of precepts that are not recognized as absolutely indispensable; *mnp* the curve of utility of the individual, who begins suffering a damage at *A*, then attains a benefit, which becomes greatest at *n*, the benefit thereafter diminishing and becoming a loss at *B*.

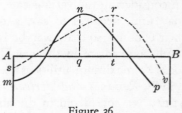

Figure 36

Similarly, let *srv* be the curve of the utility deriving to society from the fact of the individual's more or less faithful observance of the precepts. The social utility is greatest at *r*. At the point *q*, intermediate between *A* and *B*, we get for the individual the maximum of utility *qn*. At the point *t*, also intermediate between *A* and *B*, we get *tr* as the maximum of utility deriving to the community through the individual's conduct.[1]

2139. Instead of considering a single individual, one may take a number of individuals having approximately the same curve of utility, *mnp*. Then the curve of utility *srv* of the group to which the individuals belong will be the curve resulting from the conduct of those individuals. Instead of mere violations of the norms obtaining in a society, we may consider transformations and reforms of them that take place in that society. In many cases *t* will be much closer than *q* to *B;* in other words, as regards certain individuals it will be advantageous to society that the reform be greater than the reform which would bring them the maximum utility. People who are already rich and powerful oftentimes have little to gain from innovations, whereas society may benefit greatly by them. Or again, for individuals inclined to quiet, unruffled living *t* will be much nearer than *q* is to *B;* in other words, any innovation, however beneficial to society, will be distasteful and troublesome to them. For "speculators," on the other hand, *t* stands much farther removed than *q* does from *B*—and "speculators" tend much more readily to change than is necessary for the good of society. If we go on considering the various categories of individuals in that way, we may find, needless to say, a certain amount of compensation in their conduct, so that, everybody pulling for himself, a position will result somewhere in the neighbourhood of the point *t*, where the society's maximum utility is located.

2140. *Residues and derivations in relation to utility.* Above, in § 2123, we considered in the abstract certain things that might influence the social equilibrium. Now let us be specific and consider residues and derivations chiefly.[1]

2138 [1] When the ethical norms are violated by a government, the locations of the points *q* and *t* are in many cases very much as pictured in Figure 36. When the norms are violated by members of the subject class, the relative location of points *q* and *t* will be inverted, the point *q* standing closer than *t* to *B*.

2140 [1] We were dealing with a similar subject when we asked in §§ 1825 f. what measures were suitable for achieving a given objective. At that time we were con-

2141. As a preparation for our inquiry, let us forget human society for a moment and assume that we have two extreme types of abstract societies: 1. A society where sentiments hold absolute sway, without reasonings of any kind. Animal societies seem to approximate that type quite closely. 2. A society in which logico-experimental reasonings hold absolute sway. Going back to Figure 29 (§ 1869), we may say that in the first case individuals move from h to m instinctively, without reasoning, without holding an ideal, T, in view, there being therefore no tangent, hT. In the second case they move from h to m by reasoning solely, and there is again no tangent, since any such line would be an arc of the curve hm.

2142. In a case of the first type, the form of the society is determined if the sentiments are given, and the external circumstances (environment) in which the society is situated; or if the circumstances only are given, but the sentiments are regarded as determined by the circumstances. Darwinism, carried to the extreme, gave the complete solution of that problem with its theory of the survival of the individuals best adapted to environment (§§ 828, 1770). Yet not even in that very simple case was the fog that drapes these questions entirely dispelled. In the first place, one could ask: How comes it that so many varieties of animals are to be found on one same soil? One of the species should have been better adapted to it than the others and therefore have destroyed them. Furthermore, behind the phrase "better adapted" lurk the same difficulties that we encountered when we came to the term "utility." The animal that is "better adapted" as far as its own individual prosperity is concerned may not be "better adapted" as regards the prosperity of the species. If rats survive, that fortune is due solely to their extraordinary fertility. Suppose certain rats were better adapted than others to escape the traps set by human beings but at the same time were less prolific. Escaping the traps, they might in time replace other rats, but in view of their reduced fertility the species might become extinct.[1]

sidering the problem qualitatively and could not go very far with it, since we were not equipped with any definition of utility (§§ 2111 f.). Virtual movements were considered in their relation to an objective in general, and only secondarily in their relation to utility. Here we are thinking of this last in particular.

2142 [1] There have been numbers of books, favourable or unfavourable, on the subject of social Darwinism, which now and again, even without being directly mentioned, has inspired important works such as those of G. de Molinari. The criticisms

2143. In a case of the second type where logical thinking prevails, the form of the society is by no means determined when the external environment is given. It is necessary further to indicate the end to which logico-experimental reasoning is to be the means. Be it said in all deference to our estimable humanitarians and positivists, a society determined exclusively by "reason" does not and cannot exist, and that not because "prejudices" in human beings prevent them from following the dictates of "reason," but because the data of the problem that presumably is to be solved by logico-experimental reasoning are entirely unknown (§§ 1878, 1880-82). Just there the vagueness of the notion of utility again puts in an appearance, the same vagueness that fell in our way as we were trying to define utility (§ 2111). The concepts various individuals have of what is good for them and good for others are essentially heterogeneous, and there is no way of reducing them to unity.

2144. That fact is denied by people who think they know the

that we are here making of social Darwinism in no wise tend to depreciate its importance, a caution that might well be repeated for many other doctrines on which we touch in these volumes (§ 41). This treatise on general sociology is neither an exposition nor a history of sociological, philosophical, scientific, and other doctrines. We are concerned with them only incidentally, according as they provide examples which enable us to distinguish this or that derivation from experimental reality or to clarify some point in one of our scientific investigations. We would not be called upon to give this warning had the science of sociology reached the level of other logico-experimental sciences. A reader of Poincaré's *Les méthodes nouvelles de la mécanique céleste* does not expect to find in that book an exposition or a history of astronomical theories from Hipparchus to our day; and a reader of Paul Tannery's *Recherches sur l'histoire de l'astronomie ancienne* does not expect to find in it a treatise on celestial mechanics. In my *Systèmes socialistes,* my intention was to make a study of the derivations that are known under the names of such systems. One critic observed that I had stopped at forms, without getting to the bottom of things, and he went on from there to deliver a sharp condemnation of the book. The observation was sound, the condemnation deserved—at least as deserved as a criticism that might be made of Tannery for not dealing with celestial mechanics in the book just alluded to. The deficiency in my *Systèmes socialistes* is of quite another nature, arising from the fact that when I wrote that book I did not as yet have at my disposal the theory of derivations that I develop in this treatise: I was forced to apply it in advance before I had attained a thorough-going conception of it, and the result was a certain wavering. That study ought now to be recast in the light of the more exact theories which I have been expounding here. It would also be useful to have similar studies of political, philosophical, and other theories, in short, of all the various manifestations of the intellectual activity of human beings, which, the doctrines of socialist systems among them, go to make up the vast mass of social

absolute. They reduce all human opinions to their own opinion, eliminating the others by those processes of derivation of which we have given many examples; but the elimination is valid only for themselves and their followers, other people remaining of the differing opinions.

2145. Social reformers as a rule also fail to notice, or at least they disregard, the fact that individuals entertain different opinions with regard to utility, and that they do so because they get the data they require from their own sentiments. They say, and believe, that they are solving an objective problem: "What is the *best* form for a society?" Actually they are solving a subjective problem: "What form of society best fits my sentiments?" The reformer, of course, is certain that his sentiments have to be shared by all honest men and that they are not merely excellent in themselves but are also in the highest degree beneficial to society. Unfortunately that belief in no way alters the realities.[1]

doctrines. I have not dealt with them, and quite deliberately so, in these volumes.

No one must infer from that that I am so absurdly presumptuous as to imagine that I owe nothing to such doctrines as they have been expounded in the past (§ 41). One might as well say that a man of the Stone Age was in as good a position to discuss a scientific subject as a trained scholar living in a society as intellectually advanced as ours. The influence of one doctrine on another makes itself felt not only in the points where they stand in agreement one with the other, but in their points of divergence as well. Aristotle owes something to Plato even when he criticizes him. If there had been no Euclidean geometry, we should perhaps never have had non-Euclidean geometries. Newton's theory of universal gravitation would probably never have existed had there not been the earlier theories that it contradicts. Just what was their influence on Newton's mind and what the influence of direct experience? We do not know, and Newton himself knew no better than we, and perhaps not so well. Very keen must the person be who can successfully specify the shares belonging to each of the very numerous and varied influences that bear upon an author. Such researches may be important for psychology or for anecdotic history. They have very little significance in the logico-experimental study of the laws of social phenomena. [All the same, in a work of a million words with not a few asides, and containing not a few strictures on great writers of past and present, a few hundred words more might not have come amiss to describe what Pareto in particular owed, for his general method to Auguste Comte, for his theory of derivations to Bentham (some of whose categories Pareto adopts verbatim), for his theory of class-circulation to Gaetano Mosca, for his theory of residues to Frazer and others, and for a number of phrases and items of detail even to Hegel, William James, and many others.—A. L.]

2145 [1] From the strictly objective standpoint the term "best" as used in their theorem needs defining (§ 2110 [1])—it is essential, that is, to state exactly what the term is supposed to stand for. That is like determining exactly which one of the

2146. Human society falls somewhere between the two extreme types just noted (§ 2141). Its form is determined—aside from external environment—by sentiments, interests, logico-experimental reasonings used for satisfying sentiments and interests, and, in a secondary way, by derivations, which express and sometimes intensify sentiments and interests and serve in certain cases as instruments of propaganda. Logico-experimental reasonings play an important rôle when the objective is known and the quest is for the means best suited to reaching it. They are therefore used with conspicuous success in the arts and crafts, in agriculture, industry, and commerce; and so, in addition to the many technical sciences, it has been possible to constitute a general science of interests, the science of economics, which assumes that logico-experimental reasonings exclusively are used in certain branches of human activity. They are effective also in war, where they have produced strategy and allied sciences. They might conceivably be effective in the science of government, but so far in history they have been used in that connexion rather as an individual art by this or that statesman than as a means of building up an abstract science, since the objective is not known or, being known, is better kept secret. For those reasons and others still logico-experimental thinking has played a very minor part in the organization of society. There are, as yet, no scientific theories bearing on that subject, and in everything pertaining to it human beings are moved much more by sentiment than by thought. A certain number of individuals are clever enough to take advantage of that circumstance to satisfy their own interests, in doing which, at this or that moment, case by case and as occasion requires, they use empirical and to some extent logico-experimental reasonings.

2147. Almost all the reasonings that are used in social matters are derivations. Not seldom the most important element in them is left unexpressed, implicit (§ 1876), or is at best remotely suggested. If one goes looking for it, if, that is, one tries to discover on just what principles the conclusions may be logically based, one may in many

numberless states X (§ 2111) one elects to consider. The ambiguity in the term is a favourite one with reformers and the many other people of their kind. It arises in the mistaken notion that there is one state X only. As a matter of fact there are an infinite number of states X.

cases succeed in discovering the sentiments and interests that explain the acceptance of the conclusions to which the derivations pointed the way. The better to understand the character of such derivations, suppose we consider two examples. We shall be able to examine only a few of the principles that one might legitimately assume to be implicit in them; for if one set out to deal with them all, one would be obliged to consider all the infinitude of motives that determine the opinions of men.

Example I. Let us take the celebrated parable of Bastiat on the use of a carpenter's plane,[1] and see how Bastiat applies it in his controversy with Proudhon. It is a story of two imaginary carpenters, James and William by name. James makes a plane; William borrows it, and in return for such "service" agrees to give James one of the boards he makes with it.[2]

The derivation puts in an appearance in the very statement of the issues in debate, the question as to whether interest on capital is or is not "legitimate." [3] It occurs neither to Bastiat nor to Proudhon to try to define the term "legitimate." For Bastiat it seems to mean "in accord with my sentiments," which, through a very common derivation (§§ 591 f.), become the sentiments of all men. Proudhon too entertains the same notion, but he supplements it with many others in order to harmonize his theories with the sentiments of the

2147 [1] *Œuvres complètes,* Vol. V, pp. 43-63: *"Le rabot"* ["The Plane"].

2147 [2] *Ibid.,* Vol. V, pp. 119-20. "There you have a man who wants to make boards, but he will not make one in a year's time, for he has nothing but his ten fingers to work with. I lend him a saw and a plane, two tools, remember, that are products of my labour and which I could use to advantage myself. Instead of one board he makes a hundred and gives me five. So I have enabled him, by depriving myself of property belonging to me, to get ninety-five boards instead of one—and you come and tell me that I am robbing and abusing him! Thanks to a saw and a plane that I have made with the sweat of my brow a hundredfold product has issued, so to say, from void, society enters into possession of a centupled enjoyment, a working-man who could not make a board makes a hundred, and now, sir, when, voluntarily, of his own free-will, he gives me a twentieth part of his *surplus* (*excédent*), you picture me as a tyrant and a thief!"

2147 [3] Bastiat to Proudhon, *Ibid.,* Vol. V, p. 133: "You are asking me seven questions, sir. Kindly remember that we are concerned just here with only one: 'Is interest on capital legitimate?'" Proudhon to Bastiat, *loc. cit.,* p. 148: "You press me then: 'Is interest on capital legitimate—yes or no? And answer please without paradox, without quibbling!' So I answer: 'Let us, if you please, distinguish cases. Yes—interest on capital may have been considered legitimate at one time. No, it cannot be legitimate at another time.'"

public he is addressing (derivation, Class III—accord with sentiments).[4] He finds no great difficulty in doing that, since the accord has to be established between things that are left indefinite and can therefore be stretched as far as one wishes in whatever direction. The two both agree that the loan is a "service."[5] Neither of them, however, defines at all exactly what he understands by the term, and the result, of course, is that they both draw different conclusions from the accepted premise. Pre-eminent in Bastiat's mind is the notion that a person who renders a "service" has a "right" to a remuneration. With Proudhon, the dominant feeling is that the individuals in a society render mutual "services" and their "rights" therefore offset one another. Those propositions may be true or false according to the meanings of the terms that are used. They are of a piece with propositions based on "natural law." Proudhon goes on to hint at a practical manner of effecting such offset in remunerations. That does not interest us here in itself; but one might note the implicit assumption that first one has to decide in what form of social organization "justice" and "right" reside, and then, secondarily, how that organization is to be established.[6] Had that

2147 [4] The controversy took place in 1849 at a moment when republican enthusiasms were rising high. Proudhon to Bastiat, *Ibid.*, Vol. V, pp. 120-21: "The February revolution aims, in the domains of politics and economics, to establish the absolute freedom of the man and the citizen. The watchword of the Revolution is, in the political sphere, the organization of universal suffrage—in other words, the absorption of power by society, and in the economic sphere, the organization of circulation and credit, in other words the absorption of the capitalist's status by the worker's status. That formula does not of course, all by itself, give a complete picture of the system. It is only its point of departure, its aphorism. But it suffices to explain the Revolution in its immediateness, its actuality. It justifies us, consequently [The "consequence" is worth a gold mine in Peru.], in saying that the Revolution is and can be nothing but that."

2147 [5] Proudhon to Bastiat, *Ibid.*, Vol. V, p.. 125: "On the one hand it is true, as you yourself categorically assert, that the loan is a *service*. And since every service is a *value* [What does that mean?], since, consequently, it is in the nature [Our greetings to this old friend of ours!] of every service to be recompensed, it follows that the loan must have its *price,* or, to use the technical expression, must *bear interest.*"

2147 [6] That is clearly evident in all the writings of Bastiat and Proudhon. As regards the former, the following will suffice: *Ibid.*, Vol. VI, p. 201: *Harmonies économiques: Richesse:* "It must be recognized, in the first place, that the impulse which drives us towards wealth comes from nature [Most illuminating! Does not the impulse that impels one to commit a crime also come from nature?], is of providential creation [What on earth is that?], and therefore *moral.* It lies in that

principle been stated explicitly, the many problems connected with multiple utilities would have come to the fore at once, and the many relationships between such utilities and the norms of conduct—be they what one will—to which the terms "justice" and "right" are applied. Both Bastiat and Proudhon vaguely sense the existence of such problems and exert themselves to demonstrate—with scant success, to tell the truth—that "justice" and "right" are identical with some vaguely defined "utility." [7] Bastiat uses the very common derivation of offering a hypothetical example as proof (§ 1409). An example may have its place in a logico-experimental argument provided it is adduced merely to clarify a writer's thoughts. It can never serve as proof. The complete syllogism would be: "Assuming that a situation A exists, the consequence will be B. The situation in reality is, in the pertinent respects, equivalent or

primitive and general destitution which would be the lot of us all did it not inspire us with a resolve to be free of it. And it must be admitted in the second place that the efforts men make to lift themselves from that primitive impoverishment are, provided they are kept within the bounds of justice [But the location of those bounds is the very point in dispute between those who assert and those who deny that in taking a part of the worker's product the capitalist oversteps the bounds of justice.], altogether estimable and respectable, since they are universally esteemed and respected. [Class II derivation—authority.] There is no one who does not agree that labour has quite by itself a moral status. . . . Thirdly, one must admit that the desire for wealth becomes immoral when it is carried to the point of inducing us to overstep the bounds of justice. [But who sets those bounds? They are evidently not the same for people who claim that "property" is "theft" and for those who claim that "property" is "legitimate."] . . . That is the judgment passed not by a handful of philosophers but by the universality of men. [People who do not agree with Bastiat are not "men."] On that I rest." How many words just to describe how he feels. He might have done that in the first place without such a long detour.

2147 [7] Bastiat's work as a whole is devoted to that very thing, and that is his purpose especially in his *Economic Harmonies.* Many other writers have also argued the identity of the conclusions of economic science and "morality"—Proudhon, the identity of his economic ideas and "justice." In almost all writers the identity is not between economics and morality as they actually exist in human societies, but between some future economics and some future morality, between economics and morality as they will be when the writer's ideas are adopted or as they will be at the end—a little known quantity, to tell the truth—of an historical evolution. Usually the identity obtained in that manner seems self-evident, for it is assumed implicitly that economics and morality have to be, or are going to be, logical inferences of certain given premises; and it is undeniable that the various logical consequences of the same premises cannot be discordant. The theories of final causes, of the providential organization of society, of social Darwinism, and other theories of the sort, all lead to the same conclusions.

similar to *A*. The consequence therefore will be *B*." But in offering
the hypothetical example, "the consequence of *A* will be *B*," the
proposition that most requires demonstration—that "the real situation is equivalent or similar to *A*"—is suppressed, and the conclusion
is left unstated to avoid calling attention to the suppression (§ 1406).
The example offered by Bastiat is the parable of the plane. He, however, cannot be charged with suppressing the proposition that the
example is a faithful copy of reality. He states as much in un-
equivocal terms.[8] What one can say is that he is mistaken, that
reality is not as he pictures it. Bastiat reduces the parties involved
to two: a man who has a saw and a plane, and another who wants
to make boards. That is too violent a simplification to bear any
resemblance to the real situation. One would come closer to the
truth by considering three men, one of whom uses the boards while
the other two produce them, the one having only his hands to work
with, the other owning the saw and the plane. That slight modification in the hypothesis is enough to change Bastiat's conclusions entirely, even if we accept his method of drawing them. They stand
only as regards a consumer in his relations to the two producers as
a group. They cease to be valid when the producers come to
dividing the fruits of their labour. As a matter of fact the workman
has no use for his boards. It is idle therefore to remind him that if
he had no plane and no saw he could produce hardly one board in
a year's time, whereas as it is he is producing a hundred. The problem to be solved is a different one. The working-man and the
capitalist are producing, and what we want to know is in just what
proportions the product *ought* to be divided. That problem is unsolvable unless the term "ought" is strictly defined, and Bastiat's
apologue gives not the slightest help in that connexion. Those who
think the product *ought* to go to "capital" will regard as unfair
anything that goes to the working-man beyond what is absolutely
necessary to keep him in condition to work: and the logic of that is
slavery. Those who think the produce *ought* to go to "labour" will
regard as unfair anything taken by capital—they will call it "surplus

2147 [8] *Op. cit.*, Vol. V, p. 46: "I claim in the first place that the bag for the
wheat [Another of his examples.] and the plane are types, models, symbols, of all
capital and faithfully represent it, just as the board and the five measures of wheat
are types. models, symbols, faithful representations, of all interest."

value," and the work corresponding to it "surplus labour." Those who think the product *ought* to go not to the individuals who produce it, but to society, which provides them with the environment without which they could never produce, will maintain that the product belongs to society to distribute as society thinks best. Those who think that the product "ought" to be distributed according to certain norms—norms of free competition, for instance—will hold that the working-man and the capitalist should be left to fight out the problem of division between themselves. And so on and on, there being as many solutions as there are meanings attachable to the term "ought." Still others we get if we assume that the term "ought" envisages realization of certain purposes of social utility. One might try to decide what norms of apportionment correspond to a maximum of political and military power for a country, what to a maximum of comforts for a given group of people, and so on and on. None of those solutions can be called intrinsically "true" or intrinsically "false." Only after the exact meaning of that blessed term "ought" has been declared can one ask whether the proposed solution is, or is not, a consequence of the definition.

Still to be solved, after that, are no end of problems as to the manners of determining who is the consumer, who the working-man, who the capitalist, and the consequences of those various manners. There may be inflexibly closed castes of individuals of the statuses in question, or, again, it may be possible to move from one caste to another, and then it still remains to be seen to what extent what is legally possible actually occurs (§ 2046). There is the very important problem of inheritance. Is James's plane to go to his son or not; or is it to go to someone else of James's chosing? [9] It would

2147 [9] It is sometimes thought that the problem is solved from the standpoint of utility on the ground that "the institution of inheritance is beneficial because it encourages individuals to be saving and not squander their fortunes." But even if we accept such an assertion hypothetically, the problem is solved qualitatively and not quantitatively. All other utilities still have to be considered and their resultant found. In practice, moreover, constantly increasing inheritance-taxes run counter to the principle stated. In that connexion some economists try to draw a further distinction, disregarding inheritance-taxes completely and refusing to allow them to enter the discussion. So long as inheritance subsists in name, inheritance-taxes may in the fact take almost everything away and those economists reverently will bow their heads and say nothing. But that brings the whole question down to a mere matter of words. So many are opposed to protective duties on wheat, but make no ob-

be difficult indeed to assert that all these manners are immaterial so far as economic effects are concerned; yet, after all, if someone insists on taking that point of view, he may, provided only the fact be stated explicitly. And unless the idea is to cut off any solution of the problems that arise from facing the economic consequences of the various manners in which circulation takes place among the social classes, those problems have to be frankly faced, and one's attitude regarding them made clear. The difficulties that arise in those connexions are commonly avoided in the manner just described—by separating, that is, the economic problem entirely from other social problems, without going on to explain too clearly what the reciprocal effects of the various solutions would be.

To balance the explicit declarations of Bastiat that we noted above, there are plenty of propositions that are left unstated in his argument. When he has James and William make a contract for the use of the plane, he implicitly assumes that they are free to make the contract, whereas the very question in dispute is whether they should or should not have that freedom. To dissemble the suppression he falls back on "morality"; but on what system of morality? To the system current in societies where freedom of contract in part prevails! And so he gets out of it only what was already there, going round in a circle. But since our society admits freedom of contract only in part, its "morality" also contains premises counter to such freedom, and from them Bastiat's adversaries could, with equal soundness, draw opposite conclusions to the ones he draws.

Speaking in general terms, let A and B stand for two societies where the norms for apportioning product between capital and labour differ. If one considers the problem strictly from the economic standpoint, one implicitly assumes that the difference in apportionment has no effect on the social order and so has no reaction from

jection to so-called revenue taxes, which in their effects amount to the very same thing. The prevalence of such derivations is due to an inclination on the part of many economists not to become involved in political quarrels of too great bitterness. So they reverently accept the fiscal and political policies of the governments that happen to be in power, and ask only that they be let alone to argue about their theories in the abstract. In view of their hostility to *bourgeois* governments, Socialists are usually immune to that particular cause of error. Therefore they scornfully refuse to sever the economic aspects of a situation from its social, political, and fiscal aspects, and so manage to keep closer to realities than the economists. mentioned.

the social order back upon the economic order (§§ 2203 f.). That may be true, but if so, it has to be demonstrated, for it also might not be true; and should it in fact prove not to be true, hosts of problems would have to be solved of which Bastiat's argument takes no account whatever and which therefore it implicitly regards as negligible. Bastiat's derivations are, as is usually the case, essentially qualitative, and disregard composition of residues and derivations (§§ 2087 f.). But with that matter we shall be better able to deal in connexion with the example following.

Example II. Towards the end of the year 1913 at Zabern, in Alsace, a conflict arose between military and civil authorities, and the military acted independently of the latter to maintain order. Just here we are not interested in the substance of the incident, which is a particular case of the general problem of the use of force that we shall come to in due time (§§ 2174 f.); nor are we concerned with the question as to the legality or illegality of the conduct on either side. We are interested exclusively in the derivations to which the incident gave rise.[10] On the whole they had their points of similarity with the derivations provoked by the Dreyfus affair in France (§ 1779), but their effects were very different, because the solid fibre of conservative forces in Germany (§ 2218) prevented any such upheaval in society as the dispersion of those forces permitted in France.[11] In both cases, substantially, people who

2147 [10] It is in point to recall here a remark we made above in § 75. In a work in which derivations are used, it is all very well to leave implicit propositions that are ordinarily left implicit; and so if a writer shows that it is absurd to draw a certain conclusion, *Q,* from the premises *P,* it is justifiable in a great many cases to assume that he considers the conclusion *Q* itself absurd. Not so in a work that pretends to be strictly scientific. In a scientific argument nothing is to be assumed. There is no going beyond the assertion that the argument connecting *P* to *Q* is unsound, since *Q* may stand independently of any such connexion. Take the proposition: "The circumference of a circle cannot be commensurate with its diameter because it has no angles." Now if someone should say that that demonstration is unsound, one would have no right to assume that in so saying he was holding that the circumference is commensurate with its diameter. It is easily possible to offer a demonstration that is false of a theorem that is true.

2147 [11] In the Dreyfus affair, besides, Semitism and anti-Semitism certainly played a considerable rôle, though not so great a rôle as would appear at first glance and as many still believe; for in not a few cases the pro- and anti-Semitism were merely masks for other sentiments and interests. In the Zabern incident Semitism and anti-Semitism did not figure at all—they were absolutely foreign to it; yet all the Dreyfusard newspapers in France came forward with one voice to manifest

wanted political chicanery and revolutionary agitation to prevail over the military power of the government came to a clash with those who did not want that to happen.[12]

Suppose we designate those two conditions, those two states, by *A* and *B* respectively. If a person chooses one of them merely out of faith in certain abstract principles, he deserts the logico-experimental field thereby, and we are excused from concerning ourselves further with him here. To be sure we shall have to attend to him if he comes prancing back to that field with the assertion, for instance, that his solution guarantees some of the various utilities of the individual and society. That is a proposition over which logico-

their hostility to the military authorities in the Zabern incident. That shows that along with such pro-Semite sentiments as some of them may have had regarding Dreyfus, there were other sentiments that they all had and which first impelled them to side with Dreyfus and then afterwards to side against the German military authorities at Zabern. That is all that the Dreyfus affair and the Zabern incident had in common.

Now let us turn to the differences, which chiefly arose from differences in the social and political institutions of France and Germany. They are well stated in the following article in the *Gazette de Lausanne*, Jan. 26, 1914: "When the Zabern incident occurred, liberal papers all over Europe began to predict that Germany was

2147 [12] That is flatly denied oftentimes in the derivations to which the Dreyfus affair continues to give rise: The "Dreyfusards" say that their opponents were inspired solely by a desire to have an innocent man sent to prison. The "anti-Dreyfusards," in their turn, say that the one concern of their opponents was to have a traitor acquitted. Both those positions implicitly assume as solved the very question that is in debate. Some of the anti-Dreyfusards certainly considered Dreyfus a traitor. They might therefore have been accused of holding a mistaken opinion, but not of trying to have an innocent man sent to prison. Conversely, some Dreyfusards certainly thought that Dreyfus was innocent. They might be called mistaken, but they could not be charged with favouring a traitor. But another fact, meantime, is overlooked, and it is much more important from the scientific standpoint: people do not know, or pretend not to know, that among both the Dreyfusards and the anti-Dreyfusards there were individuals who ignored the question as to whether Dreyfus was innocent or guilty. Their reasoning was somewhat as follows: "The Dreyfus case has by this time become a flag leading towards a goal which, if attained, will prove disastrous according to the anti-Dreyfusards, beneficial according to the Dreyfusards, to the country, or even just to our party." To meet such thinking with questions of legality, respect for court decisions, or of some other such principle, is to assume that the many difficult problems stated in §§ 1876 f. have been solved. To consider them solved by mere declamations against the conviction of an "innocent" man is childish, unless one desires to go to an extreme of asceticism and abstain from any defence of one's country on the grounds that war sends thousands upon thousands of "innocent" men to their graves.

experimental science has exclusive jurisdiction, and in order to discuss it one has to solve problems such as those stated in §§ 1897 f. Now those problems are either ignored or solved implicitly [12a] in the derivations. If a person asserts that the acts of the military authorities are to be condemned simply because they are contrary to legality, the "rights" of individuals, Democracy, Progress, he implicitly asserts either that those entities are the only things to be considered, the various utilities being disregarded, or else that conduct in conformity with those entities would coincide with the conduct that would be required by the utilities he is asked to consider. And similarly for those who approve of the acts of the German military

going to have her Dreyfus affair. Those papers did not know their Germany. A Dreyfus affair has long been impossible in Germany, though militarism has been far more powerful and far more aggressive in that country than it was in France in the last years of the past century. The French Chamber of Deputies primed the charge for the Dreyfus explosion in France. Now even if the Reichstag were disposed to do so, it would not have the power to arouse any such agitation for the review of the Strasbourg verdicts as proved so completely successful in France. For that matter, the majority in the Reichstag already seems to be tiring of its attitude of opposition. The National Liberals and the Centrists are asking for nothing better than a chance to step over to the majority side. Tomorrow it will be all over. On the disorderly rout of the *bourgeois* parties, *Vorwärts* very soundly observed last Saturday that 'Force and struggle are two words that are not to be found in the dictionary of the German middle classes.' Those classes are the most docile of all classes. Respectful, timid, they like nothing better than to be led blindfold by those wielders of force whom William II has called 'the backbone of the nation.' Like the wife of Sganarelle, the *bourgeoisie* across the Rhine sees nothing but caresses in the acts of violence that are inflicted upon it by the powers above. One has to have the disastrous capacity for self-deception of a Jaurès, or the appetite for dreams of the editor of *Humanité,* an internationalist who is blind on all international questions, to believe that the Reichstag has any mission in Germany or any influence on German destinies. To hail the incident that has just taken place in Germany as a guarantee of peace between that country and France is to coddle a dangerous error. A number of French Socialists who are still imbued with the revolutionary spirit of '48 are nourishing that illusion. It may prove fatal not only to France but to all Europe." On the other hand a good (Swiss) Dreyfusard wrote from Paris to his paper: "Naturally people here are following political events in Germany with the keenest interest. There is general delight that an immense majority in Germany is rising against a brutal militarism. Some perhaps may be exaggerating the happy consequences as regards Franco-German relations that may result from this conflict between what the *Temps* calls 'the two Germanies.' " They were more than an exaggeration of the influence of the "immense majority of German opinion"! That influence amounted to plus or minus zero!

2147 [12a] [Pareto said "explicitly," a slip for "implicitly."—A. L..]

authorities at Zabern simply because those acts happen to accord with certain principles of theirs.[13] To all that the derivations make not the slightest reference, the solutions of the problems being either entirely disregarded or else implicitly assumed. To give a form somewhat more concrete to these reflections, suppose we consider just one of the utilities involved, the military strength of a country, and consider the two conditions that at the present time might be called Germanic and Latin respectively, though if we were talking of the times of the battle of Jena, terms would have to be inverted (§ 2474). In the Latin condition, it is agreed that the military authority must be humble servant to the civil authority; in the Germanic condition, that the military authority is the superior. In France the prefect has precedence over the general; in Prussia not only the general, but any army officer, has precedence over all civil authorities.[14] In the Latin condition, the feeling is that if revolutionary or merely mob force comes into conflict with the military power of the government, the mob has all the rights and the military all the duties, and the duty in particular of submitting to everything before resorting to arms. Obscenities, fisticuffs, stones—everything is excusable if it comes from the mob; but retaliation is absolutely forbidden to the armed forces of government. There is always an excuse for "the People." The mere presence of soldiers

2147 [13] Bismarck well derides the use of such entities as "rights," "democracy," "Progress," in statesmanship. Busch, *Tagebuchblätter,* Vol. III, p. 231 (English, Vol. II, p. 417), Apr. 7, 1888: " 'In 1877 when the Russo-Turkish war was in the offing, England kept urging us to use our influence at St. Petersburg to prevent it, "in the interests of humanity," as the *Times* demonstrated. Queen Victoria urged us to do so in a letter to the Emperor, which was delivered to him through Augusta, who added her own intercession, and in two others to myself [Bismarck]. "Humanity," "Peace," "Liberty"! Those are always their pretexts when they cannot by way of a change use Christianity and the extension of the blessings of civilization to savage and semi-barbarous peoples. [French version erroneous.—A. L.] [By believing in those big words, Napoleon III, Ollivier, Favre, Simon, among others, ruined their country. By taking no stock in them Bismarck made his country great and strong.] In reality, however, the *Times* and the Queen wrote in the interests of England, which had nothing in common with our interests. It is in the interest of England that the German Empire should be on bad terms with Russia.' "

2147 [14] Busch, *Ibid.,* Vol. I, p. 127 (English, Vol. I, p. 96), Aug. 30, 1870: "[Bismarck] cautioned me later on that when officers saluted us as we drove past, I [Busch] should be careful not to return their salute. 'They salute me,' he said, 'not as Chancellor or minister, but as a general officer. Soldiers might be offended if a civilian seemed to think their salute was also intended for him.' "

gets on its nerves, and that justifies it in surrendering to any impulse. The police, however, must be possessed of inexhaustible patience. Smitten on one cheek they turn the other. Soldiers are expected to be so many saints, so many ascetics—indeed no one can understand why they were ever given rifles and bayonets instead of rosaries and prayer-books of the religion of Progress.[15] The Germanic condition is just the reverse. The military power demands absolute respect from everybody. People whose nerves are affected by the mere glimpse of a soldier had better stay indoors—otherwise they will learn to their sorrow that, as Bebel used to say to his followers, "bullets hit and swords cut." Retaliation for insult and assault is not only permitted the public forces, it is required of them. An army officer is disgraced if he allows his cheek to be grazed by the slightest blow without striking back. The patience has to be exercised by those who are insulting the public power; when the latter is striking back, its one concern is to enforce respect on the part of its enemies. The rosaries and prayer-books of the religion of Progress are absolutely unknown to the Prussian, and even to the German, army. Officers and soldiers know that if they carry arms it is to use them whenever necessary and in order to command respect. Absolutely inconceivable in Germany would be anything similar to what occurred in France when the Minister of Marine, M. Pelletan, visited an arsenal, riding in a carriage with an admiral, while arsenal employees shouted after them at the top of their voices: ". . . And our bullets are to be for the admirals!" The Germans may be wrong, but they do not admit it.

Now are national defence and military power equally well guaranteed by both of the conditions mentioned? And if not, which of

2147 [15] That fact transpires in the derivations that turn up on the floors of the Latin parliaments every time a conflict occurs between the police and strikers or rioters (§ 2147 [18]); and it is the characteristic manner of people who would do the act but not say the word. The Syndicalists, instead, make word and deed consistent and so come much closer to realities. They say that they intend to use force because they are at war with the *bourgeoisie*. Now that use of force can be met only with the use of force in the counter-direction, not with the fatuous and inconclusive reasonings of our "speculators," who are tireless in their efforts to lure the Syndicalists from the field where force is used, and where they know, or fear, they will not prove the equals of their adversaries, into the field where chicanery and intrigue are the main reliance, and where they are certain that they can have no competitors.

the two conditions is the more favourable to them? Those problems are not among the outstanding ones in the derivations used to defend the Latin condition. They hold first place, instead, but are solved *a priori* in the derivations used to justify the Germanic condition.[16] The difference probably is to be explained by the fact that one readily gets the impression that the Germanic condition is favourable to the military power of a country, while it is not so easy to get

2147 [16] Following on the Zabern incident and the debates relative to it in the Reichstag, a society was founded in Berlin for the defence of the Prussian system. *Journal de Genève,* Jan. 21, 1914: "Berlin, Jan. 19: The new Prussian League (*Preussenbund*) held its first convention yesterday in Berlin. The purpose of the association is to maintain and strengthen the hegemony of Prussia in the Empire, and especially the preponderance in Germany of Prussian aspirations, Prussian methods, Prussian manners of thinking. Its tendencies are essentially conservative, its policy, reaction against the gradual democratization of the Empire. The Zabern affair had, among other indirect consequences, the effect of aligning Prussia against the Empire. The Prussian League is the outcome of the conflict. Its membership is recruited from among high officials, army officers, conservative Deputies, and the League of Landowners. During these last weeks many symptoms have indicated that the organization of the Prussian League is viewed with satisfaction in higher circles. 'The speeches delivered at the convention yesterday deserve,' says the *Temps,* 'most attentive inspection. They are altogether characteristic of a certain state of mind that prevails at this moment in the higher reaches of power.' Herr Rocke, president of the Chamber of Commerce at Hanover, delivered the opening address. 'Prussia,' said he, 'is the bulwark of the Empire. The Empire must not develop at the expense of Prussia.' The second speaker was Herr von Heydebrandt, who said in part: 'Many people are wondering whether the moment has not come to defend Prussia, the Prussian spirit, the Prussian form of living, in Germany. What are the characteristic traits of the Prussian? They are a sense of orderliness, a sense of duty, love for the army, fidelity to the dynasty. It would be a catastrophe with no morrow if that Prussian spirit were to lose control of the country.' General von Wrochen delivered a eulogy of Colonel Reuter. 'The Colonel's conduct was cheering to all of us. He deported himself like a Prussian of the old stock. We shall have such men as long as the army continues to be monarchical. The verdict of January 10 was a well-deserved box on the ears for those who had talked too loudly.' General von Rogge followed him on the platform. He deplored democratic tendencies within the Empire. 'The mission of Prussia,' he said, 'has not ended. German blood still requires a strong injection of Prussian iron.' An inspector of churches, Herr von Rodenbeck, declared that the mission of Prussia as guardian of Germany had been willed by Providence. He then launched a rebuke against the peoples of the Rhineland whose 'wine-drinking had gone too much to their heads.' Before adjourning, the convention unanimously adopted the following resolution: 'It is the sense of the first convention of the Prussian League that certain tendencies of our time in the direction of an increasing democratization of our institutions are weakening the foundations of the monarchy. Prussia can fulfil her mission in Germany only if she is strong and free from all encumbrances that might result from too close a union with the Empire. All assaults of democracy on Prussia and on the inde-

that impression of the Latin condition. In spite of the different impressions one could not, strictly speaking, assert *a priori* that the Latin condition is not as favourable to the military power of a country as the Germanic condition, or even more so. But before such an assertion could be accepted, at least some suggestion of a proof would be required, and no trace of any such proof is to be found in the derivations justifying the Latin condition.[17] And that

pendence of the confederate states must be energetically repelled. It is imperatively necessary therefore that all those who are resolved to defend Prussia from the attacks of democracy should unite and labour with one accord.' "

2147 [17] On Dec. 4, 1913, after a debate on the Zabern incident the Reichstag passed by a vote of 293 to 5 a resolution censuring the Chancellor of the Empire. The Chancellor did not see things that way. He remained at his post, and army organization did not experience the remotest effects from the incident. On December 2, the French Chamber defeated by a vote of 290 to 265 the Delpierre Bill, a government measure designed to provide tax immunity for government securities about to be issued, and the ministry fell. The real cause of its defeat was its insistence on strengthening the army and its having forced the passage of the Three Years' Service Bill. That is why it occurred to Deputy Vaillant, a prominent anti-militarist, to shout when the result of the vote on the Delpierre Bill was announced: *"A bas les trois ans!"* The *Gazette de Lausanne,* Dec. 3, 1913, summarizes French editorial opinion on the incident as follows: "The *Petite République* writes: 'In saluting the fall of the ministry with the cry "Down with the Three Years!" Deputy Vaillant emphasized the real significance of the vote in a way that will prove very humiliating to not a few individuals.' The *Éclair* suspects that part of the Deputies saw fit to get their revenge for the Three Years' Law by refusing to appropriate money absolutely required if the effort to build up the army again is to be a success. The *Matin* says that the adversaries of M. Barthou will be fair enough to him to recognize that on the question of French prestige he fell with honour. The paper foresees that the new cabinet will be a ministry of union and cooperation among Republicans. The *Gaulois* interprets M. Caillaux's victory as the Bloc's revenge for the Congress of Versailles. Next in order, perhaps, will be his revenge on the man elected at that Congress. The *République française* rebukes the cry of 'Down with the Three Years!' 'But,' it goes on to say, 'it is altogether logical that the men who did not quaver about exposing France to ruin should go on and disarm her in the face of invasion.' *Action* wonders how long the coalition will last between revolutionary demagoguery and that Radical plutocracy which has just overthrown M. Barthou with cries of 'Down with the Three Years.' The *Écho de Paris* says that the Radicals 'have committed an unpardonable sin not only against the public credit by marching hand in hand with the Unified Socialists, but also against the power of the nation. If it is true that a new majority is to be organized, it will be organized against France.' The *Journal* notes that the adversaries of the Three Years' Law chanced to find themselves united against the election-reform bill and tax-exemption for the new securities. The *Libre parole* believes that dividing the spoils is the only concern of yesterday's majority. The leaders will be offered posts in the government. Some will get a sop in the election-reform bill, others in the Three Years' Law. The *Homme libre* writes: 'Every mistake is

fact clearly shows how readily derivations can dispense with logic: the same Frenchmen who pitied the peoples of Alsace and Lorraine because of their conquest by Germany do all they can to destroy the military power of their country, which amounts to preparing the way for further German conquests. They bewail an evil and do their best to make it greater. The logical fallacy in the derivations would be corrected if they asserted implicitly or otherwise that they envisage not a present but some future advantage and, further, that a conquest may be a temporary evil and a future blessing. Examples are available in the history of Roman conquests—such a thing is therefore not impossible. What is required is proof that a conquest by Germany is going to be a blessing this time. Other utilities might also be envisaged, the utilities of certain groups, for instance. It is clear enough that the Latin condition is favourable to groups that are disposed to resist the law or the authority of the government: all they seem to need in order to enforce their will is the courage to get out into the streets and fight. The Germanic condition is favourable to orderliness and respect for law, and also to arbitrary conduct and even crimes on the part of individuals in power. There too derivations figure. On the side of those who would overthrow the present social régime, conduct in that sense is regarded as inevitably "good," and that belief is justified by the myths of St. Democracy, just as, if rôles were inverted and the revolutionaries were aristocrats or monarchists, they would justify their beliefs with the myths of Sts. Aristocracy and Monarchy. On the side of those who wish to maintain the present system and are reaping benefits from it, fewer derivations are used, because people who are in the saddle do not need derivations to spur their retainers to action, and resort to them only when it seems advisable to justify their conduct, or in order to weaken opposition on the part of people who bite at such bait. In this case, as usual, their derivations aim at showing that the maintenance of law and order, which is aptly identified with the arbitrary will of the rulers, is a "highest good" for which everything else must

paid for in the end. A long series of political blunders has caused financial difficulties that can be surmounted only if all Republicans return to discipline and self-sacrifice.' " As a result the direction of the French army and navy again fell to ministers who were more concerned with satisfying cliques and political followings than with preparations for national defence.

be sacrificed. Or else the resort is to the principle that the end justifies the means—and for a person in the saddle what better end can there be than staying there and enjoying the fruits of such eminence? [18] If then, as in cases such as the Zabern incident, a conflict arises between different nationalities, no citizen of the dominant nation would dare doubt that the maintenance of its dominion is the supreme good. In that respect the nationalist faith is very like the Moslem, the Christian, the Democratic, and all the other faiths there are. And myths in enormous numbers are manufactured, all of which make it as clear as the noonday Sun that the dominant nation is deserving of its dominion, while the subject nation deserves nothing but oppression. From the time when ancient Rome proclaimed the legitimacy of her dominion over

2147 [18] Another type of derivation is very very widely used. The purpose of each of the contending parties is to look to its own convenience, its own interest, even in the face of accepted norms that there is a pretence of respecting. The comedy is played as follows: From the standpoint of the "outs": *Act I. While the conflict between themselves and public authority is raging.* Government forces must not use their weapons. Give "the People" (the strikers, the revolutionaries) a free hand. If—just to imagine the case—a crime is committed, there are courts to punish it. The job of the government is to bring citizens before the courts. Farther than that it must not go. Such crimes, or most of them at any rate, are certainly not capital offences; yet the penalty of death would actually be inflicted on anyone struck down by the fire of the police. It is not fair to use guns on people who are merely throwing paving-stones. (In Italy *carabinieri,* on being forbidden to use their arms, have been known to pick up the stones that were thrown at them and throw them back.) The police power, in a word, can offer only a patient and passive resistance. Such derivations soothe the feelings of the people who would not be satisfied if strikers or other insurgents who rob, maim, and sometimes kill were to go entirely unpunished. *Act II. After the battle.* Bygones are bygones. What is needed is an amnesty (release on bail or probation is not enough) to erase all memory of civil discord and stifle animosities in the name of love of country. The public memory is not long. It has soon forgotten the crimes of yesterday. The dead are dead, and the living—have to live: they want quiet, and still more, money, without worrying very much about the past or the future. They are therefore satisfied with such derivations, which suit their requirements perfectly. *Act III. The consequences.* The crimes mentioned have not been prevented or punished by force, for the punishment was to be attended to by the courts. The courts cannot attend to it because of the amnesty. As a result delinquencies in the past are left unpunished, and the prospect is that they will not be punished in the future. And that was the very thing that the derivations in question were designed to accomplish all along.

From the standpoint of the ruling class: *Act I. While efforts are being made to impose something by force.* This is not the moment to decide whether such a measure is legal or illegal, just or unjust. Let the citizen obey, and then if he

conquered peoples down to our own day, when so-called civilized nations "demonstrate" that it is legitimate, just, proper, necessary— and Christians add, ordained of God—that they should rule, exploit, oppress, and destroy the nations they call uncivilized, derivations of the sort mentioned have been evolved in fabulous numbers, all of them repeating virtually the same things in different words.

Both the defenders of the Latin condition and the defenders of the Germanic condition entirely disregard the quantitative problem (§§ 2174 f.). The forces and ties that determine the state A are possible, just as the forces and ties that determine the state B are possible, since both states are observable in reality. But are the forces and ties that would determine an intermediate state, C, also possible? If they are not, to find out where the maximum of utility lies, it is sufficient to compare A and B.[19] If they are, then to determine that maximum A, C, B have to be compared. That leads, in the special case we are here examining, to asking to just what extent, in order to realize specified purposes, it is advisable to give consideration and power to the army as against the civil authority. And if that inquiry

thinks he has been wronged he can appeal to the courts. This derivation and others like it quiet the alarm of people who would assent with reluctance to arbitrary acts and injustices at the expense of private citizens. There can be nothing arbitrary or unjust, for after all the courts are there to pass judgment on anything that happens. *Act II. After the fact.* If some simple-minded soul follows the advice that has been given him and turns to the courts, he is told that they have no jurisdiction and that he should go to the governmental authorities, who are sole judges of the conduct of their agents. If his simple-mindedness goes so far as to allow him to do that, he learns, at his own expense, that wolf does not eat wolf and that that is that. Such conduct is justified because the public peace, the majesty of the State, the reign of law, have to be safe-guarded. The public interest has to prevail by hook or by crook over private interests. These derivations are accepted on sentiment by people who believe that public authority must not be embarrassed by the whims of individual citizens and who realize how essential it is to the public welfare that order be maintained. *Act III. The consequences.* The governing class has acted arbitrarily and illegally and come off scot-free, and it will be able to do so again whenever it chooses. And that was the thing the derivations were designed to accomplish.

It should be remembered, however, that neither in this case nor in the other are the derivations the main cause of what happens. They are for the most part mere veilings that mask the forces which actually produce the phenomena.

2147 [19] A person holding that view might reason as follows: "If the Chancellor had fallen from power as a result of the Reichstag's vote of censure, Germany would have taken the course that *inevitably* (or just *very probably*) leads to having a minister such as Lloyd George in England, and, what is worse, to handing the

is prosecuted, results will begin appearing which at first sight will seem paradoxical—that the Latin condition, which is defended by lovers of democracy, might in the last analysis be disastrous to democracy either by inviting foreign conquest or by leading democracy towards anarchy, which has been the tomb of so many democratic systems in the past; and likewise that the Germanic condition, which is defended by the monarchists, might in the last analysis be disastrous to monarchy. An intermediate state, C, might perhaps better than A or B assure the attainment of the purposes aimed at by defenders of the two extremes. If one would treat the question scientifically, one would have to consider some at least of these and other similar problems; and the more of them one considers, the better, from the logico-experimental standpoint, one's reasoning will be. On the other hand, if one's aim is to persuade people and spur them to action, one must refrain from inquiries of that sort, not only because they cannot be grasped by the public at large, but also because, as we have said so many times, they incline one in the direction of scientific scepticism that is incompatible with the vigorous and resolute action of the believer; and the fewer the scientific problems one considers and the greater the skill with which one evades and conceals them, the better one's talk will be as regards the effectiveness of its derivations.

2148. *Composition of utilities, residues, and derivations.* To determine the complex utilities that result from the composition of residues and derivations, we shall follow out the argument we began in § 2087, where we considered the influence of residues and

army and navy over to ministers like André and Pelletan in France, who would make a shambles of their organization, and as a result Germany would be exposed to defeat and destruction in a war with her enemies. To such a tremendous misfortune we prefer the relatively slight evil of allowing a few acts of insolence on the part of the military to go unpunished. We do not care to take a course that leads over the precipice: *principiis obstat.*"

The weak point in this argument can lie only in the terms "inevitably" and "very probably." In other words, those who would refute it must show with convincing evidence that the analogy between a possible movement in Germany and the movements actually observable in England and France does not hold, and that once on the road to an omnipotent Reichstag, Germany would not go on to the Latin condition, but would stop at some point intermediate between the Latin condition and the prevailing Germanic condition. But to meet such an argument with the abstract principles of some faith or other is as fatuous, from the scientific standpoint, as going to consult the oracle at Delphi.

derivations taken as a whole. The subject is not an easy one, and no help is to be refused, even if it be lent by imperfect analogies. Let us therefore, as we have so often done before, appeal to a visual graph (§ 1869), not to prove anything, of course, for that would be a grave mistake, but just to make an argument that is quite abstract more intelligible. To have the advantage of a graph in three dimensions, let us assume that the state of an individual is such that it can be represented by a point h on a surface of which the ordinate on a

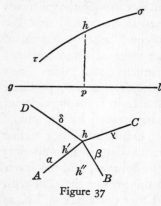

Figure 37

horizontal plane represents the index of the ophelimity that the individual enjoys. In horizontal projection the state of the individual is represented, therefore, by the point h. If we draw a vertical section passing through the point h, we get the straight line, gl, which is the section of the horizontal plane of projection; then the curve, $\tau\sigma$, which is the arc of the surface, and the ordinate ph, which is the index of the utility enjoyed by the individual (§ 1869). The point h is impinged by forces (*i.e.*, residues) moving in the directions A, B . . . with intensities α, β . . . as explained in § 2087, and must always hold a position on the surface that we have premised and which is determined by ties.

2149. Now let us forget the ophelimity of the individual, and think of the *utility* of a community, and assume that Figure 37 is valid for the community too. Suppose the point h is located in the position of the maximum utility of the community. It may be that somewhere on the straight line hA there is a point, h', at which the utility of the community would be greater than it is at h; and so the idea naturally enough arises that it would be a good thing to intensify α in order to get the community to the point h'. That is the ordinary manner of reasoning in social matters.

2150. But if equilibrium were possible at h', the hypothesis that h is a point of maximum utility of the community would no longer stand. According to that hypothesis no equilibrium is possible at any point in the vicinity of h where the utility of the community would be greater. It is therefore not possible at h'. To augment the pressure α therefore would not transfer the point of equilibrium to h', but to some point such as h'', where the collective utility is not so great. That is the case because the intensification of α occasions modifications in β, γ. . . . And in that we have a case of interdependence of residues, second type (§ 2088).

2151. The argument we have just outlined in no way depends on the hypotheses we posited in order to picture the position of the

point h in a three-dimensional space, nor indeed upon any other graphic representation of the kind. It may therefore be restated in abstract terms, and the conclusion will be valid for the general case of utility dependent on residues.

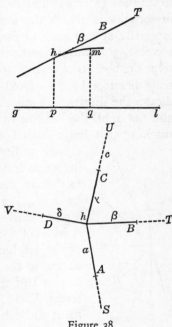

Figure 38

2152. Let us now consider derivations as well and continue in general the argument we developed for a particular case in § 1896. We again use Figure 37 (§ 2148), but adding to it the derivations S, T, U, V . . . or, if you will, the myths, the ideals, that prompt human beings to conduct in the directions A, B, C . . . under pressure of the forces α, β, γ . . . . The vertical section is now cut along hBT. The pressure β moving along hB arises in the aspiration of people towards the imaginary ideal, T, and if it were acting all by itself, it would carry the individual to the point m. But if equilibrium is attained at the point h, the effect of the force β is offset or nullified by the effects of other forces. That is the case whether h is a point of maximum utility or any point at all, provided it be a point of equilibrium.

2153. We may now repeat what we said above in § 2088, adding the consideration of utility. 1. If there is reason to believe that B operating by itself would increase utility, it in no sense follows that operating in opposition to other residues and subject to ties, its effect would still be an enhanced utility.[1] 2. The variation in utility depends on the effects of the resultant of forces manifested by the residues, not upon the imaginary resultant—if such there be—of the derivations. The real resultant is quite different: it indicates the direction in which individuals in the society where the derivations prevail are moving, and a course in that direction may lead much closer to reality than the derivation taken by itself would lead one to suppose (§ 1772); and so for the utility. That is in fact the case in societies in which the activities of individuals are aimed more especially at real than at fantastic goals, and prosperity is on the increase. 3. Quite insignificant is the fact that the derivation oversteps the bounds of reality, and points to a goal that is fantastic and may therefore be considered dangerous. The derivation merely indicates the direction in which the movement is tending to develop, and not at all the limit to which the individual will be carried. On reaching that limit, indeed, the movement may prove to have increased utility, whereas the utility might lessen and become a frank detriment if the individual went any farther in the direction in which the derivation is headed. 4. Let A, B . . . represent certain residues of a given class—Class I, let us say; P, Q, R . . . other residues of another class, say Class II; X, the resultant of the residues A, B, C . . . of Class I; Y, the resultant of the residues P, Q, R . . . of Class II, and so on; and finally Ω the total resultant of all the forces X, Y . . . which determines the real movement and consequently the utility. If we do not get the utility—or the detriment—that would result from considering the residues A alone, that is not because A is not doing its work, much less because a derivation corresponding to A has been effectively refuted, but because of the counter-actions of B, C

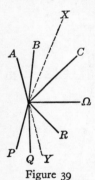

Figure 39

2153 [1] [All the evils of alcoholism could be corrected by absolute prohibition (B), but prohibition has to operate subject to ties—among them, the desire of many people to drink, the fact that other people can make money by selling them drinks, the fact that public officials can make money by selling the right to sell drinks. Prohibition, therefore, does not correct all the evils of alcoholism, but produces new evils, bootlegging, graft. The application therefore of the principle that may be logically sound may produce, in view of the ties, not an enhanced but a diminished utility.—A. L.]

. . . P, Q. . . . Furthermore, in virtue of the fact that the whole of a class A, B . . . has the peculiarity of remaining virtually constant, A may diminish very considerably, or even disappear, without any great variation in X, and consequently without any great variation in the resultant Ω and in the utility which that resultant entails. Variations in Ω and the corresponding utility are much more readily appraised by watching variations in X, Y . . . than variations in any one of the residues A, B . . . P, Q. . . .

2154. Likewise applicable to the matter of utility is what we said in § 2086 of the varying derivations T, T', T'' . . . corresponding to one same residue, B. 1. Since it is the residues, chiefly, that affect the equilibrium, the presence of one of the various derivations T, T', T'' . . . throws little or no light on the question of utility. 2. To replace T with T' can amount to little or nothing as regards modifying the utility. 3. But the fact that the person who is performing the conduct considers the derivation, T, which he accepts, as very beneficial and other derivations very harmful (or, in more exact terms, the sentiments he manifests in that way) may be of the greatest utility. Indeed, apart from a few ascetics, human beings are most reluctant to distinguish utility from what they consider "good"; so if they really regard the derivation T as "good," they will also consider it "beneficial," and if that should not happen to be the case, it would be a sign that they have no great faith in the derivation. Anything fantastic, impractical, or harmful in the belief will then be corrected by other beliefs that are also prevalent in the society that happens to be involved (§§ 1772, 2153).[1] 4. If, intrin-

2154 [1] Physicians are inclined to think of society as a flock of sheep of which they are the well-paid and devoutly esteemed shepherds. Reasoned opposition to such oppression and exploitation often comes to naught because people are frightened by the fairy-tales of the medical fraternity, just as Molière's imaginary invalid trembled in his boots at the threats of Dr. Cathartic. Sometimes, on the other hand, their prattle may be effectively met with other prattle of the same variety, such as "Christian Science," or "Natural Medicine." In the year 1913, in order to reduce recalcitrant Swiss cantons to obedience, the doctors and their allies proposed an amendment to the federal constitution that would have authorized the federal government to dictate legislation affecting large numbers of diseases, certain non-contagious diseases included. When the measure was put to popular vote, the only effective opposition, virtually, came from the devotees of "Natural Medicine." *Journal de Genève*, May 8, 1913: "As was the case in the eastern cantons, the constitutional amendment on 'federal diseases,' so called, has encountered a silent but determined opposition. Two or three districts in the Canton of Zurich have rejected

sically, from the logico-experimental standpoint, one derivation seems better calculated than others to augment utility, one cannot infer on that account that it would actually do so in practice. It might even prove that the derivation which seems more beneficial intrinsically corresponds to sentiments that are less beneficial than those expressed by derivations that seem less beneficial intrinsically. All the propositions just stated are at variance with common opinion, but observation of reality shows that they accord with the facts.

2155. From what we have been showing it also follows that the problem of utility is quantitative and not qualitative, as is commonly believed. One must determine in what proportions the consequences of a given derivation, S (Figure 38), or of the principle that it propounds, may when combined with the consequences of other derivations, $T, U, V \ldots$ prove beneficial to society; and not, as is commonly done, try to decide whether S is in itself beneficial or detrimental to society, a problem that can have no meaning. Derivations fail as a rule to take any account of these quantitative considerations, for the reason, as we have so many times said, that they are inclined to envisage absolutes (§ 1772); and when a derivation proclaims some principle or other, almost always implicit in it is the assumption that the principle is to be striven for in an absolute manner, without reservations as to degree or anything else.

It will probably help if we supplement these abstract considerations with illustrations of a more concrete nature, and clarify the general propositions with examples of particular cases. Suppose we begin with an interesting case in which contemplations of ideal ends, T, and real ends, m, are thrown together without such ends being at all clearly distinguished; and then go on to look at a number of cases of compound utilities.

it. The reason is that in those parts of our country there are large numbers of people who approve of 'natural' therapeutic methods, take no stock in official medical science, and are in fact afraid of its encroachments. They are worried lest the proposed amendment open the door to compulsory measures to which they are unalterably opposed, obligatory vaccination, for instance." Opponents of vaccination against smallpox are probably wrong; but when champions of vaccination in Italy go so far as to haul into court a scientist who has voiced an honest scientific opinion on the subject, one is forced to conclude that in resisting the "establishment" of an official science through the penal code, anti-vaccinationists are performing a useful social function.

2156. *History.* We have seen (§ 1580) that the compositions which go under the name of "history" are as a rule compounds of factual observations of one kind or another supplemented by derivations and ethical considerations, without any distinctions being drawn between ideals and myths, T, and real facts, m (Figure 29). In general one may say that history has so far been a history of derivations rather than of residues, a history of concepts, T, rather than of the forces of which those concepts are but manifestations.

2157. That is all well enough, when "history" is more or less a composition designed to influence the sentiments of human beings (§ 1580), when preaching is more or less interwoven with experimental observation; but it is not only not beneficial, it is positively harmful, when the purpose of history is to describe real facts and the relations between them.

2158. If ideas, ideals, myths, are the only things considered and they are taken intrinsically and for their own sakes, we get systems of ethics, metaphysics, and theology. If real facts are alone considered, and ideas, ideals, myths, are taken extrinsically only, as objective facts, we get researches in experimental science or, to give them a name, *scientific history* (§§ 1580, 2576).

2159. The compositions that best serve for purposes of persuasion, for arousing sentiments and urging people along a given line of conduct, are combinations of the categories above; because the human mind requires the ideal and the real in varying dosage. The proportions vary at given times and in given localities according to individuals; and taking the average of individuals in different times and localities, they vary according to a certain rhythm, as is the case with virtually all social phenomena.

2160. In our Western countries in our times, theological histories have fallen into desuetude, but metaphysical and ethical histories continue to enjoy a wide-spread vogue that gives no indication of subsiding.[1] Sometimes the ethical or metaphysical outlook is ex-

2160 [1] Fustel de Coulanges, *Questions historiques,* p. 8. "If you look for the principle that gives that unity and that life to German scholarship, you will notice that it is love for Germany. We claim here in France that science knows no country. [That is too high a tribute to France.] The Germans frankly hold the opposite view. 'It is a false doctrine,' says Herr Giesebrecht [Making the usual abuse of the terms "false" and "true," nobody knowing just what they mean.], 'that science knows no country, that it overleaps frontiers. Science ought not to be cosmopolitan.

pressly declared by writers; but that is a rare occurrence in our day. More often they fail to distinguish the various elements that go to make up their "history" (§ 1582), relying on the ambiguity of the term "historical truth" (§ 1578) to spread a veil over the mixture. They rarely state categorically their conviction that derivations determine the forms of society, allowing that fact to be tacitly inferred from the proposition, which they deem axiomatic, that the conduct of human beings is a consequence of their beliefs.

2161. How do such writings compare with logico-experimental science? If a writer ascribes a supernatural origin to religion he is at least respecting formal logic in regarding religion as the prime cause of social phenomena. But if he ascribes an earthly origin to religion, he must, even to keep to the field of merely formal logic, explain how and why religion is a cause and not an effect. When adversaries of religion lay the responsibility for the fall of the Roman Empire upon Christianity, they still have to explain why the spread of Christianity was the cause and not the effect of that dissolution and also why the two phenomena cannot be taken as merely simultaneous. If a person asserts that moral concepts are engraved on the human mind by the hand of God, he may take them outright as the prime cause of social phenomena, and he is,

[The usual abuse of the term "ought"—what does it mean? And what if someone were to snap his fingers at the "duty" laid upon him by the never-sufficiently-praised Lord Almighty Giesebrecht?] It ought to be national! It ought to be German! Germans all worship their country, and they take the word "country" in its true meaning [Twenty-one guns for our old friend True!] as the fatherland, the land of our forefathers, the *terra patrum,* our country such as our ancestors knew it and made it. They never speak of it save as a sacred thing.' " Not otherwise did the Athenians speak of the Sun and wroth were they at the impiety of Anaxagoras who said that it was just a red-hot stone. P. 9: "Scholarship in France is liberal. In Germany it is patriotic." Liberal scholarships and patriotic scholarships may both be beneficial or harmful to a country, but they are both different from the scholarship that aims to be strictly experimental. Fustel de Coulanges was writing under the impression of the War of 1870, p. 16: "But we are living today in wartime. It is almost impossible for science to preserve its old serenity. [Fortunately for scientific history, Fustel de Coulanges possessed just that sereneness in many of his writings, which, for that reason, come very close to experimental history; and despite the emotions that were stirring within him, he had the strength of character to write:] In spite of the Germans, we continue to claim that scholarship knows no country." To be strictly exact, however, he should have said "scientific scholarship," to emphasize the difference between the experimental attitude and the scholarship that aims at some social utility.

furthermore, under no obligation to inquire whether, when, and to what extent it is better for human beings to conform to them. They are obeying ordinances of God and that is the whole story: they need consider nothing else. But if a person ventures from that fortress, which is impregnable to formal logic, he must—as in the preceding case, if he would take morality as the cause of social phenomena—first explain why morality is a cause and not an effect or something merely simultaneous, and then go on to state just what solution he intends to give to the question raised in § 1897—state, that is, just what relationship, in his opinion, obtains between observance of certain moral or other norms and social utility. No such declaration is required of a person who is examining cases of conscience, or of persons examining social phenomena strictly, without making them in any way dependent on cases of conscience. But if the two things are mixed in together, the relationship between them has to be declared, the bridge specified that is to be built in order to get from one to the other.

2162. Historians commonly abstain from giving any such explanation because they are in no hurry to undertake the difficult, not to say impossible, task of justifying the solution that they accept. They rest content with the implicit assumption that observance of the norms of morality always leads to social benefit (affirmative solutions, §§ 1903-98); and they win general assent because that proposition is true, on the whole, as regards the conduct of private individuals and because, owing to group-persistences, it can be plausibly extended to public affairs. So to distinguish the various elements in the social complex and tacitly to assume solutions for the elements not considered has the great advantage of making it easier for a writer to study the element with which he is dealing, since he may take it all by itself. Furthermore, it makes his conclusions more readily acceptable to the public, in that they take for granted certain solutions that are very generally accepted. For that reason that method is followed not only by historians but by economists (§ 2147) and other investigators of social phenomena as well. From the logico-experimental standpoint the first part of the procedure, the separation of the various elements in the social complex, is permissible, is indeed indispensable, for without such a simplification no inquiry would be possible. Science, as we have so many times repeated, is essentially analytical. But the second part—the assumption for elements not considered of implicit solutions that nearly always accord with public sentiments—belongs to the field of derivations, and takes one completely outside the logico-experimental field, where unstated propositions dictated by sentiment have no place and where only facts and inferences from facts can properly stand. Logico-experimental science, accordingly, altogether rejects those implicit solutions based on sentiment of which derivations make, and have to make, lavish use, and replaces them with explicit solutions obtained by considering facts and nothing else.

It is also a common practice of historians to expatiate on ethical and legal judgments of the conduct of public individuals, usually without declaring just what ethical norms and laws underlie their verdicts. In that too premises are left implicit and are likewise accepted because, in virtue of group-persistence, they overreach the domain where the norms and laws that regulate the relationships between individuals apply. To do that is, on a very much smaller scale, something like extending juridical norms that are established for human beings to animals. It has been long debated whether Caesar had or did not have the "right" to cross the Rubicon. For the study of history and social phenomena, to solve such a problem today is about as significant as solving the celebrated query that used to be posed in the Middle Ages: *Utrum chimaera bombinans in vacuo possit comedere secundas intentiones*—though it might be a useful exercise in the abstract study of Roman public law.

2163. With many historians it is an article of faith that Napoleon III committed a "crime" in making the *coup d'état* that brought him into power. That may, or may not, be so, according to the meaning one attaches to the term "crime." In relations between individuals, that term is defined by a penal code, by law; but what code, what law, is to be used in passing judgments on political events? The answer has to be stated. It is not enough to say, as many do, that it is a crime to overthrow any "legitimate" government; for then one would have to define just what a "legitimate" government would be. As a matter of fact, from Louis XVI down to Napoleon III, and then on down to the Third Republic, there was a continuous succession of governments each of which arose by overthrowing another that called itself legitimate and then proceeded to assert that it was as legitimate as its predecessor, and even more so. No decision is possible until we are told what norms are to be used in settling such disputes; and even if we were told and had rendered our judgment with reference to them, it is still not clear just how such a judgment could add in the slightest to our knowledge of social phenomena and their interrelationships. We were discreet enough to stop, notice, with Louis XVI. We could just as well have gone farther back and questioned the "legitimacy" of the royal authority that rose on the ruins of feudalism, the "legitimacy" of the authority of Pepin, of the Frankish kings, of the Roman conquerors of Gaul, and so on back to Adam. One can remedy the absurdity of such inquiries by conceding the existence of the norm, but the limit of its validity still has to be fixed. Shall we make it thirty years, as France does for private property, or a longer or shorter period? Then from just what authority does it emanate? What means does said authority possess for making head-strong recalcitrants obey? Considered in the light of the norms of private law and morals, the morals of Catherine II of Russia were reprehensible and the things she did to win her throne, criminal. But such a judgment has, after all, very little bearing on social phenomena and their relationships; and it would be of little help in trying, for example, to determine whether it would have been to the advantage of Russia that her husband, rather than she herself, should have ruled.[1] Elizabeth of England was concerned to seem chaste, and seems not to have been. What bearing can that have had on the social development of the England of her time? Facts of that sort have a bearing on history not through the ethical value which

2163 [1] Waliszewski, *Le roman d'une impératrice, Catherine II*, p. 190. There is still some doubt as to whether the Emperor Peter was assassinated by Orlov or by Tieplov: "Orlov or Tieplov? The question may seem incidental and of scant importance. But it is not. If Tieplov instigated the crime, it means that Catherine was ultimately responsible for it, for how conceive that he could have acted without her consent? The case is different as regards Orlov. He and his brother Gregory were, and for some time still were to remain, to a certain extent masters of a situation that they had created. . . . They had not taken Catherine's advice in beginning the *coup d'état*. They may well not have consulted her on a hundred other occasions." It is very essential to solve that problem if an ethical judgment is to be passed on Catherine, but in no way important if one is estimating the social effects of the incident. It is not apparent how answering the question in one sense or the other could have the slightest bearing on the prosperity of Russia.

they possess intrinsically, but as circumstances concomitant with certain happenings or determining certain others. Among such circumstances one may count extrinsic ethical values, as for instance the judgment passed on certain acts by the persons participating in events. But even in doing that one has to proceed cautiously and warily, for very often it is not so much the judgment that influences events as the events that influence the judgment, which, for that matter, may be lenient or severe according to the sentiments this or that person entertains towards those under judgment. The *Affaire du collier* did a great deal of harm to Marie Antoinette, though she seems really to have had no part in it; yet down to that time, scandals far more serious and far better authenticated had done no harm whatever to scions of royalty in France. In politics, particularly, scandal harms the weak and causes little worry to the strong. Examples to that effect can be counted every day of the week.

2164. In discussing Taine's third volume, of which he quotes the celebrated preface, M. Aulard brings two criticisms against the author of the *Origines,* accusing him of insufficient accuracy and of disregarding a number of documents. As regards social history, neither criticism stands. The inaccuracies mentioned are in no way substantial. They may at times be important for passing ethical judgments on individuals. They have slight bearing, if any at all, on the history of social phenomena.[1] The documents quoted by

2164 [1] Cochin, *La crise de l'histoire révolutionnaire: Taine et M. Aulard,* pp. 16-17: "Suppose we draw the sum of [M. Aulard's] inventory [of Taine's mistakes]. Among the 550 references quoted on the 140 pages of the 'Spontaneous Anarchy,' M. Aulard notes 28 substantial errors, which are really 15, 6 mistakes of copying, 4 mistakes in page numbers, 2 in dates and 3 misprints—a very creditable average, after all, and one that M. Aulard himself, at least as regards his book on Taine, is far from equalling, since he errs in his rectifications at least one time in two. . . . Taine was the first to open those files in the archives. He found a virgin forest before him and gathered up facts and documents by the armful. He did not have time to be pedantic or exhaustive. Did he, to be accurate? His friends never dared to be too sure. His enemies said no, very loud and often. M. Seignobos [Who was incapable of distinguishing the fancies of his democratic theology from scientific history.] finds Taine 'probably the most inaccurate historian of our time.' M. Aulard's book refutes that estimate by M. Seignobos. Taine's work has had the rare good fortune of receiving its baptism of fire from an adversary as partisan as he is learned. [M. Cochin is being exceedingly courteous.] It wins thereby the one patent of soundness that it still lacked: the thirty years of scholarship of M. Aulard. Every statement of Taine will henceforth have two counter-proofs: the learning of Taine himself, and the fact that a critic's spleen has not dared to dispute it."

Taine are, to tell the truth, even too numerous. No such body of proof is necessary to show that, in the French as in many another Revolution, politicians stole right and left and rid themselves of their enemies by putting them to death. One has only to glance at the conduct of politicians in times of peace to see quite readily that their conduct in times of revolution betrays the existence of forces which differ only in intensity from those which manifest themselves under peaceful conditions. Taine, instead, seems to believe that the differences are in the main qualitative, and would ascribe to the statesmen of the French Revolution sins of which politicians of all times and countries cannot plead innocence; and furthermore —a more serious mistake—he tries to attribute the crimes to the mistaken theories of those statesmen.

2165. M. Aulard disregards such criticisms, and others of the kind, that can be brought against Taine's results, and probably because, at bottom, he follows the same road as Taine, the only difference being that Taine passes an unfavourable ethical judgment on the Jacobins, whereas M. Aulard is kindly disposed toward them. But history is not concerned with such ethical judgments, whether in one sense or in another.[1] Read.in succession Machiavelli's *Prince*, *The Ancient City* of Fustel de Coulanges, then Cicero's Philippics, and Taine's third volume, especially the preface; and it will be apparent that the first two and the last two stand in altogether different classes that can be in no way confused. The two former examine relationships between social facts, the latter aim chiefly at ethical judgments.

2166. The admirers and the critics of the French Revolution are substantially in agreement as to the facts; but the antis hold that the revolutionists were inspired to do the things they did by de-

---

2165 [1] Cochin, *Op. cit.*, pp. 99-100: "Shall we see the end of this crisis [in the writing of histories of the French Revolution]? I think we shall, but on two conditions: first, that we stand on better guard against that curse of all curiosity— indignation . . . and, second, that criticism should at last rid us of that revolutionary fetish, the People, send it back to politics the way Providence has been sent back to theology, and restore apologetic history to a place in the museum of religious myths that it should never have been allowed to desert. If our historians have not attended to that hitherto, it must be because the anthropomorphism of the People is more recent and more specious than that of Providence. It could still fool people in days when the workings of the social machine and the laws of practical democracy were still but vaguely discerned on the reverse side of 'principles.' Taine and M. Aulard are historians of that era. They are historians of an—Old Régime!"

pravity of character; the pros that they were provoked by the resistance and wickedness of their adversaries.[1] As regards the history of social phenomena, to solve that problem is about as important as knowing whether Caesar, Augustus, Cromwell, and other such men were honest, moral individuals, or dishonest, immoral. Taine thought he was writing of the French Revolution like a zoologist describing animals. He was mistaken. His history may be something like Buffon's history of the animal kingdom, a work of literature, but never like the *Traité de zoölogie concrète* of Delage and Hérouard, a scientific treatise. Quite like the latter instead is Machiavelli's description of Valentino's campaigns.

2167. Ethical disputes about the French Revolution possess not even the merit of novelty. They are in all respects replicas of the disputes that have raged, and will forever rage, about every political, social, or religious revolution. Those favouring a revolution will say that it is "justified" by the evil machinations of its enemies; those hostile to it will condemn it because of the evil machinations of the revolutionists. There is no way of deciding who is right and who wrong until we are told what norms are to apply in condemning or absolving; and then, on the assumption that we are told, such judgment may give us a certain ethical satisfaction, but it will show

2166 [1] Every now and then, in cases of conflict between public authorities and strikers where there are casualties, one notes facts and judgments that are altogether similar, though on a much smaller scale. Defenders of the police say that the "guilt" lies with the strikers, in that they were trying to do things that the police were in duty bound to prevent. Defenders of the strikers say that the "guilt" rests with the police, who were not sufficiently patient and tried to interfere with the strikers. Before we can determine who is right and who wrong, we have to know what meaning is to be attached to the term "guilt." If it be granted that orders from the police must always be respected and that people venturing to disobey them do so at their own risk and peril, the defenders of the police are right. If it be granted that people on strike are to be at all times respected by the police and that anyone venturing to do them violence is committing a crime, the defenders of the strikers are right. But in either of those cases we have solved an ethical problem, not a problem of relationships among social phenomena, and we still have to learn what sentiments and interests underlie the conduct of the two contending parties and what the consequences of the various solutions that might be given to the conflict would be, as regards the social order and the various other utilities. The police power is used in all countries to enforce measures that may be classified under two headings: (*A*) measures favourable, or at least irrelevant, to the welfare of the community; and (*B*) measures detrimental to the community's welfare. If one holds that resistance to the police force is *always* detrimental to the

absolutely nothing as to the relationships of one political or social fact to another, or about the uniformities that may be inferred from them (§ 2166[1]).

2168. Among the many reasons why historians of the French Revolution—in that not differing from historians in general—have followed the ethical method we must here touch on two in chief, the one subjective, the other objective. The subjective reason we have just explained in part. In view of it historians give a miscellany of ethical dissertations, sermons, exhortations, along with observations of fact and of relationships between facts. In the very best case, these latter represent only one of the purposes with which the historian is concerned, and frequently enough they are not even a purpose, but a means for realizing other purposes. The subjective reason is a general one, and figures in almost all historical writing.

2169. The objective reason is also general, but it comes out with special prominence in the histories of the French Revolution. It arises in the fact that each of the contending parties in the Revolution in order to fight and win used the phraseology of the other party, so that identical derivations disguise differing residues; with the result that if one stops at derivations one can know nothing of

community, he thereby holds either: (1) That A cannot be separated from B, and that the utility of A is greater than the harm done by B; or else (2) that A can always be separated from B in some other way than by offering resistance to the police power. This latter proposition is contradicted by history. Many transformations that have proved beneficial, indeed exceedingly so, to society have been effected only by meeting the police power with opposing force.

Conversely, if one expresses oneself as in all cases favourable to resistance to the police power, one holds either: (1) That A can in no way be separated from B and that the harm done by B overrides the utility of A; or else (2) that A can never be separated from B in any other way than by resistance to the police power. This latter proposition is in its turn contradicted by history, which shows that many transformations that have proved beneficial, and sometimes in the highest degree, to society have been effected otherwise than by resistance to the police power.

It follows, therefore, that such problems cannot be solved a priori in one sense or the other, but that each particular case has to be examined quantitatively to determine in which direction the utility or the detriment lies. It is the peculiar characteristic of ethical derivations that in such cases they substitute a priori a single and qualitative solution for the multiple and quantitative solutions that experience furnishes a posteriori. That is why ethical solutions are more acceptable to the public than experimental solutions. They are simpler, and they are easier to understand without long and fatiguing compilations of multitudinous facts (§ 2147[18]).

the forces which were really at work in the Revolution. In some cases such inconsistencies between the derivation and the conduct are so evident that they have not escaped historians; so, if they find that Augustus founded the Empire on pretence of restoring the Republic, and that Robespierre, opposing capital punishment, made extensive use of it, they get out of the difficulty by passing ethical judgments on those men in view of their inconsistencies. It may well be that Augustus was lying when he pretended to be restoring the Republic and that Robespierre was lying when he posed as a humanitarian. But if we are interested in getting at the facts we cannot stop at that. Two problems at once emerge, the one of slight, the other of very great, importance. The first lies in determining whether Augustus and Robespierre were sincere or insincere, since it might easily be, as has been seen to happen in many other cases, that both of them sincerely believed in the derivations they used in order to mislead others.[1] The second problem, which is the only one of the two that has any significance for history, lies in determining how and why the sentiments and interests cloaked by the derivations in question had the success they had. Does anyone really think that the Romans were duped by Augustus, and the French by Robespierre, much as a customer is tricked by a jeweller who sells him a piece of glass on the assurance that it is a diamond? Such a thesis is untenable. Indeed the personalities of Augustus and Robespierre themselves disappear, in part at least, in reality, and we are obliged to say that the sentiments and interests that were represented by those individuals prevailed over the sentiments and interests represented by other individuals. What took place was the resultant of all the social factors, among which the derivations did, to be sure, have their place, but not a very important place (§ 2199).

2170. *The use of force in society.* Societies in general subsist because alive and vigorous in the majority of their constituent members are sentiments corresponding to residues of sociality (Class IV). But there are also individuals in human societies in whom some at least of those sentiments are weak or indeed actually missing. That

2169 [1] Many people have perceived and stated a fact which Barras well describes in his *Mémoires,* Vol. II, p. 446: "So great is the deceptive power of the passions that when they are most concerned with a private interest, they often imagine that they envisage only the public interest."

fact has two interesting consequences which stand in apparent contradiction, one of them threatening the dissolution of a society, the
other making for its progress in civilization. What at bottom is there
is continuous movement, but it is a movement that may progress in
almost any direction.

2171. It is evident that if the requirement of uniformity (residues
IV-$\bar{\beta}$) were so strongly active in all individuals in a given society as
to prevent even one of them from breaking away in any particular
from the uniformities prevalent in it, such a society would have no
internal causes for dissolution; but neither would it have any causes
for change, whether in the direction of an increase, or of a decrease,
in the utility of the individuals or of the society. On the other hand
if the requirement of uniformity were to fail, society would not hold
together, and each individual would go his own way, as lions and
tigers, birds of prey, and other animals do. Societies that endure and
change are therefore situated in some intermediate condition between those two extremes.

2172. A homogeneous society might be imagined in which the
requirement of uniformity would be the same in all individuals,
and would correspond to the intermediate state just mentioned. But
observation shows that that is not the case with human societies.
Human societies are essentially heterogeneous, and the intermediate
state is attained because the requirement of uniformity is very strong
in some individuals, moderately strong in others, very feeble in still
others, and almost entirely absent in a few. The average is found
not in each individual, but in the group comprising them all. One
may add as a datum of fact that the number of individuals in whom
the requirement of uniformity is stronger than the average requisite
of the intermediate state in which the society is situated is much
greater than the number of individuals in whom the requirement is
weaker than that average, and very very much greater than the
number in whom it is entirely missing.

2173. For the reader who has followed us thus far it is needless
to add that, in view of the effects of this greater or lesser potency
of the sentiments of uniformity, one may foresee out of hand that
two theologies will put in an appearance (§ 2147, Example II), one
of which will glorify the immobility of one or another uniformity,
real or imaginary, the other of which will glorify movement, prog-

ress, in one direction or another. That is what has actually happened in history. There have been popular Olympuses where the gods fixed and determined once and for all how human society was to be; and then, too, Olympuses of utopian reformers, who derived from their exalted minds conceptions of forms from which human society was never never more to deviate. On the other hand, from the days of ancient Athens down to our own, the lord gods of Movement in a Certain Direction have listened to the prayers of their faithful and now sit triumphant in our latter-day Olympus, where Progress Optimus Maximus reigns in sovereign majesty. So that intermediate situation of society has usually been attained as the resultant of many forces, prominent among them the two categories mentioned, which envisage different imaginary goals and correspond to different classes of residues (§§ 2152 f.).

2174. To ask whether or not force ought to be used in a society, whether the use of force is or is not beneficial, is to ask a question that has no meaning; for force is used by those who wish to preserve certain uniformities and by those who wish to overstep them; and the violence of the ones stands in contrast and in conflict with the violence of the others. In truth, if a partisan of a governing class disavows the use of force, he means that he disavows the use of force by insurgents trying to escape from the norms of the given uniformity. On the other hand, if he says he approves of the use of force, what he really means is that he approves of the use of force by the public authority to constrain insurgents to conformity. Conversely, if a partisan of the subject class says he detests the use of force in society, what he really detests is the use of force by constituted authorities in forcing dissidents to conform; and if, instead, he lauds the use of force, he is thinking of the use of force by those who would break away from certain social uniformities.[1]

2175. Nor is there any particular meaning in the question as to whether the use of violence to enforce existing uniformities is beneficial to society, or whether it is beneficial to use force in order to

2174 [1] In the Zabern incident the same newspapers evinced the greatest indignation at the "browbeating" by the military authorities (§ 2147) but were very lenient towards the "browbeating" and the acts of "sabotage" for which the strikers were responsible at the same time. Conversely, newspapers that approved the use of force by the military waxed indignant at acts of violence on the part of their adversaries.

overstep them; for the various uniformities have to be distinguished to see which of them are beneficial and which deleterious to society. Nor, indeed, is that enough; for it is further necessary to determine whether the utility of the uniformity is great enough to offset the harm that will be done by using violence to enforce it, or whether detriment from the uniformity is great enough to overbalance the damage that will be caused by the use of force in subverting it (§ 2195); in which detriment and damage we must not forget to reckon the very serious drawback involved in the anarchy that results from any frequent use of violence to abolish existing uniformities, just as among the benefits and utilities of maintaining frankly injurious uniformities must be counted the strength and stability they lend to the social order. So, to solve the problem as to the use of force, it is not enough to solve the other problem as to the utility, in general, of certain types of social organization; it is essential also and chiefly to compute all the advantages and all the drawbacks, direct and indirect (§ 2147, Example II). Such a course leads to the solution of a scientific problem; but it may not be and oftentimes is not the course that leads to an increase in social utility. It is better, therefore, if it be followed only by people who are called upon to solve a scientific problem or, to some limited extent, by certain individuals belonging to the ruling class; whereas social utility is oftentimes best served if the members of the subject class, whose function it is not to lead but to act, accept one of the two theologies according to the case—either the theology that enjoins preservation of existing uniformities, or the theology that counsels change.

2176. What we have just said serves to explain, along with the theoretical difficulties, how it comes about that the solutions that are usually found for the general problem have so little and sometimes no bearing on realities. Solutions of particular problems come closer to the mark because, situate as they are in specific places and times, they present fewer theoretical difficulties; and because practical empiricism implicitly takes account of many circumstances that theory, until it has been carried to a state of high perfection, cannot explicitly appraise.

Considering violations of material conformities among modern civilized peoples, we see that, in general, the use of violence in repressing them is the more readily condoned in proportion as the violation can be regarded as an individual anomaly designed to attain some individual advantage, and the less readily condoned in proportion as the violation appears as a collective act aiming at some collective advantage, and especially if its apparent design be to replace general norms prevailing with certain other general norms.[1]

2177. That states all that there is in common between the large numbers of facts in which a distinction is drawn between so-called private and so-called political crimes. A distinction, and often a very sharp distinction, is drawn between the individual who kills or steals for his own benefit and the individual who commits murder or theft with the intent of benefiting a party. In general, civilized countries grant extradition for the former, but refuse it for the latter. In the same way one notes a continually increasing leniency towards crimes committed during labour strikes or in the course of other economic, social, or political struggles. There is a more and more conspicuous tendency to meet such aggressions with merely passive resistance, the police power being required not to use arms, or else permitted to do so only in cases of extreme necessity. Such cases never arise in practice. So long as the policeman is alive, the necessity is held not to be extreme, and it is bootless, after all, to recognize the extremity after he is in his grave and no longer in a position to profit by the considerate permission to use his revolver. Punishment by judicial process is also becoming less and less vigorous. Criminals are either not convicted or, being convicted, are released in virtue of some probation law, failing of which, they can still rely on commutations, individual pardons, or general amnesties, so that, sum total, they have little or nothing to fear from the courts (§ 2147 [18]). In a word, in a vague, cloudy, confused sort of way, the notion is

---

2176 [1] It would be hardly in point here to review the whole history of the use of force from ancient down to modern times, or to go into too many details. We shall confine ourselves to the present, and try to find a formula that will give a rough and general picture of the facts observable. If we were dealing with a recent past, we should have to regard violations of the norms of intellectual uniformity as on a par with violations of a material order. Not so long ago they were actually so regarded, and often indeed the former were regarded as more serious than the latter. But in our day, barring some few exceptions, proportions have been inverted, and the norms of intellectual uniformity that public authority sets out to enforce are relatively few. They may therefore be better considered apart from norms of a material order. We shall deal with material uniformities first, coming to violations of an intellectual order farther along (§§ 2196 f.).

coming to the fore that an existing government may make some slight use of force against its enemies, but no great amount of force, and that it is under all circumstances to be condemned if it carries the use of force so far as to cause the death of considerable numbers, of a small number, a single one, of its enemies; nor can it rid itself of them, either, by putting them in prison or otherwise.[1]

2178. What now are the correlations that subsist between this method of applying force and other social facts? We note, as usual, a sequence of actions and reactions, in which the use of force appears now as cause, now as effect. As regards the governing class, one gets, in the main, five groups of facts to consider: 1. A mere handful of citizens, so long as they are willing to use violence, can force their will upon public officials who are not inclined to meet violence with equal violence. If the reluctance of the officials to resort to force is primarily motivated by humanitarian sentiments, that result ensues very readily; but if they refrain from violence because they deem it wiser to use some other means, the effect is often the following: 2. To prevent or resist violence, the governing class resorts to "diplomacy," fraud, corruption—governmental authority passes, in a word, from the lions to the foxes. The governing class bows its head under the threat of violence, but it surrenders only in appearances, trying to turn the flank of the obstacle it cannot demolish in frontal attack. In the long run that sort of procedure comes to exercise a far-reaching influence on the selection of the governing class, which is now recruited only from the foxes, while the lions are blackballed (§ 2227). The individual who best knows the arts of sapping the strength of the foes of "graft" and of winning back by fraud and deceit what seemed to have been surrendered under pressure of force, is now leader of leaders. The man who has bursts of rebellion, and does not know how to crook his spine at the proper times and places, is the worst of leaders, and his presence is tolerated among them only if other distinguished endowments offset that defect. 3. So it comes about that the residues of the combination-instinct (Class I) are intensified in the governing

2177 [1] This formula states in the abstract what is actually happening in the concrete. It is met with a number of theories that state what, according to their authors, "ought" to happen. With those theories we shall deal farther along (§§ 2181 f.).

class, and the residues of group-persistence (Class II) debilitated; for the combination-residues supply, precisely, the artistry and resourcefulness required for evolving ingenious expedients as substitutes for open resistance, while the residues of group-persistence stimulate open resistance, since a strong sentiment of group-persistence cures the spine of all tendencies to curvature. 4. Policies of the governing class are not planned too far ahead in time. Predominance of the combination instincts and enfeeblement of the sentiments of group-persistence result in making the governing class more satisfied with the present and less thoughtful of the future. The individual comes to prevail, and by far, over family, community, nation. Material interests and interests of the present or a near future come to prevail over the ideal interests of community or nation and interests of the distant future. The impulse is to enjoy the present without too much thought for the morrow. 5. Some of these phenomena become observable in international relations as well. Wars become essentially economic. Efforts are made to avoid conflicts with the powerful and the sword is rattled only before the weak. Wars are regarded more than anything else as speculations (§ 2328). A country is often unwittingly edged towards war by nursings of economic conflicts which, it is expected, will never get out of control and turn into armed conflicts. Not seldom, however, a war will be forced upon a country by peoples who are not so far advanced in the evolution that leads to the predominance of Class I residues.

2179. As regards the subject class, we get the following relations, which correspond in part to the preceding: 1. When the subject class contains a number of individuals disposed to use force and with capable leaders to guide them, the governing class is, in many cases, overthrown and another takes its place. That is easily the case where governing classes are inspired by humanitarian sentiments primarily, and very very easily if they do not find ways to assimilate the exceptional individuals who come to the front in the subject classes. A humanitarian aristocracy that is closed or stiffly exclusive represents the maximum of insecurity. 2. It is far more difficult to overthrow a governing class that is adept in the shrewd use of chicanery, fraud, corruption; and in the highest degree difficult to overthrow such a class when it successfully assimilates most of the individuals in the subject class who show those same talents, are adept in those same arts, and might therefore become the leaders of such plebeians as are disposed to use violence. Thus left without leadership, without talent, disorganized, the subject class is almost always powerless to set up any lasting régime. 3. So the combination-residues (Class I) become to some extent enfeebled in the subject class. But that phenomenon is in no way comparable to the corresponding reinforcement of those same residues in the governing class; for the governing class, being composed, as it is, of a much smaller number of individuals, changes considerably in character from the addition to it or withdrawal from it of relatively small numbers of individuals; whereas shifts of identical numbers produce but slight effects in the enormously greater total of the subject class. For that matter the subject class is still left with many individuals possessed of combination-instincts that are applied not to politics or activities connected with politics but to arts and trades independent of politics. That circumstance lends stability to societies, for the governing class is required to absorb only a small number of new individuals in order to keep the subject class deprived of leadership. However, in the long run the differences in temperament between the governing class and the subject class become gradually accentuated, the combination-instincts tending to predominate in the ruling class, and instincts of group-persistence in the subject class. When that difference becomes sufficiently great, revolution occurs. 4. Revolution often transfers power to a new governing class, which exhibits a reinforcement in its instincts of group-persistence and so adds to its designs of present enjoyment aspirations towards ideal enjoyments presumably attainable at some future time—scepticism in part gives way to faith. 5. These considerations must to some extent be applied to international relations. If the combination-instincts are reinforced in a given country beyond a certain limit, as compared with the instincts of group-persistence, that country may be easily vanquished in war by another country in which that change in relative proportions has not occurred. The potency of an ideal as a pilot to victory is observable in both civil and international strife. People who lose the habit of applying force, who acquire the habit of considering policy from a commercial standpoint and of judging it only in terms of profit and loss, can readily be induced to purchase peace; and it may well be that such a transaction taken by itself is a good one, for war might have cost more money than the price of peace. Yet experience shows that in the long run, and taken in connexion with the things that inevitably go with it, such practice leads a country to ruin. The combination-instincts rarely come to prevail in the whole of a population. More commonly that situation arises in the upper strata of society, there being few if any traces of it in the lower and more populous classes. So when a war breaks out one gazes in amazement on the energies that are suddenly manifested by the masses at large, something that could in no way have been foreseen by studying the upper classes only. Sometimes, as happened in the case of Carthage, the burst of energy may not be sufficient to save a country, because a war may have been inadequately prepared for and be incompetently led by the ruling classes, and soundly prepared for and wisely led by the ruling classes of the enemy country. Then again, as happened in the wars of the French Revolution, the energy in the masses may be great enough to save a country because, though the war may have been badly prepared for by its ruling classes, preparations and leadership have been even worse in the ruling classes of the enemy countries, a circumstance that gives the constituent members of the lower strata of society time to drive their ruling class from power and replace it with another of greater energy and possessing the instincts of group-persistence in greater abundance. Still again, as happened in Germany after the disaster at Jena, the energy of the masses may spread to the higher classes and spur them to an activity that proves most effective as combining able leadership with enthusiastic faith.

2180. These, then, are the main, the outstanding phenomena, but other phenomena of secondary or incidental importance also figure. Notable among such is the fact that if a ruling class is unable or unwilling or incompetent to use force to eradicate violations of uniformities in private life, anarchic action on the part of the subject class tends to make up for the deficiency. It is well known to history that the private vendetta languishes or recurs in proportion as public authority continues or ceases to replace it. It has been seen to recur in the form of lynchings in the United States, and even in

Europe.[a] Whenever the influence of public authority declines, little states grow up within the state, little societies within society. So, whenever judicial process fails, private or group justice replaces it, and *vice versa*.[1] In international relations, the tinselling of humani-

2180 [a] [This casual allusion to the phenomena of lynch-law does not reflect the full light that Pareto's theories throw upon them; nor does it altogether square with the facts. Lynchings occur in fairly law-abiding communities in the United States (California). They fail to occur in fairly lawless communities (New York, Chicago). They are not correlated therefore with the greater or lesser efficiency of law enforcement as such. I would state the Paretan uniformity as follows (strictly, the problem belongs to what Pareto calls "special sociology, and therefore does not fall within the purview of this work). A lynching develops in three stages. 1. A revolting crime causes a violent shock to Class V residues connected with the social equilibrium. 2. Activity residues (Class III), at once come into play, and meeting no great check in combination-residues (Class I) as consolidated and made permanent by persisting abstractions (residues II-δ), vent themselves to the full. 3. The activity residues having spent their force the social equilibrium is at once restored and life resumes its normal course. The protests, editorials, sermons, that follow a lynching have little effect, because they themselves are in large part manifestations of the activity residues aroused in stages 1 and 2. In the Paretan theory the vigor of conduct is correlated with the numbers of sentiments involved in an act and their intensities, as "composed" in a resultant by the number and intensity of conflicting or opposite sentiments. Activity residues are checked in the North by the strength of persisting combinations, and the absence of lynchings is therefore interdependent with the strength of industry, commerce, popular education, prosperity and so on. Lynchings occur in the South from the relative and proportionate weakness of the combination-residues (very significant the falling off in the numbers of lynchings during the "boom" years, 1923-29). Another thing: lynchings preferably occur when the combination of Class V and Class III residues is reenforced by Class VI residues (sex) and by IV-β residues (sense of uniformity—colour). There is an interesting proof of the comment on the reactions of protest, above. Some very brutal lynchings (one the burning of a negro woman) occurred during Mr. Hoover's administration. The President at that time said nothing. He was moved to a wholly sentimental and unobjective outburst by the very orderly lynching of the San José kidnappers in 1933. That shows that he too had been profoundly stirred by the Lindbergh case and by the ensuing wave of kidnapping crimes and, owing to the *boutade* of the late Governor Rolfe, had at last found a way to vent his activity residues. Of these latter the famous manifesto of Governor Rolfe was a pure and unadulterated expression. This analysis throws the whole matter of lynchings into the sphere of non-logical conduct, and shows that just as lynchings have not disappeared after a century of preaching, they will not disappear as long as the present structure of American society endures. They can only be prevented in the given case by an application of force; but there again, as history also shows, the application of force is prevented by the very forces that cause the lynchings.—A. L.]

2180 [1] Examples from the past are too numerous and too familiar to require mention here. Suppose I note just one very recent example. In the year 1913, at

tarian and ethical declamation is just a dressing for an underlying force. The Chinese considered themselves the superiors in civilization of the Japanese (§ 2550 [2]), and perhaps they were, but they lacked a military aptitude that the Japanese, in virtue of a surviving

Orgosolo, in Sardinia, a number of individuals replaced the defective action of the police and the courts with their own group action. The incident is worth recounting as typical of the past and illustrative, with due allowances as to procedures and forms, of what can at any time be the future.

Two families, the Cossus and the Corraines, became involved in a feud for private reasons. The Cossus succeeded in winning the support of government officials and therefore of the police and the courts. The Corraines, considering themselves unfairly treated in view of that, flew to arms. *Giornale d'Italia,* Oct. 5, 1913: "*Orgosolo, Oct. 3.* The band of brigands that has been infesting the territory about Orgosolo has committed another atrocious crime. In the La Mela district the bodies of two property-owners and their hired man were found this morning, all three of them slain by the brigands in question. The dead: Giuseppe Succu, Giovanni Succu, their hired man, Michele Picconi. The three bodies were riddled with bullets and knife-cuts and horribly mutilated. One of Picconi's ears was cut off. Giovanni Corraine is keeping his promise: the more vigorously the army and the police try to run him down, the more emphatic the evidence he will give of his power and his resolve on vengeance. Today's crime had been foreseen about town. Your correspondent has interviewed Egidio Piredda, one of the chief victims of the persecution. Signor Piredda confessed that every person in the Cossu clan rose from bed this morning in terror of not seeing sundown. And he added in the presence of officials that despite the protection accorded his party by the police, despite the escorts of *carabinieri* that are being provided every time a Cossu clansman goes out of doors, the Cossus were all resigned to their fate. The man's features were overspread with anguish, the anguish of a man living under a relentless menace, and aware of the uselessness of struggling against a diabolical power that is utterly his superior. Piredda was right. On the night when the *carabinieri* fell upon the Corraine house and arrested the mother and her young and beautiful daughter, Giovanni Corraine stood only a short distance away under cover of the darkness and, clutching his rifle, he took oath to avenge them. The incident is well known. It was recounted to me by Giovanni Corraine's brother on the day when, with the pale drawn face of a sickly child, he told me in an unfaltering voice that justice would be done on those who had sent two innocent women to prison with the connivance of 'friends in high places.' That conviction is deeply rooted in the bandits, and also in all the townsfolk of Orgosolo, who would sacrifice their blood and their liberty to aid the Corraines. They firmly believe that the Cossus, sworn enemies of the Corraines [and allies of the Succus] are able to bully and mistreat the Corraines through political influence and that, as the Corraines also think, they are obstructing the orderly procedure of justice. That was their conclusion the day when a jury at Oristano acquitted the murderer of one of the Corraine brothers. That, again, was their conclusion on the night when the police, hoping to cut the bandits off from their bases of supply by wholesale arrests among the Corraine faction, dragged its outstanding figures to prison at Nuoro. And the curse uttered by Medda Corraine, the prettiest girl in Orgosolo, as she was passing the Cossu house in handcuffs and under police escort, voiced the fierce and tragic warning

remnant of feudal "barbarism," possessed in abundance. So the poor Chinese were attacked by hordes of Europeans—whose exploits in China, as Sorel well says, remind one of the feats of the Spanish *conquistadores* in the Americas. They suffered murder, rapine, and

that has had its bloody epilogue today: 'God will curse you for the wrong you are doing to our family. God will not suffer you to benefit by such a life of infamy. . . .' And so saying she lifted her fettered wrists in an unearthly gesture of imprecation. Today her brother hearkens to her curse and commits murder. Today's dead are the two brothers, Giuseppe and Giovanni Succu, members both of a wretched family that is dotting the small, lonely cemetery of Orgosolo with dozens of crosses. One by one they are falling, all of them, under the bullets of the bandits that never miss. The town looks on at the slaughter in silence and continues sending bread, ammunition, money, to 'the able-bodied' as they call them, to the men who are living like wild beasts in the woods, breathing the air of vengeance." Four days later, Oct. 9, 1913, the same newspaper published an interview with one of the "personages in high place." The official explained the situation very lucidly: " 'The bitter hatred that divides the now notorious families of Orgosolo and has already resulted in a long list of crimes is due to a number of causes. For the sake of clearness suppose we begin by explaining that the "menaced" families are the Cossus, the Succus, the Pineddas, the Poddas, and the Pisanos. The families to which the bandits belong, or by which they are supported, are the Corraines, the Moros, and the De Vaddises. [Names, as Pareto remarked in a note, are badly confused in the news articles which he quotes. I uniformize them to make the narrative coherent.—A. L.] Now what are the causes that really and immediately determined these crimes? The first and remotest cause is to be sought in some obscure disagreement over an inheritance, which is now too involved for anyone to make head or tail of. But there is a cause more serious and less remote: an offer of marriage made in behalf of a girl in the Cossu family, which was rejected by the Corraines. Soon afterwards the affront was returned. A youth belonging to the second "group" of families sued for the hand of a girl belonging to the first "group." He was rejected in his turn. Hatred between the two clans flared up. And soon there was worse. A man of the Corraine family was found drowned in a well. The police and judicial authorities were in full agreement, after a formal inquest, that Corraine had committed suicide. But the Corraines and their adherents held, and still hold, that their kinsman was murdered by their enemies and that the authorities, as a favor to the Cossus, their henchmen, invented the little story of suicide. Sad inspiration of clannish passions!

" 'But there came another such inspiration, I will not say sadder, but stranger. In a skirmish between the *carabinieri* and some fugitives from justice who were evading arrest, one of the De Vaddis boys was killed, whereupon the De Vaddises and their adherents held, and continue to hold, that their kinsman was slain by the Cossu "group" and that the authorities, again to protect the Cossus, invented this time the story of a fight with the *carabinieri*.' 'But why should the authorities— granted that it is a mistaken impression on the part of the Corraines or the others— be favouring the Cossus?' 'That suspicion is based on the mere fact that the Cossus were the wealthiest and most influential family in Orgosolo. I say "were," because the family is now all but destroyed. Its men and its possessions have been wiped out, and Antonio Cossu, the old man, has had to take refuge in Nuoro, where

pillage at European hands, and then paid an indemnity into the bargain; whereas the Japanese came off victorious over the Russians and now exact respect from everybody. A few centuries back, the subtle diplomacy of the Christian lords of Constantinople did not

carabinieri stand constantly on guard about his house trying to protect him. But let us go on with the story. The Corraine "group" now had two new grievances to avenge in addition to the old ones: two murders, in other words, for nothing will ever convince the Corraines that their two kinsmen were not murdered by their enemies.

" 'So the terrible work of vengeance began. Barns were burned, timber lands were set on fire, live stock was stolen or hamstrung, children were kidnapped, men were killed.' 'It was then that the Corraines took to the woods?' 'Exactly, and for that reason. A month or so ago the police authorities, who had been doggedly pursuing the fugitives, made a wholesale raid on their accomplices and arrested thirty in all, what with women and men. The Corraine 'group' boiled with indignation, and saw in that another abuse on the part of the authorities, because all the individuals arrested were members of their group. Nor was it of any use to remind them that the accomplices in their own crimes were certainly not to be sought in the families of their victims, who were by this time so terror-stricken that not one of them any longer dared to go out of doors.' 'And were the arrests upheld?' 'Yes. After a long and detailed "instruction" the judicial authorities decided to remand them for trial as members of a criminal association. That was the last straw. It unleashed the whole fury of the Corraines. The two months during which the inquiry had been in progress were months of truce: no word was said of individuals evading arrest. There were no personal assaults, no thefts on the farms. Evidently the "group" backing the individuals in custody hoped that the warrants would be quashed and did not care to prejudice the judges against the defendants. But when it transpired that they were to be remanded, the storm broke. For a fortnight past crime has followed on crime. . . . And the police are powerless to avert them or punish them.' 'And what might be the cause of that helplessness?' 'Many causes, but the chief one this, that everybody in the Orgosolo district, every man, woman, and child, is on the side of the fugitives.' 'And why that?' 'Because they are all convinced that in the beginning these men, or rather, the families of these men, did not get fair treatment; that they are therefore not criminals, but victims of oppression taking justice into their own hands. Moreover, in Sardinia, and especially in the vicinity of Nuoro, "procuring justice for oneself" by whatever means and at whatever cost is never considered dishonourable in anyone. So it comes about that the *carabinieri* receive no aid and are unable to get a scrap of information concerning the movements of the bandits from living soul in the country, which contains, unquestionably, a large number of reputable people; whereas the fugitives are kept perfectly and promptly informed of every movement on the part of the police and are constantly being supplied with food and ammunition. And you who know, if only from a casual visit, the country about Nuoro, cannot but understand that the police are facing difficulties that are truly insuperable.' "

And now let us listen to what is said not by the poor and ignorant peasants of a remote rural district, but by the magistrates themselves, who are entrusted with the execution of justice. *Giornale d'Italia,* Sept. 20, 1913, reporting a convention of Italian judicial magistrates in session at Naples: "His Honour Justice Giulio Cag-

save them from ruin under the impact of the fanaticism and might of the Turks; and now, in this year 1913, on the very same spot, the victors show that they have deteriorated in their fanaticism and in their power and, in their turn reposing illusory hopes in the diplo-

giano, continuing his report on the break-down of service in the courts, in the following tenor: 'History teaches that any enfeeblement or break-down in the organs of justice spells a reversion, be it a slow reversion, to primitive conditions of barbarism, that the Teppa, the Camorra, the Maffia, brigandage, are forms of collective crime that originate in distrust of official justice. The best-framed laws become mere hoaxes, like the famous "cries," or proclamations, of Don Rodrigo's time [Allusion to the villain in Manzoni's novel, *The Betrothed*.], unless there are organs to enforce respect for them and obedience to them. Nor must we overlook a side light on the question, which has a more direct bearing on the prestige of our order. If a portion of the public is capable of understanding that it is not because of the incapacity or laziness of our judges that the break-down in justice is becoming more and more alarming, the majority of the public does not hesitate to attribute it bluntly to indolence, incompetence, or lack of interest on the part of persons.' " The public also believes, and rightly, that not seldom interference by politicians and government ministries in behalf of one friend or another deprives court decisions of all status as law and justice. In serious cases, the virile, unspoiled inhabitants of Sardinia and Sicily resort to their rifles, while the milder populations on the Continent bow their heads resignedly. Even in highly civilized regions private justice on occasion replaces public administration. *Liberté,* Nov. 3, 1913: "*Fatal Gesture:* It was to be foreseen. Sooner or later an act of violence had to be the answer to one or another of those incomprehensible whims for which the jury system has been distinguishing itself for some years past. The fatal gesture has been made in open court at the Criminal Assizes of the Cher. An individual is accused by his two sons of murdering their mother. Her body has been found in a well with a rope about the neck. The jury declares the defendant not guilty and the court dismisses him from the bar. The youngest of the two sons rushes at his father and fires a revolver at him point-blank, inflicting a slight wound. 'You can acquit that rascal,' he cries. 'I won't, ever!' In the tumult the spectators throw themselves upon the self-appointed executioner with cries of 'Lynch him!' Court attendants manage to rescue him and lead him away to prison while the acquitted defendant signs the dismissal docket and strides from the court-room. . . . So there we are! In open court an individual takes it upon himself to reverse a verdict of fumbling justice, while a crowd of court-room spectators take it upon themselves to replace justice in punishing an assault. . . . The incident is of too serious an import not to merit the attention of all law-abiding citizens who may fancy they are living in an organized society. Let us state the bald truth: If such things are possible, the responsibility undeniably lies with the countless acquittals juries have been making in cases where punishment has obviously been required. Not a few such cases have been downright scandals and have served to lend piquant force to the remark of a lawyer who summarized a long experience in the courts with the reflection that 'if he were guilty, he would certainly demand a jury trial.' " The analysis is sound only in part. The "fault" in such cases—perhaps we had better say the cause of such things—does not lie only in the jury system. Judges are oftentimes worse than juries. Nor does it lie altogether in the judicial system, for

matic arts, are defeated and overthrown by the vigour of their sometime subjects. Grievous the hallucination under which those statesmen labour who imagine that they can replace the use of force with
unarmed law. Among the many examples that one might point to
are Sulla's constitution in ancient Rome and the conservative constitution of the Third Republic in France. Sulla's constitution fell
because the armed force that might have compelled respect for it
was not maintained. The constitution of Augustus endured because
his successors were in a position to rely on the might of the legions.[2]
When the Commune had been defeated and overthrown, Thiers
decided that his government ought to find its support rather in the
law than in armed force. As a result his laws were scattered like
leaves before the hurricane of democratic plutocracy.[3] We need say
nothing of Louis XVI of France, who thought he could halt the
Revolution with his royal veto, for his was the illusion of a spineless
weakling who was soon to lose what little head he had (§ 2201).[4]

after all the judicial system is no better or worse than it is made by the individuals
who administer it. It lies chiefly in the fact that through a combination of many
circumstances the public authority is failing in its function of guaranteeing justice.

2180 [2] There is an anecdote about Sulla in Appian, De bellis civilibus, I, 104.
Having abdicated the dictatorship, and still being respected by everyone because of
the fear that he continued to inspire, Sulla was finally insulted by a young man,
and he commented on the incident to the effect that "the act of that young fellow
would keep any other man who held such power as he had had [the dictatorship]
from ever resigning it. And shortly after, that very thing happened to the Romans,
for Caius Caesar refused to lay down his command." The anecdote was probably
invented to explain Caesar's conduct, but those who invented it and those who felt
its force clearly perceived the weak spot in Sulla's achievement. In fact, as soon as
he died, the Romans returned to their customary quarrelling, and the two consuls
assailed each other furiously. That is what usually happens, and it shows that where
the force of government fails, the force of individuals and factions takes its place.

2180 [3] Humanitarians are fond of repeating the aphorism: "On peut tout faire
avec des baïonnettes excepté s'asseoir dessus." ("One can do anything with bayonets
except sit on them"); but it would be interesting if they would tell us whether, in
their opinion, the power of Augustus and his successors did or did not rest to an
extent at least on the power of the praetorians and the legionaries. To be sure, the
praetorians used swords and not bayonets, but if that is not pap, it is pudding.

2180 [4] Aulard, Histoire politique de la révolution française, pp. 177-79: "On November 29, 1791, the Legislative Assembly passed, among other measures, a bill requiring ecclesiasts who had refused to accept the civil constitution within a week's
time to take the civic oath, or oath of allegiance to country, law, and king. . . .
The King refused to sign the bill. So he had opposed his royal veto to a bill of
November 9 carrying threat of death to fugitives abroad who did not return home
at once and continued plotting against the country. . . . A devious policy of watch-

2181. All such facts as a rule present themselves in the guise of derivations. In one direction we get theories that condemn the use of violence by the subject class in whatever case, in the other direction theories that censure its use by public authority (§§ 2147[18], 2174).

2182. Ruling-class theories, when the requirement of logic is not too keenly felt, appeal simply to sentiments of veneration for holders of power, or for abstractions such as "the state," and to sentiments of disapprobation for individuals who try to disturb or subvert existing orders (§ 2192). Then when it is deemed advisable to satisfy the need of logic, the effort is to create a confusion between the violation of an established uniformity for the individual's exclusive profit and a violation designed to further some collective interest or some new uniformity. The aim in such a derivation is to carry over to

fulness and intrigue both at home and abroad was masked by a ministry that was at odds with itself, had no program, and was made up of intriguers and downright counter-revolutionists. . . . The King consented to disband the Swiss Guard, but he refused to sign the law on priests and on the army." Sulla's policy was different. He cared little for the temples, stripping them of their valuables in order to pay his soldiers, and refusing to obey an order of the Senate demanding the demobilization of his legions. When he marched upon Rome, as Duruy, *Histoire des Romains,* Vol. II, p. 576 (Mahaffy, Vol. II, p. 588), aptly notes: "Once he had decided to draw the sword on people who had only a plebiscite to defend them, success was certain." Later on, Julius Caesar also trusted to his sword and won in the face of decrees by the Senate. M. Aulard certainly cannot be suspected of monarchical bias. He confesses, *Ibid.,* p. 187, that after the riots of June 20, 1792, "there was a recrudescence of royalism in the *bourgeoisie* and in certain districts in France. Twenty thousand petitioners and departmental administrations in large numbers protested against the insult that had been done to the royal majesty and which was represented as an attempt on the King's life." Petitions? Petitions were not enough! The call was for arms! Are humanitarians so obtuse that they can learn nothing from history? M. Aulard goes on to tell the story of the famous *baiser de Lamourette* (July 7, 1792) and concludes, p. 188: "So, all the defenders of the *bourgeois* régime stood grouped in one accord to defend the throne, prevent a repetition of the scenes of June 20, and punish those responsible for them." A fine defence! Words, intrigues! What those good souls lacked was faith in force, the energy to fight, the courage to fall face to the foe and weapon in hand—nothing more! P. 189: "As we have seen, the legislative assembly had disbanded the royal guard and the King had signed that bill. After depriving the King of his means of defence against a popular insurrection it had itself tried to organize a military force to checkmate the plans of the King or his entourage." Then what always has happened, happened: those who possessed the force defeated those who could not bring themselves to use it; and that was fortunate for France at that time, as it had been for other peoples in the past, for the rule of the strong is generally better than the rule of weaklings.

the social or political act the reprobation that is generally visited upon common crime. Frequent in our day are reasonings in some way connected with the theology of Progress. Not a few of our modern governments have revolutionary origins. How condemn the revolutions that might be tried against them without repudiating the forefathers? That is attended to by invoking a new divine right: Insurrection was legitimate enough against governments of the past, where authority was based on force; it is not legitimate against modern governments, where the authority is based on "reason." Or else: Insurrection was legitimate against kings and oligarchies; it is never legitimate against "the People." Or again: Rebellion is justifiable where there is no universal suffrage, but not where that panacea is the law of the land. Or again: Revolt is useless and therefore reprehensible in all countries where "the People" are able to express their "will." Then finally—just to give some little satisfaction to their Graces, the Metaphysicists: Insurrection cannot be tolerated where a "state of law" exists. I hope I shall be excused if I do not define that very sweet entity here. For all of most painstaking researches on my part, it remains an entity altogether unknown to me, and I should much rather be asked to give the zoological pedigree of the Chimaera.

2183. Again as usual, no one of these derivations has any exact meaning. All governments use force, and all assert that they are founded on reason. In the fact, whether universal suffrage prevails or not, it is always an oligarchy that governs, finding ways to give to the "will of the people" that expression which the few desire, from the "royal law" that bestowed the *imperium* on the Roman Emperors down to the votes of a legislative majority elected in one way or another, from the plebiscite that gave the empire to Napoleon III down to the universal suffrage that is shrewdly bought, steered, and manipulated by our "speculators." Who is this new god called Universal Suffrage? He is no more exactly definable, no less shrouded in mystery, no less beyond the pale of reality, than the hosts of other divinities; nor are there fewer and less patent contradictions in his theology than in theirs. Worshippers of Universal Suffrage are not led by their god. It is they who lead him—and by the nose, determining the forms in which he must manifest himself. Oftentimes, proclaiming the sanctity of "majority rule," they resist "majority rule" by obstructionist tactics, even though they form but small minorities, and burning incense to the goddess Reason, they in no wise disdain, in certain cases, alliances with Chicanery, Fraud, and Corruption.

2184. Substantially such derivations express the sentiments felt by people who have climbed into the saddle and are willing to stay there—along with the far more general sentiment that social stability is a good thing. If, the moment a group, large or small, ceased to be satisfied with certain norms established in the community of which it is a part, it flew to arms to abolish them, organized society would fall to pieces. Social stability is so beneficial a thing that to maintain it it is well worth while to enlist the aid of fantastic ideals (§§ 1879, 1875) and this or that theology—among the others, the theology of universal suffrage—and be resigned to putting up with certain actual disadvantages. Before it becomes advisable to disturb the public peace, such disadvantages must have grown very very serious; and since human beings are effectively guided not by the sceptical reasonings of science but by "living faiths" expressed in ideals, theories such as the divine right of kings, the legitimacy of oligarchies, of "the people," of "majorities," of legislative assemblies, and other such things, may be useful within certain limits, and have in fact proved to be, however absurd they may be from the scientific standpoint.

2185. Theories designed to justify the use of force by the governed are almost always combined with theories condemning the use of force by the public authority. A few dreamers reject the use of force in general, on whatever side; but their theories either have no influence at all or else serve merely to weaken resistance on the part of people in power, so clearing the field for violence on the part of the governed. In view of that we may confine ourselves to considering such theories, in general, in the combined form.

2186. No great number of theories are required to rouse to resistance and to the use of force people who are, or think they are, oppressed. The derivations therefore are chiefly designed to incline people who would otherwise be neutral in the struggle to condemn resistance on the part of the governing powers, and so to make their resistance less vigorous; or at a venture, to persuade the rulers themselves in that sense, a thing, for that matter, that is not likely to have any great success in our day save with those whose spinal columns have utterly rotted from the bane of humanitarianism. A few centuries ago some results might have been achieved in our Western countries by working with religious derivations upon sincere Christians; and, in other countries, by working upon firm believers with derivations of the religion prevailing in the given case. Since humanitarianism is a religion, like the Christian, the Moslem, or any other, we may say, in general, that one may sometimes secure the aid of neutrals and weaken resistance on the part of people in power by using derivations of the religion, whatever it may be, in which they sincerely believe. But since derivations readily lend themselves to proving the pro and the contra, that device is often of scant effect even when it is not a mere mask for interests.

2187. In our times conflicts are chiefly economic. If a government therefore sets out to protect employers or strike-breakers from violence by strikers, it is accused of "interfering" in an economic matter that does not properly concern it. If the police do not allow their heads to be broken without using their weapons, they are said to have "shown poor judgment," to have acted "impulsively," "nervously." Like strike-breakers, they must be denied the right to use arms whenever they are attacked by strikers, for otherwise some striker might be killed, and the crime of assault, assuming but not conceding that there has been such a crime, does not deserve the penalty of death (§ 2147 [18]). Court decisions are impugned as "class decisions"; at any rate, they are always too severe. Amnesties, finally, must wipe out all remembrance of such unpleasantness. One might suppose that since the interests of employers and strike-breakers are directly contrary to the interests of the strikers, they would use the opposite derivations. But that is not the case, or if they do, they do it in a very mild, apologetic way. The reason is, as regards the "strike-breaker," the "scab," that he has, as a class, very little spirit. He is not inspired by any lofty ideal, he is almost ashamed of what he is doing, and does it with as little talk as possible. As regards employers of labour, the reason is that many of them are "speculators" who hope to make up for their losses in a strike through government aid and at the expense of consumer or taxpayer. Their quarrels with strikers are quarrels between accomplices over the division of the loot. The strikers belong to the masses, where there is a wealth of Class II residues. They have not only interests but ideals. Their "speculator" employers belong to a class that has grown rich in its aptitude for combinations. They are well supplied, over-supplied, with residues from Class I and so have interests chiefly, and few or no ideals. They spend their time in activities that are far more lucrative than the manufacture of theories. Among them are not a few plutocratic demagogues who are artists at the trick of turning to their advantage strikes that are in all appearances directed against them.[1] There are general considerations, furthermore, that apply to both domestic and international conflicts. They come down, in brief, to an appeal to sentiments of pity for the sufferings that are caused by the use of force, disregarding entirely the reasons for which the force is used and the utility or the harm that results from using or not using it. They are often filled out with expressions of reverence, or at least of compassion, for the proletariat, which can never do wrong or at the very least is excusable for whatever it does. In a day gone by, similar derivations, corresponding to the very same sentiments, were used in favour now of royal, now of the-ocratic, now of aristocratic, rule.

2188. It is interesting, as in keeping with the essentially senti-mental character of derivations, that theories that would be the soundest from the logico-experimental standpoint are as a rule neg-lected. In the Middle Ages an excellent argument might have been put forward in favour of the ecclesiastical power at a time when it was at war with imperial, royal, or baronial powers—the fact that it was virtually the only counterbalance to those other powers, and al-most the only refuge of intelligence, science, and cultivation against ignorant brutal force. But that argument was seldom, if ever, used. People preferred to rely on derivations based on the doctrine of rev-elation and quotations from Scripture (§ 1617). Now employers who

2187 [1] In Italy it is a recognized practice for the government to pay to the manu-facturers who supply railroad equipment a price equal to production-costs plus a reasonable profit. If, therefore, costs rise as the result of a strike, the taxpayer pays the difference and the manufacturer sits back and takes his profit. Time and again not only railway-supply companies but others, and notably ship-building concerns, have been known to provoke strikes or threats of strikes in their factories as a means of exerting pressure upon a ministry and so securing new orders at suitable prices. The Socialist cooperatives that contract for public works do the very same thing, dispensing with the mediation of "capitalists."

themselves enjoy economic protection manifest great indignation at strikers for trying to rid themselves of the competition of non-union workers. The rejoinder is never made that they are trying to keep others from doing what they are doing themselves, and that they fail to show how and why free competition is good for the working-man and bad for the employer of labour. An individual tries to slip across the Italian frontier with a few bags of saccharin. Customs officers come running and violently prevent such competition with Italian manufacturers of beet-sugar, going, on occasion, so far as to use their guns and sometimes to kill the smuggler whom nobody mourns. All the same it is owing to just such violence and such murders that not a few Italian "sugar men" have managed to amass considerable fortunes and win public esteem, national honours, and even seats among the law-makers. One still has to be shown why violence cannot be used in the same way to increase wages.

2189. It may be objected that the violence that safe-guards the interests of the employer is legal and the violence used by the strikers on "scabs" illegal. That transfers the question from the utility of the violence to the utility of the manner in which violence is applied—a matter of considerable importance, no one will deny. Legal violence is the consequence of the norms established in a society, and in general resort to it is more beneficial or at least less harmful than resort to private violence, which is designed as a rule to overthrow prevailing norms. The strikers might answer, and in fact sometimes do, that they are using illegal violence because they are cut off from using the legal variety. If the law were to constrain people by use of legal violence to give them what they demand, they would not need to resort to illegal violence. That same argument would serve in many other cases. People who use illegal violence would ask for nothing better than to be able to transmute it into legal violence.

2190. But the matter is not yet exhausted, and we now come to the salient point in the question. Let us set the particular case aside and look at the problem in its general form. The dispute is really as to the relative merits of shrewdness and force, and to decide it in the sense that never never, not even in the exceptional case, is it useful to meet wits with violence, it would be necessary first to show that the use of cunning is always, without exception, more advisable than the use of force (§ 2319). Suppose a certain country has a governing class, *A,* that assimilates the best elements, as regards intelligence, in the whole population. In that case the subject class, *B,* is largely stripped of such elements and can have little or no hope of ever overcoming the class *A* so long as it is a battle of wits. If intelligence were to be combined with force, the dominion of the *A*'s would be perpetual, for as Dante says, *Inferno,* XXXI, vv. 55-57 (Fletcher translation):

> "For if the machination of the mind
> To evil-will be added and to might,
> Of no defence is competent mankind."

But such a happy combination occurs only for a few individuals. In the majority of cases people who rely on their wits are or become less fitted to use violence, and *vice versa.* So concentration in the class *A* of the individuals most adept at chicanery leads to a concentration in class *B* of the individuals most adept at violence; and if that process is long continued, the equilibrium tends to become unstable, because the *A*'s are long in cunning but short in the courage to use force and in the force itself; whereas the *B*'s have the force and the courage to use it, but are short in the skill required for exploiting those advantages. But if they chance to find leaders who have the skill—and history shows that such leadership is usually supplied by dissatisfied *A*'s—they have all they need for driving the *A*'s from power. Of just that development history affords countless examples from remotest times all the way down to the present.[1]

2190 [1] Almost always writers study such incidents from the ethical standpoint and so are blinded to uniformities that nevertheless stand out as plain as day. When a historian is writing the history of a revolution, his chief concern is to decide whether it was "just" or "unjust"; and since those terms are not definable, the inquiry turns into a mere question as to the impression that the facts make upon him. In the best case, if a writer chances to have no particular bias to which he deliberately subordinates history, he lets himself be guided by some metaphysical conception as to what is "just" and "unjust" and bases his appraisals on that. More frequently he has a faith that he is at no pains to conceal. If he is favourable to monarchy or oligarchy, he will say that the rebels are in the "wrong"; and, conversely, if he is a "democrat," that the rebels are in the "right." When it occurs to him—a thing that does not always happen—to look into the causes of an uprising, he will halt, one may be sure, at a set of ethical causes. If he is against the masses, he will say that they have been roused to insurrection by the misleading wiles of demagogues. Favourable to them, he will say that they were oppressed by intolerably abusive laws that were

2191. In general terms, a revolution of that type is beneficial to a community—more so when a governing class is tending more and more towards humanitarianism, less so when it is made up of individuals who are tending more and more to use combinations instead of force, especially if the combinations result, even indirectly, in the material prosperity of the community.

Let us imagine a country where the governing class, *A,* is inclining more and more in the direction of humanitarianism, is fostering, in other words, only the more harmful group-persistences, rejecting the others as outworn prejudices, and, while awaiting the advent of the "reign of reason," is becoming less and less capable of using force and is so shirking the main duty of a ruling class. Such a country is on its way to utter ruin. But lo, the subject class, *B,* revolts against the class *A.* In fighting *A* it uses the humanitarian derivations so dear to the *A*'s, but underlying them are quite different sentiments, and they soon find expression in deeds. The *B*'s apply force on a far-reaching scale, and not only overthrow the *A*'s but kill large numbers of them—and, in so doing, to tell the truth, they are performing a useful public service, something like ridding the country of a baneful animal pest. They bring with them to the seats of power a great abundance of group-persistences;[1] and little it matters, if it matters at all, that these group-persistences be different in outward forms from the old.[2] The important thing is that now they are functioning in the governing class and that owing to them the social fabric is acquiring stability and strength. The country is saved from ruin and is reborn to a new life.

If one judges superficially, one may be tempted to dwell more especially on the slaughter and pillaging that attend a revolution, without thinking to ask whether such things may not be manifestations—as regrettable as one may wish—of sentiments, of social forces, that are very salutary. If one should say that, far from being reprehensible, the slaughter and robbery are signs that those who were called upon to commit them deserved power for the good of

forced upon them by the governing class. How much paper and ink have been wasted in repeating such brainless clatter over and over and over again!

2191 [1] [Reading, in Pareto's Italian, *persistenze* for *persistenza*.—A. L.]

2191 [2] [I take *"essi"* in Pareto's Italian as referring to *"aggregati."* The passage can also be rendered with *"essi"* referring to the *B*'s.—A. L.]

society, he would be stating a paradox, for there is no relationship of cause and effect, nor any close and indispensable correlation, between such outrages and social utility; but the paradox would still contain its modicum of truth, in that the slaughter and rapine are external symptoms indicating the advent of strong and courageous people to places formerly held by weaklings and cowards.[8] In all that we have been describing in the abstract many revolutions that have actually occurred in the concrete, from the revolution which gave imperial rule to Augustus down to the French Revolution of '89 (§§ 2199 f.). If the class governing in France had had the faith that counsels use of force and the will to use force, it would never have been overthrown and, procuring its own advantage, would have procured the advantage of France. Since it failed in that function, it was salutary that its rule should give way to rule by others; and since, again, it was the resort to force that was wanting, it was in keeping with very general uniformities that there should be a swing to another extreme where force was used even more than was required. Had Louis XVI not been a man of little sense and less courage, letting himself be floored without fighting, and preferring to lose his head on the guillotine to dying weapon in hand like a man of sinew, he might have been the one to do the destroying. If the victims of the September massacres, their kinsmen and friends, had not for the most part been spineless humanitarians without a particle of courage or energy, they would have annihilated their enemies instead of waiting to be annihilated themselves. It was a good thing that power should pass into the hands of people who showed that they had the faith and the resolve requisite for the use of force.

The advantage of the use of force to a society is less apparent when the governing class is made up of persons in whom the combination instincts are prevalent, and within certain limits there may be no advantage. But when a governing class divests itself too com-

2191 [8] Critics of the French Revolution accuse it of making extensive use of force. Its admirers try to excuse it on that same score. Both are right if the purpose is to find derivations to influence people who feel an instinctive and unreasoned repugnance to the infliction of suffering (residues IV-γ2). They are wrong if they are objectively considering the conditions determining social utility. From that standpoint it has to be admitted that the use of force was one of the chief merits of the French Revolution, not a fault.

pletely of the sentiments of group-persistence, it easily reaches a point where it is unfit to defend, let alone its own power, what is far worse, the independence of its country. In such a case, if the independence is to be deemed an advantage, it must also be deemed an advantage to be rid of a class that has become incompetent to perform the functions of defence. As a rule it is from the subject class that individuals come with the faith and the resolve to use force and save a country.

2192. The governing class, *A*, tries to defend its power and avert the danger of an uprising of the *B*'s in various ways (§§ 1827, 1838, 2377 f.). It may try to take advantage of the strength of the *B*'s, and and that is the most effective policy. Or it may try to prevent its dis-affected members from becoming leaders of the *B*'s, or rather, of that element among the *B*'s which is disposed to use force; but that is a very difficult thing to achieve. And the *A*'s use derivations to keep the *B*'s quiet (§ 2182), telling them that "all power comes from God," that it is a "crime" to resort to violence, that there is no reason for using force to obtain what, if it is "just," may be obtained by "reason." The main purpose of such derivations is to keep the *B*'s from giving battle on their own terrain, the terrain of force, and to lead them to other ground—the field of cunning—where their defeat is certain, pitted as they will be against the *A*'s, who are immensely their superiors in wits. But as a rule the effectiveness of such derivations depends largely upon the pre-existing sentiments that they express, and only to a slight extent upon sentiments that they create.

2193. Those derivations have to be met with other derivations of equal effectiveness, and it will be better if some of them play upon sentiments that are acceptable to people who imagine that they are neutral, though in reality they may not be, who would prefer not to take sides with either the *A*'s or the *B*'s but to think solely of what is "just" and "honest." Such sentiments are chiefly available in the group manifested by residues of sociality (Class IV) and more especially the sentiments of pity (IV-γ1, IV-γ2). For that reason, most of the derivations favouring the use of violence by the subject class defend it not so much directly as indirectly—condemning resistance on the part of the governing class in the name of sociality, pity, and repugnance to sufferings in others.[1] These latter sentiments are almost the only ones that are exploited by many pacifists who can think of no other way to defend their thesis than by describing the "horrors of war." Derivations relating to the social struggle often have recourse, further, to sentiments of asceticism, which sometimes influence individuals among the *A*'s and so prove to be of no mean advantage to the *B*'s.[2]

2194. At bottom all such derivations express, in chief, the sentiments of individuals who are eager for change in the social order, and they are therefore beneficial or harmful according as the change is beneficial or harmful. If one is going to assert that change is

2193 [1] Sorel, *Réflexions sur la violence,* pp. 33-35, 176, 27 (91-94, 271, 83; Soule, pp. 74-76, 220, 68), has well shown the fatuity of such derivations: "One finds it difficult to understand proletarian violence when one tries to reason with the ideas that *bourgeois* philosophy has spread abroad in the world. According to that philosophy, violence would be a remnant of barbarism that is destined to disappear as enlightenment progresses. . . . The parliamentary Socialists cannot grasp the purposes of the 'new school.' As they conceive it, the whole of Socialism comes down to a search for the means of getting into power. [They are just individuals who are in process of assimilation into the governing class. The name "Transformists" which they sometimes affect fits the substance of the thing.] A shrewdly manipulated agitation is extremely profitable to parliamentary Socialists, who boast before the government and the wealthy *bourgeoisie* that they know the trick of exorcizing the revolution. That enables them to engineer the business enterprises in which they are interested, and get incidental favours for large numbers of influential vote-getters. [And, in Italy, procure governmental subsidies for Socialist cooperatives.] . . . The ferocity of the old days is tending to give way to cunning, and many sociologists think that that is a real progress. Some philosophers who are not in the habit of following the opinions of the flock do not see very clearly how that can represent any great progress from the standpoint of morals. . . . Quite a number of working-men understand perfectly well that all the claptrap of parliamentary literature [Derivations.] serves merely to dissemble the real considerations that determine the policies of governments. The protectionists get along by subsidizing a few big party leaders [And here and there a little one, and not only with money, but by flattering their vanities, nudging a newspaper to praise them, getting them decorations and posts of influence.] and supporting newspapers which in turn support the policies of those party leaders. The workers have no money, but they have at their disposal a far more effective means of action: they can *frighten*."

2193 [2] It was the surpassing merit of Georges Sorel that in his *Réflexions sur la violence* he threw all such fatuities overboard to ascend to the altitudes of science. He was not adequately understood by people who went looking for derivations and were given logico-experimental reasonings instead. As for certain university professors who habitually mistake pedantry for science (§ 1749 [6]), and, given a theory, focus their microscope on insignificant errors and other trifles, they are completely destitute of the intellectual capacities required for understanding the work of a scientist of Sorel's stature.

always for the worse, that stability is the supreme good, one ought to be ready to show either that it would have been to the advantage of human societies always to have remained in a state of barbarism, or that the transition from barbarism to civilization has been achieved, or *might have* been achieved (§§ 133 f.), without wars and revolutions. This latter assertion is so grossly at variance with the facts as we learn them from history that it is absurd even to discuss it. So only the first is left, and it might be defended by giving a special meaning to the term "utility" and adopting the theories that have sung the joys of a "state of nature." If one is unwilling to go as far as that, one cannot hold to the first proposition either; and so one is forced by the facts and by logic to admit that wars and revolutions have sometimes been beneficial (which does not mean that they have always been so). And once that is admitted for the past, no basis whatever remains for showing that things will be otherwise in the future.

2195. So there we are again, and as usual, driven from the qualitative field, where derivations predominate, into the quantitative field of logico-experimental science. One cannot assert in general that stability is always beneficial or that change is always beneficial. Every case has to be examined on its particular merits and the utility and the detriment appraised to see whether the first overbalances the second, or *vice versa*.

2196. We have already found (§ 2176) that in many cases stability is beneficial. We should find cases no fewer in number where violations of existing norms have also proved beneficial, provided we consider norms of an intellectual order along with norms of a material order. But keeping them separate, it will be apparent that— especially as regards violations by small numbers of individuals— many are the cases where violations of intellectual norms by individuals or by a few individuals prove advantageous, few the cases where violations of norms of a material order prove beneficial. For that reason, the implications of the formula stated in § 2176, whereby violations of norms of a material order should be the more vigorously suppressed, the more exclusively they are the work of individuals, the less so, the more they are the work of groups, do not in many cases take us too far astray from the maximum of social utility, as they would do if the formula were applied to violations of norms of an intellectual order. That, substantially, is the chief argument that can be advanced in favour of what is called "freedom of thought" (§ 2348).

2197. Derivations do not run that way. Dissenters defend their opinions because they are "better" than the opinions held by the majority; and it is a good thing that they have that faith, for it alone can supply them with the energy they need to resist the persecutions that they almost always incur. So long as they are few in numbers, they ask just for a little place in the Sun for their sect. In reality they are panting for the moment when they can turn from persecuted to persecutor, a thing that infallibly happens as soon as they have become numerous enough to enforce their will. At that moment the advantage of their past dissent is at an end, and the detriment resulting from their new orthodoxy begins to assert itself.

2198. In considering the use of force there is a stronger temptation than in other social connexions to think only of relationships of cause and effect; nor in many cases do we go very far wide of the mark in that. After all, in the sequence of actions and reactions that confronts one, the action of this or that force as producing this or that effect occupies a very considerable place. However, it is better not to stop at that, but go on to see whether phenomena that are more general should not be taken into account.

2199. Just above, for instance, in § 2169, we compared the revolution in Rome at the time of Augustus with the revolution in France at the time of Louis XVI; and we saw that to understand those two events we had to look beyond the derivations to the sentiments and interests that the derivations represented. Advancing one step further, one notes that both in the fall of the Roman Republic and in the fall of the French monarchy, the respective governing classes were either unwilling or unable to use force, and were overthrown by other classes that were both willing and able to do that (§ 2191). Both in ancient Rome and in France the victorious element rose from the people and was made up in Rome of the legions of Sulla, Caesar, and Octavius, in France of the revolutionary mobs that routed a very feeble royal power, and then of an army that vanquished the very inefficient troops of the European potentates. The leaders of the victors spoke Latin, of course, in Rome, and French in France, and no less naturally used derivations that were suitable to the Romans and the French respectively. The Roman people was fed on derivations conforming with a feeling that substance might be changed so long as forms were kept (§§ 174 f.), the French masses, on derivations inspired by the religion of "Progress," a faith surpassingly dear to the French of that day. Not otherwise, in the day of the Puritan Revolution, did Cromwell and other foes of the Stuarts use biblical derivations.

2200. The French derivations are more familiar than the Roman not only because more documents have come down to us, but also, as seems very probable, because they were supplied in greater abundance. Had Octavius long continued in his rôle as defender of the Senate, he might have made very lavish use of them; but when, before Bologna, he came to an understanding with Antony and Lepidus, his fortunes came to rest altogether on the might of his legions; so he laid his derivations away in his arsenals as weapons no longer needed, not taking them out again till after his victory, when it was a question of smoothing the fur of old-timers in Rome, which might have been ruffled by the change in régime.[1] Something of the same sort took place in France as regards Napoleon I; but before his time the Jacobins, who opened the road for him, found it impossible to play only the lion and had to resort to the tricks of the fox. With his own prestige as commander, Octavius had made sure of the support of an armed force, and at first with his own money, later on with the money that he was in a position to extort by force from others. The French revolutionary leaders were unable to do anything like that, in the beginning. They had to recruit their

---

2200 [1] The three triumvirs were enemies, but each had a number of legions at his disposal, while the Senate had none. They were therefore readily convinced that it was to their advantage to come to an agreement with each other and make the partisans of the Senate pay the various "considerations." Says Duruy to this point, *Histoire des Romains,* Vol. III, p. 458 (Mahaffy, Vol. III, pp. 446-47): "In line with that inexorable fatality of expiation in history to which we have so often called attention in the course of this narrative, the Senatorial party was about to come under the law that it had made for its adversaries. [Duruy prudently says nothing about the proscriptions of Marius.] The proscriptions and confiscations of Sulla were about to begin again, but this time the nobles were to pay with their heads and fortunes for the crime of the Ides of March and for the rivers of blood with which the oligarchy had flooded Rome and Italy forty years before." If Duruy were a worshipper of Jupiter Optimus Maximus, one might easily guess the agent he trusts with the task of executing his "inexorable fatality"; but since he never resorts to theological considerations of that type, one is forced to the conclusion that his "in-

revolutionary army with derivations, which, expressing as they did the sentiments of many of the government's enemies, brought them in a flock to their standards, and, expressing also the sentiments of almost all members of the ruling classes, further served as an opiate to their already listless vigilance, and broke down their already feeble resistance. Later on, as soon as the revolution got possession of power, its leaders imitated the Roman triumvirs and many other masterful men of the same type, distributing among their followers the money and property of their adversaries.

2201. If the effects of derivations are much less considerable than the effects of residues, they are not, as we have many times seen, altogether without influence, serving primarily to give greater strength and effectiveness to the residues that they express. It would not therefore be exact to say that the historians who have made the derivations of the French Revolution their exclusive or at least their main concern have dealt with an entirely irrelevant aspect of that episode. They may be said to have erred in regarding as primary an aspect that was merely secondary. It has been a more serious error on their part not to consider the rôle played by force and the reasons why force was used by some parties, and not by others. The few who have considered the rôle of force at all have gone astray in assuming that this or that man in power refrained from using force in deference to derivations, whereas both derivations and the aversion to use of force had a common origin in the sentiments of those men. And yet—if one examines closely—the whole thing seems clear,

exorable fatality" is just a metaphysical entity, which, to tell the truth, seems not a little mysterious both in itself and in its workings. All the same, if anyone desires to get some inkling of its nature, one need only turn to the ancient writers who give the facts to which Duruy alludes. Appian, *De bellis civilibus*, IV, 3, says that after the triumvirs struck their bargain, they decided to "promise the soldiers, as the prize of victory, in addition to gifts, eighteen Italian cities to be occupied as colonies, all first-class towns as regards opulence, soil, and buildings—said cities, with the territories surrounding, and all real estate, to be divided among the soldiers as though they had been conquered from a foreign enemy." And *cf.* Dio Cassius, *Historia Romana*, XLVI, 56; Tacitus, *Annales*, I, 10; Velleius Paterculus, *Historia Romana*, II, 63; Florus, *Epitoma de Tito Livio*, II, 16, 6 (IV, 6, 6; Forster, pp. 305-07). Might it not be, therefore, that Duruy's very pretty "fatality" comes down to a matter of buying and bribing individuals who represent physical force, and then using them in one's own interest? This Dame Fatality of Duruy's must have had a whole litter of children, for no other ancestors can be imagined for the deity who protects our latter-day politicians in keeping their hold on power by buying votes.

with the proof and the counter-proof. Louis XVI fell because he was unwilling, unable, incompetent, to use force; the revolutionists triumphed because they were willing and able and competent. Not by any cogency in their theories but by the sheer might of their followings did now this and now that revolutionary faction climb to power. Even the Directory, which had saved itself by resorting to force in conflicts with weaker factions, succumbed to force in its struggle with Bonaparte, made the man of the hour by his victorious troops. And Napoleon lasts until he is worn down under the superior force of the Allies. And then—over again: a succession of régimes in France, each falling because unwilling, unable, incompetent, to use force, and others rising on the use of force.[1] That was observable on the fall of Charles X, on the fall of Louis Philippe, on the advent of Napoleon III; and one may go on and say that if the government of Versailles in 1871 managed to keep its feet in the face of the Commune, it was because it had a strong army at its disposal and knew enough to use it.

2202. But at this point a question arises of its own accord: Why have certain governments used force and others not? And it is evident that on the step that we have taken above in explaining things other steps must now follow. And it is further evident that we are not strictly exact when we say, as we have just said, that this or that government fell "because" it did not use force; for if there should prove to be facts on which the failure to use force depended, those facts more properly would be the "cause" of the outcome, the failure to use force being merely the apparent cause. It might also be that those facts in their turn depended, in part at least, upon the failure to use force, and so our relationships of cause and effect would have to be amended into broader relationships of interdependence. Nor is

2201 [1] Ollivier, *L'Empire libéral,* Vol. XVI, p. 1: "Study of the facts in history has led me to this experimental conclusion: that no government was ever overthrown by its enemies. Enemies are like the buttresses in a Gothic church: they hold up the edifice. There is only one way for a government to die: suicide. [That is a little too sweeping. A government can succumb to superior force, as happened to Pompey, Charles I of England, and many others whom it would be superfluous to mention.] Since 1789 all the governments in France have destroyed themselves: the Constituents bar themselves from their own work; the Girondins surrender; the Jacobins slaughter each other; the leading Directors put their republic up at auction; Napoleon I abdicates twice; Charles X abdicates and goes abroad; Louis Philippe abdicates and takes to his heels."

that all. If it is true that governments which are incompetent or unable to use force fall, it is also true that no government endures by depending entirely upon force (§ 2251). From all of which it is apparent that we have examined only one side of the situation and must therefore broaden the scope of our researches and look at it in a much more general way. Suppose we do that.

2203. *Cycles of interdependence.* Let us go back and think once more of the elements upon which the social equilibrium depends; and since, unfortunately, we cannot consider them all and take their interdependences into account in all strictness, suppose we follow the course suggested above in §§ 2104 and 2092, and consider a restricted group of elements, to be selected, naturally, from among the more important, gradually enlarging the groups thereafter so as to have them include as many elements as possible. As for the interdependences, we will use method *2a* instead of method *2b,* as indicated in § 1732, keeping always in mind the pitfalls sign-boarded in § 2092 [1].

2204. An element of a given group acts upon elements in other groups, either apart from the other elements in its own group or in conjunction with them. Suppose we call the effect it has when considered apart from the other elements in its group the *direct* effect; the effect it has in virtue of its combination with other elements in its group, the *indirect* effect. In so doing we shall be continuing the analysis we began in § 2089. There we divided facts into two categories: 1. The fact of the existence of a society. 2. The facts observable in that society, in other words, the elements from which the fact of its existence results. Let us now first divide this second category into groups, and then go on to select one element from each group and try to determine the effect that it has, as a distinct unit, upon the elements in other groups (*direct* effect) as well as the effect it has upon them when it is considered as operating in conjunction with the other elements in its own group (*indirect* effect).

2205. And now let us turn to the matter of interdependence among the groups. To be as brief as possible, suppose we indicate the following elements by letters of the alphabet: Residues, *a;* interests, *b;* derivations, *c;* social heterogeneity and circulation, *d.* If one could use mathematical logic, the interdependence of the elements could be expressed in equations (§ 2091); but since that cannot be done in the present state of knowledge and we are compelled to use ordinary language (§ 2092), we have nothing left but to consider the interdependence in another form—in the form of actions and reactions among the elements—and to follow the course indicated in § 2104.

2206. We may say, accordingly: (I) That *a* acts upon *b, c, d;* (II) that *b* acts upon *a, c, d;* (III) that *c* acts upon *a, b, d;* (IV) that *d* acts upon *a, b, c.*

From what we have been saying in the previous chapter, it is evident that Combination I yields a very considerable portion of the social phenomenon; and those writers who have regarded ethics as the foundation of society may have had a remote and inadequate perception of that fact. In it also lies the modicum of truth that is to be found in metaphysical doctrines which make facts dependent upon "concepts," since "concepts" reflect, though very confusedly, residues and sentiments corresponding to residues. It is Combination I also that assures continuity in the history of human societies, since the category *a* varies slightly or slowly.[1]

Combination II also yields a very considerable portion of the social phenomenon, and it too varies but slightly and slowly and contributes to the continuity of human societies. The importance of Combination II was noticed by the followers of "economic determinism"; but they fell into the error of substituting the part for the whole and disregarding the other combinations. Combination III is the least important of all. Failure to perceive that fact has rendered the lucubrations of humanitarians, "intellectuals," and worshippers of the goddess Reason, erroneous, inconclusive, fatuous. However, to a greater degree than any of the others it is known to us through literature, and a far greater importance is commonly attached to it than it really has in society. Combination IV is of no mean importance, a fact remarked of old by Plato and Aristotle, to say nothing of other ancient writers. In our day the studies of Lapouge, Hamon, and others, incomplete and marred by errors as they may be, have had the great merit of throwing that very important relation into relief, while failure to take account of it fundamentally vitiates so-called democratic theories.

2206 [1] Of that we shall speak more fully further along.

2207. It must not be forgotten that actions and reactions follow one on another indefinitely and, as it were, in a circle (§ 2552 [1]): that is to say, beginning with Combination I one goes on to Combination IV and from IV back again to I. In Combination I the element *a* was acting upon *d;* in IV the element *d* is acting upon *a;* then one goes back again to Combination I, so that *a* is again acting upon *d,* and so on. In virtue, therefore, of Combination I a variation in *a* causes variations in the other elements, *b, c, d;* and just to make the situation more manageable in language, we will give the variations in *a, b, c, d* that are effected in virtue of Combination I the name of *immediate effects.* But in virtue of the other combinations, variations in *b, c, d* also effect variations in *a;* and because of the circular movement this variation reacts upon Combination I and gives rise to new variations in *a, b, c, d.* To these variations we will, again for mere purposes of convenience, give the name of *mediate effects.* Sometimes it is necessary to consider two or more combinations simultaneously. Farther along (§§ 2343 f.) we shall see an example of great significance in which effects are so intertwined that we are obliged to study Combinations II and IV together. The state of concrete equilibrium observable in a given society is a resultant of all these effects, of all these actions and reactions. It is therefore different from a state of theoretical equilibrium obtained by considering one or more of the elements *a, b, c, d* instead of considering all. Political economy, for instance, deals with category *b,* and one of its branches is pure economics. Pure economics yields a theoretical equilibrium that is different, still within category *b,* from another theoretical equilibrium yielded by applied economics; and different from other theoretical equilibria that could be obtained by combining *b* with some of the elements *a, c, d;* and different, again, from the theoretical equilibrium that most nearly approximates the concrete and is obtained by combining all the elements *a, b, c, d* (§ 2552).[1]

2207 [1] Many literary economists are inclined to consider the cycle *bc—cb* exclusively: from study of the interests, *b,* with which their science pre-eminently deals, they draw certain conclusions, *c,* and then go on to imagine that the economic activity, *b,* can be modified by disseminating the doctrines *c.* A most striking example would be free trade. Studying the economic situation, *b,* one derives the demonstration, *c,* of the desirability of free trade. When, then, the doctrine, *c,* becomes widely accepted it is taken for granted that it cannot fail to modify the economic situation,

2208. This will all be clearer if we give a less abstract form to what we have just been saying, and at the same time proceed from particular cases to more general ones, following the inductive method. Suppose we locate the protection of industries by import duties in the group *b*. We first get its economic effects, direct and indirect; and these are the concern primarily of economics, which is the science of the group *b*. We shall not go into them here, but merely note certain effects that we find it necessary to consider for our purposes. Among these we shall have to consider economic effects that have so far been more or less neglected by the science of economics. As a rule, champions of free trade have considered low prices, implicitly at least, as an advantage to a population at large, whereas champions of protection have regarded low prices as an evil. The first view is readily acceptable to anyone thinking chiefly of consumption, the latter to anyone thinking chiefly of production. From the scientific standpoint they are both of little or no value, since they are based on an incomplete analysis of the situation.[1] A

b, and make free trade a concrete reality. In general when economists come upon some sentiment, *a*, that they are obliged to consider, they usually assume that it exists of itself, without any relation to *b*. The "just" and the "unjust," for instance, are absolutes, and have no bearing whatever on *b*. Marx noted the existence of the relation between *a* and *b*, and so came quite close to a logico-experimental result; but he erred in mistaking it for a relation between a *cause*, *b*, acting upon an *effect*, *a*, whereas if *b* acts upon *a*, *a* reacts in its turn upon *b*. Among the many reasons why Combination IV is very frequently ignored is the habit of regarding sentiments, interests, and derivations absolutely, independently of individuals. That yields abstractions, and not properties of given individuals; and it is therefore assumed that the manner of variation of classes of individuals does not have to be considered.

2208 [1] The following derivations were also widely used. Taking their stand in the field of ethics, free-traders said: "Protection is an evil because it robs the unprotected in favour of the protected"; and protectionists replied: "That evil can be corrected by according equal protection to everyone equally." To which the free-traders rejoined that equal protection to everyone was equivalent to protection for nobody—which is an admission that two identical positions of equilibrium are possible with different prices (§ 2207 [1]). Both free-traders and protectionists, deliberately or unwittingly, substituted derivations for considerations of realities. In order to keep within the logico-experimental field, free-traders should have said: "Thanks to a destruction of wealth, protection transfers a certain amount of wealth from certain individuals to certain other individuals, and that transfer is precisely what you protectionists are trying to effect. You are therefore contradicting yourselves when you talk of equal protection for everybody; for if equal protection were possible, there would be no reason left for your being protectionists. When you speak of equal protection for everybody you mean, though you do not say so, equal protection not for all citizens, among whom mere owners of savings would have to be

forward step along the scientific path was taken when the theories of mathematical economics supplied a proof that, in general, the direct effect of protection is a destruction of wealth.[2] If one were free to go on and add an axiom, which is implicitly taken for granted by many economists, that any destruction of wealth is an "evil," one could logically conclude that protection is an "evil."[3] But before such a proposition can be granted the indirect economic effects and the social effects of protection have to be known. Keeping to the former for the moment, we find that protection transfers a certain amount of wealth from a part, *A*, of the population to a part *B*, through the destruction of a certain amount of wealth, *q*, the amount

counted, but equal protection for the whole of a given class of citizens, which will be found to comprise a more or less extensive number of manufacturers, farmers, and land owners. That is the thing which we regard as detrimental to the country." To which protectionists should have replied: "The facts are as you describe them. Our aim is indeed to transfer wealth from one part of the population to another. We know that such a transfer entails a certain destruction in wealth. All the same, we regard it as a good thing for the country." After that, experience alone could have shown which of the two parties came the closer to realities. But before consulting experience, it would have been essential to know more exactly what the terms "detrimental" and "a good thing" were supposed to designate.

2208 [2] That proof and another more general one were given for the first time in my *Cours*, §§ 862 f., 730. And *cf.* the Appendix to my *Manuel* [but more especially, pp. 506-19.—A. L.]

2208 [3] My *Cours* contains errors of that sort, at least by implication. I tried to avoid them in my *Manuale*. In the preface to the latter, pp. vii-viii, I say: "Here and there in my *Cours* erroneous manners of statement are to be noted. Such errors arise from two sources, chiefly: first, an incomplete synthesis, in one's hurry to get back from scientific analysis to concrete doctrine. [It was, in fact, my recognition of the necessity of a synthesis less incomplete that led me to undertake the long research the results of which appear in these present volumes.] I was aware of the necessity of a complete synthesis, but then, unconsciously, I came partially to disregard it, if not explicitly, at least by implication. Typical of all such cases would be the matter of free trade and protection. It can be shown scientifically that as a rule protection occasions a destruction of wealth. Examination of facts past and present shows that protection is for the most part established through the influence of persons who profit by it to appropriate other people's goods. But is that enough to condemn protection in the concrete? It is not. Other social consequences of the institution have to be taken into account. [But to do that one had to have a theory of the sort we are here developing, and judgment had to be postponed until that research had been completed.] I believe that I would have given that same answer at the time of my *Cours*, so that the error is not explicit in so many words. All the same, I often expressed myself as though, in the concrete, free trade were in every case a good thing and protection in every case a bad thing, and such statements presuppose assumptions that are marred by the error mentioned."

representing the costs of the operation. If, as a result of this new distribution of wealth, the production of wealth does not increase by a quantity greater than q, the operation is economically detrimental to a population as a whole; if it increases by a quantity greater than q, the operation is economically beneficial. The latter case is not to be barred *a priori;* for the element A contains the indolent, the lazy, and people, in general, who make little use of economic combinations; whereas the element B comprises the people who are economically wide-awake and are always ready for energetic enterprise—people who know how to make effective use of economic combinations. Going on, then, to consider in general not only economic but social effects, one has to distinguish between dynamic effects, which ensue for a brief period of time after protection has been established, and static effects, which ensue after protection has been established for a certain length of time. A distinction must further be drawn between the effects on productions that are readily susceptible of increase, such as manufactures in general, and the effects on productions not so susceptible of increase, such as the agricultural. The dynamic effect is more considerable in the case of the manufacturer than in the case of the farmer. When protection is established those manufacturers who already own factories for protected goods, and persons who are shrewd enough to anticipate protection or to go out and get it, enjoy temporary monopolies, and these come to an end only when new manufacturers enter the field to compete with established firms—that takes time, and often not a short time. Farmers, on the other hand, have little to fear from new enterprise, and for them, therefore, the dynamic effect is not so very different from the static. Furthermore, protection may encourage new industries and so increase, if not the profits, at least the numbers, of manufacturers. That may also happen in agriculture, though on a very much smaller scale, and the ordinary effect of agricultural protection is merely to replace one kind of acreage with another. The static effect, on the other hand, is less considerable on the profits of manufacturers than on the profit of the farmer. It increases the earnings of the farmer, while competition cuts down the earnings of the manufacturer from his temporary monopoly. For that very reason industrial protection usually destroys more wealth than agricultural protection, for with the latter the new earnings, which represent a mere transfer of wealth, are saved from destruction.

2209. Let us look at the *immediate* effects on the other groups.

Combination II. The most perceptible effects are on *d,* that is to say, on social heterogeneousness. The dynamic effects of industrial protection enrich not only individuals who are endowed with technical talents, but especially individuals who have talents for financial combinations or gifts for manipulating the politicians who confer the benefits of protection. Some individuals possess such endowments in conspicuous degree. They grow rich and influential, and come to "run the country." The same is true of politicians who are clever at selling the benefits of protection. All such persons possess Class I residues in high intensities, and Class II residues in fairly low intensities. On the other hand, people in whom endowments of character are more notable than technical or financial talents, or who lack the gift for clever political manoeuvring, are pushed down the ladder. Deriving no benefit from protection, they are the ones who pay its costs. The static effects are not identical—they are analogous in that, though they enrich far fewer persons, they nevertheless open new fields for the activities of individuals who have endowments of talent and cunning, and they increase the industrial population, often at the expense of the agricultural. In short, to put the situation briefly, when account is taken, in making up the governing class, of the imaginary examinations that we used for illustration in § 2027, the higher grades have to be given to individuals in whom Class I residues are numerous and intense and who know how to use them in garnering the fruits of protection; and the lower grades, to individuals in whom Class I residues are few and feeble, or, if they are numerous and strong, are not skilfully exploited. So it results that industrial protection tends to strengthen Class I residues in the governing class. Class-circulation, furthermore, is accelerated. In a country where there is little industry an individual born with a good assortment of combination-instincts finds far fewer opportunities for using them than an individual born in a country where there are many industries and where new enterprises are starting every day. The very art of manipulating protectionist favours offers a wide field of activity for people whose talents lie in that direction, even though they do not use them directly in industry. Carrying on the analogy suggested, one may say that the examinations for purposes of discovering the candidate best equipped with Class I residues are held more frequently and attract larger numbers of aspirants.

2210. No very appreciable effects are apparent on residues, *a,* if only for the reason that residues change but slowly (§ 2321). On the other hand, effects upon derivations, *c,* are very considerable, and one notes a rank florescence of economic theories in defence of protection, many of which are comparable to the dedications and sonnet sequences that were addressed to wealthy feudal lords in a day gone by as bids for pensions (§ 2553).

2211. *Combination III.* Derivations act feebly, or not at all, upon residues, *a,* feebly upon interests, *b,* a little more potently upon social heterogeneity, *d,* for in any society persons who have the knack for praising people in power find ready admission to the governing class. Schmoller might never have been named to the Prussian House of Lords had he been a free-trader; on the other hand English free-traders win favours from a so-called "Liberal" government. That gives us an indirect effect outside our categories: the interests, *b,* acting upon derivations, *c,* and they in turn upon social heterogeneity, *d.*

2212. *Combination IV.* Here again we get effects of great importance, not so much in the influence of heterogeneity upon residues—in view, as usual, of their relative stability—as in the influence of interests.

2213. Indeed, considering Combination IV in general, the indirect, or "mediate," influence of interests on residues is far from negligible and if continued over long periods of years, may even be very considerable. In a country that concentrates almost exclusively on economic interests, combination-sentiments are stimulated, exhilarated, and sentiments corresponding to group-persistences are attenuated. In those two classes of residues, certain genera, and especially the forms in which residues are expressed, are modified, and therefore also derivations. Perfection is located in the future instead of in the past. The god Progress is enthroned on Olympus. Humanitarianism triumphs because interests are now better safe-guarded by chicanery than by force. It becomes a habit and a principle to circumvent obstacles instead of pushing them aside by brute force. In the long run such practices sap strength of character, and cunning in all its forms comes to reign supreme.

2214. Such things have been perceived in all periods of history, but the writers whom they have chanced to interest have as a rule soon deviated from the study of facts to turn to ethical considerations, to praise or to blame; and to discovering some way of realizing this or that ideal.[1]

2215. Going back now to the particular case of protection: After interests have, thanks to protection, brought into the governing class individuals richly endowed with Class I residues, those individuals in their turn influence interests and stimulate the whole country in the direction of economic pursuits and industrialism. The thing is so noticeable that it has not escaped even casual observers, or people who wear the blinders of mistaken theories, and it has often been described as an "increase in capitalism" in modern societies. Then going on, arguing as usual *post hoc, propter hoc,* the "increase in capitalism" has been taken as the cause of a decline in moral sentiments (group-persistence).

2216. That, really, is a case of an indirect, a mediate, effect: interests, in other words, have influenced heterogeneity; the latter, in its turn, now reacts upon interests; and through a sequence of actions and reactions, an equilbrium is established in which economic production and class-circulation become more intense, and the composition of the governing class is profoundly modified.

2217. The increase in economic production may be great enough to exceed the destruction of wealth caused by protection; so that, sum total, protection may yield a profit and not a loss in wealth; it

2214 [1] Speaking strictly from the standpoint of the correspondence of theories with facts, one may say that many economists have been handicapped in that inquiry by failure to understand that in a state of free competition the *entrepreneur* on the average shows neither profit nor loss, if due account is taken of interest on capital and his wage as an individual. But when the *entrepreneur* has a monopoly, his transactions may on the average show a profit over and above such interest and wage. Many Socialists also have been handicapped by confusing the interest on capital with the *entrepreneur's* profit. Such a profit materializes, on the average, only under conditions of temporary or permanent monopoly. So a number of observations by Socialists that are true as applied to profit cease to be when they are extended to interest on capital. Socialists have been further handicapped by failing to keep two kinds of persons distinct (§§ 2231 f.), thinking of them all together as "capitalists."

may therefore prove (though not necessarily so) that the economic prosperity of a country has been enhanced by industrial protection.

2218. That, notice, is a *mediate* effect, coming about through the influence of industrial protection upon social heterogeneity and class-circulation, which go on in turn to react upon the economic situation. It is possible for that reason to suppress the first link in the chain; and so long as the second is kept, the effect will follow just the same. For that reason, again, if protection were to act in a different wise upon social heterogeneity and class-circulation, the effect also would be different; and that is what actually happens, as a rule, with agricultural protection. Halting, therefore, at the point in the cycle where we now stand, we may say that it will be possible to get the indirect, the *mediate,* effect of an increase in economic prosperity either through industrial protection or through a free trade that removes a burdensome agricultural protection. This latter is, roughly, what took place in England at the time of Cobden's League. Abolition of agricultural protection had strong effect; an effect much less strong was the abolition of industrial protection, for at that time English industry led the world, and the effects were especially due to the first measure. In England, furthermore, class-circulation was already intense and became more so through a number of political measures. On the other hand, when Germany turned to protectionism class-circulation was sluggish and largely came about for other than economic considerations. Agricultural protectionism could have had little if any effect upon a circulation already slow in itself; whereas industrial protectionism stimulated it marvellously. The effects therefore were effects largely of industrial protectionism. Observable in England also were effects depending upon the abolition of agricultural protection, and the country moved rapidly forward towards a state of demagogic industrialism, which cannot prevail in Germany so long as the Junker element remains strong and vigorous under the shelter of agricultural duties. In Italy, after the establishment of the new kingdom protectionism in finance and public works had already exerted upon social heterogeneity the influence that we have elsewhere seen attaching to industrial protection; so that when the latter was established, along with a strong dosage of agricultural protection, it had indirect, *mediate,* effects of slight importance—with some exceptions per-

haps in Northern Italy, whereas in the South agricultural protection was virtually the only kind that had any effect. As a consequence, the mediate effects were on the whole almost unnoticeable,
the economic effects of the destruction of wealth alone striking the
eye, until, as time went on, they were obscured by a coating of
beneficial effects resulting from a period of prosperity general
throughout the civilized world.[1]

2219. Knowledge of the causes of these various effects, which are
none the less economic, could not have been supplied by political
economy alone. That science had to be combined with another
more general science that would show how to throw off the spell
of the derivations on which mistaken theories were commonly
erected, and emphasize the multiplicity and great variety of the
forces that were really determining phenomena which, though
strictly economic to all appearances, actually depended upon other
social phenomena.

2220. It must not be forgotten that so far we have been very
roughly sketching a first picture of the situation. A great deal still
remains to be done in filling in the secondary details. This is not
just the place to do that (§§ 2231 f., 2310 f.); but we are obliged
to eliminate one other imperfection in it that is due to our stopping
at a certain point in the cycle, whereas actually we have to go on
and look at further mediate effects that are quite different.

2221. If no counter-forces stood in the way, and the cycle of
actions and reactions were to go on indefinitely, economic protection and its effects ought to go on becoming progressively greater;
and that is what is actually observable in many countries during the
nineteenth century. But as a matter of fact counter-forces do develop, and increasingly so. Speaking now not of the particular case
of protection, but in general, such forces may be noted in the modi-

2218 [1] Prussia has a populous small-propertied nobility. Government officials and
army officers are recruited in large part from that class, and that accounts in the
main for the high honesty of the Prussian bureaucracy and the soundness of the
Prussian army. Somewhat the same situation prevailed in Piedmont before the foundation of the Kingdom of Italy, and similar effects were observable. These at the
very least declined with the gradual decline of the cause, under the new kingdom.
From that it would follow that agricultural protection, which is favourable to proprietary classes, had far different effects in Germany and in Italy, Italy having no
proprietary class corresponding to the Junkers of Prussia.

fications that the *élite* undergoes, and in variations in the circumstances that make the cyclical movement possible (§ 2225). History shows that when the proportions between Class I and Class II residues in the *élite* begin to vary, the movement does not continue indefinitely in one direction, but is sooner or later replaced by a movement in a counter-direction. Such counter-movements often result from wars, as was the case in the conquest of Greece by Rome, Greece at the time possessing Class I residues in very great abundance, while in Rome the advantage lay with the residues of group-persistence (Class II). Then again, the counter-movement to a movement that has been in progress for a fairly long time has resulted from internal revolutions, a striking case being the change from the Republic to the Empire in Rome, which was primarily a social revolution and profoundly altered proportions of residues in the ruling class. Considering the two processes together we may say, in general and roughly, that when the counter-movement does not come from wars, it comes from revolutions, much as when the fruit is ripe on the tree either it is plucked by a human hand or it falls naturally to the ground, but in either event is removed from the tree. The cause just mentioned—modifications in the *élite*—is among the major ones determining the undulating form that the movement assumes, and of that we shall see notable examples as we proceed (§§ 2311, 2343 f.).

2222. In many countries we find industrial protection combined with agricultural protection; in fact, at the present time in Europe, they nowhere appear singly; and since they have effects that are, to an extent at least, opposite, it is apparent that pressure of facts will lead empirically minded statesmen as it were by instinct to follow a middle course. In general, protections of the industrial and the agricultural types, when combined in varying degree, yield varying corresponding proportions of Class I and Class II residues in the governing class, along with the various effects resulting from that fact (§ 2227).

2223. All that we have been saying may readily be extended to any other type of protection, economic or otherwise. The protection of the military classes that arises when individuals acquire wealth, eminence, and power chiefly through war acts no less than economic protection upon social heterogeneity, but in a different direction, tending rather to strengthen Class II residues in a ruling class. Like economic protection, military protection intensifies circulation, and permits individuals with bellicose instincts to rise from the lower strata of society to the ruling class. In such cases one notes very appreciable effects on residues—so far as such effects are possible, considering their relative stability. Wars tend to enhance intensities in Class II residues. As usual, effects on derivations are also considerable, though to no such extent as in economic protections; for war has little or no need of theories—the better to see that in an extreme form, one need only compare Sparta and Athens. For that reason too, derivations have but little influence on social heterogeneity, though a little more on residues. Finally, thinking especially of Combination IV, one finds that protection of interests connected with war encourages a nation towards military pursuits—and that again would be an effect that is *mediate*.

2224. Military protections also develop forces that tend to produce a movement in a direction counter to that of the cycle. We saw, as regards ancient times, that wars cut wide swaths in warrior aristocracies. So on the one hand frequent wars draw men of bellicose instincts into the governing classes, but on the other hand they destroy them. All things considered, the two movements in contrary directions may, according to the case, either enrich or impoverish a ruling class as regards fighting elements, and so either increase or diminish its fund of Class II residues. As regards modern times, wars require not only men but also huge expenditures in money, which can be met only by intensive economic production, so that if wars in themselves increase the warrior element in governing classes, preparations for war reduce it, drawing industrial and commercial elements into the seats of power. This second effect is the preponderant one at the present time in France, England, and Italy. It is much less marked in Germany.

2225. As for the circumstances that make the cycles in question possible (§ 2221), the war-cycle requires a supply of rich peoples that may be exploited by conquest, whereas the industrial cycle finds it helpful, though not indispensable, that there be economically backward peoples who can be exploited by industrial production. Here we come upon a point that has so far been inadequately stressed. Industrialism, in order to expand, needs a populous class of savers, whereas industrialism generally tends to diminish the saving instinct and encourages individuals to spend all they earn (§ 2228).

In general and for all periods of history, the movement of the war-cycle encounters greater obstacles within itself than the movement of the industrial cycle. In fact, up to a certain point, the industrial cycle is self-sufficient and produces the wealth it consumes. As the poorer peoples that are exploited increase in prosperity, they consume more and more goods, and the wealthy industrial peoples make greater profits in consequence. The trouble cannot begin till later on, when the poorer peoples come closer to standing on an equal footing with the richer. As regards savings, we know that residues change very slowly; so that the effects of the industrial cycle upon the sentiments underlying saving do not materialize all at once, and savings may continue to increase for a long time, so removing the danger of any immediate failure of the exploitable material that is indispensable to the continuance of industrialism. But to profit by the arts of war a nation has to be in position to practise them on peoples of considerable wealth, and if the supply of such peoples gives out, the essentially warlike nation dies of inanition. Exceptional was the case of ancient Rome, where the mediate effects of wars of conquest endured over long periods of years. But that was due, in the first place, to the fact that it was a long long time before the supply of conquerable countries gave out; and in the second place, to the fact that conquests were not alone responsible for the material prosperity of Rome, commerce and industry contributing not a little. So it came about that Rome attained her maximum prosperity towards the end of the Republic and the beginnings of the Empire. Then came failure both in the supply of wealthy peoples to be conquered and exploited and in commercial and industrial prosperity. Conquests of barbarous territories could net profits in no wise comparable to those yielded by conquests of wealthy lands such as Greece, Africa, and Asia; while stagnation in class-circulation and the ever increasing destruction of wealth dried up the fountain-heads of economic production.

2226. Carthage and Venice owed their prosperity in part to the exploitation of economically backward peoples, as is to some extent the case with the industrial and commercial states of our day. Some of these countries do not produce grain in sufficient quantities to feed their populations, and in order to get along, they are obliged to have relations with agricultural countries that have a surplus in grain production. What would become of England if all the countries on the globe had just enough grain for their own consumption? Certainly the conditions at present observable in England would have to undergo a profound change. The prosperity of Carthage broke to pieces on the military power of Rome, just as the prosperity of Venice was seriously impaired by the conquests of the Turks. The prosperity of modern industrial nations does not seem to be menaced, at least for the present, by dangers of that kind. In general, if a country moving through one of the two cycles mentioned (war, industrialism) happens to encounter a country that is traversing the other cycle, the one or the other may succumb, according to the stage that has been reached in the respective evolution. Modern countries conspicuous for their industrial development conquer, subjugate, or destroy barbarous or semi-barbarous countries that are still backward in the war cycle. On the other hand, the countries of the Mediterranean basin that were farthest advanced economically were conquered by Rome, and the Roman Empire was overthrown in its turn by Barbarians. Among the civilized countries of our time there are but slight differences in cyclical stage, and so the influence arising from disparities in evolution is, though still considerable, not decisive.

2227. Among the effects resulting from changes in the proportions of Class I and Class II residues in the ruling class (§ 2221), deserving of special attention are those which tend to break down the resistance of that class as against the subject class.[1] To get a first

2227 [1] A governing class often brings on its own ruin. It readily accepts individuals who are well supplied with Class I residues and devote themselves to economic and financial pursuits, because such people as a rule are great producers of wealth and so contribute to the well-being of the governing class. In the days of absolute monarchy they supplied the sinews for the extravagances of the kings; nowadays they provide the wealth for the extravagances of democracy; and often they may benefit a whole country. The first effects of their coming to power are therefore favourably felt by many people and they strengthen the hold of the governing class; but gradually, as time goes on, they prove to be borers from within, by divesting the class of individuals who are rich in Class II residues and have an aptitude for using force. So the "speculators" (§ 2235) in France encompassed first the triumph of absolute monarchy and then its ruin (§ 2384 [1]). In our day in a number of countries they have contributed to the triumph of the régime that is called democratic (and might better be called pluto-demagogic) and are now preparing its ruin.

rough conception of these very important phenomena, one might observe that, very loosely speaking, the ruling and subject classes stand towards each other very much as two nations respectively alien. A predominance of interests that are primarily industrial and commercial enriches the ruling class in individuals who are shrewd, astute, and well provided with combination instincts; and divests it of individuals of the sturdy impulsive type richly endowed with instincts of group-persistence (§ 2178). That may also happen through other causes, and speaking of them in general (considering Combination IV, that is (§ 2206)), one might guess that if cunning, chicanery, combinations, were all there was to government, the dominion of the class in which Class I residues by far predominate would last over a very very long period and come to an end only with the senile degeneration of the stock itself. But governing is also a matter of force (§ 2174), and as Class I residues grow stronger and Class II residues weaker, the individuals in power become less and less capable of using force, so that an unstable equilibrium results and revolutions occur, such as the Protestant revolt against the ruling classes of the Renaissance, or the uprising of the French masses against their governors in 1789; and such revolutions succeed for very much the same reasons that a rude and crude Rome was able to conquer a civilized and sophisticated Greece. An exception that proves the rule would be Venice, who long endured in her one political system because her aristocracy managed to preserve those sentiments of group-persistence which are required for the use of force. The masses, which are strong in Class II residues, carry them upwards into the governing class either by gradual infiltrations (class-circulation) or in sudden spurts through revolutions (§§ 2343 f).

2228. In our modern countries that are economically advanced industry, commerce, and even agriculture require large amounts of capital. Furthermore the governments of such countries are very expensive, since they must make up with chicanery, and with the money that that costs, for the force in which they are deficient. They conquer by gold, not by steel. For that reason those countries where the industrial cycle is developing at an ever accelerating speed require savings in vast amounts (§ 2317). But the virtues of thrift are more compatible with Class II than with Class I residues.

Adventurous individuals, people who are for ever on the look-out for new combinations, are not savers. So a governing class that is pre-eminently industrial and commercial must have a substratum of people of a different type who save. If it does not find them in its own country, it has to look for them abroad. That is the case with the governing class in the United States, which draws extensively on European savings. The class governing in France finds the savings it needs at home and in great abundance, owing, chiefly, to the French women, in whom Class II residues still predominate. But let the French women become like American women, there being no compensation somewhere else to offset the change, and the quantity of savings that France provides for its own ruling class, and for other countries, may very materially diminish (§§ 2312 f.).

2229. With the social sciences constituted as they are at present, not having as yet attained the level of the logico-experimental sciences, the predominance of Class I residues actually means the predominance not only of interests, but also of derivations and in-tellectual religions, and not of scientific reasonings; and often-times those derivations are much farther removed from realities than the non-logical conduct of the mere empiricist. Before there was any science of chemistry the dyer's art was more safely en-trusted to the dyer who knew his trade by rule of thumb than to alchemists who played with the theoretical lucubrations of magic and other such nonsense. The "intellectuals" of Europe, like the mandarins of China, are the worst of rulers, and the fact that our "intellectuals" have played a less extensive rôle than the mandarins in the conduct of public affairs is one of the many reasons why the lots of European peoples and the Chinese have been different, just as it explains in part why the Japanese, led by their feudal chieftains, are so much stronger than the Chinese. "Intellectuals," to be sure, may be held aloof from public affairs even when Class I residues predominate in a ruling class, and that was the singular good fortune of Venice; but, in general, the predominance of Class I residues in the ruling class inclines that class to avail itself extensively of the services of "intellectuals," who are, on the other hand, rebuffed by people in whom "prejudices"—to use the jargon of our Continental humanitarians—in other words, Class II residues, predominate.

2230. In §§ 2026 f. we suggested a general classification of social strata and in § 2052 we alluded to the relations of that classification to the classification of aristocracies. That is not all there is to the matter. It may properly be the subject of many other considerations, one among which is of the first importance.

2231. It is of an economic character. Writers have confused and persist in confusing under the term "capitalists" (1) owners of savings and persons who live on interest from property and (2) promoters of enterprise—"*entrepreneurs.*" [1] That confusion is a great hindrance to an understanding of the economic phenomenon and an even greater hindrance to an understanding of human society. In reality those two sorts of "capitalists" often have interests that are different. Sometimes indeed they are diametrically opposed and stand in even greater conflict than the interests of the classes known as "capitalist" and "proletarian." From the economic standpoint it is to the advantage of the man of enterprise, the *entrepreneur,* that the interest on savings and other capital that he borrows should be the lowest possible. It is to the interest of the savers that it be as high as possible. The promoter of enterprise profits when the goods he produces go up in price, while rises in the prices of other commodities are of slight importance to him if he finds a compensation in the profits netted by his own goods. But all such increases in prices are to the loss of the mere saver. Tax imposts on the goods that he produces do little harm to the *entrepreneur*—in fact they are sometimes an advantage, in that they scare off competition; but they are always injurious to the consumer whose income derives from the lending of savings at interest. In general, the owner of an enterprise can always pass on to the consumer the increase in costs that results from heavy taxes. The mere saver almost never can. So rises in wages as a rule cause only temporary inconvenience to the manufacturer—to the extent, that is, of standing contracts, since he can offset them by raising prices in future contracts. The mere owner of savings loses by wage-increases, usually without being able to recoup. In such cases, therefore, owners of enterprises and their employees have a common interest, which is in conflict with the in-

---

2231 [1] The "capitalists" and "*entrepreneurs*" of ordinary language are not the capitalists and "*entrepreneurs*" considered by pure economics (see Pareto, *Cours,* § 87 and *passim*) or, in general, by scientific economics. Scientific analysis separates the compounds that are observable in the concrete.

terests of mere owners of savings.[2] The same may be said of employers and employees in protected industries. Agricultural protection frequently has contrary effects and is therefore opposed by industrial workers, who are inclined to act on impulse; whereas it is shrewdly favoured by manufacturers, since they see in it a way of maintaining industrial protection.

2232. No less pronounced are the conflicts from the social point of view. *Entrepreneurs* as a class are recruited from individuals in whom the combination-instincts indispensable to success in enterprise are highly developed. Individuals in whom the Class II residues predominate remain among the mere owners of savings. *Entrepreneurs* are in general, therefore, adventurous souls, hungry for novelty in the economic as well as in the social field, and not at all alarmed at change, expecting as they do to take advantage of it. The mere savers, instead, are often quiet, timorous souls sitting at all times with their ears cocked in apprehension, like rabbits, and hoping little and fearing much from any change, for well they know of bitter experience that they will be called upon to foot the bill for it (§ 2316). The inclination to an adventurous and extravagant life, like the inclination to a quiet and thrifty life, is in great part a matter of instinct and only to a very slight extent a matter of reasoned design.[1] They are like other inclinations in human beings,

2231 [2] That fact was sensed by economists in setting "consumers" over against "producers"; but it was soundly objected that in reality those two classes oftentimes merge, and that the majority of individuals are at once consumers and producers. The difference that was sensed in those terms is really the difference between the person who passively experiences the effects of the economic, political, and social movement and the person who uses his wits to take advantage of it.

2232 [1] If that fact has not been perceived by numbers of economists, the failure is due to their being led astray by their eagerness to find a principle from which a theory of savings could be logically derived, and also, once they were on that road, to their deserting the field of experimental observation for excursions into the realm of theoretical speculation. It would be helpful to theory if the quantity of savings accumulated in a given unit of time were exclusively, or at least chiefly, a function of the interest obtainable on savings. But unfortunately that is not the case, and one cannot, out of sheer love of theory, shut one's eyes to the plain facts, nor replace what anyone with eyes may see with theoretical juggling of statistics. Statistics as to savings are woefully incomplete. They not only cannot keep track of the amounts, to a very considerable total, that small manufacturers, merchants, and farmers use in their private enterprises; they cannot even give anywhere near the exact figures for the surplus savings that are invested in government or other securities. Finally— and this is the chief reason why they mislead in the matter here in point—they

like courage, cowardice, the passion for gambling, concupiscence, fondness for this or that bodily exercise, this or that intellectual pursuit. All such inclinations may be modified to some extent by incidental circumstances; but beyond a doubt they are in the main individual traits on which reasoning exercises little or no influence. To try by reasoning to convert a coward into a brave man or a spendthrift into a saver, to persuade a gambler to give up his gambling or a rake his women, is, as everybody knows, nearly always—and one might say always—a waste of breath; and that is not to be gainsaid by marshalling statistics, as people have tried to do in order to show that saving is an essentially logical act and that the amount of savings is determined primarily by the interest that is to be had on them. In such cases, to use statistics of very complex phenomena in place of the direct observation of simple phenomena

relate to a very complex situation in which many forces besides individual tendencies to saving are at work. What influence could possible interests from savings ever have had on the saving instinct in the days when people tucked gold and silver coins away and secreted them in their houses? Or in the days when people in France were always talking of the "woollen stockings" of the frugal peasantry? And even now—go to the good French housewife who lays money away a penny at a time and then takes her little hoard to the savings-bank, and ask her if she would save any more if the interest-rate at the bank were raised! You would be lucky if she understood what you meant, and if by some chance she did, she would laugh at you as a simpleton. And it is ridiculous to describe as "auto-observation" observations that are made in such fashion on others. If, now, statistics when skilfully manipulated say the opposite, it simply means either that they are wrong or that they have been unsoundly handled, like statistics which might show that people walked on their hands and not on their feet. Avarice is thrift carried to extremes. From ancient down to modern times the type of the miser has been over and again described by men of letters. But what writer ever dreamed of putting the miser's saving in relation with the interest he could make on his money? Nothing of the kind, certainly, is to be seen either in Theophrastus or in Molière. The miser saves all he can, and he extorts all he can as interest on the money he lends, and the two maxima are in no way correlated. In the day of Theophrastus there were no statistics, and they cannot, therefore, prove of a certainty whether the Athenians ate, drank, and wore clothes; but it seems probable that they did, just as it is probable that there were provident and improvident individuals among them; and the descriptions of a keen observer such as Theophrastus are worth infinitely more than the nebulous disquisitions of certain of our statisticians. In describing the man given to sordid hoarding ("The Penurious Man," *Characters*, 10 (11), Jebb, pp. 146-49) Theophrastus does not so much as intimate that there was any relation between his savings and the interest he might have made on them. It is evident that saving is an instinctive act manifesting a passion for accumulating money. And so is the saving that figures in the counsels of Cato the Censor, who knew a thing or two about

that one is trying to understand can only lead astray.[2] All human conduct based on instinct may be more or less modified by reasoning, and it would be going too far to assert that that does not apply also to conduct based on the instinct for saving. But that does not prevent that instinct from being the primary element in saving, which remains none the less a non-logical act.[3]

2233. The facts just mentioned put us in the way of making a more general classification in which the preceding classification would be included and to which we shall have frequent occasion to refer in explaining social phenomena hereafter (§§ 2313 f).[1] Suppose we put in one category, which we may call *S,* individuals whose incomes are essentially variable and depend upon the person's wide-awakeness in discovering sources of gain. In that group, generally

thrift and miserliness on his own account. I noted in my *Cours,* § 30, that savings do not have—and in that differing from other economic goods—an elementary ophelimity that diminishes as quantity increases. There too direct observation shows that many persons who have no savings at all feel no need of thrift, while the need develops and grows stronger in them when they have made savings to some amount. It is a well-known fact that a gift of a bank-book to a working-man who has no savings is frequently a way to induce him to save. But it is useless to go on mentioning facts so well known, and which anyone who chooses may verify. Those who refuse to recognize them may stick to their opinions like Don Ferrante in Manzoni's "Betrothed," who showed with learned theory that the plague raging in Milan could not exist save as a malign influence from the celestial bodies, and then caught it and died of it, shaking his fists at the stars. *Cf.* Pareto, *Cours,* § 419, and *Manuale,* Chapter VIII, § 11.

2232 [2] Two scientists of great and deserved reputation, Bodio in Italy and De Foville in France, have very soundly shown how much prudence, discretion, and caution are required in using statistics. Such warnings should be kept constantly in mind.

2232 [3] Among the better-authenticated cases where logic interposes to determine saving is the case where a person "retires" from a profession when he has saved as much as he needs to live comfortably for the rest of his life; and it is interesting that in that case the logical conduct is the reverse of what one would expect if quantity of savings increased with potential interest. Even in that very simple case the situation is complex. The amount of savings required for "retiring" depends not only on interest on savings, but also on costs of living and one's standard of living at the moment of retirement. Then come other circumstances having to do with family situation, the usages and customs of the times, and so on. All such things are adjuncts to the non-logical conduct, not substitutes for it. The spendthrift does not need to worry about interest-rates—he has no savings. The miser, too, ignores them—he is busy accumulating with might and main. Individuals in the intermediate stages are influenced partly by instinct and partly by reasoning.

2233 [1] The classification in question was first suggested in my *"Rentiers et spéculateurs,"* in *Indépendance,* May 1, 1911.

speaking and disregarding exceptions, will be found those promoters of enterprise—those *entrepreneurs*—whom we were considering some pages back; and with them will be stockholders in industrial and commercial corporations (but not bondholders, who will more fittingly be placed in our group next following). Then will come owners of real estate in cities where building speculation is rife; and also landowners—on a similar condition that there be speculation in the lands about them; and then stock-exchange speculators and bankers who make money on governmental, industrial, and commercial loans. We might further add all persons depending upon such people—lawyers, engineers, politicians, working-people, clerks—and deriving advantage from their operations. In a word, we are putting together all persons who directly or indirectly speculate and in one way or another manage to increase their incomes by ingeniously taking advantage of circumstances.

2234. And let us put into another category, which we may call R, persons who have fixed or virtually fixed incomes not depending to any great extent on ingenious combinations that may be conceived by an active mind. In this category, roughly, will be found persons who have savings and have deposited them in savings-banks or invested them in life-annuities; then people living on incomes from government bonds, certificates of the funded debt, corporation bonds, or other securities with fixed interest-rates; then owners of real estate and lands in places where there is no speculation; then farmers, working-people, clerks, depending upon such persons and in no way depending upon speculators. In a word, we so group together here all persons who neither directly nor indirectly depend on speculation and who have incomes that are fixed, or virtually fixed, or at least are but slightly variable.[1]

2234 [1] Monographs along the lines of Le Play's would be of great use in determining the character of the persons belonging in our S group, and those belonging to our R group. Here is one such, contributed by Prezzolini: *La Francia e i francesi del secolo XX osservati da un italiano.* I know it as quoted by E. Cesari in the *Vita italiana,* Oct. 15, 1917, pp. 367-70. The person in question is a well-known member of the French parliament—we suppress the proper name: for us here, he is not a person, but just a type. The figures given by Prezzolini are those publicly declared by the member himself, Monsieur X. X's fixed income yields a total of 17,500 francs, of which 15,000 are salary as a member of the parliament and 2,500 interest on his wife's dowry. Only the latter sum belongs in category *R*—the salary belongs rather in category *S,* because to get such a thing one must have the ability and the good

2235. Just to be rid of the inconvenience of using mere letters of the alphabet, suppose we use the term "speculators" for members of category S and the French term *rentiers* for members of category R.[1] Now we can repeat of the two groups of persons more or less what we said above (§ 2231) of mere owners of savings and *entrepreneurs,* and we shall find analogous conflicts, economic and social, between them. In the speculator group Class I residues predominate, in the *rentier* group, Class II residues. That that should be the case is readily understandable. A person of pronounced capacity for economic combinations is not satisfied with a fixed income, often a very small one. He wants to earn more, and if he finds a favourable opportunity, he moves into the S category. The two groups perform functions of differing utility in society. The S group is primarily responsible for change, for economic and social progress. The R group, instead, is a powerful element in stability, and in many cases counteracts the dangers attending the adventurous capers of the S's. A society in which R's almost exclusively predominate remains stationary and, as it were, crystallized. A society in which S's predominate lacks stability, lives in a state of shaky equilibrium that may be upset by a slight accident from within or from without.

Members of the R group must not be mistaken for "conservatives," nor members of the S group for "progressives," innovators, revolu-

---

fortune to be elected. X's expense-account shows a total of 64,200 francs, divided as follows: household expenses, 33,800; office expenses, 22,550; expenses for his election district (avowable expenses), 7,850. There ought, therefore, to be a deficit of 45,700 francs; but the deficit is not only covered but changes into a surplus in view of the following revenues: contributions to newspapers and other publications, 12,500 francs; honorarium as general agent of the *A.B.C.* Company, 21,000 francs; commissions on sales, 7,500. In this connexion, Prezzolini notes that X, reporting on the war budget, enters 100,000 francs for supplies delivered to himself, as general agent of the *A.B.C.* Company: that gives X his "sales commissions." Finally, because of the influence that he enjoys, our member, X, receives a stipend of 18,000 francs from a newspaper. In all, these revenues, which clearly belong in the category S, yield a total of 50,000 francs. Prezzolini adds that the member in question is not the only one, nor the least, of his species. He is just a better-known and an honester type.

2235 [1] It might be well to repeat that our use of such terms is not based on their ordinary senses, nor upon their etymologies. We are to use them strictly in the sense defined in §§ 2233-34, and the reader must refer to those definitions whenever he encounters them in the remainder of this volume. [I keep the term "speculator." English ordinarily analyzes the matter embraced under Pareto's term, especially in slang. Pareto's "speculator" is our "hustler," "man of pep," "wide-awake individual," "live-wire," and so on.—A. L.]

tionaries (§§ 226, 228-44). They may have points in common with such, but there is no identity. There are evolutions, revolutions, innovations, that the *R*'s support, especially movements tending to restore to the ruling classes certain residues of group-persistence that had been banished by the *S*'s. A revolution may be made against the *S*'s —a revolution of that type founded the Roman Empire, and such, to some extent, was the revolution known as the Protestant Reformation. Then too, for the very reason that sentiments of group-persistence are dominant in them, the *R*'s may be so blinded by sentiment as to act against their own interests. They readily allow themselves to be duped by anyone who takes them on the side of sentiment, and time and time again they have been the artisans of their own ruin (§ 1873). If the old feudal lords, who were endowed with *R* traits in a very conspicuous degree, had not allowed themselves to be swept off their feet by a sum of sentiments in which religious enthusiasm was only one element, they would have seen at once that the Crusades were to be their ruin. In the eighteenth century, had the French nobility living on income, and that part of the French *bourgeoisie* which was in the same situation, not succumbed to the lure of humanitarian sentiments, they would not have prepared the ground for the Revolution that was to be their undoing. Not a few among the victims of the guillotine had for long years been continually, patiently, artfully grinding the blade that was to cut off their heads. In our day those among the *R*'s who are known as "intellectuals" are following in the footprints of the French nobles of the eighteenth century and are working with all their might to encompass the ruin of their own class (§ 2254).

Nor are the categories *R* and *S* to be confused with groupings that might be made according to economic occupation (§§ 1726-27). There again we find points of contact, but not full coincidence. A retail merchant often belongs to the *R* group, and a wholesale merchant too, but the wholesaler will more likely belong to the *S* group. Sometimes one same enterprise may change in character. An individual of the *S* type founds an industry as a result of fortunate speculations. When it yields or seems to be yielding a good return, he changes it into a corporation, retires from business, and passes over into the *R* group. A large number of stockholders in the new concern are also *R*'s—the ones who bought stock when they thought they were buying a sure thing. If they are not mistaken, the business changes in character, moving over from the *S* type to the *R* type. But in many cases the best speculation the founder ever made was in changing his business to a corporation. It is soon in jeopardy, with the *R*'s standing in line to pay for the broken crockery. There is no better business in this world than the business of fleecing the lambs—of exploiting the inexperience, the ingenuousness, the passions, of the *R*'s. In our societies the fortunes of many many wealthy individuals have no other foundations.[2]

2236. The differing relative proportions in which *S* types and *R* types are combined in the governing class correspond to differing

2235 [2] Many people conclude that such facts are enough to condemn our social organization, and hold it responsible for most of the pains from which we suffer. Others think that they can defend our present order only by denying the facts or minimizing their significance. Both are right from the ethical standpoint (§§ 2162, 2262), wrong from the standpoint of social utility experimentally considered (§ 2115). Obviously, if it be posited as an axiom that men *ought,* whatever happens, to observe certain rules, those who do not observe them necessarily stand condemned. Trying to put such a reasoning into logical form, one gets as its premise some proposition of the type mentioned in §§ 1886, 1896-97. If one goes on to say that the organization so condemned is in the main injurious to society, one must logically fall back on some premise that confuses morality and utility (§§ 1495, 1903-98). On the other hand, if premises of those types are granted and one would, notwithstanding, still defend or approve the organization of our societies, there is nothing left but to deny the facts or say they are not significant. The experimental approach is altogether different. Anyone accepting it grants no axioms independent of experience, and therefore finds it necessary to discuss the premises of the reasonings mentioned. On so doing one soon perceives that it is a question of two phenomena that do indeed have points in common, but are in no sense identical (§ 2001), and that in every particular case experience has to be called in to decide whether one is dealing with a point of contact or a point of divergence. An instant's reflection is enough to see that if one accepts certain conclusions one adopts by that fact the premises to which they are indissolubly bound. But the power of sentiment and the influence of habitual manners of reasoning are such that people disregard the force of logic entirely and establish conclusions without reference to the premises or, at the very best, accept the premises as axioms not subject to discussion. Another effect of such power and such influence will be that in spite of the warnings we have given and over and over again repeated, there will always be someone to carry the import of the remarks that he is here reading on the *R*'s and *S*'s beyond the limits we have so strictly specified, interpreting all that we have been saying against one of those groups as implying that the influence of the group is, on the whole, harmful to society and the group itself "condemnable"; and all that we have been saying in its favour as a proof that the influence of the group is, in general, beneficial to society and the group itself worthy of praise. We have neither the means nor the least desire to prevent the fabrication of such interpretations. We are satisfied with recognizing them as one variety of our derivations (§ 1419, I-β).

types of civilization; and such proportions are among the principal traits that have to be considered in social heterogeneity.[1] Going back, for instance, to the protectionist cycle examined above (§§ 2209 f.), we may say that in modern democratic countries industrial protection increases the proportion of S's in the governing class. That increase in turn serves to intensify protection, and the process would go on indefinitely if counter-forces did not come into play to check it (§ 2221).

Before we can go any farther along this line, we must have a better understanding of a number of other phenomena.

2237. *Government and its forms.* Among the complex phenomena that are observable in a society, of very great importance is the system of government. That is closely bound up with the character of the governing class, and both stand in a relationship of interdependence with all other social phenomena.

2238. Oftentimes, as usual, too much importance has been attached to forms at the expense, somewhat, of substance; and the

2236 [1] As usual, one may raise the query: "If this social phenomenon is of such great moment, how comes it that people have not remarked it hitherto?" The answer, again as usual, is that people have indeed noticed it, but have proceeded to cover it over again with a cloak of derivations. The substratum underlying anti-Semitism is a movement against speculators. It is said that the Semite is more of a speculator than the "Aryan" and the Jew is therefore taken as representing the whole class. Consider the case of department-stores and bazaars in Europe. They are the targets, especially in Germany, of the anti-Semites. It is true that many such stores are owned by Jews, but plenty of others are owned by Christians, and in either event are equally harmful to the small retailer, whom the anti-Semites would protect—anti-Semite in this case meaning "anti-speculator" and nothing more. The same may be said of financial syndicates and other characteristic forms of speculation. Socialists pick their quarrel with "capitalists," and theoretically it is a good thing that for once the "capitalist" is not confused with the "speculator"; but practically, the mobs that follow Socialist leadership have never grasped head or tail of Marx's pretty theories as to "surplus value"; they are inspired solely by an instinctive impulse to take for themselves at least a part of the money that is going to "speculators." Theorists, too, when dealing with "capitalism" in history, confuse it, to some extent at least, with "speculator" rule. Finally, if anyone is inclined to go farther back in history, he may find ample traces of remarks and doctrines that reflect the conflict between speculators and the rest of the public. In the case of Athens the people in the Piraeus are at outs with the farmers, and Plato (*De legibus,* IV, 705) would place his republic far from the sea to keep it safe from the influence of speculators. In that he is a predecessor of the anti-Semites of our time. Speculators may be found at work in all periods of history. Various the ways in which their influence manifests itself, various the names that are applied to it, various the derivations that it provokes; but the substance is ever the same.

thing chiefly considered has been the form that the political régime assumed. However, in France, especially during the reign of Napoleon III, and more particularly among economists, a tendency developed to ascribe little or no importance to forms of government, and not only that, to substance as well. That was going to another extreme, and exclusively "political" theories of society were met with exclusively "economic" theories, among them the theory of economic determinism—the usual mistake of disregarding mutual correlations in social phenomena (§§ 2061 f.).

2239. Those who attach supreme significance to forms of government find it very important to answer the question, "What is the best form of government?" But that question has little or no meaning unless the society to which the government is to be applied is specified and unless some explanation is given of the term "best," which alludes in a very indefinite way to the various individual and social utilities (§ 2115). Although that has now and then been sensed, consideration of governmental forms has given rise to countless derivations leading up to this or that political myth, both derivations and myths being worth exactly zero from the logico-experimental standpoint, but both of them—or, rather the sentiments that they manifest—having, it may be, effects of great consequence in the way of influencing human conduct. It cannot be doubted that the sentiments manifested by the monarchical, republican, oligarchic, democratic, and still other faiths, have played and continue to play no mean part in social phenomena, as is the case with the sentiments underlying other religions. The "divine rights" of the prince, of the aristocracy, of the people, the proletariat, the majority—or any other divine right that might be imagined—have not the slightest experimental validity. We must therefore consider them extrinsically only, as facts, as manifestations of sentiments, operating, like other traits in the human beings that go to make up a given society, to determine its mode of being, its form. To say that no one of these "rights" has any experimental foundation does not, of course, in any way impugn the utility to society with which it may be credited. Such an inference would be justified if the statement were a derivation, since in such reasonings it is generally taken for granted that anything that is not rational is harmful. But the question of utility is left untouched when the statement is rigorously logico-experimental, since then it contains no such implicit premise (§ 2147).[1]

2240. Here, as in dealing with other subjects of the kind, we stumble at the very first step on difficulties of terminology. That is natural enough: the objective investigations that we are trying to make require an objective terminology, whereas the subjective discussions that are commonly conducted can get along with the subjective terminology of ordinary parlance. Everyone recognizes that in our day "democracy" is tending to become the political system of all civilized peoples. But what is the exact meaning of the term "democracy"? It is even more vague than that vaguest of terms, "religion." We must therefore leave it to one side and turn to the facts that it covers.[1]

2241. One observes at the outset a pronounced tendency on the part of modern civilized peoples to use a form of government where legislative power rests largely with an assembly elected by a part at least of the citizens. One further notes a tendency to augment that power and increase the number of citizens electing the assembly.

2242. In Switzerland, by way of exception, the legislative powers of the elective assembly are limited by the popular referendum, and in the United States they are to some extent checked by the federal courts. An attempt to limit them by plebiscite was made in France at the instance of Napoleon III. It met with no success, though one could not definitely assert that that was due to any inherent defect in the scheme itself, since the government that was created by it was destroyed by the armed forces of a foreign enemy. The tendency to increase numbers of voters is general, and along that road, for the time being, there is no going back. The franchise is continually being extended. After giving it to adult men, the idea is now to grant

2239 [1] The study of forms of government belongs to *special* sociology. Here we are concerned with them only incidentally in connexion with our quest for the substance underlying derivations and for the relationship between types of ruling-class composition and other social phenomena.

2240 [1] The best government now in existence, and also better than countless others that have so far been observable in history, is the government of Switzerland, especially in the forms it takes on in the small cantons—forms of direct democracy. It is a democratic government, but it has nothing but the name in common with the governments, also called democratic, of other countries such as France or the United States.

it to women. It is not beyond the range of possibility that it may be extended as regards age.

2243. Underlying such forms, which are more or less the same with all civilized peoples, there are great differences in substance, like names being given to unlike things. The power of the legislative assembly varies all the way from a maximum to a minimum. In France both the Chamber of Deputies and the Senate are elective. For the purposes of our investigation, therefore, they may be regarded as a single assembly, which is, one may say, absolutely sovereign and has no limits to its power. In Italy, the power of the Chamber has a theoretical check in the Senate, an actual check in the monarchy. In England, once upon a time, the power of the House of Commons found in the House of Lords an actual check that is now very much attenuated, and in the monarchy another that has likewise become largely nominal. In the United States the President is elected independently of the Congress and effectively limits its power. In Germany the States' Council and, to a still greater extent, the Emperor, supported by the military caste, constituted very considerable checks on the power of the Reichstag. So gradually we come to Russia, where the Duma has very little power, and to Japan, where the elective assembly has almost none at all. We may overlook Turkey and the republics of Central America, where the legislative assemblies are more or less fanciful entities.

2244. We need not linger on the fiction of "popular representation"—poppycock grinds no flour. Let us go on and see what substance underlies the various forms of power in the governing classes. Ignoring exceptions, which are few in number and of short duration, one finds everywhere a governing class of relatively few individuals that keeps itself in power partly by force and partly by the consent of the subject class, which is much more populous. The differences lie principally, as regards substance, in the relative proportions of force and consent; and as regards forms, in the manners in which the force is used and the consent obtained.

2245. As we have elsewhere observed (§§ 2170 f.), if the consent were unanimous there would be no need to use force; but that extreme is unknown to fact. Another extreme has a few concrete illustrations—the case where a despot keeps himself in power by armed force against a hostile population (such cases all belong to the past); and then the case where a foreign power holds a re-luctant people in subjection—of that there are still quite a few examples in the present. The reason why the equilibrium is much more unstable in the first case than in the other has to be sought in the prevalence of differing residues. The residues working in the satellites of the despot are not essentially different from those work-ing in the despot's subjects, so that there is no faith available to inspire, and at the same time to restrain, the use of force; and as was the case with the praetorians, the janissaries, and the Mame-lukes, satellites are readily tempted to make capricious use of their power, or else to abandon defence of the despot against the people. The ruling nation, on the other hand, generally differs in usages and customs, and sometimes in language and religion, from the subject nation. There is a difference in residues, therefore, and so plenty of faith to inspire use of force. But there may be plenty of faith in the subject nation to inspire resistance to oppression; and that is how, in the long run, the equilibrium may chance to be upset.

2246. It is in fear of that very outcome that conquering peoples try to assimilate their subject peoples, and when that can be done, it is by all odds the best way for them to assure their dominion. They often fail because they try to change residues by violence instead of taking advantage of existing residues. Rome had the faculty for this latter in pre-eminent degree, and so was able to assimilate the many peoples about her in Latium, Italy, and the Mediterranean basin.

2247. We have had incidental occasion already to remark that the policies of governments are the more effective, the more adept they are at utilizing existing residues (§ 1843), the less effective, the less skilful, and in general total failures when they set out to change residues by force; and to tell the truth, almost all explanations as to the success or failure of certain policies of this or that government come down in the end to that principle.[1]

2247 [1] Practical men often sense this fact, but are kept from acting on it by pseudo-theoretical considerations or by obstacles they chance to meet in doing so. Busch, *Tagebuchblätter,* Vol. I, p. 103 (English, Vol. I, p. 80), Aug. 24, 1870 (in question, just what territories Germany might find it advisable to take away from France): "Von Alvensleben, for his part, was for taking everything as far as the Marne. Bismarck said that he had another idea but that unfortunately it could not be carried out. 'My ideal,' said he, 'would be a sort of German colony, a neutral state of eight or ten million people exempted from all military service but paying

2248. Many people are prevented by derivations from recognizing the principle. If *A,* for instance, is the derivation that expresses certain sentiments of the subject class, another derivation, *B,* is readily found, which at bottom expresses the sentiments of the dominant class but which the latter regards as a valid and convincing refutation of *A.* In that confidence it concludes that it will be an easy matter to force *B* upon the subject class, since that will be a mere question of opening their eyes to a truth so obvious. So the conflict between sentiments becomes a conflict between derivations or, in other terms, a mere battle of words. Others see the realities a little more clearly but use sophistries. They dwell at length on the advantages of a people's having unity of faith in certain matters, but neglect entirely to consider whether that can be accomplished without incurring very serious disadvantages that would offset or more than offset the advantages. Still others implicitly assume that for a person to take advantage of the sentiments of others without sharing them, he must necessarily have a purpose that is dishonest and detrimental to society, and so they condemn such conduct outright as worthy only of a wicked hypocrite.[1]

2249. To utilize the sentiments prevalent in a society for attaining a given purpose is in itself neither beneficial nor detrimental to society. The utility, or the detriment, depends upon the result achieved. If the result is beneficial, one gets a utility; if harmful, a detriment. Nor can it be said that when a governing class works for a result that will be advantageous to itself regardless of whether it will be beneficial, or the reverse, to its subject class, the latter is necessarily harmed. Countless the cases where a governing class working for its own exclusive advantage has further promoted the welfare of a subject class. In a word, utilization of the residues prevailing in a society is just a means, and its value the value of the results achieved.

2250. Along with residues, considered as instruments of govern-

taxes, which, after the satisfaction of local needs, would go to Germany. In that way France would lose a province from which she gets her best soldiers and would never be a menace again.' " Compare that far-sighted outlook with the oppressive measures resorted to by present-day governments with a view to changing the sentiments of subject peoples, often in altogether insignificant respects.

2248 [1] However, that mode of reasoning is peculiar to a small number of moralists. One rarely notes it in practical men.

ing, come interests, and at times these are the only available agents
for modifying residues. It is important, however, not to forget that
naked interests alone, taken apart from sentiments, may indeed be
a powerful instrument for influencing individuals showing a predominance of Class I residues and so for influencing numerous elements in a governing class; but that taken in that way by themselves, apart from sentiments, they have very little influence upon
individuals showing a predominance of Class II residues, and consequently upon the subject class as a whole. One may say, in general
and speaking very roughly, that the governing class has a clearer
view of its own interests because its vision is less obscured by sentiments, whereas the subject class is less aware of its interests because
its vision is more clouded by sentiments; and that, as a result, the
governing class is in a position to mislead the subject class into serving the interests of the governing class; but that those interests are
not necessarily opposite to the interests of the subject class, often in
fact coincide with them, so that in the end the deception may prove
beneficial to the subject class.

2251. Consent and force appear in all the course of history as instruments of governing. They come forward in the legendary days
of the *Iliad* and *Odyssey* to make the power of the Greek kings
secure. They are discernible in the legends of the Roman kings.
Later on, in historical times, in Rome they are busy under both Republic and Empire; and it is by no means to be taken for granted
that the government of Augustus enjoyed any less support in the
subject class than the various governments the last years of the Republic managed to secure. And so coming on through the Barbarian
kings and the mediaeval republics down to the divine-right potentates of two or three centuries ago, and finally to our modern democratic régimes, we find all along the same mixture of force and consent.

2252. Just as derivations are much more variable than the residues
that underlie them, so the forms in which force and consent express
themselves are much more variable than the sentiments and interests in which they originate; and the differences in the relative proportions of force and consent are in large part due to varying relative proportions of sentiments and interests. The parallel between
derivations and forms of government goes farther still. They both

have less influence upon the social equilibrium than do the sentiments and interests that underlie them. That fact has also been perceived by many scholars, but they have tended to go a little too far in asserting that forms of government are altogether matters of indifference.

2253. A governing class is present everywhere, even where there is a despot, but the forms under which it appears are widely variable. In absolute governments a sovereign occupies the stage alone. In so called democratic governments it is the parliament. But behind the scenes in both cases there are always people who play a very important rôle in actual government. To be sure they must now and again bend the knee to the whims of ignorant and domineering sovereigns or parliaments, but they are soon back at their tenacious, patient, never-ending work, which is of much the greater consequence. In the Roman *Digesta* one may read truly splendid constitutions bearing the names of very wretched Emperors, just as in our day we have very fair legal codes that have been enacted by fairly brainless parliaments. The cause in both cases is the same: The sovereign leaves everything to his legal advisers, in some cases not even divining what they are having him do—and parliaments today even less than many a shrewd leader or king. And least of all King Demos! And such blindness on his part has at times helped to effect betterments in conditions of living in the face of his prejudices, not to mention much-needed steps in behalf of national defence. King Demos, good soul, thinks he is following his own devices. In reality he is following the lead of his rulers. But that very very often turns out to the advantage of his rulers only, for they, from the days of Aristotle down to our own, have made lavish use of the arts of bamboozling King Demos.[1] Our plutocrats, like those

2253 [1] Jouvenel, *La république des camarades,* pp. 57-60: "Of course, people insist on having platforms and programs, in deference probably to a long-ingrained habit of mind; but it is rare for anyone to care very much about carrying them out. . . . That is because platforms are rarely written with the idea that they are to be carried out. The principles of the republican *bourgeoisie* go back to '89, of Marxian Socialism to '48. The Radical platform dates from 1869. Rest assured that they will wear for a long time still! Struggle between these various stationary conceptions nevertheless goes to make up what is called 'modern politics.' . . . A program that chanced to be carried out would cease by that fact to exist. . . . Almost all our important laws have been submitted for debate to the parliament by ministers who did not believe in them, or who were already on record as uncompromising oppo-

of the late Roman Republic, are at all times busy making money, either on their own account or to sate the hungry maws of their partisans and accomplices; and for anything else they care little or nothing. Among the derivations which they use to show that their rule is to the advantage of a country, interesting is the assertion that the public is better qualified to pass on general questions than on special ones. The fact, in reality, is the precise opposite. One has to talk only for a very brief time with an uneducated person to see that he grasps special questions, which are usually concrete, much more clearly than general questions, which as a rule are abstract. But abstract questions have the advantage for people in power that whatever the answers that are given them by the public, they will be able to draw any inference they choose from them. The people sends to parliament men who are pledged to abolish interest on capital and "surplus value" in industry, and check the "greed" of the "speculators" (general questions); and those representatives now directly,

nents of them. [But since, after all, they are intelligent men and not a little shrewd, we are obliged to conclude that there must be some powerful force that is driving them into the course they follow. That force can be located nowhere else than in a social organization that has put the government into the hands of "speculators."] Read the confessions of Waldeck-Rousseau. He will tell you that after he had prosecuted before a high tribunal a plot that he was not sure had ever existed, he forced through the old-age pension bill from which he expected nothing and the income-tax bill from which he feared everything. 'We were condemned,' he writes, 'to adopt as a rule overriding everything else the necessity of not falling from power. We were obliged to make concessions on points of principle, while doing our best to prevent our principles from being carried out.' " But why all that? Because he wanted to rehabilitate Dreyfus! And why did he want to rehabilitate Dreyfus? Because an intense excitement, fanned in part by a press liberally subsidized by men who expected to get their money back, had laid hold on the country, and the speculators wanted to turn it into profits, just as they turn discoveries of mines or new inventions into profits. That was the start of the current that had gripped Waldeck-Rousseau—already the long-standing champion and friend of the speculators—and his friends, and which lifted on its silt-laden waves a ship packed with modern Argonauts who sailed away to conquer a golden fleece and came home with power, honours, and many a side of bacon. Jouvenel continues, p. 60: "A Premier who did not believe in the separation of Church and State made that separation inevitable. Another Premier signed the bill that made it law, and he had never favoured it. Most of our Radical Senators today have at one time or another fought for the abolition of the Senate. Many of our colonial Deputies were opponents in their youth of colonial representation. The Senate was almost unanimous against the repurchase of the 'Western' [railway] and against the income-tax. It has now voted the repurchase of the 'Western' and will vote the income-tax." And that because it was the ransom paid to public sentiments for lucrative operations conducted by shrewd

now indirectly by helping others, increase the public debt beyond all bounds and consequently the interest paid to capital, maintain and in fact increase the "surplus value" enjoyed by manufacturers (many of whom fatten on political demagoguery), and put the government of the nation into the hands of speculators such as Volpi, who concluded the Peace of Lausanne, or of cabinet ministers such as Caillaux and Lloyd George.

2254. The governing class is not a homogeneous body. It too has a government—a smaller, choicer class (or else a leader, or a committee) that effectively and practically exercises control. Sometimes that fact is visible to the eye, as in the case of the Ephors of Sparta, the Council of Ten in Venice, the favourite ministers of absolute sovereigns, or the "bosses" in parliaments. At other times it is more or less hidden from view, as in the "caucus" in England, the political convention in the United States, the cliques of "speculator" chieftains who function in France and Italy, and so on.[1] The tendency

financiers, promoters, and other speculators. In Italy a Chamber that opposed extension of suffrage, and rejected the very moderate extension proposed by Luzzatti, approved the much more radical measure proposed by Giolitti, and that because it could not stand out against a man who was so expert in protecting trusts and in manipulating electoral patronage. As for Giolitti himself, he favoured an extension of the franchise to pay for the support of Transformist Socialists and other democrats, and that, in order to lessen the opposition they might offer to his own enterprises, among which we must reckon the Tripolitan War, which, in turn, he had not favoured at first, but which was forced upon him by sentiments prevailing in a large part of the public.

2254 [1] The situation is excellently described in a speech made by M. Briand at St.-Étienne, Dec. 20, 1913: "There are feverish impatiences in our democracy, there are demagogic plutocrats who are rushing towards Progress at such a frenzied pace that we lose our breath in trying to keep up with them. They want everything or nothing, those men. At the very time when they are amassing fortunes with scandalous ease, they are grasping at wealth with a demeanour so menacing, so exaggerated, so unrestrained, that we have a right to wonder whether it is really to get it and not rather to protect it." All the same the financiers M. Briand has in mind let others do the talking while they go on making money. Of their breed Carducci wrote "On the Fifth Anniversary of the Battle of Mentana" (*Poesie,* p. 483):

> ". . . Se il tempo brontola,
> finiam d'empire il sacco!
> Poi venga anche il diluvio—
> sarà quel che sarà. . . ."

("If the storm begins rumbling, let us hurry and fill our pockets; then let a deluge come, and what will be will be.") The thing is of all times and places whenever and wherever speculators hold the upper hand. *Liberté,* Apr. 14, 1913: *"Banker*

to personify abstractions or merely to think of them as objective
realities inclines many people to picture the governing class as a
person, or at least as a concrete unit, and imagine that it knows what
it wants and executes by logical procedures designs which it had
conceived in advance. In just such terms do anti-Semites think of
the Jews, and many Socialists of the *"bourgeoisie"* (though others,
coming closer to realities, think of the middle class as a "system"
functioning to some extent quite aside from any design on the part
of its members). Ruling classes, like other social groups, perform
both logical and non-logical actions, and the chief element in what
happens is in fact the order, or system, not the conscious will of individuals, who indeed may in certain cases be carried by the system
to points where they would never have gone of deliberate choice. In
speaking of "speculators," we must not think of them as actors in a
melodrama who administer and rule the world, executing wicked
designs by stratagem dark. Such a conception of them would be no
more real than a fairy-story. Speculators are just people who keep
their minds on their business, and being well supplied with Class I
residues, take advantage of them to make money, following lines
of least resistance, as after all everybody else does. They hold no
meetings where they congregate to plot common designs, nor have
they any other devices for reaching a common accord. That accord
comes about automatically; for if in a given set of circumstances
there is one line of procedure where the advantage is greatest and
the resistance least, the majority of those who are looking for it will
find it, and though each of them will be following it on his own
account, it will seem, without being so, that they are all acting in
common accord. But at other times they will be carried along by
the sheer force of the system to which they belong, involuntarily,

Carbonneau and His Friends the Politicians: Every time the police manage to collar
some financier of dubious status, they cause a great pain to a certain deputy in the
Bloc, who, as it inevitably turns out, is friend and legal adviser to all promoters of
blue-sky enterprise. There are, to be sure, a number of specialists of that type; but
there is one in particular whose name comes to mind every time a Carbonneau goes
to the lock-up. When the Duezes, the Martin-Gauthiers, the Rochettes, the Carbon-
neaus need a good legal adviser they turn instinctively to the Hon. M. X——, because they know in advance that as legal adviser he will not prevent them from
fleecing investors, and that as a Deputy enjoying far-reaching influence in the
Chamber and in the Chamber galleries (lobbies), he will screen the boat and its
pilots behind his flag." And see § 2256 [1].

and indeed against their wills, following the course that is required of the system. Fifty years ago "speculators" had no conception whatever of the state of affairs that prevails today and to which their activities have brought them. The road they have followed has been the resultant of an infinitude of minor acts, each determined by the present advantage. As is the case with all social phenomena, it has been the resultant of certain forces operating in conjunction with certain ties and in the face of certain obstacles. When we say that at the present time our speculators are laying the foundations for a war by continually increasing public expenditures, we in no sense mean that they are doing that deliberately—quite to the contrary! They are continually increasing public expenditures and fanning economic conflicts not in order to bring on a war, but in order to make a direct profit in each little case. But that cause, though an important one, is not the main cause. There is another of greater importance—their appeal to sentiments of patriotism in the masses at large, as a device for governing. Furthermore, the speculators in the various countries are in competition with each other and are using armaments to exact concessions from rivals. Other similar causes are operating, and they all are leading to increases in armaments without that's being in any sense the consequence of preconceived design. Not only that. Those men who are rich in Class I residues sense intuitively, without needing to reason or theorize, that if a great and terrible war should occur, one of its possible consequences might be that they would have to give way to men who are rich in Class II residues. To such a war they are opposed in virtue of the same instinct that prompts the stag to run from the lion, though they are glad to take on little colonial wars, which they can superintend without any danger to themselves. It is on such interests and sentiments, not on any deliberate, premeditated resolve, that their activities depend, and these accordingly may eventually carry them to some objective that they may be aiming at, but also quite as readily to points where they would never have dreamed of going. Some day the war they have made way for but not wanted may break out; and then it will be a consequence of the past activities of the speculators, but not of any intent they have had either at that time or ever. So the speculators of ancient Rome brought on the fall of the Republic and the dictatorships of Caesar and Augustus, but without knowing that they were headed in those directions and without the slightest desire to reach those goals.

In dealing with speculators, as with other elements in the social order, the ethical aspect and the aspect of social utility have to be kept sharply distinguished. The speculators are not to be condemned from the standpoint of social utility because they do things that are censured by one or another of the current ethical systems; nor are they to be absolved from any given ethical standpoint because they have proved socially beneficial. The utility depends upon the circumstances in which the activities of the speculators are carried on, and specifically upon the relative proportions of speculators to persons strong in Class II residues, either in the population at large or in the governing classes. To determine and appraise such utility is a quantitative, not a qualitative, problem. In our day, for instance, the enormous development of economic production, the spread of civilization to new countries, the remarkable rise in standards of living among all civilized peoples, are in large part the work of speculators. But they have been able to do that work because they came from populations in which Class II residues were numerous and strong: and it is doubtful, indeed it is hardly probable, that benefits such as these could be realized if there were any great decline in the Class II residues in our masses at large or even merely in our governing classes (§§ 2227 [1], 2384 [1]).

2255. To have a concrete instance of the applications of the instruments of governing just described, one might consider the case of Italy during the Depretis régime. How could that politician ever have been master of the Italian Chamber and the country for so many years? He was not the leader of a victorious army. He had none of the eloquence that stirs the emotions of men. He had none of the prestige born of high achievement. He was not forced upon the country by a king. What, then, the source of his strength? Only one answer is possible: He was a past master at utilizing the sentiments and interests then prevailing in the country, and more especially the interests, and so becoming really the leader of the syndicate of speculators that was then ruling the country and to a large extent holding the substance of the power of which he enjoyed only the semblance. He made many speculators rich men by protective tariffs, railway deals, government contracts in which the state was robbed right and left, banking irregularities that were later exposed. Never was bandit chieftain more lavish towards his confederates in pillage and plunder. Crispi was an interlude. His was an administration that set out to modify residues and cared little for the interests of speculators. He aspired to creating sentiments of nationalism in a people that had no sense of country, and his work, like the work of all men who have tried what he tried, came to nothing. Instead of using the Socialists, he fought them and so had their more intelligent and active leaders against him. And hostile or indifferent were the speculators, to whom he tossed few if any bones to pick. In a word, the conditions of the economic period in which he ruled were all in his disfavour (§ 2302). He fell incidentally as the result of a defeat in Abyssinia, but he could not have lasted long in power in any event. Remarkable the contrast between him and his successor, Giolitti, who was truly a master in the art of using interests and sentiments. He, no less than Depretis, made himself the leader of the speculator class and the protector of "big business"; and since money was required for helping the latter, and the banks had their money tied up in government loans, he provided the government with funds by founding the insurance monopoly, so making the money in the banks available for "big business." [1] Sentiments he had

2255 [1] Pantaleoni, *Cronaca* (on the news), pp. 260-64: "The monopoly guaranteed the Institute [of Life Insurance] has a double purpose. On the one hand, the state is given control of the life-insurance industry; on the other, the state is provided with an *instrument for having considerable financial resources at its disposal* for many years to come—the premiums that will be paid in by the insured, and which will not have to be paid back till many years hence when the policies mature. [And then the state will or will not pay them back according to the way the people then in power happen to feel, and according to the surplus available in the budget.] That aspect of the situation has not been advertised before the parliament and the taxpayers, and with good reason, for it is unwise to divulge the creation of a debt not accounted for in the budget. [Even if it had been divulged, things would have been the same: a demagogic plutocracy worries little about the future.] . . . Parliamentary government has countless virtues, but also not a few defects; among which, three in particular: For one thing, the rank and file of Deputies in the parliament are woefully deficient in political education. . . . Then again that the Chambers should split up into parties of a very low moral stature is a rule without exception. In view of that division, every proposal of a ministry that is calculated to surmount some serious political difficulty is not discussed from the general and comprehensive standpoint of national interest . . . but is studied as a propitious and far-reaching opportunity for overthrowing or blackmailing that ministry. Finally, publicity of debate is a rule of parliamentary procedure. . . Those traits in the parliamentary

a gift for using in a truly marvellous way, never overlooking a single one. Crispi had striven to create nationalist sentiments in the country, and he had striven in vain. Giolitti found them ready-made, and exploited them lavishly and ever with success. He never dreamed of fighting Socialism. He billed and cooed with its leaders till he got them—as he himself said—to "pack Marx away in the attic." Others he tamed to such an extent that they came to deserve their nickname as "the King's Socialists." He lavished money on the Socialist co-operatives, and that he was in a position to do, because economic conditions were in his favour (§ 2302), just as they had been unfavourable to Crispi; and those same conditions allowed him to carry the Libyan adventure to a successful conclusion and defer to the Greek calends the liquidation of the huge public debt that was incurred in connexion with his policies. Friendly with the Socialists, at least with such among them as were not too savage and staunch, he was not unfriendly to the Clericals, and if he did not tame them, he at least made them more tractable, and could depend on them extensively at election time. Taking advantage of an enthusiastic public consensus in sentiments of nationalism, he broke up the close-knit body of Republicans and reduced that party to a small nucleus of zealots blindly keeping faith with their principles. He extended the franchise to strike terror into the hearts of the *bourgeoisie* and make himself its protector, meanwhile doing his utmost to look like the patron of the popular parties. In a word, there was not a sentiment nor an interest in Italy of which he failed to make clever use for his purposes, so piling success on success and going through with the Libyan enterprise, which was something far more costly and dangerous than the Abyssinian venture that had proved so fatal to Crispi (§ 2302). It is said that he did not want the war with Turkey and fought it only as a sop to certain sentiments, using it as an in-

system occasioned no great inconveniences so long as the Chambers exercised mere financial supervision. . . . But now they necessarily make ministries either unwilling or unable to declare frankly what their purposes are, forcing them to conceal the instrumentalities they are using and to pay toll now to this, now to that, parliamentary group or, to speak even more frankly, to pay blackmail."

However, Pantaleoni approved of the insurance measure on the ground that it might serve to provide funds for a future war. But if it might have served that purpose, it did not actually do so, for the insurance premiums went into the pockets of the cliques that were then ruling in Italy, while the army and the navy continued in a state of utter unpreparedness.

strument of governing. Like all men preponderantly endowed with Class I residues, he could use sentiments, but he did not understand them. He could never see how they could still be strong in the masses at large when they showed themselves so pliant in the popular leaders whom he flattered and cajoled. He therefore had no accurate perception of their social significance. That was no great hindrance to him in his deft manoeuvres from moment to moment; but it prevented him from having any broad view of the future that he was meantime preparing. But that, after all, did not worry him greatly—his eye was wholly on the present. In fighting the Libyan War, he was striking a grievous blow at the Ottoman Empire and so bringing on the Balkan War, and as a result profoundly altering the balance in Europe. Yet he made no efforts to strengthen the military and naval forces of his country with a view to oncoming wars. He refused to increase army and navy appropriations in the degree required because he did not care to exasperate the taxpayers, and especially because he needed the votes of the Socialists. On the other hand, he made loud boast of the fact that in spite of his war he had maintained or increased expenditures on public works and in subventions of various kinds to voters. He concealed the amounts the war had cost by disguising them in his budget reports, postponing payment of them to the future. He increased the public debt clandestinely by issuing long-term treasury bonds, so filling the coffers of commercial and savings-banks but with grave risks of danger to come. By such devices he made ready to have his war and yet conceal its costs. The policy was momentarily convenient, for by those devices he was able to satisfy both the elements who wanted the war and the elements who were unwilling to shoulder its inevitable consequences. But it postponed and aggravated the difficulties that it failed to solve.

In this particular case one sees, as under a magnifying lens, the kind of thing that speculators generally tend to do. The great predominance of Class I and the virtual absence of Class II residues in Giolitti and his followers first was a great help and then ended by being a great handicap to their power, which was all but shattered by fifty or more Socialist Deputies who were sent to the parliament by the elections of 1913 and who were strong in Class II residues. Before that campaign the Socialist party had had to choose between "transformism" and "intransigence" (non-compromise), in other words, between following a course more particularly featured by Class I residues and a course prevailingly featured by Class II residues. As usually happens with both nations and parties, the Socialist leaders were inclined to follow the first course; but a great tidal wave came surging up from the masses and bore new leaders to the fore, and then swept them, with a few survivors from among the old, along the second course, where sentiments predominated. That was fortunate for the Socialist party, for it was in that way placed in a favourable position for giving battle to a government that had no convictions and no faith. And in that we have a particular instance of a development that is general and with which we shall have to deal at some length. In other words, we discover that the greatest strength of a party lies not in the exclusive predominance of Class I residues or of Class II residues, but in a combination of residues from the two classes in certain relative proportions.

2256. The interlude provided by the administration of Luzzatti confirms these inferences. Luzzatti had been of great help to elements that profited by protective tariffs, but they had no further need of him when he became Prime Minister—at that time protection was in no danger, and once water has gone over the dam it comes no more to the mill. Furthermore, Luzzatti was far from being as good a representative of the speculators as Giolitti had been, nor did he have Giolitti's faculty for using sentiments without sharing them. For that reason Giolitti remained the actual "boss" during Luzzatti's turn in power and took power away from him with the greatest ease when he judged the moment opportune. Likewise Sonnino, who is far superior to many another statesman in Italy so far as education and political thinking are concerned, has never been able to last long in power, because he lacks either the ability or the inclination to act as a faithful agent of the band of speculators. In France, Rouvier was frequently "boss" of the parliament simply because of his merits as leader of a similar band, and his last ministry came to an end not because of difficulties at home but because of difficulties abroad. Caillaux's strength lies altogether in the speculators who are gathered about him. But it would be wiser for us not to stop at these names or any other list of the kind and imagine that we are dealing with situations peculiar to certain individuals, certain political systems, certain countries. They are closely bound up with a social system in which speculators make up the governing *élite*.[1] In England the election campaigns against the House of Lords were backed financially by speculators led by so-called Liberal ministers.[2] In Germany the great manufacturing and financial interests

2256 [1] Descriptions given by technicians who follow the ways of empiricism without any cluttering of theory are very useful for getting facts in a clear light. Such men are immune to the ever present danger of reshaping fact to conform with theory, even unwittingly. I will quote in point such a description from the *Financial Times*, Mar. 27, 1914. It relates to the things that we have just been discussing. I will merely note that the description applies not only to France, but to other countries where speculators are in the saddle. As regards the United States, a good deal would have to be added to the description, but nothing taken away. *"Paris, March 24.* We have heard a good deal of late about 'plutocratic democrats' and 'democratic plutocrats,' by which is meant either a wealthy financier who becomes a demagogue for the sake of political influence rather than from any real conviction or, as is more widely the case in France, a demagogue who has no objection to becoming a wealthy financier if circumstances permit. M. Barthou, M. Briand, and their friends have freely used the expression in connexion with M. Caillaux, to whom they are politically opposed, and it is a fact that certain prominent Republican politicians belonging to all sections of the Republican party have of late years turned their political influence to considerable personal advantage." A long account follows of things various statesmen had done in collusion with financiers. We omit it because we prefer not to cite proper names, their presence easily diverting attention from general uniformities to considerations of ethics, party, or particular sympathies or antipathies. The conclusion of the article takes us back to facts of general bearing, which are of greater importance in a scientific study. *"Need of a political protector:* As a matter of fact, it has long been the fashion with French financial and other companies to provide themselves with a *'paratonnerre'* or 'lightning-rod,' in the shape of a person of political influence who can act more or less as a mediator in high places, and who, on occasion, can help to shield financiers who may be liable to get into trouble, or protect interests that may be in danger from threatened legislation. As a rule politicians are very chary of being openly connected with any but concerns of very high reputation; but there are others. Thus, there are many barristers who are both clever pleaders and brilliant politicians. Many are the concerns that willingly pay huge annual fees to a political barrister in order to secure his services as 'legal adviser.' The legal adviser is paid quite as much for his political influence as for his legal advice, and he runs no risk, not being openly connected with the concern. It is natural, perhaps, in a country where kissing goes by favour—and show me the country in which it does not!—that people interested in important business schemes should endeavour to obtain a hearing with the powers that be by securing as influential a political intermediary as they can get, but the practice undoubtedly has its drawbacks." And see § 2254 [1].

2256 [2] Guglielmo Emanuel, *Corriere della sera*, Feb. 9, 1914: "Characteristic of the [English] system is an incident of which I heard the story one evening as told in a political address by a Liberal who, being both a Member of Parliament and the recipient of a knighthood, certainly knew whereof he spoke. Before the elections of

reach the very foot of the throne, though that choice spot is still to some extent disputed by the military caste. In the United States Wilson and Bryan went into power as professed and probably sincere opponents of trusts and financiers, but actually they worked in their favour in maintaining anarchy in Mexico with a view to securing a President there who would be subservient to American finance. And those pacifists carried their self-composure to the extent of inviting Mexico to attend the Peace Congress at The Hague at the very moment when the American navy was attacking Vera Cruz, killing men, women and children! The recent past is very much like the present. In France Louis Napoleon Bonaparte was able to become Napoleon III only because he had become the leader of the speculators, while in Italy administrations of the past have fallen

1906, which gave the majority and the government to the Liberals, he was discussing with a friend who later became a minister what a scandalous thing it was that the Unionist ministry which was at the time in power should be 'selling' titles. Being still an innocent young man and ignorant of the ways of politics, he exclaimed emphatically: 'When we get into power we must put an end to such a disgraceful thing!' 'Really?' answered the future minister calmly. 'I believe that when we get into power we shall have to sell as many titles as we can in order to replenish the party's treasury.' If one is to believe what the Opposition newspapers are now saying, it would seem that the idea of the prospective minister has been carried out to the letter. Wagging tongues assert that a price-list has actually been agreed upon. A knighthood cannot be bought for less than £5,000 sterling; a baronetcy requires a contribution of at least £25,000; and a peerage, not less than £60,000. . . . The money derived from such 'sales' goes into the 'war budget,' where it is administered by the 'chief whip.' "

And there we have the "ethical state" or "the State of Law" so greatly admired by simpletons! The same situation is to be noted in other countries. Austria-Hungary does a rushing business in decorations and titles. In every civilized country government ministries have considerable subsidies at their disposal for election purposes. *Liberté*, May 10, 1914: "Ingenuous people imagine that the government has at its disposal for 'making' the elections only the slender item of a million and a quarter accounted for in the budget under the 'secret fund.' The 'black box' is infinitely better lined than that. A man who has been minister of agriculture in the Bloc is quoted to the effect that he had thirty millions a year to distribute, as he saw fit and without making any accounting, for the requirements of ministerial politics. The pretext in that case was subsidies to farmers. Then there is the income from gambling (card-playing clubs and horse-racing). Now the government has absolute control, outside the budget, of that real gold-mine. In 1912 income from casinos and race-track betting yielded twenty-four millions (francs) for application to purposes of public charity. The total was larger for 1913. This public charity has a bearing on elections, primarily, a fact that allowed the Hon. M. X—— to say to the voters in his district: 'Why, in eight years' time I have secured a good million in relief for you!' " And see § 2557 [1].

through unawareness of the importance of speculators or through disregarding or neglecting them. It would perhaps be going too far, though not very much too far, to say that if the governments of the King of Naples and his other neighbours had made a concession of the "Railways of the South" to private interests, and promoted other similar enterprises, they would not have been overthrown. For years and years French and Italian liberals have tired our ear-drums with their praises of the English parliamentary system, which they have held up as a model before the whole world. Some of them may possibly have been ignorant of the extraordinary corruption which features that system and has been so excellently described by Ostrogorski. But others must certainly have known of it, and if they have held their peace, it has been in deference to the principle that wolf does not eat wolf.

2257. For purposes of maintaing its power the governing class uses individuals from the subject class, who may be grouped in two divisions corresponding to the two principal instruments for holding power secure (§ 2251). The one group uses force, and is made up of soldiers, police of one sort or another, and the *bravi* of a day gone by; the other uses skill, and ranges in character and in time all the way from the clientage of the old Roman politicians to the clientèles of our contemporary politicians. Those two groups are always with us, but never in the same actual proportions, nor, much less, in the same visible proportions. One extreme is marked by the Rome of the praetorians, where the chief *de facto* instrument of governing, and even more so the visible instrument, was armed force. The other extreme is represented by the United States of America, where the chief actual instrument of governing, and to a somewhat lesser extent the apparent instrument, is the political "machine." These cliques work in various ways.[1] The principal way is the least conspicuous. The administration in power "looks after"

2257 [1] A study of such procedures technically, from the standpoint of efficiency and costs and containing no ethical ramblings, no quest for "remedies," and no sermons—which are about as productive of results as a sermon that might be preached to the Phylloxera exhorting them to stop devastating our vineyards—is still a desideratum. We cannot occupy ourselves with it here. The reader will find valuable information as to Anglo-Saxon ways in Ostrogorski's classical work, *La démocratie et les partis politiques;* and on the same thing in Italy in Giretti's excellent study: *I trivellatori della nazione* ("The art of scuttling the country").

the interests of the speculators, and often without any explicit understanding with them. A protectionist government, for instance, gets the confidence and the support of the manufacturers it protects without having to come to explicit terms with all of them, though it may have some agreement with outstanding individuals. The situation is the same with public works, though agreement with the big contractors is becoming the rule. Other ways are better known—they are less important from the social standpoint, but are commonly regarded as more important from the ethical standpoint. Among them is the bribery of voters, elected officials, government ministers, newspaper-owners, and other such persons, which has its counterpart under systems of absolutism in the bribery of courtiers, favourites, male and female, officials, generals, and so on—an old form of corruption that has not altogether disappeared.[2] Such means

2257 [2] Direct purchase of votes was a practice widely followed in days gone by (§ 2557 [1]), and it still is, though perhaps not to the same extent as formerly. People who are beaten by such practice condemn it bitterly and often perhaps sincerely. Those who profit by it sometimes pretend to condemn it, but sometimes also openly vouch for the benefits it brings to the public. Here is an example: *Rivista popolare*, June 15, 1913. Discussing the election for which preparations were in progress at Cuneo [Giolitti's home town], the review prints a passage from a government newspaper, quoted in Salvemini's *Unità*, May 16, 1913: "Quite apart from any notion of vote buying, a thing of which we are unable even to conceive (*sic*) [interpolation of Salvemini] it is a fact that general elections put a great deal of money into circulation. [That sounds much better than the word "bribery."] And when money circulates, it circulates for everybody. It is therefore desirable that this rain of manna should continue for a certain length of time. We understand, of course, that it means sacrifices, and very burdensome sacrifices, because they are of a financial character. But a noble ambition to serve one's country properly implies some sacrifice. Furthermore there is no law obliging our politicians to run the chances involved in an election. If they have no money and cannot procure any, if they have money but do not care to spend it, let them stay indoors at home. No one, we repeat, compels them to make a bid for the spot-light. The Honourable Giolitti, in accord with the Head of the State, will call for the new elections at what he judges to be the proper time; and whatever he does will be well done. For our part—and we are confident that we speak for the vast majority in the country—we hope that the campaign will be a long, a very long, one. There will be a lot of talk, but there will also be a lot of money put into circulation, and it will circulate down to the humblest levels in society; and so—to come to the point—candidates old and new need not worry as to the precise date of the elections. Let them rather take to heart the admonition of the Divine Master: *Estote parati!* Let them be prepared, for they shall know neither the day nor the hour when the famous decree cometh. Let them be ready—that is to say, let them come supplied with everything and especially with the viaticum."

That newspaper might have added that the statesmen who control it get their

have been employed in all periods of history, from the days of ancient Athens and republican Rome down to our own; but they are really the consequences of government by a class that forces its way into power by cunning and rules by cunning. And that is why the numberless attempts which have been made to "purify" politics have been failures and still remain such. Witch-grass may be cut as often as one chooses, but it sprouts only the more rankly if the roots are left untouched. Our democracies in France, Italy, England, and the United States are tending more and more to become demagogic plutocracies and may be following that road on the way to one of those radical transformations that have been witnessed in the past.

2258. Barring some few exceptions, chief among them the conferring of honours and decorations by governments (§§ 2256², 2257²), money has to be spent to secure the support both of armed

viaticum from the taxpayers, whereas the Opposition have to produce their viaticum from their own pockets. An honest man, and of such there are still a few, pays his money and that is the end of it; but the man who is not so honest—and of such the numbers are legion—considers his campaign contribution as an investment that is to bear dividends when he is elected, and to that end he sometimes comes to terms with the man who was his enemy a few days earlier.

Money is not used in all cases of corruption. The most economical form of corruption is to confer honorific titles or other such favours; and sometimes they can be sold for money and the money then used for direct corruption. A case that may serve as typical came to public notice in Austria in 1913. It is excellently reported by Achille Plista, a correspondent of *Liberté*, Dec. 26, 1913: "M. Stapinski, leader of the Popular party in Poland, received from M. Dlugosz, a member of the cabinet as minister from Galicia, large sums of money to be used for party campaign publicity and other election expenses. The charge was made by M. Dlugosz himself. But it turns out that M. Stapinski is much less blameworthy than was at first believed. M. Dlugosz is also a Pole and a sympathizer of the Popular party. He is a man of some wealth. In applying to M. Dlugosz for help for the party, M. Stapinski was acting quite properly. The money he received came, he supposed, from a man of the same political faith, a wealthy Polish patriot, generous and devoted to 'the cause.' That, however, was not the case. M. Dlugosz took advantage of his membership in the cabinet to procure the money from the Premier. It was provided out of secret funds. M. Stapinski did not know that. He did not know, either, that M. Dlugosz paid him less than he had received from the secret fund. The situation of the Premier, though beyond criticism on the side of personal integrity, is hardly less embarrassing as regards the propriety of his conduct in office. He has used the secret fund for purposes of legislative corruption. To tell the truth, it is perfectly well known that the government has its resources for influencing Deputies and parliamentary groups. But that is known and yet not known. So much the worse, then, for the minister who lets himself be caught red-handed in an operation of that type. Only one course is open to him: disappearance. The incident has been the occasion of a long debate in the course of which the Chamber heard some

force and of political "machines." It is not enough, therefore, to be willing to use such instruments—one has to be able to. That capacity is correlated with the production of wealth, and the production of wealth, in its turn, is not independent of the manner in which armed force and the political following are utilized. The problem therefore is a complex one and has to be considered synthetically

blunt truths. M. Daszynski testifies, for instance, that during the past seven years elections in Galicia have cost the secret fund of the Ministry of the Interior four millions. Now the Interior has a credit of only 200,000 crowns a year under that rubric. In seven years, therefore, 1,400,000 crowns! Where did the other 2,600,000 come from? A voice from the floor answered the question: 'How about philanthropies?' The remark has the following background. At moments of crisis in ancient Rome a dictator was created. Here they create a baron. Barons are made out of financiers and manufacturers, if they are rich enough. The decree mentions as justifying the nomination: 'Services rendered to the national economy, national industry, national commerce'; or else, 'philanthropies.' Deeply rooted here is the belief that the services which receive most signal recompense are not mentioned in the decree. That explains the enormous discrepancy between the liberalities of the secret funds of the Interior or of Foreign Affairs and the very moderate normal budgets allowed those two departments for their inexpensive operations. Has it not been shown that a single newspaper, the R——, has cost the Interior a hundred thousand a year more than the total allowance for the secret fund? I keep to the Interior alone. For if one were to go into the activities of the other department, we would be carried too far afield, perhaps even abroad! Deputy Tusar remarked quite appositely that for some time past every day had been wash-day for dirty linen. That is true. After the Prohazka scandal came the gambling scandal in Hungary, with a whole flock of others, notably the 'Canadian-Pacific' scandal, which was one of the most astonishing that ever came to light here. In that one the Austrian public servant appears in an attractive, honourable, even touching rôle. The Austrian Ministry of Commerce sees the port of Trieste boycotted and Austrian shipping strangled by a powerful combination of German companies that are working for Bremen and Hamburg and with the brutal matter-of-factness of a Lieutenant Forstner and his colonel ["heroes" of the Zabern affair]. So, to break that monopoly, an agreement is reached with an English concern that is strong enough to stand the strain of battle—the Canadian-Pacific, which is to favour Trieste by steering emigrants to that port. 'I take it'—protested a section chief of the ministry at the investigation—'I take it that an Austrian official has a right to serve Austrian interests!' But the powerful German syndicate sets a newspaper, the *Reichspost*, to work, and also emissaries who win the support of the military authorities. By an army order all the representatives of the Canadian-Pacific are arrested, its offices closed, its sailings cancelled. As a result foreign interests came to triumph over Austrian interests, and the Austrian Army, doubtless unwittingly, was made the tool of a German syndicate against the Austrian Government! The Chamber had to interfere with a parliamentary investigation, before the Army, which had been fooled by the *Reichspost* and other agents of the great German group, could be brought back to the right road. What was the rôle of stupidity, what of venality, in all that? Those who know may tell, but not everything can be ascribed to in-

(§ 2268). Analytically, one may say that armed force in many cases costs less than the "machine," but in certain other cases the "machine" may prove to be more favourable to the production of wealth; and that has to be taken into account in striking the balance (§ 2268).

2259. Evolution towards "democracy" seems to stand in strict correlation with the increased use of that instrument of governing which involves resort to artifice and to the "machine," as against the

experience and simple-mindedness. The case of the innocent Deputy Stapinski, who was bribed without knowing it, must be fairly rare in this hard-boiled age of ours." In England the election campaign conducted by the Asquith ministry to strip the House of Lords of its power cost enormous sums, and the money was supplied in large part by manufacturers and business men. In Italy and to an even greater extent in France, the distribution of decorations is an instrument of governing that has the advantage of costing nothing. The *mérite agricole,* which is frequently conferred on individuals who could not tell wheat from barley, the *palmes académiques,* which are oftentimes conferred on individuals who have fought heroically in a war with French syntax, and other honours of the kind, have saved the country millions and millions of francs. In Italy an administration can also take advantage of its power to grant or withhold licences for bearing arms, granting them to members of its party, refusing it to its adversaries. And—chiefly at election-times in districts where the battle is hottest—it grants licences to professional criminals who help the government candidate in ways not always legitimate, and withholds them from the honest citizens who show themselves favourable to an opposition candidate. Between the days when Aristophanes was exhibiting the corruption of Athenian politicians on the stage and the days when the Panama investigation and other scandals were shedding a flood of light on the ways of contemporary politicians, centuries and centuries have elapsed, countless treatises on morality have been written, sermons without end have been preached, to induce men to behave themselves in an honest and upright manner; and since all that has been in vain, it is obvious that ethical theories and the sermons that go with them have been absolutely powerless to eliminate or even to reduce political corruption, and it is very very probable that they will be just as ineffectual in the future. The things that really influence the situation are of a quite different character. It is interesting, however, that our knowledge, now authentic and voluminous, of countless instances of political corruption does not serve to shake the faith of certain "intellectuals" in the "ethical state," nor the faith of the masses at large in governments that have to thank their existence and their power, in part at least, to such corruption. So in the Middle Ages the simony and the immorality of many Popes in no way shook the Catholic faith—Boccaccio, as we have seen, in his story of the converted Jew (§ 1937 [1]), shows by a pretty derivation that such things very properly strengthened it. At every step we take we stumble on facts of the same kind, and they all go to show that in people at large there are two currents, a current of logical or pseudological reasoning, and another current of non-logical conceptions, beliefs, faiths, of the inconsistencies of which people are not aware; or which, if they do perceive them, they immediately brush aside as nuisances, and forget. The two currents flow in parallel channels, never mixing their waters, ever remaining, to an extent at least, independent.

instrument of force. In ancient times that was clearly observable towards the end of the Republic in Rome, where there was a conflict between precisely those two instrumentalities, force winning the final victory in the Empire. It is even more apparent in our own day, when the régimes in many "democratic" countries might be defined as a sort of feudalism that is primarily economic (§ 1714) and in which the principal instrument of governing is the manipulation of political followings, whereas the military feudalism of the Middle Ages used force primarily as embodied in vassalage. A political system in which "the people" expresses its "will"—given but not granted that it has one—without cliques, intrigues, "combines," "gangs," exists only as a pious wish of theorists. It is not to be observed in reality, either in the past or in the present, either in our Western countries or in any others.[1]

2259 [1] A library of thick volumes would not be big enough to hold even an insignificant fraction of the available documents. From a host of examples I will quote just one from Italy: the construction of the Palace of Justice in Rome. For the particulars, see Eugenio Chiesa, *La corruzione politica, discorsi alla Camera dei Deputati,* with the preface by Napoleone Colajanni. Among the findings of the commission that conducted the inquiry, Number 4 is as follows: "Interference on the part of public authorities with work on the building was very active and very harmful even during the period when the work was on a money-saving basis, 937,328 lire being spent at that time, nominally to pay for work of preservation, but actually to give employment to four hundred labourers who were so faithful and so inactive on their jobs that they came to be called 'hod-carriers of state.'" It is amusing to note that those lines were written under an administration whose chief device for governing lay in holding the support of the Socialists by subsidizing a number of cooperatives, which, if those workmen deserved the nickname of "hod-carriers of state," could only have been called "revolutionists of state" (§ 2261 [1]). The widow of his late Excellency, Ascanio Branca, who came in for censure at the hands of the Commission, very justly wrote to the *Giornale d'Italia,* Apr. 30, 1913: ". . . Allow me . . . to protest vigorously against the strictures brought by said Commission against my late husband, Ascanio Branca. I well remember that at the time when he was Minister of Public Works he was forced to append his signature to the contracts in question under pressure from the then Minister of the Interior, the Marquis di Rudinì, who, with a sense of his responsibility for the maintenance of the public peace and [When force cannot be used, one has to use one's wits.] in order to avoid a very serious strike, thought it his duty to regulate his political conduct in that manner." In similar terms the son of the late Minister Ferraris soundly defended his father, alleging and proving that all sorts of pressure had been brought to bear upon Signor Ferraris, at the time Keeper of the Seals, in connexion with the Courts' Building. Interesting one of the letters written by the Keeper of the Seals to the Prime Minister on July 11, *Giornale d'Italia,* May 3, 1913: "Before yielding, as your Excellency says and truly, may I be allowed to speak my mind

2260. Such phenomena, long the subject of remark, are usually described as aberrations, or "degenerations," of "democracy"; but when and where one may be introduced to the perfect, or even the merely decent, state from which said aberration or "degeneration" has occurred, no one ever manages to tell. The best that can be said is that when democracy was an opposition party it did not show as many blemishes as it does at present; but that is a trait common to almost all opposition parties, which lack not so much the will as the chance to go wrong.

2261. It is further to be noted that the defects in various systems of government may differ from each other, but, taking things as a whole, it cannot be held that one type of régime is very different in that respect from any other. The criticisms that are levelled at modern democracy are not greatly different from those that were lev-

on the housing and construction question in Rome. From as far back as 1879 the national and municipal authorities have been deceived, or at least have chosen to be deceived—certainly they have deceived the parliament and the country. [Really, it was not deception, but just the consequence of a certain method of governing.] Instead of resolutely taking upon itself both the expense and the management of the works required for modernizing the capital . . . the state placed or pretended to place the responsibility on the shoulders of the city government. The city assumed the responsibility, not realizing altogether just what it was doing; all the more so because meantime it was accepting assistance from the state, leaving the question of balancing accounts open. At any rate, the city accepted the assistance, and the state, either in connivance or out of impotence, gave it more rope. . . . The city proceeded to mismanage everything and it *will always* be unable to do otherwise; because it has no traditions; because politics figures in everything [And what of the national government? Politics not only figures in everything—it *is* everything!], because the real interests of the city are not considered at election-time, in a word because it is forced to go wrong either through connivance, or through weakness, or through incompetence. [Exactly what the investigation showed had been the case with the national government.] The last straw was the enactment of July 20, 1890. Now I see that the same mistakes are being made over again, with this one in addition. The government is eager to keep, and is trying to keep, the goodwill of the city authorities; it is eager, and is trying, to avert a municipal panic: it has neither the program nor the courage to make an issue of the labour question and answer it once and for all. [Artifice still substituting for force.] The result is that they are all like persons sinking in the mire [Mire is the element in which eels and politicians live and grow fat.]: the more they struggle, the deeper they sink; and meantime the city authorities, the contractors, the labour agitators, are feathering their nests. . . . Having said that much, I, who am of opinion contrary to the view I see prevailing in the cabinet, yield. I yield for many reasons, in fact for every reason; but to ask me to name a Roman office-holder as my personal representative is going too far. In view of the pressure that had been brought to bear upon me [A Minister of State is speaking, remember, the titular head of a national magis-

elled at ancient democracies, the Athenian, for instance; and if there
are cases of corruption in democracies old and new, it would not be
difficult to find cases just as bad in absolute and constitutional monarchies, in oligarchical governments, and in any other sort of régime
(§§ 2446 f., 2454).[1]

tracy! The pressure is bearing upon such a man! Imagine the pressure that must
bear on a mere judge when some political service is required of him!], I had
already issued instructions to Councilman Gargiulo. I shall excuse him. But I will
appoint no one in his place. It is for your Excellency to indicate whom I shall
name, and I will name him, in full conscience at any rate that I shall be in no
way responsible for what he does or fails to do as my appointee."

The file copy of this letter is in Ferraris's personal hand. It is a pity that we
do not have all the letters that Ministers of State in France and England have
written to one another in connexion with "business." There would certainly be
some like the above. There are honest people in abundance in every country,
but they are powerless to resist the manoeuvres of the politicians—they are ground
to bits in a powerful machine: the political system. Among the countless documents
that might be quoted, see *Atti della Commissione d'inchiesta parlamentare sulle
banche, Roma, 1894: Interrogatorii* (testimony of Pietro Antonelli, pp. 8-11; and of
Carlo Cantoni, pp. 38-39). But in general, for that matter, politicians and newspaper men may be seen buzzing about the banks like flies about honey.

2261 [1] So for political parties: The difference between them lies in the opportunity,
not in the will. Examples are legion. *Iniziativa,* Apr. 19, 1913: "Everybody remembers the chorus of protests that arose from the Socialist camp—the *Avanti* leading the music—when a few voices made themselves heard anent the degeneration
manifest in the Socialist cooperative labour movement. Everything was denied, even
things that spoke for themselves, namely, that in accepting contracts for public
works the Socialist cooperatives were making the Socialist Deputies tools of the administration. And, in fact, so strong today are the ties between parliamentary Socialism and Giolittian government, and so close the relations between the Socialist cooperatives and the Ministry of Public Works—which naturally misses no opportunity
for favouring the Socialist cooperatives, in contempt of every norm of fair play—
that breaking them will be absolutely out of the question. It will also be a vain
hope that the Socialist Deputies, even those to be returned by unlimited suffrage,
will ever go back to an earnest and staunch anti-ministerialism. Well says the *Unità*
of Florence, calling attention to a declaration by Nino Mazzoni, who has recognized,
for once at least, the degeneracy in the cooperatives that Socialism, official and non-
official, has brought about in Italy: 'The most pernicious influence is the fact that
the cooperatives force Deputies in the parliament, or candidates for the parliament, to wear their shoes out on the stairways of the various ministries, first to
procure a decision to do some public job, then to have it done immediately, then
to have it awarded to this or that cooperative even against the judgment of the
consulting experts, then, while the work is in progress, to obtain all the advances in
money that from day by day prove necessary but which have not been stipulated
in the contracts, and so on and so on [§ 2548]. Can a Deputy upon whom that
kind of livelihood is forced ever be anti-ministerial in earnest? And will not the
contemplated "Bank of Labour" be a source of moral corruption, of subservience of

2262. Political parties usually approach these facts from the ethical standpoint and use them to fight one another. The ethical aspect is also the aspect that most impresses the public, and so the adversary in religion or politics is generally accused, rightly or wrongly, of not living up to the norms of morality. Oftentimes morality means sex

Deputies and cooperatives to cabinets in power, of a chronic and unavoidable ministerialism? For every loan that has to be obtained, for every payment that has to be deferred, how many times will the Deputies not be compelled to kotow before the president of the Bank of Italy, or seek the intercession of the Minister or Undersecretary of Finance, and make tacit promise of some act of baseness?' " *Corriere della sera,* Jan. 6, 1914. The Executive Committee of the Milanese Chamber of Labour passed the following resolution: ". . . The Chamber of Labour registers vigorous protest with the Federation of Cooperatives of Production and Labour of Milan, for its efforts, in contempt of the self-respect of organized labour, to obtain contracts for public works in Libya, which are tossed out as 'biscuit' by the Government under the vulpine pretext of desiring to help cooperatives of working-people, but actually with the design to discredit the vigorous opposition of the labouring classes to colonial enterprise, and draw its teeth."

The favours obtained by cooperatives in the Southern provinces were not as lavish as the favours showered upon cooperatives in Romagna for the purpose of taming the Socialists there; so Deputies from the South were very bitter in their comments on expenditures in Romagna. Deputy Tasca di Cutò, also a Socialist, alluded to them in a speech in the Chamber on Mar. 4, 1914—verbatim report in the *Giornale d'Italia*—as follows: *"Tasca di Cutò:* 'The state cannot, from considerations of an electoral and doctrinal character, continue to be one vast laboratory of orthopedic accessories for the various cases of economic rickets that require attention; nor can it be allowed to hold the bag for privileged individuals, whether these belong to high finance, or to certain labour groups who are already settling back on their haunches in a shabby economic cooperativism. While the number of our emigrants is increasing in alarming proportions, the state has become a regular subsidizer of unsound speculations, emanating now from groups of workers, now from groups of capitalists connected with high finance. (*Loud applause. Exclamations. Protests from a few seats at the extreme Left.*)' " The rest we take from the *Corriere della sera:* "Marchesano *(to the Socialists):* 'The government gives favours only for favours received!' (*Catcalls.*) Tasca di Cutò: 'Must not some limit be put to this system where so-called civil expenditures are gradually coming to look like those other disbursements which I have just described as "unproductive"? I ask if we are to go on with a policy of public works that is an end in itself and is determined by considerations of electoral advantage and public peace, a policy which, under pretext of relieving unemployment, is intensively promoting unemployment itself. (*Vigorous applause from the Majority benches. Loud protests from the Socialists.*)' "

Shortly before this there had been a tumultuous session in the Chamber to determine whether a promise made by Minister Sacchi to aid land-reclaiming schemes in Northern Italy to the tune of thirty or forty millions a year, to be taken from the Cash-on-hand and Loan Fund, was binding or not on the new cabinet. The principal purpose of the expenditures for said "improvements" was to provide good

morality (§§ 1757 f.), which is the kind that rouses the greatest emotion in many people. That sort of accusation was widely used against the powerful in days gone by, and it still serves, on occasion, as a political weapon in England. It was on charges of that variety that the political career of Sir Charles Dilke was cut short. History shows no correlation between such shortcomings—or even greater ones—and an individual's political worth. The correlation seems more plausible when the sins involve appropriations of other people's property, or bribery. Yet even in those regards the individuals who rise to prominent places in history are generally far from being free from blemish, and the differences, if we choose to keep to the field of ethics, are differences in forms rather than in substance. Sulla, Caesar, Augustus, brutally distributed the property of private citizens among their veterans. Modern politicians distribute them more artfully and more pleasantly among their partisans by favouritism, patronage, and other similar devices.[1]

Consideration of the situation from an exclusively ethical standpoint prevents perception of the uniformities in correlations of facts that obtain in it. Suppose we have a certain social system in which the uniformity obtains that in order to govern those in power have to grant favours and protect the interests of financiers and promoters

contracts for certain cooperatives and to reduce agents in the parliament to subservience to the Government.

In France expenditures for similar political purposes go under a different name, but they are not smaller in amount; in fact, they are larger. The case of state management of the Ouest-État railways is sufficient proof, the main purpose there being to provide votes for the Radical-Socialist party then in power. *Liberté*, March, 1914, takes the figures on the deficits incidental to state management from the report by Deputy Thomas. They are, in millions of francs, for the year 1909, 38; 1910, 58; 1911, 68; 1912, 76; 1913 (estimated), 84. *Liberté* adds: "The system of state management of railways necessarily leads to ruin by waste. . . . It is not by any means the fault of the technical engineers. . . . They are prisoners of a system that is itself nothing but an expression of graft, mistakes, and political interests. In that system the party that it is most important to satisfy is not the public that is served but the employees whose votes must be held. Of course it is the duty of the company to look after the welfare of its agents. . . . But in the 'Western,' not labour and service are most lavishly recompensed, but work at election-time, where the Deputies are at once creditors and debtors, now to this person and now to that. And these are the debts that are paid with greatest generosity." In Italy the very same causes help, among others, to explain poor railway service, late trains, frequent accidents, and thefts of freight and baggage.

2262 [1] There is an actual difference in substance between the two modes of action, but it has to be sought in another field (§ 2267).

of economic production, and, in their turn, must receive favours and patronage from them. The relation between rulers and speculators will as far as possible be kept dark. Still, every so often to some the connexion will come to light—it will be proved, that is, that certain *A*'s, who are in power, have had relations of that kind; and almost always it will be certain *B*'s, adversaries of the *A*'s, who reveal the scandal.[2] That much granted, procedure in accord with the methods

2262 [2] Take for a concrete example the Rochette affair in France, which may serve as typical of a very large class of facts. However, we must persuade ourselves deliberately to ignore a number of things in connexion with it: 1. The country in which it occurred—for similar occurrences abound in other countries. 2. The form of government—for monarchies and republics are on a footing in such respects. 3. Political parties, for there are few differences between them. 4. Individuals, for if the things in question had not been done by those particular individuals, they would have been done by others, since they are really consequences of the social system.

To be certain we are getting our information from a source above suspicion, let us take the summing up of the spokesman for the Parliamentary Investigating Commission: *Journal officiel, Chambre des Députés,* 2d session, Apr. 3, 1914, p. 2282: "It has been established that in March, 1911, between the twenty-second and the thirtieth—for my part dates are of little consequence, the fact alone being important [An answer to derivations designed to obscure the main issue by arguing about incidental questions of date.], M. Monis, Minister of the Interior and Premier, at the request of his colleague M. Caillaux, asked M. Fabre, State's Attorney-General, to come and see him. M. Monis, Premier and Minister of the Interior, and stranger to matters of the courts by the very constitution of the ministry to which he belonged, communicated to M. Fabre—call them orders, call them instructions, call them a mere expression of personal views, I am not interested in such niceties— [Again an answer to derivations designed to obscure the main issue by irrelevancies] remarks that gave M. Fabre to understand that the government was concerned to find some way to postpone the Rochette case, a matter that had already been dragging along for four years. [During which years Rochette, thanks to the protection of politicians, was continuing to organize fraudulent corporations and pocketing money, most of which, however, trickled on to the press and to one politician or another.] . . . What was the point of attack in 1911? What was the criticism? Fault was being found with the brutal and uncalled-for action of the police in the bodily seizure of Rochette with the help of a paid and pretended witness. [The *A*'s against the *B*'s. In the second act of the drama it will be the *B*'s against the *A*'s.] *M. Jules Delahaye* [from the floor]: Yes, the magistrates were sharply criticized for too great haste, and for needless brutality, as you say. . . . But it has to be yes or no: Was the stock exchange given a 'tip,' or was it not, with a view to causing a crash in the Rochette securities? Is it true or not true that five days before the warrant for Rochette was issued, that 'tip' had been delivered by *M. Y. D.*—since certain brokers were informed in advance of the arrest? . . . *The Commission* (through its spokesman) [He reads Fabre's digest of his conversations with Monis.]: 'On Wednesday, March 22, 1911, I was sent for by M. Monis, the Premier. He wanted to see me about the Rochette case. He told me that the government was

of experimental science would be as follows: 1. *With regard to real movements,* to determine whether the case were accidental, exceptional, or one of a large class of similar cases. In the latter event, one would have to determine what uniformity was indicated by that class of cases and in what correlation the uniformity stood with

anxious not to have the case come to trial on April 27, a date long since agreed upon; that it might embarrass the Finance ministry, which already had the liquidation of the religious congregations on its hands, the matter of real-estate credits, and others of the same sort. [The sort where certain individuals appropriate public monies with the well-compensated assistance of politicians and newspapers.] The Premier ordered me to have the presiding justice of the Chamber of Correction put the case over till after the court vacations of August-September. I protested vigorously. . . . The Premier stuck to his orders. . . . I felt certain that that incredible thing was all a put-up job of Rochette's friends. . . . I sent for the presiding justice, M. Bidault de l'Isle, and with some emotion stated the predicament in which I had been placed. Finally M. Bidault de l'Isle consented to the postponement out of consideration for me. That evening, Thursday, March 30, I called on the Premier and told him what I had done. He seemed very much pleased. . . . In the Premier's waiting-room I had seen M. du Mesnil, editor of the *Rappel,* a newspaper that was defending Rochette and from time to time insulting me. He was there, doubtless, to find out whether I had submitted.' [The spokesman for the commission continuing:] That is the situation, and I have a right to say that when one reads that document and notes the feelings of the Attorney-General in penning it, one inevitably gets the impression that that is an accurate statement, describing the facts just as they were. . . . M. Bidault de l'Isle . . . yielded. He granted the postponement, and you already know what followed. Rochette was enabled to continue his operations, to go on plundering the national savings . . . from April, 1911, to February, 1912, and more generally down to the time of his flight abroad. There you have the brutal fact, the material fact, which has been so long denied in the lack of any proof, but which is today as clear as the light in this room. . . . In my judgment, what is urgently demanded of Republicans at this moment, and my judgment is the judgment of a Republican of the Left, is to establish the independence of the courts."

And that, precisely, was what was not done, even to the slightest extent, because it could not be done without a far-reaching change in the social system! Not once from the day when Attorney-General Bulot proclaimed that the magistrate had to bow to the *"fait du prince"* (§ 1824), has anything, anything whatever, been done in France to secure independence for the magistrate; and that shows the strength of the forces that are working against a reform of that kind. M. Briand remarked before the Commission, p. 2288 of the same report, and very soundly: " 'Oh, the courts are not free? But where does the trouble lie, gentlemen? How can you expect our judges to be altogether free? Their appointments, their promotions, their dismissals, their careers, their lives, are all in our hands!' *M. Maurice Violette* (from the floor): 'But you have been in power yourself a number of times!' [Derivation: actually, the *B*'s are no better than the *A*'s. The spokesman for the commission hints, p. 2282, at the reasons why magistrates have to take orders from politicians, who in turn are tools of the financiers:] But there you are: all our judges are not

other uniformities prevailing in the society in question. 2. *With regard to virtual movements,* assuming that it is considered desirable to prevent the recurrences of such cases, to determine what ties, among those susceptible of elimination (§ 134), have to be eliminated or modified in order to achieve the desired result.

heroes! I will even add, to be quite fair, that not all of them are required to be, and that some of them, men with large families, may be so situated as not to be able to make a practice of heroism. M. Fabre may have remembered the fate of one of his predecessors, M. Bertrand, who fell victim to his courageous resistance to governmental pressures. And besides it was not the first time pressure had been brought to bear upon him. He had met similar difficulties, notably at the time of the troubles in the Champagne [*Cf.* § 1716 [5]]. M. Bidault de l'Isle, for his part, was nearing the end of his career and did not care to compromise or jeopardize the position and the future of the Attorney-General."

After all that, one might imagine that the spokesman for the commission would have gone on and concluded that the incidents that it condemned were a consequence of leaving power with a ministry to issue orders to a court judge. But no—he says: "It is just another case, gentlemen, of the drawbacks inherent in that sense of loyal comradeship that prevails among us." That again is one of the usual derivations, designed to divert attention, by stressing the secondary and leaving the main untouched.

The same *Journal officiel,* p. 2291: *"M. Maurice Barrès* . . . 'Among the members [of the commission investigating the Rochette affair] were men who were bound, tied, controlled, commanded, by sentiments of friendship and loyalty in misfortune. On those I shall make no comment. Others judged that in making himself a mouthpiece for the desire of a lawyer, his friend, M. Caillaux had meant to be obliging, had merely given vent to a spontaneous good nature, to a sense of *camaraderie:* that in yielding to M. Caillaux's request, M. Monis had merely responded in the same feelings of goodwill, *camaraderie,* eagerness to be accommodating. But those same commissioners found that the Briands and the Barthous were great rascals, mercilessly abusing instinctively good souls, such as Caillaux and Monis, who had been led into difficulties by their sheer good nature. [Derivation serving for the counter-attack of the *A*'s upon the *B*'s.] "Let's help each other along." That was the feeling uppermost in the minds of the commission [Not that commission only, not in one country more than another, but in all the men who make up the general staff of speculation and in all countries where speculation is supreme.], and it was in singular accord with the definition that Anatole France gave of our régime as a "system of mutual accommodation": *"C'est le régime de la facilité."* The problem is not a simple ordinary problem. You are not called upon to judge individual shortcomings. You are asked to pronounce and decide whether you accept the failure of our present system.' *M. Jules Guesde* [from the floor]: 'Not of the republican system. The same sort of thing goes on in monarchical England and imperial Germany. It is the capitalist system that is at fault.' " There is some truth in Guesde's remark, but only if the phrase "capitalist system" be amended to read "a system ruled by 'speculators.' " "Speculators" could perfectly well hold the reins in a Socialist system, and in fact their influence reaches deep down into the Socialist press and among Socialist leaders.

That manner of reasoning is hardly ever—one might say never—followed.[3] And that, in the main, for two reasons: first, that, human beings as we have repeatedly noted, commonly prefer derivations, and especially ethical derivations, to logico-experimental reasonings; and second, that the few who might be capable of seeing things as they really are have an interest in diverting public attention from

2262 [3] Occasionally someone takes a step along the road that would lead to a scientific solution, but he very soon halts, in fear of shocking this or that principle, this or that dogma. The same *Journal officiel*, p. 2308: *"The President of the Commission [Jaurès]*: '. . . I have a right to denounce in the name of the country this universal conspiracy of silence and equivocation. To it you owe the fact that instead of solving this mystery at the proper time two years ago and settling it through a commission appointed by you, it has dragged along from intrigue to intrigue, furnishing those whom the Attorney-General has called "enemy brothers" with means for mutual negotiation and intimidation. [The battle between the *A*'s and the *B*'s, in which, Jaurès forgets to add, his Socialists also took a hand and likewise in the interests of financial powers.] Well, gentlemen, I say that the time has come for the country to be freed of this system of intrigues by groups and cliques. . . . The time has come for us squarely to face the great and formidable danger that is threatening it. A power that is not new but is growing in strength is hovering over it, the power called finance—high finance, low finance. . . . [The promoters and owners of business should not be forgotten, nor the fact that the power in question has a strong prop in the conduct of the Socialists. After comparing the power of modern finance with the power of the old feudalism Jaurès continues:] This new power is as subtle as it is formidable. It conquers silently. [Even the Socialist press and the Socialist associations succumbing.] It makes its way into interests and consciences [Not excepting Socialist interests and consciences.], and a time comes when a nation that believes itself sovereign and solemnly celebrates the rite of the ballot [One of the dogmas cluttering the quest of the orator for experimental facts.] is suddenly led away into captivity by the power of money. That power triumphs in the disintegration of our political parties. [A statement that is contradicted by the facts.] It triumphs in a swarming of newspapers which, resting on no central ideas, can live only by clandestine subsidies. [Even the press of well-defined parties considers it useful and helpful to have its share in the largess distributed by the financial powers and the politicians. At this point Jaurès abandons his quest for experimental causes, leaves the solid earth, and goes soaring away into the clouds.] No! Organized democracy must [Must! But it doesn't!] rise against organized finance [Just now it is kotowing to finance, not fighting it. When will the change come?] but it must [Again an expression of a hope or desire instead of a search for relations actually existing between facts.] be an active organization having its centre in an idea, its flame in a conviction and a faith, its rallying force in a doctrine and a program. [*Sunt verba et voces et praeterea nihil.* What follows is a quotation by Jaurès of the testimony of the Attorney-General before the Investigating Commission, in which he used the words "enemy brothers" (*frères ennemis*)]: "I have served under thirteen Ministers of Justice. May this thirteenth one not bring me bad luck! Do you think it an easy matter to live and hold on among a host of statesmen who are tearing at one another? [While the *A*'s and *B*'s

them. The *B*'s, remember, are in no sense trying to prevent *everybody* from doing the things they complain of, but only the *A*'s. Their object is not so much to change the social system as to turn it to their own advantage by unseating the *A*'s and taking their places. From that standpoint it is better to represent the facts as consequences not of the social system, but of the rascality of the *A*'s. The so-called subversive parties, which contemplate the destruction

are fighting it out, the third party fattens.] I held my ground as best I could among these "enemy brothers." ' " *Liberté,* Apr. 20, 1914: "The Friendly Association of Magistrates, at a convention attended by 400 delegates representing a membership of 1,900, has adopted a number of recommendations, notable among which some dealing with the moral and material situation of the judge and the need of protecting the administration of justice from interference by politicians. Two hundred magistrates attended the banquet that closed the convention, grouped about M. Bienvenu-Martin, Keeper of the Seals. In a loudly applauded after-dinner speech, M. Braibant discussed the deeply regrettable interference of the legislative authorities with the orderly administration of justice. It was a legend, he said, in the magistracy that to obtain advancement and reach a satisfactory situation a judge needed to be a diplomat, surround himself with friends, and not be afraid to join the followings of high and powerful patrons. 'The Friendly Association of Magistrates,' cried M. Braibant, 'was organized for the express purpose of providing our colleagues with guarantees against such interference from the executive and legislature powers.' M. Willm, Deputy from the Seine, also alluded to the incidents that cost M. Fabre his post as Attorney-General: 'He resigned,' he said, 'with the esteem and respect of all his colleagues.' 'But that,' interrupted M. Bienvenu-Martin, 'is a criticism of my personal policy.' M. Willm denied that any such criticism of the Keeper of the Seals had been intended and concluded amid great applause: 'Justice must be above influence, outside of and above all parties, and the best way to save the Republic is again to give those who are seeking justice the impression that the courts know no such thing as weakness.' " Jouvenel, *La république des camarades,* pp. 178-79: "Besides, if the magistrate needs the government, the government often needs the magistrate. The whole scandalous history of the Third Republic comes down to a series of compromises and conflicts between the executive power and the judiciary authorities [§ 2548]. The Union Général crash, Panama, the Dreyfus, Humbert, and Rochette affairs, have been mere episodes in the back-stage life of the Seine courts during these last thirty years. . . . When a Minister of Justice asks an Attorney-General to appoint an investigating judge or court president who will be 'reliable,' he knows very well how the request will be interpreted. A judge who has just been promoted is as a rule much less 'reliable' than one waiting for an advancement. A judge who is approaching the age of retirement is more independent than a man exposed to dismissal without pension. [In Italy there is also the danger of being transferred from a desirable location to some second-rate or out-of-the-way place. That exerts a powerful influence on judges who are not heroes, and heroes have never been very numerous at any time in history.] Not a file of any magistrate [in the archives of the Ministry of Justice] but contains at least a dozen recommendations from politicians. Ministers order promotions and transfers in the courts by weighing one such recommendation against another."

of the present social order, ought, it might seem, to follow a different tack. As a matter of fact they do not, because the changes they desire are not, on the whole, of a type that would prevent recurrences of the scandals in question. So they follow the lines of the ethical derivation, merely adding that the rascality of the A's is occasioned by the "capitalist" system that they are trying to destroy. The A's and B's welcome such derivations, for they centre attention on remote and very improbable eventualities, and divert it from causes much closer to hand and far easier to deal with.[4]

So the argument rambles on, stressing ethical considerations more and more, and the best derivations, from the standpoint of the people who are using them, are those that divert attention from what are the danger points for them. In most common use are the following: 1. Since it is the B's who have brought the misdeeds of the A's to light, friends of the A's take the offensive against the B's, and say that after all they are no better than the A's—and in that they are altogether right and are therefore believed by many persons in all good faith. So the very ticklish question as to whether the existing political system may not in some way be accounting for the misconduct of the A's and B's, which is duly brought to light—of the A's by the B's and of the B's by the A's—is worked over into a harmless question as to the relative moral worth of the A's and the B's. That question is virtually unanswerable, so after a season of talk

2262 [4] In just that way the French Socialist Sembat saved his Radical friends who were compromised in the Rochette affair. *Gazette de Lausanne,* Apr. 6, 1914 (reporting the session of the Chamber where the resolution on the Rochette affair was adopted): "The findings of the Investigating Commission were replaced by a fairly anodyne text which stopped at 'taking cognizance' of those findings and denouncing the interference of politics with the courts, such interference having been one of the principal industries of the Majority that felt called upon to denounce it before adjourning for the day. The text of the resolution had the advantage of ignoring MM. Briand and Barthou and of dealing with MM. Monis and Caillaux in the most impersonal and general terms. That was where M. Sembat interfered with an altogether superior dexterity. He clearly perceived the discredit that the Socialist party might incur by supporting the 'whitewashing' policy of M. Jaurès. He therefore demanded criminal prosecutions—only, he named four defendants: MM. Caillaux, Monis, Briand, and Barthou. That was a sure device for getting nobody into trouble and also for saying afterwards that the Socialist party had held out for punishment. M. Sembat is an ingenious, clever fellow." In England Lloyd George and Lord Murray were saved by charitableness on the part of the leaders of the opposing party, who counted naturally on similar indulgence being shown to their friends.

the great excitement over the "scandal" involving the A's simmers down to nothing. 2. A variation on the preceding. It is shown that in calling attention to the misdeeds of the A's, the B's are prompted by purely partisan interests. Many other derivations of that kind are available, the purpose of them all being to stress the question, "How and why has the misconduct of the A's been brought to light?" instead of the question, "Has there been misconduct, and if so, what is the cause of it?" 3. Other derivations that do not compare the A's with the B's but take them separately. As regards the A's, there is the trick that works so effectively for the defence in trials by jury. One goes into the past life of the defendant in great detail, so that the accusation is lost sight of in the mass of data. The A's have been good patriots. They have served their party loyally. And no end of other such things are brought out, though they are altogether irrelevant to the charge in point. One derivation that is widely used is to assert, truly or falsely, that the A's have derived no *direct* pecuniary benefits from the alleged misconduct, with no allusion to the profits direct or indirect—or to intangible profits such as distinctions, influence, and other benefits of the kind—which have accrued to their relatives, friends, supporters, voters, and so on. Nothing, further, is said of the indirect profit they have enjoyed by winning and holding power through the help of the persons whom they have benefited and of the press which has been paid or directly favoured by financiers who have had protection.[5] But even if it could be shown

2262 [5] It is not easy to determine just how much money the press collects from financiers for showing goodwill towards them and towards the politicians who are their friends. The Panama *exposé* mentioned figures that were exceedingly large, and plenty of other evidence goes to show that that was by no means an exceptional case. So-called publicity outlays are very considerable in the cases of certain firms. A publicity agent, M. Rousselle, was on the stand before the commission investigating the Rochette affair, and his testimony has to be taken into serious account as one of the very few available declarations betraying facts that are unknown, or not very well known, to the public. "*M. de Folleville:* 'You are a publicity agent? Specifically, you were connected with the Rochette enterprises?' *M. Rousselle:* 'I did publicity for the Rochette enterprises, as for any number of other bankers. When a banker wants to issue securities or introduce new stocks on the market, it is as necessary for him to advertise their advantages as it would be for any ordinary commodity. To do that he resorts to newspaper publicity. The publicity agent discusses the conditions on which the papers can be induced to help, the conditions, that is, on which the information furnished will be published. A remuneration is agreed upon as results begin appearing (*en cours de publicité*). The publicity agent pays the sum stipulated. The manner of payment varies according to the bank's

that in doing the things they did the *A*'s were inspired by sentiments of the purest and loftiest morality, that would not show that they did not do the things they did and that the public was not injured by their misconduct. And that, as usual, means replacing the question as to the fact and the damage with the irrelevant question as to the moral value of the *A*'s. Similar derivations are used, *mutatis mutandis,* against the *A*'s. Instead, that is, of proving the fact and the damage of the misconduct of which they are accused, it is shown that the *A*'s are of little or no account morally—an entirely different question. There are similar derivations for dealing with the *B*'s, with similar substitutions of problems. 4. Many derivations urge hushing everything up lest harm should be done to friends, the party, the

credit.' *M. de Folleville:* 'How large were Rochette's expenses for publicity?' *M. Rousselle:* 'A certain number of Rochette enterprises, so called, are posterior to his arrest. For the real Rochette enterprises, those antedating his arrest, I disbursed, I should say, roughly, two millions (francs). In the later enterprises, a million more or less.' *M. de Folleville:* 'You kept books for such disbursements?' *M. Rousselle:* 'In matters of financial publicity I act as a personal representative. When the work is over, I report back to my banker as to how I have used the sums entrusted to me and give him the papers bearing on the various transactions.' *M. de Folleville:* 'Do you keep books in such a way as to show what use you have made of the money?' *M. Rousselle:* 'These matters are too old to allow me at this late date to reconstruct them in detail. I could give totals. As regards beneficiaries, I very much doubt.' *M. Leboucq:* 'Do you deal directly with the newspaper editors?' *M. Rousselle:* 'As a rule I do not deal with the political editor of a paper, but with someone representing him.' *M. Leboucq:* 'You are a publicity agent on your own account? What is your procedure when you are dealing with a paper?' *M. Rousselle:* 'Certain newspapers deal directly. Others lease their space. The tendency at the present time is towards leasing (*affermage*). At the time of Rochette, that was rather the exception.' *M. Leboucq:* 'When you are discussing terms, do you have a quota fixed in advance—so much for each paper?' *M. Rousselle:* 'Yes.' *M. Leboucq:* 'In connexion with the Rochette enterprises, did you raise the perquisites of any particular newspaper?' *M. Rousselle:* 'Prices on the whole were the same that I gave for enterprises that were not Rochette enterprises.' *M. Leboucq:* 'What was the percentage of such disbursements as compared with the gross totals of the enterprises?' *M. Rousselle:* 'Three per cent.' *M. Delahaye:* 'It has been said 10 per cent.' *M. Rousselle:* 'Apart from publicity in newspapers, Rochette spent a good deal on circulars and in publishing special newspapers.' *M. Leboucq:* 'Do you not find the discrepancy of 7 per cent somewhat large?' *M. Rousselle:* 'One would have to see the books. Rochette used mail publicity as part of his method for launching paper.' *M. de Folleville:* 'Did he use many bond-salesmen?' *M. Rousselle:* 'I imagine he did. He had branch offices in various parts of the country. He had banks that were working for him on the side.' " The simple-minded public pays for all that, admires and cheers those who fleece it in that fashion, reposes its faith in the newspapers that defend them, and calls the state that encourages them the "ethical State."

country. Such arguments come down in substance to the contention, more or less attractively veiled, that it is not so important to prevent corruption as to prevent its becoming known.[6] 5. Finally come procedures that are tricks rather than derivations, the idea being to embrace as many individuals as possible under the accusation of misconduct. That is a very easy matter, since corruption is the rule rather than the exception in certain governments. The measure is very effective, because, as Machiavelli in his day wrote, *Mandragola,* Act IV, scene 6: "When a thing concerns the many, it behooves the many to keep watch over it." Sometimes one stands amazed to see the *B*'s at the moment of victory, when they are pushing the *A*'s over the precipice, suddenly halt, begin to hedge, and end by resting content with half a victory. But there is a reason for that. They know perfectly well that their own tail is made of straw and that someone may touch a match to it. The many honest ingenuous souls who are ignorant of the real nature of things are attended to with

2262 [6] Testimony of M. Barthou before the Rochette Commission: "I said to M. Caillaux: 'Things that greatly astound me are going on at the Ministry of the Interior. The Premier sent for the Attorney-General and told him to have the Rochette case continued.' M. Caillaux answered that he had himself asked M. Monis to request a continuance. He told me that Rochette had the list of his expenditures in launching one or another of his earlier enterprises, that he intended to publish it, that the publication would cause a sensation, and that he had seen M. Monis to tell him to prevent the revelation." Testimony of M. Monis: "M. Caillaux added that if the continuance were refused, Rochette's attorney would make a startling opening address alluding to issues of securities that had involved losses to savings-banks and had not been prosecuted." So then: There are a certain number of pirates, and the official appointed to destroy all pirates saves one of them that the others may rest secure from punishment. *Journal officiel,* p. 2288: "M. Aristide Briand . . . 'The Rochette affair once out of the way, my intention was to send for the Attorney-General. I would have asked him for the original of the document. Then I would have taken my own copy of it and burned the two papers in his presence, and that is that! Someone will say to me: In so doing, you would have prevented the country from knowing the truth about a matter of grave importance. Gentlemen, that matter did not entail the juridical consequences which I feared. But it might have assumed, without any possible justification, the proportions of a scandal. I congratulate myself on not having occasioned it. [*Applause. "Hear! Hear!" from the Centre and the Left.*] I congratulate myself as a man in the government, as a Frenchman, as a Republican. And I have congratulated myself all the more since I have been reading the newspapers abroad and have become aware of the importance that is attached to such things outside our country.' " Such sentiments are shared by many people. We may safely conclude therefore that only a very few facts of that kind come to light. What we can know at best is a few typical cases of a body of fact that is exceedingly extensive.

derivations in endless variety that serve to conceal the real causes of corruption under veils of tolerance of human frailties, pity, community pride, patriotism, and the like.

2263. The men who make earnings at all extensive through political and financial manipulations may be divided into two categories. First come those who spend about all they earn, and take advantage of that circumstance to point out that they can have made nothing by way of political and financial intrigue, since they are not rich men. Then come individuals who have made not only enough to cover huge expenditures, but large fortunes besides. Into these two groups fall the new-comers in the governments of our modern countries, while owners of hereditary fortunes gradually disappear from the governing class. In some rare case the manipulations of this or that group of speculators are discovered, and the revelations turn to their harm. But the number so caught represents a very small fraction of the numbers actually engaged in such activities. The majority escape all penalty, all reproach, and some of them, in numbers relatively few but absolutely not so few, achieve great wealth and high honours and come to govern their countries. In Italy almost all the great fortunes made in recent decades have come from government concessions, railway construction contracts, and enterprises subsidized by the state or protected by customs tariffs; and not a few individuals have climbed over those routes to the highest honours within the gift of the kingdom. That is why the whole system looks to the clever politician like one great lottery offering premiums now great, now not so great, now quite insignificant, and which, alas, even involves the professional risk of ruin. But that risk is no greater, after all, than the risks of loss or ruin incidental to most professions.

2264. It sometimes happens that the merchant who fails in business is more honest than the man who makes a fortune. Just so, in some cases, the politician who is found out is one of the less culpable. Luck may have been against him, or he may have lacked the ability, the energy, the effrontery in corruption, required for saving himself. "Seldom," says Machiavelli (§ 1704), "do men know how to be altogether evil or altogether good." In these battles between politicians it is often the worst who come off best. It is comical at such times to see them sit in judgment on people less guilty than they and hand out sentences in the name of virtue and morality; and one thinks of the scathing witticism of Diogenes who, "once seeing some magistrates taking one of the treasurers who had stolen a bottle to prison, remarked, 'Lo the big thieves taking the little one to jail.' " [1] Certain it is that if justice lies in "giving to each his due," many of these convictions are not "just," because the victims are getting more than their due.[2]

2264 [1] Diogenes Laertius, *Diogenes*, VI, 45 (Hicks, Vol. II, p. 47): Θεασάμενός ποτε τοὺς ἱερομνήμονας τῶν ταμιῶν τινα φιάλην ὑφῃρημένον ἀπάγοντας ἔφη: 'οἱ μεγάλοι κλέπται τὸν μικρὸν ἀπάγουσι.' The ἱερομνήμονες were a kind of magistrate that is often referred to in Greek literature under one name or another.

2264 [2] In Italy in 1913 the Palace of Justice Investigation (§ 2259 [1]) unearthed a document that summarizes the norms which, so long as the present system endures, have to be followed by any concern that intends to make contracts with the state. The document is summarized in the *Rivista popolare*, May 15, 1913, as follows: "It would be to the interests of the concern: (1) To continue putting up with things, as it is doing today, (2) meantime dropping all questions at issue—they can be taken up again at some other time! (3) To get acclimated with the personnel at the ministry. By appealing to the minister the concern precludes his being interested and makes a leap in the dark. Will the minister be so honest, so far above any attack, as to protect the concern against all contingencies and against all the individuals who are stalking it? . . . 4. To examine: in case the work is to be carried on as it is today, what the financial results would be if the concern granted demands and made none. For not honest firms, but *only dishonest ones* can have dealings with the government, concerns which, strong in the damage they have suffered, sit tight, and watch for a mistake or a strait on the part of the bureaucracy, in order then to 'go in and argue matters.' "

The *Rivista* goes on: "The investigating commission styled this 'diabolical plan' a 'reprehensible scheme, not at all ethical.' [If the commission did not know that that plan is the plan that is followed and has to be followed by any concern having dealings with the state, it was displaying the greatest ignorance; if it did know, it was displaying no little hypocrisy.] That was the least it could say. [No, it could and should have added that the fault lay not with the person who jotted down in that plan things that everybody knows, but with the system which made such a plan inevitable.] But in his own defence, Deputy Abignente asserted, with rare courage, that one had only to read it to grasp its spirit and its propriety. His assertion, we repeat, is proof of the Deputy's daring. [The daring required to repeat in public things that everybody is saying in private.] But he is uttering the truth when he adds after finishing his reading of the document: 'This sketch is the history of all enterprises connected with public works in this country. [That is the truth, the whole truth, and nothing but the truth.] They have been carried on in that fashion because of defects in our organization'—defects that Deputy Abignente denounced before the Chamber, as he states, on June 5, 1905." One ought to add, however, that the present organization cannot be abandoned without replacing it with another of the same sort, because such things are necessary if politicians and their partisans are to make any money. Deputy Abignente's constituency understood that one man could not properly be blamed for faults inherent in the system;

2265. Small countries such as Switzerland, with very honest populations, may remain outside this current which has come down in a muddy torrent from the past to the present and is flooding all the great civilized countries today. It has often been remarked that the absolutist régime in Russia was not less corrupt nor less corrupting than the ultra-democratic system of the United States. Free-traders used to say that there was one cause for both cases—the protective tariffs, which prevailed in both countries; and there is some truth in that, for it cannot be disputed that protective tariffs open a wide field for corruption. But there are other causes also, since political corruption is just as conspicuous in free-trade England. The modicum of truth would be made larger if instead of protective tariffs one were to say economic protection—protection of business. Yet even if economic protection were eliminated, there would still be other fields for corruption, such as military supplies and munitions, fortress construction, ship-building, public works, state concessions (§ 2548), the administration of justice (on which Deputies and other politicians have so much influence), the distribution of favours and honours within the gift of the state, apportionment of taxes, "social" legislation, so called, and so on and on.[1]

2266. As a few typical proofs of these assertions, suppose we take different countries under varying systems of government for the first six months of the year 1913. We find: for Russia, the usual charges of corruption in the army and navy departments; in Hun-

and so when he had resigned in consequence of censure at the hands of the commission and the Chamber, he was re-elected not only to the same session of the parliament, but again to the next session in the general elections of 1913.

2265 [1] In September, 1913, *Iniziativa,* asking the how and the why of facts of the kind, wrote: "It is not so much that the Deputies are bad; it is because the voters, and especially the local 'bosses' (*grandi elettori*) are as bad as possible. It is the method of selecting and electing Deputies that is defective. An article in *Avanti* dwells on the criteria that govern the announcement and promotion of candidacies in many places. 'Among people in the South,' writes the Socialist organ, 'the conviction is wide-spread (or at least behaviour conforms with such a conviction) that even when one requests the mere recognition of a right of any government bureau, one needs . . . support from one's Deputy, or a letter from some influential person [§ 2268 [2]]. Naturally that is a system that is patented and guaranteed to produce Deputies who will be 'ministerial' to the last ditch! In fact, even if on assuming representation of a district the Deputy has intentions of being honest and independent, he is obliged after a time to bind himself hand and foot to the administration and is forced by his very constituents to accept that vassalage by their perpetual requests for 'influence' and 'letters.' 'I could,' adds the writer,

gary, banking scandals, the banks contributing millions to the campaign fund of the party in power; and a gambling scandal, a syndicate contributing 1,500,000 crowns to the party campaign fund and 500,000 crowns to political intermediaries for the right to open a casino on Margarita Island. In England, the wireless telegraph scandal; in France, gambling scandals (licences for casinos); in Italy, the Palace of Justice scandal, to say nothing of the Libyan war-supplies scandal; in Germany, armament and army munitions scandals.

All these cases except the last involved primarily members of parliaments and precisely because, in all the countries mentioned except the last, members of parliaments hold the power and manage by intrigue to exert pressure upon the men in power when they are not filling executive posts themselves. Wherever Deputies can make and unmake ministries, there generally one may look for parliamentary corruption. Now thinking rather of times and parties: in France under Napoleon III, the Republicans made a great to-do over corruption in the imperial government; yet when later on they came to power themselves they showed in the Panama affair and similar scandals that on the score of corruption they could go it as fast as their predecessors. When the Right was governing in Italy the various Lefts raised a great hullabaloo over the corruption of their adversaries; and then when they got into power, they behaved as badly as their predecessors and in fact much worse. Now, it seems, we are to look forward to a golden age when *"bourgeois* corruption" will

'give the names—since they are well known to everybody in parliamentary circles—of electoral districts that have sent delegations to Rome to look for some candidate who would be equipped not with a political faith or program, but with an entrée that would assure them district influence with the administration. Other districts in the South have actually requested candidates of the ministry, requests that, it seems, were granted on a number of occasions by the famous Commendatore Peano, the *alter ego* of the Honourable Giovanni Giolitti, who rightly considered that a small price to pay for abject consciences. It is only natural that the political deputation of a region that recruits many of its representatives in just such a spirit should contain a number of unscrupulous men and now and then a plain ordinary rascal. But one has no right to be amazed at or to find fault with such a thing, especially if one has done nothing to put an end to such a lamentable situation, but has rather made one's own deliberate contribution towards bringing it on and perpetuating it.' " [The Commendatore Peano mentioned above is the original in life of the inimitable portrait of "the Commendatore" which Guglielmo Ferrero drew in the first two volumes of his *Terza Roma,* which appeared in English as *The Seven Vices.*—A. L.]

stand aside for "Socialist honesty," but one may doubt whether that promise will be kept any better than the many similar promises that have been made in the past.

2267. If we look at all these facts from the outside, trying as far as possible to free our minds of the ties of sectarian passions, prejudices of country and party, utopian perfections, ideals, and so on, we see that, substantially, and whatever the form of government, men holding power have, as a rule, a certain inclination to use that power to keep themselves in the saddle, and to abuse it to secure personal gains and advantages, which they sometimes fail to distinguish clearly from party gains and advantages and almost always confuse with the gains and advantages of country. Wherefrom it follows that: 1. Individuals holding power behave in more or less the same way under the various systems of government. The differences come in the substance, in other words, in the sentiments that prevail in the given population: the more (or less) honest the population, the more (or less) honest the government. 2. Uses and abuses of power will be the greater, the more extensive the government's interference in private business. As raw material increases, the amount that can be earned from it increases. In the United States, where the government tries to enforce morality by law, one notes gross abuses that are not observable in countries where there are no such restrictions or where restriction is on a smaller scale.[1] 3. The governing

2267 [1] The corruption of the New York police department is partly the result of foolish efforts to enforce virtue by law. Without the purchased goodwill of a police that knows how to keep one eye shut, life in New York would become impossible. The famous Mayor Gaynor, at one time so much talked about and in no favourable sense, certainly, did not want to allow New Yorkers even to dance. *Liberté*, Apr. 6, 1913: "*An orgy of vulgarity:* Such the description, according to Mayor Gaynor of New York, that fits the disease that is afflicting high society in America at the present time. The engrossing tango, the despotic turkey-trot, are so furiously rampant this season in the land of the Transatlantics that public orderliness in the metropolis has been seriously compromised, and the evil, in an epidemic form, weighs on the mind of his Honour the Mayor like a veritable nightmare. The fad of 'tango suppers'—suppers that were usually protracted till dawn—had become so rapidly dangerous to the maintenance of good morals that Mr. Gaynor recently felt called upon to resort to Draconian measures to deal with the scourge. He ordered midnight closing for all-night restaurants and applied the decree with pitiless rigour. Some days ago a number of the more notorious feasters who had set out to flout the law were expelled *manu militari* on the dot of closing-time. The police, hard-hearted fellows, refused to allow them even to get their hats and coats, which were delivered to them on the sidewalk. Night suppers being now

class sees to appropriating other people's property not only for its own use, but also to share with such members of the subject class as defend it and safe-guard its rule, whether by force or by fraud—the support the client lends to the patron. 4. In the majority of cases neither patron nor client is fully conscious of violating the moral norms that prevail in their society, and even when they are, they justify themselves either on the ground that after all others would like to be doing as they do or on the convenient pretext that the end justifies the means—and from their point of view what better end can there be than to keep in power? In fact, not a few of them in all sincerity identify that end with the best interests of their country. There may even be persons who believe that they are up-holding honesty, morality, and the public welfare, whereas in point of fact their activities are but a cloak for the intrigues of men who are out to make money.[2] 5. The government machine consumes, at any rate, an amount of wealth that is correlative not only with the total amount of wealth belonging to the private enterprises in which the government interferes, but also with the instruments that the governing class uses to keep in power, and consequently with the relative proportions of Class I and Class II residues in the ruling class and in the class that is ruled.

2268. As regards the various parties within the governing class, we may distinguish two sorts of persons in each of them: *A*. In-

impossible, the Americans, and especially their women, are falling back on the 'five o'clock.' Between five and seven in the more popular resorts, curtains are carefully drawn, lights are turned on, and that artifice creating an illusion of night-time, the dancers give themselves up to the excitements of the turkey-trot and the 'grizzly-bear.' Mayor Gaynor has had such establishments watched by his agents, and police reports have revealed horror upon horror, it seems. Deeming that such offhand morals are not consistent with the régime of democratic austerity that Mr. Wilson has inaugurated in the White House, Mayor Gaynor yesterday urged upon the legislature of the State of New York a bill calculated to strike a death-blow at these eccentric dances. Henceforth dancing is to be forbidden in all public places. However, the unhappy Mayor is still not at the end of his pains. There is one last refuge for the tango—the private home. In one of the more worldly drawing-rooms in Washington a new fad has just been launched that will drive the Mayor to despair. Lights are extinguished and the dancing goes on in utter darkness. To find their way about the couples have no guide save a little pocket flash-light carried by the male partner. It gives a very curious effect and is the very latest vogue."

2267 [2] Late in the year 1913, Huerta was President of Mexico. The government of the United States was showing itself intensely hostile to him, while the Eng-

dividuals who aim resolutely at ideal ends and unswervingly follow certain personal rules of conduct. *B*. Individuals whose purpose in life is to strive for their own welfare and the welfare of their associates and dependents. Such individuals may be in turn divided into two categories: *B-α*. Individuals who are content with the enjoyment of power and honours, leaving the material profits to their fellows. *B-β*. Individuals who pursue material benefits, generally in the form of money, both for themselves and for their henchmen. People who are kindly disposed towards a party will call the *A*'s in that party "honest men" and sing their praises. Adversaries of the party will call them "fanatics" and "sectarians," and hate them. The *B-α*'s are generally considered "honest" by friends, while they are

lish Government, which had begun by befriending him, was now deserting him, just to avoid difficulties with the United States. The conflict at bottom was exclusively a matter of business interests. While he was President of Mexico in 1900, Porfirio Diaz had granted oil rights over an extensive territory to Henry Clay Pierce, and Pierce had sold them to the very powerful Standard Oil Company. An English concern, the Eagle Oil Company (Compañia Mexicana de Petroleo Aguila) had come to be a competitor of the Standard Oil. President Madero succeeded Diaz. He had favoured the American company—and not without personal profit—and had thought of decreeing a nullification of the concessions to the English concern. Huerta, on the contrary, confirmed them, and that made him the object of wrath on the part of the Standard Oil, of the Standard Oil's friends and customers, and of other American companies or trusts, which were all desirous of exploiting Mexico with the help of the United States Government. Wilson, the President of the United States, said nothing of all that. He said that he could not recognize Huerta because Huerta had not been "regularly" elected, and he showed great indignation that Huerta had come into power through a revolution, so violating the sacrosanct dogma of election by popular vote. In that way Wilson was substantially defending American trusts abroad, though at home he was posing as an enemy of the trusts. That is not all. Wilson had been elected as a pacifist and an anti-imperialist. In trying to intervene in Mexico he entered upon a policy that spelled war and imperialism. There is no way of determining whether he was or was not conscious of the inconsistency. On the one hand it is hard to admit that he alone was ignorant of what everyone else knew about the rapacious designs of American trusts upon Mexico; and if the attempt to force a government of American choice upon an independent country like Mexico is not imperialism, it is hard to imagine what imperialism could be. On the other hand we have already seen that there may be such things as war-pacifists (§§ 1705 f.), and abundant proofs are available to show that the faith of certain democratic humanitarians is so great as to blind their eyes to facts that are glaringly obvious and induce them to embrace views that are in the highest degree absurd and veritable rubbish. Wilson may be one of that type. We have no way of knowing. That problem, however, is of interest only to moralists. It has no bearing whatever on the quest for the uniformities prevailing among social facts.

viewed with indifference as regards "honesty" by their opponents. When the existence of the B-β's is discovered, they are called "dishonest" by everyone; but friends try to prevent the fact of their existence from becoming known, and to attain that end they are capable of denying that daylight is daylight. As a rule the B-α's are more costly to a country than the B-β's, their veneer of honesty facilitating all sorts of intrigues that are designed to appropriate other people's property for distribution within their political cliques. One might specify that tucked away among the B-α's are not a few individual's who take nothing for themselves but are careful to enrich their families.[1] The relative proportions of these types depend very largely on the relative proportions of Class I and Class II residues. In the A's, Class II residues by far predominate, and so they may be called "honest," "fanatical," or "sectarian," according to the point of view. Class I residues predominate in the B's, and that makes them better fitted to exercise power. When the B's get into power, the A's are a dead weight on their hands, though they do serve to give the party a certain complexion of respectability. This latter purpose, however, is served far better by the B-α's, who are a fairly rare commodity and are very much sought after by all political parties (§ 2300). The relative proportions of Class I and II residues in the following of the party, in the party members who are not actually administering power, and in its voters, correspond to, without being identical with, the relative proportions of those residues in the governing element, in the general staff. Only a party rich in Class II residues can elect any great number of A's; but such a party also elects, unwittingly, a certain number of B's, since they are shrewd, circumspect individuals, deft in the arts of combinations, and they readily deceive ingenuous voters who are rich in Class II residues. In our political

---

2268 [1] Jouvenel, *La république des camarades,* pp. 135-36: "There are long-faced ministers who consider themselves honest men because they have never turned a sou for themselves, but who have literally pillaged the budget to the profit of their families and intimates. [And add: their constituents, the press, and their friends in finance.] For a touching circumstance, public sympathies are often with them. They win almost equal gratitude for never having stolen anything for themselves and for spreading joy all about them. That kindly disposition towards them has most unfortunate consequences, for, in spite of everything, the needs of a politician have their limits, and there are families we know in Gascony that have needs with no limits at all. A law that would result in quite regularly substituting prevarication for nepotism would be a very good law."

systems in the West political parties fall into two general classes: I. Parties that alternate in governing a country, so that while one is in power the others stand in opposition. II. Intransigent parties, parties of lost causes, that never get into power. It follows from what we have been saying that the former (the parties that alternate in power) will contain a minimum of A's and a maximum of B's, and the intransigent parties, a maximum of A's and a minimum of B's. The situation may be stated in different language by saying that parties which never attain power are frequently more honest, but also more fanatical, more sectarian, than parties which do. That is the meaning of a common aphorism in France to the effect that "the Republic was a fine thing under the Empire." All that, essentially, is a result of the system. In the parties that get into power a first selection is made at election-time. Barring exceptions—and they are few—a person cannot be elected Deputy unless he pays and is willing to grant, and more lavishly still to promise, governmental favours. That makes a mesh which lets very few A's get by. Candidates who are wealthy enough to buy seats in the parliament, thinking of them as luxuries, amount almost to A's; and it is strange, yet nevertheless true, that next to the A's they are the most honest of politicians. They are getting to be few in number nowadays, because the sums required for buying an election are rising to unheard-of heights, and those who pay them out of their own pockets are concerned to get them back in earnings, while those who either cannot afford them, or do not care to, charge them up to the administration to be paid in the form of concessions and favours of various kinds. The competition in this field is terrific, and to come to the top a person has to be exceptionally well supplied with combination-instincts (Class I residues).

A second and more thorough-going sifting of the raw material takes place in the choice of ministers. Candidates for the parliament have to make promises to the voters. Ministerial candidates have to make promises to the Deputies and be able to assure them that they will look after them and their political followings.[2] Ingenuous souls

2268 [2] Session of the Italian Chamber, Mar. 8, 1915, *verbatim* report in the *Giornale d'Italia:* The Honourable Bevione speaking on Tripoli: "The Arab population is ruled in an oligarchical, in fact a patriarchal, fashion. It obeys certain chiefs devotedly, almost superstitiously. . . . The chiefs back their dependents, help them in their dealings with the authorities, accord them hospitality, give them

imagine that to do things like that a man needs merely to be a rascal. They are wrong. Rare gifts of acuteness and aptitude for combinations of every kind are absolutely necessary. Ministers do not have strong-boxes that they merely have to open to get money by the handfuls to scatter among their partisans. They have to look over the field of business with a discerning eye to discover subtle combinations in economic favouritism, neat ways of doing favours to banks and trusts, of engineering monopolies, manipulating tax assessments, and so on; and in other domains, influencing courts, distributing decorations, and the like, to the advantage of those on whom their continuance in power depends. And meantime one has to do one's best to keep the A's in other parties from getting together. A person with a faith opposite to the faith of the A's will not get very far with that; but if one has no faith at all, no convictions, if one has almost no residues except residues of combinations (Class I), one will find it easier to influence the A's, nay, take advantage of their very convictions to get them on one's side, or at least to draw the teeth of their opposition. We may therefore be certain that in the parties which alternate in governing a country, Class I residues by far predominate; and the system being what it is, matters cannot be otherwise; and for that reason our system is tending more and more towards becoming a demagogic plutocracy. The various parties are for ever accusing each other of dishonesty back and forth. They are right or wrong according to the point of view. Almost all parties have their B-β's, so that if one considers that element only, one may justly accuse a party of dishonesty. Parties also have their B-α's, so that if one thinks of these exclusively, one may or may not accuse a party of dishonesty, according to the meaning that is attached to the term. Few the parties, finally, that do not have their

letters to other chiefs when they travel abroad, and in return receive blind homage and obedience from them." And shortly thereafter he adds: "The simplest things— which were obtained in the days of the Turks by the recommendation of some notable (and my honourable colleagues will observe that notables in Tripoli perform, or at least used to perform, towards the local bureaucracy the same lubricating functions that we Italian Deputies perform in relations between the public and the bureaucracy of the kingdom)—are now obtained only after months and months of pressure and delay." Interesting this comparison between the Italian social system and a quasi-feudal system, because it is made by a person who is describing the facts without letting himself be carried away by preconceptions and theories (§ 2307 [1]).

A's, and considering them exclusively one will say that a party is honest. Thinking rather of relative proportions between A's and B's in a party, one will certainly find parties in which the A's predominate and which may therefore be called "honest." But in a great many other cases, one cannot make out whether there is any great difference in the relative proportions of A's and B's. In the various parties contending for power all that one can say is that the A's are mighty scarce. Meantime the lower classes are still rich in their Class II residues; so that administrations which are in reality inspired by purely material interests must at least pretend that they are inspired by ideals, and the politicians have to shroud themselves with veils—often very transparent veils—of honesty. When one of them is caught with his hand in the bag, the opposition party makes a terrible outcry, trying to take advantage of the mishap for its own purposes. The party of the alleged culprit tries at first to defend him; and then, if it finds that task impossible or too difficult, it throws him overboard, much as a storm-tossed ship unloads ballast. The public looks on very much like an audience at a play; and if there chances to be a touch of human interest or of the sex interest, it has the time of its life and free of charge. Insignificant side-lights crowd out main issues, and the real issue, in other words, the social and political system that breeds such scandals, is altogether ignored.[a] If a minister is caught dictating a court decision, the country begins to shout at the top of its lungs, but no one ever demands that magistrates be made really independent by being freed of ministerial control. That too has its reasons. The opposition parties are eager, to be sure, to use the incident to pull their rivals down from power, but are firmly resolved, when they get there themselves, to do the same things. And then again, the public grasps only the concrete, particular fact and never manages to get interested in abstract, general questions. So "scandal" follows on "scandal," each leaving the same weather it found. While one is breaking out, the other is ripening to break out in its turn, and people are shocked at each new case, regarding as the unusual what is the absolute usual and the conse-

2268 [a] [In all the literature devoted during the years 1932-33 to the case of Mayor Walker of New York, I doubt whether one will find as trenchant an analysis of that whole phenomenon as is contained in these three sentences penned twenty years in advance of it.—A. L.]

quence of a system that they have willed or tolerated. Moralists assume that the scandal is due to the accidental rise of a "dishonest" man to power, that it is altogether parallel to the case of a cashier embezzling from his employer. That is not at all the case. It is no fortuitous chance that raises a man of that stamp to power. It is a matter of selection, the choice being dictated by the nature of the system. To validate the comparison with the dishonest cashier, one would have to assume that the cashier was not chosen in the usual way, but that the employer went out to look for him among the persons most likely to rob a till and best qualified to do so by gifts of light-fingeredness and other such talents.[3]

2268 [3] Sometimes the *B*'s split into quarrelling factions, and when that happens, their recriminations throw light on intrigues that would otherwise remain in the dark. Among our contemporaries in Europe, the rise of nationalism provoked just such a split. In his *La Germania alla conquista dell' Italia,* pp. 66-82, Preziosi describes under one of its particular aspects a situation that is general. Noting the large number of manufacturing concerns in Italy that were subsidiaries of the Banca Commerciale, he continues: "If we go on from the economic question to the political, it becomes apparent that all the concerns mentioned, and others besides, with factories of varying size and importance scattered all over Italy and providing work for tens of thousands of hands, are in effect gigantic election agencies, their activities being coordinated with the activities of the many branch offices of the shipping-companies that are likewise sprinkled all over the country. The influence of such companies on political and administrative elections is exerted, naturally, in their own interests. That explains why so many Italian politicians and men otherwise prominent in public life are directly or indirectly hitched to the chariot of the Banca Commerciale and indirectly to German policies. In Italy, as in all other countries living under parliamentary régimes, the Deputies are, with few exceptions, the most humble and obedient servants of their constituencies and cannot free themselves from local influences. One may readily guess from that what efforts Deputies dependent for their elections upon such concerns have to make and the compromises to which they are obliged to lend themselves. The concerns are well aware that money is today more than ever the backbone of the political contest. They therefore vie with one another in making campaign contributions and so assure themselves of the considerate remembrance of the parliamentarians that are so gratified." Preziosi goes on to quote, p. 75, a passage from the *Rivelazioni postume alle memorie di un questore,* published in 1913 by a former police chief of Milan, and points out that newspapers made no allusion to the passage. It reads: "The Banca Commerciale . . . is known for the immeasurable influence it has always exerted on the political, economic, and financial life of the nation. For many years past, owing to the assiduous labours of the late Senator Luigi Rossi, it has managed to have a say, directly or indirectly according to circumstances, about the make-up of the successive ministries. It imagined at any rate that it had them under its patronage. [Just such a condition of demagogic plutocracy was observable towards the end of the Roman Republic. We shall consider it in Chapter XIII.] . . . Unfortunately

2269. We cannot do without some conception of the economic resuts of the various types of government (§ 2258). As regards expenditures, it has been assumed that they could be known from the amounts levied in the form of taxes, or otherwise acquired by the state. But that figure and others of the kind represent only a fraction of a country's expenditures, for account has to be taken of the costs of economic and political favouritism, of the wastage resulting from so-called social legislation, and in short of all other measures involving expenditures and waste, even if they do not figure in the state budget. After the cost of the government plant has been determined in one way or another, its product has to be computed. That is a very difficult problem, and in fact it cannot be solved in all its numberless ramifications. Approximate solutions have had to be adopted, therefore. One such is nowadays in great vogue. It is not, however, ordinarily presented as approximate, but as an absolute. It is obtained by assuming that the government provides for "public needs," and does so by levying taxes. That is a way of balancing the two sheets in the socio-economic ledger of the state, and the value of product is automatically equalized with cost.

2270. Theoretically that solution has the advantage of lending itself to easy calculations for arranging expenditures and income in the most convenient way. To put the situation very briefly, a certain requirement, A, is taken for granted; the cost is put at a, and an amount equivalent appropriated from revenue and apportioned among the taxpayers. Then, to satisfy the need for logical developments, a series of derivatives are put forward to show the "need" and to justify the apportionment that "ought"—so it is preached—to

even the press is very largely under the influence of the Banca Commerciale. A goodly number of Italian newspaper-writers are dependents of the bank and its subsidiaries. The fact is too generally known to require any great amount of proof. Who is not aware that that organ [At that time, the *Tribuna*.—A. L.] which is so constantly faithful to all ministries of whatever colour as they succeed each other in power is largely inspired by a well-known corporation lawyer connected with the Banca Commerciale, the shipping-companies, and the steel trust of Terni? *Ab uno disce omnes!* The system that the bank follows is always the same. Each of the subsidiaries must underwrite a part of the capital of a given newspaper or periodical, which in consequence finds itself with its hands tied as regards both the firm that is one of its coproprietors and other firms allied with it. In addition newspapers receive subsidies in one form or another, most often in the form of advertising accounts, with the industries that are located in the regions where they are published and read. . . . Some industries own their own newspapers besides." And see § 1755.

be made, according to the sentimental principles of one or another
of the many social moralities current. In that way one gets the solution most compatible with the sentiments of the author of the theory
and of his followers, but not the solution that best pictures the facts
as they are.[1]

2271. Noteworthy among such derivations is a pseudo-scientific
variety obtained by extending the notions of pure economics to the
social "needs" of a people. It is assumed that such "needs" are satisfied by the "state"; then by consideration of marginal utilities, one
derives the norms of a certain equilibrium between "needs" and the
"sacrifices" required for satisfying them. So one gets theories that
may conform to formal logic in certain cases but which are so far
removed from realities as at times to have nothing in common with
them. The divergence arises in any number of ways. Suffice it here
to specify the following: 1. The concept of "needs" is in no way
definable, and cannot therefore serve as a premise for strict reasoning. The economists were called upon to deal with a difficulty of
that type, and they found no way of surmounting it, except to draw a
distinction between an objective utility that they decided to ignore,
and a subjective utility (ophelimity) that they made the sole basis
for determining the economic equilibrium. But that was not the end
of it. They were further obliged to admit, in the first place, that the
individual is the sole judge as to whether or not the subjective utility
exists, and in the second place, that he is the sole judge of its
amount. All that could have a meaning, as applied to a community,
only if the community could be considered as a single person
(§ 2130), with unity of sensations, consciousness, thinking; but since
that assumption does not square with the facts, neither can the inferences drawn from such a hypothesis square with the facts. The
concept of "public need" is used in order to eliminate artificially
the difficulties that arise from the necessity of considering, if one
would keep in touch with realities, the various sorts of *utility*
(§§ 2115 f.).

2. Even assuming that the concept of "need" is definable, we have
still not eliminated all the major causes of error, and one in par-

---

2270 [1] [The use of the term "derivative" in this paragraph is so exceptional,
and in fact so unique, that one may almost regard it as a lapsus for "derivation."—
A. L.]

ticular forces itself upon us as of great importance. The reasoning based on public "needs" assumes that human beings satisfy them by logical procedures. Now that cannot stand. Non-logical actions figure very very largely in the situation. It is true that they also play a certain part in concrete economic phenomena, but that part as a rule is relatively small and may be disregarded in a first approximation. A theory assuming that human beings act logically in procuring economic property yields conclusions which are verified by experience, at least in great part. Things stand quite otherwise as regards concrete social phenomena. In some of them—and a very important group it is—non-logical conduct prevails to such an extent that a theory envisaging nothing but logical conduct fails to yield even a first approximation, but leads to conclusions that have little if anything to do with realities.

3. Reasonings, finally, of the kind we are here examining disregard very important by-products of the government plant—the effects on class-circulation, for instance. It is true that the term "public needs" is so elastic that, if one chooses, one may crowd anything into it, and say that class-circulation of a given type and to a given degree of intensity is a "public need," just as one could also cram into it a "need" of stability in government, a "need" of revolution, or a "need" of replacing one governing class with another, and so on *ad infinitum*. But it is also true that a term that may mean so many things ends by meaning nothing and that an argument in which it serves as premise strays away into mere talk.

2272. Practically, the doctrine of "public needs" (§ 2270) is useful to the governing class, or a class aspiring to power, as justifying its control and having it more readily accepted by the subject class. Suppose the governing class, *A,* desires to pass a certain measure, *X,* which will be all to its own advantage. Evidently, something will be gained by calling *X* a "social need" and trying to make the subject class, which is to derive no advantage from it, yet is to provide the funds, imagine that it is designed to satisfy one of its "needs." If then someone says that he is not conscious of any such need, he is told at once that he "ought" to be. National defence is commonly classified among the "public needs." A country, *G,* is holding a province, *A,* in subjection. The inhabitants of *A* feel no need whatever of being united to *G;* indeed they feel the opposite "need" of breaking with G and combining with the country F. The country G taxes all its citizens, including the people living in the province A, in order to increase armaments against the country F and so to hinder the province A from seceding to F. It would be accurate to say that the tax serves the advantage of those who are holding the province A, or, if you will, satisfies a "need" of theirs. But the preference is to say, in flat defiance of the fact, that the tax satisfies a "public need" of all the inhabitants, including the inhabitants of A; for in such language the fact of the oppression that is being suffered by A is made less apparent. In the same way, here is a country where a Socialist or Syndicalist party says that it feels no "need" at all of a war that the rest of the population wants. It helps to say that the war satisfies a "national need," for so one conceals, attenuates, over-passes, disaccord between those who feel the "need" of the war and those who, so to speak, feel a "need" of not having it. Sophistries of that kind are dissembled by the intentional ambiguity of the term "public need" (derivations, IV-γ). It may mean no less than four distinct and different things: 1. An actual need of all the members of a community. 2. An actual need of certain members of the community, and also certain specific "needs," such as the "need" felt by "honest men," "patriots," followers of a given faith, and so on. 3. A need that an actual majority of the community declares to be a "need of the community." 4. A need that the majority of a certain assembly, or of certain individuals legally designated to functions of governing, or of individuals who have acquired them by cunning, force, or otherwise, declare to be a "need of the community." Usually arguments designed to show the utility of satisfying such needs consider only 1, while the conclusions are calculated to cover 2, which, thanks to the indefiniteness of the language, turns out to be simply what the author of the derivations considers desirable; or to cover 4, which is, at bottom, a mere expression of the will of the group in power.[1]

2272 [1] Speculators are generally opposed to local liberties and variety in legislation, because they find it easier under centralized and uniform legal systems to ply their trade and force their will upon a country. But they do not state that motive. They use derivations. If A and B are two parts of the same country, they merely exclaim at the absurdity of A's having one set of laws and B another, without giving any reason for their amazement and without specifying whether their theory is to be extended to different countries, so leading to uniform legislation for the whole

2273. In what is called the science of finance we often get, there-fore, two kinds of derivations: 1. Derivations that aim at drawing inferences from certain ethical or sentimental principles and which may go far wide of realities. 2. Derivations that aim at giving a the-oretical tinge to results which have been arrived at in an entirely different manner. These reach conclusions that accord with reality, but for the simple reason that the conclusions have been determined in advance. If one keeps to the naked facts, it is readily apparent that governments try to get all they can out of the public and are never embarrassed by lack of "needs" to satisfy. Their one check is resistance on the part of the taxpayer. The practical financial science of a minister of state in no sense lies, therefore, in a quest for the-oretical demonstrations of this or that theorem or for the logical implications of this or that principle. It comes down altogether to finding ways and means for overcoming the taxpayer's resistance, for plucking the goose without causing too much honking. That science—or art, as one chooses—has been brought to great perfec-tion in our day, so that in the ministries of the various countries there are now certain traditional norms for extracting money along lines of least resistance. There are ways of taking advantage of mo-ments of great excitement that may arise in a country; ways of esti-mating the forces prompting expenditures and originating in in-dividuals who are to profit by them, and the forces running counter to new taxes and originating in individuals who will be damaged by them; ways, finally of stimulating forces of the one type and of diminishing the others. It is after all such circumstances have been taken into account that ministers of finance decide upon new ex-penditures and new taxes. There can, moreover, be no harm in covering such designs with a coating of derivations that will trans-figure them as logical consequences of this or that sentiment. That, in fact, may help; for there are people who are not greatly, if at all,

world. Of late they have come forward with another interesting derivation. They say: "The aim nowadays is to save energy. There must therefore be no talk of new political duties for citizens. We must get rid of all the political complications that are still left and get a purely commercial state with uniform laws." It is something like a safe-crackers' convention passing a resolution to the effect that "The prin-cipal aim nowadays is to save energy. Dogs and night-watchmen should therefore be abolished. All strong-boxes, furthermore, should be of the same make in order to promote efficiency in safe-cracking, for in that case a burglar who has learned to crack one safe will be able to crack them all."

affected by the eagerness for new expenditures or by resentments against new taxes, and such persons may be fooled by a well-conceived derivation. A government is never short of such sophistries, and theorists are always available to provide new ones. It should not be forgotten, however, that the derivations are consequences of the government's policies, never the policies consequences of the derivations.[1]

2274. If we would solve the problem stated in § 2258 (relative costs of government by armed force and by political "machines"), we must first get rid of all the derivations of which we have just seen examples, and then, bearing the complexity of the situation in mind, look for the aspects that are essential in it. Among these, certainly, will be those which we have already considered—the effects on economic and social prosperity, on defence against possible attacks from abroad, on public safety, on speedy and impartial justice, on public services, and on many other government functions. But of equal if not greater importance will be, further, effects on class-circulation and on the stimulus or depression indirectly experienced by the national economy in correlation with those respective manners of government. It must not be forgotten that oftentimes a ruling class will aim at certain results but indirectly occasion others, some of which will be unforeseen and unwanted. People in power may, for instance, establish protective tariffs in order to benefit

2273 [1] Pantaleoni, *Cronaca,* pp. 262-63: "Who does not remember the Old Age Pension Fund manoeuvre? The government owes the pensioners a yearly income, an annual amount that is chargeable, under a well-ordered finance, to ordinary budget revenues. Such the first position in which the political prestidigitator finds himself. Now comes the second: 'Since that annual amount is, roughly speaking, always the same, or again, since it is easy to predict what the total maximum amount is going to be so long as the pension-list remains the same, let us capitalize that amount by banking enough debt-certificates for the interest to cover that annual amount exactly. The item is now funded.' Then comes the third motion: 'Let us now sell those certificates and use the revenue for railways, highways, harbour improvements, fortifications, and retirements of treasury-bonds, which in their turn have served a hundred different purposes, and recover the pension annuity by charging it off to ordinary budget revenues, where they ought to be anyhow.' The three steps require, of course, a certain length of time. They are not taken by the same ministry nor even by the same Chamber. And the press, which called the man who consolidated the pension annuity a great financier, now calls the man who reverses that process an even greater one. But, really, cannot such operations be managed without all the sundries incidental to the clandestine detour? Apparently not! *Mundus vult decipi.*"

members of their clique, but incidentally and as a result in no way intended, stimulate class-circulation. From an ethical standpoint a measure may be judged apart from all other social phenomena, but from the standpoint of social utility that cannot be done; the effects of the measure on the equilibrium as a whole have to be considered. A measure that is reprehensible from the ethical standpoint may be altogether commendable from the standpoint of social utility; and, *vice versa,* a measure commendable from the ethical point of view may be deleterious from the standpoint of social utility. But in that connexion it is better for the subject portion of the population to believe that there is an exact identity between the ethical value of a measure and its social utility.

It would be a long and difficult task to consider this matter, even keeping to the essential details. Let us barely touch upon it, just to get a very general notion of it, and for that purpose we might consider certain types of governments known to us from history.

I. *Governments relying chiefly on physical force and on religious or other similar sentiments.* Examples would be the governments of the Greek cities in the age of the "tyrants," of Sparta, of Rome under Augustus and Tiberius, of the Venetian Republic during the last centuries of its existence, of many European countries in the eighteenth century. They show a governing class made up of individuals with Class II residues predominating over Class I residues. Class-circulation is generally slow. They are not expensive governments. On the other hand they fail to stimulate economic production, whether because they are conservative by temperament, recoiling from new enterprise, or because they put no premiums in class-circulation on individuals distinguished by instincts for economic combinations. If, however, such instincts survive in the population at large, the country may enjoy a moderate economic prosperity (Rome in the days of the High Empire) provided the government sets no obstacles in the way. But in the long run the obstacle usually arises, because the ideal of governments of that type is a nation that is crystallized in its institutions (Sparta, Rome in the day of the Low Empire, Venice of the Decadence). They may grow wealthy through conquests (Sparta, Rome); but since no new wealth is produced in that manner, the prosperity is necessarily precarious (Sparta, Rome). Furthermore, in times past, such régimes have tended to degenerate into government by armed mobs (praetorians, janissaries), which can do nothing but squander wealth.

2275. II. *Governments relying chiefly on intelligence and cunning.*

II-*a*. If the intelligence and cunning are used chiefly to influence sentiments, the result is some type of theocratic government. The type has entirely disappeared in our Western countries and on it therefore we need not linger. The governments of the ancient kings in Greece and in Italy may have approximated the type, in some respects at least; but we know too little of their history to be warranted in so asserting.

II-*b*. If the intelligence and cunning are used chiefly to play upon interests—which, however, does not necessarily imply disregard of sentiments—the result is governments like the demagogic régimes in Athens, the rule of the Roman aristocracy at various moments under the Republic, the governments of many mediaeval republics, and finally the very important type of government flourishing in our day—government by "speculators."

2276. All governments of the II type, even governments confining the use of intelligence and cunning to playing upon sentiments, have governing classes in which Class I residues predominate as compared with Class II residues. For to play artfully, shrewdly, and with success upon both interests and sentiments requires a governing class possessing combination instincts in high degree and unencumbered with too many scruples. Class-circulation is generally slow in the subtype II-*a*, but rapid, sometimes very rapid, in subtype II-*b*. It attains its maximum velocity under the system of our contemporary speculators. Governments of the II-*a* type are usually inexpensive, but they produce very little. They stupefy their populations, moreover, and kill every stimulus to economic production. Making no great use of force, they cannot make up for deficiencies in home production by wealth acquired through conquests abroad. In fact they fall ready prey to neighbour countries expert in the use of force and so disappear either by conquest or by internal decay. II-*b* governments are expensive, oftentimes very very expensive, but they produce actively and sometimes enormously, so that there may be such an excess of production over costs as to assure great prosperity. But there is no guarantee that as expenditures increase the surplus will not shrink to much lower proportions, disappear, and perhaps even change to a deficit. That depends on numberless conditions and circumstances. Such régimes may degenerate into government by shrewd but cowardly individuals who are easily overthrown by violence, whether from abroad or from within. That was the case with many democratic governments in Greek cities, and it played no inconsiderable part in the fall of the Roman and Venetian republics.

2277. In the concrete one finds combinations of these various types, with now the one, now the other, predominating. Governments in which the II-*b* type in moderate proportions is combined with a considerable dosage of the I type may endure for a long time on a foundation of force, and without sacrifice of economic prosperity. This mixed type is represented more or less closely by the earlier Roman Empire. It runs the risk of the degeneration peculiar to type I, and of a progressive dwindling in the proportions of the II-*b* type. Governments in which the II-*b* type in considerable proportions is combined with the I type in small proportions may also last for a long time, because they have a certain capacity for self-defence while achieving very considerable economic prosperity. They risk the degenerations peculiar to the II-*b* type and a progressive diminution of the type I element; and that almost inevitably exposes them to danger of foreign conquest. That development played its part in the destruction of Carthage and in the conquest of Greece by the Romans.

2278. Governments that rely chiefly on force in their relations represent combinations of the I and II-*b* types. That was more or less the case with the government of the Roman aristocracy in the heyday of the Republic.

2279. *Economic periodicity.* Rhythmical movements in one group of elements have their repercussions upon movements in the other elements, the resultant being the movement that is observable in the complex unit formed by the sum of the groups. Notable among such actions and reactions is the interplay between the economic and other groups.

2280. The economic status of a country may be qualitatively estimated by considering the observations of writers as to increase or decrease in its wealth. That method is exceedingly imperfect. Unfortunately it is the only one at our disposal as regards the distant past. We can see that Athens became a rich city after the Persian

Wars and poor after the disaster in Sicily, that Sparta was prosperous when she held the hegemony in Greece and poor after the battle of Leuctra. In the case of Rome, undulations are even more marked, and we can follow them all the way along from ancient, almost legendary, days down to the Middle Ages. In times nearer our own phenomena become much more general, undulations tending to be the same in several countries at one time—a result of their economic interdependence.

2281. Wherever economic statistics, however imperfect, are available, it becomes possible to replace qualitative with quantative estimates, and the substitution is always advantageous even if there are imperfections in the method used, for at the very worst the road is opened to perfecting results either by better statistics or by sounder methods of using them.

2282. In attempting to solve the problem as to the relations between movements in population and economic conditions, economists tried to discover at least the indices of such conditions. For predominantly agricultural countries the sizes of harvests might have been taken as indices, but the crop-yields not being known directly for periods in the past, indices were sought in the prices of wheat, the leading staple among our Western peoples. That index was accepted by Marshall as more or less accurate for England until down towards the middle of the nineteenth century, when that country became a predominantly manufacturing country. After that, indices were taken from movements in international trade and the amounts settled at the clearing-house. Clement Juglar noted, in studying economic depressions, that several other indices agree, and it is that agreement which goes farthest towards showing the general trend in an economic development. Various combinations of economic indices have been tried, to obtain a picture of the general economic movement in a given country, but so far little or nothing has been accomplished along that line.[1] The main difficulty lies in the method of combining indices, and if their sum is taken, in finding coefficients for each. To put all indices on a footing with a coefficient of unity is impossible. That would mean offsetting increase in some very important economic department with decrease

---

2282 [1] An excellent study on the subject is available in Bachi's *"Metodi di previsioni economiche," Rivista delle scienze commerciali,* Nos. 8-9.

in some department that is insignificant. What is needed is a coefficient that will stand in at least some remote relationship to the "importance" of the phenomenon. Not only is it difficult to find such a coefficient. Just what constitutes "importance" is not very clear. In point of fact there are as many "importances" as there are objectives that may be envisaged.

It might seem natural to say that the "importance" of a bond is its actual value. Suppose we are considering a hundred millions in public-debt certificates and a hundred millions in industrial stocks. The value of bonds and shares being equal, we assign an equal index to both. So, if the certificates go up to the value of one hundred and ten millions, and the shares fall to ninety millions, there will be perfect compensation. And that is all well and good if we want to know effects on the total capital of public debt plus stock values. But it is not so appropriate if we are trying to determine the economic trend. It is known that at times of business depression, public-debt securities rise in price while industrial stocks go down. We should be coming nearer to realities, therefore, though still being left at a good distance from them, if, instead of balancing the ten-million rise against the ten-million drop, we were to change the sign of the depreciation from minus to plus, add it to the appreciation, and take the sum of twenty millions as the index of the change in economic status. When many indices are added together with different coefficients we often get a precision that is misleading, and until science is farther advanced than it is now, much farther, it is better to keep to mere general indices, such as, in the case of England, the amounts settled at the clearing-house, or to other indices of the kind.[2] Variations in the numbers of individuals in a given population are generally slight. They may therefore be disregarded as compared with fairly considerable economic variations, such as the variation, within brief spaces of time, in the amounts of clearing-house settlements, or the variations in international trade.

2282 [2] The same thing is observable in many technical calculations. Engineers know that it is useless to have a merely formal approximation. Suppose we are trying to determine the diameter of a tree-trunk and so take its circumference, which we assume to be a perfect circle, with a piece of string. In making our calculation it would be the height of absurdity to use a π carried to ten decimals. We might just as well take π as 22/7, offhand, and in fact do even better by dividing the circumference, as obtained with the piece of string, by three.

But there is a more important reason for taking the total of international commerce directly, and not that total divided by the number of individuals constituting population. What, after all, we are looking for is an index for the country's economic prosperity; and it is evident that if every individual continues to have the same income, and to produce the same quantity of economic commodities, the country's economic prosperity increases with increase, and decreases with decrease, in population. Suppose that in England the *per capita* average of international commerce and clearing-house settlements remains constant and that the population decreases by half. We would have to assume that England's economic prosperity had decreased. Otherwise, we should be carried to the absurd conclusion that if only one individual were left in all England and he made, trading in the furs of the wild animals that would then be flourishing in the island, an income equal to the *per capita* average now prevailing, England's economic prosperity would not have decreased. *Vice versa,* an increase in population—the *per capita* average for production and trade remaining the same—represents an increase in a country's economic prosperity.[3]

2283. Of great importance for variations in economic conditions in a given country are the inflow of monetary metals into it and, in our time, the production of gold, since all civilized countries are in extensive commercial communication and gold has become the international medium of exchange. Without giving too strict an

2282 [3] The same holds for the prices of commodities that figure in international trade. We need not insist on the point that estimates of such prices are imperfect and very unreliable. Even if they were perfect, we should not, in trying to obtain an index of economic prosperity, divide the totals of trade in those commodities by their prices. It is well known that periods of industrial prosperity are also periods of high prices and, *vice versa,* that periods of economic depression are periods of low prices. There are particular cases, besides, in which that relationship becomes more obvious. If we want an index of Brazil's prosperity, we have to consider the total price of the coffee exported. If we divide that total by the price per unit of weight, we get the quantities of coffee exported, which are far from being in the same relation to the country's prosperity as the total price. Similarly, as regards the prosperity of the Cape diamond mines, it is much more important to get a high total sales-price than to sell many diamonds for a low total. For that reason the mines there have combined in a syndicate to take appropriate measures for selling diamonds at prices that will yield high totals. One may presume that they have a better understanding of the standards of their own economic prosperity than certain writers show in making a not very intelligent use of statistics.

application to the quantity theory of money, since the thing undergoes too many perturbations, it is none the less certain that any considerable increase in the influx of monetary metals exerts a powerful influence on prices. That hypothesis has been verified in too many cases, from ancient times down to our own, to be explained as a merely fortuitous coincidence; and it is very largely a relationship of cause and effect—in no way barring the possibility that prices may react on the influx of monetary metals and on their production. In our day, further, the various methods of settling financial and commercial transactions without recourse to metallic media also influence prices extensively; but it should not be forgotten that such practices make the effects of any increase in a definite quantity of gold more appreciable, since that quantity becomes a more considerable fraction of the gold remaining in circulation. Issues of paper money—inflations, so called—affect social phenomena in some respects like the supply of precious metals.

2284. Many studies have been made on the history of the production of precious metals and on concomitant variations in prices, as well as on certain social effects of such phenomena. Attention has centred more particularly on the changes that variations in prices have occasioned in the situations of creditors and debtors and therefore also of the richer and poorer classes; and since price-variations have often been upwards, the rise in prices has been the case most thoroughly studied. However, other phenomena of equal and sometimes greater importance have been neglected, and notably variations of intensities in class-circulation and the ensuing political consequences. Very common, also, has been the error of substituting relations of cause and effect for relations of interdependence. The inflow of monetary metals or, in general, the production of precious metals, the consequent variations in prices, and the readjustments of monetary systems are all things arising under our category *b* (§ 2205), in other words, they come under "interests," and they have to be considered as aspects of the cycles in the reciprocal influence of social elements that we studied in §§ 2206 f.

2285. It must not be forgotten that the elements in category *b*— the body of interests—operates in the cycles for the most part as a whole, and that the phenomena depending upon inflow of precious metals are only a part of that whole. The effects of such things may therefore be partially offset by counter-effects from other phenomena, just as they may be intensified.

2286. Observable, in times ancient and modern, are many co-incidences between abundance of money in a given country and the country's economic and political prosperity, though one is unable to determine very clearly just what is cause and what effect. It would at any rate be a grave mistake to assume that an influx of currency metals necessarily induces prosperity. Athens was pros-perous while tribute was coming in from her allies and while she was mining silver to large amounts in the Laurium. As for the allied tribute, it was, to be sure, a cause of prosperity; but it was also an effect, since it was exacted by Athenian power. The silver from the mines was predominantly a cause but also in part an effect; for had the Athenians been a poor and weak people, they would not have had the slaves and other capital required for operat-ing the mines. Ancient Rome knew her greatest prosperity at a time when conquests were bringing gold, silver, and copper into the city from the territories conquered in Asia, Africa, and Europe. In that case the influx of currency metal was predominantly an effect of the conquests. Modern nations need gigantic sums of money to provide armaments that were not needed by ancient peoples, so that if Rome's monetary wealth may have been of some little service, directly, to her conquests, it was certainly not the main cause of the victories of the Roman people. In those days, it follows, Combi-nation I (§ 2206—residues influencing interests, *etc.*) was of much greater importance than Combination II (interests influencing resi-dues, *etc.*), whereas there may be no such difference in the case of modern peoples. Combination III (derivations on residues, in-terests, *etc.*) was, as usual, of little importance. As for Combination IV (class-circulation on residues, *etc.*), it worked in a direction counter to Combination I, tending to augment, or to conserve, Class I residues; and that was one of the causes of decline under the Empire (§§ 2550 f.).

2287. Different is the case where influx of precious metals is not a consequence of foreign conquest or of some other contingency extrinsic to the economic field, but is in part an effect of prosperity itself, prosperity enabling a people to procure the metal. That was strikingly the case in a number of the mediaeval communes and republics, where good money and economic prosperity went hand in hand in a relationship of mutual dependence.

2288. Those few cases excepted, the Middle Ages were a period of material and intellectual poverty, and also a period of monetary poverty. One cannot say that the latter was the cause of the former; but it would be rash to say that it was altogether irrelevant, since their correlation was strikingly emphasized by developments in the period following.

2289. The discovery of America was one of those many unforeseen and unforeseeable events which suddenly occasion great and far-reaching changes in our category *b*—in interests. The discoveries made by industrial science in the course of the nineteenth century were another; but they were consequences of prosperity to a much greater extent than the discovery of America, which was achieved with a scanty, in fact an insignificant, outlay. Between the last decade of the fifteenth century, when America was discovered, and the middle of the seventeenth century, two very interesting periods coincide in Europe: a period of economic, intellectual, and political prosperity, and a period of great abundance in money and of extraordinary rises in prices. Phenomena in the two periods seem to be much more strictly correlated than they do in the cases of Rome (§ 2286) or the Middle Ages (§ 2288). In fact, if the first impetus was given by a fortuitous incident, the discovery of America, the movement continued with accelerated intensities because conditions in Europe became more and more favourable to the production of wealth; and that was chiefly a result of the gradual rise to predominance of Class I residues and of the uses to which the sentiments corresponding were turned, people now applying themselves by preference to the arts and sciences rather than to theology or magic. The first impetus came, therefore, from Combination I (residues on interests, *etc.*), but the movement went on in response to Combination II (interests on residues, *etc.*); and it would be difficult to say which was on the whole the more important of the two combinations. Combination IV (class-circulation on residues, *etc.*) seems to be just as important, and it operates in the same direction as the first two. And that is the case also with Combination III (derivations on residues, *etc.*), which, however, though not a negligible quantity, has little influence on the trend of events.

2290. From the middle of the seventeenth century down to about 1720, we get, very roughly speaking, a quiet period as regards economic prosperity and a period in which the production of precious metals shows no great variations. But between 1720 and 1810, roughly, comes a period of rapid increase in the production of precious metals and a period of economic prosperity, which is chiefly apparent in England, the Continent being engrossed in the wars of the French Revolution. The Revolution seems to be connected primarily with Combination IV, as a phenomenon of class-circulation. From 1810 on we begin to get statistics, very imperfect at first, but gradually and continually improving, so that we are able to bring our findings to much greater exactness.

2291. The description that we have so far been giving is very much like drawing a line on a map to represent a chain of mountains. In reality there is no line called the Apennines, dividing Italy into two parts, nor a line called the Alps that gives a northern border to that country. All the same, that general and very crude picture has its uses.

2292. Even today, though statistics help to bring us closer to what is real, we are still forced to keep to generalities and look for comprehensive pictures that ignore details.[1]

2293. Let us take, as an example, the movement in French foreign trade.[1] Drawing a graph from the statistics available, and attentively observing the curve so obtained, we note, in chief, three types of variation: 1. Accidental variations. 2. Short-period variations. 3. Long-period variations.

1. *Accidental variations.* They interrupt the general trend but very briefly, the curve at once resuming its former trend. Notable, for instance, the break in the year 1848, and even more so, in the year 1870. So long as the forces determining the dynamic equilib-

2292 [1] We have already indicated the method for studying these things in general (§ 1718). We now have to apply it to the particular case with which we are here dealing. The study here is taken in part from my study entitled: *"Alcune relazioni tra lo stato sociale e le variazioni della prosperità economica,"* Rivista italiana di sociologia, XVII, Nos. V-VI, September-December, 1913. The reprints of the article were issued in September, 1913, before the appearance of those numbers of the Rivista, and even before that an advance summary had appeared in the Giornale d'Italia, Aug. 3, 1913. § 2293 is reproduced verbatim from the article in the Rivista.

2293 [1] For statistical tables see Appendix II to the article just mentioned (§2292 [1]). Here we give nothing but conclusions.

rium continue to function, that equilibrium, if an accidental force chance to disturb it, is at once re-established (as soon, that is, as the disturbing force is removed—§ 2068), and the development resumes its normal trend.

2. *Short-period variations.* These have often been perceived and partially studied under the name of "crises." Notable the crisis of the year 1881. The curve shows an ascending section along which accidental variations are observable, and a descending section of the same type. Characteristic the transition from the ascending to the descending section; it is not gradual, it is abrupt. An unusual spurt in prosperity often presages a drop in the near future.

3. *Long-period variations.* They have not so far been studied, chiefly for lack of the requisite statistical data. Taking the curve of the trade trend as a whole, and trying to disregard the short and accidental variations, one observes that its progress is not uniform. Periods of rapid increase are followed by periods of slight increase or depression, which are followed in turn by periods of increase. For instance, between the years 1852 and 1873 there was a period of rapid increase interrupted by the war of 1870-71 and followed by a period of slight increase, or even depression, extending from the years 1873 to 1897. Then comes another period of rapid increase extending from 1898 to 1911. Similar periods are observable, though on a much smaller scale, in the past. From 1806 to 1810 there is a decline. Then from 1816 to 1824 comes a period of depression, and then a period of increase between the years 1832 and 1846.[2]

2294. If similar graphs are drawn for England, Italy, and Belgium, we get similar conclusions. Distinguishable in all those countries are three long-period variations extending roughly from 1854 to 1872, from 1873 to 1896, and from 1898 to 1912. Emigration statistics in Italy, clearing-house settlements in London, and theatre-ticket sales in Paris confirm these inferences.[1] We are evidently deal-

2293 [2] That method of viewing things is not a little crude, and ways must be found for attaining greater exactness. That may be secured by interpolating the curve obtained, by determining, that is, the line around which it fluctuates. The results of these calculations are also to be found in Appendix II to the article mentioned in § 2292 [1].

2294 [1] Since that time many new verifications have been obtained. See my *"Forme di fenomeni economici e previsioni,"* *Rivista di scienza bancaria,* Rome, August-September, 1917.

ing therefore with a phenomenon of a fairly general character.

2295. After 1870, as is well known, the production of silver became so great that that metal could not continue to be used as real money, and in civilized countries it eventually came to be coined only as a form of fiduciary currency. So, whereas down to the nineteenth century we considered the combined production of gold and silver, beginning with the nineteenth we have to consider gold-production only, gold gradually becoming the sole coinage for real money.

2296. The annual average of gold-production that stood as low as 189,000,000 francs in the decade from 1841 to 1850 became 687,000,000 francs in the five years between 1851 and 1855, and remained in that neighbourhood until the end of the half-decade between 1866 and 1870. We therefore note a certain correspondence between a period of economic prosperity extending from 1854 to 1872 and a period of great gold-production. In the five years 1871-75 average annual gold-production falls to 599,000,000 francs. Beginning with 1875 we get statistics for separate annual productions. There is a period of decreasing or constant production ending about 1891. Very fair the correspondence between that period and the period of economic quiet between 1873 and 1876. Beginning with 1892, when gold-production stood at 750,000,000 francs, and coming down to 1912, when it stood at 2,420,000,000 francs, there is a period of great and rapid increase in gold-production roughly corresponding to a period of great economic prosperity from 1898 to 1912.

2297. The correlations mentioned must not, we again caution, be interpreted in the sense that the increase in gold-production was the *cause* of the economic prosperity. It certainly figured as a cause in its effects on prices and, to an even greater extent, on class-circulation, but it was also beyond any doubt an effect of the prosperity. At the present time gold is no longer being obtained in major part from alluvial soils, as was the case at first in California and Australia. It is dug in mines requiring very costly underground operations and very expensive machinery. Gold-production, accordingly, is now possible only after enormous outlays of capital and so depends on economic prosperity itself, the latter becoming cause after having been effect. It is further to be noted that gold-production results in increased prices, but that these in turn react upon gold-production by increasing the cost of mining. There are many mines of low-percentage ores that cannot be operated at the present time at current costs of labour and machinery and which could be exploited the moment those costs dropped ever so little. That will probably be the case as mines with high-percentage ores are exhausted.

2298. These correlations all pertain to the economic category, to interests (element *b*, § 2205). They serve to show how the structure of the complex *b* is made up in its various elements. But we must not stop at that point, but go on and examine its influence upon other categories and their reactions upon it. That we have already done in the particular case of protective tariffs, and we made it our point of departure for a discussion of economic favouritisms and, even more generally, of cycles of action and reaction between the various categories of elements (§§ 2208 f.). In that case we deliberately ignored undulations. But what we said at that time will serve, with slight additions and modifications, to give us an understanding of the phenomenon even when undulations are considered.

2299. Suppose we keep to the economic and social status of the civilized peoples of the West from the beginning of the nineteenth century down to the present time. The most important Combinations (§ 2206) are II (interests on residues, *etc.*) and IV (class-circulation on residues, *etc.*). In fact, looking first at the most important element in the situation, we may consider, for a first approximation, a restricted cycle in which interests *b* influence class-circulation *d* and, then again, class-circulation reacts upon interests. It would be difficult, not to say impossible, to separate the two elements in the cycle, so it is better to consider the latter as a whole.

2300. If one were to state in a few words the differences obtaining between the social state, *M*, before the French Revolution and our present state, *N*, one would have to say that the difference lies chiefly in a present preponderance of economic over other interests and in a greatly accelerated circulation between classes. In our day the foreign policies of the various countries are almost exclusively economic (§ 2328), and domestic policy comes down more than anything else to economic conflicts. Furthermore, not only have obstacles to class-circulation disappeared, barring some few restrictions in Germany and Austria, but such circulation has become very intense in the fact, owing to assistance from economic prosperity. Nowadays almost anybody who possesses a good supply of Class I residues and knows how to use his talents in industry, agriculture, commerce, and the arts; in organizing financial enterprises, honest or dishonest; in duping the good-natured producers of savings; in obtaining licence to exploit less clever neighbours by political influence, customs tariffs, or other favours of all sorts and kinds—is certain, unless he has very bad luck indeed, not only to amass wealth but to win honours and power, to become, in a word, a member of the ruling class. The men who get to be leaders of that class (still barring exceptions as, to some extent, in Germany) are those individuals who best manage to serve the economic interests of the ruling class. They get their pay sometimes directly in cash, sometimes indirectly by money given to members of their families or to friends, while then again they sometimes rest content with power and the honours that go with power, leaving the filthy lucre to their henchmen. Individuals of that sort are in greater demand than others for governing a country. And, in truth, they are safe from the shafts of the opposition, which, in order to be understood by the good-natured public, has to use the language of derivations and therefore stands constantly on watch to discover some venomous charge of "immorality" that it can hurl at its adversaries. The art of scandalmongering has been brought to high perfection, and a politician who too naïvely appropriates a few thousand dollars is easily thrown out of office if he is not rescued by the "machine" that he has benefited; whereas the politician who takes nothing for himself, but gives millions, even hundreds of millions, of the public's money to his henchmen, retains his power, mounts in public esteem, and goes on to new honours (§ 2268).

2301. Class-circulation at the present time, therefore, raises to membership in the ruling class large numbers of persons who destroy wealth, but even larger numbers who produce wealth; and certain proof that the activity of the producers prevails over the activity of the wasters is ready to hand in the fact that the economic prosperity of our civilized peoples has increased enormously. In the years following 1854 in France, at the time of the fever for railway-building, not a few dishonest financiers and no fewer politicians made fortunes and destroyed vast amounts of wealth; but immeasurably vaster amounts of wealth were produced by the railways, so that the net result of the operation was a great increase in French prosperity.[1]

2302. In periods of rapidly mounting economic prosperity (§ 2294) governing is much easier than in periods of depression. The fact can be determined empirically by comparing political conditions and social conditions during the economic periods distinguished in § 2293. The successful period of the Second Empire in France coincides with the period of economic prosperity that began in 1854. Difficulties began appearing later on, and it is probable that even had there been no war in 1870 the Empire would have encountered very serious dangers in the period from 1873 to 1896. There were plenty of troubles for the governments ruling in that period, not only in France, but in other countries. More or less everywhere in Europe that was the heroic age of Socialism and Anarchism. In order to govern at all Bismarck himself, as powerful as he was, needed "exceptional laws" to deal with the Socialists. In Italy the period culminates in the revolt of 1898, which was quelled only by force. Then again, from 1898 down to the present time [1913], we get another period of easy government or, if one wish, of government not too difficult, which culminates as regards Italy in the year 1912 in the collapse of the opposition parties and an easy dictatorship for Giolitti; while in Germany, the Socialists in the Reichstag—how times do change!—approve new and huge appropriations for armament; and in England the pacific successors of the Fenians of 1873-98 easily obtain "Home Rule."

Compare, if you please, the effects in Italy of the Abyssinian War that occurred in the 1873-98 period, and the effects of the Libyan War that occurred in the 1898-1912 period (§ 2255). For the moment we are not considering causes and effects, nor even relations of interdependence—we are merely noting coincidences, which may even be fortuitous. Whatever may have been the causes, it is certain, very very certain, that the Italian public took the Abyssinian War and the Libyan War in very different ways. The so called subversive

2301 [1] We are not called upon to determine here whether that result might not have been attained just as well without wasting so much money on financial, political, and other parasites, for we are considering real, not virtual, movements. We are describing things that have happened and are happening and choose not to go beyond that. That caution has to be kept in mind in all that hereafter follows in this volume.

parties rose against the Abyssinian War with energies carried to an extreme. The Libyan War they accepted, either approving or in resignation; and only by hook and by crook could a party hostile to the Libyan War, which called itself the Official Socialist Party and was short, to tell the truth, in influential leaders, manage to secede from Socialism as it had been up to that time. And for France one may compare the opposition to colonial enterprises in the days of Jules Ferry (within the 1873-98 period) with the assenting or resigned acceptance of the Morocco venture (falling within the 1898-1912 period), which was far otherwise costly and hazardous. The contrast surely is just as marked as in the case of Italy. And compare, again, the excitement in the French public following the discovery of the Panama embezzlements by various politicians with the calmness and indifference it manifested toward the no less dishonest and no less considerable peculations that accounted for the notorious "billion of the Congregations." It really seemed in this latter case as though many people, in thinking of such pirates, were saying to themselves: "Poor devils, they took a great deal of money, that is true; but after all there is money enough to go around, for us as well as for them." But before such tolerance can become the rule, the melon has to be big enough to provide, in addition to the big slices that go to the "statesmen," the smaller slices that go to the politicians, and at least a sliver apiece for many minor individuals. For one of the amazing things in this world is the ferocious zest for honesty, morality, and all the other fine things that a slim diet will inspire in a politician. Compare, finally, the furious conflicts that raged around the Dreyfus affair, which may be said to have amounted to a great revolution, with the much more pacific politico-social conflicts of the 1898-1912 period, and one will be forced to grant that something has changed in the atmosphere of political society.

2303. It would be easy to marshal many other facts of the kind from the present, nor would it be hard to find their parallels in the past. It is a trite observation that in remoter times poor harvests and famines spread ill humour among subject classes and readily impelled them to revolt; and, in times nearer our own, crop-failures and famines were not irrelevant to the course of events in the French Revolution. It is hard to admit that so many coincidences should be merely fortuitous. Some relation there must be between phenomena that are so regularly found in company.

2304. That conclusion is confirmed by analysis, which also gives us an insight into the character of the correlation. Evidently it may vary as social conditions vary. Famines used to drive peoples to revolt just as hunger drives the wolf into the open. But the relation between economic conditions and the temper of a people is something much more complex in peoples of high economic development, such as those of our time.

2305. In their cases, as stated above (§ 2299), it is better to consider in the main the restricted cycle in which *b* (interests) influences *d* (class-circulation) and *vice versa*. One might say briefly that since modern governments are keeping in power less and less by resort to force and more and more by a very expensive art of government, they have a very urgent need of economic prosperity in order to carry on their activities, and that they are also much more sensitive to any variations in prosperity. To be sure, even the older governments, which relied mainly on force, began to totter whenever want cruelly asserted itself; for then their force was met by another and greater force born of despair. But they could feel safe until changes in economic conditions reached that limit, whereas every change in economic prosperity, even no very great change oftentimes, makes itself felt on the far more complex and protean organization of governments that rely chiefly upon the costly arts of economic manipulation. To drive a despot's subjects to revolt economic sufferings far more serious were required than are required to cause a government nowadays to lose an election. It is readily apparent, therefore, that if the economic periods that we distinguished in § 2293, and which did not reach limits of abject poverty, had occurred under governments relying mainly upon force, they would have coincided with social and political situations far less widely contrasting than the situations that are actually observable under governments relying largely upon the art of economic combinations.

2306. In arranging for the combinations that are indispensable to their existence modern governments commonly spend in a given period more than their revenues would allow, covering the difference by contracting overt or secret debts. That enables them to have the benefits of the money now and shoulder the burden of payment off upon the future. That future becomes more and more remote, the more rapidly economic prosperity increases; for in virtue of that increase, the yield from current imposts increases without any increase in taxes themselves and future state surpluses are expected, in part at least, to make up for past deficits. Our governments have gradually become accustomed to that state of things, which is so convenient and profitable for them, and they now regularly discount future surpluses to pay for present expenditures. That is happening in many countries and in many ways, notable among which the keeping of special or extraordinary budgets parallel with general or ordinary budgets; the entering of proceeds from new debts as state revenues; the charging off of expenses incurred by specific administrative departments of the state as debts owing to the state and therefore as credits, the state so becoming debtor and creditor at the same time, and items that are really liabilities being represented as assets. Then when, in virtue of such tricks and others still, an actual deficit has been changed into a fictitious surplus, well-paid journalists are commissioned to broadcast to the world the glad tidings of the country's prosperous financial condition; and if someone ventures to question such sleight-of-hand in accounting, he is accused of "discrediting the country."[1]

2306 [1] Secreting debts was a trick extensively used in Italy under Magliani's ministry [years 1879-88]; then the practice declined, though it was never altogether abandoned. It came into great vogue again during the Libyan War. The Honourable Edoardo Giretti exposed the trick of transforming debits into credits by manipulations in accounting. Luigi Einaudi showed how an artificial budget surplus can be manufactured from an actual deficit. Finally, Feb. 14, 1914, the Honourable Sidney Sonnino exposed all the tricks of budget-making with admirable clarity in a speech before the Italian Chamber. The speech would deserve quotation in its entirety, because it goes far beyond the particular case and deals with the general methods of budget manipulation. However, just a few very significant passages here: "Let me state my position clearly. I am not raising questions of legality or illegality, nor inquiring whether at this moment we are facing a surplus or a deficit, and how large. I am exclusively concerned with a question of clarity and frankness in our national finance. Today on the strength of a series of enactments that have been slipped as riders into no end of nondescript special bills and on the strength of interpretations more and more far-fetched of such enactments, we have reached a point where the Minister of the Treasury has *de facto* absolute discretion over the allotment of large numbers of appropriations, accounting for them under any department of state he chooses, and frequently under whatever classification he chooses, and indeed without reference to them in the general accountings, as presented to the Chamber, of the services for which they were appropriated. In his

2307. Such procedure occasions no serious difficulties in periods of rapidly mounting economic prosperity. Natural increases in budget revenues cover the manipulations of the past, and the future can be relied on to take care of those of the present. The difficulties come

financial report he takes no account of such expenditures in his first computations of the totals of their administration, and he is so enabled always to report the existence of large effective surpluses, and thereupon to charge against each apparent surplus whole series of new and larger expenditures that may themselves have been already contracted for and paid. And so it comes about that in the face of a grand budget total that shows a deficit in Classification I of 257,000,000 lire and which, even if we eliminate all Libyan expenditures from it, still shows a deficit of more than 7,000,000, the country is still being given the false impression that the fiscal period of 1912-13 ended with an actual surplus of a hundred or more millions and that the ordinary budget was able in that year to pay off forty-nine or more millions of Libyan War debts. For the last three years tricks in budget-accounting have become so numerous that it is now very difficult for the parliament to get a clear conception of the real state of things. In the first place, in the budgets of the various ministries there appears today a long list of actual expenditures to meet which the minister is authorized to draw upon current accounts either with the Cassa Depositi or with specified local banks or trust-companies or upon so-called Treasury advances; and only a fixed annual expenditure is entered for a longer or shorter term of years, while in the actual administration of that service the money is spent within a much shorter term. . . . There are, besides, a number of important categories of extraordinary expenditures on the allotments of which, as established by various bills, the minister, in special bills of authorization (or even in some unnoticed section of a budget bill), has gradually reserved authority to draw in advance by ministerial decree. In the Navy Budget Bill for the year 1914-15 there is even a request for authorization to do the same for the list of *ordinary* expenses for fleet-maintenance up to 20,000,000 a year, so anticipating appropriations for fiscal periods posterior by four years. Is it not a little silly to charge by law an expenditure that *has already been* allotted, and even paid, to an eventual surplus of a given service, instead of charging it purely and simply to that service itself? What does it mean to enter a sum among receipts for the year 1914-15, representing it as drawn from a former appropriation, and of counterbalancing it, in the expense column, with a corresponding sum designated as reimbursement for a pretended 'Treasury advance,' a reimbursement, in other words, for an unconfessed deficit, or an overstated real surplus from an earlier account? No meaning whatever, given the principles upon which our budget regulations are based! They are empty forms, mere devices for depriving entries and totals of all clarity. Magliani, in his time, invented ultra-extraordinary expenditures for public works that were to be met by increases in the public debt, and in that way he managed to withhold such expenditures from his computations of surpluses and deficits. Today all that sort of thing seems primitive and antiquated, and far more specious and refined methods are in vogue. An article is voted into some law or other, even the Budget Law, or is ordained by decree, stating, more or less explicitly, that such and such expenses will be met by drawing upon the Cassa, or by the ordinary resources of the Treasury, or by the current account with the Cassa Depositi. From that moment it is possible, if one wishes, to incur all those expenses without accounting for them in totals of the service to which

in periods of depression, and they would be far worse if a depression at all protracted were to supervene. The social order is at present such that probably no government could remain unaffected during such a period; and tremendous catastrophes might occur and in

they are allotted as presented in the financial reports. So one is enabled to declare a surplus in the budget in question, and then to apply that surplus either to new expenditures or to reimbursements of the Treasury for advances made under some other form.

"So, further, the trick of the *rotating* surplus is also made easier. Suppose we imagine a sequence of several fiscal periods for which extraordinary expenditures are authorized, for example, 150,000,000 for building ships, to be paid in five equal instalments. For the first year, let us say, the Treasury Minister succeeds in one way or another in claiming an effective surplus of 30,000,000. After announcing such a surplus, he proceeds to draw in advance on the allotment of the following year, charging it off against that first surplus. So the account in question is lightened by 30,000,000 and if—just for a hypothesis—it would have balanced without the advance, with the advance it will present a favourable margin of 30,000,000. The minister proceeds accordingly to announce a second actual surplus of 30,000,000 for the following year as well, going on to draw again in advance on the allotment for the next succeeding year; and so on from year to year, so that with a single generous initial surplus of 30,000,000, the minister is able to announce in his financial reports five successive surpluses totaling 150,000,000, whereas it is only 30,000,000 at the end of five years—granting that the original surplus was real in the first place. In case he does not succeed in charging off the first advance on future allotments, as determined by special bills, against a real surplus in Category I, he can resort with just as great advantage to the trick of 'Treasury advances'—by charging off the advance drawing against the first fiscal period in Category I, but counterbalancing it by entering in the receipts column of Category III a corresponding sum as drawn on the Cassa Depositi. That procedure has a number of advantages, in addition to the advantage of satisfying anybody who wants to know about expenditures: 1. The advantage of not altering general totals for purposes of Treasury accounting in summing the totals of the various categories. 2. The advantage of not accounting for the expenditure in question in the next ensuing financial report to the damage of the net surplus, on the specious argument that it is a mere question of an advance on an allotment. 3. The advantage of being able to represent the corresponding levy the following year to reimburse the Treasury in Category III as an improvement in national resources. In a word, as regards the stage-setting, so to speak, in the parliament, the expenditure in question never appears in its true essence and substance at any time either before or after it is made. . . . I have done! And let no one, *more solito,* try to hush criticism, however honest and dispassionate, on the ground that it will impair the nation's credit abroad."

Minister Tedesco made a reply to Sonnino not denying the facts, which were after all undeniable, but pointing out that procedures analogous to his own had been the rule since 1910—and in that he was not wrong, the only question being of a more or a less. From the standpoint of parliamentary politics, the question that Signor Tedesco raises is of interest as permitting praise or blame of this or that individual. It has slight if any bearing on the research for uniformities that is our one concern here. Substantially Signor Tedesco's defence confirms the uniformity we have de-

magnitudes far greater than any that history has hitherto recorded.[1]

2308. But leaving such hypothetical contingencies aside and keeping to real movements, we now see one of the reasons for the coincidences noted in § 2302—the fact that in periods of economic depression a government has to demand greater sacrifices of the governed, while the benefits it can bring to the public and to its own supporters are fewer and smaller. On the one hand, it has to pay for past extravagances to meet which it had relied on increasing revenues that have now failed; and on the other, if the period of depression is prolonged, it becomes increasingly difficult to get money to spend by mortgaging the future.

2309. Economic circulation stagnates and so does class-circulation; for no means are available for rewarding, either naturally as a consequence of the existing system, or artificially by direct fiat of the government, those individuals who give evidence of possessing in high degree aptitudes for those economic and political combinations upon which our governments depend. Governing cliques find it difficult to tame their adversaries because of the scarcity of sops to

scribed. Speaking before the French Senate, M. Ribot made similar strictures on the French budget, nor could he be refuted by the ministers in the cabinet. But that too is not important. Such situations arise not through fault of this or that politician, but chiefly as consequences of the pluto-demagogic system that is nowadays called democracy. M. Ribot all along has lovingly hoed and watered the plant. Now that it is bearing its fruits he raises a cry of alarm and astonishment. No one can see just why.

2307 [1] Pietri-Tonelli, *Il socialismo democratico in Italia*, pp. 22, 24-25: "It is uniformly observable in all modern democratic régimes that the decisive political power is distributed variously among the bureaucratic classes, which include office-holders high and low, both civil and military, and politicians high and low. These two categories of persons are so closely bound by ties of mutual assistance to one another and to speculators of all kinds as to form an indissoluble trinity. Success and advancement in office are nearly always facilitated by the support of politicians [§ 2268 [2]]. The outcome of elections is largely influenced by the administration in power through support of various kinds, business men providing the necessary funds [§ 2268 [3]]. Politicians moreover are the more influential in proportion as they are successful in obtaining favours for their constituents and to the extent of their backing by men of affairs. . . . For that matter, in places where the Socialists or the Popular party control local administrations, favouritism in awarding and even in creating salaried positions has not diminished—only the colour of the individuals favoured has changed: once they were black, now they are red. Sometimes . . . the same persons have changed in colour, provided the opportunity has offered, and provided they have never declared any pronounced political colouring other than that of the party in power. That posts have been created everywhere to the limits

throw them; and even if there is enough to go round among the leaders, the rank and file has to be left with empty maws, and it makes a noise and refuses to follow them. Differing circumstances in the budget forbade Crispi and allowed Giolitti liberally to subsidize cooperatives and other Socialist organizations as well as the manufacturing and banking trusts. That certainly was one of the causes, important or unimportant as it may have been, of the differing fortunes of those two statesmen (§ 2255). And when, in 1913, there was a first touch of economic depression in Italy the rank and file in the Socialist party refused to follow leaders who had been tamed of yore, and turned to others who ran in the elections on platforms frankly hostile to the Libyan War and to military expenditures. The old leaders in growing so tame had forgotten that the masses still cherished the ideals that they themselves had lost either of their own accord or in deference to favours from the government. Those popular ideals the government could not combat by appealing to selfish interests in the masses through lavish ex-

of the possible is beyond question. In fact, speaking to that very point, the head of a city administration controlled by the Popular party candidly remarked to me not long ago that if only he were able to create some twenty new offices to hand out every year, he could certainly succeed in silencing opposition not only from individuals in his own party but from opposing parties." That, in fact, is pretty much the way governments are run, not only in Italy, but in other countries. But that method of governing requires money, a great deal of money. A particular case, the case of war, has been studied by Federico Flora in a book called *Le finanze della guerra* (*War and Finance*). He concludes: "It is begun with cash on hand, it is sustained by loans, and finally paid for by taxes." It is evident that the situation will be different according as the liquidation takes place during a period of rapid increase in economic prosperity, or during a period of reduced increase or, what is worse, of depression. Governments trusting too far to future liquidations may some day find themselves in a serious predicament. Michels, *Zur Soziologie des Parteiwesens*, p. 255 (Paul, p. 267): "Every time the labour party founds a cooperative or a savings-bank that offers intellectuals a secure livelihood and an influential position, one observes flocking to it a host of individuals who have no Socialist sentiments whatever and are looking for nothing but a good bargain." In Italy, and not only in Italy, such cooperatives and people's banks can prosper only with the help of politicians. As a result not only individuals who benefit by such institutions, but others who hope to, join the followings of the politicians, support them, defend them, procure honours and power for them, and receive the favours they receive by way of compensation. That system is very expensive. Oftentimes in order to enable a favourite to make a mere pittance the state has to spend large amounts that are more or less wasted. [*Cf.* the amusing description of such manoeuvring in the intrigues required to win a title for Signor Alamanni in Ferrero's novel, *The Seven Vices.*—A. L.]

penditures. So opposition to the government and to the leaders who had become its instruments became more wide-spread and more intense.

2310. We are now in a position to complete our survey of the contrasts between the "speculator" and the *"rentier"* (§§ 2234 f.). Periods of rapid increase in economic prosperity are favourable to speculators, who grow rich and win places in the governing class if they do not already belong to it, but unfavourable to people who live on incomes more or less fixed. These latter drop behind, either because of the natural rise in prices or because they are unable to compete with the speculators in securing the favours of politicians or public. Effects are just the reverse in periods of economic depression.[1]

2311. It follows that when periods of rapid increase in economic prosperity are more the rule than periods of depression, the governing class gets richer and richer in speculators, who contribute Class I residues to it in powerful dosage (§§ 2178 f.); and poorer and poorer in "gentlemen"—in people living on virtually fixed incomes —in whom Class II residues are generally the more powerful. That change in the composition of the governing class tends to incline a people more and more to economic enterprise and to increase economic prosperity until new forces come into play to check the movement (§§ 2221 f.). The opposite is the case when the periods of economic depression or, what is worse, of economic retrogression, are the rule. The first situation is exemplified by our modern civilized peoples. Examples of the second would be the peoples of the Mediterranean basin under the declining Roman Empire down through the Barbarian invasions and into the Middle Ages.[1]

2312. In civilized societies producers of savings perform a function of very great importance (§ 2228). They remind one of the bees that gather the honey in the honeycomb, and of them one may say: *Sic vos non vobis mellificatis, apes!* It is no exaggeration to assert that a people's civilization stands in direct ratio to the quantity of savings that it possesses or puts into use. If economic prosperity increases, the quantity of savings used in production likewise increases.

2310 [1] That is to be taken as holding true only in a rough and very general way. In not a few individual cases the course of events may be different.

2311 [1] These effects on the constitution of the governing class are not the only ones observable in the respective periods of prosperity and depression. We shall meet others further along in §§ 2343 f.

If economic prosperity wanes, there is a decrease in the quantity of savings devoted to production.

2313. Before we can go farther along this line we must refer back to the two groups, S and R, considered in §§ 2233-34 and which for mere purposes of convenience we decided to name "speculators" and *"rentiers."* When savers get their requirements for living from their savings, they belong in great part in the R group—the class of people, that is, who have fixed or virtually fixed incomes. They are people of quite opposite traits to the people in the S group, to the "speculators" (§ 2232). They are, in general, secretive, cautious, timid souls, mistrustful of all adventure, not only of dangerous ventures but of such as have any remotest semblance of not being altogether safe. They are very readily managed and even robbed by anyone deft in the opportune use of sentiments corresponding to Class II residues, which are very strong in the R's.[1][2] Speculators, on the

---

2313 [1] One notes nowadays a tendency to put into the R group small stockholders in corporations, who are exploited especially by executives and directors and a few large stockholders. Various devices are used, according to the country, and always, of course, with the complicity of the legislator. In England the trick of "reorganization" is in great vogue. It consists substantially in dissolving a corporation and then immediately reorganizing it under another name, stockholders in the old corporation receiving stock in the new provided they pay a certain quota. They are thus given the alternative of either losing everything or spending more money, the unwilling stockholder not being allowed simply to demand the return of his share in the old corporation's assets. Certain corporations have "reorganized" several times in that manner. The directors set up a certain number of "the boys" who "underwrite" or "guarantee" the operation; that is to say, in consideration of a bonus, which frequently reaches considerable figures, they undertake to redeem on their own account such stock as shall not have been taken up by the old stockholders. There are corporations that have never paid a penny in dividends to their stockholders but which every two or three years yield very fair profits to their directors in that manner. In some few cases the operation may be advantageous to the stockholders at large; but they are not allowed to distinguish between such cases and others, for the law does not reserve to the individual stockholder the right to withdraw at any moment and get back his share in the assets. In Italy the legislator at first made the "mistake" of granting that right, but he soon hastened to correct the error in deference to high lords of finance who were friends of the politicians. *Avanti,* Mar. 12, 1915: *"Great bank speculations.* We are informed that three large banks have merged in the course of the last few days. . . . To facilitate the operation the government took the appropriate measures for side-stepping the civil and commercial code by introducing a bill in the parliament to suspend for the period of one year the right of stockholders in corporations to withdraw." Even when such a right obtains, the difficulties in the way of exercising it are so numerous and the costs so great that nearly always it remains a dead letter. So all roads are closed whereby the simple producer or possessor of savings might escape the pursuit of the

other hand, are usually expansive personalities, ready to take up with anything new, eager for economic activity. They rejoice in dangerous economic ventures and are on the watch for them. In appearance they are always submissive to the man who shows himself the stronger; but they work underground and know how to win and hold the substance of power, leaving the outward forms to others. No rebuff discourages them. Chased away in one direction,

speculators. The bill alluded to by *Avanti* was passed by the parliament and became law. *Giornale d'Italia*, Apr. 1, 1914: *"Report of stockholder's meeting, Bank of Rome* (Stockholder *T* speaking): 'Last year conditions in the bank were excellent. What has become of the millions that are now confessed lost? The only excuse that he [the President] can think of is the loss incidental to investments in Libya. But is that a loss of the past year or of the years before that? You have been doing a patriotic work in Libya, and as an Italian I congratulate you warmly. But I am not only an Italian. I am also a modest saver and I ask you: what use have you made of my savings? . . .' When, said the speaker, the question of merging the three banks came up, his heart warmed to the thought that he could avail himself of his right to withdraw, 'but changes made in the commercial code . . .' *The President* (interrupting): 'I feel called upon to declare that the Bank of Rome had nothing whatever to do with the steps that were taken to obtain a modification in the law of withdrawal.'"

2313 [2] As regards the susceptibility of the *rentier* to hoodwinking by sentimental appeals, one of the most amusing inspirations on the part of Latin speculators has been anti-Clericalism. They have shown a veritably master hand in taking advantage of sentiments of antipathy to the clergy that were prevalent in the masses in order to divert attention from their own lucrative "operations." While a simple-minded public was arguing itself hoarse over the temporal power, the infallibility of the Pope, the religious Congregations, and other such matters, the speculators were quietly filling their pockets. In that they were helped by the ingenuousness of their adversaries, who met them with anti-Semitism, not observing that in so doing they were keeping to a ground altogether favourable to the speculators and helping them to distract public attention from their exploits. In all the years that the anti-Semites have been fighting, what have they gained? Nothing, absolutely nothing! And what have their adversaries gained? Power, money, honours! Anti-Clericalism is sometimes just a pretext for favours and reprisals on the part of politicians. *Liberté,* Mar. 13, 1915: " 'Raggings, injustices, irritations, insults, sufferings!' Such the terms in which M. Barrès epitomizes the picture of the scandals to which the assignments of indemnities to the families of men at the front are giving rise all over France. Local feuds, political animosities, election manoeuvres, inspire most of the officials or deputy officials appointed by the Prefecture. 'The commission,' writes a woman of the Jura district, 'has informed me that I shall receive nothing because my husband was a practising Catholic. My request has been rejected because my husband did not belong to the Mayor's party.' So writes a woman from the Ariège. ' "You are for the priests," they answered.' That from a woman of the Lot! A Socialist newspaper prints a whole list of such complaints this morning and draws this conclusion: 'So free-thinkers are suffering at

they come buzzing back, like flies, from some other. If the sky darkens, they take to their cellars, but out they come the moment the tornado has blown over. With their unfaltering perseverance and their subtle art of combinations they override all obstacles. Their opinions are always the opinions most useful to them at the moment. Conservatives yesterday, they are Liberals today, and they will be Anarchists tomorrow, if the Anarchists show any signs of getting closer to power.[3] But the speculators are shrewd enough not to be all

the hands of Clerical officials.' Which proves, in any event, that the distribution of war-relief is occasioning scandal and protest on all sides without distinction as to parties."

2313 [3] At the time of the Dreyfus affair in France the French speculators were almost all Dreyfusards, and less out of any love for the Jews than from an instinct they had that their advantage lay in fighting for Dreyfus. It is interesting to note the great prevalence of group-persistences in the anti-Dreyfusards, along with a great deficiency in the combination-instincts—in political skill. The anti-Dreyfusards fought on such terms that victory could have brought them little if any advantage, and defeat utter ruin, as was in fact the case. In truth, in the event of victory all they could have won would have been the satisfaction of keeping an unfortunate, and perhaps an innocent, man in prison; and in the event of defeat, they could only look forward to oppression at the hands of their adversaries. Their agitation would have become intelligible if prosecuting Dreyfus had been conceived as a means of securing the help of the army in making a *coup d'état*. It is unintelligible as an end in itself. Evidently, they were not able and, in their lack of any courage, were unwilling, to overthrow the régime, and consequently they were left groping in the dark. They were not even shrewd enough to spend the "billion of the Congregations," but jealously guarded it for their enemies to pilfer at their leisure. People who are timid and cherish great respect for the law have no business to be toying with such adventures.

The influence of residues of group-persistence is clearly apparent in those individuals who believed Dreyfus guilty, closed their minds to all else, and faced every danger so only he were kept in prison, not considering that when so many guilty persons escape it matters little really whether one more or one less goes free. Then again, among their adversaries there were individuals who could see nothing but the presumed innocence of Dreyfus and sacrificed everything so only an innocent man were saved. The difference between the two groups lay solely in the fact that different people were using them. The anti-Dreyfusard forces were destitute of any leadership even remotely comparable to the very astute leadership that the speculators supplied to the Dreyfusard party. To mention just one of the many individualities that might be pointed to—what leader on the side of the anti-Dreyfusards could compare in ability with Waldeck-Rousseau, who led the Dreyfusards to victory like the shrewd and unscrupulous lawyer he was, indifferent as to the means he used for his client? Waldeck-Rousseau is the ideal type of the leader the speculators like to get for themselves. He had always been an enemy of the Socialists—and he became their ally. He had always been a patriot, and he handed his country's army over to an André and its navy over to a Pelletan. He had always defended the sanc-

of one colour, for it is better to have friends in all parties of any importance. On the stage one may see them battling one another, Catholics and pro-Semites, monarchists and republicans, free-traders and Socialists.[4] But behind the scenes they join hands, speculators all, and march in common accord upon any enterprise that is likely to mean money. When one of them falls, his enemies treat him mercifully, in the expectation that if occasion requires they too will be shown mercy. Neither the R's nor the S's are very adept in the use of force, and both are afraid of it. The people who use force and are not afraid of it make up a third group, which finds it very easy to rob the R's, rather more difficult to rob the S's; for if the S's are defeated and overthrown today, they are back on their feet and again in power tomorrow.[5]

tity of private property, and he dangled the "billion of the Congregations" as booty before the eyes of his partisans. He had always been a conservative, and he came forward as leader of the extremest revolutionaries; in very truth, neither sentiments nor scruples ever laid any obstacle in his path, nor did they distract him ever from the pursuit of his own advantage.

2313 [4] The novels of "Gyp" contain many keen observations of fact in this connexion. Cotoyan, in *Un mariage chic,* is the type of a very large class of living creatures.

2313 [5] Jouvenel, *La république des camarades,* pp. 53-54; 45-46: "Above all cliques and parties [among the Deputies], all rivalries between man and man, there is one imperious sovereign rule: to respect the traditions of the house and do no comrade any harm. Among comrades there can be differences, but never hatreds—fights, but with soft gloves. Angry as one may be, one cannot forget that one's anger is at a colleague [*Read:* accomplice.]. Even when an argument grows discourteous, it is never without its touch of brotherliness. The circumstances that place you at swords' points today will change tomorrow when you will need one another—why then utter the irreparable word? [The writer elsewhere describes the relations between ministers and Deputies, and what he says applies to conditions in Italy as well as in France and every other country that has a parliamentary form of government.] When a Deputy has passed his forenoon soliciting favours in the offices of the ministers, he spends his afternoons checking up on them. Half his day for asking favours, the other half for securing guarantees! When he gets a good stock of guarantees, he is not less exacting as regards the favours. When he has had a lot of favours, he is sometimes less severe as regards the guarantees. That is only human." *Avanti,* Mar. 1, 1915: "*The election budget.* It is, of course, the budget of the Ministry of Public Works plus the budget of the Ministry of Posts and Telegraphs. One Deputy wants a bridge, another a road, another a railroad, another a trunk-line for automobiles . . . each reserving the right to complain later on that expenses are mounting and the works that are executed are useless—though never with the sincerity to confess that they serve to increase the prestige of the Deputy in the eyes of his half-witted constituents, who grant that he may be a great scoundrel, but hold that all the same he does not neglect 'local needs' " (§ 2562 [1]).

2314. Very clear proof of the scant courage of the *rentier* is the supine and stupid resignation with which he accepts fundings of public debts in the various countries. At the time of the first conversions, there might have been some doubt as to the advantage of accepting them or not. But by this time, after no end of examples in which bonds have sunk below par after conversions, acute intellectual blindness is required in order to hope that a new conversion can have any different result. At the time of the last conversions it is inconceivable that the holders of English and French bonds should not have learned enough from the past to foresee what was in store for them. In 1913 English "consols" dropped to 72 and French "consols" to 86. If, in the course of the next few years, those bonds should again rise above par, holders would be very stupid or very cowardly to accept a new conversion. All that would be needed to block any sort of funding would be an agreement between a fairly small number of holders. But it would be easier to induce a flock of sheep to attack a lion than to get the slightest trace of vigorous action out of such people. They simply bow the head and let their throats be cut.[1] French savers allow themselves to be fleeced by their government precisely like a flock of sheep. The French Government grants or denies to foreign governments the privilege

2314 [1] Investors sometimes hail conversions with joy. All sellers of merchandise lament drops in the selling-prices of their wares. The one exception is the producer of savings, who rejoices when the interest-rate on money falls—in other words, the value of the commodity he produces. If anyone tried to reduce the wage of a given group of workers from 4 to 3.50 lire, they would raise an outcry, go on strike, defend themselves; but when, by a conversion of bonds, the saver gets 3.50 instead of 4 lire from the state, he does not lift a finger to defend himself and all but thanks the statesmen who fleece him. Interesting is another strange illusion peculiar to savers: They cheer whenever there is a rise in the prices of public-debt certificates that they purchase with their savings, and wear long faces whenever there is a drop; whereas the purchaser of bonds ought to be eager to get them at the lowest price possible. Among the causes of the illusion, the following is perhaps to be reckoned. Let us imagine a saver who already owns certificates of public debt to the value of 20,000 lire and saves 2,000 lire annually, investing them in more bonds. If the exchange price of public-debt bonds rises 10 per cent the saver's 20,000 lire become 22,000, and he imagines that he is the richer by 2,000 lire. But that would be the case only if he were to sell his bonds; if he keeps them he is worth not a penny more and draws the same annual income. Furthermore, the 2,000 lire that he saves every year and invests in public-debt certificates net him less income; for he receives 10 per cent less than he would have received had the exchange price of the bonds not risen. In a word, he is worse off than he was before.

of floating loans in France not with a view to protecting the nation's savings but with an eye to its own political conveniences, which sometimes incidentally go hand in hand with the private conveniences of certain plutocratic demagogues, and at other times are nothing else. Add to that the various taxes on the buying and selling of bonds, stamp-duties and the like—all of which bear upon the investor. Some savers in France, it is true, are now beginning to look after their own interests and are sending their money abroad; but such foreign investors represent but a very small fraction of the total as regards both their number and the amount of their savings.

2315. Another example of a lesser but far from negligible importance is the conduct of French investors of Clerical leanings in the years preceding the suppression of the religious congregations and the confiscation of their property. It was known beyond any doubt that sooner or later, and sooner rather than later, that was going to happen; yet the owners of that kind of property did not succeed in devising the flimsiest combination to avoid the impending loss. On the contrary they saw to it that it should be all the graver through their mania for owning real property—by giving to their wealth, in other words, the form most readily susceptible of confiscation by a government. And yet it would have been the easiest thing in the world to prevent, at least to a large extent, a robbery foreseen and foretold. The cash and the paper could have been deposited abroad for safe-keeping. As for the real estate, if the French investors were really bent on owning it, they could have assigned the deeds to a corporation, holding the majority of the voting stock themselves, but selling a few on the exchanges in London, Berlin, and New York—just enough to bring anybody minded to rob the corporation into complications with England, Germany, and the United States.

2316. But such stupidity is in no wise peculiar to our contemporary French Clericals. From the days when the Oracle at Delphi was plundered down to our own, one notes an unbroken stream flowing from the producer or holder of savings into religious institutions, which governments proceed to rob exactly the way an apiarist [a] makes annual extraction of honey from the hive that the worker

§ 2316 [a] [*Agricoltori*, misprint for *apicoltori*.—A. L.]

bee tirelessly keeps filled for him.[1] That is just a particular case of something much more general: In human societies, as known in historical times, the producers and holders of savings are continually being robbed of them. As regards means: The thing is done by

2316 [1] Bouché-Leclerq, *Histoire de la divination dans l'antiquité,* Vol. III, pp. 158-59. Towards the year 590 B.C., "the Oracle at Delphi was getting to be the biggest bank in the world. All around the temple rose 'Treasures' filled with votive offerings from one people or another, from princes, cities, winning athletes, reformed criminals, rich philanthropists eager to do something for the temple, notoriety-seekers of all sorts who were concerned to get their names before the public. With the income from gifts of real estate, with the fines that were imposed, with the interest that accrued, the Oracle came to own an enormous capital, which was being rapidly increased by intelligent management. Furthermore, since there was not in all Greece a safer place than Pytho, governments as well as individuals were in the habit of depositing precious documents there, testaments, contracts, promissory notes, even specie, and the priests took charge of such deposits, rewarding the trustfulness of the depositors by honorific privileges and distinctions. . . . So the Oracle came to hold enormous interests in its hands and showed itself disposed to increase its extensive clientèle. . . . Means of acquisition there were in plenty; but since it was as important to hold as to have, a superstitious terror was inspired in individuals who might be tempted to despoil the god. Visitors to Delphi were shown the statue of a wolf that was said to have revealed just such a thief to the prophets— another story was that it had eaten the thief in question."

The history of the spoliation of the temple begins with legends that, most probably, as is usually the case, relate to the past impressions belonging to the times in which they originated. Among such thieves was Hercules, no less. Bouché-Leclerq, Vol. III, p. 109, quotes a legend that alludes to a wrestling-match between Hercules and Apollo for possession of the prophetic tripod; but another legend mentions robbery outright: "And he set out to rob the temple": Apollodorus, *Bibliotheca,* II, 6, 2: τόν τε ναὸν συλᾶν ἤθελε. [Frazer, Vol. I, p. 241: "As the Pythian priestess answered him not by oracles, he was fain to plunder the temple, and, carrying off the tripod, institute an oracle of his own."] A legend quoted by the scholiast of the *Iliad,* XIII, v. 302 (Dindorf, Vol. II, p. 15) after Phereses, shows the Phlegyae burning the temple at Delphi and being destroyed by Apollo for that crime. In historical times, the series of "Sacred Wars" fought to punish attacks on the temple and the god's property begins with the wars against the Chrysseans, 600-590 B.C. The Second Sacred War was declared against the Phocians, during the years 355-346 B.C. Philomelus, leading a troop of highly paid mercenaries, occupied Delphi (Diodorus Siculus, *Bibliotheca historica,* XVI, 28, 1-2, and XVI, 30, 1-2; Booth, Vol. II, pp. 103-04). He began by laying taxes on the richer inhabitants. Shortly, not satisfied with such sources of income, he extended his depredations to the treasures belonging to the temple, asserting, perhaps in good faith, that it was just a loan; and just as probably, as is the case in our time, there were innocent souls who took his promises at their face value. Grote observes in that connexion, *History of Greece,* Vol. XI, p. 252, note 3: "A similar proposition had been started by the Corinthian envoys in the congress at Sparta, shortly before the Peloponnesian War; they suggested as one of their ways and means the borrowing from the treasures of Delphi and Olympia, to be afterwards repaid (Thucydides, *Historiae,* I,

violence—war, plunder, individual assaults; or by trickery and deceit—special tax-laws aimed at holders of savings; issues of fiat money and certificates of public debt that are sooner or later repudiated in whole or in part; monopolies and protective privileges;

121, 3). Perikles made the like proposition in the Athenian Assembly; 'for purposes of security, the property of the temples might be employed to defray the cost of war, subject to the obligation of replacing the whole afterwards' . . . (Thucydides, *Ibid.*, II, 13, 5). After the disaster before Syracuse, and during the years of struggle intervening before the close of the war, the Athenians were driven by financial disasters to appropriate to public purposes many of the rich donatives in the Parthenon, which they were never afterwards able to replace." The promises made by the French Government to honour the *assignats* of the Revolution, and similar promises made by other governments, have had at one time or another a similar fate.

Curtius, *Griechische Geschichte,* Vol. III, p. 423 (Ward, Vol. V, pp. 74-75), remarks that the strength of Philomelus rested on hired troops: "In the circumstances it would have been a miracle if Philomelus had managed to adhere to the moderateness of which he had made a formal law. [The very same thing happens to modern governments that depend for their strength on the advantages they can procure for their supporters.] The temptation was too strong. There they were, absolute masters of the richest treasure in Greece! When their money gave out were they to hand the country over to their bitterest enemies? To tell the truth, after having gone that far there was no choice left. So a Treasury was created (Diodorus, *Op. cit.,* XVI, 56; Booth, Vol. II, pp. 126-27), and on its responsibility the funds in the temple were tapped, at first, no doubt, in the form of loans, though as time went on the procedure became bolder and less scrupulous. [As is the case, in modern times, with issues of fiat money and public loans.] Objects that had reposed for centuries 'under the threshold' of the temple were scattered to the four winds of heaven. Not only was the gold melted down into coins, but holy relics were confiscated, and jewels coming down from the heroic age could be seen sparkling at the throats of the mistresses of the officers.

"It was said that 10,000 talents (to a value of about 11,000,000 dollars) were put into circulation in such ways. The money was used not only to pay wages to the soldiers, but also abroad to win the support of influential people, such as Dinikha, wife of Archidamus, King of Sparta (Theopompus, *Hellenica, Fragmentum* 258; mentioned by Müller, Vol. I, p. 322. Pausanias, *Periegesis,* III, *Laconia,* 3, 2, accuses that royal pair of accepting bribery), and to work upon opinions in the enemy camp."

Onomarchus, and Phailus after him, as successors to Philomelus, did even worse. At last the Phocians, overcome by Philip of Macedon, were condemned to pay an annual fine to a large amount. So a compensation between the theft and its punishment was established from the ethical standpoint, but not from the economic standpoint; for the mercenaries never paid back the money they had received in high wages, and the fine was paid to some slight extent in the form of restitutions, but more largely by fresh assaults on private property.

The Third Sacred War, 339-338 B.C., has no bearing on our present interests.

We have no information as to the occupation of Delphi by the Locrians and the Aetolians in the year 290 B.C. In the year 278 B.C. the Gauls attacked Delphi, to be defeated, according to Greek tradition, the god being interested in defending his

measures of all sorts designed to alter the prices and conditions that would prevail under free competition; and so on. The simplest form is the direct spoliation by violence of certain numbers of savers, often selected by chance and with a view only to their wealth. That

sanctuary, successfully, according to another tradition reported by Livy, *Ab urbe condita,* XXXVIII, 48, 1: "Even Delphi, from time immemorial the common oracle of the human race, the navel of the world, did the Gauls despoil" (*"Etiam Delphos, quondam commune humani generis oraculum, umbilicum orbis terrarum, Galli spoliaverunt"*).

After each new robbery the treasury at Delphi was refilled by the piety of the faithful (§ 2316 [5]). Sulla, accordingly, found it in flourishing condition when he took possession in his turn (Plutarch, *Sulla,* 12, 3-5; Perrin, Vol. IV, p. 363). At the time of his campaign in Greece, "since he was in need of large amounts of money for purposes of war, he violated the sacred asylums of Greece and sent for the richest and most beautiful offerings at Epidaurus and Olympia. He wrote to the Amphicthyons at Delphi that it would be well to put the treasures of the god in his safe-keeping; for he would guard them most carefully and, should he use any of them, give them back intact."

That is what the powerful, in general, say when they are raising loans either by love or by force. Sometimes they keep their promises; sometimes they forget them, or haggle and hedge. Sulla behaved, on the whole perhaps, a little better, though not so very much better. After the battle of Chaeroneia (Plutarch, *Op. cit.,* 19, 6; Perrin, Vol. IV, p. 391) "he put aside half of the [Theban] territory and dedicated it to the Pythian Apollo and the Olympian Zeus, ordering that the income from those lands be handed over to those gods in repayment of the money that he had taken." Bouché-Leclerq, *Op. cit.,* p. 197, remarks in that connexion: "Apollo surely knew what his bill against the Thebans would be worth, once Sulla had departed." These successive and repeated plunderings impoverished the temple altogether in the end. Strabo, *Geographica,* IX, 3, 8 (the text is corrupt. Strabo's French translator, La Porte du Theil, renders, Vol. III, p. 458:) "Being the object of greed, even the most sacred wealth is difficult to keep. So the temple at Delphi is now very poor; for even if the larger number of the tokens that have successively been dedicated there are still left, everything of any real value has been taken away. In olden times, however, the temple was very rich." In the Didot collection, the passage reads: "But wealth, being offensive to envy, is hard to keep, even be it sacred. Nowadays the temple at Delphi is very poor so far as monies are concerned. As regards the votive offerings, part have been taken away, though part are still there." [Jones, Vol. IV, pp. 357-59: "But wealth inspires envy and is therefore difficult to guard, even if it be sacred. At present, certainly, the temple at Delphi is very poor, at least as far as money is concerned; but as for the votive offerings, although some of them have been carried off, most of them still remain."]

The Emperor Constantine completed the ruin of the temple, carrying away such objects of art as still survived there in his day to decorate his new capital at Constantinople.

Just one example now from the hosts of operations in modern times that bear some resemblance to Sulla's loans on the treasure of Delphi. Stourm, *Les finances de l'Ancien régime et de la Révolution,* Vol. II, pp. 338-42: "After following, down to the re-establishment of order, the history of the partial bankruptcies declared each

corresponds in a certain way to the hunting of wild animals. Forms that are progressively more complicated, more and more ingenious in character, and more and more general in bearing keep appearing as we come down in history; and they correspond to the rearing of domestic animals. The analogy holds even for the consequences. The first sort of chase destroys incomparably more wealth and occasions far greater disturbances than the second.

Considered as to its manners of application, the operation that takes the savings of the savers may be more or less direct or indirect; the contribution may be forced or, to some extent, voluntary. Illustrative of the first manner would be the impost, the forced loan, the assault on inheritances, and the measures, so frequent in ancient times, that are designed to cancel or alleviate indebtedness.[2] The second manner is, in the typical case, an operation developing in two acts. In the first act, individuals give their savings to certain corporations, especially religious corporations—to temples—or they entrust them to the state or to institutions guaranteed by the state. In the

half-year by the revolutionary government on arrears in interests on the public debt, we now come to its default on the capital of the public debt that it declared in an official and final manner in 1797. How painful it is, as we turn to this failure so unpleasantly famous of the 'Consolidated Third,' to recall the proud resolution of the Constituent Assembly at the outbreak of the revolution, the bill of June 17, 1789, whereby 'this Assembly declares that, the public debt having been placed under the guardianship of French honesty and the French sense of honour, no power has the right to utter the infamous word "bankruptcy," no power has the right to betray the public faith under any form or designation whatsoever! . . .' The bill of September 30, 1797 (9 Vendémiaire, an VI), known as the law of the 'Consolidated Third,' that was voted by the two Councils, erased from the ledger for ever two-thirds of the public debt. It stipulated the reimbursement of the two-thirds mobilized in bonds and maintained only one-third of the amount of each subscription. . . . The interest on this remaining third was itself paid in fiat currency down to the year 1801." Such practice has been followed by many modern governments. You are owed 100 lire. You are given a piece of paper with a pretty engraving on it, and the figure, "100 lire." What have you to complain of? The powerful like to seem respectful of the laws of their ethics even when they are violating them; and there are always complaisant writers a-plenty to supply them with the derivations they need to justify themselves, and professors a-plenty to teach such derivations with all the authority of their chairs.

2316 [2] Pareto, Cours, § 449-53. The author of the Cours erred in not freeing himself entirely of ethical considerations. For example, he said, § 450: "One must rid one's mind of the preconception that inclines one to believe that robbery is not robbery when it is carried out in legal forms." That is a derivation of the I-β type (sentimental assertion). His mind was freer when he wrote, § 441: "There is hardly an economist who does not feel called upon to decide whether 'interest,' in other

second act, such corporations or institutions are robbed, now by a foreign enemy, now by a powerful private individual, often by a national government, which, also often, appropriates the sums that it had recognized as a debt or had undertaken to repay. Operations of the first group are altogether or chiefly voluntary. At the promptings of religious myths, which were once pagan, were then Christian, and are now nationalistic, individuals are induced to hand over their savings in the hope of winning favours from their gods, or else under the lure of promises to pay annuities, or in hopes—often mistaken hopes—that they will get back both interest and capital.[3] Operations of the second group ensue as a matter of course, following lines of least resistance. The money is appropriated wherever it happens to be, and at points where, for lack of any efficient resistance, it is least well defended.[4] It does make a difference whether a sum of money is taken through a tax or through a loan that is later to be repudiated, and whether it is taken directly or through measures of so-called protection, for in the masses those devices provoke resistance of very different kinds.

words, rent on savings, is just, equitable, legitimate, moral, or natural. Those are questions that overstep the domain of political economy and furthermore cannot possibly be answered unless one sees fit to define in advance just what such terms mean." In those last two remarks lies the germ of this present *Treatise on General Sociology*.

2316 [3] *Dictionnaire encyclopédique de la théologie catholique, s.v. Biens ecclésiastiques* (missing in Wetzer): "The Judao-Christians were unwilling, as Christians, to fall short of what they had formerly done as a matter of duty as Jews. They sold what they possessed and laid the money therefrom at the feet of the Apostles. The pagano-Christians made haste to imitate such devoted zeal, all the more since the pagan religions themselves had accustomed their believers to offering sacrifices to the gods and gifts to the priests; and since among the new converts there were many persons of wealth, considerable sums of money were thus paid into that voluntary community of property that was formed by the first Christians." In our day believers belonging to the various humanitarian, imperialistic, or patriotic sects are following the example of the faithful of paganism and Christianity.

2316 [4] Dionysius of Syracuse good-naturedly chaffed the gods he robbed. Cicero, *De natura deorum*, III, 34, 84: "Of such as bore the inscription in the old Greek style: '[property] of the good gods,' he said that he intended to put their goodness to some use (*In quibus quod more veteris Graeciae inscriptum esset, 'bonorum deorum,' uti se eorum bonitate velle dicebat.*)" According to Justin, *Historiae Philippicae*, XXIV, 6 (Clarke, p. 205), the leader of the Gauls justified the pilfering in the temple at Delphi with the words: "The gods are rich—it is well that they give to mortals"; and further: "The gods cannot be in any need of property, since they are so lavish with it to humans." Our modern pilferers doubtless feel the same way about it, but, barring some exceptions, they express themselves less cynically.

As regards time, the spoliation takes place either in the form of catastrophes coming at long intervals—of centuries in some cases—or in the form of developments recurring at briefer intervals, such as the losses inflicted on savers during "economic depressions," or again in the form of legislative or other enactments that are of continuous operation, such as the "leitourgias" (obligation to finance public rites) and the "trierarchias" (obligation to outfit a trireme) in ancient Athens and the progressive taxes of our day. In all those connexions, in a word, we get instances of those fluctuations of great, moderate, or minor scope which feature economic and social phenomena in general (§ 2293).

Largely under pressure of ethical sentiments, violent fluctuations come to look like catastrophes, and it is assumed that no account need be taken of them in considering a society that is functioning normally and regularly. That is just an illusion. Actually they differ from other fluctuations only in degree, and they are, on the whole, as regular, as normal, as any other development in human society.[5]

2316 [5] So from earliest legendary times down to our own, spoliations of sacred properties have proceeded regularly, the pilferings of pagan property finding their successors in pilferings of Christian property. One cannot help seeing in such phenomena the effects of one same identical force operating through the remotest centuries down to our time. *Dictionnaire encyclopédique de la théologie catholique, s.v. Biens ecclésiastiques* (Wetzer, *s.v. Kirchenvermögen*): "It is certain that the Church owned real properties by about the year 300, for in the year 302 Diocletian confiscated such properties and five years later Maxentius restored them. . . . The edict of Licinius, promulgated conjointly with Constantine and according unrestricted liberties to the new religion, ordered that all properties which had been taken away from Christian communities be returned. The properties of pagan temples were transferred to the Church along with certain contributions from the Imperial treasury. . . . This benevolent policy of the Emperor was on several occasions interrupted or disturbed, notably under Julian the Apostate, who stripped the Church even of her sacred vessels. But the devotion of Julian's successors compensated the Church for the losses she had suffered under him."

From that time on in history one notes an unending series of goings and comings of ecclesiastical properties, very like the ebbs and flows of the tide. Muratori, *Dissertazioni sopra le antichità italiane*, LXXIII (Vol. III, p. 436) [*Antiquitates: De monasteriis in beneficium concessis*]: "To the churches, or to their patrons and stewards, the faithful in their piety and devotion brought great affluence. . . . The remainder of their wealth and power the men of the Church got for themselves working diligently and with all their strength of brawn and brain for the advantage of the sacred places committed to their care and for their own. In every century, on the other hand, there have been other elements among Christians who could think of nothing better (*cui nihil antiquius fuit*) than to pilfer the patrimony of the Church and make it their own by every possible device. The clerics and especially

Forms, in any given fluctuation, may change, substance is constant. Formal, primarily, is the difference between the old debasings of metallic currencies and the modern issue of fiat money, between the ancient loans made from sacred treasuries and certain modern issues

the monks always shrank from labouring in the field of the laity; but the laity, on their side, left no stone unturned (*nihil intentatum relinquebant*) to gather into their own barns in the most expeditious manner possible the harvest garnered by the ecclesiasts. . . . On the causes of this unfortunate circumstance I have touched in a preceding essay. Here I will mention one other—the wicked habit of certain kings of making gifts of the lands of the Church, and especially of the monasteries, either to assure themselves of the loyalty and affection of their barons, or to encourage their mercenaries to greater efforts in war, so winning easy reputations for liberality and gratefulness by lavish spending of what belonged to others (*liberalitatis et grati animi famam facili rei alienae profusiones captantes*)." Exactly what is going on in our day.

Ecclesiastical property, however, is enriched not only by the piety of the faithful, but by the hopes they have of being compensated for their gifts either in this life or in some other. This feeling of a sort of contract with the divinity, of a *do ut des,* which was preponderant in Roman times, does not vanish with the advent of Christianity. Fustel de Coulanges, *La monarchie franque,* pp. 566, 568, 574-75: "Everybody in those days was a believer. Belief, as regarded the mass of the laity, was neither very extensive nor on a very lofty plane. There was very little thought in it and it had nothing abstract or metaphysical about it. But it was only the more cogent for that reason upon the mind and the heart. [Residues and interests with a minimum of derivations.] It came down to this, that the principal business of each individual in this world was to make a place for himself in the next. Interests private and public, personality, family, city, state—everything bowed the knee to that intellectual conception, everything gave ground before it. [But there were exceptions, just as there are today in the case of our humanitarian and patriotic religion. In every era of mankind there have been plenty of foxes to exploit the faith of other people.] Credulousness had no limits. To believe in God or the Christ was nothing . . . people wanted saints to believe in. . . . It was a very crude and material faith. One day St. Columban learned that his property had been stolen while he was busy praying at the tomb of St. Martin. He goes back to the tomb and upbraids the Saint: 'Do you think I came to pray over your bones just to get my things stolen?' And the Saint felt obligated to discover the thief and procure the return of the stolen articles. A robbery is committed in the Church of St. Columba in Paris. Eloi hurries back to the sanctuary and says: 'Listen carefully to what I have to say to you, St. Columba: if you do not have the stolen property returned to this place, I shall cause the door of your church to be barricaded with a pile of briers, and there will be no more worship of you.' The next day, the objects were returned. [§ 1321. In our day such errands would be entrusted to an "immanent Justice" or some other creature of the sort.] . . . Donations were numerous. They are explainable in the state of mind and heart then prevailing. Once a person firmly believed in a future happiness as his recompense, it occurred to him quite naturally to use all or a part of his property to obtain that reward. A dying man could well calculate that his soul's salvation was worth a piece of ground. He figured up his sins and counted off a part of his estate against them. . . . Consider the language

of public-debt certificates, between the brutal seizures made in days of yore by force of arms and the financial operations of modern politicians, between the award of booty to armed mercenaries and the concession of favours to influential vote-getters.[6] All the same

in which almost all such donations are couched: The testator declares that he intends 'to redeem (to "buy back") his soul'; that he donates a piece of land 'with a view to salvation,' 'for the remission of his sins,' 'to obtain an eternal reward.' From that it is evident that in the view of those people the gift was not gratuitous: it was an exchange—one gift for another: 'Give,' it was said, 'and unto you shall be given': *Date et dabitur."* Subscribers to certain (or rather uncertain) certificates of public debt reason in much the same way in our day.

The faithful gave, and the powerful received. The thing begins at a time when faith was profound. Gregory of Tours, *Historia ecclesiastica Francorum,* IV, 2 (*Opera,* pp. 270-71; Dalton, Vol. II, p. 117): "King Clothair had previously ordained that all the churches in his kingdom should pay a third of their income to the exchequer. All the bishops had, quite grudgingly, consented and subscribed to the edict; but the blessed Injuriosus, rising in wrath, courageously refused to subscribe, and said, 'If thou dost take away the things that are of God, the Lord will shortly deprive thee of thy kingdom. . . .' And he departed in dudgeon from the King's presence without bidding him adieu. And the King was moved, and moreover, fearing the power of the blessed Martin, he sent messengers after the bishop with gifts, and begged the bishop's forgiveness and his intercession in the King's favour with the power of the blessed pontiff Martin."

Tirelessly the Councils rained fulminations and ecclesiastical penalties upon usurpers of Church properties. A council [*read:* Synod] was held in Rome in the year 504 with that primarily in view. Re-enacting regulations of previous Councils, it decreed in its Canon I (Labbe, Vol. V, p. 513): "Whosoever in dangerous arrogance shall presume to confiscate, or appropriate, or trespass upon properties of the Church (suppressing *aut* before *sua: Quicumque res Ecclesiae confiscare aut competere aut pervadere periculosa sua infestatione praesumpserit*), unless he shall forthwith have corrected himself through satisfaction of the Church in the premises, shall be smitten with anathema. Likewise any persons who shall have withheld properties of the Church at the bidding or largess of princes or any individual of power, or by occupation, or by tyrannical seizure, and shall have transmitted them by inheritance to children or heirs, unless forthwith at the admonishment of the Pontiff and upon evidence of the truth they shall have restored the properties of God, let them be smitten with perpetual anathema." Great the shrewdness of the usurpers in question. They had thought of occupying Church properties on the pretext of safe-guarding them in intervals of episcopal interregnancy. The Council condemns them. In the year 909 a Council was held at Troslé, near Soissons: Fleury, *Histoire ecclésiastique,* Vol. XI, pp. 615-17, Vol. XII, pp. 15-18 (Labbe, Vol. XI, pp. 731-34): "The preamble to the decrees of the Council recites that 'The towns are depopulated, the monasteries ruined or burned, the open country reduced to solitudes.' . . . The decadence of the monasteries is then described: some have been ruined or burned by the peasants, others stripped of

2316 [6] See Pareto, *Cours,* §§ 344-63, barring, however, a few ethical considerations that creep in by implication here and there.

an appreciable change is observable as regards forms, in view of the gradual elimination of the more brutal procedures. There are no recurrences, in our day, of violent spoliations such as Octavius, Antony, and Lepidus perpetrated to make sure of their troops

their properties and reduced all but to nothing; those of which some traces remain are going forward with no form of regular living. . . . The Council then expatiates on the respect due to ecclesiasts, the outrages to which they were at the time being subjected, and the plundering of properties dedicated to God." And for the year 956 Fleury says: "We also have a treatise by Atton de Verceil on the sufferings of the Church. It is divided into three parts. . . . The third relates to Church properties. 'We may,' says Atton, 'overlook the fact that on the death or expulsion of a bishop, Church properties are given over to pillage at the hands of the laity. For what matters it whether they be plundered after his death or while he is alive? And what purpose does it serve to guard the Church's treasure so carefully if the barns, the cellars, and all the rest be robbed? All the crops vanish. The harvests still ungarnered are sold in the name of the new bishop, and his ordination is postponed until all has been consumed; and finally the bishopric is given to the man who offers most. With the result that no lands are so often sold and plundered as the lands of the Church.' "

The Eastern Church was treated no better than the Western. Fleury, *Histoire ecclésiastique,* Vol. XI, p. 17, *anno* 1155: "The Emperor Manuel Comnenus reproclaimed a law that his father had made prohibiting seizure of the properties of vacant bishoprics. 'We have learned,' he said, 'that on the deaths of bishops, and sometimes even before they have been buried, local officials enter their houses and carry off everything they find therein and make seizure of the landed property of their churches.' " [As late as the sixteenth century, part of the popular festivities connected with the election of a Pope in Rome was a raid on the residence of the successful Cardinal, which was thoroughly sacked.—A. L.]

If piety was not the only motive of the donation, impiety was not the only cause of the spoliation. Urgent need of cash has often been the leading consideration. Sulla may well have believed in Apollo while he was plundering the temple of that god. Pious Christian monarchs acted not otherwise, and in our times sincere humanitarians often find ways to get rich through their religion. Charles Martel was a devout prince, yet he too was accused of robbing the Church. Frantin, *Annales du moyen âge,* Vol. VI, pp. 455-56: "Charles's captains, accordingly, were his first vassals; and the new finance, if one may so say, that he created was based on the Church properties, the plunder from which he apportioned among his men. Not only Church properties, but the churches themselves, the monasteries, the episcopal chairs, fell prey to his sacrilegious liberality. 'The episcopal sees,' says a writer of the time, 'he handed over to laymen and he left no power to the bishops. After a victory one of his captains received the sees of Rheims and Trèves for himself as his recompense. The monasteries were invaded, ruined, or destroyed, the monks being driven away to live without discipline and to find refuge where they might.' 'Charles,' says another writer, 'destroyed throughout all France the little tyrants who were usurping authority: whereafter, in the intent of rewarding his soldiers, he confiscated Church properties and distributed them to his men. Such violent usurpation of the ecclesiastical patrimony took place all through the course of his long wars.' Finally, says the *Chronicle of Verdun:* 'Charles dispensed the public patrimony in unheard-of profusion to his warriors, who began to be called *soldiers* [men fighting for pay, that is], and who flocked to him from all parts of the world under lure of gain.' The pillaging of the royal treasury, the sacking of towns, the devastation of realms abroad, the spoliation of churches and monasteries, the tributes that came in from conquered lands, were hardly sufficient for his greed; and when such resources were exhausted, he seized the lands of the churches. He bestowed bishoprics on his captains whether they were clerks or laymen, and there were sees that were left without pastors for years at a time."

Legend took it upon itself to punish the plunderers of the temple at Delphi. It also took charge of punishing Charles Martel. The thieves of Delphi received their due in this world. Charles received his in the next. It was St. Eucherius of Orleans who saw the soul of Charles Martel in Hell. The bishops call the attention of Louis the Pious to that fact in a letter: *Decretum Gratiani, pars* II, *causa* 16, *quaestio* 1, *canon* 59 (Friedberg, Vol. I, pp. 780-82): "Because, in truth, Prince Charles, father to King Pepin, first among all the kings and princes of the Franks separated the property of the churches from them and divided it, for that thing alone, primarily, has he been damned eternally. For St. Eucherius, Bishop of Orleans, being in prayer and transported in rapture to the other world, among the other things that he saw by revelation of the Lord saw he Charles in torment in the nether Hell. . . . [The angel who was guiding the Saint on the excursion in question explains that Charles is suffering such punishment because of his thefts, and that the only thing to do would be to redistribute the property that he left among the churches and the poor:] Whereupon, coming to himself, St. Eucherius sent for St. Boniface and for the Abbot Fouldray (*Fuldradum*) of the Monastery of St. Denis, and, reporting what he had seen, gave them for a sign that they should go to the tomb where Charles was buried, and if they should not find his body there, they could believe that what he was saying was the truth. And they, forthwith, hastened to the monastery aforesaid, where the body of Charles had been buried, and as they opened his tomb, a dragon was seen hastily to issue from it and the tomb was found to be blackened within, as though it had been burned. We have ourselves seen the men who were eyewitnesses to this thing, they being still alive in our time, and to us they gave their word as to the things they had seen and heard. And this becoming known to Pepin, son of Charles, he called a synod at Létines-Palais (*Liptinas:* Létines-en-Cambraisis) . . . and whatsoever he was able of the ecclesiastical properties that his father had seized he tried to restore."

To this passage Master Gratian adds: "Mention of this story is also made in the Life of the Blessed Eucherius. . . . Such division as Charles had made, in this way, of ecclesiastical properties, Pepin and Charles the Emperor prohibited. Before the eighty-third enactment in that same book a heading explains: '. . . This article was issued at Aix, because laymen were accustomed to apportion the bishoprics and monasteries among themselves for their own use, leaving to no bishop, abbot, or abbess aught more than was barely sufficient for the monks and priests to live.' "

Similar things have been happening from those days all the way along to our own time, when we come upon the suppression of religious corporations in Italy and France. The property of the churches was distributed, ostensibly, among the soldiers of Charles Martel. The "billion of the Congregations" vanished into the pockets of partisans of the French politicians. In both cases the operation may have been substantially beneficial to the country as assuring the stability of a given régime.

Thorold Rogers has well described the prodigalities of Henry VIII in England

(§ 2200 [1]). So too the practice of handing the taxpayer over to the greed of an agent and then proceeding to extort the ill-gotten gain from him has almost disappeared from civilized countries, or has at least been modified.[7]

and their consequences, *The Economic Interpretation of History*, pp. 35-36: "During the whole of English history, there never was a sovereign so outrageously and wantonly extravagant as Henry. He inherited an enormous fortune from his thrifty father, as fortunes in the sixteenth century went, and dissipated it speedily. His wars and alliances in which [he] subsidized the needy Emperor of Germany . . . cost him much, but his expenditure during time of peace was prodigious. . . . He seemed to have an idea that it was splendid and safe to entertain his nobles, and he made them quarter themselves in his numerous palaces. . . . If he could have got at it, he would have spent all the private wealth of all his subjects, and he made every effort to get at it. . . . He was popular in a way, for wasteful people generally are, even when they waste what does not belong to them. [That applies just as well to the politicians of our time.] The smaller monasteries went, and he soon came to an end of their accumulations. The larger ones he spared, declaring them to be the seats of piety and religion. He pledged himself that the spoil of the monasteries [being] given him, he would ask his people for no more taxes, not even for necessary wars. Soon the greater monasteries went. I believe that, foreseeing the storm, the monks had granted long leases of the lands, so that much of his plunder was reversionary. But the accumulated treasures of ages came into his clutches. A long array of waggons carried off the gold, silver, and precious stones, which for nearly four centuries had accumulated round the shrine of Becket. This shrine was no doubt the richest in England, perhaps in Christendom. But there were others more ancient and nearly as wealthy, at Winchester, at Westminster, at a hundred sacred places. It is exceedingly probable that the accumulations of these holy places were, as bullion, equal to all the money in circulation at the time. It vanished like snow in summer. . . . The lands of the monasteries were said to have been a third of the English soil. After these exploits he seems to have hardly dared to ask his people for money. But there still remained a way in which he could most effectually attack their pockets. He began to issue base money."

To carry the analysis on to other countries would merely result in collecting more facts of the same sort. In Germany the war of the investitures, the Reformation, the secularization of ecclesiastical principalities at the time of the French Revolution; in France, the distribution of the abbeys to abbots belonging to the Court; the expropriations of the First Republic, and the more recent expropriations of the Third—all are new instances of wide fluctuations in the curve of spoliation.

2316 [7] Aristophanes, *Equites*, vv. 1147-49: *The People* (speaking): "I am forcing them [dishonest leaders] to belch out the money they have stolen from me." In Rome, towards the end of the Republic the provinces were handed over to speculators, who won the right to exploit them by showering largess upon the Roman populace. The despots of Asia and Africa had their subjects despoiled by stewards whom they in turn proceeded to strip. The kings of Christendom allowed Jews, usurers, and bankers to amass fortunes and then confiscated them. In France, the Regency allowed many individuals to get rich through scandalous speculations that it had itself promoted; then it forced them to give up the ill-gotten gains, with a few exceptions still more scandalous. On the speculations arising under Law's

The transfer of economic values that results from attacks on property may at times have the effect of increasing production. That is the case when the resources pass from the hands of people who are unable or unwilling to use them to the best possible advantage into the hands of people who make better use of them. But most often the proceeds of spoliations are wasted, the way the gambler wastes his winnings at play, and the ultimate outcome is a destruction of wealth. The veterans whom Sulla made wealthy men after a time were paupers again (§ 2577 [1]). People alive in our day are witnesses to the extravagance of individuals who grow rich in politics and to the waste in which they indulge. Taking the attack on property in conjunction with the voluntary prodigality of holders

"System," see Ferrara, *Della moneta e dei suoi surrogati* (*Money and Its Substitutes*), p. 499. Admirers of the "ethical state" and more or less gratuitous defenders of the speculators have tried to defend the system of Law and the Regent. The derivations they put forward are the ones usual in such cases. On Jan. 26, 1721, all holdings of properties connected with the "system," including annuity contracts purchased with notes, were made subjects to visa. Contemporaries of the defaults and visaings of 1716 and 1721 were well aware of the character of those confiscations. Buvat, *Journal de la Régence,* Vol. I, p. 201: "On the tenth [of December, 1716] a medal began going the rounds. It had been struck on the occasion of the prosecution of merchants and speculators by the Chamber of Justice. On one side was a portrait of King Louis XIV, with, underneath, the legend: *Esurientes implevit bonis;* and on the other was a portrait of King Louis XV, with the words: *Divites dimisit inanes."* And farther along, speaking of the visas of 1721, Vol. II, p. 273: "'Don't talk to me of a tax,' the Prince [the Duc de Bourbon] resumed. 'Everyone is only too well aware of the misapplication of funds that took place during the last Chamber of Justice; and there will be the same trouble with the Chamber there is now talk of holding. The most insignificant woman will get anything she wishes from Monsieur the Duke of Orleans in procuring the exoneration of those from whom she will expect some recompense for doing them a favour. Do not imagine I am saying that because the Duke is not here. I will maintain it to his face.'" Martin, *Histoire de France,* Vol. XVII, pp. 228-29: "Various categories were established, the losses being graduated from 1/6 to 19/20 [A system somewhat like the progressive taxes of today.], an enormous task, designed, as had been the case in 1716, to achieve a certain relative justice in the betrayal of the public trust. Five hundred and eleven thousand persons deposited to the amount of 2,521,000,000 papers, which were forthwith reduced by 521,000,000. Left were about 1,700,000,000 that were recognized as capital for life or perpetual annuities. . . . A very small part of the debt, 82,500,000, was settled in cash." Before that procedure in bankruptcy, there had been another in 1715, as to which Martin notes, Vol. XVII, p. 161: "The financial history of the Old Régime is just one alternation of depredations by the financiers upon the people and of governmental abuses of power upon the financiers. There was no escaping from that circle."

It is strange that a historian of Martin's ability should not have seen that it was a

of savings and their heirs, we get in those two things forces tending to counteract the efforts of producers of savings and considerably to restrict the accumulation of wealth.

The remarkable regularity with which the developments here in question recur in time and space leads one to the conclusion that in historical times in our societies the right of private property subsists only as tempered by behaviour and inclinations that run counter to it. We have, in other words, no example of a society in which the property-right subsists strictly without limitation. It is further apparent that one must not take one's stand on the narrow ethical ground where such attacks are viewed as unpleasant, reprehensible incidents offensive to law, justice, and equity; but on the broader

question, in all that, of a particular case of a thing that is general. Practical men often discern more clearly than thinkers. Saint-Simon, for instance, *Mémoirs,* Hachette ed., Vol. XI, pp. 274-75, *anno* 1715, grasped the point that if one were to break the circle of spoliations, one would have to prevent the inflow of the money that supplied material for the repudiations; but he was mistaken as to the efficacy of his means. He suggests bankruptcy pure and simple, and thinks it would have the good point that no one would any longer lend to the government and the latter would have to reduce expenses: "The louder the protests and the laments it [the declaration of bankruptcy] arouses, the greater the despair, through the ruin of so many people and so many families, both directly and indirectly [*par cascade,* a favourite phrase with the Duke.—A. L.], and consequently, the greater the disorder and embarrassment it occasions in the affairs of so many individuals, the more prudent the individual will be in the future. [In that Saint-Simon is wrong. Ages and ages of experience go to show that the ingenuousness of the investor is as incurable as the passion of the gambler.] . . . Whence two marvellously beneficial effects: inability on the part of the king to get hold of such immense sums for doing anything he pleases or, much more often, anything it pleases other people to put into his head to do for their personal advantage, an inability that would force a wise and moderate policy upon him, and prevent his reign from being a reign of blood and brigandage and perpetual war upon a whole Europe banded against him at all times and always in arms in the sheer necessity of defending itself. . . . The other effect of that inability would be to deliver France of a hostile race of men (*un peuple ennemi*) that is forever intent on devouring her with all the devices that greed can imagine and reduce to a deadly science [Which became the "science of finance" of our day.] by that mass of imposts [It is even greater in our time.] of one sort or another, the management, collection, and diversity of which is deadlier than the tax-rate itself, and by that horde of individuals who are withdrawn from all useful functions of society and busy themselves at naught else than destroying it, robbing private persons and upsetting intercourse of every kind." Those are words of an *R,* a *rentier,* a "man living on income." He sees one side of the medal. An *S,* a speculator, would have seen the other. [It would be profitable to reconsider the Semblançay case under Francis I in the light of this analysis by Pareto.—A. L.]

ground where they are viewed as ties that are the necessary counter-parts of the ties established by the right of private property.[8]

The proofs of that thesis are supplied by history; but it is further confirmed by numerous inferences, notable among which the corol-laries of the theory of compound interest.

It has long since been remarked that that theory, when applied to long intervals of time, yields results which are flatly belied by experience.[9] "A centime placed on compound interest at the rate of 4 per cent at the time of the birth of Christ would yield by the year 1900 a fabulous amount in francs represented by 23 followed by 29 zeros. [More exactly the figure 23,085 followed by 26 zeros.] Assuming the Earth were made entirely of gold, thirty-one such Earths would be necessary to cash that sum in gold. A result quite as absurd would be obtained by dropping money from consideration and thinking of economic values, in general, as multiplying in that progression. A value of 100,000 francs placed at an interest of 3 per cent would yield in 495 years 226,000,000,000—in other words the present wealth, approximately, of France. According to Petty, the wealth of England in the year 1660 was 6,000,000,000—let us say 8,000,000,000 for the United Kingdom. If we take the Exchequer's valuations for the year 1886 (235,000,000,000), the interest-rate re-quired to transform 8,000,000,000 into that amount in 226 years would be about 1.5 per cent. One may infer from that that only by exception can wealth increase in a geometrical progression equiva-lent to or exceeding a rate of 1.02 per cent or 1.03 per cent. . . . If the wealth of England were to increase according to the progression observable between the years 1865 and 1889, the English Govern-ment would get, within a few centuries, an altogether fabulous revenue. It is therefore certain that that progression cannot hold during centuries to come. . . .

"Life-insurance premiums are based on calculations of compound interest. They can be accepted so long as only small portions of the population and wealth of a country are involved. They would lead to utterly fantastic results if they were to apply to the whole of

2316 [8] We use the term "necessary" in this sentence in its experimental sense, without any further implication of metaphysical absoluteness or anything of the kind. We mean by it simply that within the limits of space and time known to us, one development is observed as invariably conjoined with another.

2316 [9] The passage in quotes is from Pareto, *Cours*, §§ 469-72.

a population or to any considerable fraction of a national wealth."

If a few families had placed a centime at compound interest at the beginning of our era and been able to save the wealth so produced, they would long since have absorbed all the wealth on the globe. As regards distribution of wealth, one gets results as absurd as for the total wealth.

In the face of facts so solidly established, some writers have halted at the conclusion that the theory and the computations of compound interest cannot be applied to any notable portion of a population over any very extensive period of time, a conclusion, to tell the truth, that simply restates the description of the facts without explaining them. The author of these volumes had not himself gone beyond that point as late as the year 1896.[10] The theories of sociology now

2316 [10] Why is it that a writer should first stop at such a point and later on go beyond it? If that were a mere individual case, it might not be worth while to answer the question. But it has a more general bearing, and may furnish considerations that will have their use in the investigation of social phenomena. The author of the *Cours* insists at length on the necessity of taking account of the interdependences between phenomena. The main source of his error, therefore, cannot have been any *general* oversight as to that principle. One may nevertheless say that, in the particular, he has to some extent neglected interdependences between economic phenomena and social phenomena. But his error lies primarily in the fact that whereas he is careful to subject economic situations to a strict scientific analysis, in dealing with social problems he often accepts ready-made theories and *a priori* judgments supplied by the ethics that is current in his time in the society in which he is living. That principle has been and still is the guiding principle with many economists, and it is well therefore to call attention to the error. The author of the *Cours* seems, at least by implication, to hold that anything contrary to ethics is harmful to society and that anything that is declared reprehensible by common opinion, which he adopts as his own, *ought* to be avoided. The fact illustrates the potency of residues, and specifically of the II-ζ residues (sentiments objectified). IV-$\epsilon 3$ residues (group approbation) also figure. The author studies his economic problems with all possible care. Rightly or wrongly he felt he had obtained scientific demonstrations and was standing on solid ground so far as those problems were concerned. He was indifferent to any reproach that sentiment might make of him, and to prevailing opinions save as they were justified by experience. But on entering the field of sociological phenomena, he felt that he had not as yet subjected them to a thorough-going experimental anaylsis and that the ground was insecure under his feet. He hesitated to attack certain opinions the scientific fallacy of which he was not as yet in a position to demonstrate; and in such cases he subordinated his judgment to prevailing sentiments, or to his own. So derivations came leaping forward—II-a derivations, for example (authority). Economists of great and deserved reputation had held that debasings of currency were simple frauds, crimes of immoral governments; and unconsciously under the influence of that idea, which

permit us to complete that earlier investigation. If practical results do not substantiate the implications of the theory of compound interest, the fact is due not to any defect in the theory, but to the assumption of a premise that does not square with realities. Computations of compound interest implicitly assume that wealth is to accumulate over very extensive intervals of time at rates of interest not widely different from the rates observable in our time for accumulations of brief duration representing insignificant fractions of the total wealth.

Failure of the facts to corroborate conclusions soundly derived from a given premise is sufficient proof of error, or at least of incompleteness, in the premise. That must be the case with the premise just stated. But how explain the conflict between the results yielded by theory, according as it be applied to longer or shorter periods of time, to larger or smaller fractions of the total wealth?

If one ignore the fact that the rates of interests envisaged are more or less the rates actually observable, one might infer that as wealth accumulates it becomes less and less productive, so that, in the long run, the rate of interest approaches zero. That principle is vaguely present in optimistic theories of a diminishing interest-rate. But such theories are belied by the facts, which clearly show that from the heyday of Athens down to our own times, interest-rates have risen and fallen in successive variations but have failed by far to reach

had been nurtured in him by his masters, he succumbed to III-α derivations (accords with sentiments) and perhaps even to III-ϵ derivations (metaphysical). As regards logic, for that matter, he finds in it, and soundly, an incontrovertible refutation of the patter emanating from adorers of the "ethical state." In that, too, we have a thing that is general: a derivation that is fallacious inspires a refutation which, sound enough from the standpoint of pure logic, seems to be equally sound from the experimental standpoint. Marx evolves an absurd theory of value, which is a gross exaggeration of the theory of Ricardo: the author of the *Cours* refutes it, and thinks that thereby he has refuted Marx's Socialism. That is wrong. No dispute revolving around derivations touches the experimental substance of things.

The changes observable in these volumes arise primarily in the fact that the author has now carried the experimental method into the field of sociology; that he has striven, to the best of his knowledge and ability, to accept nothing *a priori* or in deference to the most venerable authority, to trust in no wise to sentiments, whether his own or of others, to resist any intrusion on the part of metaphysical and religious beliefs of one kind or another—in a word, to subject everything to the single test of experience.

zero in our day.[11] We must therefore discard the hypothesis of a diminishing rate approaching, in the long run, zero; and we are constrained to assume, in that case, that if the accumulation of wealth that would result from real interest-rates fails to develop, it is because the accumulation is made impossible by successive destructions of wealth.

And that is exactly what observation reveals. History is replete with descriptions of numberless causes for the destruction of wealth. Some of them bear upon total wealth: wars, revolutions, epidemics, plunderings and burnings, wastage of all sorts. Others bear upon the distribution of wealth and prevent protracted accumulations in given families, given communities, not without indirect reactions upon total wealth: and such are individual attacks upon private property belonging to families and groups and transfers of wealth resulting from force or from prodigalities. So it turns out that the curves of accumulating wealth for families, communities, nations—all humanity—instead of showing the regular increase that a uniform rate of interest would yield, are undulatory lines fluctuating about an average medium curve (§ 1718). The curve for humanity as a whole shows beyond any question a certain amount of increase from the earliest historical times down to the present day, though there may have been periods of retrogression. Just as certainly there is a curve of increase for the given family, community, or race, though with periods of decrease.

The duration of the periods is long for the human race as a whole, less long for nations,[12] fairly short for communities, very brief for families. The thing is, in short, only a particular case of a very general phenomenon (§§ 2293, 2330), the fluctuations revealing and representing the various forces that affect the social aggregate as a whole.

Economic effects are not the only ones to be considered—there

2316 [11] See Pareto, *Cours,* §§ 466, 471 [1]. The description there given is such as was possible without, as yet, the assistance of a general theory positing an undulatory form for social phenomena (§§ 1718, 2293, 2330). All the same, it had the merit of disputing the optimistic theory of a diminishing interest-rate, which prevailed at the time of the *Cours,* though facts subsequently materializing took it upon themselves to refute it.

2316 [12] One such fluctuation, in the case of England, is analyzed in Pareto, *Cours,* § 471 [1].

are others just as important. As regards class-circulation, measures that are catastrophic, or violent, or merely of far-reaching scope, may, along with consequences beneficial to society, have others that are harmful to a far greater degree than effects produced by measures involving persuasion or deception and which, for that very reason, affect only certain classes of persons. In fact, measures of the violent or catastrophic type affect all individuals alike whatever the position they occupy in class-circulation whereas measures of persuasion and deception primarily affect individuals who occupy very low stations on the social ladder owing to their simple-mindedness, ingenuousness, or credulity, or their lack of courage and initiative. Measures of the first type may therefore be far more destructive to socially useful elements than measures of the second type.

If, now, one were to conclude from all the above that private property or other institutions of the sort might be abolished altogether, that would be falling into an error that is very general among sociologists and economists, and to which we have repeatedly called attention: the error, namely, of using a qualitative instead of a quantitative analysis, of overlooking interdependences in social phenomena, of imagining that in explaining social phenomena one can confine oneself to a single tie among the many ties and modify the one without touching the others.

History of course supplies facts directly counter to those we have just been considering. History shows that in societies in which private property is apparently non-existent or reduced to a minimum, in which equality seems to prevail, private property, or similar institutions, along with inequalities, tend to develop. That fact emphasizes the necessity (the *experimental* necessity) of other ties working in a sense opposite to the equalitarian ties.[18] And from that to conclude that attacks on private property, and other similar institutions, and on inequalities, can be suppressed altogether would be to go astray and fall into the same error. For such things are just another illustration of the composite character of the forces that are working upon society.

And there is, finally, one other type of error of which we must beware, the error of confusing, as is often done, real movements

2316 [18] See Pareto, *Systèmes socialistes,* Vol. I, Chap. IV, "Real Systems," and especially p. 179.

with virtual movements. The fact that history shows certain groups of simultaneous ties functioning in every age proves that those ties are interdependent (real movements) not only among each other but also with other conditions determining the social equilibrium; it does not show that the forms under which the ties in question function bring to society the maximum of any given utility that might be desired (virtual movements).

2317. Owing to their poverty of spirit, producers and holders of savings have little influence on economic developments, which are determined by the total quantity of savings far more than by any resistance that the savers might offer to those who are trying to rob them. Carrying on the analogy of the bees (§ 2316), the quantity of honey that the apiarist obtains depends on the total quantity the bees have gathered, and not on any resistance they may offer to being deprived of it.[1]

2317 [1] According to Neymarck, *Journal de la Société de statistique de Paris*, April, 1914, p. 191, at the end of the year 1912 the total value of negotiable securities in the world—government bonds, corporation stocks and bonds, and so on—amounted to 850,000,000,000 in francs. Of these 115,000,000,000 to 120,000,000,000 were held in France, 80,000,000,000 of which were in French paper. Bygones being bygones, if it were possible to do the thing in such a way that future producers of savings would not be aware of it or, after all, in such a way that they would not be frightened on their own account, the 850,000,000,000 could be taken away from their present owners without any great change in the economic productivity of the world. One would get merely a transfer of wealth from certain individuals to certain other individuals, with the perturbations that differing tastes and needs in the new owners, as compared with the old, might occasion in production. Not so if future producers of savings were to take fright; for some of them would then stop saving and the rest would hoard what they did save, so cutting off the essentials for expansion in production and bringing on economic ruin. The problem, therefore, that governments have to solve, and especially speculator governments, is to find ways to rob past producers of savings without frightening future ones. Not by way of theory, but empirically, following instinct, they have hit on the very best solution to the problem, which is to proceed very gradually step by step, taking a little nibble every so often, now here, now there, at the cake. Far from alarming future producers of savings, that system emboldens them, for the value of future savings rises in proportion as the burdens on existing savings are made heavier.

In 1913, for instance, there was talk of a tax on French government bonds. That forced a drop in the bonds on exchange. In a phenomenon so complex no exact relationship can be established between the tax-rate and the exchange quotation of a bond. Speaking hypothetically and just to give a concrete form to considerations so abstract, suppose the tax on the coupon is 5 per cent, so that instead of being worth 3 francs for every 100 francs in capital, it will be worth only 2.85

2318. In periods of economic stagnancy there is an increase in the quantity of available savings, and that is the groundwork for the ensuing "boom" when the amount of available savings will diminish and so open the way to another period of stagnancy. And so on indefinitely.

2319. Superimposed upon these two types of fluctuation is a third, of very long duration, generally to be measured in terms of centuries. Every so often, that is, those elements in a population which are able and willing to use force and are endowed with powerful residues of group-persistence shake off the yoke that the speculators or other sorts of individuals expert solely in the arts of combinations have forced upon them; and that marks the beginning of a new era, during which the defeated classes gradually return to power, to be eventually overthrown again, and so on and on (§ 2331).

2320. In studying such developments it is important to note that oftentimes in one same country there is a very extensive group of phenomena in which the evolution described is going on, and another small, perhaps very small, class in which the use of force is constant. The typical example of that would be the Roman Empire. There the evolution was going on in the civil population; but along-

francs. If the price of the bond falls from 92 francs, let us say, to 87.40, the old investors lose a certain amount, while new investors neither gain nor lose and continue investing their savings at the same interest-rate they would have had if the stock had remained at 92 without a tax on the coupon. There are two other situations: 1. If the stock remains above 87.40, old owners of savings lose less, and new ones lose a little, there being a general lowering in the earnings of capital. 2. If the stock goes lower than 87.40 the old investors lose more, and the new ones gain, there being a general rise in the earnings of capital. The first case is quite generally observable in periods of depression, the second in periods of "boom." Speaking now in general terms, in this second case the speculators gain in two ways: 1. They appropriate some of the money that they took from the old investors. 2. For their own savings, which are easily made owing to increased profits, they get a higher earning on capital. That movement cannot go on indefinitely, not because of any resistance on the part of those who are robbed, but because of the falling-off in production that results from the higher interest on capital; and further, because the ease with which speculators are making money encourages people to spend rather than to save. It is readily apparent that with a grand world total of 850,000,000,000 in savings, these consequences materialize very slowly; and before they can modify the course of events very profoundly forces of more rapid effect may interpose, such as international competitions in the advantages accorded to savings, or the use of force to deprive speculators of their prey.

side the civil population stood the relatively small group of praetorians, for whom there was no evolution and who supported the
Empire by force and gave it its leader. Something of the same kind
may be seen today in the German Empire, though on a much
smaller scale. The persons in the categories mentioned have friends,
clients, and dependents of one sort or another, with whom they are
now in accord, now in disaccord, and who have to be taken into
account in estimating the social action of such persons. Conspicuous
from that standpoint in our day are the relations between employers
and employees, and between politicians and office-holders, and so
on (§ 2327).[1]

2321. Suppose now we enlarge the restricted cycle we elected to
consider in §§ 2221 f., where we decided to confine ourselves to interests, b, and class-circulation, d, and consider the influence of those
elements upon residues, a, and derivations, c. The influence on
derivations is readily detected, because it is displayed in literature
and in numberless other ways. Not so the influence on residues,
which has to be unravelled from those various manifestations. The
common error is to assume that it is much larger than it actually is.

2320 [1] The thing is notorious and has been described times without end; but
it must not be considered apart from other aspects of the present system of government. For a century or more past little else has been heard but complaints
about the increase in the numbers and in the power of bureaucracy, yet with ever
accelerated rapidity it continues to increase, and it is now invading countries, such
as England, where it used to be unknown. Evidently, therefore, forces of great
power are at work in that direction and are strong enough to overcome all
counter-forces. The fault lies partly in a habit the various political parties have of
condemning increase in the numbers and power of office-holders in general, but of
approving and promoting partial increases in such departments of public service as
serve certain political or personal ends of their own, reserving their condemnation
for departments where their interests are not involved. In any event, in one way
or another modern governments are irresistibly driven to increase the amounts
they spend on service, in order to win the support of the people who profit
thereby and of the backers of those people. Says Treves in *Avanti,* Mar. 29,
1915: "The Colonial budget for 1915-16 sets aside 7,577,900 lire for salaries. Bureaucratic elephantiasis finds its Elysium in the colonies. That explains many things,
among others, our 'democratic' tolerance of imperialism as the saviour-redeemer
of the poverty-stricken elements in the intellectual petty *bourgeoisie* that revolves in
the orbit of high finance. It is providing such people with a dignified means of
livelihood and keeping them from joining hands with the industrial proletariat."
Generalize these remarks, which Treves shapes to the interests of a party, and one
gets a description of the situation that is at present observable in almost all civilized
countries.

Not so long ago, one might easily have imagined that the cycle *bd-db* had modified residues, *a,* very extensively in the direction of eradicating from humanity all save rational and humanitarian sentiments; but then suddenly a great wave of nationalism supervenes, and, to a lesser but still conspicuous degree, imperialism and syndicalism came to the fore; while there are revivals in the old religions, in occultism, spiritualism, and metaphysical moods, the sex religion attains extremes in a ridiculous fanaticism, and belief in dogmas new and old asserts itself under many forms; all of which goes to show that the cycle in question had exerted far greater influence upon derivations than upon residues.

2322. Something very similar happened in ancient Rome in the days of Hadrian and Marcus Aurelius. At that time the curve of prevalence for intellectualism and rationalism reached its high point. It really seemed then as though the world were thenceforward to be governed by reason. But with the advent of Commodus the curve begins to decline, not so much, as many writers are still saying, because of that Emperor's "vices" as from a natural reaction, like many other reactions observable in history; and, meantime, in the lower strata of Roman society a bounteous harvest of faith was ripening, soon to be garnered by pagan philosophy, the worship of Mithras and other cults of the kind, and finally Christianity.

2323. That in no sense implies that there has been no influence of the cycle *bd-db* upon residues, *a,* but merely that whereas within the cycle itself violent rhythmical variations, periods of pronouncedly differing traits, are observable, residues, *a,* show much more tenuous effects.

2324. The cycle *bcd-dcb* . . . is an important one. That derivations, *c,* should adapt themselves to changed conditions in class-circulation, *d,* is readily understandable; and they reflect, though to a lesser degree, changes in economic conditions; and so far as that is the case they may be regarded as effects of those causes. As the ruling class is gradually enriched in elements showing a predominance of combination-instincts (Class I) and becomes more and more disinclined to a frank and open use of force, derivations adapt themselves to such concepts of life. Humanitarianism and pacifism rise and prosper. There is talk of a world to be ruled by reason and logic. Old traditions are regarded as outworn prejudices. One has only to glance at literature—Latin literature under the Antonines; European, and especially French literature, in the latter half of the eighteenth century, and then again in the latter half of the nineteenth—and the traits described become strikingly apparent.

2325. Observable, on occasion, is the parallel development of another literature chiefly designed to effect changes in the apportionment of profits between the governing class and its adjutants: in Rome, between patricians and plebeians, Senators and knights, in the matter of war-booty and tributes from the provinces; in our countries, in the apportionment between politicians and speculators, manufacturers and working-men, in the matter of proceeds from economic favouritism and the tributes levied upon possessors of fixed incomes, small stockholders, and producers of savings. The larger the total to be apportioned, the hotter the battle and the more copious the literature it inspires, a literature that serves to show the merits and deserts, or the crimes and perniciousness, of this class or that, according to the spontaneous or well-paid predilections of the writer. Not a few "intellectuals" and humanitarians, sincere of faith and poor of spirit, gape in open-mouthed astonishment at such portentous demonstrations, and dream of a world that will some day be ruled by them; while the speculators, well aware of their fatuousness, look on approvingly, certain as they are that while people are engrossed in them and dote on them, they can go leisurely on filling their pockets.

2326. Early in the nineteenth century, either because it was richer in Class II residues than now or because it had not yet been taught of experience, the governing class by no means considered such derivations innocuous, and much less to its advantage. It persecuted them, therefore, and tried to control them by law. Gradually in course of time it discovered that they in no way constituted obstacles to ruling-class profits, that sometimes, indeed oftentimes, they were a help. The scowl changed to a smile and the law no longer punishes them. In those days rich bankers were almost all conservatives. Nowadays they hobnob with revolutionaries, intellectuals, Socialists, and even Anarchists. The most virulent invectives against "capitalism" now get into print through the subsidies of "capitalists." Capitalists who have not the courage to go that far find some cosy corner at least among the Radicals.[1] An interesting example of that sort of thing would be the celebrated Mascuraud Committee in France. It is made up of wealthy members of the manufacturing and commercial classes, who advance to the very limit where Radicalism turns into Socialism. Similar things are observable under different names in Italy, England, Austria-Hungary, Germany. Were the thing not there before one's eyes, it would seem incredible that in every country the defenders of the proletariat are not proletarians themselves, but well-to-do and sometimes very wealthy people, as is the case with certain Socialist Deputies and literary men. To tell the bald truth, the proletarians have no enemies in any party. In books and newspapers, on the stage, in parliamentary debates, all the members of the well-to-do classes declare that their one interest is the welfare of the working-man. They differ only as to the means of achieving that ideal, and it is around the various proposals that political parties are formed. But can it really be that all rich or well-to-do members of our present-day *bourgeoisie* have grown so solicitous for the welfare of others, and so indifferent to their own? Who could ever believe that we are living in the company of so many saints and apostles of renunciation? May not a Tartuffe or two, con-

2326 [1] For certain special influences that attract numbers of persons who are not speculators into the Socialist or democratic parties, see Michels, *Zur Soziologie des Parteiwesens,* pp. 251-54 (Paul, pp. 263-66): "There are kindly charitable souls, provided in abundance with all they need, who sometimes feel an impulse to devote themselves to a propaganda bearing on their special situation. . . . Not a few individuals of no great brains, and with bank-accounts to be matched in size only by their love of paradox, have conceived the fantastic notion that in view of the imminence of the revolution, they can save their fortunes only by joining the labour party in advance and so winning the influential and helpful friendship of its leaders. [They are following with no direct profit a policy that the speculators follow to very great profit.] Still others among the rich think it their duty to join the Socialist party because they regard it as a refuge against the rage of the poor. Very often, again, the rich man is brought to embracing Socialism in sheer despair of finding any new enjoyments. . . . But there are other elements also among Socialists of *bourgeois* origin: in the front rank of the phalanx, those who are malcontents out of principle; then even more numerous individuals who have personal reasons for discontent. . . . Many of them, consciously or unconsciously, hate the authority of the state because they have never been able to reach power. . . . Then there are persons more or less closely approximating the types mentioned . . . eccentrics, for instance. . . . There are people who stand at the top of the social ladder but feel irresistibly impelled to go down. . . . Then come the disappointed and the despondent."

scious or unconscious, be lurking somewhere among them? When certain men of means, such as M. Caillaux, go to such pains in fighting for the progressive income-tax, are they really and solely inspired by eagerness to give of their wealth unto others, and not in the least by the opposite thought, of bringing the wealth of others unto themselves? All things are possible, but some things seem hardly probable. Appearances may be one thing, realities quite another. When rich people pay good money to lecturers to preach to them that they should divest themselves of their goods, they might seem to be out of their heads; but they show that they are in full possession of them as they proceed to fill their pockets while others chatter. Speculators would seem to be mad in advocating and actually establishing the progressive income-tax; but their wisdom becomes apparent when, as the result of that gesture, they are enabled to work manipulations that net them much more than the tax takes away.[2]

2327. Manufacturers too once believed that every increase in wages meant a decrease in profits; but experience has now shown them their mistake, that they can increase both wages and profits at the same time, the increase coming out of the pockets of small stockholders and producers of savings, and people living on fixed incomes. The discovery was first made by manufacturers benefiting from protective tariffs. They would naturally have preferred to keep all the profits; but in time they came to see that it was to their advantage to share them with their help, and that even after deducting the working-man's share and the compensation due the politician for sending the rain of protectionist manna, a very handsome profit was still left. That is why it is much easier to settle strikes nowadays than it used to be, especially in protected industries, or industries that sell their products to the state. In fact, managers of such industries have learned how to take advantage of strikes and

2326 [2] See Pareto, *"Rentiers et spéculateurs," Indépendance,* May 1, 1911: "The 'Progressives' in France are opposed to the progressive income-tax because they know that the proceeds from it will not go to them. The 'Liberals' of Milan are in favour of it because they are in power and will spend the proceeds, the money going to them and their henchmen. The general staff of the Milanese Liberals is largely made up of speculators. The French 'Radicals' depend largely on the votes of *rentiers.* In those circumstances therefore it is only natural that the 'Liberals' should be favourable and the 'Radicals' opposed to the progressive income-tax. Under other conditions, in the case of a state or poll tax, for instance, their respective attitudes might be different."

turn them into profits (§ 2187 [1]). The man of brains can always find ways for turning apparent damage to account.

2328. The intelligence and ingenuity of the speculator transpires also in international politics. Preparations for war are profitable to speculators because of the economic activity required for the manufacture of armaments, and because they can utilize the sentiments of nationalism in their political battles. But war itself involves grave dangers to their dominion, because on the battle-field the man of courage is of more account than the man of subtle wiles, and they always pale at the thought that some victorious general may strip them of their power. So, with the assistance of their good friends the "intellectuals," they try in every way to persuade the civilized peoples that the reign of force is at last at an end, that great wars have become impossible through the deadliness of modern instruments of destruction, that it is sufficient if huge sums are spent on armaments in preparation for wars, though the wars will never occur. But when it comes to appropriations, they meet the competition of other devourers of the public budget, who want money for "social reforms" or other such purposes, and they have to come to terms with them. In their newspapers, as best fits their shrewd combinations, the financial syndicates are one day preaching peace and concord, exalting the miracles of international law and the blessings of "peace through law," and the next day they are instigating international discords and preaching defence of a nation's "vital interests," its special "rights," its "civilization." But the masses of people at large more or less second such manoeuvres, and that fact supplies an interesting example of derivations and of the way in which identical sentiments may be directed towards different goals. But not always are those who provoke a tempest able to quell it at their pleasure, and the speculator is always in danger of overreaching himself in trouble-making and bringing on the war he so greatly abhors. Today cunning is in the saddle, but that does not mean that force will not be in the saddle tomorrow, be it only for a brief ride.[1]

2328 [1] One might at this point recall what we said in § 2254, namely, that "speculators" must not be thought of as a single person performing logical actions with a pre-established purpose in view (§ 2542). What happens happens as a result of the system rather than of any deliberate intent. The Balkan War of 1912 was not wanted by the majority of European financiers, yet their policies made it inevitable. They sapped the strength of Turkey, so that that country became ready prey for any nation disposed to attack it. First among such financiers at that time were the

2329. *Oscillations in derivations in correspondence with social oscillations.* The phenomenon is of great importance. As a manifestation of ideas and doctrines, it appears in conflicts between various sentimental, theological, and metaphysical derivations, and between such derivations and the methods of the logico-experimental sciences. To write their history would be to write the history of human thought. As a manifestation of the forces that are operative in a society, it appears in conflicts between the sentiments corresponding to various residues, chiefly Class I and Class II residues, and therefore also in conflicts between logical and non-logical conduct. It is a very general thing, therefore, and under one form or another dominates the whole history of human societies. No wonder then that we should have frequently encountered it along our inductive path. Specially interesting are the two following cases. In the first place, considering doctrines transcending experience, we found ourselves confronted with the question as to how it comes about that experience works so differently in sentimental, theological, and metaphysical derivations and in scientific reasonings (§§ 616 f.); and we had to give some hint as to the answer, though deferring the more thorough-going examination to our present chapter. Then, later on, in considering derivations we had to ask ourselves how and why certain derivations, so patently false, fatuous, absurd, from the experimental standpoint, nevertheless persisted and recurred for century after century (§§ 1678 f.). That fact implied a very serious objection to our characterization of such derivations in such terms; for one could properly wonder how in the world people could have failed to perceive for that length of time that they were false, fatuous, absurd. At that time we could neither disregard that question altogether and proceed without an answer, nor yet could we completely answer it, for lack of knowledge that we could not acquire till later on. We therefore had to rest content with merely

Italian bankers who instigated the Libyan War, and so prepared directly for the Balkan Wars, the ground for which had been indirectly prepared by European financiers and speculators at large. Thereupon they proceeded and are at present [1913] still proceeding to the economic partitioning of Asiatic Turkey, and in that—indirectly and unintentionally, it may be—they are preparing the ground for a new war that will have to be fought to transform the economic apportionment into a political apportionment. Such a war may not come; but if it does, the responsibility for it will rest with the speculators, even though at the time of its outbreak a few or many of them will be against it.

broaching an inquiry that we are now to complete. Meantime, as we went on, we found the problem widening in scope (§§ 1678 f.), and it stands before us now in the form of a mutual correlation between an undulatory movement in residues and an undulatory movement in derivations, and between both those movements and other social phenomena, among which, very especially, the economic. Considering long periods of time, the relative proportions of Class I and Class II residues may vary very perceptibly, especially as regards the intellectual classes in society; and in such cases very significant situations arise in connexion with derivations.

2330. Even when stated in such terms, which are very broad, the problem is just a particular aspect of a more general problem—the problem of undulations in the various elements constituting social phenomena and of the mutual relations of those elements and their undulations.[1] In all periods of history, one may say, people have had some conception of a rhythmical, periodic, oscillatory, undulating movement in natural phenomena, social phenomena included. The notion is probably correlated with residues of group-persistence (Class II) arising from observation of the periodic alternation of night and day, the seasons, the phases of the Moon, and later on, in a day of astronomical observation, the movements of the celestial bodies. In other departments of life the attention is caught by periodic alternations of good crops and bad crops, abundance and famine, prosperity and depression.[2] Uninterrupted is the succession in

---

2330 [1] Pareto, Cours, § 925: "The molecules that, taken in the aggregate, make up the social body are in perpetual oscillation. We can, for the purposes of a given analysis, consider certain average economic situations, just as we may consider a mean level of ocean tides. But those are mere conceptions that in no case have any real existence."

2330 [2] Numberless such notions can be documented, all the way along from the dream of Pharaoh (Gen. Chapter 41), who saw seven fat cattle and seven lean ones, seven fat ears of corn and seven withered ones, down to the Jevons theory of a correlation between economic crises in the West and periods of crop-failure in India. Pharaoh saw the lean cattle and the lean ears eat the fat ones, not the reverse. So in our time many economists restrict the term "crisis" to the descending segment in an economic wave, and seem not to be aware that the ascending period leads to the descending period, and vice versa. [The allusion above is to W. S. Jevons, Investigations in Currency and Finance, pp. 217-18. Jevons's son, Herbert Stanley Jevons, The Sun's Heat and Trade Activity, pp. 15-31, correlated barometric pressures in Córdoba, Argentina, and Bombay, India, with harvests in the United States.—A. L.]

individuals, new ones replacing those who die, and one age succeeding another—childhood, manhood, senility. The notion of such
a succession suggests itself as regards families, cities, peoples, nations, all humanity, as tradition or history comes to embrace a certain expanse of time and the curiosity of the intelligent turns to
such matters. Then again the spectacle of terrestrial cataclysms
prompts, under the influence of persisting abstractions (residue II-δ),
to a more or less deliberate application of the principle of rhythmic
movement to the universe as a whole. In all these different cases,
finally, the requirement of logical elaboration (residue I-ε) and residues of persisting uniformities (II-ε), lead to the fabrication of doctrines that come into thriving vogue with metaphysical and pseudo-
experimental appendages.

What probably happens is that writers reasoning *a priori* or dog-
matically, as well as metaphysicists in great majority, instinctively
extend to the whole universe impressions they have received from
this or that body of fact, and so come to assert that everything is
subject to a rhythmical movement. There are writers, however, who
reach the same conclusion by hasty generalizations that far overstep
the facts, which for that matter they distort.[3]

2330 [3] The doctrine that the universe has undergone a series of creations and destructions seems to have been held by Anaximander, Anaximenes and Heraclitus
(*Fragmenta,* 20), though the fragments of those writers that survive have been
variously interpreted. One of them was fairly obscure even to Cicero, who remarks,
De natura deorum, III, 14, 35, that since Heraclitus has not seen fit to make himself
clear, what he says may be disregarded. After all, such matters of interpretation are
without bearing on investigations such as we are making here. We may stop at the
fact that certain ancients had the idea in question and of that there can be no doubt
in view of Aristotle, *De coelo,* I, 10, 2 (Hardie-Gaye, Vol. II, p. 279b); *Physica,*
VIII, 1, 1 (Hardie-Gaye, p. 250b) and Diogenes Laertius, *Heraclitus,* IX, 8 (Hicks,
Vol. II, p. 415). Diogenes ascribes to Heraclitus the declaration that "the world is
one, being born of fire and consumed anew in certain periods alternating from age
to age, as Destiny determines." And cf. Eusebius, *Evangelica praeparatio,* XIII, 13
(*Opera,* Vol. III, pp. 1117-18). The Stoics had a similar doctrine, whether or not
derived from earlier philosophers: Eusebius, *Ibid.,* XV, 18 (*Opera,* Vol. III, pp.
1347-48); and Cicero, *Ibid.,* II, 46, 118. So we get one of the extremes mentioned.
The other is represented by Herbert Spencer. In the second part of his *First Principles* he devotes a whole chapter to "The Rhythm of Motion." Giving a number of
examples of such rhythms, he does not halt, as experimental science would require, at the conclusion that rhythm is a fairly general phenomenon, but yielding
to his metaphysical hunger for the absolute, he concludes, p. 291: "Thus, then,
rhythm is a necessary characteristic of all motion. Given the co-existence everywhere of antagonist forces—a postulate which, as we have seen, is necessitated by

Returns are noted, for the most part, in connexion not with phenomena that are sharply defined and characterized, but with abstractions that are more or less vague, so that, with resort on occasion to the doctrine of exceptions (§ 1689 [3]), the theory can be made to fit all circumstances and never fail of verification. Even in our day, in regard to phenomena with easily measurable indices, Jevons came out with his theory of "economic crises," leaving the term "crisis" inadequately defined. On the other hand, there is often a demand for a definiteness that can only give illusory results, as, for instance, the effort to determine exactly, or on the average, the period of time that will elapse between one return and the next; all of which is in deference to the instinct that prompts many people to give concrete forms to their abstractions (residue II-ζ).

At times no limit is set to the oscillation; but then again, and more often, yielding to the instinct that prompts the human being to seek his own welfare and the welfare of his fellows, there is a more or less explicit conception of a limit, and generally it is a state of happiness. Only some rare pessimist locates the end in a state of unhappiness, or in complete annihilation.

With all deference to fanatics of the "historical method" and partisans of "complete bibliographies," a study at all extended of such theories would be of not the slightest practical use as regards any understanding of the phenomena presumably pictured by them. The effort required for such an investigation could much more profitably be devoted to objective study of the phenomena themselves or, if one prefer, of the direct testimony bearing upon them (§§ 95, 1689), along with a search for measurable indices for the phenomena and for a classification of fluctuations in order of intensity, with the object, if possible, of determining what the major oscillations are, and of discovering a few of the very numerous correlations prevailing between oscillations in different phenomena (§§ 1718, 1731, 2293). Study of the theories may, indeed, throw light on the derivations of which they are made up; and that again must always be an objective study, save that the subject-matter is not the phenomena pictured by the theories, but the statements of them, their litera-

the form of our experience—and rhythm is an inevitable corollary from the persistence of force."

ture. We have already given so many examples of such derivations that we need touch on them but very briefly here.

Plato had the vision of a perfect city, and at the same time he could not help seeing that the actual cities he knew about were not organized on his model. On the other hand, he was preaching in order to translate into reality the city of his dreams. He therefore had to admit the possibility of its existence, merely carrying it outside the present world, either backward to the past or forward to the future, or both together. So his ideal city became either an origin or a goal, or else the origin or goal of a certain evolution, which, as a result of the metaphysicist's fondness for generalization, is represented as a universal evolution.[4] Plato, of course, knowing everything, also knows the length of time each cycle will require: "As regards divine generations, the revolution is comprised in a perfect number." As regards mortal generations—human beings—Plato's specifications are so vague that none of his modern commentators have ever been able to make head or tail of them. The ancients were more fortunate, but they were not considerate enough to share their light with us, so that we are left in the dark as to just what the number was. That is a great loss indeed, though it is partly offset by the fact that other writers have given us other numbers of the same sort and surely just as probable.[5]

2330 [4] *Respublica,* VIII, 546A: "It is difficult for the city [his ideal city] so constituted to change. But since all things that are born decay, that constitution cannot abide forever: it will dissolve; and the dissolution will occur in the following manner. Not only the plants that are born of the earth, but the souls and bodies of animals that inhabit the earth, have periods of fertility and sterility, as the revolutions of each cycle are completed. Such periods are brief for short-lived species, long for long-lived species." A few lines farther on comes the sentence quoted above in the text.

2330 [5] Aristotle, *Politica,* V, 10, 1-2 (Rackham, pp. 477-79), quotes Plato's sentence and seems to have grasped its meaning. He criticizes Plato for having all things change simultaneously, even though they do not originate simultaneously. That, however, is a purely formal criticism that can readily be raised against all theories of that kind by setting up the continuous variations that are actual against the discontinuous variations which the authors of such theories envisage in order to facilitate the exposition of their doctrines. One must bear that fact in mind, and not take the exposition literally. Paulhan, *Le nouveau mysticisme,* pp. 51-52: "This latter spirit will none the less be a combination of the last beliefs prevailing and of old beliefs more or less exploded but still holding their own: it is this synthesis that gives the new spirit its newness. . . . The old state of mind does not recur; there is never any complete return to an anterior state in the intellectual life of societies,

In his *Politics,* at least, Aristotle uses less metaphysics than Plato and comes a little closer to the experimental method. He criticizes Plato's theory, though one has to admit that his strictures bear rather on forms than on substance, and are not always well taken. Of all the ancient historians Polybius comes closest to experimental reality in his investigations. He is a worthy predecessor of Machiavelli. At first blush one is astounded at seeing him (VI, Fragment III, 5), taking over Plato's theory to the extent of transcribing it as an explanation of the transformations occurring in the government of the ancient city. It may well be, however, that he thought he was recording experimental facts, his error lying chiefly in a hasty generalization that led him astray from the real world. When he comes to a comparison of various republics he discards Plato's as a fiction of the imagination.[6] In a treatise on *Generation and Corruption* that is attributed to Aristotle, one notes the concept of a continuous transformation, and it is further stated, in clarification of the notion, that the transformation has to occur in a circle (II, 11, 7). That amounts to generalizing the theory of Plato.

Many writers have worked on that common background (it has its experimental element) of unbroken oscillations. Vico's theory of "recursals" (*ricorsi*), primarily metaphysical in character, oversteps

any more than there is in their political life. The second childhood of the aged is not the childhood they knew as children. The Restoration was not the same as the Old Régime. While a reaction against the achievement of the Revolution was in progress, that achievement was to a great extent being consolidated, deriving new vigour from the older ideas with which it was associated." Such reflections imply abandonment of the notion of cyclical revolutions with discontinuous periods, and tend towards the conception of a wave-movement with continuous variations that experience actually reveals in certain phenomena. Ferrari, *Teoria dei periodi politici,* pp. 15-16: Ferrari does not fail to appreciate the difficulty "of separating one generation from the one before it"; but he thinks he can solve the problem by considering changes in government, and is carried to the consequence "that generations are renewed with governments every thirty years. Every thirty years a new plot unfolds, every thirty years a new drama appears with new characters, every thirty years there is a new *dénouement*." Such statements far overstep the results yielded by experience.

2330 [6] Farther along, Fragment VII, 57, he explains changes in republics by noting that "all existing things are subject to corruption and change." That conception, however, he need not necessarily have derived from Plato, for it is a universal notion and translates the impression that is left on all human beings by the changes that go on in the world we live in.

the limits of reality almost as far as Plato's theory.[7] For that matter, he confesses that his work reaches the same conclusions as Plato's. Vico still has admirers today, and probably will continue to have so long as the great stream of metaphysics that has come down across

2330 [7] At the beginning of Book IV in his *Scienza nuova*, Vico summarizes the matter he has expounded in his preceding chapters on the subject of "ideal eternal history" (which would be another variety of history to be added to the long list from which we gave specimens some distance back (§§ 2156-69, 1580)). Says he, p. 785 (stresses on words Vico's own): "*Soggiugniamo il corso che fanno le nazioni, con costante uniformità procedendo in tutti i loro tanto vari e sì diversi costumi sopra la divisione delle tre età, che dicevano gli Egizi essere scorse innanzi nel loro mondo, degli dèi, degli eroi e degli uomini, perchè sopra di esse si vedranno reggere con costante e non mai interrotto ordine di cagioni e d'effetti, sempre andante nelle nazioni per tre spezie di nature; e da esse nature uscite tre spezie di costumi; e da essi costumi osservate tre spezie di diritti naturali delle genti; e, in conseguenza di essi diritti, ordinate tre spezie di Stati civili o sia di repubbliche; e, per comunicare tra loro gli uomini venuti all'umana società tutte queste già dette tre spezie di cose massime, essersi formate tre spezie di lingue ed altrettante di caratteri; e, per giustificarle, tre spezie di giurisprudenze, assistite da tre spezie d'autorità e da altrettante di ragioni, in altrettante spezie di giudizi, le quali giurisprudenza si celebrarono per tre sètte de' tempi, che professano in tutto il corso della lor vita le nazioni. Le quali tre speziali unità, con altre molte che loro vanno di séguito e saranno in questo libro pur noverate, tutte mettono capo in una unità generale, ch'è l'unità della religione d'una divinità provvedente, la qual è l'unità dello spirito, che informa e dà vita a questo mondo di nazioni. Le quali cose sopra sparsamente essendosi ragionate, qui si dimostra l'ordine del lor corso.*" [This passage from Vico arouses Pareto's mirth because of its aggressive obscurity. Boven, *Traité*, Vol. II, p. 1547, virtually throws up the sponge. He transfers the passage verbally into a senseless French and then reprints Michelet's paraphrase, which is equally inaccurate. Put off the track in the first place by a misprint (*"essa"* for *"esse"*), Boven does note that Vico might have done better had he written *"franchement en Latin."* His style in fact evinces an extreme classicism, so that certain words have to be translated as though they were Latin. Taking the problems in order: *"esse"* refers to *"età,"* not to *"divisione"* as Boven guessed. *"Andante"* goes with *"ordine."* *"Uscite,"* *"osservate,"* and *"ordinate"* with their nouns are predicates of *"si vedranno."* *"Si celebrarono"* is used in the Latin sense of "practise." *"Uomini"* is the subject of *"comunicare"* and *"spezie di cose massime"* the object. *"Spezie di lingue"* similarly is the subject of *"essersi formate,"* which again depends on *"si vedranno."* *"Sètte dei tempi"* stands for *sectas temporum* and is coordinate in meaning as well as in grammar with *"spezie."* *"Professano"* is *profiteuntur*, in the sense of "declare," therefore "show," "manifest," "exemplify."—A. L.] "Then there is the course that the nations traverse, following in a constant uniformity in all their varied and multifarious traits the three distinct ages that the Egyptians said had elapsed before their time in their world, to wit, the ages of the gods, of heroes, and of men. For they will be seen to conform to those three ages in a continuous and never interrupted progression (*ordine*) of causes and effects that is for ever developing (*andante*) in the nations according to three species of temperaments

the ages flows on in its course. The "theory of political periods" of
Giuseppe Ferrari might seem to be taking us into the experimental
field, but unfortunately that appearance is deceptive.[8] Ferrari treats
facts somewhat arbitrarily, often attaching to them a significance

(*nature*); whereof [will be seen to] proceed three species of morals (*costumi*)
observing three species of natural laws of nations that are the foundations of three
species of civil governments or commonwealths. And that on attaining civilized
society men might communicate to each other all the three species of supreme
things aforesaid, three species of languages were formed and as many alphabets,
and to justify them [*i.e.,* those same supremacies] three species of jurisprudences,
supported by three species of authority and three species of reason in three species
of judgment; which jurisprudences were practised in the three manners of the
[three] ages, respectively, which the races and nations of men exemplify in the
whole course of their lives. And these three special unities [*i.e.,* of the three ages],
with many others that follow from them and which will likewise be enumerated
in this book, all lead to the general unity, which is the unity of the religion of one
provident [*i.e.,* foreseeing] divinity, which is the unity of the spirit that gives form
and life to this world of nations. These things having been but incidentally touched
upon heretofore, the order of their development will here be set forth."

We might glance in passing at the three sorts of morals (customs), p. 789:

2330 [8] *Teoria dei periodi politici,* pp. 7-11, 75, 105-13, 134, 150, 175: "In our view
the generation will be the fundamental element in every return. Like the sunrise it
is always the same and continually repeats the same drama, in all periods of history,
in all civilizations. . . . The average length of the individual life is not the average
length of the political generation. . . . The average life of the political generation
is to be calculated by taking men at the moment of their real birth, when they take
charge of their families, their governments, their armies. . . . Then their intellectual
life begins and its lasts thirty years, more or less. . . . The age of birth varies. Some
men reveal themselves between twenty and twenty-five, and they are poets, painters,
sculptors, masters of music. Others arrive at a later age, such as philosophers, jurists,
historians, who require at least thirty years to conceive their plans, execute their
many researches, apply their ideas, rectify inevitable mistakes, in a word catch the
ear of the generation that is to applaud them. . . . [Exceptional individuals have
two lives:] That is the case with Voltaire, who remained in the public eye from
1718, the year of the production of his *Oedipe,* down to 1778, the year of his death.
But he led two lives that cannot be confused." Some generations are prolonged,
others are shortened. Some are as short as nineteen years. There are preparatory,
revolutionary generations and reactionary, conclusive generations. Political periods
evolve in four times (generations): "Every new principle uses four generations,
which it dominates in such a way as to make one single dramatic episode. And
since principles are succeeded by principles, generations follow one another in
groups of four at average intervals of 125 years. It took Christianity 115 years to become established: from the advent of Diocletian, who degraded Rome, to the death
of Theodosius, which marks the fall for ever of the pagan world. France allows
four times (generations) for religious reform, from 1514 to 1620; four for the mod-
ernization of the aristocracy, from 1620 to 1750; four for the Revolution proper,
which is drawing to its close in our day."

they do not have. His main defect, which other writers under similar circumstances share, lies in his trying to force facts under inflexible rules that have an exactness which is altogether illusory. He would give rigid and immutable form to oscillations, which are

"Primitive customs, as described to us in Deucalion and Pyhrra, who came just after the Flood, were all suffused with religion and pity. The second, as exemplified in Achilles, were choleric and susceptible, the third, 'officious,' inspired by a high sense of civic duty." As for the meaning of "officious," Vico explains, p. 858, in connexion with his three periods of time: "Latin writers under the Emperors call the duty of a subject the *officium civile.*" The three kinds of alphabet are, pp. 799-802: (1) Divine characters, called hieroglyphics, which all nations used in the beginning; (2) heroic characters; (3) common characters, which go with the various vernaculars. We shall spare the reader any further divagations of this sort; but it would be a pity to make no mention of Vico's strong faith in the story of the Flood and in giants. For the giants he has experimental proof (p. 208)—the weapons of enormous length belonging to ancient heroes that Augustus, if one is to believe Suetonius, kept in his museum, along with bones and skulls of giants of old. The fact, however, is that Suetonius, *Divus Augustus, 72,* says something quite different. Alluding to the villas of Augustus, he writes: "His own villa, though small, he decorated with statues and paintings, with porticos and groves, with antiques and curios, such as bones of sea-monsters and wild animals exceptional for size, which are popularly called (*quae dicuntur*) 'giants' bones', and weapons of famous soldiers" [*arma heroum,* being that is, co-ordinate with *membra,* not the predicate of *quae dicuntur,* as Vico read it.—A. L.]. Interesting as regards derivations is Vico's use of the number 3 with the mystical properties so dear to metaphysicists and theologians.

In Book V Vico treats "of the recursal in human affairs through the renaissance of nations." Epitomizing, p. 958, the substance of the earlier books, which were devoted "to illumining with clearer light the era of the second barbarism (which had been even darker than the era of the first barbarism, which itself had been called dark by that great scholar of early antiquities, Marcus Terentius Varro, in his division of eras); and also to showing how God Greatest and Best [*Ottimo Grandissimo Dio, Jupiter Optimus Maximus*] had applied the designs of this Providence, with which He has guided the nations in all things, to the realization of the ineffable decrees of His grace . . . forasmuch as, having in superhuman ways declared and established the truth of the Christian religion against Roman power by the miracles of the martyrs and against the false wisdom of the Greeks through the teachings of the Fathers, there still being destined to arise armed nations that were everywhere to combat the true divinity of their Maker, He permitted a new order of humanity to be born among the nations to the end that it might be firmly established according to the natural course of human affairs themselves. With that eternal design He brought back times truly divine, during which everywhere, in order to defend the Christian religion of which they are protectors, the Catholic kings donned the dalmatic of the deacons and consecrated their royal persons." Finally Vico gets to a conclusion, p. 1036: "So then let us conclude this work with Plato, who makes a fourth sort of commonwealth wherein the supreme rulers are honest upright men, the which would be the true natural aristocracy. Such a commonwealth as Plato conceived Providence hath so ordained from the first be-

essentially variable, essentially protean. Under lure of that illusion, he imagines phenomena that have nothing to do with realities, such as "thinking generations," lasting on the average about thirty years, and "political periods," made up of four "thinking generations" and lasting about a hundred and twenty-five years. Metaphysicists as a rule are contemptuous of facts (§ 821): Ferrari at least pays homage to them by trying to make them fit into the plan he has drawn. For that purpose he falls back, as many writers do, upon the great resource of exceptions (§ 1689[3]). Certain individuals, such as Voltaire, Goethe, Aristophanes, Sophocles, Rossini, and others, he endows with two "thinking lives." He admits delays and accelerations in "thinking generations" and in "political periods." In the different nations he finds certain "translations" of the periods, notes their "comparative velocity," in a word, himself partially demolishes the foundations of his own theory. All the same, as compared with metaphysicists generally he has the great merit of expressing himself clearly; and in a mass of details of misleading exactness and arbitrarily organized, one notes remarks which, like Draper's theories (§ 2341[1]), come very close to experimental realities. The cases of Ferrari and Draper are like a great many others we have seen (§§ 252-53, 2214): They catch a vision of the facts through a fog of metaphysics and pseudo-experience.

2331. Slight oscillations do not ordinarily appear in correlation; they are fleeting manifestations in which it is difficult, nay impossible, to discover uniformities. Correlations in wide oscillations are more easily discernible: they are manifestations of long duration in which now and again we succeed in recognizing a law (uniformity), either for some given phenomenon considered apart from others or for given phenomena as correlated with others. Such uniformities have long been perceived, though more often indistinctly and stated in no very adequate terms. When, for instance, corre-

ginnings of Nations." The metaphysicist thinks he has also demolished all doctrines different from his own, p. 1049: "So therefore we have refuted Epicurus, who believes in chance, and his followers Obbes [Hobbes] and Machiavello. And confirmed on the contrary are those political philosophers, prince among them the divine Plato, who prove that Providence rules human affairs." Such ramblings soar so far far above the clouds that facts have become altogether invisible. They have nothing to do with the humble realities of Earth, or with any experimental fact such as the undulatory forms assumed by certain phenomena.

spondences are noted between the wealth of a country and its manners and customs, one is dealing with uniformities in interdependent oscillations; but ordinarily the temptation is to overstep experience and go wandering off into ethical reflections.

A number of errors are commonly to be noted in studies of such uniformities. They fall into two classes: *A*. Errors arising from failure to take due account of the undulatory form that phenomena assume. *B*. Errors in interpreting that undulatory form.

2332. *A*-1. The waves in a curve represent periods of intensification and decline in phenomena. They may be described as ascending or descending. If they are at all protracted, people living in them readily get the impression that a movement is to continue indefinitely in the direction observable in their time, or is at least to terminate in some stationary condition without subsequent countermovements (§§ 2392, 2319).

2333. *A*-2. That error is attenuated but not corrected when it is indeed assumed that there is a mean line about which the movement is oscillating, but it is also assumed that that mean line coincides with the line of one of the ascending phases of the movement. Never, or almost never, is it made to coincide with the line of a descending period.[1]

2334. *B*-1. It is known that, in the past, the movement has shown oscillations, but it is taken for granted that the normal movement is a movement favourable to society in the direction of a uniformly increasing good. At the most, someone will concede that it is no more than holding its own but shows no decline. The case of a downward movement uniformly unfavourable is for the most part barred. Oscillations that cannot be disputed are regarded as abnormal, secondary, accidental—each has a "cause" that *might* be (§ 134) or *ought* to be remedied, whereupon the oscillation itself would disappear. Derivations in this general form are not common; but they are very common under the form next following (*B*-2), and it is not difficult to see why; the human being has a propensity to seek his advantage and to shrink from anything that is to his harm.

2335. *B*-2. It is assumed that oscillations can be separated, keeping the favourable and eliminating the unfavourable by removing

2333 [1] We shall consider a particular case of these errors farther along (§§ 2391 f.).

the "cause." Almost all historians accept that theorem, at least implicitly, and go to great pains to explain just what this or that nation should have done to keep for ever in a favourable period without ever slipping into unfavourable periods. Not a few economists even know and are kind enough to inform the world how "crises" might be averted, the term "crisis" designating nothing but the descending period in an oscillation.[1] All such derivations are commonly used in discussions of social prosperity (§§ 2540 f.). They are favourites with a great many writers who naïvely imagine that they are doing scientific work when they are really preaching moral, humanitarian, or patriotic sermons.

2336. B-3. Merely as a reminder—for we have only too often had occasion to allude to it—let us note the error of mistaking relationships of interdependence for relationships of cause and effect. In the case here in point the assumption is that the oscillations in a given phenomenon have causes of their own independent of oscillations in other phenomena.

2337. B-4. Disregarding correlations, actually, but still resolved to find some "cause" for oscillations in a given phenomenon, a writer will seek a cause in theology, in metaphysics, or in vagaries that are experimental in appearance only. The Hebrew prophets found the cause of descending periods in the prosperity of Israel in the wrath of God. The Romans were convinced that every evil that befell their city was caused by some violation of rites in the worship of the gods. To recover prosperity one had only to discover what the violation had been and make suitable amends. Many many historians, even modern historians, seek and find similar causes, now in "corruption of morals," now in the *auri sacra fames,* now in violations of the precepts of morality, law, or brotherly love, now in the sins of an oligarchy that is oppressing a people, now in capitalism, in too great inequalities in wealth, and so on and on. Of such derivations there is an assortment varied enough to please all tastes.[1]

2335 [1] Pareto, *Cours,* § 926: "The term 'crisis' is most often kept for the descending phase of the oscillation, when prices are falling. In reality that phase is closely bound up with the ascending phase, when prices are rising. The one cannot subsist apart from the other and the term 'crisis' should be kept for their sum."

2337 [1] Pareto, *Manuale,* Chap. IX, § 82: "Causes of crises have been seen in each and every circumstance connected with them. In the ascending period, when every-

2338. In reality oscillations in the various elements that go to make up the social phenomenon are interdependent, as are those elements themselves. They are mere manifestations of changes in the elements. If one is bent on using at all costs the misleading term "cause," one may say that the descending period is the cause of the ascending period following, and *vice versa;* but only in the sense that the ascending period is invariably associated with the preceding descending period, and *vice versa*—that, therefore, speaking in general terms, the various periods are just manifestations of a single state of things, that observation shows them as succeeding one another, so that the succession is an experimental uniformity.[1] The oscillations are of various kinds depending on the length of time required for their completion. The time may be brief, very brief, long, very long. Very brief oscillations are ordinarily accidental, in the sense that they reflect the action of momentary, ephemeral forces (§ 2331); those which evolve in fairly extensive periods of time reflect forces of some duration. Owing to our scant information as to very remote eras in history and our inability to foresee the future, very long oscillations may not look like oscillations at all, but seem to be permanent trends in a given direction (§ 2392).

2339. Returning now to the particular problem we set ourselves

thing is prospering, consumption increases and business men increase production. To do that savings are transformed into frozen and liquid capital, credit expands, and circulation becomes more rapid. Now every one of those various steps has been taken as the exclusive cause of the descending period, to which the term "crisis" has been applied. The only truth in that is that those phenomena have indeed figured in the ascending period that always precedes the descending period. . . . It is fantastic to speak of a permanent excess of production. If any such thing existed there would have to be somewhere constantly increasing deposits of excess merchandise. But no such thing has ever been heard of."

2338 [1] Pareto, *Cours,* § 926: "A crisis must not be thought of as an accident interrupting a normal state of things. The normal thing is the wave-movement, economic prosperity bringing on depression, depression bringing on prosperity. In regarding economic crises as abnormal phenomena, the economist is making the mistake a physicist would be making in thinking of the nodes and internodes of a rod in vibration as accidents independent of the movements of the molecules in the rod." And Pareto, *Manuale,* Chap. IX, § 75: "The 'crisis' is just a particular case of the great law of rhythm that prevails in all social phenomena (Pareto, *Systèmes socialistes,* Vol. I, p. 30). The social system shapes the crisis; it does not affect its substance, which depends upon the nature of the human being and of economic problems in general. Crises occur not only in private industry and commerce, but in public enterprise and finance."

in § 2329, as to the interdependence of waves: It is clear that in order to solve it we have to take account of the forces that are working upon the various elements in the social phenomenon, the interdependences between which we are trying to determine. It will help if we divide such forces into two groups: 1. Forces arising in the conflict between theory and reality, in the more or less perfect adjustment of theories to realities. They manifest themselves in differences that arise between sentiments and the results of experience. That aspect of the problem we may call *intrinsic*. 2. Forces tending to modify sentiments and arising in the relationships in which such sentiments stand towards other facts, such as economic and political conditions, class-circulation, and so on. That we may call the *extrinsic* aspect of the problem.

2340. 1. Intrinsic aspect.[1] At times, for individuals in whom Class II residues (group-persistence; the thing A in § 616) have declined in vigour while the combination-instincts (Class I residues) have intensified (while experimental science has gained in prestige, we said back there, in § 616), conclusions deriving from Class II residues (group-persistence) come to seem more strikingly at odds with realities, and that circumstance gives rise to a feeling that such residues are "outworn prejudices" that had better be replaced with combination-residues (§ 1679). So, non-logical actions are mercilessly condemned from the standpoint of experimental truth and individual or social utility, and the idea is to replace them with logical actions, which are professedly dictated by experimental science, but in reality are based on pseudo-science and are made up of derivations of little or no validity. The situation is usually stated in terms of the following derivations, or others of the kind: "Faith and prejudice must give way to reason." It is held that the sentiment expressed in that derivation "demonstrates" the "falsity" of the group-persistence residues, the "truth" of the combination-residues. At other times, when an inverse trend is in progress and residues of group-persistence are acquiring new strength while the combination-residues are losing ground, contrary phenomena are observable (§ 1680). The residues of group-persistence that have weakened may

2340 [1] We began this investigation above in §§ 616 f., where it came up in the course of our induction. We touched on it again in §§ 1678 f. [in a general consideration of theories]. We are now concluding it here.

be beneficial, indifferent, or detrimental to society. In the first case, the derivations of the combination-instinct, on the basis of which the Class II residues are rejected, show themselves entirely at odds with practice, as tending to give the society forms unsuitable to it and which might even encompass its destruction. That is felt instinctively rather than demonstrated by thought; so a trend begins in a sense counter to the trend that had given predominance to Class I residues: the pendulum starts swinging in the opposite direction, and an opposite extreme is reached. Conclusions drawn from Class I residues being sometimes at odds with reality, they are said always to be—they are held, in other words, to be "false"; and that condemnation is carried on to the principles of experimental reasoning themselves, principles of group-persistence alone being regarded as "true," or at least as possessing a "higher truth." And such sentiments give rise to many derivations, among which the following: That we have within us ideas, notions, concepts, that are superior to experience, that "intuition" must take the place of "reason," that "conscience must assert its rights in the face of positivistic empiricism," that "idealism must replace empiricism, positivism, science," that "idealism is alone 'true science.'" It is firmly believed that this "true science," with its absolute, comes much closer to realities than experimental science, which is always contingent; that, in fact, it "is reality," and that experimental science, which is identified with the pseudo-science of the Class I residues, is misleading and harmful. In days gone by such opinions prevailed in all branches of human knowledge. In our day they have disappeared, or virtually so, in the physical sciences, the last noteworthy example there being Hegel's *Philosophy of Nature;* but they still persist in the social sciences. In the physical sciences they were eliminated by the progress of experimental science and because they were of no use. In the social sciences they endure, not only because experimental research in social science is still in a very rudimentary stage, but especially because of their great social utility. In fact, there are many cases in which conclusions drawn from residues of group-persistence (or, in other words, obtained by "intuition") come much closer to realities than conclusions that are drawn from the combination-instinct and go to make up the derivations of that pseudo-science which, in social matters, continues to be mistaken for experimental science. And—again in many cases—these latter derivations seem so harmful that the society which is not eager to decline or perish must necessarily reject them. But not less deleterious are the consequences of an exclusive predominance of Class II residues, not only in the physical arts and sciences, where their harmfulness is obvious, but in social matters as well, where it is perfectly apparent that but for the combination-instinct and the use of experimental thinking there could be no progress. So there is no stopping, either, at the extreme where Class II residues predominate; and a new oscillation sets in heading back towards the first extreme, where Class I residues predominated. And so the pendulum continues swinging back and forth from one extreme to the other, indefinitely.

2341. Such developments may be described in other terms that emphasize one or another of their interesting aspects. Keeping to surfaces one may say that in history a period of faith will be followed by a period of scepticism, which will in turn be followed by another period of faith, this by another period of scepticism, and so on (§ 1681).[1] Such descriptions are not in themselves bad; but the terms "faith" and "scepticism" may be misleading, if they are thought of as referable to any particular religion or group of religions. Looking a little deeper, one may say that society is grounded on group-persistences. These manifest themselves in residues which, from the logico-experimental standpoint, are false, and sometimes

2341 [1] Draper had ideas that come more or less close to that doctrine, *History of the Intellectual Development of Europe*, p. 15: "The intellectual progress of Europe being of a nature answering to that observed in the case of Greece, and this, in its turn, being like that of an individual, we may conveniently separate it into arbitrary periods, sufficiently distinct from one another, though imperceptibly merging into each other. To these successive periods I shall give the titles of: 1. the Age of Credulity; 2. the Age of Inquiry; 3. the Age of Faith; 4. the Age of Reason; 5. the Age of Decrepitude." Draper clearly has an intuitive perception of one of our wide oscillations. What he fails to see is that there is an indefinite sequence of them and that the major ones are simultaneous with any number of minor ones. Then again he lets himself be led astray by a mistaken analogy between the lives of nations and the lives of individuals. It is also strange that he should think of Socrates as initiating the "age of Faith" in Greece that was followed by an "age of Inquiry": *Ibid.*, p. 106: "The Sophists had brought on an intellectual anarchy. It is not in the nature of humanity to be contented with such a state. Thwarted in its expectations from physics, the Greek mind turned its attention to morals. In the progress of life, it is but a step from the age of Inquiry to the age of Faith. Socrates, who led the way in this movement, was born B.C. 469." Those who place Socrates among the Sophists come much closer to the facts.

patently absurd. When, therefore, the aspect of social utility predominates to any large extent, doctrines favourable to the sentiments of group-persistence are accepted, instinctively or otherwise. When, however, the logico-experimental aspect predominates, even to some slight extent, such doctrines are rejected and replaced by others that accord in appearances, though rarely in substance, with logico-experimental science. So the human mind oscillates between the two extremes, and being unable to halt at either, continues in movement indefinitely. There might be a resting-place, at least for a portion of the intellectual ruling class, if individuals here and there would consent to be persuaded that a belief may be useful to society even though experimentally false or absurd (§§ 1683, 2002). Those few who look at social phenomena exclusively or at beliefs of others —not their own—may hold that view; and in fact we see traces of it in scientists, and we find it more or less explicit, more or less disguised, in public men who approach matters empirically. But the majority of human beings, people who are neither exclusively scientists nor far-sighted statesmen, people who do not lead but are led, and think more of their own beliefs than of the beliefs of others, can hardly hold such a view, either because of ignorance or because there is a distressing contradiction between having a faith that is to inspire vigorous action and considering that faith absurd. There is no saying that such a thing could never happen; but it remains a rare exception. In fine, to summarize what we have just been saying in a few words, the "cause" of the oscillation is not only a lack of scientific knowledge but, and chiefly, a confusion between two separate things—between the social utility of a doctrine and its accord with experience. The magnitude of that error we have already had frequent occasion to stress, and the harm it does to the quest for uniformities in the social field.

2342. No such development takes place for individuals who are not called upon to consider one or the other of the extremes. Many people live satisfied with their own beliefs and are not in the least concerned with the problem of reconciling them with logico-experimental science. Some few others dwell in the clouds of metaphysics or pseudo-science and worry not at all about the practical necessities of life. Many persons occupy intermediate situations and participate now more, now less, in the oscillation.

2343. 2. *Extrinsic aspect*. What we have just been saying has one defect that might become a source of serious error. It seems to lend colour to a tacit assumption that people think logically or pseudo-logically in choosing derivations. That is what might be gathered when we say that human beings accept derivations as the logical consequence of certain sentiments. Some individuals do that, but they are very few. The vast majority adopt residues and derivations under the direct impulse of sentiments. The intrinsic aspect just examined is important for the theory of doctrines, but is of no great significance as regards the theory of social movements. Such movements are not consequences of theories—the contrary, rather, is the case. Alternating periods of faith and scepticism have to be correlated, therefore, with other facts (§§ 2336-37).

2344. Let us begin, as usual, inductively. The oscillations we are trying to understand are like oscillations in the economic field (§§ 2279 f.). They are of varying intensities. Let us disregard minor ones and keep to those of the larger magnitudes, the largest possible, in fact. That will give us a rough picture of the facts. We are looking for oscillations in residues in the masses as a whole. Oscillations, therefore, in the intellectual elements in a population—men of letters, philosophers, pseudo-scientists, scientists—are pertinent only as indices. In themselves they mean nothing; they have to be widely accepted in the masses at large before they can serve as indices of popular sentiments. The works of a Lucian, rising like an islet of scepticism in an ocean of credulity, have a significance of approximately zero. The works of a Voltaire, on the other hand, enjoyed wide acceptance. They are more like a continent of scepticism and therefore merit consideration as an important index. These are all imperfect tools, even more imperfect than are available for evaluating economic oscillations when accurate statistics are not to be had. However, we have to be satisfied with them, since we can get nothing better—for the present at least.

2345. *Athens*. Taking the situation in Athens, from the war with the Medes down to the battle of Chaeroneia, one first notes a period in which Class II residues appear in great abundance in the population in the mass, whereas the ruling class shows a great abundance of Class I residues. Let the number 1 in Figure 40 represent the date of the battle of Marathon (490 B.C.)[1] and the line *ab* the intensity of Class II residues in the population as a whole. We get striking evidences, such as the conviction of Miltiades after the Paros expedition (489 B.C.), of the differences in strength of Class II residues in the lower classes and in the Athenian leaders. Later on, as Aristotle

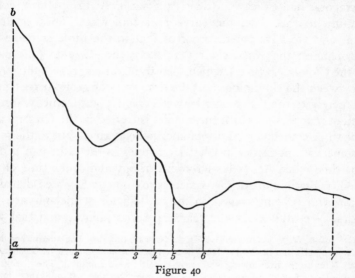

Figure 40

testifies, *De republica Atheniensium,* 25 (Kenyon, p. 46), during the seventeen years following the war with the Medes the constitution remained in the hands of the Areopagus, though it was breaking down a little at a time, till in 460 B.C. came the reform of Ephialtes, which deprived the Areopagus of its constitutional prerogatives. We have an excellent index of the intellectual movement during the period in the *Oresteia* of Aeschylus (458 B.C.). Unmistakable in that trilogy is the reflection of the struggle between those who were holding loyal to residues of group-persistence and those who were replacing them with combination-residues.[2] The former were completely defeated. The point 2, corresponding to the year 458 B.C.,

2345 [1] As late as the war with the Medes the Athenians were still believing, as more than one passage in Greek literature proves, in direct interventions by gods.

2345 [2] The *Eumenides* especially seems to have been written to defend the Areopagus and old tradition against innovations.

must therefore be located on a rapidly descending segment of the curve.[3] But the curve dropped even lower in the ruling classes. Pericles purged himself of popular "prejudices" and prepared the ground for the rise of Alcibiades to power.[4] Afterwards came a slight reaction, and the sceptical friends of Pericles were persecuted. Anaxagoras had to leave Athens (431 B.C.).[5] At the point 3, corresponding to that date, the curve rises somewhat. Then it drops again; and we have patent proof of that in the three comedies of Aristophanes: the *Acharnians* (425 B.C.), the *Knights* (424 B.C.), and the *Clouds* (423 B.C.) which, like the *Oresteia,* reflect the struggle between the champions and the destroyers of group-persistences. Not merely to the differences between tragedy and comedy are the different manners in which the conflict is treated in the *Oresteia* and in the three comedies of Aristophanes to be ascribed, but to the great differences in intensities in Class II residues in the Athenian people at the time when Aeschylus wrote his trilogy and at the time of the comedies. By the time of the comedies mythology has been defeated, and the war is being waged on the battle-fields of metaphysics and politics.[6] We must mark the year 424 B.C. as point 4, and that will

2345 [3] Justin, *Historiae Philippicae,* II, 14 (Clarke, p. 34): "The vanquished Mardonius [generalissimo of the Persians] escaped as from a shipwreck with a handful of men. The camps overflowing with royal wealth were captured. The Greeks divided the Persian gold among themselves, and that was the first time that the extravagance which goes with wealth laid hold on them."

2345 [4] Plutarch, *Pericles,* 6, 1 (Perrin, Vol. III, p. 15). Plutarch says that from his contacts with Anaxagoras Pericles derived, among other advantages, "the further one, that he seemed to have grown superior to superstition." Thucydides, *Historiae,* II, 53, 4, seems inclined to lay the blame for the progress of unbelief in Athens on the plague, but that is one of the usual errors of ethical reasoning (residues I-β4): unbelief was rife in Athens before the plague, and continued to increase after all the effects of the plague had vanished.

2345 [5] The law of Diapeithes against impiety (Plutarch, *Pericles,* 32, 1; Perrin, Vol. IV, p. 93) belongs to that time. It bore upon "those who do not recognize the gods or who speculate on celestial things," and is to be regarded as an expression of popular sentiment hostile to the prevalence of the combination-instincts, which were encouraging naturalistic studies.

2345 [6] The political conflict also ended very shortly. It no longer figures in the middle comedy, much less in the new. But already Aristophanes had been obliged to let politics alone, in deference, it has been said, to legislation forbidding attacks on magistrates or citizens on the stage. But that explanation can be only partially true. Aristophanes could very well have touched on politics without mentioning names of living people. Instead, in the *Ecclesiazusae,* mere fun-making takes the place of the fierce invectives in the *Acharnians,* the *Knights,* and the *Clouds.* We

indicate a new drop in the curve. The movement runs on down to the Melos affair (416 B.C.). That will be 5, and something very close to a minimum in group-persistences for both rulers and ruled in Athens. Never had Greeks talked so cynically, discarding all thought of religion, morals, and justice—that was the time when Alcibiades was lording it over Athens.[7] Then comes a very faint reaction: Alcibiades is accused of profaning the mysteries (415 B.C.). A still more

may disregard the *Birds* (414 B.C.) as an exception, but neither in the *Frogs* (406 B.C.) nor in the *Plutus* (409 B.C.) is there any trace of the bitter struggle that seethes in the first three comedies mentioned. It seems that by that time Aristophanes had grown resigned to a thing he could not help and began poking fun at the victors, just as at a later date the Greeks would poke fun at the Romans who had conquered their country, and just as, in modern times, the Legitimist *salons* laughed at Napoleon III, and, after the fall of the Right, the conservative *salons* at the democratic republic. Such mirth seems to be, as it were, the sour grapes of the vanquished.

2345 [7] One should read, in Thucydides, *Historiae*, V, 85-111 (Smith, Vol. III, pp. 157-75), the long colloquy between the Athenians and the Melians. The Athenians insist, substantially, that the right of the stronger is always the better and that the gods themselves support it. The Melians must surely be aware that human conflicts are decided according to justice as between equals, but that "the strong exact what they can, and the weak make the best of it." That is a sound experimental observation true for all times and places; and if, from the days of Thucydides down to our own, it is ever and anon denied in many derivations, that is because, as we have so many times noted, derivations completely at odds with experience win assent if they accord with certain sentiments. The derivations may at times be beneficial, at other times harmful. In the present case they accord with so-called sentiments of "justice," and those have oftentimes been productive of good; because in the first place, they have availed to mitigate the sorrows of many people by inspiring hopes in a better future and inducing them to live, mentally, in a "better" world than the experimental world; and because, in the second place, to express sentiments through derivations helps to reinforce them; and sentiments of justice, so called, though they are readily smothered by interests and other sentiments—such as, in the circumstances here in point, sentiments depending on Class V residues (personal integrity), notable among which, nationalism—may sometimes prompt human beings to attenuate, be it ever so slightly, the evils caused by "injustice." The Athenians use another argument that continues current in international, and especially in civil, strife. They try to show the Melians that their subjection to Athens would have advantages for both peoples. The Melians ask whether they might not be accepted as neutrals. The Athenians refuse, because, they say, that would be detrimental to them. In that, again, we get an experimental observation, valid for all places and times, from the time of the conference at Melos down to the Treaty of Campo Formio, and applying to international conflicts, and to a far greater extent, to civil conflicts. Derivations running counter to it are numerous. They win assent for reasons such as we have described; but they are usually harmful and oftentimes result in utter ruin for states and social classes, because they dissuade people from adopting the one road to salvation, which lies in preparing guns and evincing the willingness, and the ability, to use force.

pronounced reaction is evident at the time of the prosecution of Socrates (399 B.C.), which we may designate as 6.[8] After that we have no indications of any great changes in the Athenian people down to the battle of Chaeroneia (338 B.C.), which we mark with 7. That battle puts an end to the independence of Athens, and its history thereafter blends with the history of the rest of Greece down to the Roman conquest.

2346. As regards the intellectual class in Greece, the downward movement continues. It is chiefly notable at the "time of the Sophists," so called. As is usual with many other words of the kind, the term "Sophist" is so indefinite that exactly what it means is hard to say. In the course of centuries, it has come to mean an individual who twists arguments to suit his personal conveniences, and so it has acquired a strong ethical colouring. Since we are not concerned with ethics here, that definition can be of no service to us. We care not a whit whether a man took money for lessons in logic or gave them free. We are interested, however, in distinguishing individuals who aimed at undermining group-persistences, at substituting logical for non-logical conduct, at deifying Reason, from individuals who defended group-persistences, stood by tradition, were therefore favourable to non-logical conduct and burned no incense to the goddess Reason. For convenience of reference, suppose we call the former A's and the latter B's.

2347. Not a few writers contrast Socrates with the Sophists. Others say he was a Sophist too. The controversy cannot be settled unless the term "Sophist" is defined. We need not go into the matter here; but of one thing we are certain: that Socrates, and Plato

2345 [8] The trial of Socrates is merely the best known of a series of prosecutions that took place about that time and which indicate a popular reaction against unbelief in the intellectual classes. Decharme, *La critique des traditions religieuses chez les Grecs*, p. 140: "So towards the end of the fifth century one notes a wave of prosecutions for impiety of which only faint traces are to be noted in earlier ages. They bear witness to new progress in unbelief, and therefore deserve our somewhat closer attention." They show not only the progress of unbelief, but the intensity of popular sentiments reacting against it. It is interesting that in those prosecutions accusations of impiety towards the gods were not the only charges. There were complaints of a political and private character and, in general, charges of immorality. In a treatise, *De virtutibus et vitiis*, which is attributed to Aristotle, "impiety," ἀσέβεια, is defined, VII, 2 (Solomon, p. 1251a, ll. 30-32), as "guilt towards the gods, towards the *daimones,* or even towards the dead, one's parents, one's country." One might therefore say that the term designates an offence against the principal group-persistences.

too, are to be classed among our *A*'s, since both aim at undermining group-persistences in Athens and replacing them with products of their own thought. They may have differed from Protagoras, Gorgias, Prodicus, and others in the means they used; but their tendencies, whether they were aware of it or not, were the same.

2348. Writers, as a rule, wax indignant that Aristophanes should have named Socrates in the *Clouds*. They may be right from an ethical standpoint; but they are wrong from the logico-experimental standpoint as regards doctrines and social utility. Aristophanes was telling the literal truth when he says that Socrates and, to an even greater extent, Plato aimed at dethroning the Zeus of mythological tradition to transfer sovereignty to the "clouds" of their metaphysics. The daemon of Socrates is first cousin, at least, to the goddess Reason and own brother to the "conscience" of our Liberal Protestants. As for Plato, he so truly believes in the omnipotence of the goddess Reason that he trusts in her alone to create out of whole cloth a republic of human beings of flesh and bone. From the standpoint of social utility it is evident that working along that line the foundations of non-logical conduct on which society rests would soon have been demolished. Not, indeed, that the doctrines themselves could have had that effect. Quite to the contrary, they are themselves one of the effects of the social disintegration; and that is why the condemnation of Socrates was a useless thing and therefore stupid, wicked, and criminal, just as the condemnation of any man for expressing opinions deemed heretical by the people about him has been and continues to be useless and therefore stupid, wicked, and criminal.[1]

2349. At first blush, there might seem to be very great differences between the atheist Sisyphus, portrayed in a tragedy of Critias, and a devout soul such as Plato seems to be. And from the standpoint of ethics that may well be. But not from the standpoint of social utility. There the stress has to be laid on the traits common to the Sisyphus of Critias and the Socrates of Plato's *Republic*. Neither of them accepts the gods of tradition. Both refashion gods after their own patterns. Both, in other words, sap the foundations of group-persistences by transforming them. Sisyphus expresses the opinion

---

2348 [1] We have gone into that subject deeply enough in § 2196, and *passim*. Nothing more need be added here.

that in the beginning there must have been some wise and learned man "who invented the gods in order to keep men to the paths of duty." But the Socrates of the *Republic* is just such a wise and learned man. If he does not invent gods out of whole cloth, he none the less reshapes the gods of tradition to fit patterns of his own, and for the same purpose as the law-maker of Sisyphus, to make men better, that is.[1] That procedure is the more noteworthy in that it is a very general one. Our Modernists have inclinations towards it, and it is very definitely the procedure of the Liberal Protestants, who remould the Christ of history to their own taste and transform him into a creature of their own imaginations. In that we get a particular instance of the intrinsic aspect of our problem (§ 2340). When, in the minds of people of intellectual habits, traditional conceptions of certain group-persistences come into conflict with other conceptions that their pseudo-science deems better calculated to serve social

2349 [1] A long passage from the tragedy in which Sisyphus appears has been preserved by Sextus Empiricus, *Contradictiones*, IX, *Adversus physicos*, II, *De diis*, 54 (*Opera*, Vol. II, pp. 558-62). It gives the substance of the play quite clearly: "Critias, one of the tyrants of Athens, seems properly to be classed among the atheists when he says that the law-makers of old thought of God as an overseer of the virtuous or wicked conduct of men, to the end that no one should covertly offend his neighbour, in fear of chastisement from the gods." The last two lines of the harangue by Sisyphus (vv. 41-42) read: "So, I wot, in the beginning, were men persuaded to believe in the race of daemons [gods]." And just previously (vv. 24-26): "In such ways very wittily did he advocate moral laws of his own device, concealing truth under garb of fiction" [Hervet: *"verum sub umbra contegens mendacii"*]. And now suppose we listen to Plato, *Respublica*, II, 17, 377D: *"Adeimantus:* But I do not understand just what fabrications you refer to as the 'biggest.' *Socrates:* The stories that Hesiod and Homer, and the other poets for that matter, have told us; for the myths which they have told and are telling to men are naught but fictions." But since the mythology of the poets was also the mythology of the people the Socrates of the *Republic* was at one with the Sisyphus of Critias in regarding it as fiction, and they were in agreement also in their purpose, which was to have a mythology that would be helpful to men. Plato finds fault with lines in the *Iliad* for representing Zeus as a dispenser of both good and evil (379D). He would have it said that Zeus does nothing but good, and that the evils which he inflicts upon mortals are for their benefit. In that he is adopting one of the affirmative solutions (*B-1*) that we noted in §§ 1903 f. (and *cf.* § 1970); but, good metaphysicist that he is, he takes the greatest pains not to give trace of proof of his assertion, to which we are asked to assent simply because it has the assent of the speakers whom Plato himself supplies with words. Substantially he finds his proof in a "metaphysical experience," just as some of our contemporaries find theirs in a "Christian experience." Still an unfathomable mystery is why, in such egregious company, room should not be found for an "atheist experience."

utility, they follow one of two courses, both of which lead to the same goal: either they declare the traditional conceptions altogether false and fallacious; or else they modify them, transform them, make them over in their own way, not observing that in so doing they are destroying them, since the manifestations that they deem accessory are, instead, essential to the persistence of the group, and to suppress them is like depriving a man of his body and expecting him to live. The gods of Homer, with whom Plato picks his quarrel, were alive in the minds of millions upon millions of human beings. The god of Plato was never alive, and he has remained a rhetorical exercise on the part of a few dreamers.

2350. Variations in intensities in Class I and Class II residues seem to be in no way correlated with the democratic or aristocratic character of the system of government.[1] In the Athenian aristocracy we find a Nicias, who shows a predominance of Class II residues, a Pericles, who gave pre-eminence to Class I residues, and an Alcibiades, who had almost no others, in that resembling the plutocratic demagogues of our day. The régime of the Thirty was kindly disposed towards Socrates, merely reprimanding him. A democratic régime condemned him to drink the hemlock.

2351. Nor do the variations in question seem to be in any way correlated with the state of wealth. If Class II residues began to weaken when Athens was prosperous, the reactions also occurred

---

2350 [1] One must be on one's guard against the error of assuming that the cruelty of the Athenians towards the Melians was correlated with a predominance of Class I residues. Quite to the contrary, on many an occasion the Athenians evinced more humaneness than the Spartans, in whom Class II residues were uppermost. The difference lies, more than in anything else, in the character of the derivations used. They are more prolix and better compounded in the case of the Athenians; terser, less well knit, and sometimes brazenly mendacious in the case of the Spartans. Instructive from that point of view is the massacre of the inhabitants of Plataea, as recounted by Thucydides, *Historiae*, III, 52-68. The Plataeans surrendered to the Spartans on a promise by the latter that "the guilty would be punished, but none unjustly." Spartan "justice" ran as follows, *Ibid.*, 52, 4-5: The Spartans asked the Plataeans "whether in the present war they had done anything in favour of the Spartans and their allies." The Plataeans marvelled at the substitution of such a question for the promised judgment. They argued at length, and were no less patiently refuted by the Thebans; whereupon the Spartans, *Ibid.*, III, 68, 2-3, put the question to each individual Plataean; and, each in turn, being unable to answer yes, was forthwith executed. That is just one more of the countless examples that go to show that anyone promising to act "justly" promises nothing, "justice" being like a rubber band to be stretched to any length considered desirable.

while she was still holding prosperous. In her days of poverty, there is no apparent recovery in Class II residues. At the time of the Roman conquest, there was no return in Athens to the state of mind prevailing in the days of Marathon. The variations do seem to be somehow correlated with *rapid increase* in wealth, which appears conjointly with a weakening in Class II residues as well as with the ensuing reaction; but that may well be a fortuitous coincidence. Other situations would have to be studied before any certain conclusions could be reached in that connexion.[1]

2352. Variations in the intensities of Class I and Class II residues go hand in hand with variations arising from the *intrinsic* point of view (§§ 2340 f.), but what the correlations are we cannot determine. That they are not few is very probable. An Anaxagoras, a Socrates, a Plato may well have been inspired by forces of an *intrinsic* character; but it is hardly probable that such causes could have influenced a Critias or an Alcibiades, to say nothing of the Athenians who attended the conference with the Melians (§ 2345 [8]).

2353. *Rome.* Conditions in Rome before the second Punic War we cannot know with any exactness. Numberless facts go to show that one need pay little attention to the declamations by men of letters as to the "good old times." Vices there must have been in Rome, then as afterwards. They were merely less talked about, as practised on a less conspicuous stage, within narrower limits, and there were no literary men to leave record of them. Vices transpire even in the legends, though we are unable to determine their bearing on historical realities.

2354. Certain it is that in the second century before our era two

2351 [1] The situation can be better stated in mathematical language. Let p be an index of the relative proportions between Class I and Class II residues in a given population; q, an index of the wealth of the same population; t, the time. We get the equation:

$$\frac{dp}{dt} = f\left(\frac{dq}{dt}\right)$$

rather than the equation:

$$\frac{dp}{dt} = \phi\,(q)$$

Or, in order not to ascribe to our description an exactness it cannot have, we might say that $\dfrac{dp}{dt}$ depends much more on $\dfrac{dq}{dt}$ than on q. *Cf.* an analogous situation in Pareto, *Cours.* § 180 [1].

concomitant facts come to the fore in Rome: a very rapid increase in economic prosperity and a decline in the residues of group-persistence in the masses at large, but to a still greater extent in the upper classes (§§ 2545 f.). Then comes a reaction, as was the case in Athens and in other situations of the kind to which we shall come in due course, the only differences lying in the nature and the intensity of the reaction. The action and reaction appear therefore in conjunction, and it is their sum as a whole that is to be viewed as correlated with variations in wealth (§ 2351 [1]) and in class-circulation.[1]

2354 [1] Polybius is the best authority we have on this matter, provided we stop at his facts, disregarding his theories as to their causes. The facts may be epitomized more or less as follows: 1. In the day of Polybius, group-persistences were still much stronger in Rome than in Greece. *Cf.* Polybius, *Historiae,* VI, 56 (a passage of capital importance already quoted above in § 239); VI, 46 (analysis of the Cretan system); XX, 6; XVIII, 37 (on Roman chivalry); XXIV, 5. Also Plutarch, *Philopoemen,* 17 (Perrin, Vol. X, pp. 303-05) (debaucheries of the Greeks at Chalcis); Polybius, XXVIII, 9; XXXIII, 2; V, 106. 2. A rapid weakening in group-persistences is next observable: Polybius, IX, 10 (on the sack of Syracuse, Roman year 542, 212 B.C.); and XXII, 11-13, after the conquest of Macedonia (Roman year 586, 168 B.C.). Other writers of varying authoritativeness may be quoted to the same effect: Valerius Maximus, *De dictis factisque memorabilibus,* IX, 1, 3: "The end of the Second Punic War and the overthrow of Philip, King of Macedonia, gave an impulse (*fiduciam*) to rather licentious life in our city." (Roman year 558, 196 B.C.). In his *Historia naturalis,* XVII, 38 (25) (Bostock-Riley, Vol. III, p. 527), Pliny mentions a lustration that was performed by the censors in the Roman year 600 and adds: "Piso, a writer of weight, dates the decline of good morals in Rome from that time." And in XXXIII, 53 (Bostock-Riley, Vol. VI, p. 136), he relates: "In his triumph in the Roman year 565, Lucius Scipio displayed 1,450 pounds weight of chiselled silver and 1,500 in gold plate. But the thing that struck a severer blow at morals was the gift of Asia (Minor) by Attalus. The legacy from that king was deadlier than the victory of Scipio. Rome abandoned all restraints in bidding for the precious objects that were sold at the auction of Attalus. That was in the year 622. During that interval of fifty-seven years Rome had learned to admire, nay to love, exotic luxuries. Morals moreover received a violent shock in the conquest of Achaia, in that same interval, and specifically in the year 608. That victory contributed sculpture and painting, to cap the climax. That same period saw the birth of Roman luxury and the death of Carthage, and by a fatal coincidence, people had both the opportunity and the appetite for plunging into vice." Florus, *Epitoma de Tito Livio,* I, 47, 2 (III, 12, 2; Forster, p. 213), remarks, with some exaggeration, that the hundred years preceding the extension of Roman conquests overseas were years of extraordinary virtue: "The hundred years before that age had been pure, devout, and as we said, golden, without wickedness or crime, the virtues of the pastoral school still remaining innocent and unspoiled." The next hundred years, he goes on, were years of great military successes, but of serious domestic corruption, and he voices doubts as to whether the conquests were profitable to the Republic. *Ibid.,* 8 (Forster,

2355. The historians have seen the facts but, misled by the common mania for ethical interpretations, they have not managed to grasp the relations between them (§§ 2539 f.). They have used a number of ethical principles very extensively, never, however, going to any great pains to check them on the facts. There is the principle that wealth tends to corrupt morals, yet one need only glance about to see that England in all her wealth is not more corrupt than certain provinces of Russia in all their poverty; and that the morals of the prosperous Piedmontese are not in any way worse than the morals of the very poor peasants in Sardinia or the Italian South. If one prefer to limit the comparison to a given people at different times, could it be said that the morals of Milan or Venice in our day are worse than the morals of those same towns a century ago? And yet they have grown enormously in wealth.

Another principle might be stated in paraphrase of Pliny's apothegm (*Historia naturalis,* XVIII, 6, 7, 35): "*Latifundia perdidere Italiam*" (§ 2557). The growth of inequality in wealth is taken for granted—it is not proved, because no proof could be given. Some think it is made sufficiently obvious by pointing to examples of very wealthy citizens. But that is not enough. It must further be shown that wealth has not increased in the same proportions in the other classes in society—and there are facts in abundance to show that such an increase is at least possible. There is no proof, further, that a country showing numbers of rich people is necessarily in deca-

p. 215): "For what else provoked these civil upheavals than too much prosperity? The conquest of Syria first corrupted us, then the legacy of Asia bequeathed by the King of Pergamum. All that wealth, all those luxuries, ruined the morals of the age and reduced a commonwealth that was already sunk in vice to the very depths (*quasi sentina*). . . . Whence the dissension between the knights and the Senate as to the administration of the courts unless it be from greed, that the state revenues and the courts themselves should be prostituted for gain?" Velleius Paterculus, *Historia romana,* II, 1, 1: "The earlier Scipio had opened the road to Roman power, the later Scipio, the road to Roman luxury. Indeed, the fears of Carthage once removed, the rival in empire once out of the way, there came not so much a turn as a mad rush away from virtue to vice. The old discipline was abandoned, and a new one introduced. The whole city turned from vigilance to somnolence, from arms to pleasure, from industry to laziness." Cf. Dio Cassius, Fragment 227, Gros ed., II, 27: Reimar ed., Vol. II, p. 71; and Sallust, *Bellum Jugurthinum,* XLI [§ 2548 [8]], *Bellum Catilinae,* X. Then Livy, *Ab urbe condita,* XXXIX, 6, 4: "Exotic luxury was first introduced into the city by the army that served in Asia." Justin, *Historiae Philippicae,* XXXVI, 4 (Clarke, p. 261): "So when Asia became a property of the Romans she sent her vices along with her wealth to Rome." Cf. § 2548.

dence. After the Napoleonic wars one notes simultaneously in England extensive *latifundia* belonging to English lords and a very great national prosperity. The trusts in the United States today correspond exactly to the Roman *latifundia,* and they prevail side by side with a prosperity such as the world has never before witnessed. We will say nothing of "capitalism," which, explaining everything (§ 1890), necessarily explains the decline of Rome and other countries. For some writers the democratic régime was the ruin of Athens. For others, the aristocratic régime was the ruin of Rome.

2356. Duruy takes the transformation that came over Roman society after the Punic Wars as his text for a sermon (§ 2558). Says he:[1] "In accord with the wisdom of the nations, we are going to say that that wealth which is not the fruit of honest toil and of all those virtues that attend it is of no benefit to those who hold it; that ill-gotten riches depart the way they came, leaving a deal of moral wreckage behind them. And then we are going to add, with the experience of economists behind us, that gold is like the water in a river: if it overflows suddenly, it spreads devastation abroad; if it comes slowly in a gentle circulation through a thousand channels, it creates life on all hands." Therefore, dear children, to draw the moral of such a pretty fairy-story—to be perfect it needs only to be written in rhyme or set to music—be good, virtuous, and industrious, and you will live happy lives. But do not read history, for you would be put to it to reconcile what you find there with such assertions. Take, for example, Corinth. Wealth in Corinth was certainly much more the fruit of honest toil, and much less the fruit of conquest, than it was in Rome; yet Corinth was conquered and sacked by the Romans. If that wealth "which is not the fruit of honest toil . . . is of no benefit to those who hold it," Corinth should have conquered and sacked Rome. And, if it is true that "ill-gotten riches depart the way they came," and if the wealth of the Romans was "ill-gotten," how comes it that they enjoyed it for so long a time after the period that Duruy is criticizing and that they were stripped of it by the Barbarians, who acquired such wealth as they had not by honest toil, but by conquest and robbery?[2]

2356 [1] *Histoire des Romains,* Vol. II, pp. 224-25 (Mahaffy, Vol. II, pp. 228-29).

2356 [2] Duruy is excusable in his notions as to the economists. "Economists" a-plenty deliver themselves of balderdash such as Duruy describes. Political economy,

2357. All such trappings must therefore be stripped from the narratives of the historians in an effort to get at the naked facts. In doing that, one finds that the two phenomena mentioned in § 2354, rapid increase in wealth and a weakening in Class II residues, are undeniable facts, that they are the counterparts, as we have just seen, of developments in Athens, and of still others that we are shortly to encounter. We therefore have to ask whether in that we have just a series of coincidences or are dealing with a relationship of interdependence.

2358. In Rome, as in Athens (§§ 2345 f.), there were a number of reactions to the weakening trend in group-persistences, and they occasioned temporary deflections in the general course of the movement. Notable, in the case of Rome, the reaction associated with the name of Cato the Censor. It was of brief duration and soon gave way before the general trend of the curve.

2359. A special circumstance interposes to make the situation in Rome more difficult to grasp in the period between the conquest

as widely taught in Duruy's time and as still widely taught, was less an investigation of experimental realities than a sort of ethical literature. Duruy continues, *loc. cit.*, p. 225 (Mahaffy, p. 229): "Beginning with the second half of the nineteenth century, Europe has been seeing just such a flood of gold pouring in from the placers of America and Australia. But such capital has been the product of labour and has been used by Europe to modernize her industrial plant, and an enormous increase in public wealth as well as in individual welfare has resulted from it." So the machinery in European factories, the railways, and so on were made of gold from America and Australia! A pretty metamorphosis, in fact! And in that Duruy is less excusable. Even in his day, there were few, very few "economists" who were still mired in the fallacy of the old mercantile economies that mistook gold for wealth, and gold for capital. Most economists at that time were coming a little closer to realities than that. But many historians know nothing whatever of economic science, and very little of the literary economics that is commonly taught, and imagine that they can make up for the deficiency with ethical disquisitions. So when they are called upon to deal with economic matters they straddle the goat of the greatest absurdities imaginable. Duruy further continues: "Whereas Rome leapt suddenly from poverty to wealth by war, pillage, and robbery, and the gold from her conquests served merely for the unproductive extravagance of those who got possession of it." So great the power of ethical group-persistences! In that Duruy is forgetting things that he knew very well and even taught to others. He forgets that if conquest was in fact one of the primary sources of Roman wealth, commerce too was a far from negligible factor in it. Roman *mercatores* and *negotiatores* are always turning up in history, numerous, active, and rich. He forgets the public works the Romans executed, among other things their roads, which contributed their share to increasing wealth.

of Greece and the end of the Republic: the intellectual influence of Greece upon the educated classes in Rome. That prevents one from distinguishing with any assurance between spontaneous products of the Latin mind and imitations of Greek literature, philosophy, and science. If, for instance, we knew nothing but the poem of Lucretius, we could not tell just what importance should be ascribed to it as indicating the state of mind of educated Romans. But the doubt is cleared away by Cicero's essay *On the Nature of the Gods,* and by many other facts of a literary and historical character. All of them point to the conclusion that towards the end of the Republic a number of group-persistences had weakened to a very considerable extent in educated circles.

2360. They had weakened to a far lesser extent in the lower classes, and that is a general case of which there are countless examples. The lower classes in Rome were undergoing a profound transformation through the influx of elements from abroad, especially from the East, all of them contributing their own peculiar intellectual habits to Rome. In that lies one of the main causes for the differing intellectual evolutions of Athens and Rome.[1]

2361. The low-water mark in group-persistences in the educated classes in Rome—and, for all we know, in the masses at large, there being no evidence on the point—seems to have been reached in the period between Horace and Pliny the Naturalist. Thereafter a gen-

2360 [1] Friedländer, *Sittengeschichte Roms,* Vol. III, p. 423 (English, Vol. III, p. 84): "We have two sources of knowledge for the religious situation in antiquity during the first two centuries of our era. They are of a very different character and are oftentimes contradictory in many respects. One is literature, the other the monuments, and notably stones bearing inscriptions. [The contradiction vanishes once one stops to reflect that the literary sources express the states of mind more especially of the higher educated classes, the inscriptions, public sentiments as a whole, and therefore the sentiments more especially of the more numerous elements—the masses proper.] Literature derives in the main from circles that had been affected by unbelief or indifference or circles that were trying to spiritualize popular beliefs, purify them, make them over by thought and interpretation. The inscriptions, on the other hand, derive in large part at least from social strata that had been less extensively influenced by literature and dominant literary attitudes, from environments where no need was felt to express one's opinions on religious matters, and where many would have been unable to do so at all clearly. They therefore testify, as a rule, to a positive belief in the divinities of polytheism, to a faith that is as immune to doubt as it is devoid of intellectual niceties, an altogether ingenuous spontaneous faith."

eral upward trend sets in, undulating, as usual, in the detail; and it continues on into the Middle Ages.[1]

2362. In the upper classes a reaction in the direction of a strengthening in the combination-instincts or, if one prefer, of resistance to the strengthening of group-persistences occurred under the reign of Hadrian, when Greek Sophists were for a short spell in great vogue in Rome; and it continued down to the beginning of the reign of Marcus Aurelius. That invasion of the Sophistic arts parallels only in minor respects the Sophist movement in Athens (§§ 2346 f.), and primarily because in Rome it was confined to insignificant numbers of intellectuals (§ 1535). Rome had no Socrates to carry the thought of the Sophists down to the masses; or, more exactly, the Roman masses had no proclivities towards such thinking. The cosmopolitan masses in Rome at that time could in no way compare, on the score of intelligence and education, with the Athenian populace of the time of Socrates.

2363. Thereafter the general trend towards a strengthening in group-persistences becomes a torrential onrush. In the pagan writers, in other words in those individuals who stood closest to the ancestral notions of the Graeco-Latin races, it was noticeably slower than in the Christian writers, who welcomed the vagaries of the Oriental religions with open arms. Even in Macrobius, who lived in the fifth century, one notes much more balance, a far clearer sense of realities, than in Tertullian, who lived in the third, or in St. Augustine, who lived in the fourth, or in other writers of that type.

2361 [1] Friedländer, *Op. cit.*, Vol. III, p. 430 (English, Vol. III, p. 90): "Not even in the first century had people of a philosophical education assumed attitudes of actual hostility to the state religion. In the literature of that time, to be sure, as was the case in France in the eighteenth century, inclinations and tendencies hostile to faith predominate; but in no case did they enjoy that pre-eminence later than the end of the first century of our era. The tide of anti-Christian sentiment in France during the past century rapidly dropped once it had attained its high mark, and the ebb was so violent as to sweep the majority of the educated classes along with it. So it was with the Graeco-Roman world. The outstanding tendencies in the literature of the first century gave ground before a strong reaction towards positive faith that laid hold on those same circles and conquered them; and under a multiplicity of pressures, faith degenerated into a crude superstition made up of miracles, pietism, and mysticism." That is an excellent description. One slight emendation is required: the general movement developed not along a uniform line but along a wavy line.

2364. As early as the days of Polybius, and even more in the day of Pliny and Strabo, there were educated people evidently who held some perception of the possible intermediate state of mind where a faith is kept for its social utility, though it is recognized as experimentally false (§ 2341). From that point of view, the writers of that period stood much closer to experimental realities than many of our own day who go to one extreme or the other where no halting is possible. Some faint reflection of that intermediate state of mind may have encouraged a few pagan writers to a relative indifference towards the fantastic Oriental religions that were sweeping the Empire. They could not imagine how such things could ever appeal to the intellectually higher classes, and in that they might not have gone far wrong had the Roman *élite* remained as they knew it. But that *élite* was in full decadence. Oriental superstitions did not in fact rise to the higher classes. The higher classes sank to them.

2365. The main cause of the decline is to be sought in phenomena of class-circulation, to which we shall come in due time (§ 2546). If Rome had continued to increase in wealth after the reign of Hadrian, as it had been doing towards the end of the Republic and in the early years of the Empire, and if, as then, the ruling classes had remained open to individuals who were well supplied with combination-instincts and were therefore able to get rich, the Roman *élite* might have held on above the level where group-persistences came to predominate. What actually happened was that the Empire grew poorer and poorer; class-circulation came to a halt; the combination-instincts found their expression in intrigues to court favour with the Emperor or other powerful individuals; and as a result a trend developed directly counter to the movement observable under the late Republic and the early Empire. Examination of the two contrary movements leads therefore to the same conclusion.

2366. In the West, after the Barbarian invasions a glimmer of cultivation still survives, perhaps, in the clergy; but it had certainly disappeared altogether in the rest of the population, which sank eventually into utter illiteracy. Just when that intellectual poverty reached its maximum cannot be determined, for lack of documents. By the time of St. Gregory of Tours (sixth century) it seems to have been very considerable.[1] Following the usual undulating rhythm, there is a slight fluctuation in the direction of an increase in intellectual activity at the time of Charlemagne; but shortly thereafter the general downward trend is resumed.

2367. And then suddenly, towards the end of the eleventh century and the beginning of the twelfth, comes a slight intellectual renascence in the educated classes, and one notes a rapid series of violent actions and reactions with regard to group-persistences in a few countries.

The intellectual movement gives rise to Scholastic philosophy. It makes its appearance among the clergy, the clergy being at the time the only educated class. It is brought about by the forces we identified in considering the *intrinsic* aspect (§ 2340).[1] The movement for the population as a whole falls into two phases: (1) a gradual weakening in religious sentiments; then (2) a violent reaction tending to reinforce them. In the first case the movement is still chiefly an affair of the clergy, not, however, in its intellectual elements, but in the part belonging to the governing class. It is a particular case of the general phenomenon that group-persistences tend gradually

2366 [1] Guizot, *Histoire de la civilisation en France,* Vol. II, pp. 1-2: "Studying the intellectual situation in Gaul in the fourth and fifth centuries, we found two literatures, the one sacred, the other profane. The distinction was noticeable in persons and in things: laymen and churchmen studied, thought, wrote, and they studied, thought, wrote on secular subjects and religious subjects. Sacred literature was gradually gaining the ascendancy, but it did not stand alone—profane letters were still alive. Between the sixth and eighth centuries there is no profane literature left—sacred literature is the only literature produced. All the studying and writing is done by clerics and, barring some rare exception, they confine themselves to religious themes. The outstanding trait in the period is the concentration of intellectual activity within the religious sphere."

2367 [1] St. Bernard had a clear perception of this raid by the combination-instincts: *Tractatus de erroribus Abaelardi* (*Epistolae,* CXC, *Ad Innocentium II pontificem*), I, 1 (*Opera,* Vol. II, p. 1053): "We have in France a man who now from schoolmaster has turned theologian. As a youth he toyed with the arts of dialectic. Now he is lunaticizing on the Scriptures. Doctrines that had long since been condemned and laid to rest, both his own and those of others, he is now trying to revive, adding new ones of his own. Of all things that are in Heaven above and on Earth below, he never deigns to know nothing, save only of the phrase 'I know not.'" And again, *Epistolae,* CCCXXX (*Opera,* Vol. I, p. 555): "A new faith is being forged in France, the dispute raging not morally about the virtues and the vices, not reverently about the Sacraments, and not soberly and humbly about the mystery of the Holy Trinity, but against all that we have so far believed." Those, substantially, however different the forms, were the charges laid against Socrates.

to weaken in aristocracies and *élites*. In the second case the movement is characteristic, on the whole, of the subject and less cultivated classes. It too is a particular case of the general uniformity that reactions in favour of group-persistences come from the masses.

2368. Nominalism and Realism are two metaphysical theories, and therefore vague and indefinite from the experimental standpoint. Starting with an indefinite concept, differing conclusions can be drawn according to the route one follows. If we centre on the fact that in attributing "existence" to individuals only, Nominalism seemed inclined to consider only experimental entities, and press our reasoning along that line, we may think of logico-experimental doctrine as an extreme form of Nominalism stripped of all metaphysical accessories (§ 64). But other paths radiate just as well from the experimentally indefinite centre of Nominalism. One of them is indicated by St. Anselm, who complains, in allusion to the Nominalists, that there were heretical dialecticians who held "universal substances to be nothing but puffs of air"; [1] and that position of the Nominalists can be interpreted to mean that no account need be taken either of abstractions or of the group-persistences which they express. If we follow that line to the end we shall be carried to the extreme where the residues depending on the persistences will be regarded as "outworn prejudices" (§§ 616, 2340) which the rational man need consider only as childish fancies.

2369. In the same way, starting with an undefined Realism, we may, though with greater difficulty, arrive at a theory of non-logical conduct, and so come very close to realities. But much more easily one can reach the extreme where metaphysics takes the place of experience and imaginary entities are created by transforming abstractions and allegories into realities (§ 1651).

2370. The second routes, in the cases both of Nominalism and Realism, are those that bring one closest to the practical inferences which people actually drew from those doctrines. Considering the facts from that standpoint, therefore, we may say that the conflict between Nominalism and Realism made an issue between the two extremes noted in § 2340. When group-persistences hold the upper

---

2368 [1] *De fide Trinitatis et de incarnatione Verbi*, II (*Opera*, Vol. I, p. 265): "*Illi utique nostri temporis dialectici, imo dialectice haeretici, qui non nisi flatum vocis putant esse universales substantias.*"

hand, species and genera acquire metaphysical "existence," and we get the Realist solution. But that solution runs aground on the facts of experience; so thereupon the metaphysical "existence" of species and genera is denied, and it is held that only the individual "exists" —the Nominalist solution.

An intermediate solution, which, were it not entirely metaphysical, might approximate a position midway between the two extremes of the oscillation, would be supplied by Conceptualism, which recognizes the "existence" of species and genera as concepts.

2371. Cousin [1] declares that Abelard's Conceptualism is mere Nominalism, and he may be right as regards the field of metaphysics, which we choose not to enter. We are at no more pains to discuss the "existence" of the genus, the species, or the individual than to argue the beauty of the Theban Sphinx. Metaphysicists, fortunate mortals, know the meaning of the term "exist." We do not, nor have they been able to tell us, for we understand neither head nor tail of what they say, and because we fail to find any judge to settle their interminable altercations (§ 1651). We therefore ignore that type of research and confine ourselves to quarrels in which experience can act as referee.

2372. From the experimental standpoint, the Conceptualist solution contains a few more—not so very many more—real elements than the Nominalist solution, many many more than the Realist solution. Says Cousin: "Examining Conceptualism in itself, one readily sees that it is nothing but a wiser [What kind of a theory would be *wiser* than some other?] and more coherent Nominalism. In the first place, Nominalism necessarily includes Conceptualism. Abélard argues against his old master Roxellinus in these terms: 'If universals are just words, they are nothing, for words are nothing; but universals are *things:* they are conceptions.' Roxellinus might well have answered: 'Who ever dreamed of denying that? Assuredly when the lips utter a word, the mind attaches a meaning to it, and the meaning so attached is a conception of the mind. I am therefore a Conceptualist like yourself. But why are you not a Nominalist, as I am? To say that universals are mere conceptions of the mind is to say by implication that they are only words; for, in my language, words are the opposites of things [That precisely is his mistake:

2371 [1] *Ouvrages inédits d'Abélard,* Pref., p. clxxx.

words also manifest psychic states, which are "things" for those who look at them objectively.], and not admitting that universals are things, I had to make words of them. I never meant anything more than that. Rejecting Realism, I reached Nominalism, taking Conceptualism for granted.'" Probably! But, alas, what he took for granted was quite as important as what he explicitly asserted.[1]

2373. If, in fact, instead of lingering in the nebulous regions of metaphysics, Cousin had deigned to come down to the experimental earth, he would have seen that the question as to whether universals or, in general, abstractions, are or are not anything more than words is not the only question to be answered. There is the far more important problem of determining to just what psychic states such words correspond and especially whether they express group-persistences of greater or lesser power, or are mere gambols of the fancy. The "Socraticity" that the Scholastics say finds its manifestation in Socrates is only a word, just as "justice" is only a word over which people have argued for century after century without ever succeeding in defining it; but the word "Socraticity" corresponds to a metaphysical abstraction that has never had the slightest influence on the social system; whereas the word "justice" corresponds to very powerful group-persistences that are the firm foundation of human society. A modern Roman exclaims "By Bacchus!" and calls on the god Bacchus by name exactly as the ancient believer did. In both cases Bacchus is only a word, but it expresses ideas or sentiments that are essentially different. We begin to get closer to reality, there-

2372 [1] To look at a thermometer immersed in a liquid gives the "temperature," the thermic state, of a liquid, one of its characteristics: it classifies it with other liquids that are like it from that point of view. To hear "universals" or some abstract entity mentioned by certain human beings gives us knowledge of "concepts," of a psychic state, of a characteristic of those human beings—it classifies them with other human beings who are like them in that respect. One may say, if one chooses, that the expression "twenty degrees Centigrade" is, like the expression "justice," a mere *flatus vocis;* but they are both indices of states: the former an index of a thermic state in a liquid, the latter of a psychic state in a human being. The indices differ in that the former is exact, like a sharply defined nucleus, the latter is more or less vague, like a fog. The former can serve as a premise in a strict reasoning; the latter does not lend itself to that sort of thing. If instead of the temperature registered by a thermometer we were to take the abstract entity "heat," as ancient philosophers did, that entity would be altogether similar to the entity called "justice." Both are partially indeterminate, like a fog, and cannot serve as premises in strict reasonings.

fore, when we do not stop at the word but try to get at the concept that underlies it. If Roxellinus meant that nothing exists except things and words, he was to that extent departing from realities; and if that was his language, one can only say that it was the language of error. "Conceptualism" did well in making a start at least toward correcting it, but erred in halting at the opening of the road into which it had turned and not carrying the analysis further, distinguishing the various "concepts," and determining on experimental fact their nature and characteristics as a basis for their classification.

2374. The intellectual movement represented by Scholasticism is of the same type as the Sophistic movement in Greece, and there have been others still. It springs from a need of inquiry that is intensified by the strength of combination-instincts and is felt only by restricted numbers of individuals.

2375. Parallel to it, but distinct from it, is the trend towards a weakening in group-persistences in the less intellectual portions of the governing class. At that time it expressed itself in a special form. Appetites for material goods and sensual enjoyments are more or less constant forces, and they may be repressed by powerful religious sentiments. It follows that any predominance of material appetites is an indication of a weakening in religious sentiments and in the group-persistences to which they correspond. That, exactly, is what one observes in the period here in question. The clergy almost throughout had become concubinary, dissolute, grasping, simoniacal.

2376. On all that we have direct evidence; but even more abundant is the indirect testimony supplied by the bitter rebukes that were rained upon the clergy by reformers. It is an interesting fact that the action—the weakening in group-persistences in one portion of the ruling class—is known to us primarily through the reaction that it provoked in the subject class.

2377. Such movements of action and reaction are specially noticeable in Southern France (Catharists and Waldenses) and in Northern Italy (the Arnoldites of Brescia, and the Patarini of Milan). Those were districts more conspicuous than others in the Catholic world for rapid increase in wealth about that time.[1] So

2377 [1] St. Bernard was sent by Pope Innocent to correct the waywardness of the burghers in Milan, Pavia, and Cremona. Accomplishing little or nothing, he wrote

there we get another case where variations in economic prosperity go hand in hand with variations in the combination-residues, as compared with the residues of group-persistence (§ 2351 [1]). The more of such coincidences we meet, the lesser the likelihood that they are due to mere chance, and the greater the probability of a relationship of interdependence.

2378. The Roman Curia dealt with the three cases in different ways: It suppressed the Catharists and the Arnoldites, but struck an alliance, of brief duration to be sure, with the Patarini. A consistent policy underlay these apparent differences. The idea of the Church was to take advantage of prevailing residues as a means of maintaining its own power. The Archbishop of Milan was showing an inclination to deal with the Pope on an equal footing and may have been thinking of winning independence of him. Such power as the Patarini represented could therefore be used as a check on the Archbishop. Arnold of Brescia and the Catharists waged open war on the Pope and he had no choice but to fight back, defending in Provence, Brescia, and Rome the laxities among the clergy that he was condemning in Milan.

2379. In the course of his struggle with the Milanese clergy, Pope Nicholas II induced the Council of Rome, in 1059, to pass a canon forbidding the laity to hear Mass of a priest known to be living in concubinage (Labbe, Vol. XII, p. 138). That made the validity of the religious rite dependent on the personal character of the priest. But the same doctrine was later on condemned by the Church when held by the Waldenses. As we have seen, derivations prove the yea and the nay equally well.[1] So in our day many Socialist Deputies

---

to the Pope, *Epistolae*, CCCXIV (*Opera*, Vol. I, p. 520): "The Cremonese have hardened their hearts and their prosperity is working their ruin. The Milanese are a contemptuous lot and their self-conceit is misleading them. Their attention all engrossed in coaches and horses, they had none left for me, and my labours among them were in vain." [The "Patarini" were so-called from a poor quarter of Milan, the Pataria: as it were, "Slummers."—A. L.]

2379 [1] *Decretum Gratiani, pars* I, *distinctio* 32, *canon* 5, *tit.* 7 (Friedberg, Vol. I, p. 117): "*Mass shall not be heard of a priest keeping a concubine: Nicholas, Pope, to all bishops:* No one shall hear Mass of a priest whom he knows of positive information to be keeping a concubine or secretly maintaining any woman." This is Canon 3 of the Twenty-fourth Roman Council held under Nicholas II. The prohibition was re-enacted by Pope Alexander II in 1063. See Baronio (Rinaldi), *Annales ecclesiastici, anno* 1063, XXXIV, and *Decretum Gratiani, pars* I, *distinctio* 32, *canon* 6 (Friedberg, Vol. I, p. 117-19). The Magister comments, *loc. cit.*, p. 118:

inveigh against "capitalism" in order to curry favour with the electorate, and then protect the interests of "capital" in order to curry favour with the plutocrats.

2380. The reformers needed some raiment of derivation in which to garb their sentiments, and that, of course, was always very easily found. The Catharists seem to have resorted to the derivations of Manicheism, but they might have used the resources of any other heresy just as well; and had the Papacy been Manichean, they could have used derivations contrary to Manicheism.

2381. More interesting still is the case of Arnold of Brescia, who is said to have been a disciple of Abelard.[1] Far from favouring the

"These rulings seem in principle to go counter to Jerome, Augustine, and others, who declare [Augustine, *Epistolae*, XXII, 6 (*Opera*, Vol. II, p. 91; *Works*, Vol. VI, pp. 53-54)] that the Sacraments of Christ are not to be spurned (*fugienda*) whether from a righteous or a wicked person, as the case of prelates guilty of simony hereafter following amply shows. But Urban II, in a letter addressed to the Provost of St. Iventius, clears up this inconsistency by saying: 'As to [your question] whether ordinations and other sacraments may be used when celebrated by individuals guilty of such crimes as adultery, violation of monastic vows, and the like, we answer that unless they are severed from the Church by schism or heresy we do not deny that their ordinations and other sacraments are holy and to be revered, in that agreeing with Augustine.'" So Socialists who are also fast friends with plutocrats might answer a similar scruple by saying: "If the plutocrat has not been excommunicated by us, but supports us and contributes to our cause, we do not deny that his 'operations' are righteous and praiseworthy." Bernard Guidon, *Practica inquisitionis heretice pravitatis*, p. 242: "They [the Catharists] say that confessions made to priests of the Church of Rome are worth nothing because since said priests are sinners, they cannot bind and loose, and since they are unclean themselves, they cannot cleanse another person." Moneta, *Adversus Catharos et Valdenses*, V, 5, §§ 3-4 (p. 433): "*As to whether guilty priests can administer sacraments and preach, and whether they are to be obeyed, the heretics striving to sustain the negative*. . . . The heretics known as the Catharists, and also the 'Paupers' in Lombardy, hold that such priests cannot administer the sacraments on the following grounds . . . [The Scriptural passages adduced by the heretics are quoted and refuted in detail. The conclusion is reached, § 4, p. 336, that:] even though priests may be guilty as individuals, they nevertheless retain the prerogative of preaching and administering the sacraments and are owed obedience."

2381 [1] Baronio (Rinaldi), *Annales ecclesiastici, anno* 1139, X, quotes the lines that "a celebrated poet of those days," Gunther of Liguria, devoted to Arnold of Brescia:

"'*Cuius origo mali tantaeque voraginis auctor*
extitit Arnoldus, quem Brixia protulit ortu
pestifero, tenui nutrivit Gallia sumptu,
edocuitque diu. Tandem natalibus oris
redditus, assumpta sapientis fronte, diserto

reformers, who were trying to strengthen religious group-persist-ences, the theories of Nominalism tended to work against them. But derivations are of such scant importance that they may at times serve to express residues with which they would seem to be inconsistent. So Marxist theories today are not in any sense favour-able to the plutocracy at present reigning, and yet they sometimes serve to defend it.

2382. The religious reaction of the Albigenses was crushed by the Roman Church, but it provoked another religious reaction within the latter. In that we get, under varying forms, a develop-ment that is general. It recurs at the time of the Reformation and again during the French Revolution.

> *fallebat sermone rudes, clerumque procaci*
> *insectans odio, monachorum acerrimus hostis,*
> *plebis adulator, gaudens popularibus auris,*
> *pontifices ipsumque gravi corrodere lingua*
> *audebat Papam, scelerataque dogmata vulgo*
> *diffundens, variis implebat vocibus aures:*
> *Nil proprium cleri, fundos et praedia nullo*
> *iure sequi monachos, nulli fiscalia iura*
> *pontificum, nulli curae popularis honorem*
> *abbatum, sacras referens concedere leges,*
> *omnia principibus terrenis subdita, tantum*
> *committenda viris popularibus atque regenda.*
> *Illis primitias, et quae devotio plebis*
> *offerat, et decimas castos in corporis usus,*
> *non ad luxuriam sive oblectamina carnis*
> *concedens, mollesque cibos, cultusque nitorem,*
> *illicitosque thoros, lascivaque gaudia cleri,*
> *pontificum fastus, abbatum denique laxos*
> *damnabat penitus mores, monachosque superbos.'* "

(" 'Cause of the trouble, author of the great confusion, was Arnold, whom Brescia bore of baleful lineage, whom France reared at slight expense and educated in due time. Thence returning to his native land and assuming the pose of a philosopher, he began to deceive the uneducated with his glib talk, assailing the clergy in bitter hatred, showing himself a fierce enemy of the monks, and a demagogue skilful at catching the ear of the mob. The priests and the Pope himself he ventured to sear with his spiteful tongue, spreading wicked beliefs through the people, dinning all ears with a variety of doctrines: alleging that the clergy could hold no property, that the monks had unlawfully obtained their lands and estates, that sacred laws had given to no pontiff fiscal rights and to no abbot the prerogative of governing the people, that all things were subject to lay authority, and that their management was to be entrusted to men of the people. Granting the clergy the first fruits and the tithes, and such offerings as the devotion of the people might make—but for

2383. The Reformation very strikingly manifests traits that we have already observed in other oscillations of the kind. In the first place, from the intrinsic standpoint (§ 2340), the Renaissance is partly a reaction of experimental reality against religious and moral prejudices; and if it takes the form of a return to pagan antiquity, that is a merely external trait that adds nothing essential to substance, being in that respect altogether similar to the return of the Reformers to Scripture. It is a very grave mistake to imagine that the Reformation in any sense furthered freedom of thought. On the contrary, it did an immense amount of harm to freedom of thought and halted the advance the Roman Church had been making toward tolerance and liberty. The Reformed and Roman Churches may be classed together as regards the scientific content of their doctrines. They both stand quite apart from the Humanists, who were coming much closer than they to experimental reality, by however much they may have failed of attaining it. But the Humanist movement, which had permeated even the College of Cardinals, was brought to a dead halt by the Reformation and the ensuing reaction in the Catholic Church.

2384. Considered from the extrinsic standpoint (§ 2340), the Renaissance occurred in a period of economic prosperity. To that

legitimate needs of subsistence and not for lusts or delights of the flesh—he altogether condemned high living, magnificence in forms of worship, concubinage and licentious enjoyments in the clergy, display on the part of the Popes, loose morals in the abbots, worldly pride in the monks.' ") And further, quoting Otto of Frisingen, Rinaldi explains: "Arnold was an Italian of Brescia, a cleric of the Church though ordained only as a lector. He had once been a pupil of Abelard. He was a man of no mean talents, though more distinguished for glibness of speech than for soundness of judgment. A lover of the unusual, eager for anything new, he was prone, as men of such temperaments are, to fomenting heresies and dissensions. Returning to Italy from his studies in France, he donned the habit of a priest, the more readily to deceive, and began to criticize and abuse everything, sparing no one, slandering the clergy and the bishops, persecuting the monks, and showering flattery only upon the laity. [An evident reflection of the popular character of the Arnoldite movement. Fundamentally it had nothing to do with the existence or non-existence of universals.] He said that priests who held property, bishops with palaces, monks with vast possessions, could in no wise be saved, that all such things belonged to the lay prince, who in his bounty should use them for the benefit of the laity." The usual excuse put forward by rulers for robbing religious institutions! It served pagan and Christian potentates, then the French Revolution, and finally it was adopted by that ultra-moralist, Waldeck-Rousseau.

fact there is no end of testimony.[1] It was also an age of rapid rise in prices, as the result of the inflow of precious metals from the Americas. Old institutions could no longer stand the strain. Everything seemed to need reforming. The modern world was being born. And then a religious reaction sets in and, as usual, it comes from the masses. Their leaders cared little about religion save as a tool of government. But for the masses it was the chief concern, and they

2384 [1] In his history of the Reformation in Germany, *Geschichte des deutschen Volkes,* Vol. I, pp. 594-95 (Mitchell-Christie, Vol. II, pp. 288-89), Janssen sees the facts as coloured by his faith, but, substantially, his description is not a bad one. He epitomizes conditions in Germany on the eve of the Protestant outbreak as follows: "[Germany at the end of the Middle Ages]: A flourishing condition in agriculture . . . an extraordinary development in industry and trade, a great wealth of mines, a commercial prosperity that surpassed that of any other Christian nation [An exaggeration: Janssen is forgetting Italy.], had all contributed to making Germany the richest country in Europe. Working-men on the farms in the country and in industry in the cities are for the most part very well off, materially speaking, at the beginning of the sixteenth century. But gradually the state of balance and the reciprocal influence of the great groups of labour are disturbed. Commerce begins to stifle value-producing labour. [An ethical derivation serving to take account of the rise of the speculator type to importance.] Price-manipulations and cornerings of commodities take place on all hands in spite of governmental measures, and the working-classes begin to be exploited on a large scale by capital. [Another derivation of the same sort.] Wide-spread now the complaints about monopolies, forestallings, the high interest on money, the high prices of commodities of prime necessity, the adulteration of food-products, the manoeuvres of 'big' business men and capitalists [A description in terms of derivations of the predominance of speculators—they are all phenomena of our own day.], in a word, about the tyranny exercised by those who have over those who have not. [One of the symptoms by which the predominance of speculators may be diagnosed.] The effects of such abuses are all the more disastrous in that the rich parade their unbridled extravagance before the eyes of the poor. And the workers and farmers themselves feel the bad influence of the luxury that is prevailing all about them. Material prosperity has stimulated expensive living and pleasure-seeking, and these in their turn develop a growing eagerness for greater and greater profits and foster in all ranks of society a passion for owning and enjoying." That might as well have been written of what we see going on under our own eyes: it is "speculation" gone rampant.

Things were very much the same in France at that time. Imbart de la Tour, *La France moderne,* pp. 421-62: "The merchant is no longer selling on the spot a specified commodity. He is a middleman who procures and sells the most diverse products. . . . He has an eye out for everything. . . . In those circumstances there are no limits to what he may earn. . . . Owing to increased demand, a higher standard of living, a larger turnover, he can corner for his own profit all sources of wealth, and great fortunes begin to be founded on the ruins of some and the mediocre station of others. . . . The second half of the century witnesses the advent of hordes of large-scale business men, who are real speculators and manipulators of business and who are destined to drain off all the wealth produced by labour and

tried their best to enforce it now in one way, now in another. It was the objective of many of their activities. The Reformation, in short, was one of the usual reactions by which Class II residues (group-persistences) force a retreat upon Class I residues (the instinct for combinations).

2385. But since economic conditions that were stimulating Class I

by the soil. [The usual bias of the moralist: those speculators themselves produced huge amounts of wealth.] The outstanding trait in the merchant of that period is that, more than anything else, he is what is called 'the forestaller.' He deals in large quantities and gets them into his own hands. He buys to sell, and he sells what he does not yet own. [That always rouses the wrath of our moralists but, economically, it often has very good results.] In 1517, the number of fictitious markets has become so large and they are so much the rule that the scrivener of Orleans asks the public authorities to interfere. They interfere . . . but to no purpose. Nothing more spectacular than the Barjots, who had never been heard of in the Beaujolais, but who laid the foundations of their fortune in the vitriol mines and then became 'public merchants' of grains and wines, and the better to prosecute said business 'rent and hire several large benefices both secular and regular [i.e., of the Church], and the properties of several gentleman in the district.' The Barjots were not alone. Documents of the period are for ever mentioning these speculators who are swooping down on all the revenues (*fermes*) in a district and winning the exasperated jealousy and hatred of the people there. . . . Trader, speculator, collecting agent for public and private revenues, broker, banker, money-lender, as skilful at amassing money as he is at investing it, the merchant succeeds in turning to his profit that immense power which rules the world: capital. . . . Semblançay is not just an instance. He is a symbol. He epitomizes the whole history of those amazing upstarts whom a society in transformation has spouted up from its depths. Their emergence was doubtless in part the personal work of Louis XI, who liked contrasts. It was the recompense for the service they rendered, for their professional aptitude, their peculiar turn of mind. But it was also the work of circumstances that were then pushing the man of money to the fore as they had the man of war in a day gone by. [Just so in our day.] . . . But their mounting wealth also increased their influence. [Just so in our day.] Their private prosperity was bound up with public prosperity. In them royalty [In our day, democracy.] always found suppliers of funds who were pledged in advance, and they were always necessary [Just so in our day.] in the moments of embarrassment in which the Exchequer was always finding itself." At that time speculators served monarchy. In our day they serve democracy. Tomorrow they will serve Socialism, and day after tomorrow Anarchy, if necessary. They are always ready to serve anybody who will help them in their money-making; and to making money they are driven by their wealth of combination-instincts and their poverty in group-persistences (Class II residues). "*Bourgeoisie* and absolutism [Today, democracy.] grew up together, the *bourgeoisie* fed by the absolutism, the absolutism strengthened by the *bourgeoisie*. . . . They [The Caillaux's of that day.] were all the more devoted to absolutism in that in working for its interests they were working for their own." The kings who gave all that power to speculators were preparing the way for the Revolution of '89, and consequently for the fall of monarchy (§ 2227 [1]).

residues continued to prevail, those residues gradually began to regain the ground they had lost. "Reason" again set to work to demolish the edifice of "superstition," and that edifice, so far as the upper classes in society were concerned, collapsed towards the end of the eighteenth century, and perhaps a half-century earlier in England than in France;[1] and then very much the same things happened as at the beginning of the sixteenth century. Two hundred years had been enough to complete the work. The *philosophes* of the eighteenth century were the heirs of the Humanists, and like them leaned toward paganism; for that is one of the many forms which the battle between Class I and Class II residues may assume, when Class II residues are defended by Christianity. The opposite might be true if the battle were waged in a pagan society—and that may actually have been the case in the early days of Christianity.

2386. The latter part of the eighteenth century was a period of economic prosperity. At that time we witness the first dawnings of modern transformations in agriculture, commerce, and industry. That circumstance favoured, as usual, a predominance of Class I residues, and was itself favoured by that predominance. The tide of economic prosperity rose first in England, and that is why the curve for Class II residues, as regards their relative proportions to Class I residues, first shows a drop in that country; and that also is why, in virtue of the undulating movement peculiar to that curve, even with

2385 [1] Porret, *Le réveil religieux du XVIIIᵉ siècle en Angleterre,* pp. 11-12. Despite a rich saucing of theological and ethical derivations, the facts are tolerably well described: "Towards the end of the seventeenth century the 'reasonable Christianity' of the philosopher Locke, deistic in theology, sensualistic in psychology, was predominant in England. The Gospel was looked upon as a mere system of morality and a rather vulgar morality at that. . . . Bishop Hoadley openly professed Deism. According to Judge Blackstone there was no more Christianity in the sermons of the more prominent preachers in London than in the orations of Cicero. Possessed of comfortable incomes and not obliged to keep taverns to make a living, as some of their predecessors had done, clergymen who got drunk in a genteel manner were by no means rare exceptions. Some were mere idlers about the drawing-rooms of society, others devoted themselves to letters, to poetry especially. . . . Better behaved on the whole, the churches of the dissenters hardly had any greater vitality. . . . Addison notes in 1712 that 'the very appearances of Christianity had vanished' and Leibnitz says in 1715 that even 'natural religion was languishing in England.' . . . Aristocratic society was in decay. Unbelief was on the aggressive, running from the most radical rationalism to brazen atheism. Successes in the book-trade went to unbelief. Woolston's addresses against miracles sold up to thirty thousand copies and the materialism of Hobbes could count a very considerable following."

economic conditions remaining virtually constant, England was the first country to experience a reaction toward a rise in the curve.[1] So, both the action and reaction in England anticipated the corresponding movements in France. The action was "philosophic" in outward garb in both countries; the reaction, though substantially the same, assumed different forms, being Christian in England and democratic in France. The French Revolution was a religious reaction of the same type, under a different form, as the religious reaction in England, and also of the same type as the religious reaction represented by the Reformation. But it was soon to change its costume. Democratic and humanitarian in the early stages of the Revolution, it became patriotic and belligerent under Napoleon, then Catholic under Louis XVIII. The high point in the curve of the relative preponderance of Class II over Class I residues was reached, taking Europe as a whole, shortly after 1815; and the exteriors everywhere were Christian.

2387. But such movements are essentially undulatory, so that again there came a further drop in the curve—a sharp one, because it

2386 [1] Porret, *Op. cit.*, pp. 18-20: "About 1790 Edmund Burke cried: 'Not one of the men born among us within the past forty years has read a word of Collins, of Toland (author of a *Christianity Not Mysterious,* who died in 1722), of Tyndal (apostle of natural religion, hailed by Voltaire, who died in 1733), or of any of that flock of so-called free-thinkers. Atheism is not only against our reason, it is against our instincts.' What a change in outlook! Fifty years had been enough to encompass such an incredible reversal! How account for it? . . . I do not deny that Addison, the founder of the *Spectator,* which reached a circulation of 3,000 copies a week, may have exercised a salutary influence at the beginning of the century. Berkeley was a vigorous thinker and his profession of idealism was effective enough to ruin a materialism that had been just previously triumphant. Samuel Johnson must not be forgotten, later on. But it would be fantastic to ascribe a decisive influence to any one of them or to all three of them together. The religious and moral awakening in England between 1735 and 1775 is not to be explained by a few nobly inspired books. It presupposes some fact, or better some body of fact, some powerful movement [Very true.], that lays hold on souls in large numbers, tears them as it were from themselves and gives them birth to a new life [An ethico-theological derivation.], forcing those that prove refractory, if not to show love, at least to show respect. Such a change can be explained only by the influence of the moral and religious conscience as the centre of human personality. [Another ethico-theological derivation.] It can be explained only as the work of a powerful and merciful God"— a purely theological derivation. It is interesting that this writer should have seen so clearly, through the fog of his ethical and theological derivations, the power of the non-logical impulses that were responsible for the undulating movements we have been describing.

corresponded to a swift and powerful wave of economic prosperity. Economic production was in process of transformation. Large-scale industry, large-scale commerce, international finance, were coming on the scene, and prospering. The Class I residues gradually regain pre-eminence, and the "positivists," "free-thinkers," and "intellectuals" of the nineteenth century resume their time-honoured task of undermining the edifice of "prejudice," so proving themselves the legitimate heirs of the *philosophes* of the eighteenth century. They did not wage their war in the name of paganism, as did the Humanists, or in the name of "common sense," as did the *philosophes* of the eighteenth century. The banner they bore aloft was the ensign of the goddess Science. The wave that they expressed attained its peak of intensity between the years 1860 and 1870. Thereafter it begins to fall away, and in the first decade of the twentieth century a reaction sets in in favour of group-persistences (Class II residues) [neo-idealism, nationalism, *etc.*].

2388. As is usually the case, particular undulations are superimposed upon this general trend, and care must be exercised not to mistake the short waves for the general trend, that error being all the easier since it is the short wave that we have before our eyes, and in virtue of that proximity it may seem to have a greater importance than it actually has when the movement as a whole is viewed over a period of years (§ 2394).

2389. Noteworthy among such short waves is the undulation that occurred after the War of 1870 and which, though determined primarily by the conditions prevailing at that time in European societies, was also due in some small part to the personal influence of Prince von Bismarck. In his *Kulturkampf* Bismarck contributed, quite involuntarily, to the fight on Class II residues and so prolonged the predominance of Class I residues. He protected the Old Catholics for the sake of gaining momentary advantages, without perceiving that in that policy he was striking at the foundations of his imperial policy. Later on he thought better of the matter, and made his peace with the Roman Curia.

In all that department the Emperor, William II, showed himself more far-sighted than Bismarck, for he saw clearly that any conflict which tended to weaken group-persistences could in no way benefit the Empire. Bismarck, furthermore, and again for momentary requirements of tactic, protected the anti-Clerical republic in France; and the effect of that measure too was to prolong the predominance of Class I residues. On the other hand, out of aversion to *bourgeois* liberalism, of which he had more than once had occasion to complain, he extended universal suffrage throughout the German Empire, so favouring the Socialist party and reinforcing certain residues of Class II. Others were also increased in intensity through the formation of the Catholic party of the Centre, so called, and through the spread of anti-Semitism.[1]

2390. At the present time the prosperity of the Class II residues seems to be chiefly entrusted to the intensification of patriotism in one form or another, such as nationalism and imperialism. Socialism is also stimulating other group-persistences that stand in conflict with patriotism, but of late, in this year 1914, it has been showing itself inclined to political combinations and is being permeated with Class I residues, with the result that it is offering a very feeble resistance to nationalism and imperialism. Many Socialists, in fact, are changing forms of faith, and may be seen combining, on one pretext or another, with nationalists and imperialists. On a subordinate plane, we are now witnessing revivals in various religions, from the Christian down to the sex and Prohibitionist religions, while metaphysics is again having its day, and nonsensical patter that fifty years ago seemed to have been discredited for ever is coming into vogue again. This oscillation is now in its first stages. How long it will last, and how far it will go, are things not given us to foresee; but what we know of oscillations in the past justifies the prediction that it will end in a new fluctuation of opposite trend.

2391. If one considers from a standpoint somewhat detached all these phenomena that so regularly occur and recur in history from the remotest past down to the present, one can only gather the

2389 [1] Bismarck afterwards changed his mind on the matter of suffrage too: *Gedanken und Erinnerungen,* p. 645 (Butler, Vol. II, p. 338): "Around '78 or '79, the persuasion that I had been mistaken, that I had not appraised the national spirit of dynasties at its true value, that I had overestimated the value of patriotism in German voters or at least in the Reichstag, had not absolutely come over me, in spite of the bad will with which I had had to deal in the Reichstag, at Court, and in the Conservative party and its spokesmen (*Deklaranten*). Today I must offer my apologies to dynasties."

impression that such oscillations are the rule and that they are not likely to cease very soon. What is to happen years hence in a far distant future we do not know; but it is altogether probable that a course of events with a history so long is not to change in any near future.

2392. It is in no sense proved that the oscillations occur about a line, *ab* (Figure 41), corresponding to a constant proportion between Class II and Class I residues, and not, rather, about a line, *mp,* which indicates a diminishing proportion of Class II residues. Facts in great number lead one to believe that it is the latter line, *mp,* that

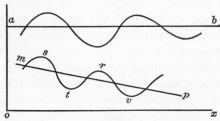

Figure 41

describes the general average movement. We have seen that classes of residues change slowly, but are not, for all of that, constant. The movement represented by the line *mp* is in no way contrary, therefore, to the properties of residues. On the other hand, if conditions in our societies are compared with conditions in Graeco-Roman society, it is readily apparent that in many branches of human activity, as, for instance, in the arts and sciences and in economic production, Class I residues and the conclusions of logico-experimental science have forced a retreat on group-persistences. In political and social activity that is less apparent, and perhaps such effect as there may be is very very slight. But those are mere branches of human activity. If we consider modern life as a whole, we may safely conclude that Class I residues and the conclusions of logico-experimental science have enlarged the field of their dominion. To that fact is largely due, indeed, the great variety of traits in our modern societies as compared with the societies of ancient Greece and Rome.

2393. It is no great mistake, therefore, to judge that "reason" is coming to play a more and more important rôle in human activity. Indeed such a view is altogether in accord with the facts. But that proposition, like all the formulas that literature substitutes for the theorems of science, is vague in meaning, and easily gives rise to not a few errors, among which one might specify the following:

2394. 1. The formula can refer only to the social complex as a whole. It has widely differing values as applied to the various departments of society, and one goes wrong in imagining that political and social activities show the traits that are observable in the arts and sciences, and in economic production.

2. It describes a mean or average trend, and the average trend must not be mistaken for the real trend, *strv.* . . . So true is it that people are most strongly impressed by the facts they have before their eyes that a person situated, for instance, on the descending segment, *st,* of the curve [when "reason" is gaining over "faith"] will imagine that that represents the mean movement, that the rest of the curve will continue indefinitely downward in the same direction, or that it will never turn upward again—not foreseeing that the rising segment, *tr,* will eventually be appearing. *Vice versa,* a person situated on a rising segment, *tr* [when "faith" is gaining at the expense of "reason"], will not foresee the drop *rv.* That happens more rarely, however, either because the general mean trend of the curve, *mp,* is contrary to that second opinion [and in favour of "reason" over "faith"] or because—the more cogent reason—the second opinion is in conflict with the theology of Progress, whereas the first is in accord with it.

3. An error of the same sort, though less serious, is to conceive of the mean curve as approximately coinciding with the trend of the short wave that is visible before one. So a person situated on the descending segment, *rv* [where "reason" is gaining over "faith"], is led to believe that the mean curve is dropping more rapidly than is actually the case [that intelligence is gaining].

4. Finally, there is the common error of viewing the contingent observation of experience as something absolute. So theologies and metaphysics of retrogression, stability, progress, come into being, and people laud, exalt, glorify, the wisdom of the ancients and a golden age that they locate in the past; or the serene immobility of the dogmas of a religion, an ethical system, or a political and social constitution; or, again, the god Progress, the blessings of "evolution," and a golden age now located in the future. Time was

when almost all writers verily believed that the men of their day were physical dwarfs as compared with the giants who had lived of yore. Nowadays not a few writers, thinking of the moral rather than of the physical, and inverting terms, firmly believe that the men of our time are to be counted moral dwarfs as compared with the moral giants who will live at some future time, when the wolf shall lie down with the lamb and there shall be "a little more justice in the world." Along such lines the experimentally verifiable segments, *strv,* of the undulations become imaginary segments, grotesquely distorted, till sometimes they end by having little if anything to do with reality.[1]

2395. Such logico-experimental errors may sometimes be beneficial to society, but we need not add anything here to the much we have already said on that subject. Keeping to the correspondence between theory and fact, we see that the purpose of the scientific study of social phenomena is to avoid just such mistakes and replace figments of the imagination with the results of experience. The imaginary and the demonstrated fact may at times have something in common; but if one would acquire a sounder and broader knowledge of natural phenomena and escape the danger of going wrong, one must trust only in the results of experience as progressively corrected and recorrected by new observations.

2396. *Society as a whole.* We have now arrived at a general conception of the social complex, not only in its static but also in its dynamic aspects, and not only as regards the forces that are actually working upon it but as regards the outward appearances, the more or less distorted forms, in which they are perceived. Some few remarks about their bearing on logico-experimental studies such as we have been trying to prosecute in these volumes may still not come amiss.

2397. A logico-experimental study merely relates facts with facts. If that is done directly, merely describing facts that are observable simultaneously, we get pure empiricism. Empiricism may serve to discover uniformities if, by observation or experiment, one succeeds

2394 [1] In general at least, such imaginary segments are largely determined by the segments, *strv* . . . , to which they correspond—and that is the relation we examined in considering what we called the *extrinsic* aspect (§§ 2343 f.). But the theories represented by such imaginary segments also act and react upon one another, and to that also we adverted in considering what we called the *intrinsic* aspect (§§ 2340 f.).

in distinguishing not more than two categories of facts that stand in correlation. Once the categories multiply and effects become involved, it proves to be very difficult, and more often impossible, to find uniformities with the tool of pure empiricism. The sum of effects has somehow to be unsnarled. In certain cases that can be done materially by experiment. In others, experiment is out of the question or else fails to unravel the complication. Then one can only resort to hypothetical abstractions, now to one, now to another, testing each in turn with the idea of solving ideally what cannot be solved materially, accepting finally that hypothesis among the many which yields results that accord with experience. The manner in which the hypothesis has been reached may be absurd. That is of little if any importance; for the value of the hypothesis is tested not by the manner in which it has been conceived, but by the verifications that can be made of it.

2398. But if the hypothesis has been inferred in the first place from certain facts, $A, B \ldots P$, that circumstance in itself is a first step toward verification; for since the hypothesis has been inferred from those facts, they certainly will appear among the results it will yield. What remains to be seen is whether it will also yield the facts $Q, R \ldots V$, which have not yet been taken into the reckoning (§ 2078 [1]).

2399. In these volumes, therefore, we might have followed a deductive method, positing our residues and derivations at the very outset as mere hypotheses, without explaining how we came by them, thence going on to show that they yielded results which accorded with the facts. Instead we elected to follow the inductive method, deriving our residues and derivations from facts in very large numbers. So, as far as those facts were concerned, the verification was made then and there, and all that remained was to extend the verification to other facts not as yet considered. That verification we proceeded to make and are still making. In a word, then, what we have been doing, and are still doing, is to establish relations between facts.

2400. There is nothing peculiar about such a method. It is the method general in all the sciences. Oftentimes in the sciences a hypothesis serves for a certain length of time and promotes progress in a particular science; then it is replaced by another, which performs the same function until, in its turn, it gives way to still a third; and so on. Sometimes a hypothesis may hold its ground for a very long time, as was the case with the hypothesis of universal gravitation.[1]

The logico-experimental sciences are made up of a sum of theories that are like living creatures, in that they are born, live, and die, the young replacing the old, the group alone enduring (§ 52). As is the case with living beings, the lifetimes of theories vary in length and not always are the long-lived ones the ones that contribute most to the advancement of knowledge. Faith and metaphysics aspire to an ultimate, eternal resting-place. Science knows that it can attain only

2400 [1] Perrin, Les atomes, p. 73. Alluding to a theory that was at first considered false and was subsequently recognized as true, Perrin remarks: "That experience emphasized to me how little stock, really, we take in theories, how true it is that we think of them as mere tools for discovering things, rather than as actual demonstrations." That is just our attitude towards the theories that are set forth in this treatise. Ostwald, Der Werdegang einer Wissenschaft, p. 150: "Following the lot of the various theories in chemistry down to our own time, what one notes very regularly is that a theory is developed in the first place in order to picture by modifications in a certain scheme the variedness of existing combinations. Naturally one scheme that is chosen harmonizes with known facts, so that all theories more or less adequately reflect the state of knowledge at their time. [That is true of sciences that are cultivated experimentally. The social sciences, however, have so far been studied in the light of sentiments, more than anything else. For them, therefore, one would more accurately say rather: "reflect the state of sentiments and interests, at their time, with larger or smaller admixtures of experimental elements."] But science is constantly adding to its fund of facts [For the social sciences: "Experience is always gaining more or less ground."], so that sooner or later a lack of accord develops between the actual multiplicity of facts and the arbitrary multiplicity of the theory. [In the social sciences the disaccord is chiefly apparent between facts and inferences from sentiments.] Most often there is a first effort to squeeze the facts into the theory, if all its possibilities can be seen at a glance and it cannot yield anything more. But in the long run, facts are tougher and more durable than theories, or at least than the men who fight for them. So it eventually becomes necessary to broaden the old doctrine so far as is required, or to replace it with new conceptions that are better adapted to requirements."

There are several types of persons who cannot understand such things, among them persons who devise, or adopt, theories in defence of their own interests (auro suadente, nil potest oratio!); those countless individuals who follow the lead of sentiments, faiths, beliefs; finally our "intellectuals" who disseminate "social science" without even knowing what an experimental science is. All such, and others still, may be socially useful, but they do not count when discovering experimental realities is the one concern (§ 2113 [1]).

provisory, transitory positions. Every theory fulfils its function, and nothing more can be asked of it.[2]

If such succession in doctrines is in great part determined by a single force, the successive stages may constantly approach a certain limit; their curve may have an asymptote (§ 2392). That is what is happening in the logico-experimental sciences. The force, and if not the only one at least the chief one, that is now influencing those sciences is the investigation of correspondences between theories and experience. Theories therefore are constantly getting closer to experimental reality; whereas in a day gone by other forces were at work and prevented attainment of that result. Economic and social doctrines are still subject to such forces, and for that reason they continue to be at variance with experimental reality, sometimes to very considerable degrees, and it is doubtful whether there be any asymptote for their oscillations.

If the succession of doctrines is determined by a large number of forces of approximately equal intensities, the movement revealed in the succession may be so complicated as to make it impossible to

2400 [2] Perrin, *Op. cit.,* pp. 290-91. Noting the agreement of the results obtained in determining Avogadro's Number *N* under widely differing circumstances, Perrin continues: "All the same, however urgently the existence of molecules and atoms forces itself upon us, we must always be in a position to state visible realities without resorting to invisible elements. And that, in fact, is very easy. We simply have to eliminate the invariant *N* from the thirteen equations that have served to determine it in order to get twelve equations that deal entirely with sensible realities and express profound relations between first-hand phenomena as completely independent as the adhesion of gases, the Brownian movement, the blue of the sky, the spectrum of the opaque body, or radioactivity. . . . But we should never be so awkward, on pretext of meticulous accuracy, as to avoid introducing molecular elements into the statement of laws that we could not have obtained without their assistance. That would not be removing a prop that had become useless for a grown plant: it would be cutting the roots that have been feeding it and causing it to grow."

Much the same may be said of our theory of residues. Residues represent a constant element in huge numbers of varying phenomena. All the same, we might say, we ought always to be able to state concrete realities without appealing to abstractions. That we can do by eliminating the invariables called *residues* from among the many many equations that we have used in obtaining our abstractions and in which they represent nothing but concrete realities. But we should not be so unwary as to avoid, on pretext of exactness, the introduction of abstract elements into statements of laws that we have obtained with their help. It is to our advantage not to dispense with the important services that they can still render until progress in knowledge has replaced them with others, which in their turn will be kept as long as they are serviceable, and so on indefinitely.

find any general expression for it. But if such forces, without being so few as one, are at least not many, there are cases in which we can discover such an expression. We may, for instance, recognize movements as oscillating about a given point, whether tending towards an equilibrium in that position or continuing on indefinitely without any tendency of the kind. We have seen movements of that sort taking place under the pressure of two forces in the main: correspondences with experimental reality and social utility (§§ 1683, 2329, 2391).

Only in a first approximation can the numberless forces operating in a concrete case be reduced to two. If, to carry an investigation farther, new forces are brought into consideration as an addition to the two main ones, we get movements that grow increasingly complicated and are harder and harder to manage (§§ 2339, 2388). In these volumes we have succeeded in taking a few steps along that road (§§ 2343 f.), but it bristles with obstacles, and they are too numerous to permit us to go as far as we should have liked.[3]

2401. Kepler's discovery that the orbit of Mars was an ellipse with one of its foci coinciding with the centre of the Sun was purely empirical, providing a summary description of the situation. In that case, owing to the imperfect observations available (§ 540[1]), it was possible to distinguish the movement of one planet with respect to the Sun from the movements of the other planets. Had the observations been more nearly exact, no such distinction could have been made, Kepler would have found no ellipse, and that would have been a serious obstacle to the advancement of astronomy.

Two cases have to be considered in this connexion:

2402. 1. As regards our solar system, the obstacle might have been overcome without great difficulty. Some scientists would have observed that if the curve traversed by Mars was not an ellipse, it was in any case not far from an ellipse; and he could have suggested the *hypothesis* that if Mars and the Sun were considered apart from the

2400 [8] Had we followed the deductive method, the things we are now saying would have come at the beginning of our first volume; but in that case, without the help of the exposition that has gradually been unfolding our theory might have been misunderstood, or even not grasped at all. The inductive approach has enabled us to establish our meaning clearly and make it readily intelligible; and the general theory, coming as it does after an examination of particular cases, is adequately explained by them.

other planets, the curve had to be an ellipse, and that if that was not the case, it was because the Sun and Mars were not considered apart from the other planets.

2403. 2. The obstacle would have been much greater and perhaps insuperable if instead of our solar system, where the central body has an enormously greater mass than any of its planets, a system of stars and planets of no very appreciable differences in mass had been in question.

2404. Sometimes, though unfortunately very rarely, the facts correlated by statistics may be brought under the first case just mentioned: that is to say, by interpolation, a certain hypothetical curve can be found from which the real curve can be inferred by assuming perturbations. But much more often the facts of economics, and to a still greater extent of sociology, are to be brought under the second case.

2405. Newton advanced a hypothesis, known as the theory of universal gravitation, whereby if the Sun is assumed to be stationary with a planet revolving around it, one gets a curve something like the curve discovered by Kepler—an ellipse.

2406. That hypothesis has one peculiar merit that is rarely met with in other hypotheses of the kind. The relation between the hypothesis and the facts can be inverted. If it be assumed that a planet is moving in an ellipse about a stationary Sun, a law of gravitation results that is Newton's law exactly. Generally, in economics and sociology, a hypothesis may indeed imply the existence of certain facts, but those facts may lend themselves to many other hypotheses.

2407. Newton's hypothesis has also another very great merit, that so far at least [1914], taking the Sun and its planets as a whole, it has been adequate for explaining all the perturbations that have been observed in the movements of the celestial bodies. If that had not been the case, Newton's hypothesis might have stood, but it would have had to be supplemented with other hypotheses, the hypothesis, for instance, that the attraction exerted by the planets upon one another is different from the attraction between the planets and the Sun.

Needless to say, neither economics nor sociology possesses simple hypotheses as widely applicable as Newton's.

2408. In political economy and sociology, therefore, it is indispensable to consider many different elements in the complex phenomena that are directly recorded by observation.[1] The simplest thing one can say in economics is that the economic equilibrium

2408 [1] Pareto, "*Économie mathématique,*" *Encyclopédie des sciences mathématiques:* "From the strictly mathematical point of view, it makes no difference as regards determining the equilibrium whether the individual's conduct is known as a function of supply and demand or by index-functions. [In note 9, p. 596:] Only gradually, as I freed myself from the notions of the old political economy, did I come to replace the concept of ophelimity with the concept of index-functions. Ophelimity is used exclusively in my *Cours;* it gives way to indices of ophelimity in my *Manuale.* It is still further generalized in my *Manuel.*" P. 606: "Cournot took $pF(p)$ as an index-function. He would have reached exactly the same result had he taken $F[pF(p)]$, F being an arbitrary function. He used index-functions without being aware of it. Cournot tried to extend his method to the case of free competition, but he was altogether mistaken in his inferences, and the consideration of indices inferred from quantities exchanged at given prices was abandoned for another method. . . . All the same, by reasoning correctly . . . index-functions can be deduced from a consideration of quantities exchanged at given prices." In my *Manuel,* p. 542, after suggesting an equation (9) that might be derived directly from experience and contains nothing but quantities of commodities, I add: "The equation (9) is the only one, strictly speaking, that we need in order to establish the theory of the economic equilibrium. Now that equation contains nothing corresponding to ophelimity or indices of ophelimity. The whole theory of the economic equilibrium, therefore, is independent of the concepts of utility (economic), usage-value, and ophelimity. It needs only one thing: to know, that is, the limits of the relationships

$$\frac{\Delta_1 x}{\Delta y}, \quad \frac{\Delta_2 x}{\Delta z} \dots$$

A whole treatise on political economy could therefore be written starting with equation (9) and other similar equations, and it may be desirable some day to do that. [In a note:] That is one of many reasons why our theories are altogether distinct from those of the 'Austrian School,' so called." And I might add that in that respect they differ also from the theories of Walras, which I followed more closely in my *Cours,* and for which the concept of "rarity" (§ 2078 [1]) was an indispensable basis. *Ibid.,* pp. 570-71: "Instead of experimenting to determine lines or varieties of indifference, suppose we experiment to find out just what quantities of goods the individual will buy at certain given prices." The required experiments are described in mathematical terms. Then comes the conclusion: "The greater or lesser difficulty, or even the impossibility, one might encounter in making these experiments practically is a matter of scant importance. The theoretical possibility of making them is sufficient for proving, in the cases examined, that indices of ophelimity exist, and for showing certain of their characteristics. So the indices of ophelimity and the laws of supply and demand are brought into correlation, and one may move back and forth from the ones to the others." *Ibid.,* p. 571 (§ 43): "The theory of the economic equilibrium might be derived directly from the experiments just indi-

results from the conflict between tastes and obstacles; but the simplicity is only apparent, since one then has to go on and take account of an intricate variety of tastes and obstacles. The complications in sociology are greater still and by far. There, in addition to
logical conduct, which is alone envisaged in economics, one has to
deal with non-logical conduct, and then again, in addition to logical
thinking, with derivations (§ 99).

2409. The laws, so called, of supply and demand cannot be deduced from statistics as to the quantities and prices of a commodity
produced or brought to market. When economists said that an increase in supply brings a drop in price, they stated the law of an
ideal situation that is rarely observable in the concrete. In working
out theories in economics it is an illusion to believe that we get any
closer to the concrete by starting with the laws of supply and demand than we do by starting with the "utility" of the early economists, or with the "marginal utility," the "rarity," or the "ophelimity," of more recent economists.[1] Whatever we do, we are re-

cated"—therefore, without resort to the concepts of ophelimity, indices of ophelimity,
or any other indices of the kind. To find the laws of supply and demand Walras
considered the exchange of two commodities only [*Éléments d'économie politique
pure*, pp. 43-106], and he was right in that, for difficulties are solved one at a time.
But then it is necessary to go on from there and solve new problems. That is what
I did in considering exchanges of several commodities, assuming first independent
consumptions ([*"Di un errore di Cournot nel trattare l'economia politica con la
matematica"*], *Giornale degli economisti*, August, 1892), then assuming dependent
consumptions (see my *Manuel*, and my article, "*Économie mathématique*," *Encyclopédie des sciences mathématiques*).

2409 [1] Pareto, "*L'économie et la sociologie au point de vue scientifique*," *Scientia*,
Bologna, 1907, p. 13: "Since the economic equilibrium was first studied on the
basis of free competition, many people have imagined that pure economics envisaged that situation only. That is very like the mistake of imagining that because dynamics began by considering the movement of one material point, it
could not deal with a system of points subjected to 'ties.' Pure economics can and
does study all sorts of economic situations in addition to the case of free competition; and in view of the exactitude of its methods it gives exact definitions for
the terms 'free competition,' 'monopoly,' and so on, which have been hitherto used
more or less loosely. Among the groups of equations that determine the economic
equilibrium there is one which contains the ophelimities of commodities consumed. That circumstance was the occasion for another mistaken impression, that
the theories of pure economics were closely bound up with the concept of ophelimity
('rarity,' 'marginal utility,' and the like) and therefore could not stand apart
from it. There is nothing to that. We can, if we choose, eliminate ophelimities from
those equations, and get a new system that will determine the economic equilibrium
just as well. This new system will contain a group of equations that will exactly

sorting to abstractions, and we cannot do otherwise. Theoretically one may start with any one of those considerations or indeed with any others; but however we start, we must use certain cautions that are overlooked by many writers who talk political economy without knowing the first thing about it. From the theoretical standpoint, again, one must not forget that consumptions of commodities are not independent, as not a few of the founders of pure economics assumed them to be.[2] Nor can the undulatory movements of economic phenomena be disregarded, nor a great many other circumstances, such as speculation, which change the simpler form of the phenomena that, for purposes of convenience, was the one considered first.

2410. All that has just been said applies *a fortiori* to sociology. Little or nothing can be inferred directly from the mere description, and in that sense the apothegm that "history never repeats itself" is very true. Concrete phenomena have to be broken up into ideal phenomena that are simpler, that we may so arrive at something more nearly constant than the complex and ever shifting thing we have before us in the concrete.[1] In these volumes we have sought

express the older, vaguer, and at times erroneous conception that was called the 'law of supply and demand.' "

2409 [2] Pareto, *Manuale*, Chap. IV, § 11: "In order to make the problems with which they were to deal more manageable, a number of the founders of pure economics were led to assume that the ophelimity of a commodity depended only upon the amount of it at the individual's disposal. They are not to be blamed for that; for difficulties have to be dealt with one at a time, and to go safely one must go slowly. But now the time has come to take another step forward and think of the ophelimity of a commodity as influenced also by the consumptions of all other commodities." That subject is discussed at length in the chapter mentioned and in my "Mathematical Appendix." The *Manuale* was published in 1906. Yet long years after that, and after the French translation of that work had appeared, a writer came along and criticized the theories of pure economics for considering only independent consumptions of commodities! Such the passion that blinds certain individuals, and such the ignorance that afflicts them! From the theoretical standpoint, the order of consumptions also has to be taken into account. A keen and very sound remark by Professor Vito Volterra led me to make a study of that subject, which I published in the *Giornale degli economisti*, July, 1906, and summarized in my *Manuel*, pp. 546-56.

2410 [1] It was in deference to that principle, precisely, and to other principles of scientific sociology that Marie Kobalinska wrote a book that we have often quoted, *La circulation des élites en France*. If the rôles of classes of residues and derivations were inverted, if, that is, residues were very variable and derivations virtually constant, the evolution of human societies would have been altogether different

these less variable, these more constant, elements in residues and
derivations. They might very well be sought in other directions.
That is not so important as to be careful that wherever one goes
looking for them, elements and forms that lead away from objective
reality are not introduced. That "history never repeats itself" identically is just as certain as it is that history is "always repeating itself"
in certain respects that we may call the main respects. It would be
inconceivably absurd to imagine that history could produce an
event identically repeating the Peloponnesian War, in the sense of
being an exact copy of it. But then again, history shows that that
war, which arose in the rivalry between Athens and Sparta, is only
one item in an endless series of similar wars that have been brought
on by similar causes, that in that sense there are numberless copies
of it that are likenesses, to some extent at least, from the wars that
arose in the rivalries between Carthage and Rome down to all the
other wars that have been fought in all periods of history between
then and now. In his *Politica,* V, 3, 7 (Rackham, p. 395), Aristotle
says: "Finally, it must be evident that those who have been the
cause of power [to a city], whether they be private citizens, magistrates, clans, or in short, any part of a people, are responsible for
insurrections." In those words he was describing one of the main
elements in the great many facts that were known to him, and he
was foreseeing a great many other facts that were to come true after
his time, the cases of Cromwell and Napoleon, to mention examples
closer to our own times.

The main element in such happenings is in fact supplied by sentiments (residues), which have varied but slightly between Aristotle's
time and our own. The same may be said of many maxims of

from what it is seen to have been, and the general remarks of historians would
have to take on a new and different form, in which, among the elements determining social phenomena, demonstrations would take the place now held by sentiments and interests. Just such a form of historical writing that strays from
realities, and sometimes very far, is represented by writers who consider logical
conduct exclusively or primarily, and by those who view their facts through the
lens of this or that system of absolute ethics. Indeed the ethics and the logic remaining constant, the derivations to which they give rise also have to be considered
constant; and the variability in phenomena becomes wholly or almost wholly dependent on an assumed variability in residues and on the experimentally verifiable
variability of the arts and sciences (§ 356), which, for that matter, is usually made
dependent on residues, including sentiments that prevent human beings from
making adequate use of reason.

Machiavelli, which hold as true today as they were in his time. Classes of residues vary but slightly and but slowly, and they may therefore be counted among the elements that determine the constant, virtually constant, or at least not very variable element in historical phenomena. The separate genera in a class of residues vary to a far greater degree and much more rapidly than the class as a whole, and we must therefore be cautious in giving them any such position. Derivations vary widely and very rapidly; and they are generally to be counted, therefore, only among the subordinate elements that determine secondary, variable, and for the most part negligible phases in a phenomenon. What we have just been saying furnishes the key also to a fact to which we have had frequent occasion to allude—that in a quest for sociological uniformities, too many facts, details too minute, may be a hindrance rather than a help; for if one dwells on all the petty circumstances that figure in a situation, one easily loses one's way, like a person travelling in a thick underbrush; one is prevented from assigning proper indices to the various elements, mistaking what is secondary for what is principal, what is very variable for what is quasi-constant, and so one ends by writing a piece of literature that is devoid of the slightest scientific value.[2]

2411. In the practice of the social sciences one must especially be on one's guard against intrusions of personal sentiments; for a writer is inclined to look not for what is and nothing else, but for what *ought* to be in order to fit in with his religious, moral, patriotic, humanitarian, or other sentiments.[1] The quest for uniformities is an

2410 [2] Excellent works in sociology have been criticized for not considering "all the facts" and all details of the facts. That is to mistake a merit for a defect. For such an objection to be valid it has to be presentable in the following form: "You fail to take account of this or that fact which exerts an important influence on the main element in the phenomena in which you are looking for uniformities; and you overlook this or that detail which is just as important." Furthermore, as regards substance, adequate substantiation of the assertions would then have to be offered. But all such things are understandable only to a person who is using in the social sciences the methods that have proved so successful in the experimental sciences. [This note repeats remarks that were made in §§ 537 [1] and 1749 [6].—A. L.]

2411 [1] And one must also be on one's guard against the eagerness, the mania, for practical applications. In my article on *"L'économie et la sociologie au point de vue scientifique,"* Scientia, Bologna, 1907, I wrote: "Most sociologies have been offered professedly as substitutions of scientific thought for religious and political prejudices, and they have ended by propounding new religions. That is strikingly the case with

end in itself. Once they have been found, they may be made to serve other purposes. But to mix the two researches is harmful to both, and is in any case a serious and oftentimes insuperable obstacle to the discovery of experimental uniformities. As long as the natural sciences had to deal with such obstacles, they made little or no progress, and only as the obstacles became fewer in number and finally disappeared did they make the marvellous progress they show today. If, accordingly, one would remould the social sciences

Auguste Comte, but it is also observable in Herbert Spencer and in the hosts of humanitarian sociologies that each passing day brings forth [§ 6]. Sometimes there is an effort to disguise it under a scientific varnish, but it is a transparent varnish, and the dogma that would be concealed is readily discernible. . . . Sociologists who never get as far as working out a religious system insist at least on getting immediate practical applications from their 'science.' Practical applications will be possible some day, but that day is still far distant. We are as yet barely glimpsing the uniformities that the mutual dependencies of social phenomena present. An enormous amount of labour will still be necessary before we shall have acquired sufficient knowledge of those uniformities to enable us to predict with any assurance the social effects of any change in a given order of facts. Until that time, the synthetic empiricism of the statesman will still be far more trustworthy, as regards practical results, than the most scholarly analysis that can be made by the sociologist."

That was written in the year 1907; yet there are still people who imagine that the purpose of the scientific researches in which we are engaged is to be able to prophesy, in unchivalrous competition with Madame de Thèbes. So in days gone by there were those who expected political economy to prophesy commodity-prices. Similar opinions were ventured when mathematical economics first appeared and there were those who asked, "With all your calculations, can you tell what the price of wheat is going to be next year?" Such people are unable to distinguish between a virtual movement and a real movement, between a logico-experimental reasoning and a derivation, between a scientific proposition and a prophecy.

The form a logico-experimental reasoning takes with regard to virtual movements is: "Given the circumstances $A, B, C \ldots, X$ will occur." The requisite at bottom is that $A, B, C \ldots$ shall actually be experimental facts and the reasoning associating them with X strictly logical. If from observation of the past it seems reasonably certain that $A, B, C \ldots$ will recur in the future, one may guess, with the same degree of probability, that X also will recur. That is a scientific forecast (§ 77), a consequence of the uniformity associating $A, B, C \ldots$ with X, but remaining altogether distinct from that uniformity; so much so that the uniformity will hold even if the forecast with regard to X fails to materialize; and that would happen not because of any failure in the connexion between $A, B \ldots$ and X, but because of the mistaken forecast that $A, B \ldots$ would recur in the future.

If the reasoning just noted is kept in form, but changed in substance, whether because $A, B \ldots$ are not, in some respect, experimental, or because the reasoning that associates them with X is not strictly logico-experimental, we get a derivation. Such derivations have not the slightest validity as demonstrations and fail to in-

on the model of the natural sciences, one must proceed in them as in the natural sciences, reducing highly complicated concrete phenomena to simpler theoretical phenomena, being exclusively guided all the while by the intent to discover experimental uniformities, and judging the efficacy of what one has done only by the experimental verifications that may be made of it.

Many such verifications we have furnished in these volumes with regard to particular cases. We must now go on to a few others bearing on more general cases.

crease in the slightest the probability of the bald assertion that "X will occur." If the assertion is the non-logical "hunch" of a practical man, it may have a high degree of probability in its favour. If it is the prophecy of a believer who lives in the clouds or of some individual who is exploiting the credulity of others, little reliance is to be placed on it—it must be packed off to keep company with the prophecies of those estimable seers who foretell lottery drawings.

If with the price of public-debt certificates at 81, the demand for them exceeds the supply, an economist can say that the price is going to rise. That would be a particular case of a uniformity studied by his science. If you want to know what the quotations on those bonds are going to be a fortnight hence, do not go to an economist—he can tell you nothing on the subject. Go rather to a statesman who is willing to share his "inside" information with you. That will enable you to infer, to a greater or lesser degree of probability, whether the demand is to increase or diminish as compared with the supply. Or else you might seek the counsel of a seasoned stock-broker, who may hit the nail on the head or miss by a mile. If he has often won money in speculations, he will more probably be right than wrong; but in any event it will be a probability that has nothing whatever to do with economic science. If, then, you go to a man who "has abiding faith in the destinies of the country" and therefore concludes that the quotations on its bonds must "necessarily" rise, kill two birds with one stone and ask him also what lottery numbers he has dreamed, for they will bring you good luck, and remember that his prophecies will be worthy of a distinguished place among the prophecies of Nostradamus or Madame de Thèbes. Of that sort also are the assertions of many "sociologists" who naïvely imagine that they are proclaiming sociological uniformities when they voice their desires or their sentiments, or retail the visions of their humanitarian, patriotic, or social religions.

CHAPTER XIII

The Social Equilibrium in History

2412. We are to proceed, henceforward, to further experimental verification of the theories we have been expounding, by examining new facts, new relationships between facts.

2413. We have time and again been led to recognize that one of the principal factors determining the social equilibrium was the relative proportions of Class I and Class II residues in individuals. In a first approximation, that proportion may be considered from three points of view, by making the comparison: (1) between populations of different countries, or populations of a given country in different periods of history; or (2) between social classes, and more particularly between the governing class and the class that is governed; or finally, (3) as bearing on class-circulation within a population.

2414. Meantime we must be on our guard against two mistakes. First, the error of regarding the relative proportions of such residues as a "cause" and the social phenomena as an "effect."[1]

2415. Second, the error of regarding the prevalence of certain relative proportions of such residues in such correlations as the only determining factor and, what is worse, of regarding such a condition, even though it is a necessary condition, as a necessary and sufficient one. Furthermore, as a first approximation and for the sake of brevity, we are confining ourselves here to Class I and Class II residues, but obviously the other residues have to be considered too. However, not a few residues of sociality, personal integrity, and so on, have their counterparts among the group-persistences, so that they are taken account of indirectly in appraisals of Class II residues.

To make this point clearer, suppose we consider some analogous situations. If one is to get a good crop of wheat, the soil has to contain assimilable phosphorus and nitrogen in certain relative proportions. But that, evidently, is not enough. To say nothing of many

---

2414 [1] We have all too frequently warned the reader against the error of mistaking relationships of interdependence for relationships of cause and effect. We need not expatiate further on the matter here.

other indispensable conditions, weather has to be considered. If weather conditions are unfavourable, a soil containing the proper proportions of phosphorus and nitrogen may yield a poorer crop than a soil not so well provided with substance but enjoying more favourable weather conditions. However, in the long run there is a certain balance between bad-weather seasons and good-weather seasons, and on the average the soil containing the proper proportions of phosphorus and nitrogen will yield the larger crops. For that reason, chemical analysis of soils is far from being a useless thing. It is, in fact, the basis of modern agriculture.

Another example: In the case of a modern army probabilities of victory stand in correlation with certain relative proportions of artillery to other arms. Now that condition is not the only one; there are many others, in particular the condition that the army be well provided with food and munitions. Then again, though the condition specified may in certain cases be essential, it is never sufficient. A proper proportion of artillery to other arms is not by itself enough: ability to use one's equipment is also necessary. Just so, other residues besides those of Classes I and II have to be considered. One must consider whether or no the artillery has the necessary horses and sufficient quantities of ammunition, and is manned with good soldiers and competent officers commissioned and non-commissioned. So it is not enough that a governing class possess Class I and Class II residues in the proper proportions; it is also necessary that proper use be made of them. It is evident that if the combination-instinct expresses itself in devising magical incantations instead of in economic or military activities, it will not amount to much; and if it is wasted on parlour intrigues instead of being applied to efficient government, it will amount to little indeed.[1] If group-persistences exhaust themselves in ascetic, humanitarian, or other antics, they will

2415 [1] Paul Bosc, *Souvenirs de l'Assemblée nationale,* p. 339, note: "On the train that was taking the members of the National Assembly back to Paris for the last time, M. Laurier . . . delivered the funeral oration of the Majority. 'We are done for,' he said. 'Those rascals the Republicans are going to get our places. That's what we get for asking at every crucial moment when a decision has to be made, "But what will Duchess So-and-So say?"—and then doing something foolish. We should have said, "Never mind the Duchess," and then followed sound policy. We would not be where we are today if we had paid less attention to ball-room opinion.'" It is a notorious fact that the old French aristocracy prepared the ground for the first Revolution that was to destroy them in their drawing-rooms.

be socially as efficient as wooden cannon in a military campaign. All
the same, in the long run, if the different arms in a military establishment are used with average ability and proper equipment, the
advantage of proper relative proportions in the various arms will
be apparent. So when residues are functioning in a manner on the
whole conducive to social prosperity, the advantage of proper proportions in them will be apparent in the long run.

That is the theory we are now setting out to test on the facts.

2416. Suppose we take the mass-populations of different countries.
On the axis *oz* (Figure 42) we will put indices of the economic, mili-

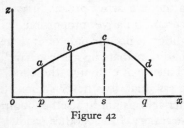

Figure 42

tary, and political prosperity of the
countries; on the axis *ox*, the various respective proportions of Class
I and Class II residues (residues of
other classes can also be considered). It will not be difficult to find
countries, *p*, in which that proportion is small, in which residues of
combination (Class I) are relatively few (*op*) as compared with
group-persistences (Class II). We also find countries, *q*, where Class
I residues greatly predominate (*oq*) over Class II residues. Then
there will be other countries, *r*, that show an intermediate proportion, *or*. In a great many cases we notice that the indices of prosperity, *pa*, *qd*, are lower than the indices *rb*, and from that we
conclude that the curve of the indices of prosperity very probably has
a maximum, *sc*, corresponding to a proportion, *os*, which we cannot
determine exactly, but which we do know stands somewhere between *op* and *oq*.

2417. Now instead of comparing different countries, suppose we
compare the various situations in one country at different times. In
this case, we can learn very little from considering the relative proportions of Class I and Class II residues in general. Taking a population as a whole residues change very slowly, and the effects of
varying proportions may remain indistinguishable in the mass of
effects of other more variable phenomena. But we can distinguish
such effects from other effects by fixing our attention on proportions of residues in the governing class, for proportions in governing
classes sometimes vary very rapidly. However, that variation is

strictly correlated with variations in class-circulation. So oftentimes we are able to determine nothing more than total effects, without being able clearly to distinguish the respective share that belongs to proportions of residues and to phenomena of class-circulation.

2418. Furthermore, the index of social utility depends not only upon proportions of residues in the governing class, but also on proportions of residues in the subject class. The actual situation therefore has to be pictured in a three-dimensional space. In Figure 43

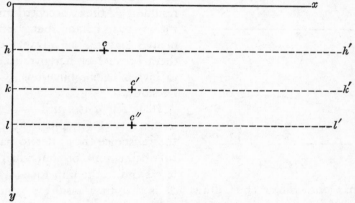

Figure 43

the plane xy, taken as horizontal, is the plane of the figure. The axis oz, which is taken as vertical and is therefore not represented in the figure, will be the axis of indices of utility. On the horizontal plane the axis ox will be the axis of relative proportions of residues in the governing class, the axis oy the axis of such proportions in the subject class.

Now let us cut various vertical sections, hh', kk', ll' . . . parallel to the plane oxz (Figure 43). In each of those sections we find (Figures 43 and 44) maximum points, c, c', c'' . . . , and, comparing the various maxima, $sc, s'c', s''c''$ . . . , we find one, c'', which will be greater than the others and will therefore indicate the most suitable proportions in the governing class and in the subject class.

2419. Ancient Greece was a laboratory of social and political experiments and it provides a rich storehouse of observations. The moment one approaches the phenomena alluded to in § 2416, one thinks of Sparta and Athens as illustrating the indices *pa* and *qd* in Figure 42. The great predominance of Class II residues in Sparta and of Class I residues in Athens is too obvious to require documentation. But it will be worth while to show in some detail how those two extremes in proportions kept the two communities from attaining the maximum of prosperity, *sc*. Sparta rebuffed innovations because of her overbalance in favour of group-persistences (Class II residues). Athens accepted innovations out of hand, but she was unable to take full advantage of them because of her overbalance in favour of combinations (Class I residues).

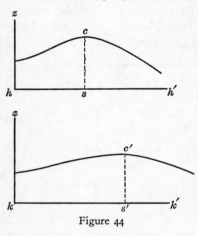

Figure 44

2420. The chief utility of the sentiments of group-persistence is the resistance they offer to harmful inclinations of individual interest and to the impetuous sweep of passions.[1] Their chief drawback is that they inspire a conduct that is logically consistent with them but detrimental to society. To perform their first, their conservative, function such sentiments have to be very strong. When they lose their vigour to any considerable extent they are unable to resist powerful interests and aggressive passions, and vent themselves in effects of the second sort only—those which are detrimental to society.

2421. That is what one observes in various episodes in Athens, and a typical example would be the case of Alcibiades. Alcibiades succeeded in persuading the Athenians, against the better judgment of the conservative Nicias, to undertake the Sicilian expedition. Had

2420 [1] Curtius, *Griechische Geschichte,* Vol. III, p. 52 (Ward, Vol. IV, p. 79): "The moral health of a Hellenic city depended primarily on the fidelity of the living generation to past traditions, its faith in the gods of the fathers, its devotion to the commonwealth, its scrupulous respect for what custom and legislation had laid down as the rule of community life." That is true provided it be applied not to rulers and ruled alike, but primarily to the ruled. Otherwise the Athenians under a Nicias, who followed the program Curtius describes to the letter, should have enjoyed greater prosperity than under a Pericles, who cared nothing for tradition and for the gods. As is well known, the exact opposite was the case.

sentiments of group-persistence been at all strong in the Athenians, they would have followed the view of Nicias, or would at the most have been satisfied with sending a small expedition that would have been no great tax on their resources. That, exactly, is what Sparta did, when, shortly afterwards, in her turn falling under the spell of Alcibiades, she sent Gylippus, but no one else, to the aid of Syracuse, with what few ships she could secure from Corinth. The Athenians, instead, sent a powerful army to Sicily, and it drained Greece of her strength to a very considerable extent. The Athenians, then, might at least have been sufficiently persevering in their re- solve to disregard every little incident that arose to interfere with an enterprise so perilous and so critical. But they were too weak in Class II residues to attain that degree of devotion, while those resi- dues were still strong enough in them to induce them to insist that Nicias, because he was considered an honest and a religious man, should serve as coleader of the expedition with Alcibiades and then to recall Alcibiades at the moment when his work in Sicily was most needed. The Spartans, too, later on, were eager to be rid of Alci- biades, but they did not dismiss him till they thought, rightly or wrongly, that they no longer needed him, and suspected that he was betraying them.

As will be remembered, while the fleet was making ready to sail from Athens, it was discovered one morning that the Hermic pillars about the streets of the city had been smeared with filth. The city was horrified at the ominous sacrilege, and evinced sentiments of group-persistence such as would have been manifested in other Hellenic cities.[1] But strong as such sentiments may have been, they were not strong enough to overbalance the combination-instincts; and the Athenians kept Alcibiades in command of the fleet, though he had been accused of the sacrilege and though he himself, desiring

2421 [1] Grote, *History of Greece*, Vol. VII, pp. 172-73: "Amidst the mournful dismay spread by the discovery of so unparalleled a sacrilege, it appeared to the Athenian people—as it would have appeared to the Ephors at Sparta, or to the rulers in every oligarchical city of Greece—that it was their paramount and im- perative duty to detect and punish the authors. So long as these latter were walk- ing about unknown and unpunished, the temples were defiled by their presence, and the whole city was accounted under the displeasure of the gods, who would inflict upon it heavy public misfortunes." Well and good; but had such sentiments been at all powerful in the Athenians, they would have dropped the notion of an expedition to Sicily, and so have escaped far-reaching disasters.

an immediate trial for purposes of his own, remarked that "it would be wiser not to send him at the head of so great a fleet while such an accusation was hanging over him and before he had been purged of it." [2] The combination-instincts therefore prevailed at that time, the Athenians thinking only of what a wonderful idea it was to have Alcibiades in command of the expedition. And even so, had they stuck to their decision, the expedition might perhaps have succeeded. But there they were, suddenly changing their minds and, at the very moment when it is most important to keep Alcibiades in Sicily, they send a trireme from Salamis to bring him back to Greece to answer a charge of profaning the Eleusinian mysteries; and that was the cause of the flight of Alcibiades to the Spartans, where he began to plot the ruin of Athens. [3]

2422. Something of the sort happened in France at the time of the Dreyfus affair. The Eleusinian mysteries had been profaned at Athens. In France judicial guarantees had been profaned to the disadvantage of a man presumably innocent. That seemed to be a sufficient excuse for disorganizing and weakening all the institutions of national defence; for naming officers and generals not on the basis of their military merit, but for their knack at a low form of political intrigue; for entrusting the ministry of war to an André and the ministry of the navy to a Pelletan, all of which, had Germany attacked France at that moment, as Sparta attacked Athens, would have brought upon France a disaster of no lesser magnitude than the ruin of the Athenians in the expedition to Syracuse. [1] The controversies that raged at Athens over the profanation of the Hermic pillars and the Eleusinian mysteries, and the quarrels that

2421 [2] Thucydides, *Historiae*, VI, 29, 2: Καὶ ὅτι σωφρονέστερον εἴη μὴ μετὰ τοιαύτης αἰτίας πρὶν διαγνῶσιν πέμπειν αὐτὸν ἐπὶ τοσούτῳ στρατεύματι.

2421 [3] Curtius, *Griechische Geschichte,* Vol. II, p. 676 (Ward, Vol. III, p. 410): "The Athenians threw themselves into a hazardous enterprise which called for a determined, skilful, unscrupulous leader, and then of the one man who possessed those qualities they proceeded to make an enemy of the city, bent upon the ruin of his own work, entrusting the task of carrying on the war to a god-fearing general [Such as Napoleon III at Sedan.] sick of body and not believing in the expedition, and setting out to meet a more dangerous enemy than they had ever met before."

2422 [1] In December, 1908, Admiral Germinet declared in a public statement: "Most of the ships in the fleet have not enough munitions to sustain a battle three hours long." The government of plutocratic demagogues that had reduced the navy to that state took steps, not to fill the magazines on the ships with ammunition, but to relieve Admiral Germinet of his command.

raged in France over the Dreyfus affair, were largely masks and pretexts to cover passions and interests. But they had their effect as masks and pretexts, because they were not recognized as such by many people, but were supposed to be genuine expressions of sentiments; and the people who so accepted them were influenced by sentiments corresponding to certain residues of group-persistence (Class II).

2423. It would have been to the advantage of France had she been strong enough in group-persistences to withdraw from all adventures depending upon the combination-instinct. But that instinct prevailed in France as it had prevailed in Athens. France set out to establish her dominion in Morocco, forgetting, as Athens had forgotten in recalling Alcibiades, that wars are not fought with the chatter of politicians, the insipidities of "intellectuals," the underhanded combinations of plutocrats, but with the ability of generals and the devotion of soldiers. France escaped disaster at that time because there was no second Bismarck in Germany to play the rôle that Philip of Macedon played against Athens.

As we shall see more clearly (§§ 2449, 2434), lessons of that sort are of little or no avail in preventing the recurrence of such mistakes; and that is another proof of the non-logical character of the conduct in question.[1]

2423 [1] On Nov. 28, 1913, a Radical-Socialist Deputy, André Lefèvre, declared without rebuttal in the Chamber: "Following the Tangiers incident we have had to submit to an injunction because the French army had only 700 rounds per gun. There are economies that come very high! If we had had an army and navy corresponding to our foreign policy we would not have been brought to the pass in which we find ourselves at present." The Prime Minister, M. Caillaux, replied: "It is, alas, true that the efforts required have not always been made, and that we have had to make up for lost time." G. Berthoulat comments on Lefèvre's speech as follows, *Liberté,* Nov. 30, 1913: "M. André Lefèvre is no friend of ours, politically, but it is only fair to say that when he talks he always has something to say—a compliment that is rarely deserved by our Deputies in the parliament at the present time. M. Lefèvre delivered a peerless speech on the Army Reform Bill. His remarks yesterday were no less to the point, and no moment could have been better chosen for proving to the Chamber, while the country was listening, that if the ministers of the Bloc had not at all times treated national defence in an offhand manner, France would not be required to make such a great military and financial effort today. The bewildered indignation of our Jacobins in the face of his proof was truly comical. But was it so much of a revelation after all? Doesn't everybody know that at the time of Algeciras, M. Rouvier, out of his wits, let M. Delcassé down in the matter of the German ultimatum by remarking to a group

2424. Going back again to the Athenians, it is apparent that they learned nothing from the first recall of Alcibiades, for they repeated the same mistake. By leaving Sparta in the lurch, Alcibiades had restored the fortunes of Athens in a most unexpected manner. Obviously there was nothing to do but to allow him to proceed. But against the express orders of Alcibiades, his lieutenant, Antiochus, joined battle with Lysander on the sea and was defeated. That was a new excuse for the enemies of Alcibiades. On one of the usual charges of sacrilege they had him removed from command, and that was a second step towards ruin for Athens. It is plain enough that what was lacking in Athens was such a balance between the combination-instincts and the residues of group-persistence that while the combination-instincts encouraged to adventure, the group-persistences would supplement them with the perseverance and firmness of resolve required for success in the schemes imagined.

2425. A similar lack of balance in the proportions of the two sorts of instincts is to be noted in Sparta, but with terms inverted. The Spartans certainly were not short in perseverance and steadfastness of purpose. What they lacked was the combination-instinct that would have enabled them to turn those traits to good account. Had Alcibiades not counselled the Spartans to go to the relief of Syracuse and occupy Decelea, no one knows how long Athens might have held out and whether the outcome would not have been unfavourable to Sparta. But once the opportune combinations of Syracuse

of Deputies in the corridors in my presence, that 'since there was no French army or navy left, thanks to André and Pelletan, France had to back down?' And is it not also a part of history, vouched for by M. Bertaux himself, that at that time feverish efforts had to be made to provide for the most elementary needs of a ruined equipment and to use two hundred millions from the secret funds for that purpose? M. Lefèvre was therefore saying nothing new, but he was the first to be courageous enough to raise the question on the floor of the Chamber. That story of the 700 rounds told by a man of the Left who set country higher than party was a cruel thrust for the survivors of the 'abject régime.' The *Radical* made a delicious comment on the episode: It reminds M. Lefèvre of 'certain proprieties.' But what proprieties? The proprieties those responsible have been observing? A reminder of the truth would be more serviceable! M. Lefèvre's indictment is irrefutable. And evidently it should fall more especially upon the man whom the *Radical* calls 'the leader of the Republican party,' since every time M. Caillaux has been minister of finance he has collaborated diligently in the wastage of the food policy, all the savings he has made being at the expense of the army—savings, in other words, that he should never have made and which, added together, make up the lion's share of the present deficit." And *cf.* § 2465 [1].

and Decelea were set before the slow-thinking Spartans, they carried those enterprises out with perseverance, consistency, and shrewdness.

2426. Characteristic of Spartan character is the anecdote recounted by Herodotus, *Historiae,* IX, 52, of Amompharetus. That soldier, at the battle of Plateia, refused to execute a strategic retreat which his chief, Pausanias, had ordered, because it would have caused him to give ground before the Barbarians, and that would have been dishonourable in a Spartan.[1]

2427. The phenomena we are here examining are more strikingly conspicuous in the art of war, for there we get definite indices. Of all historical events, victories and defeats are the best known to us. In considering the activities of Alcibiades among the Spartans we encountered, without going to the trouble of looking for it, a most interesting fact that demonstrates how desirable it is that combination-instincts should predominate in leaders and the instincts of group-persistence in subordinates.[1] At bottom it was because Alci-

2426 [1] Amompharetus, according to Herodotus, was the leading citizen of Pitana. Speaking of common historical errors, Thucydides, *Historiae,* I, 20, 3, remarks that there never was such a place as Pitana. [Actually what Thucydides says is that there never was a "Pitana company" in the Spartan army.—A. L.] That would cast doubt on the whole story in Herodotus. However, even if it were legendary, in whole or in part, that would make no difference as regards our purposes—to determine Spartan sentiments. Evidently a legend that is accepted as history has to accord with the sentiments it exemplifies.

2427 [1] Curtius, *Griechische Geschichte,* Vol. III, pp. 132-33 (Ward, Vol. IV, pp. 191-92). Without in the least contemplating any such theory as ours, Curtius supplies another example, from the story of Xenophon's Ten Thousand: "In those men obsession with present dangers kept up a state of constant exhilaration and it had destroyed all love of their home land in them. [Specific residues have weakened, but the loss is offset by other residues.] But how devotedly they remained attached to their oldest traditions! Dreams and portents sent by the gods determine, as in Homer's camp, the most crucial decisions [§ 2440 [1]]. It is with most pious fervour that they sing their paeans, light the sacrificial fires, build altars to the gods who have saved them, and celebrate games, at last, when the longed-for sea comes into view and their drooping strength and courage rally. Tribal rivalries can be discerned in the Ten Thousand; but the sense of community, the consciousness of national unity, holds the upper hand, and the rank and file has enough good sense [*Read:* enough Class II residues.] and abnegation [There the residue, as it were, in person.] to be obedient to those whom their experience and their intelligence [Class I residues.] indicate as the ones fit to command. And, miraculous as it seems [Not at all miraculous: it was the logical consequence of the residues Curtius is describing.], in all that motley horde of Greeks it is the Athenian who surpasses everyone in capacity and becomes the real saviour of the army. [As was

biades had men like the Spartans to execute his combinations that he was able to be of greater service to Sparta than to his native city, Athens. That fact suggests that the first distribution of residues is more efficient than the second, and much more efficient than still a third, where a Nicias is in command, while those who elect him and accept his leadership are strong in the combination-instincts. Of all that we shall shortly be seeing further and more striking examples.

2428. At the battle of Leuctra the tactical formation of the Spartans was still the one that had been in use at the time of the Persian Wars, whereas the progress made by the Athenians in that respect between the time of Miltiades and the time of Iphicrates had been enormous.[1] But that was of little benefit to Athens. The Spartans could not get away from precedent. The Athenians could not take advantage of the innovations that came to them so easily, deficient as they were in the perseverance and steadfastness indispensable to victory. Athens stood to Sparta in some respects as Pyrrhus and Hannibal, in their time, stood towards Rome. But the analogy fails as we turn to Sparta. The Romans learned the art of war from Pyrrhus and Hannibal and used what they learned to good purpose. Sparta learned nothing from Iphicrates, and nothing from Chabrias and other able adversaries.

2429. It would have been easy therefore to foresee that both Sparta and Athens would succumb if ever they chanced to join issue with a people possessing ability to innovate combined with ability to make the proper use of novelties, a situation that arises in countries where our Class I residues predominate in the leaders and Class II

the case with Pericles at Athens, Epaminondas at Thebes, Philip in Macedonia.] . . . The Athenian alone had the higher cultivation of mind required to maintain order and discipline among those soldiers who had been brutalized by selfishness and to serve them under the most varied circumstances now as orator, now as general, now as diplomat. To him more than anyone the credit was due if, in the end, in spite of indescribable sufferings, among hostile peoples, over barren snow-capped mountains, and after losing their way many times, eight thousand Greeks at last reached the sea-shore." More exactly, and following Curtius's own words, it was due to the combination-instinct in Xenophon working in unison with the group-persistences in his soldiers. These latter are admirably described by Curtius.

2428 [1] Curtius, *Ibid.*, Vol. III, p. 291 (Ward, Vol. II, pp. 412-13): "In spite of some scattered reforms, military art among the Spartiates was still based on the old arrangement by lines. They advanced upon the enemy with their old phalanx, a line of battle of equal depth throughout."

residues in the subject classes. That contingency arose in Thebes at the time of Epaminondas, and in Macedonia at the time of Philip and Alexander the Great (Figure 45).[1] In those two countries improvements in the art of war were at once adopted, and they bore fruit as applied by leaders who were endowed with combination instincts in high degree and commanded peoples who had the group-persistences required for steadfastness of purpose. They bore better

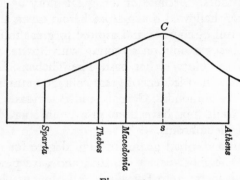

Figure 45

fruits for Macedonia than for Thebes because, through a greater intensity in their Class II residues, the Macedonians stood by their leaders more consistently than the Thebans did.

2430. Theban power rose and declined in a very short space of time. The case is interesting to us here in that the interval was exactly the interval when the conditions indicated in § 2429 were fulfilled. The first of those conditions failed with the death of Pelopidas and Epaminondas. Thereupon the power of Thebes declined. The situation is worth examining more in detail.

2431. The rise of Thebes to power was altogether unforeseen. At the Congress of Sparta peace was made between all the Greek states except Thebes. Xenophon reports that, in view of the isolation of Thebes, "people in Athens were of opinion that the Thebans would be decimated, as the common talk was, while the Thebans themselves

2429 [1] It seems that in the battle of Cannae Hannibal anticipated modern German tacticians (see Schlieffen, *Cannae,* pp. 1-4). The Romans were not inventive, but they knew how to take advantage of the experience of others. So also they profited by the naval skill of the Carthaginians.

left [the Congress] utterly downhearted."[1] And then, forthwith, the Spartans, under their king Cleombrotus, invaded Boeotia. The Thebans were terror-stricken and feared that their capital would be utterly destroyed.[2] Such alarm was justified, considering the great strength of the army under Cleombrotus and the reputation of Sparta, which up to that time had never known defeat.

2432. To the rescue of Thebes came "prejudices" corresponding to Class II residues. "Because of the great glory of its forefathers, which had been hallowed down from heroic times, the city of the Thebans rose full of courage and aspired to great things."[1] So far, however, Thebes was only on a footing with Sparta, who was also thrilling with the glory of her past. The Thebans, Diodorus continues (*loc. cit.*), "had leaders of great courage, outstanding among whom, three: Epaminondas, Gorgias, and Pelopidas." But there too the Spartans could not have been greatly inferior, for they had Agesilaus and Cleombrotus.

2433. Epaminondas had genius in high degree for military combinations, but Cleombrotus was no fool, and gave proof of that by his tactic in advancing into Boeotia. The Boeotians were expecting him to come along the regular highway from Phocis. He attacked instead over the difficult passes of Thisbe, and reached Creusis.[1] The

2431 [1] *Hellenica*, VI, 3, 20: . . . οἱ μὲν Ἀθηναῖοι οὕτως εἶχον τὴν γνώμην, ὡς νῦν Θηβαίους τὸ λεγόμενον δὴ δεκατευθῆναι ἐλπὶς εἴη, αὐτοὶ δὲ οἱ Θηβαῖοι παντελῶς ἀθύμως ἔχοντες ἀπῆλθον. Diodorus Siculus, *Bibliotheca historica*, XV, 51, 2-3 (Booth, Vol. II, p. 40): "The Lacedaemonians, accordingly, decreed to attack the Thebans, who stood so deserted by everyone, and reduce them to slavery. And since it was known that the Lacedaemonians were making huge preparations for war and that no one was doing anything for the Thebans, everyone assumed (ἅπαντες ὑπελάμβανον) that the Thebans would be crushed with no great difficulty. Those, therefore, who were friendly to them grieved at their plight, foreseeing the calamities that were in store for them, while their enemies were jubilant."

2431 [2] Plutarch, *Pelopidas*, 20 (Perrin, Vol. V, p. 389).

2432 [1] Diodorus Siculus, *Bibliotheca historica*, XV, 50, 6 (Booth, Vol. II, p. 40): Ἥ τε πόλις τῶν Θηβαίων διὰ τῆς τῶν προγόνων ἐπιφανείας ἐν τοῖς ἡρωικοῖς χρόνοις φρονήματος ἦν πλήρης καὶ μεγάλων ὠρέγετο πραγμάτων.

2433 [1] Grote, *History of Greece*, Vol. X, p. 176: "That prince [Kleombrotus], with a degree of military skill rare in the Spartan commanders, baffled all the Theban calculations. Instead of marching by the regular road from Phokis into Boeotia, he turned southward by a mountain-road scarcely deemed practicable, defeated the Theban division under Chaereas which guarded it, and crossed the ridge of Helikon to the Boeotian port of Kreusis on the Crissaean Gulf. Coming upon this place by surprise, he stormed it, capturing twelve Theban triremes which lay in the harbour."

difference lay in this, that in Sparta innovations had to remain within the circle of Spartan institutions, group-persistences being so strong in the people that they would tolerate no innovation that overstepped traditions. At Thebes the military commanders could deploy their army as they thought best, the strength or, if one prefer, the character of the Class II residues in the people not prohibiting departures from old customs.

2434. Before the battle of Leuctra the Spartans had had plenty of warnings as to the desirability of changes in their tactical formations. In the year 390 B.C., through a clever manoeuvre with his peltasts, the Athenian Iphicrates had destroyed a corps of six hundred Spartan hoplites under the walls of Corinth.[1] But Spartan inertia was not in the least stirred on that account, nor was it shaken by the tremendous defeat at Leuctra. Free to do as he pleased, Epaminondas altogether changed the battle-order then in use not only among the Spartans but among all the other peoples in Greece. He anticipated the strategy of Napoleon that lay in so manoeuvring as to be overwhelmingly superior to the enemy at a given moment at a given point. It had been customary with the Greeks to begin battle, as far as possible, over the whole front of an army. Epaminondas deployed his troops obliquely, so that the left, headed by the

---

2434 [1] Xenophon, *Hellenica*, VI, 4, 12 (Brownson, Vol. II, p. 59). Nepos, *Iphicrates*, 1: "Iphicrates, an Athenian, won his glory not so much through the magnitude of his achievements as through his expertness in military tactics. As a general there was no one in his time who could be compared with him, nor was his superior to be found among those before him. He had long experience in warfare, often commanding armies, never suffering a defeat through fault of his own, and often winning by sheer skill. He introduced many things that were new in the art of war, and made great improvement in things that were old." Grote, *Op. cit.*, Vol. IX, p. 335, considers it legitimate to base the following description of the improvements introduced by Iphicrates on the references in Cornelius Nepos and Diodorus Siculus: "He lengthened by one half both the light javelin and the short sword, which the Thracian peltasts habitually carried; he devised a species of leggings, known afterward by the name of iphikratides; and he thus combined, better than had ever been done before, rapid motion—power of acting in difficult ground and open order, effective attack either by missiles or hand to hand, and dexterous retreat in case of need." As a result, p. 337, "the successes of his light troops were remarkable. Attacking Phlius, he entrapped the Phliasians into an ambuscade, and inflicted on them a defeat so destructive that they were obliged to invoke the aid of a Lacedaemonian garrison for the protection of their city. He gained a victory near Sikyon and carried his incursions over all Arcadia to the very gates of the cities; damaging the Arcadian hoplites so severely, that they became afraid to meet him in the field."

"Holy Battalion," was held by the hoplites fifty ranks deep, a formation unheard of up to that time.[2] So he would be in a position to
attack the Spartan right, where the King and the chief commanders
were stationed, in overwhelming force, and the crushing rout there
would give him a complete victory. Things turned out as the Theban captain had foreseen. "As the battle was joined, both sides fighting furiously, matters were even. But gradually the men under
Epaminondas prevailed owing to their valour and their close formation, and many of the Peloponnesians were slain; for they were not
strong enough to withstand the fierce attack of those picked soldiers; but of those who resisted some fell and some were wounded,
all receiving their wounds in front." [3] Later on, in the battle at
Mantineia, Epaminondas again used the tactic he had found so successful at Leuctra;[4] and the Lacedaemonians, who had learned
nothing from their defeat, stuck to their old formation to their great
loss.

2435. The "prejudices" that saved the Thebans by giving them

2434 [2] Xenophon, *Hellenica,* VI, 4, 12, says that the Spartans had deployed the
enomotias [companies of twenty-five, thirty-two, or thirty-six men, according to different writers] in three ranks [Brownson: "three files abreast"], which made their
army twelve men deep, at the most, while the Theban army was nowhere less than
fifty shields deep. Centuries later Vegetius was to describe with praise a battle-forma-
tion of the same sort, *De re militari,* III, 20 (Clarke, pp. 143-44): "There are seven
manners or kinds of battle order in a pitched battle (*cum infesta ex utraque parte
signa configunt:* when the hostile standards come together from each side). One is
on a long front, with the army in a square, the way battles are almost always fought
nowadays. However, experts in arms do not consider that order of battle the
best. . . . A second is the oblique line, which is the one many experts prefer. With
this line, even if you have only a few troops but are on the proper terrain, you can
win a victory against a foe superior in both numbers and training (*virtute*). The
procedure is as follows: Just as the opposing lines are coming together in battle-
array, you draw back your left from the enemy's right quite a distance (*longius*)
so that neither missiles nor arrows can reach it. But with your right you join
with the enemy's left, and open the battle there. Using your best cavalry and your
most experienced troops, you attack and outflank his left, driving it back or overrunning it so that you reach his rear. Once you have begun to rout the enemy
from that point of vantage you will surely win, since your reserves will keep coming
up, and the part of your line that you have held off from the enemy will be in no
danger."

2434 [3] Diodorus Siculus, *Ibid.,* XV, 55, 4 (Booth, Vol. II, p. 44).

2434 [4] Polybius comments, *Historiae,* XII, 25, 4 (Paton, Vol. IV, p. 379): "The
affair at Mantineia occasioned a display of great variety and great science in gen-
eralship."

courage to resist the Spartans almost ruined them before the battle began, because of their fear of certain omens; but the quick-wittedness and good sense of Epaminondas came to the rescue, changed the evil omens into good ones, and even supplemented them with some specially good ones, which were provoked for the occasion. As a result, instead of being handicapped the Thebans were greatly benefited by their faith in presages.

2436. As they were marching out of Thebes the army encountered a crier leading a blind slave [1] and proclaiming a decree that the man must not be allowed to leave the city. The words were interpreted as a bad omen for the departure of the army. But Epaminondas immediately recited a line from Homer (*Iliad,* XII, v. 243), to the effect that "to be fighting for one's country was the best of omens." A worse omen supervened. "The camp scribe," Diodorus continues, "was marching along in front holding aloft a lance with a ribbon on the end, so publishing the orders of the captains to the army. It chanced that a gust of wind blew the ribbon loose from the lance and it fell on the shaft of a memorial monument on a spot where some Spartans and Peloponnesians, who had fought under Agesilaus, were buried. Again the older soldiers fell to begging their captains to lead them no farther, the gods having given manifest evidence of their disapproval." Diodorus states that Epaminondas marched on, contemptuous of the presage, but one of his subsequent remarks lends greater credibility to the account given by Frontinus, to the effect that Epaminondas twisted the presage in his favour by an ingenious interpretation (§ 2439 [1]).[2]

Moreover, to turn the superstition of his soldiers to good account,

2436 [1] Diodorus Siculus, *Ibid.,* XV, 52, 3 (Booth, Vol. II, p. 41).

2436 [2] Diodorus Siculus, *Ibid.,* XV, 52, 7 (Booth, Vol. II, p. 41), notes that for doing that "Epaminondas, who had been instructed in philosophy and was putting into practice the wise teachings he had received in his youth, incurred reproach from many." That goes to show that prejudices were active in the masses at large, but gave ground before the prestige of Epaminondas. And *cf.* Plutarch, *Pelopidas,* 3-4. Frontinus says, *Strategematon,* I, 12, 5 (Bennett, p. 83): "The soldiers being depressed because the wind had torn off an ornament on his lance [A slightly different circumstance from the one mentioned by Diodorus.] that was the ensign of his office and blown it upon the tomb of a certain Spartan, Epaminondas, the Theban, cried: 'Have no fear, soldiers. That means ruin for the Spartans. Their tombs are being decorated for their funerals.'" And Frontinus goes on to relate two other incidents of the same sort.

he was ingenious enough to go on and invent favourable omens out-right—many of them, and such good ones that no one could have wished more or better.

Xenophon was alive in those times and he must certainly have had opportunities for talking with veterans of Leuctra. He says, *Hellenica,* VI, 4, 7-8, that the Thebans gained great self-confidence from an oracle which foretold that the Spartans were to be defeated on a spot at Leuctra where two young girls, on being violated by certain Spartans, had taken their own lives (§ 1952). Moreover, the gates of temples in Thebes opened of themselves and the priestesses declared that in that the gods were promising victory. Nor was that all. It was further reported that the vases in the Temple of Hercules had vanished, which signified that Hercules had gone off to war. Xenophon, pious and credulous soul, adds: "Some say, how-ever, that all those things were but tricks of the captains." [3]

2436 [3] οἱ μὲν δή τινες λέγουσιν ὡς ταῦτα πάντα τεχνάσματα ἦν τῶν προεστηκότων. Things were just the other way round with the Athenians; and that shows how important it is to consider quantities in residues. At first the Athenians were handi-capped by the fact that their Class II residues were too weak to induce them to heed the prudent counsels of Nicias and refrain from the Syracuse venture, yet strong enough to induce them to name Nicias as one of the commanders of the expedition. Grote, *History of Greece,* Vol. VII, pp. 351-52, fails to make that dis-tinction, and therefore involves himself in a gross error. Quoting the kindly judg-ment that Thucydides passed on Nicias, he continues: "Thucydides is here the more instructive, because he exactly represents the sentiment of the general Athenian public towards Nikias during his lifetime. They could not bear to condemn, to mistrust, to dismiss, or to do without, so respectable and religious a citizen. [Class II residues. That applies very well to the second half of the work of Nicias—to his command in the Sicilian expedition, but not to the first half; for he tried to dis-suade the Athenians from undertaking the expedition and was not listened to.] The private qualities of Nikias were not only held to entitle him to the most indulgent construction of all his public short-comings [His advice against going to Sicily was certainly not one of them.], but also insured to him credit for political and military competence altogether disproportionate to his deserts. [True, if applied only to his conduct of the Sicilian expedition; untrue, if applied to his advice against undertaking it.] . . . Never in the political history of Athens did the people make so fatal a mistake in placing their confidence. [The same stricture is in point here. The fact gives Grote occasion to justify the demagogues:] No dema-gogic arts or eloquence would ever have created in the people so deep-seated an illusion as the imposing respectability of Nikias. [Yet Grote refutes himself in ex-plaining how the eloquence and the wiles of Alcibiades created in the Athenians the illusion that the Sicilian expedition would be a good thing against the better judgment of Nicias, who foresaw disaster.] Now it was against the overweening ascendancy of such decorous and pious incompetence, when aided by wealth and

2437. Diodorus probably drew his information from the writings of Ephorus, now lost. He bluntly alleges a trick and gives further details.[1] According to his story, Epaminondas bade certain travellers who came from Thebes report that the weapons hanging in the Temple of Hercules in that city had disappeared. That implied that the heroes of old had taken them to join in the battle on the side of the Boeotians. Another traveller, returning from the cave of Trophonius, said that the god had bidden him admonish the Thebans to institute public games in honor of Zeus-the-King at Leuctra, after their victory. "This stratagem [on the part of Epaminondas] was furthered by a Spartan, Leander, an exile from Lacedaemonia,

family advantages, that the demagogic accusatory eloquence ought to have served as a natural bar and corrective." That would, to be sure, have been a great thing as regards the second half of the work of Nicias. The great misfortune for Athens was that it happened for the first half. Grote himself says, *loc. cit.,* p. 159: "The position of Nikias in reference to the measure is remarkable. As a dissuasive and warning counsellor, he took a right view of it; but in that capacity he could not carry the people along with him." Grote asserts, it is true, that the Sicilian enterprise would have been profitable to Athens had it been properly managed, but there are no proofs for any such hypothesis. Furthermore, as regards faith in presages, it may be advantageous if a far-sighted leader can use it to induce a people to undertake and carry out a profitable enterprise; it may be disastrous·if the leader shares the same sentiments as the people and the presages are taken as intrinsically meritorious instead of being used as means to ends. The presages were favourable while the Sicilian expedition was in preparation, and the Athenians complained bitterly of that when things turned out badly. Thucydides, *Historiae,* VIII, 1, 1-2. Euripides, *Helena,* vv. 744-60 (Coleridge, Vol. I, p. 345), makes himself the mouthpiece for Athenian sentiments of scepticism and contempt for prophecies. He concludes: "Sound judgment and discernment are the best of seers." Nicias perhaps lacked the wit—he certainly lacked the will—to interpret the oracles and prophecies in his own favour as against undertaking the expedition. He would have done that had he been like Epaminondas, and the Athenians would have believed him had they been like the Thebans. Presages again put in an appearance when the Athenians have to decide whether their navy should leave the harbour at Syracuse (§ 2440 [1]), and apparent again are the disastrous consequences of Nicias's belief in them.

2437 [1] *Op. cit.,* XV, 53, 1-4 (Booth, Vol. II, pp. 42-43). Polyaenus, *Strategematon,* II, 3, 8, also hints broadly at trickery. Noting that the Thebans were terror-stricken, he adds: "Epaminondas won them over by two devices." And he tells of a message from the cave of Trophonius predicting victory for the side that should be the first to attack; and he says further that Epaminondas went with his soldiers to the Temple of Hercules, where, following orders that had been given him, the priest had furbished the weapons and left the temple doors open. That was interpreted as a presage of victory. And *cf.* Frontinus, *Strategematon,* I, 11, 16 (Bennett, p. 78).

and at the time serving as a soldier in the Theban army. Summoned to the assembly, he asserted that the Spartans had an ancient oracle to the effect that they were to lose their hegemony when they should be defeated by the Thebans at Leuctra. To Epaminondas there also came certain rustics, interpreters of oracles, who said that a very grievous misfortune was to overtake the Lacedaemonians near the tomb of the daughters of Leuctrus and Scedasus, and for the following reason. Leuctrus was the man for whom the plain had been named. His daughter and the daughter of a certain Scedasus, both young girls, had been violated by Lacedaemonian emissaries. Unable to endure the unspeakable insult, invoking curses on the country that had sent the odious legates, they took their lives with their own hands." Nor was that yet all. Plutarch relates that a most timely dream came to Pelopidas, ordering him to sacrifice a "virgin with auburn hair" to the young girls violated by the Spartans, and that, after some debate and other doings calculated to have their effects on the soldiers, the auburn-haired virgin was recognized in the person of a bay colt, and the colt was forthwith sacrificed.[2]

2437 [2] *Pelopidas,* 20-22 (Perrin, Vol. V, pp. 391-95): "Situated on the plain of Leuctra are the tombs of the daughters of Scedasus, who are called Leuctridae after the place. [A slight alteration of the story as told by Diodorus, but it agrees with the account of Pausanias.] . . . It was therefore continually predicted to the Spartans in oracles and prophecies that they should beware of the 'Leuctrian wrath,' a prediction that was not at all understood by the Spartan multitudes, who were not even certain of the place so designated, there being in Laconia also a small city by the sea called Leuctris and, further, in Arcadia, near Megalopolis, a place of the same name. So Pelopidas, while asleep there in the camp, dreamed that he saw the young maids weeping about their graves, cursing the Spartans, and that he saw Scedasus himself, who bade him sacrifice a maid with auburn hair to his daughters if he would vanquish the enemy." He communicated his dream to the soothsayers and the captains, some of whom would have had the command executed to the letter; and they mentioned many examples of that kind of sacrifice. "But others were of opposite opinion, that not one of the beings so superior to us and of a nature so much better than our own could take pleasure in a sacrifice so barbarous and cruel. . . . While the principal leaders were disputing on these matters and Pelopidas was more than any other uncertain and perplexed, a mare colt that had escaped from her herd came galloping through the camp and halted before them. The others all marvelled at the flame-red colour of her mane . . . but Theocritus, the soothsayer, clearly understanding, raised his voice before Pelopidas and cried: 'Behold, O happy man, the victim! Let us await no other virgin, but do thou receive and sacrifice this, which hath even now been offered thee of the god!' They therefore took the mare and led her to the graves of the maids; and having made the supplications, and crowned the mare, they sac-

2438. Pelopidas and his friend Epaminondas had a profound knowledge of the human heart. Had Pelopidas merely dreamed of sacrificing a mare outright, the dream would have made a far slighter impression on the soldiers than the anguish of a terrible human sacrifice, happily avoided by an ingenious interpretation. The Romans, less civilized than the Greeks and perhaps in greater terror, resorted in similar circumstances to the human sacrifice and would have no substitutes (§758).

2439. Adroitness in combinations in Epaminondas and Pelopidas, and perhaps in other Theban leaders, had given a good account of itself when coupled with a moderate quantity of group-persistences in the Theban masses.[1] The same combination, with a greater distance separating rulers from ruled, was to give a still better account of itself in the case of Philip of Macedon and his subjects.

2440. At the time of the Persian wars as well, aptitude for combinations in Themistocles, combined with a moderate supply of group-persistences in the Athenians, gave evidence of its efficiency when Themistocles induced the Athenians to abandon their city and

rificed her there to the joy of all, and the vision of Pelopidas and the sacrifice were the talk of the camp." Pausanias, *Periegesis*, IX, *Boeotia* 13, 5 (Dindorf, p. 451), knows the names of the two girls, Molpia and Hippo, and in all good faith recounts the presages as actual happenings.

2439 [1] Curtius, *Griechische Geschichte*, Vol. III, p. 365 (Ward, Vol. IV, p. 514), compares Athens and Thebes, Pericles and Epaminondas: "The ascendancy of those two individuals is to be explained by their high and varied culture. [That cannot stand. Both in Athens and Thebes ignorant demagogues enjoyed the full confidence of their fellow-citizens. Curtius comes closer to experimental realities in what follows:] In Thebes also we find an altogether aristocratic leadership functioning in the full midst of a democratic system [Different words for the combination we mentioned.], personal power vested in an individual of outstanding intelligence [Better: combination-instincts]. Epaminondas, like Pericles, also governs his country as a man trusted by the people [Who have little understanding and by not re-electing him "boeotarch" place the country in danger again.] as general (*strategos*) re-elected from year to year. [The very great disadvantage of a combination in itself a good one.] In that position, like Pericles too, he had to suffer from the fickleness of the citizenry and the hostility of an opposition that saw in his rule a violation of the equality guaranteed by the constitution. Men like Meneclidas at Thebes play the part of Cleon at Athens. [The terms of the combination are now inverted: individuals who have the talents for obedience are now governing those who have the talents for commanding—a situation that is ruining Athens and greatly endangering Thebes; Macedonia is still safe, not being stricken with that malady.] Epaminondas put up with all attacks and humiliations with the equanimity that great souls manifest. In war he had, like Pericles, been invariably successful

repair to Salamis. Inverting terms, we get bad results from a distribution of residues whereby Nicias, commanding the Athenians, was induced by his group-persistences to place his trust in oracles and so led the army under him to complete ruin.[1] Those instances

in all enterprises of importance, because he had combined the greatest shrewdness with the utmost energy and especially because he had the gift of rousing the enthusiasm of his soldiers and animating them with his own spirit. [But to an even greater extent because he knew how to take advantage of their sentiments.] He taught them, as Pericles taught the Athenians, how to master their superstitious prejudices." At that point Curtius quotes Diodorus, *Op. cit.*, XV, 53, on the episodes preceding the battle of Leuctra (§ 2437). But that account in no way shows that Epaminondas taught the Thebans how to master their prejudices. It shows that he fomented them in order to use them for his own purposes. He did not tell his soldiers that the oracles were silly prattle; he met bad omens with better ones. Diodorus speaks clearly enough in the very passages that Curtius quotes. He says, XV, 53, 4 (Booth, Vol. II, p. 42): "Seeing that the soldiers were filled with superstitious terrors in view of the presages, Epaminondas strove to remove their fears by intelligence and strategy" (Miot translates, Vol. IV, p. 529: "in his enlightened intelligence and his military conceptions"): Ὁ δ᾽· Ἐπαμεινώνδας ὁρῶν τοὺς στρατιώτας δεισιδαιμονοῦντας ἐπὶ τοῖς γεγονόσι σημείοις, ἐφιλοτιμεῖτο διὰ τῆς ἰδίας ἐπινοίας καὶ στρατηγίας [strictly: military device] μεταθεῖναι τὰς τοῦ πλήθους εὐλαβείας. And Diodorus goes on to recount the tricks Epaminondas used.

This mistake on the part of a historian as able as Curtius is noteworthy as arising in the mania historians have for ethical sermons, instead of keeping to descriptions of fact and relationships between facts. Quite unwarily the historian is now and again convinced that he is called on to assert the superiority of knowledge over ignorance, of virtue over vice. Curtius therefore unqualifiedly glorifies the intelligence of Epaminondas, without observing that his success was due to the ignorance of the people whom he led and manipulated. Grote, *Op. cit.*, Vol. X, p. 347, describes the despair of the soldiers after the death of Epaminondas at Mantineia: "All the hopes of this army, composed of such diverse elements, were centred in Epaminondas. All their confidence of success, all their security against defeat, were derived from the idea of acting under his orders. All their power, even of striking down a defeated enemy, appeared to vanish when those orders were withdrawn. We are not indeed to speak of such a proceeding with commendation." And there we are back again in the field of ethics! Ignoring the question of praise or blame, which has nothing to do with the matter in hand, we note simply that such sentiments in the Theban soldiers show the strength of their group-persistences, which in this particular case take the form of an unlimited faith in their captain, almost of worship for him. And in that we find corroboration for our theory, that the maximum of utility is realized when the leader has the combination-instincts required for command, and his soldiers the sentiments and prejudices that make a religion of obedience.

2440 [1] Had the Athenians left the harbour of Syracuse they would have escaped the total ruin that later overtook them. Everything was in readiness for the departure, which could easily have been made. "But early in the evening on the day before the time set for the departure, there was an eclipse of the Moon. Nicias, accordingly, who was superstitious by nature and all the more nervous in view of the pestilence in the army, referred the matter to the soothsayers. Their response

show that oracles are good things if they are used by rulers, who perhaps have no faith in them, as means of persuading their subordinates, but harmful if they are taken at face value by rulers and used as an end in themselves, not as means of persuasion. To make

was that it was customary to wait three days before setting sail. Demosthenes [who was in favour of getting away] and those who were with him had to consent in deference to the gods." Thucydides, *Historiae*, VII, 50, 4: "A majority of the Athenians, in deference to conscientious scruple, exhorted the generals to postpone [the departure]. Nicias, as a man, was even too superstitious and prone to such things. He said that no decision as to breaking camp should be taken before they had waited, as the soothsayers prescribed, three times nine days." And *cf.* Polybius, *Historiae*, IX, 19, 1-4 (Paton, Vol. IV, p. 45).

Had Nicias been as free from prejudice as Epaminondas or Pelopidas, he could readily have found derivations adequate for convincing the army that the eclipse was favourable to retreat. They were found after the fact to save the face of the prophecies. Plutarch, *Nicias*, 23, 5 (Perrin, Vol. III, p. 293): "For the presage [of the eclipse], as Philochorus says, was not unfavourable to anyone obliged to flee, but exceedingly favourable rather; for darkness is the ally of those who are acting in fear, and light is their enemy."

In similar circumstances Dio, and, after him, Alexander the Great, found ways to interpret eclipses to their own advantage. Plutarch, *Dio*, 24 (Perrin, Vol. VI, pp. 49-51) (Dio being about to advance against Dionysius): "After the libations and the customary prayers, there was an eclipse of the Moon; whereat Dio was not in the least surprised, for he knew that eclipses recurred at fixed periods and that the shadow that darkened the Moon came from the interposition of the Earth between the Moon and the Sun. But the soldiers were terrified, and since they needed somehow to be reassured, the soothsayer Miltas came forward and said that they should be of good cheer and look forward to the greatest successes; for the gods were showing by that sign that some luminous thing was to suffer an eclipse, and since there was nothing more luminous to the eye than the tyranny of Dionysius, it was that glare that they would eclipse the moment they set foot in Sicily."

While Alexander was advancing on Darius an eclipse of the Moon occurred, but Alexander straightway sacrificed to the Moon, the Sun, and the Earth, and found or commandeered individuals to help him. Arrian, *De expeditione Alexandri*, III, 7, 6: "Aristander found that the eclipse of the Moon was favourable to the Macedonians and Alexander, that the battle would be fought during the month, and that the sacrifices presaged victory for Alexander." Rufus Curtius, *De rebus gestis Alexandri Magni regis Macedonum*, IV, 10 (Cambridge, pp. 100-01): The soldiers, worried by the lunar eclipse, were grumbling: "Things were getting to the point of mutiny, when he, undaunted [whether at the presage or at the panic of the soldiers: *ad omnia*], bade the officers and commanders of the soldiers to gather at headquarters (*praetorio*) and ordered the Egyptian soothsayers, who he thought were very expert in matters touching the weather and the stars, to state their views. Now they knew perfectly well that the heavenly bodies (*orbes*) fulfil predestined cycles of time and that the Moon is eclipsed (*deficere*) either when it gets under the Earth or is overshadowed by the Sun. However, they did not explain to the untutored crowd the reason that they knew. They said that the Sun stood for the

the proposition general, and so applicable to times that know no oracles, one need merely replace the term "oracles" with the term "group-persistences" (§ 2455). Furthermore, it will be just as well if the doctrine here stated be not very generally known to the masses who are to be influenced, for the artifice, to be fully efficient, has to remain concealed. It loses little if any of its efficiency, however, if it is known to some few scholars; for daily experience shows that people continue to believe assertions that stand in flattest contradiction with the known results of logico-experimental science.

2441. Philip of Macedon lived at Thebes in his youth and learned the art of war from Epaminondas.[1] Had he been a citizen of Sparta

Greeks and the Moon for the Persians, and that whenever there was an eclipse of the Moon it portended ruin and slaughter for the Persian hordes. And they enumerated ancient examples of kings of Persia who had been shown by eclipses of the Moon to have fought under the disfavour of the gods. Verily nothing exerts a more powerful influence upon the multitude than superstition, though the mob is impotent, savage, undependable, when its fancy is caught by some fatuous belief."

Our "intellectuals" forget this message from the experience of the ages. Nowadays no one believes that lunar or solar eclipses have the slightest influence on the fortunes of war, but many people do believe that they are influenced by the "justice" or "injustice" of the cause that is committed to arms. Modern rulers are no longer called upon to worry about eclipses; but it is just as well if they go to some pains to make people believe that the cause for which they are fighting is "just"; and it is not bad either if they are not too sure of that themselves, if, that is, they follow the example, not of Nicias, who believed in the influence of lunar eclipses, nor of Napoleon III and his minister Ollivier, who placed their reliance on the "justice" of their cause; but, rather, of Themistocles, Epaminondas, Dio, and Alexander, who knew how to use omens for the furtherance of their plans; or even of Bismarck, who listened while other people chatted about justice, but as for himself saw to it that he was the strongest in guns; and when he began tinkering with the Ems despatch, he did not ask the advice of a moralist, but inquired of Moltke and Roon whether the army was ready and able to win.

2441 [1] Plutarch, *Pelopidas,* 26 (Perrin, Vol. V, pp. 405-07): "Pelopidas . . . received Philip, the king's brother, as a hostage, along with thirty other young men from prominent families and took them with him to Thebes. . . . That was the Philip who later on made war upon the Greeks to subjugate them. At that time he was still a boy and was reared at Thebes in the house of Pammenes. It seems accordingly that he began by emulating Epaminondas, having perchance been impressed by his activities in military science and in the conduct of armies, the which were but a small part of that great man's talents. As for the temperance, the justice, the magnanimity, the good manners, for which Epaminondas was truly great, Philip partook in no way of them whether by nature or by emulation." Grote, *Op. cit.,* Vol. XI, p. 209: "His mind was early stored with the most advanced strategic ideas of the day, and thrown into the track of reflection, comparison, and invention, on the art of war."

or Athens he could have accomplished little, for opposite reasons. But he was called upon to lead a people in whom prejudices were strong enough to assure their obedience to their king, yet not strong enough to prevent the reforms that he set out to introduce. The Macedonian kingdom was not an absolute monarchy, but it was much stronger than the Spartan. Had Epaminondas not been slain at Mantineia but lived a few years longer, he might successfully have checked the rising power of Macedon. Such the rôle of chance in human affairs! Certain forces persist over long periods of time, others are accidental and of brief duration. In the end the former prevail, provided they last.

2442. At another extreme, Athens had generals of the greatest ability at that time, but she could neither keep them nor take advantage of them. Timotheus and Iphicrates seem to have been in no way inferior to Philip, but to their misfortune, they had to work with Athenians, who were enamoured of novelties, doted on court trials and prosecutions, and were incapable of the serious discipline that is made possible by group-persistences. An indictment and a trial disposed of Timotheus and Iphicrates at one fell swoop and left the city defenceless against the formidable power that was rising in Macedonia.[1]

2443. Where sentiments of group-persistence are not very strong, people readily surrender to the momentary impulse without giving adequate thought to the future, forgetting the larger interests of the community under the sway of uncontrolled appetites. The Mace-

---

2442 [1] Though he is an undiscourageable panegyrist of Athenian democracy, Grote cannot refrain from deploring the loss of the best generals in Athens, who were stupidly discarded by the Athenian public, *Op. cit.*, Vol. XI, p. 230: "The loss of such a citizen as Timotheus [He went into exile.] was a fresh misfortune to her [Athens]. He had conducted her armies with signal success, maintained the honour of her name throughout the Eastern and Western seas, and greatly extended the list of her foreign allies. She had recently lost Chabrias in battle; a second general, Timotheus, was now taken from her; and the third, Iphikrates, though acquitted at the last trial, seems, as far as we can make out, never to have been subsequently employed on military command. These three were the last eminent military citizens at Athens; for Phokion, though brave and deserving, was not to be compared with either of them. On the other hand, Chares, a man of great personal courage, but of no merit, was now in the full swing of reputation. The recent judicial feud between the three Athenian admirals had been doubly injurious to Athens, first as discrediting Iphikrates and Timotheus, next as exalting Chares, to whom the sole command was now confided."

donians obeyed Philip in everything, and after him Alexander. The Thebans followed the lead of Epaminondas. Then they indicted him, though he issued victorious from the trial. The Athenians cared little for their generals. They tormented them, persecuted them, condemned them, lost them through fault of their own. The lessons taught by past experience are of no avail for the future, there being no sense of group-persistence.

2444. Phenomena altogether similar are observable in a comparison between Germany and France from the time of the Second Empire down to our day [1914] (§§ 2469 f.). Germany in a way resembles Macedonia or Thebes, France suggests Athens. The force of group-persistences makes up for deficiencies in that logico-experimental knowledge whereby the individual citizen might understand that his indirect utility is sacrificed when the utility of the community is sacrificed beyond a certain point. Those Athenian citizens who paved the way for the defeat at Chaeroneia [1] and those French citizens who paved the road to the capitulation at Sedan, did so to their own individual damage.

2445. Such phenomena are often examined from the single standpoint of forms of government—democratic, oligarchic, or monarchical. All the woes of Athens have been laid at the door of the Athenian democracy, and there have been efforts to acquit democracy of such blame. It is undeniable that forms of government do have their influence on social phenomena; but it must not be overlooked that in the first place, such forms are, in part at least, products of the character-traits of the peoples involved, the traits, therefore, being far more important as causes of the social phenomena; and that in the second place, identical forms of government may yield entirely different results, a thing that clearly proves the presence of more powerful causes that assert themselves regardless of forms.

2446. To the fact that Macedonia had a monarchical form of government we must attribute the circumstance that after his total defeat by Onomarchus, Philip of Macedon none the less retained his power and was so enabled to even the score. Had he been a general of the Athenian republic, he would probably have been condemned to death, an eventuality that might have nipped the rise of Macedon in the bud. Had he been a general of the Theban republic, he

2444 [1] [*Coronea* misprint for *Cheronea.*—A. L.]

would have been dismissed, as was the fate of Epaminondas, and that again would have been a serious loss to Macedonia. From that one might be led to the conclusion that owing to the stability of command which it provides, the monarchical form is favourable to a country's prosperity; and the conclusion may hold in many cases. But it does not hold in others. Stability of command is a good thing when the command is good—in the hands, for instance, of an Epaminondas or a Philip. Of that there can be no doubt. It is also a good thing when the leadership is just average. The harm that is done by changing horses in midstream may far overbalance the advantage of removing a man of little talent from power. But it is certainly disastrous if it keeps absolute incompetents, such as many of the Roman Emperors were, in power.[1] The conduct of the Athenians

2446 [1] Interesting among the derivations used in defence of the monarchical form of government is the rebuttal that is offered to the objection that history shows many instances of harm done by that type of régime. It is answered that the harm would not have been done had the king been a "good" king, capable, and fitted to command. Of that, in truth, there can be no doubt. But that is not the objection. The objection is that monarchy cannot guarantee that the monarch will have those qualities nor that, possessing them, he will keep them all his life long. In his *Souvenirs d'un vieil homme*, pp. 178-79, Dugué de la Fauconnerie tries to acquit the imperial government in France of responsibility for the terrible disaster of 1870, and argues: "To assert his personal authority the Emperor would have had to be the emperor he had been at the time of the Constitution of 1852, or at least to have remained what he had been in 1863. . . . But that water, alas, had gone over the dam. The poor Emperor had gradually yielded to the pressure of the parliament and with the sole result of finally resigning the authority he held from the nation into the hands, let alone of an Ollivier, of Orleanists such as Buffet and Daru. Nothing could now be done." Suppose we ignore the question of fact and take the statements at their face value. Dugué de la Fauconnerie refutes his own thesis by picturing an emperor who held absolute power and the force to maintain it, and yet allowed himself to be dispossessed by parliamentary politicians. If, as the writer would have it, the evils ensuing were attributable to those intrigues, the first responsibility lies with the weakness of the sovereign who handed power over to them; and since the imperial form of government offers no guarantee that an emperor of that type will not come along every so often, the responsibility oversteps the individual, Napoleon III, and rests with that form of government. That is all hypothetical, of course, keeping strictly within the scope of the statements of Dugué de la Fauconnerie. The excuses Ollivier himself finds for his ministry are of the same sort. First of all, the bad faith of Bismarck and the Hohenzollerns, as though the chief business of a Prime Minister were not, precisely, to keep the bad faith of an enemy from harming his country. Then the opposition of the Right, which prevented him from knowing the true state of the Emperor's health and therefore led him to consent to the Emperor's taking the field as commander-in-chief of the army —as though it were not the business of a Prime Minister to keep informed on such

and Thebans towards their generals was by no means a necessary consequence of the republican form of their governments. There was a republican form of government in Rome when after the defeat at Cannae all orders of citizens in the state marched forth to meet the defeated consul on his home-coming to tender him their thanks for not having despaired of the Republic.[2] Republics are not necessarily obliged to listen to men like a Cleon in Athens, a Meneclidas in Thebes, or a Caillaux in the present-day French Republic.

2447. Von der Goltz remarks,[1] anent conditions in Prussia before the battle of Jena: "In France the civil authority always defers to the army, whereas in Germany the prevailing spirit in the civil government, as well as in the public at large, is always to block the military authority. [Now the terms are precisely inverted: what could then be said of Germany can now be said of France, and *vice versa*.] That, in brief, was the opinion of Scharnhorst, and he used to add: 'It has been said, and rightly, that the French with a republican government are governed monarchically, while the Allied Powers, with their monarchical governments, are managed like republics.' "

2448. After power in France passed into the hands of people of the state of mind manifested in the Dreyfus affair, the French Re-

essential matters, and his duty to resign if he is placed in a position where he cannot do the things required for the country's defence.

Equally untenable, as regards Italy, were the self-justifications of Lamarmora after Custozza and Baratieri after Adua. A leader has to know and foresee, and the man who does not know and foresee had better leave the task of exercising command to someone else and quietly return to his fireside. Ollivier shows the harm done to France by the regency of the Empress during the War of 1870. No republican government would ever dream of putting a country's fate into the hands of such a woman. Rochefort wrote in the *Lanterne,* Aug. 8, 1868, p. 34: "Her Majesty the Empress of the French presided at the Cabinet meeting yesterday. How surprised I should be were I to hear that Mme. Pereire had presided over the Directors' meeting of the Crédit Mobilier!" One may sometimes receive good advice from an enemy. If Napoleon III had heeded that very sound remark by Rochefort, he might have averted the fall of his government, or at least made it less probable. As Ollivier said, the Second Empire committed suicide, the Empress-Regent aiding and abetting.

2446 [2] Livy, *Ab urbe condita,* XXII, 61, 14: "At that time patriotism in the city was at such a high pitch that when the consul who was largely responsible for the disaster came home, *obviam itum frequenter ab omnibus ordinibus sit et gratiae actae quod de republica non desperasset.*" And Livy adds: "Had he been a Carthaginian general, no punishment would have been great enough for him."

2447 [1] *Von Rossbach bis Jena und Auerstadt,* p. 517.

public greatly neglected national defence. But the Empire had neglected it almost as badly. On the other hand the conservative Republic, after 1871, made defence its chief concern. No correlation can be detected, therefore, in the French case, between forms of government and efficiency in providing for national security.

2449. As we have had frequent occasion to point out, in the quest for social uniformities, past and present throw a reciprocal light upon each other. Facts from the present are better known in the detail and so afford a clearer understanding of the past. And when the past parallels the present in one relationship or another, it forms the groundwork for our induction that those relations constitute a uniformity—are a law.

2450. If, for instance, one would clearly understand what happened in ancient Athens, one must consider what happened in France beginning with the ministry of Waldeck-Rousseau. The French disasters in the War of 1870 were very considerably due to the stress on political instead of on military considerations. Political were the reasons for the march on Sedan, political the reasons for Bazaine's inactivity at Metz. It would seem as though a country that had received such tremendous lessons would banish politics from military matters for ever after. But what do we see actually? Waldeck-Rousseau verily deserves a niche beside the worst demagogues in Athens. He set out to disorganize the whole military establishment of France for political reasons, and in furtherance of a policy so disastrous to his country he handed the Ministry of War over to General André, who spent his time in vulgar political intrigues, altogether neglecting national defence and to such an extent that when, in 1905, there was danger of war with Germany, it was necessary to improvise on the spur of the moment the prime essentials for a defence of the German frontier, which André had left deliberately unprotected as a favour to his political accomplices.[1]

2450 [1] Sorel, *La révolution dreyfusienne,* pp. 72, 41, 42: "In order to keep afloat until election-time, Waldeck-Rousseau was obliged to accept a number of compromises that must have seemed very painful to the sometime partner of Jules Ferry. It cost him some effort to allow the gendarmes who had had a collision with strikers at Chalon to be tried by a court-martial. Yet he had to give that satisfaction to the Socialists in the parliament, for they were afraid of being accused of treason by their district committees and their votes were necessary to hold a governmental majority during those trying days. After Gallifet's resignation, Waldeck-Rousseau was willing enough to retire, and he may have stayed only in the hope of getting more than

2451. Nor is that all. In France as in Athens the same mistakes were repeated, for, the same causes operating, the same effects ensue. In 1911 a new threat of war made the French authorities aware that General Michel, who had been entrusted with the supreme command for political considerations, was not the man to exercise it.[1] His chief merit was his subservience to the politicians. Colonel Picquart had been made a general for the services he had rendered in the course of the Dreyfus affair. In the manoeuvres of 1910, it seems, his work had not been of the highest grade; but in order to avoid saying as much, which would have embarrassed the politicians, General Michel, contrary to long-established practice, did not publish his review of manoeuvres at once, but temporized, and eventually delivered himself of the gentlest and mildest criticism possible.

2452. Under threat of war General Michel had to be replaced. Everybody recognized that on the basis of military merit, General Pau was entitled to Michel's post. But Pau would assume command only on condition that he be given the deciding voice in nominations of generals and that they be chosen solely for military merit, quite apart from political influence. That condition the government could not accept, and it rummaged about for another commander who would be more malleable in political hands.[1]

even with his enemies in the elections. Certainly he was aware of the military ineptitude of André, who had become a general only through pressure from Brisson. However, he accepted that caricature as Minister of War because Brisson and Léon Bourgeois both demanded it (Joseph Reinach, *Histoire de l'affaire Dreyfus,* Vol. VI, p. 121), and Bourgeois had saved the ministry in the session of May 28. Time was when the resignations of the chief of staff and the commander-in-chief would have frightened Waldeck-Rousseau, who had in common with all the Gambettists a deep interest in army matters. Now he had to let the Radicals have their way, along with the 'beplumed cephalopod' (words of Clemenceau) who was their favourite minister. [Luckily for France and the Latin countries, Germany had no Bismarck and no William I at that moment.] A deal of corruption was required to hold that provisory majority together till election-time. Waldeck-Rousseau had selected as general secretary to his ministry a man who would wince at no scruple. There was a mad scramble for melons, and in the rush the Socialists in the parliament were not the least cynical." Yet there are still people who believe in all sincerity that the ministry of Waldeck-Rousseau represented the triumph of political and social righteousness.

2451 [1] As early as 1866 Stoeffel, speaking of Moltke (*Rapports militaires,* Oct. 25, 1866, p. 39), had remarked on the advantage of having a powerful and competent chief of staff.

2452 [1] *Gazette de Lausanne,* Aug. 3, 1911: "Speaking of a reform designed to give the controlling voice in the High Council of National Defence to civilians, the writer says: 'What was required was not that commanders of land and sea forces

2453. Read now what Isocrates has to say, *Antidosis,* 26-27 (Norlin, p. 261), as to the causes underlying the conviction of Timotheus at Athens, and it will be apparent that both causes and effects are constant. He tells how he warned Timotheus: "You see what the mob is like, how bent it is upon pleasures (Norlin: "how susceptible it is to flattery") and therefore leans more to those who wheedle its appetites than to those who act honourably, more to those who pleasingly and amiably deceive it than to those who labour for its benefit in all earnestness and wisdom." He advises him to manoeuvre in such a way as to have the politicians with him. Timotheus replies (Norlin, pp. 263-65) that the counsel is undoubtedly sound, but that he cannot change his nature and stoop to the level of those who cannot tolerate people with qualities superior to their own—cannot, in a word, resign himself to what Faguet, in our day, has so well called the "cult of incompetence."

2454. What Isocrates says is said also by many writers, though oftentimes in the futile and fallacious form of the moral sermon, or in that other form, equally futile and fallacious, of the attack on this

should be admitted to the Council as extra members, but that all members of the higher councils of army and navy should be admitted on a par with everybody else.' 'A lean toward reaction!' cries M. Messimy. 'An effort to drown the government under a flood of generals and admirals!' Perhaps, in view of that, I may in my turn denounce this incorrigible mistrust that is hypnotizing people of the Bloc as regards the dangers professional military men represent for this wretched civil power that is for ever in danger. So long as such alarms go no further than merely spoiling the sleep of those who feel them, there is no great harm. But it becomes more serious when they inspire measures that may weaken our national defence. It was probably under the influence of the same democratic suspiciousness that M. Messimy proposed suppressing the title, not of generalissimo, for that title never existed, but of vice-president of the High Council of War. Everyone admits that in such matters questions of person take precedence over all others. With General Pau, the army would have accepted any title, however cacophonous, and any order of precedence. With General Joffre it might have asked permission to think twice. There is no doubt today . . . that considerations of the basest political character were responsible for General Pau's refusal. It seems that that energetic and distinguished soldier insisted on a decisive voice in nominations of corps commanders, not only as regarded the future but as regarded the past; and he made no secret of the fact that he contemplated a number of executions, that notably of a general officer, as scandalously incompetent as crudely self-conceited, whom the caprices of politics have placed in command of one of our principal army corps. That had to be prevented at any cost, and nothing of the sort was to be feared from General Joffre, a man of distinguished intelligence, but a bit of an intriguer too, and, as I am also informed, a Freemason. Luckily intelligence makes up for a lot of things!" That was not all. The politicians wanted more and better. They hit upon a most ingenious combination whereby, by

or that form of government (§ 2261). It was not, as some would have it, the democratic form of the Athenian system that was responsible for the defects in question. Both the democracy and the defects were products of the Athenian temperament taken in conjunction with all the circumstances in which Athens was situated at that time.[1] Comparisons between one nation and another, or between various epochs and circumstances in a given nation, serve to bring out the effects of permanent forces, disengaging them from the effects of contingent ephemeral forces, chief among them such

laying a responsibility that was their own on the general staff, they could get command of the army into the hands of their henchmen. On July 13, 1914, Senator Charles Humbert, reporting for the Army Commission, laid before the Senate the lamentable inadequacy of French armaments. A debate also took place in the Chamber. *Liberté,* July 17, 1914: "After M. Humbert's charges, the Chamber understood that it could do nothing but share the pained surprise of the Senate. Nothing is said before the higher assembly that the Deputies do not know. . . . The Chamber, or rather the Radical majority that has been governing the country uninterruptedly for fifteen years, was so little in need of opening an investigation on the inadequacy of war-materials that it was itself responsible for that condition. It has continually refused to vote the appropriations asked for by the General Staff. . . . The facts, the dates, the figures can be quoted. Three Ministers of War, who have embodied majority sentiments with peculiar fidelity, have not feared to side against their own department in order to play the game of the anti-militarists and keep them in the majority in the cabinet." Deputy Driant revealed in the Chamber the background of the move made in the Senate: "What astonishes one is the astonishment in the Senate, and if anything can be more astonishing, it is the indignation of M. Clemenceau. He has served three years as Prime Minister. He gave us a weak and incompetent Minister of War. The campaign that is now opening is designed to effect a change in the high command and replace the present incumbents with a politico-military clique." That was not denied by anyone. Deputy Lefèvre figured that between the years 1900 and 1912 France had spent 1,056,000,000 less than Germany on armaments. On that point *Liberté* remarks: "In 1898 our army was without a peer. . . . About 1900, policies change, and we get War Ministers whose names were General André and General Picquart. From that time on, all army requirements have been systematically cut, while the German army has been enlarged at an annually growing rate."

2454 [1] In general "speculator" governments are not only deficient in certain Class II residues, but also fail to take advantage of high-powered group-persistences in their subjects; and that comes about because people are inclined to judge others by themselves and have no clear comprehension of sentiments they do not themselves possess. The war that Italy fought in Libya furnished a remarkable instance of that. Giolitti, at the head of a speculator government, did not want any such war. Driven willynilly into it by powerful public sentiments corresponding to Class II residues, he prepared the country for it in a political, not in a military, sense with consummate skill and in a manner truly worthy of a master of the art of combinations (Class I). But he was not able to conduct the war in such a way as to strengthen

as depend upon the character of the individuals whom chance elevates to the seats of power.[2]

That is why we have examined the case of France at some length, as providing three very striking examples: first the Empire, which neglects national defence and dares not require of the country the sacrifices that are indispensable to security; then the conservative republic, which, immediately after the War of 1870, requires those sacrifices, the country cheerfully assenting; finally, after 1900, a democratic republic that dares not, and cannot, demand sacrifices of an unwilling country. If one keeps to the comparison between the Radical republic and the Conservative republic, the blame might be laid on the spread of democracy. But that inference fails to stand

the public sentiments in question, nor to obtain the necessary sacrifices from the country without resistance. He gave the atmosphere of an economic enterprise—the only type of enterprise the speculator thoroughly understands—to what should have been an enterprise grounded on national sentiments, a type that is in great part stranger to the speculator mind. If his government had demanded pecuniary sacrifices of the country at a time when war enthusiasms were at their height, the sacrifices would have been joyfully made, and far from cooling public ardour for the new enterprise, they might even have enhanced it; for in circumstances of that kind the case is not rare where love of country warms in proportion to the sacrifices that are demanded of it. Such a thing is inconceivable to the speculator. He cannot believe his ears when he is told that there are people who judge an enterprise otherwise than by a computation of profit and loss. And so, with their own minds preoccupied solely with such matters, the Italian speculators were convinced that the only way to interest the Italian public in the Libyan War was to persuade the country that it was an excellent economic "deal," that it could be carried to a conclusion without new taxes, without any decrease in expenditures on public works, without the least damage to the state budget. To do that they resorted to one trick or another, even reporting budgets that were "doctored" so as to show surpluses where there were really deficits (§ 2306 [1]). They were further steered in that direction by another attribute of the speculator temperament, an inclination to worry only about the present, never about the future. Such tricks worked for a time, to be sure, but they did all the greater harm when at last the truth could no longer be kept concealed. In all that policy the speculators failed to take proper advantage, as they might have done, of the great forces embodied in the country's enthusiasms and, being neglected in that fashion, the enthusiasms gradually cooled.

2454 [2] In Athens forms of government at the time of Themistocles and at the time of Demosthenes, though both democratic, were to some extent different; but the differences were not great enough to explain why the Athenians resolutely embraced the very severe sacrifices counselled by Themistocles in order to resist the Persians, while they failed to make the much lighter sacrifices recommended by Demosthenes in order to resist Philip of Macedon. The explanation is to be found only in the different relative proportions of Class II residues in the Athenians at those different times.

once the comparison is extended to the Empire, which, without
being democratic, behaved exactly as the Radical republic behaved.
In the same way, if the comparison is confined to the Empire and
the Conservative republic, one might, as many have done, ascribe
the disasters of 1870 solely to personal absolutism. But that conclusion fails to stand the moment the comparison is made between Empire and Radical republic. In the latter there is no personal absolutism, but there is the same unpreparedness that led to defeat in
1870. Everything, on the other hand, becomes perfectly clear if one
centres on intensities in Class II residues. Where those residues are
strong and are kept stimulated by a prudent government that is
skilful in taking advantage of them, a population willingly assumes
the burdens of preparedness for war. Where they are weak or are
weakened by a government that is concerned solely with certain
material interests and does not look forward to the future, the population refuses to assume the burdens of national defence.[3] If history
be studied attentively, one sees that nations on the road to defeat
and ruin have very rarely failed of warning signs that should have

2454 [3] Whenever a nation, A, in which Class II residues have weakened and in
which, accordingly, material and momentary interests prevail, is threatened by a
nation, B, in which Class II residues are strong and which in consequence is inclined
to sacrifice material and momentary prosperity to future and more abstract interests,
the nation A may properly be warned in the words that Demosthenes addressed to
the Athenians in just such circumstances.

In order to keep the funds in the Theoria (the Athenian budget for public spectacles) intact and spend them on public festivals, the Athenians were neglecting
military preparations against Philip and paving the way for the defeat at Chaeroneia.
Modern countries, in order to make sure of "social" and other "reforms" that provide leisure and material enjoyments for the followings of politicians, neglect expenditures that would be essential to the maintenance of national independence.
Demosthenes, *Philippicae*, II, 3: "In all cases where a man is inspired by a desire
for dominion he must be met with works and deeds, not with words; and we orators are the first to refrain from urging deeds upon you, O men of Athens, in fear
of your wrath against us." *Ibid.*, IV, 55: "If one chances to speak of the doings of
Philip, straightway someone rises to say that one must not lose one's head and suggest war. And then he goes on to portray the delights of living in peace and the
annoyances of maintaining a large army; and he adds: 'There are people who are
trying to get the money for themselves' and other fictions that wear the false face of
truth."

The chief defect in the derivations that are used by people who shrink from the
sacrifices necessary for their country's defense to justify their indolence and their
greediness for material pleasures, lies in their forgetting that war may be forced
upon a people that does not want it, and that if it is unprepared, it faces utter ruin.
Grote, *History of Greece*, Vol. XI, p. 290: "Demos at home had come to think that

counselled a change of course, and that few, very few, have had governments so lacking in vision as not to foresee the impending doom. Forces adequate for spurring the nation to look to its defence have been there; but they have been more or less effective according to their intensities, and the intensities have depended primarily on the intensities of Class II residues in the governing classes, and they have been offset by greater or lesser resistance according to the greater or lesser intensities of those same residues in the subject classes. The Roman people conquered the Greeks and the Carthaginians chiefly because those sentiments of group-persistence that are known as love of country, and those other sentiments that supplement and reinforce love of country, were more intensely felt in Rome than in Greece and Carthage, her rulers meantime possessing Class I residues in abundance so that proper advantage could be taken of the residues in the masses.

2455. The utility of certain combinations of residues of Classes I and II is apparent, even if one considers only small groups of people, or even one or two individuals. It was, perhaps, owing to the fact that Bismarck and William I were called upon to work together

the city would march safely by itself without any sacrifice on his part, and that he was at liberty to become absorbed in his property, family, religion, and recreations. And so Athens might really have proceeded, in her enjoyment of liberty, wealth, refinement, and individual security—could the Grecian world have been guaranteed against the formidable Macedonian enemy from without." Were it not known that Grote wrote his history long before the War of 1870, one could not be too certain that he was not thinking of France during the last years of the Empire when he wrote of the Athenians, *Ibid.*, Vol. XI, p. 278: "The superiority of force was at first so much on the side of Athens [of France during the war of 1866] that if she had been willing to employ it, she might have made sure of keeping Philip at least within the limits of Macedonia [Prussia within the boundaries she had had before the war with Austria]. All depended upon her will; upon the question, whether her citizens were prepared in their own minds to incur the expense and fatigue of a vigorous foreign policy [whether Napoleon III were disposed to follow such a policy instead of dreaming along in his fanciful humanitarianism]—whether they would handle their pikes, open their purses, and forego the comforts of home, for the maintenance of Grecian and Athenian liberty against a growing, but not as yet irresistible destroyer. To such a sacrifice the Athenians could not bring themselves to submit; and in consequence of that reluctance, they were driven in the end to a much graver and more irreparable sacrifice—the loss of liberty, dignity, and security." The disaster that France suffered in 1870 was not so grave as the disaster that overtook Athens in the war with Macedon, but there is no telling how serious another such disaster might be if, in a near future, the same causes still holding, similar effects should ensue.

that they were able to do great things. A well-known story that Bismarck used to tell [1] clearly shows how "prejudices" (group-persistences) in King William I saved the Prussian monarchy in 1862. At that time the quarrel between the King of Prussia and his parliament had reached a very serious pass. The King was returning discouraged from Baden to Berlin, and Bismarck rode out to meet him in order to persuade him. Says he: "Still under the influence of his talk with his wife, he was visibly depressed, and when I asked his permission to report on what had happened during his absence, he interrupted with the words: 'I see perfectly how it is all going to end. Down there, in the Opern Platz, under my windows: first your head and, not so very long thereafter, mine!' I guessed—and eyewitnesses were later to confirm the impression—that during his week's sojourn at Baden he had been tormented with variations on the themes of Polignac, Strafford, Louis XVI. When he had finished I asked simply: 'And after that, Sire?' 'Why, after that—we shall be dead!' 'Yes,' I resumed, 'after that we shall be dead. But we are going to die sooner or later anyway, and could we possibly die in a more glorious manner? . . . Your Majesty is called upon to make a fight. Your Majesty cannot capitulate. You must resist the violence that is being done you, even at the risk of your person.' The longer I talked in that tone, the higher the King's spirits rose and the more he looked and talked like the military man he was, fighting for monarchy and country. [Group-persistences, Class II residues.] When facing 'external,' personal dangers, whether on the battle-field or from the would-be assassin, he was a man of a rare intrepidity that came natural to him. . . . He was the ideal type of the Prussian officer carried to the highest degree of perfection, the officer who, in the service, marches to certain death without regrets, without fear, with the simple words, 'Yes, Commander,' but when called upon to act on his own responsibility, fears criticisms on the part of his superior and the world at large more than he fears death. [Absence of Class I residues: but Bismarck had what King William lacked.] . . . Now . . . the upshot of our talk there in that badly lighted compartment on the train was that he came to look upon the rôle which the situation was creating for him from the standpoint of the army officer. Once more he was the soldier, above all

2455 [1] *Gedanken und Erinnerungen,* pp. 266-67 (Butler, Vol. I, p. 315).

else the soldier, and he saw himself in that situation as an officer who had been ordered to defend the post assigned him to the death, come what may."

Had Charles X, Louis Philippe, MacMahon, thought and acted in that manner in France, they would not have been overthrown so readily.

2456. The Italian war of 1859 had shown to the governors of Prussia on the one hand, and to the people ruling in France on the other, the urgent necessity of improving their military establishments. Both countries applied themselves to the task, but with quite different outcomes. William I, who had far less power and far greater opposition in his country than Napoleon III had in his, attained his purpose fully. Louis Napoleon failed. Why? Sustaining the erroneous thesis that France was perfectly prepared for war in 1870, Émile Ollivier admits, in self-contradiction, that preparations could not be completed either in 1860 or in 1867 (§ 2461).

2457. We have already seen (§ 1975[3]) what his excuses were as regards preparations after 1860, and we examined them in their bearing on the problem as to the accord between virtuous conduct and happiness. Now let us look at the facts he gives from the standpoint of the relative proportions of Class I and Class II residues in ruling and subject classes respectively. Though formally differing, the two aspects substantially coincide; for acceptance of the ethical principles on which Ollivier based his conduct depends, in fact, upon Class II residues, which may be beneficial or harmful according as they prevail, in the main, in rulers or ruled.

2458. Napoleon III appears in history in two outstanding guises: as the unwitting leader of a band of "speculators" (§§ 2465[1], 2463[1]) who used him as their tool; and then as a kindly upright soul with a prevalence of Class II residues (§ 1975[3]).[1] It was of no mean ad-

---

2458 [1] Busch, *Tagebuchblätter,* Vol. I, p. 569 (English, Vol. I, p. 315), Dec. 23, 1870: "Conversation at table turned on Napoleon III. The Chief [Bismarck] regarded him as a man of limited intelligence. 'He is much more good-natured and much less acute than is ordinarily supposed,' he said. 'Why,' Lehndorff interrupted, 'that is just what someone said of Napoleon I—"a good honest fellow, but an idiot."' 'No, seriously!' replied the Chief. 'Whatever one may think of his *coup d'état,* he is really kind-hearted, sensitive, sentimental, but his intellect is not brilliant, and his education limited.'" Bismarck was wrong as regards Louis Napoleon's education, or at any rate he chose to be wrong. Napoleon III was a well-educated man, much better educated than Bismarck; but he was a humanitarian, a dreamer, the tool of a

vantage to him that his government began with a period of increasing economic prosperity (§ 2302) and covered it.

2459. The central idea in Ollivier's history, *L'Empire libéral,* is to contrast a good, honest, virtuous sovereign (Napoleon III) with a king who was a wicked, evil-minded bandit (William I); and Ollivier is so deeply engrossed in his moral theme as not to observe that the praises he heaps on the sovereign he is defending are the worst accusations conceivable, making him out an inept individual altogether destitute in far-sightedness. If Napoleon was the man Ollivier represents him as being, he may have been a perfect gentleman, but he was a no less perfect idiot (§ 1975 [3]). If he did not comprehend what was going on in Germany, he could have comprehended nothing at all; and one can only laugh at a man who is enough of a dreamer to imagine that a sovereign can enjoy a "moral supremacy" without asserting a supremacy of force. Later on he was to meet Bismarck. Had he asked him what he thought of such a preposterous idea, he would certainly have given the Chancellor a moment's keen amusement.

2460. But whatever, after all, the causes of the Emperor's inertia, the explanation given by Ollivier might be sound, and we have to examine it. All we know of the character of that humanitarian daydreamer who came to be called Napoleon III shows that some little truth there was in the cause alleged by Ollivier, though it cannot be the only cause, nor even the main one, since when in time it lapsed, the alleged effects continued.

2461. Ollivier himself supplies the proof, Vol. X, pp. 347-48. In 1867 everyone could foresee that war was possible.[1] The childish

group of men who were amassing wealth by speculation. What is the use of having brains if they are to be used to one's own undoing, as Napoleon III used his when he conceived the astonishing idea of lending assistance to the various nationalities that were organizing in Europe—the best conceivable policy for leading his own country to ruin? A less intelligent sovereign would have clung to tradition (Class II residues) and done everything in his power to keep neighbours of France, which had been a united country for centuries, disunited. One might imagine that if Bismarck had had the temperament of Napoleon III, and *vice versa,* the destinies of Prussia and France would have been reversed. But that would be an erroneous inference. In a country like Prussia a Napoleon III in Bismarck's shoes would have amounted to little or nothing, and a Bismarck in the Emperor's place in France would have amounted to little more.

2461 [1] Maupas, *Mémoires sur le Second Empire,* Vol. II, p. 188, says that at the time of Sadowa "the Emperor was obsessed, and everybody knows how much, with

dream of a "moral supremacy" seemed to have vanished, and Napoleon III appointed a "High Commission made up of eminent individualities from all orders in his government, to find ways and means for putting our national forces in a position *to guarantee the defence of our territory and the maintenance of our political influence.*" [2] Marshal Niel drafted a bill for strengthening the army. The Legislative Body appointed a commission that was opposed to asking of the country the sacrifices that were required. The Emperor resisted, and even threatened to dissolve the Legislative Body. But the commission held obdurate. "The Emperor thought at first that he would pick up the glove that had been thrown at him and re-enact in France the struggle between William I and the Prussian parliament. Rouher developed as much vehemence in dissuading him from that as he had used in intimidating the High Commission. . . . Marshal Niel yielded in his turn . . . 'It would have been better to get more; but what we are getting will be sufficient.' And without even awaiting orders from the Emperor he began negotiating with the commission, agreeing that whole classes of young men would not be enlisted, but only annual contingents to be fixed by the Chamber. The Emperor was painfully surprised at that concession on the part of his minister. When he was told of it he buried his head in his hands and sat silent for some moments, crushed. Deserted by everyone, there was nothing for him to do but be resigned." [3]

2462. Here we are on the way to finding the real explanation. William I was surrounded by men like Roon, Moltke, and Bismarck. Napoleon III was surrounded by men like Randon, Niel,

the idea that we were destined sooner or later and inevitably to have a war on the Rhine."

2461 [2] *Op. cit.,* Vol. X, p. 382. Ollivier devotes a whole chapter (pp. 264-79) to "The Inevitability of War with Prussia." Granier de Cassagnac, *Souvenirs du Second Empire,* Vol. III, p. 256: "No one will deny that war was a foregone conclusion from the end of the year 1866, after the defeat of Austria at Sadowa."

2461 [3] Something of the kind may one day be written of Poincaré as President of the French Republic. Towards the end of 1913, he had to resign himself to accepting the Doumergue ministry, which was bent on disorganizing national defence. As regards persons there is the difference that Napoleon III could, and would not, while Poincaré could not and there is no knowing whether he would or would not; but certainly as regards forms of government, Empire and Republic were in the same boat in their results.

and Rouher. But that is not all. The circle of the governing class has to be widened. In Prussia one finds a hereditary monarchy supported by a loyal nobility: Class II residues predominate; in France one finds a crowned adventurer supported by a band of speculators and spenders: Class I residues predominate.

2463. The democratic Opposition in France was no better than the Imperial party. Under one form or another a single idea came to the surface everywhere: "We want to get rich and enjoy life; we do not want sacrifices." [1] Apparent in that again are the effects of weakness in Class II residues, which are among the strongest forces inspiring human beings to self-sacrifice. And the same weakness is again apparent when a Radical-Socialist government granted its voters a reduction of the term of military service to two years; and still again, in 1913, when the Three Years' Service Bill was fiercely opposed, though the change was absolutely necessary in view of the

2463 [1] Ollivier, *Op. cit.,* Vol. X, pp. 382, 351-53, 558: "We were to think only of enjoying the blessings of quiet, of getting rich. We were to see no other enemy than tuberculosis, grim product of the vices of peace which in a year's time claimed more victims than months of war. No ideal anywhere, in any form! How ask a people trained to such doctrines to have the military spirit and bless the good fortune of being confined to a barracks? To defend the country's independence? No one could believe that it was threatened. Besides, a vague fear grounded on no tangible reality is not enough to kindle in souls inured to pleasures a passion for the slaveries and sacrifices of military life. . . . Garnier-Pagès used to say: 'The influence of a country depends on its principle. Armies, rivers, mountains have had their day. The real frontier is patriotism.' All these themes were taken up and enlarged upon in the talk one heard. Who could be most eloquent in disparaging standing armies that were soon to be abolished (Magnin, Sept. 20 and 21, 1867), which create in our midst a race of men who are cut off from the rest of their fellow-countrymen (Jules Simon, Dec. 19, 1867)? Who could denounce most loudly that armed peace which, with all its nervous strain and its sacrifices, was worse than war, 'since it never ends and fails to give the one thing capable of compensating for struggle on the battle-field, the manly energy of peoples that are soaked in blood they have shed' (Jules Simon, Dec. 23, 1867)? According to Garnier-Pagès, neither soldiers nor munitions were necessary. The *levée en masse* would be enough. 'The time the country got aroused,' he would say, 'we whipped Prussia and went to Berlin. When the Prussians got aroused they came to Paris.' (Dec. 24, 1867). Jules Favre would say: 'You talk of frontiers; but they have been abolished, frontiers! And what has wiped them out? The hands of our engineers, that line of double steel that goes winding through the valleys—civilization!' " By the time that estimable phrase-coiner went to Versailles to whimper in Bismarck's presence, he must have learned that in addition to "civilization" another thing called "force" had a little something to say about national boundaries. Bismarck used to laugh at tomfooleries of that variety. Busch, *Tagebuchblätter,* Vol. II, p. 145 (English, Vol. I, p. 408), Feb. 4, 1871: Of the ag-

enormous and formidable growth in the German army; and finally when the Barthou ministry was overthrown to the cry of "Down with the three-years law!" which Deputy Vaillant at least had the courage to raise while others were doing without saying.

2464. Marshal Niel begged the voluptuaries of the Majority to make some sacrifice for the army, but with little success. Said he: "'If you compel me to go too far with the numbers of men on furlough, we shall have regiments of inadequate complements with officers discouraged and sergeants and corporals absent on leave. The new system will seem to be a disgraceful thing and you will have caused its failure when it ought to triumph.'" [1]

2465. One gets an altogether different picture on turning to Prussia. Stoeffel was struck with it and warned his government to be on its guard, but to no avail. In France the army was subordinate to finance; in Prussia, finance to the army.[1] Not that opposition was

gressive anti-German platforms of candidates running for the French National Assembly, Bismarck said: " 'Too much rhetoric! . . . They remind me of Jules Favre. On two or three occasions he tried that grand language on me. But it did not last long. I always brought him down to earth with a jesting remark' " (§ 2470 [1]). Yet that man came to head the country that he had done his part to ruin. The same absurdities were again audible in 1913 in opposition to defence measures made necessary by the increase in German armaments; and it was again preached that the enemy was to be met not with arms, but with humanitarian and pacifist principles. As an extreme concession there was again talk of the "armed nation," twin sister to the *levée en masse* before 1870, while again as then Frenchmen could be heard preaching disarmament and peace in their own country while the enemy was arming formidably for war. And all such things should occasion no surprise. Derivations are, and have to remain, what the crowds who heed them and esteem them like to hear. The charlatans of today use the same devices that were used by the charlatans of ancient Greece and Rome, just as our demagogues today are, to the letter, the demagogues of Rome and Greece.

2464 [1] Ollivier, *Op. cit.,* Vol. X, p. 565.

2465 [1] It seems that at the time of Sadowa Napoleon III and his minister, Drouyn de Lhuys, thought of sending an observation corps to the Rhine. That might have changed the outcome of the war. Says Maupas, *Mémoires sur le Second Empire,* Vol. II, pp. 189-90: "For a moment . . . there was reason to hope that the policy of far-sightedness and energy, which were openly favoured by M. Drouyn de Lhuys and Marshal Randon, had finally prevailed at the Tuileries. On July 5, the decrees convoking the Chambers and ordering the mobilization of our army had been drawn up and possibly signed, and they were about to be sent to the *Journal officiel* when influence highly placed and enjoying access to the Sovereign essayed one last effort upon him. Among the outstanding individualities who played a part in the final hour of that moving episode was M. Rouher. . . . What, then, could have been the motive of the Minister of State, in particular, in opposing the despatch of an ob-

lacking in Prussia. There was violent opposition; but it was possible to overcome it, owing to the traditions and prejudices active in a people that at that time had been hardly at all industrialized and to no great extent commercialized, and was little affected by the speculator temperament. Some of the contrasts prevailing between Macedonia and Athens in Philip's time have their counterparts in the antithesis between Prussia and France before 1870. "Members of the wealthiest families," says Stoeffel,[2] "all the most prominent names, serve as officers, submit to the hardships and exigencies of military life, preach by example; and, at such a spectacle, one is moved not only to esteem such an earnest and hardy people, but almost to fear the power that such institutions give to its army. . . . I have already said that in Prussia all the honours, all the advantages, all the favours, go to the army or to those who have seen service. The man who for one reason or another has not been a soldier cannot attain to any position in public life, and in town and country alike he is the butt of taunts from his fellow-citizens." In France, even after the terrible lesson of 1870, the army remained subordinate to the politicians. Just as Machiavelli, mistaking the part for the whole, talked of "religion" (§ 2532) where one has to think of Class II residues, so Stoeffel talks of "morale" where, again, one must think of Class II residues: "I must further call attention to a quality that is very peculiarly characteristic of the Prussian nation and contributes to enhancing the morale of its army: the sense of duty. It is developed to such a degree in all classes in the country that one never fails to marvel at it in studying the Prussian people. It not being to the point here to consider the causes of the thing, I content myself with noting it.

servation corps to the Rhine? The causes must not be sought in considerations of any higher order. . . . M. Rouher yielded to the influence of certain fanatical friends of Italy with whom he was intimate; and he was also subject to the pressure of the group of financiers and big manufacturers who had danced attendance upon him ever since his assumption of the Ministry of Public Works. In those men the passion for business paralyzed sentiments of patriotism. In the despatch of an observation corps to the Rhine, which would logically follow the mobilization of our army, they saw prolonged interference with the 'boom' in business. And they had succeeded in convincing M. Rouher that the real interests of the country lay in absolute neutrality, in inaction." Something similar occurred in 1905 when Rouvier, a worthy representative of the "lobbyists" (*affairistes*), dismissed Delcassé in obedience to an injunction from Germany. The same paralysis was also one of the reasons why Giolitti did not take to the notion of a Libyan War.

2465 [2] *Rapports militaires*, Apr. 23, 1868, pp. 101-04.

The most remarkable proof of this attachment to duty is supplied by the personnel of all ranks in the various departments of the monarchy. Paid astonishingly low salaries and burdened with large families more often than not, the men on the departmental staffs work all day long with indefatigable zeal, without complaining, without seeming to aspire to more comfortable posts. 'We are at great pains not to tamper with these men in any way,' Bismarck said to me the other day. 'This hard-working, underpaid bureaucracy does the best of our work for us and represents one of our main sources of strength.'" Something of the same sort was observable in Piedmont before 1859, and was not the least of the causes contributing to that country's successes.

2466. But all such things are impossible when Class I residues hold any great predominance, and speculation, business, finance, commerce, claim all talents of intelligence and industry. Before 1870 Prussia was poor and strong. Today she is certainly wealthier. But she may possibly be weaker unless the intensification of Class II residues in the subject classes, as manifested in Pan-Germanism and other phenomena of the kind, has offset the increase in Class I residues and, conversely, if it has more than offset it in the ruling classes. As for France, the situation today is very much what it was before 1870. If Class I residues have not increased, they certainly have not fallen off. But meantime Class II residues have also been intensified in the lower classes, as attested by revivals in religion and metaphysics and by an increasing virulence in nationalism. One is left in doubt therefore as to the direction in which the relative proportions between Class II and Class I residues may have varied.[1]

2466 [1] If A is the index of the force of the sum of Class I, and B the similar index for Class II, residues, our task is to discover, be it in roughly approximative terms, the variations in the equation:

$$q = \frac{A}{B}.$$

One of the greatest difficulties in the way of doing that lies in the fact that it is not enough to know that B has increased in order to conclude that q has increased; for A may have increased enough to offset the increase in B, so that there will be little if any change in q; or indeed the variation in A may have been such as to cause an increase in q, or, again, a decrease. One must therefore consider variations not only in one index, but in both, and try to evaluate them as best one can. We are most favourably placed for such an investigation when we can find phenomena directly dependent upon q and therefore giving some inkling as to the manner of its variations.

2467. One must not forget, however, that in such reiative proportions, it is always a question of mores or of lesses, not only as regards the subject classes, but also as regards the governing class, and that the maximum of political and military power is not attained at either extreme. In the years before 1866, Hanover had fallen completely asleep and, satisfied with her tranquillity, was making no provisions against possible eventualities. In one of his speeches Bismarck observed in that connexion: [1] "The Honourable von Vincke has contended, with apparent soundness, that the Hanoverians had eaten their white bread first, as the French proverb says, that for a long time they had given no thought to the defence of their country, and that had they acted as their duty required, they would not have made those economies. Assuredly, gentlemen, a bad organization of national defence brings its own punishment. Because of neglecting defence, Hanover lost her autonomy, and the same fate awaits any country that neglects defence. That is the price one pays for it."

2468. The case of Hanover serves to show that the differences between France and Prussia in 1870 were not due to differences in race, as between Latin and Germanic. And not only that. Prussia herself was beaten in the Jena campaign for the same reasons, by and large, that France was defeated in 1870.

2469. What does Von der Goltz say? In many places in his book [1] one has only to change "Prussia" to "France" to get a description of what happened in 1870: "In those campaigns [on the Rhine] Prussia had put only a part of her forces into commission; because, as Clausewitz said, 'she desired to adhere to the mandates of a prudent caution.' She could console herself with the thought that if she chose to bring all her resources into play in a determined campaign, she could easily triumph over an inexperienced France." The French Government had had its warning from Stoeffel before 1870 and disregarded it. The Prussian Government had similar warnings before Jena and also disregarded them. "Connexions with the French armies had always been maintained. There had been no lack of opportunities for studying them, nor any lack of official reports as to their manner of being. As early as May 12,

2467 [1] *Ausgewählte Reden,* Vol. I, pp. 385-86 (Feb. 4, 1868).
2469 [1] *Von Rossbach bis Jena und Auerstadt,* pp. 378, 395-96.

1798, Minister von Alvensleben had stated his view of Prussia's situation in a very remarkable memorandum: 'To fight the French with advantage we must adopt their ways and methods, otherwise we shall always be in a situation of inferiority. . . . To procure equal resources we must do as the French do—pillage our whole country before casting the dice. To get recruits we must draw on all our provinces.' Von Alvensleben was not unaware of the radical character of his proposal. He even feared that its adoption might provoke a revolution. Unfortunately he could suggest no middle course except an alliance with France." [2]

2470. Put Bismarck for Napoleon and Prussia for France and we get in Von der Goltz, *Op. cit.,* p. 407, a description of the diplomatic events leading up to 1870: "Napoleon had completely fooled Prussia. But statesmen were not the only ones to fall into his trap. Many people in the public at large took the assurances of the *Journal de Paris,* August, 1806, as cash in advance: 'France and Prussia,' said that editorial, 'are bound by ties of closest friendship.' The most surprising thing about those days is that, when war was the threat of every moment, a great many Germans sat philosophizing not only on the abolition of standing armies, but on the possibilities of universal peace, which they thought was near at hand. *'Never have circumstances so conspired to make an epoch more propitious for the realization of that great ideal which will mean happiness for mankind.'* So declared a scientist, in the news from Berlin, on May 9, 1805. . . . The mistake of the diplomats was the mistake of many others. The graver the danger grew, the sounder the slumber of people in their sense of security." Exactly as happened in France on

2469 [2] So say the French pacifist-Socialists of 1913: "We cannot prepare for war without abandoning outlays for 'social' improvements. That we do not care to do. Let us therefore make an alliance with Germany, putting aside all grudges as to the loss of Alsace-Lorraine." Those estimable individuals forget that every so often history shows a verification of the proverb, "Play the sheep and you will be eaten by a wolf." The self-abasement of Carthage before the Romans did not save her from utter ruin. The remissiveness of Venice before Napoleon had its epilogue in the Treaty of Campo Formio. English radicals of the Lloyd George type say that war expenses should be paid by the rich, because they alone derive profit by it through the defence of their properties. As though the plain people in territories occupied by an enemy were not exposed to losing their lives as well as their wages, not having the money required for taking to their heels! But such utterances are mere derivations, designed to hide an eagerness to have the enjoyments of life at someone else's expense.

the eve of the War of 1870, when she was sending her statesmen to international peace conventions; or again in 1905, when the successors of those gentlemen were repeating the same absurdities on the eve of the Moroccan crisis (§ 2463 [1]).[1]

2471. The vogue that humanitarian derivations acquire at certain times is usually a sign of weakening in Class II and Class V (individual integrity) residues, which make for the preservation of individual and community. People who like sonorous words imagine that their declamations can take the place of the sentiments and the conduct that maintain the social and political equilibrium.

2472. Like France in 1866, Prussia, in the course of the year 1805, says Von der Goltz, *Op. cit.,* pp. 466-67, "had the most favourable opportunity for action that had presented itself since 1740. . . . Only one step was necessary—and how differently would that army, so despised for its defeats at Jena and Auerstadt, be judged today, had statesmanship taken that step! . . ." P. 473: "While public opinion was rejoicing over the maintenance of peace and enlightened intelligences were calling the policy of hesitation the shrewdest diplomacy . . . the leading ideal of the two outstanding statesmen, Hardenberg and Haugwitz, who thought that they could take advantage of the great crisis without drawing the sword [So Napoleon III, in 1866.], was an incomprehensible hallucination, given Napoleon's [Bismarck's] manner of procedure. To try to obtain a share in the booty without adopting the explicit resolve to take it from the enemy is neither honourable nor prudent. . . . The policy of fishing in muddy waters is a dangerous one. It is sound only when it is intimately bound up with a wealth of audacity and force; for

2470 [1] *Journal des Goncourt,* Vol. V, p. 59, Aug. 13, 1872: "Luncheon at Munich with Ring, first secretary of the [French] embassy at Vienna. He was the man who played diplomatic elephant-driver to Jules Favre at Ferrières. He talked of that lawyer's ingenuousness, of his confidence that he would overwhelm Bismarck with the speech he was preparing on the train. He boasted, poor lamb of the law-courts, that he would convert the Prussian to the doctrine of the brotherhood of the peoples by displaying before his eyes as the reward of moderation the popularity he would gain with future generations that would be locked in one world-wide embrace. The German Chancellor's irony threw cold water very soon on that childish illusion" (§ 2463 [1]). And there are still people who dote upon similar balderdash, which attains its maximum absurdity in the speeches of M. d'Estournelle de Constant, who at least has the merit of stating his position frankly, whereas there is considerable doubt as to the sincerity of many others who are using the derivations he uses.

no power will allow us to make a fool of it with impunity unless it is afraid of our strength. [Exactly what Machiavelli said, and what Napoleon III forgot in 1866 (§ 1975 [8]).] When, therefore, on January 24, 1806, the bulk of the army was demobilized while Napoleon was maintaining his forces on a war footing in South Germany, Prussia placed herself at the mercy of an enemy whom she had just galled and put on his guard by rattling her sword. Then, in August, 1806, she decided to make war, at a time when she could no longer deceive herself as to Napoleon's designs [Bismarck's, in 1870.], a resolve dictated by fear of attack, and possibly justified as a resort of despair. But the moment was altogether unfavourable. [Exactly as it was for France in 1870.] . . . After blunders so serious one could hardly count on a successful outcome. . . ." P. 377: "That policy, that sort of leadership, an unfortunate make-up of the general staff, numerical inferiority in forces, were the main extrinsic causes of the catastrophe." The same may be said of France in 1870. It is useless for Ollivier to lay the blame on the generals. They may have done badly, very badly indeed; but had they been under the orders of a Moltke and a William I, had they been working in a different political atmosphere, they would have done as well as the German generals.[1]

2473. Not a few people imagine that humanitarian sentiments are a product of democracy. That is a mistake. Humanitarianism may just as well prevail under monarchical or aristocratic forms of government. Democracy *de facto* must not be confused with the ideal democracy of the humanitarians, just as science *de facto* must not be confused with the fantastic "science" of the anti-Clericals.

2474. "The army," says Von der Goltz, *Op. cit.*, pp. 512-14, "was anxiously watched to keep it from manifesting any signs of discontent. However tranquil Prussia seemed to be, and though confidence in the army was unshaken, the governing classes were not exempt from a secret fear of revolution. [So the monarchical, semi-feudal Prussia of 1800 presents the same phenomena as the republican, democratic France of 1900.] Mollendorf never ceased urging upon garrisons and patrols that when called upon to disperse gatherings,

2472 [1] [This passage from *Rossbach und Jena,* to which Pareto refers in French translation, appears much rewritten in Von der Goltz's revised version of 1906, Chap. XII. The substance, however, is the same.—A. L.]

or, in general, to maintain the public peace, they should at all times act with patience and discretion and resort to moderate severities only when conciliatory measures had proved fruitless. The civil population was not to be incited to aggressiveness or resistance to authority by conduct or word of mouth on the part of the military. It should not be given any occasion for such things. The troops were absolutely forbidden to mistreat a trouble-maker in arresting him. He was to be dealt with with every consideration. Funk moreover recounts the following in his diary: 'Saxony had enjoyed peace for almost thirty years and an administration from which the military element had almost everywhere been eliminated. The bailiffs and burgomasters looked proudly down from very exalted heights upon the higher army officers, certain that in case of trouble the soldier would be convicted in any court.' What is here said of Saxony applies to Prussia as well, although to a lesser degree." Those are all dogmas of our present-day humanitarians. That is what is happening now (1913) in France, and what happened in Italy before the Libyan War. It is a specific trait of weak governments. Among the causes of the weakness two especially are to be noted: humanitarianism and cowardice—the cowardice that comes natural to decadent aristocracies and is in part natural, in part calculated, in "speculator" governments that are primarily concerned with material gain (§ 2480 [1]). The humanitarian spirit is to be classed among the Class II residues; but as we have already explained (§ 1859), it is among the weakest and least effective of them. It is a malady peculiar to spineless individuals who are richly endowed with certain Class I residues that they have dressed up in sentimental garb.

2475. Von der Goltz, *Op. cit.*, p. 522, quotes a poem that was written in the year 1807. " 'In days gone by,' it ran, 'a hero's greatest glory was to die in battle for country and king. But since world and men have been cultivating civilization and philosophy, fighting to the death has come to be called 'organized murder.' So civilization brings us to sparing even the blood of our enemy." [1] That exactly

2475 [1] From *Minerva*, Vol. I, 1807, p. 554:

> "Sonst freilich war, fürs Land und für die Majestät
> In deren Dienst man focht, das Leben zu verlieren
> Des Helden höchster Ruhm; doch seit Humanität,
> Philosophie, die Welt, die Menschen kultivieren,

is what our humanitarians are saying now. Von der Goltz concludes: *"Beyond question, therefore, the spirit of the age was the main cause for the intrinsic weakness of the Prussian army."*

2476. That was the conclusion reached by a practical man. It coincides exactly with the conclusion we reach by a theory that associates social phenomena primarily with sentiments (residues), and it is apparent once again that the damage resulting from an overstress of Class I residues is the same regardless of differences in nationality (Prussia in 1800, France in 1870). Whether the deviation from the relative proportions corresponding to the maximum of utility be in one direction or another, there are countries to show the harm that results from it.

2477. After this glance at the equilibrium in different countries, suppose we consider the equilibrium in various social strata, examining, that is, examples of class-circulation. It would be a good idea to begin by considering virtual movements, asking, that is, what means a governing class has at its disposal in order to defend itself by eliminating individuals who might conceivably overthrow it (§§ 2192, 1838) as possessing superior talents of a type likely to be dangerous to its rule.

2478. 1. *Death.* The infliction of death is the surest means, but also the most harmful to an *élite*. No race, either of men or of animals, can long endure such a selection and destruction of its best individuals. This device was extensively used by ruling families in the past, especially in the Orient. The individual who ascended a throne often exterminated all close relatives who might become pretenders to power. The Venetian aristocracy also made some little use of death to anticipate or punish the plots of individuals who showed a disposition to alter institutions in the state; or merely to eliminate some citizen who had grown too influential through ability, character, or power.

2479. 2. *Persecution not carried as far as capital punishment: imprisonment, financial ruin, exclusion from public offices.* This tool is not very efficient. It produces martyrs who are often more dangerous than they would have been if let alone. It is of slight or no ad-

Heisst fechten auf den Tod 'den Mord organisieren.'
So schont die Aufklärung sogar des Feindes Blut."

[This last verse does not scan, but was so printed.—A. L.]

vantage to the governing class, but it does no great harm to the *élite* considered as a whole made up of a governing and a non-governing element. It may in fact sometimes be beneficial, since persecution tends to stimulate qualities of energy and character in the non-governing element—the very qualities that may be lacking in an aging *élite;* and the persecuted elements may end by replacing the governing element.

2480. The effect just noted for conflicts between the two elements in the *élite* is a particular case of a much more general effect, which is very frequently observable in conflicts between a governing and a subject class. One may say, that is, that a governing class offers effective resistance only as it is disposed to go to the limit in resistance, without hesitation, using force and resorting to arms whenever necessary.[1] Otherwise it is not only ineffective; it may even benefit

2480 [1] In June, 1914, revolutionary disturbances broke out more or less everywhere in Italy, but particularly in Romagna. They give an excellent example, on a miniature scale, of the principles here in point. At the moment when the revolt was at its height, on June 10, Premier Salandra sent the following circular to the Prefects: "Regrettable incidents have occurred in some cities of the kingdom. All hearts are saddened. It is supremely important to prevent recurrences of them. You are to devote all your efforts and your whole zeal to that end. The government is not an enemy. It has duties to fulfil, chief among which is the maintenance of the public peace. But in maintaining order it would have the resort to force, if indispensable, not untempered with greatest caution. In its task of restoring quiet it trusts that it will have the assistance of all citizens who love their country and believe that the common weal is best furthered by a common respect for the law and for public liberties."

With this humble and submissive utterance from the head of the government, who seems to be apologizing to his opponents for venturing to resist them, compare the article printed in *Avanti,* the official Socialist organ, on June 12: *"Armistice.* The general strike that came to an end yesterday was the severest popular uprising that has shaken the Third Italy since 1870. Compared with the revolt of 1898 this strike has cost fewer lives, but it surpassed that 'Tragic Maytime' in scope and in depth. Two essential elements distinguish the recent general strike from all its predecessors: its extent and its intensity. There is just one gray page in the story of these days of fire and blood, and the General Federation of Labour took it upon itself to write it by suddenly and arbitrarily ordering the cessation of the strike, without consulting the Executive Committee of the Party. Another dark paragraph was written by the railway men, who learned that the strike was on three days late, and then learned of it only—not to strike. But all that does not injure the beauty of the uprising in its general outlines. We understand the pains and fears of reformism and democracy as they face a situation that will grow steadily more difficult for them. Premier Salandra, who is a liberal Conservative, and Sacchi, who votes against him, for us stand exactly on a par. We state the fact with a touch of the legitimate joy the craftsman feels as he contemplates his handiwork. We of course

its adversaries, and sometimes very greatly. The best example would
be the French Revolution of '89, where royal authority resisted just
long enough to strengthen the rebellion, and then ceased at the exact
moment when it could have crushed it. Other less striking examples
could be found in other revolutions in France and one country or
another, and also in the petty disturbances that sometimes occur in
civilized countries. In 1913-14 the English Government imprisoned
the "suffragettes" and freed them as soon as they went on hunger-
strike. That solved the problem of finding the form of resistance
that has a minimum of efficiency in favour of the government and a

lay claim to our share of the responsibility for the events that have occurred and
for the situation that is now taking shape. If, to imagine the case, Bissolati had
been Premier instead of Salandra, we would have done our best to make the general protest strike even more violent and more decidedly insurrectionary.

"Another period of truce in the social war has been in progress since last evening.
Whether it is to be a long one or a short one we cannot say. We shall take advantage of it to continue our multifarious Socialist activities, to consolidate our political
organization, to recruit new workers for our trade-unions, to occupy other redoubts
in local and provincial governments, in short to prepare increasing numbers of
moral and material conditions favourable to our movement; so that when the red
clarion is again sounded, it will find the proletariat awake, ready, and resolved for
the greatest sacrifices and for the greater and more decisive battle."

That language was the language of other Socialist papers. The *Scintilla* (*Spark*),
for example, said, June 18, 1914: "The flood-gates of humanitarian sentiment have
been opened. All kind hearts are now outpouring their unctuous deprecations 'of
all violence' and their crocodilian tears of pity 'for all victims.' The newspapers
of democracy, which are above all afraid of the effects the strike is to have on their
pre-election deals, are now flooded with pathetic sermons, milk-and-water homilies
on the dogma of 'revolution by evolution,' and lamentations on the sinister fatuity
of violence. We are proud to note that the Socialist party has made and is making
no contribution to this pap of revolting hypocrisy. . . . We have nothing to repudi-
ate and no one to deny, not even the so-called *teppa!* Naturally we shall never advise, as we have never advised, anyone to throw paving-stones at police lines. We
have no love for paving-stone revolutions: they are stupid. What especially exasper-
ates us is the stupidity of people who seem to think they can meet army rifles,
'latest model,' with brick-bats. Our objection to the sling-shot rebellion is, therefore,
a purely practical one—the attack is inferior to the reaction."

The fight between the fox and the lion! The one side relies only upon cunning
to win its battle; there is not a word that betrays the virile, courageous spirit of the
man who has a faith. The other side shows the opposite traits. The government
does not care to be known as the enemy of its enemies. The latter reply that they
are, and will continue to be, its enemies and the enemies of every other government
of the kind; and not to understand them is indeed to be deaf and blind. So it is
that the men who write for the *Avanti* [the editor at the time was Benito Musso-
lini.—A. L.] show that they have the qualities of virility and frankness, the qualities that assure victory in the end and which, after all, are beneficial to the nation

maximum in favour of its adversaries.[2] In Italy the "general strikes" and the more or less revolutionary disturbances that keep breaking the peace of the country are due in large part to the fact that the government resists just long enough to irritate its opponents, induce them to patch up their differences with each other, and incite them to violence, and then stops at the point where it could crush them.[3][4] (For footnote 4 see page 1791.)

as a whole. The fox may, by his cunning, escape for a certain length of time, but the day may come when the lion will reach him with a well-aimed cuff, and that will be the end of the argument.

Meantime some of the Socialists, and notably the "Reformists," are still relying on the pity of their mild-spirited adversaries, and plead extenuating circumstances. They say that the disturbances are caused by want, that the rioters are so many good little angels, and that if occasionally they throw a paving-stone it is because they are driven to it, against their will, by provocations on the part of the government, the police, the *bourgeoisie*. In general the strength of a government or an opposition party corresponds to the derivations it uses; so that the derivations may be taken as a gauge of the strength. The greater the strength, the fewer the appeals to the pity of opponents or neutrals, and *vice versa*. The Italian Government fled before mob violence and it fled again before the violence of a slender minority in the parliament. Salandra had made the taxation measures proposed by Giolitti his own. By sheer obstructionism some thirty Socialist Deputies held up a majority of many more than four hundred. But the thirty had courage and were inspired by an ideal. The others were chiefly concerned with the interests of their confederates. The government had to come to terms with the handful of filibusters. The treaty of peace was favourable to both parties. The speculators, represented by the government, obtained authorization to impose their taxes for the moment, and that was what they were after—for the rest they cared not a hang. The Socialist minority secured the great advantage of proving their own strength and showing that it had become impossible to govern without their fiat.

2480 [2] The weakness of a government that does not dare to keep a "suffragette" on hunger-strike in prison is one of the main causes for the continuance of the "suffragette" rebellion. At the time of the disturbances of June, 1914, in Italy, English newspapers went looking for reasons more or less fantastic to explain them. But they could have found the explanation by just gazing about at home. The main cause of the insurrectionary outbreaks in Italy was the main cause of the "suffragette" outbreaks in England. Such things are not going on in Germany, for where the cause fails to operate the effect fails to appear.

2480 [3] On June 7, 1914, at Ancona in Italy, a handful of individuals were leaving a private meeting that had been held in place of a public meeting which the police had forbidden. The police tried to keep them from proceeding to the Piazza Roma, where a band-concert was in progress. The result was a riot. Three of the rioters were killed and five wounded. Seventeen *carabinieri* were wounded. That was the signal for a series of uprisings all over Italy in which several persons were killed and many wounded, and which the government could not and would not suppress. So then: It interfered with a promenade that might have been harmless, or perhaps at the worst have caused some slight disorder, and refused to interfere effectively

And the government follows that course not from ineptitude, but because like all governments in the civilized countries of today, it represents speculators, and can follow no other course. Speculators want quiet above all else, for quiet is what they need to carry on their profitable enterprises, and quiet they are ready to buy at any price. They are interested in the present and worry little about the future, not in the least scrupling to sacrifice their champions to the

with acts of open rebellion *armata manu*. It displayed great force when dealing with defenceless individuals, and great cowardice when dealing with armed mobs.

On June 9 Premier Salandra explained to the Chamber that he had forbidden the meeting at Ancona because "its obvious intent was to incite the military to mutiny and rouse public contempt for the army. The fact that 'Constitution Day' (the anniversary of the *Statuto*) had been chosen as the date for the meeting revealed an intent to interfere with the civil and military ceremonies that customarily mark that holiday." So then: The Premier offered armed resistance to individuals intending to insult the army by word of mouth, and then, without using sign of force, allowed army officers to be clubbed and disarmed, and a general even to be captured, with absolute impunity. Could the speeches that had been foreseen possibly have been more insulting to the army than the acts that followed? The minister forbade "disturbance of civil and military ceremonies," and allowed public buildings to be sacked and burned. Is "disturbing a ceremony" a more serious crime than robbery or arson?

2480 [4] The *Corriere della sera*, June 13, 1914, remarked very soundly: "So then we can only wonder whether this cowardice on the part of the *bourgeoisie* is a means, a system, a device, a manoeuvre, or just a humiliating disposition to leave the destinies of Italy in the hands of an insignificant minority [But not so much smaller than the minority actually governing the country.] that has grown ultra-powerful through its own audacity and the supine bewilderment of its adversaries. [Really one should say, "through the art of governing by manipulation, avoiding the resort to force."] Must we really grant, in order to hush the clamours of the Socialists in the parliament, that the presence of the police in places that are overrun by mobs previously aroused by the utterances of orators in public meetings, is a provocation? That it is a provocation to expose police and soldiers for three or four days running to hisses, insults, paving-stones? [Yes, all that has to be granted by anyone not willing to resort to force, the *ultima ratio* in settling conflicts.] What evidence is there of that? Public forces in Romagna were very slender. For three days (and it seems that the spectacle has not yet ended) crime has reigned in that province. [The usual exaggeration of calling one's adversaries "criminals." Really, in every revolution, including the revolt of the Italian *bourgeoisie* against the old governments, "criminals" came forward and tried to fish where the water was muddy.] A police commissioner who was trying to reason, who was pleading for calm, has had his skull fractured. Wounded soldiers have been cruelly mistreated. Fire has been set to historic churches. [In every revolution, as in every war, public monuments suffer.] A general and two officers have been—let us call a spade a spade—taken prisoners. [Things like that do not happen in Prussia. Why not? Because Prussia has a different sort of government from Italy and France. There is no reason why rebels should not make prisoners of their opponents.] Pistols have been liberally used, not to mention the time-honoured knife. [But how else are wars fought, if not with weapons?] All that will be something to boast of in Socialist war-songs; and from their point of view they are right [A very sound remark, sufficient all by itself to save this whole editorial.]: those who will have the end must have the means. There are no revolutions in Arcady. [In Arcady people write circulars like the circular that Premier Salandra wrote (§ 2480 ¹).] Except that when it is a question of ascertaining, in the particular, who fired the shot, it is never the rioter who did the killing. And that too is natural. The revolutionary hero now makes way for the crooked lawyer. [Whereas the other side *always* sticks to the crooked lawyer.] But why do we have to build the defences of our very lives in Arcady? Well we know that such words cannot be uttered without our hearing from our adversaries, and especially from that portion of the *bourgeoisie* which wants to go on with its petty business [And also with its medium-sized, big, and very big business.] even in the country's most serious crises *et ultra,* cries of reaction, 'gallowsism,' 'a return to '98,' and so on."

It seems that that "portion of the *bourgeoisie*" must in fact have been heard from, for two days later the same paper changes its editorial line and justifies the government's weakness. *Corriere della sera,* June 15, 1914: "Premier Salandra did not deny that more energetic measures might have averted some of the violence of the revolutionists. 'What we are trying to do in Romagna,' he explained to the Chamber, 'is to restore order with the greatest caution. My colleagues understand that it would be easy to restore order by force. But if the measures taken by the government have not produced immediate effects, that is due, precisely, to the moderation with which force has been used.' . . . That makes Premier Salandra's line of policy perfectly clear. He tried to avoid bloodshed at all costs." For once it may have been all right, but certain it is that in the long run the "line" in question is a "line" that leads to defeat and destruction. The newspaper goes on to speculate as to what the consequences of vigorous suppression would have been: "Would we have avoided a much longer, more wide-spread and more violent general strike than the one we have gone through? [Exactly what "that portion of the *bourgeoisie*" which wanted to go on with its petty "business" was interested in avoiding.] Would we have avoided a railway strike more general, more complete, and more disastrous to national prosperity [And for the prosperity of the speculators.] than the one that has occurred?"

Those are the usual arguments of people who want to stop midway, and who dread going to the limit as the greatest of misfortunes. So the fox always reasons—but not the lion; and that is the chief reason why the lion kills the fox in the end. The newspaper concludes by expressing its full and unqualified approval of Salandra's policy; and such approval is proper enough if one admits that the prime function of government is to safe-guard orderliness in economic production, disregarding everything else. But one must not overlook the consequences of that policy in other fields.

They are well set forth in the *Giornale d'Italia,* June 16, 1914: "The purpose was a political revolution, a real revolution; and what is more serious, a successful revolution, though not for more than twenty-four or forty-eight hours and not without its ridiculous aspects. One may in fact call successful a movement that upsets towns and the country roundabout, that sets out to change forms of government, obliterates, smothers, the authority existing and replaces it with another both in the semblance and in the substance of power. Consider also that the movement was planned and premeditated, and not without a certain technical skill.

"It began with the isolation of every city or town, with the destruction of means of transport for troops by rail, with the cutting of telephone and telegraph wires. That prepared the ground for spreading the most false and absurd rumours. Assaults on armories, seizures of markets, confiscations of automobiles and the gasoline supply, completed the fact of revolution. The make-up of the separate individual committees, each containing simultaneously a Republican, a Socialist, a Syndicalist, and an Anarchist, bespeaks premeditated accord between the various insurrectionary groups. The police forces, small in numbers, taken unawares, constrained to let the storm pass, obliged to hand over the breeches of their guns or else to keep to their barracks, were paralyzed. And so the triumphant revolution was immediately able to pull down the royal coats of arms, raise red flags, close the streets to citizens not provided with passports of the revolutionary committees, confiscate food-stuffs, compile lists of persons who were to make contributions in money or in kind, close churches, burn railway stations and customs offices, and in some places even recruit a sort of revolutionary national guard, the embryonic militia of a new order of things. [That time it was just an attempted revolution. Some other time it may be a real revolution—and it may be a good thing for the country. Those things, the newspaper continues, were not to be taken as lightly as some people were taking them:] Think of the great loss to our national life that is represented by this red interregnum, this storm of folly which has kept one city or another in Central Italy in a nightmare for some days, cut off entirely from the rest of the world. And what prostration, what bewilderment, what prevarication, all fruits of a long period of compromise, temporization, disorganization, that have humiliated, demoralized, slowed up, all the organs of government! We pant for order, and order is held up to us—and not only by the subversives—as reaction. We desire a reasonable protection of the liberties of all on the part of the police, and the presence of soldiers is represented by a mob of agitators as a provocation! We grope our way hesitant and trembling towards the remedy, while the remedy asserts itself as urgent and clear, so that in the state to which the prestige of the law and the authority of the state have been steadily reduced during these many years, it would seem that what looks like excessive caution had now become unavoidable necessity. The moral harm, therefore, the heavy blow that has been struck at public spirit, the bankruptcy of all confidence in the authority of the state, are not less deadly than the material damage, all traces of which will disappear in the course of these next few days. . . . Things are at such a pass that now we await orders not from the law, but from the committees, leagues, federations, syndicates, labour chambers of the Socialists. In a word, when we hear Deputies expressing their satisfaction in the parliament at the issuance of an order by we forget what exalted Committee of Public Safety, bidding the subversive uprising to come to an end and the country to return to order, the conviction cannot help forcing itself upon one that, owing to some fatal degeneration, today, above the executive power and above the legislative power, we have allowed a higher commanding authority of demaguery to take root as the supreme arbiter of our national destinies. [Since the world has been the world, the strong and the courageous have been the ones to command, and the weak and cowardly the ones to obey, and it is in general a good thing for a country that that should be so.] What the consequences of this new manner of viewing neo-constitutionality in Italy are can be testified to by the populations of Romagna and the

wrath of the adversary.[5] The government punishes its officials for
no other crime than obeying orders. It sends soldiers to resist rioters,
but with orders not to use their weapons, so trying to save the goat
of public order along with the cabbages of tolerance from their less
virulent enemies.[6][7] In that way the speculators have been able to
prolong their dominion, and will continue to be. But, as often happens in social history, measures that are useful in a given direction

Marches, who have been the guinea-pigs during these past days for this practical
experiment in applying subversive ideals. And if we consider that fiscal and international difficulties will soon be demanding arduous proofs of self-sacrifice and
abnegation on the part of the country, we are led to fear that such difficulties will
prove insuperable unless meantime the prestige of the state be given a new lease on
life by reasserting the principle of authority and preferring to an artificial popularity, which has for so many years been the ministerial *porro unum*, the restoration
of the law—simply of the law." But that is absolutely impossible unless one is willing to use force. To secure respect for the law without using arms upon those who
break it is a humanitarian dream corresponding to nothing in the real world. The
"fiscal difficulties" alluded to are in great part due to government by speculators,
who bleed the country of as much money as they can. They are masters at cunning,
but they lack the spirit and the courage to defend themselves by force. [This editorial aroused wide comment at the time in Italy. It was thought to be in part "inspired." And I remember that the allusion to "international" difficulties was taken
as a hint that something exciting was in store in the European field. This was twelve
days before the affair at Sarajevo. After the fact it was taken as evidence of a
démarche by Austria to Italy long in advance of the troubles with Serbia.—A. L.]

2480 [5] If they thought of the future they would easily see from history what lies
at the end of such roads. In the long run the agents of a government, its troops,
become weary of being perpetually sacrificed, and so come to defend it without
enthusiasm or even not at all. Occasionally some of them come to see their advantage in turning against it and joining its adversaries. Many revolutions have come
about in just such ways, and that may be the way in which the dominion of the
governing class at present in power in almost all civilized countries will terminate.
However, that certainly is not going to happen very soon. Our speculators, therefore, give little or no thought to it. So people speculating on exchange are keenly
interested in the next day's quotations, the quotations of the days after that, but
not at all in what prices are to be some years in the future.

2480 [6][7] To grasp the extent to which humanitarian sentiments and cowardice in
responsible rulers may impair the strength of an army, one may consider the following incidents that took place in Italy in June, 1914. *Corriere della sera,* June 11:
"Genoa, June 10. . . . A column of Syndicalists and strikers yesterday disarmed a
lieutenant and a captain of infantry." *Ibid.,* June 13: "Parma, June 12. The following is the official version of the incidents that occurred last evening:
"About nine o'clock three second lieutenants from the training-school were returning from a walk home with a comrade. They were made the butt of catcalls,
stones, revolver-shots. The three second lieutenants turned to fight back but found
themselves followed by a crowd of young men. They deemed it prudent (*sic*), therefore, to go on to the Piazza Garibaldi, where they told officers they met of what had

for a certain length of time eventually come to work in an opposite direction, and so encompass the ruin of governments that place their reliance on them. That has been the case with many aristocracies. If the day comes when "speculator" governments, instead of being useful, become harmful to society, it will then be possible to say that it was a good thing for society that the speculators should have per-

happened." A number of details follow that are of no great interest here; then ". . . they were greeted with stones and shots, which they answered by firing into the air." Those volleys naturally were not taken seriously. Soldiers came up and, as usual, fired into the air, with no results: "The soldiers and the police advanced, under a shower of insults and pistol-shots. . . ." Orders were that soldiers and *carabinieri* must not resort to arms or, when obliged to, should shoot into the air.

In several places in Italy they lost patience, and since they were forbidden to use their guns, they picked up the paving-stones that had been hurled at them and threw them back at the mobs. It seems that such fighting on equal terms was not forbidden by orders. Senator Garòfalo observed in the Senate that "in Italy the custom of leaving soldiers defenceless against mob violence is now deeply ingrained." Senator Santini remarked that "when an army has to be ordered to submit to abuse and insults . . . it had better be kept in barracks" (*Corriere della sera,* June 11).

No Deputy dared go so far in the Chamber. On the contrary a Conservative Deputy—the stress is on the "Conservative"—recounted a number of episodes where the soldiers had given evidence of truly angelic forbearance, and added: "The officers have been mentioned here. Well, I heard from a lieutenant that he had been spat upon repeatedly and yet had stood there, revolver in hand, though he was boiling inside. (Voices from the Right: "They are heroes!") These poor soldiers have been admirable for their forbearance, unselfishness, and spirit of sacrifice." And all present, ministers included, applauded!

No scene even remotely similar has ever been enacted in the German Reichstag. No Minister of War in Germany would have tolerated such praise, which might pass for a saint or a friar, but is grossly insulting to an army officer or a soldier. Such differences between the Italian and German governments arise in the fact that speculators have much greater power in the former than in the latter. Interesting the case of General Agliardi. The story is given in the version of the Minister of War, in answer to an "interpellation" from the floor of the Senate. *Giornale d'Italia,* June 12, 1914: "On the morning of the eleventh, General Agliardi and his staff were on their way from Ravenna to Cervia for staff manoeuvres (manoeuvres which, in the circumstances, should have been cancelled, the responsibility for that resting upon others). They were held as hostages for five hours, and, what is worse, the General and the other officers surrendered their swords to their captors."

General Agliardi had given plenty of proof of bravery in the Libyan War. He did not hand over his sword for lack of courage. For punishment he was merely placed on the retired list. Had he defended himself with arms against his aggressors, he might easily have killed one or more of them. In that case his punishment would have been more severe. He had therefore no avenue of escape from the misfortune that threatened him. A government that will not have weapons used against assailants, and at the same time will not have them surrendered, would

sisted in measures conducive to their ruin. From that standpoint present-day humanitarianism may, in the last analysis, prove beneficial to society, the way certain diseases that destroy enfeebled and degenerate organisms rid human communities of them, and so prove a blessing.

2481. 3. *Exile and ostracism.* These are moderately efficient. In modern times exile is about the only penalty for political crimes that nets those who use it in defence of their power greater advantages than disadvantages. Athenian ostracism resulted neither in great benefits nor in great losses. Such measures do little or no harm, as regards the evolution of traits in the *élite*.

2482. 4. *Admission to membership in the governing class of any individual potentially dangerous to it, provided he consents to serve it.* The qualification must not be overlooked: "provided he consents to serve it." Take it away and we get a mere description of class-circulation that means nothing else than the admission to the *élite* of elements extraneous to it, the new members bringing in their opinions, traits, virtues, prejudices. But when such elements change colour and character and turn allies and servants where they had been enemies, we get an entirely different situation in which the essentials of class-circulation are absent.

2483. The device has been resorted to in many countries in many different periods of history. Nowadays it is virtually the only resort of the demagogic plutocracy that controls in our present-day so-

---

seem to be inconsistent; for the only way not to surrender them is to use them. But the inconsistency disappears the moment one reflects that the sole purpose of the government is to get along quietly, and that it sacrifices everything to that end. The Minister of War answered the question as to General Agliardi in the Senate, because he knew that in that body there was no danger of any spirited debate. Premier Salandra refused to answer similar questions in the Chamber, because there an uproar would have been certain.

One notes signs already that the defenders of the present régime are to some extent beginning to tire of such annoyances. Missiroli in *Giornale d'Italia,* June 15, 1914, writes: "The Agliardi incident reminds me of another something like it. A year ago during the strikes in the foundries at Imola, the strikers were replaced by non-union men who had to be protected by troops. The soldiers could think of nothing better in the line of performing their duty than to advise the non-union men to leave town, threatening them, during the night, in cases of refusal. And the free workers left. In cases of general strikes nowadays it is quite the rule for the police to compel merchants to obey the strikers and close their shops."

cieties; and it has demonstrated its effectiveness for maintaining it in power. It is harmful to an *élite,* as tending to intensify traits that already prevail to excess in it. Furthermore, along with the corruption that is inseparable from it, it debases character and provides an opening for those who have both the will and the power to use violence in shaking off the yoke of the ruling class.

2484. Governing classes that are rich in Class II residues but short in combination-instincts (Class I residues) need new elements in which those proportions are reversed. Such elements would ordinarily be supplied by normal circulation. But if, instead, the governing class opens its doors only to individuals who consent to be like it, and are indeed driven by their ardour as neophytes to exaggerate in that direction, the already harmful predominance of certain residues is carried further still and the road to ruin is thrown open. Conversely, a class, such as our plutocracy, that is woefully lacking in Class II residues and overrich in Class I residues would need to acquire new elements that are weak in Class I and strong in Class II residues. Instead, by opening only to those individuals who betray faith and conscience in order to procure the benefits which the plutocracy so lavishly bestows on those who devote themselves to its service, it acquires elements that in no way serve to supply it with the things it most needs. It does, to be sure, deprive the opposition of a few of its leaders, and that is very helpful to it; but it acquires nothing to replenish its own inner strength. So long as cunning and corruption serve, it is likely to keep winning victories, but it falls very readily if violence and force chance to interpose. Something of that sort happened in the declining Roman Empire.[1]

2485. When, in a country, classes that for any reason have long remained separate suddenly mingle or, in more general terms, when a class-circulation that has been sluggish suddenly acquires an intensity at all considerable, almost always observable is an appreciable

---

2484 [1] For a significant symptom consider the ease with which threats of violence in Ulster checkmated the English demagogic plutocracy in 1914; and for another of less significance, but by no means negligible, how violence on the part of the "suffragettes" earned them impunity in setting fire to buildings and so inflicting damage to an amount of millions of pounds. In Italy the violence of farm-laborers in Romagna overawed the government and enabled them to set up a state within the state, with laws of its own that were better obeyed than the laws of the Italian state. Another example would be, again, the uprisings in Romagna in June, 1914 (§ 2480).

increase in intellectual, economic, and political prosperity in the country in question. And that is why periods of transition from oligarchic to more or less democratic régimes are often periods of prosperity. Examples would be Athens in the time of Pericles, republican Rome after the victories of the plebs, France after the Revolution of '89. But one could go on. There would be England in the time of Cromwell, Germany during the Reformation, Italy after '59, and Germany after the War of '70.

2486. If the prosperity in question were due to different systems of government, the prosperity should continue as long as the new régime endured. But that is not the case. The florescence lasts for a certain length of time and then comes a decline. The Athens of Pericles declined very soon, while the form of government was becoming more and more democratic. The "boom" in the Rome of the Scipios had a longer life, but the decline is conspicuous towards the end of the Republic. Prosperity returns for a brief space with the Imperial régime, which in its turn is soon in decadence. The France of the First Republic and Napoleon becomes the France of Charles X and Louis Philippe. To picture the situation one might imagine as separated two substances that effervesce when combined. The effervescence takes place as soon as the separation ends, but it does not last indefinitely.

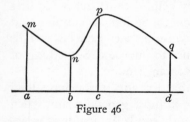

Figure 46

2487. After all we have been saying, the explanation is not difficult. During the period *ab* (Figure 46) class-circulation slackens, and prosperity declines from the index *am* to the index *bn,* because the governing class is declining. In the brief space *bc* comes a revolution, or some other event that stimulates class-circulation, and the index leaps from *bn* to *cp*. But the *élite* again proceeds to decline, and the index drops from *cp* to *dq*.

2488. Both the slackening and the speeding-up in class-circulation may affect quantities as well as qualities. In Athens the two things went hand in hand, for the Athenian citizenry was a closed or virtually closed caste to which resident aliens had no access, and military merit availed little to elevate individuals to the governing class.

In Rome the freedmen came after a few generations to restore the free-born class, but towards the end of the republic intrigue and corruption were the main sources of power. With the Empire better qualities again became influential on accessions to the governing class, but another and more serious decline again supervened. Our modern plutocracy sets no limit to circulation as regards numbers, and that is why the prosperity which it has brought about has had a longer life; but it banishes force and energy of character from the qualities that give access to the governing class, and that, among other things, will probably cause the present curve of prosperity, *pqr,* which is now rising along the segment *pq,* to decline hereafter along the segment *sr.*

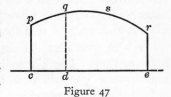

Figure 47

2489. After these few theoretical remarks, suppose we turn to some concrete examples.

Ancient Sparta and modern Venice are examples of closed or semi-closed aristocracies. They show declines in their respective aristocracies, but on the other hand substantiate the theory that the use of force avails, in spite of the decline, to preserve the dominion of an aristocracy over the lower classes in a population. And so too they refute the claims of moralistic historians that the higher classes keep themselves in power only by realizing the welfare of their subjects. It would be pleasant for the subject classes if matters stood that way. Unfortunately they do not.

2490. In the heyday of Sparta, its population was divided into three classes: the Spartiates, who were the governing class; the *perioikoi,* who were a class of freemen, but subordinate to the dominant class; and the helots, who were serfs bound to the soil. The first dates of Spartan chronology cannot be determined exactly, but we should not be going very far wrong, probably, in putting them as far back as 750 B.C. The Spartan oligarchy, with various ups and downs, kept in power from that time down to the year 227 B.C., when Cleomenes III destroyed the Ephors—a dominion, therefore, of about five centuries. The methods that enabled it to do so have their points of resemblance with the methods used by the Venetian oligarchy. An occult and terrifying power anticipated or suppressed every attempt, or suspicion of attempt, on the part of the subject classes to improve their lot.

2491. Much has been written of the *crypteia* (secret service). According to Plutarch, *Lycurgus,* 28 (Perrin, Vol. I, pp. 289-91), it was a veritable helot-hunt. That opinion seems now to be discredited, though even writers most favourably disposed towards the Spartiates grant that the *crypteia* was harsh and cruel to the helots.[1] There are besides undeniable facts that more clearly show Spartiate cruelty—for example the slaughter of helot warriors recounted by Thucydides, as occurring at the time when the Athenians were occupying Pylos.[2]

2492. It cannot be said that the Spartiates maintained their power for lack of resistance. Aristotle well notes, *Politica,* II, 6, 2-3 (Rackham, p. 133): "The Thessalian *penestae* (serfs) have often inflicted harm on the Thessalians, as have the helots on the Lacedaemonians; indeed they stand watching for every opportunity to profit by their masters' misfortunes." The Spartan aristocracy remained in the sad-

2491 [1] Schoemann, *Griechische Alterthümer,* Vol. I, p. 196 (Hardy-Mann, Vol. I, p. 195): "These raids (κρυπτεία) were directed especially against the helots, and more than once, doubtless, individuals whose plots were feared were done away with without a suggestion of legal process. Writers of a later date took occasion from such patrols to say that a helot-hunt took place every year and that it was a butchery. That is an exaggeration too absurd to require contradiction." P. Girard in Daremberg-Saglio, *Dictionnaire, s.v.* Κρυπτεία: "Very probably it was a police service designed to preserve order in Laconia. That the young men engaged in it as supervisors and watchmen of the territories often came to blows with helots and showed themselves on occasion very severe and cruel toward them is also very probable."

2491 [2] *Historiae,* IV, 80, 3-4: "The Lacedaemonians had already taken many precautions against the helots; and since the helots were many in number, and many of them young and therefore a cause of alarm, the Lacedaemonians resorted to a trick. They had it cried abroad that those among the helots who claimed to have been bravest in war on behalf of the State should stand apart from the others and they would be made free men. But that was just a device to discover who they were, for they thought that those who should presume to be first in obtaining their freedom would also be the bolder in attacking them. So two thousand such were chosen, and they led them, crowned with garlands, from temple to temple, as the custom was with men who were set free from slavery; but soon after they made away with them and no one knew by what death they had perished." Diodorus Siculus, *Bibliotheca historica,* XII, 67, 4 (Booth, Vol. I, p. 477): "Two thousand having inscribed their names, the most powerful [citizens] were commanded to slay them, each one in his own house." Had the Spartiates been humanitarians, like the French aristocrats towards the end of the eighteenth century, the helots would have killed the Spartiates.

dle only because it was stronger than its menials, and it took war with other states finally to break its power. The Messenians were freed not because they were strong enough to claim their freedom, but because the Thebans won at Leuctra. Aristotle again very soundly notes that the Cretans had no troubles from the hostility of their slaves, because the different states on the island, even when at war with one another, refrained from favouring slave rebellions, since they all had slaves of the same kind.

2493. Wherever, on the other hand, the power of the masters failed, the slaves changed status and replaced their masters. Equilibrium seems to have been specially precarious in the island of Chios, now the ones, now the others, prevailing. About the year 412 B.C., being at war with the aristocracy ruling in Chios, the Athenians invaded the island and were the cause of serious trouble there, "forasmuch as the slaves of Chios, who were many and had been increased in numbers disproportionate to a single city [or: "where there were more slaves than in any other city"], except possibly the capital of the Lacedaemonians, and for that reason were the more difficult to control in their mischief, deserted for the most part as soon as they judged, in view of the strength of its fortifications, that the Athenian army had secured a strong foothold. And since they knew the country well, they inflicted great damage." [1] The occupation of Pylos by the Athenians had similar effects upon the Spartan helots, as did the Spartan occupation of Decelea upon the slaves of Athens. The Athenians, it should be noted, treated their slaves with a great kindness that was judged excessive by the author of the *Anonymous Republic,* so called, I, 10 (Kalinka, p. 69). In the days of a certain Nymphodorus, the slaves on Chios took to the hills and fought with such success on both the offensive and defensive that their masters had to come to terms with them until their leader was treacherously slain.[2] Later on Mithridates reduced the Chians to slavery and handed them over to their own slaves. The fact gave the moralists their chance to expatiate on the propriety of the punishment, the Chians having been the first to buy slaves.[3]

2493 [1] Thucydides, *Historiae,* VIII, 40, 2.
2493 [2] Athenaeus, *Deipnosophistae,* VI, 88-91.
2493 [3] And that, says Athenaeus, was the source of the proverb: "Chios bought its master": Χῖος δεσπότην ὠνήσατο.

2494. The case where aristocracies begin by being open and end by being closed, or trying to be, is fairly general. It is observable also in the Spartans. Aristotle, *Politica,* II, 6-12 (Rackham, p. 139), relates, as tradition (λέγουσι), that in order to avoid danger of depopulating the state through long wars, the first kings of Sparta granted rights of citizenship to foreigners.[a] But Ephorus, as quoted by Strabo, is positive on the point. He says that "all the inhabitants living in the neighbourhood of the Spartans submitted on condition that they be their equals and sharers in the citizenship and in public office."[1]

2495. Access to the privileged class was, however, soon cut off. Herodotus, *Historiae,* IX, 35, says that only Tisamenus and his brother, Hegias, had received Spartan citizenship. In the Spartan aristocracy we therefore get a type of the closed or, more exactly, the semi-closed class, and it remained such down to the days of Cleomenes III. An attempt at reform had been made about 242 B.C. by Agis IV, but it failed, and the oligarchy still had enough vigour left to cling to its power.[1]

2494 [a] [Rackham reads, not "in order to," but "with the result that."—A. L.]

2494 [1] Strabo, *Geographica,* VIII, 5, 4. The passage follows a lacuna. Jones translates, Vol. IV, p. 135: "Though the neighbouring peoples, one and all, were subject to the Spartiatae, still they had equal rights, sharing both in the rights of citizenship and in the offices of state." The explanation of the measures as a provision against the danger of too serious a reduction in the number of Spartiates is suspect. It was probably thought of after the fact; but that does not affect the plausibiliy of the traditions that there were such measures.

2495 [1] According to Plato, *De legibus,* I, 629A (Bury, Vol. I, p. 17), Tyrtaeus also had Spartan citizenship conferred upon him. It is of little importance whether those were just the facts. Evidently, award of Spartan citizenship was an altogether exceptional thing. Plato and Herodotus were thinking, besides, only of foreigners. No class can succeed in being absolutely closed for any great length of time. Schoemann, *Griechische Alterthümer,* Vol. I, pp. 209-10 (Hardy-Mann, Vol. I, pp. 208-09), describes the situation excellently: "It is expressly stated, and we are obliged to assume, that at first the Spartiates willingly admitted to their number the non-Spartans whom they met in Laconia—the Achaeans, in other words. . . . Not till they had consolidated their rule did they adopt a more exclusive attitude. The right of citizenship, which set up a class apart as compared with the rest of the inhabitants, was so rarely granted from then on that Herodotus mentions as the one known exception the naturalization of two Elians. . . . There is no reason to suppose that the Spartiates were more liberal with it in the period that followed the death of Herodotus. Citizenship, as we have seen, was denied to *neodamodes* [serfs liberated as a reward for services in war]. The *mothaques* [adopted illegitimates born of helot mothers] sometimes obtained it. They were illegitimate off-

2496. Entrance to the privileged class was barred, but not egress. The best elements in the remainder of the population could not rise to it, but inferior elements were thrown out. To hold a place in the dominant class known as the "peers" (ὅμοιοι), it was not enough to be of Spartiate origin. Strict performance of the difficult and rigorous duties of the class was also requisite. Alluding to that law as having been made by Lycurgus, Xenophon says clearly: "He

spring of Spartiates who had been recognized and legitimized by their fathers. They obtained the honour only if, in addition to meritorious conduct, they had ample means. It seems that at a time when education was greatly neglected in other places, non-Spartans had their children reared at Sparta. Some of these young people managed to gain admittance afterwards to the ranks of the citizenry, but they had to have shown themselves worthy of it, and for those who had not succeeded in establishing themselves permanently at Sparta and in acquiring property there, it was a sterile honour that carried none of the essential rights with it." On the other hand, Curtius, *Griechische Geschichte,* Vol. I, p. 182 (Ward, Vol. I, p. 218), is evidently overstating a little when he writes: "The legislator of Sparta had wisely provided ways for the Spartiate community to replenish itself by recruits of a different blood and untapped energies [That certainly was not the case. There is no question that in historical times the Spartiates dwindled in numbers.] It was possible even for individuals not born of pure Dorian unions, for children of *perioikoi* (native rural) or helot stock, if they had conscientiously completed their military education, to be admitted into the Dorian community and provided with vacant lands. But the consent of the kings was required for such promotion and the formal adoption of a candidate by a Dorian who had attained his majority took place in their presence. So the state was provided with new citizens. [Very few, at best.] To that institution Sparta owed a goodly number of her best generals. Education, discipline, made the Spartiate, not ancestral blood." For his proof Curtius quotes Plutarch, *Instituta Laconica,* 22 (Babbitt, Vol. III, p. 439), and Xenophon, *Hellenica,* V, 3, 9; but really those texts show very little. Plutarch is speaking of legendary times and is not any too positive: "Some say that any foreigner who consented to live according to the customs of the city was, in pursuance of a law of Lycurgus, admitted to a share in the original division of the territory [Babbitt: "might become a member of the division assigned to him at the beginning."]." As for Xenophon, he says that King Agesipolis was sent against Olynthus with thirty Spartans, who were voluntarily joined by resident aliens and bastards (νόθοι) of high character and some training under Spartan discipline. The fact that Xenophon names them apart from the Spartans is evidence enough that they did not have full status as Spartiates.

Of the abortive revolt of Agis, Droysen, *Geschichte des Hellenismus,* Vol. III, p. 423, remarks: "Democracy, tyranny, foreign rule, revolution, did not, at Sparta, as it did in most of the other states, sweep away a confused mass of irrational institutions that had no actual value and leave the ground free for a new power." That at bottom means stagnancy in class-circulation. A better fate attended the *coup d'état* by Cleomenes in 227 B.C., because it was carried out partly with the support of mercenaries. But the new order did not last very long. Six years later Antigone re-established the authority of the oligarchy at Sparta. Cleomenes abolished

[Lycurgus] ordained that if anyone neglected doing well the things prescribed by the law, he should no longer be of the 'peers.'" [1]

2497. Among the things prescribed by the law was participation in the common meals, each paying his own share. Anyone unable to do that because of poverty was dropped from the class.[1] In like manner individuals deficient in military or civil capacities, or failing to preserve their ancestral fortunes, were dropped—in a word, therefore, most of the decadent elements. That circumstance was most conducive to the maintenance of efficiency in the oligarchy, and was probably one of the main causes of its long life. Unhealthy, instead, was the unwillingness to admit new members. As a result of that the governing class constantly diminished in members, dropping from ten thousand to two thousand, it is said—and still there was no disposition to replenish it with new and better elements.

2498. However—and that was another favourable circumstance—the need of new elements was less urgent than elsewhere, there being no necessity for stimulating Class II residues in the governing class. The Spartan system of education, the maintenance of military discipline in time of peace, hostility to literature, science, philosophy, and the liberal or manual arts, the fact, finally, of continuous war, made the Spartan oligarchy immune from many of the forces that operate in decadent aristocracies to attenuate group-persistences and intensify instincts of combination. Humanitarianism, which is the bane of decaying ruling classes, never infected the Spartans, even when they had fallen away from their ancient virtue. One need only think of the custom of flogging young men to the quick at the altar of Artemis Orthia. The origin of the custom has been much debated but, like so many questions of origins, that question is of little if any interest to sociology. There the important thing is to know what sentiments the custom reflected. We have already seen (§§ 1190 f.) that a notable part must have been played in it by sentiments of asceticism, which are a hypertrophy of senti-

---

four of the five ephorates, keeping one for himself (Plutarch, *Agis et Cleomenes,* 10; Perrin, Vol. X, p. 69). That reminds one of the Roman Emperors who kept the *tribunicia potestas* for themselves, account being taken in both cases of the intensity of group-persistences in the masses at large.

2496 [1] *Lacedaemonium respublica*, X, 7: Εἰ δέ τις ἀποδειλιάσειε τοῦ τὰ νόμιμα διαπονεῖσθαι, τοῦτον ἐκεῖνος ἀπέδειξε μηδὲ νομίζεσθαι ἔτι τῶν ὁμοίων εἶναι.

2497 [1] Aristotle, *Politica*, II, 7, 4 (Rackham, p. 151).

ments that spur the individual to self-sacrifice in behalf of the community's interest. The long survival of such a barbarous custom is also an obvious indication of the absence in the Spartans of humanitarian sentiments, let alone sentiments even of merest pity. Otherwise the custom, whatever its origin, could not have held its own for so long a time. In Cicero's day Sparta had lost her independence, yet the custom was still in vogue. And it still flourished in the day of Pausanius, a writer of the second century of our era. It bears witness, further, to the extraordinary strength of group-persistences in the Spartans.[1]

2499. On the other hand the Spartan aristocracy was handicapped by its lack of combination-instincts, even in its one special field of activity, warfare; and to an even greater extent in politics and diplomacy. In that department the nimble frivolousness of the Athenians and the slow-moving conservatism of the Spartans had untoward consequences that were not very different.

2500. In Venice we get another example of the closed aristocracy. Down to the year 1296 access to it was free, and those were days of great prosperity for Venice. Between 1296 and 1319 comes the change leading up to the Closure of the Grand Council (*Serrata del Maggior Consiglio*), which barred additions to the governing class; and it remained closed for more than four centuries.[1] In the year 1775 it

2498 [1] Cicero, *Disputationes Tusculanae*, II, 14, 34: "At Sparta boys are flogged at the altar so severely that 'from the flesh the blood doth spurt in streams,' and not rarely, as I heard when I was there, they die of it, yet no one of them has ever cried out or uttered a groan." That is testimony of an eyewitness.

2500 [1] Sandi, *Principi di storia civile della repubblica di Venezia*, Pt. II, Vol. I, Bk. V, pp. 1-10: "The entire century covered by this book is much more significant from the standpoint of domestic reform than of achievement abroad. . . . And, indeed, what matter of government could be more momentous than the establishment of an aristocracy essentially hereditary through the male line, whereby the dominant nobility was perpetuated in time and kept pure in blood? . . . The fact, accordingly, that the Grand Council had changed every year for almost fifty years . . . had called attention to the desirability of reform in it. But the discussion continuing down to about the year 1286 [*read:* 1296], it was finally conceived that there could be no wiser way of avoiding intrigue, faction, and other civic improprieties than by forming at that time a first fixed Council made up of the best-qualified citizens, and in numbers so comprehensive as, without destroying or transforming the original design of aristocratic government by an excessively large membership, to satisfy the common desires of the people living at the time; which Council so formed would thereafter be definite, stable, and permanent. With that

was decreed that the Book of Gold should be kept open for twenty years and that nobles of the Venetian mainland to the number of forty could inscribe their names in it. But the mainland counts seem not to have taken very enthusiastically to the concession.[2]

2501. The Venetian governing class did not shrink in numbers as the Spartan did, but it declined to extremes in character and vigour. The difference was chiefly due to the different sorts of activities in the two aristocracies, civil for the Venetians, military for the Spartans. In Venice, possession of an aggressive personality was good ground for keeping a man in private life, and the State Inquisitors carefully extirpated any plant that gave promise of too exuberant growth. In Sparta only those individuals remained among the "peers" who had the energy and the physical strength to endure the heavy burdens of military discipline. In Venice noble rank was indelible, and was retained even by the decadent. In Sparta incompetents were extruded by the "peers" by automatic elimination. Of the two obstructions to free class-circulation, the one—the non-admission of new elements—was common to both Venice and

in view, there could have been no safer and more tranquil procedure than to declare the prerogative of sitting in the Council an original characteristic and essence in the legitimate descendants of the first nobles by the male line, with perpetual succession. . . . Finally on the last day of February of that Venetian year the Doge moved and the Council accepted the famous law of 1296, which has commonly and traditionally been known as the Closure of the Grand Council, to which, in truth, the Republic owes its survival."

2500 [2] [As a matter of fact nine families accepted. The system in Venice was not as rigid as Pareto represents it. The Venetian citizenship at large was at all times liberally extended to foreigners. Furthermore, under the class of patricians registered in the Book of Gold came the order of "originary citizens," which largely monopolized the bureaucracy of the state. The "second nobility" was open to any family that had not practised a manual trade for three generations. The citizens in turn could become patricians on invitation and by money payments. Around 1651, to replenish a treasury greatly depleted by the Turkish wars, the patriciate made an active propaganda to enroll citizen families on payment of 100,000 ducats. Few, if any, accepted, and largely in deference to sentiments of group-persistence: respect for the old traditions of the Republic, good taste. There was, instead, a rush of "speculators" to assume the new privileges: the Naves, rich paper manufacturers, the Benzons, silk merchants, the Griffonis, bakers, the Gallos, tanners, etc. For ample data on this matter see Molmenti, *Storia di Venezia nella vita privata,* Vol. III, pp. 37-39, and Vol. I, pp. 71-78. For the strength of prejudices against upstarts in the patriciate see my *Vita veneziana nel '600,* Venice, Calegari, 1913, pp. 45-47.— A. L.]

Sparta. The other—failure to eliminate decadent elements—had more far-reaching effects in Venice than in Sparta.[1]

2502. Common again to both Sparta and Venice was the use of force for maintenance of power, and to that their long survival was mainly due. They both succumbed, not to internal transformations, but to *force majeure* coming from without.[1] There were also some differences in their manner of using force. The Venetian governing class grasped the fact that the masses by themselves could do nothing unless they were led by elements from the governing class; and it aimed primarily at preventing such elements from becoming available. How effective that policy was is evidenced by the long survival of the Venetian aristocracy in power, even during times when it had lost all vigour except in the traditional habit of striking in time at every possible leader of a future upset. The Spartan governing class did not, to be sure, neglect that method of governing, and time and again the Ephors showed themselves the equals of the State Inquisitors of Venice. But whether because of Sparta's military activity, or for other reasons, they were much less effective than the Venetian Inquisitors; and that is why Sparta had better captains than Venice. The Spartans were defeated not from any lack of bravery, but by shortcomings in strategic science. In the days of her decline Venice was deficient in both respects.

2503. Sparta would probably have improved her governing class by recruiting individuals distinguished for combination-instincts (Class I residues). Venice, on the other hand, would have fared better had she strengthened her patriciate with individuals distinguished by instincts of group-persistence (Class II residues). There is no way of knowing whether the Spartan population contained the elements required by the governing class. Venice surely

2501 [1] [In Venice, as is well known, the resort for penniless aristocrats was to the dole. The relief was distributed in the square at San Barnaba, and those who received it came to be known as "Barnabots."—A. L.]

2502 [1] That is strictly true in the case of Venice. In the case of Sparta the mercenaries of Cleomenes figure to some extent. Polybius, *Historiae,* IV, 41, 12-13, soundly notes: "So, after Lycurgus had established his laws, the Lacedaemonians had an excellent republic and very great power down to the battle of Leuctra. After that, fortune now turning against them, their republic went from bad to worse. In the end, many troubles, many civil seditions, afflicted them. They suffered many new divisions of lands, and many exiles, and they dwelt in direst slavery down to the tyranny of Nabis."

had them. Speaking of the days when the Republic was tottering, Malamani well observes: "However, in the midst of that orgy, that pagan funeral-banquet at which most of the Venetian aristocracy were feasting, the populace, more tenacious of its traditions than any other class, was still clinging almost entirely to the uncompromising purity of its time-honoured customs. . . . Rarely did corruption make its way into the humble homes of the working-people. . . . They lived to themselves, forming a society apart, with their own customs, their own laws. Under crude exteriors they still kept the worship of the family alive."[1]

2504. Venice evinced strong-hearted patience in her misfortunes. She lacked boldness in her day of prosperity. It has been said over and again that Venice was ruined by the discoveries of America and the Cape of Good Hope, which diverted trade that had formerly been conducted through her harbour. But at the time of those discoveries, Venice was the leading maritime power on Earth. Why could she not have made conquests in the Americas, the East Indies, and the Sunda Islands, as did Spaniards, Portuguese, Dutch, French, and even Danes? No reason, except lack of initiative on the part of the Venetian patriciate, which, perchance, had it been reinvigorated by new stock from its people, might have mustered greater daring and greater interest in new ventures.

2505. In the victory at Lepanto a leading rôle was played by the Venetian galleys, which carried guns of a power at the time unequalled. The combination-instinct had not yet deteriorated, therefore, in Venice.[1] What was lacking was the energy to profit by it.

2503 [1] *La satira del costume a Venezia nel secolo XVIII*, p. 122. Like almost all present-day historians, Malamani mistakes the morals of a class for energy and, what is worse, sex morality judged according to Christian standards. But aside from that easily removable defect, his book contains much that is sound.

2505 [1] Giustiniano, *Dell' historie venetiane*, pp. 668-721: "And in the first encounter [at the battle of Lepanto] the heavy galleys of the Venetians attacked the enemy impetuously, and through their valour was the road opened to the victory of the Christians. For as the galleys of the enemy came together in close formation to fall upon ours, they were so battered and discomfited by the artillery fire from the heavy galleys, which delivered terrific broadsides, that the lines of the Barbarians were broken, and on that side took virtually to flight; for seeing the damage that six galleys only were doing, they began to foresee what the others could do, something which the Turks had never imagined. . . . But of the captains of the Venetian fleet . . . Francesco Duodo, commander of the heavy galleys, won most special and singular glory. . . . For having broken the Turkish lines with his

After the victory at Salamis the disproportion between the power of Athens and the power of the "Great King" was greater than the inferiority of Venice to the Sultan. But the Athenians were daring. Their fleet swept the seas in pursuit of the Persians. After Lepanto the Venetians cautiously repaired to Corfù, and their inaction cost them all profit from their victory, which remained a sterile gesture. The last years of the Republic were years of extreme decay and great poverty. Not even on the sea did Venice preserve a shadow of her power.[2]

2506. The Spartan aristocracy won a well-merited fame for its fortitude in the face of reverses. In the Venetian aristocracy the underhanded tyranny of the State Inquisitors extinguished even sentiments of personal integrity. When the Venetian aristocracy was still young and could boast greater vigour, it produced a Marin Falier. Had the conspiracy which he attempted, along with an energetic commoner, succeeded, the Venetian aristocracy might have had a less inglorious end. But one cannot say that populace and *bourgeoisie* would have been happier and not more unfortunate had they been driven out upon the stormy seas of revolution and exposed to the usual evils of political and social unrest. Owing to the different origins of the respective governing classes, religious preju-

artillery (as I said above), he was of great assistance in winning the victory, as is witnessed by the patents awarded him by Don Juan of Austria and Marco Antonio Colonna. . . . Many master workmen from the Arsenal were sent from Venice to Pola, where the said heavy galleys had been beached, to repair them, for those galleys have great power at sea. And the old Venetians designed those naval machines, for they were very skilful in maritime matters; and in designing seagoing vessels the Venetians surpass all other nations abroad."

2505 [2] Daru, *Histoire de la république de Venise,* Vol. V, pp. 216-17: "At that time the forces of the Republic amounted, as regards seaworthy craft, to eight or ten ships of the line, some few frigates, and four galleys. A score of vessels more or less were in process of construction, but the Venetians could not manage to get them finished. When the French entered Venice in 1797, they found thirteen ships and seven frigates on the ways, not enough materials being available to complete them. Of the thirteen ships, two had been laid down in 1752, two in 1743, two in 1732. These last were sixty-five years old before they were ready to enter the water! All that ship-building equipment was a device for keeping up a mere illusion. The vessels were all of light timbering, carrying only twenty-four-pounders in their lower batteries. They could not get out of the harbour with the guns aboard, and had to be armed outside. The officers had long been without any opportunity to acquire experience, and a merchant marine that kept not more than four or five hundred vessels busy could not supply enough sailors to man a formidable fleet."

dice was very strong in Sparta, but it was weaker in Venice, in the various periods of her history, than in other states. In 1309 the Venetians let themselves be excommunicated by the Pope, but snatched Ferrara from him all the same. Later on, on May 25, 1483, Pope Sixtus IV again excommunicated the Venetian Republic. The Council of Ten did not see things that way, and ordered the clergy to continue services as though no excommunication had been heard of, and the Council was scrupulously obeyed.[1] No better fate awaited the bull issued by Pope Julius II against the Venetians, who were defeated by the temporal arms of the League of Cambrai, not by the spiritual weapons of the Church.[2] With a monitory of April 17, 1606, Paul V threatened to excommunicate both the Doge and the

2506 [1] Macchi, *Storia del Consiglio dei Dieci,* Vol. IV, pp. 30-33: "In spite of such great precautions the bull of excommunication reached Venice by way of Mantua. It should be said, however, that in deference to government orders, the patriarch, Maffeo Gerardo, sent the despatch still sealed and unopened to the Council of Ten. Following his example, the majority of the clergy swore obedience to the government, and such few as felt obliged by conscience to submit to the Pope's order were banished. Venice appealed to a General Council, whereupon the Pope replied with another monitory. . . . The Venetians, to tell the truth, took little notice of such excommunications." In a note Macchi paraphrases the *Diary* of Marin Sanudo: " 'The bull was sent by the Pope to Don Maffeo Girardo, patriarch of Venice, that he should publish it, *sub poena excommunicationis, maledictionis, suspensionis, et interdicti.* Hearing which the Seigniory, together with the leaders of the Council of Ten, *auctoritate sua,* ordered seizure of the letter of excommunication, and forbade that it be in any way seen or published. And seeing that such an unjust excommunication was not of the kind to be obeyed, the Heads (*capi*) of the Ten gave orders that sacred offices be celebrated as usual in all churches "under pain of our displeasure." ' " Malipiero, *Annali veneti,* pp. 282-83: "Not many days passed before the Pope sent one of his mace-bearers specially to Don Maffio Ghirardo, patriarch of this city, with a letter of his commanding him to serve the interdict upon the Doge and the Seigniory. . . . The Patriarch feigned illness and informed the Doge and the Heads of the Ten of what had happened, and the Patriarch was ordered to keep the whole thing secret and that it should not be executed in any particular. . . . An appeal was put in official form in three copies, and laid before the Doge and the Seigniory, which sent it to Rome by Traversin Bergamasco, a very trustworthy courier, with orders to post one of the copies on the door of the Church of St. Celsus. The courier went, and diligently executed the commands that had been given him, and by the ninth of July was home again. On the morning of July 3 the Pope was told of the Seigniory's protest, which had been posted the night before, and he was also told that the whole city of Rome was astir with excitement. And for all the diligence that was used, no one found out how the thing had happened until long after."

2506 [2] Daru, *Op. cit.,* Vol. III, p. 331: "All such threats were nothing but empty formulas, objects of contempt even on the part of the clergy."

Senate unless they satisfied the demands of the Pope within twenty-four days. "And if the Doge and the Senate should persist three more days after the twenty-four, 'he will place the whole dominion under interdict, so that neither masses nor divine offices may be celebrated. . . .' On the publication of the monitory at Rome Venice began by appealing to divine aid. . . . Then all ecclesiastical prelates were commanded not to publish the monitory or allow it to be posted in any place. Anyone possessing a copy of it was bidden to deliver it, under penalty of death, to the magistrates in the city of Venice and to rectors in the Dominion. . . . The monitory so being taken as null and void, it was thought sufficient to 'protest' with printed letters to be posted in public places. . . . Thereupon, of the religious orders, the Jesuits, the Capuchins, the Theatines, the Reformed Franciscans, departed from Venice. . . . But no other orders left. Divine offices were celebrated as usual. The city and the people remained very calm at the will and through the foresight of the Senate, no blood being shed and no life lost." [3] That was possible only because there was no fanaticism either in clergy or people, a circumstance that assured the government of obedience during its controversy with the Pope. [4] Venice favoured no schism, no heresy.

2506 [3] Sandi, *Op. cit.*, Pt. III, Vol. II, Bk. XX, Chap. VII, § 3.

2506 [4] Daru, *Op. cit.*, Vol. IV, pp. 216-19: "Only one man in the whole Republic, the Grand Vicar of Padua, ventured to reply to the Podestà, who called on him to serve the orders, that 'he would do as the Holy Spirit should inspire him'; to which the Podestà replied with a warning that 'the Holy Spirit had already inspired the Ten to have anyone disobeying the order hanged.' " The Venetian Senate did not disdain derivations suitable for refuting the Pope, and to be sure that plenty were available it created the office of Consulting Theologian, naming Fra Paolo Sarpi as the first incumbent. Even the powers of the Inquisition were confined within strict limits by the Venetian government. On that subject Sarpi wrote, by order of the Doge, his "Discourse on the Origin, Form, Laws and Practice of the Office of the Inquisition within the City and Dominion of Venice" (*Discorso, etc.*). He speaks very freely (pp. 34, 35, 47, 55) of the Roman Curia: "The most Serene Republic of Venice could not (*puote*, misprint for *potè*) be induced by the requests made by Popes Innocent, Alexander, Urban, and Clement, and the seven succeeding other Popes, to recognize the Office of the Friars Inquisitors, instituted by the Pope. She rested satisfied with the secular inquisition established by herself and with good outcome in the service of God. They [the Venetians] had before their eyes the frequent disorders that arose because of the new Office in the other cities where it was, because the Friars Inquisitors roused the people by their sermons, turning them into Crusaders, so that they rioted with great disturbances; for many of the Crusaders took their vengeance upon their enemies as heretics, and other innocent

She concerned herself with her temporal interests and gave little or no thought to theology. That may have been shrewd policy on the part of the government as a way of avoiding offence to the Roman Curia, but to no small extent it was also a matter of indifference to religion, of weakness in Class II residues.[5]

2507. The example of Venice is an excellent one for getting a clear picture of the composition (§§ 2087 f.) of social forces, of the necessity of considering them quantitatively and not merely qualitatively, and of the heterogeneous character of the various sorts of utility.

The custom followed by the Venetian Government of entrusting command of forces on the mainland to foreigners to the exclusion of native patricians was a source at once of military weakness for the Republic and of strength in its civil institutions, which were not exposed to the danger of being overthrown by some victorious general. Scarcity of Class II as compared with Class I residues assured the Venetians a happy existence for generation after generation, over many centuries—something altogether contrasting with

people were oppressed under that name by individuals who coveted their goods. . . . But when Nicholas IV was elevated to the pontificate . . . he insisted so urgently that it was resolved to recognize the Office, but under this limitation: that it should cause no disturbance. . . . Here we must stop and observe that the Office of the Inquisition in this Dominion is not dependent upon the Roman Curia, but upon the Most Serene Republic, and that it is independently established and constituted by the same." Sarpi goes on to mention several instances in which the Popes abused their spiritual power to attain temporal ends, and concludes: "Which things make it evident that since some individuals maliciously avail themselves of that Office to advance secular and dishonest interests, the manner of its exercise has to be carefully supervised that no pretext be given for abuse of it. . . . For hundreds of years ecclesiastics have had no other purpose than to usurp temporal jurisdiction, much of which they have usurped to the serious disruption of governments."

2506 [5] Daru, Op. cit., Vol. IV, pp. 174-75: "To be perfectly safe from encroachments on the part of the ecclesiastical power, Venice began by being careful to give it no pretext for interfering in state affairs, and remained uniformly faithful to dogma. None of the new opinions ever found the slightest favour in Venice. No heresiarch ever came from Venice. Church Councils, church quarrels, religious wars, took place without her ever participating in the slightest way. Steadfast in her faith, she was not less consistent in her policy of toleration. Not only did her subjects of the Greek faith retain their bishop, their priests, their forms of worship, but Protestants, Armenians, Mohammedans, Jews, all religions, all sects, that had believers in Venice, had their churches also, and burial in the churches was not at all denied to heretics." That was the policy of the Roman People under the Republic; and we must again repeat in this connexion what we have said many

the hardships, disasters, massacres, that fell upon the unlucky inhabitants of countries where Class II residues predominated and
fanaticism was a curse upon men. But the same scarcity was also, to
an extent at least, a cause of the fall of the Venetian Republic. And
the question arises: Is it better, or not better, to purchase a happiness
of many centuries, of many many generations of people, with the
loss of a country's independence? There would seem to be no answer
to such a question, for it implies comparisons between two heterogeneous utilities. The problem is set to almost every country in all
periods of history, and is solved now in one sense, now in the other,
according to the value sentiment attaches to the present or to the
future utility, to the utility of the individuals living or of those
who are to come after them, to the utility of individuals or to the
utility of the nation.

One might ask: Could both extremes not be avoided and some
middle course found that would reconcile the utility of living generations with the utility of generations to come? This second prob-

times heretofore, that the art of government lies in using existing residues and not
in essaying the difficult and often desperate task of changing them. Daru adds:
"There is a story that once a foreigner in the presence of a Venetian was reproach-
ing the government of the Republic for keeping priests in such an insignificant
position, and accusing the nation, or at least the patricians, of unbelief and irre-
ligion. 'Why,' he said, 'they believe in the mystery of the Holy Trinity, at the very
most!' *'E ve par poco, signor?'* the Venetian interrupted ('Isn't that believing
a-plenty, sir?')." Sarpi, *Op. cit.,* Chap. 24: "They shall not allow the Office under
any circumstances to take action against Jews, or against any other kind of infidels
of whatever sect, on accusation of crimes committed by word of mouth or by
deed. . . ." Chap. 25: "Likewise they shall not allow the Office of the Inquisition
to take action against any person of a Christian nation that as a whole has its own
rites, different from ours, or is ruled by its own prelates, such as the Greeks and
other such nations, even though the accusation were against articles held by one
party or the other." Sarpi goes on, Chaps. 24-25, to give the reason for these provisions: "Infidelity is not heresy, and of the violations that infidels commit to
the offence and in contempt of our Faith no cognizance can be taken by the
Church. . . . The Office of the Inquisition outside of this state claims authority to
try Oriental Christians on any article whatsoever, even if the nation as a whole dis-
sents from the Roman Curia. In this Most Serene Dominion, having regard to the
protection that the Prince accords to the Greek nation, the Inquisitors do not
carry their claims so far. They merely say that the Greeks may be tolerated as to
those three opinions in which they dissent from the Western Church; but that if
any one of them should hold an improper opinion on those articles upon which
their nation is in accord with us, that is within the jurisdiction of the Inquisition.
That distinction is superfluous, and no less inconsistent with the protection of
the Prince than if such persons were tried on the three matters of difference."

lem is no easier to solve than the other. In the first place, the difficulty of comparing the heterogeneous utilities of the present and
the future is attenuated, to be sure, but not removed; for to evaluate
the middle course it will also be necessary to affect a composition
of the two utilities, and according as sentiment prefers the one or
the other, the middle course will be bent towards one extreme or
the other. Then again, the new problem carries us into the difficult
field of virtual movements, and in order to solve it we must first
solve another intricate problem as to whether it is possible (§ 134)
to remove certain ties and establish certain others.

Such difficulties are not, in general, perceived by writers on
social or political matters, since they solve problems not according
to data of experience, but according to their own sentiment and
the sentiment of people who agree with them. Their reasonings,
therefore, have little if anything in common with logico-experimental science. They are derivations, more or less, of the type of
metaphysical and theological theories and little more than mere
manifestations of sentiment. As such they are to be classed with
the derivations that we have already examined in general; they follow their oscillations and present, from the extrinsic standpoint of
social utility, their merits and their defects. Their oscillations, like,
in that respect, the fluctuations in ethics, are much less extensive
than oscillations in mere theories, since considerations of social
utility prevent their straying very far from the extreme where
sacrifice of one's own advantage to the advantage of others, of the
individual to the community, of the present generation to the
future, is preached. They almost always voice sociality sentiments
(Class IV residues) that are much more vigorous than anything their
authors, or those who approve of them, actually feel. They are, as
it were, a vestment that it is decorous to be seen wearing.

2508. In Athens the governing classes may be thought of in two
ways. We have, in the first place, the Athenian citizenry, which was
a governing class with respect to slaves, aliens, and the inhabitants
of territories under Athenian dominion. Then within this class, we
get a new division, with an *élite* that actually governed.

2509. The first class, the class of Athenian citizens, remained as
exclusive as possible. That the money which they had extorted from
the allies might be enjoyed by as few as possible, the Athenians, at

the instance of Pericles, decreed in the year 451 B.C. that only individuals both of whose parents had been Athenian-born should be Athenian citizens.[1] Generally speaking, in the heyday of the Republic, the Athenians awarded the citizenship with very considerable reluctance. Says Beauchet: "In the first half of the fourth century (B.C.), two bankers, Pasio, and his successor, Phormio, famous through their associations with Demosthenes, might be mentioned among freedmen who were made citizens. . . . However, the rarity of such allusions in Greek texts shows that citizenship must have been accorded quite grudgingly to aliens and freedmen."[2]

2510. The effects of such obstacles to class-circulation were attenuated by the salutary fact that, sporadically, sudden mass-admissions of great numbers of citizens took place, although these can in no wise be taken as corresponding to the selection that results from normal circulation in classes.

2511. After the fall of the Pisistratides, Cleisthenes conferred citizenships in large numbers, probably with the idea of strengthening the plebeian party of which he was leader.[1] It is not at all clear that these new citizens were selected elements. The inhabitants of Plataea, who had been driven from their own city and, later on, the slaves who fought in the battle of the Arginusae, obtained limited rights of citizenship. In a word, there was never any circulation in the strict sense of the term.

2512. On the other hand, within the body of citizens a governing class with free circulation had been formed as early as the days of Solon. The Areopagus comprised the best elements in the population and, like the Roman Senate at one time or another, and the English House of Lords, it constituted an aristocracy of magistrates.[1] Aristotle states unequivocally that when the Athenians restored the

---

2509 [1] Aristotle, *De republica Atheniensium,* 26 (Kenyon, p. 49).

2509 [2] *Histoire du droit privé de la république athénienne,* Vol. I, p. 488.

2511 [1] Aristotle, *Politica,* III, 1, 10 (Rackham, p. 181): "He enrolled many foreigners, resident aliens, and slaves among the citizens." And *cf. Id., De republica Atheniensium,* 26 (Kenyon, p. 35).

2512 [1] Daremberg-Saglio, *Dictionnaire, s.v. Areopagus:* "The Areopagites transmitted rules of honour and uprightness to one another and to them new-comers hastened to conform. Aeschylus was not exaggerating when he described that august Senate [*Eumenides,* vv. 700-06] as 'envied of the Scythes and Pelopides, a true bulwark of the land, which it protects from anarchy and despotism, an assemblage of unselfish, austere men, dignified, respected.'"

Areopagus to its ancient authority after the battle of Salamis, they enjoyed excellent government.[2]

2513. Even Grote, who is a great admirer of the Athenian democracy, grants that Athens attained her maximum prosperity at the time of the outbreak of the Peloponnesian War; and, without having the remotest inkling of our theory, he notes that before that time literature, the arts, and philosophy had been backward (indicating weakness in Class I residues), while thereafter "although the intellectual manifestations of Athens subsist in full or *even increased vigour,* the energy of the citizens abated" (prevalence of Class I over Class II residues, which are gradually failing)—a notable instance, therefore, where a maximum of prosperity is yielded by a certain proportion between Class I and Class II residues, an excess in either proving alike harmful.[1]

2514. Another interesting example would be the case of the

2512 [2] Aristotle, *De republica Atheniensium,* 23 (Kenyon, p. 43): "As a result of that service [the service rendered just before the battle of Salamis] they [the Athenians] deferred to it [the Areopagus] and were governed excellently and to their great advantage."

2513 [1] Grote, *History of Greece,* Vol. VI, pp. 150-51 (in question the famous oration on the war-dead of Athens that Thucydides, *Historiae,* I, 140-44; Smith, Vol. I, pp. 238-53, puts into the mouth of Pericles, § 541): "Connected with this reciprocal indulgence of individual diversity, was not only the hospitable reception of all strangers at Athens, which Periklês contrasts with the xenêlasy, or jealous expulsion practised at Sparta—but also the many-sided activity, bodily and mental, visible in the former [Class I residues.], so opposite to that narrow range of thought, exclusive discipline of the body, and never-ending preparation for war [Class II residues.], which formed the system of the latter. . . . So comprehensive an ideal of many-sided social development . . . would be sufficiently remarkable, even if we supposed it only existing in the imagination of a philosopher; but it becomes still more so when we recollect that the main features of it at least were drawn from the fellow-citizens of the speaker. It must be taken, however, as belonging peculiarly to the Athens of Periklês and his contemporaries; nor would it have suited either the period of the Persian war, fifty years before, or that of Demosthenês, seventy years afterwards. At the former period, the art, the letters, and philosophy [adverted to with pride by Periklês], were as yet backward, while even the active energy and democratical stimulus, though very powerful, had not been worked up to the pitch which they afterwards reached: at the latter period, although the intellectual manifestations of Athens subsist in full or even increased vigour, we shall find the personal enterprise and energetic spirit of her citizens materially abated." Grote tries to explain that by the Peloponnesian War, but the main cause, really, was the disappearance of the old aristocracy, which had been replaced by an aristocracy of demagogues and sycophants. No Peloponnesian War forced the Athenians to bestow the succession of Pericles upon a Cleon!

Albigenses. The cloaking they used for their sentiments, their doctrine, seems to have been an offshoot of Manicheism, and ideas of that sort were current in a number of countries; but the movement thrived primarily in countries that were economically prosperous, in other words, in Italy, where there were not a few heresies (well diluted by the usual Italian scepticism), in Flanders, and most notably, in Southern France. In the twelfth century Provence was more flourishing in both material and intellectual domains than other Latin countries. People there had grown rich, and their literature, earlier than the Italian, was the first of our literatures in the vernacular. The contrast with Northern France, a poor, ignorant, uncouth region, is very striking. In the South Class I residues predominated, in the North Class II residues held the lead by far (Paris, with its university, was an exception).[1] As often happens in such cases, one notes in the South, on the one hand an absence of religious sentiments, and on the other, religious fanaticism; on the one hand extremely loose morals, on the other, excessive strictness. In the Courts of Love, matters of sex were treated mirthfully. In the meetings of the heretics licentious gaieties were mercilessly condemned.

2515. Schmidt gives an excellent description of conditions in Southern France in the twelfth century, which, after all, were very much like what was again to be witnessed during the Renaissance in Italy and in other economically prosperous countries.[1] There is no

2514 [1] Guillaume de Puy-Laurens, *Chronique,* pp. 206-07: "Now some of the heretics were Arians, others Manicheans, others Waldenses or of the heresy of Lyons. Though they were not at one among themselves, they were nevertheless all agreed in conspiring against the Catholic faith for the damnation of souls. The Waldenses argued very shrewdly with the others, whence it comes that these were tolerated by a few stupid priests out of hatred for the Waldenses. [The combination-instinct applying itself to theology. The Crusaders, who came from the North, did not dream of arguing about such matters.] Moreover priests were so roundly despised by the laity that their name was used in oaths as though they were Jews. So, when one says: 'I would rather be a Jew than do such a thing,' they say: 'I had rather be a priest.' "

2515 [1] *Histoire et doctrine de la secte des Cathares ou Albigeois,* Vol. I, pp. 66-68, 188-90: "The higher classes in society had attained a degree of cultivation that was without parallel in all Europe. Chivalry was flourishing as nowhere else. Many powerful lords were spending their days amid the risks of combat and the most frivolous gaieties of genteel flirtation. At the urge rather of an overpowering hunger for unusual adventures than of any deep religious enthusiasm, they not seldom took the Cross for the Holy Land and came home again with religious

lack of testimony to the shrewdness of the Provençaux of the twelfth century. Raoul de Caen dévotes a whole chapter to a description of the capers of the men of the South on Crusade. They had brighter wits than the French of the North, but were also less courageous; whence the saying: *"Les Français pour les combats, les Provençaux pour les vivres."* He tells how they would slyly wound a horse or mule in the intestines in such a way that the wound could not be seen, and the animal would die. The French, good souls, would be nonplussed at such a thing and cry: "Let us away! Forsooth, the Devil hath blown upon this animal." Then "like crows the Provençaux would gather about the carcass and cut it in pieces, each of

emotions no keener but with their fancies stimulated by the splendours of the East. . . . The clergy itself had been caught by the light, frivolous spirit of the nobles. . . . In the towns things were very much the same. After a long and spirited fight to rid themselves of feudal domination, the burghers had on the whole triumphed over their sometime oppressors by the end of the twelfth century. Enriched, some by commerce with the East, others by industry, the towns were proud of their prosperity and defended their municipal liberties with ever-increasing success. The burghers imitated the manners and morals of the nobles, rivalling them in courtesy and bravura. They too were poets and could become knights and gentlemen if they chose. . . . All that had resulted in an atmosphere of freedom and religious tolerance that had its counterpart in no other country of Christendom at that time. Any opinion could be expressed without untoward consequence. . . . At the close of the twelfth century, the social and political situation in the South of France was still the same as at the time when the Catharist Church threw off all mystery and publicly organized in those territories. . . . Increasing prosperity in the towns had developed an increasing sense of freedom in the inhabitants. Strong in their municipal institutions, they were resolved to defend their independence against anyone who should try to encroach upon it. In the courts of the princes, in the castles of the nobles, in the towns, politeness and good manners had acquired a polish that filled the Southerners with pride, whereas the poorer and cruder barons of the North could look only with envy upon the joyous poetic life of the chevaliers of Provence and upon the opulence of the Southern burghers. The more advanced civilization of the South, combined with an ingrained assuetude to civic and political liberty, had given rise to the spirit of religious toleration that had so extensively favoured in previous generations the propagation of doctrines counter to the dogmas of Rome. That spirit was so much the order of the day that not only was there a Catharist Church quite peaceably existing side by side with the Catholic; but the Waldenses had also succeeded in organizing flourishing communities. There were noble families, such as the Counts of Foix, where members of the two sects met. . . . The gay worldly life of the laity had found its imitators in the clergy. . . . The Pope and the provincial synods continually complained of such decadence, but their protests had no effect. . . . Anarchy had gone so far that on the eves of the saints' festivals, people danced and sang profane songs in the churches. . . . For the greatest scandals prelates themselves were responsible."

them carrying a share away, either to eat it themselves or to sell at market." [2]

2516. To see a merely religious war in the Albigensian Crusade would be to stray far from realities. Looking at derivations, one may well point out that the doctrine of the Catharists was a form of Manicheism, admitting two principles, one good and one evil. But in advancing to the conquest of the rich and blossoming lands of the South the Crusaders from the North were not in the least concerned whether there were one, two, or sixteen principles, and most probably they would not have understood head or tail of those complicated and fantastic arguments. They were interested in the booty, the pretty women, and the fertile lands that were soon to be theirs; and, as always happens, those who had wealth, but not the courage to defend it, saw it taken from them by those who were poor but had the energy to fight and win.[1]

2515 [2] *Histoire de Tancrède,* pp. 129-30: "Just as the hen is in all respects the opposite of the duck, so the Provençaux differ from the French in morals, intelligence, habits, and manner of living. . . . In times of famine they rendered much better service by their activity than men of other stocks who were better fighters. . . . They went much too far, however, in just one thing, and in a way very discreditable to them—their greed; for they would sell dog-flesh as hare and donkey-meat for goat-meat." (Then comes the story of the horse and mule.)

2516 [1] Writers altogether favourable to the Crusaders from the North cannot overlook their greed and their cruelties, though as usual laying the blame on human frailty. Guillaume de Puy-Laurens, *Chronique,* pp. 264-65: "The following winter, Foucaud de Brigier and John, his brother, with a number of other knights, again ranged the same country they had pillaged once before and made much booty there. . . . This Foucaud was a very cruel man, full of pride. He had made it a rule, it was said, to put to death any prisoner of war who would not pay him a hundred sous in gold, torturing him by starvation in a subterranean dungeon and then when he was brought before him dying or dead, ordering him to be thrown into a cesspool. . . . For that matter, one ought not and could not recount all the infamies that the servants of God committed. Most of them had concubines and kept them publicly. They carried off the wives of other men by brute force and committed such crimes and a thousand others of the same sort with impunity. Now they did not act that way, surely, in the spirit that had brought them thither. The end did not square with the beginning. They did not offer in sacrifice the tail along with the head of the victim. In a word, they were neither hot nor cold, but merely lukewarm. Wherefore the Lord began to vomit them forth from His mouth, and to drive them from the country which they had conquered." Yes, but meantime He had allowed them to conquer it. Martin, *Histoire de France,* Vol. IV, p. 204: "The pontifical 'pardons' consisted of a remission of all the sins the Crusader had committed since his birth, and further in an authorization to withhold payment of interest on all debts for the duration of the campaign. Hope of escaping their debts

2517. So among the nobles in the South, who were kindly disposed towards the Albigensian heresy, there may have been some few who were prompted by soulful theological conceptions, but the motives of many of them were more material and tangible.[1] Something very similar was observable during the Reformation, when many German princes were rather more attentive to appropriating Church properties than to interpreting the Scriptures, ever regarding as the soundest text the one that brought the desired goods into their hands with the least trouble.

2518. The masses, as usual, were inspired by envy of the comforts of the higher classes, and that sentiment was much more powerful than any ingenious theological theory. Traces of that fact are discernible in many writers, among others in Étienne de Bourbon, who had judged the Albigensians as an Inquisitor and was thoroughly acquainted therefore with their ways of thinking. Again as usual, a wave of asceticism and religious ardour was rolling up from the lower social strata and threatening to engulf the whole of society.[1]

2519. The prelates of the South were leading luxurious lives. Lovers of culture and of cultivated society, they were gradually divesting themselves of the intolerance of the more barbarous prel-

and especially of pillaging the beautiful manor-houses and the rich towns of the Languedoc was more than enough to set in cry all the adventurous nobles of Christendom. One may judge of the power the lever of fanaticism would have when reinforced by such a cogent motive. All the passions of greed and blood-thirstiness of which the human heart is capable were let loose with terrifying violence."

2517 [1] Guiraud, *Cartulaire de Notre-Dâme de Prouille,* Vol. I, Preface, p. cclxiv: "Antagonism reigned between the ecclesiastical and the lay nobility, the latter trying to rob the former, the former trying to recover at the first opportunity the properties that had been usurped to their loss. The Albigensian heresy profited by that fairly general state of things."

2518 [1] *Anecdotes historiques,* § 251: "I have heard from the friars in Provence that when the heretics in the Albigensian districts are being persuaded by Scripture and reasons, they have no stronger argument for defending their error and misleading the simple-minded than the bad deportment of Catholics and especially of the prelates. At a loss for other arguments, they keep hammering on this point: 'See what these and those are like, and especially the prelates! See how they live! See how they strut! Not as the ancients, not as Peter, Paul, and the others, do they walk!'" And *cf. Ibid.,* § 83. Those good souls who found fault with such of the clergy as enjoyed life were later imprisoned, tortured, and burned by a clergy that better conformed to their ascetic notions. Great was their profit by the change!

ates, who were poor, ignorant, fanatical, and enforced their authority cruelly, as such people always will.[1] A similar situation arose in the sixteenth century in the conflict between the fanaticism of the Reformation and the sophistication of a Leo X. From the standpoint of a certain ethics, the immorality of the clergy of those days marked a lowering in the level of civilized living; from the standpoint of intellectual freedom, tolerance, comfort, progress in the arts, it marked a rise in that level.[2] Humanity would have been

2519 [1] Guiraud, *Op. cit.,* Preface, pp. cclviii-ix: *"Looseness in the Higher Clergy:* To tell the truth the looseness of morals and lack of discipline in the higher clergy favoured the spread of the heresy much more than any more or less hypocritical adherence on their part to its doctrines. The efforts the Councils made to effect reforms show the full extent of the evil that had to be remedied in order to restore to the Church, along with her supernatural powers, the means of resisting the moral ascendancy which the Perfects enjoyed over the masses. . . . *Chaplains and Heretics:* Another chaplain, the Chaplain of Cadenal, lived with a Perfect, Squire Pons, for two years, taking all his meals with him. He knew very well that he was breaking bread with a full-fledged heretic, but little he cared! A priest serving as boon companion to a Perfect! Interesting indeed!" Had it not been for the Albigenses and the reaction that they provoked, people in Southern Europe at least would probably have been enjoying from those early days a liberty of conscience that has hardly been won in our own.

Whyte, *Histoire des langues romanes,* Vol. II, p. 193: "The conduct of the prelates was not only a flagrant violation of all principles of morality. It manifestly showed, further, that they regarded Christianity as a simple ritual of ceremonies, as a mask for the vilest hypocrisies, as a store-house of specifics for the execution or absolution of all crimes." Yet under those prelates there was little if any persecution for beliefs, whereas under their ultra-moral successors persecutions went to terrifying extremes of cruelty. As for the crimes, they seem to have been fewer under the old ones than under the new ones. At any rate, there are no signs of any decrease. [Pareto says "increase"—evidently the opposite of what he means.—A. L.]

2519 [2] Daru, *Histoire de la république de Venise,* Vol. IV, p. 181: "To judge by its policy, the government seemed to believe that if they were to be more manageable, the people of the Church had better have some leeway. They were therefore allowed a freedom in morals which all the population of Venice at all times enjoyed." In a note Daru quotes from a *relazione* by a foreign ambassador: "The clergy indulge in conduct that is quite inconsistent with their status and would not be tolerated in them in any other country. They evade obedience to their superiors, who cannot restrain them, and the authority of the apostolic nuncios over them is brought to nought. . . . If at the time of the interdicts (§ 2506) all the clergy in the Republic had been observers of their rules and obedient to their superiors, not only would they [the Ten] have been unable to force them to conduct divine offices, but there would have been hundreds of priests ready to rouse the people with sermons and protests. Yet, with the above-named allegiance null and void, all the friars and priests in the Republic sided with the government."

spared an enormous amount of suffering had such tides of religious feeling not flooded those promised lands (§ 1701).

2520. We have already learned from facts on facts that derivations are of little importance from the standpoint of the logical consequences that may be drawn from them, but of great importance from the standpoint of the residues of which they are symptoms, the sentiments that they express. The humanitarian and ascetic trends in the Catharists have to be considered from that point of view. As theories they have no importance; as symptoms of manners of feeling in the people who had those humanitarian, those ascetic inclinations, they serve to explain why the doughty warriors of the North defeated the spiritless Southerners.[1] So the declamations of a Tolstoy, who went about preaching non-resistance to evil and other such insipidities, have not the slightest importance as theories, but great importance as indications of the state of mind of people who admire them, and so they serve to reveal one of the causes of the defeat suffered by the Russians in their war with Japan. Says Tocco:[2] "And along with riches, he [the Perfect] condemns honours and power, for which mankind in fatuous yearning strives, not sparing bloody wars or the wiles of fraud to attain them. But war is a thing of violence, which followers of the Evil One may desire and require in their fury, but not assuredly meek creatures of the good God, who always condemn war, even when it is provoked by others or waged

2520 [1] Pierre de Vaulx-Cernay, *Histoire de la guerre des Albigeois,* pp. 8-11: "Of the Roman Church almost as a whole they said that it was a den of thieves and the prostitute mentioned in the Apocalypse. . . . Confirmation and confession, they said, were two silly things and altogether fatuous, and the sacrament of marriage a prostitution, no one who begat sons or daughters in marriage being able to be saved. . . . Certain of the heretics were called 'Perfects' or 'Good Men,' others 'Believers.' The Perfects dressed in black, falsely pretended to be observers of chastity [The "falsely" seems to be a mere slander on the writer's part.], spurned the use of meats, eggs, and cheese, and pretended never to lie. . . . Those who were called 'Believers' lived in the world, and although they did not strive to imitate the Perfects, they hoped to be saved by the faith of those saints. . . . There were other heretics called 'Waldenses' (Vaudois), from a certain Waldo (Valdo), a man from Lyons. . . . Not to enter into the detail of their many errors, one may say that these lay chiefly in four points—wearing sandals after the manner of the Apostles; saying that under no circumstances was it lawful to take an oath or to kill; and, especially, affirming that the first comer among them could, in case of need and for urgency, consecrate the body of Christ without having received orders from the hand of the bishop—provided, always, one wore sandals."

2520 [2] *L'eresia nel medio evo,* pp. 88-89.

in self-defence. And no less than war do they condemn taking human life, going so far as to deny that public authorities have a right to put law-breakers to death. These heretics preached the abolition of capital punishment in the full midst of a violent blood-thirsty society." [3] And that is why they perished by fire and sword, nor could it have been otherwise.

2521. When a society is weakening through lack of Class II residues, through humanitarianism, as a result of a failing in the energies that encourage the resort to force, a reaction often occurs in a part—it may be a small part—of that society. But it is interesting to note that instead of tending to stimulate residues that would contribute to reinvigorating the society, as would be the case if it were a logical reaction, the reaction is chiefly manifest in an intensification of residues that have no bearing, or very little, on the preservation of the society, and it so betrays its non-logical origins.

Among the residues so stimulated nearly always observable are the residues of the sex religion, which are the ones least beneficial to society and indeed may be called altogether useless. The fact is easily explainable if one but consider that those residues are active in moderate intensities in almost all human beings and that an increase or decrease in them may in many cases serve as a thermometer for gauging intensities in other classes of residues, among which those that are beneficial to society. It then comes about that, in trying to provide a logical vesture for their non-logical impulses, people take the symbol for the thing and imagine that by influencing the sex religion they can influence the residues of which it may be serving as a symptom. That procedure, which is very widespread among human beings and in connexion with other religions besides the sex religion, is like imagining that one could get summer

2520 [3] Tocco annotates the quotation with comments as follows: "*Not sparing bloody wars:* From Moneta, *Adversus Catharos et Valdenses*, V, 13, Pt. I, § 3 (p. 513): 'Those heretics disapprove of all war as unlawful and say that it is not lawful to defend oneself. . . .' P. 515: 'They also point to Matt. 5:38-39: "Ye have heard that it hath been said, An eye for an eye and a tooth for a tooth. But I say unto you that ye resist not evil." ' P. 517: 'And Matt. 22:7: "And he destroyed those murderers." ' 'And Matt. 5:44: "Do good to them that hate you." ' *Abolition of Capital Punishment*: From Sacconi's *Summa* [?], p. 486: 'They say that secular authorities sin in punishing criminals or heretics by death.' And Évrard de Béthune [*Adversus Waldensium sectam*, XV (Migne, Vol. XXIV, p. 1556Bg)] reports that the heretics commonly quoted the line: '*Dictum est: non occides.*' "

heat in winter by adding enough mercury to the tube in a thermometer to make it register the number of degrees desired.

2522. A weakening in those non-logical sentiments that make for the preservation of society provoked in the days of the Perfects a reaction characterized by an extraordinary sex asceticism; then similar reactions during the Renaissance, such as Savonarola's campaigns; and in our own day the stupider reactions to which we have many times alluded. All of them are and have been not only not beneficial, but positively harmful, to society, as affording a certain amount of satisfaction to the instincts of social preservation and thereby preventing them from turning in a direction where alone they could do effective service towards strengthening the residues of group-persistence (Class II), which latter constitute the foundations of society and stimulate the belligerent spirit that preserves it.[1]

2522 [1] Schmidt, *Op. cit.,* Vol. II, pp. 68-69, describes the strange beliefs of the Catharists: "The best-accredited opinion was that the souls of the first men had been angels. The Devil shut them up in material bodies in order to prevent them from returning to Heaven. But a means also had to be found to chain them in perpetuity to the wicked world, and that means the Evil One thought he had found in the propagation of the human species by the sexual union. He conceived the plan of seducing Adam through Eve, and designed to trap them both into sinning in order to make them for ever his slaves and snatch them from the heavenly world. Introducing them therefore into his false Paradise and forbidding them, the better to excite them, to eat of the tree of knowledge, he himself took possession of a serpent and began by misleading the woman—whence the awakening of the will to evil, of carnal concupiscence and all its consequences. According to the system of mitigated dualism, the forbidden fruit was nothing but the commerce of man with woman. . . . The sin of the flesh, the *fornicatio carnalis,* is the truly original sin, and the greatest of sins, for not only was it committed by free-will, thereby constituting a deliberate revolt of the soul against God, but it was also the means of perpetuating a wicked race and so enlarging the kingdom of Satan. Towards the end of the twelfth century in Italy, some few partisans of mitigated dualism believed that after creating Eve the Devil had intercourse with her and that Cain was their son. Of the blood of Cain sprang the race of dogs, whose devoted attachment to men proves that they were of human origin." Worthy predecessors, those, of our modern sex-reformers. Moneta, *Adversus Catharos et Valdenses,* I, 1, § 2 (p. 111): "Now we are to see what the sin of Adam was (*Adae* genitive of *Adam*), according to them. . . . They say that Sathan shut up another angel in a female body made from a rib of Adam while he was asleep. It was with this woman that Adam sinned. The sin of Adam, they assert, was carnal [*i.e.,* actual, not spiritual] fornication. They also say that he [*i.e.,* Sathan] courted Eve *et cum cauda corrupit eam,* and from his embrace with her Cain was born." Moneta quotes, *loc. cit.,* note 8, Moses Bar-Cepha: "Some of them think that what Adam tasted of was not [the fruit of] a tree, but the amorous embrace he had with his wife." Moneta continues, *loc. cit.: "Dicunt etiam quod mulier in luxuria assuefacta ad Adam ivit et*

2523. The Counts of Toulouse were destroyed not because they were immoral, but because they lacked faith and courage. Compare the scepticism of Raymond VI and his son, Raymond VII, with the shrewd fanaticism of Simon de Montfort. In 1213 the Provençaux and the Aragonese were besieging Muret. Simon led his army to the relief of that stronghold. He had many fewer soldiers than the enemy, but faith and courage made up for that. Disdaining all suggestions that he avoid a battle, he attacked, and won; and at last, as befitted the brave man he was, he fell at the siege of Toulouse, struck in the head by a stone and pierced by a number of arrows.[1]

2524. The unlucky Counts of Toulouse could never make up their minds as to the policy to follow. By fits and starts they would try resistance; then they would lose courage and give up the fight, throwing themselves on the mercy of Pope and King, humbly begging forgiveness.[1] They never grasped the fact that to win a victory

qualiter cum ipsa coiret ostendit et suasit, et sicut Eva suasit ei, sic Adam opere complevit, et istud esse esum ligni scientiae boni et mali asserunt." Similar derivations are to be found among Catholic writers as well. Strangest among the strange is the notion that certain sex sins were the cause of the Flood: Sanchez, De sancto matrimonii sacramento disputationes, IX, disp. 16 (p. 215).

2523 [1] Pierre de Vaulx-Cernay, Histoire de la guerre des Albigeois, pp. 269, 341-42: "Now all our men, counting knights and mounted men, did not number more than eight hundred, while it seemed as though the enemy were a hundred thousand. We had besides very few footmen, in fact almost none, and such as we had the Count had forbidden to go out during the battle. [The author's figures are certainly exaggerated. He means simply that there was a great disproportion in numbers between Montfort's army and the Provençaux and Aragonese.] When the enemy began that sortie, a messenger rushed to the Count, who . . . was hearing Mass, and urged him to go at once to the rescue of his men. 'Suffer me,' he replied, 'to attend divine service.' He had barely said the words when another messenger came." But the Count chose to remain till Mass was over. Then he said: " 'Come now, and if necessary, let us die for Him who deigned to die for us.' "

2524 [1] Guillaume de Puy-Laurens, Chronique, pp. 281-82. In 1229 Count Raymond VII threw himself on the mercy of the Franco-Papal legate, and accepted a treaty of peace which was so humiliating to himself that the writer could only believe it due to God's watchfulness over the Kingdom of France: "I must not fail to say that the kingdom having fallen to a woman with her children, as King Philip, the grandfather, had feared would happen after the death of his son, the surrender of Raymond happened only by will from Above and the goodness of the King of Heaven, protector of the French. [And Guillaume might have added, "of assassins and thieves."] Indeed, as the first auspices for the reign of the young prince, God willed so to honour his childhood on the occasion of such a long war with the said Count, that of the several clauses contained in the treaty each would alone have been sufficient ransom had the King met the said Count on

one must be ready to die weapon in hand, and so became worthy predecessors of the pitiable Louis XVI of France, who also, instead of fighting, threw himself upon the mercy of his enemies and delivered his friends to them, the way the Counts of Toulouse delivered their loyal subjects into the hands of the Inquisition. Force of arms is what decides who is to be saved and who to perish, who is to be master and who slave. Tyrtaeus had told them that in verse long long before.[2] On the terrible trials that the Spartans inflicted upon the Messenians at the end of their first war, he says: "Their backs bending under the loads they bear like beasts of burden, they carry to their masters one-half the crops of their fertile fields. . . . The men and their wives must dress in mourning and weep and wail if baneful Atropos snips the life-thread of any of their conquerors."

2525. The Southerners in France were defeated by the warriors from the North for the same reason that the Athenians were defeated by the Macedonians, and the Carthaginians by the Romans: because their instincts of self-preservation were too weak as compared with their combination-instincts.

2526. The contingency of contact and of the use of force between peoples possessing Class I and Class II residues in differing relative proportions is a factor that must not be overlooked. If for any reason force is not or cannot be used, a people widely varying from the relative proportions that assure the maximum of power in a struggle does not succumb to the people that has proportions more closely approximating that maximum. And the same may be said of the different social classes. The position of equilibrium varies according as force figures to a greater or a lesser extent.

2527. If one compares the French populations in the North and the South as they stand today, the relative proportions of Class II and Class I residues are seen to be not so very different from what they were at the time of the Albigensian Crusade. But since now-

the field of battle and made him prisoner. [Nor was that all:] The Count was reconciled with the Church on Easter Eve [April 12, 1229] and at the same time those who were with him were relieved of excommunication. And it was a pity to see such a great man, who had managed to hold out against so many great nations for so long a time, led to the altar in his shirt-tail and with arms and legs bare."

2524 [2] Pausanias, *Periegesis,* IV, *Messenia,* 14, 5 [and see Edmonds, *Elegy and Iambus,* Vol. I, p. 67.—A. L.]

adays force no longer figures in the relations between the districts, which are now two sections of one same political unit, a safe guess would be that the situation would be the reverse of what was observable in the days of the Albigensian Crusade, and that the South, where Class I residues by far predominate, would be the one to master the North, where Class II residues predominate. That exactly is what we observe. It has been many times remarked that the majority of the ministers and politicians who are at present governing France hail from the South. Where shrewdness is the outstanding requirement in society, Class I residues have a value they do not have, and by far, where force is the primary consideration. And conversely for Class II residues.[1]

2528. China was for long years exempt from pressure emanating from external force and was able to get along with a very exiguous

2527 [1] *Journal de Genève,* July 17, 1911 (a review of a study of the birth-rate in Gascony by Emmanuel Labat, with quotations): "There is less interest in getting on in the world than in enjoying life. There is very little worry about the destiny of the family property, about the future of the next generation. [Class II residues.] People think very much about themselves. The woman, even the peasant woman, dreads the restraints, the fatigues, the dangers, of motherhood. [Because those things have remained much the same, while the sentiments that used to offset them have lessened in intensity.] The man shuns worries and burdens. Each person is inclined to live for himself, to utilize for his own advantage the time and resources he has at his disposal. [Once Class II residues have lapsed, those are the only interests that are left.] If one's life is on a modest plane, or even cramped, one can still manage. The life that is easy, full, devoid of risks, is the life that seems desirable." And now Labat: "It is difficult to see nothing more than a coincidence in the weakening of morality and the simultaneous falling-off in the religious sentiment [The ordinary way of bringing in Class II residues.] unless one puts facts aside or distorts them in some way or other. The different centres of the psychic life, the various modes of the soul's activity, are too closely correlated for such important changes to take place simultaneously in them apart from some mutual dependence. People in Gascony have never been very pious. But in spite of everything [down to very recent years] religious permeation was general, deep, decisive. A life that was poor and rough was embellished, inspired, illumined, by an ideal that betrayed its religious origin and character not only at the solemn moments, such as death, marriage, birth, but also in the conception of the family and the general conception of duty, in fidelity to contract, respect for the sworn oath, deference to the aged, hospitality to the poor. [A literary description of Class II residues.] . . . The lack of moral cultivation in the young is a disquieting thing. . . . Particularly unexpected and distressing is the contrast between intellectual advance [Class I residues.] and moral retrogression. [Class II residues.] The soul of the humble peasant presents the spectacle of a field half of which is under cultivation while the other half is virtually fallow soil." [Disproportion between Class II and Class I residues.]

proportion of Class I residues. Stimulated now by the example of Japan, she is beginning to innovate—to increase her supply of Class I residues (§ 2550[2]).

2529. Even more remarkable than the case of the Albigenses is that of the Italians during the Renaissance. Towards the end of the Middle Ages Italy was so far superior to the other European countries in every branch of human activity that one can hardly imagine how she should have failed of restoring the Roman Empire and have undergone instead a new era of barbarian invasions. Italy surpassed all other countries in wealth. Her bankers were lending money to individuals and governments the world over, and names such as "Lombard Street" and the "Boulevard des Italiens" survive to our day as fossil witnesses to an age that is past. Literature, science, the arts, were flourishing in Italy while they were still in their infancy in other countries. Italians were scurrying hither and thither over the whole terrestrial globe. A Marco Polo was visiting unknown regions in Asia, a Columbus was discovering America, an Amerigo Vespucci was giving it its name. Venetian diplomacy was the first in the world. Lorenzo de' Medici in practical statecraft, Machiavelli in theoretical statecraft, had no peers.

2530. But was it only in the arts of civic life that Italians were distinguishing themselves? By no means! They were showing their talents in the arts of war as well. Francis I of France and Charles V of Austria both competed for the services of Andrea Doria as commander of their fleets. Piero Strozzi became a marshal of France; Leone and Filippo Strozzi served honourably in the French armies. The *condottieri* may have had many vices, but great captains were to be counted among them.[1]

2531. Why, then, when circumstances were so favourable, was Italy herself conquered instead of being the conqueror? The answer

---

2530 [1] Burckhardt, *Die Cultur der Renaissance in Italien,* p. 91 (Middlemore, pp. 115-17): "Italy . . . was the first to use the system of mercenaries. . . . She first relied on Germans, but during the period of the Renaissance some good Italian soldiers were trained among the foreign mercenaries. . . . New inventions meantime [firearms] made their way forward, and every advantage was taken of them. The Italians became the teachers of all Europe in matters pertaining to ballistics and military engineering. There were princes such as Federico d'Urbino and Alfonso d'Este of Ferrara who acquired in those special branches a superiority that dimmed even the reputation of Maximilian I. Italy was the first to make warfare a science, and a complete and rational art."

comes at once: Because she was divided. But why was she divided? France and Spain had also been divided, but they had achieved their unity. Why had that not happened in Italy? For the very reasons that had brought her the many blessings of wealth, intellectual prosperity, and a subtle refinement in the arts of war and statesmanship. Because in her case combination-instincts far surpassed group-persistences in importance. Other nations where relative proportions in residues diverged less widely from the combination that assures a maximum of power necessarily had to invade and conquer Italy once they established contact with her. That is exactly the case of Rome and Greece.[1]

2532. The evils that befell Italy as a result of her shortage in the instincts of group-persistence were, to an extent at least, perceived by Machiavelli, who "like an eagle soareth" over the multitude of ethical historians (§ 1975). He uses, it is true, the term "religion," but as designating any religion, a fact which—along with his considering religions quite apart from any intrinsic truth they may have, quite apart from their theological content, as Polybius, Strabo, and others already had done—clearly shows that Machiavelli was thinking of the instincts that are manifested through religious derivations, in other words, Class II residues. Like all other writers, Machiavelli's manner of expressing himself premises the assumption that the conduct of human beings is entirely logical and a consequence of the residues functioning in them. But that does not affect the substance of the reasoning in his case, for whether the derivations act directly or are mere symptoms of the residues in which they originate, the conclusions remain unaltered. In the same

---

2531 [1] Burckhardt, *Op. cit.,* p. 89 (Middlemore, p. 113): "There is no feudal system in Italy such as there is in the North, with rights founded on theories that are respected. [Derivations from Class II residues.] The power an individual possesses, he possesses as a rule in the fact and entire. There is no domestic nobility working to maintain in the prince's mind the concept of an abstract point of honour with all its strange implications. [More Class II residues and their derivations.] The princes and their counsellors are agreed that one is to act strictly according to circumstances and with reference to the objective that is to be attained. [Class I residues and their derivations.] As regards one's subordinates or allies, whatever their origin, there is none of that pride of caste that intimidates and holds aloof. The fact that there is a class of *condottieri,* where the question of origin is a matter of supreme indifference [Absence of group-persistences.], itself makes clear that power is something concrete, something real."

way, one cannot blame Machiavelli for accepting the old Roman legends at face value. They were taken as history by everybody in his time. And that again does not detract from the force of his reasonings, for, after all, what he says of Romulus he understands as applying to military institutions in general, and what he says of Numa, as applying to religious, and other kindred institutions.

2533. In the *Deca*, I, 11-12, he writes: "If one consider the Roman histories attentively, apparent is the great advantage that lay in religion for disciplining the armies, holding the people in hand, keeping men good, and shaming the wicked; so that if one were to debate to which prince Rome owed the greater debt, whether to Romulus or to Numa [If one were to debate whether the greatness of Rome depended on her military institutions or on the sentiments manifested in what the Romans said of religion.], I believe that Numa would obtain the first rank, for where there is religion arms can readily be introduced, but where there are arms but no religion, it is a difficult matter to introduce religion. . . . And if one were to found a commonwealth in these times one would undoubtedly find it easier to do so among people of the hills, who are not civilized [Who are rich in Class II and poor in Class I residues.] than among people who are accustomed to living in cities, where civilization is corrupt." [A lapse into one of the usual moralistic derivations.]

2534. "Those princes," he continues, "or those republics which would endure uncorrupted, must above all keep religious ceremonies intact and hold them always in veneration." Machiavelli, notice, says "ceremonies," not "dogmas," and, nominally a Christian, he is speaking of the religion of the pagans. That is coming very close indeed to a theory of Class II residues.

2535. But Machiavelli states his thought even more clearly: "The leaders of a republic or a kingdom must therefore maintain the foundations of the religion which they profess [Derivations are of little, residues of very great, importance.]; and if they do that it will be an easy matter for them to keep their state religious [With a proper proportion of Class II residues.] and consequently, sound and united. And all things that come up in favour of religion they must second and promote even though they believe them false." In that Machiavelli is talking like a scientist, not like a fanatic.

2536. Of Italy he goes on to say, I, 12: "And since some are of opinion that the welfare of Italy depends upon the Church of Rome, I would state against that view such reasons as occur to me, and in particular two very strong ones, which, in my judgment, admit of no rebuttal. The first is that owing to the wicked ensample of the Court of Rome this country (*provincia*) has lost all devotion and all religion, which thing carries with it no end of disorders. For where there is religion the existence of all that is good may be taken for granted, and so where there is no religion, the contrary may be presumed. We Italians therefore stand in debt to the Church and the priests for this, that we have become without religion and wicked. But we owe them a still greater debt, which is the cause of our ruin —that the Church has kept and is keeping this country of ours divided."

2537. There Machiavelli stops at the surface of things. It may well be that the Papacy was keeping Italy divided; but why did Italians tolerate such a thing? Why did they call the Papacy back, when it had found a home in Avignon? Why did they not allow it to remain there, or object to its coming back to be a nuisance to them again? Certainly not for religious reasons—they had no religion; but because the presence of the Papacy in Rome favoured certain of their combinations; because their Class I residues prevailed over their Class II residues.

2538. The Reformation in Germany was a reaction on the part of people strong in Class II residues against people strong in Class I residues—a reaction of German force and devoutness against Italian intelligence, cunning, rationality. Since the appeal was to force the Germans won. Had there been no resort to force, the Italians might have won. Had the mediaeval German Empire survived to our time and continued to include Italy, the Italians of our day would probably be governing Germany, the way Frenchmen of the South are ruling France.

2539. *Rome.* The social evolution of Rome has as usual to be sought out behind the derivations that obscure it in the histories. First we must rid ourselves of ethical derivations, which not only appear in the histories of Rome and other countries, but beset us in daily life as well (§§ 2161 f.). Then we must be on our guard against religious derivations. They are conspicuous and explicit in Bossuet, for instance, and figure more or less disguised in many other Christian writers, who never can speak of Roman history without cluttering their pages with comparisons between Christian manners and morals and pagan manners and morals. Many modern writers are not so concerned with Christian theology; but the gain is small, for they merely replace it with other theologies, democratic, humanitarian, or the like. We may ignore the theology of sex, which we have elsewhere discussed at sufficient length. It may be responsible for a good many absurdities, but has led to no very serious distortions of the history of Rome.

2540. In the particular case of Rome we again meet in their general forms the errors we identified above (§§ 2331 f.). All such derivations have a common cause—the fact that we look at events through glasses that have been coloured by our sentiments. A few writers who are at some pains to be impartial, and succeed after a fashion in being so, use lenses of the brighter tints. The majority revel in the stronger colours, and sometimes select their dyes deliberately, more especially dyes of religion and dyes of patriotism. To believe certain German writers and their imitators in other countries, patriotism ought never to be missing. Such writers habitually regard history as a study of the evolution of a very pretty metaphysical entity of their own invention that they have baptized with the name of "State," which, they say, was born and spent its infancy in Rome but did not, needless to say, attain full-grown perfection till the present German Empire came along. Another colouring, imperceptible though rarely absent, arises in the implicit assumption that every "evil" recorded by history could have been avoided had proper measures been taken to deal with it (§§ 2334-35). Underlying that assumption is another that, roughly, human society would by nature be prosperous, happy, perfect, were its normal development not disturbed by occasional causes that it would be *possible* (§ 134) to remove. That doctrine is very like the doctrine that the cause of human misfortunes lies in original sin, but it is less logical; for the original sin being still operative, it is easy to see why the evils that result from it continue to subsist, whereas if all the evils of society are ascribable to causes which it is *possible* (§ 134) to remedy, one cannot understand why not one, at least, of the many societies known to us through history has managed to show a continuous and uninterrupted prosperity. In the same way one might say that if it is *possible* to make the human being immortal, it is exceedingly strange that all the human beings of whom we have so far had any knowledge have died. Actually the normal development of prosperity in human societies is along an undulating curve; and abnormal—so abnormal that no example of it has ever been witnessed—would be a line representing a prosperity that is at all times uniform, or uniformly increasing or diminishing (§ 2338).

2541. When historians of the school mentioned consider the decline of the Roman Republic, they take it as axiomatic that the decline had a "cause," the problem merely being to find it in the conduct of the Romans living at that time, and that said cause must essentially be something different from the "cause" of the prosperity of the Republic, opposite conditions necessarily having opposite causes. It never occurs to them that successive situations, although opposites to each other, have a common "cause," an identical origin (§ 2338). If one is going to use the term "cause" in that way, one may say, as regards the individual, that life is the "cause" of death, since life is certainly followed by death; and, as regards the species, that death is the "cause" of life, since, so long as the species survives, the deaths of certain individuals are followed by the births of others. And just as birth may be said to be common "cause" and origin both of life and of death, certain facts may be said to be common "cause" and origin first of prosperity and then of decline in a human society, and *vice versa.*[1]

2542. Another pitfall to be avoided is an oversimplification of extremely complex situations. In its general form, this error is frequently dissembled under derivations involving personifications, whereby we are tempted to consider as a single person presenting uniform interests and sentiments a group of persons presenting diverse and even contrary interests and sentiments (§§ 2254, 2328 [1]). We may legitimately speak of the things that "Rome" or "Macedonia" did, provided those names are used for the mere resultants of the various forces that were at work in those countries. We begin to go wrong when we forget the great multiplicity of such forces,

---

2541 [1] We are not saying that that is the case in all situations. We mean merely that it may be the case in some situations and that any axiomatic solution of the problem of historical causes must be avoided, and the solution sought in a strictly experimental investigation of the facts (§§ 2331 f.).

and assume that "Rome" or "Macedonia" had one will or intent much as an individual has one will or intent. We know that in Rome, in the year 200 B.C., a number of Romans wanted war with Macedonia and a number of other Romans did not want any such war (§ 2556). As a way of stating the gross fact we might say that "Rome" did not at that time want war with Macedonia. Roughly to suggest some of the different elements that figured in the resultant, we could specify that the "Senate" proposed the war and that the "People" voted against it. Going on in that fashion, we could specify other elements in the resultant. It would be ridiculous and insufferably pedantic absolutely to avoid all such modes of expression, and we are on safe ground so long as we think of the things those names stand for. The error creeps in with the personification, develops with the development of the personification, and attains its maximum when the personification is complete. "Rome" did not have any single will with regard to war with Macedonia, in the sense in which some individual Roman might have had such a will. Nor did the "Senate" have any such will, nor the "speculators" who favoured the war, nor even various factions that might be mentioned in those groups. If we start with the complex "Rome" and gradually increase the number of elements we consider, we get closer and closer to reality, without, however, being able ever to attain it altogether. We get, in other words, a number of approximations. We cannot dispense with using them, and they cannot lead us astray so long as we take them for what they are and do not go beyond their particular significance.

It is a somewhat similar error to assume, be it implicitly, that the same name indicates the same thing at different moments in history. The names "Senate" and "People" remain all through Roman history. The things they designate change altogether from moment to moment. That was a common mistake with some historians in the past. Others avoided it. On the whole, it is less to be feared, because less insidious, than the error of personification, which continues to flourish in our day in writings too numerous to count that deal with "Italy," "France," "England," as though those countries were individual persons.

2543. But at this point two sand-bars rise in our course, and of them it might well be said: *Incidit in Scyllam cupiens vitare*

Carybdim. Hardly a century has gone by since people were writing history without caring about details, save for more or less romantic anecdotes that were dwelt on at length. Today the inclination is to gather every minutest detail and argue endlessly over matters of no importance. That is helpful as regards the preparation of materials, but not as regards using them. It is the work of the quarryman who cuts the stone, not of the architect who builds the edifice. When one is looking for uniformities, details big or little are to be thought of as means, not as ends. And one must abandon any hope of at once completing the theory one is in process of building, clearly understanding that only successive approximations can bring one to the desired goal. The main lines of a phenomenon are first drawn, then one goes on to the secondary, and so on, so contributing to the perpetual advancement of knowledge.

2544. All such lines are ideal and are obtained by abstraction; in other words, by looking for certain main elements in the concrete phenomenon that goes under a single name, though it is actually a composite of numerous elements. So we give the name of "clay" to a compound of a number of chemical elements, and the name of "humus" to a compound of a still larger number of chemical elements. That fact was not held in mind by writers who have dwelt at length on the struggle between "republican liberty" and "imperial despotism" in Rome, or by those who saw a struggle between the aristocracy and the masses in the ancient struggles between patriciate and plebs, whereas we now know well that it was a battle between two aristocracies. In times less remote the conflict between Senators and knights was by no means a simple phenomenon, as many have imagined; and adequate proof of that is the fact that Senators and knights stood shoulder to shoulder, in view of common interests, against the agrarian laws.

The lines alluded to are not geometrical, any more than the lines that separate the land from the waters of the ocean are geometrical. Only a presumptuous ignorance can insist on an exactness that the science of the concrete cannot attain. The terms of such a science must correspond to reality, but that is possible only within certain limits. No rigorous definition of "humus" or "clay" can be given, nor can one tell the exact number of years, days, hours, that separate youth from manhood. But that does not prevent experimental science from using such terms, as qualified by the approximations to which they are subject. One attains the maximum of possible rigour in taking such approximation into account. Mathematicians themselves are obliged to follow that course in order to take advantage of so-called irrational numbers.[1]

2545. Let us try therefore to get a first rough notion of the matter in hand. We have already discovered that in social phenomena the manner in which human beings obtain the things required for living, and also for comfort, wealth, honours, power, is of great importance as regards both interests and sentiments, and we saw that from that standpoint it was helpful to divide people into two categories (§ 2233). Let us now see whether we encounter any uniformities along that route. If we do, we shall go on; if we do not, we shall turn back.

2546. In studying a number of different elements it is best to begin by classifying them. In the matter of class-circulation in Rome we must consider the following elements:

A: Norms regulating movement from one class to another.

A-1: Legal norms regulating movement from one class to another. In times bordering on the prehistoric there were serious legal obstacles to circulation. The early conflicts between patricians and plebeians were fought to remove them. Gradually they were abolished as regarded Roman citizens, and mitigated as regarded freedmen. Towards the end of the Empire, closed or quasi-closed classes reappear.

A-2: Actual movements from class to class. They depend primarily upon the ease with which wealth can be amassed in one way or another. They are very considerable towards the end of the Republic and under the early Empire.

B: Characteristics of the new élite.

2544 [1] The terms of experimental science correspond to realities within more or less extensive limits. The terms of theology and metaphysics correspond to no realities whatever or, if one prefer, do so within such vast limits that approximation is a matter of illusion. There is no doubt that things corresponding to the term "clay" exist, just as individuals who are "young" or "old" or belong to "social classes" exist. The doubt arises only as to the limits outside of which given things no longer belong to the category "clay," given individuals to the category "young," a given "social class," and so on. But as for "Zeus," "justice," "the good," all correspondence with experimental reality fails, and there is no question of limits.

B-1: From the ethnic standpoint.[1] At first the new elements are Roman, Latin, Italian—the *élite* is rejuvenated without change in ethnic character. In the end they are predominantly Oriental—the *élite* changes completely in character. In the same way the relative proportions—differing in the various periods of history—of urban and rural elements in the governing class have to be considered. Belot probably attached too great an importance to such proportions, but there is some truth in what he says. He did, however, mistake the symptom for the thing. The material fact that a person lives in city or country is not the important fact. The important fact is the differences in sentiments and interests that are revealed thereby. With such sentiments and interests, therefore, we shall be concerned here, primarily.

B-2: From the standpoint of Class I and Class II residues. When the *élite* is in part retimbered from the newly rich, when agricultural occupations give way to financial and commercial enterprise, the governing class increases its stock of Class I residues and there is a falling-off in Class II residues. Towards the end of the Republic, a condition is reached where the ruling class is rich in Class I, poor in Class II, residues, while the subject class, especially in elements living far from the capital, is rich in Class II residues. With the Empire a movement in the opposite direction sets in as regards the ruling class, which increases in Class II residues to such an extent as to end, in that respect, on a level with the subject class.

B-3: From the standpoint of the aptitude for using force and the use actually made of it. In the beginning the citizen is indistinguish-

2546 [1] The term "ethnic" is one of the vaguest known to sociology. We use it here merely to designate a state of fact, going in no sense into the question of explaining the fact. We are not concerned with determining whether or no there are different human races, and if so, how many, nor with ascertaining how they are made up, how they combine, how they disappear. In ancient times there were human beings who called themselves Romans, Samnites, Italians, Hellenes, Carthaginians, Gauls, and so on, and were so called by others. In our day there are people who call themselves, and are generally called, Italians, Frenchmen, Germans, Slavs, Greeks. That and no other is the fact we mean to designate when we speak of ethnic differences. Each one of those names indicates a certain number of individuals who usually, and to a greater or lesser extent, share certain sentiments, certain ideas, a certain language, sometimes a certain religion. Here we accept the fact as it is, altogether disregarding causes and origins. We repeat the caution, because the reader must bear it constantly in mind, so as not to ascribe to the term "ethnic" a different meaning from the one in which we use it.

able from the soldier. The *élite* is homogeneous in that respect. It can use force and does so. Gradually the citizen becomes distinct from the soldier. The *élite* falls into two parts: a minority ruling primarily by force, a majority neither able nor inclined to use force.

2547. Phenomena succeed one another in time with very gradual modifications; but to describe them at all we are obliged to divide them off into groups corresponding to periods, fractioning, disjoining, a unity that is continuous. Yielding to that necessity, we shall consider the following periods of time, to which we set definite boundaries for the mere sake of convenience, much as we speak of youth, manhood, old age, in reference to human life, which passes as a single continuity with very gradual changes: I. From the Second Punic War down to the end of the Republic. II. From the accession of Augustus down to the Antonines. III. From the Antonines down to Gallienus.

We must never lose sight of the interdependence of the various elements in the social state, the elements *a* (residues), *b* (interests), *c* (derivations), *d* (social heterogeneity), as explained in § 2206.[1]

2548. I: *From the Second Punic War down to the end of the Republic.* We may disregard earlier periods. Their history is uncertain and still more so their chronology. In the period indicated, the political, military, and financial power of Rome is on the increase and attains its maximum, and so for the manifestations of Roman intelligence (§§ 2354 f.). Economic freedom is very considerable.

A-1. Class-circulation as law:

Very appreciable at first, legal obstacles to class-circulation disappear as regards citizens.[1] There is a tendency towards equality between the rural and the urban populations. Descendants of freed-

---

2547 [1] The evolution of economic institutions in Rome I have discussed at length in my *Cours,* §§ 802-08, so that I need touch upon it but briefly here, devoting the main attention to other elements. At the time that chapter in the *Cours* was written I was as yet unequippèd with the theory of the interdependence of waves in social phenomena that is set forth in the present volume (§§ 2552-53). The development of the Roman corporations has to take account of that theory.

2548 [1] Mommsen, *Römisches Staatsrecht,* Vol. III-1, pp. 500-01: "[Under the Republic] any individual, whatever his birth, might, as a matter of law, aspire to status as a knight. As a matter of custom, the equestrian horse was preferably bestowed on children of the old families. . . . The law and the fact subsist unchanged under the Empire."

men of the second generation, exceptionally even of the first, obtain *ingenuitas,* or status as "well-born," and are admissible to the *élite.*

A-2. Class-circulation in the fact:

War, commerce, and, in the end, collections of taxes open up many sources of wealth.[2] Class-circulation, in the fact, is intense without, however, being too rapid, on the whole, at least.[3] It is the

2548 [2] Mommsen, *Ibid.,* Vol. III-1, pp. 510-11: "The *ordo publicanorum* is never identified with the *ordo equester* and cannot be, but both groups issued from that middle class which was formed by the exclusion of Senators from the public markets and of the equestrian centurias from the Senate. The leaders of both classes were largely the same individuals. In that sense, the politico-commercial leadership of the knights belonged to the publicans, and the unity of the publicans as a class made them specially adaptable to the organization of large business concerns." (Quotation continued in § 2549 [8].)

2548 [3] It begins with the slaves, continues with freedmen, travellers from abroad, and residents of foreign birth, goes on through the knights and Senators, then reaches as high as the Emperors. Towards the end of the Republic a slave could acquire his freedom within a few years. Cicero, *Philippicae,* VIII, 11, 32: "Since, O Conscript Fathers, we have conceived the hope of freedom after six years, after enduring servitude for a longer time than diligent and honest slaves usually serve . . ." We must not take this six-year term literally. Cicero merely found it a convenient simile for the theme of that oration. All the same, he would not have used it had the length of time in which a sober and industrious slave could win his freedom been a very long instead of a short one. Another passage in Cicero shows the rapidity of circulation in general: *Pro Lucio Cornelio Balbo,* 7, 18: "Before I come to the claims of Lucius Cornelius from the legal standpoint, it seems advisable for me, in order to eliminate all ill will from this case, to advert briefly to the common condition of us all. If, O judges, each of us had to remain from birth to old age in the station in which he was born or was placed by fortune, and if all those whom fortune has raised or who have distinguished themselves by their efforts and achievements were to be punished, it would not seem a more grievous rule or condition for Lucius Cornelius than for many another sagacious and energetic man. But if, instead, many men have risen by virtue, intelligence, and competence from the lowest levels of birth and fortune and acquired not only friendships and wealth, but honours, glory, public respect, the highest praise, I do not see why envy should offend the worth of Lucius Cornelius rather than that your fairness should manifest itself in behalf of his modesty." Mommsen excellently explains the character of Roman nobility: *Römisches Staatsrecht,* Vol. III-1, pp. 462-65: "The *nobilitas* is not, to be sure, a right of birth, as the patriciate is, but it too is hereditary. It is an acquisition of the person but it is passed on to the agnatic descent of the first acquirer, or rather it begins with his descendants. The person who does not enter the circle by right of inheritance, the 'new man' (*homo novus*), is not himself *nobilis,* but he ennobles his descendants. . . . When the ordinary curule magistracies in the city . . . became open to plebeians . . . the magistrate acquired with his office for himself and his agnatic descent . . . the body of rights designated by the term *nobilitas.* The 'new man' made of his posterity a new family of the Roman nobility. The most important advantage the *nobilitas* procured was also one that was least suscep-

norm—with, to be sure, various exceptions according to the times —and it will remain the norm down to the fall of the Empire, that a family can rise but gradually in social station. A slave may become a freedman. His grandchildren are free born—*ingenui*. If they attain public office they can enter the equestrian order, and their descendants can acquire *nobilitas*. The same individual—providing always the norm be observed—can obtain public offices only in a prescribed order. The general movement, slow at first, is accelerated towards the end of the Republic. Then we get a period of anarchy in which rules are not at all strictly observed.

B-1. Ethnic character of the élite:

The whole or virtually the whole *élite* is made up of native elements. Towards the end of the republic, however, come great and sudden changes in the citizenry and in the *élite*.[4] The Social War

tible of being legally determined. It lay in the fact that descendants of the 'new man,' as belonging to the hereditary nobility, could compete on a footing of equality with the nobles for appointments in the various magistracies and pontificates."

2548 [4] Records of only a few cases have come down to us, but the probability is that there were many such. Plutarch says of Sulpicius, *Sulla*, 8, 2 (Perrin, Vol. IV, p. 349), that "he sold the Roman citizenship to freedmen and foreigners, openly counting the money on a table that stood in the Forum." Marius conferred citizenship upon a thousand of the inhabitants at Camerinum at one time. Reproved for that, he said that "he could not hear the voice of the law for the rattling of so many swords" (Plutarch, *Marius*, 28, 2; Perrin, Vol. IX, p. 541). Sulla and Pompey conferred citizenship upon anybody they chose. Appian, *De bellis civilibus*, I, 100: "He [Sulla] added to the People more than ten thousand slaves belonging to individuals whom he had proscribed, selecting them from among the youngest and most promising. In giving them their freedom he made them Roman citizens, and they were called 'Cornelii' after himself"—he being their patron, they his clients. A law decreed (Cicero, *Pro Lucio Cornelio Balbo*, 8, 19) "that those who had individually been made citizens by Pompey, on recommendation of his Council, should be Roman citizens." In that connexion Cicero stresses the advantage to the Roman People of conferring citizenship upon men who showed themselves worthy of it. He was met with the objection that allies could not be made citizens except with the consent of their nation. Replying, he says, among other things, that it was a pity that allies could not be rewarded in that way, while the citizenship was being conferred upon so many others: "For we see the citizenship being conferred on many tributaries from Africa, Sicily, Sardinia, and other provinces, and we know that deserters from the enemy to our generals have been given the citizenship if they have performed great service to the state, and even slaves, who are of the lowest order as regards social station and before the law, have been in many cases rewarded with freedom, and therewith citizenship, for distinguished service to the country." Specifying many instances where Roman citizenship had been awarded, he incidentally drops the remark: "Many of those who have been admitted to citizenship from free and allied peoples have been freedmen." In the *Pro Archia*, 10,

finally ended in the issuance of Roman citizenship to certain numbers of citizens in the Italic cities.

B-2. Proportions of Class I and Class II residues:

Some of the new citizens were doubtless rurals and may have contributed a certain dosage of Class II residues to the Roman People; but the majority, we may be sure, were of the shrewd type, rich in combination-instincts, since only such had the talent for manoeuvring in the stormy waters of those days and procuring the rights of citizenship from the powerful. The same may be said of the slaves who won their freedom. A comparison drawn by Dionysius of Halicarnassus between the freedmen of the old days and those of his time indicates that the latter teemed with Class I

25-26, he says: "If Archias had not been a Roman citizen by law, could he not, I wonder, have arranged to be made one by some general? When Sulla was bestowing the citizenship on Spaniards and Gauls, could he have rejected a petition from this man? . . . Could he not have obtained it for himself or for the Luculli from Quintus Metellus Pius, an intimate friend, who bestowed citizenship on many people?" Appian, *Op. cit.,* I, 53, notes that at the end of the Social War all allies obtained citizenship except the Lucanians and the Samnites, and they got it later on. He also states that new citizens were more numerous than the old. Florus, *Epitoma de Tito Livio,* II, 6, 1-3 (III, 18, 1, Forster, p. 233), very soundly remarks that the allies and the Romans by that time constituted one people: "Since the Roman People has mixed Etruscans, Latins, and Sabines together and made one blood of them all, it has made one body of those members and is a unit made up of them all." Not all the cities, however, accepted rights of citizenship; and there were others where only a few individuals complied with the formalities required for securing them. Brundisium, for instance, must have been left out, for on his return from the war with Mithridates, Sulla exempted that city from paying taxes (Appian, *Op. cit.,* I, 79). Carbo also created new citizens: Livy, *Ab urbe condita,* LXXXIV (*Epitome*): "The right to vote extended to the new citizens by a decree of the Senate." Throughout all this period, probably, citizenship was obtained for the most part by intriguers, "speculators," and their henchmen. The quiet, industrious elements, the small property-owners, probably did not go to the trouble required for obtaining it. Caesar dispensed citizenships and honours very freely: Suetonius, *Divus Julius,* 76, 3: "He admitted to the Curia men on whom he had conferred citizenship, and some of them were semi-barbarian Gauls." The triumvirate of Octavius, Anthony, and Lepidus elevated many allies, soldiers, descendants of freedmen, and even slaves to the Senate (Dio Cassius, *Historia Romana,* XLVIII, 34, 4). Later on, becoming sole master under title of Augustus, Octavius decided to limit the number of slaves to whom liberty could be granted, that being an item in his program for reviving ancient customs in Rome (Dio Cassius, *Ibid.,* LV, 13, 7; Suetonius, *Divus Augustus,* 40). In his will he advised Tiberius not to be too lavish in liberating slaves, nor in granting citizenships (Dio Cassius, *Ibid.,* LVI, 33, 3). Such counsel, however, did not prevent the movement from continuing under his successors.

residues much more conspicuously than the former.[5] They were also increasing, as compared with residues of group-persistence, in the governing element, which was taking in speculators in greater and greater numbers. The movement towards creating new citizens has to be kept distinct from the movement modifying the *élite;* and in this latter movement we have to distinguish a number of different aspects. There is, as yet, no shortage in warriors. After a few abortive attempts soldiers, in fact, are to seize power and establish the Empire. Speculators represent the majority in the *élite.* They may be seen forever shifting in the direction from which the wind seems likely to blow most favourably, now intriguing in the Forum, buying votes in the comitia as long as they find it profitable to do so, now switching with the greatest ease to the warriors if they see a chance of deriving some advantage from them. They are most conspicuous among the equestrians, but they are far from wanting in the other classes. Finally comes a class of timid and often honest souls who believe in the efficacy of the law against force of arms. They are constantly declining in vigour, and are busy digging their own graves. In written history such people appear chiefly among the Senators, among whom, however, not a few speculators are to be counted (§ 2542).[6]

We have already observed, for the general case (§ 2338), that causes which produce first prosperity and then decline are the same.

2548 [5] *Antiquitates Romanae,* IV, 24 (Spelman, pp. 193-94): "In the old days the slave most often secured his freedom gratuitously by reason of his courage and probity, and that was the best way of escaping from the control of the master. Some few paid their own ransoms, earning the money by lawful and honest toil. Not so in our day. Now everything is so confused and the morals of the Roman Republic have become so shameless and debased that some get the money required for purchasing their freedom (and straightway becoming Roman citizens) by thieving, pilfering, prostitution, and other crimes. Others become the accomplices and witnesses of their masters in poisonings, murders, and crimes against the gods and the Republic, and so [by blackmail] are rewarded by their owners with freedom."

2548 [6] Worthy predecessor of the Imperial Senate was that Republican Senate of which Marcius Philippus said that with such a body no government was possible. Cicero, *De oratore,* III, 1: "When Lucius Crassus returned to Rome on the last day of the public games, he was deeply impressed by a speech that Philippus was reported to have delivered before the People, and in which he had said that he [Crassus] would have to see about getting some other counsel, since he could never run a government with that Senate." Speculators and regular routineers who are satisfied with their present state are alike in the one respect that they both shrink from the use of force.

When an infant is born one may foresee approximately what he will be like when he has reached old age. So when circumstances are known, one may foresee the general lines of development that will be followed by aristocracies such as the Spartan or the Venetian, by peoples that hold apart from others, such as the Athenians or the Chinese, and by peoples whose ruling classes will be replenished with new elements, by military conquests and speculations, such as the Romans. A few brief words of Florus give the synthesis of the situation at the end of the Republic. He is impressed by the evils in which plutocracy had resulted.[7] But at first plutocracy had been a blessing, not a curse, for Rome. Polybius saw the good side. He knew Rome at a time when the causes that were later to bring on the collapse of the state were still contributing to its power and prosperity. He was struck with the fact that the whole population seemed engrossed in economic and financial activities. Substantially, under the somewhat different forms, the situation was in great part similar to what is observable in our day in our modern civilized countries. Polybius, *Historiae*, VI, 17, 1-4 (Paton, Vol. III, pp. 307-09), notes, in particular, manipulations of public contracts by the censors, especially the farming of taxes, and he remarks that virtually everybody was engaged in it. "Some," he says, "get the contracts from the censors themselves, others are in partnership with them, others are bondsmen, others mortgage their properties as bonds." There, in its cradle, is the creature that will one day be

2548 [7] Towards the end of the Republic the equestrian order was for the most part made up of "speculators." Its power and its robberies in the provinces are familiar themes. Says Florus, *Epitoma de Tito Livio*, II, 5, 3 (III, 17, 3, Forster, p. 229): "The Roman knights had such great power that by embezzling the taxes they despoiled the state in their own right, as though they possessed the rank and station of emperors." And *cf.* § 2354 [1]. Cicero, *In Caium Verrem*, III, 72, 168: "Certainly there would have been no escape for this man had the publicans, in other words the knights, been his judges." And *Ibid.*, 41, 94: "In former days, when the equestrian order was a judicial body, even dishonest and rapacious magistrates in the provinces respected the publicans and paid honour to all who worked with them. Any Roman knight whom they met in a province they showered with favours and liberalities. . . . The knights thought at that time, I know not how, as it were by common consent, that anyone who had ventured to affront a Roman knight should be judged by the whole order as worthy of an evil fate." That is very much the situation with the plutocrats of our time, who are coddled and abetted by the parliaments, governments, and courts that depend on them (§ 2262 [1]).

named Plutocracy. An infant weakling, it remains subordinate. Once it gets its growth and its muscle, it will claim dominion. In the transition from the one situation to the other, it will bring power and prosperity to Rome. The people whom Polybius saw about him were busy exploiting the conquests of Rome, and their successors were to exploit them still more busily; and all the countries of the Mediterranean basin, even countries over which Roman rule did not as yet extend.[8][9] To all of them might more or less be applied what

2548 [8][9] Sallust, *Bellum Jugurthinum*, 41, 7: "In military and domestic matters decision was taken at the arbitrary will of the few. The treasury, the provinces, public offices, the glories and triumphs, were in their hands. The people [Those who were neither speculators nor accomplices of speculators.] were burdened with military service and poverty. The generals, with a few others, laid hold on all the booty of war, and meantime the relatives and children of the soldiers were turned out of their homes if they chanced to be neighbours to someone more powerful. So with power came greed [Mere ethical declamation. Where did they get that power? They bought it in the *comitia!*] without bound or limit to usurp, despoil, pillage everything and to stop at nothing [More ethical declamation.] till at last it wrought its own undoing." At last a fact. According to Diodorus Siculus, *Bibliotheca historica*, XXXVI, 3, 1 (Booth, Vol. II, p. 551), when Marius applied to Nicomedes, King of Bithynia, for auxiliaries to be used in the expedition against the Cimbri, he was told that the majority of the subjects of that king had been bonded in slavery to publicans. Cicero, *Pro lege Manilia*, 22, 65: "It is difficult, fellow-citizens, to describe in words how hated we are of the nations abroad because of the abuses and the greed of the men we have sent with plenary powers to rule them during these past years. What shrine in those lands do you think has been inviolate in the eyes of our officials, what citizenship sacred, what private house adequately locked and fortified? There is a search for rich and prosperous cities against which some pretext for war can be found in order to sate their thirst for plunder." In that oration Cicero is flattering Pompey. In another, *De provinciis consularibus,* he is trying to win the good graces of Caesar and defends the publicans who, he says, are being abused by Gabinius. But in so doing, he himself indirectly testifies, 5, 10, to the power of such speculators: "The poor publicans (and poor me—so deeply do I feel the hardships and tribulations of those deserving men) he (Gabinius) has reduced to servitude to Jews and Syrians, races born to servitude. [In Cicero's time evidently the Jews and Syrians were commonly regarded as born to be slaves and therefore proper subjects for exploitation at the hands of the publicans. Nowadays civilized nations feel the same way about the so-called backward countries, and hand them over to our modern speculators.] He began by deciding every case that came before him against the publicans and he held to that policy. He cancelled contracts that contained nothing abusive. He abolished their body-guards. He exempted many people who were paying taxes in money or in kind. He forbade any publican or publican's agent to stay in a town where he was or which he intended to visit." Cicero concludes that the Senate ought to go to the rescue of such estimable public servants, in spite of the poverty of the Treasury—*"in his angustiis aerarii."* For the rest, Cicero was well acquainted with the character of his good friends the publicans;

Cicero says of Gaul, *Pro Marco Fonteio,* V, 11: "Gaul is crowded with merchants, crowded with Roman citizens. No Gaul transacts any business save under the eye of a Roman citizen, nor does a piece of money circulate in Gaul without being entered in the ledger of some Roman citizen." And great in very truth was the economic and financial prosperity of those days, something similar, making the due allowances, to the prosperity of the modern civilized countries in the early years of the twentieth century. Then as now prices

and in a letter to Quintus he says that if the thing could be done without stirring up a hornet's nest, he would like to see a limit set to their rapacity—the letter, for all the world, is one that a gentleman of our time might write to some public official of his intimacy, advising him to "clean up"—but for Heaven's sake, no scandal! *Ad Quintum fratrem,* I, 1, 2: "As I think of the welfare of our allies, as I do my best to resist the shamelessness of many of our traders. . . ." *Ibid.,* I, 11, 32 (Williams, Vol. III, pp. 421-23): "Your good intentions and your devotion meet a serious obstacle in the publicans. If we go against them we alienate both from ourselves and from the state an order that deserves well at our hands and which through us is bound to the state. On the other hand if we yield to them in everything, we allow those whom it is our duty to help and protect to be utterly ruined." (§§ 2300, 2268, 1713 [4], 2178). *Loc. cit.,* 33: "I have heard from many citizens of the bitterness our allies are feeling on account of the publicans." Livy, *Ab urbe condita,* XLV, 18, 7, alludes to the difficulties involved in collecting taxes in Macedonia and specifically the tax on mines: "For they cannot be collected without the publican, yet if the publican is there, that is the end either of the public's due or of the liberty of our allies." Money was needed to buy votes in the *comitia,* and it had somehow to be procured whether by "voluntary" gifts on the part of the provincials or through robbery, cunning, force, usury, and so on. Not to buy votes at Rome was a strange exception. Cicero approves of certain liberalities, and if he condemns others, he seems to do so the better to stress such exceptions, among them his own case. In *De officiis,* II, 17, 58-59, he begins by saying that any suspicion of stinginess of character must be avoided: *"Vitanda tamen est suspicio avaritiae."* The ideal of the time in fact was the speculator who earned much and spent freely—the plutocrat of our day. Cicero mentions the case of one Mamercus, who was rejected for the consulate because he had not first stood for the aedileship, an office that called for far greater expenditures. He concedes that one may even venture on liberalities that are not approved of by the best opinion: "If a thing is demanded by the people, it is the part of wisdom to do it, even if it be a thing of which honest men do not approve but which they nevertheless condone—always, however, within one's means, as we [I] did ourselves [myself]; and so likewise if some greater and more useful advantage is to be acquired by popular largess, as was the case with Gnaeus Orestes, recently, who won great honours by giving dinners in the streets on pretext of paying a religious tithe." Lucius Philippus, he says, and Cotta, and Curio, used to boast that they had obtained their first honours without money. "And I too," he concludes, "might in some degree make the same boast, for considering the amplitude of the honours that I attained with unanimous votes . . . the expense of my aedileship was trifling."

were rising and luxury was on the increase.[10] Evidently such numerous and important interests on the part of the populous class of speculators represented a power that would be strong enough to gain the upper hand in public affairs, unless it were offset by another force of equal or almost equal weight (§§ 2087 f.). In the day of Polybius shrewd politics were still adequate for that purpose. Polybius notes, *Historiae*, VI, 17, 5, 6, that all the contracts handled by the censors depended upon the Senate: "and there are many cases indeed where the Senate can greatly damage or, on the other hand, benefit farmers of taxes or managers of public enterprise." [11] And lo, in that, a force which, whether as help or hindrance, has to be reckoned with by the plutocrats, whose activities consequently will be more beneficial, indeed far more beneficial, than harmful to the Republic, and at the same time an obstacle, surmounting which corruption and violence will have a free hand until a greater force, the force of arms, supervenes to check them! A person so placed as to be able to be of help or hindrance to other people is the target of either corruption or violence. That is observable in all periods of history (§ 2261 [1]), present and past explaining each other mutually. A political body endowed with such powers is also a target for the rivalries of people who aim at overthrowing it and getting its power into their own hands. Furthermore, people who depend on such a body, or on its rivals, sooner or later perceive that it would be better not to depend on anyone; and then the plutocracy begins to take over power. It might have been foreseen that the Senate would not be left in peaceful possession of its prerogatives; that corruption and violence would change in forms according to the body in power,

2548 [10] Plutarch, *Marius*, 34 (Perrin, Vol. XI, pp. 555-57), relates an incident that is altogether parallel to things that go on in our day and which shows the great rise in values of real estate, an ever infallible symptom of mounting economic prosperity. The dictator owned a beautiful house near Misenum. It had been bought from one Cornelia for 75,000 drachmas and was resold soon afterwards to Lucius Lucullus for 2,500,000 drachmas. "So suddenly did sumptuousness increase and to such degree did prosperity tempt to extravagance."

2548 [11] Cato the Censor (Plutarch, *Cato Major*, 18-19; Perrin, Vol. II, pp. 355-57) picked his quarrel with the speculators on ethical grounds, and as usually happens in such cases, got nowhere. The Senate stood by the speculators, just as parliaments and legislatures do in our time. Cato lowered prices paid on contracts for public works and raised percentages on the tax-farmers. The Senate annulled his contracts, and the tribunes imposed a fine on Cato!

and meantime grow gradually more obstreperous with the increase in the rewards expected and realized from them. It also fell to Polybius to observe one of the ways in which the Senate managed to cling to power—its prerogative of sitting in judgment in cases arising under both private and public law. And it might therefore readily have been foreseen that the battle would be joined about that privilege, as was in fact the case, as everybody knows.

B-3. *Use of force:*

The *élite* is still in great part a military class, but a growing distinction between military and civil functions is already manifest.[12] The army, furthermore, which had at first been largely made up of property-owning citizens, rich, therefore, in Class II residues, tends to become in part a collection of paid soldiers, of men therefore who are the tools and the supporters of leaders rich in Class I residues.[13]

2548 [12] Mommsen, *Römisches Staatsrecht,* Vol. I, pp. 505-06: "In the day of Polybius, early in the first century B.C., the law required at least five years of service of an applicant for the military tribuneship (cadetship), and at least ten for a civil magistracy, the quaestorship in particular. Since that was the general length of obligatory service in the cavalry and the people who aspired to those offices served without exception in the cavalry, one may say that no one could begin a political career till he had completed his military service." The ten years did not have to be spent all in actual service. According to Mommsen, p. 508, "Since the age of forty-six marked, in principle, the limit for obligatory military service, proof of completion of service was not demanded of a man above that age, and consequently anyone who had not completed the ten years, or even who had not served at all, was eligible from then on." Military service ceased to be required by law towards the end of the Republic, though, p. 509, "it was still customary . . . for aspirants to a political career not to shirk military service altogether." For a comparison of this state of things with the situation under the Empire, see § 2549 [9].

2548 [13] The trend sets in under Marius, who recruited his legions in large part from proletarians. Sallust, *Bellum Jugurthinum,* 86, 2-3: "He enrolled his soldiers not according to ancient custom nor from the registered citizens (*ex classibus*) but taking anyone who chose to join him and many men without property or civil status (*capite censos*). He did that, some say, because of a lack of reputable men, according to others from motives of ambition, for he gained in fame and power from that sort of people; and surely to the man who is seeking power the pauper will prove most useful, for the pauper has nothing to lose and so has no worries about property, and everything that promises gain to him seems honourable." That seed was to sprout and yield the Empire as its crop. Stopping at the fact that Marius, as a proletarian leader, opened the army to proletarians and in that was the predecessor of Caesar, one readily gets the impression, which at one time generally prevailed, that the Empire represented the triumph of the Roman masses in their war on the aristocracy. And if, in the same way, one stops at the fact that Augustus stripped

2549. II: *From the accession of Augustus down to the Antonines.*
We are still close to the maximum observable in the previous period,
but a decline is setting in. Government by manipulation has given
way to government by force. It is no longer necessary to bribe the
comitia, for they have been stripped of their power and will soon be
disappearing. Violence in the *comitia* will soon give way to the violence of the praetorians. But under Augustus and Tiberius the praetorians are still under the control of the Emperor; they are tools of
government, not themselves government. Speculators are held in
leash—they can still do a great deal of good and not so very much
harm. We get a period very like the days when they were checked
by the prestige of the Senate and the weight of the rural citizenry.
But just as the old form of government produced a period of prosperity and then a period of decline, so the new form of government
is to show a similar evolution; and just as the earlier period had
revealed first the good points and then the bad points of a government depending primarily on cunning (Class I residues), the new
period is to show first the good points and then the bad points of a
government resting primarily on force (Class II residues).

A-1. Class-circulation and the law:

As regards the legal norms bearing on class-circulation a tendency towards crystallization sets in in this period.[1] We find a no-

the *comitia* of all power and set out to revive ancient customs, one gets the impression that the Empire represented a reaction against popular liberties. But if one
refuses to stop at surfaces and looks a little more deeply into those very complex
developments (§ 2542), it is readily apparent that the showering of rewards on the
proletarians were means, not ends, with the military leaders, and that such means
were used by a democrat, Marius, an aristocrat, Sulla, and by a Caesar and an
Octavius, who were neither democrats nor aristocrats. The military leaders used for
their purposes mercenaries, proletarians, the Senate, the knights—in short anybody
and everybody who could be of any help to them and would consent to be used.
If in so great a flux of changing fact we would fix on something that is at all constant, we have to find it in the conflict between speculators on the one hand and,
on the other, individuals both able and willing to use force. The speculators triumphed in the days when Cicero suppressed the revolt of Catiline. The strong arm
triumphed first in Caesar and then in Augustus.

2549 [1] Mommsen, *Römisches Staatsrecht,* Vol. III-1, p. 459: "The old system,
where all public offices were open to all citizens, was overthrown. The magistracies
and pontificates were completely closed to individuals not belonging to one of the
two nobilities [The *nobilitas,* which was hereditary, and the equestrian order,
which was personal, in other words, the *ordo senatorius* and the *ordo equester,*
which together constituted the *uterque ordo.*]; and as between the two nobilities,

bility that is showing an inclination to be more and more exclusive—an *ordo senatorius* and an *ordo equester*.[2] These phenomena are correlated interdependently with the intensification in Class II residues. The number of citizens is increasing—sons of freedmen obtain the *ingenuitas,* or status as "well-born." Naturally, as the value of citizenship diminishes it is granted more and more liberally.

A-2. Class-circulation in the fact:

Commerce and industry continue to enjoy under the High Empire the freedom that had been theirs under the Republic and still provide many persons with opportunities for accumulating wealth—in fact they are utilizing some of the energies that were formerly wasted in the political intrigues of the Forum.[3][4] (For footnote 4 see page 1850.) So in our day economic enterprise in Germany

only half the magistracies and pontificates were open to each. . . ." P. 466: "The *nobilitas* [under Augustus] became a hereditary peerage, a senatorial order that was closed by law. . . ." P. 467: "Under the Julian-Claudian dynasty the old *nobilitas* of the Republic lived on in the fact beside the senatorial order. But the old families rapidly died out or else were destroyed. . . . Beginning with the Flavians the republican *nobilitas* has a place in the Roman state that was even more limited than the one the old patriciate had occupied under the late Republic. . . ." P. 487: "Former military tribunes were still playing an important rôle in the class of knights in the last years of the Republic before the reform of Augustus." Waltzing, *Études historiques sur les corporations professionelles chez les Romains,* Vol. II, p. 7: "The Roman bureaucracy was almost entirely a creation of the Empire. Even in the days when the Republic was in control of the Roman world, it had no administration. Its officials or financial agents were few in number. . . . Under the Empire bureaucracy took a rapid and vast development."

2549 [2] Charles Lécrivain in Daremberg-Saglio, *Dictionnaire, s.v. Senatus:* "Augustus permanently and officially founds a senatorial order, a sort of hereditary peerage which has a monopoly of the ancient magistracies and is opened only through award of the laticlave, by *allectio.* The new *nobilitas* acquires a special title probably toward the middle of the first century, and officially at any rate in the period of Marcus Aurelius and Verus. It is the title *clarissimus* . . . that is applied to men, women, and children. This nobility comprises Senators and their wives and agnatic relatives down to three degrees."

2549 [3] Waltzing, *Op. cit.,* Vol. II, pp. 255-58: "For a long time [between the first and the third centuries] the gilds *(collegia)* were formed exclusively on private initiative, even gilds of public officials. The state came to interfere gradually, first to encourage, then itself to establish corporations. [Much the same thing is observable in our civilized societies in the nineteenth century and the early years of the twentieth.] . . . Two periods are to be distinguished: a period of freedom lasting about two centuries, another period of servitude that begins in the course of the third. [Ascending and descending arcs in a wave-movement, such as are observable

is utilizing a small part at least of the energies that other countries are wasting on parliamentary intrigues. Class-circulation *de facto* is still fairly active.[5]

B-1. *Ethnic character of the* élite:

The invasion of foreign elements, which had set in as early as the end of the Republic, and affected the *élite* as well as the citizenry, increases in intensity and further and further impoverishes, in respect of ancient Roman or even Italic stock (§ 2546[1]), a people that still continues to call itself Roman, and its leaders.[6] These for-

in our time.] . . . For two or three centuries the state used no constraint: the gild was primarily a private institution, organizing in virtually complete freedom. . . . In a word, the distinctive trait of the period is a service that is freely accepted, the absence of any sort of force."

2549 [4] Marquardt, *Das Privatleben der Römer,* pp. 171-72: "Senators were forbidden to engage in commerce under ancient law and money-lending was in ill repute, but Cato the Elder had interests in shipping and anyone who had money lent it at interest. By this time earnings even of the basest sorts had ceased to involve loss of esteem. However, they were managed through commission agents (farmers), freedmen, or slaves, and thanks to those intermediaries, the capital of the rich was finding profitable outlets hitherto unknown. That may be one among other reasons . . . why industrial and commercial activity was concentrated almost wholly in the hands of slaves and freedmen under the Empire. . . . Greeks and Orientals had a very special aptitude for business activities. The 'fortune of a freedman,' the *patrimonium libertini* (Seneca, *Epistulae,* XXVII, 5), became proverbial" (§ 2597[2]).

2549 [5] Duruy, *Histoire des Romains,* Vol. V, pp. 329, 636-37 (Mahaffy, Vol. V, pp. 317, 602-03): "In the social hierarchy many free-born inhabitants are going down, many slaves are rising, and they meet half-way between servitude and freedom: decline for the ones, progress for the others. . . . Inscriptions, signs over shops, sometimes formless débris, bear witness to the transformations of the farming society of Cato the Elder into the industrial society of the Empire. [Duruy is forgetting the knights and *negotiatores,* who were already flourishing towards the end of the Republic.] It was nothing less than an economic and therefore a social revolution [Not a revolution—just a gradual evolution.] and it occasioned profound modifications in civil law. The same revolution was going on in the provinces. The Saint-Germain Museum harbours a multitude of funerary monuments of artisans, which excavations in Gaul alone have so far yielded. Those relics attest two things: the fact that mere working-men were able to afford costly tombs, and the pride of those representatives of free labour." Dio Cassius, *Historia Romana,* LII, 37, 8, imagines Maecenas as saying to Augustus: "Pay honour to craftsmen and those who do useful work."

2549 [6] Friedländer, *Sittengeschichte Roms,* Vol. I, pp. 77-79, 89, 91 (English, Vol. I, pp. 34-36, 43, 45): "Down to the time of Vitellius the freedmen had more or less of a monopoly of the offices at court, and since the time of Caligula that monopoly had transferred almost all power into their hands. Vitellius was the first to bestow some of those perquisites on knights. . . . The corps of servants at the Imperial

eigners are bringing in Class II residues in great abundance. A little tree is sprouting. Some day it will bear fruit in an incursion of Oriental religions, in the growth of Mithraism, and in the triumph of Christianity.

B-2. Proportions of Class I and Class II residues:

There is no great change in the ways in which slaves win their freedom. The selection of individuals rich in Class I residues continues, therefore, but it is now being made in an environment strong in Class II residues. If one picks the tallest individuals in a population of dwarfs, one gets men of smaller stature than would be the case if the selection were made from a population of normal people, and very much smaller than if it were made from a race of giants. So with the Roman *élite*. It is attained during this period by individuals who are skilful in the arts of the speculator and through the Emperor's favour.[7] That tends to expand its stock of Class I residues. But ethnic origins are contributing many Class II residues. On the whole, therefore, there is at first little change in relative proportions—there is a certain parity between present and past. Then gradually Class II residues gain the upper hand. The govern-

palace, as well as in the great mansions in Rome, were almost exclusively recruited during that period in the Eastern countries—Greece, Syria, Asia Minor, Egypt. While the Emperors entrusted their personal protection to body-guards made up of men of the North and West, they preferred Greeks and Orientals for their personal service and for the management of their affairs. Continually appearing, in consequence, at the summits of power were individuals hailing from the stocks that Roman pride had most sincerely despised. The reason was, as one of their race, Herodian, *Historiae,* III, 8, 11, saw fit to proclaim, that they were cleverer. . . . The wealth that flowed into the hands of freedmen as a result of their privileged positions was one of the main sources of their power. Certainly, at that time, when the opulence of the freedmen had passed into proverb, few private individuals could rival, as regards power and wealth, the servants of the Imperial house as a class. . . . Quite aside from what lucrative posts brought in, the freedmen in the provinces as well as in Rome, in the fiscal departments as well as in the private service of the Emperors, had a thousand opportunities to swell their fortunes by taking shrewd advantage of circumstances without resorting to measures that could be bluntly called plunder or extortion. . . . Owning such enormous wealth, the freedmen of the Imperial house eclipsed all the grandees of Rome in display and magnificence."

2549 [7] Mommsen, *Römisches Staatsrecht,* Vol. III-1, p. 504: "In order to participate in the profitable service of the legionaries under the Empire the holder of the equestrian horse had to surrender it. That often took place under the form of an immediate award of the legionary centurionate to individuals who resigned from the privileged class in order to obtain it."

ing class becomes a class of government office-holders with all the narrow-mindedness peculiar to people of that type.[8]

B-3. Use of force:

The gap between civil and military functions widens, though they are not as yet distinct.[9][10] The military class rules through the Emperor. It represents a brute force—it is not an *élite*. The *élite* is increasingly civilian. It has neither the will nor the brains to use force, nor the force to use.

2550. III: *From the Antonines to Gallienus.* The great predomi-

2549 [8] Mommsen, *Ibid.,* Vol. III-1, p. 511 (continuing the quotation in § 2548 [2]): "Under the principate, the legal status of the publicans remained on the whole the same, but their practical situation underwent a complete change. The monarchical reorganization of the state made an office-holding class out of the leaders of the order of knights, and its financial reorganization enabled the state, in principle, to dispense with intermediaries in collecting revenues as well as in making disbursements, and cut the ground from under the large-scale speculation that the equestrians had practised under the Republic."

2549 [9][10] Mommsen, *Ibid.,* Vol. III-1, p. 553: "The jealous exclusion of the senatorial order from military service that is characteristic of the Empire under the Severuses, and after, is something foreign to the system of Augustus." *Ibid., loc. cit.,* pp. 542, 560-62: "Augustus very probably stripped the *contubernales* (cadets), 'companions' [*Cf.* medieval *comes,* count.], who were still in evidence under the late Republic, of such military status as they still had. . . . We have shown that, as regards the requirement of military service in the theory of eligibility for service as a magistrate, service as a 'cadet' (*contubernales*) held on as late as Caesar's time. But it must have lost more and more of its military character, not only because the service of a knight who never entered the ranks could hardly be taken seriously, but because the 'cohort of friends' (*cohors amicorum*) was more and more largely made up of individuals who were not even nominally soldiers. . . . For a long time under the principate, service as an army officer was the only road leading to equestrian office . . . but in course of time a civil road was opened alongside the military. There is no proof of any such thing in the first century, but after Hadrian's time, administrative service from the bottom of the ladder up may lead to the higher offices without military service. . . . The objections that were still made under Antoninus Pius to the appointments of scribes and lawyers gradually die away. The day when a preliminary course in military training was required of office-holders in the bureaucracy was no more." *Ibid.,* Vol. I, p. 513: "The military tribunate had effectively lost its military importance under the Empire, and . . . if it is not a purely nominal title, it designates a bureaucratic function rather than any real command. . . . The language used in framing the *Lex Iulia Municipalis* . . . shows that residence in the provinces with a governor fulfilled the requirements of service. . . . The strict association of the political career with military service as an officer is more apparent than real under the Empire. Military service and the exercise of command were much more essential elements in the political career under the Republic, even under the late Republic, than under the Empire." Marquardt, *Römische Staatsverwaltung: Militärwesen,* pp. 356-57: "The military

nance of Class II residues is showing its effects more and more positively. The political, military, financial, and intellectual decline of
Rome is becoming more marked, economic and social institutions
more and more rigid. The Barbarians are invading the Empire.

A-1. Class-circulation as law:

The crystallization of society increases to totality. Alexander Severus closes the corporations of crafts and trades. The decurionate
becomes an onerous obligation (§ 2607 [2]). Roman society is getting
to be a society of castes.[1]

tribunate [under the Empire] was a sort of honorary office that carried equestrian
rank with it. The Emperors very understandably conferred that dignity on persons
who had no intention of devoting themselves to a military career. They contented
themselves with six months of service—the *tribunatus semestris*—and then returned
to private life with the title they had earned in that manner." [So Brissaud, whose
French version Pareto had before him. Marquardt's German: *"Diese Standes-
bezeichnung wurde die Veranlassung, dass die Kaiser den Tribunat auch an Per-
sonen verliehen, welche gar nicht beabsichtigten, sich dem Militärstande zu wid-
men, sondern nach einer halbjährigen Dienstzeit (tribunatus semestris) sich im
Genusse des erworbenen Titels in den Privatstand zurückzogen."*—A. L.]

2550 [1] From some of them, such as the gild of the decurions and the corporations,
withdrawals are prohibited, since they carry very heavy burdens in the state. The
decurions enjoy judiciary privileges and honours, but towards the end of the Empire
they shun the Curia so far as they can. The movement begins early, with the crystallization of society. Ulpian, *Digesta*, L, 2, 1, and Paulus, *Ibid.*, L, 2, 7, § 2 (*Corpus
iuris civilis*, Vol. I, p. 948; Scott, Vol. XI, pp. 214, 217): "When decurions are found
to have left their seats in the cities to which they belong and moved elsewhere, governors of provinces shall see to it that they are sent home to attend to their proper
duties." "A man who is not a decurion cannot function as a *duumvir* or in other
offices [of that class], for plebeians are not allowed to exercise the prerogatives of
decurions." Waltzing, *Études sur les corporations professionelles chez les Romains*,
Vol. II, p. 7: "If the Emperors broke with the traditions of the Republic, they did
so because they were obliged to. Administration depends on political constitution.
[Relations of interdependence represented as relations of cause and effect.] Now
the revolution that was present in germ in the reforms of Augustus, though it took
three centuries to reach its full development, or rather to free itself of its semi-
republican semblances, may be summarized in two words: All powers are concentrated in the hands of the Emperor." P. 260: "The absence of economic freedom
in Rome was a consequence of the absence of political freedom. Despotism and
overcentralization killed freedom of labour." It by no means follows that absence
of economic freedom results from absence of political freedom, as witness the civilized countries of our day, where political freedom is increasing, while economic
liberty is on the decrease (§ 2553 [1]). Our demagogic plutocracy has learned how to
turn political "freedom," and for that matter anarchy, into profits. Many writers
of our time are inclined to lay the responsibility for the decline of the Roman
Empire on imperial "despotism," for that distracts attention from a similar decline
to which our demagogico-plutocratic system may easily lead. The closed corporations

A-2. Class-circulation in the fact:

De facto circulation becomes less and less extensive. Closure of the corporations and the growth of poverty throughout the Empire are drying up the sources of energy that produce new elements for the *élite,* so that it is now taking in only a few speculators and a few favourites of Emperors. The division into castes is even more a matter of fact than of law.

B-1. Ethnic character of the élite:

The *élite* is by this time made up in great majority of foreign elements. The Emperors themselves are foreigners.

and the state monopolies of the Roman Empire were an evil! The obligatory unionizing that is being forced upon labour nowadays, and the state monopolies that are becoming more and more numerous, are a blessing! The difference lies in Imperial "despotism"! The scapegoat has been found!

Waltzing, p. 17, refutes his own theory that the system was forced on the Empire by Imperial despotism: "Are we to say that service in these gilds (*collegia*) was a labour forced by law, required much as taxes are required? No! The system developed gradually. [Rome was moving along the downward segment of one of the waves we describe in § 2553.] In the early centuries municipal dignities were not compulsory either: they were sought because the honours that went with them made up for the trouble and money they cost (§ 2607 [3]). In the case of the gilds too, advantages at first overbalanced burdens, and their members willingly accepted service for the state or for their cities either as groups or as individuals, and they consented to fulfil special functions that the state could have exacted of all taxpayers." If they "accepted" that order of things, if they gave it their "assent," it cannot be said that it was forced upon them by Imperial "despotism." In our day too citizens "accept," in fact seek, ties that the demagogic plutocracy uses to its own advantage. What Waltzing says, p. 261, of the Empire during its decline may be repeated word for word of the situation towards which our civilized countries are at present headed: "Gradually that powerfully organized administration which had its agents everywhere [Compare that with the enormous growth of the number of office-holders in our modern governments.] and had its finger in everything [However, it never tried to tell citizens what they should eat and drink. Prohibitionism is an altogether modern malady.] covered the whole Empire. The whole population became subject to officials who had no very serious responsibilities. Interfering in everything itself, the Imperial bureaucracy began by killing the little private initiative that the social state of the Romans still made possible, for where the public power does everything the citizen does nothing and washes his hands of everything. . . . Then it annihilated all freedom, because persons and property were at its mercy. [Just as they are at the mercy of present-day parliamentary majorities manipulated by demagogic plutocrats.], and it facilitated that terrific financial depression which has remained famous." And which may be outstripped by the depression in store for our present-day societies. But Waltzing is in error in one respect. It was not imperial bureaucracy that deprived the citizens of liberty; it was because liberty had disappeared that such a bureaucracy could go on existing. Tiberius had an inkling of what was in the offing, when, if we are to believe

B-2. Proportions of Class I and Class II residues:

As the supply of speculators and other similar elements for replenishing the *élite* gives out, the stock of Class I residues in the *élite* diminishes, while Class II residues increase inordinately, the new elements being for the most part superstitious Orientals and Barbarians.

B-3. Use of force:

The severance of the civilian *élite* from military activities is absolute. By this time the *élite* is a herd of weaklings, fit subjects for conquest by the Barbarians.[2]

Tacitus, *Annales,* III, 65, he "made it his habit to exclaim in Greek as he left the Curia: 'O what men! How ready for slavery!'" Liberty dies on the day when citizens accept chains or ask for them, not when what they have asked for is thrust upon them or when at last they suffer its consequences. Among the forces that play upon the human being there is one that impels him to preserve his freedom of action, and then many others that impel him to shackle himself with ties for one reason or another—considerations of interest, asceticism, desire for uniformity in laws, customs, and so on. Nations enjoy more or less freedom according to the greater or lesser intensity of such forces. If ascetics and jurists have been and still remain among the greatest destroyers of freedom, that is because citizens allow themselves to be led astray by a hankering to force a uniform type of life upon everybody, at the cost of any amount of physical and moral pain. They do not know, or at least refuse to see, that the oppressors of today are the oppressed of tomorrow.

2550 [2] Striking the similarities between the social situation in the Roman Empire at this time and the situation in China at the time of the Tatar conquest. But the Tatars were assimilated by the people to a far greater extent than the Barbarians who invaded the Roman Empire. They adopted Chinese institutions instead of destroying them and putting an end to the senile ossification of the nation. That is why China continued to be a pacific country, and it in part explains the present lot of China, which is so different from that of Japan. Europeans of our time who go about dreaming of "peace through law" and imagining a social condition in which "civilization, justice, and law" will make nations secure against oppression by other nations, without their being called upon to defend their independence by force of arms, may find in the histories of the decline of the Roman Empire, and especially of the Eastern Empire and China, not a few indications of the real character of the situation towards which they are trying to lead their countries. The Chinese, like our pacifists, thought a nation should be proud rather of its civilization than of its military prowess. So their legendary history tells of nations that were submissive to China not by constraint of arms but out of respect for the virtues of the Chinese government. Moyriac de Mailla, *Histoire générale de la Chine,* Vol. I, pp. 49, 221, 274, 316: "In the fifth year of the reign of Yao, Yuei-chang-chi, ruler of a country in the south of China, solely at the reputation of the Emperor and fascinated by the great things he heard said of him, deemed it a glory to come and offer submission to him and recognize him as his sovereign. . . . In the sixth year of the reign of Cao-Tsong, six foreign kingdoms of a language unknown to China sent ambassadors, each

2551. All these traits grow more and more accentuated down to the fall of the Western Empire.[1] At that time the Barbarians shatter a crystallized Roman society. That is their chief contribution to the new order of things. Even more superstitious than the peoples they are conquering, they add a stock of Class II residues that is already overwhelming and so contribute to the ruin of civilization. In their ignorance they smash the mechanism of Imperial institutions, which for that matter they are eager enough to preserve but are incompetent to manage, so sowing the seed of a new civilization. In fact, as time goes on, points are here and there discernible where Class I

with an interpreter, to pay homage to Cao-Tsong and submit to his rule." Legend would also have it, p. 105, that there were bandits who surrendered in deference to ungarnished virtue. A certain Yeou-miao rose in revolt against the Emperor, who sent Yu against him with an army: "Yu set out at the head of his troops, and thinking to avoid bloodshed by avoiding combat, went no farther than to besiege Yeou-miao in his government. More than a month passed without any signs of Yeou-miao or of any disposition on the part of the rebels to surrender, and that was a source of great pain to Yu, noticing which, Pe-y, who was attending Yu on this expedition, addressed him as follows: 'Virtue alone can move Heaven, for there is no place however distant that it reacheth not!' [Our humanitarians today use identical language except that they mention "law," "justice," or "democracy" instead of "Heaven."] Touched by the nobility of the words, and to show Pe-y the impression they had made upon him, Yu straightway ordered his troops to withdraw and encamped them in a place at some distance from Yeou-miao. [That is what our humanitarians do in cases of industrial strikes today, but reality usually treats them less kindly than the legend treated Yu.] In seventy days' time Yeou-miao and the other rebels came and surrendered." In times more historical—in the year 731 of our era—King Tsan-pu sent an embassy to the Emperor Hiuen-Tsong to ask for the sacred books of China. *Ibid.,* Vol. VI, p. 220: "Yu-hiou-liei, custodian of the books, observed in reply on that occasion that though the Prince of Tong-ping was a close blood relative of the Hans, they had refused him the histories that he asked for. With all the more reason, therefore, should they refuse them to the Prince of Tou-san, who was an enemy of China; for to do so would be to supply him with the means of learning the art of good government and put weapons into his hand against the Empire. Halted by that objection, Hiuen-Tsong brought the matter before his Council, which advised him to give the books to the king, Tsan-pu, that he might profit by the words of wisdom which they contained, and opined that not only did nothing stand in the way of giving the books, but that it was the thing to do, to the end that that prince might imbibe from them the great principles of uprightness, good faith, and virtue, which it is one's duty to impart to everybody. And the Emperor followed the advice of his Council." This controversy as to the capacities of books of ethics to guarantee prestige and power to a nation is worthy of our "intellectuals," who merely replace the books of the Chinese with the rules of their "international law," or others such.

2551 [1] Waltzing, *Op. cit.,* Vol. II, pp. 263, 303, 318: "The upward thrust that meant renewal and maintenance of the middle and upper classes had spent it-

residues and commercial activities increase, the ones stimulating the others back and forth (§ 2609). In just such ways Athens, Rome, and other ancient Greek and Italian cities had originated in their time. Different circumstances lead to differences in forms of development but, underneath, substances are the same. In districts such as Provence or Italy, where commerce, the crafts, industry, give speculators opportunities to accumulate wealth and rise to the *élite,* bringing with them a supply of Class I residues that are so lamentably deficient, political, military, financial, and intellectual prosperity returns—we have reached the age of the Communes.

2552. The general movement in all this has been in the form of an undulating curve, of which we have already seen many examples, and we might at this point repeat all that we have said in §§ 2330-39.[1] As usual we have to consider theories, or derivations, *c* (§ 2205), and the facts corresponding, *a, b, d.* Suppose, for purposes of convenience, we call the sum of such facts *s.* We have already examined (§§ 2203 f.) the general case of interdependence between the elements *a, b, c, d* . . . and the cycles observable in them. Now we come to the particular case of their fluctuations in time and to the relations of interdependence that obtain between the fluctuations.

self. . . . Soon [after Constantine] men will everywhere be bound to the status in society they occupy with their property and their families. The curials, we may guess, were the first to become subject to that law, but gradually it was extended to all callings. [So in our day, the start has been made by exploiting the wealthy and the well-to-do. Other classes will be brought under exploitation as time goes on.] A man was now a curial, a member of a gild, an office clerk, a private in a cohort, a tiller of a field, by birth. He was obliged to succeed to the functions his father had filled. Almost everybody in the Empire was subject by birth to a specified status: *obnoxii condicioni, condicionales originarii.* [That was the law but not the fact. Imperial favouritism made a certain amount of circulation possible.] . . . Imperial favours could not have been of rare occurrence, as proved by the numerous edicts in which the Emperors forbade applications for such rescripts [which granted exemption from compliance with the law]. They were obtained from the Emperor through 'influence' [Today through the influence of politicians.], the Emperor yielding to the urging of individuals of high place, or allowing himself to be deceived by the intrigues of the gild members or their patrons."

2552 [1] After trying to account for the development of extravagance in Rome by reflections on morals (§ 2585 [3]), Tacitus voices a doubt which brings him very close to realities, *Annales,* III, 55: "*Nisi forte rebus cunctis inest quidam velut orbis, ut quemadmodum temporum vices ita morum vertantur. Nec omnia apud priores meliora.*" ("Unless perchance it be that all things move in cycles, so that manners change like the seasons. Not all things were better among our predecessors!")

Study of successive states in the economic and social order leads to a consideration of the successive undulations in the categories b (interests) and d (circulation), to which, if we so desire, we may add undulations in sentiments, a, which for that matter, as we know, assume proportions at all considerable only over fairly extensive periods of time. With that qualification we may say that we are considering undulations in the complex s. Conceptions of the states of s and of the theories, c, corresponding to them appear more or less vaguely in the terms "free trade" or "protectionism," "individualism" or "collectivism" (*statismo*), as used in ordinary language. The first two terms have more or less exact meanings and may be used after a fashion in a scientific reasoning. The latter two are altogether indefinite, like the terms "religion," "morality," and so on, and cannot be used unless their vagueness is at least to some extent remedied.

In the first place theories have to be distinguished from facts. If a person assumes that all conduct is logical and, inventing his own history, imagines that theories and derivations determine human conduct, he may, with no great harm, keep theories and facts mixed and dispense with distinguishing the theories, c, of "individualism" and "collectivism" (*statismo*) from the facts, a, b, d, to which they correspond. Not so the person who appreciates the importance of the part played in social phenomena by non-logical conduct. He cannot, if he would reason with any experimental exactness at all, confuse c with the sum of a, b, d (which we also designate by s).

So we distinguish c from s. But that is not enough. Roughly speaking, we can tell whether a theory, c, is "individualistic" or "collectivistic" (*statista*), just as we can tell whether a given theory stands closer to Nominalism or to Realism. But it is much more difficult to specify to just what facts, s, the facts designated as "individualism" or "collectivism" (*statismo*) correspond. To achieve precision in such terms is as desperate an enterprise as to try to get definitions of the terms "religion," "morality," "law," and so on. If we are to classify the states s it is better therefore to follow some other method. We can get a certain amount of definiteness by considering the strength of the ties that regulate the conduct of the individual. If ties are weak, we get something more or less like the state described as "individualism." If ties are strong we approximate the condition described as "collectivism" (*statismo*).

In the second place economic ties, which belong to b (interests), have to be distinguished from ties of class-circulation, d. Ties of both those types may be weak, as was the case towards the end of the Roman Republic and in the early years of the Empire; or they may be strong, as they were when the Empire turned definitely towards decline. Ties of the first type may be weak and ties of the second strong, as was the case in the days following the Barbarian invasions. Finally, ties of the first type may be strong and ties of the second exceedingly weak, as is more or less the case with our present-day societies. Proceeding as we did in § 2339, we get an intrinsic and an extrinsic aspect both for undulations in the derivations, c, and for undulations in the social facts, s. Working from the first standpoint, we keep c and s distinct and consider first for c and then for s an ascending period as influencing a subsequent descending period, then an influence of the latter upon a following ascending period, and so on. Working from the second standpoint we take c and s together and consider the influence of the undulations in one of the two categories upon undulations in the other.

We have, therefore, to consider the following aspects:

> I. Intrinsic aspect:
>> I-α. Derivations, c
>> I-β. Sum of the social facts, s
>
> II. Extrinsic aspect:
>> II-α. Influence of c upon s
>> II-β. Influence of s upon c
>> II-γ. Influence of the various elements in c
>> II-δ. Influence of the various elements in s

We need give no special attention to this last problem here, since it is a part of our general investigation of the forms of society. Let us look at the others.

2553. I-α: *Intrinsic aspect of derivations.* In the social "sciences" almost all authors of theories have hitherto been primarily inspired by faith in some ideal; so they have considered only such facts as seemed to accord with that ideal, disregarding contrary facts almost entirely. Even when such theories ape experimental forms, they tend to be metaphysical in character. The derivations of "individualism" and "collectivism" may be put on a par with Nominalism and Realism; and, though the analogies are not so striking, even the derivations of "free trade" and "protectionism" are not so very different from metaphysical theories. In this respect, therefore, the case that we are now studying is very like the case we analyzed in §§ 2340 f. (alternations of "faith" and "reason"). But between the two there is also a considerable difference, in that in the present case the dissonance between theory and fact has little or no influence; and hence there is no temptation to combine successive periods, as was the case in § 2340. That comes about because, though in matters pertaining to the natural sciences it is difficult, in fact almost impossible, to side-step conflicts between derivations and experimental realities, that is as easy as can be in matters pertaining to the social "sciences." In these latter, theories are judged by their accord with sentiments and interests rather than by their accord with experimental realities. We may therefore conclude that, in the present case, the intrinsic aspect of c is of little importance.

I-β: *Intrinsic aspect of the sum of the social facts.* Here, on the other hand, the intrinsic aspect is of great importance. A period of "individualism" (when ties are weak) paves the way for a period of "collectivism" (when ties are strong), and *vice versa*. In the first stage private initiative assembles the materials that the rigidified institutions of the state will utilize in the second; and in this latter condition the increasing damage resulting from the crystallization of society paves the way for decadence (§§ 2607 f.), which only a revival of flexibility and freedom of private enterprise can change into progress (§ 2551). Experience shows that undulations may be of different magnitudes, different durations; but it does not show civilized countries where such oscillations do not occur at all. For the time being at least, we must consider it hardly probable that social states free from fluctuations can exist. A society in which individuals rich in Class I residues move about as they please gives an impression of disorganization. What is more, a certain amount of wealth is undoubtedly wasted in sterile enterprise, so that when crystallization sets in, society seems not only better organized, but also more prosperous. The stiffening in Roman society under the Low

Empire was not only forced by the government; it was desired by the population itself, which saw in it an amelioration in living-conditions. To bind the husbandman irrevocably to the soil, the craftsman to his trade, the decurion to his bench, not only helped the government, which was so enabled to get a better-organized society and one more advantageous to itself, but also pleased the lawyers and the "intellectuals," who could only admire such attractive symmetry. And it was desired and demanded by the landowners, who could keep a hold on their farm labour; by the corporations, which could be sure of the services of such workers as were shrewder and abler and could otherwise have taken the wealth they created to other places; and by people in towns who were exploiting their decurions.

The situation can be better grasped if we look at certain aspects of our own times that are to some extent similar. The prosperity of our modern countries is due to the freedom—be it only a limited freedom—of economic and social activity that was enjoyed by the various elements in our populations during a portion of the nineteenth century. Now crystallization is setting in, precisely as happened in the case of Rome. It is desired by the public and in many cases seems to increase prosperity.[1] To be sure, we are still far dis-

2553 [1] As we have frequently pointed out, the present helps to understand the past, and *vice versa*. For that reason the current example of Switzerland is interesting. The remarkable thing about that federalized country is the way it has succeeded in making three races elsewhere hostile, the German, the French, and the Italian, live together in perfect peace and concord. That has been due not only to the morals of the people, which are the soundest in Europe, but primarily to the independence of the Cantons, which has obviated the friction that arises between different nationalities in other countries, allowing each to live according to its own tastes, without being shocked by the preferences of the others. But for some years past a movement has been in progress, with ever increasing acceleration, towards political and administrative centralization. The liberties of the Cantons and of individuals are being curtailed. The federal government is erecting monopolies and entering business. Judicial, economic, and social institutions are becoming less flexible. This movement is in some ways similar to the movement that is going on in France, England, and Italy, under the auspices of and in favour of the demagogic plutocracy. As yet only its first effects are visible in an increasing prosperity for those countries, since it is drawing on the wealth of social and economic energies that were accumulated during the era of freedom by the efforts of private individuals. In virtue of those effects, the movement is welcomed gladly and favoured by the majority of people, upon whom meantime it is imposing new ties.

Looking back upon the Roman Empire in the days of its decline, we may have some doubt as to whether the same were the case, and we may wonder whether the

tant from the state in which the working-man is definitely bound to his craft; but labour-unions and passport restrictions upon movements from one country to another are leading in that direction. The United States of America, which has grown up on immigration and owes its present prosperity to immigration, is now trying in many ways to keep immigrants out, and other countries, Australia among them, are doing the same. Labour-unions are tending to keep non-union labour from working, and on the other hand, are far from willing to admit everybody who applies for membership to the unions. Governments and municipalities are every day extending their interference in economic matters, driven to that by the public will and often to the apparent public advantage. In Italy the municipalization of public utilities was so eagerly desired by the public that the government granted it and used the measure as an election "issue." Already other analogies are emerging that may be more strikingly apparent as time goes on.[2] The Imperial authority in the days of the decline gave chase to the curials to force them back to their burdensome offices (§ 2607). The democratic plutocracy ruling in our societies gives chase, if not to the well-to-do, at least to their purses. To escape unbearable burdens, taxpayers are

ties were not imposed by the Emperors governing by force of the legions. Looking about at France, England, or Italy, the doubt is dispelled in part, though not altogether; for one may make the point that our parliaments do not represent public inclinations exactly. In the case of Switzerland no doubt whatever is possible. In Switzerland no change can be made in the federal constitution unless it is approved by the majority of voting citizens and by a majority of the Cantons. It is therefore with full consent of Cantons and citizenry that the old order, which brought so much prosperity, so much peace, such great harmony, to the country, is being demolished and a new order instituted, which, if the movement holds in the same direction in which it is headed—as it still may not—would end in a centralized state governed by a majority, in other words, by the German element, and a governmental system modelled on the pattern of the present German Empire, and in the end, perhaps, creating an irredentist myth, which so far has been altogether stranger to the country.

Such things, which are going on under our very eyes, strengthen us in the conclusion to which we are led by a direct examination of the history of the Roman Empire in decline, namely, that the movement towards rigidified institutions was desired, or at least assented to, by the public at large, rather than imposed from above by the Imperial government.

2553 [2] Remote but not to be overlooked is the analogy between the way in which certain Roman Emperors bought power from the praetorians and legions and the ways in which politicians buy power of the voters in our contemporary demagogic

sending their funds to other countries, and the governments under which they live grow indignant and try to reach them in various ways. And so agreements of mutual aid have been reached—and they may well be called conspiracies between exploiters—between the governments of the democratic plutocracies in France and England; and the French Government has tried, though in vain, to enlist the aid of the Swiss Government in running down such tax-evaders. There is a tendency in our societies to have taxes voted by the great majority that does not pay them, and to lay the burden on a small minority. As regards the exploiters there is, to be sure, a great difference between our present condition and the situation under the Roman Empire, where the Imperial authority fixed the tax to be paid by the well-to-do. But the difference is much smaller as regards the victims, for after all it matters little to them whether their money goes to fatten the henchmen of an Emperor or the henchmen of a demagogic plutocrat. In point of fact, the legions of an Alexander Severus, who was so liberal in paying his soldiers, cost much less money than it costs to buy votes for the party of a Lloyd George. Moreover the legions at least defended the country, whereas these "Liberals" defend nothing but their present comforts and pleasures.[3] In a word, we are very apparently moving along a

plutocracy. In our day, of course, such operations are at least draped with a veil. In Rome all reticences were brutally brushed aside, as when, on the assassination of Pertinax, the praetorians put the Empire up at auction. Dio Cassius, *Historia Romana,* LXXIV, 3: "Then happened a shameful thing, disgraceful to Rome. The city was put up at auction, along with the whole Empire, as in a market in a public square." The highest bidder on the occasion was one Didius Julianus, who, Dio says, *loc. cit.,* 2, "was always busy with some new thing." A speculator, in other words. (Cary, Vol. IX, p. 143: Julianus "was always eager for revolution": νεωτέρων τε ἀεὶ πραγμάτων ἐπιθυμῶν.)

2553 [3] Liberal spending was characteristic of the whole Lloyd George administration. Luzzatti, *Corriere della sera,* Sept. 3, 1915: ". . . When Lloyd George was Chancellor of the Exchequer he made no economies. He taxed readily, but at the same time inordinately expanded administration and the civil service. It was he who ruled that of the £400 received as salary by members of the House of Commons £100 should be exempted from the income-tax, a measure that was defeated in Italy. Then expenditures for ministers were also increased considerably: instead of one, two ministerial posts were created at salaries of £5,000. . . . Curious cases are mentioned, things somewhat similar to the expenditures made for equalizing land-taxes in Italy. The commission which is estimating incomes from property for the purpose of taxing incomes derived not from labour or capital but from favouring circumstance has so far cost £676,000, and it has collected an amount of

curve such as Roman society traversed in its day after the founding of the Empire and showing first a period of prosperity and then, as it was prolonged, a period of decline. History does not repeat itself. Unless one chooses to believe in some "yellow peril" there is little likelihood that the next period of prosperity that is to come will originate in another Barbarian invasion. There would be more plausibility in the guess that it will come from some internal revolution which will transfer power to individuals who are strong in Class II residues and are able and willing to use force. But predictions as to such remote and uncertain contingencies belong rather to the realm of fancy than to experimental science.

II-α: *Extrinsic aspect: Influence of c (derivations) on s (social complex)*. Such influence is not out of the question, but it is usually of scant importance. The more significant thing to notice is that after originating in the social complex, s, c (derivations) reacts upon s and strengthens it. Expressing a state of mind, c intensifies it and invigorates it. Expressing sentiments of integrity (Class V residues) to some extent, c reconciles them with sentiments of sociality (Class IV residues). As disguising interests, c serves to conceal and shelter them from those who do not share them. Dissembling brute facts, c "justifies" them and reconciles them with the prevailing "morality" and, in general, with group-persistences (Class II residues). In addition c satisfies the need human beings feel for "explaining" things (residues I-ε), and so distracts them from experimental investigations that might result in some modification, however slight, in s. As a sum of pleasing fictions, c satisfies the desires, quiets the longings, of people who are eager to forget the misery and the ugliness of the real world and take refuge in the realms of the fanciful and the ideal, so disarming active enemies of existing conditions and

£50,000! [The purposes of such commissions is to give friends an opportunity for making money and to provide some satisfaction for demagogic instincts. From those points of view the commission in question accomplished its purpose to the full.] On June 29 that scandal was brought up before the House of Commons and debated, but to no conclusion. [Because wolf does not eat wolf.] Local governments are imitating the national government. For example—an excellent thing in itself, but not for war-times such as these—whole networks of independent automobile roads are being built, and the sum paid by the state into this budget is almost £1,500,000 a year."

maintaining the social complex, s, intact or without too great change.[4]

II-β: *Extrinsic aspect: Influence of s on c.* Evidently, undulations in derivations, c, that make up the theories of "free trade" or "protectionism," "individualism" or "collectivism," follow undulations in the complex s very closely; and that leads to the conclusion that undulations in c correspond to undulations in s rather as results than as causes. Theories favourable to free trade are developed and come into vogue when interests and class-circulation are favoured by free trade, and so for theories of protection and for theories of "individualism" and "collectivism" (§§ 2208 f.). The fluctuations in s are therefore the main thing, and the importance, after all, of the undulations in c lies almost entirely in the picture they give of the undulations in s.

II-γ: *Extrinsic aspect: Influence of the various elements in c.* The logico-experimental thinking that is done in empiricism, practice, and science has, if not a great, at least some little, influence on the derivations that are used in social connexions, whether by individuals or by communities. Aristotle, the naturalist, gets closer to realities in his utterances on social matters than does Plato, the metaphysicist. Machiavelli had long experience with the reasonings of empirical statesmanship. He comes very very close to things as they are. Bismarck goes not very far wrong for the same reason, and for opposite reasons the humanitarian dreamer known to history as Napoleon III went very far wrong indeed. As regards communities, the economic theories of Adam Smith and Jean Baptiste Say, which more closely coincide with experimental reality than anything that had been written before their day, appeared at a time when prog-

---

2553 [4] Foscolo may have had some such idea in appraising the work of Machiavelli in his *Sepolcri*:

> "Io quando il monumento
> vidi ove posa il corpo di quel grande
> che temprando lo scettro a' regnatori
> gli allor ne sfronda ed alle genti svela
> di che lagrime grondi e di che sangue."

("Then saw I the tomb that holds the body of that great man, who stayed the upraised sceptre of those who rule, stripped it of its laurels and revealed to the peoples with what tears and blood it drips.") The same may be said of other experimental researches of the Machiavellian type.

ress in the natural sciences was rapid and far-reaching; and, conversely, the vagaries of the historical school, with its childish denials of the uniformities (laws) of social science, come on the scene at a time when a State-worshipping mysticism and a morbid patriotism are severing all contacts between the far-advanced natural sciences and a literature that is usurping the name of social science.

2554. What we have done is to sketch, in the case of Rome, the main outlines of the evolution of the complex s as regards sentiments, interests, and class-circulation, disregarding many details that might have obscured our synthetic view of the whole. We had now better consider at least a few of such minor details in order to get a closer and more adequate picture of what actually occurred.

The origins of the Roman Senate are obscure, nor are we required in any event to dwell on the question here. It may be that, as tradition says, Senators were first appointed by the king and at a later date by the consuls. In historical times (about the Roman year 442), Senators were appointed by the censors, who confirmed the status of Senators already enrolled and designated new ones when they took the census. There was little choice, in the fact; for certain magistrates were regularly enrolled as members of the Senate in the census next following the expiration of their terms in office. The numbers of such officials kept increasing during the whole period of the Republic. So long as the Senate continued to play an important part in the government, in other words, down to about the time of Marius and Sulla, the governing class was, more or less roughly speaking, the senatorial class. Down to that time military and civil functions, prominent among which latter the judiciary, went hand in hand; and that fact, along with the fact that public offices were obtained by popular election and that no salaries went with them—in short, the manners and customs of the time—tended to keep the class filled with individuals possessing some military aptitude, some little native intelligence, some experience in public administration, some knowledge of the law, some familiarity with the combinations whereby popular favour is secured and held, and finally, some wealth. The class, therefore, must have had a certain balance in the relative proportions of Class I and Class II residues. It was something very similar to the Areopagus in Athens, or the House of Lords, or the House of Commons, in England at the time of the wars against Napoleon I. Considering, then, that below was a subject class strong in Class II residues, but still with enough combination-instincts to execute the combinations devised by the governing class, one readily understands how a maximum prosperity came to be attained during the period extending from the Second Punic War down to the conquests of Greece and Asia.

2555. Wealth and speculation seem never to have been wanting in Rome from the very dawn of historical times, and they must have served indirectly to provide access to the governing class for at least the descendants of the newly rich. In spite of that they had no direct power until the conquest of Greece and Asia.

2556. In the year 200 B.C. the Roman People rejected a proposal to declare war on the King of Macedonia. Livy, *Ab urbe condita*, XXXI, 6, says that "the citizens were tired of a long and hard-fought war and voted that way of their own accord in a spirit of surfeit with fatigues and dangers. Quintus Bebius, furthermore, as tribune of the people, taking advantage of the time-honoured privilege of calling the Conscript Fathers to account, accused them of evolving one war from another so that the people could never enjoy a moment's peace." Easily to be read between those lines is the eternal conflict between the two classes of people, the *R*'s and the *S*'s, described in § 2235; in other words, between people who live on virtually fixed incomes and people with whom fortune has its ups and downs. Small property-owners in Rome were ruined by wars unless they participated in the "booms" that followed them. People who plundered the conquered provinces and otherwise speculated grew rich. Such the conflict that Livy describes as a conflict between Senate and People (§ 2542). He himself furnishes the proof. When the Third Macedonian War was being worked up in the year 171 B.C., reasons for rejecting it were far more weighty than had been the case thirty years before; yet the People voted for it without opposition, and volunteers were available in plenty for the campaign, "for they saw that those who had participated in the previous Macedonian war, or in the war against Antiochus in Asia, were now wealthy men." [1]

2556 [1] Livy, *Ibid.*, XLII, 32, 8: ". . . *et multi voluntate nomina dabant, quia locupletes videbant qui priore Macedonico bello, aut adversus Antiochum in Asia, stipendia fecerant."*

2557. So the balance in the population of Rome kept gradually shifting. The numbers and the influence of individuals of variable income deriving from plunder and speculation was increasing by leaps and bounds. Such people were at first abetted (in view of a common interest in preserving that order of things) and later on opposed (when the time came for dividing the spoils) by the urban plebs, which shared in such enterprises either directly, or by selling their votes, or otherwise, and by those elements in the rural plebs which were abandoning the plough to find lucrative employment in the army; nor could the increasing multitude of clients have been without influence in the same direction.[1] Meantime that portion of the rural population which lived by tilling the soil was growing smaller and smaller. Not the *latifundia* caused Italy's ruin, but that complex of facts in which the *latifundia* themselves, in part, originated (§ 2355). The Roman wars of conquest had the same effects in those days as, in our day, the expansion of industry and the opening-up of new territories in Asia, Africa, and the Americas. In our modern countries speculators have greatly increased and are still increasing in numbers and power, and they are now supported (in view of a common interest in preserving the present demagogico-plutocratic order), and now sometimes opposed, as in strikes or

2557 [1] Cicero, *Epistulae, Ad Atticum,* IV, 15, mentions an instance in which the competition in vote-buying caused a rise in interest-rates: "Follow me now to the battle-field [*i.e.,* the Forum]. Bribery is going on apace! To give you some idea, I will say that by the middle of July interest on money had doubled from 4 to 8 per cent. 'I can make it at that,' you may be saying, and 'Oh, what a man I am! Oh, what a self-sacrificing citizen!' " (§§ 2256 [2], 2257 [2].) Plutarch, *Sulla,* 5, 2 (Perrin, Vol. IV, p. 335): "On one occasion when he [Sulla] was praetor, he had a quarrel with Caesar and angrily averred that he would use the power of his office against him. Caesar answered smiling: '*Your* office? Well said, for truly, you bought it!' " [No one, so far as I know, has ever pointed out that the famous Roman pasquinade on the simony of Rodrigo Borgia in selling his seat as Cardinal when he became Pope Alexander VI may be a rephrasing of this retort of Caesar to Sulla in Plutarch: "Alexander is selling the keys, the altars, Christ! Well, why not? He bought them!":

"Vendit Alexander claves, altaria, Christum:
emerat ille prius, vendere iure potest."

See Morandi's introduction to Belli, *Sonnetti romaneschi,* Vol. I, p. clxiv.—A. L.] Marius too was accused of buying votes to obtain the praetorship: Plutarch, *Marius,* 5, 2 (Perrin, Vol. IX, p. 473). Appian, *De bellis civilibus,* II, 19: ". . . and the voters appeared in the Forum as a sort of goods for sale on the market." And *cf.* § 2548 [8].

otherwise, by the urban population that participates in their enterprises either directly or else indirectly through political intrigues, and by that portion of the rural population which deserts the farm for the city at the lure of higher wages and pleasanter work. And they are supported also by many elements in the *bourgeoisie* itself— lawyers, accountants, engineers, physicians, and so on—who are munificently paid for their services by the speculators, who make money easily and are as generous towards their henchmen as the padroons of old were to their clients. Meantime lamentation over the deserted farms grows shriller and shriller, and small-property acreage shrinks smaller and smaller. If slavery or serfdom prevailed today, the *latifundia* would again become the rule. It is a most significant fact that far from resisting this tendency, the Socialist populace in Europe is praying for it and in various ways manifesting its hostility to small property and even more so to tenant systems. As regards Italy, Romagna has been the scene not only of strikes, but of armed conflicts, aiming at effecting a change in the existing property system so that there would be nothing but property-owners on the one hand and hired labour on the other, and that system would bear every resemblance to the Roman *latifundia* of old. The speculators who are governing today in modern Rome are doing nothing, just as their predecessors who ruled in the Rome of the dying Republic did nothing, to resist this trend, and in fact they aid and abet it as they aided and abetted it of yore whenever they needed the votes of the masses. What is going on in our time gives a clearer understanding of what went on in ancient Rome, and shows that the *latifundia* were in many cases effects of conditions of which they have been taken as causes, or better yet, that they stood in a relationship of interdependence with those conditions.

2558. Moralists have expatiated at length on the "corruption" that was the "consequence" of the increase of wealth in Rome, repeating with numberless variations a motif that was expanded in his day by Diodorus Siculus.[1] Some picked their quarrel with wealth in gen-

2558 [1] *Bibliotheca historica*, XXXVII, 2, 1 (Booth, Vol. II, p. 558). Diodorus is speaking of the Marsic War: "Prime cause of the war was the fact that the Romans had abandoned the orderly, frugal, continent lives, by which they had so greatly prospered, for a disastrous luxury and a habit of insolent self-assertion." That is the refrain in every age when a people has grown wealthy. Dante harps on it in the *Paradiso*, XV, vv. 97 f., and says Boccaccio, *Decameron*, VI, 10: ". . . for

eral, some just with the wealth born of the "crime" of war and the extortions resulting from war. In general declamations on the virtuous poverty of the past, as contrasted with the debilitating wealth of the present, hide the fact of a change in the relative proportions of individuals living on virtually fixed incomes and rich in group-persistences, and individuals of variable incomes rich in the combination-instincts.

2559. Some have blamed the concentration of wealth (§ 2355), others, the *latifundia* (§ 2557), others, capitalism (§ 1890), others, the wickedness of the Roman "aristocracy" in oppressing and bleeding the virtuous masses, others, slavery, which, they say, was the "disgrace" of those times; still others, defects in the political organization of Rome, which—had it been, according to some, more "democratic"; had it provided, according to others, for a parliament with representation of subject peoples; had it, according to still others, more nearly approximated the perfect organization of the present German Empire—would have assured Roman power a long, a very long, perhaps an eternal, prosperity. Such writings may make as pleasant reading as the historical novels of Dumas; but they go very wide of realities.

2560. So cogent are the facts that they force their way through the very derivations in which such writers would bury them (§ 2356). Says Duruy: "A century of wars, plunder, and corruption [Merely the transformation resulting from new sources of wealth—a segment of our cycle *bd-db* (§ 2321).] had devoured the class of small landowners [Why devoured? Those people had simply changed occupations! From living on virtually fixed incomes they had become speculators, or henchmen of speculators.] to whom Rome had owed her strength and her liberties." [1] Duruy should have said that the prosperity had been due to a favourable balance between that class and the other class in which Class I residues prevailed; and that the

as yet only a few of the refinements of Egypt had come overseas into Tuscany, just as later on they came in great numbers, to the ruin of all Italy."

2560 [1] *Histoire des Romains,* Vol. II, pp. 283-84 (Mahaffy, Vol. II, p. 291). Duruy continues: "There you have the basic fact in this period and the cause of the great overturn that is to follow [All right, provided by "overturn" one means a change in the relative proportions of *S*'s and *R*'s.], for with that class patriotism died, and the orderliness and austerity of the old customs passed away." An ethical derivation hiding a grain of truth—a hint at a predominance of Class I residues.

prosperity failed when the relative proportions of residues became unfavourable. It is interesting that, without our looking very far, as much may be gathered from what Duruy himself says just previously, p. 282 (Mahaffy, p. 291): "Prodigies were still as numerous as ever, still as fantastic; in other words, the people and the soldiers were still as uncouth, as credulous. [Predominance of Class II residues.] Generals still vowed temples—but, like Sempronius Gracchus, adorned them with tablets recounting their exploits, or with paintings depicting their triumphs. They still sacrificed great flocks of victims before battle, but only, as Paulus Aemilius did, to curb the impatience of their soldiers and bide the propitious moment. Gravely they studied the heavens before and during a vote at election-times, but only to have an excuse for dissolving the assembly, for evoking the *obnuntiatio,* if the voting seemed to be going against the Senate."

2561. Then he observes very soundly, p. 293 (Mahaffy, p. 298): "So needs were increasing daily, and daily also, at least for the poor man who faced the perils but had no share in the lasting benefits of conquest, the means of satisfying them were diminishing." So the people whom Duruy calls "the poor," and who really were people living on virtually fixed incomes, were forced to become speculators or henchmen of speculators. The same thing is observable in our own time. The "upstarts and sudden gains" that Dante speaks of had the same effects in Rome that they have had everywhere and in all periods of history.[1] Deloume comes very close to the truth as

2561 [1] Marquardt, *Das Privatleben der Römer,* pp. 382-83: "While the acquisition of new territories was causing this agricultural crisis in Italy, it was giving a new and extraordinary impetus to the money business and speculation. The Romans had always had a fondness for profits of that sort. Judge them odious and disgraceful as they might, they could not help finding them attractive. . . . With all the more reason were such scruples quieted when the provinces were opened to that type of exploitation. The moment a new territory was conquered, Roman speculators would alight upon it in clouds. . . . The nobility made fortunes by governing provinces, the knights by contracting for tax-collections and then collecting them by atrocious extortions. Big and little, they bled the conquered countries white. Speculation was further encouraged by contracts and concessions that were opened by the censors in the name of the state or even by local governments or private individuals. Collections of revenue, construction of temples, roads, bridges, sewers, aqueducts, repairs on public buildings, supplies for public worship and public games, then private enterprises of all sorts—construction of houses, harvestings of crops, settlements of estates, bankruptcy sales and adjustments,

regards the situation that prevailed after the conquest of the Mediterranean basin and shortly before the fall of the Republic.[2] That period bears not a few resemblances to the present time. Guizot's comparison with England, which Deloume adopts, is altogether in accord with the facts, and it is interesting that it carries over to our time. It was the "country squires," the small landowners, who saved the country at the time of the Napoleonic wars. Afterwards their share in running the country progressively declined, while the speculators came into their own. Well known the fact that at the present time [1913] Asquith has many such millionaire speculators in his majority, and they are among those who most loudly applaud the invectives his party hurls at "the rich." Their battle with the Lords corresponds exactly to the struggles that went on in Rome in the last years of the Republic between knights and Senators.

funerals—all such things were awarded on contract and spelled rich profit for the speculator who undertook them."

In that Marquardt falls into the common mistake moralists make in imagining that the hated "speculator" always makes his profit. Such enterprises do, it is true, bring profits and prosperity to the skilful speculator, to the adept at combinations; but they spell loss and ruin for the unskilled speculator, the man who cannot learn to devise and utilize combinations. So a process of selection goes on. Individuals rich in Class I residues, individuals of talent and ingenuity, rise in the social scale. Others are eliminated.

2561 [2] *Les manieurs d'argent à Rome,* pp. 45-46: "Knights, especially, who had some capital and were not halted by aristocratic prejudices, got rich on state enterprise or tax-collecting, which they took on contract. The gold of the vanquished poured in unending streams into the coffers of the publicans and *negotiatores.* Patricians of breeding who stood loyal to the old customs and were becoming fewer and fewer every day, were reduced to the bare income from their lands, and they were everywhere outstripped. Day by day, after heroic resistance and prodigies of skill, they surrendered some new privilege to the *plebs.* [Really, to the "gangs" captained by "speculators."] Their inheritances lost all value, relatively, and the rights that had belonged to birth now went to wealth in the fact of everyday custom as well as in law. So the location of prestige and influence shifted from the patricians to the newly rich, the *homines novi.* The ethics of interest was in danger of being no longer tempered by traditions of family and race. [Change in relative proportions of Class I and Class II residues.] So to the political assemblies in Rome one might have applied what M. Guizot wrote of the English Houses: 'In one of the first Parliaments of the reign of Charles I it was noted with surprise that the House of Commons was three times richer than the House of Lords. Plain gentlemen, freeholders, merchants, men who were exclusively busied with utilizing their lands or their capital to the full, were growing in wealth and in influence, combining more closely from day to day, and bringing the whole people under their sway.' In Rome the revolution was more far-reaching than in England."

2562. The conquest of the Mediterranean basin opened up sources of great profits for the victors—for any of them who had a knack for combinations. By a wise spending of money in Rome, one could get the right to exploit a province and cover one's expenses, with plenty to spare. It was a type of speculation that exactly parallels the protectionist lobbying that goes on today with the purchasing of votes and legislators.[1]

2562 [1] Marcus Aemilius Scaurus would be the type of the Roman speculator. *Mutatis mutandis,* he is the exact counterpart of the speculator of our day. He was Sulla's stepson and seems not to have abused that relationship in amassing his fortune. Asconius, *Enarratio in Scaurianam, Argumentum* (Cicero, *Pro Marco Scauro*), p. 18: "Marcus Scaurus, son of that Marcus Scaurus who had been president of the Senate, was stepson to Sulla. When Sulla triumphed and was showing himself most lavish towards his comrades in victory, Scaurus very laudably asked nothing for himself, nor did he buy any confiscated property at the auctions." So it is with some of our speculators who are honest enough in private matters. When he came to be aedile he behaved like other Roman speculators, and like our own: he sowed in order to reap. "He administered his aedileship with consummate brilliancy, spending a vast fortune he already had and contracting heavy debts." Roman speculators spent their own money, ours spend the money of the taxpayer; but in that they had a predecessor in Pericles: Aristotle, *De Republica Atheniensium,* 27 (Kenyon, p. 51), says that since Pericles was not rich enough to compete in liberality with Cimon (the usual conflict between the upstart and people with ancestral fortunes), he found a way to shower the citizens with gifts which they paid for with their own money. Pliny, *Historia naturalis,* XXXVI, 24 (Bostock-Riley, Vol. VI, pp. 349-51), describes the magnificence of a temporary theatre that Scaurus built while he was aedile. Contrarily to Cicero's account, he seems to think that Scaurus got his start from his relationship to Sulla: "I shall not allow those two Neros to enjoy even that glory, for I can show that their extravagant madness was surpassed by the private enterprises of Marcus Scaurus. I could not say whether the term he served as aedile was not more destructive to Roman morals than anything else ever was [Again the particular fact for the general, the anecdote for the uniformity, the cause-and-effect relation instead of interdependence.], nor whether Sulla did not do more harm through the great power he gave to his stepson than he did through the proscription of so many thousands. During his aedileship Scaurus executed [for a temporary purpose] the greatest building that was ever reared by human hand even as a bid for eternity. It was a theatre." And sowing one reaps: Asconius (*Argumentum cit.*): "As propraetor he obtained the province of Sardinia [There the reaping begins.], a post in which he was thought to have deported himself with too little restraint and very tyrannically. That trait he seems to have imitated from his father, though his industry in other directions was in no sense on the same level." Indicted on that account in Rome, he was defended by Cicero, who knew he was guilty and, while preparing the defence, wrote to Atticus, IV, 15 (Winstedt, L. C. L., pp. 308, 311), that if Scaurus failed of election as consul he would be in a pickle. The trial took place, and Scaurus was acquitted by a large majority [65 votes to 8] (Asconius, *Ibid.,* p. 28). Remembering his past liberalities and perhaps hoping for

2563. The situations, then and now, are alike in many ways—yet there is also a difference, and a very important one, which determined the form of organization the Roman state was to take under the Empire. The henchmen of the Roman speculators were in part civilians and in part soldiers, and the soldiers in the end turned on the speculators. The henchmen of our present-day speculators are nearly all civilians.

2564. Many individuals had no access to the characteristic sources of wealth under the Republic and no aptitude for the combinations required to exploit them; but they were not short in energy and courage—Class II residues. Such people enrolled for longer or shorter periods of time under leaders who were ingenious, daring, and especially fortunate, and made up the armies of Marius, Sulla, Caesar, Antony, Octavius. If one counts only the tillers of the soil, the Roman middle class was decreasing at that time; but the farmers were replaced by professional soldiers, and later on, the Italic races by Greeks and Orientals.

2565. As we have several times indicated, the weak point in speculator rule is in the speculator's lack of courage and his scant aptitude for using force. Speculator governments therefore are usually destroyed by people who do know how to use force, whether they come from the same country or are foreigners. They succumb, that is, now through civil, now through foreign wars. As regards internal revolutions, the final catastrophe is often preceded by attempts at revolt that are successfully suppressed.

2566. Those who think of human conduct as exclusively logical are inclined to judge such abortive attempts as separate incidents and look for the causes and effects of each. Ordinarily the cause is found in the sufferings of the subject class, and since such sufferings are never wanting and differ from time to time only in intensities, the cause is always readily found. If it were possible to establish the theory that attempts at revolution are the more frequent and have greater chances of success in proportion to the amount of suffering,

future ones, the People were all for him. Asconius, *Ibid.*, p. 29: "Cicero made the usual motion to prosecute the accusers of Scaurus, and since many from among the People were pointing to them, Cato, the praetor, yielded to the ignorant mob and the following day opened prosecutions against the plaintiffs on charges of slander." So nowadays do voters pamper our plutocrats, in gratitude for past favours and in hopes of favours to come (§ 2262).

the force of the cause could be estimated by measuring the intensity of the suffering. But things do not stand that way. Experience from most ancient times shows that revolts often take place when conditions among the masses are very good, and it was actually a maxim of government in a day gone by that nations were the less docile in proportion to the ease of their circumstances—a dictum sound up to a certain point, but not beyond.[1][2] There is the opposite theory

2566 [1][2] The pamphlet known as *The Political Testament* of Cardinal de Richelieu contends, I, 4, 5 (p. 179), that "All masters of statecraft are agreed that if peoples were too prosperous, it would be impossible to hold them to the observance of their duties." Comparing the revolt, known as the Jacquerie, of 1358, with the French Revolution of 1789, one cannot believe that the sufferings of the people were greater in the latter case than in the former. That does not prove that general misery was not one of the forces determining revolt. It does show that it was not the sole, nor the most cogent, cause. Another point of difference between the two revolts was in the use of force on the part of the governing class. Force was applied lavishly and in all self-confidence in the Jacquerie, feebly and hesitatingly in the Revolution. And that again does not mean that force alone is enough to suppress a revolt; it does mean that force is one of the most effective means for suppressing one. What would have happened had the ruling class of 1789 fought with the vim of the ruling class of 1358? We cannot say with certainty (§ 139), but we can say that their chances of winning would have been better than they were in view of the supine and cowardly resignation which they actually manifested. All history goes to show that those who put up a good fight may win or lose, but that those who lie down are certain to lose, and ever and anon verified is the proverb: Be a sheep and you will meet a butcher. As regards the Jacquerie, see Luce, *Histoire de la Jacquerie*, p. 141. Luce gives a description of the truly incredible sufferings of the subject class and the unspeakable cruelties of the rulers. Of the battle for Meaux he writes: "If we are to believe Froissart [*Chronique, Œuvres*, Vol. VI, pp. 54-59], from the beginning to the end of the conflict, the one thought of the nobles was to slaughter without running the least danger themselves. Never did soldiers strike to kill with greater desperation and greater contempt of human flesh. One has to read the *Chronicles* oneself to get the full vividness of the picture Froissart draws of that frightful butchery. . . . However, the victory would seem to have been more dearly bought than Froissart indicates, for the attack reached the barricade [of the market-place], and beyond that, and not a few nobles were slain. [Luce gives a list of names.] . . . Furthermore, a goodly number of the footmen from Paris as well as of the burghers of Meaux managed to escape, as is attested by the many pardons that were issued to them later on for their part in the battle for the market-place at Meaux. In any event, after the struggle was over, the nobles were not less blood-thirsty in their vengeance than they had been in the battle itself. The whole town was sacked, and not only private dwellings but the very churches were pillaged. Nothing of any conceivable value was left in them. Many of the inhabitants of Meaux were massacred, and those who were not slain were shut up as prisoners in the citadel. Soulas, the mayor, was hanged, and then the town was set on fire. The burning lasted for two weeks. The royal château was burned and many houses, among them

that a governing class can safe-guard its power only by assuring the welfare of its subject class. That theory too contains an element of truth—no more than that—and those who adopt it are probably led to do so, unconsciously it may be, by their preference for one of the affirmative solutions noted in §§ 1902 f.—by a desire to show that a person who does good is necessarily rewarded, or that that, at least, is to be the rule of the future if it has not been true of the past.[8]

the canonry. All the serfs found in the houses were locked in and they perished in the flames. . . . Such barbarities might, it would seem, have sated the wrath of the nobles. But they were far from appeased. They rode madly about the neighbouring country, killing every serf on whom they could lay hands and burning all their villages. To believe one chronicler, the nobles caused more ruin in the kingdom on that occasion than the English, born enemies of France, could ever have inflicted." This slaughter of the peasantry by the nobles can be matched with the "September massacres" of the nobles by the revolutionaries in the French Revolution. We must, to be sure, refrain from reasoning *post hoc, propter hoc,* but such associations and contrasts in events must not be disregarded, especially since history records them in goodly numbers.

2566 [8] Tocqueville and Taine try to show that the French governing class brought on its own ruin in the Revolution by clinging to its privileges and neglecting its "duties." The thesis contains a modicum of truth, but it is none the less at variance with another thing that is shown by experience: that ruling classes maintain their power by oppressing their subjects. Tocqueville supplies plenty of arguments against his own thesis: *L'Ancien Régime et la Révolution,* p. 33: "One thing surprises at the very outset. The main object of the Revolution was everywhere to abolish remnants of the Middle Ages, but it did not break out in countries where those institutions were best preserved and therefore made their severities and annoyances most conspicuous, but in countries where they were doing least harm. The mediaeval yoke therefore was found least endurable in places where really it was least heavy. Hardly anywhere in Germany at the end of the eighteenth century had serfdom been altogether abolished, and almost everywhere the people were positively bound to the soil, as had been the case in the Middle Ages." Taine correlates good works and rewards very definitely: *L'Ancien Régime,* Bk. I, Chap. IV, sec. 6 (Vol. I, p. 131): "An effect as proper as it is fatal [Ethical derivation.] of the privilege that one exploits for one's own profit instead of using it to the advantage of others! To say 'sire' or 'lord' is to say 'the patron who feeds,' 'the elder who advises and guides.' [Verbal derivation.] On that basis, and in return for that service, one cannot [Who cannot?] give him too much, for no function is more exalted or more difficult to fulfil. But he has to fulfil it, otherwise in the hour of danger he is deserted. [As a matter of plain fact, the armies of Sulla, Marius, Caesar, Octavius, and others too numerous to mention, wanted money and land more than anything else.] Indeed, long before the hour of danger, his people are not really his. If they march, they do so as a mere matter of routine. They are just a mass of individuals, not a disciplined force. [Taine forgets that that very "mass of individuals" can be governed by the person who has a few men at his disposal, for they stand loyal to him because they are well paid with the money he and they can take from the mass of individuals.] Even before the final crash France

2567. As regards the effects of attemped revolts, many people consider every revolt that is defeated and suppressed harmful, or at least useless, to the subject class; and in that they would be right if that fact could be taken apart from other facts and regarded as a logical act, since undeniably it is harmful, or at least not to one's best advantage, to expose oneself to a defeat. But in reality matters stand otherwise. Such unlucky attempts at revolt have to be re-

was a disorganized country, and the disorganization was due to the fact that those who enjoyed privileges had forgotten their status as *public servants.*" If what Taine says were an experimental uniformity, the Jacquerie should have won; for the nobles of that time were far more neglectful of their "duties" towards their subjects than the nobles of pre-Revolutionary days. Luce, *Histoire de la Jacquerie,* pp. 33-39: "Whatever their causes these repeated defeats [at Poitiers, Courtrai, and Crécy] had disastrous consequences for the French nobles. In the first place they stripped them of a prestige that represented a large part of their power—prestige in arms. [A sound remark, according with the experience of all countries at all times.] In the second place, captured in large numbers in the various battles, the lords had been obliged to resort to heavy levies on their vassals to provide the large sums required for their ransoms, and that had exasperated their subjects. [Another experimentally sound remark.] Already disesteemed, they now became objects of hatred. [The force that was holding the vassals to obedience had weakened, the force impelling them to revolt intensified.] The nobility furthermore was not even able to pretend unselfish sacrifice in behalf of the country. Now beginning to live far from their castles in attendance on the king, the knights were acquiring the servile mercenary attitude of courtiers. They were now refusing to serve without pay. . . . By a strange coincidence, the nobles chose a moment for exacting a payment that was out of the ordinary when they least deserved help in view of their military blunders and failures. . . . 'After the battle of Poitiers,' says the second continuator of Nangis, 'affairs in the realm took a turn for the worse. The state fell prey to anarchy, banditry became rife on all hands. The nobles redoubled in their hatred and contempt for the serfs [A fine way to fulfil their duties! In 1789 there was neither hatred nor contempt. It was an era of humanitarianism.], and made short shrift of the interests of the Crown and of those of their vassals. They robbed and oppressed the men in their homage and country-dwellers generally.' . . . Oftentimes, without coming into too intimate relations, gentlemen and brigands went into partnership and divided their booty half and half. . . . 'At that time,' says the chronicler, Guillaume de Nangis, 'those who should have been protecting the people inflicted no less vexatious wrongs upon it than open enemies.'" And those responsible for such rascalities won the war! They saved themselves and destroyed their enemies! Their successors in 1789, who deported themselves humanely, honestly, kind-heartedly, were defeated, overthrown, destroyed. From the standpoint of social utility, probably it is wiser not to stress the contrast; but experimentally it cannot be denied.

Ideas of the sort espoused by Taine are to be noted in large numbers of contemporary writers. Just one example: Missiroli, *Satrapia,* pp. 13-14: "To reassert, even at the cost of sacrifice—especially by sacrifice—the claims of duty and moral freedom [Metaphysical derivation.] is to solve the economic problem to the extent

garded as manifestations of a force that, at first inferior to the forces that stand against it, in the end may triumph over them in the final reckoning. It may well be that the abortive attempt weakens the force it expresses, or at the best has no considerable effect upon it; but it may also enhance its intensity. Which of those two possibilities is actually verified depends upon circumstances. Finally, the attempted revolt may, and in fact very often does, reflect the maximum intensity of the force it manifests. In that case it is idle to expect any increase in the intensity of that force before the final catastrophe occurs and to expect that ineffectual revolts will not go on recurring.

2568. The catastrophe occurs oftentimes not so much because the force expressed in the abortive revolt has increased to the point of overcoming the counter-forces that serve to maintain the social equilibrium, but because, in increasing, it has modified the action of other forces and especially of the military power, which itself comes to overthrow the established order, now by ceasing to resist revolutionary elements, now by joining hands with them, or, still again, by replacing them, stealing their thunder. In such cases the overthrow is due, not directly but indirectly, to the operation of the force manifested in the abortive revolt; but the latter does not, for that reason, cease to be dependent on it.

2569. Even worse than the method of viewing human conduct as strictly logical is the temptation to judge abortive revolts by norms of legality, law, equity, ethics, religion.[1]

that economic goods depreciate in value when they are considered as means and not as ends. [Derivation: a golden age located in the future.] As long as all life is made to unfold within the economic category and the category of personal interest [The *auri sacra fames* rebaptized as "the economic category."], the economic problem will be the main problem and an unsolvable one. [It has been that from the earliest times of which we have any record, and will probably continue to be for some little time to come.] All human beings will want to share in material pleasures and replace one another in the possession of power. [The history of that is what history is.] Human history cannot, fortunately, end in nothing more than an exchange of pocket-books. [History stops at the record of facts.] But who ought [Metaphysical derivation.] to set the first example? Evidently, those who are at the top of the social ladder—the middle classes. I am carried back, despite myself, to the ideas I expressed at the beginning. The *bourgeoisie* has to revise the concept of property and consider property as a responsibility rather than as a right; and it must accept all the sacrifices, all the pains, that go with that new attitude."

2569 [1] Such derivaions we have already analyzed at length in §§ 2147 [18], 2181 f.

2570. As regards legality, it is evidently violated not only by any act of revolution—by any *coup d'état*—but also by any act preparatory to an overturn of the existing order. Argument on that point is therefore altogether idle. Yet that is the point which is most hotly debated both by those who are defending, and by those who are trying to subvert, a given social order. The defenders are trying to take advantage of sentiments of disapproval for any act contrary to legality, and therefore fail to see, or at least pretend not to see, that the legality is the very thing the revolution is trying to change. Assailants of the social order, the better to destroy it, try to take advantage of the forces engendered by that order and therefore make every effort to show, in the face of all evidence, that acts which are undoubtedly acts of revolt are "legal" and that they therefore ought not be and "cannot" be punished by defenders of the order.[1]

2571. As for the principles of law, equity, ethics, and religion, they are appealed to because there is nothing else to appeal to, once one has deserted the logico-experimental field, and because they have the great merit of proving anything one desires to prove. Religious principles, except of course the principles of the now dominant religion of democracy, have lapsed into desuetude. Still vigorous and fresh are the principles of law, equity, and ethics; and they are used to judge not only domestic but international conflicts.

2572. Juridical principles may be more or less exact and therefore yield (provided they are used in conflicts between private citizens in societies in which they are generally accepted and in which they therefore reflect common sentiments) conclusions that more or less accord with reality (§§ 1772 f.). But such provisos fail when one portion of a population rises against another. In that case the accord of the principles with reality also fails in consequence; and the principles can no longer be used unless they are viewed as having an absolute value that oversteps the experimental field. The same is to be said of their application to international conflicts. They may yield

2570 [1] Those derivations turned up on the occasion of the uprisings in Romagna in June, 1914. The speculators and their satellites, gravitating around the sun of legality, spoke of the riots as criminal activities on the part of enemies of the country, or at least on the part of poor misguided individuals inspired by the leaders of the "subversive parties." The subversive parties on the other hand called the riots "a well-justified move on the part of an oppressed proletariat to claim its *rights.*"

conclusions that are not greatly at variance with realities provided they are used between nations that assent to them as expressing common sentiments; but again the proviso fails if such common assent and sentiments are lacking. Ethical principles also are devoid of any definiteness, and those who use them in the cases here in question are merely investigating the bearing of the facts on their own sentiments, not the relationship of fact to fact, not experimental uniformities. But sentimental research is the more easily carried out, and the literary lucubrations it produces are more readily grasped by the masses at large. That is why it is the one more generally resorted to.

2573. The history of the decline of the Roman Republic yields several instances of attempts to overthrow legal institutions either from below or from above. Suppose we consider one of those attempts in some detail, in view of its resemblances to revolutionary, anarchistic, and other such disturbances that are going on in our time.

Famous in history is the conspiracy of Catiline. The description that Sallust gives of it in his *Bellum Catilinae,* is so ridiculously rhetorical as hardly to pass as a cheap melodrama. He begins, I-XIII, by declaiming against greed and the lust for gold. Then he picks a quarrel with ambition and explains how it comes more nearly to being a virtue than greed. Then he sheds a tear over the grave of virtue and waxes wroth at immorality. Finally in sheer goodness of heart he remembers that he is supposed to be telling about Catiline's conspiracy, and after his beautiful prologue states clearly what its causes were, XIV, 1: "Catiline gathered about him as it were for a body-guard, a thing easy to do in a city so great and so corrupt, a conglomeration of all conceivable infamies and crimes." [1]

2573 [1] [Rolfe: "troops of criminals and reprobates."] Sallust goes on, XV, 3-4, to accuse Catiline of killing his own son and suspects that remorse must have hastened his attempt: "And that [the murder of his son], it seems to me, must have been the original cause of his conceiving such a plot; for the guilty soul that is harassed by thought of gods and men alike can find no peace either when awake or in slumber. So did conscience devastate the terrified soul of this murderer. That explains his pale face, his shifting gaze, his walking by fits and starts, for madness was written patently on every lineament of his features." Sallust says nothing of Cicero's Fourth Oration against Catiline and slides over Cato's attacks on Caesar. Appian also, *De bellis civilibus,* II, 2, mentions the charge that Catiline had killed a son. And *cf.* Valerius Maximus, *De dictis factisque*

2574. Fortunately we have other accounts of the conspiracy. The story by Appian (*loc. cit.*), being the soberest of all, would seem to come closest to facts as they were. That Catiline was a bit of a rascal is averred by all authorities in unison, and that seems plausible enough. But it is also apparent that that not very honest man was not an adept at the astute ingenuities that raised men no more honest than he was to power and wealth, while he, on the other hand, had the courage that disinclines people to resigned acceptance of oppression. Around him gathered individuals of identical temperaments. If, with what would probably be excessive severity, one chooses to regard them all as criminals, we may say that their conflict with the governing class was a battle between thieves by violence and thieves by adroitness; and that may explain why Caesar had for them the benevolence people commonly feel for men who are fighting those whom one despises even more; or, rather, that may explain why Caesar, who cared little about honesty of means so only they attained his ends, conceived then and there the scheme of using the thieves by violence to undo the thieves by adroitness, and so to be left with the wealth of the whole Roman Empire in his own hands.

2575. Appian records the fact that Catiline stood for the consulate and failed of election—essayed, in other words, the battle of wits and lost because he had no aptitude for that type of game: "Whereafter he refused to take any part in public affairs [As uncompromising anti-parliamentarians do in our day, and for identical reasons] because politics led neither promptly nor surely to absolute power but was full of brawls and hatreds." [1] By no means the idiot that Sallust would expose to our gaze! Cicero himself relates that Cati-

memorabilibus, IX, 1, 9. Plutarch, *Sulla*, 32 (Perrin, Vol. IV, p. 431), accuses Catiline of murdering a brother, and still another person, one Marcus Marius.

2575 [1] *De bellis civilibus*, II, 2: Αὐτὸς δὲ πολιτείαν μὲν ὅλως ἔτι ἀπεστρέφετο ἐκ τοῦδε, ὡς οὐδὲν ἐς μοναρχίαν ταχὺ καὶ μέγα φέρουσαν, ἀλλ' ἔριδος καὶ φθόνου μεστήν. The word πολιτεία is probably to be taken, as explained by Plutarch, *De unius in republica dominatione*, II, 826 (Goodwin, Vol. V, pp. 395-98), to signify participation in the government of the Republic. The passage therefore means that Catiline did not run again for any office. Dio Cassius, *Historia Romana*, XXXVII, 29, 2, mentions a decree of the Senate which Catiline believed—and rightly, according to Dio—to have been framed against him, and says that it induced him to attempt to overthrow the *comitia* by force.

line's grave was decorated with flowers and that funeral honours were celebrated upon it.[2]

2576. Moralists who like to make a novel of history consider it their duty either to condemn or absolve Catiline. Those who condemn him see in him an enemy of his country; those who absolve him make him out a friend of "the People" in its effort to shake off the yoke of an "oligarchy." Others in plenty follow a middle course and rule Catiline's purpose just, but his means mistaken and reprehensible.[1]

The facts are much more complex than any such poetic fancies. Catiline seems to have been an ambitious man without trace of scruple, and altogether similar in that respect to Marius, Sulla, Crassus, Pompey, Caesar, Octavius, and others too numerous to count, who had no scruples to speak of. He was looking for his own road and found it, as usually happens, in the direction of least resistance. Had he been more skilled at political intrigue he would have used political intrigue. He tried to do so, in fact; he failed, and he was shrewd enough to see that that was not crust for teeth such as his. A man of intrepid spirit, fiery, ever ready to use force, he sensed, perhaps without clear inner perception of what he was doing, that his course lay in the direction of force, and he followed it.

2577. He might have been one of the many obscure rebels of whom history makes bare mention; but, as fate decreed, many other individuals happened to find themselves in his own situation, and in that situation, rather than in some other, because the speculators held the upper hand in the governing class in Rome. As a result of that, the episode assumed more considerable proportions and has

2575 [2] *Pro Lucio Flacco,* 38, 95: "Caius Antony was convicted . . . and on his condemnation the grave of Catiline was strewn with flowers and there was a celebration with funeral banquets attended by a general gathering of desperadoes and public enemies, and funeral rites were performed for Catiline."

2576 [1] [Napoleon III], *Histoire de Jules César,* Vol. I, pp. 338-39: "Certainly Catiline was guilty in trying to overthrow the laws of his country by violence, but in that he was only following the examples of Marius and Sulla. He dreamed of a revolutionary dictatorship, the downfall of the oligarchy, and, as Dio Cassius says, *Historia Romana,* XXXVII, 30, 3, a change in the constitution of the Republic and an uprising of the allies. It would have been unfortunate had he succeeded. No abiding good ever comes from impure hands." How pure were the hands of Octavius, who founded the Roman Empire? How pure the hands of Caesar, who preceded him? It is beyond belief that sentiment could so befog human eyesight!

received more attention from history. Catiline attracted former veterans of Sulla, men accustomed to violence because of their background, and with no skill in the subtle arts of the politician.[1] To him came other men of faction, individuals who had lost their money, were burdened with debts, and desired to improve their status by resort to violence. Among them there may well have been some few specimens of the social refuse that floats on the surface of every revolution. But the fact that men like Caesar were suspected of being with them shows that the movement included people of quite another sort—people who had been beaten at the political game and panted for another test of strength where the victory would go to the man of brawn rather than to the trickster, to the man of fearless courage rather than to the man of versatile wits.[2][3]

2577 [1] Appian, *Op. cit.*, II, 2: "He sent about all over Italy to find soldiers of Sulla who had squandered the booty they had obtained by violence and asked nothing better than to do the same thing over again." The point is confirmed by Sallust, *Bellum Catilinae*, XVI, 4. Alluding to the troublesome elements that were gathered about Catiline, he adds: "Trusting in such friends and associates, Catiline conceived the plan of overthrowing the Republic, because meantime there was a huge debtor class throughout the land and because many soldiers who had served under Sulla, and had spent their wealth too lavishly, remembering their former victories and all the plunder they had brought them, were anxious for another civil war." Plutarch, *Cicero*, 14 (Perrin, Vol. VII, p. 115), also speaks of Sulla's veterans as "again desirous of plunder and pillage." Dio Cassius, *Historia Romana*, XXXVII, 30, 2, makes the same point. Either documents have suddenly lost all value or it is impossible not to see in testimony so varied and of such weight traces of a conflict between force and the methods of political manoeuvring.

2577 [2][3] Cicero, *Pro Marco Coelio*, 4, 10: "Coelius's intimacy with Catiline is held against him . . . though many altogether respectable persons were attracted to that worthless and wicked man." Farther along (5, 12; 6, 13, 14), Cicero awards to Catiline a praise that Caesar also deserved: "He had about him many allurements to licence, but also many encouragements to industry and effort. He was a man of countless debaucheries, but he had a keen interest in military matters. . . . What man was ever more charming for his distinguished associates, what man more closely affiliated with the worst elements? By that varied and complex nature he had gathered all the most desperate and wicked characters about him from all quarters: but he also fascinated many good and sensible men with a certain false face of talent."

Some day, when our present plutocratic régime has been overthrown by the Anarchists, or the Syndicalists, or the militarists, or by any party, in fine, whatever its name, which will meet the cunning that is now triumphant with force, the world will perhaps remember words such as Sallust, *Bellum Catilinae*, XX, 8-10, puts into the mouth of Catiline: "So all influence, all power, all honour, all wealth is theirs [Of the powerful of his day, counterparts of the speculators of ours.] or of those on whom they choose to bestow them. To us they have left the dangers,

2578. How firm their resolve, how great their might, transpires from the fact that when the Senate promised immunity from prosecution and a reward of two hundred sesterces to anyone supplying information with regard to the conspiracy, not one traitor appeared; and more clearly still from the manner of their dying at the battle at Fiesole. All their wounds were in front and most of them covered in death the spots of ground on which they had fought alive.[1]

2579. Sallust, *Op. cit.*, XXXIII, 1, had them say that they had taken up arms not against their country but to defend themselves against the money-lenders, who had deprived many men of their country and all men of honour and wealth. On the other hand it was the speculators, in other words the knights, who defended Cicero, stood guard about the Senate, and threatened armed violence upon Caesar, who was suspected of being one of Catiline's accomplices.[1]

2580. In those days in Rome, as in all Europe in our day, the increase in wealth had raised the cost of living, so that people disposed to rest on their ancestral fortunes were soon overreached, forced into debt, ruined. Those only saved themselves (or in fact often accumulated great wealth) who sought new earnings in politics and speculation. More cowardly than the Romans, our modern losers for the most part sit resigned. The more impetuous Roman

the defeats, the exiles, the poverty. How long will you endure such things, O men of heart? Is it not better to die bravely than to lose a wretched and contemptible life in ignominy, after making sport for the insolence of others? Of course it is, by the faith of gods and men! Victory is within our grasp. Youth is our strength, courage our watchword. And they? They are weaklings and dotards, sapped by age and high living."

2578 [1] Sallust, *Op. cit.*, XXXVI, 5: "Not one among the hosts of conspirators was induced by the reward offered by the Senate in two decrees to make any revelations as to the plot, nor was one deserter to be counted from Catiline's camp." And LXI, 1: "What courage and what spirit prevailed in Catiline's army one could see after the battle was over. For almost every man covered with his dead body the spot he had elected to defend while alive. Some few in the centre had been driven back a little by the praetorian cohort [that is, the general's personal command], but all of them had fallen with their wounds in front."

2579 [1] Sallust, *Op. cit.*, XLIX, 4: "A number (*nonnulli*) of Roman knights stood guard with drawn swords about the Temple of Concord [the Senate building], inspired whether by the magnitude of the peril or by noble ideals. That their loyalty to the state might shine the clearer they threatened Caesar with their swords as he issued from the Senate." Suetonius, *Divus Julius*, 14, adds other details, among them that Caesar had voted against the death-sentence that had been passed upon

losers elected to make the test of arms before resigning. Force not seldom avails to break the flimsy, however flexible, meshes of shrewdness and cunning.

2581. Says Plutarch, *Cicero*, 10, 4 (Perrin, Vol. VII, pp. 107-09): "All Etruria was rising in rebellion, and likewise a large part of Cisalpine Gaul. Rome stood in gravest danger of a total overturn because of the inequalities in wealth [The usual error, repeated by many moderns, of assigning to inequalities in wealth effects that are due to other causes.], since men who were most eminent for their achievements and character had ruined themselves in lavishing money on theatres, banquets, election campaigns, and public buildings [They were the muddlers at the political game. The clever ones more than made up for costs by exploiting provinces or in speculations, as Crassus did.]; so that wealth had passed into the hands of the low-born and the worthless [Able politicians, rather, men endowed with combination-residues to the exclusion virtually of all other residues.] and anyone who had dared might have overthrown a state that was in itself already tottering." In other words, anyone venturing to meet cunning with force would have had a good chance of winning. Catiline failed of victory. Success smiled for a time on Caesar, and rested permanently with Augustus.

Catiline's accomplices. Then he adds: "And he did not cease his opposition till an armed band of Roman knights, who were standing about the Senate as a guard, threatened him with death . . . striking at him with their drawn swords, so that those seated about him ran from him with one accord, while a mere handful strove to protect him by throwing their arms about him and covering him with their togas. He was so thoroughly frightened that he not only left the Senate but did not return thither for the remainder of that year." Had the knights continued to use force in that manner, they and not their enemies would have been the victors. But they were against that by temperament, having fundamentally the temperament of all speculators. And *cf*. Plutarch, *Caesar*, VIII (Perrin, Vol. VII, pp. 459-61). In his oration *In toga candida* (*Opera*, Vol. VII, pp. 376-77), of which a few fragments have been preserved by Asconius, Cicero declares that Catiline could ask the consulate neither of the leading citizens, who would have none of his candidacy, nor of the Senate, which had condemned him, nor of the equestrian order, which he had tried to slaughter: *"Ab equestri ordine, quem trucidasti?"* On that point Asconius remarks, *Enarratio in orationem 'In toga candida,'* p. 89: "The equestrian order had stood with Cinna's faction against Sulla and had stolen much money, because of which they were known as *saccularii* (pickpockets). Many of them were slain after Sulla's victory, in view of their unpopularity on that account." That gives a clear picture of the speculators who filled their pockets and could be checked only by force. *Cf*. Quintus Cicero, *De petitione consulatus*, II (pp. 527-28).

2582. Says Napoleon III:[1] "Cicero thought he had destroyed a whole party. He was mistaken. He had but foiled a conspiracy and rescued a cause [For Louis Napoleon, bless his heart, the "cause" was the cause of democracy versus oligarchy.] from the hands of irresponsible individuals who were compromising it. The unlawful execution of the conspirators rehabilitated their memory." And with that we go back to the moralistic romance! Cicero's "mistake," according to Napoleon III, lay in his not having stuck to the law! How faithfully Caesar and Augustus stuck to the law![2] If one must say that Cicero made a "mistake" it would be the rather stupid mistake of believing that eloquence, or if one prefer, reason and righteousness, can serve as substitutes for force.

2583. Catiline's conspiracy was just one of the many attempted rebellions that preceded the final catastrophe. It was an episode in the civil wars that marked the end of the Republic and they were all, to some extent at least, struggles between people who were rich in Class I residues and people who were rich in residues of group-persistence (Class II). The latter finally won out with Octavius and he, as Augustus, tried, though in vain, to restore the religion, the morality, the manners, the customs of the days of old. That, with the support of the military, gave stability to the Roman Empire for a short time at least.

2584. The victory on which the Empire was founded was not, however, a victory of force exclusively; for Caesar and Augustus used a lavish supplement of cunning, and Caesar further enjoyed extensive support from the plutocracy. Then, as is the case in our day, the plutocracy turned in the direction where it saw the greater probabilities of profit. In France it burned incense to Napoleon III, author of a *coup d'état;* then, after 1870, it idolized Thiers; today it makes prostrate obeisance to the Radical-Socialists. As long as the

2582 [1] *Histoire de Jules César,* Vol. I, p. 339.

2582 [2] Against our view Napoleon III contends, *Op. cit.,* p. 339: "Legality may legitimately be violated when society is rushing to its doom and a heroic remedy is indispensable for saving it, when, in other words, a government is supported by the bulk of the nation and becomes the representative of its interests and desires. [Exactly what Cicero thought with regard to suppressing Catiline's conspiracy, and as Napoleon III thought with regard to his own *coup d'état.*] But when a country is split up into factions and a government represents only one of them, it must cling to the most scrupulous observance of the law in dealing with any conspiracy."

profits are there it little cares what flag covers the goods. Towards the end of the Republic speculation in provincial taxes was the prevalent type; but there was also a speculation of the modern type that was applied to economic production, with an adjunct of political manipulation. The Empire weakened that tie, and to its good fortune got a type of speculation that was in the main economic.[1]

2584 [1] Crassus was the type of the plutocrat-politician of the last years of the Republic, very much like the plutocrat-politician of our day. He differs from the modern type in that he was a man of senatorial origins, whereas our plutocrat-politicians generally emanate from the middle or lower classes. Conspicuous in him as in the moderns is the overwhelming abundance of Class I residues and a virtually total absence of Class II residues. Crassus came of a line of speculators, as do numbers of our plutocrats today. Pliny, *Historia naturalis*, XXXIII, 47(10) (Bostock-Riley, Vol. VI, p. 129): "Later on they [the Crassi] acquired the epithet of 'Rich' (*Dives*) as a family name, though it is notorious that the first of that name got his money by defaulting his debts. Marcus Crassus, who was of that line, denied that anyone was a rich man unless he could maintain a legion on his annual income." Mommsen draws a magnificent portrait of Crassus, *Römische Geschichte*, Vol. III, pp. 14-16 (Dixon, Vol. IV, pp. 13-15): "As regards mental endowments, literary culture, military talent, he was far in the rear of many men of his class, but he surpassed them all in tireless activity and in his stubborn resolve to own everything and be in the forefront in everything. [Traits of the modern plutocrat as well.] He threw himself headlong into speculation. [That is the way plutocrats get to be plutocrats.] Purchases of real estate during the revolution lay at the base of his enormous fortune [The wealth of our modern plutocrats generally originates, when not in protective tariffs, in government supplies, government contracts, and other favours that are bought of politicians.], though he did not neglect other forms of money-making. He built houses in Rome that were as shrewdly situated as they were pretentious. With his freedmen [They correspond to the modern plutocratic clique.] he acquired interests in commercial firms and enterprises. He had banks in Rome and other places, with or without partners or agents. He lent his money to his colleagues in the Senate [As Berteaux did to Deputies in the French parliament.], acting as their 'dummy,' as occasion offered, in obtaining public contracts and buying support for them in trials before the *collegia*. [In our time, the plutocrat buys the politician who in turn influences court decisions.] . . . Carefully judging his conduct in such way as to avoid open conflict with the criminal judge, he knew the art of living simply, unostentatiously, like the true man of wealth he was. Starting with an ordinary senatorial inheritance, he was known within a very few years to have amassed an enormous treasure. Just before his death, in spite of unprecedented and unexpected outlays, his fortune was still estimated at 170,000,000 sesterces ($10,000,000). . . . He spared no pains to extend his influence. . . . Most of the Senators were in his debt. [In France many deputies owed Berteaux money. In Italy the bank investigations showed that many members of the parliament were in debt to members of the plutocracy.] He had hosts of prominent men dependent on him. . . . A business man above all else, he lent money without regard to political affiliations, and had interests in all parties. [Exactly as our plutocrats do. They lend even to the most

2585. This economic activity enabled men who got rich to rise to higher classes.[1] So elements from below attained the governing class, enriching it in combination-instincts; but they rose slowly, so that the combination-instincts had time to strike a balance with group-persistences. The Empire was organized in distinct and separate social classes, which were reached by hereditary right but also by class-circulation, some individuals mounting on the social ladder, others dropping to lower rungs, but, with some few exceptions due largely to Imperial favour, the advance in station was not sud-

blood-thirsty enemies of financiers, capitalists, the *bourgeoisie*.] His purse was open to anyone who was solvent or who could be useful to him. As for leaders of parties and factions, whose attacks spared no one, they were very careful to keep hands off when it came to Crassus. . . . Ever since Rome had been Rome, money had played a powerful rôle in the state, but by this time gold was the road to everything, along with the sword. [To make that fit our day the word "sword" has to be deleted.] Then it was that a Crassus—a symptom characteristic, alas, of the time—who was a very ordinary orator and a worse general, a politician full of activity but short on energy [A good description of the plutocrats who govern our modern civilized countries.], a man of boundless greed but of no great ambition, getting along on nothing save his colossal fortune and his skill in finance, could be seen extending his influence everywhere, acquiring full control of the all-powerful influence of the cliques of intriguers [For our plutocrats one has to add the newspapers.], considering himself the equal of the greatest generals and statesmen of his age, and vying with them for the possession of the highest palms to which the greed of the climber can aspire." Plutarch, *Crassus*, 2, 27: "At the outset he possessed not more than 300 talents [A talent was $10,000.]. Later on, when he came into power, he contributed the tenth part of his fortune to the Temple of Hercules, gave the people a banquet, and provided grain for three months for each citizen. Nevertheless, before starting out on his expedition against the Parthians, he made an inventory of his fortune and found that it amounted to 7,100 talents." He bought houses that were in need of repairs at low prices and rebuilt them. He owned silver mines and agricultural properties yielding large revenues, "yet all such would seem little as compared with the sums of money that he derived from the labour of slaves, of whom he had huge numbers and of every sort: readers, copyists, metal-workers, stewards, table-servants." Crassus posed as a democrat, much as our own plutocrats pose as Socialists. Like our plutocrats, further, he knew the road to the good graces of the powerful. When Caesar was about to start for Spain, he freed him from his creditors, standing bail for him in the amount of 830 talents. Noting that there were three factions in Rome following Pompey, Caesar, and Crassus respectively, Plutarch continues: "Crassus steered a middle course [between the other two factions], making use of them both. Changing political

2585 [1] Marcus Seneca, *Controversiae*, II-2, I (Bouillet, pp. 171-72): "Property evaluation climbs the stairs to the Senate, distinguishes the Roman knight from the plebeian, assures promotion in the army, selects the judges in the law-courts." And *cf*. § 2548 [3].

den, but gradual, so that several generations were required for climbing at all high.[2] So long as it was the fact as well as the law that wealth gave entrée to the class next above, and so long as the class that was so entered actually had some share, however small, in public affairs and was not merely honorific, the Empire was economically prosperous, even though military virtues in the dominant class were languishing. The maximum of prosperity was realized in the early days when the civilian element was producing wealth and a military class was maintaining order at home and abroad.[3]

colour according to the ebb and flow of fortune in Rome, he was neither a faithful friend nor an implacable enemy, putting away his benevolence or his wrath as best suited his convenience. [Exactly as our plutocrats do.] He was often to be seen, in short spaces of time, now defending, now opposing the same men or the same laws." So Caillaux manoeuvred with regard to the income-tax, and Giolitti with regard to universal suffrage. And the Italian Chamber, immediately after rejecting as exaggerated the modest extension of suffrage proposed by Luzzatti, approved the far greater extension proposed by Giolitti. Plutocrats and their representatives are interested in money. For other things they care not a hang.

2585 [2] Fustel de Coulanges, *L'Empire romain,* pp. 279-80: "All these social distinctions were hereditary. Each individual was fully entitled to the rank in which birth had placed him. However, he could sink in station if he lost his money, or rise higher step by step as his wealth increased. To climb in that social hierarchy was the ambition of everybody who could boast activity and energy. The Imperial government offered no resistance to that continuous ascent which was the objective of all efforts. Its main concern was that it should not be too rapid. It fixed the conditions and the rules under which it could be allowed. It sought especially to prevent, so far as possible, a family's advancing more than two stages in one lifetime. Buying his complete freedom the slave could become a plebeian, but he was forbidden to rise as high as a curial. The plebeian could take his place in the Forum if he came to own twenty-five acres of land and was able to pay his quota of municipal taxes. The curial could in his turn become a *principalis* [entitled to hold public office], if he was rich enough to bear the burdens of a magistracy and if he could get his fellow-citizens to vote for him. However, the Imperial government insisted that he should fill all the lower offices before he could stand for the higher, and that was a first obstacle and spelled long delay for the upstart." Fustel bases this analysis on the Theodosian Code. That may well have been the law of the matter. In the fact there were many exceptions. *Cf.* § 2551 [1], and Tacitus, *Annales,* XIII, 27. Fustel continues: "When the municipal career had been entirely traversed, then, and not till then, could a family aspire to senatorial rank. There too wealth was necessary, but it was not enough. The rule required that a Roman magistracy should be awarded by the Emperor."

2585 [3] Extravagant living was still astounding in Rome in the day of Tiberius. Tacitus, *Annales,* II, 38. In III, 52, he says: "Caius Sulpicius and Decimus Haterius followed as consuls. It was a year of quiet abroad. At home it was foreseen that measures would be taken against extravagant living, which had gone out of bounds in regard to everything on which money could be squandered." The aediles were

The Empire drooped towards decline because beyond the frontiers no wealthy people were left to be exploited by conquest, and because at home the crystallization in economic institutions, the progress in "organization," after producing a brief period of prosperity led to the usual economic depression. Production held its own for the reason stated in § 2553, that it tends to show improvement as society begins to rigidify after a period of flexible initiative—in this case the costs of maintaining stability at home and defending the frontiers of the Empire being reduced to a minimum, or being, at any rate, insignificant as compared with the squanderings of the demagogic plutocracy during the last years of the Republic. The wages of the praetorians, who upheld the government and assured quiet under Tiberius, were a pittance as compared with the fortunes spent by politicians towards the end of the Republic in purchasing votes from the people (§ 2562).[4] But such a state of things had to

minded to prohibit such wastage and the Senate asked Tiberius to decide what was to be done. Tiberius pointed to the difficulty of doing anything, *Ibid.,* 53: " 'What indeed should first be forbidden? What shall we try to bring back to olden customs? The great villas? Shall we prescribe the number and nationality of slaves? The weight of silver and gold that may be used on our tables? What about the wonders in bronze, and the pictures? Shall we fix the styles of dress for men and women, and especially for women, since they are transferring our substance to foreigners and enemies to buy gems?' " Disregarding the usual crusting of derivations, one must say that, substantially, Tiberius was right. *Ibid.,* 54: " 'From victories abroad we learned to squander the properties of others, from our victories at home we have learned to squander our own.' " Tiberius was for letting things take their course, and Tacitus remarks, *Ibid.,* 55, that in spite of that there was a diminution in extravagance, and he assigns the credit to a new *élite* that was coming Romeward from the provinces, and to the good example set by Vespasian. He then ventures his theory of the cycle to which we alluded in § 2552 [1]. The causes he mentions may be reckoned among the secondary, certainly not among the primary, causes, for after Vespasian's time the Romeward movement of population had produced every possible effect and the second was entirely missing, for, to say nothing of others, Commodus, Caracalla, and Elagabalus, among Vespasian's successors, were not just the ones to set examples of parsimonious living. Yet money-spending by private citizens and economic prosperity continued to fall off.

2585 [4] Marquardt, *Römische Staatsverwaltung: Das Finanzwesen,* Pt. II, Bk. II, p. 96: "The praetorians, who were organized in nine cohorts of 1,000 men, were paid, at the time of Tiberius, 720 *denarii,* but without supplies. These were added to their pay beginning with Nero." The total cost of twenty-five legions, the praetorians, and the urban cohorts was, according to Marquardt, 46,710,000 *denarii* or $10,105,000. But there were other expenses, not least among them the *donativa,* which cannot be estimated and which increased as time went on. [The *donativa* were "tips" paid by the Emperor to soldiers on festive occasions of importance, especially his birthday.—A. L.]

change, by normal evolution, into decline for the Empire (§ 2541):
the ascending period was closely knit to the descending period
(§ 2338); the youthful prosperity of the organism gradually changed
to the hardships of old age. As society progressively crystallized production gradually diminished (§§ 2607 f.), while wastage of wealth
increased. Imposing more and more upon the civil authority and
changing in character and methods, the military power became a
source of weakness to the government to which it had formerly lent
stability, substituting intimidation for the obedience it had once paid
its generals, so exploiting the social system for its own profit, causing wastage of wealth (§ 2608), and finally weakening and destroying the military power of the army itself (§ 2606).

2586. The Empire's main reliance had been the army, but it was
not in the army that the major portion of the governing class originated. The legions could easily make an Emperor, but they did not
develop any great number of administrators, very few in fact, and
so were not a rich source of new materials for replenishing the *élite*.
The governing class became more and more a class of office-holders,
with all the merits and shortcomings peculiar to that sort of people,
and military capacity gradually vanished from it.

2587. Most illuminating from that standpoint are the events following the death of the Emperor Aurelian. The legions asked the
Senate for an Emperor. The Senate refused to name one. But the
legions held out, and as a result the Empire was left without a head
for six months. Finally the Senators were virtually forced to designate one of their number. And whom did they elect? A general,
perchance, or at least a man of energy? Not at all! An old man of
seventy-five! The incident shows the dearth of combination-instincts
in the legions, and in the Senate the dearth of military vigour. The
first defect might have been remedied had the choice of the legions
chanced to fall on an individual rich in instincts for political combinations. For the second defect there was no remedy, and to it were
in great part due first the ruin of the *élite* and then the fall of the
Empire.[1]

2587 [1] Vopiscus, *Divus Aurelianus,* 41, gives an account of the death of Aurelian,
the interregnum, and the reign of Tacitus. He quotes (41, 2) the letter in which the
legions requested the Senate to select an Emperor: "Send us some one of your
number to be Emperor, but a man in your judgment worthy." Tacitus, a consul at
the time, thought that a dangerous honour was being paid the Senate and said

2588. What we are told of the election of Tacitus shows that the disease of humanitarianism that is at present raging in our modern countries was spreading wreckage far and wide in that early day.

2589. Inspired as they are by ethical prejudices against wealth, luxury, "capital," most writers centre on those circumstances alone in the history of Rome, whereas more illuminating in their bearing on the social equilibrium would be the modifications in the sentiments (residues) prevailing in the governing class.

2590. Traces of class-circulation in the early days of the Empire are abundant; and if they are not as abundant as one might wish, the fact is due to the feeling that such details were hardly worthy of mention in dignified history, so that we are left with merely incidental allusions. What we have is adequate, however, to show what was going on.[1] The parvenu Rufus, of whom Tacitus, *Annales*,

(41, 13-15): " 'I think this matter of choosing an Emperor should be referred to the army itself. For in making a choice of this kind, unless the action of the Senate is ratified it will be dangerous for the man chosen and a source of unpopularity for those who choose him.' "· The Senate adopted that view but, both sides holding firm, the Senate finally yielded, nominating Tacitus himself: " *'Probata est sententia Taciti: attamen cum iterum atque iterum mitterent, ex S. C., quod in Taciti vita dicemus, Tacitus factus est imperator.'* " In his *Tacitus,* 2, 1, Vopiscus says: "Therefore—a thing most strange and embarrassing—the Senate and Roman People had to put up with the fact that for six months the state should be without an Emperor while a good one was being sought." But the army had to have a commander, and the Consul, Gordianus, remarked before the Senate, *Ibid.,* 3, 4: " 'An Emperor has to be elected. The army cannot go on any longer without a commander and the necessity is urgent, for the Germans are said to have broken the frontier across the Rhine.' " Rome found no demagogue along the lines of Jaurès, Caillaux, or Lord Grey, to assure her that she need have no fear of the attacking Germans; but that was little gained, for the Conscript Fathers, good humanitarians that they were, thought that the invaders could be held off by private and public virtues. And yet poor Tacitus, declining the honour they were forcing upon him, observed with much wisdom, *Ibid.,* 4, 5-6: " 'I am surprised, O Conscript Fathers,

2590 [1] For instance, Pliny, *Historia naturalis,* XIV, 5(4) (Bostock-Riley, Vol. III, pp. 234-35): "Acilius Sthenelus, a man of the freed plebs, rose to the greatest eminence. He got his start by developing a vineyard of 60 jugera [about 35 acres], not more, in the Nomentum district and selling it for 400,000 sesterces [$16,000]. Vetulenus Aegialus, also a freedman, of Liternum in Campania, won great fame and a popularity greater still, for developing a farm on the estate which Scipio Africanus had occupied in exile." Most famous of all was Rhemmius Palaemon, a Greek tutor, who bought a vineyard for $25,000, with the help of the freedman Sthenelus mentioned above, developed it till it was earning $16,000 a year and then resold it to Annaeus Seneca for $100,000. Pliny alludes to another millionaire freedman, a Thessalian eunuch, in XII, 5 (Bostock-Riley, Vol. III, p. 106).

XI, 21, draws a portrait, manifests all the traits of the ingenious baseness that were characteristic of the new *élite* and which were conspicuous in other individuals. Says Tacitus: "Of the origins of Rufus, who some say was the son of a gladiator, I would not speak falsehood, and yet I am loth to speak the truth. . . . Become a man, he scraped an acquaintance with the quaestor in Africa. Being at Adrumentum and walking alone in the porticos one day at noon, he had a vision. A woman of supernatural semblance appeared to him and said: 'Rufus, thou shalt come here one day as proconsul!' Taking heart from the prodigy, he hastened to Rome, and thanks to an alert mind and loans from friends, he became quaestor and later on, by favour of the Emperor Tiberius, praetor, a post that belonged to men of noble birth. Tiberius said, in excuse of the man's low birth: 'I am sure Rufus was his own father.' He lived a long life. With the great he was a craven flatterer, with inferiors an arrogant bully, with equals merely a disagreeable bore. He obtained consular authority, the honours of a triumph, and finally Africa, where he died, the prophecy so being fulfilled."

2591. The Trimalchio of Petronius, *Satyricon,* 76-77 (Mitchell, pp. 139-40), though he may have been a character of fiction, undoubtedly was drawn from real life. Eliminating the pornography and replacing the gluttony with other forms of indulgence, the man is quite the counterpart of certain exotic millionaires of our day. How does Trimalchio acquire his huge fortune? He loads five ships with wine and despatches them to Rome. They founder at sea, but he does not lose heart on that account. He outfits a new fleet with ships

that you could think of choosing an aged man as Emperor in the place of Aurelian who was a commander of great merit.' " A Senator of consular rank suavely breathed the humanitarian poetry that counselled choice of a Tacitus, *Ibid.,* 6, 2: " 'We have elected Emperor a man who is our elder and who can counsel us all as a father would. [Clemenceau would have said: "a man who is a 'pure' republican."] Nothing rash, nothing impulsive, nothing harsh is to be feared from such a man. . . . He knows the sort of Emperor he has always desired for himself, nor can he exhibit to us anything that he does not desire and approve of.' " It all sounds like an idyll. Nothing is missing save the shepherdess and a flock of lambs with ribbons around their necks. The good soul warmed the throne for half a year. *Ibid.,* 13, 5: "He achieved nothing of importance because of the briefness of his reign; for after six months he was murdered, according to one story, by a group of conspirators among the soldiers. According to another he died a natural death. One thing is certain, that he had neither intelligence nor courage, and succumbed to the many factions."

bigger, better, and luckier than the first, and cargoes this time of wine, pork, beans, perfumes from Capua, slaves. That makes him 10,000,000 sesterces—$250,000—at one scoop. He continues trading, always luckily, and then quietly settles down to the business of lending money to freedmen. His real inclination would have been to retire from business altogether; but he was dissuaded from that by a fortune-teller. Could a modern parvenu do better than Trimalchio when he turns to one of his guests and exclaims: "Take my word for it: if you have a penny, you are worth a penny; if you have a million, it is hail! hail! That friend of yours—he was once a bullfrog! Look at him now! He's a king!"[1] Trimalchio will have his say on matters of philosophy and literature,[2] and he knows as much about them as one of our moderns, who thinks that now that he has made his money he is an authority in every field. Trimalchio (*Satyricon,* 67) parades his wife's jewels before his guests and will have them know their precise weight. Not a few modern parvenus could do as well.

2592. But from the economic standpoint of the husband, Trimalchio's wife is far superior to the women of our plutocracy. Our modern wives, when they get rich or even reach moderately easy circumstances, disdain the cares of the home and become mere luxuries, devourers of wealth and savings. The good Fortunata devotes herself in all earnestness to domestic economy, and once when her husband had been ruined (*Ibid.,* 76) she gave him her jewels—in that too differing, quite, from many women in our plutocracy, who make haste to divorce men who cease to be able to keep them in luxury.[1]

2591 [1] *Satyricon,* 77 (Mitchell, p. 141): *"Credite mihi: assem habeas, assem valeas: habes, habeberis. Sic amicus vester qui fuit rana nunc est rex."*

2591 [2] *Satyricon,* 59 (Mitchell, p. 115). Trimalchio also gives a lecture on mythology. Says he: "Diomed and Ganymede? They were two brothers. Helen was their sister. Agamemnon carried the lass off and gave Diana a doe to call it quits. Now what Homer is trying to tell is why the Trojans and the Parentines are fighting all the time."

2592 [1] *Satyricon,* 67 (Mitchell, p. 125): " 'But tell me, Gaius, please—why doesn't Fortunata join us?' 'What?' said Trimalchio. 'She? She wouldn't stop to take a drink of water till she has laid away the silver and given the children their supper.' . . . But at last Fortunata came, wearing a yellow sash over her cherry-red tunic, gilt anklets and gilt shoes . . . and wiping her hands on a towel that was thrown over her shoulders."

2593. Petronius has other parvenus besides Trimalchio. He mentions the sexvir, Habinna, a sculptor or at least a stone-carver, who also gives his wife costly jewels, and a barrister, Phileron, who has risen to great wealth.[1] A number of freedmen who had been Trimalchio's comrades in servitude are also now rich.[2] So commerce, in person of Trimalchio, industry in Habinna, learning in Phileron, produce the new-comers. They are laughed at, but the laugh proves that they are there. Martial chafes a cobbler who had given a gladia-

2593 [1] *Satyricon,* 65 (Mitchell, p. 123): "Meantime a lictor banged on the doors of the dining-room and a new guest entered, clad in a white toga and attended by a huge retinue. Abashed at such an impressive sight, I thought that at the very least a praetor had come, and made an effort to rise from my couch and get my bare feet on the floor. Agamemnon laughed at my fright. 'Stay where you are, idiot! That is just Habinna, the sexvir. He is only a stone-cutter, but, they tell me, a good one—for gravestones!' " The sexvirs were the presidents of the six guilds of knights. They were drawn largely from the class of freedmen. They had to be men of some means, since their posts called for heavy expenditures in connexion chiefly with public games and anniversary celebrations, the anniversary in particular of the march of Octavius on Rome. Marquardt, *Organisation des römischen Reichs,* pp. 206-07: "It was the duty of the sexvirs (or sevirs) to see that ordinary sacrifices were provided for and to look after holiday celebrations, the expenses being covered by the money the sexvirs had paid in, when the decurions had not already spent it on public buildings of one sort or another." The sexvirs at Narbonne (Orelli, *Inscriptionum . . . collectio,* no. 2489), celebrated sacrifices twice a year, and four times a year supplied all colonists and residents with incense and wine. De Ruggiero, *Dizionario epigrafico, s.v. Augustalis,* quotes an inscription from Panormus, *Corpus inscriptionum Latinarum,* Vol. X, no. 7269 (p. 753): "*Aram Victoriae Sex. Pompeius Mercator VI vir Aug. praeter summm pro honore d.d.p.s.p.* [*pro honore decurionum decreto pecunia sua posuit*]" ("This altar to Victory Sextus Pompeius, merchant, Augustal sexvir, erected by decree, and with money paid in addition to his decurion's honorarium.") The allusion is to the *honorarium decurionatus,* which the sexvir paid on assuming office. By a chance that is strange indeed in its bearing on the passage in Petronius, an inscription has survived mentioning a stone-cutter (*marmorius*) who was a sexvir. Other trades too are mentioned in such inscriptions, a broker (*negotiator*), a pork-merchant, a silver-worker, a haberdasher (*vestiarius tenuiarius*), a manufacturer of purple dyes, a miller. They all indicate wealth on its way upward from the lower classes. [This note has been rewritten.—A. L.]

As for the lawyer, Petronius says, *Satyricon,* 46 (Mitchell, p. 98): "And there you see Phileron, the lawyer. Had he not studied law, he would not know where his next meal is coming from. A short time ago he was peddling in the streets with a pack on his back. Now there he is stretching in the face of Norbanus! He is a treasure-store of learning and there is no end to his craft."

2593 [2] *Satyricon,* 38 (Mitchell, p. 86): "But don't underestimate his other ex-comrades in servitude. They all have their piles today. Do you see that fellow at the end of the table? Today he has his million—and he started with nothing."

torial show at Bologna, and a fuller who had done the same at Modena.[3]

2594. Juvenal too aims the lash of his satire at the newly rich. Making lavish allowances for poetic exaggeration on his part, one still cannot believe that his anecdotes are altogether in contradiction with what everyone knew and could see in Rome. Twice he speaks of a barber he had patronized as a very rich man. The particular fact may not be history. The type surely was true to life.[1]

2595. The invasion of Rome by foreigners is also well remarked by Juvenal. He shows, on the one hand, I, vv. 102-11, the "descendants of the Trojans" fallen on evil days and begging dole, and, on the other, a rich freedman who wants a place in the line ahead of the Romans. "Let him who recently came to this city with whitened

2593 [3] *Epigrammata*, III, 59, vv. 16-17:

> "Sutor cerdo dedit tibi, culta Bononia, munus.
> Fullo dedit Mutinae. Nunc ubi caupo dabit?"

("A cobbler, Bologna the learned, hath given thee a show, and a fuller one at Modena? Where, next, a brothel-keeper?")

> "Das gladiatores, sutorum regule cerdo,
>   quodque tibi tribuit subula, sica rapit.
> Ebrius es: nec enim faceres id sobrius unquam,
>   ut velles corio ludere cerdo tuo."

("So you are giving us gladiators, O kinglet of cobblers? What an awl earned, a dagger takes away! You are drunk, surely, for who ever heard of a sober cobbler having fun at the expense of his own hide?") Tacitus, *Annales*, IV, 62, 2, also speaks of a freedman named Atilius who had given a gladiatorial spectacle: "*Atilius quidam libertini generis . . . quo spectaculum gladiatorum celebraret . . .*"

2594 [1] *Saturae*, X, vv. 225-26:

> "Percurram citius quot villas possideat nunc,
>   quo tondente gravis iuveni mihi barba sonabat."

("Rapidly must I trip over the many villas now possessed by a man who, when I was young, heard my heavy beard sing under his razor.") The scholiast notes: "*Quo tondente gravis:* 'Licinius the barber got to be a Senator.'" And again: "*Percurram citius,* the many villas the barber who used to shave me has, now that he has become a Senator." And cf., *Ibid.*, I, vv. 24-25:

> "Patricios omnes opibus quum provocet unus
>   quo tondente gravis iuveni mihi barba sonabat."

("All patrician wealth is challenged by a man who, when I was young, heard my heavy beard sing under his razor.")

feet not yield precedence to consecrated office."[1] Of the Greeks who
had come to Rome, Juvenal says, III, vv. 92-93: "We too can praise
as they do—but they persuade." And farther along, vv. 119-20:
"There is room for no Roman where a Protogenes, a Diphilus, or a
Hermarchus rules." Then, vv. 131-32: "The youth free-born must
yield the sidewalk to some rich man's slave." And earlier he had
said, vv. 60-66: "I cannot endure, Quirites, a Rome that is Greek,
though, after all, how small a part of it this refuse of Achaea makes!
For a long time now has the Syrian Orontes been pouring its
language and its customs into the Tiber."[2] And he might have
added: its religion. He no doubt is exaggerating, though none the
less with a kernel of fact, when he says of the seats for the equestrian
order at the theatre, III, vv. 153-58: "He whose property sufficeth not
the law will depart, if he hath not lost all shame, from these equestrian cushions; they are for the haunches of sons of panderers, born
of this or that brothel, who sit applauding between the scions of

2595 [1]　　　　　"... Prior, inquit, ego adsum:
　　　　Cur timeam, dubitemve locum defendere, quamvis
　　　　natus ad Euphraten, molles quod in aure fenestrae
　　　　arguerint, licet ipse negem? sed quinque tabernae
　　　　quadringenta parant: quid confert purpura maior
　　　　optandum, si Laurenti custodit in agro
　　　　conductas Corvinus oves? ego possideo plus
　　　　Pallante et Licinis! Exspectent ergo tribuni,
　　　　vincant divitiae, sacro nec cedat honori
　　　　nuper in hanc urbem pedibus qui venerat albis."

(" 'I was here first,' he said. 'Why should I fear or hesitate to hold my place just
because I was born on the Euphrates (as the holes in the lobes of my ears would
show, even though I tried to deny it)? My five brothels bring me in their forty
thousand. What profits a higher purple, if Corvinus, the patrician, tends hired
sheep on a Laurentian farm? Am I not richer than a Pallas and a Licinus? So let
the tribunes wait! Gangway for wealth, say I. Let him who came to this city with
whitened feet not yield precedence to consecrated office.' ") [Pallas was a rich freedman, favourite to the Emperor Claudius. Licinus was imperial barber to Augustus.
—A. L.] "Five brothels," "Five taverns," has been interpreted, on no very good
grounds, as a place-name. When a recently imported slave was for sale his feet
were kept whitened with chalk.

2595 [2]　　　　　"... Non possum ferre, Quirites,
　　　　Graecam urbem: quamvis quota portio faecis Achaei?
　　　　Iam pridem Syrus in Tiberim defluxit Orontes
　　　　et linguam et mores."

some trim auctioneer, or the polished cubs of some gladiator, or trainer of gladiators." [3]

2596. Many upstarts there must have been in a society that did not brand as stupid and absurd a satire that ran, *Ibid.*, III, vv. 29-39: "We had better withdraw from this country of ours and leave it to these sly individuals who make contracts for building temples, cleaning rivers, harbours, sewers, carrying corpses to the pyre, selling slaves at auction. People who once blew the horn in rural arenas and have made reputations for bugling as criers, today are giving shows of their own and so only they win popularity, will kill anyone desired at the turning-down of thumbs. Then once out of there, back they go to the latrines they keep for the public. And why not? Are they not they whom Fortune in sarcastic mood is raising from low to high estate?"

2597. Imperial favour picked certain freedmen and lifted them from nothing to the highest honours. Claudius was completely under the control of such people; but they were still few in number and most of them advanced by merit in administrative offices imperial and private.[1] Dio Cassius, *Historia Romana*, LXXIX, 13, 2, shows

2595 [3]   ". . . Exeat, inquit,
si pudor est, et de pulvino surgat equestri
cuius res legi non sufficit, et sedeant hic
lenonum pueri quocunque in fornice nati.
His plaudat nitidi praeconis filius inter
pinnirapi cultos iuvenes iuvenesque lanistae."

A scholiast note on *pinnirapi:* "Gladiators were plumed with peacock feathers when they paraded in the opening procession."

2597 [1] Belot, *Histoire des chevaliers romains,* Vol. II, pp. 385-87: "The Emperor Claudius went farthest in raising his freedmen to power under guise of fiscal agents. Plaything in the hands of a clique, he issued orders that the decisions of his freedmen should be respected as though they emanated from his person. That meant putting into their hands that personal and extra-legal justice which he saw fit to set up in place of the courts. Charges of peculation and embezzlement (*de repetundis*), which had occasioned so many party conflicts in the days of the Republic, were now settled behind closed doors by the comptroller, Pallas, who had succeeded another freedman, Menander. The armies and the provinces felt the effects of this new importance that had come to freedmen. A freedman, Felix, was named cohort-tribune and wing-prefect in the cavalry, and on resigning those military commands he went as governor to Judea, a province that Claudius ruled with procurators who were now knights, now freedmen, without distinction. . . . Tacitus mentions other provinces that were in the hands of procurators at the time of Nero's death: the two Mauretanias, Rhaetia, Noricum, and Thrace. Shortly after that, the Maritime Alps and Cappadocia came under the pacific rule of procurators."

Macrinus sending Agrippa as his lieutenant to Dacia, and Decius Triccianus to Pannonia. The former had been a slave; the latter an ordinary soldier, footman to the governor of Pannonia. Seneca dwells on the wealth of freedmen, and Tacitus shows them permeating the whole governing class despite the resistance of freeborn citizens.[2] During Nero's reign the Senate debated the frauds of freedmen, who "were dealing as equals with their masters," and required putting in their places. "It was said in rebuttal that the guilt of the few should fall upon the few, and not upon a body which, taken as a whole, was so large that in the majority the gentes, the decuriae, the assistants to the magistrates and priests, the urban cohorts, to say nothing of countless knights and Senators, came from no other source, for, leaving out descendants of freedmen, the number of other free-born citizens would be scant indeed. . . . And Nero directed, in a rescript to the Senate, 'that individual complaints against freedmen be given satisfaction, but that there be no measure taken against them in general.'" And not long afterwards Paris, entertainer to Nero's aunt, Domitia, was taken from her by virtually civil process, not without discredit to the Emperor at whose instance he had been declared free-born.[3] Nero gave his patronage to the newly rich and Suetonius represents him as preferring to get the personnel for his government exclusively from such men.[4]

2597 [2] Seneca, *Epistulae*, 27: "Calvisius Sabinus was a rich man, within the memory of those now living. He had the wealth of a freedman and the talents." *Ibid.*, 86: "So far I have been speaking of the water-systems of ordinary people. What would I have to say of the baths of freedmen?" *De beneficiis*, II, 27: "Gnaeus Lentulus, the augur, was the outstanding example of wealth before the freedmen made him look like a pauper." [Lodge: "before his franklins waxing wealthie and great made him seem poor."] *Naturales quaestiones*, I, 17: "These débutante daughters (*virgunculis*) of freedmen spend more for a looking-glass than the Roman people gave Scipio as a dowry for his daughters (*dos . . . quam dedit Scipioni:* better reading: *quam dedit pro Scipione*)." Tacitus, *Annales*, II, 48, 1, tells of a rich freedwoman, Aemilia Musa, who died intestate. Tiberius directed that her fortune be given to Aemilius Lepidus, to whom she seemed to have belonged as a slave.

2597 [3] Tacitus, *Annales*, XIII, 27.

2597 [4] *Nero*, 37, 3. Nero, according to Suetonius, said that he intended to abolish the senatorial order "and hand over the armies and provinces to freedmen and Roman knights." Of Vitellius, Tacitus, *Historiae*, I, 58, observes that he "bestowed on Roman knights imperial services which had been commonly exercised by freedmen." Pliny the Younger praises Trajan for not emulating a number of his predecessors in kotowing to freedmen, *Panegyricus*, 88: "Not a few Emperors, though

2598. On the other hand, war and impoverishment were extinguishing the patriciate. Dio Cassius notes, *Historia Romana,* LII, 42, that in order to keep up the sacrifices, Augustus had to create new patricians to replace the many who had perished in the civil wars.[1] Tacitus, *Annales,* III, 55, 4, also speaks of the many upstarts from the municipia, the colonies, and even from the conquered provinces, who had entered the Senate, and tells how Claudius admitted Gauls to the Senate over the vain protests of the Senators.[2] And Vespasian,

masters of the citizens, were slaves to their freedmen, acting at the beck and call of such men, hearing with their ears, speaking with their tongues. The praetorships, the priestly offices, the consulates, were sought by them and through them. You hold your freedmen in highest honour, but for what they are, and you think that it is enough for them if they be honest and useful as men." Capitolinus, *Antoninus Pius,* 11, 1 (Magie, Vol. I, p. 127), says that Antoninus "as Emperor, used his friends not otherwise than he had done as a private citizen, for not even his friends could influence him in any respect through his freedmen, with whom, indeed, he was very severe." And of Pertinax the same Capitolinus notes, *Helvius Pertinax,* 7, 8-9 (Magie, Vol. I, p. 331), "that he had the freedmen who had belonged to Commodus resold as slaves, and afterwards many of those whom he had ordered sold he took into his personal service as menials, and that amused him as an old man, since under other Emperors they had been reaching even senatorial rank."

2598 [1] Dio adds, *loc. cit.,* 5, that "civil wars are to nothing more fatal than to nobility." The War of the Roses had just that effect in England.

2598 [2] *Annales,* XI, 23, 2-6. It was objected that "Italy was not so sick that she would be unable to supply a Senate for her capital; that in olden times natives had sufficed for our kindred peoples, that there was no occasion to be ashamed of the old Republic and that still remembered were the examples of virtue which Roman character had handed down to glory through its ancient morals. Did the fact that Venetians and North Italians (Insubrians) had broken into the Curia mean so little that a conglomeration of foreigners should be inflicted upon it as a form of bondage? What further respect would there be for the remnants of the nobility, if indeed some poor man from Latium might be left in the Senate? For the rich were overrunning everything, men whose grandfathers or great-grandfathers had been leaders of hostile nations and had destroyed Roman armies in war." But Claudius was obdurate and concluded his rescript with the words (*Ibid.,* XI, 24, 11): *"Omnia, patres conscripti, quae nunc vetustissima creduntur, nova fuere; plebei magistratus post patricios, Latini post plebeios, ceterarum Italiae gentium post Latinos. Inveterascet hoc quoque, et quod hodie exemplis tuemur inter exempla erit."*—("All things that are now supposed to be very ancient were once, O Conscript Fathers, new. Plebeians succeeded patricians in the magistracies, Latians the plebeians, people of Italic race the Latians. The things of our time will also be some day old, and what we are testing today on precedent will itself some day be precedent.") The Emperor's rejoinder is an excellent description of class-circulation in Rome.

again, is called upon to restore a senatorial order deficient in both numbers and quality.[3]

2599. Circulation, therefore, is very clearly apparent, and not only in Rome as between the lower and the higher classes. Slaves were herded to the city from all parts of the Empire and even from countries beyond the frontiers. Those among them who were the richest in Class I residues, Greeks and Orientals especially, easily won their freedom. Still in virtue of a predominance of Class I residues, their descendants accumulated wealth, climbed the social ladder, and became knights and Senators. So Latin and Italic blood was eliminated from the governing class, and the new *élite,* for many reasons, not least among them its origins in slavery and in Asiatic cowardice, became more and more alien to the military spirit.

2600. It was encouraged in that direction by the emperors themselves, who feared it. Dio Cassius, *Historia Romana,* LII, 14-40, alludes to that attitude in his time in a discourse, altogether unhistorical probably, which he has Maecenas deliver to Augustus advising him as to his manner of government.[1] The principle was faithfully adhered to by the successors of Augustus, until finally Gallienus went so far as to forbid Senators to enter any army camp; and Severus in his time had discontinued the custom of recruiting praetorians from Italy, Spain, Macedonia, and Noricum, and brought them on from all other sections of the Empire, even from the most barbarous countries.[2]

2598 [3] Suetonius, *Divus Vespasianus,* 9: "The two highest orders, which had been exhausted by a varied slaughter and contaminated by long-standing negligence, he purged and recruited anew by a revision of the census of Senators and knights, removing unworthy members of those classes and making new elections of Italians and provincials of reputable character." Aurelius Victor, *De Caesaribus,* 9: "At the same time, taking a census in the old-fashioned way, he removed all discreditable characters from the Senate, and by an election of distinguished men from hither and thither, he scraped together a thousand patrician families (*gentes*—Causabon) where he had found a bare two hundred, so many having perished in the cruel persecutions of the tyrants."

2600 [1] Dio is simply stating, as through Maecenas, the ideals of the Empire as conceived in his time. He also stresses the advantages of complete separation between civil and military functions, *Ibid.,* LII, 27, 4-5.

2600 [2] Dio Cassius, *Historia Romana,* LXXIV, 2. Dio adds that that spelled ruin for young men in Italy, in that they turned to brigandage and the gladiatorial profession as a result. And *cf.* Marquardt, *Organisation des römischen Reichs,* p. 557.

2601. The development may be pictured roughly in these terms: under the Republic obligation of actual military service on the part of members of the *élite;* in the early years of the Empire, a merely formal obligation, actual service not being forbidden; in the latter periods, complete legal disqualification from actual military service.

2602. The case of Pliny the Younger illustrates what military service was like for young knights in the transition period. He spent his term of service in the commissary. On the other hand he praises Trajan for having seen actual service.[1] According to Suetonius, *Divus Claudius,* 25, 1, Claudius "instituted a sort of nominal military service, which he called 'supernumerary' and which was designed to provide military credit for men who had seen no service."

2603. Augustus forbade Senators to leave Italy without his permission, exception made for Sicily and the Narbonese, "the people in those parts being unarmed and peacefully inclined."[1] Senators were not allowed to set foot in Egypt on any condition,[2] and that prohi-

---

2602 [1] *Epistulae,* VII, 31. He is speaking of his acquaintance with one Claudius Pollio, whom he had met while in the service: "I came to know this man very well while we were in the service together, and not merely as a fellow-soldier. He was in command of a wing-division [cavalry and allies]. I was ordered by the consular legate to examine the supplies accounts of the wing-forces and cohorts." He also seems to have found time to devote to philosophy and literature. In *Ibid.,* I, 10, he alludes to the philosopher Euphrates: "I met him first in Syria when I was a mere boy doing my term of service. I got to know him intimately and thoroughly. I did my best to win his close acquaintance, though that was no great task [with such an affable person]." Of another philosopher he says, *Ibid.,* III, 11: "I made a close acquaintance with Artemidorus at the time when I was serving as tribune in Syria." Those who chose, however, were at liberty to do otherwise, and, like Trajan, actually serve in the army: *Panegyricus,* 15: "You were not content merely to have seen a camp and rushed, so to say, through a brief service. You took your cadetship so seriously that you could have been a general at once." Tacitus, *Agricola,* 5, praises Agricola for not emulating young men who spent their terms of military service in riotous living: "Nor did Agricola apply his title and inexperience as a tribune [cadet] licentiously, after the manner of young men who turn their periods of service to lustful indulgences, nor did he idle his time away in pleasures and furloughs (*commeatus*)."

2603 [1] Dio Cassius, *Historia Romana,* LII, 42, 6. According to Dio, *Ibid.,* LIII, 12, 4, the real consideration underlying the distribution of the provinces between Augustus and the Senate was the Emperor's concern to be the only one to have soldiers at his command. Senators sent to govern provinces, furthermore, were forbidden (LIII, 13, 3) to wear swords and military uniform, though he granted that privilege to his own governors.

2603 [2] Tacitus, *Annales,* II, 59: "Among the other secrets of his scheme for holding power (*inter alia dominationis arcana*) Augustus segregated Egypt, forbidding

bition was regarded as so important that it was reinforced with religious sanctions.[3] Under Alexander Severus, according to Borghesi, under Aurelian, according to Kuhn, the provincial governments were divided into two branches, with a *praeses* for the civil branch, and a *dux* for the military.

2604. The constantly widening gap between the soldier and the civilian progressively crippled the military spirit in the latter and made him more and more helpless and more and more incapable of defending himself *armata manu*. When Septimius Severus marched through Italy with his legions, the cities were terror-stricken, "for the Italians had long since left all use of arms and military discipline, devoting themselves to agriculture and a peaceable course of life."[1] That was a good indication of the supineness with which they would deal with the Barbarian invasions.

2605. Nevertheless in the days of Gallienus, the grave and imminent peril of such a catastrophe seemed to bring the Romans back to some signs of life, though for a brief moment. "The Emperor Gallienus was engaged beyond the Alps with the Germans. Perceiving the dire peril, the Roman Senate armed all soldiers in the city and supplied weapons to the most able-bodied men among the people, so raising a force that was larger than the army of the Barbarians; and they, fearing the outcome of a battle, withdrew from the neighbourhood of Rome."[1] But the military oligarchy that was exploiting the Empire soon come to the rescue. Fearing that the optimates might seize power, Gallienus ordered the Senate

Senators or Roman knights of any consequence to enter that country without his permission. That was to prevent anybody who might chance to establish himself in that province and get possession of the key-points by land or sea, even be it with a small garrison as compared with great armies, from cutting off the food supply of Italy" (*ne fame urgeret Italian—fama* misprint for *fame*).

2603 [3] Trebellius Pollio, *Tyranni triginta*, 22, 10-14: "When he [Lucius Mussius Aemilianus] decided to confer the proconsulate [of Egypt] upon Theodotus he was forbidden to do so by the pontiffs, who declared that it was unlawful for consular fasces to enter Alexandria. . . . It is said that a gilded column at Memphis bore an inscription in Egyptian characters to the effect that Egypt would be free when once Roman fasces and the bordered toga of a Roman Senator (*praetexta*) should enter it."

2604 [1] Herodian, *Historiae*, II, 11. Herodian further notes the contrast between the Italians of the Republic and the Italians of the days of Septimius Severus, remarking that Augustus had been responsible for disarming them.

2605 [1] Zosimus, *Historia nova*, I, 37-38 (Reitemeier, pp. 49-50; Davis, pp. 20-21).

to disband its militia and prohibited Senators from entering any army camp.[2] Alexander Severus used to say that "soldiers had their proper trade, exactly as literary men had theirs," and that it was "the duty of every man to do the thing he was fitted for."[3] Arrius Menander says bluntly, *Digesta,* XLIX, 16, 2, §1 (*Corpus iuris civilis,* Vol. I, p. 940; Scott, Vol. XI, p. 188): "For a man to join the army when he has no right to do so is a serious crime; and, like other crimes, it becomes the more serious in view of the importance and dignity of the army."

2606. So the army of the Empire ended by being an agglomeration of the worst elements, and it became necessary to find soldiers among the Barbarians—a way of inviting the enemy into the house. Vegetius, *De re militari,* I, 7 (Clarke, p. 15), gives a vivid picture of the situation: "Never has time served to improve an army that has been careless in its choice of recruits, and that we have learned

2605 [2] Aurelius Victor, *De Caesaribus,* 33: "*Quia primus ipse metu socordiae suae* [alarmed at the consequences of his own mistake], *ne imperium ad optimos nobilium transferretur, senatum militia vetuit etiam adire exercitum.*" The severance of optimates and army became increasingly strict thereafter. *Codex Iustiniani,* X, 31 (32), 55 (*Corpus iuris civilis,* Vol. II, p. 652; Scott, Vol. XV, p. 123): "The August Emperors Theodosius and Valentinian to their provost Isidorus: If any decurion or any subject of the curia has presumed to undertake any military service, let him not be provided with a regular enlistment but be returned at once to his proper status, lest he or any children born to him after such service be enabled to shirk the duty he owes to his country." The order was issued in Constantinople, April 8, *anno* 436 A.D. And *cf. Ibid.,* XII, 34(33), 2 (*Corpus iuris civilis,* Vol. II, p. 749; Scott, Vol. XV, p. 277), and the *Codex Theodosianus,* VIII, 4, 28 (Haenel, p. 711). Other classes of the population were also barred from military service. *Codex Iustiniani,* XII, 34(33), 1 (*anno* 528-29) (*Corpus iuris civilis,* Vol. II, p. 571; Scott, Vol. XV, pp. 279-80): "The Emperor Justinian to his provost Mena: Superintendents of workshops in this mother-city or in the provinces we prohibit from undertaking any military service from this date forward." However, he excepts business men, barring them only from the armed militia, and also armourers, because of their usefulness to the army: "Merchants shall be ineligible for service of this kind from the date of this edict. Those who ply their trade for the production of arms shall not be denied admittance to service compatible with their trades, meanwhile continuing to practise the latter." Rural farmers could not be accepted for the army. *Ibid.,* XII, 34(33), 31 (*Corpus iuris civilis,* Vol. II, p. 749; Scott, Vol. XV, p. 277): "The August Emperors Arcadius and Honorius to Pulcher, commander of both services: Your Highness (*sublimitas tua*) will observe with watchful care that neither farmers nor foresters shall be accepted for military service either as volunteers or as conscripts." [In other texts this edict is attributed to the Emperors Diocletian and Maximian.—A. L.]

2605 [3] Aelius Lampridius, *Alexander Severus,* 46, 1 (Magie, Vol. II, p. 271).

from our own practice and experience. To that have been due all the defeats which our enemies have inflicted upon us at one place or another, since they can be attributed only to the great negligence and indifference with which our soldiers have been selected in view of a long peace and the rush for civilian offices on the part of our better citizens (*honestiores*), and the fact that, by favour or fraud of recruiting officials, the army accepts from the owners whose duty it is to supply them only men for whom their masters can have no possible use." [1]

2607. Roman society was stiffening and class-circulation, whether legal or actual, began meeting all sorts of obstacles. If now and again imperial favour would overleap them in the case of some individual, that only meant that the governing class was being peopled to that extent with individuals not very worthy of places in it. Alexander Severus organized into gilds all the crafts and trades, so giving legal status to a system that most probably already existed in the fact.[1] That system grew and prospered thereafter, approximating a

2606 [1] Farther along, *Ibid.*, I, 28 (Clarke, p. 44), Vegetius returns to the attack: "The security of a long peace has inclined men partly to the enjoyments of leisure and partly to civilian occupations. So we see that interest in military training first declines into carelessness, then into mere pretense, and finally into oblivion." Conditions to an extent similar have been observed in China, and are observable today, in this year 1913, in a number of our modern countries (§ 2423 [1]) that are manifesting their real temperaments through the symptoms of democratic humanitarianism.

2607 [1] Lampridius, *Alexander Severus*, 33, 2 (Magie, Vol. II, pp. 241-43): "He organized wine-sellers, greengrocers (*lupinarii*), shoemakers, and all the other trades, into gilds, and gave them defenders from their own numbers and specified the judges before whom each should come." See Pareto, *Cours,* § 803: "In general terms and without attaching too much importance to dates that are not very certain, one may distinguish one period that runs from Augustus to Alexander Severus. During that period the gilds are authorized by the government but membership is free. The Emperors now and again interpose to encourage certain gilds that are organized for purposes of public utility. A second period begins with Alexander Severus, who organized or perhaps reorganized the gilds. . . . In a third period that extends from Constantine to Theodosius, the element of constraint in gild organization is more conspicuous. Equilibrium has broken down. Privileges no longer compensate for burdens. Finally between Theodosius and Honorius, the gilds represent a form of slavery, and people do their utmost to escape from them. Membership in them is now compulsory. As Serrigny well says, *Droit publique et administratif romain,* Vol. I, p. 170: 'The interdiction laid on change of occupation is one of the most distinctive features of imperial legislation. It was applied to a large number of trades or professions and may be taken as a general rule for the bulk of the inhabitants of the Roman Empire.' "

social organization such as is proposed today in the obligatory labour-union.[2] Gradually the craftsman is bound to his trade, the farmer to the soil, the "Augustal" to his gild, the decurion to the Curia. They all tried to wriggle free and escape, but the government gave chase to shirkers and unless they were saved by grace of the Emperor or some powerful influence, they were returned to their posts, to which they and their descendants were to remain bound forever.[3]

2608. Production of wealth diminished and wastage increased, owing to the many burdens laid upon the rich. On the other hand the wealthier classes had ceased to be the governing classes, and membership in them entailed more honour than power. The Emperors were named by an uncouth and corrupt army blessed with no remotest conception of statesmanship. There were no revolutions on the part of the non-military, civilian element that would have

2607 [2] That from the standpoint of production, which is the matter here in question. As regards distribution of wealth the comparison would not hold. A system in which the corporations are exploited is altogether different from a system in which the gilds hold the power and do the exploiting.

2607 [3] The *Augustales* were just below the order of the decurions in the social scale. De Ruggiero, *Dizionario epigrafico, s.v. Augustalis:* "From the third decade of the second century on, a radical transformation takes place in the institution of the *Augustales,* extending especially to those communities which theretofore had had annual 'colleges' of the *sexviri Augustales.* . . . But even in such communities as had as yet known only *Augustales* . . . a goodly number of *sexviri Augustales* organized in corporations now appear in their stead. . . . Even in places where the cult of Augustus had not at first been accepted by the people at large . . . there now arises a corporation organized as a gild, and designated as the 'college of the *sexviri Augustales.'* " In the prosperous days of the Empire, it had been a much-prized honour to belong to the sexvirs. In the days of the decline it became an unbearable burden which people tried in every way to avoid. Bouché-Leclercq, *Manuel des institutions romaines,* p. 558 (quoted by Brissaud in an appendix to his translation of Marquardt, *Le culte chez les romains,* Vol. II, pp. 233-34): "Like all honours under the Empire, the office of sexvir was burdensome and came to be nothing more than a tax added to other taxes. . . . The gild was reinvested with certain rights that it had lost in losing its status as a private association, notably civil rights, the right, that is, to receive legacies and gifts, the right to manage its own funds and to choose its own treasurers. . . . That was a way of giving a little vitality to an institution that was menaced with atrophy. And yet, towards the end of the third century, it became necessary to apply to that priesthood the system of compulsory investiture by which the municipal councils and municipal corporations were kept full (*Corpus inscriptionum Latinarum,* Vol. X, no. 114, p. 16; and Vol. II, no. 4514, p. 604). So the decurions who appointed the sexvirs came to exercise upon others the same compulsion to which they were themselves subject."

mixed classes, started class-circulation afresh, and brought individuals distinguished by Class I residues to posts of leadership. Montesquieu very aptly compares the Roman Empire in decline with the regency in Algiers in his own time.[1] But Algiers did not have a bureaucracy, like the Roman bureaucracy of the decline, to sap every source of individual activity and initiative. Roman society declined economically and intellectually under the curse of a stupid military caste and a cowardly and superstitious bureaucracy.

2609. In the West this ossified social order was shattered by the Barbarian invasions (§§ 2551 f.). They brought anarchy, but they also brought a certain amount of flexibility and freedom. To proceed directly along a line *ac* (Figure 48) from the corporations of the dying Empire—in other words, from a situation, *ma,* where ties are very strong,

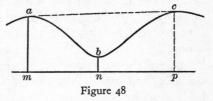

Figure 48

to the gilds of the Middle Ages, or, in other words, a situation, *pc,* where ties are also strong, is to miss the real line, *abc,* and disregard the situation *nb*—the anarchy resulting from the Barbarian invasions, in which ties were few and weak. That error has been to an extent perpetuated by the common failure to distinguish between the state of fact in a country and the state of law. Where liberty is not explicitly granted by law it is assumed that freedom does not and cannot exist; whereas freedom may very well result from the absence of laws or—as is the more frequent case—from failure to enforce, or efficiently to enforce, existing laws. So the crystallization in a country is often less complete than would appear from its law, the law picturing the factual situation very loosely. Corruption of public officials also serves in many cases as an effective remedy for the oppressiveness of a legislation that otherwise would be unbearable.[1]

2608 [1] *Considerations sur les causes de la grandeur des Romains et de leur décadence,* Chap. XVI (*Œuvres,* p. 287; Baker, p. 329).

2609 [1] Guizot gives a terse but excellent description of the state of society in the days of Gregory of Tours: *Grégoire de Tours,* Vol. II, p. 265: "The condition of administration in those days of confusion might be imagined even if one knew nothing of the documents. The institutions emanating from the central power have lapsed. Municipal institutions have in part been preserved by the cities, which could

2610. In the Western Empire the crystallization in society was broken by the Barbarian invasions. In the Eastern Empire it held on intact and all the effects of "planning" ("organization") carried to an extreme became manifest.[1] An anecdote that has come down to us from the Byzantium of those days serves to give a vivid picture of the conditions that prevailed in Attila's time. The historian Priscus Panites, author of a *Historia Byzantina,* in large part lost, was on the staff of Maximinus, who had been sent by Theodosius on an embassy to Attila. In the Hun camp he happened on a Greek who was living at the time among the Scythians and had acquired great wealth. The man told him his story, *De legationibus ad Attilam,* pp. 86-87, 77, 97. He had been taken prisoner in a battle and given as part of the booty to Onegisius, next to Attila the greatest man among the Scythians. "He fought valiantly against the Romans and the tribe of the Acatzires and, giving his Barbarian master the booty which he had won in the field, he obtained freedom according to the law of the Scythians. He married a woman of the Barbarians, raised a family, and having obtained a seat at the table of Onegisius, he thought that he was enjoying a better living than he had ever had. For those who live among the Scythians lead quiet lives after a war, each enjoying his own goods unmolested by anyone. Those,

not exist without them, and tolerated by the new masters. These latter have gathered up a few scattered fragments of the great administrative machine which the Romans had created, and used them, but with modifications necessarily resulting from contact with Germanic habits. Disorder has spread from administrative institutions to the geographical units which correspond to them."

2610 [1] Pareto, *Cours,* § 802: "The bad economic organization of the Roman Empire, the systematic destruction of liquid capital, further and further affected production. Instead of trying to make head against the current that was leading to such deadly results, there was an ever growing trend towards greater protection, and the government tried to 'plan' economic production. The first step was to give privileges to the arts and trades gilds. The last step was to reduce them to virtual slavery." One has only to read *The Book of the Prefect or the Edict of Emperor Leo the Wise on the Gilds of Constantinople (Le livre du préfet, etc.),* edited by Nicole, to see the limits to which "planning" (organization), in other words, social crystallization, could be carried in those days, and so to get some distant conception of the similar limits towards which our present-day societies are advancing. [It should not be forgotten that these lines were written in the year 1914.—A. L.]

The description of the economic evolution of the Roman Empire given in the *Cours* is not exempt from the errors pointed out in §§ 2334-35. That is an interesting fact, because my theory of economic crises not only avoids those errors, but reveals them. That fact stands in some relation, perhaps, to the following (§ 2547 [1]): 1. I succumbed, to some extent at least, to a common preconception among economists

however, who live among the Romans run ready risk of destruction in war, for they must repose their hopes of personal safety in others, their tyrants not allowing them to bear arms; and to those who do, the ineptitude of their generals proves fatal, for they mismanage everything. And the burdens they bear in times of peace are harder to endure than the evils of war, owing to harsh taxes and abuses from the wicked, for the laws are not the same for all. If the law-breaker is a man of wealth, his crime goes unpunished; if he is a poor man, inexperienced in intrigue, he is given the penalty sanctioned by the law, provided he does not lose his life before sentence is passed, because of the long protraction of processes at law and the great costs in money. There is indeed a most iniquitous manner of obtaining by bribery what should be adjudicated by law; and it is the fact that no tribunal will give redress for the injustices one has suffered unless money is lavished on judges and officials." In rebuttal Priscus sings the praises of Roman administration; but it is noteworthy that the very embassy on which he was serving illustrates the cowardice and corruption of that government. Maximinus was an honest man, one of those individuals whom governments in every age use to mask corrupt and dishonest practices (one of our A's: §§ 2268, 2300); but with him went Edecon and Vigilias

that the economic factor can be isolated from other social factors. Not till I had completed the investigation presented in these volumes did I become altogether aware of that error, which meantime kept me from taking the short step that leads from the particular theory of economic crises to the general theory of social phenomena indicated in §§ 2330 f. 2. I also succumbed, without any very clear perception of doing so, to a common inclination of economists and sociologists not to confine themselves to a quest for the uniformities (laws) that obtain in the relationships between facts, but, though equipped with a very limited and imperfect knowledge of the facts, to imagine that they know the goal towards which society "ought" and can advance; and that their thinking has some mysterious power to change the facts and make that goal attainable. Not yet having managed to give a moderately passable statement to the problem of real movements (§ 129), they imagine they can handle the much more difficult problem of virtual movements (§§ 130, 2552-II-a). Not content with attending to the business of science, they have the further hankering to counsel and preach. Striving to substitute scientific experience for faith in every department of my work, I did not perceive that I was still infected with one shred of faith that finds its expression in a certain sentimental leaning in favour of freedom. That leaning is not consistent with pure experience, which is interested in the relationship between facts altogether apart from any preconceptions.

This little incident is noted here as supplying an example of the obstacles that are for ever interposing to hinder the search for experimental truth in the social sciences.

with orders to devise ways and means for assassinating Attila. The Imperial government could "plan" anything, even assassination! On that occasion, things did not turn out well. Attila got wind of the plot, and sent ambassadors to upbraid the Emperor with words that cut to the bone, reminding Theodosius that in paying tribute to him, Theodosius had made himself his slave, and he added: "Improperly therefore doth he conduct himself who plotteth like a faithless slave against his better and one whom Fortune hath made his master." [2]

2611. One among countless anecdotes might be mentioned to show how people climbed to the governing class under Byzantine "planning." Synesius was an individual who lived about a century before Priscus's Greek. He writes to his brother: [1] "It is hardly likely that Chilas the panderer can be unknown to very many people in view of the fame he won at his trade; for Andromache the mime, the most beautiful woman living in our time, was of his troop. After spending his youth in that handsome profession, and getting on toward middle age, he thought it altogether consistent with his

2610 [2] If the current period of our demagogic plutocracy continues to hold on the ascent for some time longer and comes to give greater scope to a movement that we are now witnessing in its early beginnings, one may readily imagine some individual who has managed to escape from the oppression of that future time and taken refuge with a certain people, X, repeating with few changes the words of the Greek with whom Priscus talked: "People who live among the X's lead quiet lives after they have worked and put aside a few savings, each enjoying his own goods unmolested by anyone; whereas in his former country he was robbed and oppressed, now by fair means, now by foul. There he had to pay heavy taxes, which were imposed by the votes of a majority that did not pay them and were paid by fewer and fewer people, so mounting beyond all limits in order to meet the enormous costs of government by a demagogic plutocracy. And he had further to suffer annoyances from those who run such government, or their accomplices. There the laws are not the same for all. If a law-breaker is in some way connected with the ruling element, his crime goes unpunished; if he is someone, such as the humble smuggler, who flouts the fiscal privileges of that class, he suffers the penalty sanctioned by the law. No better fate awaits the innocent man falsely accused, who wrongs no one and would suffer no wrong himself; for litigations are long-drawn-out and cost fortunes owing to the whims of 'kind-hearted judges' and the intrigues of others who curry favour with the politicians and with 'outstanding members of the bar.' There is indeed a most iniquitous manner of obtaining by 'influence' what ought to be adjudicated by law—by placing oneself at the disposal of those in power and helping them in the elections, from which they derive their power."

2611 [1] *Epistulae*, CX (*Opera*, pp. 252-53; Fitzgerald, p. 205). And cf. *Ibid.*, CXXVII (*Opera*, pp. 262-63; Fitzgerald, pp. 216-17), for an account of a certain Euctalius, prefect of Egypt, and a first-rate thief.

former estate that he should win renown in arms. He has been here now for some time, on his appointment by the Emperor to the command of our brave Marcomanni. The Marcomanni have always been a doughty lot, but now that they have a general so illustrious, one may guess that they will provide us with miracles." And how did this Chilas the panderer win Imperial favour? Through the good offices of two individuals, one named John, the other Antiochus, who seem to have had antecedents as creditable as his own. With a governing class being built up in such a manner, one readily understands how the provinces of the Empire were one by one lost, and in the end the capital itself. But such things are nothing peculiar to the Byzantine bureaucracy; they are general, and nearly always feature the senile period of bureaucracies. They have been and are still observable in China, Russia, and other countries. So social "planning" begins with a "boom," and ends in disaster (§ 2585).[2]

2611 [2] In the European War of 1914 the Russian bureaucracy made the same identical blunders it had made in the Russo-Japanese War. It seemed to have learned nothing from experience. A speech delivered in the Duma on Aug. 14, 1915, by M. Maklakov, brother to a former Minister of the Interior, gives in a particular form a general view of the social state in question: *Journal de Genève,* Sept. 3, 1915: "That brings us to the thorniest question in our political life. It is no secret to anyone that Russia, alas, is the classic model of a state where many people are not where they belong (*Approval from Left and Centre*). [The senile stage of a bureaucracy that was a good one in its time.] It is a country where there is general complaint about the lack of good men but where no attention is paid to the good ones there are. We know only too well, unfortunately, that in Russia the man who succeeds is the pleasant fellow, the amiable nobody (*Voices of approval*), the agreeable conversationalist, the man who knows how to drift with the current or guess the direction of the next puff of wind, while the man who does not succeed is the man of character, of purpose, of real competence. [A description by a practical man of a problem in class-circulation.] Things have come to such a pass, gentlemen, that a rapid and sometimes brilliant career is a discredit to a man. We know that such a career means not talent, merit, achievement, but accommodation, complicity, favouritism, patronage. (*Approval from Left and Centre.*) Appointment after appointment constitutes a public scandal, a challenge to public opinion, and when the mistake is discovered it is too late to remove the appointee, the prestige of power forbidding. This new government has the task of beating Germany. It will soon see that the harder task will be to vanquish the resistance of its subordinates. The great sand-bar on which all initiative runs aground in Russia is the make-up of the bureaucracy." A Socialist orator had laid the blame for Russia's unpreparedness on the "despotic" régime. M. Markov replied very appositely: "M. Adjemov has very soundly remarked that in this terrible conflict Germany was ready. He has also said in a tone of reproach that France was too. The French, really, were worse prepared than we, and the war has shown that the strongest of the Allies is Russia. We hear

2612. As we have said many times and again repeated just above (§ 2553), undulations in derivations follow undulations in social facts. That is why, about a century ago during an ascending period of freedom, it was fashionable to condemn the rigid and restrictive institutions of the Byzantine Empire. Now that we are in a descending period of freedom and an ascending period of "planning," the same institutions are admired and praised, and it is proclaimed that the European countries owe a great debt to the Byzantine Empire for having saved them from the Moslem invasion, forgetting that brave warriors of Western Europe succeeded time and again in defeating and repelling the Arabs and the Turks and that they very easily occupied Constantinople before any Asiatic peoples conquered that city. Byzantium shows how far the curve along which our societies are now moving may lead. Anyone who admires that future is necessarily led to admire that past, and anyone who admires that past will in all consistency admire that future.

from the Left that we were not ready because freedom has been in chains. But the French, English, and Belgian governments were not in chains, and yet they were not ready—they were less ready than Russia." And it should not be forgotten that the government of Catherine the Great was more rather than less autocratic than the Russian régime under Nicholas, yet it was victorious in a number of wars.

APPENDIX

Index-Summary of Theorems

Index-Summary of Theorems [1]

I. GENERAL SUBJECTS

I-*a*

There is nothing absolute about the norms that are followed in a scientific work (see II-*l*, below); they are determined with reference to the purposes of that work itself. Statement of the norms that are followed here (Chap. I, *4, 5, 6, 70, 71*; and see Sociology [in Index-Bibliography following]).

I-*b*

For mere convenience in studying them, we divide the facts that are observable in human societies into two categories:

M. Manifestations, verbal or through conduct, of instincts, sentiments, inclinations, appetites, interests, *etc.*, and the logical or pseudo-logical inferences that are drawn from such manifestations. This category therefore comprises both logical and non-logical conduct (Chap. II). The part that is made up of non-logical conduct may be further subdivided into two categories:

1. A part, *d,* that does not give rise to verbal manifestations
2. A part, *c,* that does give rise to verbal manifestations (*851-54, 1690, 2083*).

N. All other facts that are observable in the world in which human societies appear.

This classification of facts is strictly experimental. The two categories *M* and *N* have nothing to do with the "inner" and "outer" worlds of the metaphysicists (*95*, and see Concepts). They are just groups of facts. Animals do not have any part *c;* they have only the part *d* (see Actions, non-logical). Human beings often fail to realize, they do not know, they disregard, the fact that many of the verbal manifestations that go to make up *c* are mere manifestations of instincts, inclinations, *etc.* (see Actions, non-logical, Derivations). One of the purposes of this work is to strip realities of such veilings of sentiment (Chaps. II-V).

---

[1] [Pareto's own Index-Summary with his own references, accurate or inaccurate as they may be. Number references are to paragraphs in the text. Word references are adapted to the Index and Bibliography following. Numbers that Pareto starred as important are printed in italic.—A. L.]

I-*c*

The element *c* is outstanding in human beings, for they are wont to express their instincts, sentiments, *etc.* in verbal form, and they are prone to embellish them with logical or pseudo-logical developments. The element *c* readily and spontaneously detaches itself from the facts of which it is a mere manifestation and seems to possess an existence of its own (1690, and see III, below: *Language*). The element *c* is divisible into two further parts:

a. A part that varies but slightly (residues)

b. A part that is much more variable (derivations) (*798-841*, Chaps. V, VII-X).

I-*d*

We have to consider the following relations between the categories of facts designated as M and N:

a. Mutual relations between M and N

β. Relations of M and N to theories, doctrines, propositions

γ. Relations of M and N to the make-up of human societies.

As a first approximation, the M group may in many cases be taken simply as *c,* especially in an examination of theories (Chaps. II-V).

I-*e*

a. Mutual relations between M *and* N: There is a certain relation, which is not a relation of exact correspondence, between M and N, and likewise between the various groups in M and N, or, in other words, between various groups of facts (see Interdependence). Every living being adapts itself in some way or other to the world in which it lives, and therefore depends in some way or other on that world, both as regards material forms and in respect of instincts, sentiments, and so on. Instinct, for example, in predacious animals is correlated with the existence of the prey on which they feed (1768-70). More briefly one might say that there may be certain correspondences between the groups of facts in M and the groups of facts in N. Here we are to concern ourselves more especially with correspondences between *c* and N. The groups designated as *c* may be thought of as nebulous masses made up of a nucleus surrounded by a halo of fog. In the case of some such nebulae there may be a rough correspondence between the nucleus and the facts N, but there is no such correspondence as regards the fog. Sometimes there is no correspondence either for nucleus or fog (1767). In other words, a *c* group is sometimes a bad photograph of *N* (*1778*[1], and see below, III-*f*); then again it has no bearing on *N* at all (Chaps. XI-XII).

I-*f*

Among *c* groups that have no bearing on *N* at all are such as wholly pertain to a supernatural or metaphysical—in short a non-experimental—world. With them are also to be classified such as show a merely partial correspondence. The logico-experimental sciences are not concerned with such relations (see below, II-*g*, II-*h*, II-*i*).

I-*g*

β. *Relations of* M *and* N *to theorie*s. Suppose we consider *c* instead of *M*, in a first approximation. From the standpoint just indicated [I-*f*], the group of facts *c* [i.e., facts giving rise to verbal manifestations], may be subdivided into two other groups:

*c*1. Facts pertaining to the author of the theory

*c*2. Facts pertaining to the human beings with whom he is connected.

These sub-groups, *c*1 and *c*2, will be found to have elements in common. Any theory, evidently, depends on *c*1. Differences between theories arise from differences in the character of that dependence and from the manners in which account is taken of *c*2 and of *N* (see Objective-subjective, Derivations, Residues; Chaps. I, III-V).

I-*h*

The fact that among the facts present in the author of a theory (*c*1) are facts that are present also in other individuals in the group to which he belongs (*c*2) is the source of the illusion that in arguing from *c*1, one argues impersonally and, overreaching the relative and contingent, attains the absolute (see Derivations, Mind, Consensus).

I-*i*

γ. *Relations of* M *and* N *to the make-up of human societies.* From this point of view, *M* may be subdivided into two elements:

Ms. Instincts, sentiments, *etc.* (see Residues)

Mr. Reasonings (see Derivations).

In theory, at one extreme one would get societies determined exclusively by *Ms* and *N*. Animal societies, probably, are of that type. At the other extreme one would get societies determined exclusively by *Mr* and *N*, but such societies do not exist in the concrete (2143). Belief that they can exist is one of the dogmas of the religion that makes a deity of Reason or of "Science" (see Science, Reason, Theology of Science).

Actual human societies fall into intermediary stages (2146). So far as we can know, M and N together seem to determine their make-up (Chap. XII).

I-*l*

Prominent among the relations of M and N to the forms of human societies is their relation to utilities of one sort or another, utilities of individuals, of groups and societies, of all humanity, and so on (see Utility). Of such relations logico-experimental science can take account only through examination of the facts (see below, II-*b*). Non-logico-experimental sciences usually establish such relations *a priori,* in whole or in part. Very often they reduce them to an identity between certain utilities and something that they call "Truth" (Chaps. XI-XIII, and see Utility-truth, Metaphysics, Theology).

I-*m*

Human society is heterogeneous. The theology of equality denies that fact, much as Christian theology in a day gone by denied the existence of antipodes. Logico-experimental science ignores all such theologies when it is looking for uniformities in the facts which they disguise. It is interested, however, in knowing how they arose and to just what facts they correspond (see Derivations, Residues). In a first approximation one may consider certain average phenomena for a given society, but in a second and finer approximation some account almost inevitably has to be taken of social heterogeneity; and if we would not stray too far from realities, certain phenomena must from the outset be considered in their bearing on social heterogeneity. As a step in that direction we may divide society into various classes or strata, now from one point of view, now from another. Such classes or strata have to be considered not only as in a static condition but as in a dynamic condition and that requires a study of class-circulation, the circulation, that is, within *élites* of people who have fixed, or virtually fixed, incomes, as compared with people who have variable incomes (and other sorts of people have to be considered too). In a word, the peculiar characteristics of the various classes have to be taken into account if one would understand the forms that society as a whole assumes, and its evolution in history (see below I-*r;* then: Classes [social], Democracy, Movements [rhythmical], Residues [proportions of], Utility-Truth, Speculators, Rentiers).

I-*n*

Human society is viewed as a system of molecules (2066), which, in space and in time, possess certain properties, are subject to certain ties, subsist in certain relationships. The reasonings (derivations), theories, beliefs that are current in the mass of such molecules are taken as manifestations of the [psychic] state of that mass and are studied as facts on a par with the other facts that society presents to view (below, II-*e*). We look for uniformities among them, and try to get back to the facts in which they in turn originate. We are in no wise engaged in setting up one derivation against another derivation, meeting one faith with another faith. We are concerned to discover in just what relations, in time and in space, derivations and beliefs stand towards each other and towards all other facts (see Apostolates, Applications [practical], Actions, Society as a whole, Economics, Elements, Equilibrium [social, economic], Experience, Uniformities, Maximum of Utility, Method, Ethics, Objective-subjective, Residues, Derivations, Sentiments, Sociology, History, Theories, Speculators).

I-*o*

Social phenomena as a rule develop in waves. Waves are of various types and of varying intensities. They may therefore be classified into groups which mark periods in given phenomena (Movements [rhythmical], Periodicity).

I-*p*

Interdependence. The molecules in the social system are interdependent in space and in time. Their interdependence in space becomes apparent in the mutual relations that subsist between social phenomena. Let the letters *A, B, C* . . . stand for the various parts into which we decide to divide the social mass as a whole for mere convenience in studying it. The logico-experimental science that deals with *A* (economics, for instance) takes direct account of the interdependence of the molecules in *A*. So for the logico-experimental sciences that deal with *B, C* . . . (see Interdependence). Then the logico-experimental science that studies *A* and *B* together, or *A, B, C* together, or *A, B, C, D*, has to take account of interdependences between *A* and *B*, or *A, B* and *C*, and so on. That situation may be described by saying that logico-experimental science distinguishes between analysis and synthesis and supplements analysis by synthesis (see below, II-*q*); or again by saying that the science that deals with *A* cannot by itself yield an exhaustive theory of the concrete phenomena of which *apparently A* is made up (see below II-*r*). Really *A* is made up of mere abstractions that have been drawn from the phenomena in question, by eliminating from them all parts depending on *B, C, D* . . . The synthesis that follows on the analysis aims at restoring such parts to their original situations. Those who follow the methods of the non-logico-experimental sciences in the field of the social sciences, do not grasp that fact, for they deal with concepts (94, 95) rather than with facts, and concepts are not only simpler than facts, but also seem to be much more independent (see Just-unjust, Morality-immorality, Theory and practice, Precepts). From this limitation on the part of such writers it results that when they become aware that the logico-experimental theory that deals with A fails to explain a concrete phenomenon that apparently belongs in A, they conclude that that science should be abandoned, whereas all that it requires is filling out with the results of other sciences (II-s, below). Or perhaps they do worse still and put forward a verbal derivation that betrays a gross ignorance of realities on their part. They assert that economic and social laws have exceptions and fail to perceive the ridiculousness of asserting that there can be uniformities that are not uniform (109, 1689[1], 1792).

I-q

Interdependence. As we consider the phenomena in question in point of time, the above remarks have to be supplemented with still others. Social phenomena assume essentially undulatory forms (I-o). A given phenomenon, A, presents a sequence of waves, and so do the phenomena B, C, D . . . Account therefore has to be taken: 1. Of the interdependences of the undulations in A, and so for the undulations in B, C, D, each phenomenon being taken by itself. 2. Of the interdependence of the undulations in the various phenomena (2552). This latter research stands closer in character than the first to the study of interdependences considered from the standpoint of space (I-p). The influence of earlier upon succeeding waves might become apparent in the course of a study of the whole movement, if such a study were conducted by a method that posited an undulatory form in phenomena (2585). Many writers are deterred from doing that because they are looking for a *cause* for the maladies of society, with the idea of removing that cause (2541); or because they are less interested in studying facts as they are than in preaching in order to change them; or because they are writing ethical, theological or some other sort of history instead of logico-experimental history (see History). Really, in many departments of social life, waves follow one on the other very much as the various ages succeed each other in the individual life (2541). Just as birth may roughly be taken as the origin of boyhood, and boyhood of manhood and then of old age and death, so the earlier periods in social phenomena may in a sense be regarded as the origin of the periods that follow, and certain given facts may at first stimulate prosperity and then decadence (2541, 2585). All the above runs counter to the results that are yielded by non-logico-experimental histories and theories that pretend to arrive at absolute judgments (II-*m*) as to the *values* of facts on the basis of some ethical, metaphysical or theological principle (see Theories, Religion, Metaphysics, Sociology).

I-*r*

Proportions of residues in the various social strata. Among the many, many elements that have a bearing on social forms and on the development of those forms in history, evidently outstanding are the relative proportions in which residues are to be found functioning in the various social strata and especially the proportions of Class I to Class II residues in the ruling and subject classes respectively. History shows that a first rough outline of developments may be obtained by centering the main attention on those proportions, other circumstances of importance being considered in subordination to them (Chaps. XII-XIII).

II. LOGICO-EXPERIMENTAL AND NON-LOGICO-EXPERIMENTAL THEORIES

(Saving specification to the contrary, "experience" means "experience and observation.")

II-*a*

If a dispute is to be decided, there has to be a judge (*17,* 27, 28, 961). In the logico-experimental sciences, that judge is objective experience, which alone has the prerogative of supplying *proofs* (16, 17, 42, 69-7, 475). In the non-logico-experimental sciences, any number of other judges may be available, such as sacred books, in the case of believers in this or that religion, "conscience" in the case of some metaphysicists, "introspection" in the case of others, "necessary principles" for still others, and so on (see Truth, Introspection, Liberal Christianity, Natural Law, Right Reason, Nature, Good [the], Metaphysics). Very frequently the non-logico-experimental sciences use a mere accord of sentiments as their judge (42, 49, 581; see Logic of Sentiments, Persuasion). Often considerations of utility are brought in, a doctrine finding its "truth" in the fact that it is considered "beneficial" (see Truth—423, 473, 474, 475, 581, 593, 594, 961; see Sociology).

II-*b*

Logico-experimental theories accept guidance only from the facts. They are made up of descriptive propositions that assert experimental uniformities and of the consequences that follow from those propositions (see Theories). Non-logico-experimental theories strive to exercise control over the facts, and they contain propositions that overstep experimental uniformities in one direction or another (55, 56, 521, 524; see Uniformities, Principles, Metaphysics).

II-c

The logico-experimental sciences derive principles from the facts (2078 [1]) and such principles are at all times subordinate to those facts. The non-logico-experimental sciences posit certain principles *a priori* and the facts depend on those principles (10, 11, 22, *23, 24, 54-56, 57, 63,* 90-93, 343, 514, 521, *638, 642-43,* 665, 976, 1532, 2397, 2398).

II-d

Logico-experimental theories argue from facts, that is to say, from the categories c_2 and N, as defined in I-g above. They take account of c_1 merely as so many facts, never as sentiments that have to be deferred to. Their exclusive concern is with putting facts in relation with other facts (see Explanation). Everything that lies beyond experience is foreign to them (Chaps. IV, V). Abstractions are nothing but elements common to certain numbers of facts. Non-logico-experimental theories argue from sentiments (c_1) that their authors have (I-g), and more particularly, indeed, from the impressions that certain words make on them (see Language). They are concerned not only with facts but with certain entities that lie beyond experience (Chaps. IV, V) and they try to bring facts into some sort of relation with those entities. For them, abstractions are not mere compendia of certain definite groups of facts, but have an independent existence all their own. The difference between logico-experimental theories and theories that are not such, lies mainly in the fact that logico-experimental theories try to reduce the exclusive dominion of c_1 as nearly as possible to zero (*2411,* Chap. I), whereas non-logico-experimental theories, often implicitly, and sometimes explicitly, ascribe a more or less preponderant rôle to c_1 (*see* Classification, Theories). At one extreme one finds theories that strive to do away with the influence of the c_1 group, and to keep strictly to c_2 and N—at least as far as possible, for it is exceedingly difficult to keep clear of c entirely. At the other extreme stand theories that give full rein to the sentiments expressed by c_1—again as far as possible, for it is just as difficult to ignore c_2 and N completely (*142,* 143, 170, and see 9, 16, 69, 75, 76, 108, 170, 514 [2], 521, 803, *977-979,* 2411, Chaps. I, III-V; and see Objective-subjective, Hypotheses, Economics, Sociology).

II-e

The logico-experimental sciences examine the theories, doctrines, propositions, *etc.*, that are observable in society as mere social facts (I-*n*), even if they are not logico-experimental, even if they are altogether fantastic or absurd (7, 12, *69-6*, 81, 145, 466, 514 [2], 838, 843, 845). Analogies with philological studies (346, 468, 469, 659, *879-883;* see Derivations).

II-f

Speaking from a chronological standpoint, the non-logico-experimental sciences as a rule precede the logico-experimental (57).

II-g

The domain of logico-experimental theories is entirely distinct from the domain of non-logico-experimental theories, and has no points of contact with it. Study of the experimental world has nothing to do with study of the non-experimental world (16, 43, *69-2*, 70, 97, 474, 477, 481, 973). Each of the two researches is sovereign in its own domain and neither can be granted the right to invade the domain of the other (16, 43, *69-3*, *70*, 477).

II-h

Gods and deified entities dwell beyond the boundaries of experimental reality, as do metaphysical (see Metaphysics, Theology) and pseudo-experimental abstractions (see Theories, Liberal Christianity). From the standpoint of logico-experimental science a metaphysical abstraction is neither better nor worse than a deified abstraction (1667; see Gnosis). As regards proximity to experimental reality, the entities and principles of metaphysical systems, the entities and principles of the theologies, in fact, non-experimental entities and principles in general, all stand on a par (67, 616, 928, 1667, 1767; see Entities, Metaphysics, Religion). One religion cannot be more or less scientific than another (16 [2], 43, 309, 377, 569, 570, 616, *630,* 765, 928, 1533, 1767; see Liberal Christianity, Modernism). Metaphysics is not more "scientific" than theology, nor does it come any closer to reality (67, *378,* 928, 1533, 1538; see Imperatives [categorical], Right Reason, Nature).

II-i

Logico-experimental science cannot accept theorems that establish relations between things that lie in whole or in part outside the experimental world (479, 1667). Neither can it accept, short of experimental verification, theorems that relate things that do belong to the experimental world, but where the correlation is established by the elimination of non-experimental entities (479, *480-482*, 1540, *1607, 1608*). In the same way it rejects any conclusion that might be drawn from the fact that such theorems are or are not verifiable by experience as to the existence or non-existence outside the experimental world of the entity so eliminated (*481*, 487, 516; see Religion, Prophecy, Miracles, Entities, Elimination of non-experimental *X*). All the theorems just stated are implications of II-*g* above.

II-*l*

Since there is no basis of comparison between logico-experimental studies and non-logico-experimental studies, one cannot say in any absolute way that one is better or worse than the other. One can make such a statement in a relative sense by designating the objective that one is trying to attain (*70, 71*; see Casuistry, Truth, Ideals).

II-*m*

The logico-experimental sciences are in all respects relative, contingent. The non-logico-experimental sciences envisage the absolute (see Absolute). The former offer no conclusions as "certain," "necessary" (1531), "absolute." They halt at probabilities, perhaps very great probabilities (see Certainty-probability). Their conclusions are put forward under the qualification "within the limits of time and space that are known to us" (69-5). The non-logico-experimental sciences offer conclusions as "certain," "necessary," "absolute," and without qualifications of any kind (47, 69-5, 97, 408, 529 [2], 976, 1068, *1531*, 1532, and above, I-*r*).

II-*n*

The logico-experimental sciences do not possess principles that are "certain." The non-logico-experimental sciences do, and they call them "natural" or "necessary" principles, or else "laws" (which are different in their eyes from experimental uniformities), or axioms, metaphysical or theological (55, 56, 90, 91, 642, 1068; see Uniformities, Metaphysics, Religion).

II-*o*

Practitioners of the non-logico-experimental sciences do not as a rule grasp the relative, the contingent character of the logico-experimental sciences and speak of them as though they did envisage some "absolute" or other which would be merely a different absolute from the absolute that is envisaged by the non-experimental sciences (973). They therefore imagine that the logico-experimental sciences have dogmas, such as, for instance, the dogma that the "truth" can be known only through experience (16); the dogma that experimental "truth" is of a higher quality than other sorts of "truth" (26, *46*, 69); the dogma that the theorems of the logico-experimental sciences yield a "certainty" that gives us knowledge of "laws" and not mere experimental uniformities; or the dogma that "everything" can be explained by experience (determinism)—and try if you please to get it into their heads that the very form of such a theorem shows that it cannot be of a logico-experimental character, since a logico-experimental theorem can never recognize the absolute that is implied in the word "everything" (88, *528-532*, 976, *1531;* and see Uniformities, Derivations, Truth, Determinism).

II-*p*

Logico-experimental theories are in a state of continuous development and they advance by successive approximations. Non-logico-experimental theories usually arrive in one bound at a state which those who accept them believe must *obviously* be immutable, though as a matter of fact it varies from writer to writer, from believer to believer (*69-9*, 91, 92, 106, 107, 144, 826, *1531*, 2410; see Approximations [successive], Facts, Movements [rhythmical]).

II-*q*

The logico-experimental sciences distinguish analysis from synthesis (I-*p*). Each of such sciences is essentially analytical, breaking the concrete phenomenon up into various parts and studying those parts one by one. A synthesis is then made by bringing certain of the conclusions together (I-*p*). Real movements are always considered independently of virtual movements—the study of what is is kept distinct from the study of what ought to be (ought to be, if a given purpose is to be realized). The non-logico-experimental sciences tend to combine analysis and synthesis, to blend them one with the other, the writers themselves not always being aware that they are two different things. They fail to keep real and virtual movements distinct, or at least fail adequately to distinguish them (see Movements). All such sciences claim to know directly and completely all about this or that thing, and when that claim is shown by experience to be unfounded, they resort to devices that are often childish, such as quibbling over the meanings that should be given to certain words (see Value); or they declare, or at least imply, that if a thing does not exist, it at least *ought* to exist; or indeed they openly boast that they are interested only in what *ought* to be. The non-experimental element, in such cases, lies in the term *ought,* which is used in an absolute sense, without specification as to any experimental purpose (10, *28-32,* 33-40, *69*, 253, 265, 277, 279, 297-299, 346, 483, 518, 605, 613, 701, 711, 804,

817, 818, 845, *966-75,* 1459, 1687, 1689, 2016, 2017, 2147, 2214, 2219, 2411; see Duty, Empiricism, Theory and practice, Applications [practical], Absolute).

II-*r*

Economics cannot by itself yield a theory for "value," "capital," "interest," "protection," *etc.,* if such terms are taken as referring to concrete phenomena. Its results have to be supplemented with the results yielded by other sciences (I-*p*). So the science of accounting, taken by itself, cannot yield a theory of business in a concrete, nor thermo-dynamics a theory of steam engines in the concrete. And so for other sciences (35, 36, 38, *2022-24, 2219*).

II-*s*

Since, in the logico-experimental sciences, synthesis has to follow on analysis if the concrete phenomenon is to be known, it follows that when it is found that one of the logico-experimental sciences fails to give an exhaustive explanation of a given phenomenon, it has to be filled out with other theories, and not thrown away; nor should one try to save its face by a surreptitious synthesis such as changing meanings in the terms it uses or straying away into some non-experimental field. That, however, is the usual recourse with people who are not versed in thinking with the methods of the logico-experimental sciences, and even with people who are, but who succumb to sentiments or to interests the moment they enter economic or sociological spheres (*33-39, 2017-2024;* see Derivations).

II-*t*

Logico-experimental theories strive to attain the perfection of the quantitative method, of measurement. Non-logico-experimental theories are as a rule qualitative (108, *144, 2091-2104,* 2107, *2122, 2155,* 2175, 2467 f.; see Quantitative-qualitative).

II-*u*

Experimental reality and social utility are entirely different and sometimes flatly contradictory things. The theorems of the logico-experimental sciences harmonize with the former, but may not harmonize with the latter. The theorems of the non-logico-experimental sciences usually do not harmonize with the former, but they may harmonize with the latter. In a word, a theory may be in accord with experience and yet be harmful to society, or in disaccord with experience and yet beneficial to society (see Utility-truth, Religion, Metaphysics, Reason, Ethics, Ideals).

III. LANGUAGE AND DEFINITIONS

A. LANGUAGE

III-*a*

Scientific language and ordinary parlance (*108*, 109, *113*-118, 245, 266, 331, 366, 396, 408, 815, *960*, 1545, 2240).

III-*b*

In the logico-experimental sciences the aim is to make language as exact as possible. Terms are the better the more definite they are in meaning. In the non-logico-experimental sciences the aim is to leave language vague and indefinite in order to profit by those traits in it, and terms are the better in proportion to their vagueness (9, 18, 21, 26, *69*-6, 108, 171, 408, 499-506, *507*, 508, *515*, 586, 595, *596*, 640, 965, *1546*, 1552-1554, 1686; see Derivations [contradictory], Persuasion, Logic).

III-*c*

From the logico-experimental standpoint, any discussion is futile if nobody knows to what things the terms that are used in it actually correspond (*27*, 69, 108, 119, 380, 442, 490, 965, and see II-*i* above).

III-*d*

The logico-experimental sciences never quarrel about names. They quarrel about the things that the names stand for. A logico-experimental argument retains its full value if the names it uses are replaced by letters of the alphabet or by numbers. If things are designated beyond possibility of doubt or misunderstanding, the names that are given to them matter hardly at all. The non-logico-experimental sciences quarrel over names, and it is better for them that they should, for the terms they use, when they do not stand for altogether fanciful things, at least add a non-experimental something to the things they are trying to designate. That adjunct is very frequently an adjunct of sentiments deriving either from the writer or from somebody else (II-*d*). The conflicts of the non-logico-experimental sciences tend therefore to become battles of words. They lose value and sense if the ordinary words they use for things are replaced with numbers or with letters of the alphabet, since such symbols do not make the appeal to sentiments that ordinary words make (16, *21*, 113, 114, 115, *116*, 119, 124, 128, 380, 514, 580, *642*, 2002).

III-e

Since language, in the logico-experimental sciences, is altogether arbitrary, it does not have the slightest influence upon things. In the non-logico-experimental sciences language, seeming to exist independently of things, may seem to have a greater or lesser influence upon them, and it certainly does have an influence on the theories that are devised to explain them. Both influences may be now slight, now great, and they may even be carried to an extreme where words seem to acquire some occult power over things (magic), or where, at least, they serve for the construction of theories that have no bearing whatever on realities (metaphysics, theology) (see Concepts, Derivations, Religion—*182,* 183, 227, 514, 958-65; Words-things, 658, 660, 691, 698, 1548, 1686).

III-f

Language, at best, reflects facts of the outer world much as a bad photograph reflects them—and in the worst case, a very bad photograph, or a photograph that is a complete botch. To argue from words therefore is like pretending to derive from a botched photograph accurate knowledge of the things it was intended to picture (108 [1], 118, 690, 691, 694-95, 1767, 1769, 1772).

III-g

Ordinary language may permit one to construct a very rough theory, just as the bad photographs mentioned may give some very vague hint as to the things they were supposed to picture. Ordinary language, for one thing, is usually synthetic, so that in using it one does take account, roughly and inadequately to be sure, of certain interdependencies in phenomena. That may be very helpful in cases where no better instruments are available (108-09, 117, *118,* 1767).

III-h

Ordinary language is much more serviceable in practical everyday life than in the elaboration of theories, for the reason that the adjunct of sentiment that it appends to things (III-*d*) is a very important element in practical decisions (*113,* 815, 817; see Empiricism, Theory and practice, Derivations).

III-i

The consequences that follow from the vagueness of ordinary parlance (266-67, 365-66, 376, 1545, *1546,* 1552, 1556, 1797, 1857, 1904-12, 1937, 2240).

III-*l*

Language as a manifestation of non-logical impulses (*158;* see III-*h* above).

III-*m*

Since the logico-experimental sciences use a language that is objective and exact, one must never take it to mean more than it actually states. One must reject every extension in its meaning that sentiment would incline us to make. Since the non-logico-experimental sciences use a language that is in part subjective and indefinite one may take it as meaning something more than what it literally states, or something different. The additions and modifications that are thus introduced in the light of sentiment often fit in exactly with the modifications and extensions that the writer was concerned to make in things themselves. In such cases, therefore, the loose interpretation comes closer than the exact interpretation to what the author may have had in mind (*41, 74-75,* 171, 311, 1678 f.; see Theory and practice).

B. DEFINITIONS

III-*n*

In the logico-experimental sciences, given the thing one may select the name for it quite arbitrarily (III-*r* below). In the non-logico-experimental sciences, the name is usually given and one goes looking for a thing to which the sentiments that the name arouses will correspond. If no such thing can be found among real things, one resorts to imaginary things (26, 109, *118,* 119, 150, 371, 578, 638-39, 686-91, 960-63, 965).

III-*o*

It follows from all the above that, barring involuntary slips and mistakes, the logico-experimental sciences use terms that correspond to real things, while the non-logico-experimental sciences use terms that, now by deliberate choice of the writer, now as a result of the principles he is applying, fail to correspond to anything that is real, or else correspond to things that are altogether fanciful (108-09, 171, 371, 408, *442,* 509-11, 515, 579-640).

III-*p*

In the logico-experimental sciences definitions are mere labels that help us to keep track of things. In the non-logico-experimental sciences, definitions contain a non-logico-experimental element that very often has its basis in sentiment (*119,* 150, 236, 245, 577-78, 638, *642, 798, 868, 960,* 965; see Definitions).

III-*q*

In the logico-experimental sciences, definitions are arbitrary, barring certain considerations of convenience (III-*r*). They must not contain anything that should be stated in the form of a theorem [that has to be proved] 381, *382-88,* 442, *963*).

III-*r*

Requisites for logico-experimental definitions (387, *388*).

INDEX AND BIBLIOGRAPHY

Index and Bibliography

[Numbers refer to paragraphs and notes in the body of the work. Words in parentheses relate to the one number immediately following. Abbreviation L. C. L. stands for Loeb Classical Library. Personal names aim to identify persons and sharpen outlines that were left vague in the Italian original. Bibliographical entries give the specific work or edition to which references in the notes are made. The occasional comment that is interspersed among the various entries is by the editor.]

A, see Psychic state *A; A-a,* elements (principles in theories), and *a,* element (residues) in social equilibrium, see Elements; *A's* (and *B's*) in politics, 2268

Abbés, 1390

Abd ul Hamid II of Turkey, 933, 1702 [1]

Abdul-Hassân (*Arabian Nights*), 738

Abel, Eugen, *Scholia recentia in Pindari Epinicia* (2 vols., Berlin, 1891-93), 188 [2], 1382 [2]

Abel, Niels Henrik, mathematician, 1441

Abelard, Peter, 1671, 2367 [1], 2381; *Ouvrages inédits* (see Cousin, Victor), 1651 [1], 2371-73

Abicht, Johann, see Scherzer

Abignente, Giovanni, 2264 [2]

Abishay the Shunamite, 1627 [4]

Abolitionists (prostitution), 1388

Abraham, biblical, 1627 [4], 1662 [1]; the Recluse, 1180 [1]

Absence, L', est à l'amour . . . , 1832 [2], see Bussy, in Addendum

Absinth, 1695 [1]

Absolute, the, 6, 10, 19, 22, 26, 58, 67, 69 [5], 70, 108, 112, 119 [1], 408, 447, 459, 528, 616, 857, 1402, 1471 [2], 1501, 1519, 1531-32, 1536, 1585, 1596 [4], 1626 [1], 1697, 1778 [2], 1886, 1878, 1893, 2025 [3], 2110 [1], 2115, 2129 [1], 2155, 2207 [1], 2330 [3], 2400, 2572

Absolutism, 1507, 1695 [1], 1713, 2227 [1], 2253, 2257, 2261, 2265, 2384 [1], 2454

Abstinence (meat, wine, sex), 1166-67, 1182, 1326-27, 1374 [2], and see Asceticism, Prohibitionism

Abstraction, capacity for, 177, 177 [1], 701 [1], 809. Abstractions, 13, 63-64, 90-92, 245, 336-37, 525 [1], 575-779 *passim,* 927-28, 993-94, 1227, 1231, 1356, 1511-32, 1670, 1677, 1689-91, 2400 [2], 2409; metaphysical (derivations, III-β), 1533-42, 1649, 1651; personified, 306, 332-46; deified, 176-81, 1460-63; powers of, 698-711, 701 [1]; their power to punish, 331-38; persistence of (residue II-δ), 1065-88, 1157, 1243; need of new (residue I-θ), 1086-88, 1677

Absyrtus myth, 1253-55

Abuse (Lagrange), 384-87

Abyss (god), 1645 [2], 1646-50, 1647 [2], 1651 [2], 1652 [1], 1668-69, 1671, 1673

Abyssinia, 2255, 2302; see Adua

Academy, French, 1436, 1471 [3], 1715 [2], 1751 [1]; see Crusca

Acarnanians, 1925

Acatzires (Barbarians), 2610

Accord, with experience, 14-15, 50, 52, 57-58, and *passim;* and see Experience, Theories, logico-experimental; with facts, 52, 55, 59, 86 [1], 304, and *passim;* with interests (derivations III-β, III-γ), 1477-1500; with principles (derivations III-δ, III-ε, III-ζ), 1501-42; with sentiments (derivations III-α), 1465-76; 14, 41-42, 69-7, 75, 78, 514, 963, 965-2, and *passim*

Accuracy (scientific), 537 [1]; see Exact, Facts ("all the facts")

Achaeans, 1975, 1983, 2495 [1]

Achilles, 939, 1059-60, 1231 [1], 1321, 1321 [1], 1963, 1971 [2], 1983, 2330 [7]

Acre, 1381 [4]

Acron, Helenius (*i.e.* Pseudo-Acron), *Pseudo-Acronis scholia in Horatium vetustiora,* Otto Keller ed., in Leipzig, 1902-04 (also in *Opera Q. H. Flacci,* Paris, 1519), 1382 [4], 1550 [1], 1980 [1], and see Porphyrio

Acropolis, 919 [1], 957 [1]

Acta et decreta sacrosancti et oecumenici concilii Vaticani (Freiburg-im-Breisgau, 1871), 605, and see Schaff

Acta pontificia et decreta SS. RR. Congregationum (Rome, October, 1907), 1630 [5]

Action-reaction, see Interdependence. Actions (human conduct), 145 [1], 145-48; logical, 13, 147-52, 157; otherwise follow: nonlogical actions, definition, 13, 149-50, 161; classification, 147-51; importance in society, 153-54; in animals (insects), 155-57; language as, 158; relations to psychic state, 162-68; as viewed by writers, 254-304; devices for rationalizing, 160, 305-67, 410; rôle in non-experimental theories, 574-841 *passim;* relations to elements *a, b, c* in theories, 798-803, 809-10, 824; general: 69 [3], 146, 159-60, 175 [1], 176, 176 [1], 180-81, 183-84, 190, 211-12, 217-18, 220, 223, 235, 242, 249-53, 579, 581, 583, 603, 636-40, 642, 661, 694, 696, 698, 705-07, 709-10, 741, 748, 753, 756-59, 794, 842-45, 883, 889, 892-93, 897, 899, 903, 905, 929, 950, 952-54, 965-5, 972-75, 982-84, 1000, 1021, 1053, 1059-64, 1079, 1083, 1095-97, 1118-20, 1121-25, 1127, 1129, 1136, 1138, 1144 [1], 1146, 1152, 1161-62, 1176-77, 1188, 1190-91, 1217-19, 1221-22, 1225-26, 1231-32,

Beautiful, beauty, 334, 515, 970, 1042, 1429, 1474, 1551, 1578 [3], 1601, 1905, 1905 [1], 2067 [1]
Bebel, Ferdinand A., 1322 [2], 2147
Bebius, Quintus, a tribune, 2556
Becket, Thomas à, 2316 [5] (p. 1661)
Bede, the Venerable, 1196 [1]
Beechey, Frederick William, *Narrative of a Voyage to the Pacific and Beering's Strait* (London, 1831), 1008 [1]
Bees, 155, 928 [1], 1506, 1602, 1602 [3], 2312, 2316-17
Beet-sugar, 2188
Beggars, royal, 921
Béguines, 1814 [2]
Being, 471; "Being creates being," 597; see Existence, Metaphysics
Beleth, Jean (Johannes Belethus), *De quadam libertate decembris* in *Divinorum officiorum rationale*, Lyons, 1568 (and Migne, *Patrologia*, Vol. 202, pp. 12-166, see pp. 125-26), 737 [2]
Belgium, 1050, 1050 [1], 1696 [1], 1751, 1755 [7], 1843 [2], 1975 [3], 2294, 2611 [2]
Belief, beliefs, 1008; social importance of, 81; see Faith, Religion
Belin, J. P., *Le commerce des livres prohibés à Paris de 1750 à 1789* (Paris, 1913), 1749 [1], 2048 [1]
Bell, Henry C. P., article on hill paddy (rice), 175
Bellarmino, Roberto Francesco Romolo, 1948 [1]
Bellerophon, 1971 [2]
Belli, Gian Gioacchino, *I sonetti romaneschi*, Morandi ed. (Città di Castello, 1896), 1851 [1], 2557 [1]
Belot, Emile Joseph, *Histoire des chevaliers romains* (Paris, 1869), 2546, 2597 [1]
Benecke, E. F. M., translator, Comparetti, *Vergil in the Middle Ages* (New York, 1895)
Benedict of Norcia, Saint, 1311 [1]
Beneficial, see Utility
Benefit-detriment, 14 [1]; see Utility; of clergy, 1159
Benevolence, 1149-52, 1155; see Altruism
Bentham, Jeremy, 450 [1], 1397 [2], 1486-92, 1552 [1], 1883; *Tactique des assemblées législatives; Traité des sophismes politiques*, text of Etienne Dumont (Paris, 1822), 1397 [2], 1435 [1]; *Traité de legislation civile et pénale* (Dumont text) (Paris, 1820) (and see Atkinson), 1486, 1486 [2], 1490; *Deontology*, Bowring ed. (London, 1834), 1486 [2], 1488-92; *Works*, John Bowring ed. (Edinburgh, 1843), 1489 [2], 1490 [2]
Béranger, Pierre Jean, *Chansons* (Paris, 1821); *Procès faits aux Chansons de P. J. Béranger* (Paris, 1828), 1749 [1]
Bérenger, Senator René, 6, 6 [1], 208, 570,

625 [1], 1127, 1180 [1], 1341 [1], 1344-45, 1352, 1370, 1379 [2], 1553 [1], 1715
Berg, Lodewyk W. C. van den, *De beginselen van het volgens de imâm's Aboe Hânitat en Sjefeï* (Batavia, 1878). References to French trans.: *Principes du droit musulman* (Algiers, 1896), 16, 19 [1]
Bergaigne, Abel, *Les dieux souverains de la religion védique*, Paris, 1883 (Part IV, Vol. III of *La religion védique d'après les hymnes du Rig-Véda*, 4 vols., Paris, 1878-87), 784 [1]
Bergerat, Emile, *Théophile Gautier, entretiens, souvenirs et correspondance* (Paris, 1879), 1719 a [1]
Bergier, Nicolas Sylvestre, *Dictionnaire de théologie* (with notes by Gousset) (6 vols., Besançon, 1848), 1470 [1]
Bergk, Theodor, *Poetae lyrici Graeci* (Leipzig, 1882), 1980 [4]
Bergson, Henri, 69 [3], 132 [1], 616, 1702 [4]
Berkeley, George, 2386 [1]
Berlin, 1695 [2], 1696 [1], 2147 [16], 2315, 2455, 2463 [1], 2470
Berlin, University, 1436, 1580 [3]
Berliner Post, 1708; *Tageblatt*, 1580 [3]
Bernard le Trésorier, *Chronique*, see Mas Latrie
Bernard of Clairvaux, Saint, *Opera omnia* (Paris, 1854), 1617, 1617 [1], 1629, 1629 [2-3], 2367 [1], 2377 [1]
Bernard Guidon, Fra, *Practica inquisitionis heretice pravitatis* (Paris, 1886), 1012 [1]
Berne, 717, 1502 (p. 957), 1641 [2]
Berosus, 744 [2]
Berriat Saint-Prix, Jacques, *Rapport et recherches sur les procès et jugements relatifs aux animaux* (*Mémoires de la Société royale des Antiquaires de France*, Vol. VIII, Paris, 1829), 1502, 1502 [1]
Bertaux, Henri Maurice, 1152, 2423 [1], 2584 [1]
Berthoulat, Georges, 466 [2], 1713 [3], 1716 [2], 2423 [1]
Bertinoro, Obadiah (Yareh), 444, 1267 [1], 1279 [2]; see Mishna
Bertrand, Joseph L. F., *Les fondateurs de l'astronomie moderne* (Paris [1865]), 540 [1]; *Calcul des probabilités* (Paris, 1889), 557, 558
Besse, Dom J. M., *Les moines d'Orient antérieurs au Concile de Chalcédoine*, [anno] 451 (Paris, 1900), 1168 [2], 1180 [1]
"Best," 2110 [1], 2145, 2145 [1], 2239
Bestiality (law), 1381, 1382 [6]
Bethlehem, 1484 [1], 1948 [1]
Bevione, Giuseppe, 2268 [2]
Biart, Lucien, *Les Aztèques* (Paris, 1885), 735
Bias, 170, 818 [1], 1412
Bible, general, 43, 67, 70, 198, 204, 204 [1], 206-07, 366, 377, 379, 430 [2], 485, 489,

Gaudentius the Donatist, 1576 [1]

Gaul, Gauls, 189 [1], 243, 652 [1], 654 [2], 668 [1], 731, 758-59, 866, 927 [5], 1006, 1070 [1], 1318, 1318 [1], 1339 [3], 1344, 1379 [1], 1934 [1], 2025 [3], 2163, 2316 [1], 2316 [4], 2366 [1], 2546 [1], 2548 [4], 2548 (p. 1845), 2549 [5], 2581, 2598; Gallia personified, 1070 [1]

Gaulis, Georges, "La révolte des Albanais" (article in Journal de Genève, May 7, 1910), 932 [1]

Gauss, Johann Friedrich Karl, 69 [5], 503 [5]

Gauthier le Chancelier, Bella Antiochena, reference to partial French translation by Michaud, Histoire des guerres d'Antioche (in Michaud, Bibliothèque des Croisades, Vol. I, pp. 104-23), 1381 [4]; Gautier, Lucien, Introduction à l'Ancien Testament (Lausanne, 1914), 1454 [1], 1627

Gaynor, Mayor William J., 1345 [1], 2267 [1]

Gazette de Lausanne, 466 [2], 947 [1], 1128 [1], 1330 [3], 1463 [1], 1714 [1], 1749 [3], 1883 [1], 2147 [11], 2147 [17], 2262 [4], 2452 [1]

Gedik (Gediccus), Simon, Defensio sexus muliebris (The Hague, 1638, new ed., 1707), 1821, 1821 [1]

Geissbühler, J. U., 1641 [2]

Gellius, see Aulus

Genera, existence of, 2368-74

General, delivery, 1297; questions (politics), 2253; sociology, see Sociology; will (Rousseau's), 1608; generalization (residue II-ε), 1068; see Generic

Generations, cyclical, 2330 (p. 1681); divine, 926-28, 1356, 1965 [1], and see Birth; Ferrari's, 2330 [5], 2330 [8]; succession of, 1859

Generic combination (residue I-a), 888, 892-909

Genesis, Book of, 774, 927 [2], 963, 1370, 1541-42, 1570, 1623, 1646, 1650 [1], 1695 [1], 2330 [2]

Geneva, 544, 1079, 1341 [1], 1440 [2], 1441 [1], 1697 [2], 1701, 1716 [1]; Congress of, 1559 [1]; Lake of (Leman), 256 [1], 1502 [3]

Gennadius, St., 1187 [4]

Genoa, 1199 [1], 1436 [1], 1710 [1], 1713 [3], 2480 [6]

Gens, γένος, 1023-36, 1041

Gentile, Giovanni, La riforma della dialettica hegeliana (Messina, 1913), 1686 [1]

Gentiles (not unclean), 1278-79

[Gentillet, Innocent], Discours sur les moyens de bien gouverner et maintenir en bonne paix un royaume ou autre principauté . . . Contre Nicolas Machiavel florentin ([Geneva], 1576), 1975 [1]

Gentiloni, Conte Vincenzo Ottorino, 1713 [3], 1913

Grabe, Johann Ernst, 1646 [1]

Geodesy, 1731, 2011

Geography, 37, 489, 564 [1], 594 [1], 1695, 1776, 2099

Geology, 50, 99, 536 [1], 619 [1], 1695 [1], 1792, 2002, 2014, 2060

Geometry, 4-5, 90, 108, 374-75, 491 [1], 505, 570, 1444, 1511, 1551 [1], 1604 [5], 1630, 1686, 1767, 2011, 2018-19, 2079, 2142 [1], 2147 [10]; national, 2019; Non-Euclidean, 4-5, 2079, 2142 [1]

Geoponicon, see Cassianus Bassus

Georgia (U. S.), 299 [1]

Gerasenus, see Nicomachus

Germanicus, Caesar, 1323

Germany, Germans, character, 932 [1]; "Germanic condition," Latin condition, 2147-II and notes; ancient, 1148, 1379 [1], 1462, 1462 [1]; Middle Ages, 1199 [1], (Crusades) 1106 [1], (witchcraft, witches) 212 [1], 217-5, 927 [5], 928 [1], (flagellants) 1200; Reformation, 2384 [1]; birth-control, 1345 [2]; classcirculation, 2053; education, 1564 [4], (scholarship, science) 75 [1]; Ems affair, 1922-23; Kulturkampf, 1843; language, 781; militarism-pacifism, 1129, 1799; politics, 1552, 1751, 1764; population in, 77; religion, 1204; sex hypocrisy, 75 [1], 1330, 1330 [2], 1330 [3]; Socialism, 541 [4], 1416, 1703 [1]; compared with France, Sparta, etc., 2444-76, 2450 [1], 2452 [1]; Germania personified, 1070 [1]; unclassified: 217, 927 [3], 1006, 1044, 1050-51, 1051 [1], 1070 [2], 1106 [1], 1148, 1200, 1297, 1440 [2], 1441, 1462, 1522-29, 1552, 1553 [2], 1564 [4], 1567 [2], 1580 [1], 1580 [3], 1703, 1708-09, 1715 [3], 1728 [1], 1751, 1755 [2], 1799, 1843, 1853 [2], 1881 [1], 1922-23, 1929, 1950-51, 1951 [1], 1975 [3], 2004 [1], 2014, 2053, 2108, 2147-II, 2160 [1], 2179, 2218, 2224, 2236 [1], 2243, 2247 [1], 2256, 2257 [2], 2262 [2], 2266, 2268 [3], 2300, 2302, 2315, 2316 [5] (p. 1661), 2320, 2326, 2389, 2422-23, 2423 [1], 2455, 2480 [2], 2480 [6], 2480 [7], 2485, 2517, 2530 [1], 2538, 2540, 2549-A2 (p. 1849), 2553 [1], 2559, 2566 [3], 2587 [1], 2605, 2611 [2]; see Pan-Germanism

Germinet, Admiral, 2422 [1]

Gerson, Jean Charlier of Gerson, called, 1202, 1436 [2]

Gesta Romanorum, Dick ed. (Innsbruck MS.), Erlangen-Leipzig, 1890; Swan's translation, 2 vols. (London, 1824), 674 [1], 1993 [1]; and see Brunet

Gethsemane, 1484 [1], 1948 [1]

Gheel (Belgium), 927 [6]

Ghengis Khan, 441

Ghisleri, Arcangelo, 1705 [1]; Le razze umane ed il diritto nella questione coloniale (Savona, 1888), 1051 [1]

Ghosts, 184 [3], 561-62, 584, 699, 709, 710, 921 [1], 1054, 1304-08, 1439 [2], 1698 [1]; Holy, see Spirit

Giacomo, Salvatore di, 1329 [1]

Giants, 664, 927 [2], 1288 [3], 1927 [1], 2330 [7], 2394; "giants' " bones, 2330 [7]

Textes de droit romain, pp. 72-79), 231 [2], 2549, notes 9-10

Leyden, John of, 1757 [1]

Liabeuf case, 1136

Liao-Yang, battle, 1703 [2]

Libations, 1057-64, 1254, 1304-10

Libentius of Bremen, St., 1311

Liber, god, 177 [3], 192 [1], 684, 960 [9], 1107 [1], 1339 [3], 1343 [1] (p. 830), 1344 [3]

Liberal, liberals, liberalism, 934, 1341, 1524, 1554, 1555 [1], 1561, 1564, 1702, 1702 [3], 1703-04, 1715 [3], 1755 [5], 1823, 1843 [1], 2147 [11], 2211, 2256, 2256 [2], 2313, 2326 [2], 2389, 2553 (p. 1863). Liberal, Christians, 337-38, 337 [1], 592, see Protestants, Liberal, Modernism; Protestants, see Protestants. Liberality (Cicero on), 1211

Liberté, La (newspaper, Paris), 466 notes, 690 [1], 1050 [1], 1127 [1-2], 1136 [2-3], 1142 [1], 1301 [2], 1330 [3], 1345 [1], 1580 [3], 1638 [1-2], 1696 [1], 1713 [1], 1713 [3-4], 1716 [2], 1716 [4-5], 2180 [1], 2254 [1], 2256 [2], 2257 [2], 2261 [1], 2262 [3], 2267 [1], 2313 [2], 2423 [1], 2452 [1]

Libertines, 1341, 1341 [1], 1471 [3], 1749 [2], 1937

Liberty, 298, 1341 [1], 1490, 1564 [4], 1625 [1], 1686 [1], 1686 [3], 2147 [13], 2544; as free initiative, 2550 [1]; "true," 961

Libya, Libyans, 594 [1], 1559 [1], 1560, 1704, 1728 [1], 1760 [1], 1776 [1], 2313 [1]; Libyan War, see Italy

Licinius (Valerius Licinius Licinianus), 2316 [5]; the barber of Augustus, 2594

Life, as catchword, 1686 [5]; insurance, 2255 [1], 2316 [9]

Light, 115, 504, 506, 511, 1623; creation of, 1542 [2]

Lightning (omen), 925

Liguria, 274

Liguori, Saint Alfonso Maria de, *Theologia moralis summatim exposita,* Ninzatti ed. (Turin, 1892), 1387 [1]

Likes, combinations of, see Similars

Likeness to God, 1556 [1]

Lille, 1716 [5]

Lime-juice, 950 [2]

Limit, -states (in evolution), 375-82, 517, 2111, 2213, 2330 (p. 1680), and see Type-religions, *etc.;* theory of limits, 831-33, 1018-19

Lindau, Rudolf, 1755 [2]

Lindemann, Franz, ed., *Pauli Diaconi excerpta et Sexti Pompeii Festi fragmenta* (Leipzig, 1832, Vol. II of *Corpus grammaticorum Latinorum veterum*)

Lingams, 1181 [1], 1272 [1]; see Phallus

Lions, 256, 661, 715-17, 716 [1], 793, 912 [1], 939, 939 [3], 1145, 1285 [1], 1301 [1], 1359 [1], 1471, 1770; crucifixion of, 1501 (p. 953), 1501 [7]; lions and foxes, 2178, 2480 [4]; lion-grass, 917

Lipsius, Justus (Joest Lips), *Politicorum sive*

civilis doctrinae libri sex (Leyden, 1589, Lyons, 1594), 1934 [1]

Liptinae, 2316 [5], see Létines

Lisbon, 927 [3]

Litanies (Church), 1002

Literalism (in biblical interpretation), 1450-57

Literature, 545, 1017-19, 1074-76, 1084, 1164, 1321, 1334, 1345, 1415 [1], 1450-57, 1674, 1719 a [1], 1733-34, 1761-67, 1881 [1], 1892, 1926, 1937, 1999-2000, 2008, 2206; as expressing ideals, 1876-95; influence of, 971, 1761-65, 2048 [1]; as history, 543-45; obscene, 1129, 1333-34, 1351-52, 1380, 1380 [1], 1381, 1381 [4] (p. 863); radical, toleration of, 2325-26; see France, Greece, Italy, Rome; literary, criticism, 541, 855-56, 859, 1739; science, see "Science"

Littré, Emile, translator, *Histoire naturelle de Pline* (Paris, 1850), 179 [1]

Liutprand, 660, 1381 [4] (p. 865)

Livia Drusilla, wife of Augustus, 925

Living, "living one's own life," 1462; "living" ("dead"), 1686; persistence of relations between living and dead (Residue II-β), 1052-55

Livingstone, David, 793

Livy (Titus Livius), 651, 664 [2], 1567; *Ab urbe condita* (commonly, the *Annales*), 182 [6], 225 [1], 230 [2], 231 [2], 237, 313 [1], 757, 758 [1], 925 [4], 926 [1], 930 [2], 960 [10], 1074 [2], 1109, 1382 [2], 1567, 1921 [1], 1934 [1], 2316 [1], 2354 [1], 2446 [2], 2548 [4], 2548 [8], 2556

Lizards, 175, 914 [1], 1264 [4]

Lloyd George, David, 1152, 1713 [5], 1755 [5], 2147 [19], 2253, 2262 [4], 2469 [2], 2553 [3]

Loadstone, 1438 [1]

Loans, foreign, 2314

Loathing, 1346

Lobachevski, Nicolai Ivanovich, 5, 6

Lobbying, 2562

Lobsters, 1571 [2]

Locke, John, 365, 1495; *An Essay concerning Human Understanding* (*Works,* 10 vols., London, 1812, Vols. I-IV), 460; *The Reasonableness of Christianity as delivered in the Scriptures* (*Ibid.,* Vol. VII, pp. 1-158), 2385 [1]

Locris, Locrians, 1074 [2], 1980, 2316 [1]

Logarithms, 77 [3], 558

Logic, logical, 7, 12-14, 20, 42, 76-77, 168, 463, 477, 514, 514 [1], 559, 563 [1], 626, 637, 971-75, 1079, 1127, 1315, 1345, 1399, 1405-13, 1416-17, 1435, 1438, 1497, 1529, 1542-43, 1546, 1550, 1556, 1560, 1607, 1621, 1624, 1686 [3], 1689, 1755, 1768, 1771-98 *passim,* 1802-03, 1822, 1843, 1982-83, 2016, 2079, 2161, 2410; logic and experience, 29, 45-48, 69 [3], 76, 607; hunger for logic, see Residue I-ε; necessity of conclusion in syllogism, 29, 41-42,

1986 THE MIND AND SOCIETY

97; objective-subjective logic, 155; pure logic, 69-5; value of logic tested by experience, 29; logical interpretation of nonlogical conduct, 217-6, 249-367 passim, and see Action

Logos, Gnostic, 1645 [2]

Loi des suspects, 1012

Loiseleur Deslongchamps, Louis (Auguste Louis Armand), translator from Sanskrit, Manava-Dharma-Sastra: Lois de Manou, comprenant les Institutions religieuses et civiles des Indiens (in G. Pauthier, Les livres sacrés de l'Orient, Paris, 1840, pp. 331-460), 1261 [1], 1263 [1]

Loisy, Abbé Alfred, 618 [2], 777 [3], 1570 [1], 1630, 1660; Simples réflexions sur le decret du Saint Office "Lamentabili sane exitu" et sur l'encyclique "Pascendi Dominici gregis" (Paris, 1908), 774, 1630 [4]; Autour d'un petit livre (Paris, 1903), 776-78, 1630 [3]; Le prologue du quatrième Evangile (in Revue d'histoire et de littérature religieuses) (Vol. II, Paris, 1897, pp. 249-267), 1570 [2], Etudes sur la religion chaldéenne-assyrienne (7 installments in Vols. II-IV, in Revue des religions, Paris, Nov. 1890-April, 1892), 1571; Etudes bibliques (Paris, 1903), 1571 [2]; L'Evangile et l'Eglise (Paris, 1902), 1630 [1]

Lombardy, Lombards, 652 [1], 1180 [1], 1381 [4] (p. 865), 1502 [3], 1617, 1839 [1], 1975 [3], Lombard Street, 2529

Lombroso, Cesare, 1439

London, 95, 1011 [1], 1053, 1217 [1], 1393 [1] (p. 880), 1508 [1], 2018-19, 2294, 2315, 2385 [1]; Congress of (1913), 1508 [1]

Long (short), 1550; long-period oscillations, 2319

Loosli, Carl Albert, 1641 [2]

Lord, the: His ways inscrutable, 1902, 1976 [1], 1979 [1], 1995-98; Lord's Day observance, 1554; see Sunday; Prayer (in magic), 215, 954 [1]

Los Angeles (Cal.), 1345 [1]; Times, 1345 [1]

Lot (biblical), 1343 [2]

Lottery, 615, 621-22, 892, 934, 982, 1579, 1823, 1823 [1], 1977, 2411 [1]

Loubat, William [sic], 466 [2]

Louis (of France): IX (St. Louis), 1127, 1381 [4] (p. 863), 1383, 1383 [1], 1383 [3], 2316 [5]; XI, 1975 [2], 2384 [1]; XII, 1975 [2]; XIV, 931, 1574-75, 1748 [1], 1974 [1], 2027, 2316 [7]; XV, 1747 [1], 2027, 2316 [7]; XVI, 49, 1747 [1], 2059, 2163, 2180, 2191, 2199, 2201, 2524; XVIII, 1747 [1], 1751 [1], 2386; Louis-Philippe, 1152, 1638, 1747 [1], 1951 [2], 2201, 2201 [1], 2455, 2486

Love, 1627; Christian, 1757 [1]; Courts of, 2514; thy neighbour as thyself, 1772; philtres, 185 [2], 212; love-hatred, 1357; love-interest (literary), 1324-96

Lower classes, 1858, 1930-32, 1933, see Classes

Lowrie, Judge (England), 1127 [2]

Loyson, Charles (Father Hyacinthe), 1086 [1], 1355 [2]

Lubbock, Sir John William, The Origin of Civilization and the Primitive Condition of Man (New York, 1873), 1095, 1112 [1]

Lucan, Marcus Annaeus, De bello civili, commonly, Pharsalia, 194 [1], 296 [1], 654 [2], 931 [1]

Lucania, 2548 [4]

Lucca, 1381 [3]

Luce, Siméon, Histoire de la Jacquerie (Paris, 1895), 2566 [1], 2566 [2]

Lucerne, 947

Lucian, 189 [2], 310, 1681, 1685 [1], 1763-64, 2344; Opera Graece et Latine (9 vols., Leipzig, 1822-31), English-Greek, Harmon ed., 4 vols. only (L. C. L.), 184 [3], 684 [2], 926 [1], 1184 [3], 1189 [1], 1194 [2], 1305, 1439 [1], 1695 [2]; see Fowler

Lucretius (Titus Lucretius Carus), 207, 471, 521, 1537 [2], 1681, 2048 [1], 2359; De rerum natura (Rouse ed., L. C. L., 1928), 487 [2], 615 [1], 1438 [1], 1567 [2], 1890

Ludwig IV, the Bavarian, Emperor, 1817 [6]

Luke, St., 215 [1]; see Gospels

Lupercalia, 233 [1], 763 [1], 1111, 1191-93, 1203, 1203 [1]

Lusitania, 927 [3]

Lustration, 1246 [4], 1259 [1], 1287, 2354 [1], see Baptism

Lutetia, 654 [2]

Luther, Martin, 927, 927 [6], 1242 [1], 1701, 1821 [1], 1856; Lutherans, Lutheranism, 379, 624 [2], 1553 [2], 1856

Lutz, Premier, 1843 [1], 1843 [2]

Lux, Baron de, 1949

Luxury, in Rome, 2585 [3]; cause of "corruption," 2558-59

Luzel, François Marie, Légendes chrétiennes de la Basse Bretagne (2 vols., Paris, 1881), 1993 [1]

Luzzatti, Luigi, 1152 [2], 1823, 2253 [1], 2256, 2553 [3], 2584 [1]

Lyall, Sir Alfred Comyn, Asiatic Studies, Religious and Social (London, 1882), 1082-84, 1090, 1092

Lycophron of Chalcis, Cassandra (Alexandra), Potter ed., with scholia of Tzetzes (Oxford, 1697) (Mair ed., L. C. L.), 684 [2], 927 [4]

Lycurgus of Sparta, 313 [2], 1190, 1195, 2496, 2502 [1]; of Athens, 883 [1]

Lydia (Asia), 1253

Lyman, D., The Moral Sayings of Publius [read Publilius] Syrus (Cleveland, 1856)

Lynceus, 652 [2]

Lynchings, 1050 [1], 1134, 2180, 2180 [a]

Lyodesma, goddess, 1191

Lyons, 466 [2], 1292 [1], 2514 [1], 2520 [1]

Residues, 119, 357, 383 [1], 397, 407, 514 [4], 642, 675 [1], 2020; 1. [This item is arranged *seriatim*, not analytically] [The concept of residues is present in Pareto's early writings, even before he hits on that term. One might bear in mind a rather verbose and cumbersome form of expression that he is constantly using: "There is (exists) in us a preconception (*preconcetto*, prejudice, sentiment) that inclines us to believe that . . ."]

I. Inductively considered, under other names: as manifestations of the psychic state *A*, 161-70; as a constant element in non-logical actions (to be distinguished from a variable element, derivations), 189-248, and see 965-*I*, 1690; as related to conduct and theories, 269; as principles of non-logical actions, and rationalized, 306-67; as principles in non-logico-experimental theories, 397, 407-08, 416, 445, 513-14; as figuring in the logic of sentiments, 575-769 *passim* and more particularly: 579 (opposite conclusions from same principle, and see also 1474 and Pro-contra), 587, 591, 596, 640-42, 651, 658, 740; as the "element *a*" in "theories *c*," and compared with a logico-experimental "element *A*," 797-804, 815-20, 824-41, 848-54, 861-70, 874-78, 880, 886-87 (also 1768-70, 1773)

II. Deductive exposition: 869-70, 874; relation to sentiments, 875, 1401; composite residues, 876, 966-71, 1353; derivatives taken as residues, 877, 1449; compared with word-roots in language, 879-84; chronological relations to derivatives, 886-87; classification, 888; classified analysis, 889-1396, for which see Particular Residues; cumulation of residues, 927; and see 1556, 1556 [1], 1606, 1635; residues and derivations (here and hereafter, Pareto uses the terms "residue" and "sentiment" interchangeably): 1397-1686

Chap. II; and it develops that if some conduct, the conduct that corresponds to the practical side of life, to interests, is largely logical, in the other domains of life non-logical conduct prevails, 154-248. This fact has been generally sensed by observers of human history; but few if any have grasped its full import. That is because non-logical conduct most often appears as more or less logicalized, or rationalized, in theories, Chap. III. Classification and study of the means by which this rationalization is effected, 306-367. Equipped now with the concepts of non-logical actions and of rationalization, one can resume the search begun in § 13, examining theories, that is, as to their substantial elements, and as to the quality, logical or fallacious, of the nexus that holds them together, 467, 472, 473. Elements in theories, 470-518. Character of the nexus, 519-796. As for the elements, theories may contain experimental and non-experimental elements, and that yields a triple classification: theories that combine experimental elements with non-experimental elements (logico-experimental theories); theories that combine experimental with non-experimental, or non-experimental with non-experimental, elements (non-logico-experimental theories), 474-518. Examination of the nexus yields a triple classification, 523: descriptive propositions (having no nexus at all they can hardly be called theories), 525; assertions of logico-experimental laws, 526-73; theories that overstep or ignore the logico-experimental domain. In this last category we get huge numbers of theories that fall into two groups, 575: theories that overtly vaunt a super-experimental majesty (trans-experimental theories), 576-632, and theories that more or less covertly mix and mingle experimental and non-experimental principles (pseudo-scientific theories), 633-796.

But the interest in all this has been not in theories as such, but in theories as revealing the forces (8, 466 [at end]) that determine the forms of human society. Having now looked over the whole field of theories, can one advance another step toward that goal? Theories are merely what people say about the things they do or experience. Comparisons of actions and comparisons of theories show that while the forces that prompt human conduct remain fairly constant, the reasons people give for doing as they do vary widely. We can therefore gain by changing the form of the research and considering theories, *c,* as made up of that constant ele-

ADDENDA

Bussy-Rabutin, Roger de, *Maximes d'amour* (in *Histoire amoureuse des Gaules,* Cologne, 1716. The maxim, *L'absence est à l'amour, etc.,* is on p. 219), 1832 [2].

Dorens, 1172 [1]. This, however, is an error on Pareto's part. The line *Gardez-vous bien, etc.,* is by the Sieur Du Laurens (Jacques Du Laurens or Lorens), *Les Satyres,* Paris, 1624, *Satyre I* (see Fleuret-Perceau, *Les satires françaises du XVIIme siècle,* Paris, 1923, Vol. I, p. 279).